Syntax – Theory and Analysis
HSK 42.1

Handbücher zur Sprach- und Kommunikationswissenschaft

Handbooks of Linguistics and Communication Science

Manuels de linguistique et des sciences de communication

Mitbegründet von Gerold Ungeheuer
Mitherausgegeben (1985–2001) von Hugo Steger

Herausgegeben von / Edited by / Edités par
Herbert Ernst Wiegand

Band 42.1

De Gruyter Mouton

Syntax – Theory and Analysis

An International Handbook

Volume 1

Edited by

Tibor Kiss
Artemis Alexiadou

De Gruyter Mouton

ISBN 978-3-11-020276-2
e-ISBN (PDF) 978-3-11-037740-8
e-ISBN (EPUB) 978-3-11-039423-8
ISSN 1861-5090

Library of Congress Cataloging-in-Publication Data

A CIP catalog record for this book has been applied for at the Library of Congress.

Bibliographic information published by the Deutsche Nationalbibliothek

The Deutsche Nationalbibliothek lists this publication in the Deutsche Nationalbibliografie; detailed bibliographic data are available on the Internet at http://dnb.dnb.de.

Typesetting: Meta Systems Publishing & Printservices GmbH, Wustermark
Printing and binding: Hubert & Co. GmbH & Co. KG, Göttingen
Cover design: Martin Zech, Bremen
♾ Printed on acid-free paper

Printed in Germany

www.degruyter.com

MIX
Papier aus verantwortungsvollen Quellen
FSC® C016439

This handbook is dedicated to the memory of our dear friend Ursula Kleinhenz (1965–2010).

The light that burns twice as bright burns half as long.

Preface

When our friend Ursula Kleinhenz approached us during the annual meeting of the German Linguistic Society (DGfS) in Mainz in 2004, it was not to piece together the events of the previous evening. Being without the benefit of a screenwriter and a director, we usually had to figure out the events from the nebula of a hangover ourselves (but we never woke up next to a tiger). Ursula was just as hilarious as she was professional and could switch between these personas just as easily as she could be both simultaneously. If any consolation can be found in her premature death, it is only because her life was as intense as that of two others. Ursula's proposal was that we should edit the *syntax handbook* in the HSK series. Like other handbooks in the series, the syntax handbook had a predecessor (published in 1993 and 1995), but Ursula (and de Gruyter) thought that it was about time to take a fresh look. Presumably, she also had a deeper insight in the process of conceiving, compiling, and editing such a handbook. Perhaps she could even foresee how much time would pass until the idea became a published book.

With its present structure, the handbook aims to provide a valuable source not only for the professional syntactician but also for the linguist who wants to gain information about the current state of the art in syntax; in particular it should facilitate the advanced student's way into syntax.

Syntax can look back on a long tradition. The term itself is ambiguous. On the one hand, it is understood as a means of structural and descriptive analysis of individual languages using clearly defined instruments. Naturally, syntactic analyses can be comparative, spanning several languages. On the other hand, *syntax* is understood as syntactic theory, the aim of which is to decide which instruments can be sensibly applied to syntactic analysis. Syntactic theory thus defines the aims of syntactic research. Especially in the last 50 years, however, the interaction between syntactic theory and syntactic analysis has led to a rapid increase in analyses and theoretical suggestions. This increase has been accompanied with the impression that syntax is a fragmented discipline. This impression is not wrong in so far as syntactic theory cannot be traced back to one school, but rather to a great number of approaches in competition with each other. It should, however, not be forgotten that the competitive situation in most cases was triggered by empirical problems and that complex problems may be approached in more than one way. Precisely this situation has led to very decisive progress in syntactic analysis in the last 50 years. This result would probably have never been achieved if syntax had been limited to just one dispute about theory or method.

This handbook – which is spread out over three volumes, containing 61 articles in nine sections – adopts these unifying perspectives and places at the fore the increase in knowledge that results from the fruitful argumentation between syntactic analysis and syntactic theory. To reflect this, the handbook contains articles on syntactic phenomena from two different angles: one perspective is mainly descriptive, allowing linguists to grasp what is at issue when a particular phenomenon is subjected to sometimes heated debate. Thus Section III (Syntactic Phenomena), which covers the bulk of Volume I of the handbook, contains descriptions of a set of phenomena that are called *syntactic*. The phenomena comprise the argument-adjunct distinction, negation, agreement, word order, ellipsis, and idioms, among others. We would like to note that the phenomena were not selected on the basis of the personal preference of the editors. Instead, we asked our colleagues around the world to take part in a survey in order to determine which phenomena should be dealt with in such a handbook.

Four of the phenomena are taken up again in Section VI (Theoretical Approaches to Selected Syntactic Phenomena) and receive theoretical analyses. The reader of the handbook may thus approach syntactic phenomena from the perspective of what is in need of an analysis. We assume that a description can be provided prior to (even if it is not entirely independent of) an analysis since the phenomena are natural – at least in parts. Alternatively, the reader may approach syntactic phenomena from the perspective of what has been, and also what has not been, covered by an analysis. We believe that those issues in particular that have been omitted from current analysis provide good starting points for future syntacticians to gain access to the syntactic community. Such gaps in analysis should thus not been seen as flaws but as open questions to be dealt with promptly.

As for the structure of the handbook as a whole, the first volume (Sections I–III) is devoted to the position of syntax in linguistics (including its interfaces to other linguistic domains), to the syntactic tradition prior to the advent of structuralism and generativism, and – as already mentioned – to syntactic phenomena.

The second volume (Sections IV–VI) begins with a survey on the dominant syntactic theories and frameworks (in the Introduction to the handbook we deal with the perennial question of why we have more than one theory (cf. 1)), and continues with a detailed description of the relationship between syntax and its major interfaces. Considering the relationship of syntax to other neighbouring disciplines, we note that, right up to the 1990s, an artificial comparison between formal models and models dealing with content was postulated, for example using the key phrase of "the autonomy of syntax". However, it has become clear in the meantime that syntax based on formal options interacts with other components of linguistic knowledge, for example through correspondence rules or through defined interfaces. The chapters in Section V (together with the overview on Syntax and its interfaces in Section I) provide a picture of syntax as placed among the other linguistic domains.

The second volume closes with theoretical analyses of several of the aforementioned phenomena.

The third volume (Sections VII–IX) provides syntactic sketches of various languages, language types, and language families (the Bantu language family, Bora, Creole languages, Georgian, German, Hindi-Urdu, Japanese, Mandarin, Northern Straits Salish, Tagalog, and Warlpiri). It then deals with the cognitive environment of syntax, covering language acquisition, language disorders, and language processing, and finally deals with the broader role of syntax when dealing with corpora, lexicographic resources, stylistics, computational linguistics, the development of reference grammars and the documentation of (endangered) languages, and finally, what role syntax might play in the classroom.

In conclusion, this handbook highlights syntax as a mature discipline, whose state of knowledge concerning the languages of the world has rapidly increased.

This brief preface cannot and should not be concluded without an expression our gratitude to the various groups of people without whose participation this handbook would have been an even more impossible mission.

We thank our authors, which are not named here, as their articles speak for themselves.

Each article has been subjected to an anonymous review process, and individual articles as well as the handbook as a whole profited enormously from the comments and the suggestions made by these reviewers. We would like to thank Peter Ackema, Susan Bejar, Eva Belke, Adriana Belletti, Miriam Butt, Katharina Colomo, Jeroen van Craenenbroeck, Berthold Crysmann, Holger Diessel, Laura Downing, Stanley Dubinsky, Susann Fischer, Bart Geurts, Kook-Hee Gill, Michael Hahn, Hubert Haider, Daniel Hole, Joachim Jacobs, Jaklin Kornflit, Beth Levin, Terje Lohndal, Anke Lüdeling, Stefan Müller, Timothy Osborne, Eric Potsdam, Beatrice Primus, Frank Richter, Norvin Richards, Björn Rothstein, Vieri Samek-Lodovici, Florian Schäfer, Sabine Schulte im Walde, Frank Seifart, Wolfgang Sternefeld, Jesse Tseng, Marc de Vries, Helmut Weiß, Martina Wiltschko, and Niina Ning Zhang.

We would also like to thank Barbara Karlson, Birgit Sievert, Anke Beck and Wolfgang Konwitschny at Walter de Gruyter for their assistance and their gentle way of midwifery. We also thank Nils Hirsch and Patrick Lindert for editorial assistance. Many thanks to Miriam Butt and Gereon Müller for discussions early on in the process of structuring the content of this handbook.

Finally, a very special thank you to Alicia Katharina Börner. Without her rigorous and thoroughgoing assistance in the preparation of the final manuscripts, we would perhaps still be awaiting the publication of the handbook.

Contents

Volume 1

I. Introduction: Syntax in Linguistics

II. The Syntactic Tradition

III. Syntactic Phenomena

Volume 2

IV. Syntactic Models

V. Interfaces

VI. Theoretical Approaches to Selected Syntactic Phenomena

Volume 3

VII. Syntactic Sketches

VIII. The Cognitive Perspective

IX. Beyond Syntax

Indexes

I. Introduction: Syntax in Linguistics

1. Syntax – The State of a Controversial Art

Abstract

This article provides a broad introduction to Syntax, as it is conceived in this handbook. We will present a number of assumptions that have been considered to constitute common ground for all syntacticians. But they are as fundamental as they are controversial for syntactic theory and analysis. In fact, approaches to syntactic analysis as well as syntactic theories quite often take controversial positions, leading to the apparent conclusion that syntactic research is fractured. It is not our goal to offer a band-aid to patch up what better should be kept separate. Our conclusion is that many issues might indeed be controversial within syntactic research but that such controversy should be seen as the driving force behind progress in syntax.

1. Introduction

Perhaps the simplest way to approach syntax is to define it as the linguistic component that relates sound and meaning, and thus fulfils this crucial task in mapping the two intelligible sides of the Saussurean sign. Syntax must thus be able to break up the continuous flow of sound signals into elementary tokens, must be able to provide a structure for the tokens, and enable the semantic component to access the tokens – and the larger parts made of them in order to account for the interpretation of complex units. It goes without saying that the same story could be told if we started with the interpretational component, letting syntax map meaning to sound.

A grammar consists of a complex formal unit that requires analysis, a rule system relating atomic and complex units to the complex formal unit under analysis, and a characterization of the atomic or elementary elements, and how they relate to the rule system. Typically, the sentence (S) is the formal unit that requires analysis, there are all kinds of rule systems resulting in a sentence, and the lexical units are taken to be the atomic elements, which are assigned appropriate categories so that the rule system can make use of them. This characterization seems to be uncontroversial, and it owns its uncontroversial status to its relative abstractness, e.g. the lack of detail concerning the rule system, the use of categories, and more or less everything else required to actually carry out a syntactic analysis.

When it comes to detail, however, syntax is mostly conceived as fractured. It is often forgotten that, within the broader realm of Saussurean linguistics, proper syntax started as a straggler, coming to maturity only approximately 60 to 70 years ago, and that it has achieved quite a lot in this short lifetime. And yet, a necessary precondition of syntax seems to be that the linguist becomes a member of one of the many different schools of thought. Schools that sometimes are engaged in fierce fights (giving rise to terms like "Linguistics Wars", cf. Harris 1993), and sometimes are content with peaceful coexistence, or mutual neglect. In fact, one realizes soon that "schools" are partitioned in various dimensions, as for instance formal in opposition to functional or cognitive, formal in opposition to descriptivist, and so forth. Deep within syntax, different views pertain to the structures that are actually used to carve up the continuous flow of sound signals (be they tree structures, dependency arcs, grammatical relations, derivations etc.). This situation may leave those who want to study syntax in a state of confusion, about which school to choose, or whether to choose one at all, or more than one. (In addition to confusion, students may also feel pressured since syntax is interfacial by definition, and hence it will become necessary for the apprentice to be familiar with one of the major components with which syntax interfaces.) It should be noted, however, that disagreement is not pertinent to syntax alone, but can be observed in other areas of linguistics as well (or linguistics as a whole), cf. the discussion following the influential article of Evans and Levinson (2009).

The goal of the present article is twofold: On the one hand, we would like to address several issues that seem to be controversial within syntax as a research area, and shed some light on real or apparent controversies. On the other hand, we would like to make clear that controversy in itself does not mean that a field is unripe or uninteresting, but to the contrary that disagreement is an expression about the relative maturity of syntax. In doing so, we will take recourse to Henk van Riemsdijk's presentation of a set of background assumptions "which (...) virtually every linguist (...) shares" (van Riemsdijk 1984: 1).

Writing in 1984, van Riemsdijk believed that the assumptions presented were widely shared. We have chosen a selection from van Riemsdijk's assumptions, the ones that we believe to have the strongest bearing on current research. Relating current positions to the positions held back then when van Riemsdijk presented them also allows us to evaluate the progress made in syntax and syntactic theory. In fact, we take controversial issues in syntax to be an indicator of scientific progress. So, it is good that there is controversy.

2. Syntax relates sound and meaning

While the very idea of syntax relating sound and meaning has to be considered uncontroversial, with syntax breaking up the stream of sounds into units which accordingly receive an interpretation, it is at least unclear whether sound and meaning are relevant to syntactic operations or not. Mainstream generative grammar has assumed from Chomsky

(1965) onwards that the syntactic component of the grammar is "generative" (we will come to this term below), while the other components are "interpretative", i.e. work on structures provided by syntax. This position has been challenged by a variety of frameworks. HPSG (Pollard and Sag 1994; cf. S. Müller, this volume) assumes that syntactic and semantic properties receive the same formal representation, and interact in agreement and anaphoric binding (the reader is referred to Wagner's contribution to this handbook to discuss the relation between syntax and phonology). Pustejovsky's generative lexicon (Pustejovsky 1995) raises the question of how syntactic categorization is influenced by lexical semantics to account for coercion processes.

These are just two proposals that challenge a model of syntax, in which syntax is taken to differ fundamentally even from the linguistic components with which it shares an interface (cf. also Mycock, this volume).

3. Sentence grammar differs from extra-sentential (or sub-sentential) modes of combination

Riemsdijk (1984: 2) states that "[the structure of the sentence] is determined by rules and principles sui generis". As often when contemplating questions about syntax, the statement seems to be clear and intuitive at the outset, but invites further considerations after second thoughts. What we can assume is that there are sentence internal operations (rules and principles), whose application to units that consist of sentences would be nonsensical, i.e. would not lead to plausible results. Case marking might be a case in point, as well as reference to syntactic arguments or grammatical relations as discourse relations. But the composition of sentences may also rely on rules, which do not exclusively apply within a sentence. Pronominal agreement can serve as an illustration. Consider the examples in (1).

(1) a. *John told Paula$_i$ that she$_i$ would have to apply for the dean position on Monday the latest.*

b. *John spoke with Paula$_i$ about the dean position. She$_i$ understood that she would have to apply on Monday the latest.*

To begin with, we are talking about one sentence in (1a), but two sentences in (1b). And yet, the relationship between the object of *tell/speak* to the subject of the embedded sentence and the subject of the second sentence, respectively, seems to be similar. In particular, we see agreement in gender, person, and number. Going further, we may assume that the agreement is a consequence of Principle B of Binding Theory (Chomsky 1981; Pollard and Sag 1994) in (1a). Since identification of the indices of antecedent and pronoun implies agreement of antecedent and pronoun in number, person, and gender, the observed agreement can be deduced from a condition on syntactic elements within a clause. In (1b), however, the agreement may come about because the discourse referent of the antecedent is identified with the discourse referent of the pronoun, as this is usually done in Discourse Representation Theory (Kamp and Reyle 1993). Since they are identical, and since discourse referents either cannot be formally distinguished from indices (as in the analysis of Pollard and Sag 1994) or bear the very same features, once again agreement emerges because two indices are identified, and hence the features that make up the indices are identified as well. At this point, we may ask whether index identification is a syntactic rule *sui generis.* It would be possible to argue that index identification started as rule of sentence grammar and spread into the rule system for discourses. If this interpretation is assumed, we may consider van Riemsdijk's view as uncontroversial. The statement would have to be translated to the effect that rules of sentence grammar might form the basis for rules outside of sentence grammar, but that the reverse is not likely to happen. The reader may decide whether this characterization still allows the maintenance of the position that the structure of the sentence is formed by rules *sui generis.*

We would like to note that there is a second interpretation of Riemsdijk's statement. Even if we take it that the rules within a sentence are different from the rules outside of it, we may still ask whether the rules are restricted in their application to atomic units or whether the sentence is the smallest unit to which specific rules apply. This question translates into the relationship between syntax and morphology, or more generally into the relationship between syntax and the lexicon (for the latter, cf. Alexiadou, this volume). One position has been initiated by *lexical integrity* (Bresnan and Mchombo 1995). According to the lexical integrity hypothesis, morphological processes and syntactic rules form two separate domains of linguistic rule systems. Interestingly, the lexical integrity hypothesis has not only been attacked from the position of syntactic access to sub-syntactic units, but also by *lexical rules* that seem to affect syntax and morphology (for a recent vindication of lexical rules against constructional analyses, cf. Müller and Wechsler 2014). Another position gives up the distinction between morphology and syntax (cf. Harley, this volume).

Can morphology for instance be taken to be word syntax? This question requires careful investigation as well, and sometimes, we find surprising evidence. Consider the relationship between syntactic combinations and morphological composition. If morphological composition crucially differs from syntactic modes of combination, the former should not be able to satisfy requirements imposed by the latter. But this does not seen to be correct. It is well known that morphological operations – such as composition and derivation – affect the valency of lexemes, but one sometimes even finds that modification is mirrored in morphology. As an illustration consider mass terms in German that may only appear together with an indefinite determiner if they are internally modified, as illustrated with *Stahl ('steel')* in (2).

(2) a. *Dies ist ein Stahl *(von besonderer Güte).* [German]
this is a steel of particular quality
'This is a high-quality steel.'

b. *Dies ist ein Gütestahl.*
this is a quality.steel
'This is a high-quality steel.'

The combination with an indefinite determiner is ungrammatical without internal modification in (2a), and similarly in (2b). But in (2b), the modifier is realized as part of a compound. If (morphological) composition and (syntactic) modification are aspects of modification within sentence grammar, the observation in (2) would not be surprising. If morphological operations are separated from syntactic operations, the observation is in need of an explanation.

The analysis of polysynthetic languages forms another challenge for the distinction of syntactic and sub-syntactic rule systems. With regard to polysynthetic languages, some researchers argue to give up a distinction between morphology and syntax (cf. Evans and Levinson 2009: 432). Eventually, the analysis of polysynthetic languages will form a touchstone for the relation between syntax and morphology, and will thus allow to answer the question whether syntactic rules are rules *sui generis* when compared to super-syntactic operations, or perhaps also when compared to sub-syntactic structure building.

With these provisos given, one could still say that the vast majority of syntacticians agree that the sentence is the unit within which syntactic relations must be established. By the same line of reasoning, syntacticians assume that syntactic relations are not employed to describe relations between sentences. The clear distinction between rule systems affecting the sentence and rule systems affecting super-sentential units gives the sentence a psychological reality, as well as a formal definition.

4. There are (no) universals

The concept of universal grammar, and with it, the concept of a syntactic universal has always been controversial. Van Riemsdijk was well aware of this. He thus simply states that "universals are there to be found". He goes on and says: "we all think we must find them". Nowadays, this view is contested from various points of view. Evans and Levinson (2009) argue against it from the perspective of linguistic typology. Construction Grammar (cf. Fried, this volume) rejects the idea of a universal from the perspective of syntax being derived in a bottom-up fashion from individual instances.

Let us restrict ourselves to the term *universal* (we will come back to the term *universal grammar* below), and let us further restrict ourselves by explicitly excluding the Greenbergian concept of a universal from further discussion. One reason for excluding this concept is that it is not the entity that most syntacticians have in mind when using the term *universal.* Another reason is that the Greenbergian concept is controversial in itself. As an illustration, consider Dryer's (1988) refutation of the conditional universal relating verb object and adjective noun orders. Even under this restriction, it is amazing to observe the sheer magnitude of misconceptions that the term *universal* invites. Chomsky (1965: 27–30) initiated the debate. It is thus instructive to look at Chomsky's introduction of the terms of *substantive* and *formal* universals. The former are characterized as follows: "A theory of substantive universals claims that items of a particular kind in any language must be drawn from a fixed class of items." (Chomsky 1965: 28) *Formal universals* receive the following introduction: "The property of having a grammar meeting a certain abstract condition might be called a *formal* linguistic universal, if shown to be a general property of natural languages. Recent attempts to specify the abstract conditions that a generative grammar must meet have produced a variety of proposals concerning formal universals (…) For example, consider the proposal that the syntactic component of a grammar must contain transformational rules (…) mapping semantically interpreted deep structures into phonetically interpreted surface structures, or the proposal that the phonological component of a grammar consists of a sequence of rules, a subset of which may apply cyclically to successively more dominant constituents of the surface structure (a transformational cycle …)" (Chomsky 1965: 29).

Criticism has focussed much more on substantive than on formal universals. Within the generative syntactic tradition, criticism has also been encouraged by undertaking research into the identification of universals only sparsely. The most advanced attempt to provide such universals, within the Theory of Principles and Parameters (Chomsky and Lasnik 1993), has failed by general consensus within and outside of generative linguistics. With regard to formal universals, there has been an extended debate between 1979 and 1994 (approximately) on whether transformational rules are formal universals or not for the reason that their very existence has been called into question (cf. Gazdar 1981; Gazdar et al. 1985). But this debate has not broadened our understanding towards the concept of formal universals. Evans and Levinson (2009: 430–431) have a clear idea what substantive universals should be, but are much less clear in their characterization of formal universals. We would doubt that *subjacency* would actually be considered a formal universal (cf. Evans and Levinson 2009: 436–437).

But discussions of the term *substantive* universal suffer from problems as well. Evans and Levinson (2009: 432) make the following claim with regard to the existence of apparently substantive universals despite their superficial absence in individual languages: "The differences (…) are somehow superficial (…) This (…) is wrong, in the straightforward sense that the experts (…) do not agree that it is true." This conclusion seems to suggest that an assumption is proven to be wrong because not every expert agrees on its truth. There might be something that escapes us here, but major scientific breakthroughs have quite often been accompanied by denials of experts. So it seems that the existence of universal categories that are not attested in every language is controversial, and not that their existence has been falsified. But controversy can lead to research results, even if these results falsify the initial assumptions of the researcher. Consider the discussion around the claim that well-established syntactic categories (such as noun, verb, adjective, or preposition) form part of the inventory of every language. Pinker and Bloom (1990) claim – perhaps somewhat prematurely – that all languages employ the aforementioned categories. Evans and Levinson (2009: 434) adduce arguments to show that adjectives and adverbs may not exist in all languages and that certain languages may even relinquish the distinction between noun and verb. (Northern) Straits Salish is usually cited as a language that does not make use of a noun/verb distinction. The current discussion, however, as also presented in Czaykowska-Higgins and Leonard (this volume), suggests that the distinction between verbs and nouns is present in Northern Straits Salish. Here, Evans and Levinson (2009) apparently underestimate the insights that syntacticians can gain from pursuing such assumptions. We argue that it might be premature to assume the universality of lexical categories that we have taken over from Latin and Greek grammarians. But the true nature of lexical categories can only be revealed once we have at least shown negatively that we cannot work with these purported categories. In this respect, a claim about the universality of a lexical category, while proven wrong in further research, opens a venue to refine our understanding of the concept of a lexical category in itself. But such claims are always couched in linguistic (syntactic) theories. A modest syntactic theory may at least offer a means to adduce evidence that an entity considered to be a prerequisite does not exist, with the usual repercussions for the theory.

More concrete entities usually abound in the controversies about syntactic universals. More abstract categories or rules are not typically the subject of such debates, and with it the existence of more abstract (possibly formal) universals is not often discussed.

We would like to illustrate this point with three examples: the *exhaustive constant partial order* (ECPO) property of ID/LP grammars in GPSG as an example of a universal that is directly derived from the formal properties of the grammar, the presumed universality of endocentricity (a.k.a. *Merge* in Minimalism), and the terminological non-universality of relative clauses.

The ECPO property of ID/LP grammars states that constraints on ordering must be context-insensitive insofar as an ordering must neither depend on the mother under which the ordering takes place, nor on the head of a phrase. This property has been introduced as a general property of grammars that separate dominance and linear precedence in GPSG (Gazdar et al. 1985). It should be noted here that other grammar models that assume this distinction do not take over the ECPO, as e.g. HPSG (Pollard and Sag 1994). The ECPO predicts that languages that require contextual ordering as mentioned above do not exist. The ECPO is thus a strong candidate for a formal universal. Gazdar et al. (1985: 49) carefully note that imposing the ECPO restricts the possible languages analysed by a GPSG severely, and hence that they would even be surprised "if ECPO turned out to be a linguistic universal". Nevertheless, Gazdar et al. (1985: 49) are "committed to the rather strong claim that it turns out to be universal".

In discussing the ECPO from hindsight, it is not really important that it became clear rather soon that it could not be a universal. With regard to this point (but not actually addressing the ECPO), Haider (1993) noted that unmarked orders between German complements depend on the verbal head of which they are complements. Hence, it had to be admitted that German violates the ECPO (with regard to the ordering constraints in German, (cf. Frey, this volume)). What is important is that the ECPO is even more abstract than a formal universal in that it provides a property that is directly derived from the formal apparatus of GPSG. ID/LP grammars of the form presented in GPSG must obey the ECPO. It seems to us that uncovering potential formal universals like the ECPO is more rewarding than collecting indicators that a particular syntactic category does not occur in a language – even if the potential formal universals are refuted eventually.

Let us now turn to the treatment of complementation, which perhaps is sometimes considered an operation so ubiquitous that its character is not even mentioned. We will illustrate the problem with the treatment of complementation in HPSG, but similar considerations apply to the operation *Merge* in syntactic Minimalism. HPSG (Pollard and Sag 1994; cf. the introduction by S. Müller, this volume) assumes that Immediate Dominance Schemata form part of Universal Grammar. One such schema is the head-complement-schema, which combines a head with one or more complements, and which is a subtype of endocentric phrases. They illustrate their analysis mostly with English (and thus invite criticism by linguistic typologists), but the very point in question can already be made clear by adding another related language (German) to the picture. For English, Pollard and Sag (1994) introduce Schemata 1 and 2 as instances of the head-complement-schema. They are instances of the head-complement-schema for English (the first combining sole arguments with phrasal projections, the second combining all arguments save one with lexical entities), and as such could not be used to analyse German, where it seems much more plausible to assume that complementation is instantiated by a single schema, which yields uniformly binary branching structures. Schema 1 and Schema 2 as well as the purported schema for German are instances of complementation, but complementation is a universal mode of combination (cf. below for a qualification), and as such requires a formal representation within the model.

It turns out that a schema more general than Schema 1 and Schema 2 in English, as well as more general than the schema employed for German cannot be easily defined. Still, the combination of a head with its argument(s) seems to be a plausible candidate for a universal rule, which may even apply to free *word* order languages (Evans and Levinson 2009: 441), i.e. languages that are not apparently confined by phrasal boundaries. Latin is a familiar instance of a free word order language, as opposed to languages employing free order of phrases. Evans and Levinson (2009: 441) illustrate for Latin that tree-like structures may not be appropriate to describe the relations between the verb and its subject, or between an adnominal modifier and the head noun of the subject, as illustrated in (3).

(3) *ultima* *Cumaei* *venit* *iam* *carminis* *aetas* [Classical Latin]
last.NOM Cumae.GEN come.3SG.PST now song.GEN age.NOM
'The last age of the Cumaen song has now arrived.'
Evans and Levinson (2009: 441)

We can observe that the adjective *ultima* is severed from the noun *aetas,* and the relationship between this subject (last age) and the verb *venit* is interrupted by an adverbial and the postnominal genitive *carminis Cumaei.* An analysis in terms of non-branching trees is presumably not easily provided for (3). What we can say, however, is that endocentricity plays a crucial role in this example, just as it does in structures that can be described more easily in tree structures: *aetas* is the head of the subject, and *ultima* is its adjectival modifier, and the featural make-up (nominative) must be related to the head, and not to the postnominal complement of the head. One can say that the discontinuity of *ultima* and *aetas* becomes a discontinuity only because they are conceived as a unit at some level of representation, that they together fulfil the subject argument slot of the verb, and as such that they together are subject to complementation.

While there may not be evidence for continuous phrases, there is clearly evidence that features target the 'right' elements, which must be achieved somehow, and is usually achieved by invoking endocentricity.

So while Pollard and Sag's Immediate Dominance Schemata translate into more usual phrase structures for German and English, this does not have to be the case, and structures akin to Dependency Grammar (cf. Osborne, this volume) may be the result. Still, we would like to maintain for Latin that the head-complement-schema is at work, and more generally that either the schema or the concept of endocentricity count as a universal. The universality of complementation is not entirely undisputed. Koenig and Michelson (2012) discuss Oneida and suggests that the head-complement-schema is not employed in this language. Even if this conclusion turns out to be correct, we would still require a formal concept of complementation to begin with.

Van Riemsdijk (1984: 2) also takes structure dependence to be an uncontroversial tenet of syntactic theory, but ignores the fact that structure dependency invites the question which kind of structure is required. It might well be that not all languages of the world can be analysed by employing tree-like structures – in fact, it strikes us that tree-like structures are more often used as a *lingua franca* of dialects of syntactic theories than as basic building blocks of the theory, consider Categorial Grammar (Baldridge and Hoyt, this volume) and Minimalism (Richards, this volume) in this respect – but it still seems plausible to assume that syntax adduces structure, be it for the simple reason that semantic interpretation works more nicely, if structure is adduced. The question whether tree-like structures or dependency structures (or functional structures, as employed in LFG, cf. Butt and King, this volume) or something entirely different will be appropriate can only be determined by making strong claims that stand the test against the diversity of natural languages. Linguists criticising syntactic universals often adhere to diversity as a means in itself, but it strikes us that only the interplay between claims embedded in syntactic theories and the diversity of natural languages may eventually allow linguistics to become a mature science. With regard to the complementation schema discussed above, we would like to assume that language specific complementation schemata are formally represented as instances of a more abstract, and possibly universal complementation schema, which forms an instance of endocentricity (with a modification schema as another instance of endocentricity, and further instances as well). Couched within the respective theory, the relation between the universal and the language-specific schemata should be represented as simply as possible (if it turns out that the appropriate definition may only refer to dependencies, tree-like structures employed in German or English may be viewed as epiphenomena). Ideally, language-specific schemata should be represented as more specific instances of universal schemata; the specific schemata are still abstract (for instance, they do not make reference to particular categories), and yet they are much more concrete than their universal super-types.

Imposing a concept like complementation requires its formal representation within syntactic theory. Hence, it becomes a prerequisite for determining the adequate modelling in the theory, and a touchstone for the theory itself. The quest for formal universals has thus an immediate bearing on determining the competition of syntactic theories, and clearly cannot be established outside the realm of a theory (which may lead to the confusion that is e.g. expressed in Evans and Levinson (2009: 436–437)).

With this background, let us enter unto a discussion of what we see as misunderstood universal categorizations. We assume that most (if not all) linguists would agree that a term like *relative clause* is much less a universal category than a pure means of description. It is less clear whether a relative clause is an instance of a more general operation, where a phrasal modifier is related to a modified element through a marker (the marker itself may be present or not, and may be more or less abstract). Gil (2001: 107–108) tries to show that clausal association to nominals in Hokkien Chinese, as illustrated in (4), should not be confused with the concept of a relative clause in English or German.

(4) $a^{44(>44)}$*-beŋ*^{24} *bue*^{53} $e^{24>22}$ p^{h}*eŋ*$^{24>22}$*-ko*^{53} [Hokkien Chinese]
Ah Beng buy ASSOC apple
'apples that Ah Beng bought'
(Gil 2001: 107)

Because the attributive marker e^{24} (the superscript indicates a tone; x > y indicates tonal sandhi) is not only used in Hokkien to establish a relationship between a clause and a nominal, but is also required to establish relations between adjectives and nouns, PPs and nouns, and further adnominal elements and nouns, Gil (2001: 108) concludes that the concept *relative clause* should not be used in Hokkien grammar. While this may be correct, it also seems trivial. However, it seems plausible to assume that the attributive construction in Hokkien and relative clauses in other languages share a common core in that a nominal element is formally linked to another phrase, and establishes a restrictive interpretation through the combination. A relative marker (not to be confused with the relative pronoun, and hence possibly without phonetic signature) in English or German establishes what is established by e^{24} in Hokkien. If we abstract over this particular property and indicate that we are not calling a *relative clause* a universal, we might be able to identify a possibly universal mode of combination (cf. for instance, Kayne 1994 and subsequent work).

With regard to the question raised in this section, and the current state of affairs regarding its answer, it seems to us that syntactic research should focus on identifying or rejecting more abstract universals as part of syntactic theories (as e.g. complementation). In addition, it seems that at least some rather basic universals (such as employing noun and verb as categories) have survived recent iconoclastic attempts to demolish them (once again, the reader is referred to the language sketch of Northern Straits Salish in Czaykowska-Higgins and Leonard, this volume). So, the nature of linguistic universals is controversial, but it is a fruitful controversy.

5. What is the object of study?

After Saussure's introduction of the distinction between *langue, parole* and *faculté de langage*, every syntactic theory must position itself with regard to its actual object of study. Saussure made it clear that the object of study is mesmerizingly difficult: "Quel est l'objet à la fois intégral et concret de la linguistique? La question est particulièrement difficile" (Engler 1968: 123). Van Riemsdijk (1984: 1) states that "we regard the object which we study as a real object, a mental organ as Chomsky has put it. From this it also follows that what we study is the grammar, not the language." Van Riemsdijk concludes that language acquisition is the central problem of syntactic theory. This position has been attacked from various perspectives – not the least one being that there seems to a conflation of a variety of concepts. For instance, there can be real objects without being related to a mental organ. In their introduction to one of the strictest attempts to provide a formal analysis of natural language, Gazdar et al. (1985: 5) state that "[o]ur linguistic theory is not a theory of how a child abstracts from the surrounding hubbub of linguistic and non-linguistic noises enough evidence to gain a mental grasp of a natural language." Other syntacticians attack the idea that grammar comes first and that language is derived from grammar. At least some versions of Construction Grammar (cf. Fried, this volume) assume that the grammar is induced from language data. It seems uncontroversial, however, that language in general is a bio-cultural hybrid, partly the product of biological evolution, but also partly the product of our own making, but this characterization applies to human beings in general, and may thus not be a specific property of language, or a property only in the slightly circular sense that it is human language we are dealing with.

The objects of syntactic study have been delimited by means of various distinctions that prove to be problematic in themselves. There is the celebrated distinction between competence and performance, as introduced in Chomsky (1965), and later supplanted by a distinction between *internal* and *external* language in Chomsky (1986). Here, van Riemsdisk (1984: 3) remarks that "everyone lives by it". We are not so sure that this is actually correct. The latter distinction has been utilized to separate theories into those that address internal and those that address external language. But even if we followed this direction and assumed that Gazdar et al. (1985) investigated external language, while Chomsky (1986) was concerned with internal language, we cannot be sure that the separation actually yields different objects, as it is purely noumenal. Drawing such an arbitrary distinction will lead to confusion at best, and will weaken the field as a whole at worst. In any case, there are many syntactic models that are agnostic to the distinction, as well as to the distinction between competence and performance.

Similarly, the object under syntactic study was delimited by the distinction between core and periphery within the Theory of Principles and Parameters. If one goes through the discussions of the past 20 years, however, one easily detects that today's periphery might become tomorrow's core and vice versa. Müller (2013) discusses *Exceptional Case Marking* (ECM, more familiar in traditional grammar under the rubric 'accusative-cum-infinitive construction') as an illustration for this tendency: Chomsky (1981: 70) assigned ECM to the periphery, but 15 years later, ECM became a building block of case assignment in specifier-head-configurations.

The morale to be drawn here is threefold. Firstly, it seems to us that the distinctions (competence/performance, core/periphery, etc.) have been useful in the past since it allowed syntactic research to start somewhere without being constantly endangered by requests to also account for other, presumably related phenomena. In this sense, early syntactic theories had to be reductionist, and introduced distinctions to this end. Syntax in its current guise should give up reductionism.

Secondly, it seems that these distinctions have failed to provide an instrument to gauge whether syntactic models make headway or not. If we take a fixed concept of a core that has to be described or explained by syntactic theory, then we can assume that a model should be abandoned (or at least very critically scrutinized) that does not provide analyses for phenomena that unequivocally belong to a "core". Progress could be characterized by accounting for an agreed-upon set of phenomena, and could be gauged by consecutively extending the core that is covered in this way, until it becomes clear that further extensions would lead to analyses of phenomena that form part of the periphery because they emerge as cultural artefacts that have no biological basis. It would also allow syntactic analysis to establish a canon of analysed phenomena (where a canon is understood in the sense of engineering and natural science, i.e. as foundational part that has already been successfully covered), and to proceed from this canon to areas of syntactic research that still await detailed scrutiny. Yet, syntactic theories often have not developed in this way. As a striking illustration consider the treatment of negative placement in inverted English sentences.

(5) a. *Can John not leave?*
    b. *Will John not leave?*

Almost 25 years after their celebrated analysis in *Syntactic Structures* (Chomsky 1957), Lasnik (2000: 151) admits that "[t]here are about a dozen really fancy ways in the literature to keep [the sentences in (5)] from violating the [Head Movement Constraint].

To the best of my knowledge, not one of them really works." One does not have to understand the workings of the *Head Movement Constraint* to see that any syntactic analysis blocking the derivation of the examples in (5) may be in need of refurbishment. While such renovations took place, they were not initiated by indications of prior failure and did not lead to an overall improvement.

What are the conclusions here? It sounds awkward to assume that negative placement in English belongs to the periphery, and even absurd to delegate it to issues of performance. But it might very well be that syntactic theories should not generalize from rather singular language-specific properties to propose universal constraints. Perhaps the general ignorance towards this construction has to do with the conclusion that the construction is in fact peculiar – but a distinction between competence and performance, or core and periphery adds little to this insight.

Thirdly, and finally, it should be noted that the distinction between competence and performance also provides the ground for the distinction between grammaticality and acceptability (the former only affected by competence, the latter affected by factors of performance as well). This is important insofar as psycholinguistic experimentation, which seems to be the most plausible methodology to arrive at conclusions about the biological side of syntax, can only access acceptability, i.e. is always "blemished" by performance (cf. Schütze 1996 and Felser, this volume).

In light of the problems mentioned, it seems wise to consider the question of the object under study with a bit of agnosticism. Currently, it is a majority view that the objects of study are real objects (but one also finds the position that language is principally a cultural creation), but it does not follow that all syntacticians agree in investigating a mental organ, and moreover that it remains unclear how such an organ could be assessed in the first place.

6. Generative grammar

With the term *generative grammar,* we seem to have arrived at a completely uncontroversial spot, given the definition provided by van Riemsdijk (1984: 2): "anyone is a generative grammarian (…) who holds that the grammar must be a finite rule system which explicitly characterizes an infinite set of sentences." Even linguists who would not characterize themselves as generative grammarians agree to versions of this statement, as e.g. Martin Haspelmath (2010: 666): "To describe a language, one needs categories, because it is not possible to list all the acceptable sentences of a language."

7. There is more than one way to do it (presumably)

The final quote from Henk van Riemsdijk's list serves to illustrate that syntactic research has indeed progressed considerably in the past 30 years: "Modern linguistic research is characterized by a comparative freedom of strict methodological imperatives. In this sense, it is clearly different from corpus linguistics, (…) and the statistical straight-jacket of the social sciences. (…) most grammarians will tend to have most faith in serious introspection." (van Riemsdijk 1984: 3) This statement is interesting insofar as linguistics (syntax in particular) strives to become acknowledged not as part of the humanities, but as part of the natural sciences. Whatever one might say about this, it should be clear that the methodological constraints within the natural sciences might be even more rigid than the ones of the social sciences (with the usual proviso that we should not forget the lesson learned by Paul Feyerabend's *Against Method).* But the quote reflects the time when syntax had to work with the resources that were available. Without proper computing machinery, the development of corpora was problematic, syntactic annotation was practically unknown, and hence data analysis was much less a question of methodological orthodoxy than of impossibility. All this has changed. In addition, we have a much better understanding of the limits of introspection, and may also use controlled experiments to arrive at conclusions about data. So, from hindsight, it appears that 30 years ago, syntactic research was free from one particular methodological imperative for the simple reason that the methodology was still in its infancy. With the advent of advanced computing devices and a deeper understanding of controlled experimentation, the current syntactic researcher has not only much more freedom to decide whether data should be derived from introspection, from corpus search, or from experimentation. We also understand now that data sometimes cannot be assessed through introspection, just as scarcely occurring data cannot easily be assessed through corpus-based methodologies (for a case study, cf. Meurers and Müller 2009). It is thus handy that more than one method is at our disposal.

While methods flourish, other – more practical, as well as socio-economical – constraints affect syntactic research (as well as linguistics in general). Linguistics remains a rather small field, the subject under study, however, provides an abundance of data that in many cases resist automated analysis and thus requires human analysis (in this respect, we fully agree with Evans and Levinson 2009). It would be ideal if all languages could receive the same degree of attention, but syntactic research is not often recognized as a goal in itself.

Finally, there is not only more than one way to do it method-wise, but also with regard to the different frameworks that the syntactician may employ. More often, syntacticians do not choose from these frameworks because they belong to schools, but because they see that for the questions at hand, different frameworks may allow different entry points, which eventually may lead to similar conclusions, or even similar ways of analysing syntactic data. As an illustration, consider the treatment of long distance dependencies. When Gazdar (1981) proposed that certain long distance dependencies could be handled without transformations but by employing complex (SLASH) categories, Chomsky retorted that GPSG (under which name the new transformationless framework became known) was just a notational variant of the current version of transformational grammar. While it seems illogical to call something a "notational variant" that employs less machinery than the theory of which it is considered a variant, the lesson learned was that "notational variants" are to be dodged, if only because they are superfluous. If one compares the current-day treatment of long distance dependencies in certain versions of Minimalism (cf. Richards, this volume) with the treatment of long distance dependencies in HPSG (S. Müller, this volume, HPSG in this sense is an offspring of GPSG), one is tempted to assume that the treatment must be very different for the very reason that the first framework calls itself derivational, while the second is termed representational. Closer scrutiny reveals, however, that the strictly local representational treatment (in terms of local trees) is mirrored in strictly local versions of derivational Minimalism. It does not matter whether an analysis is based on representations or derivations, if both are strictly local. Just as a syntactician cannot look "into" a local representation, he or she cannot look into the history of a local derivation. In this light, the so-called *uniform-path* analyses in derivational Minimalism cannot be distinguished from SLASH-based analyses in representational HPSG (cf. Alexiadou, Kiss, and Müller 2012: 30). What is more, a replacement of *uniform-path* analyses in favour of *punctuated-path* analyses, which would not be "notational variants" of SLASH projection, cannot be justified by observable consequences (i.e. empirical differences) (again, cf. Alexiadou, Kiss, and Müller 2012: 30–31).

The new lesson to be learned is that it may perhaps be not only be useful to attack problems from different vantage points, but also to observe what the other camp is doing. If the results gained are similar, they are so not because they are "notational variants", but perhaps because they represent the limit of current expertise in the worst case, and the true nature of the object under investigation in the best.

1. Acknowledgements

This article has benefited from comments by Stefan Müller, for which we are grateful.

8. References (selected)

Alexiadou, Artemis, Tibor Kiss, and Gereon Müller
2012 Local modelling of non-local dependencies in syntax: An introduction. In: Artemis Alexiadou, Tibor Kiss and Gereon Müller (eds.), *Local Modelling of Non-local Dependencies in Syntax*, 1–48. Berlin/Boston: Walter de Gruyter.

Chomsky, Noam
1965 *Aspects of the Theory of Syntax.* Cambridge/London: The MIT Press.

Chomsky, Noam
1986 *Knowledge of Language. Its Nature, Origin, and Use.* New York: Praeger.

Engler, Rudolf (ed.)
1968 *Ferdinand de Saussure, Cours de Linguistique Generale.* (Édition critique par Rudolf Engler, tome 1.) Wiesbaden: Harrasowitz.

Evans, Nicolas, and Stephen C. Levinson
2009 The myth of language universals: Language diversity and its importance for cognitive science. *Behavioral and Brain Sciences* 32: 429–492.

Gazdar, Gerald, Ewan Klein, Geoffrey K. Pullum, and Ivan A. Sag
1985 *Generalized Phrase Structure Grammar.* London: Blackwell.

Gil, David
2001 Escaping Eurocentrism: fieldwork as a process of unlearning. In: Paul Newman and Martha Ratliff (eds.), *Linguistic Fieldwork.* Cambridge: Cambridge University Press, 102–132.

Harris, Randy Allan
1993 *The Linguistics Wars.* Oxford: Oxford University Press.

Haspelmath, Martin
2010 Comparative concepts and descriptive categories in crosslinguistic studies. *Language* 86: 663–687.

Koenig, Jean-Pierre, and Karin Michelson
2012 The (non)universality of syntactic selection and functional application. In: Christopher Piñon (ed.), *Empirical Issues in Syntax and Semantics* 9: 185–205. [http://www.cssp.cnrs.fr/eiss9/]
Müller, Stefan, and Stephen Wechsler
2014 Lexical approaches to argument structure. To appear in *Theoretical Linguistics 40.*
Pollard, Carl, and Ivan A. Sag
1994 *Head-driven Phrase Structure Grammar.* Chicago: University of Chicago Press.
Riemsdijk, Henk van
1984 Introductory remarks. In: Wim de Geest and Yvan Putseys (eds.), *Sentential Complementation*, 1–9. Dordrecht: Foris Publications.
Schütze, Carson
1996 *The Empirical Base of Linguistics: Grammaticality Judgments and Linguistic Methodology.* University of Chicago Press.

Tibor Kiss, Bochum (Germany)
Artemis Alexiadou, Stuttgart (Germany)

2. Syntactic Constructions

Abstract

The term construction *is widely used descriptively in discussing grammar, and is still used informally in most theoretical work for characteristic formal patterns of syntactic categories or features, usually associated with a meaning and/or function. Modern linguistic theories employ a range of formal devices to produce or characterize surface constructions; they may be rules, or schemata, or constraints. It is usually assumed that competence in a language consists largely of these formal devices together with a lexicon; the constructions themselves are epiphenomenal. As such, constructions are an abstraction over the data which linguistic theory must analyze; insight in syntax is achieved through discovering generalizations across constructions.*

1. Introduction

The term *construction* is ubiquitous in contemporary syntactic literature, being used informally to refer to linguistic expressions in a variety of ways. The term also has a technical sense in the theory of Construction Grammar, as detailed in Chapter 28.

The term construction is widely used to characterize certain kinds of form–meaning pairings, as when we refer to "possessive constructions" or "the verb–particle construction" to refer to examples like those below.

(1) Three examples of possessive constructions
  a. *Seymour's new friend*
  b. *a new friend of Seymour's*
  c. *Seymour has a new friend*

(2) Three examples of the verb-particle construction
  a. *We picked up a lamp at the flea market.*
  b. *We picked a lamp up at the flea market.*
  c. *What did you pick up at the flea market?*

In general, linguists would not refer to the three examples in (1) as comprising a single possessive construction, because they are too different in their syntax; in (1a) the possessor precedes the possessed noun, in (1b) the possessor follows the possessed noun, and in (1c) the possessor is expressed as a distinct argument outside the possessed noun phrase. These differences represent three different ways of expressing the concept of possession, in English.

In (2), on the other hand, many linguists would be inclined to refer to all three sentences as manifesting a single verb-particle construction, on the basis of the perceived similarity of the syntax of the three cases. There is a very large class of verb–particle pairings which allow the ordering alternation shown in (2a)–(2b), where the order reflects no apparent difference in meaning (such as *drop off, smash up, fix up, turn on, leave out*). In such cases, the object can systematically be the focus of a question, as in (2c); so the general consensus would be that these three sentences illustrate the verb-particle construction.

On this view, (1) illustrates three different form–meaning pairings, even though one component of the meaning is shared across all three, while (2) illustrates one form–meaning pairing, even though independent factors distort the shared form (and the correct characterization of the meaning component may be elusive).

At the same time, (2c) illustrates a *wh*-question construction, in addition to the verb-particle construction. Since the properties of the *wh*-question construction (e.g. *wh*-expression in clause-initial position, auxiliary in second position) are independent of the verb-particle construction (e.g. the predicate includes a particle like *up, down, out*, etc.), there is no motivation for formulating a distinct "verb-particle *wh*-question construction."

1.1. Toward a definition

The term construction is not a technical term (outside of Construction Grammar), and consequently it is difficult to define. As an approximation, it can be defined as follows.

(3) A construction is a characteristic formal pattern of syntactic categories or features, usually associated with some meaning and/or discourse function.

The use of the word *pattern* here is an attempt to be as theory-neutral as possible; a pattern might be a structure, or a template, or the output of a rule. The notion *formal* is meant to include aspects of form which are of significance to grammar. In some theories word order is a primitive of grammar, while in other theories word order is derived from structure, such that structure, but not linear order, would count as a formal property (see Chapters 17 and 40 on Word Order).

The notion *syntactic categories* is intended to include major parts of speech but also minor or functional categories such as the class of English verb-particles, or the class of determiners. The notion *syntactic features* in the definition is meant to include morpho-syntactic features such as the past participle or dative case but also semantico-syntactic features such as negation or "wh" (borne by interrogative expression like *what* and *who*). Together *syntactic categories or features* includes function words such as infinitival *to* and bound formatives such as possessive *'s*, on any analysis.

The definition in (3) is meant to exclude phonology and surface exponence, which do not characterize constructions as the term is ordinarily used in mainstream syntax. For example, we would not expect to find a construction which necessarily involved words beginning with the phoneme /w/, even if we speak loosely of various kinds of *wh*-constructions. Similarly, if there is more than one formal category in English which is spelled out by the suffix *-ing*, then we expect a construction to be identified by the underlying features which are being spelled out (e.g. progressive, or gerund), not by the phonological form of the exponent doing the spelling out. Though we might descriptively call something an Acc-*ing* construction, for example, in a more careful statement of its characteristics, we would distinguish the feature or category that *-ing* manifests.

Thus, the definition offered above is intended to stress syntactic form, not phonological form. This is in accord with the usual use of the word construction in syntax. An idiom like *kick the bucket* meaning 'die' requires the lexical items *kick* and *bucket*, and hence makes direct reference to exponents with phonological content (see Chapter 23 on Idioms). As such, ordinary usage would not make reference to a *kick the bucket* construction (Construction Grammar, however, is different here: idioms are considered to be constructions).

In this way, more or less functional elements like the interrogative pronoun *what* and the light verb *do* are treated together with syntax as opposed to lexical items like *kick* and *bucket*. Thus is it not controversial to speak of a construction of the form *What's X doing Y?* meaning roughly 'Why is X Y?,' where X is a subject and Y is a predicate. For example: *What's the newspaper doing in the bushes?* or *What are you doing leaving without your shoes?* This construction requires *what* and *do* as well as the progressive with an appropriate form of *be*.

The definition offered in (3) also suggests that a construction is usually associated with some meaning and/or discourse function. The importance of meaning is somewhat loosely applied in practice. Thus, it is not usually considered necessary to have a rigorous statement of the meaning of a possessive construction like the one in (1a) in order to call it a construction, if it has a clearly defined syntactic form. But if there are two disjoint meanings involved, then it is common to think of them as involving two distinct constructions. For example, in English, the auxiliary inverts with the subject when a *wh*-item is fronted, but also when a negative element is fronted, as in (4) (cf. Chapter 12, on V2).

(4) a. *Which of them would he recommend?*
 b. *None of them would he recommend.*

Even if the syntax of the inversion is identical in the two cases, it would be most natural here to speak of subject-auxiliary inversion constructions in the plural, rather than a single subject-auxiliary inversion construction which was indifferent to whether the initial element was a negative or an interrogative phrase–though practice varies somewhat here (and in Construction Grammar, there is no limit to how abstract a construction can be).

The notion of discourse function in (3) is intended broadly, to include various pragmatic inferences and affect. For example, the *What's X doing Y?* construction is only used when there is some sense that it is incongruous or inappropriate for X to be Y (as discussed by Kay and Fillmore 1999). Thus the question *Why are men rebelling?* can be asked in a range of contexts, but *What are men doing rebelling?* can only be asked if there is some salient sense (perhaps the speaker's opinion, but not necessarily) that it is inappropriate, incongruous, or outrageous for them to be doing so.

1.2. Applying the definition

Returning to the examples in (1)–(2), we can apply the definition offered in (3) to show that it is harmonious with the common intuition that (1) illustrates three different possessive constructions while (2) represents three different manifestations of a single construction.

According to (3), a class of phrases or sentences must share a characteristic formal pattern in order to belong to a single construction. The formal differences among the three examples in (1) are fairly clear; (1a) lacks *of* and the possessor precedes the possessum, while (1a) contains the function word *of*, and the possessor follows the possessum. Furthermore, in (1a), the possessum is understood as definite, while in (1b), the possessum is indefinite. The example in (1c) is predicative, and contains the verb *have*. So the fact that the three expressions describe the same semantic relation is not normally taken to imply the existence of a single possessive construction. Thus it seems that the definition appropriately picks out each of the three as a construction.

Turning to (2), we can first address the question of whether (2c) represents a different construction from the other two. Of course it does, as it involves *wh*-movement, but this is irrelevant to the verb–particle construction. The interrogative construction simply applies to a clause that has a verbal particle in the predicate, just as it does in an ordinary transitive clause.

The second question is whether there is motivation to treat examples like (2a) and (2b) as distinct constructions. This cannot be conclusively determined without formal analysis. By and large, the two are distinguished only by word order, not by meaning, nor by functional categories or features. There are some differences, for example (2b) allows the object to be pronominal (*We picked it up*), but (2a) does not (**We picked up it*). If such differences can be independently explained, then an analysis can be motivated in which there is a single construction with some flexibility of order, that is, a single 'characteristic formal pattern of syntactic categories or features' in which whatever determines the placement of the particle before or after the internal argument is not characteristic, or is not a syntactic feature. This is the usual consensus (see Ramchand and Svenonius 2002 for one such account), though alternative analyses exist in which the two represent distinct constructions (see Farrell 2005).

2. Examples of constructions

To further illustrate the notion of construction, several examples of constructions are listed in this section. No detailed characterization or analysis is attempted. The examples serve simply to give an impression of a small part of the range of syntactic constructions.

2.1. Argument structure, grammatical functions

A number of constructions involve valency, argument structure, and grammatical functions (see Chapter 8 on Grammatical Relations). For example, a passive construction involves the demotion of the external argument, compared to the active use of the same verb (see Chapter 22 on Voice). In English, the demoted external argument can be expressed in a *by*-phrase or left implicit, and the verb appears in a past participle form, with a form of the auxiliary *be*. The implicit argument can control a purpose clause, as illustrated in (5b), just as with the active construction in (5a). English also has a middle construction, in which the external argument cannot appear in a *by*-phrase, and is not syntactically active as diagosed by a purpose clause, as illustrated in (5c).

(5) a. *The owner sold the house (to pay off debts).*
  b. *The house was sold (by the owner) (to pay off debts).*
  c. *Houses sell easily (*by the owner) (*to pay off debts).*

In a conative construction, illustrated in (6b), the internal argument is oblique and is not as fully affected as in a regular transitive construction, compare (6a). In a benefactive construction, illustrated in (6c), an indirect object derives some benefit from the action, or comes into possession of the direct object (see Chapters 9 and 37 on Arguments and Adjuncts).

(6) a. *The baker cut the bread.*
  b. *The baker cut at the bread.*
  c. *The baker cut me a piece of bread.*

Resultative and depictive constructions involve secondary predicates, as illustrated in (7a) and (7b) respectively.

(7) a. *They drank the bar dry.*
  b. *They ate the bread dry.*

Control, raising, and so-called Exceptional Case Marking (ECM, or accusative-with-infinitive, or subject-to-object raising) constructions usually involve infinitive complements in which arguments are, descriptively speaking, shared across the two clauses (see Chapters 14 and 38 on Control).

(8) a. *Ian wants to stay at the house.* (control)
b. *Ian seemed to stay at the house.* (raising)
c. *We believed Ian to stay at the house.* (ECM)

English provides many more examples of constructions involving various configurations of arguments, and other languages provide yet more. In some cases, the availability of a construction may be tied to the availability of a lexical item; for example, it may be that if a language has an ECM construction if and only if it has a verb with the selectional properties exhibited by English *believe* in (8c). However, in other cases, the availability of a construction in a given language does not seem to be connected to lexical items. An example is the resultative construction illustrated in (7a), which many languages lack, despite having verbs and adjectives which are otherwise like the ones used in the English resultative construction (Snyder 2001).

2.2. Unbounded dependencies

There is a range of constructions which have been analyzed as involving displaced constituents, or filler-gap dependencies. These include (in the order in which they appear in [9]): *wh*-questions, embedded *wh*-questions, clefts, pseudoclefts, relative clauses, comparative constructions, and (contrastive) topicalization (for some discussion of some of these and related constructions, see Chapter 12 on V2, Chapter 13 on Discourse Configurationality, and especially Chapter 21 on Relative Clauses and Correlatives).

(9) a. *Which book did you read?*
b. *I asked which book you read.*
c. *It was this book that I read.*
d. *What I read was this book.*
e. *The book that I read was long.*
f. *She read a longer book than I read.*
g. This *book, I read.*

These constructions have in common that the dependency can cross finite clause boundaries.

(10) a. *Which book did your mother think you read?*
b. *I asked which book your mother thought you read.*
c. *It was this book that my mother thought I read.*
d. *What my mother thought I read was this book.*
e. *The book that my mother thought I read was long.*
f. *She read a longer book than my mother thought I read.*
g. This *book, my mother thought I read.*

In this respect they contrast with passive, as illustrated in (11a), and for example raising, as illustrated in (11b) (compare [12]).

(11) a. **The house was thought (by his mother) the owner sold.*
b. **Ian seemed stayed at the house.*

(12) a. *It was thought the owner sold the house.*
b. *It seemed Ian stayed at the house.*

In fact, the constructions in (9)–(10) can cross indefinitely many finite clause boundaries, and for this reason are known as unbounded dependencies.

(13) a. *Which book did you think your mother thought you read?*
b. *I asked which book you thought your mother thought you read.*
c. *It was this book that I thought my mother thought I read.*
d. *What I thought my mother thought I read was this book.*
e. *The book that I thought my mother thought I read was long.*
f. *She read a longer book than I thought my mother thought I read.*
g. This *book, I thought my mother thought I read.*

The availability and properties of unbounded dependency constructions can vary somewhat from one language to the next. For example, sometimes there is a resumptive pronoun in the gap position, and in other cases there is no displacement on the surface, with the filler element remaining *in situ*. Unlike the case with argument structure alternations, this kind of variation tends not to be dependent on lexical items, though it may be connected to the properties of functional elements such as *that* and *which*.

In fact, it has been proposed that properties of constructions are largely determined by the properties of their heads. This is explicit in the name of the theory Head-Driven Phrase Structure Grammar (see Chapter 27 on HPSG), but is also a common assumption in other theories (e.g. Borer 1984). For example, the properties of a relative clause could conceivably be entirely determined by the cluster of features contained on its (possibly abstract) head. The head would be a kind of C[omplementizer] taking a finite TP complement, attracting a suitable nominal element to its specifier, and projecting a category which could be used as a nominal modifier.

2.3. Complex constructions

In this regard, constructions like the *What's X doing Y?* construction mentioned above are complex, as they appear to involve an interdependency of several heads. Mainstream theory would probably treat a construction of this kind as a special kind of idiom.

Construction Grammar, in contrast, holds that there is no principled difference between a fully general construction and a highly idiomatic one, or even between a fully general abstract construction and a lexical item; each is a pairing of form with function, broadly construed.

3. Constructions and syntactic theory

Traditional descriptive grammars may characterize and exemplify a list of constructions in a given language. They may organize the constructions according to perceived similarities, and may attempt to state generalizations which transcend the individual constructions. This much is extremely useful in a reference grammar (see Chapter 59 on Reference Grammars).

Modern syntactic theory necessarily goes further, and is based on the assumption that higher-level generalizations are necessary in order to achieve what Chomsky (1964) called explanatory adequacy, a model of language which accounts for how individual languages are learnable by children.

Traditional grammar posited rules to characterize or generate constructions, such as passive and relative clauses. Generative grammar took this as a starting point and went on to abstract properties from classes of rules, such as elementary transformations and different kinds of formal conditions constraining them. Generative grammar in the 1970's explored the ways in which the properties interacted in rule systems, and sought to discover constraints on them.

For example, Emonds (1976) observed that transformational rules did not produce structures unlike those which had to be base-generated ("structure preservation"), suggesting that the full power of transformations was unneeded. Chomsky (1977) showed that the class of unbounded dependencies displayed highly uniform properties, suggesting that they were not produced by distinct rules.

Subsequent work has increasingly focused on higher-level generalizations over rule types, shedding much light on the nature of grammar.

Thus, generalizations about constructions involving valence and argument structure led to those being analyzed in Lexical-Functional Grammar as the output of lexical rules (see Chapter 25 on LFG), accounting, for example, for their structure-preserving properties and their relative sensitivity to lexically listed traits of individual verbs. Similarly, generalizations about the class of unbounded dependencies as a whole led to the development of Move-α in Government-Binding Theory (Chomsky 1981), and the SLASH feature as used in Head-Driven Phrase Structure Grammar (see Chapter 27 on HPSG).

The development of Principles and Parameters theory (Chomsky 1981) involved rethinking the nature of rules entirely; once deconstructed into a system of invariant universal principles interacting with parametric points of variation, there are no rules per se. This is expressed in the following quote from *Lectures on Government and Binding*: "The notions "passive," "relativization," etc., can be reconstructed as processes of a more general nature, with a functional role in grammar, but they are not "rules of grammar"" (Chomsky 1981: 7).

Since constructions were the output of rules in the traditional conception of grammar, the elimination of rules from the theory means that in a Principles and Parameters framework, constructions are epiphenomenal, as reflected in the following quote, also from Chomsky but a decade later: "A language is not, then, a system of rules, but a set of specifications for parameters in an invariant system of principles of Universal Grammar (UG); and traditional grammatical constructions are perhaps best regarded as taxonomic epiphenomena, collections of structures with properties resulting from the interaction of fixed principles with parameters set one or another way" (Chomsky 1991: 417).

Since that time, although the notion of parameter has been substantially rethought, mainstream syntactic theories continue to regard the notion of construction, like the notion of rule or transformation, as a descriptive stepping stone on the path to greater understanding rather than as an analytic result in its own right.

Work in Construction Grammar, too, recognizes that insight does not come from simply listing the individual surface constructions in a language, and therefore, like other theories, seeks generalizations over constructions; the difference between Construction Grammar and other theories mentioned here is that in Construction Grammar, the generalizations are themselves modelled as abstract constructions. Nor is this just a terminological distinction: the claim in Construction Grammar is that the generalizations have the same kinds of properties as the constructions themselves, at a suitable level of abstraction.

4. Conclusion

I have characterized a construction as a characteristic formal pattern of syntactic features, usually associated with some meaning or discourse function. The way constructions are characterized in descriptive work tends to combine morphological, syntactic, and semantic facts. Purely phonological facts, however, tend not to be significant for the characterization of constructions. The precision of the syntactic characterization is usually taken to be more important than the semantic description of the meaning of a construction (e.g. even if two possessive expressions had exactly the same meaning, substantially different syntaxes would usually lead to them being classified as distinct constructions).

Some such notion is descriptively indispensible in syntactic work. Descriptive grammars must contain detailed characterizations of surface properties of constructions, and all careful empirical work makes reference to numerous construction types, as will be seen in the other chapters in this work.

Linguistic theory advances through the careful examination of the properties of constructions. Ultimately, principles are sought which transcend the individual constructions themselves, and the construction itself can be taken to be a taxonomic artifact.

5. References (selected)

Borer, Hagit
1984 *Parametric Syntax*. Dordrecht: Foris.

Chomsky, Noam
1964 *Current Issues in Linguistic Theory*. The Hague: Mouton.

Chomsky, Noam
1977 On wh-movement. In: Peter Culicover, Thomas Wasow, and Adrian Akmajian, (eds.), *Formal Syntax*, 71–132. New York: Academic Press.

Chomsky, Noam
1981 *Lectures on Government and Binding*. Dordrecht: Foris.

Chomsky, Noam
1991 Some notes on economy of derivation and representation. In: Robert Freidin (ed.), *Principles and Parameters in Comparative Grammar*, 417–454. Cambridge, Massachusetts: MIT Press.

Emonds, Joseph E.
1976 *A Transformational Approach to English Syntax: Root, Structure-Preserving, and Local Transformations*. New York: Academic Press.
Farrell, Patrick
2005 English verb-preposition constructions: Constituency and order. *Language* 81 1: 96–137.
Kay, Paul, and Charles J. Fillmore
1999 Grammatical constructions and linguistic generalizations: The *What's X doing Y?* construction. *Language* 75 1: 1–33.
Ramchand, Gillian, and Peter Svenonius
2002 The lexical syntax and lexical semantics of the verb-particle construction. In: Line Mikkelsen and Christopher Potts (eds.), *Proceedings of WCCFL 21*, 387–400. Somerville, Massachusetts: Cascadilla Press.
Snyder, William
2001 On the nature of syntactic variation: Evidence from complex predicates and complex word-formation. *Language* 77: 324–342.

Peter Svenonius, Tromsø (Norway)

3. Syntax and its Interfaces: An Overview

Abstract

The notion that knowledge of language comprises separate modules or levels is central to linguistic research, though the precise subcomponents of grammar, their rules and primitives, the extent to which they overlap, and the nature of the architecture of which they are a part are still the subject of intense debate. Investigation into interface phenomena necessarily straddles the traditional boundaries of linguistic enquiry and thus provides an important perspective not only on specific empirical issues, but also on broader theoretical matters including the organization of the grammar itself. The focus of this chapter is the interaction of syntax with other modules of grammar which have been posited: the lexicon, morphology, phonology, semantics, and pragmatics. Each section explores a different syntactic interface through discussion of contemporary empirical and theoretical research undertaken in a variety of frameworks.

1. Introduction

The aim of work on syntax and its interfaces is to identify the basic properties which other modules share with syntax and thus the precise domain of syntax within the grammar. In this respect, there are three central questions to be answered: How is syntax distinct from other components of the grammar? To what extent do syntactic processes operate within the grammar? How is syntax related to other levels of linguistic representation? Addressing these issues has implications for fundamental aspects of the grammatical architecture. Any theoretical framework will ultimately be judged on the extent to which it is able to capture the relevant generalizations about syntax and its interfaces with regard to the autonomy of posited components, the input–output relations which exist between them, and language structure versus usage.

The issue of autonomy naturally precedes any discussion of the interfaces which link modules of the grammar. With respect to syntax, the question is to what extent its primitives and operations influence aspects of linguistic structure which might otherwise be treated as belonging to another component of the grammar, and vice versa. For instance, debate continues regarding whether morphology exists as an autonomous component of the grammar with its own combinatory principles. It has been argued that positing a separate part of the grammar to account for apparently morphological phenomena is unmotivated and unnecessary because the features of complex word formation are consistent with independent syntactic principles. Data which indicate that the relationship between morphology and syntax is not always isomorphic undermine the claim that morphology can be reduced entirely to syntax. Some approaches imply that syntax itself is not an independent component, raising the question of whether syntax represents an abstraction of the linguist or a natural object. For example, Head-Driven Phrase Structure Grammar (Pollard and Sag 1994) includes a single level of structure SYNTAX-SEMANTICS.

Any approach which posits autonomous components of the grammar must also define the input–output relations which connect them. Precisely how syntax interacts with each component in terms of whether the relationship is serial or parallel, unidirectional or bidirectional is still the subject of much debate. For instance, a strictly serialist conception of the interface between syntax and phonology, according to which the former serves as input to the latter, predicts the influence of syntax on phonology and excludes the possibility of interaction in the opposite direction. Data which appear to show that prosodic weight may influence syntax represent a challenge to such a unidirectional characterization of the syntax–phonology interface. The nature of the links between different components of the grammar continues to be the focus of research. Even the standard assumption that the lexicon serves as input to syntax has been challenged (Borer 2005).

Finally, there is the matter of how the architecture of the grammar reflects a structural as opposed to a usage-based approach to language, an issue perhaps most clearly illustrated by the interaction between syntax and pragmatics. For instance, Mandarin Chinese is claimed to be a language whose syntax is organized in terms of the distinction between topic (that which is being discussed) and comment (what is being said about the topic) rather than grammatical relations such as subject and object (Li and Thompson 1976). Accounts of such interaction in terms of the organization of the grammar will contribute to the wider debate on the relative merits of a structural versus a usage-based model of language.

Research into syntax and its interfaces thus has implications for the architecture of the grammar which are relevant across theoretical frameworks and sub-disciplines.

2. Syntax and the lexicon

2.1. Introduction

While it is often posited that the lexicon exists as a separate part of the grammar, this has not always been the case, nor is it true of all current theoretical frameworks. In those approaches which distinguish the lexicon from the syntactic component, the issue of where the boundary between the two lies has consequences for the interface between them, as well as the organization of the grammar as a whole.

In early generative work such as Chomsky (1957), lexical items and morphemes were those units which could be inserted at the terminal nodes of Deep Structure trees by phrase structure rules. Despite their unique status, these elements were not initially treated as members of a component distinct from syntax with its own rules and types of structure. The lexicon was identified as a part of the syntactic Base Component in Standard Theory (Chomsky 1965) and defined as an unordered list of entries containing information only about a lexical item's idiosyncratic features (cf. Bloomfield 1933). However, subsequent research has indicated that at least some word-formation processes may differ in key respects from those which form syntactic structure, prompting a reassessment of the contents of the lexicon and its nature. Today, the Lexicalist Hypothesis (Chomsky 1970) still lies at the heart of the debate on the relationship between lexical items and syntax (Section 2.2), as the different analyses of processes such as causative formation (Section 2.3), undertaken within a variety of theoretical frameworks, illustrate.

2.2. The Lexicalist Hypothesis

Chomsky (1970) identified regularities in the relation between a nominal and the verb from which it had been derived (1a), but noted that this nominalization process had idiosyncratic features such as restricted productivity (1b), which made it incompatible with syntactic rules characterized as applying without exception.

(1) a. *John* ***criticized*** *the book.* V
John's ***criticism*** *of the book* N

b. *John* ***amused*** *(interested) the children with his stories.* V
John's* ***amusement* *(interest) of the children with his stories* N
(Chomsky 1970: 187–189)

To account for such data, Chomsky argued for the inclusion of some operations in the lexicon. Under this lexicalist view, the lexicon served not only as a repository for lexical items, but also as a generative component in its own right. Wasow (1977: 331) contrasted lexical rules with syntactic ones in terms of five criteria; the former and not the latter affected structure, could relate items of different categories, were local, could have exceptions, and applied before any syntactic rules. These distinctions, and the last criterion in particular, assume an architecture of grammar in which the lexicon interacts in a limited way with syntax, providing the minimal units manipulated by syntactic operations. These assumptions underlie the Principles and Parameters model (Chomsky 1981), in which the lexicon is no longer treated as a part of a syntactic component, but rather has equal status with syntax and the other independent levels of linguistic structure posited (Logical Form and Phonetic Form).

Central to all formulations of the Lexicalist Hypothesis is the notion that syntactic operations, which follow those responsible for word-formation, are blind to the internal structure of lexical items. This principle distinguishes lexicalist from non-lexicalist approaches to grammar and thus is an important one with far-reaching consequences. Systematic regularities in word-internal structure are accounted for in terms of lexicon-internal processes that are fundamentally different to syntactic ones. The Lexicalist Hypothesis has often been revised, and both strong and weak forms of it have been advocated, the difference being whether inflection is classed as a syntactic operation along with derivation and compounding or not.

Within transformational theory, the Lexicalist Hypothesis has been challenged by Baker (1988), who proposed that the incorporation of a noun into a verb is a word-formation process that is not lexical but syntactic (Section 3.2). This syntactic analysis has been used to account for other word-formation processes such as causative formation (Section 2.3.3) as well. Some researchers go further and reject the Lexicalist Hypothesis entirely, claiming that primitives and processes relevant to lexical items and word-formation are wholly syntactic (e.g. Ramchand 2008). Other work broadly compatible with the Minimalist Program, by contrast, adopts some version of the Lexicalist Hypothesis (e.g. Ackema and Neeleman 2004).

In contrast to approaches such as the Minimalist Program, which seek to relate syntactic structures via transformational operations and hence are derivational, many lexicalist theories are non-derivational. The latter provide a framework within which to explore grammaticality in terms of how constraints on the correspondences between different levels of linguistic structure, which are simultaneously present, can be satisfied. Such correspondence theories include Head-Driven Phrase Structure Grammar (HPSG; Pollard and Sag 1994), Lexical-Functional Grammar (LFG; Bresnan 2001), Role and Reference Grammar (Van Valin and LaPolla 1997) and Culicover and Jackendoff's (2005) Simpler Syntax. Construction Grammar (e.g. Fried and Östman 2004) takes a different overall approach, treating the relationship between the lexicon and syntax as a continuum on the basis that both lexical and syntactic constructions represent pairs of form and meaning which simply differ in terms of internal complexity. The relationship between syntax and the lexicon has been explored in each framework through analysis of a variety of interface phenomena. In addition to the issue of the relationship between morphology and syntax (Section 3), research has centred on accounting for the realization of arguments and argument structure alternations, for example the dative alternation (Goldberg 1995), unaccusativity (e.g. Alexiadou et al. 2004; Levin and Rappaport Hovav 1995), aspect (e.g. Erteschik-Shir and Rapoport 2005) and incorporation (Baker 1988). The different analyses of causativization which have been proposed serve to illustrate the major differences between these approaches with regards to a particular valency-changing operation.

2.3. Causative constructions: lexical or syntactic?

The English sentence (2) is an example of a periphrastic causative in which Charlie is the causer, Lily is the causee, and the caused event is Lily laughing. This sentence describes two separate events expressed by two different verbs, each in a different clause, with the cause of the second event being given in the first clause. Each verb is a separate lexical item that corresponds to a separate syntactic predicate.

(2) *Charlie caused Lily to laugh.*

Not all causative constructions are formed in this way though, and the variation that exists brings to light issues which have a direct bearing on the status of lexical items and their interaction with the syntactic component of the grammar. In a Romance language such as Catalan, the causative construction consists of two verbs, but in contrast to its English counterpart, tests show that it is not biclausal but monoclausal. For example, while the logical subject of *llegir* 'read' is realized as a grammatical subject in (3a), in (3b) it appears as an object expressed as a prepositional phrase which must follow the other object noun phrase *un poema* 'a poem' (Alsina 1996: 190, 210). This is consistent with the cause (the boy) being the third argument of a single syntactic predicate ('make-read') in a simple clause.

(3) a. *El nen llegeiz un poema.* [Catalan]
the boy read a poem
'The boy is reading a poem.'

b. *El mestre fa llegir un poema al nen.*
the teacher makes read a poem to.the boy
'The teacher is making the boy read a poem.'
(Alsina 1996: 190)

In the Catalan monoclausal causative construction therefore two separate verb forms combine to give a single syntactic predicate, demonstrating that the overt form of a verb and its function can be separated in this instance.

In Japanese, the productive causative formation process involves affixation of the morpheme *-(s)ase* to the verb, as in (3b).

(4) a. *Akira-ga it-ta.* [Japanese]
Akira-NOM go-PST
'Akira went.'

b. *Hiroshi-ga Akira-o ik-ase-ta.*
Hiroshi-NOM Akira-ACC go-CAUS-PST
'Hiroshi made Akira go.'

This process would be classed as occurring in the syntax according to Wasow (1977) because it is productive. I refer to this construction in theory-neutral terms as the productive *sase* causative.

Kuroda (1965), amongst others, argues that the productive *sase* causative construction exemplified in (4) consists of two clauses rather than one, even though the verb is a single word. Evidence for this analysis includes the fact that the inclusion of a manner adjunct, which can be interpreted as modifying either the grammatical subject or the logical subject in a biclausal sentence, also results in ambiguity in a productive *sase* causative construction, as (5) shows. Hence, productive *sase* causative constructions are biclausal.

(5) *Jon-wa muriyari sono ko-ni sono kutsushita-o ooyorokobide* [Japanese]
John-TOP forcibly the child-DAT the socks-ACC happily
hak-ase-ta.
put.on-CAUS-PST
'John forcibly made the child put on his socks happily.'
[ambiguous as to who was happy]
(Matsumoto 1998: 9)

In a sense, the productive *sase* causative in (4b) is the mirror image of the Catalan causative in (3b): in the Japanese construction, a single verb form corresponds to two syntactic predicates; in Catalan, two verb forms correspond to a single syntactic predicate. Thus, data show that there is not necessarily a one-to-one correspondence between function and verb form.

In addition to the biclausal productive *sase* causative construction in Japanese, a certain group of transitive verbs form a monoclausal structure when the causative *-(s)ase* morpheme is added. For example, the causative form of *nomu* 'to drink' (*nom-ase-ru*) in (6) means 'to feed/give a drink to'.

(6) *Hahaoya-wa akachan-ni miruku-o nom-ase-ta.* [Japanese]
mother-TOP baby-DAT milk-ACC drink-CAUS-PST
'The mother fed the baby with milk (from a bottle).'
(Matsumoto 1998: 5)

This process would be classed as occurring in the lexicon according to Wasow (1977) because it is not fully productive. I refer to this construction as the non-productive *sase* causative.

In contrast to a biclausal productive *sase* causative construction like (5), the interpretation of adverbials is unambiguous in the case of a non-productive *sase* causative construction such as (7). This and other data indicate that non-productive *sase* causatives are monoclausal.

(7) *Jon-wa sono netakirino roojin-ni sono kutsushita-o* [Japanese]
John-TOP the bedridden old.man-DAT the socks-ACC
ooyorokobide hak-ase-ta.
happily put.on-CAUS-PST
'John happily put the socks on the feet of the bedridden old man.'
[unambiguously John who was happy]
(Matsumoto 1998: 9)

However, if the productive *sase* causative is formed in the syntax, as per Wasow (1977), and the lexicon provides the input for the syntax, Manning et al. (1999) note that data such as (8) are problematic. In this sentence, a lexical process (nominalization via suffixation of *-kata* 'way') has applied after the formation of a productive *sase* causative.

(8) (?*kodomo-e-no*) *hon-no* *yom-ase-kata* [Japanese]
child-DAT-GEN book-GEN read-CAUS-way
'the way to cause (the child) to read a book'
(Manning et al. 1999: 44)

Any analysis of the productive *sase* causative must account for (8), as well as the different syntactic structures (monoclausal vs. biclausal) of the two *sase* causative constructions. Three different approaches could be adopted: (i) both causatives are formed by a syntactic process, but differ in terms of their syntax (Section 2.3.1); (ii) both are formed by a lexical process, but differ lexically (Section 2.3.2); or (iii) the two processes are fundamentally different because one is lexical and the other is syntactic (Section 2.3.3). Comparing these approaches, each with distinct theoretical consequences, provides an insight into a range of issues concerning the relationship between lexical items and syntax and how they have been addressed.

2.3.1. Syntactic approaches

Harley (2008) analyses causativization in purely syntactic terms within the framework of Distributed Morphology (Halle and Marantz 1993; see also Section 3.2), a theory in which there is no lexicon and (syntactic) principles apply to both morphology and syntax. The main semantic feature shared by different types of causatives is defined syntactically: the head CAUSE of a verbal projection is common to all causative constructions. The two Japanese *sase* causatives are analysed as differing in terms of the structural complexity of their syntax. In the case of the non-productive *sase* causative, *-(s)ase* appears in v°, immediately adjacent to a verb root which cannot have a subject of its own. By contrast, in the biclausal productive *sase* causative, *-(s)ase* is the head of a verbal CAUSE projection which subcategorizes for a clause with its own subject.

The possibility that the same morpheme may attach to a "high" or "low" projection, and that this may correlate in a systematic way with the differences between them, is common to a number of analyses. For example, Travis (2000) distinguishes different types of causatives in Malagasy and Tagalog on the basis of the syntactic position that the causative morpheme occupies. Travis (2000) states that the Event Phrase marks the boundary between l(exical)-syntax and s(yntactic)-syntax; causatives formed in the domain of l-syntax (causative morpheme occurs below E, the head of the Event Phrase) are non-productive, while those formed in s-syntax (causative morpheme occurs above E) are productive. This approach to the issue of causativization, as well as those outlined by Harley (2008) and Ramchand (2008: 150–192), treats syntax as a generative component with respect to word formation.

However, data from languages other than Japanese challenge a uniform syntactic analysis of causativization cross-linguistically. For example, Horvath and Siloni (2010) argue that a productive causative construction in Hungarian is not biclausal but monoclausal (see also Pylkkänen 2008: 107). The productive/non-productive distinction thus does not appear to correlate with the proposed difference in syntactic structure. Another issue for a syntactic analysis is that in order to account for the data in (8), *-kata* nominals must be derived in the syntax, as Harley (2008: 48, fn. 8) notes.

2.3.2. Lexicalist approaches

Analyses such as Manning et al. (1999), working in the framework of HPSG, and Matsumoto (1996, 1998), working in LFG, seek to account for the two Japanese *sase* causatives in terms of a lexical distinction. In both cases, the causative verb is derived from the base verb in the lexicon. The monoclausal/biclausal distinction is generally dealt with as a difference in structural complexity relating to the mappings between different types of linguistic structure. For example, Matsumoto (1998: 5–6) captures the fact that productive and non-productive *sase* causatives in Japanese share some features by proposing that they are both monoclausal at f(unctional)-structure, a level of syntactic structure at which grammatical relations such as subject and object are represented. Non-productive *sase* causatives involve a single predicate – the verb stem and causative morpheme together have a single argument structure – and are "purely monoclausal" (Matsumoto 1998: 5), i.e. at the level of a(rgument)-structure as well as at f-structure (9).

(9) Non-productive *sase* causative, e.g. *nom-ase-ta* 'fed/gave a drink to' in (6)

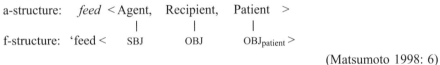

a-structure: *feed* < Agent, Recipient, Patient >

f-structure: 'feed < SBJ OBJ OBJ$_{patient}$ >

(Matsumoto 1998: 6)

By contrast, productive *sase* causatives are biclausal at the level of a(rgument)-structure. The causative morpheme introduces a separate predicate CAUSE with its own argument structure. The patient of CAUSE and the agent of the embedded predicate are fused together in a-structure, as indicated by the dashed line in (10), the result being that two thematic roles are shared by a single "fused" argument (Alsina 1992).

(10) Productive *sase* causative, e.g. *nom-ase-ta* 'caused to drink'

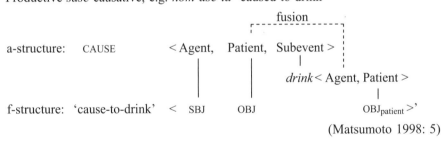

fusion

a-structure: CAUSE < Agent, Patient, Subevent >

drink < Agent, Patient >

f-structure: 'cause-to-drink' < SBJ OBJ OBJ$_{patient}$ >'

(Matsumoto 1998: 5)

Thus two different a-structures may map to the same f-structure, cf. (9) and (10), and the observed monoclausal/biclausal contrast is analysed as a reflex of argument structure. The fact that the productive *sase* causative can be nominalized by suffixation of *-kata*, as exemplified in (7), supports this lexicalist analysis because both are proposed to be formed in the lexicon.

Accounting for the possibility of disjunction of sub-word constituents under the scope of causation (Kuroda 2003: 455–458) and the causativization of raising verbs (Horvath and Siloni 2010: 168) have been identified as challenges to the lexicalist analysis of the productive *sase* causative.

2.3.3. Mixed approaches

A third possible approach to the two *sase* causatives would be to assume that they are inherently different, one being formed in the lexicon and the other being formed in the syntax. Baker (1988) represents a framework broadly consistent with the Weak Lexicalist Hypothesis within which to explore this possibility. According to this approach, the underlying structure of both causative constructions is the same because according to the Uniformity of Theta Assignment Hypothesis (UTAH; Baker 1988: 46), there is a one-to-one correspondence between syntactic positions and thematic roles as assigned by a specific type of predicate. The productive *sase* causative is formed in the syntax: the base verb is head of a lower VP that moves to SpecC' before its head is adjoined, via Incorporation (Section 3.2), to *-(s)ase* which is the head of a higher VP. The non-productive *sase* causative, on the other hand, is formed in the lexicon and represents a single verb in the input to the syntax. Harley (2008: 33) criticizes this type of Incorporation analysis for failing to account for the systematic relationship which exists between the productive and non-productive *sase* causatives. For discussion of other problems with an Incorporation analysis of causatives, see Alsina (1992).

Horvath and Siloni (2010) propose an analysis which does not seek to define causative formation in purely syntactic or lexical terms either, defining the difference in terms of the setting of the Lexicon-Syntax Parameter (Reinhart and Siloni 2005), which states that valency-changing operations including causativization apply either in the lexicon or in the syntax in a language. In Japanese, causativization is claimed to apply in the syntax; non-productive *sase* causatives are hypothesised to be underived lexical items or relics and therefore irrelevant to the language's parameter setting. It remains to be clarified how data such as (8), which shows that a syntactic causative can be the input to nominalization, is dealt with under such an analysis.

2.4. Conclusion

The causative construction has been the focus of much research and its study continues to raise issues of importance. This and other data concerning the realization of arguments are key to understanding and defining the relationship between lexical items and syntax. A closely related issue is the interface between syntax and morphology.

3. Syntax and morphology

3.1. Introduction

Different theoretical approaches account for the part which syntax plays in the formation of complex words in distinct ways. Defining the nature of morphology is an important consideration in itself. A key proposal that cuts across lexical and syntactic approaches to the syntax–morphology interface is the Separationist Hypothesis (see Beard 1995, amongst others), which advocates divorcing the meaning or morphological function of a morpheme from its form. For example, an abstract L(exical)-derivation rule of pluralization changes the features of an English singular count noun thus: [−Plural, +Singular] → [+Plural, −Singular] (Beard 1995: 160). The form of the plural is determined in a separate morphological spelling (MS) component. MS-rules include suffixation, e.g. *dog–dogs*, and umlaut, e.g. *man–men*, which accounts for the multiple exponence of the morphosyntactic category 'plural' in English. This approach is often adopted in the analysis of inflection, and has also been extended to derivation by some researchers (see Beard 1998).

For those who do not subscribe to the view that syntax subsumes morphology (Section 3.2) and instead adhere to a strong or weak version of the Lexicalist Hypothesis (Section 3.3), the challenge is not only to identify those primitives and operations which are uniquely morphological in their nature and define them, but also to characterize the interface between syntax and morphology (Section 3.4). Key data are examples of phenomena which exhibit a combination of properties that appear to be neither wholly morphological nor wholly syntactic. These include cliticization (e.g. Anderson 2005; Halpern 1995; Zwicky 1994), incorporation (e.g. Baker 1988; Mithun 1984) and inflection (e.g. Anderson 1992; Steele 1995; Stump 2001). Indeed, approaches to morphology can also be classified according to the relations they posit between the morphology and morphosyntactic properties of an inflected word (lexical vs. inferential and incremental vs. realizational). See Stump (2001).

The proposed analyses of incorporation, undertaken in a variety of frameworks, provide a useful insight into some major issues.

3.2. Syntax subsumes morphology

Noun incorporation is a productive process found in a number of languages including Classical Nahuatl, a North American language. The two sentences in (11) are very similar in meaning and include the same morphemes, but in (11b) the direct object *naca* 'meat' is part of the verb *qua* 'eat', the only word in the sentence.

(11) a. *ni-c-qua* *in* *naca-tl.* [Classical Nahuatl]
1SG.SBJ-3SG.OBJ-eat DET meat-ABS
'I eat (the) meat.'

b. *ni-naca-qua.*
1SG.SBJ-meat-eat
'I eat meat.'

(Iturrioz Leza 2001: 715)

The process involved in forming (11b) is productive and may be the usual way to convey a particular meaning. This is reminiscent of a syntactic process, though the result of this noun incorporation is a single word. As Mithun (1984: 847) states, such noun incorporation is "perhaps the most nearly syntactic of all morphological processes".

Baker's (1988) influential approach to noun incorporation is an example of how word formation can be analysed as a syntactic process: syntax is argued to manipulate morphemes to form words in cases such as (11b). Specifically, complex words are formed by head movement, a syntactic operation restricted by the Head Movement Constraint (Travis 1984: 131), or possibly the Empty Category Principle (Chomsky 1981: 250) or Relativized Minimality (Rizzi 1990), as shown in (12). This type of derivational rule is known as Incorporation.

(12)

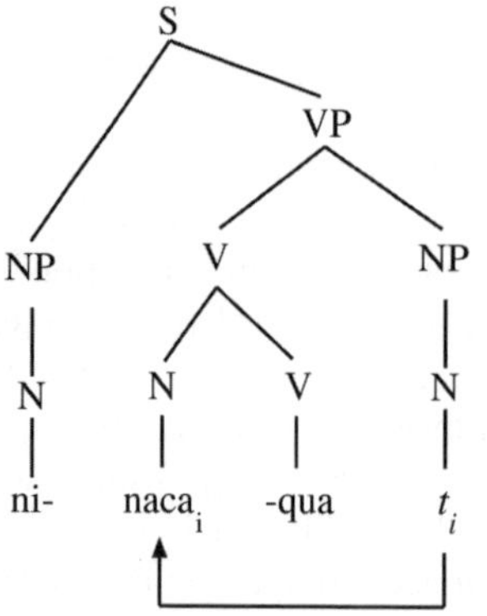

Noun incorporation, a way of forming a complex word, is thus analysed in terms of established principles of derivational syntax. In this way, syntactic operations are proposed to be responsible for generating structure below as well as above word level. Other syntactic analyses of noun incorporation are presented in van Geenhoven (1998), Koopman and Szabolcsi (2000) and Massam (2001). Baker (2009) compares his head-movement analysis to these approaches in the context of the Minimalist Program (Chomsky 1995).

Baker (1988) also uses Incorporation to account for other morphosyntactic phenomena, including passivization and applicativization, two processes in which affixation may accompany a change in argument structure. Baker (1985: 375) further claims that grammar is constrained by the Mirror Principle: "morphological derivations must directly reflect syntactic derivations (and vice versa)". The order of affixes relative to each other and the base is thus predicted to reflect the order in which the relevant syntactic operations applied in the derivation of a complex word. If syntax subsumes morphology entirely, the Mirror Principle should always constrain word-internal structure. However, while it represents a strong tendency, the Mirror Principle does not appear to be inviolable, as Hyman et al. (2009) show. For example, when an applicative is passivized, the order of syntactic operations is applicative then passive, so the applicative morpheme should be affixed closer to the base than the passive one according to the Mirror Principle. This is the case in the example from the Bantu language Ndebele in (13a). However, when a passive is subject to applicativization in Ndebele, and hence the order in which the syntactic operations apply is reversed, as in (13b), the same morphemes appear in the same order as in (13a).

(13) a. Passivized Applicative [Ndebele]
abantwana b-a-phek-el-w-a *ukudla*
children they-PST-cook-APPL-PASS-FS food
'The children were cooked food'

b. Applicativized Passive
ukudla kw-a-phek-el-w-a abantwana
food it-PST-cook-APPL-PASS-FS children
'The food was cooked (for) the children'
(Hyman et al. 2009: 298)

Thus, morphology does not reflect syntactic derivation in (13b). This undermines one of the strongest types of argument for a purely syntactic analysis of such productive complex word formation because in these cases the processes involved in syntactic and morphological structure building do not appear to be exactly the same.

Baker himself does not advocate a syntactic analysis of all complex word formation (Baker 1993: 588) and Incorporation could not be straightforwardly extended to cover morphological processes which are non-concatenative. Others go further though, assuming that there is no separate part of the grammar which generates morphological structure. Lack of isomorphism is an issue which syntactic approaches to morphology must address.

Lieber (1992) seeks to capture complex word formation in terms of independent principles of syntax and phonology. Under this approach, syntactic rules based on revised principles of X-bar theory may apply to form a word from morphemes contained within the lexicon. In this linear model, the sole interaction between morphology and syntax is insertion of lexical items into syntax, at which point structure above and below word level is built. Lieber's (1992) analysis rests on definitions of head and non-heads intended to apply both above and below word level, and the proposal that direction of headedness is a parameter set once for a language and thus that the order of syntactic units and morphemes will be identical, all things being equal. In support of this claim, Lieber (1992) notes that, for example, English is largely a head-final language with right-headed morphology (i.e. suffixation, Lieber 1992: 49–64, the head of a word being the part that determines its category) while Tagalog is largely a head-initial language with left-headed morphology (i.e. prefixation; Lieber 1992: 40–49). There are languages such as Warlpiri (Simpson 1991) though which exhibit freedom of word order and a rigid morpheme order that would be difficult to account for in terms of a headedness parameter.

A purely syntactic analysis must account for complex word formation in terms of independently motivated syntactic principles. However, Lieber (1992) finds it necessary to adapt X-bar principles to account for word-internal structure, indicating that it does differ in some respects from syntactic structure (see Borer 1998).

Distributed Morphology (Halle and Marantz 1993; Harley and Noyer 1999; Marantz 1997) is another syntactic approach to morphology, according to which "all derivation of complex objects is syntactic" (Embick and Noyer 2007: 290), and therefore syntactic and morphological structure are fundamentally the same. Distributed Morphology is an attempt to incorporate Separationism in a model which in effect eliminates morphology altogether. Instances in which there is a lack of isomorphism between the two are accounted for by differences in the complexity of the derivation involved or the application of readjustment rules post-syntactically (Embick and Noyer 2007: 305–310).

Distributed Morphology, in common with other syntactic treatments of morphological phenomena, is argued to be preferable on the grounds of parsimony: by having the syntactic component subsume some or all complex word-formation, it is possible to reduce or eliminate the need for morphology as a separate part of the grammar. However, if it is necessary to posit new or revised operations which are not motivated on independent syntactic grounds and may never apply in the syntax, or to add powerful post-syntactic stipulations in order to account for morphological processes, the parsimony argument in favour of a syntactic analysis is undermined.

3.3. Lexicalist approaches

Contrasting with syntactic approaches to morphology are those such as Aronoff (1994) which maintain that the formation and structure of complex words is distinct from that of phrases and hence morphology is a separate component of the grammar.

The Strong Lexicalist approach (e.g. Halle 1973), in which specific rules of word formation apply in one component of the grammar and feed into a separate syntactic component, has generally been rejected on the basis that inflection exhibits features consistent with syntactic principles. This is the weak lexicalist position found in the work of Aronoff (1976), whose word-formation rules (WFRs) account only for derivational morphology. According to the Weak Lexicalist Hypothesis, derivational processes apply in the lexicon, whereas "inflectional morphology is what is relevant to the syntax" (Anderson 1982: 587). Thus in English, nominalization by addition of *-ion* (derivational morphology) is analysed as being inherently different from affixation of *-s* to a verb stem indicating third person singular subject agreement (inflectional morphology) as the latter is integrated with the syntax. Inflectional processes such as agreement and case marking are characterized as a set of adjustment rules which serve to harmonize the output of the syntactic and morphological components in a Weak Lexicalist framework. Kiparsky's (1982) Strong Lexicalist analysis, by contrast, relates the distinction between derivation and inflection to the cyclic ordering of rules of affixation relative to each other within the lexicon. Morphology is thus kept separate from syntax in this Lexical Phonology/Morphology model, but the price is to situate morphological and phonological rules in the lexicon.

The process of incorporation is open to a lexicalist analysis, as work by Di Sciullo and Williams (1987), Mithun (1984) and Rosen (1989) shows. Under such an analysis, noun incorporation is the result of a verb combining with one of its arguments, similar to an English verbal compound such as *horse riding*. This is a lexical rather than a syntactic process. (Not all noun incorporation appears to be the same in this respect. Rosen 1989 identifies a type of incorporation, Classifier NI, which involves incorporation of a noun that is not selected as an argument by the verb.)

Anderson (2000: 135), concurring with Baker, notes that "the syntactic and lexical theories of Noun Incorporation are 'tied' in that each can be said to account for roughly the same range of phenomena the other can", but goes on to discuss data which are problematic for a purely syntactic analysis. Specifically, Anderson (2000) discusses instances of morphosyntactic agreement in noun incorporation constructions. Baker (1996: 307–329) claims that when the syntactic operation of Incorporation has applied, a trace is left which occupies the position in which the incorporated noun was base generated, as in (12). There should not be marking on the verb of agreement with this trace because it does not possess any of the features of the moved element. Anderson

(2000) though cites data which show that such agreement can occur. In sentence (14) from Mohawk, the marker *-hi* may signal agreement with the incorporated noun.

(14) *Wa'-ke(-hi)-kstʌ-hser-áhset-e'* [Mohawk]
FACT-1SG.SBJ-M.SG.OBJ-old.person-NOM-hide-PUNC
'I hid the old person (the old man)'
(Anderson 2000: 137)

The agreement in (14) is unexpected if the incorporated noun's original position is occupied by a trace. Under a lexicalist analysis, on the other hand, this agreement is accounted for because *pro* (rather than a trace resulting from movement) is posited to be one of the noun-verb compound's arguments (Anderson 2000). Baker et al. (2004) revise the syntactic approach, suggesting that a trace may retain some (non-phonological) features of the incorporated noun, in line with copy theory (Chomsky 1995), which explains the different agreement patterns found in languages with noun incorporation. The issue of whether incorporation is a syntactic process or not thus continues to be debated, and analysis of this phenomenon still represents an important line of research into the syntax–morphology interface.

Ackema and Neeleman's (2004) approach is also consistent with the weak lexicalist hypothesis because, while they claim that the systems which generate hierarchical phrasal and word-internal structure are part of the same module of the grammar, within this SYNTAX macromodule there are separate submodules of phrasal syntax and "word syntax" (morphology). Word syntax and phrasal syntax, though distinct, share features and principles of the SYNTAX macromodule of which they are both a part, including the notions of head and c-command (Ackema and Neeleman 2004: 6). This approach therefore avoids duplication within the grammar. Syntax and morphology are characterized as being in competition; when all is equal, syntactic combination wins over morphological combination. Morphological combination must be triggered by information stored in the lexicon. This is the case when affixation occurs. As a result, morphological derivation by affixation correlates with semantic irregularity, while syntactic derivation correlates with semantic regularity. However, Lieber and Scalise (2007) point out that data do not always support this distinction: the results of affixation are not always semantically unpredictable, for example *-er* affixation (e.g. *work–worker*) and the formation of synthetic compounds such as *truck driver* exhibit semantic regularity. Lieber and Scalise (2007: 16) conclude that the proposed alignment of semantic predictability and derivation in different submodules of the grammar, which is crucial to Ackema and Neeleman's (2004: 48–88) concept of competition and thus their account of the data, is arbitrary. Lieber and Scalise (2007: 16) therefore reject competition as a way to "breach the firewall" which is assumed to divide morphology and syntax. The nature of this interface is an issue that must be addressed by any approach which assumes that the two are separate components (or subcomponents) of the grammar.

3.4. Interfacing autonomous morphology with syntax

While many approaches which posit a separate morphological component characterize its interface with syntax in terms of an extremely limited, linear output–input relation (words feed syntactic rules and lexical integrity is a consequence of the structure of the grammar), this is not the only possibility.

Sadock's (1991) Autolexical Syntax approach was a direct response to the challenge of accounting for the syntactic and morphological properties of noun incorporation. Sadock (1991) proposes a model of grammar in which separate syntactic, morphological and semantic components exist in parallel. The three are related by principles which constitute an interface subsystem that governs the well-formedness of the representations generated by each independent module. Under this approach, incorporation is evidence of a mismatch between syntax and morphology: syntactically, an incorporated noun is distinct from the verb (and thus is equivalent to its non-incorporated equivalent in terms of syntactic structure), but morphologically, it is part of a single word along with the relevant verbal affix. Such mismatches are constrained by mapping principles. This accounts for those instances in which there is a lack of isomorphism between morphology and syntax.

Such a parallel architecture assumes that morphology and syntax are not ordered with respect to each other at all. However, Borer (1988) provides data which indicate that words may be formed after syntactic structures. For example, in Modern Hebrew a construct-state noun such as (15b), i.e. a complex noun phrase consisting of a definite noun, cf. (15a), modified by another noun, is constructed in the syntax, the formation process involved being productive and its meaning being compositional (Borer 1988). However, construct-state nominals behave like a single word with respect to definiteness marking and interpretation, indicating that post-syntactic word formation has occurred. Note that *ha-* can only be affixed to the non-head NP *yalda* 'girl' in (15b) and that both the head and non-head NPs are interpreted as definite.

(15) a. *ha-caʕif* [Modern Hebrew]
the-scarf
'the scarf'

b. *caʕif ha-yalda*
scarf the-girl
'the/*a scarf of the/*a girl'
(Borer 1988: 47–48)

Accounting for such data is problematic when co-analysis of morphology and syntax occurs simultaneously in a parallel architecture. Borer's (1988) own model of Parallel Morphology includes conditions that determine whether word-formation operations apply before or after the formation of syntactic structure, the latter possibility being in violation of the strong version of the Lexicalist Hypothesis. This accounts for (15b), as well as similar examples: construct-state nouns are formed by a compounding operation when its input is syntactic rather than lexical.

As well as the output of syntax feeding word formation processes, as in (15b), there is evidence that the relationship between morphology and syntax more generally may be, to some extent, bidirectional. For example, given the Lexical Hypothesis and assuming that the principles of syntax govern inflection, a syntactic head should not agree with part of a word as syntax cannot access word-internal structure. However, Corbett (1987: 300) notes that in Upper Sorbian the case marking on the possessive pronoun *mojeho* 'my' in (16) shows agreement not with the possessed plural noun *dźěći* 'children', but with the masculine singular stem *bratr* 'brother' of *bratrowe*, the possessor noun. Such data indicate that word-internal structure is not always opaque to syntax.

(16) *mojeho* *bratrowe* *dźěći* [Upper Sorbian]
my.GEN.SG.M brother.NOM.PL children.NOM.PL
'my brother's children'
(Michałk 1974: 510; cited by Corbett 1987: 300)

There are also examples in which syntax seems to manipulate morphology, in apparent violation of the Lexical Hypothesis. Harris (2000, 2002) discusses Udi endoclitics, person markers which may not only affix to words (17a), but also appear inside them (17b).

(17) a. *yaq'-a-**ne*** *ba-st'a* [Udi]
road-DAT-3SG in-LV.PRS
'On the road he opens it.'
(Harris 2002: 3)

b. *zavod-a* *aš-**ne**-b-sa*
factory-DAT work-3SG-DO-PRS
'She works in a factory.'
(Harris 2000: 598)

Such data does not necessarily spell the end for the Lexicalist Hypothesis. Lieber and Scalise (2007), for example, argue for a reformulation of it which not only permits syntax access to morphology, but also vice versa. Anderson (2005), meanwhile, preserves the Lexicalist Hypothesis and admits the possibility of bidirectional interaction by reframing it in terms of a family of violable (though usually highly ranked) Integrity constraints in his Optimality Theoretic approach to the analysis of clitics.

3.5. Conclusion

While some researchers have argued that some or all features of morphology in the world's languages are distinct from those of syntax, others have argued for approaches ranging from a blurring of the distinction between syntax and morphology to an outright rejection of the assumption that a separate morphological component of grammar exists. Through its interaction with not only syntax but also phonology and semantics, morphology provides important insights into the nature of linguistic knowledge and its organization.

4. Syntax and phonology

4.1. Introduction

Research into the relationship between syntax and phonology focuses on the extent to which the structure and ordering principles of syntax constrain the domains in which phonological processes apply post-lexically, and how best to model the mapping between the syntactic and phonological components. Approaches to this interface can be divided broadly according to whether they posit Direct Reference (Section 4.2) or Indirect Reference (Section 4.3) between syntax and phonology. (The proposal that phonological processes apply in domains at a separate level of structure is also found in Chomsky and Halle 1968; see Hayes 1989: 203–205 for an overview of the 'boundary symbol' approach to the syntax–phonology interface and issues with it.) Approaches may also differ in terms of how they characterize the correspondence between syntax and phonology, and therefore how the grammar is organized (Section 4.4).

4.2. The Direct Reference approach

Under the Direct Reference approach, phonological output is determined by syntactic phrasing (cf. Pāṇini's conception of the architecture of grammar). This means that post-lexical phonological rules such as *raddoppiamento sintattico* in Italian, tone sandhi in Ewe, and French liaison are posited to apply in domains defined in terms of syntax alone (Kaisse 1985). Phonological processes are assumed to make direct and relatively free reference to a sentence's syntactic representation without any other level of structure mediating between the two.

This characterization of the syntax–phonology interface has not been widely adopted, though the work of Odden (1990, 1995) is an exception. Odden (1995) argues that the domain of application of certain phrase-level phonological processes in Bantu languages must be defined in terms of specific syntactic relations in similar, syntactically defined domains. To give one example, in Kimatuumbi, vowel shortening affects long stem vowels in words which are syntactic heads when they are followed by other phonetic material, i.e. when they are not the final element in an XP. Compare the form of *kįkóloombe* 'cleaning shell' as it appears in (18a), in which it is the only word in the NP and the final word in the VP, and in (18b), in which it does not occupy XP-final position and shortening therefore applies. (The vowel affected is given in bold.)

(18) a. [*akįtwéetį* [*kįkóloombe*]$_{NP}$]$_{VP}$ [Kimatuumbi]
he.took cleaning.shell
'he took a cleaning shell'

b. [[*kįkól**o**mbe* [*kįkeéle*]$_{AP}$]$_{NP}$ *chaángu*]$_{NP}$
cleaning.shell red mine
'my red shell'

(Odden 1995: 50)

(19) Shortening

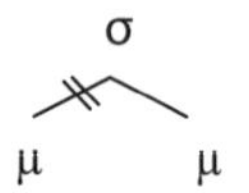

/ [XP[X __ X] Y XP] (Y contains phonetic material)

(Odden 1995: 51)

Note the reference to syntactic information (XP, Y) in (19). At the interface, the hierarchical structure of syntax and phonology is taken to be identical. (See Truckenbrodt 1999 for an alternative, Indirect Reference analysis of Kimatuumbi data within an Optimality Theoretic framework. Seidl 2001 provides a critical assessment of Truckenbrodt's proposals.)

In addition to segmental processes such as that exemplified in (18), analyses of suprasegmental processes have been proposed. For example, Cinque (1993) claims that, by default, main phrasal stress is assigned to the most deeply embedded constituent on the basis of a sentence's syntactic representation. (See also Culicover and Rochemont 1983; Zubizarreta 1998.)

However, some interface phenomena indicate that syntactic and phonological domains are not isomorphic. For instance, in the example from Shanghai Chinese (20) the domain for post-focus tone deletion (underlined) is *ʔnjiaw 'geq 'dou khe*, which is not a syntactic constituent. Chen (1987) and Bošković (2001) make the same point with respect to tone sandhi in Xiamen Chinese and cliticization in South Slavic languages respectively.

(20) [Shanghai Chinese]

[[*'zaw* [[*'oN*]$_{AP}$ *'geq* [[*ʔnjiaw*]$_{NP}$ *'geq* *'dou*]$_{NP}$]$_{NP}$]$_{PP}$ *khe* [*tshjaN*]$_{NP}$]$_{VP}$
( )( )(________________________________)( )
toward red bird head open gun

'shoot at the red head of the bird'

(Selkirk and Shen 1990: 330)

As Pak (2008: 51) points out though, Direct Reference does not necessarily mean defining phonological rule domains solely in terms of syntactic constituency: such domains can, in principle, be defined by reference to other types of syntactic information such as the head-complement relation. Examples like (20) therefore do not necessarily force the rejection of all formulations of this type of approach.

This approach has also been argued to miss generalizations about data which show that different phonological processes target the same domain of application (see e.g. Hayes and Lahiri 1991 on Bengali). This is because the (syntactic) domain of application is uniquely defined for each rule, and so cases in which distinct phonological rules converge on the same domain are a matter of coincidence rather than a consequence of the theoretical framework.

4.3. The Indirect Reference approach

The lack of isomorphism between syntactic and prosodic constituents, as exemplified by (20), has been cited as evidence of a separate level of prosodic structure with its own constituent structure. Under an Indirect Reference approach, syntax and phonology are related via a mediating level of prosodic structure (e.g. Gussenhoven 1984; Hayes and Lahiri 1991; Nespor and Vogel 1986; Pierrehumbert and Beckman 1988; Selkirk 1978, 1986, 1995; Truckenbrodt 1999). Prosodic structure (also referred to as phonological constituent structure) is posited to consist of a finite number of hierarchically organized prosodic units which are universally available (the Prosodic Hierarchy). These prosodic constituents, which function as the domains of application for phonological rules, are systematically related to syntactic constituents by a mapping algorithm, but are not necessarily isomorphic with them. Syntactic structure therefore influences rather than defines phonological structure. This is more restrictive than an approach which assumes direct reference because phonology only has access to certain syntactic information via prosodic structure.

Two independent strands of research exist within the Indirect Reference literature, one primarily concerned with the domain of application of segmental rules (e.g. Nespor and Vogel 1986; Selkirk 1986) and the other with the domain of application of non-segmental intonational rules (e.g. Frota 2000; Grice 1995). Overviews are provided in Jun (1998) and Shattuck-Hufnagel and Turk (1996). These two approaches differ with respect to how prosodic constituents are defined. Generally within research into segmental phonology, prosodic units are defined on the basis of syntactic structure, the emphasis being on how to predict prosodic boundaries. The hierarchy of prosodic units assumed in the segmental approach is given in Figure 4.1.

(21) Utterance
Intonational Phrase
Phonological Phrase
Prosodic Word

Fig. 4.1. The Prosodic Hierarchy: segmental approach (see e.g. Selkirk 1978)

Within research into intonational phonology, by contrast, prosodic constituents are defined with reference to informational markers and the emphasis is on how to identify prosodic boundaries. The hierarchy of prosodic units assumed in the non-segmental approach is given in Figure 4.2.

(22) Intonation Phrase
Intermediate Phrase
Accentual Phrase

Fig. 4.2. The Prosodic Hierarchy: non-segmental approach (see e.g. Beckman and Pierrehumbert 1986)

Regardless of which Prosodic Hierarchy is assumed, a well-formed prosodic structure is consistent with the Strict Layer Hypothesis (Nespor and Vogel 1986: 7; Selkirk 1981, 1984: 26), which requires exhaustive parsing of a sentence into non-recursive prosodic constituents grouped in layers corresponding to each category of the Prosodic Hierarchy. Any prosodic constituent is thus parsed into a prosodic constituent or constituents belonging to the level of the hierarchy directly below. (The units of the Prosodic Hierarchy in Figure 4.1 are used in [23] for the purposes of exposition.)

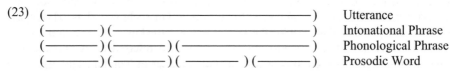

(23) (————————————————————) Utterance
(————)(————————————————) Intonational Phrase
(————)(————)(——————————) Phonological Phrase
(————)(————)(————)(————) Prosodic Word

Fig 4.3. An illustration of exhaustive parsing of prosodic units consistent with the Strict Layer Hypothesis

Given that both claim to represent the hierarchical organization of prosodic structure, the question arises of whether the domains of post-lexical segmental rules (Figure 4.1) and non-segmental rules (Figure 4.2) are the same, i.e. does a single homogeneous prosodic hierarchy exist? Hayes and Lahiri (1991) identify a single domain to which a segmental rule (voicing assimilation) applies and which is also key to intonational (non-segmental) phonology in Bengali. Domain convergence has also been identified in European Portuguese (Frota 2000) and Korean (Jun 1998), suggesting that one homogenous Prosodic Hierarchy exists which is universally available. Gussenhoven (1992) opposes this view and argues that the two hierarchies cannot be unified because they represent separate but related types of phonological structure which do not always coincide. The extent to which there is cross-linguistic evidence of a universally available hierarchy of prosodic units is an important research issue.

The Indirect Reference approach in general has been criticized by Seidl (2001), who cites data which indicate that the domains to which different phonological rules apply are not consistent with the existence of a Prosodic Hierarchy or the Strict Layer Hypothesis. For example, in Oyo Yoruba the domains in which a tonal obligatory contour principle (OCP) phenomenon and vowel harmony apply are different, even though both consist of a clitic and its host. Tonal OCP applies in only one environment: it deletes the high (H) tone on an object enclitic when it attaches to a verb which also bears a H tone, as in (24).

(24) () = tonal OCP domain [Oyo Yoruba]
ó=(kọ́=mí) → *ó=kọ́=**mi***
he/she/it=taught=me
'he/she/it taught me'
(Akinlabi and Liberman 2000: 39)

Regressive tonal vowel harmony applies when a subject proclitic attaches to a verb, as in (25). It cannot apply in the environment verb plus object enclitic.

(25) [] = vowel harmony domain [Oyo Yoruba]
[ó=lọ] → *ọ́=lọ*
he/she=went
'he/she went'
(Akinlabi and Liberman 2000: 54)

The two phonological rules apply to different types of clitic-host domains and thus may overlap rather than converge, as in (26).

(26) *[ó=(kọ́=]=wá)* → *ọ́=kọ́=**wa*** [Oyo Yoruba]
he=taught=us
'he taught us'
(Seidl 2001: 53)

Overlapping domains are not expected if prosodic constituents are organized hierarchically and obey the Strict Layer Hypothesis. One possible way to deal with such domain paradoxes would be to reformulate the Strict Layer Hypothesis as a set of violable constraints (see Selkirk 1995).

Data which indicate that certain phonological rules must refer to syntactic information such as category membership or syntactic function, and thus that the relationship between the two components is in at least some cases more direct than indirect, also represent a challenge. For example, in Hausa a long vowel at the end of a verb is shortened when it is immediately followed by a direct object which is a full noun phrase. One suggestion is to treat such processes as fundamentally different from other phonological rules and thus distinct in terms of their domains of application (see Hayes 1990).

Given the issues with the Indirect Reference approach which have been identified, research has continued into the possibility of characterizing the syntax–phonology interface in terms of direct interaction between the two. Seidl's (2001) Minimal Indirect Reference model is more constrained than Kaisse's (1985) original Direct Reference approach. Seidl (2001) proposes that phonology has access to syntax through the level of morphosyntactic representation, which in turn has a direct relationship with syntax. Phonological domains are derived directly from theta-domains via the Phonological Domain Generator which maps morphosyntax to prosody, with prosodic ("late") rules applying to domains in which theta roles are assigned, and morphosyntactic ("early") rules applying at the edges of phases (see e.g. Chomsky 2000, 2001 on phases). Phonological processes may therefore apply at more than one stage. Domain convergence and domain paradoxes fall out of this model as a result of this distinction between early and late rules and also the types of domains to which they may apply (morphosyntactic vs. prosodic). For example, Seidl (2001: 22–33) accounts for the different domains of tone sandhi and consonant mutation in Mende, the former being smaller than the latter, by analysing tone sandhi as applying at an earlier stage than consonant mutation.

Seidl's (2001) approach involves a much more restricted notion of indirect reference than that posited by, for example, Selkirk (1986, 1995) or Nespor and Vogel (1986) because it assumes a greater degree of structural isomorphism. However, the scope of Seidl (2001) leaves room for further investigation. For instance, as Elordieta (2007: 147) points out, Seidl (2001) does not discuss phonological processes which apply to domains smaller or larger than theta-domains.

4.4. Defining the mapping between syntax and phonology

Whether direct or indirect reference is assumed, modelling the nature of the mapping relation between syntax and phonology is a key issue in interface research. Four main theoretical approaches can be distinguished: relational (e.g. Frota 2000; Nespor and Vogel 1986), end-based (e.g. Chen 1987; Truckenbrodt 1999), arboreal (e.g. Zec and Inkelas 1990) and cyclic (e.g. Kratzer and Selkirk 2007; Wagner 2005).

Under the relational approach, phonology has access to information about a variety of syntactic relations including c-command, dominance and the head/complement distinction. The sisterhood relation in particular is crucial, and two fundamental types of parametric variation, Type 1 and Type 2 in Table 4.1, are predicted (Hayes 1989; Nespor and Vogel 1986).

However, English is problematic: it behaves like a Type 2 language except when a complement branches, in which case the branching complement maps to a separate phonological phrase (Zec and Inkelas 1990). The effects of branching on the syntax–

(27) Tab. 4.1 Parametric variation in the syntax–phonology mapping under the relational approach

	Syntactic structure	Prosodic structure	Example (Nespor and Vogel 1986: 179–182)
Type 1	head and complement	separate phonological phrases	stress assignment in Chimwi:ni
Type 2	head and complement	a single phonological phrase	liaison in colloquial French

phonology mapping do not follow straightforwardly from the relational approach and must be stipulated. Nespor and Vogel (1986: 173) propose an optional restructuring rule which incorporates a non-branching phonological phrase containing a complement within the phonological phrase which contains its head. This approach could be argued to describe rather than account for the observed variation.

End-based mapping offers a more restrictive view of the interface. Phonology is posited to have access to only two types of syntactic information: X-bar constituency and the location of X-bar constituents' edges. The syntax–phonology mapping aligns one edge of a phonological domain with that of a syntactic constituent. Languages are predicted to vary in terms of how many phonological phrases a syntactic constituent maps to depending on (i) the position of the syntactic head (initial or final), and (ii) the setting of the edge parameter (left or right). However, English presents the same challenge to an end-based approach as it does to a relational one. To cover the optionality relating to the phrasing of branching complements, it is necessary to add a stipulation about branchingness (see e.g. Cowper and Rice 1987: 192).

In work by Selkirk (1995) and Truckenbrodt (1999), the end-based approach is reformulated in Optimality Theoretic (OT) terms as a set of violable constraints. Ranked together in a single hierarchy, faithfulness constraints, which apply to the mapping between syntactic and prosodic structure and serve to align the edges of both types of constituents, interact with constraints that determine the well-formedness of structure in the two separate modules, including prosodic domination constraints which preserve the Strict Layer Hypothesis. A consequence of an OT analysis which ranks interface and prosodic dominance constraints in a single hierarchy is that this type of end-based approach does not face the same challenges as one which assumes inviolable strict layering.

While it does not fall out naturally from either the relational or the end-based approach, branching – specifically, the syntactic relationship between sisters – is fundamental to Zec and Inkelas' (1990) arboreal approach, according to which syntactic sisters are mapped to a single phonological phrase. However, this approach makes strong predictions which are wrong in the case of Chimwi:ni (syntactic sisters map to separate phonological phrases) and French (branching is of no consequence to the mapping). Lack of sensitivity to branching must be introduced if the arboreal approach is to cover the data referred to in Table 4.1. This mirrors the stipulations regarding sensitivity to branching which must be added to the relational and end-based approaches in order to address precisely the opposite problem.

A fourth approach characterizes the syntax–phonology interface as a single operation of Spell-out, which applies cyclically to connect these two components of the grammar. Cyclic analyses are theoretically compatible with both Direct and Indirect Reference approaches (cf. Pak 2008 and Ishihara 2004 respectively), but are inherently derivational, adopting key theoretical assumptions of the Minimalist framework. Within Minimalist theory, the operation Spell-out applies to a syntactic representation to give the input to the phonological component. As Spell-out occurs in cycles, phonological processes may apply to spelled-out material, which need not correspond to syntactic constituents, at various stages during a derivation. This captures the predominantly hierarchical nature of phonological domains. Even setting aside the assumption of a derivational theory of grammar, a number of theoretical issues arise with respect to the cyclic approach which remain to be explored fully, including the precise form of the input to phonology and how it is derived.

In characterizing the nature of the mapping between syntax and phonology, it is also necessary to account for its direction. A straightforward serialist view of the interface, which models syntactic structure as the input to a component whose final output is the phonological representation of an utterance, predicts the influence of syntax on phonology, in line with the principle of phonology-free syntax (Zwicky 1969; cited by Zwicky and Pullum 1986: 71) which states that "no syntactic rule can be subject to language-particular phonological conditions or constraints". Bidirectional interaction between syntax and phonology is therefore ruled out by a strictly serialist approach.

However, Zec and Inkelas (1990) argue that the behaviour of some heavy dislocated constituents is evidence of how phonology may affect syntax, the relevant concept of weight relating to prosodic rather than syntactic branching: "a prosodic constituent is heavy iff it branches" (Zec and Inkelas 1990: 373). For example, in Serbo-Croatian, a syntactically branching prepositional phrase (28a) is not heavy enough to be a topic, in contrast to a prepositional phrase which also forms a complex prosodic constituent, such as the branching phonological phrase in (28b). (Brackets indicate prosodic constituency.)

(28) a. **((Sa Petrom)) razgovarala=je samo Marija.* [Serbo-Croatian]
with Peter talk.PST=AUX only Mary
'To Peter, only Mary spoke.'

b. *((Sa tim) (čovekom)) razgovarala=je samo Marija.*
with that man talk.PST=AUX only Mary
'To that man, only Mary spoke.'
(Zec and Inkelas 1990: 374)

The interface as characterized by, for instance, Selkirk (1995) and Truckenbrodt (1999) does not preclude possible interaction between syntax and phonology in both directions, and Zec and Inkelas (1990) explicitly propose a bidirectional model. Pullum and Zwicky (1988: 275–276) counter that heaviness effects are probably indicative of a processing-based preference for long or complicated constituents to appear non-finally, rather than evidence of some grammatical rule having applied though.

4.5. Conclusion

Accounting for syntax–phonology interface phenomena is a concern of researchers working in many different theoretical models (e.g. Kiaer 2006, Dynamic Syntax; Klein

2000, HPSG; Butt and King 1998, LFG; Szendrői 2003, Minimalism). It is clear that such research is key to increasing our understanding not only of the precise nature of the interaction between syntax and phonology, but also of grammar and its organization.

5. Syntax and semantics

5.1. Introduction

Using finite mental resources, a native speaker is able to determine for any one of an infinite number of sentences (i) whether it conforms to that language's syntactic requirements and thus is well formed, and (ii) what its meaning is. Accounting for a speaker's ability to associate a novel phrase or sentence with the appropriate meaning is a key issue in the study of the relationship between syntax and semantics. Debate has centred on how to define and delimit syntax, semantics and their interaction in accordance with the Principle of Compositionality (Section 5.2), whose interpretation and formalization in turn has important implications for the architecture of the grammar.

A wide variety of phenomena have been examined in light of proposals made concerning the interaction of syntax and semantics. As well as determining how the two are related, research has focused on where the boundary lies between syntax and semantics. For example, with regards to argument structure, there is debate over whether explanations should be framed in terms of syntactic or semantic relations (see e.g. Baker 1997; Goldberg 1995; Grimshaw 1990; Hale and Keyser 2002; Van Valin 2005). Other key topics include anaphora (Heim 1998; Reinhart 1983), coordination (Partee and Rooth 1983; Steedman 2000b), tense and aspect (Giorgi and Pianesi 1997; Guéron and Lecarme 2004), interrogatives (Comorovski 1996; Ginzburg and Sag 2000) and ellipsis (Dalrymple et al. 1991; Kennedy 2003).

In order to illustrate some of the issues faced by theories of the syntax–semantics interface, Section 5.3 reviews two approaches to the analysis of quantifier scope, a subject which has provided significant insights and continues to be the focus of research.

5.2. Compositionality

Also referred to as Frege's Principle (though attribution of the modern version has been questioned; see Cresswell 1973: 75, fn. 97; Janssen 1997: 420–421; Pelletier 2001; amongst others), the Principle of Compositionality (29) underpins a variety of theoretical approaches to the syntax–semantics interface.

(29) The Principle of Compositionality:
The meaning of a complex expression is a function of the meanings of its parts and of the way they are syntactically combined.
(Partee and Hendriks 1997: 20)

The Principle of Compositionality accounts for the productivity and systematicity of language in terms of the mind's finite resources: a speaker knows the meaning of smaller pieces of language and the rules which combine them to form larger, potentially novel pieces of language; the meaning of the whole is composed of the meaning of its parts as they are put together in the syntax. Syntactic structure and semantic interpretation are thus proposed to be closely linked.

Precisely how the Principle of Compositionality should be interpreted continues to be debated because it is not framed in terms of a specific theory of either syntax or semantics, nor does it precisely define the nature of the relationship between the two (see e.g. Pagin and Westerståhl 2001). Theoretical approaches to compositionality may be distinguished on the basis of whether they characterize all syntactic-structure building as preceding semantic-structure building (the interpretive approach) or posit that syntactic and semantic structure are built in tandem (direct compositionality, also referred to as the "rule-to-rule" or "rule-by-rule" linking of syntax and semantics, e.g. Bach 1976; Partee [1984] 2004).

An interpretive theory (e.g. Heim and Kratzer 1998), assumes that semantics has access only to the fully assembled syntactic structure of a complex expression. As the basis for semantic composition is a completed syntactic structure, it is not the case that all expressions which act as input to syntactic operations, or indeed syntactic operations themselves, should have semantic relevance. This approach is usually framed within a transformational theory of grammar which posits that an expression's syntactic structure is interfaced with its semantic interpretation via Logical Form, a separate level of representation that is derived from the pronounced (overt) syntactic structure and consists of all and only the syntactic information relevant to interpretation. The interpretive approach has been criticised for involving unnecessary complexity because syntax and semantics are posited to operate on the same types of objects, the former applying before the latter. Jacobson (2002: 609–611) argues that it is not clear why this should be the case when syntax and semantics are assumed to be distinct combinatory systems.

Under direct compositionality, semantics operates in parallel with syntax. Directly compositional approaches such as Steedman (2000b) analyse the construction of a complex expression's syntactic and semantic structure as occurring simultaneously because "for every syntactic operation there must be a corresponding semantic operation" (Barker and Jacobson 2007: 1). Direct compositionality therefore requires every syntactic object and operation to have a semantic counterpart. The interaction between these two components of the grammar follows from this assumption of homomorphism. Modelling the interface in this way is not without its problems though. If the rules of syntax and semantics apply in tandem, the semantic structure of a complex expression is expected to reflect exactly its syntactic structure and how it was assembled. This is the case in (30). (Throughout, structures have been simplified for the purpose of exposition.)

(30) *John met Alice.*

a. Syntactic structure

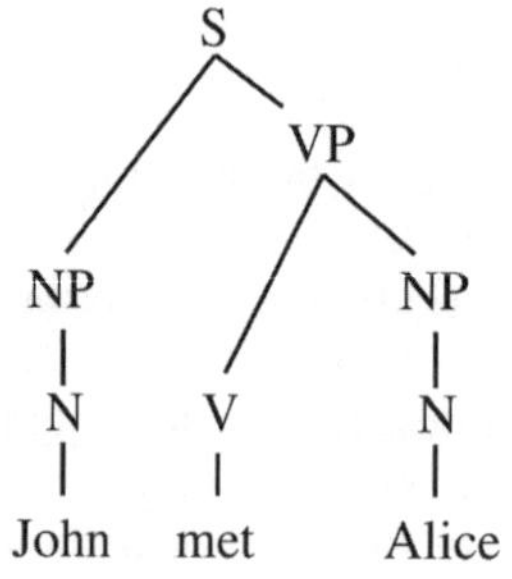

b. Semantic structure
$\lambda y.\lambda x.$meet(x, y)(alice) [syntax: object NP + V = VP]
$\lambda x.$meet(x, alice)(john) [syntax: VP + subject NP = S]
meet(john, alice) [syntax: S]

However, examples such as (31), which include an object quantifier phrase (*every student*), indicate that it is not always possible to account for the relationship between syntactic and semantic structure in terms of such a straightforward correspondence. In the sentence's syntactic structure (31a), the quantifier phrase *every student* combines with the verb *met* to form a verb phrase; the quantifier phrase thus occupies a lower syntactic position than the subject *John*. By contrast, in the sentence's semantic structure (31b), the quantifier phrase combines with the rest of the sentence to give its meaning and thus the quantifier takes scope over the individual *john*.

(31) *John met every student.*
a. Syntactic structure

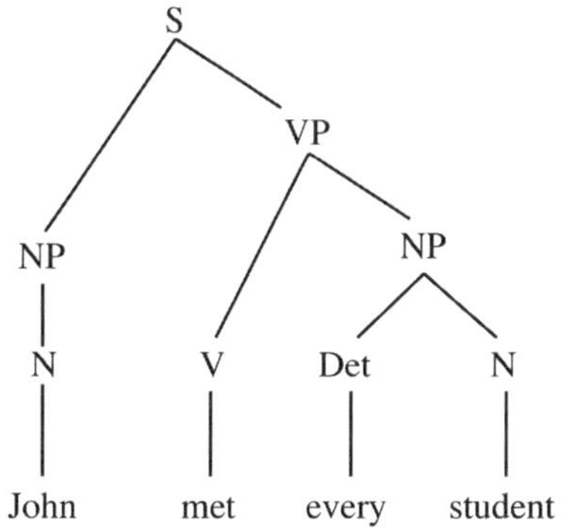

b. Semantic structure
every(student, $\lambda y.$meet(john, y))

The differences between the syntactic and semantic structures in (31) are problematic for a directly compositional analysis because the object quantifier is not interpreted in situ, which runs contrary to the assumption that the syntactic and semantic combinatory systems operate in parallel. Some additional mechanism is therefore required to account for the interpretation of object quantifiers, increasing the complexity of a directly compositional analysis.

Directly compositional theories vary in terms of how strictly compositionality is assumed to apply. In its strongest interpretation (see e.g. Jacobson 1999), the Principle of Compositionality is taken to require that a strict homomorphism maps the structure of syntax onto the structure of semantics, and thus no reference can be made to a constituent's internal structure. It follows that complex expressions are constructed in the syntax only by the concatenation of strings (Barker and Jacobson 2007: 4).

Under a weaker version of compositionality, on the other hand, the internal structure of syntactic and semantic constituents can be accessed. This weakening is motivated by the need to account for examples of ambiguity which are not the result of lexical or syntactic ambiguity, as in cases of quantifier scope ambiguity (Section 5.3). The extent to which access is permitted varies, meaning that a number of different theories exist which can be characterized as adopting weak direct compositionality. For example, at one end of the scale are approaches like that of Bach (1979, 1980) in which concatenation is augmented only by an infixation operation (Wrap). This requires a slightly weakened notion of compositionality because in identifying any point of infixation, reference must be made to the internal structure of the expression.

While a weaker version of direct compositionality permits reference to internal structure, it is not the case that such an approach must rely on a hierarchical conception of syntactic structure, such as that in (31a). The glue semantics approach (Dalrymple 1999) captures weak compositionality in a formally precise way without assuming that meanings are constructed in a rigid order on the basis of phrase structure alone. According to this theory of the syntax–semantics interface, meanings are assembled by linear logic (Girard 1987), which acts as the "glue" connecting an expression's syntactic structure and its semantic interpretation. Each word contributes a meaning, specified in logical terms; syntactic rules and parts of the syntactic structure may also contribute meanings. These meanings are combined by standard inference to give the meaning of the whole sentence. Syntactic structure thus constrains semantic composition without determining its order. Like the Principle of Compositionality itself, glue semantics is independent of the theoretical frameworks used to capture semantic composition and syntactic structure, and is therefore compatible with a range of syntactic and semantic formalisms. For example, glue analyses have been proposed within a standard Montague-type predicate logic (Dalrymple 2001) and Discourse Representation Theory (van Genabith and Crouch 1999), within LFG (Dalrymple 1999) and HPSG (Asudeh and Crouch 2002).

Interpretive theories and those which observe some version of direct compositionality are generally framed as opposing theories of the syntax–semantics interface, with the former offering a syntactic solution and the latter a semantic solution to the issue of apparent mismatches, though Barker (2007) argues that the two approaches can coexist within the grammar without introducing redundancy and proposes a grammar with the property of direct compositionality on demand.

5.3. Quantifier Scope

The test for any theoretical approach to the interaction between syntax and semantics is to provide an analysis of interface phenomena. One of the classic problems which must be addressed is accounting for quantifier scope construal.

5.3.1. Object quantifiers and quantifier scope ambiguity: the data

An intransitive verb such as *smiled*, which denotes a property, requires an argument such as *Al*, which refers to an individual, to give a sentence *Al smiled* whose meaning is a proposition and which can be represented as in (32).

(32) *Al smiled.*
smile(al)

A quantifier such as *every student* does not refer to an individual or a set of individuals (see e.g. Heim and Kratzer 1998: 131–177), but is analysed as representing a property of properties, a higher-order property. For instance, in the meaning of the sentence in (33), *every student* describes that some property applies to every student, in this case the property of having smiled. (Contrast this with the meaning represented in [32], in which having smiled is a property which applies to the individual referred to by the subject *Al.*)

(33) *Every student smiled.*
$\text{every}(\text{student}, \lambda x.\text{smile}(x))$

Complications arise when a quantifier appears in object position, as in the sentence *John met every student* in (31), because of the mismatch between syntactic structure and semantic interpretation. In the syntactic structure in (31a), the object *every student* combines with the predicate *met*. However, the sentence's semantic structure, given in (31b), does not reflect this. The transitive verb *met* denotes a relation between individuals (e.g. *John met Alice*, as in [30]), but a quantifier like *every student* combines with a property to give a proposition, as in (33). Hence, it does not appear to be the case that the meanings of *met* and *every student* combine to give the meaning of the VP *met every student* in (31), in violation of the Principle of Compositionality.

A related issue is quantifier scope ambiguity. When two quantifiers appear in the same sentence, as in (34), two readings are available for a single syntactic structure (34a) in English because the relative scope of the quantifiers may differ. (This does not hold in all languages though. For example, Kiss 2001 shows that German is an exception.)

(34) *Everybody met somebody.*

a. Syntactic structure

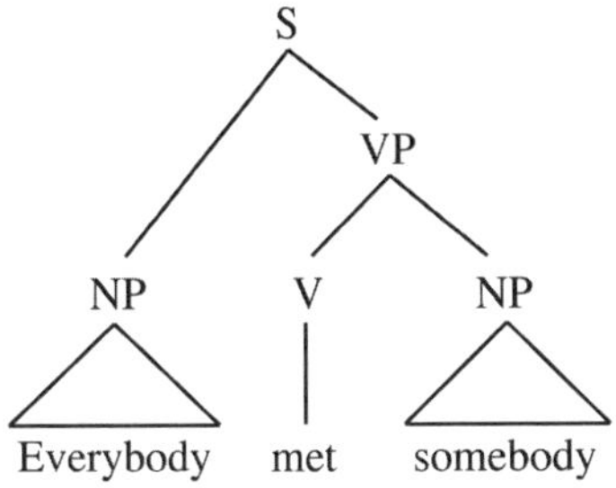

b. Reading 1: 'for each person, there is at least one person that he/she met'
everybody takes scopes over *somebody*
$\text{every}(\text{person}, \lambda x.\text{some}(\text{person}, \lambda y.\text{meet}(x, y)))$

c. Reading 2: 'there is at least one person that was met by everyone'
somebody takes scopes over *everybody*
$\text{some}(\text{person}, \lambda y.\text{every}(\text{person}, \lambda x.\text{meet}(x, y)))$

Sentences like (34) are problematic because according to the Principle of Compositionality there should only be one semantic structure associated with any single syntactic structure. A theory of the syntax–semantics interface must account for such instances of ambiguity and the different quantifier scope relations involved in data from a variety of languages, on the importance of which see Bach et al. (1995a, 1995b) and Matthewson (2001, 2008).

In Sections 5.3.2 and 5.3.3, two different theoretical approaches, one compatible with an interpretive analysis and one with direct compositionality, are reviewed in order to give an idea of how issues relating to quantifier scope have been addressed. Other approaches to quantification and the syntax–semantics interface, which are not covered for reasons of space, include Montague's (1974) "Quantifying In", Cooper Storage (Cooper 1975; Keller 1988) and continuations (Barker 2002).

5.3.2. The interpretive approach and quantifier raising

A widely adopted interpretive approach to quantification is that outlined in Heim and Kratzer (1998), in which a level of Logical Form is assumed and quantifier scope is accounted for in terms of syntactic movement of the quantifier from the position in which it was generated (where it leaves behind a trace *t* with which the quantified phrase is co-indexed) to a position consistent with the sentence's proposed semantic structure. This Quantifier Raising creates a structure at Logical Form within which the quantifier binds a variable that is located in the position originally occupied by the quantifier (Chomsky 1976; May 1977). A quantifier's scope corresponds to its c-command domain (see Reinhart 1976). In this way, the local and global aspects of a quantifier's interpretation are accounted for.

The Logical Form representation of the sentence in (31) is derived via Quantifier Raising as shown in (35). It is this Logical Form representation, rather than the initial syntactic representation, which is the input to semantic interpretation. Interpretation of a quantifier therefore occurs after Quantifier Raising has occurred and its scope has been determined, i.e. ex situ, meaning that although the VP *met every student* is a syntactic constituent, it does not have a corresponding semantic interpretation.

(35) *John met every student.*

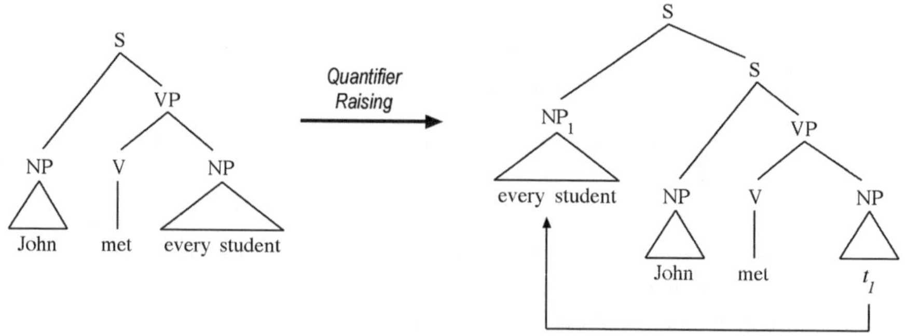

The quantifier scope ambiguity exemplified in (34) is accounted for thus: *Everybody met somebody* represents a single syntactic structure from which two different LF representa-

(36) *Everybody met somebody.*

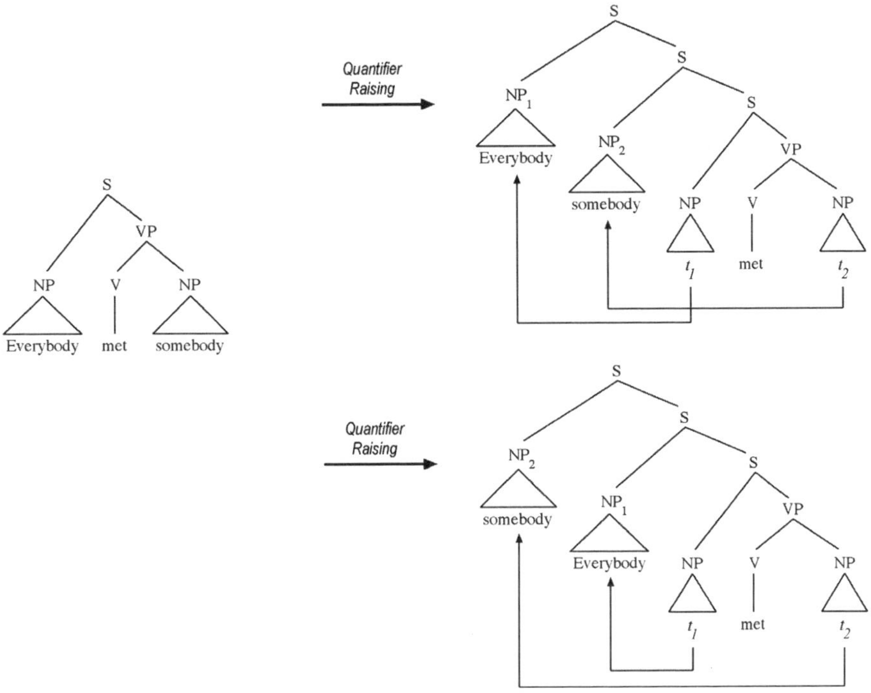

tions, each associated with a different meaning, may be derived depending on the order in which quantifier raising applies, as shown in (36).

Quantifier Raising deals with the mismatch between syntactic and semantic structure by increasing the complexity of the syntax. It is claimed that this is justified given independent evidence of movement and observed parallels between the covert movement of quantifier phrases and overt movement of elements such as question ("wh") phrases (see e.g. Aoun and Li 1993; May 1985). However, if they are instances of the same phenomena, the syntactic constraints which restrict the scope of quantifiers (see Heim and Kratzer 1998: 209–238) and those on movement should be identical. Ruys and Winter (2011) discuss data which indicate that at least one syntactic condition on movement, the Subjacency Condition (Chomsky 1973), does not apply to Quantifier Raising in the same way that it does to question words. Such divergence undermines a unified account of movement and Quantifier Raising, which is one of the main motivations for the Quantifier Raising analysis.

5.3.3. Direct compositionality, flexible types and type shifting

Hendriks' (1993) flexible types approach is a semantic solution to mismatches at the syntax–semantics interface, compatible with direct compositionality, which builds on Partee and Rooth's (1983) proposal that predicates are semantically ambiguous. Under this approach, transitive verbs do not uniformly denote relations between individuals;

this is simply their minimal type. Rather, the semantic type of a verb is flexible and type-shifting rules may apply to systematically change it depending on the context in which the verb occurs. This flexibility resolves the mismatch issue exemplified in (31) as sketched in (37). In a sentence such as *John met every student*, type-shifting rules apply to lift the type of the object position of the transitive verb *met*, so that the verb denotes a relation between an individual and a quantifier (a property of properties) and the object position has scope over the other argument position. In this way, the object quantifier can combine with the meaning of the transitive verb in such a way as to capture the facts about scope in accordance with direct compositionality. It is not necessary to posit any syntactic operation such as Quantifier Raising to account for these data. (Another possibility is type-shifting of the quantifier phrase; see Heim and Kratzer 1998: 180–182.)

(37) *John met every student.*

a. *met* = $\lambda y.\lambda x.$meet(x, y)

$\Downarrow$ TYPE LIFTING

met = λP.$\lambda x.$P($\lambda y.$meet(x, y))

b. *met every student* = $\lambda x.$every(student, $\lambda y.$meet(x, y))

c. *John met every student* = every(student, $\lambda y.$meet(john, y))

With respect to quantifier scope ambiguity, the different versions of a verb's meaning which are available license the different scope relations that may exist between quantifiers in its argument positions. The order in which type-shifting rules apply ultimately determines which of the two quantifiers takes scope over the other in a sentence such as (34), thus accounting for the semantic ambiguity. In the case of Reading 1 (34b), a type-shifting rule applies to lift the type of the subject argument before the object argument and hence the object quantifier is in the subject quantifier's scope; in the case of Reading 2 (34c), the order in which this type-shifting occurs is reversed, and consequently so is the relative scope of the quantifiers.

A flexible types approach therefore addresses the issue of mismatch at the syntax–semantics interface at the cost of increasing the complexity of the semantics. It relies on the assumption of widespread polysemy and the introduction of type-shifting rules. Type-shifting is a powerful mechanism; it must be constrained in a principled manner in order to avoid overgeneration. Another concern is that a flexible types approach may be inconsistent with the self-reliance which is characteristic of direct compositionality according to Barker (2007: 106) because, rather than being self-contained, interpretation of a constituent can depend on looking ahead in the semantic analysis to relations that will exist between a constituent and some external element.

Under a glue semantics analysis (Section 5.2), the semantic ambiguity in (34) arises as a result of there being two possible ways in which the same semantic objects can be combined. No type-shifting rules are necessary; the flexibility is inherent in the combinatory mechanism. See Asudeh and Crouch (2002).

5.4. Conclusion

Accounting for quantifier scope construal represents a challenge for any theory of the syntax–semantics interface. The different approaches outlined, which take the Principle of Compositionality as their starting point, each continue to contribute to our understanding of syntax, semantics, and the organization of the grammar as a whole, as well as the systematic and productive nature of human language.

6. Syntax and pragmatics

6.1. Introduction

It has been argued that to understand syntax and pragmatics, the two cannot be divorced as "pragmatics without syntax is empty; syntax without pragmatics is blind" (Huang 2007: 271), an allusion to Kant's (1781: 51) statement that "Gedanken ohne Inhalt sind leer, Anschauungen ohne Begriffe sind blind" ['thoughts without content are empty, intuitions without concepts are blind']. Discussing the syntax–pragmatics interface is complicated by the difficulties in defining pragmatics itself, as Levinson's (1983: 5–35) review of the term and its scope indicates. For the purposes of this overview, which can deal with only some of the relevant issues in general terms, pragmatics is regarded as the study of a sentence's meaning in context, and thus its interface with syntax is explored with regard to the effect that context may have on sentence structure and its acceptability.

The acceptability of sentences is not simply a matter of their being syntactically well formed or interpretable, as the examples in (38) illustrate. While the passive constructions in (38a–b) are both grammatical, (38b) is infelicitous in the context given in (38d); (38a), on the other hand, can appear in a similar context (38c).

(38) a. *He will be succeeded by Ivan Allen Jr.*
b. *The mayor will be succeeded by him.*
c. *The mayor's present term of office expires on January 1. He will be succeeded by Ivan Allen Jr. ...* (Brown Corpus)
d. *Ivan Allen Jr. will take office January 1. # The mayor will be succeeded by him.*

(Ward and Birner 2004: 169–170)

Ward and Birner (2004) account for the infelicity of the passive construction in (38d) in terms of the relative discourse status of the syntactic subject, *the mayor*, and the logical subject *him* (Ivan Allen Jr.) which appears in the postverbal *by*-phrase. They claim that in this and other such argument-reversing constructions, the syntactic subject must represent information which is at least as familiar as that represented by the logical subject in the *by*-phrase within the context of the discourse. In (38c) the mayor, the antecedent of the syntactic subject *he*, is old information, having been given in the first sentence, while Ivan Allen Jr. is new information; as a result, the passive construction is felicitous. In (38d), by contrast, the mayor (the syntactic subject) is new information while Ivan Allen Jr. (the antecedent of the logical subject *him*) is old information, having been mentioned in the first sentence; as a result, the passive, though grammatical, is infelicitous. (38d) thus exemplifies a mismatch at the syntax–pragmatics interface.

Passivization is only one example of a wide range of phenomena covered in the literature on the syntax–pragmatics interface. Other topics include ellipsis (Cann et al.

2007), evidentiality and logophoricity (Speas 2004), scalar implicatures (Chierchia 2004) and anaphora (Huang 2000). To highlight some of the relevant issues, Sections 6.2 and 6.3 focus on one aspect of the interaction between pragmatics and syntax: information structure.

6.2. Information structure

Information structure has been the focus of research in various sub-disciplines of linguistics and within a range of different theoretical frameworks. For example, the relationship between intonation and information structure is discussed by Büring (1997), Downing (2006), Mycock (2006), Skopeteas et al. (2009) and Steedman (2000a), while the relationship between semantics and information structure is the subject of work by, e.g., Heim (1988), Kamp ([1981] 1984), Krifka (1992), Rooth (1985, 1992), Strawson ([1964] 1971) and von Stechow (1991). The key issue is why it should be possible to express fundamentally the same meaning in a variety of ways. Languages with free word order illustrate this point well. Slovene, for example, has highly flexible word order: the grammatical function of a constituent is usually marked morphologically; grammatical functions do not appear to be associated with particular syntactic positions. Derbyshire (1993: 122) provides two versions of the same two-word sentence which vary in terms of their word order and precise interpretation. (Focus is indicated by small capitals in the translation.)

(39) a. *Moram brati.* [Slovene]
must.PRS.1SG read.INF
'I must READ.'

b. *Brati moram.*
read.INF must.PRS.1SG
'I MUST read.'
(Derbyshire 1993: 122)

While the sentences in (39) may both be translated into English as *I must read*, this does not capture the fact that the relevant information is packaged in a particular way which results in subtle differences in emphasis and possible usage. As Ward and Birner (2004: 153) observe, "the speaker's choice of constructions (…) serves to structure the informational flow of the discourse". Thus, the syntax reflects pragmatic factors. The effects that such packaging of information may have on syntax are not arbitrary and are attested in a wide range of languages. For example, the most common ordering of grammatical functions in Slovene is SVO according to Greenberg (2006: 124), Herrity (2000: 333) and Priestly (1993: 428), inter alia. However, this tendency is likely to be a consequence of a stronger ordering restriction best expressed in terms of discourse functions rather than grammatical functions such as subject and object. A number of proposals have been made with regard to the organizing principles and primitives of information structure which have consequences not only for syntax, and thus the analysis of data such as (39), but also for the architecture of grammar as a whole.

6.2.1. Information structure primitives

Information structure (Halliday 1967), sometimes also referred to as information packaging (Chafe 1976), is broadly concerned with how linguistic structures serve to indicate the relationship of an utterance and its contents to the wider discourse context. Establishing what the primitives of information structure are has been a concern at least since Mathesius ([1929] 1983), whose work has been followed up by linguists such as Daneš (1974), Firbas (1964) and Sgall (1967) within the Prague School tradition, and has influenced many others, including Bolinger (1965), Kuno (1972) and Vallduví (1992). The primitives of information structure continue to be the subject of debate and a range of different definitions, terminology, and divisions exist in the literature, as the summary provided by Kruijff-Korbayová and Steedman (2003: 254) and the inventories provided by Erteschik-Shir (2007) show. Even so, key to many accounts of information structure and its interaction with syntax are two concepts which are usually referred to as topic and focus. While it is not within the scope of this section to provide a comprehensive summary of all the relevant definitions in the literature, it is possible to outline what is broadly meant by these two terms.

Topic and focus relate an utterance to the wider discourse context and reflect the communicative requirements of the discourse participants. A topic specifies what an utterance is about; the rest of a sentence or utterance represents the speaker's comment on that topic. It is widely assumed that for an element to be a topic, and thus for it to be available for comment, it must be given or old, that is it must represent an entity whose meaning the speaker and the addressee can retrieve, for example, from previous experience or from the immediate discourse context. (Gundel and Fretheim 2004 review the given-new distinction and claim a more fine-grained analysis is required to account for attested differences; see also Prince 1981 for more on the given/new distinction.)

Focus has also been defined in terms of givenness: focus represents information new to the addressee, presented in terms of its relation to information that is (or can be assumed to be) given or old to him/her (background information). Any topic is old in this sense too, so the focus/background and topic/comment dichotomies may overlap, as the answer to the question in (40) shows. (Vallduví 1992 conflates topic/comment and focus/background into a trinomial hierarchical articulation of the information structure of an utterance.)

(40) Q: *What did Charlie bring?*
A: *He brought chocolate.*

TOPIC	COMMENT	
He	*brought*	*chocolate*
BACKGROUND		FOCUS

The standard test for focus/background involves a constituent ("wh") question, as in (40), because the answer constituent represents information new to the addressee and hence the focus of the utterance. Tests for topic status are less clear-cut, as Erteschik-

Shir (2007: 19–22) shows. In (40) though, it is clear that the question requires the answer to be about Charlie and because he has been mentioned in the question, Charlie is given information. The pronoun *he* in the answer has properties of givenness and aboutness, consistent with it being a topic.

In some languages, there is a particularly close relationship between syntax and information structure. Hungarian is an example of such a discourse-configurational language (É. Kiss, this volume): there is syntactic marking of aspects of discourse structure, but otherwise word order is relatively free. In Hungarian, a single focused item appears immediately preverbally and is preceded by any topics, as in (41).

(41) [*Anna*]$_{\text{TOPIC}}$ [*Péter-nek*]$_{\text{TOPIC}}$ [*könyv-et*]$_{\text{FOCUS}}$ *adott.* [Hungarian]
Anna.NOM Peter-DAT book-ACC give.PST.3SG
'To Peter, Anna gave a BOOK.'
(Lipták 2001: 10)

Aspects of the canonical order of constituents in Hungarian are therefore best expressed in terms of their information structural status rather than their grammatical function. This is also the case in other languages. For example, the fact that SVO is the most common ordering of constituents in Slovene (Section 6.2) is likely to be related to the more general cross-linguistic tendencies for old information to precede new information and for the subject to be the default topic (Lambrecht 1994; Li and Thompson 1976; Reinhart 1982).

Huang (2007: 271) states that the degree to which there is interaction of pragmatics and syntax varies typologically. He asserts that in pragmatic languages such as Chinese, Japanese and Korean, principles of language usage rather than rules of grammatical structure are key to understanding some phenomena which have been analysed purely in terms of syntax. This indicates that the precise location of the border separating syntax from pragmatics may differ from language to language, undermining universalist syntactocentric conceptions of grammar.

Even in a language in which canonical word order can be captured in terms of grammatical functions such as English (SVO), the effects of the interaction between information structure and syntax can be identified, as in (42).

(42) a. Topicalization (O S V)
G: *Do you watch football?*
E: *Yeah.* [*Baseball*]$_{\text{TOPIC}}$ *I like a lot better.*
(Ward and Birner 2004: 161)

b. Inversion (ADJ V S)
We have complimentary soft drinks, coffee, Sanka, tea, and milk. Also complimentary is [*red and white wine*]$_{\text{FOCUS}}$.
(Ward and Birner 2004: 171)

Thus, the information structure status of constituents may be the reason for their occurrence in a non-canonical position.

6.3. Analyzing information structure

Theoretical approaches to information structure and, more generally, to pragmatics can be divided into two main types based on whether the architecture of grammar is posited to be multi-level. The architecture assumed in the Minimalist Program (Chomsky 1995) has the syntactic computation interact separately with Phonetic Form (PF) and Logical Form (LF). There is no separate level of pragmatics; information structure which has an effect on the syntax is thus part of the syntactic computation itself. Non-canonical word order is the result of the movement of constituents, which is triggered by the need to check and delete uninterpretable features (by having them matched with interpretable features) before PF and LF in the fine structure of the clause's left periphery, outlined in an influential paper by Rizzi (1997) and pursued in the cartographic approach (e.g. Benincà 2001; Rizzi 2004; for a different theoretical approach within the Minimalist framework, see Reinhart 2006.) For example, Rizzi (1997: 297) proposes the articulated structure for the complementizer system in (43), which includes recursion of Topic Phrases (indicated by the asterisks), to account for ordering constraints in a clause's left periphery.

(43)

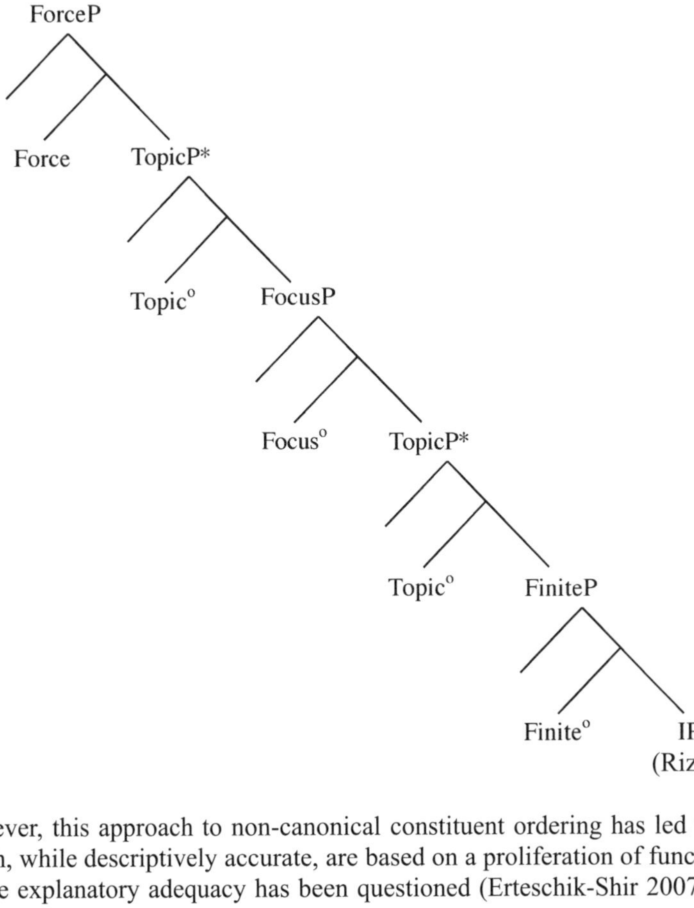

(Rizzi 1997: 297)

However, this approach to non-canonical constituent ordering has led to some analyses which, while descriptively accurate, are based on a proliferation of functional projections whose explanatory adequacy has been questioned (Erteschik-Shir 2007: 86–101).

Huang (2007: 271) points out that constraints on syntax which are rooted in pragmatics tend to be general and violable and thus appear to be fundamentally different from the rules of syntax themselves. He suggests that OT syntax may offer a way forward for modelling the interaction between syntax and pragmatics in the Chomskyan generative tradition.

The idea that pragmatics and syntax are distinct is modelled straightforwardly in those approaches which posit a multi-dimensional grammatical architecture. Such multi-level systems can be further divided into those which posit that information structure, with its own rules and primitives, represents an independent level of linguistic structure (LFG; Erteschik-Shir's 1997 focus-structure theoretical framework) and those which do not (Construction Grammar, Dynamic Syntax, HPSG, RRG).

In the non-derivational framework of LFG, those features of information structure which result in non-canonical syntactic constructions are represented as grammaticized discourse functions at the level of f(unctional)-structure (Bresnan and Mchombo 1987). Discourse functions overlay grammatical functions such as subject and object, in order to relate an element to the wider discourse context. The discourse functions topic and focus are integrated into the meaning of a sentence by binding an element which bears an argument function (the Extended Coherence Condition; see e.g. Dalrymple 2001: 390). Thus at f-structure the value of two functions may be the same subsidiary f-structure. As focus and topic cannot necessarily be straightforwardly defined in terms of syntactic constituents – if they affect the syntax at all – researchers including Butt and King (1997), Choi (1999) and Mycock (2006) have argued for a separate level of i(nformation)-structure in the LFG parallel architecture. If an independent i-structure representation is part of the grammar, King (1997) points out that the issue arises of whether any information about discourse functions should be included at f-structure at all. This point remains to be fully explored.

The argument function of a constituent in a non-canonical syntactic position cannot be determined directly by reference to local information such as subcategorization frames. It is therefore necessary to resolve the grammatical role of the constituent in non-canonical c-structure position. At the syntactic level of c(onstituent)-structure, the relevant node, which is annotated with functional equations, associates that c-structure position with (i) the appropriate discourse function, and (ii) a grammatical function (GF) at f-structure. In (44), for instance, the functional equation $\downarrow \in (\uparrow \text{FOCUS})$ associates the immediately preverbal c-structure position with the function FOCUS at the levels of f-structure and i-structure simultaneously (every grammaticized discourse function bearing the corresponding discourse function at i-structure by definition), while the functional equation $(\uparrow \text{GF}^*) = \downarrow$ associates it with a grammatical function at f-structure (in this case, object). This means that the value of the grammatical function OBJ and the discourse function FOCUS is the same at f-structure in (44); the structure sharing involved is represented by a solid line linking the two functions. The relations between the immediately relevant levels of linguistic structure are represented in (44) by arrows; the correspondence function φ relates c-structure nodes to f-structures, and the correspondence function ι relates c-structure nodes to i-structures (see Dalrymple 2001).

(44) [*János*]$_{\text{TOPIC}}$ [*Mari-t*]$_{\text{FOCUS}}$ *hív-t-a* *fel.* [Hungarian]
John.NOM Mary-ACC call-PST-DEF.3SG VM
'John called MARY.'

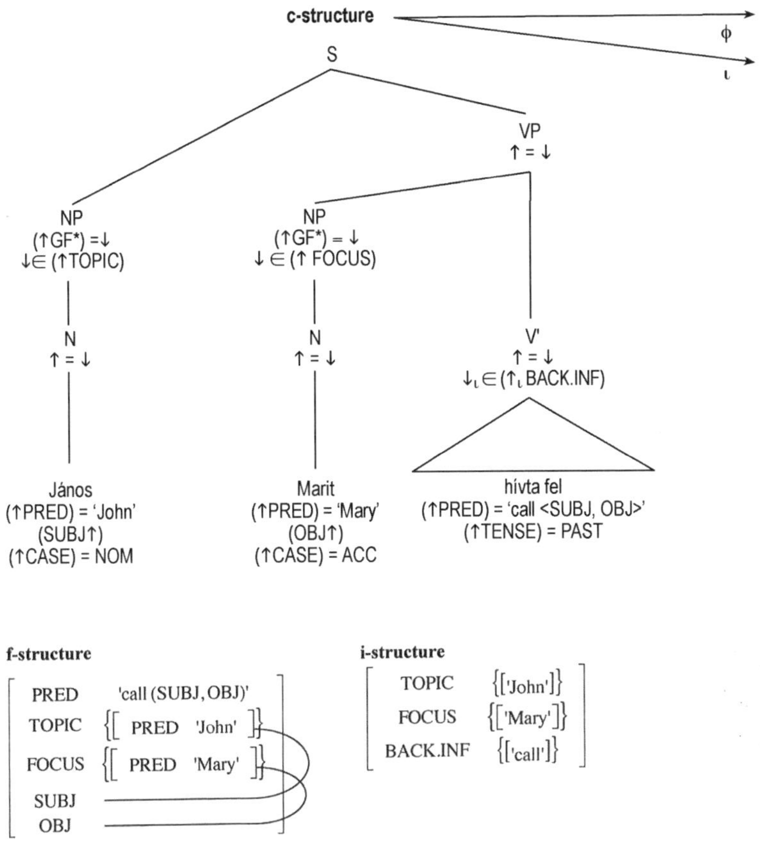

As Mycock (2006: 81, 90–91) notes, the possible values of functions such as FOCUS at i-structure and how exactly information-structure relates to semantic-structure in LFG's parallel, correspondence-based architecture remain to be determined.

Choi (1999) also investigates information structure within the LFG framework, but provides an OT analysis of the universal mapping principles which link syntax and information structure. Choi (1999) argues that word-order variation is due to the interaction of syntactic constraints, which are responsible for canonical word order, and information structuring constraints. The two are ranked relative to one another, with the exact ranking determined on a language-by-language basis. This captures the insights that the influence of information structure on word order varies cross-linguistically and that pragmatic constraints tend to be violable rather than absolute (cf. Huang 2007: 271).

Role and Reference Grammar (RRG; Van Valin and LaPolla 1997; Van Valin 2008) adopts a different approach to the syntax–pragmatics interface and therefore information structure. The communicative functions of grammatical structures are central to this approach, according to which syntactic knowledge is stored in constructional templates specified for morphosyntactic, semantic and pragmatic properties. According to RRG, which builds on the approach to information structure outlined in Lambrecht's (1994) influential work, a construction is assigned a focus structure which, like the constituent projection and the operator projection, is represented as a separate projection of the

(45)

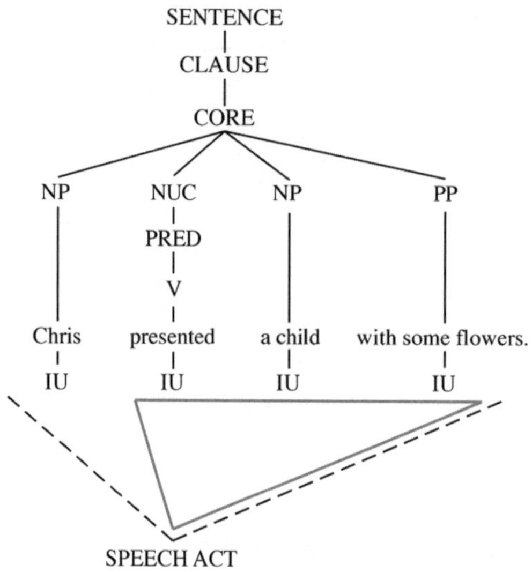

(Van Valin 2005: 77)

clause. Focus structure is analysed in terms of syntactically defined, information structural units (IUs), following Lambrecht (1994). For example, in (45), *Chris* functions as the topic while the remainder of the sentence functions as the comment, referred to in RRG as the focus domain. The speech act node acts as an anchor for the focus structure projection, within which the Potential Focus Domain (dashed lines) and the Actual Focus Domain (the grey triangle) are represented. The Actual Focus Domain is determined in relation to the utterance in question.

A distinction can be made between specialized and unspecialized constructional templates. In the case of the latter, assignment of the appropriate focus structure to a sentence is to some extent context dependent, as is the case in (45). When a specific sentence type is associated with a particular focus structure though, as in the case of constituent ("wh") questions (Van Valin 2005: 171), the two are stored together as a specialized template.

Erteschik-Shir (2007) discusses some issues which remain to be addressed in future work on the syntax–pragmatics interface within the framework of RRG. She points out that the mapping from syntax to focus structure in RRG may be stipulated rather than motivated, and without constraints it would be too permissive (Erteschik-Shir 2007: 147). There is also the issue of whether it is always possible to define information (focus) structure solely in terms of syntactically defined units.

6.4. Conclusion

Much progress has been made but as research continues into the wide range of phenomena, including information structure, which exemplify the interaction between syntax and pragmatics, Bar-Hillel's (1971: 405) words of warning are still relevant: "Be more careful with forcing bits and pieces you find in the pragmatic wastebasket into your favorite syntactico-semantic theory. It would perhaps be preferable to first bring some order into the contents of this wastebasket". The analysis of non-canonical syntax and its relation to context is key to defining and understanding the scope of pragmatics, the scope of syntax, and the organization of grammar as a whole.

7. Conclusion

This chapter has given an overview of syntax and its relationship with other components of the grammar. The modules which are proposed to comprise the theoretical construct of the grammar could be taken to define and delimit domains of enquiry and hence subdisciplines of the field of linguistics. However, the issue of interfaces shows that this cannot always be the case. In this sense, interfaces are the theory-internal correspondent of the wider matter of inter-disciplinarity. Providing as it does insights into a wide range of empirical and theoretical issues, not least the structure of linguistic knowledge itself, investigation into the interfaces of syntax with other modules of the grammar represents an important area of contemporary research that will continue to stimulate debate between linguists from across the field working within a variety of frameworks.

8. Abbreviations

BACK.INF	background information
DO	direct object
FACT	factual
FS	final suffix
LV	light verb
PUNC	punctual
VM	verb modifier

3. Acknowledgements

This work was supported by a British Academy Postdoctoral Fellowship. I would like to thank Miriam Butt, and Susana Afonso, Mary Dalrymple, Bethwyn Evans, Tibor Kiss, Aditi Lahiri, Atsuko Masuda, Yo Matsumoto, Sandra Paoli and Nigel Vincent for their time, insights and comments on drafts of this chapter.

9. References (selected)

Ackema, Peter, and Ad Neeleman
2004 *Beyond Morphology: Interface Conditions on Word Formation*. Oxford: Oxford University Press.

Alsina, Alex
1996 *The Role of Argument Structure in Grammar: Evidence from Romance*. Stanford, CA: CSLI Publications.

Anderson, Stephen
2000 Some lexicalist remarks on incorporation phenomena. *Lexicon in Focus, Studia Grammatica* 45: 123–142.

Anderson, Stephen
1982 Where's morphology? *Linguistic Inquiry* 13: 571–612.
Aronoff, Mark
1994 *Morphology by Itself.* Cambridge, MA: MIT Press.
Bach, Emmon
1980 In defense of passive. *Linguistics and Philosophy* 3: 297–341.
Bach, Emmon
1979 Control in Montague Grammar. *Linguistic Inquiry* 10: 515–531.
Baker, Mark
1996 *The Polysynthesis Parameter.* Oxford: Oxford University Press.
Baker, Mark
1988 *Incorporation: A Theory of Grammatical Function Changing.* Chicago: University of Chicago Press.
Baker, Mark
1985 The Mirror Principle and morphosyntactic explanation. *Linguistic Inquiry* 16: 373–415.
Bar-Hillel, Yehoshua
1971 Out of the pragmatic wastebasket. *Linguistic Inquiry* 2: 401–407.
Barker, Chris, and Pauline Jacobson
2007 Introduction: direct compositionality. In: Chris Barker, and Pauline Jacobson (eds.), *Direct Compositionality*, 1–19. Oxford: Oxford University Press.
Beard, Robert
1995 *Lexeme-Morpheme Base Morphology.* Albany: SUNY Press.
Beckman, Mary E., and Janet B. Pierrehumbert
1986 Intonational structure in Japanese and English. *Yearbook of Phonology* 3: 255–309.
Bolinger, Dwight L.
1965 *Forms of English: Accent, Morpheme, Order.* Cambridge, MA: Harvard University Press.
Borer, Hagit
1988 On the morphological parallelism between compounds and constructs. *Yearbook of Morphology* 1: 45–65.
Bošković, Željko
2001 *On the Nature of the Syntax–Phonology Interface: Cliticization and Related Phenomena.* Amsterdam: North-Holland.
Bresnan, Joan
2001 *Lexical-Functional Syntax.* Oxford: Blackwell.
Bresnan, Joan, and Sam A. Mchombo
1987 Topic, pronoun, and agreement in Chichewa. *Language* 63: 741–782.
Büring, Daniel
1997 *The Meaning of Topic and Focus: The 59th Street Bridge Accent.* London: Routledge.
Butt, Miriam, and Tracy Holloway King
1997 Null elements in discourse structure. ms, University of Konstanz.
http://ling.uni-konstanz.de/pages/home/butt/
Chafe, Wallace L.
1976 Givenness, contrastiveness, definiteness, subjects, topics and points of view. In: Charles N. Li (ed.), *Subject and Topic*, 25–55. New York: Academic Press.
Choi, Hye-Won
1999 *Optimizing Structure in Context: Scrambling and Information Structure.* Stanford, CA: CSLI Publications.
Chomsky, Noam
2001 Derivation by phase. In: Michael Kenstowicz (ed.), *Ken Hale: A Life in Language*, 1–52. Cambridge, MA: MIT Press.

Chomsky, Noam
1995 *The Minimalist Program*. Cambridge, MA: MIT Press.
Chomsky, Noam
1981 *Lectures on Government and Binding*. Dordrecht: Foris.
Chomsky, Noam
1970 Remarks on nominalization. In: R. Jacobs, and P. Rosenbaum (eds.), *Readings in English Transformational Grammar*, 184–221. Waltham, MA: Blaisdell Publishing.
Chomsky, Noam, and Morris Halle
1968 *The Sound Pattern of English*. New York: Harper and Row.
Cooper, Robin H.
1975 Montague's semantic theory and transformational syntax. Ph.D. thesis, University of Massachusetts, Amherst.
Corbett, Greville G.
1987 The morphology/syntax interface: evidence from possessive adjectives in Slavonic. *Language* 63: 299–345.
Culicover, Peter W., and Ray Jackendoff
2005 *Simpler Syntax*. Oxford: Oxford University Press.
Dalrymple, Mary
2001 *Lexical Functional Grammar. Syntax and Semantics, Volume 34*. London: Academic Press.
Di Sciullo, Anna Maria, and Edwin Williams
1987 *On the Definition of Word*. Cambridge, MA: MIT Press.
Downing, Laura
2006 The prosody and syntax of focus in Chitumbuka. *ZAS Papers in Linguistics* 43: 55–79.
Embick, David, and Rolf Noyer
2007 Distributed Morphology and the syntax–morphology interface. In: Gillian Ramchand, and Charles Reiss (eds.), *The Oxford Handbook of Linguistic Interfaces*, 289–324. Oxford: Oxford University Press.
Erteschik-Shir, Nomi
2007 *Information Structure: The Syntax–Discourse Interface*. Oxford: Oxford University Press.
Fried, Mirjam, and Jan-Ola Östman
2004 Construction Grammar: a thumbnail sketch. In: Mirjam Fried, and Jan-Ola Östman (eds.), *Construction Grammar in a Cross-Language Perspective*. 11–86. Amsterdam: John Benjamins.
Frota, Sonia
2000 *Prosody and Focus in European Portuguese: Phonological Phrasing and Intonation*. New York: Garland Publishing.
Goldberg, Adele E.
1995 *Constructions: A Construction Grammar Approach to Argument Structure*. Chicago: University of Chicago Press.
Gundel, Jeanette K., and Thorstein Fretheim
2004 Topic and focus. In: Laurence R. Horn, and Gregory Ward (eds.), *The Handbook of Pragmatics*, 175–196. Oxford: Blackwell.
Gussenhoven, Carlos
1992 Intonational phrasing and the prosodic hierarchy. In: Wolfgang U. Dressler, Hans C. Luschützky, Oskar E. Pfeiffer, and John R. Rennison (eds.), *Phonologica 1988: Proceedings of the 6th International Phonology Meeting*, 89–99. Cambridge, UK: Cambridge University Press.
Gussenhoven, Carlos
1984 *On the Grammar and Semantics of Sentence Accents*. Dordrecht: Foris.

Halle, Morris
1973 Prolegomena to a theory of word formation. *Linguistic Inquiry* 4: 3–16.
Halle, Morris, and Alec Marantz
1993 Distributed Morphology and the pieces of inflection. In: Kenneth Hale, and Samuel Jay Keyser (eds.), *The View from Building 20: Essays in Honor of Sylvain Bromberger*, 111–176. Cambridge, MA: MIT Press.
Halliday, M. A. K.
1967 Notes on transitivity and theme in English: part 2. *Journal of Linguistics* 3: 199–244.
Harley, Heidi
2008 On the causative construction. In: Shigeru Miyagawa, and Mamoru Saito (eds.), *The Oxford Handbook of Japanese Linguistics*, 20–53. Oxford: Oxford University Press.
Harris, Alice C.
2002 *Endoclitics and the Origins of Udi Morphosyntax*. Oxford: Oxford University Press.
Harris, Alice C.
2000 Where in the word is the Udi clitic? *Language* 76: 593–616.
Hayes, Bruce, and Aditi Lahiri
1991 Bengali intonational phonology. *Natural Language and Linguistic Theory* 9: 47–96.
Heim, Irene
1988 *The Semantics of Definite and Indefinite Noun Phrases in English*. New York: Garland Publishing.
Heim, Irene, and Angelika Kratzer
1998 *Semantics in Generative Grammar*. Oxford: Blackwell.
Hendriks, Herman L. W.
1993 Studied flexibility: categories and types in syntax and semantics. Ph.D. thesis, University of Amsterdam.
Horvath, Julia, and Tal Siloni
2010 Lexicon versus syntax: evidence from morphological causatives. In: Malka Rappaport Hovav, Edit Doron, and Ivy Sichel (eds.), *Lexical Semantics, Syntax, and Event Structure*. 153–176. Oxford: Oxford University Press.
Huang, Yan
2007 *Pragmatics*. Oxford: Oxford University Press.
Hyman, Larry M., Sharon Inkelas, and Galen Sibanda
2009 Morphosyntactic correspondence in Bantu reduplication. In: Kristin Hanson, and Sharon Inkelas (eds.), *The Nature of the Word: Studies in Honor of Paul Kiparsky*, 273–309. Cambridge, MA: MIT Press.
Inkelas, Sharon, and Draga Zec (eds.)
1990 *The Phonology-Syntax Connection*. Chicago: University of Chicago Press.
Jacobson, Pauline
2002 The (dis)organization of the grammar: 25 years. *Linguistics and Philosophy* 25: 601–626.
Jun, Sun-Ah
1998 The Accentual Phrase in the Korean prosodic hierarchy. *Phonology* 15: 189–226.
Kaisse, Ellen
1985 *Connected Speech*. London: Academic Press.
Kiparsky, Paul
1982 From Cyclic Phonology to Lexical Phonology. In: Harry van der Hulst, and Norval Smith (eds.), *The Structure of Phonological Representations (Part I)*, 131–175. Dordrecht: Foris.
Krifka, Manfred
1992 A compositional semantics for multiple focus constructions. In: Joachim Jacobs (ed.), *Informationsstruktur und Grammatik*, 17–53. Opladen: Westdeutscher Verlag.

Kuno, Susumu
1972 Functional sentence perspective: a case study from Japanese and English. *Linguistic Inquiry* 3: 269–320.
Kuroda, S.-Y.
2003 Complex predicates and predicate raising. *Lingua* 113: 447–480.
Lambrecht, Knud
1994 *Information Structure and Sentence Form: Topic, Focus, and the Mental Representations of Discourse Referents*. Cambridge, UK: Cambridge University Press.
Levinson, Stephen C.
1983 *Pragmatics*. Cambridge, UK: Cambridge University Press.
Li, Charles N., and Sandra A. Thompson
1976 Subject and topic: a new typology of language. In: Charles N. Li (ed.), *Subject and Topic*, 457–489. London: Academic Press.
Lieber, Rochelle
1992 *Deconstructing Morphology: word formation in syntactic theory*. Chicago: University of Chicago Press.
Lieber, Rochelle, and Sergio Scalise
2007 The Lexical Integrity Hypothesis in a new theoretical universe. In: Geert Booij, Luca Ducceschi, Bernard Fradin, Emiliano Guevara, Angela Ralli, and Sergio Scalise (eds.), *On-line Proceedings of the Fifth Mediterranean Morphology Meeting*, 1–24. Bologna: Università degli Studi di Bologna. http://www3.lingue.unibo.it/mmm/
Lipták, Anikó
2001 *On the Syntax of Wh-items in Hungarian*. Utrecht: LOT.
Manning, Christopher D., Ivan A. Sag, and Masayo Iida
1999 The lexical integrity of Japanese causatives. In: Robert D. Levine, and Georgia M. Green (eds.), *Studies in Contemporary Phrase Structure Grammar*, 39–79. Cambridge, UK: Cambridge University Press.
Marantz, Alec
1997 No escape from syntax: don't try morphological analysis in the privacy of your own Lexicon. *Proceedings of the 21st Annual Penn Linguistics Colloquium: Penn Working Papers in Linguistics* 4: 201–225.
Mathesius, Vilém
[1929] 1983 Functional linguistics. In: Josef Vachek, and Libuše Dušková (eds.), *Praguiana: Some Basic and Less Known Aspects of the Prague Linguistic School*, 121–142. Amsterdam: John Benjamins.
Matsumoto, Yo
1998 A reexamination of the cross-linguistic parameterization of causative predicates: Japanese perspectives. In: Miriam Butt, and Tracy Holloway King (eds.), *Proceedings of the LFG98 Conference*, The University of Queensland, Brisbane, Australia. Online: CSLI Publications. http://www.stanford.edu/group/cslipublications/cslipublications/LFG/3/matsumoto.ps
May, Robert
1985 *Logical Form: Its Structure and Derivation*. Cambridge, MA: MIT Press.
Mithun, Marianne
1984 The evolution of noun incorporation. *Language* 60: 847–893.
Montague, Richard
1974 The proper treatment of quantification in ordinary English. In: Richmond H. Thomason (ed.), *Formal Philosophy: Selected Papers of Richard Montague*, 247–270. New Haven: Yale University Press.
Mycock, Louise
2006 The typology of constituent questions: a Lexical-Functional Grammar analysis of "wh"-questions. Ph.D. thesis, University of Manchester, UK.

Nespor, Marina, and Irene Vogel
1986 *Prosodic Phonology.* Dordrecht: Foris.
Odden, David
1995 Phonology at the phrasal level in Bantu. In: Francis Katamba (ed.), *Bantu Phonology and Morphology*, 40–68. Munich: LINCOM.
Partee, Barbara H., and Herman L. W. Hendriks
1997 Montague Grammar. In: Johan van Benthem, and Alice ter Meulen (eds.), *Handbook of Logic and Language*, 5–91. Amsterdam: Elsevier.
Pierrehumbert, Janet B., and Mary E. Beckman
1988 *Japanese Tone Structure*. Cambridge, MA: MIT Press.
Pollard, Carl J., and Ivan A. Sag
1994 *Head-Driven Phrase Structure Grammar.* Chicago: University of Chicago Press.
Prince, Ellen F.
1981 Toward a taxonomy of given–new information. In: Peter Cole (ed.), *Radical Pragmatics*, 223–255. New York: Academic Press.
Pullum, Geoffrey K., and Arnold M. Zwicky
1988 The syntax–phonology interface. In: Frederick J. Newmeyer (ed.), *Linguistics: The Cambridge Survey, Volume I,* 255–280. Cambridge, UK: Cambridge University Press.
Reinhart, Tanya
2006 *Interface Strategies: Optimal and Costly Computations*. Cambridge, MA: MIT Press.
Reinhart, Tanya
1982 *Pragmatics and Linguistics: An Analysis of Sentence Topics*. Bloomington, IN: Indiana University Linguistics Club.
Rizzi, Luigi
1997 The fine structure of the left periphery. In: Liliane Haegeman (ed.), *Elements of Grammar: Handbook of Generative Syntax*, 281–337. Dordrecht: Kluwer.
Rooth, Mats
1992 A theory of focus interpretation. *Natural Language Semantics* 1: 75–116.
Rosen, Sara Thomas
1989 Two types of noun incorporation. *Language* 65: 294–317.
Sadock, Jerrold M.
1991 *Autolexical Syntax: A Theory of Parallel Grammatical Representations*. Chicago: University of Chicago Press.
Seidl, Amanda
2001 *Minimal Indirect Reference: A Theory of the Syntax–Phonology Interface*. London: Routledge.
Selkirk, Elisabeth
1986 On derived domains in sentence phonology. *Phonology Yearbook* 3: 371–405.
Selkirk, Elisabeth
1984 *Phonology and Syntax: The Relation between Sound and Structure*. Cambridge, MA: MIT Press.
Selkirk, Elisabeth
1978 On prosodic structure and its relation to syntactic structure. *Nordic Prosody* II: 111–140.
Selkirk, Elisabeth, and Tong Shen
1990 Prosodic domains in Shanghai Chinese. In: Sharon Inkelas, and Draga Zec (eds.), *The Phonology-Syntax Connection*, 313–337. Chicago: University of Chicago Press.
Shattuck-Hufnagel, Stefanie, and Turk, Alice E.
1996 A prosody tutorial for investigators of auditory sentence processing. *Journal of Psycholinguistic Research* 25: 193–247.
Skopeteas, Stavros, Caroline Féry, and Rusudan Asatiani
2009 Word order and intonation in Georgian. *Lingua* 119: 102–127.

Stechow, Arnim von
1991 Current issues in the theory of focus. In: Arnim von Stechow, and Dieter Wunderlich (eds.), *Semantics: An International Handbook of Contemporary Research*, 804–825. Berlin: de Gruyter.
Strawson, P. F.
[1964] 1971 Identifying reference and truth-values. *Theoria* 30: 96–118. Reprinted in: P. F. Strawson *Logico-Linguistic Papers*. 75–95 London: Methuen.
Travis, Lisa
2000 The l-syntax/s-syntax boundary: evidence from Austronesian. In: Ileana Paul, Vivianne Phillips, and Lisa Travis (eds.), *Formal Issues in Austronesian Linguistics*, 167–193. Dordrecht: Kluwer.
Truckenbrodt, Hubert
1999 On the relation between syntactic phrases and phonological phrases. *Linguistic Inquiry* 30: 219–255.
Vallduví, Enric
1992 *The Informational Component*. New York: Garland Publishing.
Van Valin, Robert D., Jr. (ed.)
2008 *Investigations of the Syntax–Semantics–Pragmatics Interface*. Amsterdam: John Benjamins.
Van Valin, Robert D., Jr., and Randy J. LaPolla
1997 *Syntax: Structure, Meaning, and Function*. Cambridge, UK: Cambridge University Press.
Ward, Gregory, and Betty Birner
2004 Information structure and non-canonical syntax. In: Laurence R. Horn, and Gregory Ward (eds.), *The Handbook of Pragmatics*, 153–174. Oxford: Blackwell.
Wasow, Thomas
1977 Transformations and the Lexicon. In: Peter W. Culicover, Thomas Wasow, and Adrian Akmajian (eds.), *Formal Syntax*, 327–360. London: Academic Press.

Louise Mycock, Oxford (United Kingdom)

II. The Syntactic Tradition

4. The Indian Grammatical Tradition

Abstract

The history of grammar in India begins with the Aṣṭādhyāyī of Pāṇini ($5^{th}/4^{th}$ century B.C.). The Aṣṭādhyāyī is a system of rules explaining the derivation of words and word forms of Sanskrit. Syntax is a part of this system in as much as syntactic categories are involved in the derivation of most word forms from the very beginning of the derivation process. Of fundamental importance are the categories of action and the means of realizing the action, which are the kārakas. Pāṇini introduces six kārakas – point of departure, recipient, instrument, locus, object, and agent. The kārakas are defined in semantic terms; the agent, for example, is defined as "that which is independent", the object as "that which the agent most desires to reach".

In Pāṇini's derivational system, case endings are introduced after noun stems to denote the kārakas. The accusative, for example, is introduced to denote the object, the instrumental to denote the agent. The agent and the object, moreover, are denoted also by the endings of the verb: When the verbal ending represents the agent, the verb is in the kartari prayoga (active voice); when it represents the object, the verb is in the karmaṇi prayoga (passive voice).

The rules which introduce case endings after noun stems can only be applied if the kāraka to be denoted is not already expressed elsewhere. On account of this restriction, the accusative cannot be introduced to denote the object in the karmaṇi prayoga (passive voice), where the object is represented already in the verbal ending. Neither can the instrumental be introduced to denote the agent in the kartari prayoga (active voice), where the agent is represented already in the verbal ending.

As in other Indo-European languages, the agent in the active voice and the object in the passive voice are represented by nouns ending in the nominative. Yet, Pāṇini has no rules which assign the nominative to the agent in the active voice or to the object in the passive voice. The nominative can only be introduced in these cases in order to denote the meaning of the nominal stem as such.

This feature of Pāṇinian syntax forms a marked contrast with traditional European syntax. What appears as the subject from a European perspective, is not introduced as the representation of a kāraka at all – neither as a representation of the agent in the active voice nor as a representation of the object in the passive voice. Consequently, the categorial meaning of the verb does not change in the active or passive voice.

In traditional European syntax, on the contrary, we find the doctrine that the verb denotes action or suffering according to whether it is used in active or passive voice. The ultimate source of this doctrine is the conception of the object as a patient who passively experiences the action of the agent. This conception is foreign to Pāṇinian syntax. Pāṇini defined the object of the action not as a patient, but as an entity which the agent most desires to reach. This entity is an agent in its own right, who along with the principal agent and other kārakas contributes to the success of the action.

1. Pāṇinian grammar

The *Aṣṭādhyāyī* of Pāṇini (5th/4th century B.C., cf. Scharfe 2009: 28) is the foundation of a grammatical tradition, which has been preserved in India for more than 2000 years. The *Aṣṭādhyāyī* is usually referred to as a grammar of Sanskrit. Yet the word *saṃskṛtam* which occurs three times in this text (A 4.2.16, 4.4.3, 4.4.134) is used there only in the sense of 'prepared' (with reference to items of food) and 'purified with water' (with reference to an object which is used for ritual purposes). Pāṇini nowhere uses the word *saṃskṛtam* to refer to the language which is the object of his grammar. When Pāṇini refers to his object language, he uses either the expression *chandasi* 'in meter' or *bhāṣāyām* 'in language'. With the first expression, he denotes the Vedic hymns, with the second the language of ordinary communication.

Both varieties of Pāṇini's object language are phenomena of oral speech; the Vedic hymns, in particular, were not committed to writing originally, but only orally transmitted. The same is true for Pāṇini's grammar itself: "Pāṇinis Grammatik wurde für die mündliche Rede geschaffen. Sie geht an keiner Stelle von den Konventionen der Schrift aus" [Pāṇini's grammar was created for oral speech. It does nowhere rely on the conventions of writing] (Falk 1993: 257).

Pāṇini's grammar contains about 4000 rules (*sūtras*), which are arranged in eight chapters (*adhyāyas*); hence the Sanskrit name of the grammar – *Aṣṭādhyāyī* 'the eight chapters'. In addition to the text of the *sūtras*, the grammar contains a list of sounds (*pratyāhārasūtras*) at the beginning and two appendices at the end – a list of verbal roots (*dhātupāṭha*) and a list of nominal stems (*gaṇapāṭha*).

The *sūtras* of the grammar were formulated with utmost brevity by systematically leaving out informations which can be inferred from the context, by the use of artificially created technical terms, and by the use of special phonetic symbols as carriers of grammatical informations. All this made the grammar inaccessible to the uninitiated. Thus, there arose at an early time the need for commentaries.

The earliest commentators whose works are extant are Kātyāyana (3rd century B.C.) and Patañjali (2nd century B.C.). Being of equal rank as Pāṇini, the two commentators together with Pāṇini form a triad which is denoted as *munitraya* 'the three sages'. According to their functions, the three *munis* are characterized as follows: Pāṇini is the *sūtrakāra* 'composer of *sūtras*', Kātyāyana the *vārttikakāra* 'composer of *vārttikas*', and Patañjali the *bhāṣyakāra* 'composer of *bhāṣyas*'.

The *vārttikas* of Kātyāyana are composed in nominal style; they comment on selected *sūtras* of Pāṇini's grammar. The *bhāṣyas* of Patañjali comment either on Kātyāyana's *vārttikas* or directly on selected *sūtras* of Pāṇini; they are composed in colloquial language reflecting the situation of scholarly debates. The *bhāṣyas* and the *vārttikas* are both contained in Patañjali's *Mahābhāṣya* 'the great commentary'.

According to what we read in the *Vākyapadīya* (Rau 2002: 2.481–488) of Bhartṛhari (5th century A.D.), the grammatical tradition declined after Patañjali since the high level of linguistic sophistication which was reached in the *Mahābhāṣya* could not be maintained by later grammarians. Then, a revival was brought about, the culmination of which is marked by Bhartṛhari's *Vākyapadīya* itself. This great work provides a philosophical approach to the study of Pāṇini's grammar (cf. Aklujkar 2008: 216–218); it is also known as *Trikāṇḍī* since it consists of three parts – the *Brahmakāṇḍa*, which contains the principles of Bhartṛhari's linguistic monism; the *Vākyakāṇḍa*, which explores different views on the nature of the sentence; and the *Padakāṇḍa*, which deals with the semantic and grammatical categories of words.

The grammatical tradition which was built on the work of the three *munis* was not the only grammatical tradition which developed in South Asia. Schools of non-Pāṇinian grammar came into existence after Pāṇini; they were devoted to Sanskrit as well as to other Indian languages (Middle Indo-Aryan and Dravidian). Yet, in the field of Sanskrit studies, the grammar of the three *munis* was the most successful. It grew in strength throughout the centuries until "the *munitraya*'s absolute authority on the Sanskrit language" was established by Bhaṭṭoji Dīkṣita in the 16th/17th century (Houben 2008: 573).

The focus of the present survey is on syntax as it appears in the grammar of the three *munis*. In spite of its general importance for syntax, Bhartṛhari's philosophy of language has not been dealt with here systematically; only a few verses of the *Vākyakāpadīya* were adduced at particular points. Later developments of the Pāṇinian tradition of grammar after Bhartṛhari as well as non-Pāṇinian traditions of grammar in India have not been considered here (for the development of grammar after Pāṇini, see Scharfe 2000; for grammars of Indian languages other than Sanskrit, see the short overview in Aklujkar 2008: 197–198; for the tradition of Tamil grammar, which is the most important among the non-Sanskrit traditions, see Chevillard 2000a, 2000b, 2000c).

In presenting the grammar of the three *munis*, the original texts have been followed as closely as possible, particularly in case of the *Mahābhāṣya*, where the argument structure of the selected passages has been preserved as much as possible in order to give a lively picture of Patañjali's dialectic method, which consists in identifying a grammatical problem, offering a solution to it, out of which again a new problem arises, for which again a solution is sought, and so on.

Because of frequent references to the original texts, the following abbreviations are used: A [references to chapter, section, and *sūtra*] for Pāṇini's *Aṣṭādhyāyī,* Bh [references to volume, page, and line] for Patañjali's *Mahābhāṣya,* and VP [references to part, (section), and verse] for Bhartṛhari's *Vākyapadīya* (see 5). All other texts are quoted according to the bibliography. Translations from Sanskrit sources are mine.

The kind of presentation adopted here necessitated a quite extensive treatment of the selected topics so that only the most fundamental aspects of Pāṇinian syntax could be covered. The present survey, therefore, is essentially concerned with the semantic and morphological structure of elementary sentences such as *devadatta odanaṃ pacati* 'Devadatta cooks rice', which served as a favorite example among Indian grammarians.

2. Grammar and syntax

At first sight, Pāṇini's grammar appears to be a grammar of words, not of sentences. In fact, Pāṇini does not even define the term *vākya* 'sentence', which he uses several times in his grammar, whereas the linguistic unit of the word, which is called *pada*, and its constituents are well defined.

On the other hand, words are not derived as isolated units in Pāṇini's grammar, but as units which are semantically connected with other words in the sentence. This is explicitly recognized by Pāṇini's rule (A 2.1.1):

(1) *samarthaḥ padavidhiḥ*
[An operation on words [takes effect only] when the words are semantically connected.]

Pāṇini's notion of semantic connectivity was elaborated by Kātyāyana, who gave the first definitions of the sentence in two consecutive *vārttikas* (Bh 1.367.10 and Bh 1.367.16):

(2) *ākhyātaṃ sāvyayakārakaviśeṣaṇaṃ vākyam*
[A sentence consists of a finite verb together with indeclinables, *kārakas* and qualifiers.]

(3) *ekatiṅ*
[A sentence has one finite verb.]

Both, Pāṇini's concept of semantic connectivity and Kātyāyana's definitions of the sentence do not exhaust the potential of syntax in Pāṇini's grammar. Syntax plays a fundamental role in Pāṇini's grammar in as much as syntactic categories are involved in the derivation of most words from the very beginning of the derivation process. Pāṇini's idea of syntax, therefore, "cannot be understood from isolated rules, but only from rules as they are interrelated for the derivation of words" (Roodbergen 1974: vi). Because of this interrelationship, there is no proper syntactic component as clearly distinct from those parts of the grammar which deal with morphology and word formation. Both, syntax on the one hand and morphology and word formation on the other, were integrated within one system of knowledge, the objective of which was defined in the very beginning of the *Mahābhāṣya* as *śabdānuśāsana* 'instruction in words', whereas the system itself was named *vyākaraṇa*, which is usually translated as grammar.

Vyākaraṇa arose as one of the six limbs of the Veda (*vedāṅgas*), which include among others the disciplines of phonetics (*śikṣā*), etymology (*nirukta*), and prosody (*chandas*). As a limb of the Veda *vyākaraṇa* was established already before Pāṇini's grammar came into existence. Pāṇini himself bears witness to the existence of a grammatical tradition before him since he mentions in his work ten other grammarians, which might have been his predecessors, as proponents of alternative views.

A major achievement of the grammatical tradition before Pāṇini was the segmentation of the text of the Rigveda into a sequence of isolated words, called *padapāṭha*, which is attributed to the grammarian Śākalya. In the original form of the text, called *saṃhitā* or *saṃhitāpāṭha*, the words of a metrical unit are joined together according to the rules of sandhi whereas in the segmented form of the text the words of a metrical unit appear in their pausa forms. Splitting the connected form of the text into a sequence of isolated words is not just a matter of phonological analysis, but presupposes a knowledge of syntactic structures since due to the influence of sandhi, the word boundaries are often not visible in the connected form of the text.

2.1. *Vyakaraṇa* as grammatical differentiation

Generalizing the idea of splitting the connected form of a Vedic text into a sequence of isolated words, Sāyaṇa, the medieval commentator of the Vedas, defined grammar as follows (Sontakke and Dharmadhikari 1970: 538):

(4) *tasyāṃ vācy etāvad ekaṃ vākyaṃ, tasmin vākye 'py etāvad ekaṃ padaṃ, tasmin pade 'pīyaṃ prakṛtir ayaṃ pratyaya ity evaṃ vibhajya sarvataḥ karaṇaṃ vyākaraṇam*
[Grammar is that process by which division is carried out everywhere [by recognizing]: In this speech, so much is one sentence; in this sentence then, so much is one word; in this word then, this is the base and this is the suffix.]

In defining grammar that way, Sāyaṇa availed himself of the etymology of *vyākaraṇa* – *vyākaraṇa* means 'division' since it is derived from the verb *vy-ā-kṛ*, which means 'divide, differentiate'. Yet he viewed the grammatical process of differentiation as taking place on the level of audible speech only since both, the connected form of the text, the *saṃhitā*, and the linguistic units which resulted from the successive division of the *saṃhitā*, are phenomena of audible speech. This restriction to the level of audible speech, however, is not necessary in order to understand *vyākaraṇa* in the sense of division or differentiation. *Vyākaraṇa* can also be understood as differentiation if the starting point of the differentiation process is not located on the level of audible speech, but identified with the initial state of speech in the mind of the speaker.

Evidence for this understanding of the grammatical process is a verse from Bhartṛhari's *Vākyapadīya* (VP 1.52), in which the process of speech production is compared with the process in which a living organism develops out of a germinal state:

(5) *āṇḍabhāvam ivāpanno yaḥ kratuḥ śabdasaṃjñakaḥ | vṛttis tasya kriyārūpo bhāgaśo bhajate kramam ||*
[The energy called 'word' has assumed the nature of an egg. It develops in the form of an action and realizes itself as as a sequence of parts.]

From the context of this verse, it is clear that the linguistic energy "which has assumed the nature of an egg" is the inner word in the mind of the speaker. In the process of speech production, this inner word, which is not yet differentiated into parts, unfolds into a sequentially ordered linguistic structure, which can be communicated to others.

This unfoldment of the inner word is essentially a process of *vyākaraṇa* in the sense of differentiation. Yet, Bhartṛhari does not use in the description of this process a word derived from the root *vy-ā-kṛ*. That Bhartṛhari, nevertheless, views *vyākaraṇa* as a process in which a unitary and unmanifest state of language is differentiated into manifold structures, can be seen from another verse of the *Vākyapadīya* (VP 1.22), which is characteristic for Bhartṛhari's linguistic monism (*śabdādvaita*):

(6) *yad ekaṃ prakriyābhedair bahudhā pravibhajyate | tad vyākaraṇam āgamya paraṃbrahmādhigamyate ||*
[Because the one is divided in manifold ways through the different grammatical derivations, the supreme Brahma is attained, when grammar is attained.]

The supreme *Brahma* is attained when grammar is attained since the grammatical process in which a unitary and unmanifest state of language is differentiated into manifold linguistic structures is of the same nature as the ontological process in which the one universal reality, called *brahma*, is differentiated into a variety of phenomena.

2.2. *Vyakaraṇa* as syntactic differentiation

In the two verses of the *Vākyapadīya* quoted above, the grammatical process of differentiation is described in an abstract way, without reference to any particular grammatical category. This is different in another description of the grammatical process, which is given in Vyāsa's *Yogasūtrabhāṣya* (on *Yogasūtra* 3.17; Aranya 1981: 283; cf. also Cardona 1997: 568–569). In this description, Vyāsa uses the verb *vy-ā-kṛ*, from which *vyākaraṇa* is derived, with explicit reference to a grammatical process, and, furthermore, presents this process as a process of syntactic differentiation, in which two fundamental categories are involved – action (*kriyā*) and the means of realizing the action, which are the *kārakas*.

The categories of action and *kārakas* are presented by Vyāsa as being mutually dependent on each other so that in a word representing a *kāraka*, the complementary category of action is implied and vice versa. This mutual dependence of action and *kārakas* is the binding force which holds the words of a sentence together.

The force of the sentence exists in a single noun like 'tree' since in this case the verb 'exist' is supplied, as Vyāsa (Aranya, loc. cit.) maintains:

(7) *vṛkṣa ity ukte 'stīti gamyate na sattāṃ padārtho vyabhicaratīti*
[When 'tree' is uttered, it is understood that it exists since the meaning of a word cannot deviate from existence.]

This is a replica of Kātyāyana's (Bh 1.443.5–6) doctrine that the verb 'exist' (*asti*) in the third person of the present tense is understood when a noun in the nominative occurs without a verbal predicate. According to this doctrine, "there are no purely nominal sentences" (Deshpande 1991a: 37); every sentence is reduced to a verbal sentence.

As there is no agent without an action, so there is no action without the *kārakas,* as Vyāsa (Aranya, loc. cit.) further specifies:

(8) *tathā na hy asādhanā kriyāstīti tathā ca pacatīty ukte sarvakārakāṇām ākṣepo niyamārtho 'nuvādaḥ kartṛkarmakaraṇānāṃ caitrāgnitaṇḍulānām iti*
[And there is no action without the means of realizing it so that, when 'he cooks' is uttered, all the *kārakas* are implied; the explicit expression of the agent, instrument and object like Chaitra, fire and rice is for the sake of determination.]

3. Syntax and semantics

The *kārakas* are introduced in a block of 33 *sūtras* of the *Aṣṭādhyāyī* (A 1.4.23–1.4.55). Pāṇini recognizes six categories as *kārakas*; they are introduced in the following order: point of departure (*apādānam*), recipient (*saṃpradānam*), instrument (*karaṇam*), locus (*adhikaraṇam*), object (*karma*), and agent (*kartā*). For each of these six categories, Pāṇini has a general definition in terms of semantic features:

(9) *dhruvam apāye 'pādānam*
[That which remains stable when moving away is the point of departure.] (A 1.4.24)

(10) *karmaṇā yam abhipraiti sa sampradānam*
[That whom he [the agent] approaches with the object is the recipient.] (A 1.4.32)

(11) *sādhakatamaṃ karaṇam*
[That which is most efficient is the instrument.] (A 1.4.42)

(12) *ādhāro 'dhikaraṇam*
[The substratum is the locus.] (A 1.4.45)

(13) *kartur īpsitatamaṃ karma*
[That which the agent desires most to reach is the object.] (A 1.4.49)

(14) *svatantraḥ kartā*
[That which is independent is the agent.] (A 1.4.54)

A special variety of the agent is the causative agent, who acts as the instigator of another agent; in addition to being an agent, the causative agent is categorized as *hetu* 'cause' (A 1.4.55).

The six *sūtras* which define the *kārakas* in general terms do not follow each other immediately, but are interspersed with other *sūtras*, in which the general definitions of *kārakas* are either extended or restricted to particular cases.

The first of the block of the 33 *sūtras* is the *sūtra* (A 1.4.23):

(15) *kārake*
[If it is a *kāraka*.]

This *sūtra* is a governing rule; it has to be read into each of the following 32 *sūtras*. In this way, for example, *sūtra* (9), which defines the point of departure as "that which remains stable, when moving away", has to be rephrased as "that which remains stable when moving away is the point of departure if it is a *kāraka*".

By adding *sūtra* (15) to each of the following *sūtras* of its domain, it is ensured that the semantic features which are specified in the subsequent rules are only valid as definitions of particular *kārakas* if that which is defined by them is, in fact, a *kāraka*. This means that the definitions of the particular *kārakas* are not by themselves sufficient to define a *kāraka*; they are only valid as subcategorizations of the general notion of *kāraka*.

In order to correctly assign particular *kārakas* to entities of the semantic structure of a sentence, one has to know, therefore, the meaning of the word *kāraka*, of which they are subcategorizations.

3.1. The agent and the *karakas*

The meaning of the word *kāraka* is discussed at length in the *Mahābhāṣya*'s commentary on *sūtra* (15), which we shall briefly summarize (an in-depth study of grammatical problems involved in this analysis is Scharf 2002).

At the beginning of his commentary, Patañjali states that *kāraka* is introduced as a technical term in *sūtra* (15). If *kāraka* is introduced as a technical term, however, its meaning should be defined as it is the case with other expressions which serve as technical terms in the grammar. Yet, the meaning of the term *kāraka* is defined nowhere in the grammar. In order to justify Pāṇini's procedure of introducing a technical term without defining it, Patañjali assumes that the term *kāraka* has to be taken as a lengthy term, which needs not to be defined as such since its meaning can be understood from its grammatical derivation.

Kāraka is an agent noun, which is derived from the root *kṛ* 'do, make' according to rules A 3.1.133 and A 3.4.67. Hence, the meaning of *kāraka* as it appears from its grammatical derivation is 'that which acts' (Bh 1.324.9). As that which acts, the term *kāraka* has the same meaning as the term *kartā*, which denotes the agent, since *kartā*, too, is derived as an agent noun from the root *kṛ*. On account of this synonymy, *kartā*, the agent, is rightly classified as a *kāraka*. Yet, a problem arises with regard to the *kārakas* which are different from the agent since it cannot be explained why a *kāraka* which is not the agent is classified by using a word, viz. *kāraka*, which is synonymous with the agent. This difficulty is pointed out in Kātyāyana's *vārttika* (Bh 1.324.10):

(16) *anvartham iti ced akartari kartṛśabdānupapattiḥ*
[If the term *kāraka* is taken in its literal meaning, it cannot be explained why a word signifying the agent is applied to what is not an agent.]

3.1.1. Agents of constituent actions

In order to solve the problem which has been raised in *vārttika* (16), Kātyāyana (Bh 1.324.13) assumes that *kārakas* like the locus and the instrument are agents of constituent actions, into which the main action can be subdivided. Taking the action of cooking as an example, Kātyāyana explains the subdivision of the main action into constituent actions as follows.

The main action is the cooking of the agent, who is qualified as the principal agent (*pradhānakartā*) in order to distinguish him from the agents of the constituent actions. The cooking of the principal agent consists in putting the pot on fire, pouring water into the pot, putting rice into the pot, and providing sticks of fire wood. By acting in this way, the principal agent creates the conditions that the pot, which serves as the locus of the action, and the sticks of firewood, which serve as the instrument, can start their activity.

The activity of the pot consists in taking in and holding a certain quantity (*droṇa* or *āḍhaka*) of rice; it is because of this activity that one can say of the pot (Bh 1.324.21):

(17) *droṇaṃ pacaty āḍhakaṃ pacati* [Sanskrit]
droṇa:ACC cooks āḍhaka:ACC cooks
'It cooks a *droṇa* or an *āḍhaka*'

The activity of the sticks of fire wood consists in burning; it is because of this activity that one can say (Bh 1.325.1):

(18) *edhāḥ pakṣyanti* [Sanskrit]
sticks:NOM will:cook
'The sticks of fire wood will cook'

In this way, Kātyāyana demonstrated that the locus and the instrument are agents of constituent actions. The term *kāraka*, therefore, can be applied to both *kārakas* in its literal meaning so that the problem which was raised in *vārttika* (16) is solved. Yet, the problem is solved only for the locus and the instrument, not for the point of departure and the recipient as Kātyāyana admits (Bh 1.325.13). In the next sentence (19), for example, it is not possible to transform the point of departure into the agent of a constituent action on the model of (17) or (18) since the formal result of this transformation, which is shown in (20), denotes a completely different scenario:

(19) *grāmād āgacchati* [Sanskrit]
village:ABL he:comes
'He comes from the village'

(20) *grāma āgacchati* [Sanskrit]
village:NOM comes
'The village comes'

In order to demonstrate for all non-agent *kārakas* that they are agents themselves and, hence, *kārakas*, Kātyāyana (Bh 1.325.16) has recourse to a more powerful strategy, which pretends to resolve the difficulty stated in *vārttika* (16):

(21) *na vā svatantraparatantratvāt tayoḥ paryāyeṇa vacanaṃ vacanāśrayā ca saṃjñā*
[Or, rather, [this difficulty does] not [arise] because of independence and dependence. Both [independence and dependence] are alternately expressed, and [the assignment of] a technical term depends on the [alternate] expression.]

3.1.2. Independence and dependence of *karakas*

According to this *vārttika*, *kārakas* which are different from the agent may be presented alternately as dependent and independent. If they are presented as independent, they will receive the designation *kartā* 'agent' on account of *sūtra* (14), which defines the agent as that *kāraka* which is independent. If they are presented as dependent, on the contrary, they cannot be transformed into the agents of constituent actions.

In this way, it becomes clear that the impossibility of transforming the point of departure into an agent is not due to the particular nature of the *kāraka*, but only due to the particular mode of presenting it as dependent. If it can be presented as dependent, it can also be presented as independent since the mode of presenting it depends on the intention of the speaker. Patañjali (Bh 1.325.19–20), in fact, manages to find an example where a point of departure appears to be presented as independent since it can be transformed into the agent in the same way as a locus can be transformed into the agent:

(22) *balāhakād vidyotate* [Sanskrit]
cloud:ABL is:lightening
'It is lightening from the cloud'

(23) *balāhako vidyotate* [Sanskrit]
cloud:NOM is:lightening
'The cloud is lightening'

The alternate assignment of independence and dependence, which is conceded by *vārttika* (21), however, creates a new problem since in the section of the *Aṣṭādhyāyī* where the *kārakas* are introduced alternate assignment of terms is not allowed. When there is a conflict between two rules of this section to the effect that different terms would be assigned to a given item at the same time, the rule which is posterior in the order of the rules of the *Aṣṭādhyāyī* will prevail (A 1.4.1–2).

According to this principle, a *kāraka* which can be presented either as independent or as dependent should always be classified as *kartā* (agent) since *sūtra* (14), which defines the agent as the independent *kāraka*, is the last rule in the *kāraka* section of the *Aṣṭādhyāyī* and, therefore, overrides the rules in which the other *kārakas* are defined. There would be, thus, no chance that a non-agent *kāraka* like the point of departure could be classified as such.

Patañjali (Bh 1.325.24–25) somehow manages to solve this problem. Yet, the discussion of the problem, has opened a new perspective. So far, the intention of Kātyāyana's argumentation was to present the *kārakas* which are different from the agent as independent; from now on, the goal of investigation will be to demonstrate in which way they are dependent. Patañjali (Bh 1.326.1–2) introduces the new topic by directly addressing himself to Kātyāyana:

(24) *yathā punar idaṃ bhavatā sthālyāḥ svātantryaṃ nidarśitaṃ saṃbhavanakriyāṃ dhāraṇakriyāṃ ca kurvatī sthālī svatantreti kvedānīṃ paratantrā syāt*
[[But you did not demonstrate the dependence of the pot] in the same way, sir, as you have demonstrated the independence of the pot by stating that the pot, which performs the activity of taking in and holding, is independent. In which way, now, may it be dependent?]

The pot is independent with regard to the constituent action of taking in and holding a certain quantity of rice; but it must also be assumed that it is dependent with regard to the main action of cooking. As independence is needed to categorize the pot as the agent of a constituent action, so dependence is needed to categorize it as a *kāraka* which is different from the agent. In his attempt to demonstrate in which way the pot may be dependent, Patañjali presents three hypotheses.

In his first hypothesis, Patañjali (Bh 1.326.2–5) tries to demonstrate the dependence of the pot by identifying it as the object of preparatory actions such as washing and turning round, with regard to which it appears as dependent. This hypothesis is immediately rejected by pointing out that it is not for the purpose of being washed and turned round that the pot is used by the agent of cooking, but for the purpose of taking in and holding a certain quantity of rice. With regard to these actions, however, it has already been shown that the pot is independent. So still it has to be demonstrated in which way it is dependent.

In his second hypothesis, Patañjali (Bh 1.326.5–6) explains the alternation between dependence and independence as being due to the intention of the speaker: If the activity of the pot is being expressed, the pot appears as independent; if the activity of the agent is being expressed, the pot appears as dependent. The validity of this criterion, however, is questioned with the following argument: Even when the activity of the agent is being expressed, the pot still performs the actions of taking in and holding, with regard to which it is independent. Again, the question remains in which way it is dependent.

In his final attempt to answer the question, Patañjali (Bh 1.326.7–10) uses the presence of the agent, who is now explicitly referred to as the 'principal' (*pradhāna*) *kāraka*, as the criterion of differentiation between dependence and independence: In the presence of the agent, who acts as the principal *kāraka*, the pot is dependent; in his absence, it is independent. This is illustrated with an example from political life: If the ministers act in the presence of the king, they act in dependence; if they act in the absence of the king, they act in independence. Yet, also this hypothesis gives rise to the question (Bh 1.326.10–11):

(25) *nanu ca bhoḥ pradhānenāpi vai samavāye sthālyā anenārtho 'dhikaraṇaṃ kārakam iti*
[Is it not, sir, that even in the presence of the principal [*kāraka*], the fact is that the locus is a *kāraka*?]

The argument is the same as before: Even in the presence of the principal *kāraka*, the locus still functions as a *kāraka*, that is, as an agent, since it performs the action of taking in and holding, with regard to which it is independent. Yet, even if the argument is the same as before, it does not serve the same purpose as before since Patañjali, after having presented it, does not ask anymore "in which way the pot is dependent".

By identifying the pot as a locus, it has already been recognized that the pot is dependent; by demonstrating that the pot is a *kāraka* even in the presence of the principal *kāraka*, it has also been recognized that the pot is independent. Since it has been recognized, thus, that the pot is dependent and independent at the same time, there is no longer an alternation between dependence and independence, as it was stipulated in *vārttika* (21), but a simultaneity: Whenever the pot is dependent, it is also independent, which is a contradiction.

At this point of the commentary, it becomes clear that *vārttika* (21) can no longer be used in support of the view that non-agent *kārakas* are agents in their own right. It has to be accepted that the notion of *kāraka* is independent of the notion of a non-agent *kāraka* like the locus and vice versa. This mutual independence of both notions is identified by Patañjali (Bh 1.326.11–12) as the ultimate reason for the failure of the previous argumentation:

(26) *na hi kārakam ity anenādhikaraṇatvam uktam adhikaraṇam iti vā kārakatvam*
[Neither is the notion of the locus expressed by the term *kāraka* nor is the notion of *kāraka* expressed by the term *locus*.]

Both categories qualify each other because they reside in one and the same substratum. This is illustrated by Patañjali (Bh 1.326.13–15) with the case of a man who bears the composite name *gārgyo devadattaḥ*, where *devadatta* is his first name and *gārgya* his family name. Neither is his first name conveyed by calling him *gārgya* nor his family name by calling him *devadatta*. Both names qualify each other because they reside in one and the same substratum.

After having demonstrated that the general category *kāraka* and the special category of a non-agent *kāraka* like the locus are mutually independent of each other, Patañjali (Bh 1.326.15–16) is prompted to give a new and final definition of the term *kāraka*:

(27) *evaṃ tarhi sāmānyabhūtā kriyā vartate tasyā nirvartakaṃ kārakam*
[If it is so, then there is a unified action; a *kāraka* is its producer.]

The notion of *kāraka* which is defined here does not presuppose the splitting of the action into constituent actions, but the existence of one unified action which is brought about by the joint effort of all the *kārakas* involved. In this way, action and *kārakas* are recognized as mutually dependent terms. Since one term implies the other, *sūtra* (15) may alternately be taken to mean either 'if it is a *kāraka*' or 'if there is an action' as Patañjali suggests.

3.2. The object

The *kārakas* are 'means of realizing' (*sādhanas*) the action; hence, *sādhana* is used as an alternative term to denote the *kārakas*. Bhartṛhari (VP 3.7.1) defines this term as follows:

(28) *svāśraye samavetānāṃ tadvad evāśrayāntare | kriyāṇām abhiniṣpattau sāmarthyaṃ sādhanaṃ viduḥ ||*
[*Sādhana* is the capibility to accomplish actions which are inherent in their own substratum or in another substratum.]

In this definition, a distinction is made between two classes of *kārakas* according to whether their capability of performing actions is inherent in the respective *kāraka* or not.

According to Helārāja's commentary (Subramania Iyer 1963: 231), *kārakas* of the first sort are the agent and the object; *kārakas* of the second sort are the remaining *kārakas* (instrument, locus, point of departure, and recipient). The actions which *kārakas* of the first sort accomplish are inherent in the respective *kāraka*; the actions which *kārakas* of the second sort accomplish are not inherent in the respective *kāraka*, but in the agent or the object; it is through the agent or the object that these *kārakas* accomplish their actions.

By setting the agent and the object apart from the other *kārakas*, the object is accorded the same rank as the agent: it has the same capability of performing actions on its own as the agent has. Assigning to the object the capability of acting on its own is, of course, reminiscent of Kātyāyana's strategy of dividing the main action into constituent actions with regard to which non-agent *kārakas* can be established as agents (see above, 3.1.1). In the whole discussion of *sūtra* (15), however, the object was not mentioned at all. According to Nāgeśa Bhaṭṭa (Sharma no year: 243), the author of a subcommentary on the *Mahābhāṣya*, this omission is due to the fact that the capability of the object to act on its own is rather obvious since it is implied in a syntactic concept of Pāṇini's grammar, which is known as the object-agent (*karmakartā*).

3.2.1. The object-agent

The object-agent is defined in the following *sūtra* (A 3.1.87):

(29) *karmavat karmaṇā tulyakriyaḥ*
[An agent who performs the action in the same way as an object is treated as if it were an object.]

The existence of an agent whose action is of the same sort as the action of an object presupposes the existence of an object which has the capability to act on its own. Such an object performs his action irrespective of whether the agent is expressed or not. If the agent is expressed, the action of the object is hidden under the action of the agent; if the agent is not expressed, the action of the object is no longer hidden, and the object itself appears in the role of an agent. The transition from the one to the other scenario is illustrated by the following sentences:

(30) *devadattaḥ kāṣṭhaṃ bhinatti* [Sanskrit]
Devadatta:NOM firewood:ACC splits
'Devadatta splits the firewood'

(31) *kāṣṭhaṃ bhidyate svayam eva* [Sanskrit]
firewood:NOM splits self alone
'The firewood splits all by itself'

In (30), the firewood (*kāṣṭha*) is the object of the action performed by Devadatta; in (31), where Devadatta is not expressed, it is the agent itself. Nevertheless, the firewood performs in (31) the same action as in (30): Devadatta can only split the firewood if the firewood is splitting itself or lending itself to being split. The firewood of (31), thus, fulfills the condition of *sūtra* (29) – it is an agent who performs the action in the same way as an object does. By virtue of *sūtra* (29), therefore, the firewood is categorized as an agent who is treated grammatically as if it were an object.

Since the agent of (31) is treated as if it were an object, the verb which is related to it is treated as being related to an object. The grammatical consequence of this treatment of the object is that in (31) the verb is derived as *bhidyate* 'splits' according to the rules of Pāṇini's grammar whereas in (30) it is derived as *bhinatti* 'splits'.

In (30), the verb (*bhinatti*) is in a syntactic construction which is termed *kartari prayoga* 'the use of the verb to denote the agent'. This construction, which corresponds to the active voice of European grammar, is opposed to the *karmaṇi prayoga* 'the use of the verb to denote the object', which corresponds to the European passive voice. Yet, the European notion of passive is foreign to Pāṇinian grammar; as we shall see in 4.3.

In (31), the verb (*bhidyate*) has the form of a verb in the *karmaṇi prayoga*; yet, it is not in the *karmaṇi prayoga* itself since the object which it refers to is in reality an agent who is only treated as if it were an object. Neither is the verb of (31) in the *kartari prayoga* or active voice since it appears in the form of a verb in the *karmaṇi prayoga*. The verb of (31), thus, is neither in the *kartari prayoga* nor in the *karmaṇi prayoga*; it is in a hybrid construction, which is termed *karmakartari prayoga* 'the use of the verb to denote the object-agent'.

With regard to the grammatical interpretation of sentences like (31), however, there is no unanimity among the *munitraya*. Kātyāyana and Patañjali (Bh 2.68.11–22) propose an alternative interpretation, in which Pāṇini's object-agent is taken to be a genuine object. According to this interpretation, the verb in (31) is used to denote the object and nothing else; it is, therefore, in *karmaṇi prayoga*. Since the former agent has been eliminated, a new agent in form of the reflexive noun *ātmā* 'self' can be introduced in (31) on the model of a sentence like:

(32) *devadattaḥ ātmanā hanyate* [Sanskrit]
Devadatta:NOM self.INS is:killed
'Devadatta is killed by himself'

A sentence like (31), then, can be re-analyzed as a sentence in the *karmaṇi prayoga*, where the noun *ātmanā*, which denotes the agent, has been deleted (cf. Deshpande 1985: 9–16).

In any way, the transformation of (30) into (31) differs from the transformations of non-agent *kārakas* into agents of constituent actions as they were defined by Kātyāyana (see above, 3.1.1). Whereas the latter transformations do not affect the syntactic construction of the verb, which remains in the *kartari prayoga* or active voice, the transformation of (30) into (31) involves a change of the syntactic construction – either from *kartari prayoga* to *karmaṇi prayoga* (according to Kātyāyana) or from *kartari prayoga* to *karmakartari prayoga* (according to Pāṇini). In Kātyāyana's interpretation, the semantic status of the object is not changed under this transformation; in Pāṇini's view, on the contrary, the former object is transformed into the object-agent.

3.2.2. Actions inherent in the object and actions inherent in the agent

The transformation of the object into Pāṇini's object-agent is not universally applicable. According to a *vārttika* of Kātyāyana (Bh 2.66.15), it is restricted to

(33) *karmasthabhāvakānāṃ karmasthakriyāṇāṃ ca*
[verbal roots denoting dynamic being [*bhāva*] inherent in the object and verbal roots denoting action [*kriyā*] inherent in the object]

The root *bhid* 'split', for example, denotes an action which is inherent in the object since the result of the action is seen in the object, not in the agent. The transformation of the object of this action into the object-agent, therefore, is possible; the resulting sentence was shown already in (31): 'the firewood splits by itself'.

An example where the restriction of *vārttika* (33) inhibits the transformation of the object into the object-agent is the sentence:

(34) *devadattaḥ grāmaṃ gacchati* [Sanskrit]
Devadatta:NOM village:ACC goes
'Devadatta goes to the village'

In this sentence, the village (*grāma*) is the object of Devadatta's action since it satisfies Pāṇini's definition (13) of the object as that which the agent most desires to reach. Yet, the village is not affected by Devadatta's action at all; it is the agent who is affected by the action. The root *gam* 'go', thus, denotes an action which resides not in the object, but in the agent. According to *vārttika* (33), therefore, the transformation of the object into the object-agent is not possible; if attempted, it would result in the ungrammatical sentence:

(35) **gamyate grāmaḥ svayam eva* [Sanskrit]
is:being:gone village:NOM self alone
*'The village is being gone all by itself'

In *vārttika* (33), the verbal roots for which an object-agent is defined are specified twice – as verbal roots denoting dynamic being (*bhāva*) and as verbal roots denoting action (*kriyā*). The later grammatical tradition attempted to view this contrast as a semantic contrast between different classes of verbs amounting to something like a contrast between different aspects or aktionsarten (cf. Sharma 1995: 308–310).

In the light of another passage from the *Mahābhāṣya* (Bh 1.253–259), where the meaning of the verbal root is discussed at length (see below, 3.3), the double specification of verbal roots in *vārttika* (33), however, appears not as a semantic contrast between different classes of verbs; *bhāva* and *kriyā* are not mutually exclusive, but compatible terms with *kriyā* as the more general term. The difference between verbs denoting actions and verbs denoting dynamic being, therefore, will be disregarded in the present context, and the more general term *kriyā* 'action' alone will be retained in referring to *vārttika* (33).

In his commentary on *vārttika* (33), Patañjali (Bh 2.66.16) explicitly opposes roots which denote actions inherent in the object to roots which denote actions inherent in the agent. The former are called *karmastha* 'residing in the object', the latter *kartṛstha* 'residing in the agent'. This contrast is relevant only for actions which are directed to an object different from the agent, that is, for actions which are denoted by transitive verbs. For intransitive verbs, which denote actions without an external object, the contrast of *karmastha* and *kartṛstha* actions is neutralized; intransitive verbs can, by definition, only denote actions inherent in the agent.

3.2.3. Objects of *karmastha* actions

Objects of *karmastha* actions are further subcategorized into objects which are to be produced and objects which are to be modified by the action. The distinction between these two classes of objects was arrived at by Patañjali in his attempt to analyze the simple sentence:

(36) *odanaṃ pacati* [Sanskrit]
rice:ACC he:cooks
'He cooks rice '

The problem which Patañjali (Bh 1.332.14) saw in this simple sentence was that the word *odana* actually does not mean 'rice', but 'cooked rice'. If this meaning is assigned to *odana* in (36), the sentence would mean that somebody cooks cooked rice; in this case, something different from cooked rice would be produced, as Patañjali ironically remarks. In order to justify the ordinary understanding of (36), Patañjali (Bh 1.332.15) assumes that *odana* does not denote cooked rice here, but the uncooked rice grains, which are normally denoted by the word *taṇḍula*. This assumption implies a metonymic shift in the meaning of *odana*: The rice grains (*taṇḍula*) are denoted by a word which denotes that which the rice grains are meant for, namely, cooked rice (*odana*). Yet, this strategy of justifying the expected reading of (36) fails in case of the sentence:

(37) *taṇḍulān odanaṃ pacati* [Sanskrit]
rice:grains:ACC rice:ACC he:cooks
'He cooks rice grains into cooked rice'

In this sentence, both words, *odana* and *taṇḍula*, co-occur so that one word (*odana*) cannot be taken as a denotation of the meaning of the other (*taṇḍula*). In order to explain the syntactic function of *odana* in (37), Patañjali decomposes the meaning of the verb *pacati* 'he cooks' into two components – cooking and producing, which are related to *taṇḍulān* 'rice grains' and *odanam* 'cooked rice', respectively. This analysis is substantiated by the paraphrase:

(38) *taṇḍulān pacann odanaṃ nirvartayati* [Sanskrit]
rice:grains:ACC cooking rice:ACC he:produces
'By cooking rice grains he produces cooked rice'

The distinction between the two meanings of the verb *pacati* gives rise to an analogous distinction between two kinds of objects – *nirvartyakarma* 'the object which is to be produced' and *vikāryakarma* 'the object which is to be modified'. In (38), cooked rice is the object which is to be produced, and rice grains are the object which is to be modified by the action of cooking.

3.2.4. Objects of *kartṛstha* actions

As objects of *karmastha* actions, the *nirvartyakarma* and the *vikāryakarma* undergo a perceptible change in the course of the action. Objects of *kartṛstha* actions, on the contrary, are not subject to such a change; they typically serve as the goal of movements as in (34) or as the object of perceptions as in:

(39) *ādityaṃ paśyati* [Sanskrit]
sun:ACC he:sees
'He sees the sun'

(40) *himavantaṃ śṛṇoti* [Sanskrit]
himalaya:ACC he:hears
'He hears the [rumble of the] Himalaya'

Patañjali (Bh 1.445.19–20) quotes these examples in order to demonstrate the futility of the view that a true object is an object in which a difference is produced by the action. As Patañjali (Bh 1.445.20) argues, the objects in (34), (39) and (40) are as natural as the objects in sentences like *kaṭaṃ karoti* 'he makes a mat' or *śakaṭaṃ karoti* 'he makes a cart'. In Patañjali's (Bh 1.445.14–17) view, even nouns in the accusative denoting a period of time or a distance in space are natural objects and, hence, subject to passive transformation (see below, 4.3.1.) as in:

(41) *āsyate māsaḥ* [Sanskrit]
is:being:sat month:NOM
'A month is spent sitting'

(42) *śayyate krośaḥ* [Sanskrit]
is:being:slept krośa:NOM
'A krośa [measure of distance] is covered [while] sleeping'

An interesting border-line case is introduced in the following *vārttika* (Bh 1.333.1):

(43) *īpsitasya karmasaṃjñāyāṃ nirvṛttasya kārakatve karmasaṃjñāprasaṅgaḥ kriyepsitatvāt*
[If the term *karma* [object] denotes that which is most desired, it would not be applicable to a thing which has been produced, even if it is a *kāraka*, since [in this case] the action is that which is desired.]

The meaning of this *vārttika* is illustrated by Patañjali (Bh 1.333.4) with the example:

(44) *guḍaṃ bhakṣayati* [Sanskrit]
sugar:ACC he:eats
'He eats (brown) sugar'

Brown sugar (*guḍa*) is neither a *nirvartyakarma* nor a *vikāryakarma*. It is not an object which has to be produced by the action of eating since it already exists; neither is it an object which has to be modified by the action. Even though the sugar will be chemically modified through the action of eating, this modification is not what the agent actually wants to achieve. What the agent really wants is to eat the sugar, not to modify the sugar. Since eating the sugar is what is most desired by the agent, the sugar itself cannot be categorized as an object according to Pāṇini's definition (13) of the object as that which the agent most desires to reach.

Kātyāyana solves the problem he raised in *vārttika* (43) by conceding that not only the action of eating the sugar, but also the sugar itself is to be regarded as that which the agent most desires to reach since someone who wants to eat sugar will not be satisfied if he eats a piece of mud instead. The sugar and the action of eating it are of equal importance to the agent. Therefore, Pāṇini's definition of the object can be applied to the sugar.

Objects which fall neither in the category of *nirvartyakarma* nor in the category of *vikāryakarma* are only negatively characterized; they are objects which the agent most desires to reach, and nothing else. Hence, Patañjali does not use a special designation to refer to them in the discussion of the above examples. In the later grammatical tradition from Bhartṛhari (VP 3.7.51) onward, they are denoted as *prāpyakarma* 'the object which is to be reached'. This term again does not imply more than what is already contained in Pāṇini's definition of the object (13).

The *nirvartyakarma*, the *vikāryakarma*, and the *prāpyakarma* are three kinds of objects, which equally satisfy Pāṇini's definition (13). Nevertheless, there remains a difference between the *nirvartyakarma* and the *vikāryakarma*, on the one side, and the *prāpyakarma*, on the other, since the former are objects of *karmastha* actions whereas the latter is the object of *kartṛstha* actions. On account of *vārttika* (33), therefore, only the *nirvartyakarma* and *vikāryakarma* are eligible for the transformation into the object-agent. For the *prāpyakarma*, this transformation is not possible since the associated action is not inherent in the object, but in the agent (cf. Das 1990: 107, 187; Kudo 1994: 113).

3.3. Action and dynamic being

The difference between the *nirvartyakarma* and the *vikāryakarma* will remain when the respective objects are transformed into the object-agent since the action which is performed by the object-agent is the same as the action which is performed by the object prior to its transformation into the object-agent (see above, 3.2.1). Actions which are performed by the object-agent, thus, can be subdivided into actions through which the object-agent is produced and actions through which the object-agent is modified.

A more refined subdivision of actions, which is valid not only for the actions of an object-agent, but for all actions denoted by intransitive verbs, is provided by the six modifications of dynamic being (*bhāva*), which are enumerated in the *Nirukta* of Yāska (Sarup 1967: 1.2) as follows:

(45) *jāyate 'sti vipariṇamate vardhate 'pakṣīyate vinaśyati*
[being born, existing, changing, increasing, decreasing, perishing]

The six modifications of dynamic being (*bhāva*) are introduced in the *Nirukta*, however, not as subdivisions of intransitive verbs, but as subdivisions of verbs in general since dynamic being is recognized in the *Nirukta* (Sarup 1967: 1.1) as the defining property of all verbs.

Besides this doctrine, which defines the meaning of the root as dynamic being, there is another equally ancient doctrine which maintains that action (*kriyā*) is the meaning of the verbal root: In the *Kāśikā* (Tripathi and Malviya 1986: on A 1.3.1), this doctrine is ascribed to the ancient grammarians, who created the term *dhātu* 'verbal root' to denote actions. Pāṇini's definition of the root (A 1.3.1), however, does not contain any reference to the one or the other doctrine. It is an extensional definition, in which the roots are defined by enumeration:

(46) *bhūvādayo dhātavaḥ*
[*bhū* and the others are roots.]

As it was noted by Kātyāyana (Bh 1.253.13), Pāṇini's extensional definition of the root leads to the undesired consequence that expressions which are not roots themselves, but only homophonous with a root have to be considered as roots. In order to avoid this undesired consequence, Patañjali (Bh 1.254.13) suggests an intensional definition of the root such as:

(47) *kriyāvacano dhātur iti*
[*A* root denotes action.]

This definition, in turn, necessitates an inquiry into the nature of action.

3.3.1. Action as the meaning of the root

Any inquiry into the nature of action is impaired by the fact that action cannot be directly observed (Bh 1.254.15–16). Only the means of realizing the action, that is, the *kārakas*, can be directly observed; yet, the presence of the *kārakas* alone is only a necessary, but not a sufficient condition for action to take place. This is illustrated by Patañjali (Bh 1.254.17–18) with regard to the action of cooking:

(48) *sarveṣu sādhaneṣu saṃnihiteṣu kadācit pacatīty etad bhavati kadācin na bhavati*
[When all the means [of realizing the action] are present, sometimes it happens that one can say 'he cooks', sometimes it does not happen.]

If the nature of action cannot be perceived directly, how can it be known then that verbs like *pacati* 'he cooks' denote an action? Patañjali (Bh 1.254.20) gives a simple answer to this question: Verbs like *pacati* denote an action in as much as they are coreferential with the verb 'he does'.

They are coreferential with this verb when they occur in an answer to the question "what does he do?" (Bh 1.254.21). This test, however, fails in case of the verbs *asti, bhavati, vidyati*, which all denote existence. It cannot be demonstrated that verbs denoting mere existence are coreferential with the verb *karoti* 'he does' because the expression "he exists" cannot occur in an answer to the question "what does he do?" (Bh 1.255.2–3).

In this situation, Patañjali (Bh 1.256.18) considers the alternative definition of the meaning of the root as dynamic being (*bhāva*). If dynamic being is taken to be the meaning of the root, then the verbs denoting existence (*asti, bhavati, vidyati*) would automatically be included in the general definition of the root since one of these verbs (*bhavati*), precisely, is the verb from which the noun *bhāva* 'dynamic being' is derived. Yet, a new problem arises in this case with regard to roots like *pac* 'cook'. Since it was established already that *pac* and similar verbs denote actions, it has to be demonstrated now in which way roots of this type can denote dynamic being.

3.3.2. The relation between action and dynamic being

After a lengthy discussion of the pros and cons of the *bhāva* theory, Patañjali finally reverts to the theory that action is to be considered as the meaning of the root. Yet, the problem which was raised with regard to this theory has not been solved yet. It still remains to be explained in which way verbs denoting existence can be understood as action verbs. In his attempt to solve this problem now, Patañjali (Bh 1.258.11) presents a new definition of action:

(49) *kārakāṇāṃ pravṛttiviśeṣaḥ kriyā*
[Action is a special enactment of *kārakas*.]

This definition allows him to subsume the meaning of verbs like being and dying under the category of action (Bh 1.258.12–13). Being and dying, which are mentioned here as special kinds of action, are identical with two of the six modifications of dynamic being, which were introduced in the *Nirukta* (45). In fact, Patañjali quotes in his next sentence (Bh 1.258.13–14) the six modifications of dynamic being from the *Nirukta*.

By illustrating different types of action with two of the six modifications of dynamic being, Patañjali recognizes that *bhāva* 'dynamic being' and *kriyā* 'action' are compatible, if not equivalent terms since the meaning of one term (*bhāva*) is covered by the meaning of the other (*kriyā*) (cf. Cardona 1970; Deshpande 1991b: 469–470).

Yet, the complete harmonization of the two concepts is still impaired by the fact that for verbs denoting existence the coreferentiality with the verb *karoti* 'he does', which Patañjali used as a test for action verbs, could not be established (see above, 3.3.1). If dynamic being and action are not mutually exclusive, but compatible terms, it is indeed difficult to explain why verbs denoting existence cannot be used in an answer to the question "what does he do?".

Patañjali (Bh 1.258.20–21), finally, solves this problem by denying the validity of the question "what does he do?" as a criterion for singling out action verbs. From the impossibility of using the verb 'exist' in a response to the question "what does he do?" it does not follow that the verb 'exist' does not signify an action. It only means that the statement "he exists" is not the proper answer to the question "what does he do?" since:

(50) *nānyatpṛṣṭhenānyad ākhyeyam*
[One cannot answer something different from what has been asked for.]

The statement "he exists" cannot be counted as an answer to the question "what does he do?" since it is already presupposed in the very question that the person whose activity is asked for exists. So, "he exists" never can occur as an answer to the question "what does he do?" since existence is not that which has been asked for.

3.3.3. Beyond the diversity of agent and action

In the third part of *Vākyapadīya*, Bhartṛhari deals with different theories of the meaning of the verbal root from a philosophical point of view. Of particular interest is a theory in which the six modifications of dynamic being as they were enumerated in the *Nirukta* (45) – being born, existing, changing, increasing, decreasing, perishing – are reduced to two basic categories – being born and perishing, which, in turn, are equated with two more general notions – appearance and disappearance, respectively (VP 3.8.26).

Existing falls in the category of being born since it can be understood 'as birth which has assumed uniformity' (*janmaivāśritasārūpyam*) of similar moments (VP 3.8.27).

Changing exhibits both basic categories simultaneously since in any changing substance some properties appear and other properties disappear. By the same token, increasing and decreasing, which are merely quantifications of the two aspects of change, are reduced to being born and perishing, respectively.

In a further step of unification, being born and perishing are merged with their respective substrata (VP 3.8.28):

(51) *jāyamānān na janmānyad vināśe 'py apadārthatā*
[Birth is not different from that which is born and also in perishing there exists a non-entity.]

Neither can the action of being born be separated from that which is being born nor the action of perishing from that which is perishing. That which is being born is the agent of being born, and that which is perishing is the agent of perishing. The agent of being born exists already before he is born, and the agent of perishing still exists as a non-entity after he has perished.

In both cases, the agent as such remains unaffected by the action since his existence is neither created by his being born nor destroyed by his perishing. This is the conclusion which is reached in the second half of verse (51):

(52) *ato bhāvavikāreṣu sattaikā vyavatiṣṭhate* ||
[Among the modifications of dynamic being, therefore, it is being [*sattā*] alone that persists.]

According to Helārājā's commentary (Subramania Iyer 1973: 23), this being (*sattā*) has 'the nature of a great unification' (*mahāsāmānyasvabhāvā).* It is a concept beyond the opposition of the categories of agent and action. It appears as action (*kriyā*) when it is seen as a sequence of events; it appears as a means (*sādhana*) when it is seen without such a sequence. In the first case, it constitutes the categorial meaning of a verb, in the latter case the categorial meaning of a noun.

4. Syntax and morphology

From the semantic point of view, verbs and nouns appear as representations of the categories of action and *kārakas*, respectively. Yet, verbs and nouns are introduced by Pāṇini not as representations of semantic categories, but as subdivisions of the category of the word, which is defined in purely morphological terms (A 1.4.14):

(53) *sup-tiṅ-antaṃ padam*
[That which has either a nominal or a verbal ending is a word.]

Obviously, a linguistic expression which has a nominal ending is a noun, and an expression which has a verbal ending is a verb. Pāṇini's definition of the word as that which has either a nominal or a verbal ending, therefore, implies that a word is either a noun or a verb. As an Indo-European language, Sanskrit has, of course, not only nouns and verbs, but also other classes of words, which we would identify from a European perspective as prepositions, conjunctions, adverbs, and particles. Pāṇini recognizes, in fact, the existence of non-inflected words, which he denotes as *avyaya* 'unchangeable'. Yet, non-inflected words are not considered as a genuine word class by him; they are reduced to nouns by virtue of a *sūtra* (A 2.4.82), which prescribes that a nominal ending is deleted after an *avyaya*.

4.1. Nominal and verbal endings

Pāṇini's definition of the word as that which has either a nominal or a verbal ending presupposes a definition of nominal and verbal endings. This definition is given in two *sūtras* (A 4.1.2 and A 3.4.78), in which the standard forms of nominal endings (54) and verbal endings (55) are enumerated:

(54) *su-au-jas-am-auṭ-śas-ṭā-bhyām-bhis-ṅe-bhyām-bhyas-ṅasi-bhyām-bhyas-ṅas-os-ām-ṅi-os-sup*

(55) *tip-tas-jhi-sip-thas-tha-mip-vas-mas-ta-ātām-jha-thās-āthām-dhvam-iṭ-vahi-mahiṅ*

The eighteen verbal endings, which are enumerated in (55), are divided into two groups of nine endings. The nine endings of the first half are categorized as *parasmaipada*, the nine endings of the second half as *ātmanepada* (A 1.4.99–100). *Parasmaipada* and *ātmanepada* are two categories inherent in the meaning of verbal roots of Sanskrit; yet, not all the roots are capable of expressing both categories alternately. There are roots which occur only in *parasmaipada*, roots which occur only in *ātmanepada*, and roots which can be used either in *parasmaipada* or in *ātmanepada*.

Only for the last class of roots, there is a direct semantic contrast between the two categories. According to rule A 1.3.72, roots belonging to this class take *ātmanepada* endings 'if the result of the action accrues to the agent' (*kartrabhiprāye kriyāphale*). If this condition is not fulfilled, the roots of this class take *parasmaipada* endings on the further condition that the verbal endings do not denote the object or the action, but the agent; otherwise they take *ātmanepada* endings (see below, 4.3.1).

Each group of *parasmaipada* or *ātmanepada* endings is subdivided into three groups of three endings. The three groups are classified as the first, the middle and the highest person, respectively (A 1.4.101). The highest person is selected when the ending is coreferential with the pronoun 'I, we' (A 1.4.107), the middle person when it is coreferential with the pronoun 'you' (A 1.4.105), and the first person in the remaining cases (A 1.4.108), in which the ending is equivalent to the third person of European grammatical terminology (the middle person being equivalent to the European second person, and the highest person to the European first person). The three endings of each person are further categorized as singular, dual, and plural, respectively (A 1.4.102). In this way, a twofold classification is obtained for *parasmaipada* and *ātmanepada*. For *parasmaipada* this classification may be displayed in the following way (the lines contain the persons, the rows the numbers):

(56)	*tip*	*tas*	*jhi*
	sip	*thas*	*tha*
	mip	*vas*	*mas*

The analogous twofold classification is applied to the 21 nominal endings, which are enumerated in (54):

(57)	*su*	*au*	*jas*
	am	*auṭ*	*śas*
	ṭā	*bhyām*	*bhis*
	ṅe	*bhyām*	*bhyas*
	ṅasi	*bhyām*	*bhyas*
	ṅas	*os*	*ām*
	ṅi	*os*	*sup*

The seven triplets which are obtained in this classification are denoted as *vibhaktis* (A 1.4.104); as subdivisions of the nominal endings, the *vibhaktis* are simply labelled according to the order in which they are enumerated in *sūtra* (54) as the first, second, … (vibhakti). As in the classification of the verbal endings, the three endings of each *vibhakti* are categorized as singular, dual, and plural, respectively (A 1.4.103).

The seven *vibhaktis* are the counterparts of the morphological cases of the European grammatical tradition. The first *vibhakti* corresponds to the nominative case in European terminology, the second to the accusative, the third to the instrumental, the fourth to the dative, the fifth to the ablative, the sixth to the genitive, and the seventh to the locative.

4.2. *Karakas* and nominal endings

The *vibhaktis* are introduced as representations of *kārakas* by a group of *sūtras* from the third section of the second chapter of the *Aṣṭādhyāyī*. These *sūtras* have the general format: *Vibhakti* X is introduced after a nominal stem in order to denote *kāraka* Y. There is, however, no one-to-one relation between *kārakas* and *vibhaktis*. A *kāraka* may be represented by different *vibhaktis*, and a *vibhakti* may represent different *kārakas*; there are also *vibhaktis* which do not represent a *kāraka* at all. Nevertheless, for each *kāraka*, a particular *vibhakti* may be identified as its prototypical representation; these prototypical representations are specified in the following *sūtras*:

(58) *karmaṇi dvitīyā*
[The second *vibhakti* [accusative] is introduced after a nominal stem to denote the object.] (A 2.3.2)

(59) *kartṛkaraṇayos tṛtīyā*
[The third *vibhakti* [instrumental] is introduced after a nominal stem to denote the agent and the instrument.] (A 2.3.18)

(60) *caturthī saṃpradāne*
[The fourth *vibhakti* [dative] is introduced after a nominal stem to denote the recipient.] (A 2.3.13)

(61) *apādāne pañcamī*
[The fifth *vibhakti* [ablative] is introduced after a nominal stem to denote the point of departure.] (A 2.3.28)

(62) *saptamy adhikaraṇe ca*
[The seventh *vibhakti* [locative] is introduced after a nominal stem to denote also the locus.] (A 2.3.36)

The first *vibhakti* (nominative) is not introduced as the representation of a syntactic function at all. It has a purely lexical function, which is described in the following *sūtra* (A 2.3.46):

(63) *prātipadikārtha-liṅga-parimāṇa-vacana-mātre prathamā*
[The first *vibhakti* is introduced after a nominal stem when there is to be denoted nothing but the meaning of the nominal stem, its gender and number.]

Whereas the first *vibhakti* (nominative) is not introduced as the representation of a syntactic function at all, the sixth *vibhakti* (genitive) is introduced to denote syntactic relations which are not covered by the previous rules (A 2.3.50). These relations are, in particular, relations between nominal stems such as the relation between the possessor and the thing possessed.

The group of *sūtras* which introduce the *vibhaktis* is headed by the *sūtra* (A 2.3.1):

(64) *anabhihite*
[If not already expressed.]

This *sūtra* is a governing rule like *sūtra* (15) *kārake*; it has to be read into the *sūtras* of its domain to the effect that a *vibhakti* can only be introduced after a noun stem if its syntactic function is not already expressed elsewhere.

4.3. The representation of the agent and the object

In which way the syntactic function of a *vibhakti* may be expressed elsewhere, is specified in a *vārttika* of Kātyāyana (Bh 1.441.20). Out of the different possibilities which are enumerated by Kātyāyana, the possibility that a *kāraka* may be expressed in the endings of the verb is of particular relevance for syntax. A restriction, however, is laid down in the following *sūtra* (A 3.4.69) that only the agent and the object may be expressed in this way:

(65) *laḥ karmaṇi ca bhāve cākarmakebhyaḥ*
[The *lakāras* denote (in addition to the agent) also the object and, in case of intransitive verbs, the action.]

The *lakāras*, which are referred to in this *sūtra*, are the temporal and modal categories of the verb in Sanskrit; they are called *lakāras* because the single terms which denote a *lakāra* commence with the consonant *la*, for example: *laṭ* (= present), liṭ (= perfect), *luṭ* (= non-sigmatic future). In the course of a grammatical derivation, these *lakāras* are replaced by one of the verbal endings enumerated in (55) according to the *sūtra* (A 3.4.77):

(66) *lasya*
[In the place of a *lakāra.*]

Since a substitute has the same properties as its replacement (A 1.1.56), the property of the *lakāra* to denote the agent, the object or the action is transferred to the verbal ending replacing it.

4.3.1. Agent and object in verbal endings

By virtue of *sūtra* (65), three syntactic structures are defined according to whether the verbal ending expresses the agent, the object or the action. These structures are known as the three uses (*prayogas*) of the verb. The *kartari prayoga* is the use of the verb to denote the agent, the *karmaṇi prayoga* is the use of the verb to denote the object, and the *bhāve prayoga* is the use of the verb to denote the action. The three *prayogas* are illustrated by the following sentences:

(67) *devadattaḥ odanaṃ pacati* [Sanskrit]
Devadatta:NOM rice:ACC cooks
'Devadatta cooks rice'

(68) *devadattena odanaḥ pacyate* [Sanskrit]
Devadatta:INS rice:NOM is:cooked
'Rice is cooked by Devadatta'

(69) *āsyate devadattena* [Sanskrit]
it:is:being:sat Devadatta:INS
'The action of sitting is performed by Devadatta'

The *kartari prayoga* corresponds to the active voice in European terminology, the *karmaṇi prayoga* to the passive voice, and the *bhāve prayoga* to the impersonal passive of Latin or German (*curritur* and *es wird gelaufen*, respectively). As in the cognate languages, the *prayogas* affect the morphological structure of the verb.

The two verb forms, *pacati* 'cooks' and *pacyate* 'is cooked', which occur in the *kartari prayoga* of (67) and in the *karmaṇi prayoga* of (68), respectively, consist of three parts – the root *pac*, the verbal ending, which is either *ti* or *te*, and a third element, which is inserted between the root and the ending. This element, which is denoted as *vikaraṇa* 'modifier', appears as *a* in the *kartari prayoga* and as *ya* in the *karmaṇi prayoga.*

Both *vikaraṇas* contain an indirect reference to the agent and the object, respectively, since Pāṇini (A 3.1.68 and A 3.1.67) prescribes that the *vikaraṇa a* is introduced on condition that the verbal ending expresses the agent and the *vikaraṇa ya* on condition that the verbal ending expresses the object or the action.

The latter condition is also fulfilled in the *bhāve prayoga*, in which the verbal ending denotes the action. In the *bhāve prayoga* of (69), therefore, the *vikaraṇa ya* is inserted between the root *ās* and the ending *te*. The ending *te*, which is common to both, the *karmaṇi prayoga* and the *bhāve prayoga*, is not enumerated in *sūtra* (55); it is derived from the ending *ta*, which is enumerated in this *sūtra*, by the application of another *sūtra* (A 3.4.79); hence it is an ending of the *ātmanepada* group. On account of *sūtra* A 1.3.13, it is generally prescribed when the verbal endings are used 'to denote the object or the action' (*bhāvakarmaṇoḥ).*

The ending *ti* of *pacati*, on the contrary, is an ending of the *parasmaipada* group. This ending could be freely selected in (67) since the root *pac* belongs to that class of roots which can take either *parasmaipada* or *ātmanepada* endings (see above, 4.1.). By selecting the *parasmaipada* ending *ti*, it is implied that the fruit of the action accrues not to the agent, but to somebody else. This means that in (67), Devadatta does not cook for himself, but for somebody else.

4.3.2. Agent and object in nominal endings

On account of the governing rule *anabhihite* (64), the *sūtras* which introduce the prototypical representations of the object and the agent can only be applied if the respective *kāraka* is not already expressed in the verbal ending. This means that *sūtra* (58), which introduces the second *vibhakti* (accusative) as the expression of the object, can only be applied if the verb is used to denote the agent; similarly, *sūtra* (59), which introduces the third *vibhakti* (instrumental) as the expression of the agent, can only be applied if the verb is used to denote the object.

By using the terms *kartari prayoga* and *karmaṇi prayoga*, the restriction in the application of *sūtras* (58) and (59) can be stated more simply as follows: The agent is represented by the third *vibhakti* (instrumental) in the *karmaṇi prayoga* only; the object is represented by the second *vibhakti* (accusative) in the *kartari prayoga* only. Neither can the third *vibhakti* be introduced as a representation of the agent in the *kartari prayoga* nor can the second *vibhakti* be introduced as a representation of the object in the *karmaṇi prayoga*.

The cases in which the representation of the object and the agent is blocked by the governing rule *anabhihite* (64) are precisely those cases in which the respective *kārakas* are represented by a noun in the first *vibhakti* (nominative). Yet, Pāṇini teaches nowhere that the agent in the *kartari prayoga* or the object in the *karmaṇi prayoga* are represented by a noun in the first *vibhakti*. The first *vibhakti* can only be introduced in these cases on account of *sūtra* (63), 'when there is to be denoted nothing but the meaning of the nominal stem, its gender and number'.

This feature of Pāṇinian syntax forms a marked contrast with traditional European syntax. What appears as the subject from a European perspective, is not introduced as the representation of a *kāraka* in Pāṇinian syntax – neither as a representation of the agent in an active sentence nor as a representation of the object in a passive sentence. The noun in the subject position and the *kāraka* which is expressed in the verbal ending are, of course, coreferential; but there is no categorial affinity between the agent in the subject position and the active voice or between the patient in the subject position and the passive voice as we find it in traditional European syntax.

Neither is the categorial meaning of the verb affected by the selection of active or passive voice. In Pāṇinian syntax, the verb has always the same categorial meaning, which is alternately specified as action or as dynamic being (see above, 3.3). In traditional European syntax, on the contrary, we find the doctrine that the verb is 'significative of action or suffering' (*agendi vel patiendi significativum*) according to whether it is used in active or passive voice (Priscian 1961: 372).

The ultimate source of this European doctrine is a passage from Plato's dialogue *Gorgias* (476b–d), in which the concepts of agent and patient are used for the first time in the history of European linguistics. Plato arrived at these concepts in his analysis of actions like beating, burning and cutting, where he found that the action of an agent is mirrored in the experience of a patient: If somebody beats, for example, then somebody else is beaten. Plato (*Gorgias* 476d) generalized the relation which he found between the agent and the patient of these actions in the statement:

(70) *οἷον ἂν ποιῇ τὸ ποιοῦν, τοιοῦτον τὸ πάσχον πάσχειν.*
[As the agent acts, so the patient experiences.]

The Platonic concept of a patient who passively experiences the action of the agent is foreign to Pāṇinian syntax. Pāṇini defined the object of the action not as a patient, but as an entity which the agent most desires to reach. Since this entity is, furthermore, categorized as a *kāraka*, it is an agent in its own right, who along with the principal agent and other *kārakas* contributes to the success of the action (for a more detailed comparison of Pāṇinian and traditional European syntax, see Raster 2009).

5. Abbreviations

A = *Aṣṭādhyāyī* of Pāṇini (Böhtlingk 1998, Cardona 1997: 675–731)
Bh = *Mahābhāṣya* of Patañjali (Kielhorn 1985, 1965)
VP = *Vākyapadīya* of Bhartṛhari (Rau 2002)

6. References (selected)

Aklujkar, Ashok
2008 Traditions of language study in South Asia. In: Braj B. Kachru, Yamuna Kachru and S. Sridhar (eds.), *Language in South Asia*, 189–220. Cambridge: Cambridge University Press.

Āraṇya, Hariharānanda (ed.)
1981 *Yoga Philosophy of Patañjali. Containing his Yoga aphorisms with commentary of Vyāsa in original Sanskrit, and annotations thereon with copious hints on the practice of Yoga.* Calcutta: University of Calcutta.

Böhtlingk, Otto (ed.)
1998 *Pâṇini's Grammatik. Herausgegeben, übersetzt, erläutert und mit verschiedenen Indices versehen.* Delhi: Motilal Banarsidass. Reprint of the second edition of 1887.

Cardona, George
1970 Review: "Rosane Rocher: La théorie des voix du verbe dans l'école pāṇinéenne (Le 14e āhnika)". *Lingua* 25: 210–222.

Cardona, George
1976 Subject in Pāṇini. In: Verma, M. K. (ed.), *The notion of subject in South Asian languages*, 1–38. (South Asian Studies Publications Series, 2.) Madison: University of Wisconsin.

Cardona, George
1997 *Pāṇini. His Work and its Tradition. Volume One: Background and Introduction.* Delhi: Motilal Banarsidass.

Chevillard, Jean-Luc
2000a Les débuts de la tradition linguistique tamoule. In: Auroux, Sylvain, Körner, E. F. K., Niederehe, Hans-Josef, and Kees Versteegh (eds.), *History of the Language Sciences. An International Handbook on the Evolution of the Study of Language from the Beginnings to the Present*, Volume 1: 191–194. Berlin/New York: Mouton de Gruyter.

Chevillard, Jean-Luc
2000b Le Tolkappiyam et le développement de la tradition linguistique tamoule. In: Auroux, Sylvain, Körner, E. F. K., Niederehe, Hans-Josef, and Kees Versteegh (eds.), *History of the Language Sciences. An International Handbook on the Evolution of the Study of Language from the Beginnings to the Present*, Volume 1: 194–200. Berlin/New York: Mouton de Gruyter.

Chevillard, Jean-Luc
2000c Les successeurs du Tolkappiyam: le Nannul, le Viracoliyam et les autres écoles. In: Auroux, Sylvain, Körner, E. F. K., Niederehe, Hans-Josef, and Kees Versteegh (eds.), *History of the Language Sciences. An International Handbook on the Evolution of the Study of Language from the Beginnings to the Present*, Volume 1: 200–202. Berlin/New York: Mouton de Gruyter.

Das, Karunasindhu (ed.)
1990 *A Pāṇinian Approach to Philosophy of Language. Kauṇḍabhaṭṭa's Vaiyākaraṇabhūṣaṇasāra critically edited and translated into English.* Calcutta: Sanskrit Pustak Bhandar.

Deshpande, Madhav M.
1985 *Ellipsis and Syntactic Overlapping: Current Issues in Pāṇinian Syntactic Theory.* (Postgraduate and Research Department Series, 24.) Poona: Bhandarkar Oriental Research Institute.

Deshpande, Madhav M.
1991a Pāṇinian syntax and the changing notion of the sentence. In: Hans Henrich Hock (ed.), *Studies in Sanskrit Syntax. A Volume in Honor of the Centennial of Speijer's Sanskrit Syntax (1886–1986)*, 31–43. Delhi: Motilal Banarsidass.

Deshpande, Madhav M.
1991b Prototypes in Pāṇinian syntax. *Journal of the American Oriental Society* 111, No. 3: 465–480.

Falk, Harry
1993 *Schrift im alten Indien. Ein Forschungsbericht mit Anmerkungen.* (Scriptoralia 56, hrsg. von Paul Goetsch et al.) Tübingen: Gunter Narr.

Houben, Jan E.M.
2008 Bhaṭṭoji Dīkṣita's "Small Step" for a grammarian and "Giant Leap" for Sanskrit grammar. *Journal of Indian Philosophy* 36: 563–574.

Kielhorn, F. (ed.)
1985 *The Vyākaraṇa-Mahābhāṣya of Patañjali. Revised and furnished with additional readings, references, and select critical notes by K.V. Abhyankar*, Volume I. Poona: Bhandarkar Oriental Research Institute.

Kielhorn, F. (ed.)
1965 *The Vyākaraṇa-Mahābhāṣya of Patañjali. Adhyāyas III, IV and V. Third Edition revised and furnished with additional readings, references, and select critical notes by K.V. Abhyankar*, Volume II. Poona: Bhandarkar Oriental Research Institute.

Kudo, Noriyuki
1994 Why is "*jñāyate ghaṭaḥ svayam eva" not accepted? – karmakartari constructions discussed by Navyavaiyākaraṇas. In: Saroja Bhaṭe and Madhav Deshpande (eds.), *Vamanshastri Bhagwat Felicitation Volume*, 107–121. Pune: Vaidika Samshodhana Mandala.

Priscian
1961 Prisciani grammatici caesariensis institutionum grammaticarum libri XVIII ex recensione Martini Hertzii, Vol I. In: Heinrich Keil (ed.), *Grammatici Latini*, Volume II: Prisciani institutionum grammaticarum libri XVIII. Hildesheim: Olms.

Raster, Peter
2009 Der Eurotyp der Sprachen und der Sprachwissenschaft: platonische und pāṇineische Syntax im Vergleich. In: Uwe Hinrichs, Norbert Reiter and Siegfried Tornow (eds.), *Eurolinguistik. Entwicklung und Perspektiven,* 335–349. (Eurolinguistische Arbeiten, Bd. 5.) Wiesbaden: Harrassowitz.

Rau, Wilhelm
2002 *Bhartṛharis Vākyapadīya. Versuch einer vollständigen deutschen Übersetzung nach der kritischen Edition der Mūla-Kārikās*. Edited by Oskar von Hinüber. (Akademie der Wissenschaften und der Literatur, Mainz, Abhandlungen der Geistes- und sozialwissenschaftlichen Klasse, Einzelveröffentlichung Nr. 8.) Stuttgart: Franz Steiner Verlag.

Roodbergen, J. A. F.
1974 *Patañjali's Vyākaraṇa-Mahābhāṣya. Bahuvrīhidvandvāhnika (P. 2.2.23–2.2.38). Text, Introduction, Translation and Notes*. Edited by S. D. Joshi. Poona: University of Poona.

Sarup, Lakshman (ed.)
1967 *The Nighaṇṭu and the Nirukta. The oldest Indian treatise on etymology, philology, and semantics*. Delhi: Motilal Banarsidass.

Scharf, Peter M.
2002 Pāṇini, vivakṣā and kāraka-rule-ordering. In: Madhav M. Deshpande and Peter E. Hook (eds.), *Indian Linguistic Studies*, 121–149. Delhi: Motilal Banarsidass.

Scharfe, Hartmut
2000 Die Entwicklung der Sprachwissenschaft in Indien nach Pāṇini. In: Auroux, Sylvain, Körner, E. F. K., Niederehe, Hans-Josef, and Kees Versteegh (eds.), *History of the Language Sciences. An International Handbook on the Evolution of the Study of Language from the Beginnings to the Present*, Volume 1, 125–136. Berlin/New York: Mouton de Gruyter.

Scharfe, Hartmut
2009 A new perspective on Pāṇini. In: *Indologica.com – The Online Journal of the International Association of Sanskrit Studies*, Vol. 35: 3–272.

Sharma, Rama Nath
1995 *The Aṣṭādhyāyī of Pāṇini, Volume III: English Translation of Adhyāyas Two and Three with Sanskrit Text, Transliteration, Word-boundary, Anuvṛtti, Vṛtti, Explanatory notes, Derivational History of Examples, and Indices*. New Delhi: Munshiram Manoharlal.

Sharma, Shivdatta (ed.)
(no year) *The Vyākaraṇamahābhāṣya of Patañjali with the Commentary Bhāṣyapradīpa of Kaiyaṭa Upādhyāya and the Supercommentary Bhāṣyapradīpoddyota of Nāgeśa Bhaṭṭa.* Volume II: Vidhiśeṣarūpam (Beginning from Aṣṭādhyāyī, chapter I, quarter II to the end of chapter II). (The Vrajajivan Prachyabharati Granthamala, 23.) Delhi: Chaukhamba Sanskrit Pratisthan.

Sontakke, N. S., and T. N. Dharmadhikari (eds.)
1970 *Taittirīya Saṃhitā with the Padapāṭha and the Commentaries of Bhaṭṭa Bhāskara Miśra and Sāyaṇācārya,* Volume I (Kāṇḍa I Prapāṭhakas 1–4). Pune: Vaidika Saṃśodhana Maṇḍala.

Subramania Iyer, K. A. (ed.)
1963 *Vākyapadīya of Bhartṛhari with the Commentary of Helārāja,* Kāṇḍa III, Part 1. (Deccan College Monograph Series 21.) Poona: Deccan College.

Subramania Iyer, K. A. (ed.)
1973 *Vākyapadīya of Bhartṛhari with the Prakīrṇaprakāśa of Helārāja,* Kāṇḍa III, Part 2. Poona: Deccan College.

Tripathi, Jaya Shankar L., and Sudhakar Malaviya (eds.)
1986 *Kāśikā (A Commentary on Pāṇini's Grammar) of Vāmana and Jayāditya,* Volume II. (Prācyabhāratīgranthamālā 18.) Varanasi: Tara Printing Works.

Peter Raster, Essen (Germany)

5. Arabic Syntactic Research

Abstract

The Arabic Linguistic Tradition (ALT) arose phoenix-like at the end of the end of the 2nd/8th century, from its very beginning, syntactic theory playing a central role in it. Relying on the basic concepts of dependency, substitution, and grammatical function, a descriptively detailed and theoretically coherent and elaborated account of Arabic grammar was developed, whose basis till today continues to inform descriptions of Classical and Modern Standard Arabic. This summary recapitulates the descriptive breadth of the ALT, introducing key syntactic and linguistic concepts, elaborations into related pragmatic and metatheoretical issues, while adumbrating various problematic areas of linguistic analysis. The role of the ALT in the history of linguistics and its status in the western intellectual tradition are discussed.

1. Major periods

Traditionally the first grammarian is considered to have been Abu Aswad al-Du'ali (68/688; Talmon 1985; Larcher 2007a; Baalbaki 2008: 2); however, the earliest important grammarian, indeed the most important Arabic grammarian of all, was Sibawayh (for Islamic/Christian dates of Arabic grammarians, cf. bibliography). His book, *al-Kitaab* 'The Book', is the oldest surviving grammar, and in over 900 pages it defined both the basic theoretical framework and the data it was applied to. The next 140 years were a period of consolidation. Initially the data base was expanded, albeit relatively slightly, most notably in Farra's *Maʕaani l-Qurʔaan*, a three volume work of Quranic exegesis. By the end of the 3rd/9th century, grammarians, however, began increasingly to concentrate on reorganizing the data set out in the earlier works. Mubarrad's influential *Muqtaḍab*, for example, makes heavy and sometimes critical use of Sibawayh (Bernards 1997), as does Mubarrad's late contemporary Zajjaj in his *Maʕaani l-Qurʔaan*. At first there existed genuine points of difference between the grammarians, especially between Sibawayh and Farraʔ (Owens 1990; Talmon 2003), though differences are discernible in other writers as well (e.g. the *Muqaddima fiy al-Naħw*, attr. Xalaf al-Aħmar). However, the very reason for the emergence of the Arabic grammatical tradition was a systematization and codification of Arabic, initially a codification based on written and oral sources, but increasingly as time passed, one based on written sources only; these included the various versions of the *Qurʔaan* (*qiraaʔaat*), poetry and belle lettres, as well as a written standard based on Sibawayh's own grammar, so that sometime in the 3rd/9th century no new data made its way into the language corpus (Baalbaki 1995). As the data base became restricted to the Arabic attested between c. 630–800, grammarians increasingly contented themselves with refining the form and organziation of their descriptive grammars, a process that reached a climax of sorts in Sarraj's *al-ʔUṣuwl fiy al-Naħw*. Allowing for myriad local variations, this three-volume work sets the standard for all later grammatical descriptions and my expression *standard grammar* relates to a form derived to a greater or lesser degree from Sarraj. Even before Sarraj, however, linguists were devoting greater attention to another aspect of linguistic analysis, the *ʔuṣuwl* ('roots, origins', see Baalbaki 2008: 98; section 7 below). This sub-discipline, which has parallels in the legal scholarship of the day (Carter 1972; Suleiman 1999; Versteegh 2007), attempted to build an explanatory meta-theory that accounted in particular for deviations from a hypothetical norm. Further developments saw a development of methods of linguistic argumentation, as embodied above all in Ibn al-Anbari's classic work on the Basran and Kufan linguistic schools. In his *Inṣaaf* 121 linguistic disputes attributed to the early Basran and Kufan grammarians, each dealing with a simple topic, are summarized and judged. Finally, Ibn Maḍa's thirteenth century critique of the whole *ʔuṣuwl* tradition, *al-Radd ʕalaa l-Nuħaah*, should be mentioned, not for the effect it had on the ALT, which was negligible, but rather as an indication of the critical discourse which continued to accrue to the ALT. The development of the pragmatic tradition, closely intertwined with the syntactic, deserves a chapter of its own (see section 6 below; Larcher 2013).

2. An overview of basic syntactic concepts: dependency, substitution, grammatical function

The typical Arabic grammar began with syntax and treated it exhaustively. To give an idea of the detail and length involved, the entire volume I of Sibawayhi's *Kitaab*, is devoted to syntax, some 450 pages, volume II, equally long, to morphology and (morpho)phonology

The precepts of Arabic syntactic theory will be familiar to those versed in the tradition of western structural linguistics. There are three basic constructs: a dependency-based grammar, a principle of paradigmatic substitution that establishes functional equivalences between formally distinctive elements, and the attendant definition of a finite number of grammatical functions.

From its inception Arabic grammar has been a dependency one, the changing case and mode forms (see below) on nouns and verbs being explained by reference to changing governors. As Sarraj so succinctly put it "(...) case inflections are the three vowel endings (*-u, -a-, -i*) that alternate at the end of a word (...) according to a change in governing word" (*Muwjaz,* 28; see [5], [6] below for examples of case alternation due to a change in governor). On the basis of formal principles, a very consistent dependency grammar was developed (Owens 1984a, 1988: chapter 2). Sibawayh for instance notes that in

(1) *ḍarab-tu wa ḍaraba-niy zayd-un*
hit-I and hit-me Zayd-NOM
'I hit (Zayd) and Zayd hit me'

zaydun is implied object of *ḍarabtu* and overt agent of *ḍarabaniy.* He emphasizes that *zayd* is to be understood pragmatically as object of *ḍarabtu,* but that it cannot take the usual *-a* inflection of an object, and hence is not a syntactic object, "because a noun cannot be governed in both nominative and accusative case" (*Kitaab* 28.19). Sibawayh's constraint is based on formal considerations: a noun cannot simultaneously have both *-u* and *-a* inflections, **zayd-u-a* 'Zayd-NOM-ACC'. The constraint is reproduced precisely by Robinson (1970: 260), who allows a governed word to have one and only one governor.

While the governance relation was prototypically expressed in the changing vowel suffixes, the notion of governance effectively described a more abstract relation, for even words of invariable form, like interrogative pronouns (see [7], [8] below) occurred as governed items. A second prominent principle of Arabic theory was the recognition of a finite number of functional positions (Carter 1973; Versteegh 1978). Sentence parts were classified as agent, object, time object, adjective and so on. A sentence like

(2)

raʔaa	*zayd-un*	*bayt-an*	*kabiyr-an*	*al-yawm-a*
saw	Zayd-NOM	house-ACC	big-ACC	today-ACC
Verb	Agent	Object	Adjective	Time Object

Fig. 5.1: Dependency structure of a sentence

has a two-fold structure, one dependency (indicated by arrows, leading from head *raʔaa* to dependents), one in terms of the syntactic positions which the items fill. Allowing for different degrees of emphasis from different linguists, both the dependency and syntactic position constructs are discernible throughout the history of Arabic grammar. There was, however, an important methodological practice separating especially Sibawayh from later grammarians. As Carter (also Baalbaki 1979) has pointed out, Sibawayh was seeking to define the total range of syntactic constructions on essentially descriptivist principles, and a favorite analytical tool was the use of substitution techniques, whereby the structure of a more complicated construction was ascertained relative to a more basic one. For instance, Sibawayh (*Kitaab* I: 301.4.) wants to show that the bold face prepositional phrase

(3) *hal* ***min rajul-i-n*** *xayrun min-ka*
Q from man-GEN-INDF better than-you
'Is there a man better than you?'

is in the position of topic (see 4.2.1 below). Topics usually have nominative, not genitive form, however, and Sibawayh justifies his analysis by substituting the hypothetical

(4) *hal rajul-u-n xayr-u-n min-ka*
Q man-NOM-INDF better-NOM-INDF than-you
'Is there a man better than you?'

where the topic *rajul-un* 'a man' does appear in the expected nominative case. Much of Sibawayh's grammar is a cross-reference of constructions of the type: structure x has a certain analysis because it substitutes with y, which has already been shown or will be shown to have the analysis given. While later grammarians did not completely abandon the substitution methodology, by Sarraj's day, or even as early as Mubarrad's, it had become at most a more or less pedagogical device used to exemplify the nature of already defined constructions (e. g. Mubarrad I: 4, III: 172, IV: 248). Sarraj's syntactic description consists largely in running through the set of positions, as exhaustively as possible listing all the properties associated with them, as will be elaborated below.

There are in places hints of other formal organizational principles. Jurjani (*DalaaʔiI* 471/1078: q) for instance sketches a distinction between certain NP and S-level constituents, and Sakkaki's (*Miftaaħ*, 209, 244) notion of *taqyiyd* is applied to elements which effectively constitute a VP. Such concepts, however, had only a comparatively marginal function when compared to the central role of dependency and syntactic positions.

3. Basic units of syntactic theory

In this section I will outline the basic descriptive practice of an Arabic syntax. As an organizing motif, I follow the main categories treated in a short, concise summary of Arabic grammar, Ibn Jinni's *al-Lumaʕ fiy al-ʕArabiyya*. Ibn Jinni (392/1002) was one of the most significant grammarians, known in particular for his contribution to metatheoretical issues. The *Lumaʕ* (henceforth *L*) is very representative of the order as well as the grammatical categories and explanations which are found in other grammars, whether compendious or short. Of course, grammars differed in detail in the manner of presentation, though important works such as Sarraj's *al-ʔUṣuwl fiy al-Naħw*, Jurjani's *Muqtaṣid*, Zamaxshari's *Mufaṣṣal* along with Ibn Yaʕish's compendious commentary on the *Mufaṣṣal*, agree in broad thematic and organizational terms with the *Lumaʕ*. It may be noted that Sibawayh's *Kitaab* does not follow this order closely, though it does agree with it in other ways.

Turning to details, to get the syntax ball rolling, as it were, the grammars began with two morphological elements. The first is universally necessary, namely the imperative of having word classes which the syntax can operate on. Accordingly, grammars typically began with a characterization of what a word was. The twelfth century grammarian Zamaxshari had a remarkably concise characterization: "a word (*kalima*) is a form pointing to a discrete, conventionalized meaning" (*Al-Mufaṣṣal*, 6, *Al-Mufaṣṣal*, 6, (الكلمة هى اللفظة الدالة على معنى مفرد بالوضع). The form-meaning dichotomy, reemphasized in modern Linguistics through de Saussure, was a fundamental aspect of the Arabic tradition.

Three word classes were recognized, nominals (*ism*), verbs (*fiʕl*) and particles (*ħarf*). *Ism* is translated as 'nominal' since any single word which partakes of a typical nominal function is an *ism*, including adjectives, active and passive participles, quantifiers (like *kull* 'all'), relative pronouns, pronouns, and demonstratives. In Ibn Jinni's *Lumaʕ*, for instance, a nominal is characterized as a word governed by a preposition. In the category verb are finite verbs, traditionally termed perfect and imperfect, while particles were simply defined as what was left over (Sarraaj I: 40). Particles will be treated in section 3.3 below. Very broadly, nominals and verbs can be thought of as being major categories, particles as functional ones. Prototypically, word classes are held to have complementary governance properties. Nominals are case receivers, but as a rule do not govern, whereas particles and verbs are governors, but are not prototypically governed.

The second morphological element that precedes syntactic description is one particular to Arabic grammar. As seen in section 2 above, the basis of Arabic grammar from its inception was the idea of dependency relation. Since nearly every major category occurs in a governable position, morphological case, or an interpreted case form (see below) is an exponent of every syntactic relation, and hence iconically case form came to be associated with syntactic function. Indeed, the term for case/mode, *ʔiʕraab* in later usage (e.g. Al-Faariqi) came to be synonymous with 'syntactic parsing' (Carter 1981).

Nouns are classified as being inflectable for case (*muʕrab* 'inflected') or uninflectable (*mabniy* lit. 'built'). The former have three (in some cases two) case forms, nominative (termed *rafʕ*, marked by *-u*), accusative (*naṣb -a*) and genitive (*jarr* or *xafḍ*, *-i*) (see below for verbal mode inflections). Uninflectable nouns always end with the same vowel or consonant, e.g. *man* 'who?', or *tilka* 'that.F'. The basis of the inflectable/non-inflectable classification is the behavior of the nouns in syntactic environments. A noun like *al-mudiyr* 'the director', will take nominative, accusative or genitive according to the governing word, whereas *man* remains invariable.

(5) *jaaʔa l-mudiyr-u*
came DEF-director-NOM
'The director came'

(6) *raʔay-tu l-mudiyr-a*
saw-I DEF-director-ACC
'I saw the director'

vs.

(7) *man jaaʔa*
who came
'Who came?'

(8) *man raʔay-ta*
who saw-2.M
'Who did you see?'

Crucially, the difference between the inflectable and non-inflectable nouns is introduced in the *Lumaʕ* and elsewhere not in the morphology, but rather in the syntax. The supporting observation is that in alternations such as (5–6) above, the substitution of the governing element is accompanied by a change in the case marking on the noun, the case form being dependent on the identity of the governor. Merely by looking at the case form, a great deal can be read into the syntactic environment a given case form implies.

In describing the syntactic properties of nouns, the metaphor here is thus a processual, syntagmatic one, one element acting on another and changing its form (*zuwaal al-ʔiʕraab li-taɣyiyr al-ʕaamil wa intiqaalihi* "deletion and substitution of one case [for another] corresponding to a change in the governor"(*L,* 92), rather than a paradigmatic one, choosing one nominal form in a given context from a paradigmatic store of nouns inflected for nominative, accusative or genitive case.

Indeed, Ibn Jinni, in his compendious work on morphology, the *Munṣif*, defined the difference between morphology and syntax as follows. "Morphology serves to define the stable interior of words and syntax serves to define their changeable states" (*Munṣif*, 4). Morphology is based on lexically given stems which do not change under different syntactic conditions – in (5), (6) [*mudiyr*] remains [*mudiyr*] in all contexts. Syntax, on the other hand, explains the case-based alternations, the conditions under which [*-u*, *-a*, *-i*] appear in.

Given the centrality of case in the Arabic syntactic model, it was important for the grammarians to identify anomalous nominals, such as *man* in (7), (8), which lacked essential nominal properties (see 3.1), hence the introduction of the case-inflected vs. uninflectable lexical categories at the very beginning of the grammatical description.

Following this precept, the different conjugational inflectional forms of nominals were introduced. In the *Lumaʕ* for instance, these include the dual form of nouns, *-aani* 'NOM.DU', *-ayni* 'ACC/GEN.DU' (*rajul-aani/rajul-ayni* 'man-NOM.DU/ACC.DU'), the form of the suffix plural *-uwna* 'NOM-PL', *iyna* 'ACC/GEN.PL', and various irregular nouns (like *qaaḍ-i-n/qaaḍiy-a-n* 'judge NOM/GEN-judge ACC').

3.1. The sentence

Having defined the minimal morphological elements essential to following an exposition of the syntax, the basic unit of analysis, the sentence, is introduced. The elements of the sentence are functional positions, each one encapsulating a number of formal and semantic properties.

All in all, something in the range of 30 distinctive positions were recognized in the Arabic tradition. A non-exhaustive list includes the following: topic, comment, verb, agent, noun of *ʔinna*, etc., absolute object, direct object (two), comitative object, reason object, locative (time and space) objects, circumstance, specification, exception, adjective, emphasizer, appositive, coordinate, clarifying conjunct, object of preposition, vocative, condition, relative clause, and oath. The comment is described below. The verb is, of course, realized as a finite verb, and the condition and relative (and object of preposition in certain cases) by a clause. Otherwise all are realized as nominals.

The sentence is termed either *jumla* lit. 'sum, entirety' or *kalaam* lit. 'matter, word' (see Ibn Hisham *Mughni*; Talmon 1993 for different connotations and uses of the two terms). The core functional positions of a sentence are the two functions constituting a predication (the *ʕumda* 'support' of a sentence), which are also the only two which are always obligatory for a complete sentence. Two fundamental predicative types are distinguished. One consists of a verb + agent (*fiʕl* + *faaʕil*), the other of a topic and comment (*mubtadaʔ* and *xabar*). The basis of this distinction will be discussed in greater detail in section 4.2 below.

(9) Verb + Agent:
qaama zayd-un
got.up Zayd-NOM
'Zayd got up.'

(10) Topic + Comment:
Zayd-un muʕallim-u-n
Zayd-NOM teacher-NOM-INDF
'Zayd is a teacher.'

Prototypically, as seen in section 2 above, a nominal is governed by another element, putting it in a prototypical case form and where the expected case form does not occur on a nominal, its functional status is ascertained by the process of substitution. The three most common instances where this arises are prepositional phrases, sentential complements, and uninflected nominals. The case exponence of a noun governed by a preposition is always genitive, so whatever function the prepositional phrase assumes, the nominal object of preposition will not show the expected case form for that position. In example (3) above, the expected case form is nominative, which in the grammar of Sibawayh is simply asserted as a hypothetical realization. Among later grammarians, the function of the prepositional phrase was conventionally said to 'be in the functional position' of (*qaama maqaam* X, or *fi mawḍiʕ* case X, Versteegh 1978). In this formulation, *min rajul-in* is said to be in the position of a nominative noun (*fi mawḍiʕ al-rafʕ*), but its expected inflectional form is preempted by a competing functionality (*la maħall lahu min il-ʔiʕraab*). The most common positions assumed by prepositional phrases are the locative object and the direct object, the latter for verbs whose objects are considered to be the prepositional object of phrasal verbs, as in

(11) *marar-tu bi zayd-in*
passed-I by Zayd-GEN
'I passed by Zayd'.

Marra bi is a transitive verb, whose object is governed by the preposition *bi* (*Xaṣaaʔiṣ* I: 342), see below.

A second set of elements which do not have the expected case form are similar to prepositional phrases, namely dependent sentences. The nominal object of a cognitive verb like 'think' can be a dependent clause, introduced by the particle *ʔanna*.

(12) *Đanan-tu ʔanna zayd-an hunaak*
thought-I that Zayd-ACC there
'I thought Zayd was there'

ʔanna, being a particle, is not inflectable and, as noted above, particles themselves cannot be governed, so *ʔanna* cannot be the direct object. Here, the entire dependent clause is said to be in the position of the accusative case direct object.

The third category are those nominals which are uninflectable, never showing a case constrast. These include a number of high-frequency word classes, in particular the pronouns, demonstratives and question words, as illustrated in (7), (8) above.

The core sentence divides into two broad types. So-called nominal sentences (*jumla ismiyya*) are those which begin with a nominative nominal, while the verbal sentences (*jumla fiʕliyya*) begin with a verb. This distinction is a basic one, the two sentence types showing broad differences which appear at a number of places in the grammar.

Nominal sentences are characterized by a number of properties which obtain universally for the sentence as a whole, or for the constituent parts. In general (see Sarraj I: 62), the comment can be verified as true or false, the comment gives new, relevant information, and the topic is generally a definite noun; if it is definite and the comment indefinite, the order is topic-comment. Beyond these points, the comment may be any of three different types of constituent. It may be a a single noun or adjective (see [14], [15], [43]), it may be an adverb or prepositional phrase, as in (13), or it may be a complete sentence (see 4.2.1, [44]–[46]).

(13) *zayd-un fi l-bayt-i*
Zayd-NOM at DEF-house-GEN
'Zayd is at home'.

Furthermore, semantic co-occurrence restrictions were noted to obtain between the parts of the core sentence (Taha 1996; Owens 2003).

The sentential comment is bound up with conditions which will be explained in section 4.2.1 below. For the single constituent, the comment is said to be identical to the topic. If the topic and comment are both definite, the order of the elements is irrelevant, except that whatever is put first is the topic, the second element the comment (see below).

(14) Topic + Comment
Zayd-un ʔax-uu-ka
Zayd-NOM brother-NOM-your
'Zayd is your brother'.

(15) Topic + Comment
ʔax-uu-ka zayd-un
brother-NOM-your Zayd-NOM
'Your brother is Zayd'.

When the comment is adverbial, the usual order may be reversed, which happens in particular when the topic is indefinite, so that (16) is the normal order (Talmon 1993; Kouloughli 2002; Marogy 2005; Peled 2008 for detailed discussions).

(16) *fi l-bayt-i rajul-u-n*
in DEF-house-GEN man-NOM-INDF
'In the house is a man'.

Having defined the general properties of the topic/comment sentence, the grammarians noted that there were three further contexts where they were used. The first is after a set of five particles, *ʔinna* 'indeed, that', *ʔanna* 'that', *lakinna* 'but', *layta* 'if only' and *laʕalla* 'maybe'. These particles have the property of governing the "topic" of the sentence in the accusative, so that if a sentence is introduced by one of them, the "topic" will appear in accusative rather than nominative form.

(17) a. *ʔinna zayd-an muʕallim-u-n*
indeed Zayd-ACC teacher-NOM-INDF
'Indeed Zayd is a teacher'.

b. *ʔinna zayd-an fi l-bayt-i*
indeed Zayd-NOM in DEF-house-GEN
'Indeed Zayd is at home'.

c. *ʔinna fi l-bayt-i rajul-a-n*
indeed in DEF-house-GEN man-ACC-INDF
'Indeed a man is in the house'.

Since the first noun is no longer the first element, it is no longer the *mubtadaʔ*, lit. 'that with which is begun', and so it is given a new name, namely the "noun" of governing particle, in the examples here, the noun of the particle *ʔinna* (*ism ʔinna*). As the comment is unaffected morphologically and sequentially, it retains its name, so it is the comment of *ʔinna* (*xabar ʔinna*).

The particle is said to enter upon the basic topic/comment sentence, so that the properties which have already been defined for the nominal sentence are essentially carried over into the new sentence type introduced by one of the five particles. For instance, the basic order of definite topic – indefinite comment is carried over into the new sentence type (17a), the order of adverbial comment – indefinite topic = noun is maintained (17c), and so on. Special restrictions associated with this construction are noted. For instance, it is impossible for any element to be placed in front of the introducing particle (**zaydan ʔinna fi l-bayti*).

Since all of the particles in this class effect the same change on the basic topic-comment sentence, they are given the name '*ʔinna* and its sisters' (*ʔinna wa axawaat-uhaa*).

An analogous treatment is applied to the other two constructions. In one, a set of finite verbs, including *kaana* 'be', *ṣaara* 'become', *ma zaala* 'continue to be', *Đalla* 'remain', *ʔamsaa, ʔaṣbaħa* 'become', *laysa* 'be not' and *daama* 'remain'. In these, the verb is said to govern the topic in the nominative and the comment in the accusative.

(18) *kaana zayd-un muʕallim-a-n*
was Zayd-NOM teacher-ACC-INDF
'Zayd was a teacher'.

(19) *las-tu mutaʔaxxir-a-n*
be.not-I late-ACC-INDF
'I'm not late'.

Here too the topic, no longer the first element, is re-christened as the noun of the relevant predicate, e.g. the noun of *kaana*. Although the comment in this instance receives a new case form, the accusative, it continues to bear the name of comment. As with the previous class, *ʔinna*, the basic properties of the topic-comment sentence are carried over into the new sentence type, with special properties noted, and analogous to the previous class, this class is eponymously named after the verb 'be', '*kaana* and its sisters'.

The verbs in this class have a dual status. On the one hand they are normal, inflected finite verbs with perfect and imperfect variants (except *laysa* which is only perfect in form), but on the other they are held to be semantically distinct from other finite verbs, and hence are not treated within the overall framework of transitivity (see 4.1 below). The reasoning here is that a verb like *kaana* is an operator, whose only function is to impart to the basic topic and comment sentence a time element. *Kaana*, and the other of the verbs in this class, have no semantic function beyond this (*al-zamaan al-mujarrad ʕan al-ħadaθ*). In this respect they contrast with normal verbs, like *đahaba* 'go', which are said to consist of two basic components. On the one hand, like *kaana* and its sisters, they have an inherent temporal element, as manifested in the perfect/imperfect forms, and on the other they have the meaning of the typical action (*ħadaθ*) which they represent, so that *đahaba* can be broken down into the verbal noun *đahaab* 'going' and the past tense morphological pattern of *faʕala*.

Finally, the basic topic/comment sentence can be inserted as a complement of cognition verbs, termed *ʔafʕaal al-yaqiyn wa š-šakk*, 'verbs of certainty and doubt', verbs like *Đanna* 'think', *zaʕama* 'suppose' and *xaala* 'imagine'.

(20) *Đanan-tu zayd-an muʕallim-a-n*
thought-I Zayd-ACC teacher-ACC-INDF
'I thought that Zayd was a teacher'.

Here again the basic topic/comment sentence carries over its basic properties to the new construction, allowing for special conditions that accrue to the new construction, in this case, for instance, the fact that the topic, in contrast to the noun of *ʔinna* can be fronted before the verb:

(21) *zayd-an Ðanan-tu muʕallim-a-n*
Zayd-ACC thought-I teacher-ACC-INDF
'Zayd I thought was a teacher'.

Here, formal considerations lead to a different evaluation of the structural status of the "topic" and "comment". Given the fact that both elements are accusative, and accusative is the typical form of an object complement (see 4.1), this construction is assimilated into the transitivity system, with both complements considered objects. The verb *Ðanna* in this case is thus considered a ditranstive verb.

3.2. Remaining functional positions

The remaining functional positions can be highlighted briefly.

Overall, the functional positions marked by the nominative case are treated first in the grammars, and thereafter come all cases marked in the accusative, including the various classes of objects as described above. The last case-marked positions are those in the genitive. There are two main functions marked by the genitive, one the object of the preposition (22a) and the other the possessive noun (22b).

(22) a. *min al-mudiyr-i*
from DEF-director-GEN
'from the director'

b. *mudiyr-u al-maktab-I*
director-NOM DEF-house-GEN
'the director of the office'

The second example, (22b), appears to violate the precept that nouns are case receivers, but not case governors, since there is no obvious governor of the possessor noun in (22b) other than the possessed noun *mudiyr*. This inconsistency was noted by the grammarians, who held that underlying this genitive construction (*ʔiḍaafa* as it was called) were two nouns joined by an understood (*muqaddar* see section 7 below) preposition, *li* 'to, for' which regularly governs a genitive.

(23) *al-mudiyr-u li l-maktab-I*
DEF-director-NOM for DEF-office-GEN

After dealing with the nominal functions which are marked by a fixed case, the descriptive grammars move on to those nominal functions which are variably determined by agreement. These are the *tawaabiʕ*, described in greater detail in section 4.2.2 below.

Having completed the functional positions of nominals, the grammars then move to the verb, describing first the basic forms (perfect/imperfect), then the three modal forms of the imperfect, the indicative, subjunctive and jussive (JUS).

(24) a. *ya-ktub-u*
3-write-IND
'He is writing'.

b. *lan yaktub-a*
not(FUT) 3-write-SBJV
'He won't write'.

c. *lam ya-ktub-Ø*
not 3-write-JUS
'He didn't write'.

As can be seen, these three modal forms are marked in a way analogous to the noun, the indicative and subjunctive in fact being formally identical to the nominative and acusative case endings, and so they are given the same name, (*-u* = rafʕ, whether NOM or IND, *-a* = *naṣb* whether ACC or SBJV). Furthermore, the mode forms are determined in a similar way, in the case of the subjunctive and jussive by a governing word, usually a particle. The indicative is not governed, an issue discussed at length among the grammarians (for instance in Anbari's *ʔInṣaaf* question 73).

With the treatment of the verbs, including some irregular ones (e.g. the *verbs* of surprise) which generate their own special syntactic properties and the treatment of relative clauses (*al-ṣila wa l-mawṣuwl*) the basic syntactic description comes to an end.

3.3. Particles

Functional categories are the particles, an extremely heterogenous group which non-exhaustively includes the following:

(25) Functional categories
Discourse particles: *ʔammaa* 'as for', *bal* 'to the contrary' …
Question particles: *hal* 'yes-no', *ʔa* 'yes-no'
Prepositions: *fiy* 'at', *min* 'from' …
Verbal operators: *lam*, *lammaa*, *laa*, *lan*, *maa* ('not', see below), *ʔan* 'that', *likay* 'so that'
Coordinators: *wa* 'and' , *lakin* 'but', *laa* 'not', *ʔaw* 'or'…
Subordinators: *ʔinna* 'indeed, that', *ʔanna* 'that'

Whereas nouns and verbs each have their own discrete functional niches and are treated in independent chapters, particles, the third major word class, are integrated into the core grammar according to how their respective functions meld with the overall functional organization, which is built around the functions of nouns and verbs. To see how this works, it is best to take an extended example, that of the class of negative morphemes.

There are five negative particles *laa, lam, lan, maa* and *ʔin*. The last, which has a similar distribution to *maa*, is extremely rare and will not be treated here, nor is it mentioned in the *Lumaʕ* (see Larcher 2007b for overall summary). In addition there is a negative verb (see [19], [30]). *lam, lan,* and *maa* all negate verbs, while *laa* and *maa* also negate nominals.

In Ibn Jinni's *Lumaʕ* the negative particles are introduced in 5 different places, while all negators are introduced in six different ones.

Lan and *lam* occur only before imperfect verbs, the former governing a verb in the subjunctive mood, the latter in the jussive. As noted, these are introduced when the modal inflectional form of the verb is treated (*L*, 208, 213).

(26) a. *lan* *ya-đhab-a*
not(FUT) 3-go-SBJV
'He won't go'.

b. *lam* *ya-đhab-Ø*
not 3-go-JUS
'He didn't go'.

These therefore are introduced when the inflectional form of the verb is discussed, (*L* 205, Chapters 50–52)

Laa is introduced in three different places in the *Lumaʕ*. It receives a special chapter (*L* 127) since it can combine with a subject to produce a specially-marked generic negation, the so-called *laa al-nafiy li-l-jins*, as in

(27) *laa* *maal-a* *la-ka*
not wealth-ACC to-you
'You are poor'.

Laa functions as a negative conjunct, and hence is also introduced along with the other coordinators (*L*, 179, see [49c]):

(28) *qaama* *zayd-un* *laa ʕamr-un*
stood.up Zayd-NOM not Amr-NOM
'Zayd stood up not Amr.'

Laa finally is used to negate imperative verbs, and hence is introduced with the jussive verb forms (*L*, 213).

(29) *laa* *ta-đhab-Ø*
not 2-go-JUS
'Don't go'.

Besides the negative particles, there is also a negative verb, *laysa*.

(30) *lays-at* *al-bint-u* *ṭaalib-at-a-n*
be.not-F DEF-girl-NOM student-F-ACC-INDF
'The girl is not a student'.

Being a morphological verb, not a particle, it is introduced when other verbs of its class are introduced (see [19] above).

In addition, next to *laysa* there also is recorded the negative particle *maa*, which has the peculiarity in the Hijazi dialect of having the same governance properties as *laysa*, i.e. it governs the noun in the nominative and the comment in the accusative:

(31) *maa al-bint-u ṭaalib-at-a-n*
NEG DEF-girl-NOM student-F-ACC-INDF
'The girl is not a student'.

All in all, in the *Lumaʕ* negatives are introduced in the following sequence. All except *laysa* are particles.

(32) Negative morphemes in Ibn Jinni's *Lumaʕ*:
laysa, maa, laa, lan, laa, lam, lammaa

These are introduced with the following topics: *laysa*, one of the defective verbs (119), *maa* of Hijaz (123), *laa*, generic negator (127), *laa,* negative coordinator (179), *lan*, future negator (208), *laa*, *lam*, *lammaa* jussive negators (213).

Thus in the typical grammar, whether compendious or abridged, the negative is introduced in a number of different places. This arrangement is dictated by syntactic logic, where the dominant theoretical structure and organizational form is built around basic functional positions and governance categories. Except for *laysa*, none of the negators belong to the major classes and therefore are dependent for the grammar-internal existence on those functions where they occur. It follows that one and the same negator, such as *laa*, will be introduced in as many different places as there are differentiated functions it occurs in.

Here emerges a weakness in the overall descriptive system, most apparent with the negator *maa*. This is introduced in the *Lumaʕ* only because it happens to have governance properties in one dialect of Arabic, the Hijazi. In fact, *maa* is a general negator that occurs with both nominal and verbal sentences, as in (33). Since it has no governance properties in these sentences it does not merit separate attention and is not mentioned in this function in the *Lumaʕ*.

(33) a. *maa zayd-un muʕallim-un*
not Zayd-NOM teacher-NOM
'Zayd is not a teacher'.

b. *maa ya-quwm-u zayd-un*
not 3-stand.up-IND Zayd-NOM
'Zayd is not standing up'.

In more comprehensive grammars than the short *Lumaʕ*, the major sub-classes of particles will be summarized together in a single chapter, after the summary of the functional positions and after the verbs have been introduced. For instance, all of the coordinating conjunctions are summarized in a single chapter, all of the negative particles and so on (e.g. Zamaxshari *Mufaṣṣal*, 306). In Zamaxshari's *Mufaṣṣal* (305), as well as Ibn Yaʕish's commentary on it (VIII: 107–113), the six different negator particles (*ʔin*, missing in the *Lumaʕ*, is included as well) are summarized in a single chapter. At the beginning of this chapter, Ibn Yaʕish adds a general characterization of negation to the effect that a negative is the falsification or denial of the positive equivalent (*kađaab lahu*). Each of the six particles are discussed in some detail, though rather discursively, Ibn Yaʕish, in his discussion of the negative particle *maa*, slips into a lengthy discussion of the polysemy of *maa*, e.g *maa* as relative pronoun.

Still, complete lexical comprehensiveness in regards to the negators fails to be achieved, since the negative verb *laysa* will not be introduced in this chapter. It is a verb, not a particle (see e.g. [19], [30]).

Thus, while the Arabic grammars achieved a high degree of comprehensiveness, generalizations which required cross-cutting and tying together established categories were sometimes missed (Baalbaki 2008: 93).

4. Sub-components

Parts of Arabic theory are characterized by well-articulated and defined modules, such as the theory of governance and dependency. There are other parts whose essential characteristics are discretely identifiable, yet which, within the Arabic tradition itself, are not singled out as discrete theoretical objects, treated for instance in independent chapters or in individual books. Two important ones can be described here.

4.1. Transitivity, *taʕdiya*

If dependency relations bind nouns and verbs together, it is their transitivity properties which determine which elements they combine with. The Arabic designation for this domain of relationship, *taʕdiya*, lit. 'passing over', is semantically very similar to the etymology of the English term transitivity.

Transitivity relations broadly fall into three categories. There is first of all the relation between a subject and predicate, secondly the inherent classification of verbs as intransitive, bi- or tri-transitive, and thirdly there are a range of grammatical functions which occur with any predicate, i.e. are not sub-classified for verb type.

The subject-predicate relationship in and of itself is not an element of the transitivity system. As seen above in 3.1, the basic elements of a sentence are verb + agent or topic + comment and these are postulates independent of transitivity factors. Whether an intransitive or a transitive verb is chosen as predicate is irrelevant to the basic verb + agent construction. Where transitivity enters into these functions is in the treatment of passive sentences, which are marked by a characteristic passive verb form.

(34) a. *kataba ʔaћmad-u risaalat-a-n*
wrote Ahmad-NOM letter-ACC-INDF
'Ahmad wrote a letter'.

b. *kutib-at risaalat-u-n*
written.PASS-F letter-NOM-INDF
'A letter was written'.

In his original formulation of passivization (*Kitaab* I: 10), Sibawayhi distinguished active transitive verbs as verbs whose action passed over (*yataʕaddiy*, hence the term *taʕdiya*) from an agent to an object, whereas passive verbs are those in which no action passes over to an object, i.e. the object assumes the position of an agent (*al-mafʕuwl allađiy lam yataʕaddi ʔilayhi fiʕl al-faaʕil*). In later works, for instance in the *Lumaʕ* (117), the passive verb was termed the verb whose agent is not named (*maa lam yusamma faaʕil-uhu*) or, alternatively, the object about which the verb reports (*al-mafʕuwl allađiy juʕila al-fiʕl ħadiythan lahu*). The thinking among the grammarians is thus that verbal sentences normally have an active agent, but it may be removed, in which case a new agent needs to be found. The process of finding the agent of passive verbs will be described below when the other elements of the transitivity system have been introduced.

A second part of the transitivity system is the classification of verbs as intransitive, transitive by means of preposition, transitive, bi- or tri-transitive, according to whether they take no (35), one (36), two (37) or three direct objects.

(35) *đahaba zayd-un*
went Zayd-NOM
'Zayd went'.

(36) *raʔaa ʔaħmad-u risaalat-a-n*
saw Ahmad-NOM letter-ACC-INDF
'Ahmad saw a letter'.

(37) *ʔa-raa ṣadiyq-iy ʔaħmad-a risaalat-a-n*
CAUS-see friend-my Ahmad-ACC letter-ACC-INDF
'My friend showed Ahmad a letter'.

In addition, a further class of di-transitive verb was introduced above, namely the verbs of cognition (see [20]). In this case the di-transitive verbs (verbs that are transitive to two objects, *yataʕaddaa ʔilaa mafʕuwlayn*) are divided into two classes according to the parameter of obligatoriness of object. Verbs like 'give' can be used with two objects, but it is also possible to use only one:

(38) *ʔaʕṭaa zayd-un hadiyyat-a-n*
gave Zayd-NOM present-ACC-INDF
'Zayd gave a present'.

The verbs of cognition on the other hand require both. A sentence like the following is incorrect.

(39) **Đanan-tu zayd-an*
thought-I Zayd-ACC
*'I thought Zayd'.

In the Arabic metaphor, the difference is defined in terms of verbs with which one can stop (*yaqtaṣir*, 'be content with') on one object (*ʔaʕṭaa*) as opposed to those in which this is not possible.

In addition to these direct objects, there are prepositional verbs in which a function of the direct object is taken by a prepositional phrase (see [11] above).

While there are often clear derivational relationships between the morpholexical verb classes and transitivity – *ʔa-raa* in (37) contains the causative prefix *ʔa-* prefixed to the basic stem *raʔaa* in (2) for instance, and tri-transitive verbs always contain a causative prefix – the correlations between transitivity and derived verb forms were treated separately in the morphology, not in the grammar of transitivity. One reason for this is perhaps because Arabic verbal morphology while showing many broad regularities in terms of causative, stative, reflexive and reciprocal categories, equally has all the nuances and irregularities of a derivational system (see Larcher 2003), so that there are few unique one-to-one correspondences between transitivity class and verb form.

The third pillar of the transitivity system is a group of five functions which are termed objects of various sorts: direct object (*mafʕuwl bihi*), absolutive object (*mafʕuwl muṭlaq*), locative object (*mafʕuwl fiyhi* or *Ɖarf*), accompaniment object (*mafʕuwl maʕahu*) and reason object (*mafʕuwl lahu*). All of them are marked by their accusative case form.

The direct object has already been encountered above, where it was seen that verbs are sub-classified for the number and type of direct object which they take. The absolutive object is usually a verbal noun cognate with the verb, which emphasizes the action.

(40) *saara ʔaħmad-u sayr-a-n ṭawiyl-a-n*
went Ahmad-NOM traveling-ACC-INDF long-ACC-INDF
'Ahmad really traveled a long journey'.

Locative objects can be temporal, or locational/extensional.

(41) *saara ʔaħmad-u yawm-a al-jumaʕat-i farsax-ayni*
went Ahmad-NOM day-ACC DEF-friday-GEN parsang-ACC.DU
'Ahmad traveled on Friday for two parsangs'. (measure of distance)

The remaining two objects, the reason and accompaniment objects are of limited function and need not be illustrated.

The objects play a key role in determining the subject of a passive verb in the following way. The agent of a verbal sentence may be removed and the verb turned into passive form but in this case a new agent must be found in order to ensure the structural integrity of the sentence. Finding the agent proceeds as follows. If a verb has a direct object, that noun is promoted to agent, as in (34b) above, regardless of what other objects are present. If a verb has no direct object, then either of the locative or absolute objects may be promoted, there being no precedence between them, so that from (40) and (41), (42a) or (42b) may be the passive sentence.

(42) a. *siyra sayr-u-n ṭawiyl-u-n*
traveled traveling-NOM-INDF long-NOM-INDF
'It was traveled a long way'.

b. *siyra yawm-u al-jumʕat-i farsax-ayni*
traveled day-NOM DEF-friday-GEN parsang-ACC.DU
'It was traveled Friday for two parsangs'.

4.2. Agreement

A second sub-component of the grammar concerns agreement and this in turn falls into two categories, predicational and non-predicational.

4.2.1. Predicate agreement

In Classical Arabic predicational agreement is bifurcated into two types. In one, there is full agreement between topic and comment, while in the other a verb agrees only in terms of gender with its agent. The treatment of these two agreement types proceeds as follows.

To begin with the topic-comment sentence, a comment can consist of a single element (*mufrad*), like a noun (10), (14), (15) or an adjective.

(43) *al-ban-aat-u* *kabiyr-aat-u-n*
DEF-girl-F.PL-NOM big-F.PL-NOM-INDF
'The girls are big'.

Alternatively, the comment may consist of a complete sentence, as in:

(44) [[*Zayd-un*]$_{\text{Top}}$ [[[*bayt-u-hu*]$_{\text{Top}}$ [*kabiyr-u-n*]$_{\text{Com}}$]$_{\text{S}}$]$_{\text{Com}}$]$_{\text{S}}$
Zayd-NOM house-NOM-his big-NOM-INDF
'As for Zayd, his house is big'.

In (44) the inner-bracketed S is a complete sentence, 'His house is big', with its own topic (*baytuhu*) and comment (*kabiyrun*). In the case of an embedded sentential comment, there is a structural constraint such that the embedded comment must contain a pronoun co-referential (*ʕaaʔid*) with the topic, in the present example, the pronoun *-hu* suffixed to *bayt-* cross-referencing the topic *zaydun*. This pronoun can occur in any place in the embedded S, for instance the pronoun *-hu* on a possessor phrase, as in the following.

(45) [[*Zayd-un*]$_{\text{Top}}$ [[*bayt-u* *ahl-i-hu*]$_{\text{Top}}$ [*kabiyr-u-n*]$_{\text{Com}}$]$_{\text{S}}$]$_{\text{Com}}$]$_{\text{S}}$
Zayd-NOM house-NOM parents-GEN-his big-NOM-INDF
'As for Zayd, his parents house is big'.

This same analysis is applied when the comment is a verbal sentence.

(46) a. [[*al-ban-aat-u*]$_{\text{Top}}$ [[*stamaʕa*$_{Verb}$ *ʔax-uu-hunna* *ʔilaa*
DEF-girl-F.PL-NOM listened brother-NOM-their.F to
l-musiyqaa]$_{\text{S}}$]$_{\text{Com}}$]$_{\text{S}}$
DEF-music
'As for the girls, their brother listened to the music'.

b. [[*al-ban-aat-u*]$_{\text{Top}}$ [*stamaʕ-na*$_{Verb}$ *ʔilaa l-musiyqaa*]$_{\text{S}}$]$_{\text{Com}}$]$_{\text{S}}$
DEF-girl-F.PL-NOM listened-F.PL to DEF-music
'The girls listened to the music'.

In both of these cases the verb is 'listen', which heads a sentence that is in comment position. *Al-banaatu* is the topic of each. In (46a) the agent of the verb is *ʔaxuu-*, and the pronoun co-referential with the topic is the possessor of *ʔaxuu-*, namely *-hunna*. In (46b) the co-referring pronoun is considered to be the verbal suffix *-na*, signifying 3PL.F, which is also the agent of the verbal sentence. In the Arabic analysis, this *-na* is considered a pronoun, co-referential with the feminine plural topic. In general, when the topic is co-referential with the agent of the verb in the comment, the agent will appear as an inflectional suffix on the verb. In the Arabic tradition, it is the category of co-referentiality between topic and pronoun in the comment which accounts for subject-predicate agreement.

When the verb is in initial position it is invariably singular, so in this case there is no pronominal co-reference with the agent (46a), provided there is no co-referring topic.

While this is an extremely elegant solution to most aspects of agreement between verb/agent and topic/comment in Arabic, the issue of agreement in the basic sentences (14), (15) is not covered by the discussion. The problem is discussed in the specialized grammatical literature in Anbari's *Inṣaaf*. It is interesting to see how Anbari interpreted the comment in examples like (47), the following from his issue 7 (*Inṣaaf*: 55–57).

(47) a. *zayd-un ħasan-u-n*
Zayd-NOM good-NOM-INDF
'Zayd is good'.

b. *zayd-un ʔax-uu-ka*
Zayd-NOM brother-NOM-your.M
'Zayd is your brother'.

The two schools, the Basrans and Kufans, were said to be in agreement that in examples such as (47a) there is an implicit pronoun, one that co-refers to the subject (i.e. *huwa* 'he'). This being the case, the agreement with a plural subject would follow from the pronominal topicalization treatment discussed immediately above.

According to the Kufans, the same analysis was said to be applicable to (47b) as well, whereas for the Basrans, who in this as in most issues were the dominant faction, in (47b) there is no implicit pronoun.

What distinguished the two, for the Basrans, was the argument that lexical items could be arranged on a scale of verb-ness or noun-ness, as follows:

(48) Verb-noun scale

Most verb-like	Verbs
	Active participle
	Adjectives
Most noun-like	Basic nouns

Active participles are verb-like because they have verb-like meanings (e.g. perfectivity), while adjectives are said to share basic morphological form features with verbs (e.g.

gender agreement). From these similarities, other verb-like properties may be attributed to them, including a prototypical verbal property, that of having a subject pronoun in them (see [46]).

Basic nouns, on the other hand, share no formal features with verbs, and, it can therefore be inferred, they have no other verbal properties, such as having an inherent pronominal reference.

The question remains open, how the topic – comment agreement in the case of plural elements is to be accounted for (*humma ʔaṣdiqaaʔuka* 'they are your friends'). Anbari appears to have sensed this difficulty, when, in the context of another issue (*Inṣaaf*: 47), he stresses that the comment is analogous to a descriptive adjective (*yatanazzal manzilat al-ṣifa*, 'it lowers itself into the category of ṣifa'), in that a comment is referentially identical to the topic (in e.g. [47]), just as an adjective is the same as the item it describes (see [49a]). However, in the syntactic logic of the Arabic system, this analogy does not guarantee correct agreement properties, since, as seen, these are formally accounted for in terms of a pronoun in the comment co-referential to the topic.

4.2.2. Non-predicational agreement

The second aspect of agreement concerns the set of elements known, literally, as 'followers', *tawaabiʕ*, sg. *taabiʕ*. These are a set of endocentric complements, as they will be termed here, to a preceding noun, consisting of five classes, adjectives (*ṣifa*), emphasizer (*tawkiyd*), conjunct (*ʕaṭf*), appositive (*badal*) and appositive substitute (*ʕaṭf al-bayaan*). They are endocentric because all of them combine with the noun they 'follow' to create a unit of the same functional type. In the following the 'follower' is in bold face, and the agreeing categories for each sub-class listed.

(49) a. adjective (*ṣifa*)
an-nisaaʔ-u ***l-kabiir-aat-u*** (case, gender, number, definiteness)
DEF-women-NOM DEF-big-F.PL.-NOM
'the big women'

b. emphasizer (*tawkiyd*)
ar-rijaal-u *kull-**u**-hum* (case)
DEF-men-NOM all-NOM-them
'the men, all of them'

c. conjunct (*ʕaṭf*)
ar-rijaal-u *wa* *l-nisaaʔ-**u*** (case)
DEF-men-NOM and DEF-women-NOM
'the men and the women'

d. clarifying conjunct (*ʕaṭf al-bayaan*)
*haʔulaaʔi ir-**rijaal-u*** (case, number, gender)
these DEF-men-NOM
'these men'

All categories agree in terms of case. The adjective agrees in terms of number, gender and definiteness as well and the clarifying conjunct in terms of number and gender. The other categories agree only in terms of case, which suggests that originally the category was developed on the basis of case agreement (see Owens 1990: 89 on the early grammarian al-Farraʔ to this point).

The Arabic dependency treatment of these elements is interesting. The standard view (Anbari *Asraar*: 295) is that both elements are equally governed by the governing category, so for instance *raʔaytu haʔulaaʔi r-rijaal-a* 'I saw these men' would have the dependency structure:

(50)

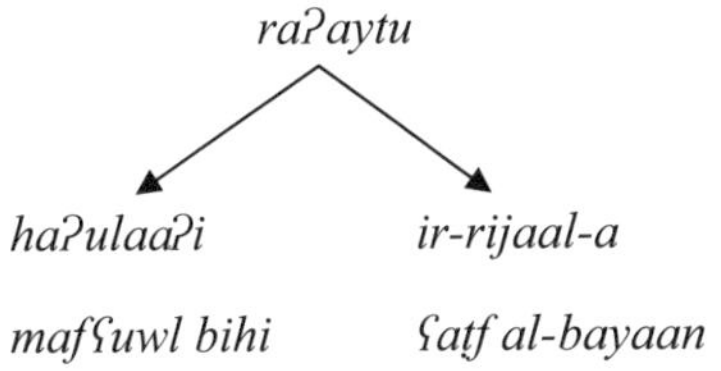

Fig. 5.2: Dependency structure among modifiers

Against some summaries (Bohas, Guillaume, and Kouloughli 1990: 58), there is no head noun here which governs the following endocentric adjunct. This follows from the dependency model assumed in which nominals do not govern other nominals directly. The confusion arises probably first because the traditional western conception of governance would consider the noun, in an example like (49d) as the governor and secondly because the explanation of case form in these constructions in fact has two descriptive clarifications. The common one is that the *tawaabiʕ* "follow the noun in terms of case" (*L*, 166). However, this formulation in the Arabic grammars has to be taken as a descriptive observation, rather than a new type of case determination, a point recognized by the grammarians when they addressed the issue explicitly. Note that the descriptions do not say that the noun governs (*yaʕmal*) the endocentric adjunct (see Suyuṭi II: 115 for further discussion).

5. Syntax and phonetics/phonology

The links between syntax and phonetics/phonology are mainly mediated via the morphology of case endings, which were seen in section 2 to be key elements of the syntax. For instance, there are a number of variants of the case endings in pausal position – lip-rounding, voicelessness, consonant doubling – which neutralize the distinction between all or some of the case endings (*Kitaab* II: 307–308). Similarly, Farraʔ (*Maʕaaniy* I: 3) describes Bedouin Quranic recitation practice in which final case vowels undergo assimilation across word boundaries. In both instances it is notable that case vowels, one of the bases of the syntactic system, are amenable to phonetic erosion.

6. Syntax and pragmatics

Leaving aside the special and to a large degree unexplored status of Sibawayh's late contemporary Farraʔ, explicit links between Arabic grammatical theory and pragmatics were not well articulated until the eleventh century. A number of scholars (e.g. Bohas, Guillaume and Kouloughli 1990; Carter 2007; Baalbaki 2008) do see in Sibawayh a broad pragmatic approach to language. However, Sibawayh never articulated a clear contrast between different levels of grammar and pragmatics in the way he did between morphology and syntax, and his overall approach was based on the sentence as a structural unit. Moreover, Baalbaki (2013: 101) himself notes that Sibawayh made up sentences for the sole sake of illustrating complex syntactic rules which "(…) have absolutely no communicative value". Similarly, while a century after Sibawayh, Sarraj formulated characterizations of the comment in discourse-based terms "what is talked about", he also did not draw explicit contrasts between grammar and pragmatics.

That the ALT operated with rigid syntactic categories is illustrated by the analyis of the two sentences, based on the basic predicatives elements, *ʔaxuuka* and *zayd*, illustrated in (14) and (15) above. Ibn Jinni notes that given the two predicative elements 'you have a free choice to make whichever one of them you want to be the topic, and you make the other the comment' (*L*, 110). So, in (14) *ʔaxuuka* is the topic, and in (15), *zaydun* is.

This analysis was not so much challenged as it was expanded in the eleventh century by the grammarian Abdu l-Qahir al-Jurjani in his book *Dalaaʔil al-ʔIʕjaaz*. While accepting the standard analyses of these sentences as in (14), (15), he observed that there are different conditions governing their use. Paraphrasing his explanations based on other examples, (14) would be appropriate when the focus is on *ʔaxuuka*, whereas (15) is appropriate when it is on *zaydun*. Appropriateness is described in terms of larger textual contexts, and thus Jurjani may be said to be the first of the Arabic grammarians to have explicitly and systematically integrated a super-sentential perspective into a sentence-based grammar. It is true that he did not develop an explicit vocabulary for this purpose, nothing comparable to foreground/background, focus/presupposition, new/available or new/old, typical categories found in today's pragmatic literature, though nonetheless his meticulous descriptions make it clear that his great interest in the *Dalaaʔil* was an exposition of the embeddedness of grammar in a larger pragmatic and discourse context. Jurjani's discussion of the following two sentences makes this perspective clear (*Dalaaʔil* 144).

<table>
<tr><td>(51)</td><td>a.</td><td>zayd-un</td><td>al-munṭaliq-u</td></tr>
<tr><td></td><td></td><td>Zayd-NOM</td><td>DEF-leaving-NOM</td></tr>
<tr><td></td><td></td><td colspan="2">'Zayd is the one leaving'.</td></tr>
<tr><td></td><td>b.</td><td>al-munṭaliq-u</td><td>zayd-un</td></tr>
<tr><td></td><td></td><td>NOM-leaving-NOM</td><td>Zayd-NOM</td></tr>
<tr><td></td><td></td><td colspan="2">'The one leaving is Zayd.'</td></tr>
</table>

Both are equally grammatical. It is only a question of appropriateness of use. Jurjani says that (51a) would be used, when the question at stake is, which person of a small set the is listener interested in. "The listener (*saamiʕ*) knows that it [that an act of leaving, j.o.] exists, but doesn't know whether it is Zayd or 'Amr". If you reply with (51a), you remove the doubt in favor of Zayd. (51b) would be appropriate if you are aware of an act of leaving but you have no idea who it is who left, "(…) you saw a person leaving from afar (…)" (*DalaaʔIl* 144). Your companion then uses (51b) to explain that the one leaving turns out to be Zayd.

While finding common analytic categories throughout Jurjani's many examples is sometimes difficult (Kamel 2006) – here for instance there does not appear to be a complete overlap with the categories of presupposed/focus or similar information-based categories in contemporary linguistic practice – Jurjani's insight was to show that choices between competing grammatical variants were governed by broader textual and, as seen in the present example, discourse considerations. Appropriateness is explained in terms of the information which the speaker wants to convey given the interlocutor's state of knowledge.

As with so many aspects of Arabic linguistic practice, here again there is a remarkable convergence between the ALT and contemporary Linguistics, this time beween Jurjani and Grice (see below).

At the base of Jurjani's thinking was a two-tiered model of language structure. On the one hand there was the classic form-meaning correspondence (*lafÐ/maʕnaa*), as illustrated for instance in the quote of Zamaxshari in section 1. This structural store encompassed not only discrete words (Saussure's *signe linguistique*), but, for Jurjani, pertained to all grammatical structure. A sentence, therefore, was more than the sum of its lexical parts, *zaydun* in section 3.1 for instance representing not only a discrete referent, but also one in a syntactic context, either topic or comment, a context which further defines Zayd by its predicative relationship with the other part of the topic/comment pair. Jurjani's approach to information structure was thus clearly modular, with grammar and the grammatical categories of topic, comment, verb, agent and all other functional categories described above having a discrete and independent existence in the language and in the speaker.

This structural store, however, manifested itself only in a token appearance. A token appearance, however, was constrained by broad contextual factors of the type described around (51).

Jurjani saw the process unfolding as follows. The speaker formulated an intention (*yaraḍ*) on a given occasion according to various contextual considerations, and accessing the structural store, uttered the appropriate sentence. Descriptively in Jurjani the operative conceptual contrasts are, beginning with meaning, *maʕnaa* 'meaning' vs. *maʕnaa fiy al-nafs* 'occasion meaning'. It is appropriate to begin here, since for Jurjani the semantic level always had priority.

The speaker has a particular meaning on a given occasion, what Jurjani termed the *maʕnaa fi l-nafs*, lit. 'meaning in the soul', which will always differ in slight detail from a meaning located in the structural store precisely because the *maʕnaa fiy al-nafs* is context dependent.

Parallel to this a contrast is drawn between the *lafḍ* and the *nuṭq*, which may be translated as 'phonological form' vs. 'occasion pronunciation'. On any occasion, the pronunciation accesses the phonological form, just as the occasion meaning, *maʕnaa fi l-nafs* accesses the underlying structrual meaning, *maʕnaa* (*DalaaʔIl* 43, see Owens 1988: 249/339; Larkin 1995). The process of sentence formation in Jurjani may be represented as follows.

(52) Tab. 5.1: Information structure in Jurjaani (based on Owens 2010)

<table>
<tr><th></th><th>structural store</th><th>activated for an intention (γaraḍ)</th><th>on-line processing</th></tr>
<tr><td>Form</td><td>lafÐ/alfaaÐ
‘form/forms’</td><td rowspan="2">⟶</td><td>nuṭq
‘occasion pronunciation’</td></tr>
<tr><td>Meaning</td><td>maʕnaa
‘meaning’</td><td>maʕnaa fiy al-nafs
‘occasion meaning’</td></tr>
</table>

It will be clear that the analogy in the western tradition which this discussion leads up to is that of Grice’s distinction between timeless and applied timeless meaning (1989: 119). For Grice, applied timeless meaning was the meaning ‘for a given occasion of utterance’.

Of course, the application of this contrast served different interests for the two scholars. Grice, for instance, used it as a basis of his conversational implicatures, while Jurjani was interested in establishing criteria for matching the appropriate grammatical variant with the correct utterance. Still, the convergence of theory is striking.

7. The *ʔuṣuwl*

The reasons for the flowering of the *ʔuṣuwl* in the 4th/10th century are undoubtedly complex and as yet little investigated (cf. Haarman 1974 for introduction). From a formal linguistic perspective I think a significant point is that having developed a compact linguistic apparatus, the creative impulses of the grammarians turned in another direction, and this was the *ʔuṣuwl*. This is essentially a metatheory which attempts to explain why the Arabic language has the form that it does. Implicit here is the assumption of an ideal form, which is described in standard grammatical terms as outlined above. Many items and constructions correspond to this ideal, but others do not, wherein lies one of the keys to the *ʔuṣuwl:* items that correspond to the ideal form are treated as “basic” or “unmarked”, *ʔaṣl* forms, those that deviate from it “secondary, marked”, *farʕ*, where this deviation is to be explained on some rational ground (*ʕilla* ‘reason’, Versteegh 1978). Anbari (*Lumaʕ*, 93) formulates the methodology very nicely.

(53) *ʔaṣl* ⟶ *ʕilla* ⟶ *farʕ*
unmarked —— departs from basic form for reason → marked

Fig. 5.3: Basic form of markedness scale

In a great many cases the *ʔaṣl* - *farʕ* distinction corresponds very well to the idea of unmarked/ marked. For instance, in the course of explaining why nouns like (inter alia) *ʔakbara* (‘bigger’) have a single accusative/genitive form, rather than the usual distinct forms (= diptotes), linguists (e. g. Sibawayh, Zajjaji) invoke a series of markedness oppositions including (unmarked/marked) SG/PL, INDF/DEF,M/F, N/V, etc. in which it is argued that nouns which have 2 or more marked properties (= the reason for the deviation) are the ones which lack distinct genitive/ accusative forms (*ʔakbara* = ADJ and resembles a verb form). Disregarding problems in the precise application of the method (Owens 1988: 210), what is striking is that the *farʕ* (marked) categories, PL, F, loan word, are precisely those which have been independently identified as marked in modern studies (Greenberg 1966). Admittedly many applications of this principle, for example Anbari's (*Asraar*: 49) attempts to explain why the nominative dual has the form *-aa* while the nominative plural is *-uw* are either arbitrary, circular or both. With this caveat, however, the method can be seen as allowing grammarians to correlate and offer explanations for phenomena which in the standard grammar appear simply as unrelated facts. Rather than a list of diptotes, for instance, this class of irregular nouns is explained relative to independently motivated criteria. The supreme example of the *ʔuṣuwl,* Ibn Jinni's *Xaṣaaʔiṣ* ranks as perhaps the most brilliant of all 4th/10th century grammatical works.

The assumption of an ideal structure opens up domains of interpretation which stretch beyond formal accounts of marked and unmarked structures. More generally it institutionalizes a disjunction between what one expects given the grammatical axioms and rules which have been assumed, and what one actually gets in a given construction. This leads into the broad domain of form and interpretation. There can be dissonance not only between formal elements, but also between formal elements and their semantic interpretations. For instance, Ibn Yaʕish (II: 38) discusses the Koranic passage

(54) a. *wa maa ʕamal-at ʔayday-hum*
and what/not did-F hands-their

This has two interpretations, each interpreted with specific syntactic and/or lexical reconstructions.

1. On the one hand the *maa* can be interpreted as an open relative pronoun 'what/ whatever'. The subject of the verb is *ʔaydayhum*, and the verb *ʕamalat*, being transitive, requires a resumptive pronoun to mark the missing object in the relative clause. This implies a sentence like (54b).

(54) b. *li-ya-ʔkul-uw min θamr-i-hi wa maa ʕamal-at-hu ʔayday-hum*
to-3-eat-PL from fruits-GEN-its and what did-F-it.M hands-their
'So that they eat from its fruit and what their hands made'.

In fact, there are two Koranic reading variants (Qiraa'aat) to this verse, one (54a), the other (54b), differentiated by the presence/absence of a resumptive pronoun.

To deal with these disjunctures the grammarians applied the technique of *taqdiyr* lit. 'estimation' (verb *qaddar*), what might be translated as '(linguistically-informed) textual reconstruction' (see Baalbaki 2008: 68; Devenyi 2007). In this the meaning of an expression is interpreted by reconstructing a text, and filling in the missing elements. In this case (54a) has the *taqdiyr* of (54b), independently of (54b) actually being attested in certain Koranic variants.

2. On the other hand, the *maa* can be interpreted as being the negative particle 'not', giving the meaning 'their hands did not work'.

(55) *li-ya-ʔkul-uw min θamr-i-hi wa lam ta-ʕmil-hu ʔayday-hum*
to-3-eat-PL from fruit-GEN-its and not 3.F-do-it.M hands-their
'So that they eat from its fruit and not (from what) their hands made'

In this case the reconstruction hinges on the lexical interpretation of *maa*. Given the negative interpretation, a different reconstruction of the target clause is necessary, the *lam* negative (see [24c]) probably being more emphatically negative than the *maa* negative. Ibn Yaʕish suggests that in the second interpretation (55) the need to reconstruct a resumptive pronoun is less strong than in (54b).

In contrast to the ʔaṣl/farʕ scheme described above, in this case there is virtually no limit on what can be interpolated, so long as it fits in broadly with Arabic grammar.

Though it has similarities to it, *taqdiyr* is not simply another word for 'paraphrase'. Typically what is reconstructed are specific elements, so that in principle after applying *taqdiyr*, another expression emerges. Circularly, though consequently, this reconstructed piece can be interpreted as the basic one, so that it will appear that a formal element – a word, a morpheme – has been deleted (*ħudifa*) from the original expression. In (54a) the *-hu* is considered to be deleted from (54b), which has the status of being the basic element.

8. Modularity and the development of Arabic linguistic thought

One way to understand the development of Arabic grammatical theory is to think of the development of discrete modules. This begins in an obvious way with Jurjani's *DalaaʔiI*. Rather than attempt to integrate information-based categories into the already existing grammatical framework, he essentially added another layer on to it, as described in section 6. A notable further step was Sakkaki's, *Miftaaħ al-ʕuluwm*, in which he distinguishes a number of sub-disciplines, including morpholology and grammar, but also what he termed the *ʕilm al-maʕaaniy*, the knoweldge of meanings, in which he systematized many of Jurjani's observations on word order, pronominalization, as well as noting the correspondence, or lack thereof, between formal sentence type and the speech acts it could be associated with (questioning, commmanding, wishing, stating, see Moutaouakil 1990; Simon 1993). He further defined a science of metaphor and word choice (*ʕilm al-bayaan, ʕilm al-badiyʕ*), and of logical structure (*ʕilm al-ʔistidlaal*).

The articulated theory of the *ʔuṣuwl* is a further module, adventitious to the descriptive grammar.

In some cases levels of linguistic analysis were added to the grammars almost surreptitiously. The thirteenth century grammarian Astarabadhi, for instance, defined grammatical categories in terms of speech acts. The past tense (*maaḍiy*), for instance was defined in terms of a time anterior to the time of speaking, while a past tense verb like *biʕtu* 'I sold' was observed on the one hand to assert a state of affairs (that I sold something), but to also be susceptible to a performative usage, 'I have hereby sold this to you', where in enunciating *biʕtu* the sale is thereby effected. In its performative sense Astarabadhi recognized that the expression was without an objective referent, the utterance bringing the situation into existence (Larcher 1991, 1992). Furthermore, pragmatics and semantics eventually developed in significant ways in the broader context of theological and legal discourse (Weiss 1966; Ali 2000).

9. Wider influences

If Arabic theory has had little direct influence on modern linguistic thinking, it was firmly embedded in an eastern Mediterranean classical tradition. Nonetheless, the degree to which it was influenced in particular by the Greek tradition remains a controversial point. There are two main viewpoints. On the one hand Carter (1972), following in the tradition of Weiß (1910), sees Arabic grammatical thinking as developing primarily under internal impetus, the influence of Islamic legal thinking and terminology playing a major role, a position which, however, has never been developed in the intervening years. On the other hand, Versteegh (1977) accords the Hellenistic tradition a greater role, though also emphasizes (1977: 7, 1980a, b) that especially the early influences came indirectly through a living hellenistic pedagogical tradition, rather than directly through the erudite writings of Greek philosophers, which became available in Arabic translations only in the course of the ninth century, well after Sibawayh had established the basis of Arabic grammatical theory. Versteegh (1977: 39) for instance, notes that the stock examples in Arabic grammars of nouns and verbs, 'man', 'horse' and 'hit', are the same as those found in the earlier Greek pedagogical literature. As Versteegh (1980a) suggests, however, such influence as there was may often have been of a piecemeal nature; no evidence indicates that the Arabic system as a whole can be explained as arising through outside influence, nor indeed can any significant isolatable sub-part. The syntactic theory sketched above must, qua theory, be regarded largely as an independent development within an Islamic-Arabic tradition.

Regarding the early development, in a number of studies, the late Rafael Talmon (1997: 2003) discerned two early schools of linguistic thought, one represented by Sibawayh and his teachers Yunus and Xalil, the other an older school which he termed the "old Iraqi school". Owens (1990) characterizes the early period, up to Mubarrad as one of heterogeneity, an era in which standardizing pressures had neither effaced earlier constructs and concepts, nor consigned non-standard (non-Basran) ideas to an intellectual sideshow.

Looking at influences emanating from the Arabic tradition, the picture is in part much clearer. The model for the establishment of Hebrew grammar, qua theoretical discipline, was clearly Arabic grammar (Bacher 1895 [1974: 166]; Hirschfeld 1926: 7). Not only did the Hebrew grammarians, beginning with Saadya Gaon (d. 942) base their organization and terminology on the Arabic, but also until ben Ezra (d. 1167) they often wrote their grammatical works in Arabic, the main language of culture from Baghdad to Spain, where the earliest Hebrew grammarians were active. If the original inspiration was Arabic, however, the Hebrew grammatical theory developed in its own way, the most original achievement (from the modern linguistic perspective) being their works on comparative semitic, Hirschfeld (1926: 18) calling Ibn Qureish (c. 1000) the "father of comparative Semitic philology" (cf. Téné 1980; Rodriguez 1983) for his comparisons of Hebrew, Aramaic, and Arabic. A high point in this genre is Ibn Barun's (c. 1100) comparative grammar of Hebrew and Arabic, where, significantly, the comparative categories are largely taken from Arabic syntactic theory (e.g. *naʕt* 'qualification', *badal* 'substitution', Wechter 1964). The Arabic tradition further had a strong influence on the Coptic, a high point in which was reached during the 13th and 14th centuries. Here again the Arabic language was the medium of description, and Arabic theory provided the basis of the terminological categories used (Sidarus 1978: 125). The influence of the Arabic tradition on early Turkish grammars is described in Emmers (1999).

Less clear are the relations between the Arabic and medieval and Renaissance European traditions, neither direct, nor indirect influences (e.g. via the Hebrew tradition) having been looked at with any systematicity (cf. Breva-Claramonte 1983: 83–96). Recalling Versteegh's work on the early influence of the Greek pedagogical tradition on the Arabic, research in this area might concentrate not only on the availability of the Arabic works to the Europeans via grammars of Arabic (Cowan 1983) and translations, but also on the structural parallels found in the two systems, parallels that might reflect a direct influence rather than mere coincidence. One thinks, for instance, of the Modistae interest in syntax in general, and in particular in its dependency-based syntax (Covington 1984: 13, 42).

10. Syntax in western studies on the history of the Arabic tradition

Arabic syntactic theory, as a part of Arabic linguistic theory in general, has had a mixed reception in the western Arabicist tradition, very different from the admiring reception accorded the celebrated Indian tradition of Panini. All in all the matter would make for an interesting contrastive study in western intellectual history (see Nekroumi 2007, for overview in Germany).

Systematic recognition of and study of the tradition began in the nineteenth century. While the grammars of the Arabic grammarians served as the basis of western grammars (e.g. Wright's still authoritative grammar of Classical Arabic [1896], based on Caspari; Badawi Carter and Gully 2004; Ryding 2005), the theoretical bases underlying them were generally either ignored, or dismissed. Dieterici, who translated Ibn ʕAqil's compendious *Alfiyya* of Ibn Malik for instance writes (1852: xi):

> Schon ein Blick auf die Eintheilung des Stoffes drängt uns zu der Ansicht hin, daß hier gar wenig auf das Wesen der Sprache Rücksicht genommen ist. Die Erscheinungen derselben sind nur ihrem äuseren nach classificiert, aber nicht ihrem Wesen nach aufgefaßt und dargestellt.
>
> [Already a glance at the organization of the material forces the conclusion that the essence of the language is given little consideration. Phenomena are simply classified according to their external form, rather than explained and represented according to their essence.]

Similarly Merx (1891) attacked the theoretical assumptions of Arabic grammar, as he understood it, calling it superannuated (['surannée'] 1891: 26). The basic failing of Arabic grammatical thinking, he asserted, was the failure to understood that grammar is based on logic (1891: 16).

This is not to say that there weren't early Arabicists who recognized the sophistication of the tradition, notably for example Gustav Jahn, who took on the massive task of translating Sibawayhi's *Kitaab* (1895, 1900). However, contemporaries such as Praetorius and Hartmann distanced themselves from these attempts, and Jahn himself, a product of nineteenth century European philological thought, often had trouble understanding Sibawayhi himself (see e.g. Carter 1973), so that it is only in relatively recent times that the Arabic tradition has been appreciated as an independent and sophisticated tradition in its own right.

Even recently the linguistic credentials of the grammarians are sometimes challenged. Kouloughli (1999), for instance, questions whether the Arabic grammarians had a theory of syntax at all (see Owens 2000b for criticisms).

More generally three broad approaches can be identified in the western treatment of the ALT. One group may be termed the *descriptivist*. A hallmark of this approach is to give a detailed account of what the grammarians said, though from a theory-neutral perspective, so that typically rather than attempt to translate Arabic terminology into another language, which implies making theoretical assessments within the target language, the Arabic terms are taken over in full. Rather than 'governor', for instance for the *ʕaamil* relation, '*ʕaamil*' will be used. In keeping with the rigidly descriptivist goals, comparative contemporary critiques are often not brought into the discussion.

A second approach might be termed the *inventionist*. Translations are used which are deemed to best fit the Arabic terminology, though these are chosen on the basis of an individual assessment of what best fits the Arabic term. For instance, *ʕaamil* in Bohas, Guillaume and Kouloughli (1990: 57) is termed "operator", probably on the basis of their translation of the term *ʕamal* as operation, a translation which is close to a more literal meaning of *ʕamila* as 'do, effect, carry out' (also Carter 1973). What I termed the *endocentric adjuncts*, Bohas, Guillaume and Kouloughli (1990) term "dependencies", though as seen in 4.2.2 there is no dependency relation in a modern technical sense.

Of course, anyone with a knowledge of the ALT will be able to follow a discussion of it, regardless of the terminology used. No terminology, within reasonable limits, is wrong. However, there is a third perspective (Owens 1988, 1995, 2000; Daniecki 1993), which explicitly attempts to link up Arabic terminology with concepts of contemporary linguistic theory. This may be termed the *comparativist* approach.

For instance, in translating the term *ʕaamil* as 'governor', explicit reference is made to the theory of dependency as developed by Tesnière (1959) Robinson (1970). The justification for this is not a philologically-perceived translation equivalence, but rather a detailed comparison of the precepts of modern dependency theory, and the Arabic linguistic practice. A well-formed dependency structure has four conditions, three of which can be cited here (Robinson 1970): one and only one element is independent, all other elements depend on another, and no item depends on more than one other. An examination of all dependency (*ʕamal*) relations in the ALT shows that these conditions are met perfectly. In this perspective, that translational equivalent will be chosen which best fits modern practice (Owens 1988: 41–52).

The purpose of such a comparison, and the corresponding choice of translation, is not to force Arabic theory into western practice, nor to suggest that only if it can be conceived of with a contemporary technical linguistic sense does it have legitimacy as an interesting concept. Rather it makes the explicit claim that linguistic concepts do not multiply ad infinitum, that linguistic theories will produce similar structures and concepts, regardless of whether they are historically related or not. By the same token the neutralist or the inventionist perspectives equally make theoretical claims about the relation between the ALT and contemporary linguistic theory, even if such claims are not well articulated. The neutralist would say that while there may be interesting correspondences, they are too difficult to discern and explain explicitly to allow translations. The inventionist, on the other hand, would claim that a homespun translation is better than embedding it in a foreign theoretical framework. Unfortunately, most who work in this latter tradition do not make explicit what their own linguistic theoretical grounding is.

From the comparativist perspective, concepts are embedded in larger explanatory schemes. A term such as 'operator' is, taken alone, as good a translation for *ʕaamil* as is 'governor'. Those who use this latter term, however, do not take the further step of showing its relevance in a larger system, and this is where 'governor' is more interesting, as it is not so much the single translation which is important, but rather a translation which accesses well-articulated theoretical constructs.

Of course, not all Arabic concepts and terms fit so readily into a western terminology. The *tawaabiʕ* discussed above for instance do not reduce to a single property that marks the entire class, other than agreement in terms of case. Choosing a covering term is thus difficult. 'Endocentric adjuncts' captures only one aspect of the grammatical relationship between noun and following word. Furthermore, in claiming that Arabic grammar is based on principles which today are applied to dependency grammar, only one aspect of Arabic syntactic theory is thereby characterized. Other aspects are comparable to other theories. Ibn Jinni's localization of grammar (writ large) in the word is, for instance, reminiscent of Hudson's (1984) theory of word grammar (see section 2). Arabic theory, being an original development, is ultimately *sui generis*; the comparativist perspective seeks to elucidate it through multiple comparisons.

A typical criticism of the comparativist perspective is that it imposes western cultural values and practices on a tradition far removed in time and culture. Of course, such a criticism may be correct, but it is not a prioristically so. Two major points can be noted here, both of them emphasizing the significant variables which need to be taken account of even to begin detailed comparison.

First, to date there are no comprehensive sociolinguistic studies either of the history of Arabic (Owens 2009) or of the Arabic linguistic tradition, so it is hard to know what social and cultural values should be postulated in order to establish differences between the contemporary world and the Arabic-Islamic world of say, the tenth century, as they impinge on the analysis of language.

Secondly, there is nothing which inherently argues against the perspective that there are essential properties of language and inherent properties of human cognition which will always make themselves manifest in similar ways when language is explicitly described (Itkonen 1991). The Arabic grammatical tradition, challenging in its own right, assumes a larger role when considered from this perspective.

11. References (selected)

al-'Aħmar, Xalaf (attributed) (180/796)
1961 *Muqaddima fiy al-Naħw.* Ed. by ʿAzz al-Din al-Tanuxi. Damascus.

al-Astarabadhi, Raḍi al-Din (686/1286)
(n. d.) *Sharħ Kitaab al-Kaafiya*. Beirut. (no editor).

Baalbaki, Ramzi
1979 Some aspects of harmony and hierarchy in Sibawayhi's grammatical analysis. *Zeitschrift für arabische Linguistik* 2: 7–22.

Baalbaki, Ramzi
1983 The relation between *naħw* and *balagha:* a comparative study of the methods of Sibawayh and Jurjani. *Zeitschrift für arabische Linguistik* 11: 7–23.

Baalbaki, Ramzi
2008 *The Legacy of the Kitaab*. Leiden: Brill.
Baalbaki, Ramzi
2013 Arabic linguistic tradition I: *Naħw* and *ṣarf*. In: J. Owens (ed.), *The Oxford Handbook of Arabic Linguistics*, 92–114. Oxford: Oxford University Press.
Bacher, W. 1895
(repr. 1974) *Die Anfänge der Hebräischen Grammatik and die Hebräische Sprachwissenschaft vom 10 bis zum 16 Jahrhundert*. Amsterdam: Benjamins.
Badawi, El-Said, M. Carter, and A. Gully
2004 *Modern Written Arabic*. London: Routledge.
Bernards, Monique
1997 *Changing Traditions: Al-Mubarrad's Refutation of Sībawayh and the Subsequent Reception of the Kitāb*. Leiden: Brill.
Bohas, Georges, and J-P. Guillaume
1984 *Etudes des Théories des Grammariens Arabes*. Damascus: Institut Français de Damas.
Bohas, Georges, J-P. Guillaume, and D. Kouloughli
1990 *The Arabic Linguistic Tradition*. London: Routledge.
Breva-Claramonte, Manuel
1983 *Sanctius' Theory of Language*. Amsterdam: Benjamins.
Carter, Michael
1972/2007 The beginnings of Arabic grammar. In: R. Baalbaki (ed.), *The Early Islamic Grammatical Tradition* (tr. From Carter 1972, Les origines de la grammaire Arabe), 1–26. Ashgate: Hants, England.
Carter, Michael
1973 An Arabic grammarian of the eighth century A. D. *Journal of the American Oriental Society* 93: 146–157.
Carter, Michael
2007 Pragmatics and contractual language in early Arabic grammar and legal theory. In: Everhard Ditters and Harald Motzki (eds.), *Approaches to Arabic Linguistics: Presented to Kees Versteegh on the Occasion of his Sixtieth Birthday*, 25–44. Leiden: Brill.
Covington, Michael
1984 *Syntactic Theory in the High Middle Ages*. London.
Cowan, W.
1983 Arabic grammatical terminology in Pedro de Alcalá. In: K. Versteegh, K. Koerner, and H.-J. Niederehe (eds.), *The History of Linguistics in the Middle East*, 121–128. Amsterdam: Benjamins.
Daniecki, Janusz
1993 The notion of *taṣarruf* in Arabic grammatical theory. *Studia Arabistyczne I Islamistyczne*, 1:7–25.
Devenyi, Kinga
2007 *Iḍmaar* in the *Maʕaani* of Al-Farra': a grammatical approach between description and explanation. In: Everhard Ditters and Harald Motzki (eds.), *Approaches to Arabic Linguistics: Presented to Kees Versteegh on the Occasion of his Sixtieth Birthday*, 45–65. Leiden: Brill.
Dieterici, F.
1852 *Ibn 'Akil's Commentar zur Alfijja des Ibn Malik*. Berlin: Ferdinand Dümmler.
Ermers, Robert
1999 *Arabic Grammars of Turkish*. Leiden: Brill.
al-Farraʔ, Abu Zakariyya (204/822)
1983 *Maʕaani al-Qurʔaan* Ed. by M. 'Ali l-Najjar, and A. Yusuf Najati. Beirut: 'Alam al-Kutub.

Goldenberg, Gideon
1988 Subject and predicate in the Arabic Grammatical Tradition. *Zeitschrift der deutschen morgenländischen Gesellschaft* 138: 39–73.
Greenberg, Joseph
1966 *Universals of Language with Special Reference to Feature Hierarchies*. The Hague. Mouton.
Gully, Adrian
1995 *Grammar and Semantics in Medieval Islam*. Richmond: Curzon.
Haarman, Ulrich
1974 Religiöses Recht und Grammatik im klassischen Islam. *Zeitschrift der Deutschen Morgenländischen Gesellschaft* 12, supplement II: 149–69.
Heinrichs, Wolfart
1984 *Isti'arah* and *badï'* and their terminological relationship in early Arabic literary criticism. *Zeitschrift für die Geschichte der Arabisch- Islamischen Wissenschaften I*: 180–211.
Hirschfeld, H.
1926 *Literary History of Hebrew Grammarians and Lexicographers*. London.
Ibn al-Anbari, Abu Barakat (557/1187)
1957 *Asraar al- ʕArabiyya*. Ed. by M. al-Bitar. Damascus.
Ibn al-Anbari, Abu Barakat (557/1187)
1971 *Al-ʔIɣraab fiy Jadal l-ʔIʕraab wa Lumaʕ al-ʔAdilla fiy ʔUṣuwl al-Naħw*. Ed. by Sa'id al-Afghani, Beirut: Dar al-Fikr.
Ibn al-Anbari, Abu Barakat (557/1187)
(n. d.) *Kitaab al-ʔInṣaaf fiy MasaaʔiI al-Xilaaf bayna al-Naħwiyyiyna al-Baṣriyyiyna wa al-Kufiyyiyna*. Ed. by M. ʿAbd al-Ḥamid. Beirut: Dar al-Fikr.
Ibn Ḥajib, Jamal al-Din (646/1248)
1982 *Al-Iyḍaaħ fiy Sharħ al-Mufaṣṣal*. Ed. by M. El-Aleeli. Baghdad: Wizarat al-Awqaf.
Ibn Hisham, Abu Muhammad (761/1360)
1969 *Muɣni l-Labiyb ʕan Kutub al-ʔAʕaariyb*. Ed. by Mazin Mubarak. Beirut.
Ibn Jinni, Abu l-Fatħ (392/1002)
(n. d.) *Al-Xaṣaaʔiṣ*. Ed. by Muħammad 'Ali l-Najjar. Cairo, 1952–56. (Reproduced, Beirut).
Ibn Jinni, Abu l-Fatħ (392/1002)
1954 *Al-Munṣif*. Ed. by Ibrahim Muṣṭafa and Aħmad Amin. Cairo.
Ibn Jinni, Abu l-Fatħ (392/1002)
1979 *Al-Lumaʕ fiy al-ʕArabiyya*. Ed. By Mohammad Sharaf. Beirut: 'Alam al-Kutub. (abbreviated as *L*)
Sarraj = Ibn al-Sarraj, Abu Bakr Muħammad (316/ 928)
(n. d.) *Al-ʔUṣuwl fiy al-Naħw*. Ed. by 'Abd al-Ḥusayn al-Fatli. Beirut: Mu'assasat al-Risala.
Ibn al-Sarraj, Abu Bakr Muħammad (316/928)
1965 *Al-Muwjaz fiy al-Naħw*. Ed. by Muṣṭafa el-Chouémi, and Salim Damerdji. Beirut: Mu'assasat Badran.
Itkonen, Esa
1991 *Universal History of Linguistics*. Amsterdam: Benjamins.
Jahn, Gustav
1895, 1900 *Sibawayhs Buch über die Grammatik*. Hildesheim: Olms.
Jurjani, ʿAbd al-Qahir (471/1078)
1978 *Dalaaʔil al-ʔIʕjaaz*. Ed. by Muhammad Rida. Beirut.
Ibn Maḍa, Abu ʕAbbas (592/1195)
1982 *Kitaab al-Radd ʕalaa l-Nuħaah*. Ed. by Shawqi Dayf. Cairo: Dar al-Ma'arif.
Kouloughli, Djamel
1999 Y a-t-il une syntaxe dans la tradition arabe. *Histoire Epistémologie Langage* 21: 45–64.

Kouloughli, Djamel
2002 On locative sentences in Arabic. *Zeitschrift für arabische Linguistik* 41: 7–26.
Larcher, Pierre
1991 Quand, en Arabe, on parlait de l'Arabe … (II) Essai sur la Catégorie de *ʔInshaaʔ* (vs. *xabar*). *Arabica* 38: 246–273.
Larcher, Pierre
1992 La particule *Laakinna* vue par un grammarien Arabe du XIIIe siècle. *Historiographia Linguistica* 19: 1–24.
Larcher, Pierre
1998 Une pragmatique avant la pragmatique: 'Médiévale', 'Arabe', et 'islamique'. *Histoire Epistémologie Langage* 20: 101–116.
Larcher, Pierre
2007 Les origines de la grammaire Arabe, selon la tradition: Description, interpretation, discussion. In: E. Ditters and H. Motzki (eds.), *Approaches to Arabic Linguistics: Presented to Kees Versteegh on the Occasion of his Sixtieth Birthday,* 113–148. Leiden: Brill.
Larcher, Pierre
2013 The Arabic Linguistic tradition II: Pragmatics. In: J. Owens (ed.), *The Oxford Handbook of Arabic Linguistics*, 185–214. Oxford: Oxford University Press.
Larkin, Margaret
1995 *The Theology of Meaning: 'Abd Al-Qahir Al-Jurjaani's Theory of Discourse.* New Haven: American Oriental Society.
Levin, Aryeh
1987 The views of the Arab grammarians on the classification and syntactic function of prepositions. *Jerusalem Studies in Arabic and Islam* 10: 342–367.
Merx, A.
1891 Reflections historiques sur l'origine de la grammaire arabe. *Bulletin de l'Institut Egyptien,* 13–26.
Moutaouakil, Ahmad
1990 La notion d'actes de langage dans la pensée linguistique arabe ancienne. In: K. Versteegh and M. Carter (eds.), *Studies in the History of Arabic Grammar II*, 229–238. Amsterdam: Benjamins.
Mubarrad, Ibn Yazid (285/898)
(n. d.) *al-Muqtaḍab.* Ed. by ʿAbd al-Khaliq ʻUḍayma. Beirut: Alam al-Kutub.
Nekroumi, Mohammed
2007 Zur Rezeption klassisch-arabischer philologischer Termini in der modernen Arabistik. *Zeitschrift der deutschen morgenländischen Gesellschaft* 157: 77–102.
Owens, Jonathan
1984a Structure, class and dependency: Modern linguistics and the Arabic grammatical tradition. *Lingua* 64: 25–62.
Owens, Jonathan
1984b The noun phrase in Arabic grammatical theory. *Al-ʿArabiyya* 17: 47–86.
Owens, Jonathan
1988 *The Foundations of Grammar: An Introduction to Medieval Arabic Grammatical Theory.* Amsterdam: Benjamins.
Owens, Jonathan
1989 The syntactic basis of Arabic word classification. *Arabica* 36: 211–234.
Owens, Jonathan
1990 *Early Arabic Grammatical Theory: Heterogeneity and Standardization.* Amsterdam, Benjamins.
Owens, Jonathan
1995 A mollusc replies to A. E.Houseman, Jr. *Historiographia Linguistica* 22: 425–440.

Owens, Jonathan
2000a The structure of Arabic grammatical theory. In: S. Auroux, K. Koerner, H-J. Niederehe, and K. Versteegh (eds.), *History of the Language Sciences*, 286–300. Berlin: Walter de Gruyter.

Owens, Jonathan
2000b On club membership: a reply to Kouloughli. *Histoire Epistemologie Langage* 22: 105–126.

Owens, Jonathan
2009[2] [2006] *A Linguistic History of Arabic.* Oxford: Oxford University Press.

Owens, Jonathan
2010 The once and future study of information structure in Arabic, from Jurjani to Grice. In: J. Owens, and Alaa Elgibali (eds.), *Information Structure in Spoken Arabic*, 1–19. London: Routledge.

Peled, Yishai
2008 *Sentence Types and Word Order Patterns in Written Arabic.* Leiden: Brill.

Robinson, Jane
1970 Dependency structure and transformational rules. *Language* 46: 259–285.

Ryding, Karin
1998 Aspects of the genitive: Taxonomy in *al-Jumal fiy al-Naħw.* In: Karin Ryding (ed.), *Early Medieval Arabic: Studies on al-Khalil ibn Aħmad*, 92–142. Washington D. C.: Georgetown University Press.

Ryding, Karin
2005 *Modern Standard Arabic*. Cambridge: Cambridge University Press.

al-Sakkaki, Muħammad (626/1228)
1984 *Miftaaħ al- ʕUluwm.* Ed. by Na‘im Zarzur. Beirut: Dar al-Kutub al-Alamiyya.

Sibawayh, Ibn ʕUthman (177/793)
1970 *Al-Kitaab*. Ed. by H. Derenbourg. Hildesheim: Olms.

Simon, Udo
1993 *Mittelalterliche Sprachbetrachtung zwischen Grammatik und Rhetorik.* Heidelberg: Heidelberger Orientverlag.

Suyuṭi, Jamal al-Din (911/1505)
1984 *Al-ʔAshbaah wa l-NaĐaaʔir.* Ed. by Z. Tarhini. Beirut: Dar al-Kitab al-Arabi.

Suyuṭi, Jamal al-Din (911/1505)
1976 *Kitaab al-ʔIqtiraaħ fiy ʕIlm ʔUṣuwl al-Naħw.* Ed. by Aħmad Qasim. Cairo.

Suleiman, Yasir
1999 *The Arabic Grammatical Tradition: A Study in Taʿlīl* . Edinburgh: Edinburgh University Press.

Talmon, Rafael
1985 Who was the first grammarian: a new approach to an old problem. *Zeitschrift für arabische Linguistik* 15: 128–145.

Talmon, Rafael
1997 *Arabic Grammar in its Formative Age: Kitāb al-ʕAyn and its Attribution to Halīl b. Aħmad.* Leiden: Brill.

Talmon, Rafael
2003 *Eighth-century Iraqi Grammar: A Critical Exploration of Pre-Xalīlian Arabic Linguistics*. Winona Lake, Ind.: Eisenbrauns.

Téné, David
1980 The earliest comparisons of Hebrew with Arabic. In: K. Koerner (ed.), *Progress in Linguistic Historiography*, 355–377. Amsterdam: Benjamins.

Tesnière, Lucien
1959 *Eléments de Syntax Structurale.* Paris: Klincksieck.

Versteegh, Kees
1977 *Greek Elements in Arabic Linguistics Thinking*. Leiden: Brill.
Versteegh, Kees
1978 The Arabic terminology of syntactic position. *Arabica* 25: 261–280.
Versteegh, Kees
1980a Hellenistic education and the origin of Arabic grammar. In: K. Koerner (ed.), *Progress in Linguistic Historiography*, 333–344. Amsterdam: Benjamins.
Versteegh, Kees
1980b The origins of the term *Qiyas* in Arabic grammar. *Zeitschrift für arabische Linguistik* 1: 7–30.
Versteegh, Kees
1993 *Arabic Grammar and Qurʔaanic Exegesis*. Leiden: Brill.
Versteegh, Kees
1995 *The Explanation of Linguistic Causes*. Amsterdam: Benjamins.
Versteegh, Kees
2007 A new treatise about the `ilal an-naħw: Ibn al-Warraq on 'inna wa-'axawaatuha. In: Lutz Edzard and Janet Watson (ed.), *Grammar as a Window onto Arabic Humanism: A Collection of Articles in Honour of Michael G. Carter*, 51–65. Wiesbaden: Harrassowitz.
Weil, G.
1913 *Die grammatischen Streitfragen der Basrer und Kufer*. Leiden: Brill.
Weiß, Joseph
1910 Die arabische Nationalgrammatik und die Lateiner. *Zeitschrift der Deutschen Morgenländischen Gesellschaft* 64: 349–396.
Wright, William
1859 [1896/1977] *A Grammar of the Arabic Language*. Cambridge: Cambridge University Press.
Zajjaji, Abu l-Qasim (337/949)
1979 *Al-Iyḍaaħ fiy ʕIlal al-Naħw*. Ed. by M. al-Mubarak. Beirut: Dar al-Nafa'is.
al-Zamaxshari, Abu l-Qasim (538/1154)
(n. d.) *Al-Mufaṣṣal fīy al-ʕIlm al-ʕArabiyy*. Beirut, Dar al-Ğil.

Jonathan Owens, Bayreuth (Germany)

6. Prestructuralist and Structuralist Approaches to Syntax

Abstract

The chapter describes in rough outline the development of the notion of syntax since its earliest beginnings in Classical Antiquity, starting with the late hellenistic Alexandrian linguist Apollonius Dyscolus, for whom syntax was mainly the study of the functions of the nominal cases in sentences. Since the modern European languages largely do without nominal case, the notion of syntax became nebulous, with the result that up to ca 1950 it was widely thought that syntax was not part of the language system but of speech, the creative use of language. This changed with American structuralism, especially with Leonard Bloomfield, who proposed a system of Immediate Constituent (IC-) Analysis, derived from Wilhelm Wundt, as the theoretical basis of syntax. This led to the question of the motivation of specific IC-analyses, which was answered, in American linguistics, mainly in two ways. One answer, given by the so-called God's truth school, was that one could somehow observe IC-structures by introspection. Another, given by the so-called hocus-pocus school, was that the correct assignment of IC-structures will result from the simplest and most compact description of the language as a whole in terms of IC-structures. This latter answer was better integrated into current philosophy of science and carried the day. It led directly to the development of Generative Grammar during the 1950s and 1960s. This whole development is treated in the broader terms of what is known as structuralism, that is, the general trend, starting in the late nineteenth century, to see mental, especially cognitive, processes as resulting from rule-governed formal rules and principles, much in the way physical nature is the result of mechanical laws: the mechanisation view of the physical world was extended to the realm of cognition. Furthermore, the notion of constituent (tree) structure, both as dependency trees (Tesnière) and as IC-trees (Wundt, Bloomfield), is considered from the point of view of formal algorithmic calculus as applied in arithmetic. In this sense, the introduction of constituent structure into the study of syntax has contributed to the formation of the notion of a formal, compositional semantics for sentences.

1. Prestructuralist syntax

The term *syntax*, in the sense of the theory of how to combine words into sentences goes back to the ancient Greek Stoic philosopher Chrysippus (third century BCE), but it did not gain currency in language studies for another five centuries, till after the publication of *Perì Suntáxeōs* [On Syntax] (see Householder's translation with commentary of 1981) by the Greek linguist Apollonius Dyscolus, who lived and worked in Egyptian Alexandria during the second century CE. The Greek noun *súntaxis* means literally 'the act of placing together' and thus occurs in different senses, such as 'composition', 'arrangement', 'organisation', 'covenant', 'treatise' and even 'state constitution' (in Modern Greek it means 'pension, retirement pay').

Apollonius's book on syntax deals with a variety of topics, in particular the use and function of the definite article and of relative and anaphoric pronouns, verbal argument structure (in particular what verbs assign what cases to what nominal arguments with what meanings), participles, prepositional constructions and adverbial adjuncts. It does not discuss but merely assumes implicitly that regular sentences consist of a subject term and a Verb Phrase, the latter consisting of a finite verb form possibly accompanied by nominal argument terms and/or prepositional or adverbial consituents. It was in this form that syntax was taught at schools and universities through the ages till well into the twentieth century, especially in connection with the Classical languages, but also with regard to those modern European languages that possess a well-developed nominal case system, such as German or Russian.

A difficulty arose with regard to the modern West European languages, especially English, Dutch, French, Italian, Spanish and Portuguese, which largely lack a nominal case system. For those languages, the notion of syntax became attenuated to the point of becoming more or less extinct. Thus, by the end of the nineteenth century, grammar books and the teachers using them, at least in western Europe, were at a loss as regards the notion of syntax. The difficulty was not felt to the same degree with respect to the Central and East European languages, with their sometimes elaborate case systems, where one simply continued in the old Apollonian tradition. The predicament that existed for the West European languages was resolved during the second half of the twentieth century, especially in the context of transformational-generative grammar, when linguists became aware of the real complexities of syntactic structures and processes, especially, but far from exclusively, in the area of sentential, clausal and participial complementation. During the intervening period, say, from 1900 till 1960, linguists, with only a few notable exceptions, tended to be at a loss as to what is involved in the study of syntax.

2. The poverty of structuralist syntax in Europe

2.1. Mainstream European structuralism

What we now call structuralism was, in fact, a very general notion regarding the workings of the human mind, which came up in the human sciences during the second half of the nineteenth century. It is probably no oversimplification to say that structuralism is best defined as the attempt to apply the mechanical notion of machine to the human mind (see Seuren 1998: 141–144). Since the seventeenth century it had been commonly accepted that the physical world as a whole, and each individual living body in particular, could be seen as a system of interrelated mechanisms. At first, it was the clock work mechanisms developed during the seventeenth and eighteenth centuries that served as the prototypical example of what was meant by mechanism, but during the nineteenth century the notion was primarily exemplified by the various kinds of transportation and production machines that came into general use in the industrialising countries of Europe.

It was thus the machine metaphor in the study of the human mind that came to define the notion of structuralism in a general sense. In Europe, the most articulate spokesman of this new philosophy was the Parisian critic, philosopher and historian Hippolyte Taine (1828–1893) who had an enormous influence on French cultural (especially literary) life during his own day and after. His influence on linguistics is not generally recognised, but, according to Aarsleff (1982: 356–371), Ferdinand de Saussure (1857–1913) derived his basic linguistic notions, such as the distinction between *langue* and *parole*, and that between diachrony and synchrony, and also his notions of *sign* and *valeur*, from Taine, with whose works he became familiar during his years in Paris previous to his appointment to a Geneva chair in 1891. Taine's thoughts on the nature of language and language use are found in his book *De l'intelligence*, first published in 1870 and reprinted many times until the beginning of the first world war in 1914. Though widely read during the *fin de siècle* in France, this book is now largely forgotten, unlike Saussure's posthumous *Cours de linguistique générale* (1916), which has been highly influential in European linguistic and literary structuralism from roughly 1935 onwards.

Other early proponents of structuralism in linguistics were the Poles Jan Baudouin de Courtenay (1845–1929) and Mikołaj Kruszewski (1851–1887), both of whom taught at Kazan in Russia. They were not inspired by Taine's very general and rather high-flown ideas, as Saussure was, but concentrated more directly on the facts of language, in particular the interpretation of speech sounds in terms of a type-level cognitive system of phonological units, which Kruszewski called phonemes. As a result, it was phonology that dominated European structuralist linguistics from the beginning until roughly 1960.

Apart from the focus on phonology, linguistic structuralism was characterised in an overall sense by an insistence on the autonomous nature of language and linguistics. Language began to be seen, though not yet in explicit terms, as an autonomous machine in the mind or brain, connected with other such machines but separated from them in that the language machine has its own internal structure and its own functional principles. Language thus began to be regarded as a kind of module in the mind, in the sense later made explicit in Fodor (1983) and other publications. Ideas about the nature or internal structure of the language module were, on the whole, rather restricted. Both in Europe and in America, the language module (Saussure's *langue*) was, for a long time, seen mainly as a collection of lexical items, idioms and a few patterns for the combination of smaller elements into larger wholes. The two continents differed in that in Europe the language module, or *langue*, was treated as an element in the conscious mind, accessible through introspection, whereby the notion of mind remained ill-defined. Across the Atlantic, by contrast, *behaviourism* reigned supreme until the early 1960s. There the language module was considered to be materially given in the brain as a set of cerebral connections established through associations of stimuli and responses having occurred in the personal history of each individual. The question of conscious access to the language system was considered unscientific and thus left out of consideration. Nowadays, of course, the dominant view is that the language system or module, though materially realised in the brain, is defined as a complex piece of brain software, inaccessible to consciousness or introspection beyond the choice of propositional content, of lexical material and of values on sociolinguistic or interactional parameters.

Remarkably, hardly any structuralist theory of syntax was developed in Europe, even though the need for such a theory was widely felt and many attempts were made at getting one off the ground. The two main problems were (a) the unclarity as regards the notion of syntactic structure and (b) the fact that no-one had a clear idea of the complexities of syntax and of the rule systems underlying syntactic constructions. In America, empirical access to syntax was achieved by the hypothesis that syntactic structure is definable as a hierarchy of immediate constituents, as will be explained in a moment. It was through this hypothesis that syntax began to open itself to linguists at large. In Europe, however, one had no grip on the problem of syntactic form, nor on the data constituting it. Notable exceptions were Bech (1955) for German (cf. Kiss, this volume) and Paardekooper (1955) for Dutch. These classic authors had a sharp eye for the baffling complexities of the syntactic structures in the languages concerned. Although they were skeptical as regards linguistic theory and even averse to it, they made vast numbers of the most acute observations and sometimes established regularities that later proved to have great explanatory power. Yet it took a long time before they were acknowledged and appreciated for what they were in the community of theoretical linguists.

In mainstream theoretical linguistics, the notion of syntax remained badly underdeveloped. Saussure, for example, took it that (1916: 30–31):

1) (...) parole is an individual act of free will and intelligence, in which we distinguish:
2) the combinations by means of which the speaking subject makes use of the language code in order to express his personal thought;
3) the psycho-physical mechanism enabling him to externalise these combinations.

What he meant by language code is explained in (1916: 172–173). Having said that *parole* is characterised by the freedom of combining words according to the thought to be expressed, he denies that all of syntax is, therefore, part of *parole*, because (a) there are fixed or idiomatic locutions, which are part of the lexicon and thus of *langue*, and (b) there are rules for combining morphemes and words into larger wholes. When these larger wholes are words, the corresponding morphological rules are unequivocally part of the language system (*langue*), but when they are word groups or phrases, then the dividing line between *langue* and *parole* is unclear. In short, Saussure's notion of the language system is strictly word-based, as a result of which he was unable to develop any serious notion of syntax. Interestingly, he was criticised for this by the American linguist Leonard Bloomfield in his review of the *Cours* (Bloomfield 1924).

Alan H. Gardiner (1879–1963) likewise failed to reserve a proper place for syntax in linguistic theory. His main publication on linguistic theory is Gardiner (1932), on the distinction between the language system (langue) and speech or language use (parole) (for discussion, see Seuren 1998: 171–177). As regards the nature and position of syntax, Gardiner had not made up his mind. On the one hand he maintained that the word is the unit of the language system, while the sentence is the unit of speech: "The smallest section or unit of speech is the sentence" (Gardiner 1932: 208). This naturally implies that syntax, or the art of combining words into well-formed sentences, does not belong to the language system but is a matter of free creative use of words. Yet he does not appear to have been quite happy with this position. In Gardiner (1932: 184) we read: "Thus there is such a thing as 'sentence form', and like all other linguistic forms, it is a fact of language, not a fact of speech.". Gardiner failed to resolve this contradiction or ambiguity. But it is clear that, whatever place he wished to reserve for it, he saw syntax as a fairly trivial list of sentence patterns. (For a clear survey of the problem of how to define a sentence and hence how to define syntax, see Bühler 1934: 356–366.).

2.2. Dependency Grammar

The only form of theory-based structuralist syntax developed in Europe is *Dependency Grammar*, also called *Valency Grammar* (cf. Klotz, this volume), developed by the French linguist Lucien Tesnière (1893–1954), whose actual theory was not published until well after his death in Tesnière (1959). Tesnière distinguished between the main functor of a sentence, the verb, and its arguments (thus deviating from the classic Aristotelian Subject-Predicate division and following the modern trend of Predicate-Argument structure). He developed a method of structural analysis known as *dependency tree*, which allows one to compute the value of a function.

This is most easily demonstrated with the help of a couple of examples from simple arithmetic. In fig. 6.1.a, one sees the computation of the function (5 × 6) + 8. This is an addition with the two arguments 5 × 6 and 8. Since the addition function requires two or more actual numbers as arguments, the number corresponding to (or the value of) 5 × 6 must be computed first. Therefore, one must start with computing the value of the multiplication function with the arguments 5 and 6. This value is 30. Then the value of the addition function with the arguments 30 and 8 is computed, resulting in the final value 38. In fig. 6.1.b, the highest function is the multiplication function × with the arguments 5 and (6 + 8). To compute this function, one first has to compute the value of 6 + 8, that is, 14. Now the multiplication function with the arguments 5 and 14 can be set to work. The final resulting value is thus 70.

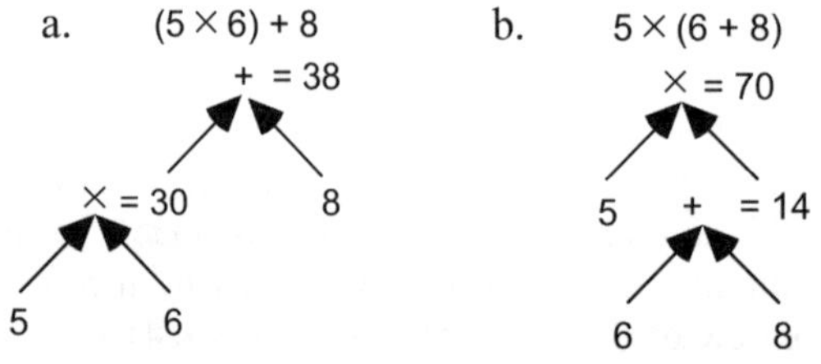

Fig. 6.1: (5 × 6) + 8 and 5 × (6 + 8) in terms of dependency trees

Tesnière applied this to sentence structure in the following way. A sentence like *The children ate sweets* is analysed as consisting of the functor word *ate* and the two argument terms *the children* and *sweets*, respectively. One may even subanalyse the phrase *the children* into the functor *the* with the single argument *children*, resulting in the referring Noun Phrase *the children.* The diagram is shown in fig. 6.2.

One may go further and say that the past tense *ate* is the result of a functor PAST with the single argument *the children eat sweets*, as in fig. 6.3.

One difference with arithmetic is that values are not automatically of the same category. In arithmetic, the arguments of an arithmetical function are numbers and every

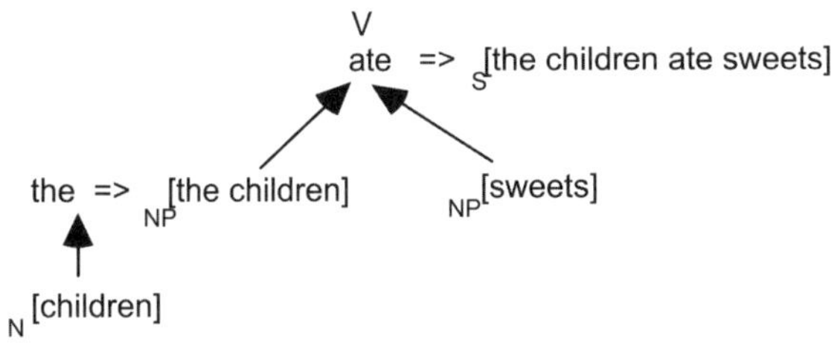

Fig. 6.2: Dependency analysis applied to *The children ate sweets*

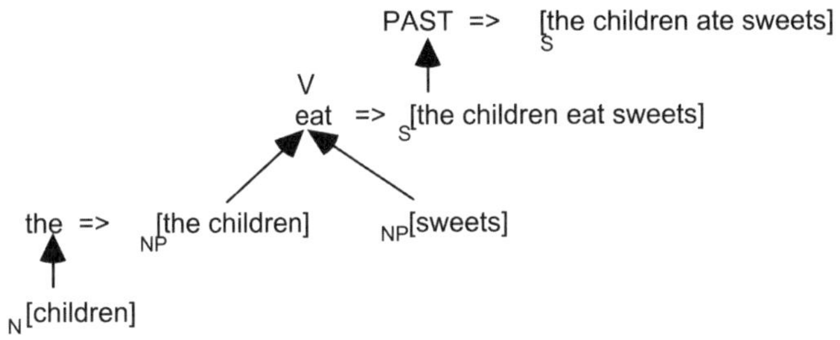

Fig. 6.3: The same as fig. 6.2, with Past Tense added

value of a function is again a number. Not so in syntax, where each value must be assigned a category and functions are thus defined for arguments belonging to specific categories. Thus, the value category of the definite article *the* can be given as N(oun) P(hrase), and the value category of the verbal function *eat* as S(entence), just like the value category of the function PAST.

A difficulty lies in the morphosyntactic form of the resulting values. For example, to get *the children eat sweets* from the arguments *the children* and *sweets* as input to the function *eat*, specific rules of syntactic arrangement are needed, which are not given by the dependency tree.

In fact, dependency trees smack more of semantics than of syntax, in that the value category of each functor stands not so much for a well-defined set of syntactic properties as for a semantic value in a model, whereby the highest value category S can be interpreted as a truth value in a model. While this can be considered to have the advantage of integrating syntactic and semantic description, it must at the same time be admitted that the formal syntactic part of the equation is not entirely transparent. Nor do dependency trees easily lend themselves to the kind of tree-transformational manipulations that are a central element in Transformational-Generative Grammar. Even so, Dependency Grammar became popular in central and eastern Europe, especially in the Prague School of linguistics and also in the Moscow school of Meaning-Text Theory (Zholkovsky and Mel'čuk 1965; Mel'čuk and Pertsov 1987).

3. Structuralist syntax in America

3.1. Constituent structure in the early Bloomfield and Sapir

A different picture arises on the other side of the Atlantic Ocean. There we see a decisive breakthrough to structuralist syntax, owing to an insistence on the notion that not the word but the sentence is the main unit of the language system. The first name to be mentioned is that of Edward Sapir (1884–1939). As he was trained in anthropological linguistics, his general ideas about language were most directly inspired by his knowledge of American Indian languages.

His most important publication in this regard is (Sapir 1921). This book is a curious mixture of traditional European thought on language and an emergent, more typically American, positivist attitude. He stresses the fact that (1921: 165) "Language exists only in so far as it is actually used – spoken and heard, written and read.". The underlying language system is actually no more than a hypothesis naturally arising in the mind of anyone who starts reflecting on language. Yet this positivism is thrown to the wind when he speaks about the sentence (Sapir 1921: 33):

> Radical (or grammatical) element and sentence – these are the primary *functional* units of speech, the former as an abstracted minimum, the latter as the esthetically satisfying embodiment of a unified thought. (…) The sentence is the logical counterpart of the complete thought only if it be felt as made up of the radical and grammatical elements that lurk in the recesses of its words.

Historically, it is interesting to see how Sapir is struggling with the concept of sentence, and how the notion of formal syntax is beginning to shape up, though still loaded with meaningless metaphors like "lurk in the recesses of words". He refuses to accept that the notion of sentence still eludes him (Sapir 1921: 36):

> We have already seen that the major functional unit of speech, the sentence, has, like the word, a psychological as well as a merely logical or abstracted existence. Its definition is not difficult. It is the linguistic expression of a proposition. It combines a subject of discourse with a statement in regard to this subject. Subject and 'predicate' may be combined in a single word, as in Latin *dico*; each may be expressed independently, as in the English equivalent, *I say*; each or either may be so qualified as to lead to complex propositions of many sorts.

While, ironically, he claims that it is not hard to define the notion of sentence, we see him fall back on purely psychological, nonpositivistic, criteria for the delimitation of this notion. And these psychological criteria are directly derived from the Aristotelian tradition, where indeed a proposition is the mental assignment of a property to an underlying, discourse-given entity. This notion was revived in the late nineteenth century by European authors like Wegener (1885), Lipps (1893) and Stout (1896), on whom Sapir relied and who distinguished a topic-comment structure in sentences-in-discourse. Yet the authors just mentioned made a clear distinction between a sentence's topic-comment structure and its overt syntactic predicate-argument structure, which in most cases does not reflect the topic-comment structure, the latter being generally manifest through an intonational overlay. This distinction between strictly syntactic and discourse-semantic (or information-structural) sentence structure was not made by Sapir, who conflated the two in an attempt to come to terms with the notion of sentence (Sapir 1921: 125–126):

> It is well to remember that speech consists of a series of propositions. There must be something to talk about and something must be said about this subject of discourse once it is selected. This distinction is of such fundamental importance that the vast majority of languages have emphasized it by creating some sort of formal barrier between the two terms of the proposition. The subject of discourse is a noun. As the most common subject of discourse is either a person or a thing, the noun clusters about concrete concepts of that order. As the thing predicated of a subject is generally an activity in the widest sense of the word, a passage from one moment of existence to another, the form which has been set aside for the business of predicating, in other words, the verb, clusters about concepts of activity. No language wholly fails to distinguish noun and verb, though in particular cases the nature of the distinction may be an elusive one. It is different with the other parts of speech. Not one of them is imperatively required for the life of language.

Interestingly, this same conflation of topic-comment and syntactic structure is found in as late a publication as Hockett (1958: 201), where one reads:

> The most general characterization of predicative constructions is suggested by the terms *topic* and *comment* for their ICs [i.e. immediate constituents]: the speaker announces a topic and then says something about it. Thus *John* | *ran away*; *That new book by Thomas Guernsey* | *I haven't read yet.* In English and the familiar languages of Europe, topics are usually also subjects, and comments are predicates: so in *John* | *ran away.* But this identification fails sometimes in colloquial English, regularly in certain special situations in formal English, and more generally in some non-European languages.

Sapir's immediate example may well have been Bloomfield's (1914) book *Language*, where we read (Bloomfield 1914: 61):

> In the primary division of an experience into two parts, the one focused is called the *subject* and the one left for later attention the *predicate*; the relation between them is called *predication.* If, after this first division, either subject or predicate or both receive further analysis, the elements in each case first singled out are again called subjects and the elements in relation to them, *attributes.* The subject is always the present thing, the known thing, or the concrete thing, the predicate or attribute, its quality, action, or relation or the thing to which it is like. Thus in the sentence *Lean horses run fast* the subject is *lean horses* and the horses' action, *run fast*, is the predicate. Within the subject there is the further analysis into a subject *horses* and its attribute *lean*, expressing the horses' quality. In the predicate *fast* is an attribute of the subject *run.*

The importance of this text lies not so much in its conceptually confused notion of sentence structure as in the fact that a linguistic structure is seen as consisting of a number of elements, later called *constituents*. In the early years of the century it was not entirely clear what this could mean, but by the 1930s some linguists were discovering the great potential of this way of looking at linguistic structures. Nowadays we are accustomed to the idea that a construction is a combination of constituents, each of which belongs to one or more given classes and which jointly form a constituent that again belongs to a given class. To us, a century after Bloomfield's (1914) book, it is a trivial insight that the highest possible grammatically relevant class is the class denoted by the symbol *Sentence* (S), but, historically speaking, it took some time for that insight to break through and become explicit.

It is not often realised in linguistic circles that Bloomfield took his notion of hierarchical constituent structure, each layer consisting of one or more immediate constituents (ICs) until the last layer which consists of ultimate constituents, from the German philosopher-psychologist Wilhelm Wundt (1832–1920), who actually drew IC-diagrams (see Percival 1976; Seuren 1998: 220–221). Wundt wrote (1880: 53–54; translation mine):

> The simplest form of a *thought*, i.e. a self-contained apperceptive representational process, occurs when a total representation ('Gesamtvorstellung') falls into *two* parts that are connected with each other. This happens in the *simple judgement.* If we use the sign $^{\cap}$ for apperceptive connections of successive representations, then $A^{\cap}B$ is the psychological symbol of the simple judgement.
>
> As soon as the total representation, the splitting up of which results in a thought process, is separated into three or more single representations the judgement is no longer simple but *composite.* In a composite judgement the connection of the single parts is never uniform, in the sense that the form $A^{\cap}B$ would extend over a larger number of members, as in $A^{\cap}B^{\cap}C$ (...). On the contrary, these apperceptive connections always proceed in such a way that first, as with the simple thought, the total representation is separated into two single representations, upon which either or both of these can be subdivided into two further single representations, and so on. Herein lies the essential difference between apperceptive and associative connections. If we use the sign $^{-}$ for the associative connection of successive representations, we see that an associative sequence $A^{-}B^{-}C^{-}D$ (...) can contain any number of members. In contrast to this, the apperceptive thought process always proceeds in forms like the following:

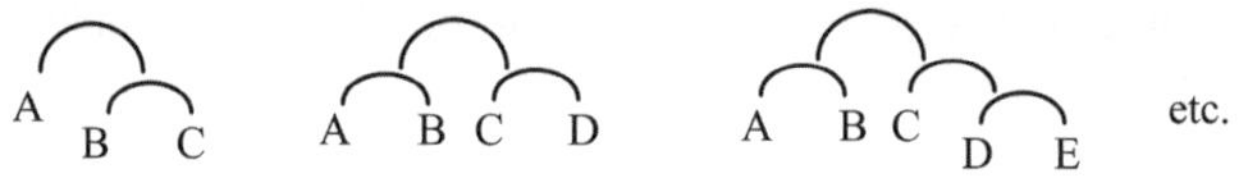

> This principle of duality or of binary connection has found its unmistakable expression in the categories of grammatical syntax. For all these categories always reduce to just *two* representations which are connected with each other. Thus we distinguish first the two main representations Subject and Predicate, which correspond with the first division of the thought. The Subject may be divided again into Noun and Attribute. The Predicate, when it is nominal, splits into the Copula and the Predicate proper, upon which the latter, like the Subject, may split into Noun and Attribute again. But if the Predicate is verbal it may split into Verb and Object, or into the Predicate proper and the supplementary Predicate.

Bloomfield (1914) is largely based on Wundt's work, and there can be no doubt that the passage just quoted from Bloomfield (1914: 61) was directly inspired by Wundt's notion of IC-analysis. Yet Bloomfield never actually drew a diagram, not even in his *magnum opus* (1933). Nor did Sapir in his (1921) book, where an elaborate IC-analysis is given of the one-word Paiute Noun Phrase corresponding to 'they who are going to sit and cut up with a knife a black buffalo'. Sapir describes this structure entirely in English prose (Sapir 1921: 31–32):

> One example will do for thousands, one complex type for hundreds of possible types. I select it from Paiute, the language of the Indians of the arid plateaus of southwestern Utah. The word *wii-to-kuchum-punku-rügani-yugwi-va-ntü-m(ü)* is of unusual length even for its own language, but it is no psychological monster for all that. It means 'they who are going to sit and cut up with a knife a black cow (*or* bull)', or, in the order of the Indian elements, 'knife-black-buffalo-pet-cut up-sit(plur.)-future-participle-animate-plur'. The formula for this word, in accordance with our symbolism, would be (F) + (E) + C + d + A + B + (g) + (h) + (i) + (0). It is the plural of the future participle of a compound verb 'to sit and cut up' – A + B. The elements (g) – which denotes futuricity – (h) – a participial suffix – and (i) – indicating the animate plural – are grammatical elements which convey nothing when detached. The formula (0) is intended to imply that the finished word conveys, in addition to what is definitely expressed, a further relational idea, that of subjectivity; in other words, the form can only be used as the subject of a sentence, not in an objective or other syntactic relation. The radical element A ('to cut up'), before entering into combination with the coordinate element B ('to sit'), is itself compounded with two nominal elements or element-groups – an instrumentally used stem (F) ('knife'), which may be freely used as the radical element of noun forms but cannot be employed as an absolute noun in its given form, and an objectively used group – (E) + C + d ('black cow *or* bull'). This group in turn consists of an adjectival radical element (E) ('black'), which cannot be independently employed (...), and the compound noun C + d ('buffalo-pet'). The radical element C properly means 'buffalo', but the element d, properly an independently occurring noun meaning 'horse' (...), is regularly used as a quasi subordinate element indicating that the animal denoted by the stem to which it is affixed is owned by a human being. It will be observed that the whole complex (F) + (E) + C + d + A + B is functionally no more than a verbal base, corresponding to the *sing-* of an English form like *singing*; that this complex remains verbal in force on the addition of the temporal element (g) – this (g), by the way, must not be understood as appended to B alone, but to the whole basic complex as a unit – and that the elements (h) + (i) + (0) transform the verbal expression into a formally well-defined noun.

Yet even though this elaborate description corresponds directly to the left-branching IC-structure of fig. 6.4, Sapir does not draw the corresponding diagram, which is presented here (as is the custom nowadays) as an upside-down 'tree' structure, with the root at the top and the branches expanding downward. Why Sapir, and with him all authors till

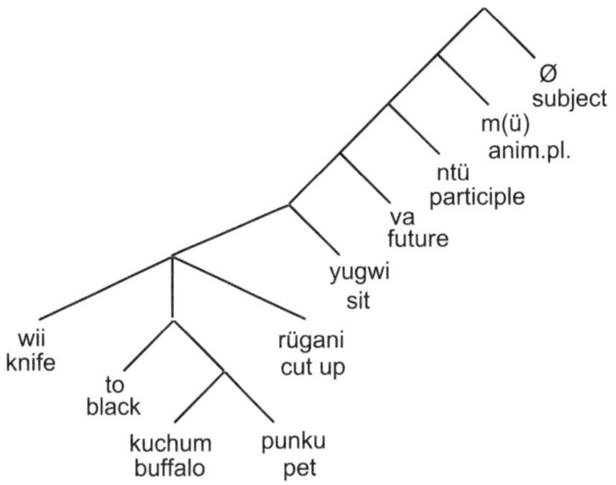

Fig. 6.4: The Paiute word *wii-to-kuchum-punku-rügani-yugwi-va-ntü-m(ü)* as a tree diagram according to Sapir (1921: 31–32)

roughly 1955, shrank from actually drawing tree diagrams will remain a mystery unless one realises that the drawing of diagrams was traditionally abhorred by scholars who worked in the human sciences and would not stoop to drawing figures, that being contrary to their strictly nonmathematical way of thinking. It took a long time for this attitude to be eliminated.

In fact (see Seuren 1998: 221–221), the first actually drawn tree diagram in the linguistic literature (with the root at the bottom end) is not found until Nida (1946: 87), shown in fig. 6.5, close to the end of the period we now identify as that of structuralist linguistics. Tree diagrams did not become common until after 1960.

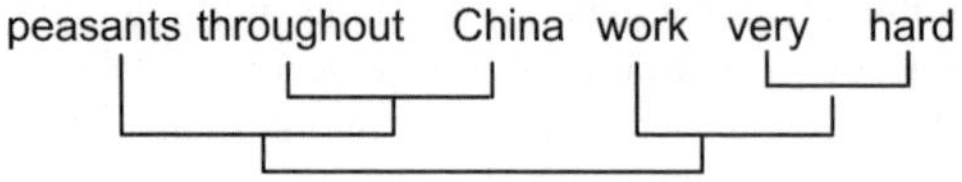

Fig. 6.5: Nida's (1946) analysis of *Peasants throughout China work very hard*

3.2. Bloomfield

The structuralist theory of syntax came to full fruition in the work of the American linguist Leonard Bloomfield (1887–1949), especially in his (1933) book *Language*. Bloomfield, whose Austrian paternal grandparents had immigrated into the United States in 1868, began as a student of Germanic philology, but he soon extended his interests to the general theory of language, taking in his stride a few American Indian languages and also Tagalog, the main language of the Philippines. In 1921 he won the chair of German and Linguistics at Ohio State University in Columbus. There he was influenced, and soon won over, by the psychologist Albert P. Weiss, who was an ardent follower of the new school of behaviourism in psychology which had started during the first world war.

In actual fact, behaviourism was much more than just a new school in psychology. It was an ideology presenting itself in the context of a positivist approach to whatever is taken be connected with the mind and hence with society. Strictly speaking, behaviourism held that (a) human beings are fully material: the mind is a fabrication based on a phenomenological delusion and on religion, (b) the main problem of psychology is to find a causal connection between stimuli impinging upon a human or animal organism and those forms of behaviour that cannot be explained by direct physical causation (such as bleeding after a cut). The simplest possible hypothesis was taken to be the assumption of a physiological transfer mechanism in the brain (conditioning), in virtue of which an existing behavioural reaction corresponding to a stimulus X, such as salivation on the sighting of food, can be prompted also by a stimulus Y provided X and Y have co-occurred with sufficient frequency in the personal history of an individual. Thus, when the sighting of food has been accompanied often enough by the sounding of a bell, salivation will occur upon the sounding of the bell even when no food is sighted. The behaviourists believed that this simplest possible hypothesis, perhaps extended with a few refinements, was adequate for the explanation of human and animal behaviour. They left no room for any genetically fixed specific predisposition for the processing of incoming stimuli, let alone for any spontaneous self-starting cognitive processes. For them, nervous systems were general purpose machines of a purely passive and associative type. During its heyday, behaviourism was extremely influential across the human sciences and even influenced US government policies. This heyday ended abruptly in the early 1960s, when the insight broke through that the explanation of human behaviour, in all its complexity, requires a far richer hypothesis than a behaviourist stimulus-response mechanism.

After his conversion to behaviourism, it became Bloomfield's aim to establish a theory of language according to behaviourist principles. The results of this resolve are found in his (1933) *Language*. Yet, although behaviourism is presented with a great deal of emphasis especially in the opening chapters of this book, its effects remain largely limited to Bloomfield's not altogether successful attempt at setting up a behaviourist semantics, according to which the meaning of a linguistic form consists in its behaviourist association with a set of physical stimuli. Other than that, fortunately, there is hardly any behaviourism to be detected in the book. The main significance of Bloomfield's express emphasis on behaviourism lies in the fact that it demonstrates his deeply rooted urge to turn linguistics into an autonomous science in the contemporary sense of the word.

His theory of syntax, in particular, has remained entirely free from behaviourist blemishes (contrary to the behaviourist psychologist Skinner's unsuccessful and unprofessional 1957 attempt at grounding a behaviourist theory of syntax). It is squarely based on the notion of IC-analysis described above, which he had derived from his study of Wundt, to whom, as will be agreed, no behaviourist tendencies can be ascribed. For Bloomfield, all linguistic products (sentences, phrases, words, morphemes) have an internal structure which is describable in terms of a layered hierarchy of constituents, as shown in the figures 6.4 and 6.5 above. He writes (1933: 161–162):

> A linguistic form which bears no partial phonetic-semantic resemblance to any other form is a *simple* form or *morpheme*. (...) From all this it appears that every complex form is entirely made up, so far as its phonetically definable constituents are concerned, of morphemes. The number of these *ultimate constituents* may run very high. The form *Poor John ran away* contains five morphemes: *poor*, *John*, *ran*, *a-...*, and *way*. However, the structure of complex forms is by no means as simple as this; we could not understand the forms of a language if we merely reduced all the complex forms to their ultimate constituents. Any English-speaking person who concerns himself with this matter, is sure to tell us that the *immediate constituents* of *Poor John ran away* are the two forms *poor John* and *ran away*; that each of these is, in turn, a complex form; that the immediate constituents of *ran away* are *ran*, a morpheme, and *away*, a complex form, whose constituents are the morphemes *a-* and *way*; and that the constituents of *poor John* are the morphemes *poor* and *John*. Only in this way will a proper analysis (that is, one which takes account of the meanings) lead to the ultimately constituent morphemes. (...) The total stock of morphemes in a language is its *lexicon*.

Clearly, this description of the sentence *Poor John ran away* corresponds to the diagram in fig. 6.6, which, however, he does not actually draw, thus following in Sapir's footsteps.

Yet he does say explicitly that each constituent deserves a name or label denoting the grammatical category, or "form class", to which it belongs (Bloomfield 1933: 165):

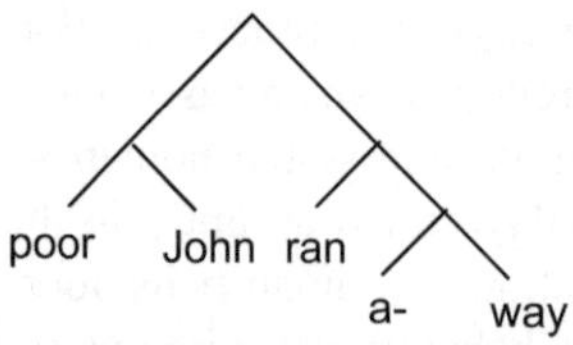

Fig. 6.6: Bloomfield's (1933) analysis of *Poor John ran away*

> The meaning of a complex form depends in part upon the selection of the constituent forms. Thus, *drink milk* and *watch John* name actions, and, as we have just seen, are infinitive expressions, but *fresh milk* and *poor John* name objects and are substantive expressions. The second constituents, *milk* and *John*, are the same; the difference depends upon the selection of the first constituent. By virtue of this difference, the forms *drink* and *watch* belong to one English form class (that of transitive verbs), and the forms *fresh* and *poor* to another (that of adjectives).

His notion of form class is still not quite clear and in any case incomplete, in that he fails to present a list of possible form classes or, as we now prefer to say, grammatical categories, arguing (Bloomfield 1933: 165): "The features of selection are often highly arbitrary and whimsical. We combine *prince*, *author*, *sculptor* with the suffix *-ess* in *princess*, *authoress*, *sculptress* (in this last case with phonetic modification of [r,.] to [r]), but not *king*, *singer*, *painter*. By virtue of this habit, the former words belong to a form-class from which the latter words are excluded.". But one may conclude that he considers that proper linguistic IC-diagrams, other than those presented by Sapir and Nida, should label their nodes by assigning them the grammatical category to which they belong. Bloomfield thus implicitly initiated the notion of labelled tree, now current in all forms of grammatical analysis, even though, as has been said, he never drew a tree diagram in any of his publications. If we anticipate the nomenclature that became current in the immediate post-Bloomfieldian period, we may rewrite fig.6.6 as the labelled tree shown in fig. 6.7 – even though no labels for the alleged morphemes *a-* and *-way* ever came into general use, and even though Bloomfield himself would analyse the finite verb form *ran* in terms of the underlying structure PAST + RUN:

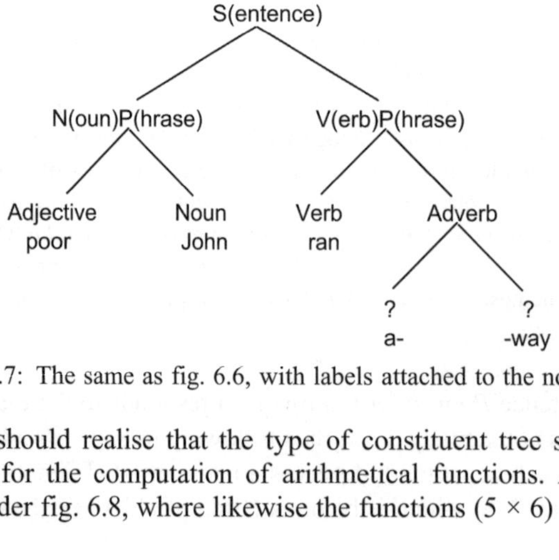

Fig. 6.7: The same as fig. 6.6, with labels attached to the nodes

One should realise that the type of constituent tree shown in fig. 6.7 can likewise be used for the computation of arithmetical functions. As a parallel to fig. 6.1 we may consider fig. 6.8, where likewise the functions (5 × 6) + 8 and 5 × (6 + 8) are computed:

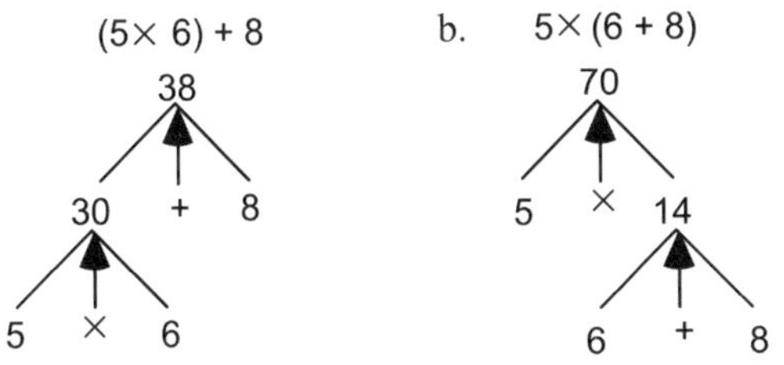

Fig. 6.8: (5 × 6) + 8 and 5 × (6 + 8) in terms of constituent trees

Here, the functor is itself a constituent of the superordinate constituent. It is necessary, for the arithmetical calculus to work, that the functor constituent be identified as such, so that it can be distinguished from its argument terms.

One problem with the type of analysis exemplified in fig. 6.7 is that it makes no distinction between morphological and syntactic structures. Bloomfield does have a definition of the notion sentence, which makes good sense in his perspective (Bloomfield 1933: 170): "An utterance may consist of more than one sentence. This is the case when the utterance contains several linguistic forms which are not by any meaningful conventional grammatical arrangement (that is, by any construction) united into a larger form.". And he defines the word as a "minimal free form" (Bloomfield 1933: 178). But what exactly distinguishes morpheme-to-word from word-to-sentence constructions remains unclear, despite Bloomfield's insistence that they differ radically (Bloomfield 1933: 183–184):

> In languages which use bound forms, the word has great structural importance because the constructions in which free forms appear in phrases differ very decidedly from the constructions in which free or bound forms appear in words. Accordingly, the grammar of these languages consists of two parts, called *syntax*, and *morphology*. (…) There has been considerable debate as to the usefulness of this division, and as to the scope of the two headings. In languages that have bound forms, the constructions in which bound forms play a part differ radically from the constructions in which all the immediate constituents are free forms.

The best he can do is in (Bloomfield 1933: 207), but no clear criterion is given:

> In general, morphologic constructions are more elaborate than those of syntax. The features of modification and modulation are more numerous and often irregular–that is, confined to particular constituents or combinations. The order of the constituents is almost always rigidly fixed, permitting of no such connotative variants as *John ran away* : *Away ran John.* Features of selection minutely and often whimsically limit the constituents that may be united into a complex form.

One notes, incidentally, that Bloomfield still appears to have no eye for the real complexities and mechanisms of syntax. It wasn't until a few decades later that syntactic phenomena became visible to linguistic observers.

Honesty forces us to admit that modern linguistic theories have equally failed to provide a criterion for the distinction between syntax and morphology, partly due to an overall failure to provide a clear definition of the notion word. All we do nowadays is classify categories (form classes) as being syntactic or morphological. Phrase and word classes are called syntactic, but stems and affixes are morphological. Differences between syntactic and morphological constructions are often commented upon, but only in an incidental way and without much in the way of general criteria.

A further serious problem with Bloomfield's IC-analysis lies in the fact that he fails to indicate on what grounds one particular possible IC-analysis is to be preferred over another. Why, for example, should we analyse *Poor John ran away* as consisting of an NP followed by a VP, and not as a tripartite structure of the kind shown in fig. 6.9?

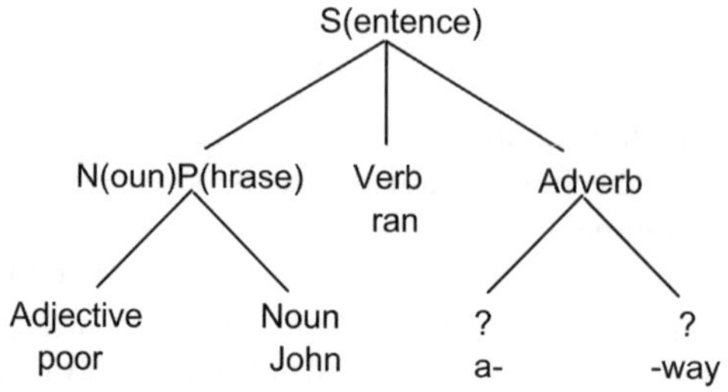

Fig. 6.9: Alternative IC-analysis for *Poor John ran away*

Bloomfield himself had no principled answer to this question, or if he had one, he merely adumbrated it. In cases where he still feels unable to encompass the notion of a complete description, as in the case of syntax, he falls back on intuitive, introspective criteria. Thus, as we saw in the larger quote given earlier from Bloomfield (1933: 161), he writes: "Any English-speaking person who concerns himself with this matter, is sure to tell us that the *immediate constituents* of *Poor John ran away* are the two forms *poor John* and *ran away.*". But when he is concerned with the restricted paradigms of morphophonemic alternation, or, in his own terms, "phonetic modification", where the notion of complete description is easier to grasp, he applies the criterion of greatest overall simplicity to the problem of how to select a "basic alternant" (Bloomfield 1933: 164): "[W]e try, of course, to make the selection of a basic alternant so as to get, in the long run, the *simplest description of the facts.*" [emphasis mine]. Or Bloomfield (1933: 211–212):

> We have not yet described, in terms of phonetic modification, the kinship of the three alternants [-ez, -z, -s] of the bound form that appears in English plural nouns. It is evident that three entirely different statements are possible, according to our choice of one or the other of the three forms as our starting point. Our aim is to get, in the long run, *the simplest possible set of statements* that will describe the facts of the English language. [emphasis mine]

What Bloomfield does not do is apply the criterion of greatest overall simplicity to the choice of immediate and remote constituents in syntactic constructions. That step was taken a decade and a half later by the American linguists Rulon Wells (1947) and especially Zellig Harris (1951).

3.3. The "God's truth" linguists (Pike)

Naturally, the question of the motivation of syntactic IC-analyses was a central concern in the schools of structuralist linguistics that developed in the wake of Bloomfield's teaching. It was, in fact, this very question that caused a radical split among Bloomfield's followers. One school followed the European trend, holding that IC-structures are psychologically real and that they are to be discovered on grounds of introspection: one somehow feels what the right structure is, for any given sentence or phrase, when one closes one's eyes and thinks very deeply about it. To get the right results it helps a great deal when the person doing the deep thinking is himself a linguist or a psychologist, since only linguists and psychologists have the "highly cultivated refinement in the description of one's own thought experiences" described and rejected as a criterion by the German psychologist Bühler (1934: 254): "Man darf den Befund nicht für alle Zeit an die Bedingung einer hochgezüchteten Feinheit des Beschreibens eigener Denkerlebnisse knüpfen, sondern muß danach streben, ihn auch weniger subtilen Augen zugänglich zu machen und noch mehr: es gilt ihn *objektiv* zu verifizieren." [One cannot ground the result for all time on the condition of a highly cultivated refinement in the description of one's own thought experiences. On the contrary, one must attempt to make it accessible also to less subtle eyes, and, what is more, one must verify it *objectively*.].

Householder (1952: 260), dubbed this school of linguistic thought the school of God's truth linguists, for two good reasons. First, for these linguists, the truth about syntactic structure was, in a sense, a question of divine or subdivine revelation, best restricted to the happy few who called themselves specialists. A second good reason for the name *God's truth linguists* was the fact that the group in question consisted mainly of protestant missionaries, who, for religious reasons, were staunchly opposed to anything that reeked of positivism or behaviourism yet were anxious to be "modern" and "scientific" but only in a strictly Christian sense. The main figures were Kenneth L. Pike (1912–2000) and Eugene A. Nida (1914–2011), both active members of the *Sumnmer Institute of Linguistics* (SIL), founded in 1934 by one W. Cameron Townsend, a devoted but linguistically naive missionary in Mexico. SIL's main aim was to have the bible translated into preliterate languages. Pike had studied with Sapir but he was also strongly influenced by Bloomfield, who was considered the chief scientific linguist of the period. Only Pike developed a theory of syntax. Nida worked on morphology but soon withdrew into bible translation.

Pike's theory of linguistic, including syntactic, structure is found in Pike (1967), first circulated in 1954. In this book, Pike presents his theory of *Tagmemics* – the term being derived from Bloomfield's rather artificial and not very well defined term *tagmeme* (Bloomfield 1933: 166), which never caught on. He starts out by stressing that language is just one aspect of overall human behaviour and that human behaviour is, in general, meaningful and cast into specific structural moulds, called *behaviouremes*. Typical behaviouremes are a church service, a football game or a breakfast. Each behavioureme consists of "emic" slots (the term *emic* is derived from the terms *phoneme* and *morpheme*, and, of course, Bloomfield's *tagmeme*), filled by "etic" material (the term *etic* being derived from *phonetic*). The breakfast behavioureme in Pike's own family is described (Pike 1954: 59–60 – section 5.2) as being preceded by pre-breakfast preparations, etically filled in by the playing of Tschaikovsky's Fifth Symphony on the family record player to get the children up, washed and dressed, followed by the calling of the children to come and sit down at the table. Then breakfast can begin. It consists of a slot for the saying of grace, followed by a slot for the drinking of fruit juice (etically filled by some drinkable substance deserving that name). Then there is a composite slot for the main meal, which includes a subslot for cereals as well as one for toast. Simultaneously there is an overall slot for conversation, filled by actual etic speech material.

In parallel frashion, speech material is divided up in emic segments called *sentences*, each of which is again divided up in emic sentence parts, each emic element being filled by etic material. The etic fillers are always the ultimate, material realisations of the emic slots. Some emic constituents are complex in that they consist of subconstituents. The emic level of description presupposes that the analysing linguist be conversant with the language (or culture) at hand: without actual knowledge of the language (or the culture), all the linguist can do is record (phon)etic material. The functional system required for emic structure is the mental property of each speaker, and it is the linguist's task to discover that inner language system by introspection. Tagmemics is thus *realist* in the sense that there is taken to be an actual emic object of investigation to be described or at least approximated by means of introspection resulting in linguistic analysis and description.

Later, this type of linguistic description was called *taxonomic* or *item-arrangement style*, in the words of Hockett (1954). Both labels are apt, because tagmemics does indeed take it for granted that morphosyntactic structures result from a taxonomy of possible morphosyntactic patterns, each pattern consisting of slots to be filled by etic material. No room was left for the thought that some such "patterns" may owe their existence to an underlying rule system for the composition of structures and that it might make sense to assume hypothetical underlying structures to be transformed according to tree-transformational processes into surface structures assigned to actually appearing utterances. Following Bloomfield, *portmanteau* etic fillers were considered in morphology, filling two or more underlying morphological slots at the time (such as etic *ate* for emic PAST + *eat*), but nothing of the sort was envisaged for syntax. No proposals were made, in this school of linguistic thought, to assume, for example, an underlying $_{S}$[$_{S}$[that John be ill] $_{VP}$[be likely]] (or: *that John is ill is likely*) for a surface structure like $_{S}$[$_{NP}$[John] $_{VP}$[be likely $_{VP}$[to be ill]]] (or: *John is likely to be ill*).

In spite of the severe limitations of this type of morphosyntactic description, hundreds of grammars were produced in this vein, mainly in the context of the Summer Institute of Linguistics. Strangely, despite the fact that it has been shown a thousand times over during the past half century that this type of taxonomic description is unable to account for the syntactic complexities of natural languages, new schools have come up lately (in particular so-called Cognitive Linguistics) which indulge in precisely this type of work, complete with appeals to introspection, simply ignoring the arguments and mountains of facts, especially regarding sentential and clausal complementation, that have been adduced over the years showing its fatal inadequacy. One cannot but conclude that linguistics is still far from having achieved the status of a mature science.

3.4. The "hocus-pocus" linguists (Harris)

It was again Householder (1952: 260) who introduced the term hocus-pocus linguists to refer to the other main post-Bloomfieldian school which came into being during the 1940s. His reason for choosing this name was the fact that the school in question showed a predilection for abstract formulaic notation and formal methods of description and analysis, strongly influenced by the rather esoteric foundational studies carried out, during the first half of the twentieth century, in the areas of mathematics and logic (see Scholz and Pullum 2007).

The school was based on the notion of overall description of a language in terms of Bloomfieldian constituency trees. The best overall description of a language was considered to be the one that covered all the facts with the help of the smallest number of IC-construction types. Minimalisation of the descriptive apparatus was the word, in accordance with the Ockhamist simplicity criterion: "postulated entities are not to be multiplied beyond necessity". The best IC-analysis in any given case is thus the one that fits into an overall description of the language that is both adequate and minimalist.

The main protagonists of this school were the Yale philosopher Rulon S. Wells (1919–2008), whose influential article (1947) was widely read, and the Philadelphia linguist Zellig S. Harris (1909–1992), who became the leader of this movement after the publication of his (1951) book *Methods in Structuralist Linguistics*, foreshadowed by Harris (1946). Both Wells and Harris proposed a method whereby substitution classes should be established for each constituent in a construction in such a way that a maximally simple overall picture would emerge, whereby it was not excluded that two or more candidates would achieve equal scores on the simplicity scale (Harris 1951: 2). But whereas Wells simply proposed the method, Harris gave it a behaviourist grounding and worked it out in minute detail for phonology, morphology and syntax. Harris, moreover, took a great interest in the foundational studies in mathematics and logic that had been and were taking place in those years and was deeply influenced by them (see Scholz and Pullum 2007) and, unlike Pike and his followers, he did not eschew abstract analyses and symbolic notations. He taught extensively about this way of doing syntax and kept publishing till well into the 1970s.

It was Harris also, who soon discovered, around 1950, that grammars will gain enormously in simplicity if one postulates a structurally regular and simple system of production rules for underlying sentence structures, supplemented with transformational rules turning the underlying or deep structures into surface structures. The true originator of what was later to be known as Transformational Generative Grammar was, therefore, Zellig S. Harris. Yet this new transformationalist approach was not incorporated into his (1951), which he had finished writing in 1947, as appears from the Preface. It gradually developed through his later publications (1952, 1957, 1965), where he also relaxed his initial strictly positivist and strictly behaviourist convictions. The transition to the transformational paradigm is not discussed in the present article, because it is felt that it marks the end of the structuralist era in American linguistics, which is characterised by taxonomic methods of classification, by an adherence to behaviourism and by a rejection of the notion of explanation in science.

Harris (1951) is a very dull book, yet it is carried by genuine conviction and real inspiration from beginning to end. It starts by saying, entirely in a positivist vein, that linguistic data consist in the sounds actually produced by people going about their business. What people understand or comprehend is not considered data because comprehension is not physically graspable. (Later, Harris gave up his strict positivism and became much more lenient with regard to semantic data.) The linguist should thus set out collecting sound samples from people in streets, trains, planes and buildings and then lock himself up with his piles of sound recordings. He should then try to sort out what minimal inventory of recurrent sound bits can be combined into units called phonemes.

This is to be done on the basis of the *distribution* of the sound bits in their various sound environments. If it turns out, as Harris said it would, that certain types of sound bit are restricted to certain environments and that these environments do not overlap, then a phoneme X can be set up as an abstract unit of description such that X has different and well-defined manifestations, called *allophones*, in each environment listed. The environment-conditioned allophones are said to be in *complementary distribution* (a notion taken from Swadesh 1934, who had introduced it in the context of the determination of phonemes). Elements in complementary distribution are open to classification as one single higher-level unit of description, in this case a phoneme. Thus we read (Harris 1951: 25):

> As the first step towards obtaining phonemes, this procedure represents the continuous flow of a unique occurrence of speech as a succession of segmental elements, each representing some feature of a unique speech sound. The points of division of these segments are arbitrary here, since we have as yet no way of enabling the analyst to make the cuts at precisely those points in the flow of speech which will later be represented by inter-phonemic divisions. Later procedures will change these segmentations until their boundaries coincide with those of the eventual phonemes.

Essentially the same method can be applied to set up higher-level descriptive units. Combinations of phonemes will be seen to form *allomorphs*, to be combined into higher-level units called *morphemes*. Morphemes again occur in constructions allowing for the setting up of ever higher-level descriptive categories until one arrives at the highest-level descriptive unit, the sentence. The book takes the reader, step by repetitive step, through all the levels proposed up till sentence level.

The notion of distribution is essential for Harris. It is considered virtually the only criterion for setting up tentative analyses, which are further tested on grounds of simplicity and generality of structure assignments (Harris 1951: 6): "The only preliminary step that is essential to this science is the restriction to distribution as determining the relevance of the inquiry.". And again (Harris 1951: 8): "It may be noted that distributional procedures do more than offer a rigorous alternative to meaning considerations and the like. Distributional procedures, once established, permit, with no extra trouble, the definite treatment of those marginal cases which meaning considerations leave indeterminate or open to conflicting opinion.".

The only concession to "meaning" is made for cases where informants are asked to repeat an utterance or to say whether two sound bits are the same or different (Harris 1951: 7): "In principle, meaning need be involved only to the extent of determining what is repetition. If we know that *life* and *rife* are not entirely repetitions of each other, we will then discover that they differ in distribution (and hence in 'meaning').".

The book is thus a massive *discovery procedure*, ideally based on a large corpus of sound recordings, for a maximally compact statement of all possible constructions in a language at the different ascending levels of phonemes, morphemes, words, phrases and, finally, the sentence. The aim is to establish an axiomatised discovery procedure for the simplest possible grammar or grammars of a language.

A grammar set up in this way is not necessarily considered to be actually present in some form in the speaker's brain but is primarily taken to be merely a way of managing, or, as Harris says (1951: 3) "arranging" the data, whereby the possible reality of an object of description is either left open or denied. Harris was thus not a realist but, entirely in the spirit of his day, an *instrumentalist* in the sense of that term current in the philosophy of science (Nagel 1961) and succinctly described in Botha (1968: 89):

> Instrumentalists regard theories as instruments, tools for calculation or computational devices for the organising of data and ordering of laws. According to this view theories are used for drawing inferences and making predictions and their statements cannot be characterised as either true or false.(…) Instrumentalists do not always agree on the question whether theoretical concepts refer to entities in reality.

A telling passage, in this respect, is Harris (1951: 3):

> The greatest use of such explicit structural descriptions will be in the cataloguing of language structures, and in the comparing of structural types. These descriptions will, however, be also important for historical linguistics and dialect geography; for the relation of language to culture and personality, and to phonetics and semantics; and for the comparison of language structure with the systems of logic.

Here, linguistic descriptions are said to be useful primarily for the setting up of taxonomies and in a secondary but ill-defined sense also for historical linguistics, dialect geography, phonetics and semantics, logic and what not, but where no mention is made of explanation or enhancement of insight.

Other than in Pike's tagmemics, which led to hundreds of actually written and published grammars, Harris's method did not lure any linguists into the activity of grammar-writing. The reason is obvious: what linguist will condemn himself or herself to such drudgery! Harris, of course, realised that. For him, the method of grammar-discovery he set out in his book was more an intellectual exercise than a practical proposal.

But then, how should a linguist who aspires to write an actual grammar of a language actually go about? Towards the end of the book, Harris proposes an answer. He first recapitulates his main purpose in writing the book as follows (Harris 1951: 366–368):

> The over-all purpose of work in descriptive linguistics is to obtain a compact one-one representation of the stock of utterances in the corpus. Since the representation of an utterance or its parts is based on a comparison of utterances, it is really a representation of distinctions. (…)
>
> The basic operations are those of segmentation and classification. Segmentation is carried out at limits determined by the independence of the resulting segments in terms of some particular criterion. (…) Classification is used to group together elements which substitute for or are complementary to one another. (…)
>
> If we were analyzing a corpus without any interest in its relevance for the whole language, we could list all the environments of each tentative segment in all utterances of the corpus, and on this basis decide the segmentation in each utterance. Usually, however, we are interested in analyzing such a corpus as will serve as a sample of the language.

Then he observes that the higher the constituent level, with "sentence" as the highest of all, the smaller the inventory of categories but the larger the set of possible fillers (Harris 1951: 369–370): "This leads ultimately to sets of few elements having complex definitions but as nearly as possible random occurrence in respect to each other, replacing the original sets of many elements having simple definitions but complexly restricted distribution.". Then, at last, light breaks through (Harris 1951: 372–373):

> The work of analysis leads right up to the statements which enable anyone to synthesize or predict utterances in the language. These statements form a deductive system with axiomatically defined initial elements and with theorems concerning the relations among them. The final theorems would indicate the structure of the utterances of the language in terms of the preceding parts of the system.

The style of his writing is abstruse, convoluted and plodding, but the message is clear. When we read "statements" as "rules" and "theorems" as "sentences", as indeed intended by Harris, we have, in essence, the concept of *generative grammar.* Not (yet) of transformational generative grammar, because what is proposed amounts to a system of rules rewriting a single given symbol as a succession of new symbols (so-called *phrase-structure* rules), without any operations performed on strings of symbols. But it did not take Harris long to realise that much greater descriptive succinctness could be achieved when one posits certain simple sentence structures as "basic" and derives more complex sentence from these by means of transformational rules, as has been said.

A similar thought had already been expressed in Harris's (1946) article *From morpheme to utterance*, where he opposed the bottom-up discovery procedure (from morphemes to sentences) to the top-down synthetic procedure now known as "generative". There we read (Harris 1946: 178):

> The [discovery] procedure outlined here could be paralleled by a series of substitutions beginning with the whole utterance and working down, instead of beginning with single morphemes and working up. In that case we would have to find formal criteria for breaking the utterance down at successive stages. This is essentially the difficult problem of determining the immediate constituents of an utterance. It is not clear that there exists any general method for successively determining the immediate constituents, when we begin with a whole utterance and work down. In any case, it would appear that the formation of substitution classes presents fewer theoretical difficulties if we begin with morphemes and work up.

In hindsight, we may sat that what is still lacking, both in Harris (1946) and in Harris (1951), is the notion of a hypothesis regarding the IC-analysis of sentences and subsequent testing, by means of an *evaluation procedure*, for greatest generality and thus greatest simplicity. Rulon Wells proposed such an evaluation procedure in 1947, but this, apparently, made little impression on Harris.

Even so, one clearly discerns the influence of foundational studies in mathematics and logic on linguistic work of this nature, and especially on Harris, who was a keen follower of these developments. This influence was pointed out and further elaborated in Harwood (1955). Scholz and Pullum (2007) point to the great influence of the work done by the mathematician Emil Post during the 1920s in the theory of algorithms as purely formal systems for the generation of strings of symbols (sentences). They also express their amazement at the fact that Post is never quoted by the linguists in question (especially Noam Chomsky), even though they owe a direct debt to him. (The same was already observed by the Dutch philosopher-logician Evert Beth in his Academy address of 1963.).

4. Conclusion

Perhaps to the surprise of beginning students of syntax, we must conclude that it was not until quite recently that the notion of syntax began to have body and soul. Prestructuralist or Apollonian syntax was heavily bound up with nominal case systems and the question of what cases are governed by what verbs with what meaning. During the period of structuralist linguistics, at least to the extent that it was theory-driven, linguists were desperately trying to get a clear notion of syntactic facts, to which the linguistic world had, on the whole, been blind. In the words of Harris (1946: 161): "(...) many grammars have carried little or no syntactic description.". Much as one may feel that the main school of transformational generative linguistics, started by Zellig S. Harris during the 1950s but quickly taken over by Noam Chomsky at MIT, soon lost its bearings and went haywire, it would seem that a sober and balanced assessment will lead to the conclusion that it was in the context of transformational linguistics that, eventually, the Apollonian view of syntax was replaced by the now current, much richer, idea of what syntax and syntactic structures amount to. What we call "structuralist syntax" was, in effect, but a stepping stone to the modern, more developed notion. To what extent this modern notion will prove fruitful and adequate, is a question which it would be premature to expect an answer to.

5. References (selected)

Aarsleff, Hans
1982 *From Locke to Saussure. Essays on the Study of Language and Intellectual History.* London: Athlone.

Bech, Gunnar
1955 *Studien über das Deutsche Verbum Infinitum, Band I.* Det Kongelige Danske videnskabernes selskab. Historisk-Filosofiske Meddelelser, 35:2 (1955) and 36:6 (1957). Copenhagen: Munksgaard. [2nd unrevised edition 1983 Niemeyer, Tübingen (Linguistische Arbeiten 139)]

Beth, Evert W.
1963 Konstanten van het wiskundige denken [Constants in mathematical thinking]. In: *Mededelingen der Koninklijke Nederlandse Akademie van Wetenschappen. Afdeling Letterkunde*, 231–256. (Nieuwe Reeks 26.7) Amsterdam: North-Holland.

Bloomfield, Leonard
1914 *An Introduction to the Study of Language.* New York: Henry Holt. [Photostatic reprint 1983, Amsterdam/Philadelphia: Benjamins]

Bloomfield, Leonard
1924 Review of *Cours de linguistique générale* by Ferdinand de Saussure. *Modern Language Journal* 8: 317–319.

Bloomfield, Leonard
1933 *Language.* New York: Henry Holt.

Botha, Rudolph P.
1968 *The Function of the Lexicon in Transformational Generative Grammar.* The Hague/ Paris: Mouton.

Bühler, Karl
1934 *Sprachtheorie. Die Darstellungsfunktion der Sprache.* Jena: Fischer.

De Saussure, Ferdinand
1916 *Cours de linguistique générale.* Edited by Charles Bally and Albert Sechehaye, with the collaboration of Albert Riedlinger. Paris/Lausanne: Payot.

Fodor, Jerry A.
1983 *The Modularity of Mind.* Cambridge, Mass.: MIT Press.

Harris, Zellig S.
1946 From morpheme to utterance. *Language* 22.3: 161–183.
Harris, Zellig S.
1951 *Methods in Structural Linguistics.* Chicago: The University of Chicago Press.
Harris, Zellig S.
1952 Discourse analysis. *Language* 28.1: 1–30.
Harris, Zellig S.
1957 Co-occurrence and transformation in linguistic structure. *Language* 33.2: 283–340.
Harris, Zellig S.
1965 Transformational theory. *Language* 41.3: 363–401.
Harwood, F. W.
1955 Axiomatic syntax. The construction and evaluation of a syntactic calculus. *Language* 31.4: 409–413.
Hockett, Charles F.
1954 Two models of grammatical description. *Word* 10: 210–231.
Hockett, Charles F.
1958 *A Course in Modern Linguistics.* New York: Macmillan.
Householder, Fred W.
1952 Review of Zellig S. Harris (1951). *International Journal of American Linguistics* 18: 260–268.
Householder, Fred W.
1981 *The Syntax of Apollonius Dyscolus. Translated, and with commentary by –.* Amsterdam/Philadelphia: Benjamins.
Lipps, Theodor
1893 *Grundzüge der Logik.* Leipzig: Dürr.
Mel'čuk, Igor A., and Nikolaj V. Pertsov
1987 *Surface Syntax of English. A Formal Model within the Meaning-Text Framework.* Amsterdam/Philadelphia: Benjamins.
Nagel, Ernest
1961 *The Structure of Science. Problems in the Logic of Scientific Explanation.* London: Routledge and Kegan Paul.
Nida, Eugene A.
1946 *Morphology. The Descriptive Analysis of Words.* Ann Arbor: The University of Michigan Press.
Paardekooper, Piet Cornelis
1955 *Syntaxis, Spraakkunst en Taalkunde* [Syntax, Grammar and Linguistics]. Den Bosch: Malmberg.
Percival, W. Keith
1976 On the historical source of immediate constituent analysis. In: James D. McCawley (ed.), *Notes from the Linguistic Underground*, 229–242. (Syntax and Semantics 7.) New York/San Francisco/London: Academic Press.
Pike, Kenneth L.
1967 [1954] *Language in Relation to a Unified Theory of the Structure of Human Behavior.* The Hague: Mouton. [First put into circulation by Summer Institute of Linguistics, Glendale, California, 1954]
Sapir, Edward
1921 *Language. An Introduction to the Study of Speech,* New York: Harcourt, Brace and Cy.
Scholz, Barbara C., and Geoffrey K. Pullum
2007 Tracking the origins of transformational generative grammar. (Review article of Marcus Tomalin, *Linguistics and the Formal Sciences: The Origins of Gernerative Grammar.* Cambridge, Cambridge University Press, 2006) *Journal of Linguistics* 43.3: 701– 723.

Seuren, Pieter A. M.
1998 *Western Linguistics. An Historical Introduction.* Oxford: Blackwell.
Skinner, Burrhus F.
1957 *Verbal Behavior.* New York: Appleton-Century-Crofts.
Stout, George F.
1896 *Analytical Psychology.* 2 vols. London: Macmillan / New York: Sonnenschein.
Swadesh, Morris
1934 The phonemic principle. *Language* 10.1: 117–129.
Tesnière, Lucien
1959 *Éléments de syntaxe structurale.* Paris: Klincksieck.
Wegener, Philipp
1885 *Untersuchungen über die Grundfragen des Sprachlebens.* Halle: Niemeyer.
Wells, Rulon S.
1947 Immediate constituents. *Language* 23.1: 81–117.
Wundt, Wilhelm
1880 *Logik. Eine Untersuchung der Prinzipien der Erkenntnis und der Methoden Wissenschaftlicher Forschung.* Stuttgart: Enke.
Zholkovsky, Aleksandr K., and Igor A. Mel'čuk
1965 O vozmožnom metode i instrumentax semantičeskogo sinteza [On a possible method and some tools for semantic synthesis]. *Naučno-texničeskaja Informacija* [Scientific and Technological Information] 6: 23–28.

Pieter A. M. Seuren, Nijmegen (Netherlands)

III. Syntactic Phenomena

7. Syntactic Categories and Subcategories

Abstract

The longstanding debate on word classes is still today far from being brought to a conclusion. The challenge approaches to word classes have to face is the need to account for both universality and cross-linguistic variation. A clear definition is further hampered by the multiplicity of criteria. In the context of a comparison of recent approaches, it is argued that the notion of word classes can only be maintained by analyzing them as lexicogrammatical categories. This article offers a survey of the debate on the basic split in full words and particles as well as on the N-V distinction and discusses various other candidates for word classes.

1. Introduction

Morphologically distinct classes of words whose membership is (more or less) identical with that of syntactically-defined word classes (in the sense that their members typically go into certain syntactic slots) and whose semantics, in addition, belong to certain typical denotational areas were first observed by the Ancient Greeks. As far as we know, Plato was the first to make a clear distinction between *onómata* and *rhêmata*, which later came to be translated as *nomina* (nouns) and *verba* (verbs). The terminology was further developed and refined by the Stoics and formalized into a system, which became the standard for Western grammatical tradition, by the Alexandrian grammarians, in particular by Dionysius Thrax (late 2nd century B.C.). In its Latin form, developed by the Roman grammarians of the post-classical antiquity, in particular Priscian (c. 500 A.D), Dionysius' system has survived as an integral part of the most recent formal grammatical theories.

The analysis of syntactic categories was familiar to the traditional grammarians under the title *parts of speech.* The early Stoics (c. 300 B.C.) distinguished between four parts of speech: "nouns", "verbs", "conjunctions" and "articles". Dionysius Thrax introduced a more elaborate system by splitting up the Stoics' classes into an eight-member inventory, consisting of "nouns", "adverbs", "verbs", "participles", "prepositions", "conjunctions", "pronouns", and "articles", which he defined in terms of a combination of denotational and morphological criteria. While the participle class was later done away with as soon as participles came to be regarded as adjectival members of the verbal paradigm, medieval grammarians added two more classes and thus came up with the ten-member system familiar to European school grammar to this day: nouns (substantives), adjectives, adverbs, numerals, pronouns, verbs, prepositions, conjunctions, articles, and interjections (for a recent concise history of parts-of-speech theories cf. Kaltz 2000; cf. also the classic article by Robins 1986). Although this systemization may be justified on formal (morphological) grounds for the Classical Languages, on the basis of which it was developed, problems have arisen from the outset with regard to the criteria underlying the definition of class membership. Early grammarians did not always clearly define the various classes formally, but tended to characterize them in terms of a mixture of morphological, syntactic, and, especially, semantic considerations. In particular, when the classical parts-of-speech system came to be applied to languages other than Latin and Greek, it proved hard to make the formal behavior of words agree with the definitional criteria of parts of speech worked out for the Classical languages. The reason is that classical parts-of-speech definitions were usually applied indiscriminately and without regard for the actual morphosyntactic phenomena observed in the language under analysis. "At least three different strands must be unravelled in the rather tangled skein which makes up the traditional theory of the parts-of-speech: the morphological, the syntactic, and the semantic" (Lyons 1977: 425). In order to find a way out of this dilemma, structural linguists replaced the traditional parts-of-speech concept by the notion of *word classes* and developed the idea that "in the grammatical analysis of languages words are assigned to word classes on the formal basis of syntactic behaviour, supplemented and reinforced by differences of morphological paradigms, so that every word in a language is a member of a word class" (Robins 1965: 227). Moreover, "where there is a conflict between syntactic and morphological classification, syntax is almost always accorded precedenc" (Robins 1965: 226). For example, the English adjectives *pretty* and *beautiful* differ in their morphological capacities, in that *pretty* is inflected for comparison (*prettier, prettiest*), while *beautiful* is invariable. Nevertheless, both words are treated as members of one class, because syntactically their relations with nouns and words of other classes in sentences are the same.

The primacy of the syntactic criterion was also accepted in the theoretical framework of Transformational Grammar and is reflected in the widely used modern term *syntactic categories*, which replaced "word classes" in more formally oriented theories of grammar. However, whereas the concern of structuralism was the development of a method to identify word classes in the course of the analysis of a particular language, Transformational Grammar took for granted that syntactic categories are undefined primitives without any semantic (let alone pragmatic) significance. The arbitrary category symbols N (noun), V (verb), A (adjective) and so on, taken over from traditional grammar without any closer examination, were regarded as innate substantive universals. Thus, there is an enormous difference between structuralist "word classes" and transformationalist "syntactic categories": the former are item classes established according to their distributive behavior, while the latter are formal symbols established by an axiomatic theory. Later varieties of Generative Grammar (X-bar-theory, LFG, and others) have modified the concept of syntactic category to the effect that the symbols N, V, etc. were now treated as syntactic features. This allowed for cross-classifications or generalizing subsumptions of syntactic categories to help avoid transformations; it was thus a theory-immanent modification born by the desire of post-TG generativists to dispense with transformations rather than based on an empirical hypothesis. The syntactic features N, V, etc. remain as undefined as their categorial predecessors.

A formal treatment of syntactic categories differing from that of Generative Grammar can be found in Categorial Grammar (cf. Schmerling 1983), which provides definitions of categories in terms of their valency. For some criticism of this early approach see Croft (1984: 56). In spite of Croft's counterarguments, Gil (2000) insists on Categorial Grammar being the most adequate framework for the typological investigation of syntactic categories.

The major problems with which both traditional and modern approaches to syntactic categories or word classes are confronted may be summarized as follows. First of all, word class systems, though similar enough in the languages of the world to suggest universal treatment, nevertheless exhibit a great deal of cross-linguistic variation. As a result, neither the transfer of the situation of Latin or a handful of Standard Average European languages to language in general, nor a preconceived formal theory can lead to any significant progress in our understanding of syntactic categories. In particular, there is a notorious confusion of lexical and syntactic categories, for instance by the use of the term syntactic categories for both, as in this article. This confusion ultimately results from the myth of the "projection line", i.e. the erroneous belief that languages universally display a perfect X:XP match (where X is a lexical, XP a phrasal category with X as its head). The problematic cases of word class-distinction discussed in section 5 show that this is not necessarily the case. A theory of word classes must therefore be backed up by intensive cross-linguistic research in order to obtain a picture of typological variation and its limits, of the universality of certain categories, of the cross-linguistic variability within a single category, etc. Secondly, a clear understanding of syntactic categories is severely hampered by the multiplicity of criteria, which has caused considerable confusion, especially in the application of the traditional parts-of-speech concept to non-European languages. The various criteria involved in the formation of word class systems must be factorized in order to obtain a methodologically and theoretically sound approach to word classes applicable to all languages of the world (for a metatheoretical evaluation of criteria for word classes cf. Knobloch and Schaeder 2000). In the following discussion we will keep both sets of problems in mind. We will first examine the different traditional criteria proposed for the definition of word classes one by one. We will then sketch some recent approaches to word classes in order to set the stage for the discussion of the current issues of research in this area; and we will finally examine the traditional inventory of major and minor syntactic categories with regard to the problem of their "universal" syntactic and lexical applicability.

Before doing this, however, let us clear up a number of terminological distinctions. Lyons (1977) makes a threefold distinction between parts of speech, form classes, and expression classes. He argues that the term part of speech should be restricted to *lexemes* and *expressions*. "We will assume that every word-lexeme is assigned, in the analysis of any language system, to one, and only one, such class" (1977: 423). In the following we will call such classes *word classes* or *categories*. By using the term category as it is traditionally applied in linguistics, we imply that class membership is *mandatorily* assigned to any given lexical item.

In Lyons' sense, word classes are primarily *lexical categories* that manifest themselves as *expressions in the syntax*. *Form class,* on the other hand, is defined in terms of syntactic equivalence: "Two forms, f_i and f_j, are members of the same form class F_x if and only if they are intersubstitutable (i.e. have the same distribution) throughout the sentences of the language (...) Given that 'come' is a verb and that *come, comes, coming* and *came* are its forms, we will say that they are all verb-forms" (1977: 424). *Expression classes* are defined in a similar way in terms of distribution ("two expressions, e_i and e_j, are members of the same expression class E_x if and only if they can be substituted one for the other throughout the sentences of the language"). The difference between parts of speech or word classes as lexical categories, and expression classes as syntactic categories, can be explained in terms of another distinction frequently found in the literature, that between *function* and *class*. An expression class comprises all expressions that share the same function, i.e. that are paradigmatically interchangeable within one functional slot. The expression class is larger than the corresponding word class and fully subsumes the latter. For instance, the expression class of nominals (it has become accepted usage to name expression classes by terms ending in *-(i)al*, e.g. *nominal*, *verbal*, *adjectival*, *adverbial*, etc.) in English contains any kind of noun phrase, so-called absolute or headless (or substantivized) adjectives, some types of constituent clause etc., but it also contains pure nouns as one of its subsets. Moreover, the word class is the most basic subset of an expression class, in other words a *prototypical* member. A prototypical member is the main member of a category on which the category type's structure and behavior is modeled.

If word classes are both lexical and syntactic categories, as Lyons' approach seems to imply, the question arises as to what to do with the many phenomena of mismatching between lexicon and syntax that are described for the languages of the world. There are at least two common types of mismatching that are particularly disturbing for a theory of word classes: (1) cases in which multiple categorization suggests itself (e.g. *iron* in *Iron melts at...* vs. *iron shackles*), (2) syntactic neutralization of lexically assigned membership in certain environments. As for (1), linguistic tradition provides a number of repair strategies: (a) the item in question is assigned multiple class membership (this practice is common in lexicography, e.g. two entries for *iron*: $iron^1$ = noun, $iron^2$ = adjective); (b) one of the senses is regarded as basic, the other(s) as derived by conversion (zero-derivation) (e.g. *iron* [noun] → *iron* [adj]); (c) underspecification (in the lexicon, category membership remains unassigned). As for (2), it is common practice to ignore syntactic neutralization, by assigning lexically-determined class membership rather than postulating syntactically-defined hypercategories.

Problematic as such cases may be even in the description of well-investigated Standard European languages, they usually concern only specific parts of the vocabulary in these languages (most frequently adjective vs. noun, adjective vs. adverb, see sections 6 and 7). Things become really explosive in certain language families such as Austronesian, where they affect all major categories and thus pertain to the entire vocabulary. Not surprisingly, dictionaries of such languages often resort to the assignment of word classes on the basis of the system of the target language. In a standard Tongan dictionary,

I have come across up to seven distinct word-class labels assigned to a single lexical item, which, as expected, neatly corresponded to the respective English translations. Moreover, when comparing dictionaries, one will be surprised at the inconsistency among lexicographers even in their application of multiple categorization (cf. Behrens 1994 on Tagalog). The results of such investigations reveal strong indications that the word class systems of these languages are far from being understood. We will come back to these issues in section 5.

2. Criteria for establishing word classes

2.1. Semantic criteria

In many popular text books and teaching grammars one finds reflections of the naive view that nouns (substantives) denote persons or things, verbs denote actions, adjectives denote properties, and so on. The German terms *Dingwort*, *Tätigkeitswort* and *Eigenschaftswort* neatly mirror such a semantically-based categorization, which, as indicated above, can be traced back to the Alexandrian grammarians. It has repeatedly been pointed out in the literature (cf. among many others especially Fries 1952 and Schachter 1985) that purely a semantic conception of word classes, however intuitively motivated and anchored in our *Sprachgefühl* it may be, fails to provide an adequate basis for establishing the word classes of a specific language. There is no language where one doesn't find an enormous amount of disagreement between semantic and lexical classes. If we take nouns as an example, it begins with the difficulty of applying the criterion of "thingness" to such immaterial entities as 'sky' and ends with total confusion with regards to abstracts and verbal nouns (How can we say that drunkenness or swimming are things?). Problems of this kind have been discussed as early as in Hermann (1928) and turned into a cliché by many authors (e.g. Palmer 1978: 39; Croft 2000: 65–66). Consequently, a criterion for establishing word classes on the basis of lexical semantic classification appears at the very outset to be neither necessary nor sufficient.

This should not prevent us from asking if a semantic viewpoint could not help us to motivate word class distinctions on a universal basis. It could be argued that the inventory of full words in the lexicon of a language, i.e. the signs that stand for the notions by which human beings classify their impressions of the real world, is divided up into various semantic groups such as individuals, materials, qualities of different sorts, states, processes, and so on (ontological categories). Such a rough language-economic semantic categorization could be taken to constitute the functional aim of the classification of lexical items into word classes at a universal level, while language-specific inconsistencies between semantic and morphosyntactic classes could remain disturbing factors yet to be worked out. Such an assumption seems to be implicit in Dixon`s brilliant article ([1977], re-issued 1982) on adjectives. Dixon suggests that the lexical items of a language fall into a number of semantic types, each of which has a basic or norm connection with a single part of speech. Subsequently, there have been several approaches concerned with further refinement of a semantic theory of word classes along these lines. For instance, Wierzbicka (1986) has shown that the difference between nouns (substantives) and adjectives can be explained in terms of categorization and description: property concepts tend to be designated by nouns rather than adjectives when characterizing an individual by a permanent and/or conspicuous and/or important quality (put in a different terminology, individual-level properties), because nouns indicate a categorization, while adjectives (or stative verbs), on the other hand, indicate a mere description and are thus suitable for the expression of temporary and/or non-conspicuous (stage-level) properties. This can be confirmed by evidence from languages totally lacking the category of adjectives (cf. below). Langacker (1987) has argued that the distinction between nouns and verbs is susceptible to notional characterization within a cognitive framework. His proposal of cognitive semantic notions for "nominal" and "verbal" concepts differs considerably from the traditional narrow notions of "thing" and "activity", but is certainly related in a more abstract sense. Special attention must finally be paid to a number of studies, beginning in the early 1980s, that limit semantic characterizations of word classes to category prototypes. Some scholars have suggested that objects are prototypical (central members) for nouns, properties for adjectives and actions for verbs (Croft 1984, 1991, 2000; Givon 1984; Hopper and Thompson 1984, 1985; and, with regard to language acquisition, Bates and MacWhinney 1982). Predecessors of the prototype approach (which has often been implicit in semantic analyses of parts-of-speech systems) are Lyons (1968: 318) and Coseriu (1987 [translation of the Spanish original of 1955]).

Though all these studies have increased our understanding of the semantics of word classes considerably, a definition of word classes in purely semantic terms continues to be problematic, if not untenable. In the analysis of a specific language even refined notions such as those of Langacker's do not provide a discovery procedure for parts of speech identification, and from a universalist point of view semantics does not suffice for understanding the motivation of the existence of word classes in language, because given the immense number of possibilities for a semantic classification of words, it is not easy to demonstrate, by mere semantic arguments, why it is this rather limited special set of classes that is so widespread among many languages, and why others do it differently (Broschart 1997).

2.2. Syntactic criteria

Another frequently discussed explanation for the existence of word classes in language is that they are primarily of a functional rather than of a categorial nature. It has been maintained (cf. especially Benveniste 1966; also Lyons 1977: 423–425; Hagège 1982: 72 for the earliest proponents of this view) that the formation of parts of speech systems is in some sense subsidiary and hence secondary to the basic syntactic relations. It is assumed that the lexical material of a language is *preclassified* in such a way that it is ready to serve certain important syntactic functions such as subject, predicate, attribute, etc. Benveniste has drawn special attention to the fact that the verb meaning always includes a component of existence ('being') which is responsible for its predicative force, and that this can be explained by the assumption that the prime task of verbs is predication. Lyons even goes so far as to say: "(...) it is generally accepted that this distinction [i.e. that between nouns and verbs] is intrinsically bound up with the difference between reference and predication" (1977: 429).

If taken as the sole criterion for establishing word classes, the syntactic argument is faced with the same problems as the semantic one. Its lack of absoluteness (nouns cannot be identified with subjects and objects – nor with arguments –, not even with referential expressions; predicativity is not confined to verbs, etc.) prevents its application as a discovery procedure in the analysis of a particular language. As far as universal (cross-linguistic) considerations are concerned, it is in fact tempting to attribute the constitution of parts of speech systems to the syntactic organization of human language – in the sense that word classes were to be defined as those subgroups of the lexicon which are likely to occur in and hence are destined for certain syntactic functions –, were it not for the fact that syntax itself is not primary, so that the syntactic relations word classes are said to be made up for are in need of explanation themselves.

Moreover, it is not seldom that authors referring to syntactic functions fail to make explicit the kind of function they have in mind. There are several candidates: syntactic slots (German *Satzglieder*), basic syntactic relations (such as argument, predicate, attribute), phrases (conceived as endocentric constructions with a unique head), and perhaps others. What kind of functions are word classes supposed to serve? When speaking of reference and predication, do we really mean syntactic functions or, rather, discourse-pragmatic operations (cf. next paragraph)? Cross-linguistically, we do not find a perfect match between formally-defined parts of speech as lexical categories and any one of the syntactic notions enumerated above.

2.3. Pragmatic criteria

Some insight into the nature of syntactic relations can perhaps be gained if one considers the fact that the structure of sentences is dependent on discourse as the larger linguistic unit they are embedded in. There have been attempts to derive the opposition of nouns and verbs from the discourse-pragmatic categories of topic and comment. This very plausible hypothesis receives support from the observation that cross-linguistically, the topic function seems to be reserved to nouns and noun-like constructions, while verbs normally form the central part of the comment. This theory has been refined in the 1980s by a number of scholars, notably Hopper and Thompson (1984, 1985). They argue that the make-up of nouns, from a discourse point of view, originates in the need of a word class that functions to introduce participants and "props" and to deploy and manoeuver them around, whereas verbs serve to report events. In their (1985) paper they introduce what they call the "Iconicity Principle", which says that "the more a form refers to a discrete discourse event, the more distinct will be its linguistic form from neighboring forms, both paradigmatically and syntagmatically" (Hopper and Thompson 1985: 151). With the help of examples from a considerable number of languages all over the world they try to demonstrate that the occurrence of the constitutive morphosyntactic characteristics of nouns and verbs is proportional to their denoting discourse-manipulable entities or events.

The discourse criterion can be taken to embrace the syntactic criterion if one accepts the view that syntactic relations merely express pragmatic relations. It has in common with the syntactic and semantic criteria the dependence on prototype analysis and inability to account for parts of speech systems in individual languages. It can nevertheless help us in understanding the general mechanisms which lead to the constitution of word classes (see below).

2.4. Morphosyntactic criteria

The language-specific difficulties discussed so far and the problem of the impossibility of a single criterion to account for them is often believed to be overcome once morphosyntactic criteria are taken into account. As noted above, it has been recognized by many scholars (particularly during the structuralist era) that the language-specific analysis of word class systems must start from the observation of formal differences in the behavior of lexical categories. Morphology (both inflectional and derivational) plays a central role here. It is only on the basis of phenomena such as declension, conjugation, motion of gender, etc. that we can speak of clear-cut form classes in Classical Languages such as Latin or Greek. In these and similar languages, each word class is established with regard to its specific inflectional make-up. We can distinguish between *category-establishing* morphology and *category-changing* morphology. The former indicates "grammemes" (grams) which have to do with the main function of the categories in question (e.g. gender, number, case for nouns, comparison for adjectives and tense, aspect, mood and person for verbs) and are therefore constitutive. The latter serves to transpose lexical material from one category to another; i.e. it is a mechanism whereby lexical items dispense with the category-establishing morphology of one category and acquire that of another category. This can be done by mere conversion (zero-derivation); or by means of derivational morphology. In the simplest case, a noun may acquire verbal syntactic behavior by taking verb morphology, or a verb may become suitable to fit into a nominal position by taking noun morphology. More often, however, category changes are connected with certain additional semantic features such as causativization, derivation of *nomina participantis* (argument nominalization: noun of agent / patient / beneficiary / instrument / location, etc.), and so on. It was this insight that led ancient grammarians to their basically morphological-cum-semantic parts-of speech definitions.

Observation of category-establishing and category-changing morphosyntactic behavior in the analysis of a particular language can thus exploited for establishing definitional characteristics for parts-of-speech classification. This would provide us with a discovery procedure to fix the word classes of a single language: we would distinguish as many word classes as different morphological behavior can be observed. In other words, we would refrain from the traditional practice of vindicating the application of the established (Eurocentric) inventory of word classes for any new language under analysis, but proceed the other way round: we would first define the distributional characteristics of word forms in a particular language and later decide whether or not we find them sufficiently similar to the established categories of other languages to justify the application of the same superordinate concept. It might thus turn out – or not – that in some cases the categories so established bear a certain family resemblance among each other, so that grouping them together as, say, "the cross-linguistic family of adjectives consisting of {Adj_{L1}, Adj_{L2}, …, Adj_{Ln}}" may hopefully lead to an interesting linguistic hypothesis.

This procedure is of course problematic, as it depends on the morphological type of a language. Conditions in isolating languages are different. In such languages, syntagmatic co-occurrence restrictions will have to serve as the sole basis of dividing lexical items into form classes. One could object that this is not a problem, given the fact that morphosyntactic criteria for establishing word classes anyhow include co-occurrence restrictions, even in languages with rich morphology. Distributional analysis must therefore be prior to morphological analysis. This view would side-step a general problem of distributional analysis: if we attempt to establish syntactic categories on the basis of distribution, we need a criterion that sets certain limits (Plank 1984; Croft 2000: 76–78; see section 3.1 below). A quick look into the literature on parts of speech in such well-investigated languages such as English and German shows that proposals range anywhere from eight to some fifty (cf. Bergenholtz 1983 on German; Jespersen 1924: 58–60 on English).

At any rate, the majority of researchers in the field today appear to agree on the importance of distributional analysis involving both morphology and co-occurrence restrictions. However, it cannot be the sole criterion and thus will meet the fate of all the other criteria discussed so far. The traditional linguistic notion of word classes has always been one of partitioning a language's vocabulary with reference to the correspondence between ontological categories and syntactic environments held to be basic and important. This is something that strongly calls for a lexical perspective in addition to a morphosyntactic one. Thus, if we want to maintain this view and not abandon word classes altogether, we must analyze them as lexicogrammatical categories, i.e. as both lexical and syntactic categories. We will come back to this issue in 3.2 below.

3. Current issues in word class research

3.1. Some recent approaches

The articles in Vogel and Comrie (2000) provide a good overview of the more recent landscape of cross-linguistic word class research and its central controversies and proposals. The most fundamental point in dispute – and unsolved to this day chiefly because of incompatible research interests and approaches – is the universality of word classes. Bhat (2000: 61) distinguishes between "two conflicting approaches to typology", which he calls "Universalistic" and "Differentiating"; "the former emphasises the similarities that occur among the languages of the world, whereas the latter emphasises the differences". He concludes: "The claims about the universality of word class distinctions (…) is now rightly being questioned by a Differentiating approach. (…) I believe that the postulation of distinctions in the sentence strategies that are in use, and the sentential functions which result (or do not result) from them, provide sufficient basis for making such a differentiating claim regarding word classes." This is echoed by Gil (2000: 174): "[C]ross-linguistic variation with respect to syntactic categories poses a serious challenge to conventional approaches to syntactic theory, underscoring the need to escape from the straightjacket of traditional Eurocentricity. However, breaking away from preconceived notions entails a reorientation of one's basic mode of investigation. Rather than asking "Is this form an X or a Y…?", the more appropriate question to ask is "What are the significant syntactic patterns in the language, and what are the categories that must be posited in order to enable the necessary generalisations to be stated?".

The notion of universality comes in several slightly different senses. One is based on the belief that there exists a universal set of holistic categories. The more rigorous proponents of such a view claim that these are anchored somewhere in the human being (where? in the bioprogram? genetically determined?) and, consequently, all languages have them, regardless of whether or not substantive evidence can be found. This approach is implicit in the earlier generativist literature, though seldom explicitly stated. A weaker hypothesis is the one that allows for cross-linguistic variation, here understood as a difference in the languages' availing themselves of the universal pot. According to this approach, some languages lack certain categories, or, in a language-specific way, lump categories together that others differentiate, or establish different hierarchies between the universal categories. A good example of the latter strategy is the family of Functional Grammar approaches to word classes (Hengeveld 1992, etc., cf. below).

A different sense of "universal" conceives of this notion as an opposite to "language-particular". This is the path pursued by Croft in his work on syntactic categories, based on the idea of typological prototypes. "Noun, verb and adjective are not categories of particular languages. (...) But noun, verb and adjective are language universals – that is, they are typological prototypes (...)" (2000: 65); more generally, "parts of speech are not grammatical categories of particular languages" (2000: 67). In the following, we will briefly sketch some of these recent approaches; for a more comprehensive overview cf. Rijkhoff (2007: 711–713).

3.1.1. Croft (1984, 1991, 2000)

Since the early nineteen-eighties, some scholars have set forth approaches which combine prototype theory with the idea that syntactic relations are nothing but formal manifestations of combined semantic and pragmatic content (Croft 1984, 1991, 2000; Hopper and Thompson 1984, 1985; Broschart 1987). Croft, who characterizes a linguistic prototype as a morphosyntactically unmarked, natural correlation, originally proposed the following chart for prototypical combinations of semantic and discourse-pragmatic features for nouns, adjectives and verbs (1984, refined in 1991, repeated in 2000):

(1) Tab. 7.1: Prototypical combinations of semantic and discourse-pragmatic features for nouns, adjectives and verbs

	REFERENCE	MODIFICATION	PREDICATION
OBJECTS	**unmarked nouns**	genitive, adjectivalization, PPs on nouns	predicate nominals, copulas
PROPERTIES	deadjectival nouns	**unmarked adjectives**	predicate adjectives, copulas
ACTIONS	action nominals, complements, infinitives, gerunds	participles, relative clauses	**unmarked verbs**

This approach combines theories of "typological markedness" with the cognitivist idea of "prototypicality". On the face of it, it does not differ significantly from Broschart (1987) and Hengeveld (1992) in its distinction between unmarked and marked constellations: in all three approaches it is assumed that the prototype reveals itself by unmarked morphosyntax, while deviations from it need special devices. Where it differs is in its emphasis on the cross-classification of discourse-semantic and lexical-semantic (in this case ontological) features. Word classes are thus defined universally as the attempt of languages (or their speakers) to partition their vocabulary with regard to the most basic discourse operations, which, in turn, are prototypically correlated with ontological categories. Category-changing morphology (or any other spectacular device such as copulas) indicates the extent to which a member of a certain word class deviates from the prototype: "derivational morphology and special syntactic constructions such as English *be* + N, A for predication (...) exist in order to signal the markedness of 'unnatural' correlations" (Croft 1984: 57). A similar view had been expressed by Hopper and Thompson.

The motivation for Croft's approach is twofold (cf. Croft 2000: esp. 72–74). On the one hand, he attempts to incorporate the insight, extensively discussed in section 2 of this article, that parts of speech are multifactor concepts that cannot be defined in terms of a single criterion. The identification of the syntactic functions of word classes does not suffice: it must be supplemented by semantic criteria. On the other hand, the model is designed to achieve cross-linguistic comparability. He argues at length that cross-linguistic comparability cannot be attained through the distributional analysis of specific languages because it "not only reveals a myriad of syntactic classes, but also reveals sometimes fuzzy category behavior at the boundaries of those classes" (2000: 81).

These considerations lead Croft to a prototype theory of parts of speech as universal categories, as outlined above. However, their connections to language-specific categorizations remain obscure: "Noun, verb and adjective are not categories of particular languages" (2000: 65). Nothing is said about how to correlate the universal prototypes with language-specific word-class systems.

3.1.2. Hengeveld (1992)

Within a Functional Grammar (FG) framework, Hengeveld (1992: 58) proposes the following typology of parts-of-speech systems (where the terms "predicate" and "term" have their usual formal logic-based FG meanings):

> A *verbal* predicate is a predicate which, without further measures being taken, has a predicative use *only*.
>
> A *nominal* predicate is a predicate which, without further measures being taken, can be used as the head of a term.
>
> An *adjectival* predicate is a predicate which, without further measures being taken, can be used as a modifier of a nominal head.
>
> An *adverbial* predicate is a predicate which, without further measures being taken, can be used as a modifier of a non-nominal head.

Superficially, this approach relies on the same idea of "typological markedness": that, which Hengeveld means by "without further measures being taken" is the unmarked morphosyntactic constellation, i.e. the one typical for the use of a given lexical item in the appropriate function. The "further measures" then indicate marked constellations (e.g. the use of copulas to signal nouns in predicative function). The fundamental difference between Croft's and Hengeveld's approaches lies in the fact that the latter does not correlate the three basic discourse-pragmatic operations with ontological categories such as objects, properties and actions, but relies exclusively on syntactic relations (predicate [of sentence or clause], head, modifier). This might be regarded as an advantage since it would open up the possibility to escape Eurocentrism and to allow for more exotic syntacto-semantic associations, but it may also constitute a drawback when leading to the neglect of semantic considerations altogether.

In addition to the definition of the four major syntactic categories, a further important cornerstone of Hengeveld's approach is his distinction between two hyper-types of language, which he calls *flexible* and *rigid* (or *specialized*). In the former, two or more categories fall together because unmarked and marked constellations cannot be distinguished by means of any formal indications, be it morphological or topological. For example, when "nouns" and "adjectives" share the same morphosyntax in all their fundamental syntactic positions, they are lumped together into a hyper-category (N/A). In the specialized or rigid type, one option is all of the major categories being distinguished, because all of them are characterized by their specific differences between normal measures and further measures, so that the full inventory is posited. The other option is two or more categories falling together because they share the normal measures and further measures typical for one of them. Category A is then subsumed under category B, and the language is said to lack category A (or, when there are some slight differences, A may be regarded as a subcategory of B). For example, when "verbs" and "adjectives" share the same morphosyntax in all their fundamental syntactic positions and, in addition, this morphosyntax is considered typically verbal, the resulting category is labeled "verb" and the language is said to lack adjectives.

Hengeveld's approach has a number of deficiencies, most of which have already been discussed in the recent literature on syntactic categories and need not be repeated in detail here. With regard to one, the basis for distinguishing between "lack of category distinction" (flexible) and "lack of a category" (rigid) is not always clear. The decision on which language falls into which type calls for strict criteria for typical morphosyntactic behavior of categories on a universal basis, which are not in sight. Another general point of criticism is that the approach is too coarse-grained and cannot cope with subtler problems of distribution, let alone semantics. For further criticism see Croft (2000).

3.1.3. Hengeveld et al. (2004)

Hengeveld, Rijkhoff, and Siewierska (2004) is a follow-up to Hengeveld's (1992) study, also cast in an FG framework. Its main concern is with the idea that the word order possibilities of a language are in part determined by the parts-of-speech system of that language. We will not go into this here. What is, however, of interest in the context of this article is the innovations of this approach vis-à-vis Hengeveld (1992). Two such innovations shall be briefly discussed below.

The two types of flexible and rigid systems are now replaced by a threefold distinction between *differentiated*, *flexible* and *rigid* systems. The differentiated type grew out of the former rigid type by splitting off those languages in which all four categories can be distinguished (differentiating) from the rest in which certain categories are lacking (rigid).

The second innovation is the postulation of a parts-of-speech hierarchy. It is said that flexibility/rigidity is gradual, and differs from language to language. "[T]he combinations of syntactic possibilities for a single lexical class in flexible languages and the lack of lexical classes for certain syntactic slots in rigid languages are not random" (2004: 533). This variation is attributed to the following hierarchy:

(2) Head of predicate phrase	>	Head of referential phrase	>	Modifier of referential phrase	>	Modifier of predicate phrase

Fig. 8.1. Parts-of-speech hierarchy

"The parts-of speech hierarchy should be interpreted in the following way: the more to the left a certain syntactic slot is positioned in the hierarchy, the more likely it is for a language to have a separate class of lexemes for that syntactic slot" (2004: 533). One of their examples is the distinction between adjectives and (manner) adverbs (positions 3 and 4 in the hierarchy): if a rigid language lacks adjectives, it will also lack manner adverbs.

Even if a number of possibly valid predictions may be borne out by this hierarchy, it still fails to account for the subtler mismatching problems mentioned in section 1. What if a language distinguishes categories A and B in certain environments but not in those held indicative of class membership? What about a possible conflict between morphological and syntactic criteria? What about unexpected overlapping (e.g. predicative adjectives and manner adverbs in German, cf. section 7)? What about cases of languages displaying a comparably weak distinction between categories at a higher level of the hierarchy while still presenting evidence for a distinction at a lower level (e.g. weak N-A distinction in Turkish despite the presence of manner adverbs, cf. section 7)?

3.2. Word classes / Parts of speech as lexicogrammatical categories

On the general idea of linguistic categorizing always being a matter of a composite lexicogrammar cf. Behrens (1995); specifically on word classes as lexicogrammatical entities see Sasse (2005).

Alexandrian grammarians pointed out as early as two millennia ago (see section 1) that Greek nouns are characterized (or even defined) by their displaying of the morphological categories of gender, number, and case, while verbs have tense, mood, and voice. Moreover, it is said that their word forms are mutually exclusive in certain basic syntactic positions, which we today would characterize in terms of "predicate" and "argument" positions. Finally, they differ in their denotational potential. Over the past 2000 years, major lexical categorizations (in the sense of word classes in lexicography) have always been categorizations between lexicon and grammar.

Word classes partition a language's vocabulary in terms of their ability to enter certain constructional slots. It follows from this that word classes have to be investigated along two dimensions: (1) the lexical dimension (word classes as lexical-semantic categories); (2) the morphosyntactic dimension (word classes as syntactic categories defined in terms of constructional slots). It will then be decided on the interactional patterns that emerge between the two. This must be done for every language separately. As far as the question of comparability is concerned, one must be ready to acknowledge not only systems that differ from the classic one in their finetuning, but also be open to the possibility that there exist systems that differ more radically in their organizational principles. It is the relationship between these two dimensions which most clearly defines the "lexicogrammatical type" of a language: given a certain slot in a construction, there will be lexical material that typically enters into that slot.

Word classes, then, are the largest and most influential lexicogrammatical categories, those which enter the most comprehensive macroparadigms, and for which the highest degree of lexical sensitivity in grammatical phenomena can be expected. Consequently, if we assume cross-linguistic differences in principles of lexical categorization, we will also have to expect different types of interaction between lexicon and grammar in each of these different systems. Thus, the division of a language's lexicon into major lexical categories or "parts of speech" penetrates its entire morphosyntactic system. And conversely, it is morphosyntactic structure that determines the partition of the lexicon into major (and even minor) lexical categories.

Summing up, the problem of syntactic categories cannot be solved by rescuing the traditional Eurocentric notions redefining them as typological prototypes. It cannot be solved either by assuming that there is a universal inventory of such categories, out of which every particular language makes its individual choice. It can only be solved by abandoning both the traditional levels of analysis (i.e. the idea that morphology, syntax, and lexicon always operate in the same way as we are accustomed from well-investigated Standard European Languages) and traditional ideas of word classes. The perspectives for future fruitful research lie in the recognition of the possibility of languages displaying a variety of lexicogrammatical types, e.g. the possibility that a different organization of morphosyntactic levels (as, for example, evident in polysynthetic languages) may go hand in hand with a different organization in lexical categories.

4. The basic split: full words vs. particles

There is no language which does not possess at least two basic types of words (cf. Hockett 1966: 21; Gleason 1961: 156–159, and elsewhere in structuralist literature). All have a class that contains items having clear semantic content, i.e. is made up of words denoting persons, things, places, states, events, properties and so on. Examples of this class in English are *boy, toy, town, know, play, beautiful*. The other class contains items which lack such concrete meanings and merely serve to mark certain syntactic functions, acting as operators of morphosyntactic categories and relations. Examples of this class in English are *the, of, by, but, and, just, when, if.* Various terms have been proposed in the literature for this distinction. The class of words having "meaning" is often called major words or content words, while the other class is called function words. Another pair of terms is *autosemantica* ('words that have semantics by themselves') and *synsemantica* ('words that acquire semantics by combination with other words'). For Nootka, Swadesh (1939) simply speaks of words and particles; this would be adequate for a number of other languages (e.g. Northern Iroquoian), too, whose particles are not necessarily function words in the strictest sense. For the present purpose I will use the neutral terminology *full words* vs. *particles*, because it is often not easy to decide where the exact boundary between "meaning" and "function" is. For instance Tagalog *mga* 'plural' and Cayuga *ó:nę̨* 'now' are clearly particles as far as the grammatical structure of the languages is concerned, but both have relatively concrete meanings.

The two classes are sometimes clearly distinct, but there are often residual forms that do not easily lend themselves to classification. The most problematic examples are adpositions (see below), which often betray their nominal or verbal origin and therefore have, to a considerable degree, concrete meanings, without, however, being susceptible to free syntactic manipulation. The reason is that function words normally arise by means of the grammaticalization of nouns or verbs (cf. the article on the origins of *synsemantica* in vol. II), in the course of which they gradually lose their semantic content and build up pure relational functions. Full words and particles are therefore discrete only on the edges of a continuum of grammaticalization. One and the same function word class in a single language may contain different strata of grammaticalization, e.g. regarding English prepositions, *of* is more grammaticalized than *under,* and this in turn is more grammaticalized than combined prepositional expressions such as *by means of.* There have been attempts to equate the distinction between full words and particles with the distinction of *open* and *closed* classes (cf. Fries 1952; Robins 1965: 230; Schachter 1985: 4–5). This is hardly tenable since it has been found that words with clear semantic content may occur in closed classes. Dixon has shown that in many languages adjectives are members of a closed class. In many Northern Australian languages, finite verbs are a closed class (Schultze-Berndt 2000) Furthermore, there are cases of very distinct closed subclasses such as locational nouns and kinship verbs (cf. Evans 2000a).

It has sometimes been claimed that there are languages which have no particles at all. Instances cited as evidence for this claim have been Eskimo and Yana (cf. Schachter 1985: 5, 23–24). In both cases the claim is unfounded; both languages do possess particles. Nevertheless, it has been proposed by Schachter that the number of particles or at least the importance of the role they play in the grammatical system of a language depends on their position in the analytic/synthetic scale of that language: highly analytic languages tend to have many particles, because they need function words in order to signal the grammatical categories they are unable to express differently due to lack of morphology, while highly synthetic languages tend to have fewer particles. Even the validity of this claim can be questioned: Northern Iroquoian, which is a group of languages of extremely synthetic character, abounds in particles. What Schachter had in mind was particles such as the English *of* ("compensating" for the "lack" of a synthetic genitive), but even if a language lacks this type of particles, there may well be particles of other types such as modal or discourse particles. In any case it is a fact that particles often compensate for a lack of morphology in analytic languages.

The difference between full words and particles also plays a role in the phenomenology of aphasia and dyslexia, cf. Garman (1990). The dropping of particles has been a long-standing defining characteristic of Broca aphasia, and visual dyslexia patients have significantly more problems with reading particles than with reading full words.

5. Noun and verb

5.1. On the universality of the N-V distinction

There has been a long-standing and heated dispute over the universality of the distinction between nouns and verbs. Hair-splitting arguments have been used to defend the different stances. Even among those scholars who admit that adjectives may not be a universal category (cf. section 6) there are many who believe in the universality of the noun-verb distinction. For the present exposition we will assume that they are not universal, at least not in the sense of universal holistic categories. As pointed out in Sasse (1993), a language's system of major syntactic categories can never be identical to that of any other language because "parts of speech" and their associated patterns of grammatical behavior observed in a given language at a given historical stage are temporary results of grammaticalization and lexicalization processes. These categories are dynamic and thus subject to continuous change and reflect a particular language's individual history. Major syntactic categories are grammatical-semantic classes, as discussed in section 3.2, rather than purely semantic classes. This alone a priori invalidates the naive reasoning, often uttered informally by advocates of the universalist hypothesis, that the distinction between nouns and verbs must be present in every language because every human must be able to distinguish between objects and situations. Cues for the ontological interpretation of lexical elements may be created in different ways, not necessarily by partitioning the content words of a language into two major classes on the basis of complementary inflectional paradigms.

Thus, we have to conclude that nouns, verbs, adjectives, etc., are types of major lexical/syntactic categories whose tokens may resemble each other in different languages due to similarities in the interaction between lexicon and grammar, even though their categorial make-up may not be identical across the languages. It may well be that the majority of languages possess comparable classes, which we then term "nouns", "verbs", and "adjectives", so that these classes represent tokens of very wide-spread, even almost near-universal types. One may speculate that this is perhaps attributable to the fact that they answer fundamental necessities of human communication along the lines of Croft's approach (such as the deployment of objects as discourse referents, the identification of subsets of objects in terms of properties, and the description of situations in which these objects are involved), which manifest themselves in a parallel morphosyntactic division, at the utterance level, into information units representing arguments, attributes, and predicates. The conclusion often drawn from these considerations is that the familiar types of categories must be universal precisely because they are based on these functional needs. Minor differences in the tokens of such universal category types are believed to be due to differences in the language-specific grammatical machinery; even if the degree of distinction is low, it is claimed that there are always some grammatical environments that render a distinction necessary. However, this view tends to obscure the understanding of the actual situation rather than contribute to deeper insights. Not only do the tokens of these types differ across the languages of the world, there also seem to be languages which simply lack grammatical macroparadigms partitioning the lexicon into major lexical categories.

To get an impression of the way such a situation is manifested in individual languages and how it leads to controversies, we will take a brief look at a group of languages for which the absence of a noun/verb distinction has been vehemently disputed in the literature. There are three geographic areas for which the noun-verb distinction has been frequently called into question, viz. Oceanic languages, Philippine languages, and certain North American languages. We will begin with Oceanic.

When we attempt to answer the question which grammatical phenomena are present that force us to subdivide the lexicon into major lexical categories corresponding to such phenomena, we are confronted with the problem that in many Oceanic languages, even upon closer inspection, it is difficult to find any reasonable differences in the grammatical behavior of "content words" (this has been argued for Tongan, Tokelau, Maori, Fijian, and other languages from that area; for references see Vonen 1997; Broschart 1997). There are no inflectional categories; Oceanic languages are stem-isolating, which means that they have a certain amount of derivational morphology. This, however, does not seem to be category-establishing or category-changing as it is for their European counterparts: any word may be combined with any affix (Broschart 1997: 146 on Tongan). Moreover, the affixes seem to be polyfunctional: the Tongan prefix *faka-*, for example, occurs in such apparently disparate cases as *faka'osi* 'finish' (from *'osi* 'finished'), *fakatangata* 'behaving like a man' (from *tangata* 'man'), *fakafonua* 'pertaining to the land' (from *fonua* 'country'), and *fakaMē* 'May celebration' (from *Mē* 'May').

If the differentiation between major lexical categories does not manifest itself in morphology, it could still be a distributional one, but this does also not appear to be the case. It is commonly reported that these languages have two major types of syntactic "phrases" occurring in fixed positions, exemplified here in Tongan with the following sentence (cf. Broschart 1997: 131):

(3) *na'e kei kata 'a e ongo ki'i ta'ahiné* [Tongan]
PST still laugh ABS ART DU small girl.DEF
'The two little girls were still laughing.'

The first phrase constitutes the main predicate and is always introduced by a member of a set of tense/aspect/mood particles, here *na'e* 'past'. This is optionally followed by a particle, mostly of temporal-adverbial character. Next comes a content word which constitutes the head of the predicate phrase (here, *kata* 'laugh/laughing'). The subsequent string, *'a e ongo ki'i ta'ahiné*, exemplifies the other type of phrase, the argument phrase. It is introduced by a case marker (here *'a* 'absolutive'), followed by an "article" (there are two of them: *e* 'specific' and *ha* 'non-specific'), a number marker (here, *ongo* 'dual'), a classifier (here, *ki'i* for small entities), and finally the head of the argument phrase. The entire argument phrase is marked as definite by an accent shift on the final syllable of the phrase, called a "definite accent". A Tongan clause may contain several such argument phrases, e.g. absolutive, ergative, and locative in the equivalent of a sentence such as 'x put y into z'.

Content words may be distributed freely in any of the available phrase types without any overt morphological change. There seem to be no lexical restrictions with regard to the fixation of a particular lexical element to the predicate or the argument phrase. Yet, the interpretation of the respective elements may be different. For example, if *lele* 'run; running' appears in the predicate phrase and *fefine* 'woman; female' in the absolutive argument phrase, we get a sentence meaning something like 'the women were running'. The opposite distribution yields 'the ones running were female'. The element *kata* corresponds to 'laugh, laughter, laughing' depending on the grammatical contexts. Some researchers on Oceanic languages have claimed that there are completely predictable patterns of interpretation correlating with the different positions in the clause, and that these interpretations constitute lexical-semantic paradigms that can be associated with semantic features, such as natural forces, provisions, nationalities, instruments, etc. Each of these classes has a typical set of "readings" for the different grammatical environments in which it occurs. For example, elements of the "food" class are interpreted as denoting the food objects in the argument phrases, and as providing the respective food in the predicate phrase (*e puaka* 'pork', *te u puaka* 'I will provide pork'); elements of the "tool" class are interpreted as denoting the tool in the argument phrases, and as using the respective tool in the predicate phrase (*e hamala* 'a hammer', *te u hamala* 'I will use a hammer'); and so forth.

Several solutions have been proposed in the literature to cope with such a state of affairs. One of them assumes that these languages do have a lexical distinction between nouns and verbs, but that there is a global rule of conversion in both directions (Vonen 1994, 1995, 1997 on Tokelau). However, this would imply that we had to assume conversion for at least adjectives and adverbs as well, because the same lexical material also appears with no formal change in attributive syntactic positions. It is not difficult to see that this would end up in highly redundant multiple class membership assignment. Moreover, proponents of such an hypothesis will find it difficult, for each lexical element in question, to prove the directionality of the conversion, a necessity assigning category values unequivocally. Another solution for such cases, usually found in more formal approaches, is the assumption of underspecification. Features [±N], [±V] are postulated, but remain unspecified in the lexicon ([αN], [αV]) and receive their value once they enter the syntactic construction. The third solution, proposed by Broschart (1997) for Tongan, assumes that no distinction between major lexical categories of the traditional type can be made; instead, it is claimed that there is a different mode of lexical categorization in terms of semantic classes which form paradigms of interpretations, depending on grammatical context. Hengeveld et al. (2004) have called the sole lexical class of such languages "contentive" (= content words).

Another language for which there had been some dispute over the N-V distinction in the literature is the Philippine language Tagalog (cf. Gil 1995; Himmelmann 1991, 2008; Behrens 1994, among many others). Tagalog has a general class of full words (contentives) which are opposed to particles. However, the semantic orientation of these words differ from that of the Tongan contentives. Putatively event-like expressions such as *sulat* 'write', *bili* 'buy', which we would expect to be verbs, are semantically conceptualized as participant-characterizing (participle-like). The language possesses an elaborate system of role-indicating morphology. There is, in principle, a four-way distinction among participant-characterizing expressions: they can be marked as actor, undergoer, instrument or place; some event-like expressions even distinguish more than these (today mostly taken to be readings of the fourth class, which was renamed "conveyance"). These types of "role orientation" are differentiated by various affixes (misleadingly called focus affixes in traditional Philippine linguistics, now gradually replaced by the term "voice"). The basic sentence structure contains a predicate slot (initial position) and a slot for a predication base (called "subject" or "topic" in the literature and marked by the referential marker *ang*, glossed as REF), joined together by simple juxtaposition (without a copula). Reference and predication are distinguished by simply shifting items from one position to the other (example from Schachter 1985):

(4) *nagtatrabaho ang lalaki* [Tagalog]
working REF man
'The man is working.'

(5) *lalaki ang nagtatrabaho*
man REF working
'The one who is working is a man.'

Again the different interpretations in terms of nouns and verbs in English are not brought about by any lexical categorizing (there is neither category-establishing nor category-changing morphology) but by their syntactic marking as predicates or referents; literally the examples (4) and (5) mean nothing but 'working (is) the man' and 'man (is) the working (one)'.

The difference between Tagalog and the Oceanic languages lies in the fact that in Tagalog, event-denoting expressions such as *nagtatrabaho* are characterized in terms of their role (hence the similarity with participles), which gives them a certain nominal touch, while the Oceanic languages do not have anything of this sort. Examples (4) and (5) demonstrate how this contributes to their semantic interpretation on the syntactic level. Note, however, that this does not have a bearing on their lexical categorization. Derivational processes run cyclically through the entire vocabulary, and any form may be freely manipulated around among the syntactic slots.

In fact, the relationship of Tagalog contentives with nouns was noted in as early as 1924, when Scheerer expressed the view that the syntactic structure of Tagalog can be explained by the assumption that verbs are nouns; he was followed by Capell some decades later (1964). The assumption that event-denoting forms may acquire a participle-like character which contributes to the lack of a sharp distributional distinction between a "noun class" and a "verb class" in the absence of finite verb forms is not unrealistic; cf. section 5.3.

There are two North American language families for which analyses have been proposed that strongly resemble the hypotheses put forward for the interpretation of the structure of Tagalog: Wakashan and Salishan. Sapir (1921: 133–134) claimed that Nootka, a language of the Wakashan family, does not distinguish between nouns and verbs until the difference is established at the syntactic level by means of definitizers or predicative markers. This idea was further elaborated upon by Swadesh (1939), who argues that the terms noun and verb are justified only if the two categories are lexically distinct from each other. That is to say, he rejects the idea of syntactic nouns and verbs in the absence of a lexical distinction of nouns and verb. He therefore posits for Nootka a general class of words as opposed to particles. He shows that there is no difference whatsoever in the morphology between words denoting nominal (thing-like) and those denoting verbal (event-like) concepts; both may occur in the argument as well as in the predicate position. One of his most famous examples is that on which Schachter's Tagalog example was modeled:

(6) *mamuuk-ma quuˀas-ˀi* [Nootka]
working-PRS:IND man-DEF
'The man is working.'

(7) *quuˀas-ma mamuuk-ˀi* [Nootka]
man-PRS:IND working-DEF
'The one working is a man.'

Jacobsen, in a widely quoted paper (1979) reexamined the Nootka data and attempted to show that Nootka does make a distinction between nouns and verbs, although this distinction is less obvious than that found in many other languages. Not all of his arguments are equally convincing. For instance, he points out that the functional ranges of notionally nominal and notionally verbal roots are not identical. One can say:

(8) *mamuuk-ma quuˀas* [Nootka]
working-PRS:IND man
'A man is working.'

but not

(9) **quuˀas-ma mamuuk* [Nootka]
man-PRS:IND working
'A working one is a man.'

This argument is weak in so far as it appeals to the language-specific conditions for definiteness, which have nothing to do with the noun-verb distinction. For example, if we suppose there are no indefinite generics in Nootka (an empirical issue that has to be tested), (9) may in fact be odd because 'being a man' is pragmatically not an extremely felicitous predicate for a specific indefinite noun. Generally, however, absence of the definite article does not change the lexical class. Indefinite generics may well constitute perfect subjects of predicates such as 'be a man', quite independent of lexical and/or syntactic category distinctions. Nothing is wrong with an English sentence such as:

(10) *Up to the 18th century, factory workers were all men.*

Even if it should turn out that Nootka – Sapir and Swadesh notwithstanding – does possess the N-V distinction, albeit in a rather weak form (on the question of degrees of distinction cf. section 5.2), what remains disturbing for a universalist theory is the fact that the same form is used to render 'he is working' and 'the one who is working' / 'worker'.

Salishan languages are no less problematic with regard to this matter. Considerable discussion has centered around this family since Kuipers (1968) and after him Kinkade (1976; 1983), Thompson and Thompson (1980), and Demers and Jelinek (1982; 1984) have made the claim that these languages do not distinguish between word classes that can be labelled noun, verb, adjective, or adverb, but rather have two kinds of words only, i.e. predicates and particles. This claim has been challenged based on the evidence of two Salishan languages, Lillooet and Lushootseed, by van Eijk and Hess (1986), whose main argument relies on the inability of so-called verbs to take the possessive prefixes, an argument that had already been used by Jacobsen (1979: 106), but invalidated by Broschart (1987). In any case, in their syntactic behavior those words that may take possessive prefixes and those that may not show the same striking similarities of function and categorizations as in Nootka.

Broschart (1987) has drawn attention to the fact that the basic semantics of what van Eijk and Hess call "verbs" in Salishan is such that they do not identify an action, but rather the object performing the action. In this respect they resemble participles or *nomina participantis*: "(...) though the Salish verbs are not grammatically identical to participles, there is a certain comparability of semantics and behavior" (Broschart 1987: 54). This similarity with participles stems from the fact that the so-called verbs of Salishan denote states of affairs in terms of the roles of their arguments, i.e. they characterize an individual in terms of a certain type of participant role it plays in a state of affairs. This is strongly reminiscent of the situation of Tagalog described above. It was claimed by Broschart that it is exactly by virtue of this property that they are able to occur both in argument and in predicate position, and it is this property which makes them resemble Indoeuropean nouns. But, at the same time, their inherent predicativity is said by Kinkade (1983: 34) to urge native speakers to translate such utterance in terms of English predicative constructions ('Johnny, look at it, that which is the little dog' = 'Johnny, look at the puppy').

The whole question is open to further investigation, not only theoretically but also empirically, as there seem to be differences between the individual languages as regards the distribution of individual contentives. Are there slight formal differences between words denoting individuals and word denoting actions in a few cases? How significant are these cases both statistically and from a general semantic point of view? And how should these differences be assessed in an unbiased theoretical linguistic approach? At any rate, the existence of phenomena such as observed the in Oceanic languages, in Tagalog, in Wakashan and Salishan not only demonstrates the possible non-universality of the traditional major categories; it also shows that there may be languages in which the intimate relationship between the organization of the lexicon and the organization of grammar leads to systems that are radically different from the one to which we are accustomed. Plank (1984: 511) had already pointed out that it remains an empirical question whether languages with radically different, albeit functionally ultimately equivalent grammatical devices can in fact exhibit comparable patterns of lexical categorization. If Broschart is right, we would have a case in point here: Tongan would in fact not possess any major lexical categories in the traditional sense. It would have a different type of lexical categories, though, namely, classes of items that can be established on the basis of rules pertaining to their semantic correspondences in the major syntactic environments.

5.2. Degrees of N-V distinction

We have so far been concerned with the possibility of a complete lack of distinction between nouns and verbs. However, it is not the case that "complete lack of distinction" and "clear-cut distinction" neatly define two linguistic types. Instead, there are many languages in which the distinction is weaker than in others, given the traditional criteria for parts-of-speech identification. Even those linguists that insisted on the N-V distinction in Wakashan and Salishan languages had to admit that the set of distinctive features is not exceedingly large.

Consequently, the N-V distinction may be regarded as a matter of degree (see Sasse 2001 for discussion of a number of scalar approaches to nouniness and verbiness). In the 1980s, when scales and continua were fashionable, several scholars tried to demonstrate that there is a continuum ranging from clear-cut distinction to (theoretical) non-distinction. Walter (1981) followed by Broschart (1987) claims that "noun-hood" and "verb-hood" are converse principles (gradients) arranged on a scale between N and V prototypes, rather than properties attached to two distinct categories. This approach borrows from a familiar idea, viz. Ross' (1972, 1973) famous "category squish" with the difference that Ross' "nouniness" squish operated in one direction (funnel direction) only (decrease of properties from verblike/gerundial expression to nouns), whereas Walter assumes that there are two funnel directions, one of decreasing nouniness and increasing verbiness, and one of increasing nouniness and decreasing verbiness. A related, but more diversified scale which takes phenomena such as the presence of articles, incorporation etc. into account was proposed by Hopper and Thompson (1984, 1985). They claim that the degree of nouniness is proportional to the degree of referentiality and the degree of verbiness is proportional to the degree of predicativity.

As far as the cross-linguistic continuum of noun-verb distinction is concerned, Walter has proposed a number of typological parameters, according to which the degree of distinction can be measured: (i) the degree of overlapping of nominal and verbal inflexion potential; (ii) the frequency of categorially ambivalent stems (which become nouns or verbs only by actualizing nominal or verbal inflexion potential such as Hungarian *fagy* 'to freeze'; 'frost', English *to jump, a jump*); (iii) the existence of a verbal inflexion for predicate nouns; (iv) the degree of overlapping of derivational potential; (v) the number of categorially threefold ambivalent (N, A, V) participles, (vi) the number of categorially twofold ambivalent (V, A) participles, (vii) the overlapping of verbal and participial inflexion. On the basis of data from three languages, West Greenlandic (G), Turkish (T), and Hungarian (H), he proposes a hierarchy for each of the parameters. For example, for parameter (i) the gradation is G > H > T, which is meant to mean that Greenlandic exhibits the highest degree of overlapping of inflexion, Turkish the lowest, and Hungarian is somewhere in between.

Broschart (1987) has pursued a different idea in establishing a noun-verb continuum. He claims that the diagnostic features of nouns and verbs must be examined in much more detail in order to determine the position of a given language on a scale. In particular, it must be demonstrated that the grammatical categories specified by the characteristic morphosyntax of nouns and verbs are closely associated with their status as "objects", participants, arguments, or reference-allowing expressions on the one hand and events or predicates, on the other. The idea is that a robust N-V distinction will always rely on grammatical categories functionally associated with one or the other. In a language with a strong N-V distinction, such as German (Broschart's example), nouniness is manifested in the categories of number (concrete objects are individualized and countable) and gender (or, in other languages, class which reflects a semantic classification of objects). Their status as participants in an event is reflected in the category of case and in the fact that nouns are combinable with prepositions. Their referential potential is reflected in their combinability with determiners of sorts (articles, demonstrative pronouns, etc.). Verbs, on the other hand, indicate tense, which is closely connected with their status as events, and *mood,* which reflects various grammaticalized aspects of their predicative force, which themselves appear in combination with further speech acts such as order, etc. Their status as terms denoting an event involving participants is reflected in their grammaticalized relationality, i.e. in valency and in person and number agreement, as well as in valency changing categories such as passive, reflexive, causative etc. and in the existence of transitivizers, etc. Morphosyntactic derivation processes are strongly marked by the presence of category-changing morphology allowing for the creation of nouns of action, nouns of agent, nouns of patient, etc. from verbs, as well as denominative verbs from nouns. In addition to the derivational mechanisms, each verb contains in its "scatter" a number of participles. A function similar to participles and verbal nouns is also fulfilled by relative clauses. Finally, there is a large inventory of syntactic rules which decouple semantic and discourse-pragmatic features when nouns are used predicatively and verbs are used referentially. For the predicative use of nouns, a *copula* must be employed as a syntactic marker of predicativity, and when events occur in argument position they form *subordinate clauses* (constituent clauses) with various degrees of nominalization for which a great variety of conjunctions is available.

Gender (class), number and case for nouns and tense, aspect and mood for verbs are the most characteristic and widespread grammatical categories among the languages of the world. We may add a few more word-class establishing categories here. Many languages make morphosyntactic distinctions along a continuum of "individuality" (human-like character) which may be roughly represented like this: Proper Names > Humans > Animals > Inanimate Tangible Objects > Abstracts ≥ Mass Nouns. Several turning points are common on this scale. The distinction between Animates and Inanimates is very widespread. Proper Names may be cut off from common nouns (e.g. Tagalog and other Austronesian languages by a special set of reference markers; Modern Greek and Albanian by specific plural forms (associatives); Dyirbal by nominative/accusative case marking as opposed to ergative case marking). Another possible division line is the line between count nouns and mass nouns. Verbs, on the other hand, very often distinguish aspect, which grammaticalizes the difference between *states* and *changes* of states, a thing of utmost importance for the communication of events. Another difference which is often formally distinguished and also reflects the fact that verbs prototypically denote events having participant frames is the difference between intransitive, transitive, and ditransitive verbs.

To sum up, the inflectional and derivational characteristics of nouns and verbs in languages with a prototypical N-V distinction are explained, in this approach, as the result of the grammaticalization of the most central linguistic aspects of their semantic and discourse-pragmatic ingredients, and hence, the degree of N-V distinction depends on how strongly these aspects are reflected in the morphology of a given language. This brings us to the next point, the historical changes that may lead to the different degree of N-V distinction.

5.3. The historical development of the N-V distinction

It may be assumed that a language can acquire or lose word-class-determining categories in the course of its historical development and that such fluctuations in connection with the reorganization of reference and predication mechanisms are responsible for the difference in the degree of N-V distinction. To bring this section to a close, I will briefly sketch the main stages of a well-attested historical change that led from a highly developed noun-verb distinction to non-distinction and back again to a very marked distinction.

Eastern Aramaic inherited a fairly sharply marked noun-verb distinction from Proto-Semitic. Semitic nouns were originally inflected for the categories of gender, number, case, and definiteness, while Semitic verbs distinguished aspect, mood and voice and had a conjugation for person with distinct (nonzero) markers for all persons in singular, plural and dual in finite verb forms. There was a remarkably well-developed system of category-changing derivations; all kinds of verbal nouns were derived from verbs, and there existed a considerable array of denominal types of verbs thanks to the derivational capacities of the verb (factitive, causative, passive/intransitive, intensive/frequentative, and various combinations thereof). Moreover, the inflectional systems of the noun and the verb were sharply distinct due to the use of external inflexion (suffixed) in the former, and a specific combination of external and internal inflexion (prefixes, suffixes, infixes and *ablaut*) in the latter. While the verbal system remained rather stable, the nominal system lost the inflexion for case and definiteness prior to the formation of Eastern Aramaic as a distinct subgroup, whereby the definiteness inflexion was replaced by a new type of definiteness marking, so that the category as such remained. By the time the dialect of Edessa (what is now Urfa in Southeastern Turkey) became the basis of the written language of the Syrian Christians under the name of Syriac (2nd century A.D.), the syntax of the language had already deviated considerably from its ancient Aramaic ancestor. The strict subject/predicate-oriented syntactic organization had been infiltrated more and more by a pragmatically guided structure. It still distinguished a nominal sentence (subject + predicate noun with zero copula, e.g. *ḥubbā nuhrā* 'love is light') from a verbal sentence (VSO order, e.g. *ḥreḇ bēṯ maqdšan* 'our sacred house is destroyed'), but the main characteristic of Classical Syriac is its considerable freedom in grouping nouns and nominal phrases around core predicates on the basis of pragmatic conditions. While the conservative written language remained at this stage until its final period, spoken varieties of Eastern Aramaic (which are not direct descendants of Syriac, but reflected in the postclassical stages, due to the fact that the Syriac of the last documents, by that time a dead language, was written by speakers of much more progressive varieties) began to show an increasing tendency to use participles instead of person-inflected verb forms. It was at that point in the development of Eastern Aramaic vernacular that the operation of predication was *disconnected* from the category of verbs and relegated to the nominal sentence where it is syntactically expressed by *juxtaposition* (zero copula). In a very short period of time the language abandoned its total inventory of finite verb forms and was left with two participles (active and passive), which took on the original aspect distinction (imperfective vs. perfective). Following an areal tendency, the language began to develop a kind of split ergativity by constructing the active participle with the actor as the subject, and the passive participle with the undergoer as the subject along with the actor as a prepositional phrase with the directional preposition *l-*. At the same time, the undergoer of an active participle was also expressed by an *l-*phrase, when animate, but by the unmarked form of the noun, when inanimate. To illustrate this system by means of imitating translation, 'Peter is kissing Mary' was expressed by 'Peter (is) a kissing (one) to Mary', while 'Peter kissed Mary' was expressed by 'Mary (is a) kissed (one) to Peter'. Although by that time no category of finite verb existed in the language, the participles had retained their nouny character (at least as much as was left of it, namely their chiefly individual-designating semantics and their overt marking of the categories of gender and number). With other things remaining the same, the system very much resembled that which we now find in Tagalog, where predicativity is not inherent in the so-called verbs, but established syntactically by the juxtapositive linking up with a predication base (subject). Soon after that period, a surprisingly dynamic and revolutionary period in the development of Eastern Aramaic began, the offshoots of which we are still witnessing in the modern Turoyo dialects of Turkey. It began with the development of an enclitic copula, which at first seems to have been cliticized to "nominal" and "participial" predicates alike. Soon the formal characteristics of the copula of canonical nominal sentences began to split off from those of participial sentences. There were two major developments: nominal sentences developed a copula form of the 3rd person, while participial sentences did not; the agglutination of the enclitic copula forms was tighter with participles than with nominal predicates. At the same time, the pronominal directive forms (consisting of the preposition *l-* + possessive suffixes) began to fuse with the passive participles to form a complex system of person agreement in the perfective forms (*nšīq lī* 'a kissed one [is he] to me' became *nšə́qli, nšīqō lī* 'a kissed one [is she] to me' became *nšiqóli,* and so forth). This was the point in the development of these dialects in which the most important step towards the reintroduction of the N-V distinction was made. There was now a strong distinction between nominal and verbal predication: nominal predication was indicated by a copula, while the verbs, due to their newly acquired inflexion for person, regained their inherent predicativity. Nouns now inflected for number, gender and definiteness and were able to take prepositions and to be constructed as heads of NPs. A rudimentary case system developed from the opposition between absolute and *l*-prefixed noun forms. Verbs inflected for aspect (due to the differences between the participles), person, and marginally for mood. While this already came very close to a prototypical N-V distinction, the recent development went even further. An elaborate prefix system was introduced, thanks to which the verbs are now able to distinguish subtle time-aspect correlations, subjunctive, jussive, resultative perfect, pluperfect and the like. Today the N-V distinction is no less manifest than it was in ancient times.

The historical development of these dialects represents a complete cycle, beginning with an extremely marked N-V distinction. Then, via a stage of non-distinction brought about by the abolishment of finite verb forms, it moved to a new period of N-V distinction being made possible by a transfer of predicativity into originally nouny types of event expressions and a gradual increase of verbal categories.

6. Adjectives

On the universality of adjectives, Dixon's classic paper (1982) was already referred to above. For a follow-up / critique cf. Backhouse (1984). For recent literature on problems of adjectives see also Bhat (1994), Wetzer (1996), Stassen (1997), and the concise but very informative handbook article Bhat and Pustet (2000). Compared to the heavily disputed universality of Ns and Vs, it is fairly widely agreed upon that a class of adjectives cannot be made out in all languages (see Evans 2000b and the literature quoted in the preceding paragraph).

The prototypical function of adjectives is believed by many scholars to be that of attribution (modification), in particular the attribution of properties (Croft, see section 3; cf. also Bhat and Pustet 2000: 757). This claim is supported by a number of languages whose adjectives occur only as modifiers, and do not occur as predicates at all (cf. Hua, Haiman 1978). Language-specifically, a class of adjectives can be defined on this basis if there is a morphosyntactically identifiable word class which prototypically serves the attribution of properties to individuals. The presence of adjectives in a language presupposes a fairly high degree of N-V distinction because it implies the formation of noun phrases (cf. word-class hierachy in Hengeveld et al. 2004 and Rijkhoff 2007). The constitutive (category-establishing) morphology of adjectives includes motion (i.e. agreement with the grammatical categories of the noun expressing the individual to which the property is attributed, especially gender or class) and comparison. The former reflects the attributive nature of adjectives, i.e. the close connection with their head nouns within the nominal phrase, while the latter reflects their semantic character as property concepts (properties can be measured in degrees). However, we will see below that comparison cannot be taken as a thumb-nail criterion for identifying adjectives in a given language.

Characteristic category-changing morphology includes the derivation of manner adverbs (see section 7), factitives (like *shorten*), inceptives ('become such and such') and *abstract nouns* (e.g. *ugliness*; such nouns serve to treat properties as arguments [e.g. subject or object], as in *I hate ugliness*). Secondary adjectives can be derived from abstract nouns (*beauty* → *beautiful*) or from verbs (*agree* → *agreeable*). Some languages also possess mechanisms for the derivation of nouns denoting individuals characterized by the properties in question (so-called absolute or substantivized adjectives) but this is often unnecessary when the character of adjectives is inherently "nouny". An example is the English language, which is forced to form such expressions by the addition of *one* (*the black one*), while other languages simply say *the black* (German *der Schwarze,* Italian *il nero* etc.).

Since the functional basis of adjectives is attribution, there is some interference with other attributive constructions such as compounds, participles, genitives and relative clauses/participles. Romance, Slavic, Modern Greek and other modern European languages often use adjectives where English and German would use a compound or a genitive construction, cf. Modern Greek *kerikes sinθikes* 'weather (lit. weathery) conditions' (German *Wetterbedingungen*), *thiikos xalkos* 'sulphate of copper' (lit. coppery s.) (German *Kupfersulfat*), *maθitiki omaða* 'a group of pupils' (lit. pupily group) (German *Schülergruppe*), etc. In some Agaw languages (Ethiopia), on the other hand, there is no difference between adjectives, genitives and relative clauses; all three represent one type of general attributive construction. Consequently, these languages cannot be said to possess a class of adjectives at all. To what degree adjectives figure in the inventory of attributive constructions of a language may well constitute a typological parameter, ranging from zero (no adjectives at all, as in Agaw) to the high percentages found in some European languages. It is important to note, however, that the functional range of adjectives, even in very adjective-dominated languages, never exceeds a certain limit. Adjectives tend to remain within the realm of non-referentiality and are not typically used for the attribution of those referential expressions, which the possessive genitives are responsible for. A *Chomskyan revolution* is not the individual Chomsky's personal revolution, but rather a revolution associated with the name of Chomsky. The adjective *Chomskyan* does not refer to Chomsky, it just includes his name and characterizes a certain entity in terms of this name. On the other hand, an expression like *Bill's father's hat* refers to Bill and his father and can not be replaced by something like *Billean fatherean hat* because this expression would imply that properties associated with Bill and his father were attributed to the hat.

We will now turn our attention to the question of how languages can be arranged on a scale of adjective-dominance. Dixon (1982), in one of the most influential studies on adjectives, points out that languages possessing adjectives fall into two groups, one which has an open class of adjectives (like English and German), and one in which adjectives constitute a closed class, often with a very small number of members. Furthermore, he sees a surprising cross-linguistic consistency in the meanings of closed-list adjectives. On the basis of a survey of 17 languages he observes that the semantic types most closely associated with a class of adjectives are dimension, age, value, and color. Languages whose adjective class is extremely small express these semantic types only by means adjectives (cf. the 8 adjectives of Igbo: 'large', 'small', 'new', 'old', 'black', 'white', 'good', 'bad'). If the class is larger, some adjectives expressing physical properties or human propensities may be added, but in general there is a tendency to express these semantic types by either nouns or verbs. The Nilo-Saharan language Acooli has about 40 adjectives, among them such physical properties as 'hard', 'soft', 'heavy' and 'light' and such human propensity adjectives as 'wise', but as a general rule physical properties are expressed through verbs and human propensity qualities through nouns (denoting the possessor of the quality). Dixon believes that there is a universal tendency to express physical properties by verbs and human propensities by nouns, but it seems that there are more factors responsible in the choice of nouns or verbs for the expression of adjectival meanings in languages which have few or no adjectives. We have already referred to Wierzbicka (1986), who suggests that the noun-verb choice is dependent on the factors of categorization (noun) and description (verb). A paradigm case in support of this assumption is Dullay, an Ethiopian language of the East Cushitic family. Dullay, which lacks a class of adjectives altogether, quite regularly uses nouns to designate individuals characterized by permanent human properties, whereas temporary states of the same qualitiy are indicated by stative verbs (an English parallel is 'drunkard' vs. 'being drunk'; cf. Amborn et al. 1980: 91–93). Givón (1984) explains these correlations in terms of time-stability. Adjectives occupy an intermediate position between nouns, which prototypically express completely time-stable "thing" concepts, and verbs, which prototypically express rapidly changing states of affairs. Thus adjectives prototypically express something which is neither time-stable nor rapidly changing, but something in between: states that are not permanent but may last for some time. One would expect, then, qualities of a more permanent nature to be expressed by nouns and qualities of a less permanent nature by verbs. Moreover, a language may have a general (language-specific or type-specific) tendency for expressing adjectival meanings by nouns or by verbs. Schachter (1985: 15–17), who considers this difference to be an important typological parameter, was the first to distinguish between *adjectival-noun languages* and *adjectival-verb languages*. The former either use abstract nouns ('kindness', 'badness', etc.) in possessive constructions to express qualities ('a person of/having kindness' = 'a kind person'), or use nouns expressing the possessor of the quality in question (like English 'a madman') in attributive or appositive constructions: 'a person (who is a) madman'. The latter typically use relativization to express the equivalent of an attributive adjective. This construction is not unfamiliar to European languages. Many languages possessing a distinct class of adjectives are nevertheless able to construct bona fide nouns, expressing persons characterized by some quality, like adjectives: Albanian *punëtor* 'worker', *njeri punëtor* 'an industrious person'. It is important to note the close relationship between predication and attribution. In spite of the nominal character of adjectives in many languages, it seems that the genesis of adjectives is often accompanied by subordination of predication, schematically *a N which is A → a N which A → a N A*.

The fact that putative nouns and putative adjectives can occupy the same slot in an attributive construction, as in the Albanian example above, has led to difficulties in the identification of categorial status in those (by no mans rare) cases in which morphology does not serve as a cue for the distinction. It comes as no surprise, then, that such cases have been a playground for hypotheses of categorial overlapping or the assignment of multiple class membership. For example, in the Classical languages, the N-A distinction is rather weak. Motion, comparison and the formation of manner adverbs may be held to constitute morphological cues for adjectives, but only on the assumption of a considerable amount of idiosyncrasy and defectivity, in so far as not all *bona fide* adjectives can unambiguously be identified in terms of these morphological categories: some do not distinguish between genders, some do not have comparatives and superlatives, and so on. On the other hand, there are many *bona fide* nouns that display motion of gender and comparison, and typically occur in attributive positions. Even a superficial check of the standard Latin and Greek dictionaries will reveal that the problem is usually solved by assigning double categorial status. Thus, Latin *senex* 'old man' and *amīcus* 'friend', and (Ancient) Greek *philos* 'friend' and *kleptēs* 'thief' are assigned two senses each, i.e. a substantival and an adjectival one. Each of the four can occur as individual-denoting entities and are therefore called nouns. But they also freely enter into attributive constructions and can form comparatives and superlatives (e.g. Latin *senior* 'older', *amīcissimus* 'the dearest friend', Greek *philteros* 'more friend', *philtatos* 'most friend', *kleptisteros* 'more thievish', *kleptistatos* 'most thievish'). Incidentally, it is typically the semantic area of human properties and social roles where such double categorization is found.

A different type of problems occurs in those languages that combine two typological features: (1) that of phrase inflexion, i.e. the phenomenon that morphological categories are indicated on the head at the end of the NP (i.e. there is no phrase-internal agreement); (2) that of a loose compound-like juxtaposition of nouns, where the left member serves to determine the right one. There is a considerable number of languages that display this combination, English being one of them. The problem of analysis that arises in such cases is that nouns and adjectives cannot be distinguished when they occur as modifiers in the prenominal position. It has been maintained for English that the prosodic difference between stress on the head and stress on the modifier may serve to disambiguate. Stress on the head is taken by some to constitute phrasal accent; the prenominal element could then be categorized as an adjective (*iron 'shackles*). Stress on the modifier is taken to be compound accent, and the prenominal element is categorized as a noun (*'iron brick*). This hypothesis does not work very well and leads to counterintuitive results: is *Gloucester* in *Gloucester 'Square* an adjective? (For detailed discussion cf. Behrens and Sasse 2003). But even if the stress criterion could be accepted for English, there are many other languages in which such a criterion is not applicable, e.g. Hungarian, Turkish, Caucasian languages, Quechua, and many others. Such phenomena significantly contribute to a low degree of N-A distinction in these languages.

7. Adverbs

In addition to nouns, verbs and adjectives, a fourth class of full words is distinguished by many linguists which is usually termed adverbs. It has proven very difficult to define the functional basis of adverbs even for those languages in which they are extremely prominent (Indoeuropean, for instance). The name *adverbium* (literal translation of the Greek term *epirrhēma* which means something like 'addition to the verb') suggests that adverbs modify verbs. However, at first glance this characterization would apply only to a small portion of what we normally call adverbs. Adverbs can modify any other part of speech: nouns (German *das Buch hier*), adjectives (*a very short article*), and other adverbs (*he slept very well*). The difficulties arise from the fact that "the label *adverb* is often applied to several different sets of words in a language, sets that do not necessarily have as much in common with one another, either notionally or grammatically, as, say, the subclasses of nouns or verbs that may occur in the language" (Schachter 1985: 20). For instance, the five words in boldface type in (11) would traditionally be regarded as adverbs in a grammar of English, though they cover a considerable semantic and grammatical range:

(11) ***Unfortunately***, *John walked* ***home extremely slowly yesterday***.
(Schachter 1985, example [47])

Given this situation, it is it is of the utmost importance that we develop a clear idea of how we should define a *word class of adverbs* as distinguished from an *expression class of adverbials* that would comprise, in addition to true adverbs, oblique case forms of nouns, adpositional phrases, etc. It seems that adverbs, more than any other class discussed thus far, owe their definition and their recognition as a distinct word class to syntactic considerations. The reason is that adverbs offer far fewer morphological clues to their identification than Ns, Vs, or As do. It is relatively easy to identify manner adverbs as long as they are derived from other word classes such as nouns and adjectives by characteristic morphology (Turkish *türk-çe* 'in a Turkish manner' from *Turk* 'Turk[ish]', or English *slow-ly* from *slow*). Adverbs of place or time such as *here* or *yesterday,* which lack such clear category-indicating markers, can be identified as adverbs only through the fact that they are believed to occur in adverbial position and cannot be identified as anything else. FG theorists have therefore restricted the word class of adverbs to manner adverbs.

But what is an adverbial position? For most of the languages known to have a class of adverbs, we can follow Schachter (1985: 20) and define the syntactic function of adverbials provisionally as "modifiers of constituents other than nouns". The rare cases of adverbs modifying nouns are clearly peripheral. Some languages do not allow them at all; in others, adverbs acting as modifiers of nouns are limited to certain types (local and temporal) and are typically distinguished from adjectival modification by their distributional characteristics. For instance, in German adverbials modifying nouns occur after the head noun, as opposed to adjectives, which occur before the head noun (*das Seminar heute* (adv.) vs. *das heutige* (adj.) *Seminar* 'today's class'). If we accept the syntactic definition of adverbials as modifiers of constituents other than nouns for the time being, we can define adverbs as a class of words, normally uninflected or at best inflected for comparison (where semantically possible), which occur in the syntactic position of the modifiers of constituents other than nouns, and cannot be identified as belonging to any other word class.

In order to set the stage for the following discussion, it is necessary to take a closer look at the reasons for their formal and functional heterogeneity. There are three sources of formal and behavioral differences: (i) differences in scope, (ii) differences with regard to possible heads, (iii) differences in meaning.

Differences in scope: There is one basic difference in the scope of adverbials which has received much attention in the literature. When we compare sentences (12) and (13),

(12) *Unfortunately, John didn't receive your letter in time.*

(13) *John wept bitterly.*

we observe that *unfortunately* and *bitterly* differ with regards to the stretch of utterance they modify. In (12), the whole sentence is in the scope of *unfortunately:* one can paraphrase (12) with *it is unfortunate that John* etc. The adverb *bitterly* in (13), on the other hand, modifies the predicate *wept* only, the subject being entirely outside its domain. Adverbials of the first type are usually called *sentence adverbials.* They do not seem to have much of a modifying function in the same sense as *bitterly* can be said to modify or determine the verb *wept.* What adverbs like *unfortunately* seem to do is set a frame for the following sentence: the entire proposition *John didn't receive your letter in time* is seen within the frame of unfortunateness. The discourse-pragmatic function of "frame-setting" seems to be fairly important for human communication, since in many languages of the world there is a syntactic slot (normally in the initial position of the sentence) where elements setting a temporal, spatial or modal frame are inserted. Note, however, that this is not necessarily done by means of adverbials: there are also many languages that use higher predicates for the purpose of frame-setting (e.g. 'It is unfortunate that ...' as in certain Cushitic languages).

Differences in head selection: Apart from verbals, there are mainly two other expression classes that occur as heads of phrases modified by adverbs: adjectivals (14), and adverbials (15):

(14) *an extremely low number*

(15) *he ran rather fast*

Both of these uses of adverbs are extensions of their predicate-modifying function. In the above examples it is basically the number's being low and the running's being fast that are modified. Compared to the number of adverbs modifying verbs, adverbs modifying adjectives and adverbs are clearly in the minority. This is explained by the relatively wide semantic range covered by verbs in comparison with adjectival predicates. One obvious detail in which properties may differ is degree: it therefore comes as no surprise that degree adverbs such as *more, most, rather, very* are perforce bound to modify adjectivals (and, in turn, adverbials) rather than verbs, because qualities are more typically measured in degrees than events. Nevertheless, there are many verbs which denote measurable states of affairs and can be modified by the same adverbs that modify adjectives/adverbs: *more beautiful* – *I love you more*; Italian *molto bello* 'very beautiful' – *mi piace molto* 'I like it very much'.

Differences in meaning: The traditional semantic sub-classification of adverbs distinguished between at least four groups: local, temporal, modal (manner), and causal adverbs (cf. *Duden* 1973: 304 for German, to quote a random example). Local adverbs indicate place: *here*, *there*, *upstairs*, *below*, etc. Local adverbials may occur as complements (16) or as adjuncts (satellites) (17):

(16) *He lives upstairs*

(17) *There was a party upstairs*

Temporal adverbs indicate time: *yesterday*, *always*, *finally*, *seldom*. They rarely occur as complements, but normally as adjuncts (satellites). Manner adverbs are in turn subdivided into various subgroups: quality (*somehow*, *quickly*), degree (*too*, *much*), contrast (*however*, *rather*), emphasis (*exactly*, *even*), and others. Causal adverbs indicate cause, instrument, condition, and a number of related circumstances. Examples of causal adverbs in this wider sense are *therefore*, *consequently*, *thereby*, *otherwise*, *nevertheless*. Some linguists distinguish more than these groups or propose differing classifications. One subgroup which is considered to belong to manner adverbs by some scholars, but taken to be a special subdivision of adverbs in its own right by others, is the subgroup of adverbs expressing the speaker's judgment of the proposition expressed by the rest of the sentence. Such "speaker's comment adverbs" may have the entire sentence or the predicate in their scope. Examples are *unfortunately*, *strangely*, *probably*, *possibly*, etc.

Several solutions suggest themselves for coping with the problem of heterogeneity. One could hypothesize that all expressions usually called "adverbs" are subsumable under a general semantic prototype, the concept of circumstantiality, the constructional correlate of which would be their preference to occur as satellites and modifiers. Whether this is enough to posit a lexicogrammatical category of adverbs in any language remains an open question: at least the correspondence between lexical characteristics and constructional slots is not as obvious as it is for verbs, nouns and adjectives in languages that have them. Another solution would be to dispense with a large category of adverbs altogether and restrict the notion of adverbs to manner adverbs. This strategy is pursued by FG research on word classes (cf. Hengeveld et al. 2004). For instance, there is a cross-linguistic tendency to develop special morphology for the derivation of manner adverbs from adjectives, while local, temporal etc. adverbs either constitute a closed set of unanalyzable words or are formed by case suffixes or other non-derivative mechanisms. Manner adverbs have often been regarded as the core group of a word class of adverbs, due to the fact that they are most obviously modifiers of the predicate. What adjectives are for nouns, manner adverbs are for verbs. It therefore comes as no surprise that there is a derivational relationship adjectives and manner adverbs: Latin regularly forms adverbs from adjectives by the endings *-e* and *-ter* (*rect-e* from *rect-us*; *liben-ter* from *liben-s*); Ancient Greek uses *-ōs* (*kalós* 'beautiful' [adj.] : *kalôs* 'beautiful' [adv.]), English *-ly* for the same purpose, and so forth. The rest of what is considered a class of adverbs, local, tempora, etc. ones, could then be relegated to a minor class of particles.

In concluding this section, let us add a few remarks on universality and problems of distinction. We will confine ourselves here to manner adverbs. The presence of a distinct class of manner adverbs is even less widespread than the presence of a class of adjectives among the languages of the world. If a language does not dispose of a productive mechanism for the derivation of adverbs, it is often said that it may possess a closed class of adverbs definable only in syntactic terms (e.g. on Dyirbal, cf. Dixon 1972: 301). If solution 2 of the preceding paragraph is accepted, we would prefer to categorize such alleged adverbs as particles. Polysynthetic languages frequently express circumstances including manner by means of affixes on the verb. Languages with more elaborate word class systems may nevertheless lack a distinct (morphologically definable) class of manner adverbs. Hengeveld et al. say that manner adverbs presuppose adjectives. This does not mean, however, that adjectives must be specifically marked when occurring as modifiers of predicates. It is therefore often said that languages may possess a syntactic slot adverbial, filled by material from other word classes. Modern Persian and Modern Armenian, for instance, lack a derivative mechanism for the formation of manner adverbs from adjectives (comparable to the English *-ly*), but use the same form of the adjective that also occurs in prenominal attributive and predicative functions. A slightly more complicated case is German, where predicative and predicate-modifier uses formally coincide (zero-marked), while the attributive adjective uses a distinct set of case endings. The consequences that such complete or partial formal neutralizations have for the postulation of a class of manner adverbs on a language-specific basis (degree of adjective-adverb distinction in a given language) have, must be carefully examined in each of these cases. The degree of noun-adverb distinction may also prove relevant, when, as in Modern Greek, non-referential bare nouns may be used as modifiers of predicates, see example 18:

(18) *i γlosa tis ðuleve roðani* [Modern Greek]
ART tongue her worked spinning.wheel
'Her tongue worked like a spinning-wheel.'

8. Ideophones

For a comprehensive bibliography of the research on ideophones cf. Voeltz and Kilian-Hatz (2001: 407–409). This volume is itself a milestone in ideophone research, comprising 28 articles on this subject dealing with a large variety of languages all over the world.

Regarded as adverbs by some scholars – cf. Samarin (1965: 118) for Gbeya and Schachter (1985: 21) for ideophones in general – but as a distinct word class by others, ideophones enjoy a special status among the "autosemantic" word classes of the languages of the world. Ideophones are clearly the least wide-spread syntactic category and, in addition, heavily restricted geographically. They have long been known as an areal characteristic of African, Australian and Amerindian languages, but occur only sporadically elsewhere: if recognized at all, they are often regarded as a special subclass of interjections. Furthermore, ideophones are the only syntactic category apart from interjections (which constitute a word class, but not a syntactic category proper, see section 12), which can be defined not only in morphosyntactic, but also in phonological terms (see below). Finally, in contrast to the other word classes discussed so far, ideophones must be defined in terms of a typical bundle of syntactic functions rather than in terms of a single "expression class".

What is an ideophone? The term was first used in African linguistics. As far as we know, it was coined by C. M. Doke (1935), who defined it as a word, "often onomatopoeic, which describes a predicate, qualificative or adverb in respect to manner, colour, sound, smell, action, state or intensity" (1935: 119). While some disagreement can be found with regard to the semantic range covered by ideophones, all scholars agree on the phonological criterion as the basic characteristic of ideophones. Some scholars have even proposed that ideophones be defined exclusively in phonological terms. "Phonologically they may violate sequence structure conditions or exhibit unusual repetitions or combinations of phonemes as in Yoruba, or even include phonemes not present elsewhere in the language, as in Nguni" (Courtenay 1976: 13–14). A rather striking feature of ideophones is their tendency towards reduplication. Cf. the following examples from Yoruba: *kọ́kọ́rọ́* 'key', *wọ́kọwọ̀kọ* 'zigzag', *pẹ́tẹpẹ̀tẹ* 'muddy, soggy', *ṣúkuṣùku* 'disorderly'; and from Apalaí (South America): *syryryry* 'gliding movement of canoe', *sororo* 'moving of canoe in shallow water', *soko soko* 'munching'. Since the characteristics described here are equally found in interjections (cf. section 12), why distinguish an extra class of ideophones? The answer can be given in syntactic terms. First of all, ideophones may be subject to ordinary word class derivation, while interjections may not. Secondly, interjections are sentence-equivalents, for the most part exclamations, which do not normally occur as constituents of sentences. Ideophones, on the contrary, typically occur as sentence constituents and are hardly found in isolation. Thus Yoruba *wẹ́ẹ́wẹ̀ẹ̀wẹ́ẹ́* 'small fragments' and *pẹ́ẹ́pẹ̀ẹ̀pẹ́ẹ́* 'trivial' may be phonologically deviant, but can be used as ordinary nouns or adjectives, respectively. They thus resemble words like German *etepetete* 'super nice, squeamish', English *la-di-da* 'id.', German *plem-plem* 'crazy', English *willy-nilly*, rather than interjections such as *aha*, *gosh,* or *ouch*.

We will now turn to the question of why we cannot distinguish a word class of ideophones in all languages. Let us first make a distinction between *ideophonic expressions* and a proper word class of ideophones. Perhaps all languages possess onomatopoeic expressions that imitate certain sounds (English *tick-tock,* German *Ticktack* 'sound of the clock'), shapes (English *zigzag*, German *Zickzack*), etc. Taking Doke's definition as a point of departure, we may consider words such as English *zigzag* ideophones; at first glance they meet all conditions mentioned in the definition. They possess a distinctive phonological shape and they occur in different syntactic functions: as predicates (*to zigzag*), qualificatives (*a zigzag* line), and adverbs (*he went zigzag*). This is true of many onomatopoeic expressions in English, including those mentioned in the preceding paragraph and many more, such as *meow*, *woof-woof*, *bow-wow*, *moo*, *blah-blah*, *buff*, *bugaboo,* etc. Upon closer examination, however, it turns out to be unnecessary to distinguish an extra word class for these expressions in English. First of all, the characteristic reduplicated form of words such as *zigzag* is confined to a relatively small number of onomatopoeic lexemes whose classification into a common category is of little functional interest. Secondly, their multifunctional syntactic behavior is not category-specific; on the contrary, it is the result of the relatively free fluctuation between word classes which characterizes the word-class structure of English as a whole. In English *zigzag* is best classified as an adverb, which may be turned into a noun, an adjective or a verb by conversion (or zero-derivation), just as *back*, a lexeme of non-ideophonic character, may occur as a noun, verb, adverb, or adjective. Even clearer is the German *Zickzack*, which is not a member of a word class of its own, but rather a masculine noun *der Zickzack.* There is no verbal derivative *zickzacken, so the idea of "zigzag" cannot be expressed in predicative position by means of this root. There is no adverbial derivation either: the adverbial 'zigzag' as rendered by the prepositional phrase *im Zickzack* literally means 'in the *zigzag*'. Finally, an adjective can be derived in German by adding *-förmig* 'having ... shape', e.g. *zickzack-förmig*. In sum, English and German have got expressions characterized by ideophonic phonological properties, but do not possess a distinct word class of ideophones.

Let us now consider what Koehn and Koehn say about ideophones in the Amazonian language Apalaí: "The ideophone is a noninflected onomatopoeic word that denotes an action that is normally expressed by a finite verb form. It is the only class of word that cannot be followed by a postpositional particle. It functions normally as a distinct sentence constituent, carrying the same meaning as that contained in the finite verb of that sentence (i.e. the basic part of the meaning, not including person, tense, etc., which are not part of the meaning of the ideophone)" (Koehn and Koehn 1986: 124–126). The following example demonstrates this adverbial character of ideophones (HIS stands for historic tense; CONTRAEXP for contraexpective; IDEOPH for ideophone):

(19) *apoi-ko repe kyry* [Apalaí]
grab-HIS CONTRAEXP grabbing.IDEOPH
'But it (the frog) grabbed him instead.'

In addition, Apalaí ideophones may occur: combined with the verb *ka* 'say; do' (*koih* or *koe koe* 'paddling', *koih ka* 'to paddle'); in isolation; functioning as an entire sentence (20); or as a substitute for a verb, cooccurring with nominals and/or adverbs to constitute a separate sentence, as in (21) and (22) (IP stands for immediate past, FRUST for frustrative).

(20) *kuto j-akuoh-no. pyhseky* [Apalaí]
frog 3SBJ1O-take.across-IP jumping.IDEOPH
'"The frog took me across," (he said). Act of jumping.'

(21) *mokyro i-nio pekã pekã pekã pekã tiwi* [Apalaí]
that.one 3-husband.POSS flap flap flap flap catch.on
'Her husband flapped (his wings, clumsily flying) then caught on (to the landing place with his beak).'

(22) *mame pokõ pokõ pokõ pokõ repe wewe po toto* [Apalaí]
then flap flap flap flap FRUST tree on 3PL
'Then away they flew quite high up in a tree'

Apalaí ideophones may be a single morpheme (as *kyry* 'action of taking hold' of in [19] above), or a sequence of reduplicated forms (e.g. *koe koe koe koe* 'action of paddling'). The number of repetitions may range from two to ten or even more. Several different ideophones may occur in sequence, e.g. *syrỹ tope topõ* 'falling into the water'. The phonological characteristics of ideophones in Apalaí include extra phonemes (a voiced implosive bilabial stop and a voiced velar fricative, for instance), and phonotactic peculiarities such as the occurrence of a glottal stop in final position where it is not permitted in non-ideophonic morphemes.

Clearly, Apalaí ideophones cannot be classified as members of any other word class, be it noun, verb or adverb, though they may occur in the functional slot of all three. They thus have, in addition to their distinctive formal behavior, a characteristic syntactic distribution which is shared by no other word class. Consequently, they constitute a separate syntactic category.

Samarin has suggested that the class of ideophones should be separately defined for each language in which they occur. Yet there are some prototypical properties of ideophones, and Apalaí is a good example for showing us what they look like. Apart from the phonological characteristics, what is most distinctive is their syntactic multifunctionality including predicative force and adverbiality, which is independent of derivation and category-changing mechanisms. If a language possesses a word class with these characteristics, this class may be identified as the class of ideophones.

9. Pro-forms

The category we will be concerned with in this section is traditionally called *pronouns* (Greek *antonymia* 'which stands instead of a noun'). On a general survey of pronouns including articles see Schwartz (2000). We use the broader term *pro-forms* here in view of the fact that an analogous relationship like that between pro-nouns and nouns also exists between "pro-verbs" and verbs, "pro-sentences" and sentences, and possibly between other forms and the categories they replace.

Pro-forms are functionally defined as substitutes which replace members of the corresponding full-word category. Actually, they do not form a single class, for which a formal characterization in terms of syntactic distribution and/or category-establishing morphemes can be provided, but rather a number of different classes, each of which normally exhibits the formal characteristics of the class it substitutes. Nevertheless, there may exist formal traits peculiar to pro-forms. Indoeuropean is a case in point; it possessed a particular set of pronominal case endings with little or no affinity to those of the noun, whose vestiges can still be seen in various daughter languages. In Latin, for instance, the genitive of pronouns has the ending *-ius*, not found anywhere else in the declensional system (*e-ius*, *cu-ius*, *null-ius*, etc.). German, as another example, has a unique ending *-m* 'dative singular' restricted to pronouns (*de-m*, *eine-m*, *welche-m*, *jene-m*, *diese-m*, etc.). Discrepancies between nominal and pronominal morphology can also be sporadically found outside Indoeuropean, e.g. Arabic *hāðā* M, *hāðihī* F (demonstrative), *allaðī* M, *allatī* F (relative pronoun), with gender affixes deviant from those of nouns.

The existence of pro-forms is probably universal, though not necessarily in the form of a distinct word class or a bundle of classes. Though all languages possess elements to express the function of pronouns, they do not necessarily all have a distinct word class of pronouns. Languages that only distinguish between full words and particles must rank pronominals among one of the two. In Cayuga (Northern Iroquoian), for instance, there are two personal pronominals, *i:* '1st person' and *i:s* '2nd person' (plural not being distinguished), and a number of demonstrative and interrogative elements (such as *so:* 'who', *nę:kyęh* 'this', *tho:kyęh* 'that', etc.), which all belong to the class of particles. In spite of the relative stability of pronouns (cf. below), the boundary separating personal pronouns and nouns may at times be rather weak, especially in the second person, where honorific forms may enter the pronominal system (the Ethiopian language Tigrinya, for example, replaced all non-first person pronouns by the noun *nass*-'soul' + possessive suffixes). Cf. also the case of Japanese referred to below. In the following we will outline the various types of pro-forms found in the languages of the world. We will begin with pronouns, which are by far the most common class of pro-forms.

Traditional grammar divides pronouns into personal, reflexive, reciprocal, possessive, demonstrative, relative, interrogative and indefinite. This sub-classification reflects the inventory of Latin and other classical Indoeuropean languages, which is perhaps the largest existing inventory of pronominal subclasses. The overwhelming majority of languages possessing a proper category of pronouns do not distinguish as many subtypes of pronouns as Indoeuropean. It will be useful in the following to proceed from a discussion of the characteristics of the various Indoeuropean subclasses. In each case we will then discuss some of the ways in which languages that lack a particular subclass express their semantic equivalent.

9.1. Personal Pronouns

The occurrence of personal pronouns is nearly universal. If a language does have a distinct class of pronouns, a set of personal pronouns will be the basic member of this class. Most of the research devoted to pronouns has concentrated on personal pronouns, with emphasis both on typological studies (early comprehensive overviews still useful today including vols. 11 and 15 of the journal *Word*, Forchheimer 1953; Maytinskaya 1969; Ingram 1978; and Wiesemann 1986), and syntactic problems of anaphora (Bolinger 1979; Borer 1986; Bosch 1983; Kreiman and Ojeda 1980; and many others).

Categories. Personal pronouns usually distinguish a number of grammatical categories, the most important of which being person. Three persons are found universally: that of the speaker (1st person), the addressee (2nd person), and one which refers to entities that are neither speaker nor addressee (3rd person). Person is a deictic category which belongs to the indexical level of language. The personal pronouns of the 1st and 2nd person point to and thereby identify the polar participants of the speech situation, while the 3rd person pronouns point to entities that do not participate in the speech situation. The 3rd person is thus a negatively defined 'non-person' (Benveniste 1956), and this fact is reflected in the absence of a 3rd person member of the personal pronoun set in many languages. For instance, the North American language families Siouan and Iroquoian distinguish only 1st and 2nd person independent pronominal elements (though affixes do exist for the 3rd person). In Dasenech (Southern Ethiopia) the pronoun of the 3rd person is replaced by the word for 'person'. In general, personal pronouns of the 3rd person are often replaced by or derived from anaphoric pronouns, which in turn are very frequently derived from demonstratives of the farthest deixis (cf. Turkish *o* '3rd person, anaphoric and demonstrative', which is the most distant of the three member set *bu* 'this', *şu* 'that', *o* 'that yonder'; Albanian *aj* '3rd person, anaphoric, and demonstrative', which is the more distant of the two member set *ky* 'this': *aj* 'that' – and many other such examples from around the world). The reason for this is obvious: demonstratives identify their referent by a local relation to a point of reference, which is normally a member of the person category (for a detailed discussion of the connection between person and demonstrative deixis see 9.5). The reference point of the distant demonstrative is always the 3rd person.

By saying that the three persons are universal, we mean that all languages somehow express the distinction between speaker, addressee, and something which is neither of these, but this does not imply that every language has three separate forms. We have already referred to a number of languages obviously lacking pronominal elements for the 3rd person. There are also reports on rare cases of neutralization of 2nd and 3rd person. Wiesemann (1986, viii) states that in Bolante (West Atlantic, Guinée Bissau) the only distinctions made are between N- (homorganic nasal) 'I', *ha-* '2nd or 3rd person singular' and *be-* 'plural persons'. On the other hand, there are many languages that distinguish more than three forms with respect to person categories. The most complex system I know of is that of Ghomala' (a Bantu language), which was published by Wiesemann and which I repeat here in full (see table 7.2.).

(23) Tab. 7.2: Ghomala': System of personal pronouns (Wiesemann 1986)

person	number	minimum	1 pl.	2 pl.	3 pl.
mono	1	gə́	pyə		
	2	o		po	
	3	e			wap
double	1 + 2	pu	pyawu	pə	
	1 + 3	pyəé	pyayʉ́		pyəapu
	2 + 3	poé		poayʉ́	poapu
	3 + 3	pué			wap
triple	1 + 2 + 3	pəayʉ́	pəayʉ́	pəayú	pəapu

This system is unique in exhausting all possible person/number combinations: *pu* 'I and thou', *pyawu* 'we and thou', *pə* 'we and you pl.', etc. The combination of 3 + 3 *pué* means 'two absent persons representing two parties'.

The most common combinations are those of 1 + 2 and 1 + 3, which give rise to the so-called 'inclusive'/'exclusive' distinction of the 1st person plural, e.g. Somali *inna-* 'we – I and thou/you', and *anna-* 'we = I and others, addressee(s) excluded'. The combinatory character of these pronouns is reflected in their etymologies; *anna* is historically *an* 'I' + *na* 'we', while *inna* is *id-* 'stem of 2nd person plural' + *na* (Forchheimer 1953: 105). The inclusive/exclusive distinction occurs in all parts of the world except Europe (especially in Africa, the Americas, and Oceania) and seems to be a feature particularly prone to areal diffusion (cf. Jacobsen 1980; Breeze 1986: 49).

Some languages possess a special pronoun for the unspecified human actor, sometimes referred to as a 'fourth person'. English *one*, French *on*, German *man*, Somali *la*, Hausa *a*, Ngizim *ndá* and comparable forms in other languages. They usually agree with the 3rd person singular, but there are languages which display special verb forms for this purpose (e.g. Navaho). In Chadic the unspecified actor markers are members of the verbal subject pronoun set, which means that one can perhaps speak of a 4th person *in statu nascendi*.

As for the category of number, a binary distinction between a singular and a plural set throughout the three persons is most common. In very few languages are personal pronouns number-indifferent (e.g. Mura Pirahã in Brazil as cited by Wiesemann (1986: viii); on Iroquoian cf. section 9), which is surprising in view of the fact that 'we' is not exactly the plural of 'I' ('I and others' rather than 'several I-s'). We may assume that in such languages the lexeme that refers to the first person simply means 'speaker included' rather than 'I'. In the second person, number indistinction is less problematic, since 'you (pl.)' can in fact be taken to represent a combination of 'addressee' + 'plural'. The difference between 1st and 2nd person with respect to number semantics is reflected formally in quite a number of languages. For instance, Modern English has given up the number distinction in the 2nd person by generalizing the form *you* in place of *thou*, but retained number distinction in the first person (*I:we*). Semitic has two unrelated lexemes for 'I' and 'we' (*'*anā* vs. **niħnu*), but derives 2nd person plural pronouns by adding plural endings to the singular forms (*'*ant-a* M, *'*ant-ī* F 'thou'; *'*ant-umu* M, *'*ant-inna* F 'you').

Dual number occurs less frequently than plural, but is not uncommon. It occurred/occurs in Semitohamitic and Indoeuropean, as well as in Amerindian, Austronesian, and elsewhere. The hierarchy of the frequency of dual marking is 3 > 2 > 1, i.e. a distinct dual form is found most frequently with 3rd person pronouns and least frequently with 1st person pronouns, with the 2nd person occupying an intermediate position. *Trial* and *quadral* numbers have been reported for New Guinea only (cf. Hutchisson 1986; Simons 1986, for instance). Whereas dual also occurs as a category of nouns, these numbers are confined to the pronominal system. The system of Sursurunga, which is displayed in the chart below, has one of the largest inventories of personal pronouns in the world. "The uniqueness of quadral pronouns is not simply the additional column on the pronoun chart which they cause (...), but also the fact that as a group, they have unique uses which are not shared by the other personal pronouns, notably that they cause skewing of number reference when used with relationship terms, and are a distinctive feature of hortatory discourse" (Hutchisson 1986: 2) (see table 7.3.).

(24) Tab. 7.3: Sursurunga: pronominal system (Hutchisson 1986: 2)

	Singular			Nonsingular			
	A	B	C	D			
				Plural	Dual	Trial	Quadral
1 + 2	-ng	i	iau	gi-t	gi-t-ar	gi-t-ul	gi-t-at
1 + 1				gi-m	gi-ur	gi-m-tul	gi-m-at
2	-m	u	i'au	ga-m	ga-ur	ga-m-tul	ga-m-at
3	-n	a	*	di	di-ar	di-tul	di-at

If there is a gender distinction in a language, it is most conspicuously indicated in 3rd singular pronouns. The best example is English, which gave up all gender distinctions in nouns but retained the difference between *he, she* and *it*. In many Afroasiatic (Semitohamitic) languages the inherent gender of nouns is only sporadically reflected in the morphological system, but the personal pronouns of the 3rd person always exhibit a marked difference by the use of sharply distinct masculine and feminine forms. As for gender distinctions in persons other than the 3rd, the hierarchy is 3 > 2 > 1. Gender-marked 2nd person forms are characteristic of Afroasiatic (Semitohamitic) languages, e.g. Cairo Arabic *inta* 'thou.M' and *inti* 'thou.F'; Berber *kai* 'thou.M' and *kəm* 'thou.F', but rarely occur outside this family. I know of only one instance of gender distinction in the 1st person: a small number of Modern Arabic dialects have differentiated the 1st person pronoun *ana* into m. *ana* and f. *ani* in analogy to the 2nd person forms *inta* and *inti* (cf. for Yemenite Diem 1973: 68). Where the language distinguishes nominal classes instead of gender, the situation is *mutatis mutandis* the same. However, there are no known instances of class distinctions in 1st and 2nd person pronouns.

Set distinctions. Many languages have two sets of personal pronouns: strong (stressed) and weak (unstressed). The former is normally made up of independent words, while the latter tends to be cliticized to verbs and may fuse with the verb stem to become conjugational morphemes (pronominal prefixes or suffixes on verbs). Functionally, strong pronouns are typically restricted to discourse-prominent positions in the sentence and occur chiefly as topic and/or focus. There is a universal tendency for strong pronouns to become weakened and cliticized in the course of the historical development of a language. A good example is French, which inherited from Latin a series of strong pronouns (still existing in Italian and Spanish, for example), weakened them to proclitic verbal person markers, and renovated them afterwards by replacing them with a new series of strong pronouns (Latin strong *ego* → proclitic *je* (cf. *je t'aime* [ʃtɛm]) and replaced by new strong *moi* from the accusative *mē*). Cyclical phenomena of this type are common in language history.

Apart from the strong/weak distinction, sets of pronouns can be found which are formed dependent on case. It is not uncommon to have a *rectus/obliquus* distinction, often with two entirely different stems. This type can be exemplified by the first person singular pronoun of Indoeuropean, which had a nominative form approaching **egō*/ **eg(h)om*, the reflexes of which continue into Greek *egô*, Latin *ego*, Old Indian *aham*, English *I* (from *ik*), etc., and an oblique stem *m-* (e.g. Latin accusative *mē*, English *me*, etc.), which formed the basis of the rest of the entire paradigm. A perfect example of a twofold stem distinction throughout the entire set of pronouns is also offered by the some 200 languages of the Afroasiatic (Semitohamitic) family, cf. Somali 1st sg. rectus *ani*, obliquus *i*; 2nd sg. rectus *adi*, obliquus *ku*, etc. The rectus/obliquus set distinction is connected to different function aspects, depending on the system of grammatical relations in the particular language (e.g. subjects vs. non-subjects in accusative languages). There may also be differences as to whether the possessive set is identical with or derived from the oblique set or whether it constitutes a set of its own.

Let us finally mention the phenomenon of the combination of pronouns with tense/aspect markers, which is especially common in Africa. Hausa, for instance, has a system of seven distinct pronoun sets, which express such verbal categories as completive, progressive, habitual, subjunctive, future, relative completive, and relative progressive, in addition to the normal set of independent pronouns. Other Chadic languages behave similarly (cf. Burquest 1986).

Honorific distinctions. Personal pronouns are universally a locus of linguistic means for the expression of esteem for the addressee or related form of polite reference. Degrees of esteem may be directly reflected in the distinctive use of different addressee pronouns. In several European languages 2nd person plural forms are employed instead of singular forms for the expression of honorific address (French, Russian, Albanian, Modern Greek, Turkish, and others). In others, the 3rd person in the singular (Italian *Lui*), or in the plural (German *Sie*), or in combination with a special honorific form (Spanish *Usted*) is used.

In many languages, an honorific form of address is paraphrased by a noun + possessive elements referring to the addressee (similarly to the titles in English, *your Excellency*, *your Majesty*, etc.), e.g. Arabic *ħadʔritak*, lit. 'your presence'. All these strategies have in common that they rely on indirectness, avoiding, in one way or another, the direct address by means of the plain 2nd person singular.

Languages having honorific distinction in the 3rd person are fewer that those with 2nd person honorifics. In general, honorific distinctions in the 3rd person follow the same basic purpose as those of addressee forms, namely to show one's esteem for the addresse (rather than for the referent of the 3rd person whose honorific pronoun is used). This is achieved here in an indirect way by using an honorific pronoun for referring to an absent person who is expected to enjoy high reputation on the addressee's part. Such forms are used in Rumanian and in Amharic, for instance. Honorific distinctions can also be made in the 1st person, for example by the use of a noun denoting a subservient concept such as 'your servant' or similar.

Sociocultural peculiarities going well beyond simple honorific distinctions are sometimes distinguished in personal pronouns. To give just one example, there may be kinship distinctions such as those found in Australian and Eastern Austronesian languages, where it is not uncommon that ego plus a certain generation is referred to by one set, while other kin relations are referred to by another set.

Historical development. Personal pronouns are among the most stable elements of basic vocabulary. The earliest attested language families such as Indoeuropean and Afroasiatic to this day use descendants of the pronoun forms reconstructed for their proto-languages. This means that we have evidence of a remarkable time-stability of pronouns over a period of at least 10,000 years. This does not imply, however, that the great similarities that can be observed among the pronominal elements of the languages of the world are necessarily due to genetic relationship. Most languages construct their pronominal systems around the five consonants *m*, *n*, *t*, *k*, and *s*, often with the same function across languages: *-n-* for the 1st person singular in Afroasiatic, Niger-Congo, Basque, Uto-Aztecan, Algonquian, and Quechua; *-m-* for the 1st person singular in Indoeuropean, Uralic, Turkic, Niger-Congo; *-k-* or *-g-* for the first person singular in Indoeuropean, Afroasiatic, Bantu, Iroquoian, and Austronesian; *-t-* for the 2nd person singular in Indoeuropean, Afroasiatic, Mayan, and Uto-Aztecan; *-k-* for the 2nd person singular in Afroasiatic, Austronesian, Quechua, and Algonquian; *-s-* for the 2nd person singular in Uralic, Turkic, Bantu, and Iroquoian – to mention just a few examples. We cannot be sure whether such similarities result from historical continuity or from the fact that pronouns, like other basic grammatical rather than content elements of language (adpositions, conjunctions, time or place adverbs), show a permanent tendency to simplify their structure and to become restricted to the most basic phonemes and syllable types.

In spite of the relative stability of pronouns, examples of drastic innovation of pronoun systems are attested. An extreme case is Japanese. It started out with a set of normal personal pronouns such as *(w)a* 'I' and *na* 'thou' in the Old Japanese period and ended up with an enormous inventory of some 40 forms in Late Middle and Early Modern Japanese (cf. Miller 1967: 342). An obvious reason for this development is to be found in the complex and rigidly graduated structure of traditional Japanese society, which led to a differentiated classification of people according to their social rank and the parallel development of equally differentiated forms of address. Marked sociocultural change may in fact be an important factor to trigger change in pronominal systems, given the close relationship between address forms and social structure.

9.2. Possessive Pronouns

Possessive pronouns are attributive forms of the personal pronoun. Their most fundamental semantic function is to express possession, i.e. the relation between speech act participants in the role of possessor and an item which denotes the possessed object. Further, they often have a general attributive function, e.g. in cases of argument inheritance in nominalized or semi-nominalized constructions (such as English *my being kissed by Mary*). There is a considerable variety of forms in which possessive pronouns can appear, which depend on the nature of attributive mechanisms in the language in question. In a number of European languages possessive pronouns appear as adjectives, e.g. Latin *meus, -a, -um*, which has retained its adjectival character in its Romance descendants; English *my*, German *mein*, Russian *moy*, etc. are also examples of possessive adjectives. Modern Greek developed enclitic forms of the possessive pronoun, e.g. *o patéras mu* 'my father', where *mu*, originally a genitive form of the personal pronoun, combines with its head *patéras* 'father' into a phonological word, without, however, becoming suffixed to it. Many languages use possessive prefixes or suffixes, which represent a further step in grammaticalization: e.g. *baba-m* 'my father'. Often possessive elements do not appear directly attached to the possessed noun, but are combined with or suffixed to a linking element. This mechanism is particularly common in gender or class languages, where the linker indicates the gender or class of the possessed noun in addition to the mere nexus of possessed and possessor. In the following examples linkers (LK) indicate m./f. gender or class: Albanian *katund-i y-t* (village-DEF:M:NOM LK:M:NOM-you) 'your village', *shtëpi-ja jo-t-e* (house-DEF:F:NOM LK:F:NOM-you-F) 'your house', Dullay *ħalhó h-áayyu* (husband M:LK-my) 'my husband', *naħté c-áayyu* (wife F:LK-my) 'my wife', Swahili *ki-tabu ch-angu* (*ki*-book *ki*-my) 'my book' (*ki*-class), *m-geni w-angu* (*m*-guest *w*-my) 'my guest' (*m*-class), Sursurunga *ka-k bor* (GENERAL CLASS-my pig) 'my pig', *a-k bor* (FOOD CLASS-my pig) 'my pork'. Finally, there is also the possibility that a language has regular genitive forms of personal pronouns which are employed as possessives.

For the categories expressed by possessive pronouns see the preceding section. Mention must be made here only of the distinction between alienable and inalienable possession, which is expressed by different forms of possessive pronouns in many languages (cf. Seiler 1983). For instance, in Sursurunga, a language of New Guinea, one says *ka-k bor* (see above) 'my pig' but *kiki-ng* (foot-POSS:1SG) 'my foot' (Hutchisson 1986: 6–7). In this language, a possessive relation with a concept not closely associated with the possessor (alienable) is expressed by possessive markers suffixed to linkers, while a possessive relation with a concept that forms an integral part of the possessor (inalienable) is expressed by possessive suffixes attached to the possessed noun directly. The degree of alienability can be arranged along a scale of inherent relationality, ranging from clear cases of inherently relational nouns such as kinship terms to clear cases of non-inherently relational nouns such as material possession (e.g. *money*). Languages having an inalienable/alienable distinction differ widely in where they put the turning point on the scale. In general, what is considered an integral part of something may well be dependent on culture or tradition. Interestingly, when the inalienable/alienable distinction is employed in the syntax of arguments (e.g. argument inheritance as a concomitant of nominalization), it is typically patients that are constructed inalienably, whereas agents use the alienable construction.

Finally, a word should be said here about the definiteness of possessive phrases. Language philosophers have often claimed that possessive phrases are inherently definite given the foolproof identifiability of their referent. Examples frequently quoted are English and German, whose possessives are used without the definite article and are therefore analyzed as determiners themselves. Nevertheless, this is a language-specific device; in Modern Greek, for instance, possessive phrases a not inherently definite and can be used with the definite, the indefinite, and the non-referential zero article.

9.3. Reflexive Pronouns

Reflexivization has been the subject of a number of substantial monographs over the last decades, notably Faltz (1977), Everaert (1986), Geniušienė (1987), Kemmer (1993), König and Gast (2008). Reflexive elements may come in a number of disguises. Many languages have morphological means of reflexivization in the form of one or more diatheses used for that purpose: there may be a reflexive voice proper or the reflexive reading is included in voice distinctions of a more general nature such as middle voice, inactive, anticausative, and the like. On the other hand, many languages also possess separate reflexive elements either instead of or in addition to the respective voice distinctions. Whether or not these should be accredited the status of "pronouns" is a matter of dispute. Kemmer (1993) makes a distinction between "light" and "heavy" elements, the light ones comprising the formatives of morphological voice distinctions, but also including some cases traditionally called pronouns such as the reflexes of Indoeuropean **se*, which continued into Romance, Germanic and Slavic languages, in various functions and stages of grammaticalization. It is an established fact that **se* both formally and functionally once belonged to the system of personal pronouns and indicated reflexivity independent of gender, number, or person. In many of the daughter languages **se* became restricted to the 3rd person (cf. Latin *se* and its Romance recurrences, German *sich*, etc.), while in the 1st and 2nd person the ordinary personal pronouns are used. In Slavic, on the other hand, reflexes of **se* retained its person-independent character and developed a tendency to become cliticized to the verb form, thus initiating something like a new reflexive voice (cf. Russian *-sja*; cf. also the similar development in Scandinavian languages).

Kemmer's heavy reflexives, on the other hand, include a number of independent ("self-standing") forms of various provenience: (1) a variable reflexive pronoun in its own right, indicating a number of grammatical categories such as person, number, gender, case, and others. Ancient Greek possessed such a pronoun: *emautón* 'myself (acc.)', *seautón* 'yourself (acc.)', etc.; (2) a nominal element 'the self' in combination or not with possessive pronouns. Clear instances of this sort are Albanian *vete*, det. *vetja* (a feminine noun) 'the self' (without possessive pronouns, e.g. *e lavdërova veten* 'I praised myself', lit. 'I praised the self'), Modern Greek *o eaftós* (*mu*, *su*, ...) 'my (your, etc.) self', Turkish *kendi-m*, *-n*, ... 'my (your, etc.) self', all of which are regular nouns. English *myself*, *yourself*, etc. is another example, though the element *self* is not as independent as the comparable lexemes of Albanian, Greek, and Turkish, so it might be suggested that the English construction is on its way to joining group 1); (3) a nominal element of a more general meaning ('head', 'body', 'soul' or similar) in combination with possessive pronouns. This type can be exemplified by Arabic *nafs* 'soul': *qatala* *nafs-a-hu* (he.killed soul-ACC-his) 'he killed himself'; (4) some subsidiary construction. In Sursurunga, reflexivity is expressed by the verb 'return': 'I hit returned to me' = 'I hit myself' (Hutchisson 1086: 19).

Theorists of grammaticalization have suggested that there is a historical continuum from heavy reflexives such as (3) via (2) and (1) which ends up with morphologically loose constructions such as the Russian one, ultimately arriving at the morphologically-marked voice distinctions that constitute the core of "light constructions" (Lehmann 1995). When looking at the attested historical development of reflexive systems, however, there is little evidence for a historical path that leads from body part terms (such as 'soul' or 'head') through the various stages postulated to morphological elements responsible for a reflexive/middle voice distinction such as the 10,000 years old *-t- in Afroasiatic.

In some languages, the simple object and possessive forms of personal pronouns have their functions extended to mark reflexive relations. The practice of many European languages to express reflexivity in the 1st and 2nd person by the normal personal pronoun may be mentioned again in this connection, but there are languages which use personal pronouns as reflexives or even reciprocals in all persons. In the Grassfields Bantu language Mundani, a sentence such as (25) has the three readings (a) 'They$_i$ are helping them$_j$', (b) 'They$_i$ are helping themselves$_i$', and (c) 'They are helping each other' (Parker 1986: 149):

(25) *bɔ́ɔ̀ ǹ-tɨ̀ŋ-á wɔ́b* [Mundani]
3PL:SBJ fact-help-IPFV OBJ:3PL

The discussion so far has not been very optimistic regarding the identification of reflexive pronouns as a cross-linguistically interesting syntactic subcategory. However, the question of what the widespread distinction between light and heavy reflexive elements, whatever their categorization parts-of-speech-wise may be, is all about, remains. Generally speaking, heavy reflexives are preferred when the reflexive element is pragmatically prominent (e.g. focused or emphasized), or when its referent can be conceived of as being somewhat independent of the antecedent's referent (as in situation like 'seeing oneself in the mirror', 'killing oneself', where the same individual can be seen as "split", as it were, in different roles). A further factor lies in the language-specific semantics of heavy reflexives, which are not seldom derived from what has been called pronouns of identity ('X personally, all by himself, without the help of others'). Another factor is the ambiguity of light reflexive constructions; e.g. do they have passive, impersonal, etc. readings? This may well influence the necessity of emphasizing the reflexive reading proper. Finally, there may be broader uses of reflexives, e.g. the difference between reflexive and anaphoric pronouns may be exploited to indicate degrees of distance and thus be employed to express certain aspects of switch reference, as in Chadic (Africa) and Chechen (Caucasus), or logophoric relations (for logophoric pronouns proper, cf. 9.5).

9.4. Reciprocal Pronouns

Recent studies on reciprocity include Siloni (2008) and Behrens (2008). It seems as if the four-way role constellation inherent in reciprocity (x on y, y on x) cognitively leads the human mind to the assumption that reciprocity involved a double reflexive relation and therefore implies an intimate relationship to reflexivity. Quite often light reflexives (cf. 9.3) also have a reciprocal reading, predominantly in the plural. Thus, when Modern Greek says *filjéme* (1SG middle voice), the default readings are either passive or reflexive; it may mean (in the passive reading) that I am being kissed by someone, or (in the reflexive reading) that I am kissing myself on some part of my body. In the 1st person plural, however, the default interpretation is reciprocal. The form *filjómaste* is usually understood to signal reciprocity 'we are kissing (each other)'. Northern Iroquoian languages have a device to disambiguate; reflexive and reciprocal readings are formally distinguished by the use of the dual prefix *te-* for the latter. It has often been claimed in the literature that reciprocity is restricted to the plural domain, but this is not the case (cf. Behrens 2007 for singular reciprocals).

Are there any candidates for reciprocals as a subcategory of pronouns? Heavy reciprocals in the sense of Kemmer (1993) would be a case in point. There are a few languages that possess reciprocal pronouns proper, such as Ancient Greek (*allēl-ōn*, *-ois*, *-ous* 'each other' in genitive, dative and accusative). Also, there is a tendency to grammaticalize transparent reciprocal constructions such as the very common 'the one … the other' into fossilized pronoun-like heavy reciprocals as in English *one another*, *each other*, German *einander*. Nevertheless, the use of specific "pronouns" does not appear to be one of the major strategies for signalling reciprocity in the languages of the world.

9.5. Demonstrative Pronouns

This subset of pronouns represents the grammaticalization of primarily spatiotemporal deixis. On deixis in relation to personal and demonstrative pronouns see among others Lyons (1977, chapter 15) and Anderson and Keenan (1985). The origin of demonstrative deixis (as well as of deixis in general) is the speech situation with its characteristic egocentric bias. "The speaker, by virtue of being the speaker, casts himself in the role of ego and relates everything to his viewpoint. He is at the zero-point of the spatiotemporal coordinates (…) Egocentricity is temporal as well as spatial, since the role of speaker is being transferred from one participant to the other as the conversation proceeds, and the participants may move around as they are conversing: the spatiotemporal zero-point (the here and now) is determined by the place of the speaker at the moment of utterance" (Lyons 1977: 638). As a result, demonstrative systems always center around an element that that points to a referent in the vicinity of the speaker. Anderson and Keenan (1985: 280) point out that, in principle, a language might possess only a single item which could function as a general demonstrative pronoun and which would simply indicate something like 'present to speaker', without referring to distance from the speaker, or to other parameters. They observe that informal varieties of Czech come close to this situation in that "the commonly used *ten* (…) may be used for items which are either close to or far from the speaker". In French, the neutralization of *ce-ci* and *ce-là* into simple *ce* also results in non-distinction with respect to distance from the speaker. A tendency towards a one-term deictic system seems to be an areal feature of Central Europe, since Colloquial German has seen the same development.

Irrespective of such rare instances of distance non-distinction, the canonical case is such that the egocentricity of the speech situation, resulting in a basic opposition between the speaker an everything else, leads to a deictic dichotomy of 'near-to-speaker' (proximal) vs. 'far-from-speaker' (distal) categories. Nearly all languages examined so far possess at least two distinct categories along the basic spatial dimension. The most familiar example of a minimal two-term system is English (*this* vs. *that*); Standard German, Semitic languages (Hebrew, Arabic), Hausa, and Iroquoian are further examples from different parts of the world.

In many languages there are three-term demonstrative systems which identify their referent by a local relation to a point of reference which is prototypically a member of the person category. As might be expected, the reference point of the near demonstrative is always the speaker, while that of the distant demonstrative is always the 3rd person. According to Anderson and Keenan (1985: 282), the systems differ in the interpretation given to their middle terms. They distinguish two major types of systems: those in which the middle term points to objects in he vicinity of the addressee (person-oriented systems), and those in which the middle term points to objects that are simply more remote than the near-to-speaker category, but closer than the most distant category. It should be noted, however, that for most languages having three-term systems it is far from clear to which of the two types their systems belong, and that a system that looks distance oriented at first sight, may still be person-oriented in its prototypical (central) instances. A rather undisputed case of a distance-oriented system seems to be Spanish, which exhibits a three-way contrast of relative distance from the speaker: close (*este*), farther away (*ese*), and comparatively remote (*aquel*). Most three-term systems seem to be person-oriented, with middle terms referring to objects in the environment of the addressee. "The Serbs say *ovo meni, to tebi i ono njemu* 'this for me, that for you, and that yonder for him', thus explicitly relating the three demonstratives to the three persons" (Greenberg 1986: xx). A rather impressive further example is Armenian, whose suffixal elements *-s*, *-d*, and *-n* indicate personal relations of the 1st, 2nd, and 3rd person, resp., on the one hand, and demonstrative relations of near, middle, and far deixis, resp., on the other, so that there is a total coincidence of personal and local deixis. Other person-oriented systems reported are those of Palauan and Japanese.

The distinction of more than three degrees of distance is not very frequent. What appears at first sight to be distance distinctions, often turns out upon closer inspection to be the addition of a further parameter, such as visibility. Asheninca, a language of Central Peru, is reported to have a four-term system distinguishing 'close to speaker', 'nearby', 'medium distance', and 'far away, out of sight' (Reed and Payne 1986: 330). Visibility also plays a significant role in the system of Kwakwa'la, with the difference that it is superimposed upon a person-oriented deictic system, yielding a six-way contrast between 'near to speaker, visible', 'near to speaker, invisible', etc. Genuine distance-oriented systems with more than three terms are Quileute (4 terms), CiBemba (5 terms), and Malagassy (7 terms), cf. Anderson and Keenan (1985: 286–288). Other physical dimensions can be superimposed on deictic systems, such as contrasts of height relative to the speaker or contrasts based on geographical features (landmarks) such as 'downhill/uphill', 'downstream/upstream'.

Since time and space are closely associated in the egocentric cognitive system (i.e. what is remote in space is also remote in time), time is often encountered as a distinctive dimension parallel to space. In English, as well as in many other languages, we can use primarily spatial demonstratives referring to temporal notions; *this month* is unambiguously the current one, while *that period* refers to a remote epoch. A few languages have extra demonstratives for time reference. In Boni (a Cushitic language of Kenya), for instance, there is a contrast between a form indicating temporal remoteness (either past or future), and an extratemporal or habitual demonstrative ('the usual x', 'the x I am habitually concerned with', or the like). From such cases of what we might call exophoric time reference it is only a small step towards endophoric (text-oriented) temporal reference. Many languages use one of the distant demonstratives for 'the aforementioned', and this is the source of the extremely common anaphoric function of distant demonstratives. Phoricity categories may thus be inherently combined with spatial functions of demonstratives. A characteristic case is Quechua, where three degrees of deixis cover the following combinations of spatial reference and phoricity: *kay* 'this' = cataphoric (forward-referring), *chay* 'that' = anaphoric (referring back to something previously mentioned), *taqay* 'that yonder' = exophoric (referring to some object in the real world) (data from the Huallaga dialect, cf. Weber 1986: 336). On the other hand, there are also languages that separate the two dimensions of distance and phoricity. In Hausa, for example, there is a special anaphoric demonstrative 'the one previously mentioned', which contrasts with a pair of cataphoric demonstratives differentiated according to a two-term system of distance ('this new one', 'that new one'). In the Niger-Congo language Yąg Dii of Cameroun (Bohnhoff 1986: 124) there are two phoricity categories in addition to the spatial deictic system, viz. 'that previously mentioned' and 'that just mentioned'. The rare case of a language having only endophoric pronouns is exemplified by the Brazilian language Maxakalí, which distinguishes *'ohõm* ~ *'õm* 'this one now being introduced' vs. *nõ'õm* ~ *nõm* 'that one already introduced'. Incidentally, Proto-Indoeuropean also had a specific anaphoric pronoun in addition to the spatial demonstratives, the stem **i-* (cf. Latin *is*, German *er*).

Before leaving the subject of demonstratives, let us briefly discuss a further phoricity function which is sometimes assumed by demonstratives, the logophoric function. "Logophoric pronouns are used to mark coreference with a participant whose speech, thoughts or feelings are being reported in a particular syntactic context" (Parker 1986: 151). Logophoric or reported speech reference is an areal feature of West African languages and has been well described for several languages of this part of the world since the 1970s (e.g. Clements 1975 on Ewe; Hyman and Comrie 1981 on Gokana; Voorhoeve 1980 on Bantu in general; for comparative treatment cf. the classic Hagège 1974 and more recently Roncador 1992: 1206). Logophoric pronouns are chiefly used in object clauses dependent on a verb of speaking, thinking, hearing, or feeling. They are coreferent with the subject of the superordinate verb and distinguish its referent from other third person referents in the sentence. In addition to the logophoric demonstrative proper, similar disambiguating functions can be fulfilled by reflexives, possessives, and other types of pronouns, which usually combine to form an entire system of logophoric marking, which may even extend its function to areas such as switch reference, subordinate clause formation, hortative constructions, etc.

9.6. Relative Pronouns

Let us define a relative pronoun as a pro-form which replaces the empty slot of a relative clause (what is commonly called the relativized element), as in English *who* in (26), which replaces the deleted subject of *wrote that*:

(26) *The man who wrote that was a genius.*

Very few languages possess relative pronouns in this sense; it is one of the minor relativization strategies to form relative clauses with relative markers that take over the grammatical categories of the relativized element. Other types of relative clause formation such as attributive markers, invariable relative markers or conjunctions, determiners of sorts, specific relative forms of the verb, or relative participles are by far more frequent. The particles involved are often called relative pronouns, but if we take pronouns in the narrow sense defined above as a replacer category, the term is inadequate in most cases. For relative clause formation in general and a detailed description of the relevant strategies cf. Lehmann (1984). Most of the languages for which genuine relative pronouns have been described are members of the Indoeuropean family, in which such pronouns derive from two different sources: interrogative and demonstrative. Interogative-based relatives may arise through the correlative *diptychon*-construction (Lehmann 1984: 147–149), such as (in imitating ungrammatical English)

(27) *which man wrote that, he was a genius*
which man wrote that was a genius

while demonstrative-based relatives develop from relative constructions with a determining/attributivizing linker:

(28) *the man, this (who) wrote that, was a genius*

For the history of relative clauses in Indoeuropean cf. Hettrich (1988).

9.7. Interrogative Pronouns

The class of interrogative elements is almost universal, although in languages that do not distinguish an extra category of pronouns, interrogatives may exist in forms other than those of the pronominals. One of the alleged exceptions to universality is Lyélé, a language of the Gur branch of the Niger-Congo family, which is purported to use demonstratives with question intonation for interrogatives (Showalter 1986: 209–210). In Godié (Marchese 1986: 231) the interrogative pronoun is not distinct from the relative, but here I would argue that the interrogative is used for the formation of relative clauses (cf. 9.6), rather than the other way around, though it seems that the element in question is derived from the demonstrative/anaphoric 3rd person pronoun. In any case, languages lacking a distinct set of elements with exclusively interrogative function are very few in number.

Interrogatives universally tend to distinguish an animate (*who*?) and an inanimate (*what*?) form, irrespective of any other types of gender distinction which may be present in the language, or of the lack of noun classification. Very few languages have been reported to lack this distinction; one example is Asheninca (Reed and Payne 1986: 322–324), which has only one general interrogative pronoun *t^sh^ika* 'who, what, where, when, ...', the more subtle differences being either inferred by the semantics of the verb or explicitly marked by verbal affixes (e.g. *t^sh^ika* + instrumental affix gives 'why').

In addition to 'who' and 'what', languages quite often also distinguish an interrogative pronoun used for giving choices and comparable to English *which*.

The interrogative pronouns 'who' and 'what' usually lack distinct plural forms, because number is normally either irrelevant or not yet specifiable in the question. There are some notable exceptions, such as Ojibwe (Schwartz and Dunnigan 1986: 302) and Modern Greek, which is also special among Indoeuropean languages by distinguishing a feminine form of 'who' as well.

The most striking syntactic feature of interrogatives is their universal tendency to occur in focus constructions. In Amharic, for instance, a constituent question is more or less obligatorily formed with the question word clefted:

(29) *yät näw yämmihedut ?* [Amharic]
where is they.are.going.REL
'Where is it that they are going?'

This corresponds exactly to the answers to such questions, which have the same structure with the questioned element in focus:

(30) *Gwändär näw yämmihedut* [Amharic]
Gondar is they.are.going.REL
'It is Gondar that they are going to.'

Cf. also French *qu'est-ce que* and many other constructions of this type around the world. There is another common syntactic rule involving interrogatives, which has received much attention in the literature (mainly because it plays such an enormous role in generativist theory), viz. that of question word fronting (WH-movement), such as in English.

(31) *What did you say?*

It may be assumed that this syntactic operation is nothing but an historical offshoot of question word focusing (cf. Sasse 1977, where focus is misleadingly called "topic"). In some languages, interrogatives are obligatorily combined with particles such as those which characterize sentence ("yes/no") questions and which usually appear combined with the focused element in such questions. This practice can perhaps be interpreted as another manifestation of the tendency to set off the question word as a separate predicative element from the rest of the sentence in order to give it discourse-pragmatic prominence, so that the syntactic behavior of interrogatives can generally be explained in terms of their inherent focus character.

9.8. Indefinite Pronouns

Very little can be said here about indefinites except that they are not a universal subgroup of pronouns. Even in the Classical languages, on the basis of which the terminology was developed, they appear to be a wastebasket category including *bona fide* pronouns side by side with nouns, quantifiers of sorts and other hard-to-determine elements. If we look into the equivalents of 'all', 'some', 'any', 'every', 'something', 'nothing', etc., in the languages of the world, we normally find a number of heterogeneous forms that have nothing in common to justify their classification into a distinct subgroup of pronouns. To give just one example, in Egyptian Arabic, all of these concepts are expressed by regular nouns: 'all' is an abstract noun *kull* 'allness'; 'someone' and 'something' are expressed by the words for 'man' and 'thing', resp., which, combined with the verb in the negative form, yield the equivalents of 'nobody' and 'nothing'. Even in familiar languages such as English, many indefinite pronouns consist of an element indicating indefiniteness and a noun of a very general "ontological category" – indicating meaning such as 'person' or 'thing'. Yet it is not uncommon for languages to possess a derived category of indefinite pronouns on the basis of interrogatives. In Quechua, the interrogatives are used to form questions when combined with the question marker (*-taq*), and indefinites when suffixed with the indefinite marker *-pis*: *pi-taq* 'who?' vs. *pi-pis* 'someone' (cf. Weber 1986: 336). In To'abaita (Oceanic), indefinites are formed by adding *bana* 'just, only' to the interrogatives (Simons 1986: 30). The traditional Indoeuropean practice is to derive indefinites from interrogatives by dropping the accent.

9.9. Other pro-forms

In principle, all instances of what has traditionally been called "pronouns in adjectival use" (possessive adjectives, demonstratives when used attributively, the interrogative adjective 'which', etc.) are *pro-adjectives*. All of these types have already been discussed in the relevant sections under pronouns.

Pro-adverbs are mainly found in interrogative, demonstrative, and indefinite functions, cf. English *where, when, here, there, how, thus, somewhere, somehow.* Pro-adverbs are extremely common in languages all over the world, but still there are some languages that lack them and instead use noun phrases (e.g. 'this place', 'some place', 'which place' for 'here', 'somewhere', and 'where', resp.) or interrogative verbs (cf. below).

Pro-numerals are interrogative, demonstrative, and indefinite quantifiers such as Latin *quotus* 'the how many-eth', etc. Quantifiers have a slight tendency to form a minor syntactic category of its own.

There may also exist *pro-verbs* of different kinds. Mandarin Chinese is known to distinguish the general form *lai* 'do it' from the demonstrative *tzemme* 'do this' and *nemme* 'do that'. There are also some languages that use interrogative pro-verbs, which may be of the 'do what?'-type (Southern Paiute *ayan·i* 'do what?, act how?' and *an·ia* 'say what?') or act as equivalents of pronominal/proadverbial question words (Yana *beema'a-* 'be where?', *beeyauma-* 'be when?').

On "yes", "no", and tag questions, which are occasionally called "pro-sentences" and "pro-clauses", cf. Schachter (1985: 32).

10. Particles and the subclasses

10.1. Conjunctions and complementizers

Particles that join clauses or parts of clauses (words or phrases) are traditionally called conjunctions. Two subclasses of conjunctions are usually distinguished, *coordinating* (e.g. *and, or, but*) and *subordinating* (e.g. *that, if, when, because, while*). Some scholars prefer a more detailed subclassification, which we will pass over here, although no doubt preferable in a language-specific analysis, concentrating instead on the question of how far conjunctions and complementizers can be taken to represent cross-linguistically comparable (minor) categories.

For early cross-linguistic studies on coordination in general, including the discussion of conjunctions and their syntactic peculiarities, cf. Brettschneider (1978), Dik (1968), Payne (1985). A recent treatment of the typology of coordination is Mauri (2008). Coordinating conjunctions assign equal rank to the elements they connect. The basic coordinating conjunction is *and*. I have heard of very few languages that do not possess an equivalent of *and* (Maricopa being a possible exception, cf. Gil 1991), though often in the form of an affix rather than a particle. Many languages have at least two *and*-s, one of which is normally restricted to clause or sentence conjoining, while the other is predominantly used for connecting noun phrases. In Somali, for example, *iyo* joins nouns an *oo* joins verbs and adjectives. Equivalents of *and* reserved for joining nouns are often identical with or historically derived from comitative elements (cf. Swahili *na* 'and' = 'with', as well as many other examples from all over the world). On the other hand, there is an intimate relationship between conjunctions joining verbs (clauses or sentences) and elements indicating a temporal sequence ('then' → 'and then' → 'and'). Aside from elements with pure connective functions, many languages possess coordinating conjunctions carrying additional semantic shades, such as selective (*or* – inclusive or exclusive), adversative (*whereas, but*), etc. The structural principles of coordination differ considerably from language to language; and the typical European trichotomy *and/or/but* is not as widespread as formerly assumed. For details cf. the literature referred to above.

In contrast to coordinating conjunctions, subordinators or complementizers are not a universal class. The presence of such elements in a language depends on the mechanism employed for clause-combining. Subordinators and complementizers are typically found in languages which use finite verb forms in both matrix (main) clauses and embedded (dependent) clauses, such as Indoeuropean and Semitic languages. On the other hand, there are languages like Agaw in Central Ethiopia (cf. Hetzron 1976), that do not have any subordinating conjunction at all, but express the subordinate relationship between a main and a dependent clause by means of a large inventory of special subordinative paradigms, correlating with a finite main-clause paradigm. Lack of subordinators in a language may also be due to the fact that its basic clause-connecting strategy is not one of subordination at all, but of juxtaposition, where the semantic relationship between the clauses is left to inference as opposed to being signaled explicitly by conjunctions.

Because of the intimate relationship between the presence of subordinators and the typology of complex sentences, subordinators are often innovated or borrowed, especially when a language shifts from one syntactic type to another (on borrowing of conjunctions see Thompson and Longacre (1985: 204–205).

10.2. Adpositions

The term adposition has been established recently in order to cover prepositions, postpositions, and circumpositions. For a general survey cf. Kahr (1975); for Indoeuropean, Delbrück (1893) and Wackernagel (1924) are also still useful. Adpositions are function words which enter a specific syntactic relationship with a noun or noun phrase and which at the same time indicate the functional role of the noun within the sentence. In English, for instance, a phrase like *on the wall* in *the picture is hanging on the wall* structurally displays characteristics of a specific type of endocentric construction, usually called prepositional phrase, while functionally it serves to express a participant role within the greater context of the state of affairs described by the verb, namely a type of location (that of contiguity).

The syntactic relationship which exists between the adposition and its noun in European languages may be described as "government"; the noun of an adpositional phrase is governed by the adposition, hence the widely used term "object of preposition". However, adpositional constructions are not always adequately described in terms of government; they are often characterized instead by some form of attributive relationship (genitive or possessive phrase), as in Turkish *Aladağın* (GEN) *ardında* 'behind the A. (GEN) mountain'. Both types of syntactic relations syntactic relations may combine in cases such as English *by means of …*

A formal parameter that has received much attention in the literature since Greenberg (1966) is that of the occurrence of prepositions vs. postpositions. It has been claimed that there is a functional relationship between the position of the adpositional element (either before or after the noun) and the basic word order of a language. The common denominator is the position of the object relative to the verb: languages with VO order tend to have prepositions, while languages with OV order tend to have postpositions (cf. Frey, this volume).

Functionally, adpositions serve to mark syntactic relations and semantic roles of arguments (complements and adjuncts). A thoroughgoing analysis of this word class in a particular language therefore necessarily presupposes the examination of their position in the broader context of case relations. In other words, adpositions, case markers, preverbs, and other types of relational markers tend to form a macroparadigm of syntactic relations which determine a family of constructions in the context of which adpositions have to be studied.

10.3. Other types of particles

Other subtypes of function words may be distinguished according to their functional and distributional peculiarities, such as *articles* and similar determiners (English *the*, *a*), *auxiliaries* (English *be*, *will*), *verb particles* (English *up* in *wake up*), *modal* or *discourse particles* (German *ja*, *doch*), etc. Sometimes such elements oscillate between subcategories of other categories and particles; e.g. in more conservative Indoeuropean languages articles display pronoun-like characteristics (cf. Schwartz 2000), while auxiliaries constitute a defective subclass of verbs. In other languages auxiliaries may be less obviously related to verbs. All these subcategories are too language-specific to justify cross-linguistic treatment here; for some generalizations cf. Schachter (1985: 40–46); on auxiliaries Steele (1978), Steele et al. (1981) and Heine (1997).

11. Numerals

Numerals have been considered a word class in the European tradition because they constitute a closed lexical set with distinct morphosyntactic behavior. They are only going to be discussed here in passing, however, because those languages in which they are a sharply distinct lexicogrammatical category, due to both their specific declensional characteristics and their specific distributional behavior, are the exception rather than the rule. In many languages, there is nothing to suggest that numerals must be classified in any other way than as ordinary nouns or adjectives. With regard to the general word-class assignment of numerals, there seems to be a universal tendency that smaller numerals are adjectival in nature and larger nominal (Greenberg 1978: 252). What makes numerals often enjoy a special status even within the major word class they are assigned to is, first of all, their property of representing a series of progression (Hurford 1975: 1), a fact that influences both their phonological and their morphosyntactic behavior, and secondly, the specific syntactic mechanisms of numeral combination (addition, multiplication, etc.), including the often curiously complicated agreement (or disagreement) rules for the combination of numeral + counted item.

In certain languages numerals belong to the larger word class of *quantifiers*, which is distinguished by specific syntactic characteristics and which, in addition to numerals, is made up of such elements as ‘many’, ‘much’, ‘few’, ‘all’, etc.

Further details about numeral systems may be found in Greenberg (2000), with further references.

12. Interjections

This word class is often treated very summarily in the grammars of individual languages as well as in theoretical parts-of-speech studies. The reason is that interjections are not a uniform category and cannot be defined as representatives of a certain syntactic constructional slot. In other words, they may constitute a word class, but not a syntactic category. They are thus at best marginal to the discussion of parts-of-speech theory. Moreover, they enjoy a special status among the word classes in so far as they cannot be strictly classified: either as full words, or as function words. Interjections are uninflectable particles that function as equivalents of entire sentences. Theoretically, they may replace any type of sentence; most of the time, however, interjections function as equivalents of exclamatory sentences. English examples of interjections functioning to replace various sentence types are the following: *uh*? (interrogative); *yeah*, *aha* (declarative); *hey*, *pst*, *shh* (imperative); *pshaw*, *oh*, *wow*, *ouch* (exclamatory).

Interjections are practically universal among the world’s languages; at any rate this author has not come across any language that lacks them. However, not only the presence, but also the main characteristic of interjections, i.e. their general tendency to display phonological behavior otherwise unknown in the language, is common for all languages. Phonological deviation may be varied. Interjections are often the only group of morphemes in which consonantal syllable nuclei are allowed: German *brr* 'stop' (said to horses), *pst* 'be quiet!', English *tsk-tsk, hm*, etc. In the Dullay languages (Ethiopia), interjections are the only elements that violate an otherwise obligatory morpheme structure rule which inhibits final consonants. Furthermore, in many languages interjections make use of sounds that are not part of the regular phonological system (e.g. a click in *tsk-tsk*).

Apart from their phonological peculiarities, interjections rarely exhibit any specific formal characteristics. They are seldom incorporated into the rest of the grammatical system. One notable exception is Albanian where interjections that function as imperatives may take plural forms, e.g. *hë* [hə] 'up!', 'let's go!', pl. *hë-ni.*

There is some affinity and perhaps a blurry dividing line between interjections and ideophones. In fact, the class of interjections often constitutes a "backdoor" through which onomatopoeic material enters the vocabulary. For instance, the Amharic interjection *k'ucc'* 'sit down!' yielded the ideophone *k'ucc'* in *k'ucc' alä* ('say *k'ucc'*'), which is presently the normal word for 'to sit'.

13. References (selected)

Amborn, H., G. Minker, and H.-J. Sasse
1980 *Das Dullay. Materialien zu einer Ostkuschitischen Sprachgruppe.* Berlin.

Anderson, S. R., and E. L. Keenan
1985 Deixis. In: T. Shopen (ed.), *Language Typology and Syntactic Description*, vol 3, 259–308. Cambridge: Cambridge University Press.

Backhouse, A. E.
1984 Have all the adjectives gone? *Lingua 62*: 169–186.

Bates, E., and B. MacWhinney
1982 Functionalist approaches to grammar. In: Eric Wanner and Lisa Gleitmann (eds.), *Language Acquisition: The State of the Art*, 173–218. Cambridge: Cambridge University Press.

Behrens, L.
1994 Alternationen – ein Schlüssel für die Universalienforschung? *Zeitschrift für Sprachwissenschaft* 13 (2): 149–200.

Behrens, L.
1995 Categorizing between lexicon and grammar: The MASS/COUNT distinction in a cross-linguistic perspective. *Lexicology* 1: 1–112.

Behrens, L.
2007 Backgrounding and suppression of reciprocal participants: A cross-linguistic study. *Studies in Language* 31 (2): 327–408.

Behrens, L., and H. J. Sasse
2003 *The Macrostructure of Lexicon-Grammar Interaction: A Study of "gold" in English and Arabic*. München: Lincom Europa Verlag.

Benveniste, E.
1956 La nature des pronoms. In: M. Halle et al. (eds.), *For Roman Jakobson*, 34–37. The Hague.

Benveniste, E.
1966 *Problèmes de Linguistique Générale.* Paris.

Bergenholtz, H.
1983 Grammatik im Wörterbuch: Wortarten. In: *Studien zur Neuhochdeutschen Lexikographie* IV 1–3/83, Bergenholtz. Hildesheim, etc.
Bhat, D. N. S.
1994 *The Adjectival Category: Criteria for Differentiation and Identification.* Amsterdam / Philadelphia: John Benjamins.
Bhat, D. N. S.
2000 Word classes and sentential functions. In: P. M. Vogel and B. Comrie (eds.), *Approaches to the Typology of Word Classes*, 47–63. Berlin: Mouton de Gruyter.
Bhat, D. N. S., and R. Pustet
2000 Adjective. In: G. Booij, C. Lehmann and J. Mugdan (eds.), *Morphologie. Ein Internationalen Handbuch zur Flexion und Wortbildung*, 757–769. (HSK 17.1, 1. Halbband.) Berlin, New York: de Gruyter.
Bohnhoff, L. E.
1986 Yąg Dii (Duru) pronouns. In: U. Wiesemann (ed.), *Pronominal Systems*, 103–129. Tübingen: Narr.
Bolinger, D.
1979 Pronouns in discourse. In: Talmy Givon (ed.), *Discourse and Syntax*, 289–309. (Syntax and Semantics 12.) New York: Academic Press.
Booij, G., Lehmann, C., and J. Mugdan (eds.)
2000 *Morphologie. Ein Internationales Handbuch zur Flexion und Wortbildung.* (HSK 17.1, 1. Halbband.) Berlin, New York: de Gruyter.
Borer, H. (ed.)
1986 *Syntax and Semantics, the Syntax of Pronominal Clitics*, vol. 19. New York.
Bosch, P.
1983 *Agreement and Anaphora. A Study of the Role of Pronouns in Syntax and Discourse.* New York.
Breeze, M. J.
1986 Personal pronouns in Gimira. In: U. Wiesemann (ed.), *Pronominal Systems*, 47–69. Tübingen: Narr.
Brettschneider, G.
1978 *Koordination und Syntaktische Komplexität. Zur Explikation eines Linguistischen Begriffs.* München.
Broschart, J.
1987 *Noun, Verb, and Participation.* (Arbeiten des Kölner Universalien-Projekts 67). Köln.
Broschart, J.
1997 Why Tongan does it differently: Categorial distinctions in a language without nouns and verbs. *Linguistic Typology* 1: 123–165.
Burquest, D. A.
1986 The pronoun system of some Chadic languages. In: U. Wiesemann (ed.), *Pronominal Systems*, 71–101. Tübingen: Narr.
Capell, A.
1964 Verbal syntax in Philippine languages. *Philippine Journal of Science* 93: 231–249.
Coseriu, E.
1987 Über die Wortkategorien. Formen und Funktionen. In: E. Coseriu (ed.), *Studien zur Grammatik*, 24–44. Tübingen. [Span. Original 1955]
Courtenay, K.
1976 Ideophones defined as a phonological class: The case of Yoruba. *Studies in African Linguistics Suppl.* 6: 13–26.
Croft, W.
1984 Semantic and pragmatic correlates to syntactic categories. In: David Testen et al. (eds.), *Papers from the Parasession on Lexical Semantics*, 53–70. Chicago: CLS

Croft, W.
1991 *Syntactic Categories and Grammatical Relations: The Cognitive Organization of Information*. Chicago.
Croft, W.
2000 Parts of speech as language universals and as language-particular categories. In: P. M. Vogel and B. Comrie (eds.), *Approaches to the Typology of Word Classes*, 65–102. Berlin: Mouton de Gruyter.
Delbrück, B.
1893 *Vergleichende Syntax der Indogermanischen Sprachen*, Teil I. Straßburg.
Demers, R. A., and E. Jelinek
1982 The syntactic function of person marking in Lummi. *Preprints to the 17th International Conference on Salish and Neighboring Languages* (ICSNL), 24–47.
Demers, R. A., and E. Jelinek
1984 Word-building rules and grammatical categories of Lummi. Preprints to the 19th ICSNL. In: *Working Papers of the Linguistic Circle of Victoria* 4 (2), 39–49.
Diem, W.
1973 *Skizzen Jemenitischer Dialekte*. Beirut.
Dik, S. C.
1968 *Coordination. Its Implications for the Theory of General Linguistics*. Amsterdam: North-Holland.
Dixon, R. M. W.
1972 *The Dyirbal Language of North Queensland*. Cambridge: Cambridge University Press.
Dixon, R. M. W.
1977 Where have all the adjectives gone. *Studies in Language* 1: 19–80. [re-issued 1982]
Doke, C. M.
1935 *Bantu Linguistic Terminology*. London: Longmans, Green and Company.
Evans, N.
2000a Kinship verbs. In: P. M. Vogel and B. Comrie (eds.), *Approaches to the Typology of Word Classes*, 103–172. Berlin: Mouton de Gruyter.
Evans, N.
2000b Word classes in the world's languages. In: Booij, G. et al. (eds.), *Morphologie. Ein Internationales Handbuch zur Flexion und Wortbildung,* 708–732. (HSK 17.1, 1. Halbband.) Berlin, New York: de Gruyter.
Everaert, M.
1986 *The Syntax of Reflexivization*. Dordrecht.
Faltz, L. M.
1977 Reflexivization: A study in universal syntax. Berkeley, CAL: dissertation.
Forchheimer, P.
1953 *The Category of Person in Language*. Berlin: Walter de Gruyter.
Fries, Ch. C.
1952 *The Structure of English*. London.
Garman, M.
1990 *Psycholinguistics*. Cambridge: Cambridge University Press.
Geniušienė, E.
1987 *A Typology of Reflexives*. Berlin: Mouton de Gruyter.
Gil, David
1991 Aristotle goes to Arizona, and finds a language without "and". In: Dietmar Zaefferer (ed.), *Semantic Universals and Universal Semantics*, 96–130. Berlin: Foris.
Gil, David
1995 Parts of speech in Tagalog. In: *Papers from the 3rd Annual Meeting of the Southeast Asian Linguistics Society*, 67–90.

Gil, David
2000 Syntactic categories, cross-linguistic variation and universal grammar. In: P. M. Vogel and B. Comrie (eds.), *Approaches to the Typology of Word Classes*, 173–216. Berlin.
Givón, T.
1984 *Syntax: A Functional-Typological Introduction*, vol. 1. Amsterdam: Benjamins.
Gleason, Jr., H. A.
1961 *An Introduction to Descriptive Linguistics*. Revised edition. New York.
Grebe, Paul, et al. (eds.)
1973 *Duden – Grammatik der deutschen Gegenwartssprache*, 3. bearb. und erw. Auflage. Mannheim.
Greenberg, J. H.
1963 Some universals of grammar with particular reference to the order of meaningful elements. In: J. H. Greenberg (ed.), *Universals of Language*, 73–113. Cambridge, MA.
Greenberg, J. H.
1978 Generalizations about numeral systems. In: J.H. Greenberg (ed.), *Universals of Human Language*, vol. 3, 249–295. Stanford: Stanford University Press.
Greenberg, J. H.
1986 Introduction. In: U. Wiesemann (ed.), *Pronominal Systems*, XVIII–XXI.
Greenberg, J. H.
2000 Numeral. In: Booij, G. et al. (eds.), *Morphologie. Ein Internationales Handbuch zur Flexion und Wortbildung,* 770–783. (HSK 17.1, 1. Halbband.) Berlin, New York: de Gruyter.
Hagège, C.
1974 Les pronoms logophoriques. *Bulletin de la Société de Linguistique de Paris* 69: 287–310.
Hagège, C.
1982 *La Structure des Langues*. Paris: Presses Universitaires des France.
Haiman, J.
1978 Conditionals are topics. *Language* 54: 564–589.
Heine, B.
1993 *Auxiliaries. Cognitive Forces and Grammaticalization.* Oxford: Oxford University Press.
Hengeveld, K.
1992 *Non-verbal Predication: Theory, Typology, Diachrony.* Berlin: Walter de Gruyter.
Hengeveld, K, J. Rijkhoff, and A. Siewierska
2004 Parts-of-speech systems and word order. *Journal of Linguistics* 40: 527–570.
Hermann, E.
1928 *Die Wortarten*. Berlin.
Hettrich, H.
1988 *Untersuchungen zur Hypotaxe im Vedischen.* Berlin: Walter de Gruyter.
Hetzron, R.
1976 The Agaw languages. *Afroasiatic Linguistics* 3/3.
Himmelmann, N.
1991 *The Philippine Challenge to Universal Grammar.* Köln: Institut für Sprachwissenschaft. (Arbeitspapier Nr. 15 N.F.)
Himmelmann, N.
2008 Lexical categories and voice in Tagalog. In: P. Austin and S. Musgrave (eds.), *Voice and Grammatical Relations in Austronesian Languages*. Stanford.
Hockett, Ch. F.
1966 The problem of universals in language. In: J. H. Greenberg (ed.), *Universals of Language*, 1–29. Cambridge, MA.
Hopper, P., and S. A. Thompson
1984 The discourse basis for lexical categories in universal grammar. *Language* 60: 703–752.
Hopper, P., and S. A. Thompson
1985 The iconicity of the universal categories ‘Noun’ and ‘Verb’. In: J. Haiman (ed.), *Iconicity in Syntax*, 151–183.

Hurford, J. R.
1975 *The Linguistic Study of Numerals*. Cambridge.
Hutchisson, D.
1986 Sursurunga pronouns and the special uses of quadral number. In: U. Wiesemann (ed.), *Pronominal Systems*, 1–20. Tübingen: Narr.
Hyman, L., and B. Comrie
1981 Logophoric reference in Gokana. *Journal of African Languages and Linguistics* 3: 19–37.
Ingram, D.
1978 Typology and universals of personal pronouns. In: J. H. Greenberg (ed.), *Universals of Human Language*, vol. 3, 213–247. Stanford University Press.
Jacobsen, W. H.
1979 Noun and verb in Nootkan. In: B. S. Efrat (ed.), *The Victoria Conference on Northwestern Languages*, 83–155. British Columbia Provincial Museum.
Jacobsen, W. H.
1980 Inclusive/exclusive: A diffused pronominal category in Native Western North America. In: Kreiman and Ojeda (eds.), *Papers from the Parasession of Pronouns and Anaphora*, 204–254.
Jespersen, O.
1924 *The Philosophy of Grammar*. London.
Kahr, J. C.
1975 Adpositions and locationals: Typology and diachronic development. In: *Working Papers in Language Universals* 19: 21–54.
Kaltz, B.
2000 Wortartensysteme in der Linguistik. In: Booij, G. et al. (eds.), *Morphologie. Ein Internationales Handbuch zur Flexion und Wortbildung*, 693–707. (HSK 17.1, 1. Halbband.) Berlin, New York: de Gruyter.
Kemmer, S.
1993 *The Middle Voice*. Amsterdam/Philadelphia: John Benjamins.
Kinkade, M. D.
1976 The copula and negatives in Inland Olympic Salish. *International Journal of American Linguistics* 42: 17–23.
Kinkade, M. D.
1983 Salish evidence against the universality of 'noun' and 'verb'. *Lingua* 60: 25–40.
Knobloch, C., and B. Schaeder
2000 Kriterien für die Definition von Wortarten. In: Booij, G. et al. (eds.), *Morphologie. Ein Internationales Handbuch zur Flexion und Wortbildung*, 674–692. (HSK 17.1, 1. Halbband) Berlin: de Gruyter.
Koehn, E., and S. Koehn
1986 Apalai. In: D. C. Derbyshire and G. K. Pullum (eds.), *Handbook of Amazonian Languages*, vol. 1, 32–127. Berlin, New York: Mouton de Gruyter.
König, E., and V. Gast
2008 *Reciprocals and Reflexives: Crosslinguistic and Theoretical Exploration*. Berlin: Walter de Gruyter.
Kreiman, J., and A. E. Ojeda (eds.)
1980 *Papers from the Parasession of Pronouns and Anaphora*. Chicago: CLS.
Kuipers, A. H.
1968 The categories verb-noun and transitive-intransitive in English and Squamish. *Lingua* 21: 610–626.
Langacker, R. W.
1987 Nouns and verbs. *Language* 63: 53–94.
Lehmann, C.
1984 *Der Relativsatz*. Amsterdam: John Benjamins.

Lehmann, C.
1995 *Thoughts on Grammaticalization.* München/Newcastle: Lincom.

Lyons, J.
1968 *Introduction to Theoretical Linguistics.* Cambridge: Cambridge University Press.

Lyons, J.
1977 *Semantics*, vol. 2. Cambridge: Cambridge University Press.

Marchese, L.
1986 The pronominal system of Godié. In: U. Wiesemann (ed.), *Pronominal Systems*, 217–255. Tübingen: Narr.

Mauri, C.
2008 *Coordination Relations in the Languages of Europe and Beyond.* Berlin: Walter de Gruyter.

Maytinskaya, K. E.
1969 *Mestoimeniya v Yazykakh Raznykh Sistem* [Pronouns in the Languages of Various Systems]. Moscow.

Miller, R. A.
1967 *The Japanese Language.* Chicago, London: University of Chicago Press.

Palmer, F. R.
1978 *Grammar.* New York.

Parker, E.
1986 Mundani pronouns. In: U. Wiesemann (ed.), *Pronominal Systems*, 131–165. Tübingen: Narr.

Payne, J. R.
1985 Complex phrases and complex sentences. In: T. Shopen (ed.), *Language Typology and Syntactic Description*, vol. 2, 3–41.Cambridge: Cambridge University Press.

Plank, F.
1984 24 grundsätzliche Bemerkungen zur Wortartenfrage. *Leuvense Bijdragen* 73: 489–520.

Reed, J., and D. L. Payne
1986 Asheninca (Compa) pronominals. In: U. Wiesemann (ed.), *Pronominal Systems*, 323–331. Tübingen: Narr.

Rijkhoff, J.
2007 Word classes. *Language and Linguistics Compass* 1/6: 709–726.

Robins, R. H.
1965 *General Linguistics: An Introductory Survey.* London: Longmans.

Robins, R. H.
1986 The techne grammatike of Dionysius Thrax in its historical perspective: The evolution of the traditional European word class systems. In: P. Swiggers and W. Van Hoecke (eds.), *Mot et Parties du Discourse*, 9–37. Leuven: Peeters.

Roncador, Manfred von
1992 Types of logophoric marking in African languages. *Journal of African Languages and Linguistics* 13: 163–182.

Roncador, Manfred von
2006 Logophoric pronouns. In: K. Brown et al. (eds.), *Encyclopedia of Language and Linguistics*, 2nd edition, vol. 7, 312–315. Amsterdam: Elsevier.

Ross, J. R.
1972 The category squish: Endstation Hauptwort. In: *Papers from the Regional Meetings of the Chicago Linguistic Society* 8: 316–328.

Ross, J. R.
1973 Nouniness. In: O. Fujimura (ed.), *Three Dimensions of Linguistic Theory*, 137–257. Tokyo: TEC.

Samarin, W. J.
1965 Perspective on African ideophones. *African Studies* 24: 117–121.

Sapir. E.
1921 *Language*. New York.
Sasse, H. J.
1977 A note on WH-movement. *Lingua* 41: 343–354.
Sasse, H. J.
1993 Das Nomen – eine universale Kategorie? *Sprachtypologie und Universalienforschung* 46: 187–221.
Sasse, H. J.
2001 Scales between nouniness and verbiness. In: M. Hapelmath et al. (eds.), *Language Typology and Language Universals. An International Handbook*, vol. 1, 495–509. Berlin.
Sasse, H. J.
2005 Lexical and grammatical categories in grammatical description. In: D. A. Cruse and P. R. Lutzeier (eds.), *Lexicology. An International Handbook*, 1585–1606. Berlin: Walter de Gruyter.
Schachter, P.
1985 Parts-of-speech systems. In: T. Shopen (ed.), *Language Typology and Syntactic Description*, vol. 1, 3–61. Cambridge: Cambridge University Press.
Scheerer, O.
1924 On the essential difference between verbs of the European and the Philippine languages. *Philippine Journal of Education* 7: 1–10.
Schmerling, S.
1983 Two theories of syntactic categories. *Linguistics and Philosophy* 6: 393–421.
Schultze-Berndt, E.
2000 *Simple and complex verbs in Jaminjung: A Study of Event Subcategorisation in an Australian Language*. Nijmegen.
Schwartz, L.
2000 Pronoun and article. In: Booij, G. et al. (eds.), *Morphologie. Ein Internationales Handbuch zur Flexion und Wortbildung,* 783–794. (HSK 17.1, 1. Halbband.) Berlin, New York: de Gruyter.
Schwartz, L. J., and T. Dunnigan
1986 Pronouns and pronominal categories in Southwestern Ojibwe. In: U. Wiesemann (ed.), *Pronominal Systems*, 285–322. Tübingen: Narr.
Seiler, H.
1983 *Possession as an Operational Dimension of Language*. Tübingen: Narr.
Showalter, C.
1986 Pronouns in Lyélé. In: U. Wiesemann (ed.), *Pronominal Systems*, 205–216. Tübingen: Narr.
Siloni, T.
2008 The syntax of reciprocal verbs: An overview. In: E. König and V. Gast (eds.), *Reciprocals and Reflexives: Crosslinguistic and Theoretical Exploration*, 451–498. Berlin: Mouton de Gruyter.
Simons, L.
1986 The pronouns of To'abaita. In: U. Wiesemann (ed.), *Pronominal Systems*, 21–35. Tübingen: Narr.
Stassen, L.
1997 *Intransitive Predication*. Oxford: Oxford University Press.
Steele, S.
1978 The category AUX as a language universal. In: J. H. Greenberg (ed.), *Universals of Human Language*, 7–45. Stanford: Stanford University Press.
Steele, S., et al.
1981 *An Encyclopedia of AUX: A Study of Crosslinguistic Equivalence*. Cambridge, MA.

Swadesh, M.
1939 Nootka internal syntax. *International Journal of American Linguistics* 9: 77–102.
Thompson, S. A., and R. Longacre
1985 Adverbial clauses. In: T. Shopen (ed.), *Language Typology and Syntactic Description*, vol. 2, 171–234. Cambridge: Cambridge University Press.
Thompson, L. C., and M. T. Thompson
1980 Thompson Salish //-xi//. *International Journal of American Linguistics* 46: 27–32.
Van Eijk, J. P., and T. Hess
1986 Noun and verb in Salish. *Lingua* 69: 319–331.
Voeltz, F. K. E., and C. Kilian-Hatz (eds.)
2001 *Ideophones*. Amsterdam / Philadelphia: John Benjamins.
Vogel, P. M., and B. Comrie (eds.)
2000 *Approaches to the Typology of Word Classes*. Berlin: Walter de Gruyter.
Vonen, A. M.
1994 Multifunctionality and morphology in Tokelau and English. *Nordic Journal of Linguistics* 17: 155–178.
Vonen, A. M.
1997 *Parts of Speech and Linguistic Typology: Open Classes and Conversion in Russian and Tokelau*. Oslo: Scandinavian University Press. [Cf. comments in Norsk *Lingvistisk Tidsskrift* 13 (1995), 211–228.]
Voorhoeve, J.
1980 Le pronom logophorique et son importance pour la reconstruction protobantu. *Sprache und Geschichte in Afrika* 2: 173–187.
Wackernagel, J.
1924 *Vorlesungen über Syntax. Mit Besonderer Berücksichtigung von Griechisch, Lateinisch und Deutsch*. Basel.
Walter, H.
1981 *Studien zur Nomen-Verb-Distinktion aus Typologischer Sicht*. München: Fink.
Weber, D. J.
1986 Huallaga Quechua pronouns. In: U. Wiesemann (ed.), *Pronominal Systems*, 333–349. Tübingen: Narr.
Wetzer, H.
1996 *The Typology of Adjectival Predication*. Berlin/ New York: Mouton de Gruyter.
Wierzbicka, A.
1986 What's in a noun? (Or: How do nouns differ in meaning from adjectives?). *Studies in Language* 10: 35–389.
Wiesemann, U. (ed.)
1986 *Pronominal Systems*. Tübingen: Narr.

Hans-Jürgen Sasse, Köln (Germany)

8. Grammatical Relations

Abstract

Despite the fact that grammatical relations, such as subject and object, have been used as descriptive terms for centuries, there is still much debate on their nature. The notions that are employed in the definition or identification of grammatical relations in various approaches will guide the organization of this chapter. First, many approaches associate grammatical relations with morphosyntactic notions such as case marking and agreement. Second, there are structural approaches to grammatical relations. Finally, there are semantic approaches linking grammatical relations to semantic roles such as agent and patient or to reference-related properties such as topicality or animacy. This chapter will show that none of these types of notions can capture the whole range of pertinent phenomena in grammar and language processing. There are two serious problems tied to grammatical relations: relational splits and multi-factor relational phenomena.

1. Introduction

Grammatical relations, such as subject, direct object, and indirect object, have been used as descriptive terms for centuries, the distinction between subject and predicate having been taken over from Ancient Greek and Roman philosophy and grammar. Alternative names are *grammatical functions* (e.g. Bresnan 2001), *syntactic functions* (e.g. Chomsky 1981) or *syntactic relations*. Common to all approaches to grammatical relations is that they have been considered to be relationships between two elements of a clause, so that *subject* is only a short term for the subject of the predicate or the subject of the clause. Traditionally, grammatical relations are primarily used for major constituents of the clause and only marginally for parts of major constituents (e.g. attribute of a noun). For this reason, this chapter will focus on grammatical relations at the major clausal level. The main issues connected to grammatical relations can be formulated as follows: (i) Are grammatical relations basic or derived notions? If they are derived notions, which are the basic underlying concepts? (ii) Are grammatical relations universal, language-specific or construction-specific notions? (iii) What are the major theoretical approaches to grammatical relations? The basic notions that are employed in the definition or identification of grammatical relations in various approaches will be the leading thread for the organization of this chapter. The next section is devoted to morphosyntactic notions associated with grammatical relations such as case marking and agreement. Structural approaches to grammatical relations will be the topic of section 3. The next two sections will present semantic factors that determine the choice of grammatical relations. Section 4 presents an overview of the basic issues concerning the relationship between grammatical relations and semantic roles such as agent and patient. Besides semantic roles, there are other semantic factors that may determine the choice of grammatical relations. These factors include, among others, referential properties related to topicality, animacy, person differences, definiteness or specificity. They are the topic of section 5. Section 6 focuses on language processing; section 7 offers a final discussion.

2. Grammatical relations, case marking, and agreement

In traditional grammars oriented on Ancient Greek and Latin, grammatical relations are associated with case marking (cf. Blake 2001: 18–19; Butt 2006: 13–15). The subject is identified with the nominative, the direct object with the accusative, and the indirect object with the dative or another oblique case. The impact of this tradition is still manifest, for example, in descriptive grammars of German as shown in (1):

(1) Grammatical relations defined by cases for German:
  a. noun phrase, nominative, actant → subject
  b. noun phrase, accusative, actant → accusative object
  c. noun phrase, dative, actant → dative object
  d. noun phrase, genitive, actant → genitive object
  (cf. Duden 2009: 809–810)

An actant is a constituent bearing a semantic participant role such as agent and patient (Duden 2009: 779). In other approaches and in this chapter, the notion of argument is used instead. In the case-based view, there are as many distinct grammatical relations as there are cases for verbal arguments, as shown in (1).

How adequate is the case-based view of grammatical relations? Let us start the discussion on the construction- and language-specific level. The case-based view explains verb agreement in German and many other languages, at least for the core patterns. Descriptive grammars (cf. Duden 2009: 811 for German), functional typology (cf. Moravcsik 1988), and Generative Grammar (cf. Chomsky 1981, 1995) converge in the view that the nominative argument is the privileged trigger of verb agreement. Moreover, verb agreement is restricted to the nominative argument in many accusative languages, for example, among the European languages in German, Latin, Russian, within the Indic group in Sinhalese, within the Altaic group in Tatar and Turkish. This is shown for German in (2):

(2) Case-based verb agreement:

Die	*Kind-er*	*seh-en*	*dich.*	[German]
the.NOM.PL	child-NOM.PL	see-3PL	you.ACC.SG	

'The children see you.'

Ergative languages are more difficult to capture in terms of case marking. In the ergative construction, which is shown in (3) below, the patient of a multivalenced predicate (P) is coded by the same case as the subject of a monovalenced predicate (S) and differently from the agent of a multivalenced predicate (A). The case of S and P is called *absolutive* (or nominative), the case of A is called *ergative*.

(3) Case-based agreement in nominal class (C) and ergative case marking:

a. *yas* *y-orč'ana.* [Avar]
girl(ABS.C2) C2-woke.up
'A/the girl woke up.'

b. *y-osana yas* *di-cca*
C2-took girl(ABS.C2) I-ERG
'I took a/the girl.'
(cf. Charachidzé 1981: 144)

The English translations of (3a, b) show the accusative pattern: S and A are coded alike by the nominative, while P appears in the accusative (or objective). So cases code different semantic roles (A vs. P) in the two types of constructions. Despite this role-semantic difference, case-based rules in ergative and accusative languages are similar. This similarity holds under the plausible assumption that the nominative and the absolutive are morphosyntactically equivalent cases, despite their different role-semantic functions (cf. for this view, among others, Sasse 1978; Dixon 1994; Primus 1999; Blake 2001). Closest to the nominative constraint on agreement mentioned so far are ergative languages in which verb agreement is restricted to the absolutive argument. In many North-East Caucasian languages, the verbal head agrees in nominal class, i.e. gender and number, with the absolutive argument to the exclusion of other case arguments (cf. for other ergative languages, Primus 1999, Chap. 6). This type of agreement is illustrated by the Avar examples in (3a, b) above. A description of verb agreement in Avar in terms of zero case (i.e. nominative or absolutive) is offered by Charachidzé (1981: 145), who adequately classifies the zero-marked argument as primary actant for agreement.

So far, the case-based approach to grammatical relations turned out to be quite successful. However, the above-mentioned nominative-absolutive constraint on agreement fails to account for some construction-specific agreement patterns. (4a) shows a construction with two nominatives in German consisting of a demonstrative pronoun in subject position and a predicative nominal. The verb fails to agree with the demonstrative pronoun *das*, which is in the privileged subject position, and agrees instead with the predicative nominal *Blumen*. (4b) shows a *there*-construction in English. In this construction, the dummy element *there*, which is in preverbal subject position, fails to agree. The verb agrees instead with the postverbal nominative argument.

(4) Construction-specific problems with case-based agreement:

a. *Das* *sind* *Blume-n.* [German]
this.NOM.SG be.3PL flower-NOM.PL
'These are flowers.'

b. *There are cows in next door's garden.*

Agreement with a predicative nominal, as in (4a), is also found in other languages (e.g. Czech, cf. Corbett 2006: 63). However, the pattern is language-specific, as shown by the

English translation of (4a), where the verb agrees with the demonstrative *these* in subject position (cf. also Engl. *It is me* with its German equivalent *Das bin* [be.1SG] *ich*). In the constructions illustrated in (4a, b), agreement is triggered by a nominative argument in a non-canonical position for subjects. But there is also agreement failure when nominative arguments appear in a non-canonical position (cf. Barlow 1992; Samek-Lodovici 2003). Cross-linguistically, case-based agreement is even less stable, since there are languages in which case plays no role in verb agreement, as discussed for Warlpiri later in this chapter.

A challenge to case-based approaches to grammatical relations and to case theories in general is Icelandic. Icelandic has various case patterns for verbal arguments. Transitive constructions with nominative subjects and accusative objects work exactly like their counterparts in other accusative European languages including English. In contrast to English, however, Icelandic also has what has become known as quirky case subjects, that is, subjects which are marked with a case other than nominative. Many studies have shown that the argument in preverbal position in Icelandic behaves like a subject irrespective of its case. Cf. the examples in (5):

(5) Quirky case subjects:
 a. *Mér er kalt.* [Icelandic]
 me.DAT is cold.
 'I am freezing.'

 b. *Mér hefur aldrei líkað Guðmundur.*
 me.DAT has never liked Guðmundur.NOM
 'I have never liked Guðmundur.'

 c. *Honum var hjálpað.*
 him.DAT was helped.
 'He was helped.'
 (cf. Barðdal and Eythórsson 2003: 754, 760)

These dative subjects have most of the properties of nominative subjects in Icelandic, except for verb agreement, which is restricted to the nominative. Thus, for instance, quirky case subjects may be the empty subject (PRO) of infinitival clauses and control an obligatory reflexive pronoun, i.e. block coreference with a personal pronoun. This is shown in (6a, b):

(6) Subject behaviour of non-nominative arguments:
 a. *Ég vonaðist til að* PRO *verda hjálpað.* [Icelandic]
 I.NOM hoped COMP PRO(DAT) was helped.
 'I hoped to be helped.'

 b. *Honum er kalt heima hjá sér /*?honum.*
 him.DAT is cold home at REFL.DAT / him.DAT
 'He is freezing at his home.'
 (cf. Thraínsson 1979: 469–471)

Correspondingly, nominative objects in Icelandic, as in (5b), have all object properties except for verb agreement. Since nominative objects are able to trigger verb agreement, this property qualifies them as morphosyntactic subjects (cf. Thaínsson 1979: 466 for some variation).

Cross-linguistically, non-canonical case marking of subjects and objects is a widely distributed pattern (cf., among others, Aikhenvald, Dixon, and Onishi 2001; Bhaskararao and Subbarao 2004). This pattern is often found for the experiencer and stimulus argument of verbs denoting a mental state (psych-verbs), which are recurrently discussed in this chapter. Languages differ as to what subject properties non-nominative experiencers accumulate, but a structural subject position in terms of basic order is one of the cross-linguistically most stable subject properties, while subject-verb agreement is less likely to be controlled by non-nominative experiencers (but there is agreement with oblique experiencers in Dargwa [North-East Caucasian], for instance, cf. Corbett 2006: 59).

Let us sum up this section. The case-based view of grammatical relations originated in Ancient Greek and Roman grammatical tradition and is still prominent in descriptive grammars of European languages. Case-based relations explain some of the phenomena that are associated with grammatical relations. This was shown for verb agreement in greater detail. However, even European languages, which are in the focus of case-based approaches, cannot be captured exhaustively as there are constructions which challenge a purely case-based treatment. For this reason, recent functional and formal approaches shifted the focus of their investigations to other types of relations. The next section will introduce structural relations as explananda for grammatical relations.

3. Grammatical relations, phrase structure, and lexical argument structure

Whereas it seems natural to associate grammatical relations with cases in languages such as Ancient Greek, Latin, Russian, or German, which have a relatively rich case system, this is less obvious for languages like English, French, and Norwegian, which have almost completely lost their case inflection. Unsurprisingly, alternative structural approaches to grammatical relations have been devised especially for languages like these. (7) shows a simple phrase structure analysis of a transitive clause in English:

(7) [$_S$ Felix [$_{VP}$ [$_V$ slapped] Rosa]]]

Subject is identified with the noun phrase that is immediately dominated by the sentence node. Object is the noun phrase that is internal to the VP. In the example (7), *Felix* is in subject position and *Rosa* in object position.

Crucially, the subject is in structural c-command of the object. This relation is usually defined as follows: from two structural positions *x* and *y* that do not dominate each other, position *x* c-commands position *y* if and only if *y* is included in all maximal projections (i.e. phrases) that dominate *x*. Since *Rosa* is included in the only phrase dominating *Felix*, namely S, *Felix* c-commands *Rosa*. C-command is assumed to be asymmetrical for grammatical relations: the object *Rosa* does not c-command the subject *Felix*, since VP is a phrase that dominates *Rosa* but not *Felix*. Ultimately, differences in the behaviour of different grammatical relations are explained by phrase-structural asymmetries in terms of c-command in this kind of approach. Thus, for example, the Icelandic reflexivization pattern shown in (6c) above can be explained by the fact that the structural position of a quirky subject asymmetrically c-commands VP-internal constituents; c-command within a local domain is the crucial condition on anaphor binding in phrase-structural approaches (cf. Chomsky 1981; Reinhart 1983; Chapter 39 in this handbook).

In later approaches, particularly in the Minimalist Program (cf. Chomsky 1995; Adger 2003), lexical heads such as V have been supplemented with functional heads such as little *v* and Tense (T, formerly Inflection I or Agreement Agr). (8) illustrates the phrase-structural positions of subject and object in the Minimalist Program for a sentence such as *Cassandra has foretold disaster.*

(8) Subject and object in the Minimalist Program (Adger 2003: 205):

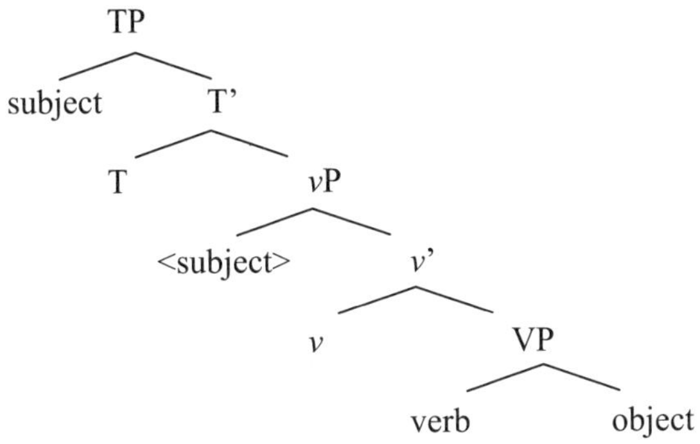

In the Minimalist Program, there are only two abstract syntactic operations, merge and move, move being a special instance of merge. Different syntactic levels such as D- and S-structure are eliminated in favour of a stepwise derivation. The relevant steps in the derivation of *Cassandra has foretold disaster* are as follows. *Cassandra* is the agent of the verb *foretold*. As such, it is merged in the specifier of little *v* and linearly follows the auxiliary *has* in T at this initial stage of the derivation. The noun phrase *disaster* is the theme of *foretold* and, accordingly, it is merged in the specifier of the lexical V-head. Merged positions at the initial stage of a derivation (formerly D-structure positions) are determined by semantic roles in this kind of approach. Principles like those in (9) map semantic roles (theta roles in the terminology of Generative Grammar) onto basic syntactic positions:

(9) a. An agent is the specifier of the higher VP [little *v*P in later approaches]
b. A theme is the specifier of the lower VP.

(cf. Baker 1997: 120)

Cassandra appears linearly in front of the auxiliary *has* in the specifier of TP, which is the surface subject position. This indicates that the subject moves to the specifier of TP and leaves a copy in the basic subject position, i.e. the specifier of *v*P, cf. the bracketed subject in (8). Crucially, the Minimalist Program introduces two subject positions in different functional phrases, as shown in (8). These two positions are motivated by quantifier floating (*the dragons have all eaten the pigs*) and by the expletive *there*-construction illustrated in (4b) above. The subject function is split up yet in another respect. Its surface realization is associated with two different types of features: EPP and nominative case. Their contribution is stated in (10):

(10) a. Finite T bears [nom] and little *v* bears [acc].
b. Finite T bears [uN*], the EPP-feature, which causes something to merge into the specifier of TP (either an expletive or a nominal phrase).
(cf. Adger 2003: 222)

The EPP-feature is reminiscent of the earlier Extended Projection Principle, which requires that every sentence has a (possibly non-overt) subject. Motivations for dissociating the nominative-feature from the EPP-feature are nominative arguments in little *v*P, as in the *there*-construction in (4b) above, and in VP, as in the Icelandic psych-verb construction in (5b) above. In these constructions, nominative-feature checking and agreement by Tense occur non-locally, namely outside TP within VP. So the nominative feature is not the sole motivation for an argument noun phrase or an expletive to occur in the specifier of TP, i.e. the surface subject position, as in earlier generative approaches. A subject in the specifier of TP can also be motivated by the EPP-feature, in which event it may not be case-marked or agreeing as a canonical subject (cf. Adger 2003, Chap. 6).

In sum, a clear tendency in the treatment of grammatical relations emerges in Generative Grammar: the clausal subject notion is decomposed in two phrase-structural relations and two subject features. Verbal arguments are structurally merged in the initial step according to their semantic roles. Surface positions of arguments or expletives are associated with the EPP and are dissociated, in principle, from case and agreement. This decomposition of the subject notion helps to improve the analysis of non-canonical subjects and objects (cf. Ura 2000; Adger 2003, Chap. 6; Mohr 2005; Bobaljik and Wurmbrand 2009 for complications and remaining problems).

One of the remaining problems of the generative approach is of greater typological relevance and will be mentioned here. Despite its enhanced flexibility, the treatment of grammatical relations in the Minimalist Program fails to dissociate nominative (or absolutive) case from agreement. However, there are languages in which verb agreement is based on argument structure and not on phrase structure or case marking. This type of agreement is found in a number of ergative languages (cf. Primus 1999, Chap. 6), including Warlpiri (Pama-Nyungan, Australian), which is illustrated here in (11):

(11) Verb-agreement based on argument structure:

a. *ngaju ka-rna wangka-mi* [Warlpiri]
I.NOM PRS-1SG speak-NPST
'I am speaking.'

b. *ngaju ka-rna-ngku parda-rni nyuntu-ku*
I.NOM PRS-1SG-2SG wait-NPST you-DAT
'I am waiting for you.'

c. *ngajulu-rlu ka-rna-ngku nyuntu nya-nyi*
I-ERG PRS-1SG-2SG you.NOM see-NPST
'I see you.'

(cf. Hale 1983: 18)

Warlpiri is a flexible constituent order language with no palpable phrase-structural asymmetries between grammatical relations. Therefore, Hale formulates the agreement rule on the basis of the following lexical structure of arguments (Hale 1983: 23):

(12) $[X_{agent} [Y_{patient} V]]$

One type of agreement marker, *-rna* in the examples in (11), is controlled by the highest argument position in argument structure. The other type of agreement marker, *-ngku* in the examples in (11), is selected by the lower argument position. For this lexical structural hierarchization, Hale adduces reflexivization facts so that his analysis of verb agreement in terms of lexical argument structure is well supported. The only remaining problem is that the semantic roles mentioned in (12) do not apply to the non-agentive verb 'see' in (11c) or to many other non-agentive verbs that pattern like those illustrated in (11). As we will see in section 4 of this chapter, this is a problem of defining semantic roles and not an argument against Hale's analysis of this kind of agreement in terms of lexical argument structure.

Returning to verb agreement in the Minimalist Program, the most advanced line of research in terms of phrase-structural relations, the explanation gap under discussion can be stated as follows. Since subject-verb agreement is associated with nominative case via Tense, this approach fails to capture an agreement pattern dissociated from case and conditioned by the position of an argument in the argument structure of the verb, which is in its turn determined by its semantic role.

Other syntactic theories are more flexible in this respect. A dissociation of case, phrase-structural, and argument-structural relations and typological motivation for these distinctions are found in Lexical Functional Grammar (cf. Mohanan 1994; Bresnan 2001; Butt 2006, Chap. 5.7) and in the functional typological approach of Bickel (2006). In Lexical Functional Grammar (LFG), there are four types of information that are associated with grammatical relations. They are organized on three structural levels: feature structure for cases and for grammatical relations taken as primitive notions, argument structure for semantic roles, and constituent structure for linear order and phrase-structural relations. The different types of information can be accessed in parallel and independently from each other.

Another non-derivational framework that accommodates parallel access to different types of information is Optimality Theory (OT). OT is compatible with several non-derivational theories, including LFG (cf. Bresnan 2000 for a LFG-based optimality-theoretical approach). In this chapter, Woolford's OT-treatment of quirky case subjects in Icelandic will be illustrated in greater detail (cf. Woolford 2001, 2003). Her approach is devised as a supplement to Chomsky's case theory in so far as basic phrase-structural conditions on cases and the distinction between structural and lexical cases are taken over. The principles for structural cases are formulated in (10a) above. Lexical cases are tied directly to semantic roles and are specified in the lexical entry of the verbal head. OT is primarily concerned with constraint interaction. Typological variation is exclusively explained in terms of different constraint rankings. Woolford (2001) introduces three case markedness constraints, which are ordered in an invariant ranking, as shown in (13):

(13) *DATIVE » *ACCUSATIVE » *NOMINATIVE

This invariant ranking establishes the following markedness hierarchy of cases:

(14) nominative > accusative > dative

Without the intervention of competing constraints, the markedness constraints universally block dative cases first and, finally, cases altogether. The competitor that is relevant to our discussion is the faithfulness constraint in (15):

(15) FAITHLEX: A lexically specified inherent Case feature must be realized.

The variation between Icelandic and English is explained by constraint re-ranking as in (16):

(16) Icelandic: FAITHLEX » *DATIVE
English: *DATIVE » FAITHLEX

OT is a competition model. The acceptability of a pattern is not exclusively determined by its own properties but rather by the question whether it satisfies the relevant higher ranked constraints better than other candidates with the same input specifications. The evaluation of competing candidates is represented in a tableau. In an OT-tableau, the input is given in the first cell, the candidates are enumerated in the first column and the constraints are aligned in the subsequent columns as specified by the ranking of the language under discussion. The tableaux 8.1 and 8.2 show the evaluation of an input with two argument noun phrases (NP) and the lexical specification of the dative case on the first NP, the subject.

(17) Tab. 8.1: Lexically case-marked (quirky) subjects in Icelandic (Woolford 2001)

V[+dat sub] NP NP	FAITHLEX	*DATIVE	*ACCUSATIVE	*NOMINATIVE
☞ a. NP-dat NP-nom		*		*
b. NP-dat NP-acc		*	*!	
c. NP-nom NP-acc	*!		*	*

Due to its high rank in Icelandic, the faithfulness constraint on lexical cases selects candidates with quirky case subjects. Additionally, the winning candidate, marked by a pointing finger, has a nominative object. The nominative is determined by the markedness constraint against accusatives, which is violated by candidates with an accusative object.

In English, dative subjects are eliminated from the competition due to the high rank of the markedness constraint against datives, as shown in tableau 8.2. The winning candidate (c) has canonical case marking.

To conclude, the main departure of OT from Chomskyan Generative Grammar is that case theory is supplemented with case constraints that are ranked according to a markedness hierarchy of cases. This hierarchy holds irrespective of phrase-structural considerations. OT shares with LFG the property of a non-derivational model that is able to access various types of information in parallel. In addition, OT is particularly well suited to

(18) Tab. 8.2: Lexically case-marked subjects in English (Woolford 2001)

V[+dat sub] NP NP	*DATIVE	FAITHLEX	*ACCUSATIVE	*NOMINATIVE
a. NP-dat NP-nom	*!			*
b. NP-dat NP-acc	*!		*	
☞ c. NP-nom NP-acc		*	*	*

explain typological variation and competing forces that shape grammars. Our examples showed the tension between faithfulness to the input, which optimizes functional expressiveness, and formal economy, which bans marked forms. There is a growing community of linguists working within this framework on topics related to grammatical relations (cf., among others, Grimshaw and Samek-Lodovici 1998 on subject universals; Bresnan, Dingare, and Manning 2001 and Sells 2001 on voice; Aissen 2003; de Swart 2007 on differential case marking; Wunderlich 2003 on case and agreement in Icelandic; de Hoop 2009 on case).

Let us sum up this section. We started our discussion with Generative Grammar, the prominent representative of a phrase-structure driven view on grammar in general and on grammatical relations in particular. One conspicuous recent development within the Minimalist Program is the decomposition of grammatical relations. Thus, the clausal subject is associated with two phrase-structure positions, specifier of Tense and of little *v*. In addition, its surface realization is determined by two features, the EPP and nominative case. This step contributes to a more adequate treatment of non-canonical subjects and objects. Nevertheless, Generative Grammar does not consider lexical argument structure, semantic roles in particular, and cases as independent types of information. They are only put to work in order to explain phrase-structural configurations. By contrast, two alternative lines of research, Lexical Functional Grammar and Optimality Theory, accommodate various types of information, which apply in parallel independently from each other. This was illustrated in greater detail by an optimality-theoretical treatment of non-canonical case marking of subjects and objects in Icelandic. As a consequence of these recent developments, grammatical relations such as subject or object play a less prominent role than in older approaches. They are short terms for other types of information, as in the Minimalist Program or in OT. In Lexical Functional Grammar, they are still used as primitive notions, but their role has decreased as a consequence of a shift in focus towards other types of relational information.

4. Grammatical relations and semantic roles

The next two sections will present semantic factors that determine the choice of grammatical relations. This section presents an overview of the basic issues concerning the relationship (linking) between grammatical relations and semantic roles such as agent and patient. Besides semantic roles, there are other semantic factors that may determine the choice of grammatical relations. These factors include, among others, referential properties related to topicality, animacy, definiteness or specificity, but also to negation, tense and aspect (cf. Hopper and Thompson 1980; Kulikov, Malchukov, and de Swart 2006; Næss 2007). Reference-related properties will be presented in the next section.

Approaches dealing with the relationship between grammatical relations and semantic roles incorporate principles that guarantee a transparent mapping, but they may differ with respect to how strictly they adhere to transparency. The strict principles in (19)–(20) characterize the framework of Generative Grammar:

(19) The Theta-Criterion: Each argument bears one and only one theta role, and each theta role is assigned to one and only one argument.
(cf. Chomsky 1981: 36)

In the Minimalist Program (cf. Chomsky 1995, Chap. 4), the Theta-Criterion is derived from principles of feature checking. Another influential principle is (20):

(20) The Uniformity of Theta-Assignment Hypothesis (UTAH): Identical thematic relationships between items are represented by identical deep structural relationships between those items.
(cf. Baker 1997: 75)

Similar principles are the Universal Alignment Hypothesis of Relational Grammar (Perlmutter and Postal 1984) and the Function-Argument-Biuniqueness Condition of Lexical Functional Grammar (cf. Butt 2006, Chap. 5.7). Arguments against such strict one-to-one mapping assumptions are discussed in Jackendoff (1990), Dowty (1991), and Culicover and Jackendoff (2005) and will be touched upon in the context of Dowty's proto-role approach later in this section.

Principles mapping grammatical relations onto semantic roles presuppose more specific assumptions about semantic roles. There are several views on semantic roles and different terminologies: *deep cases* (Fillmore 1968), *thematic relations* (Jackendoff 1990), *theta roles* (Chomsky 1981, 1995; Baker 1997), *proto-roles* (Dowty 1991), *macroroles* and *microroles* (Van Valin and LaPolla 1997; Farrell 2005, Chap. 4), among others. The different approaches can be split up basically in three lines of research. In the role-list view, semantic roles are unanalyzable entities that are listed in the lexical representation of a predicate. The other two views are decompositional. In one kind of decompositional approach, a few generalized roles are defined in terms of basic notions such as causation, motion, or sentience. In another kind of decompositional approach, roles are defined in terms of structural positions in the lexical structure of verbs. The two decompositional views can be combined (cf. Van Valin and LaPolla 1997; Primus 1999). This section will deal with role-list approaches and with Dowty's proto-role framework (cf. Primus 2009 for a comparison of different approaches).

Many influential approaches employ a list of informally defined semantic roles and a linking mechanism that is grounded on an implicitly or explicitly assumed role hierarchy. Fillmore's Case Grammar (1968) and Dik's Functional Grammar (1978, 1997) are pioneering works in this line of research. Role lists are also used in Generative Grammar (cf. Baker 1997). Baker's use of theta roles and his mapping principles for agent and theme were illustrated in (9) above. Within functional grammars, Dik's approach is representative. Dik assumes that subjects can be linked to any semantic role, in principle. However, subject and object selection is not entirely random. In nominative languages, it is restricted by the following hierarchy of semantic roles:

(21) agent > patient > recipient > benefactive > others
(cf. Dik 1978: 76)

If the subject can be assigned to some semantic role on this hierarchy, then it can be linked to any higher role on this hierarchy. Correspondingly for objects, except that objects cannot be assigned to agents. This hierarchy generalization also explains the fact that the agent is linked to the subject and the patient to the object in the basic accusative construction. As mentioned above, the ergative construction, which characterizes ergative languages, has a different linking pattern. It can be explained if the first two positions on the hierarchy in (21) are reversed so that the patient outranks the agent. The ergative construction was illustrated by Avar examples in (3) above. In this type of linking, the patient of a multivalenced predicate is coded by the same case as the subject of a monovalenced predicate and differently from the agent of a multivalenced predicate.

The linking difference between accusative and ergative constructions constitutes a major parameter within relational (alignment) typology (cf. Bickel 2011). This difference, which shows up in various ways in the grammar of the respective language types, makes a universal application of the subject and object notion questionable. This difficulty is a consequence of the mainstream European grammatical tradition that ties subject to agentivity and object to patienthood. Functional typological approaches use a relational terminology that is neutral with respect to role linking. Following Dixon (1979, 1994), many approaches use the notion of *pivot* in order to capture generalizations that are formulated in terms of subject in traditional approaches; cf. Keenan's list (1976) of subject properties. Similarly, Role-and-Reference-Grammar eliminates the subject concept in favour of the notion of privileged syntactic argument (cf. Van Valin and LaPolla 1997; Farrell 2005, Chap. 4).

Let us take a closer look at Dixon's pivot concept. Dixon and followers use S for the argument function of intransitive predicates and, in addition, A for the agentive and P for the patient-like argument of a multivalenced predicate, as already mentioned above in the context of the Avar examples in (3). On this basis, this influential line of research defines an ergative pivot as {S, P} and an accusative pivot as {S, A}. Accusative and ergative verb agreement, illustrated in (2) and (3) above by examples from German and Avar, can be analyzed in these terms as follows. In German, verb agreement works on the basis of a {S, A}-pivot; Avar has a verb agreement rule with a {S, P}-pivot.

These examples suffice to illustrate the advantage and the weakness of this kind of approach to grammatical relations. The advantage of the pivot notion or of similar concepts is that the pivot is delinked from semantic roles, at least superficially. However, semantic roles enter the definition of pivot types, thereby shifting the focus of this line of research towards semantic roles as basic explanatory notions. The problematic side is that the pivot notion obscures the explanation of purely formal, morphosyntactic rules such as verb agreement in German and Avar. As mentioned in section 2 above, case-based rules in ergative and accusative languages are similar. This similarity holds under the plausible assumption that the nominative and the absolutive are morphosyntactically equivalent cases, despite their different role-semantic functions (cf. for this view, among others, Sasse 1978; Dixon 1994; Primus 1999; Blake 2001). In both types of languages, nominative and absolutive are the least marked cases. This explains why verb agreement takes nominative or absolutive arguments as privileged targets. This explanation is not tied to the assumption of one universal markedness hierarchy of cases. Even if each language would have its own case system and its own case hierarchy, case-based agreement will target the argument with the least marked case (whichever it is) as the privileged option. The unpredictable part is that agreement is case-based, since there are languages like Warlpiri, in which agreement is based on argument structure; cf. (11) above. The predictable part is that if agreement is case-driven, the argument with the least marked case of the language will be its privileged target. Let us return to Dixon's pivot notion. Recall that in Dixon's terms, German verb agreement works on the basis of a {S, A}-pivot, while Avar has a verb agreement rule with a {S, P}-pivot. The problem is that the parallelism between German and Avar and the exact nature of the trigger (the case function) are obscured in this type of analysis.

Let us return to semantic roles. So far, I have discussed role-list approaches. Role lists are a convenient tool for preliminary role analyses and linking hypotheses. However, this kind of approach has several weaknesses. Its first weakness is that the number of individual roles exceeds by far the number of core syntactic functions, so that one-to-one mapping principles cannot be taken literally. Consider, for example, the concepts of A and P in Dixon's definition of pivot types. Within a role-list approach, A covers only agents and P only patients. Experiencer and stimulus, as illustrated in the examples (2), (5b) and (11c) above, are different roles. Obviously, this is not the way A and P are intended to work. Instead, A and P are implicitly taken to refer to two sets of roles that fall under some unspecified generalized notion of agentivity and patienthood. The same kind of criticism applies to Baker's mapping principles in (9) above, which use agent and theme to the exclusion of other roles such as experiencer and stimulus. In order to map a high number of individual roles to a small number of core grammatical relations, role-list approaches are forced to claim that many alternative roles belong together in some way that is left unexplained.

The second problem is that role lists are unstructured sets, so that additional stipulations in form of role hierarchies are needed. However, these additional stipulations do not offer a substantive explanation for the attested role asymmetries. As a result, role hierarchies and roles used in mapping principles of role-list approaches come in an unduly high number of variants (cf. Levin and Rappaport Hovav 2005: 154–183).

Decompositional approaches to semantic roles fare better. In this section, I will discuss Dowty's (1991) work as a representative of a non-structural decompositional approach. Related influential approaches are Role-and-Reference Grammar (cf. Van Valin and LaPolla 1997; Farrell 2005, Chap. 4) and the transitivity concept of Hopper and Thompson (1980). Dowty defines two superordinate proto-roles by a small set of semantic primitive properties. The agent proto-role is characterized by volition, sentience, causation, autonomous movement, and independent existence on the part of an argument with respect to its verbal head lexeme. See (22):

(22) Agent proto-role (Dowty 1991: 571):
- a. x does a volitional act: *John refrains from smoking.*
- b. x is sentient of or perceives another participant: *John knows / sees / fears Mary.*
- c. x causes an event or change of state in another participant: *His loneliness causes his unhappiness.*
- d. x is moving autonomously: *Water filled the boat.*
- e. x exists independently of the event named by the predicate: *John needs a car.*

Although most verbs select more than one proto-agent property for their subject argument (e.g. *murder, nominate,* or *give*), each of these properties may occur in isolation, as shown by the subject argument in the examples in (22). The patient proto-role is defined and illustrated by the object argument of the examples in (23):

(23) Patient proto-role (Dowty 1991: 572):
 a. x undergoes a change of state: *John moved the rock.*
 b. x is an incremental theme: *John filled the glass with water* (also stationary relative to other participants).
 c. x is causally affected by another participant: *Smoking causes cancer.*
 d. x is stationary relative to another participant: *The bullet entered the target.*
 e. x does not exist independently of the event, or not at all: *John needs a car / seeks a unicorn.*

Incremental theme is an event-related role for a participant whose degree of affectedness parallels the degree of completeness of the event. Incremental affectedness does not imply a physical change of state, cf. *read a book* and *memorize a poem*. Conversely, not every change of state or location is incremental, cf. *push a cart.*

The list of properties in (22) and (23) is preliminary for Dowty: properties can be deleted or added without changing the logic of his approach. Candidates for deletion are stationary (cf. Primus 1999: 42–43) and incremental theme (cf. Levin and Rappaport Hovav 2005: 106–110). Role properties that are neglected by Dowty include possessor (proto-agent) and possessed object (proto-patient) following, among others, Jackendoff (1990).

The specific roles of role-list approaches can be defined in terms of proto-role properties: agents by volition and possibly more proto-agent properties; instruments and causers by causation without volition; experiencers by sentience without other proto-agent properties. Thus, Dowty's generalized-role approach allows for a high number of specific roles to be subsumed under a small set of general roles. This reduces the inventory of superordinate role concepts dramatically without a neglect of finer distinctions.

The selection of grammatical relations is assumed to be sensitive to the higher or lower number of consistent role properties accumulated by an argument. Dowty's argument selection principle is given in (24):

(24) Argument Selection Principle: In predicates with grammatical subject and object, the argument for which the predicate entails the greatest number of proto-agent properties will be lexicalized as the subject of the predicate; the argument having the greatest number of proto-patient entailments will be lexicalized as the direct object.

(cf. Dowty 1991: 576)

This principle is meant to capture lexical default mappings for arguments with a high number of consistent properties such as selected by the verbs *break* and *hit*. Underspecified roles that accumulate a low number of consistent proto-role properties or none at all may have a variable realization. Psych-verbs, like those illustrated in (2), (5a, b) and (11c) above, show a considerable mapping variation within one language and cross-linguistically: they may have canonical case marking, as in the German accusative construction in (2) and the Warlpiri ergative construction in (11c), or may select non-canonical subject and object marking, as in the Icelandic examples in (5a, b). Note that there are also German psych-verbs with non-canonical marking of subject and object and Icelandic psych-verbs with canonical marking. According to Dowty (1991: 579), a psych-verb entails that the experiencer has some perception or sentience of the stimulus (proto-agent property of sentience or perception) and that the stimulus causes some emotional reaction or cognitive judgement in the experiencer (proto-agent property of causation). So each argument has a weak but equal claim to subjecthood. Psych-verbs and symmetrical predicates, such as *x rhymes with y* and *x resembles y*, which subcategorize for two arguments with properties that belong to the same proto-role, call into question mapping principles such as the Uniformity of Theta-Assignment (UTAH) mentioned in (20) above. UTAH is also problematic for the accusative-ergative distinction, since agents and themes are coded differently in these types of constructions.

For ergative constructions, Dowty assumes a reversal of proto-roles: subjects are associated with proto-patients and objects with proto-agents. However, Dowty is aware of the problem of using the notions of subject and object for the analysis of ergative languages. This problem can be omitted if one combines the basic assumptions of the approaches of Dowty and Dixon. Dixon's concepts of A and P, which are widely used in functional typology in order to define pivot-types, would be of greater typological use if they would denote proto-roles. In the combined view, the accusative construction is based on a {S, proto-agent}-pivot, while the ergative construction takes a {S, proto-patient}-pivot. These are canonical (i.e. default) mappings. Departures from a canonical mapping only occur if arguments are distinguished by a low number of consistent role-properties or not at all.

In sum, semantic roles are a major determinant of grammatical relations and of the major typological distinction between accusative and ergative constructions. There are various approaches to semantic roles. In this section, role-list approaches were compared to Dowty's generalized-role (proto-role) approach. Dowty's approach allows for a high number of specific roles to be subsumed under two general roles without additional stipulations. This reduction is necessary in order to explain the mismatch between a multitude of individual roles and the small number of syntactic argument slots. In addition, generalized-role approaches such as Dowty's are better suited to define Dixon's pivot notion or similar notions than role-list approaches. Dowty's approach is also able to explain non-canonical case marking with psych-verbs. In the next section, we will turn to parameters of variation due to referential semantic properties.

5. Grammatical relations and reference-related properties

In the reference-related view of subject and predicate, the subject is that part of a logical statement which names an entity the statement is about. The predicate is that part of the statement that states something about the subject. The German terms *Satzgegenstand,* lit. 'sentence entity', for subject and *Satzaussage,* lit. 'sentence statement', for predicate are anchored in this tradition. Similar definitions for subject and predicate are found in many school grammars of individual languages. More recent approaches interpret this distinction between subject and predicate within discourse semantics as topic (or theme) and predication (or comment). A discourse-functional view on grammatical relations characterizes a variety of functional approaches to grammar (e.g. Sasse 1978; Givón 1984; Kuno 1987; Lambrecht 1995; Dik 1997; Halliday and Matthiessen 2004). In Generative Grammar, this view is defended for discourse-configurational languages (cf. Kiss 1995). The correlation between subject and topic can be illustrated by the English example in (25).

(25) *What about Felix?*
  a. *Felix goes out with Rosa.*
  b. *Rosa goes out with Felix.*

In English (cf. Reinhart 1981: 62), there is a strong preference in discourse to interpret the grammatical subject of the sentence as its topic. Thus, (25a) is more appropriate than (25b) as an answer to the question *What about Felix? What about x* is a test question for topics. Despite this preference, the phrase-structural preverbal position associated with subjecthood in English is not restricted to topics. Recall the *there*-construction in (4b) above, in which the expletive *there* is in surface subject position but cannot be interpreted as a topic. Topics have to be referential: they have to refer to something in a real or possible world. Hence, expletives and negated quantifier phrases such as *nobody* cannot be topics.

The situation is different in discourse-configurational languages such as Rumanian, Hungarian, and Finnish (cf. Kiss 1995). In such languages, the structurally highest argument position has to be interpreted in terms of topic rather than subject. In word order typology, Rumanian, for example, has to be classified as TVX (with T for topic, V for predicate, X for any other constituent) instead of SVO (with S for subject and O for object). The problem for a theory of grammatical relations is that in Rumanian, Hungarian, and Finnish, topics do not share other subject properties, especially not obligatory nominative marking, which is responsible for most of the other subject properties in these languages. This means that, in these languages, nominative case marking competes with topicality in sharing subject properties.

Subject and object asymmetries are associated with several other referential properties in many languages. Subjects of transitive clauses are predominantly animate, for instance, up to 69 % in Norwegian (Øvrelid 2004) and up to 93 % in spoken Swedish (Dahl 2000). Correspondingly, objects refer predominantly to inanimate entities (89 % in Dahl's corpus and 90 % in Øvrelid's sample). Furthermore, in transitive clauses, definite subjects are preferred over indefinite subjects, while the reverse association holds for objects (cf. Øvrelid 2004 for Norwegian). As to person, 1. or 2. person is preferably coded as a subject and 3. person as an object (cf. Sells 2001; Bresnan, Dingare, and Manning 2001).

Soft constraints, i.e. tendencies or preferences, in one language may be inviolable hard constraints in another language (Bresnan, Dingare, and Manning 2001). This view is supported by typological findings. There are a variety of grammaticalized phenomena that are determined by reference-related properties. Three types of phenomena have been extensively discussed in the literature: voice-alternations including direct and inverse marking, differential subject or object marking, and morphological split ergativity.

In voice alternations, for example in Plains Cree (Algonquian) and Lummi (Northern Straits, Salishan), direct marking is used if the proto-agent is higher on the person hierarchy 1 > 2 > 3 or more topical than the proto-patient. Otherwise, a different indirect (or inverse) marking is used (cf. Givón 1994, Bresnan, Dingare, and Manning 2001). This corresponds to the tendency found in the more familiar European languages to use passives if the proto-patient is more topical than the proto-agent (cf. Sells 2001; Bresnan, Dingare, and Manning 2001). In Tagalog and other Austronesian languages, nearly all semantic roles compete for the principal grammatical relation and the choice among them rests on referential properties. Cf. the Tagalog examples in (26):

(26) Reference-related pivot:

a. *bumili* *ang=lalake* *ng=isda* *sa=tindahan.* [Tagalog]
PRF.AV.buy NOM=man GEN=fish DAT=store
'The man bought fish at the/a store.'

b. *binili* *ng=lalake* *ang=isda* *sa=tindahan.*
PRF.buy.OV GEN=man NOM=fish DAT=store
'The/a man bought the fish at the/a store.'

c. *binilhan* *ng=lalake* *ng=isda* *ang=tindahan.*
PRF.buy.DV GEN=man GEN=fish NOM=store
'The/a man bought fish at the store.'

(cf. Kroeger 1993: 13)

Each verbal clause in Tagalog must contain one and only one major constituent marked by the proclitic *ang*. This principal grammatical relation is variously identified in the literature under the label of topic, focus, pivot, subject, or nominative (cf. Kroeger 1993). The other constituents are marked by the proclitics *ng* (genitive) or *sa* (dative-locative), depending on their semantic role. The constituent marked by *ang* is the pivot in a number of constructions, such as conjunction reduction, relative constructions and quantifier floating. A characteristic of Tagalog and other Austronesian languages is that the semantic role of the pivot (nominative) is reflected in a verbal affix which is analysed by Kroeger (1993) as a voice marker. In the active voice of Tagalog – AV in the glosses in (26a) – the agentive role is marked by *ang*. In the objective voice – OV in (26b) –, the patient-like role is marked by *ang,* while in the dative-locative voice – DV in (26c) –, the recipient or location takes this marker. So the choice of the voice marker is jointly determined by case marking (*ang*) and semantic roles, since it varies due to the semantic role of the *ang*-marked phrase. The choice of the *ang*-proclitic is determined by two factors as well: referential properties and patient preference. The *ang*-marked noun phrase must be referential and normally definite; if a patient-like role is definite it must be marked by *ang* (cf. Kroeger 1993: 14 in conformity to other studies on Tagalog).

Referential properties also determine what is now commonly called *differential object marking* (Bossong 1985; Aissen 2003; de Swart 2007). In some languages, certain direct objects are marked by an object marker, while other objects remain unmarked. This pattern of variation is controlled by the referential property of the object noun phrase such as animacy, definiteness or specificity, or a combination of these factors. This pattern of variation is found, for instance, in Romance, Iranian, and Indic languages. Cf. the Spanish examples in (27):

(27) Differential object marking:

a. *Conozco a este actor.* [Spanish]
know.PRS.1SG OBJ this actor
'I know this actor.'

b. *Conozco esta película.*
know.PRS.1SG this film
'I know this film.'

In Spanish, the differential object marker, the preposition *a*, must be used with human noun-phrase referents, as shown in (27a). Reference-related alternations also occur on the subject in some languages, yielding a pattern of variation that is commonly called *differential subject marking* (cf. Aissen 2003; de Hoop and de Swart 2008).

Morphological split ergativity is another type of variation that is determined by referential properties in some languages (cf. Silverstein 1976; Dixon 1994, Chap. 4). For example, in many Australian ergative languages, pronouns, 1. and 2. person in particular, pattern accusatively while other types of noun phrases show ergative marking.

To conclude, reference-related variation in the realization of grammatical relations is a serious problem for any attempt at defining subject, object or pivot in one-dimensional terms because this type of variation induces a relational split. A relational split crops up whenever properties that are associated with one particular grammatical relation, for instance subject or pivot, are distributed over different noun phrases in a clause. In this section, I have shown how reference-related phenomena generate such split behaviour. Recall discourse-configurational languages such as Rumanian, Hungarian, and Finnish. In these languages, subject is split between the topic function and the nominative function. Tagalog poses another type of problem. It occurs whenever a phenomenon related to a certain grammatical relation is multi-dimensional. Recall that the choice of the *ang*-marker is determined by referential properties and can be attached to any semantic role in the clause. However, semantic roles are also relevant, since proto-patients have to be marked by *ang* if they are definite. Voice in Tagalog is also a multi-factor phenomenon. The choice of the voice marker is jointly determined by case marking (*ang*) and semantic roles, since the voice marker varies due to the semantic role of the *ang*-marked phrase. Differential case marking in Spanish is also multi-dimensional. It is jointly determined by the object function and the animacy of the verbal argument.

6. Grammatical relations in language processing

Advanced neuroscientific methods offer new perspectives on issues related to the question of how language is processed online in the brain. In parallel, an increasing number of theoretical approaches pursue a processing-driven view on grammar (cf. Hawkins 1994, 2004; Bresnan, Dingare, and Manning 2001; Culicover and Jackendoff 2005). As a consequence, there is a rapidly growing body of research devoted to language processing. This section offers a survcy of important results gained within the field of grammatical relations.

An early influential study on the processing of grammatical relations is Frazier (1987). Her experiments on Dutch revealed that an initial argument that is ambiguous with respect to its grammatical relation is incrementally interpreted as the subject of the clause. This processing strategy, which has become known as the *subject (first) preference* in psycho- and neurolinguistics, was documented for a variety of languages with various experimental methods in the subsequent years (cf. Bornkessel-Schlesewsky and Schlesewsky 2009: 170–173 for an overview). Cf. the Turkish examples in (28):

(28) Subject-first preference:

a. *Dün pilot gördüm.* [Turkish]
yesterday pilot see.1SG.PST
'Yesterday I saw (a) pilot.'

b. *Dün pilot uyudu.*
yesterday pilot sleep.3SG.PST
'Yesterday (the) pilot slept.'
(cf. Bornkessel-Schlesewsky and Schlesewsky 2009: 171)

The basic order of Turkish is subject-object-verb (SOV). In addition, a pronominal subject, particularly a first person subject, as in (28a), is usually dropped (pro-drop). Hence, an initial noun phrase in Turkish may have an unmarked object reading, which is not available in non-pro-drop languages such as Dutch and German. In (28), the temporary subject-object ambiguity is resolved by the agreement marker of the verb. In the study under discussion, critical test items, such as (28a), are contrasted with a corresponding control item that has an unambiguously marked object. The pattern of event-related brain potentials (ERPs) elicited at the disambiguating verb position indicates that speakers initially pursue a subject analysis.

There are also preferences related to modifiers and objects. There is a well-documented argument-over-modifier preference: a prepositional phrase that is ambiguous between an argument reading and a modifier interpretation is preferably parsed as an argument (cf. Bornkessel-Schlesewsky and Schlesewsky 2009: 102–103, 174–175). Studies on the interpretation of an ambiguous noun phrase as a direct or indirect object are more sparse and the findings inconclusive (cf. Bornkessel-Schlesewsky and Schlesewsky 2009: 175–180).

The experiments with verb-final structures, for instance, in Turkish, Japanese, German, and Dutch, reveal a general trait of the human language processing system (cf. Crocker 1994; Bornkessel-Schlesewsky and Schlesewsky 2009: 89–94). To fulfill the demands of effective real time communication, processing must be accomplished very rapidly and in an incremental fashion. This means that decisions must be made even in the absence of complete and certain information without waiting until the end of a construction in order to begin interpreting it. To accomplish incremental interpretation in this sense, the human processor must assign structure and meaning to the input as quickly as possible. In addition, the human processor must generate predictions. For our topic this means that a verb-dependent element is interpreted with respect to its grammatical relation, i.e. structural relation or case, and its semantic role, as soon as it is encountered even in the absence of complete and certain information, i.e., without waiting until the verbal head is presented. When two verbal dependents are encountered, they are interpreted relative to each other by using any cue that may help to identify their grammatical and semantic role. The predicted interpretations are guided by general principles such as subject-first, argument-over-modifier, subject-animate, and object-inanimate. When the interpretation of an ambiguous element turns out to be wrong, a conflict arises at the point where disambiguation towards the dispreferred reading occurs. In the Turkish example (28a) above, this happens with the first-parse subject interpretation of *pilot* when verb agreement, which enforces an object reading, is processed. The need to switch from one reading to another leads to an additional processing effort that can be identified experimentally.

In sum, the neurolinguistic experiments support the accessibility hierarchy of grammatical relations proposed by Keenan and Comrie (1977). Cf. (29):

(29) The accessibility hierarchy of grammatical relations:
subject > direct object > indirect object > other oblique arguments or modifiers

The above-mentioned neurolinguistic findings regarding the interpretation of ambiguous phrases can be summarized on the basis of this hierarchy as follows. A subject interpretation is more accessible than an object interpretation, and an argument interpretation is more accessible than an analysis as a modifier. The results for direct and indirect objects are less conclusive. This fits in well with typological work on the variant behaviour of indirect objects (cf. Dryer 1986; Primus 1998).

In the linguistic literature, the hierarchy of grammatical relations was used for the behaviour of grammatical relations, i.e. for rules, such as verb agreement, relativization, and passive. The main results can be subsumed under the schema in (30):

(30) Hierarchy-based rule schema:
a. If in a language a rule applies to a grammatical relation B, then for every grammatical relation A that outranks B on the relational hierarchy, this rule also applies to A.
b. There is at least one language where a rule applies to a grammatical relation C and for every D that is outranked by C on the relational hierarchy, this rule does not apply to D.

Let us apply the above schema to the function of the relative pronoun in relative clauses. The schema prohibits relative pronouns (or gaps corresponding to such pronouns) that are exclusively confined to direct objects. If a language has relative pronouns in the direct-object function, it must also have relative pronouns in the subject function. Additionally, rules that skip positions are blocked. For instance, no language is supposed to have relative subject pronouns and relative indirect-object pronouns to the exclusion of relative pronouns in direct-object function. The last clause of the schema, (30b), states that each grammatical relation on the hierarchy is cross-linguistically relevant.

There is an overwhelming number of psycho- and neurolinguistic studies for various languages showing that object relatives such as in (31b) lead to an increased processing cost in comparison to subject relatives such as in (31a), cf. Bornkessel-Schlesewsky and Schlesewsky (2009: 188–198).

(31) Subject vs. direct-object relativization strategy in English
a. *The managers that praised the designer examined the sketches.*
b. *The managers that the designer praised examined the sketches.*

To conclude, the processing of grammatical relations and of relation-based constructions seems to fit in well with theoretical and typological generalizations and their explanation in terms of a hierarchy of grammatical relations. However, under closer inspection, the situation turns out to be more intricate. The complexity arises due to intervening factors that lead to a split interpretation in terms of grammatical relations. This parallels the situation discussed for grammar in the previous sections. Without going into technical details of neurolinguistic methodology and theory, it suffices to mention the most important intervening factors. Sentence processing is guided by several types of information. In addition to phrase-structure and case, interpretation in terms of semantic roles plays an important role (cf. Bornkessel-Schlesewsky and Schlesewsky 2009: 134–143). Furthermore, a number of studies indicate that the processing of verbal arguments also depends on referential properties of the noun phrases such as animacy, topicality and definiteness (cf. Lamers and de Swart 2012). Finally, neurolinguistic studies suggest that the types of information are not associated as assumed in the theoretical literature. In German, for instance, there is a dissociation between allegedly "structural" case functions and phrase-structure relations (cf. Frisch and Schlesewsky 2001). In sum, the different factors that have been found to interfere with grammatical relations in grammar are also attested in language processing.

7. Final discussion

This chapter has shown that the relational interpretation of major sentence constituents is an important factor in grammar and language processing. A whole range of phenomena including verb agreement, relativization, reflexivization, basic word order, and voice cannot be captured appropriately without reference to the relational network between the verbal head and its dependents (head-dependent relations). Furthermore, there is a growing body of evidence indicating that hierarchical relations between the co-dependents of a head (co-argument asymmetries) are accessed in a way that is independent from the verbal head (cf. Primus 1998, 1999; Bornkessel-Schlesewsky and Schlesewsky 2009). Major typological parameters such as the ergative-accusative distinction also rest on relational interpretation. A challenge to all kinds of linguistic approaches is the question of the exact nature of these relationships. In this chapter, the discussion centred around the question whether grammatical relations such as subject, object, and pivot are appropriate tools to capture the relational network between major sentence constituents and its role in grammar and processing. The answer seems to be negative. This chapter has uncovered two types of serious problems tied to subject, object, pivot, and similar notions. These are relational splits (cf. for this term Ura 2000) and multi-factor relational phenomena.

A relational split occurs when behaviour or coding properties that tend to cluster for a particular grammatical relation, the subject for instance (cf. Keenan 1976), are distributed over different types of noun phrases. This leads to a situation in which each type of noun phrase accumulates some but not all subject properties that are relevant in a particular language. Recall the English *there*-construction in section 2 above, which is repeated here for convenience: *There are cows in next door's garden.* In this construction, *there* is subject in terms of surface structural position, but not with respect to case and agreement. Correspondingly, *cows* is subject in terms of case and agreement but not with respect to surface structural position. Thus, three subject properties related to case, agreement, and surface structure are split between *there* and *cows* in this type of construction. In constructions with a quirky case subject, such as in the Icelandic examples discussed in section 2 above, subject properties are split between the nominative argument, which, if present, determines verb agreement, and the highest structural argument position, which determines the function of infinitival PRO and triggers obligatory reflexivization, i.e. blocks coreference with a personal pronoun. A relational split was also mentioned for discourse-configurational languages such as Rumanian, Hungarian, and Finnish. In these languages, the highest structural argument position is restricted to topics while case marking is tied to semantic roles and determines a number of phenomena such as verb agreement. So subject is split between the topic function and the nominative function in these languages.

Multi-factor relational phenomena are also a serious problem for subject, object, and similar notions. Let us recall the determinants of case marking. In languages such as English, there are structural cases that are determined by surface phrase-structural relations, as amply discussed in the generative literature. But a structural case can also be checked in the basic position of an argument noun phrase, which is determined by the semantic role of the argument. This happens, for example, in the *there*-construction mentioned above with the structural nominative of the noun phrase *cows*. In Tagalog and other Austronesian languages, one case marker (*ang* in Tagalog) is determined primarily, but not exclusively by referential properties such as topicality and definiteness. The other factor is a proto-patient preference, as mentioned in section 5 above. Voice in Tagalog is also a multi-factor phenomenon. The choice of the voice marker is jointly determined by case marking (*ang*) and semantic roles, since the marker varies due to the semantic role of the *ang*-marked phrase. Differential case marking in Spanish, which was illustrated in section 5 above, is determined by the syntactic function (direct object) as well as by the animacy of the verbal argument.

Behavioural properties of subjects and objects are also determined by more than one factor in many languages. Verb agreement, for example, is a multi-factor rule in some languages. Hindi has attracted attention in the typological literature due to a multi-factor agreement rule that is jointly determined by the nominative case function and by argument structure (cf. Mohanan 1994: 102–106; Bickel and Yaadava 2000; Corbett 2006: 195). In Hindi, there is a tense-aspect-driven alternation between the ergative and accusative construction. In the ergative construction, the proto-patient is in the nominative, in the accusative construction, the nominative is assigned to the proto-agent. According to Mohanan, among others, agreement in Hindi is triggered by the highest argument in the argument structure of the verb that is also in the nominative. When there is no nominative argument, a default agreement marker is selected (masculine singular). Bickel and Yaadava (2000) go one step further in their claim that a combination of morphological and argument-structural notions is a general characteristic of the over-all syntax of many if not all Indo-Aryan languages. The above survey has focused on multi-factor phenomena within one language. However, from a cross-linguistic perspective, virtually all phenomena are multi-dimensional, turning any attempt towards a universal definition of grammatical relations into a fruitless enterprise. What is case-driven in one language, for instance, is motivated by structural relations in another. This was shown for case-based verb agreement in German and Avar and structure-driven verb agreement in Warlpiri.

Due to space limitation, the previous sections have selected a small range of data from the overwhelming array of critical data discussed in the pertinent literature (cf. among others, Bhat 1991; Palmer 1994; Primus 1999; Farrell 2005; Bickel 2011). Some of the critical data presented in this chapter were selected from well-studied European languages, in order to show that notions such as subject and object fail to account even for the languages these notions were primarily devised for.

The dilemma engendered by notions such as subject and pivot can be illustrated by Icelandic quirky case subjects. As suggested by this terminology, this type of argument is classified as a subject. This explains a number of facts including the structural position of this type of argument, infinitival PRO and reflexivization facts. However, verb agreement, which is triggered solely by nominative arguments in Icelandic, is left unexplained. The dilemma is that verb agreement in Icelandic could have been explained if a different, case-based subject notion would have been used instead of a structural one. The typological notions of pivot or privileged syntactic argument generate the same type of dilemma. If we apply the pivot notion to the arguments in Icelandic that are classified as subjects in alternative approaches, we cannot capture verb agreement. Conversely, if we classify the agreeing arguments as pivots in Icelandic, we fail to capture the other facts. The dilemma of any definition of subject or pivot can now be stated in general terms for the notion of subject as follows. The dilemma for other grammatical relations applies correspondingly. If we define (or identify) subject in terms of X, we capture some generalizations but miss others, which we might have captured if we had defined subject in terms of Y. But if we define subject in terms of Y, then we miss the generalizations we could have captured in terms of X. The dilemma cannot be solved, of course, by adding more correlates to the list of possible subject properties. On the contrary, the more types of correlates we find to be relevant, the clearer the dilemma becomes.

Let us summarize the solutions to this dilemma that are proposed in the recent literature. They come in two flavours: decompositional and construction-based approaches. Here again, we focus on the subject for ease of exposition. In decompositional approaches, the subject notion is eliminated and replaced by different types of relational information. This trend characterizes, for example, the Minimalist Program (MP), Optimality Theory (OT), and Lexical Functional Grammar (LFG), as discussed in section 3 above. MP is a derivational, serial model that is focused on phrase-structural relations to the detriment of other types of relations. By contrast, LFG and OT are better equipped for relational splits and multi-factor-phenomena since both theories are non-derivational and are able to access different types of relations in parallel. In recent variants of LFG, subject and object are still primitive notions, as in earlier LFG approaches, but their role has decreased in favour of other types of relational information. Another appeal of non-derivational approaches is the fact that the different types of information can be arranged on their own hierarchy, as illustrated by the case markedness hierarchy in OT in section 3 above. By this step, such approaches are able, in principle, to capture the type of function (or property) that ties different subject correlates together: a function that qualifies for a subject is the first member of a hierarchy of functions of the same kind. The notion of *nominative argument*, for instance, captures a case relation between a head and a dependent. However, when subject properties are at issue, what counts is the fact that nominative is the first member on the case hierarchy of the respective language. This carries over to other types of relational information including structural and role-semantic hierarchization. To conclude, subject, object, and pivot have to be replaced by more specific relations between a head and a dependent and, in addition, by hierarchy relations between co-dependents (cf. Primus 1998, 1999; Bornkessel-Schlesewsky and Schlesewsky 2009).

This hierarchy-based view of subject is adequately captured by the typological notions of pivot or privileged syntactic argument. However, within functional typology, these notions are one-dimensional. Recall that Dixon's pivot types are based exclusively on semantic roles, as discussed in section 4 above. This leads to a neglect of other types of relational information in this line of research.

Functional typological approaches favour a construction-based solution to the problems engendered by grammatical relations. In face of the problem that criteria for a particular grammatical relation do not converge on the same type of argument, construction-based approaches reconceptualize the notion of subject, object or pivot as the syntactic relation that an argument bears to a specific construction (or rule) rather than to the clause in which the argument is realized (cf. Croft 2001; Christofaro 2008; Bickel 2011). The variation between verb agreement in German and Avar can be analyzed in terms of the construction-based pivot notion as follows (cf. also section 4 above). In German, the pivot (or subject) for verb agreement is {S, A}. In Avar, the pivot for verb agreement is {S, P}. The problem with the construction-based pivot notion is that the parallelism between German and Avar, which can be captured in terms of the highest (alternatively primary or privileged) case function, and the exact nature of the trigger (case) are obscured in this type of analysis. More importantly, the construction-based approach to grammatical relations cannot cope with relational splits and multi-factor relational phenomena. Let us demonstrate this on quirky case subjects in Icelandic. Infinitival PRO has a {S, A}-pivot. The pivot of verb agreement must be {S, A} as well, since Icelandic has no ergative pivot of the type {S, P}. The competing relational dimensions of Icelandic, the privileged structural relation for infinitival PRO vs. the privileged case relation for verb agreement, cannot be captured by a construction-based pivot (or subject) notion. In sum, the construction-based pivot notion predicts variation where there is none, for instance, in verb agreement in German and Avar, and fails to account for variation where it occurs, for instance, among the rules (or constructions) in Icelandic.

This shows that the solution to the problem imposed by grammatical relations cannot be solved by a construction-based approach *per se*. A more appropriate solution is a decompositional approach to the notion of pivot, subject or privileged syntactic argument and a hierarchization of different types of information. This carries over to the other relational notions such as direct and indirect object. A construction-based approach is needed on independent grounds and is pursued not only in functional typological approaches. Many recent theories of grammar incorporate construction-based variation to a smaller or larger extent. Thus, among others, Culicover and Jackendoff (2005) advocate for a construction-based approach within Generative Grammar.

8. References (selected)

Adger, David
2003 *Core Syntax. A Minimalist Approach.* Oxford: Oxford University Press.

Aikhenvald, Alexandra Y., Robert M. W. Dixon, and Masayuki Onishi (eds.)
2001 *Non-canonical Marking of Subjects and Objects.* Amsterdam: John Benjamins.

Aissen, Judith
2003 Differential object marking: iconicity vs. economy. *Natural Language and Linguistic Theory* 21: 435–483.

Baker, Mark C.
1997 Thematic roles and syntactic structure. In: Liliane Haegeman (ed.), *Elements of Grammar. Handbook of Generative Syntax,* 73–137. Dordrecht: Kluwer.

Barðdal, Jóhanna, and Thórhallur Eythórsson
2003 Icelandic vs. German: oblique subjects, agreement and expletives. *Chicago Linguistic Society* 39: 755–773.

Barlow, Michael
1992 *A Situated Theory of Agreement.* London: Garland.

Bhaskararao, Peri, and Karumuri Venkata Subbarao (eds.)
2004 *Non-nominative Subjects. Volume 1.* Amsterdam: John Benjamins.

Bhat, Darbhe N.S.
1991 *Grammatical Relations: The Evidence Against their Necessity and Universality.* London/New York: Routledge.

Bickel, Balthasar
2006 Clause-level vs. predicate-level linking. In: Ina Bornkessel, Matthias Schlesewsky, Bernard Comrie, and Angela D. Friederici (eds.), *Semantic Role Universals and Argument Linking. Theoretical, Typological and Psycholinguistic Perspectives,* 155–190. Berlin: de Gruyter.

Bickel, Balthasar
2011 Grammatical relations typology. In: Jae Jung Song (ed.), *The Handbook of Linguistic Typology*, 399–444. Oxford: Oxford University Press.

Bickel, Balthasar, and Yogendra P. Yaadava
2000 A fresh look at grammatical relations in Indo-Aryan. *Lingua* 110: 343–373.

Blake, Barry J.
2001 *Case.* 2nd rev. ed. Cambridge: Cambridge University Press.

Bobaljik, Jonathan D., and Susi Wurmbrand
2009 Case in GB/Minimalism. In: Andrej Malchukov, and Andrew Spencer (eds.), *Handbook of Case*, 44–58. Oxford: Oxford University Press.

Bornkessel-Schlesewksy, Ina, and Matthias Schlesewsky
2009 *Processing Syntax and Morphology. A Neurocognitive Perspective.* Oxford: Oxford University Press.

Bossong, Georg
1985 *Differentielle Objektmarkierung in den Neuiranischen Sprachen.* Tübingen: Narr.

Bresnan, Joan, Shipra Dingare, and Christopher D. Manning
2001 Soft constraints mirror hard constraints: voice and person in English and Lummi. *Proceedings of the LFG '01 Conference.* Online CSLI Publications.

Bresnan, Joan
2000 Optimal syntax. In: Joost Dekkers, Frank van der Leuw, and Jeroen van de Weijer (eds.), *Optimality Theory. Phonology, Syntax, and Acquisition*, 334–385. Oxford: Oxford University Press.

Bresnan, Joan
2001 *Lexical-Functional Syntax.* Oxford: Blackwell.

Butt, Miriam
2006 *Theories of Case.* Cambridge: Cambridge University Press.
Charachidzé, Georges
1981 *Grammaire de la Langue Avar.* Paris: Jean-Favard.
Chomsky, Noam
1981 *Lectures on Government and Binding.* Dordrecht: Foris.
Chomsky, Noam
1995 *The Minimalist Program.* Cambridge: MIT Press.
Christofaro, Sonia
2008 *Grammatical Categories and Relations: Universality vs. Language-Specificity and Construction-Specificity. Language and Linguistics Compass.* DOI: 10.1111/j.1749818X.2008.00111.x
Corbett, Greville G.
2006 *Agreement.* Cambridge: Cambridge University Press.
Crocker, Matthew W.
1994 On the nature of the principle-based sentence processor. In: Charles Clifton, Lyn Frazier, and Keith Rayner (eds.), *Perspectives on Sentence Processing*, 245–266. Hillsdale: Erlbaum.
Croft, William
2001 *Radical Construction Grammar: Syntactic Theory in Typological Perspective.* Oxford: Oxford University Press.
Culicover, Peter W., and Ray Jackendoff
2005 *Simpler Syntax.* Oxford: Oxford University Press.
Dahl, Östen
2000 Egophoricity in discourse and syntax. *Functions of Language* 7: 33–77.
de Hoop, Helen, and Peter de Swart (eds.)
2008 *Differential Subject Marking*. Dordrecht: Springer Netherlands.
de Hoop, Helen
2009 Case in Optimality Theory. In: Andrej Malchukov, and Andrew Spencer (eds.), *Handbook of Case*, 88–101. Oxford: Oxford University Press.
de Swart, Peter
2007 *Cross-linguistic Variation in Object Marking.* Utrecht: LOT publications.
Dik, Simon C.
1978 *Functional Grammar.* Amsterdam: North-Holland.
Dik, Simon C.
1997 *The Theory of Functional Grammar.* 2nd. rev. Dordrecht: Foris.
Dixon, Robert M.W.
1979 Ergativity. *Language* 55: 59–138.
Dixon, Robert M.W.
1994 *Ergativity.* Cambridge: Cambridge University Press.
Dowty, David R.
1991 Thematic proto-roles and argument selection. *Language* 67: 547–619.
Dryer, Matthew
1986 Primary objects, secondary objects, and antidative. *Language* 62: 808–845.
DUDEN
2009 *Grammatik der Deutschen Gegenwartssprache.* 8., überarb. Aufl. Mannheim: Duden Verlag.
Farrell, Patrick
2005 *Grammatical Relations.* Oxford: Oxford University Press.
Fillmore, Charles J.
1968 The case for case. In: Emmon Bach, and Robert Harms (eds.), *Universals in Linguistic Theory,* 1–90. New York: Holt, Rinehart & Winston.

Frazier, Lyn
1987 Syntactic processing: Evidence from Dutch. *Natural Language and Linguistic Theory* 5: 519–559.
Frisch, Stefan, and Matthias Schlesewsky
2001 The N400 indicates problems of thematic hierarchizing. *NeuroReport* 12: 3391–3394.
Givón, Talmy
1984 *Syntax: A Functional Typological Introduction. Vol 1.* Amsterdam: John Benjamins.
Givón, Talmy (ed.)
1994 *Voice and Inversion*. Amsterdam: John Benjamins.
Grimshaw, Jane, and Vieri Samek-Lodovici
1998 Optimal subjects and subject universals. In: Barbosa, Pilar, Daniel Fox, Paul Hagstrom, and David Pesetsky (eds.) *Is the Best Good Enough? Optimality and Competition in Syntax,* 193–220. Cambridge/Mass: MIT Press.
Hale, Kenneth
1983 Warlpiri and the grammar of non-configurational languages. *Natural Language and Linguistic Theory* 1: 5–47.
Halliday, Michael A. K., and Christian M. I. M Matthiessen
2004 *An Introduction to Functional Grammar,* 3rd edition. London: Arnold.
Hawkins, John A.
1994 *A Performance Theory of Order and Constituency.* Cambridge: Cambridge University Press.
Hawkins, John A.
2004 *Efficiency and Complexity in Grammars.* Oxford: Oxford University Press.
Hopper, Paul J., and Sandra Thompson
1980 Transitivity in grammar and discourse. *Language* 56: 251–299.
Jackendoff, Ray
1990 *Semantic Structures.* Cambridge, Mass.: MIT Press.
Keenan, Edward L.
1976 Towards a universal definition of 'subject'. In: Charles N. Li (ed.), *Subject and Topic,* 303–334. New York: Academic Press.
Keenan, Edward L., and Bernard Comrie
1977 Noun phrase accessibility and universal grammar. *Linguistic Inquiry* 8: 63–99.
Kiss, Katalin É. (ed.)
1995 *Discourse Configurational Languages*. Oxford: Oxford University Press.
Kroeger, Paul
1993 *Phrase Structure and Grammatical Relations in Tagalog.* Stanford: CSLI.
Kulikov, Leonid, Andrej Malchukov, and Peter de Swart (eds.)
2006 *Case, Valency and Transitivity.* Amsterdam: John Benjamins.
Kuno, Susumu
1987 *Functional Syntax. Anaphora, Discourse, and Empathy.* Chicago: Chicago University Press.
Lambrecht, Knud
1995 The pragmatics of case: On the relationship between semantic, grammatical, and pragmatic roles in English and French. In: Masayoshi Shibatani, and Sandra A. Thompson (eds.), *Essays in Semantics and Pragmatics. In Honor of Charles J. Fillmore*, 145–190. Amsterdam: John Benjamins.
Lamers, Monique J. A., and Peter de Swart (eds.)
2012 *Case, Word Order and Prominence. Interacting Cues in Language Production and Comprehension*. Dordrecht: Springer.
Levin, Beth, and Malka Rappaport Hovav
2005 *Argument Realization.* Cambridge: Cambridge University Press.

Mohanan, Tara
1994 *Argument Structure in Hindi.* Stanford: CSLI Publications.
Mohr, Sabine
2005 *Clausal Architecture and Subject Positions. Impersonal Constructions in the Germanic Languages.* Amsterdam: John Benjamins Publishing.
Moravcsik, Edith A.
1988 Agreement and markedness. In: Michael Barlow, and Charles A. Ferguson (eds.), *Agreement in Natural Language: Approaches, Theories, Description,* 89–106. Stanford: CSLI Publications.
Næss, Åshild
2007 *Prototypical Transitivity.* Amsterdam: John Benjamins.
Øvrelid, Lilja
2004 Disambiguation of grammatical functions in Norwegian: Modeling variation in word order interpretations conditioned by animacy and definiteness. In: Fred Karlsson (ed.), *Proceedings of the 20th Scandinavian Conference of Linguistics.* University of Helsinki: Department of General Linguistics.
Palmer, Frank R.
1994 *Grammatical Roles and Relations.* Cambridge: Cambridge University Press.
Perlmutter, David, and Paul M. Postal
1984 The 1-advancement exclusiveness law. In: David Perlmutter, and Carol Rosen (eds.), *Studies in Relational Grammar 2*, 81–125. Chicago: University of Chicago Press.
Primus, Beatrice
1998 The relative order of recipient and patient in the languages of Europe. In: Anna Siewierska (ed.), *Constituent Order in the Languages of Europe*, 421–473. Berlin: de Gruyter.
Primus, Beatrice
1999 *Cases and Thematic Roles – Ergative, Accusative and Active.* Tübingen: Niemeyer.
Primus, Beatrice
2009 Case, grammatical relations, and semantic roles. In: Andrej Malchukov, and Andrew Spencer (eds.), *The Handbook of Case,* 261–275. Oxford: Oxford University Press.
Reinhart, Tanya
1981 Pragmatics and linguistics: an analysis of sentence topics. *Philosophica* 27: 53–94.
Reinhart, Tanya
1983 *Anaphora and Semantic Interpretation.* London: Croom Helm.
Samek-Lodovici, Vieri
2003 Agreement impoverishment under subject inversion. In: Gisbert Fanselow, and Caroline Féry (eds.), *Resolving Conflicts in Grammars. Optimality Theory in Syntax, Morphology, and Phonology,* 49–82. Hamburg: Helmut Buske.
Sasse, Hans-Jürgen
1978 Subjekt und Ergativ: Zur pragmatischen Grundlage primärer grammatischer Relationen. *Folia Linguistica* 12: 219–252.
Sells, Peter
2001 Voice in Optimality Theory. In: Géraldine Legendre, Jane Grimshaw, and Sten Vikner (eds.), *Optimality-Theoretic Syntax*, 356–391. Cambridge/Mass: MIT Press.
Silverstein, Michael
1976 Hierarchy of features and ergativity In: Robert M. Dixon (ed.), *Grammatical Categories in Australian Languages*, 112–171. Canberra: Humanities Press.
Thráinsson, Höskuldur
1979 *On Complementation in Icelandic.* New York: Garland.
Ura, Hiroyuki
2000 *Checking Theory and Grammatical Functions in Universal Grammar.* Oxford: Oxford University Press.

Van Valin, Robert D., and Randy LaPolla
1997 *Syntax. Structure, Meaning and Function.* Cambridge: Cambridge University Press.

Woolford, Ellen
2001 Case patterns. In: Géraldine Legendre, Jane Grimshaw, and Sten Vikner (eds.), *Optimality-Theoretic Syntax*, 509–543. Cambridge/Mass: MIT Press.

Woolford, Ellen
2003 Burzio's Generalization, markedness, and constraints on nominative objects. In: Ellen Brandner, and Heike Zinsmeister (eds.), *New Perspectives on Case Theory*, 301–329. Stanford: CSLI Publications.

Wunderlich, Dieter
2003 Optimal case patterns. German and Icelandic compared. In: Ellen Brandner, and Heike Zinsmeister (eds.), *New Perspectives on Case Theory*, 329–365. Stanford: CSLI Publications.

Beatrice Primus, Cologne (Germany)

9. Arguments and Adjuncts

Abstract

In this chapter it is outlined how the notions of argument and adjunct are used in syntax, and why it is considered useful to distinguish the two. First, arguments will be introduced. The distinction between syntactic arguments and semantic arguments will be outlined, as well as the possible relationships between the two. Then modifiers are introduced, and it is shown that the problem of how to integrate these into syntactic structure can lead to the notion of a syntactic adjunct. Finally, the various syntactic differences between arguments and adjuncts that have been claimed to exist are examined.

1. Arguments

1.1. The semantic notion of argument

The notion of argument as used in linguistics has both a semantic and a syntactic meaning. The two are intimately connected, as we will see, and it will be helpful to the understanding of the syntactic notion to first introduce the semantic notion.

The semantic notion of argument could be described as a participant in the event/state/relation expressed by a predicate. Predicates can be sub-divided according to how many arguments they take, their semantic valency. Thus, verbs like *laugh* or *blush* in (1)–(2) express one-place predicates (predicates taking one argument), in (3)–(4) we are dealing with two-place predicates and the verbs in (5)–(6) express three-place predicates. The elements expressing a semantic argument are between brackets.

(1) *[Mary] laughs.*

(2) *[James] blushed.*

(3) *[John] is reading [the paper].*

(4) *[Harriet] knows [the answer].*

(5) *[John] sold [me] [a copy].*

(6) *[The author] sent [his publisher] [the manuscript].*

Predicates taking more than three arguments are rare at best, but the verb *to bet* has been cited as taking four arguments:

(7) *[I] bet [you] [ten dollar] [that they will win].*

Of course, it depends on a rather more precise analysis of what a semantic argument is than saying it is a participant in the event or state expressed by the predicate to determine whether all four participants in (7) are proper arguments, but such an analysis will not be undertaken here (see Jackendoff 1990a, for instance, for extensive discussion).

From (1)–(7) it might be inferred that predicates are always expressed by means of a verb, here by forms of *laugh*, *blush*, *read*, *know*, *sell*, *send* and *bet*. However, predicates can also be expressed by other lexical categories. Thus, in (8)–(10) the predicate is expressed by an adjective, a noun, and a preposition, respectively.

(8) *[John] is* ***ill****.*

(9) *[Carla] is* ***a doctor****.*

(10) *[Simon] is* ***in*** *[the house].*

Semantic arguments can be classified in terms of their semantic content (indicating the way in which they participate in the event/state/relation). Thus, at least the following types of argument are often distinguished:

(11) a. Agent: the "doer" of the action, the causer of the event.
John *kicked the ball;* ***Mary*** *laughed;* ***The key*** *opened the door*

b. Theme: the thing undergoing the action, the thing in motion, the causee
John kicked ***the ball****; Mary read* ***the paper****; The key opened* ***the door***

c. Goal: the thing towards which the action is directed
He sold ***me*** *a copy; She gave* ***her brother*** *a present*

d. Experiencer: a sentient being that is mentally affected by the action/state:
__Mary__ fears dogs; Dogs frighten __Mary__; The outcome pleased __me__

e. Benefactives: the person/thing that benefits from the action:
I baked __John__ a cake

Exactly which argument types should be distinguished is a matter of debate, and again depends on a more precise analysis of the notion of semantic argument; see Grimshaw (1990), Jackendoff (1990a), Hale and Keyser (1993), Reinhart (2002), inter alia.

1.2. Syntactic arguments and their relationship with semantic arguments

As noted, the notion of argument introduced in section 1.1 is a semantic notion. There is a related, but distinct, syntactic notion of argument. It can be observed that certain verbs go together with just a subject (intransitive verbs), some go together with both a subject and a direct object (transitive verbs) and some take a subject, a direct object and an indirect object (ditransitive verbs), as illustrated in (12)–(14).

(12) a. *Mary laughed.*
b. **Mary laughed Bill.*
c. **Mary laughed Bill a funny book.*

(13) a. **Mary destroyed.*
b. *Mary destroyed the book.*
c. **Mary destroyed Bill the book.*

(14) a. **Mary gave.*
b. *Mary gave a book.*
c. *Mary gave Bill a book.*

The syntactic constituents that appear in the subject, direct object, and indirect object positions are the syntactic arguments of the verb, to be distinguished from the semantic arguments as discussed before. Thus, the syntactic valency of a verb is the property that determines how many syntactic arguments the verb takes, as opposed to the semantic valency of a predicate, which says how many semantic arguments the predicate takes.

The number of syntactic arguments a verb (or other lexical category expressing a predicate) can take is determined by the number of semantic arguments that the predicate expressed by the verb takes. Considering the predicates in (1)–(6) above, for example, it is clear that the one-place predicates in (1)–(2) are expressed by intransitive verbs, the two-place predicates in (3)–(4) are expressed by transitives, and the three-place predicates in (5)–(6) are expressed by ditransitives.

Nevertheless, the number of semantic arguments a predicate takes cannot simply be equated with the number of syntactic arguments that the verb which expresses that predicate appears with syntactically. This is already apparent from the example in (14b) above. Next to the case of (14c), where it appears with three syntactic arguments, the verb *give* can also appear with just two syntactic arguments. In (14b), the semantic Goal argument is left syntactically unexpressed. It is still part of the meaning of *give* (it is still implicit in 14b that there is a person or entity to whom Mary gave a book), but there is no syntactic constituent expressing it. It is an implicit argument in this case. (It is of course possible that an implicit argument is present syntactically as an empty category. There are reasons to believe, however, that this is not the case for implicit indirect objects in English as in 14b, see Rizzi 1986.) It is in fact a rather typical property of Goal arguments that they need not be expressed syntactically:

(15) a. *He sent me a letter.*
b. *He sends lots of letters.*

(16) a. *They sold us a lot of books.*
b. *They sold a lot of books last year.*

In many cases, the Theme argument of a transitive verb can also be left unexpressed:

(17) a. *Leo was eating Brussels sprouts.*
b. *Leo was eating.*

(18) a. *Heather was reading the paper.*
b. *Heather was reading.*

(19) a. *David is painting the shed.*
b. *David is painting.*

In contrast, (20) shows that in the usual case (and see below on deviations from the usual case) an Agent argument cannot be left unexpressed in a full, finite, clause in English. This might not have anything to do with their being Agents as such, but be a consequence of the fact that (overt) subjects are obligatory in English finite clauses, in combination with the canonical correspondence rule for Agent arguments mentioned in (25) below. After all, the Experiencer subject of a verb like *fear* cannot be left implicit either, as shown in (21). (However, see immediately below on the possibility of satisfying the subject requirement of languages like English by using an expletive; this would not improve the sentences in 20–21 though).

(20) a. **Was eating Brussels sprouts.* (except in topic drop/diary drop registers)
b. **Was reading.*
c. **Is painting.*

(21) **Fears dogs.*

The opposite of the situation in which a semantic argument does not seem to correspond to any syntactic argument, so a situation in which a syntactic argument does not correspond to any semantic argument, occurs as well. There can be elements that appear in a syntactic argument position that do not correspond to a semantic argument and are in fact meaningless. Clear examples of this arise in languages in which finite clauses contain a particular structural subject position that must always be filled (non-pro-drop languages). In some contexts, the semantic subject can occur in a position lower than this structural subject position, whereas in other cases there may be no semantic subject present in syntax at all. In these cases, an expletive fills up the syntactic subject position, so we have an element in an argument position that does not correspond to a semantic argument. Examples are given in (22) (22c is an example of an impersonal passive in Dutch, that is, a passive from an intransitive verb). The expletive subjects are in boldface.

(22) a. ***There*** *were a lot of mistakes in the essay.*
b. ***It*** *seems that the weather is going to improve over the weekend.*
c. ***Er*** *werd de hele avond gedanst.* [Dutch]
there was the whole night danced
'People danced the whole night long.'

So, the semantic valency of a predicate does not determine exactly how many / which syntactic arguments the category expressing the predicate appears with. The semantics of the predicate also does not determine the type of lexical categories that can realise the syntactic arguments that do occur. Predicates that are semantically very similar can impose different selectional restrictions on their syntactic arguments in this respect, see for instance Grimshaw (1979), Gazdar et al. (1985: 32), and Jackendoff (1993). However, the semantic valency of a predicate does determine the maximum number of syntactic arguments that the category expressing the predicate can appear with.

The influence of the semantic valency of a predicate on the structure of sentences in which the predicate occurs goes further than that however, at least in a language like English. Consider the examples in (23)–(24).

(23) a. *Mary saw Bill.*
b. *Bill saw Mary.*

(24) a. *The fox sold the bear the wolf.*
b. *The bear sold the wolf the fox.*
c. *The wolf sold the fox the bear.*

In both (23a) and (23b) there are two arguments, in accordance with the fact that the verb *see* expresses a two-place predicate. But not only do we know that *Mary* and *Bill* express the arguments of this predicate, we also know for sure which syntactic argument expresses which semantic argument. In (23a) *Mary* is necessarily interpreted as the Agent and *Bill* as the Theme, while in (23b) this is the other way around. Similar considerations hold for the sentences with ditransitive *sell* in (24). We know exactly what the distribution of Agent, Theme and Goal roles across the three syntactic arguments is in these sentences. Apparently, there are systematic correspondences between semantic arguments and syntactic arguments. Examples (23) and (24) illustrate the basic correspondences in (25). Possible deviations from these are discussed in section 1.4.

(25) Agent ↔ Subject
Theme ↔ Direct object
Goal ↔ Indirect object

It has been proposed (for example, by Marantz 1984) that there are languages that are fundamentally different in this respect. Such "syntactically ergative" (Dixon 1972) languages would have the correspondence rules in (26). (In contrast, morphologically ergative languages do not deviate from 25 – see for instance Bobaljik 1993 – but have a pattern of morphological case marking such that subjects of intransitives are assigned the same case as objects of transitives, while subjects of transitives receive a different case.)

(26) Agent ↔ Direct object
Theme ↔ Subject

Subsequent research has cast doubt on the existence of such languages, however, as it seems the phenomena that were taken to show that Themes occupy a structurally higher (subject) position than Agents (in object position) really relate to the notion of topic rather than structural subject (see Van de Visser 2006: 40–52 and references cited there).

A different matter is that the syntax of a language can allow for a lot more variability in word order than what is possible in English. A language can adhere to (25) while allowing various kinds of syntactic re-positionings of the subject and the objects in its surface word order. Good examples are discourse-configurational languages such as Hungarian and Finnish (see for instance Kiss 1995). Other languages may lack structural syntactic subject and object positions altogether, and express their arguments morphologically rather than syntactically (polysynthetic languages, see for example Hale 1983; Jelinek 1984, 2006; Baker 1996).

1.3. How arguments are integrated into the syntactic structure

There is some evidence that the positions in which the syntactic arguments of a verb occur are not all equal, in the sense that they are not all in the same syntactic relationship to the verb. There seems to be a hierarchy of syntactic argument positions, with the direct object position being closest to the verb, so lowest in the syntactic structure of the sentence, and the subject position furthest away from the verb, so highest in the syntactic structure. (As noted at the end of the previous section, this relates to the underlying positions of the arguments, not to their possible surface positions in all sentence types, and it may not hold at all in polysynthetic languages.) At least in a language like English, in a sentence headed by a transitive verb, the direct object and the verb seem to form a constituent that excludes the subject. Evidence for this includes the following.

First, verb and direct object together can be replaced by an instance of *do so* in English, to the exclusion of the subject, as in (27a). The subject can never be included in *do so* substitution, whether or not the object is included, as illustrated by (27b–c).

(27) a. *Mary* ***plays the guitar*** *and Deborah* ***does so****, too.*
b. ****Mary plays*** *the guitar and* ***does so*** *the trombone, too.*
c. **On Fridays* ***Mary plays the guitar*** *and when she has time on any other day* ***does so,*** *too.*

The possibility of replacing a string of words in a sentence by a single pro-form, such as *do so*, is an indication that that string forms a constituent of the sentence. Thus, (27) shows that verb and direct object form a constituent to the exclusion of the subject.

This is also shown by the fact that verb and direct object together can be put in a different position in the sentence. In particular, they can be put in first position (topicalized), as in the second of the two conjoined sentences in (28a). The subject is necessarily excluded from such topicalization, whether or not the direct object is included in it, as (28b-c) show.

(28) a. *Mary said she would play the guitar on Friday, and play the guitar she did.*
b. **Mary said she would play the guitar on Friday, and Mary play did the guitar.*
c. **Mary said she would play the guitar on Friday, and Mary play the guitar did indeed on Friday.*

If a string as a whole can undergo such displacement and be put in a different position in the sentence, then this, too, indicates that that string is a constituent. Again, then, we see that the verb plus its direct object argument appear to form a constituent to the exclusion of the subject argument.

The structure of phrases headed by a verb that takes a subject argument and a direct object argument can be represented as in (29) then. (In 29 "traditional" X-bar phrase structural notation is used, see Chomsky 1970 and Jackendoff 1977. There are, of course, other theories of phrase structure which make somewhat different assumptions, such as the bare phrase structure theory proposed in Chomsky 1995. The main point here, however, is that, in languages that are not polysynthetic, the syntactic arguments have a basic position in the sentence that is particular to them and that these positions stand in a particular hierarchical relationship to each other, such that the subject argument is higher in the structure than the direct object argument: the direct object forms a unit with the verb that excludes the subject. This point is not affected by the exact details of the phrase structure theory that is adopted.)

(29)

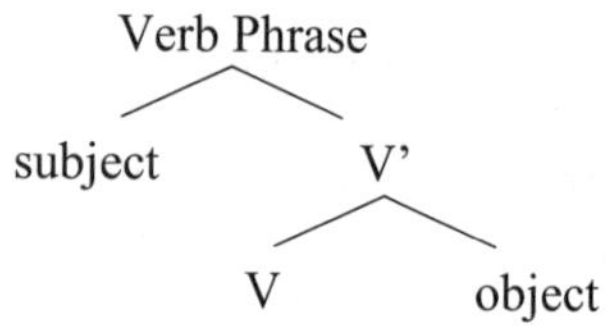

Exactly the same can be argued for Noun Phrases, as is especially clear for those NPs that are headed by a deverbal noun. Consider for example a noun like *collection*. This noun seems to combine with the same two arguments that the verb *collect* combines with, and, importantly, it seems to do so in the same way. Thus, the Theme argument appears in the complement position and the Agent argument in the specifier position in an NP like *Mary's collection of mushrooms* in (30).

(30)

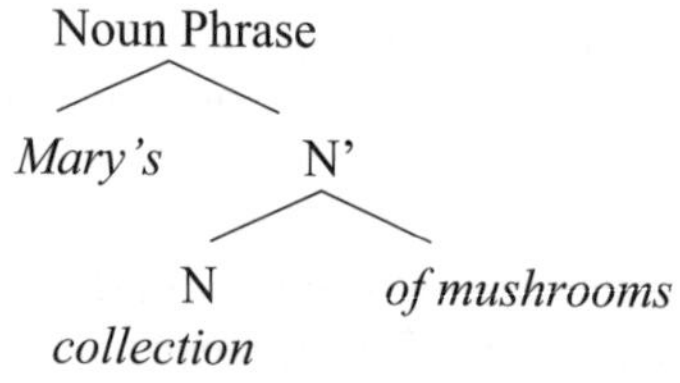

That in NPs, as in VPs, the head and the complement do indeed form a constituent (the N' in 30) that excludes the specifier can again be shown by a replacement test: a noun and its complement can be replaced by the pronoun *one*, as in (31a). Whereas the complement, if present, must be included in such *one*-replacement, as (31b) demonstrates, the specifier cannot be included in *one*-substitution, regardless of whether the complement is included or not, as shown by (31c–d).

(31) a. *Mary's **collection of coins** is not as good as Jane's **one**.*
b. **Mary's **collection** of coins and Jane's **one** of stamps.*
c. ***Mary's collection** of coins is interesting and **one** of stamps is expensive.*
d. ***Mary's collection of coins** is interesting and **one** is also expensive.*

The structure in (29) has a position for one object only, the direct object. What about the position of indirect objects in structures headed by a ditransitive verb? Although this is a matter of quite some debate, there seem to be some indications that, in such structures, the indirect object occupies a position that is hierarchically in between the position of the subject and the position of the direct object. One such indication is based on binding data. In a sentence like (32), where the meaning of the pronoun *her* is determined by the quantified expression *every girl*, in the sense that the reference of the pronoun ranges over the same set of individuals that the quantifier picks out, the quantifier binds the pronoun. (The sentence has a second reading as well, in which *her* refers to some, contextually determined, single individual, but this reading is not relevant here).

(32) *Every girl loves her mother.*

In a binding relation the antecedent must c-command the pronoun it binds. Thus, pronouns inside direct objects can be bound by the subject, as in (32) above, but pronouns inside the subject cannot be bound by the direct object, as (33) illustrates. (On the assumption that the quantified object undergoes covert Quantifier Raising, this would be a case of a Weak Crossover violation, on a par with cases that show that objects that overtly A'-move across a subject can still not bind a pronoun inside that subject: *who_i does his_i mother love*. On Weak Crossover, see for instance Postal 1971, 1993; Lasnik and Stowell 1991; Ruys 2000).

(33) **Her mother loves every girl.*

If so, the fact that pronouns inside a direct object can be bound by an indirect object (as in 34a), whereas pronouns inside an indirect object cannot be bound by a direct object (as in 34b), indicates that indirect objects occupy an argument position that is higher than that of direct objects.

(34) a. *Santa Claus gave every girl her present.*
b. **The organisers gave its rightful winner every price.*

By the same token, (35) shows that, like direct objects, indirect objects occur lower than the subject:

(35) a. *Every girl gave her mother a present.*
b. **Her mother gave every girl a present.*

Given that the order we see the arguments appear in is Subject (SU) – Indirect Object (IO) – Direct Object (DO) in English, these data would suggest that ditransitive verbs occur in a structure like (36). (When the indirect object is introduced by a preposition, it follows, rather than precedes, the direct object: *John gave a book to Mary* / **John gave to Mary a book*. On this dative alternation, see for instance Larson 1988; Jackendoff 1990b; Den Dikken 1995; Pesetsky 1995; Neeleman and Weerman 1999.)

(36)

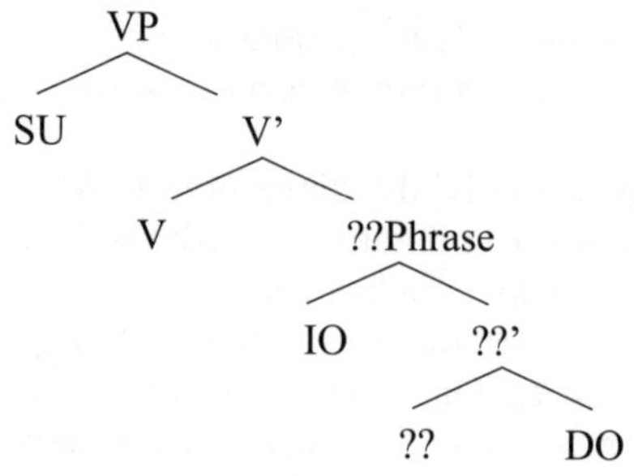

The question then is what kind of constituent the ??Phrase in (36) is. Various proposals for this have been put forward in the literature. Larson (1988), for example, proposed that what is labeled ??Phrase in (36) is actually the VP, whereas what is labelled VP in (36) is a second, higher, layer of the VP (a VP-shell). Chomsky (1995) suggests that this higher layer is actually the projection of a distinct verbal head, which he terms *v* (as opposed to V) that is specifically responsible for the introduction of the subject argument. For critical discussion and an alternative view, assuming that VPs can have a flatter structure than indicated in (36), see Jackendoff (1990b) and Culicover and Jackendoff (2005). Note that the same problem does not arise in OV languages in which the binding data and linear order between IO and DO are the same as in the VO language English, as we can simply add another argument position for the IO in the VP here, as in (37). See Neeleman and Weerman (1999) for extensive discussion of the differences between VO and OV languages in this respect.

(37)

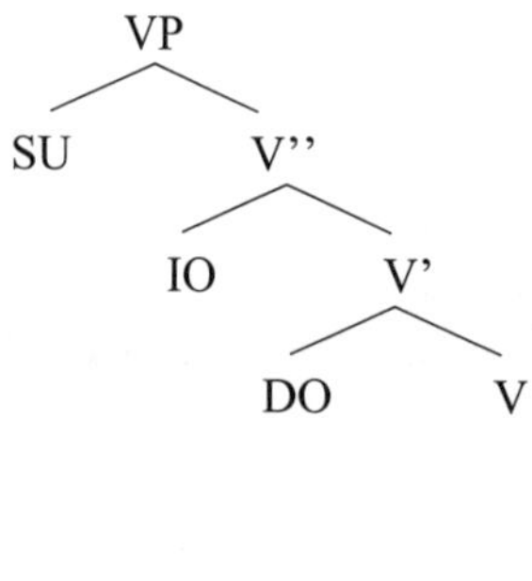

1.4. Manipulating argument structure

If the correspondences between semantic arguments and syntactic arguments given in (25) above always held, it would be possible to equate syntactic arguments with semantic arguments. But as already mentioned in section 1.2, this neat 1-to-1 correspondence does not always hold: a semantic argument need not always correspond to any syntactic argument (and vice versa). A semantic argument can sometimes be left syntactically unexpressed. There are other ways in which deviations from (25) can arise as well. The grammar of a language can provide various ways of manipulating the correspondences between semantic and syntactic arguments, so that semantic arguments can come to be associated with different syntactic arguments. Such grammatical processes, which seem to manipulate the so-called argument structure of a verb, include the ones listed in A–F below.

Before we discuss these processes, it is important to note that they genuinely affect the way in which semantic arguments are expressed by syntactic arguments. As noted before, a different matter is that syntactic arguments can sometimes occur in positions other than their usual one because the grammar can demand that constituents with a particular form or discourse function must occur in a special position in the sentence. Consider for example questions in English. Regardless of whether the questioned phrase is a subject, a direct object or an indirect object (or anything else), it must undergo wh-movement and thus come first in the sentence (*who gave Jill that book? / whom did Mary give that book? / what did Mary give Jill?*). Apparently, the grammar of English (in contrast to the grammar of a wh-in-situ language such as Japanese) specifies that questioned phrases must undergo wh-movement. But there is a crucial difference between what happens in cases of wh-movement and what happens in the processes mentioned in A–F below. When, say, a direct object that expresses a Theme argument is questioned, it does not as a result of that become the subject of the sentence; nor is another argument suppressed that is not suppressed in the non-question counterpart of the sentence. Compare *Jill read the book* and *what did Jill read*: just like in the former, in the latter the Agent argument is still the subject, and the Theme argument is still the direct object, even though it occurs in the position for wh-phrases rather than in the usual direct object position. This is very different, though, in passives for example (process A below): in a passive, the Agent argument no longer appears as the subject, and the Theme argument becomes the subject of the sentence (as witnessed by its ability to control the agreement on the finite verb, for example). This distinction is extensively discussed in the (vast) literature on A-movement versus A'-movement. Having said this, let us now consider the various argument structure alternations that one can encounter.

A. Passivization. This has the effect that the Theme (or whichever argument is the direct object argument in the active) becomes the subject, and the Agent (or whichever argument is the subject argument in the active) need not be expressed syntactically anymore (although it can optionally appear in a *by*-phrase), as illustrated in (38) and (39). There is a large literature on passives; see for example Chomsky (1981), Siewierska (1984), Jaeggli (1986), Postal (1986) and Baker et al. (1989).

(38) a. active: *Flora has fed the tigers.*
b. passive: *The tigers have been fed (by Flora).*

(39) a. active: *The Romans destroyed the city.*
b. passive: *The city was destroyed (by the Romans).*

B. Middle formation. A so-called middle resembles a passive in that the Theme argument corresponds to the subject. In contrast to a passive, however, the Agent argument cannot be expressed optionally through a *by*-phrase in a middle. Passives and middles also differ in their meaning, in that passives can express an event, while middles typically express a property of their subject (i.e. the Theme argument). Moreover, middles can distinguish themselves from passives formally as well (although in some languages they are formally identical to passives). In English, for example, middle formation does not express itself morphologically at all. Instead, the verb keeps the same form as in an active sentence. (This is why the term middle is used for such sentences: they are in between active and passive sentences in that formally they look like actives, but in their distribution of semantic arguments across syntactic constituents they are more like passives). Some examples of middles in English are given in (40b) and (41b). For discussion, see Fagan (1988, 1992), Stroik (1992), Ackema and Schoorlemmer (1994, 1995) and Steinbach (2002).

(40) a. active: *Barry read this book.*
b. middle: *This book reads well.*

(41) a. active: *The mafia bribed the bureaucrats.*
b. middle: *Bureaucrats bribe easily.*

C. The causative-inchoative alternation. Some causative verbs (verbs that have a subject argument that expresses the causer of the event or state) allow their Theme argument to become the subject. The Agent/Cause argument seems to disappear altogether in that case, even semantically. The version of the verb which has the Theme as its subject is called an inchoative verb, which means that the verb expresses a change of state of this argument. Relevant discussion can be found in Levin and Rappaport Hovav (1994), Reinhart (2002) and Schäfer (2009).

(42) a. causative: *Zoilo opened the door.*
b. inchoative: *The door opened.* (no Agent implied – the door opened "by itself")

(43) a. causative: *The sun ripened the tomatoes.*
b. inchoative: *The tomatoes ripened.* (no Agent implied – the tomatoes ripened "by themselves")

D. Reflexivization. The Theme argument of some verbs that are otherwise obligatorily transitive can remain syntactically unexpressed if this argument refers to the same entity as the Agent argument, as in (44). This phenomenon is discussed in Marantz (1984), Grimshaw (1990), Reinhart and Reuland (1993), Pesetsky (1995) and Reinhart and Siloni (2005).

(44) a. *John dresses.* (can only mean John dresses himself)
b. *Mary washes.* (can only mean Mary washes herself)

The operations in A–D above all occur in English, as the examples illustrate. Many languages have the same or similar operations, although probably none of these processes is universal. Languages that do not have passives, for instance, include Tongan, Samoan and Hungarian (Siewierska 1984). On the other hand, languages can also have yet other ways of manipulating a verb's argument structure. Two such processes are the ones in E–F.

E. Applicative. In an applicative, a phrase that is not usually an argument of the verb, but for instance an instrumental modifier (see section 2 on modifiers), becomes the direct object of the verb. An example from the Bantu language Chingoni is given in (45), from Ngonyani and Githinji (2006) (FV in the gloss stands for final vowel); note the applicative morpheme *-il* carried by the verb. Various tests show that phrases like *chipula* 'knife' in (45) indeed function as an object rather than an instrumental modifier. For example, such phrases can in turn become the subject of the sentence if the applicative sentence is passivised (compare section 3 on why this presumably indicates the phrase is an argument rather than a modifier). For discussion, see Baker (1985, 1988a, b), Mchombo (1993), Alsina and Mchombo (1993), Hyman (2003).

(45) *Mi-jokwani v-i-dumul-il-a chi-pula.* [Chingoni]
4-sugarcane 2SBJ-PRS-cut-APPL-FV 7-knife
'They use the knife to cut the sugar cane with.'

The closest thing in English to an applicative is the so-called spray/load alternation (see for instance Levin and Rappaport Hovav 1994). Verbs such as *spray* and *load* can have their Theme as object argument, in line with (25). But, as the (b) sentences in (46) and (47) show, the element expressing Location can also seemingly occur as object argument with these verbs, resembling the promotion to argument status of such modifiers in applicatives.

(46) a. *They sprayed paint on the wall.*
b. *They sprayed the wall with paint.*

(47) a. *They loaded hay onto the wagon.*
b. *They loaded the wagon with hay.*

The last process affecting argument structure to be mentioned does not involve promotion of any argument or modifier but rather the opposite. This is the following.

F. Anti-passive. In this process, the direct object of a verb gets demoted, and is either not expressed at all anymore, or at best as a phrase that carries case morphology that is typical of modifiers (cf. section 2) rather than arguments. Polinsky (2005) provides an overview of this construction. The Chukchi examples in (48) illustrate the alternation between an ordinary transitive sentence and an anti-passive (examples from Kozinsky et al. 1988: 652, cited here from Polinsky 2005; AOR in the gloss stands for aorist). Note that the ergative-absolutive case marking pattern in (48a) indicates that this a transitive sentence in which *kimitʔən* 'load' (the absolutive argument) is the direct object, whereas the absolutive-instrumental case pattern in (48b) indicates that this an intransitive sentence in which *kimitʔ-e* 'load' (with Instrumental case) acts as a modifier. The same is indicated by the presence versus absence of object agreement on the verb. Further discussion of anti-passives can be found in Marantz (1984), Johns (1987), Baker (1988a) and Bok-Bennema (1991).

(48) a. *ʔaaček-a kimitʔ-ən ne-nlʔetet-ən.* [Chukchi]
youth-ERG load-ABS 3PL.SBJ-carry-AOR.3SG.OBJ
'The young men carried away the/a load.'

b. *ʔaačekət ine-nlʔetet-gʔe-t kimitʔ-e.*
youth-ABS ANTIP-carry-AOR.3SG.SBJ-PL load-INS
'The young men carried away the/a load.'

This concludes the overview of processes that appear to change the way a predicate's semantic arguments are syntactically realized. Another question is how to analyze such processes. Roughly speaking, two approaches can be distinguished, which could be called the lexical approach and the syntactic approach.

The lexical approach assumes that the lexicon does not only contain entries for verbs (and other predicative elements) that specify their basic argument structure, but also a set of operations or principles that can manipulate this argument structure. Thus, Williams (1981) proposed there are rules like Externalise(X) and Internalise(X) where X is some designated argument of the predicate. Ackema and Schoorlemmer (1994) and Bouchard (1995) propose that when what is normally the subject argument of a predicate is not realized syntactically, the next highest argument, as determined by a particular argument hierarchy, can receive that status. For discussion see also Aranovich and Runner (2000), Spencer and Sadler (1998), Reinhart (2002), Reinhart and Siloni (2005).

According to the syntactic approach, lexical manipulation of argument structure is not possible, so the semantic arguments always correspond to syntactic arguments in exactly the same way initially (this is the tenet of Baker's 1988a Uniformity of Theta Assignment Hypothesis). Argument promotion or demotion processes such as the ones mentioned above are then considered to be the result of syntactic operations that can put constituents in a different argument position, in combination with the assumption that syntactic arguments can sometimes be realised by empty elements. See for instance Baker (1988a), Baker et al. (1989), Stroik (1992), Hoekstra and Roberts (1993).

How best to analyze a particular process depends on issues that we cannot go into in this chapter, such as the proper nature of unaccusativity (cf. Levin and Rappaport Hovav 1994; Alexiadou et al. 2003), as well as on the perceived similarities and differences between the various processes. It is conceivable that not all argument structure changing processes should be analysed in the same way. Possibly, some are the result of lexical rules on argument structure, whereas others are the result of A-movement in syntax. For example, Ackema and Schoorlemmer (1994, 1995) try to show that at least in Dutch middles are unlike passives in showing no signs of their surface subject having undergone A-movement from object position (middle verbs in Dutch behave on a par with unergatives rather than unaccusatives), so for them a lexical treatment is required. They also note that middles in some other languages seem to behave more like passives in this respect, and so might be better analysed as involving syntactic A-movement (see also Authier and Reed 1996). Detailed accounts involving such a lexical versus syntactic cross-linguistic split in middle constructions can be found in Lekakou (2004) and Marelj (2004) (for a general overview see also Ackema and Schoorlemmer 2005). Reinhart (2002) and Reinhart and Siloni (2005) propose to extend such an approach to other processes affecting argument structure as well, in particular to reflexivization. Thus, they propose the following general parameter (where thematic arity more or less corresponds to what is termed argument structure here):

(49) The lex-syn parameter
Universal Grammar allows thematic arity operations to apply in the lexicon or in the syntax.

It is probably fair to say, though, that there is no general consensus as to what the optimal overall approach to such processes is.

2. Adjuncts

In section 1, semantic arguments were introduced as participants in the event or state expressed by the predicate, and syntactic arguments as constituents expressing those. Sentences can contain more elements than the predicate and its arguments, however. In particular, they can contain constituents that provide all sorts of additional information about the event/state: where it occurred, when it occurred, the reason why it occurred, the manner in which it took place, what the emotional state of the participants was, and so on. Such information is expressed by so-called modifiers. Examples of modifiers are the phrases in boldface in (50).

(50) a. *Gerald bought a cd* ***in the megastore***.
b. *Gerald bought a cd* ***before noon***.
c. *Gerald bought a cd* ***without realizing he already had it***.
d. *Gerald* ***quickly*** *bought a cd*.
e. *Gerald bought a cd* ***to impress his friends***.
f. ***Eager to fill this gap in his enormous collection***, *Gerald bought a cd*.

The notion modifier is really a semantic notion: whereas a semantic argument is a participant in an event or state, a semantic modifier modifies the event or state in the sense that it provides some additional information about it that distinguishes this event/state from other events/states of a similar type. (Of course, much more can be said about the semantics of the relation between modifiers and predicates than the rough description just given; see chapter 37 in this volume for a thorough discussion). As such, this semantics does not tell us anything about the syntactic status of the phrases that express modifiers, such as the phrases in boldface in (50). How do these fit into the syntactic structure?

For a start, it is clear that the phrase structure for Verb Phrases adopted in section 1 does not provide enough room for constituents expressing modifiers. Even if we adopt the elaborate structure for double object constructions in (36), all specifier and complement positions in this structure are already occupied by the arguments of the verb. At first sight, it may seem that we could simply extend this phrase structure by adding another fixed position to it that would be the designated position to host modifiers. The problem with that is that, in contrast to the number of arguments, the number of modifiers that can be added to a sentence is in principle unlimited:

(51) *Eager to fill this gap in his enormous collection, Gerald quickly bought a cd in the megastore before noon to impress his friends without realizing he already had it (...)*

Because of production/processing constraints, any actually spoken sentence will have a finite length. Also, there is only so much information that can be expressed about a single event/state. For example, a single event takes place in a particular single location (ignoring quantum-effects), so once a modifier expressing this location is added it does not make sense to add another such modifier (except to make the first one more precise, but in that case again adding more modifiers is perfectly fine: *he was murdered in his house, in the bathroom, in the bath, underwater.*) But purely syntactically speaking there does not seem to be anything wrong with adding yet another modifier to any particular sentence. Thus, no matter how many fixed positions would be added to the X-bar phrase structure schema for phrases, it would never be enough in principle to accommodate modifiers. A more flexible means to integrate modifiers into the structure is required.

This is also shown by another crucial distinction between syntactic arguments on the one hand and modifiers on the other hand. This is the following: whenever a modifier is added to some syntactic category, the result is a category of precisely the same type. This is not so in the case of arguments. When we add an object argument to a transitive verb, the result is not another verb. This is apparent from the *do so* replacement test, as introduced in section 1.3. It was shown there that *do so* can replace a combination of verb and object, that is, a V'. In contrast, *do so* cannot replace a single verb without its object. This contrast, illustrated by the pair of examples in (52), shows that the combination of verb and object is a different type of constituent than the verb alone. (Intransitive verbs can seemingly be replaced by *do so*: *Karin walked and Frank did so, too*. It can be maintained, however, that *do so* can only replace a V'; in this case, the V' it replaces contains the verb and an empty, rather than filled, complement position.)

(52) a. *John* ***ate a banana****, and Geraldine* ***did so****, too.*
b. **John* ***ate*** *a banana, while Geraldine* ***did so*** *an apple.*

In turn, when we add a subject argument to a V', the result is something that is not a V' again, as shown by the fact that the resulting constituent cannot be replaced by *do so*:

(53) **Yesterday* ***Julia ate a pear*** *and today* ***did so****, too.*

In contrast, when one or more modifiers are added to a V' the result is invariably something that can still be replaced by *do so*. Apparently, then, the resulting constituent is just another V':

(54) a. *John* ***ate a banana yesterday****, and Geraldine* ***did so****, too.*
b. *Danielle* ***read the paper at home with a cup of coffee while listening to a cd*** *and Arthur* ***did so****, too.*

Note that not only *ate a banana yesterday* is a V' in (54a), but *ate a banana*, without the modifier, is still a V' just as well. The modifier can be included in *do so* replacement (as in 54a), but it need not be, as shown by (55). (The same holds for the modifiers in 54b).

(55) *John* ***ate a banana*** *yesterday, while Geraldine* ***did so*** *today.*

It can be concluded that in (54a) we have a V' *ate a banana*, and if this V' is extended by adding a modifier to it, the resulting constituent is still a V'.

The same conclusion follows from the other test showing that verb and object form a constituent to the exclusion of the subject that was discussed in section 1. Recall that verb and object can be fronted to the first position of a sentence together, whereas the subject cannot be part of such a fronted constituent. When we look at the behaviour of modifiers with respect to this test, again we see that they can partake in fronting, and be displaced together with the verb and object (as in 56a), while at the same time it is also possible for them not to partake in fronting and remain behind (as in 56b). If fronting is V' fronting, as assumed before in section 1.3, this, too, shows that verb and object form a smaller V' that excludes the modifier, while verb, object and modifier together also form a, larger, V'.

(56) a. *She said she was going to play the drums loudly, and play the drums loudly she did.*
b. *He said he was going to read that book one of these days, and read the book he did yesterday.*

To accommodate these facts about modifiers, it is assumed that a particular level of syntactic phrase structure can just be iterated when there is a modifier of the constituent at that level. Thus, a sentence like *John ate a banana yesterday* has the structure in (57). (Note that in the literature modifiers that are said to modify V' here are often assumed to modify VP; this is under the assumption that the subject is not in the specifier-of-VP position but is outside of VP. This is immaterial for the essential point here, which is that a modifier does not create a new type of constituent when it is added, hence that the notion of adjunction is required to integrate them into the structure.).

(57)

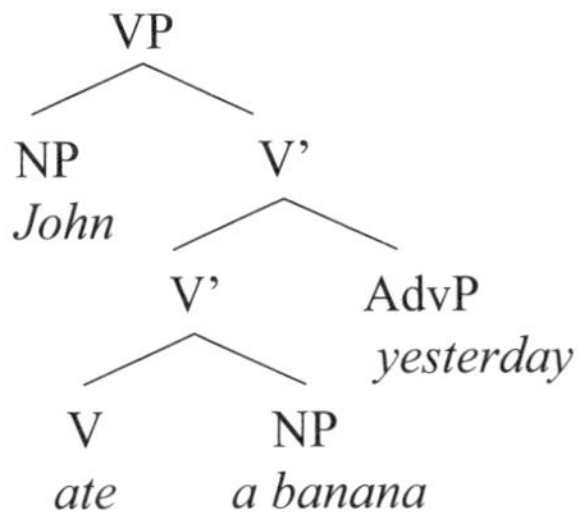

This way of integrating modifiers into the structure is called adjunction. So, when a constituent adjoins to, for instance, V', this means an extra V'-node is created immediately above the original one, and the modifier is attached to this newly created node. An element that is attached in this way is called an adjunct.

Before we proceed, it should be noted that with respect to at least adverbial phrases that function as modifier there is a complication with the notion that whenever an adjunct is added to a phrase of a particular type the result is a phrase of exactly the same type. This has to do with certain ordering restrictions between the adverbs themselves. For example, in English an adverb like *probably* can precede an adverb like *quickly*, but not vice versa: *Mary probably quickly hid the jewels* versus **Mary quickly probably hid the jewels*. Because of this, it is not strictly true that adding, for example, *probably* to a phrase results in a phrase of exactly the same type, since before *probably* is added there is a phrase to which *quickly* can be added, whereas after *probably* is added there is a phrase to which *quickly* cannot be added. The question is whether these restrictions are of a syntactic structural nature or of a semantic nature. Some authors have argued that they are an effect of syntactic structure. In particular, they argue that adverbs appear in designated positions in the structure, these positions being strictly hierarchically ordered, very much like argument positions (thus, for this type of modifier at least, the notion of adjunct is dispensed with). Detailed accounts of the syntax of adverbs along these lines are given in Alexiadou (1997) and Cinque (1999). Others have argued that such approaches lead to ordering paradoxes that cannot be resolved by allowing for a particular adverbial position to occur more than once in the structural hierarchy (as Cinque already argues is necessary), indicating that the ordering restrictions in question might be essentially semantic in nature and not related to syntactic structure per se; see for instance Ernst (2002, 2007) and Nilsen (2003) for discussion.

With this caveat in mind, it can be maintained that modifiers are expressed by a type of constituent, an adjunct, that combines with a particular phrase to deliver a phrase with the same phrase-structural status. This holds for modifiers of verbal constituents, as shown above, but it also holds of modifiers of other types of constituents. Consider NPs. As discussed in section 1.3, in these phrases, too, the head (the noun) and the complement form a constituent to the exclusion of the specifier. This was shown by the *one* replacement test, as illustrated by the data in (31) above. It was concluded that *one* can replace an N', but not an N or an NP. Looking now at the behaviour of modifiers in NPs with respect to *one*-replacement, it turns out that a modifier can be included in such replacement, but need not be. This is shown by the examples in (58). Again, then, the modifier does not change the nature of the constituent it modifies: when it modifies an N', it just forms a larger N' with it.

(58) a. *Rachel saw a* ***collection of stones worth 100 euro****, and Jack saw another* ***one****.*
b. *Rachel saw a* ***collection of stones*** *worth 100 euro and Jack saw another* ***one*** *worth 200 euro.*

The same test shows that the *that*-clause accompanying the noun in (59a) is a complement clause (an argument), whereas the relative clause accompanying the noun in (59b) is an adjunct.

(59) a. **The idea that this is bad for your health and the one that this can be treated by therapy are both wrong.*
b. *This is the idea that William liked and the one that Paul dismissed.*

So, the structure of an NP with an adjunct functioning as modifier is as follows:

(60)
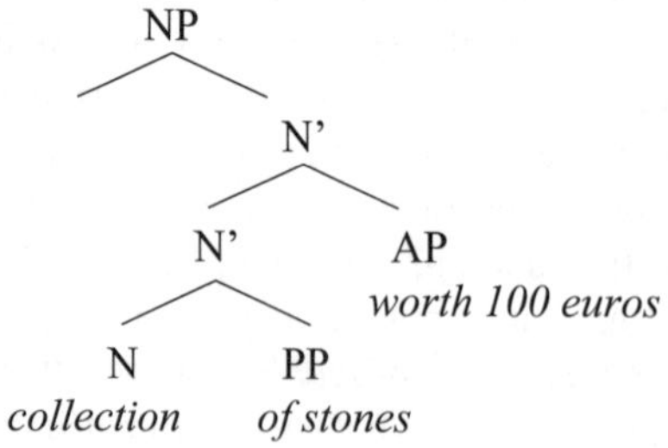

In a way parallel to what was shown for VPs and NPs, we can also distinguish arguments in complement position from modifiers in APs. Consider the following two APs:

(61) a. *Sam was proud of her dog.*
b. *Sam was proud because her dog behaved well.*

These seem quite similar. Nevertheless, another replacement test, in this case with the word *so,* shows that the phrases that accompany the adjective in (61a) and (61b) behave differently. The type of *of*-phrase present in (61a) is obligatorily included in *so*-replacement, as shown by (62a–b). A *because*-clause like the one in (61b), on the other hand, may be included in such replacement but need not be, as shown by (62c–d).

(62) a. *Sam was* ***proud of her dog****, and Lily was* ***so****, too.*
b. **Sam was* ***proud*** *of her dog, and Lily was* ***so*** *of her cat.*
c. *Sam* ***was proud because her dog behaved well****, and Lily was* ***so****, too.*
d. *Sam was* ***proud*** *because her dog behaved well, and Lily was* ***so*** *because her cat was not making a mess.*

This is typical of the distinction between complements and modifiers. Thus, the *of*-phrase in (61a) is a complement of the adjective and forms an A' constituent with it; the *because*-phrase in (61b) is a modifier that is attached to the A'-constituent and forms a larger A' constituent with it. (Note that the smaller A' constituent in 61b contains an empty complement position. This position can be filled just as well in this case, as in *Sam was proud of her dog because it behaved well*).

3. Distinguishing arguments from adjuncts

There are a number of ways in which syntactic arguments and adjuncts can be distinguished from each other, although there are various caveats to most of these tests. The different syntactic behaviour of arguments and adjuncts is the topic of this section.

Two of the defining differences between arguments and adjuncts were already mentioned in the previous section. First, there is no principled limit to the number of adjuncts that can be included in a sentence. In contrast, the maximum number of syntactic arguments that can appear seems to be three (though see 7 for a possible counterexample), namely the subject, direct object and indirect object in a sentence headed by a ditransitive verb. Second, and probably related to the first difference, adding an adjunct to a constituent results in a constituent of the same type, that is, a constituent with the same phrase structural status. This is evidenced by the fact that the constituent with the adjunct behaves in exactly the same way as the same constituent without the adjunct with respect to replacement and displacement tests. In contrast, adding an argument to a constituent gives a constituent of a different type.

A third criterion that is often used to distinguish arguments from adjuncts concerns the question whether a particular constituent occurs obligatorily or only optionally. Arguments are said to be obligatory, whereas adjuncts are optional additions to a sentence.

Arguments certainly can be obligatory. A VP headed by a verb like *destroy* or *examine*, for example, seems to be only felicitous if the direct object argument of these verbs appears. This argument cannot be omitted even if it has a generic or non-specific reading, as (63c) and (64c) show.

(63) a. *The Vandals destroyed the town.*
b. **The Vandals destroyed.*
c. **The Vandals were destroying constantly, so they became notorious for it.*

(64) a. *The doctor examined the patients.*
b. **The doctor examined yesterday.*
c. **This doctor examines for a living.*

On the other hand, in section 1 it was already shown that arguments can sometimes be left out. The direct object argument of many transitive verbs can in fact be left out quite easily:

(65) a. *David was eating Brussels sprouts.*
b. *David was eating.*

(66) a. *Harriet was reading the newspaper.*
b. *Harriet was reading.*

The criterion to distinguish arguments and adjuncts on the basis of their obligatoriness therefore must be more subtle at least: it should be that, in contrast to arguments, adjuncts are never obligatory.

Note that, according to this criterion, a locative PP, which usually expresses a modifier and is an adjunct, is actually an argument with a verb like *put*, since it cannot be left out of a sentence headed by this verb:

(67) a. *Beatrice put her bike in the shed.*
b. **Beatrice put her bike.*

The assumption that the locative phrase is an argument in (67a) is in line with the fact that it is also obligatorily included in *do so* replacement in this case (compare section 2):

(68) a. *Beatrice* ***put her bike in the shed*** *and Mary* ***did so****, too.*
b. **Beatrice* ***put her bike*** *in the shed and Mary* ***did so*** *against the railing.*

Considering arguments and adjuncts in NPs, at first sight it seems that here not even arguments are ever obligatory. Consider the contrast between leaving out the complement to verbs like *examine* or *destroy* (bad, see 63–64) versus leaving out the complement to a nominalization of these verbs, which is apparently possible:

(69) a. *Their examination of the candidates took a long time.*
a′. *The examination was difficult.*
b. *The enemy's destruction of the city was awful to watch.*
b′. *The destruction was terrible.*

However, deverbal nouns like *examination* or *destruction* have two different readings: they can either express an event, or the result of that event. For instance, *destruction* can mean "the act of destroying", but also "the result of the act of destroying". This distinction is crucial when considering what the argument structure of such nouns is, as extensively discussed by Grimshaw (1990). She points out that in the event reading the arguments are in fact obligatorily present. Indeed, in the examples in (69a') and (69b'), where the arguments are left out, the noun can only have the result reading. Perhaps, then, the result nouns do not actually take arguments, whereas with the proper event nouns the arguments are as obligatory as they are with the verb from which these are derived. With this proviso, then, it may be possible to maintain the criterion to distinguish arguments from adjuncts that says that arguments, but not adjuncts, can sometimes be obligatory, also in NPs.

However, this criterion is not without its problems. In some contexts, phrases that appear to be genuine adjuncts can nevertheless not be left out without this resulting in an infelicitous sentence. For example, in the active sentence (70a), the PP *in 1959* appears to be a bona fide adjunct, and as expected it is optional (see 70b). Nevertheless, in the passive counterpart of this sentence, given in (71a), it seems that the same phrase needs to be present to render the sentence felicitous, as illustrated by (71b).

(70) a. *Jones and Co built these houses in 1959.*
b. *Jones and Co built these houses.*

(71) a. *These houses were built in 1959.*
b. **These houses were built.*

Middle sentences (see section 1.4) are also often degraded if they do not contain a modifying adjunct phrase:

(72) a. *This book reads well.*
b. **This book reads.*

(73) a. *This is the soup that eats like a meal.*
b. **This is the soup that eats.*

It may be that the apparently obligatory presence of the adjunct in the relevant sentences is caused by pragmatic, rather than syntactic, factors. Simply put, these sentences do not seem to convey any relevant information without the adjunct. For example, since all houses are built, rather than arising out of thin air, (71b) does not provide anyone with any information that is not already part of their general world knowledge. Note that the sentence is saved by adding just any modifier that provides some new information, it need not be the time adverbial of (71a). Even expressing the Agent (rather than a semantic modifier) in an adjunct *by*-phrase is enough to render the passive felicitous:

(74) *These houses were built by Jones and Co.*

Similarly, it is a property of any (normal) book that it can be read, so (72b) is not informative. But it is certainly not a property of any book that it is easy to read, so (72a) is. When the middle sentence expresses a property of its subject that is already distinctive without the presence of a modifier, then including such an adjunct in a middle is not, in fact, always necessary:

(75) *This dress buttons (whereas the other one has a zip).*

For more discussion, see Grimshaw and Vikner (1993) on passives, and Fagan (1992) and Ackema and Schoorlemmer (2005) on middles. For problems with the pragmatic account of the obligatory presence of a modifier in most middle sentences, see Lekakou (2006).

The next criterion that is sometimes said to differentiate between arguments and adjuncts concerns the category of the phrases they are expressed by. Within VPs, the prototypical argument is an NP, whereas the prototypical adjunct is a PP or an adverbial phrase. (Within NPs, arguments are typically expressed by NPs or PPs, while typical adjuncts are APs or PPs). The reader can verify this by looking over the examples given so far in this chapter. It is clear as well, however, that there are all sorts of exceptions to this generalization.

For a start, both arguments and adjuncts can be realized by embedded clauses, rather than NPs or PPs. For arguments this is illustrated by (76a) (containing a subject clause) and (76b) (containing an object clause), whereas (77) gives examples containing adjunct clauses. (That both arguments and adjuncts can be realised by a clause in NPs as well was already illustrated by the examples illustrating the difference between complement clauses and relative clauses, see 59).

(76) a. [*That smoking is bad for your health*] *worries most people.*
b. *I never knew* [*that that song was written by Brahms*].

(77) a. *Harry met Sally* [*while he was working in a bar*].
b. *Sally likes Harry* [*because he works in a bar*].

More seriously, arguments can be realized by the categories that, according to the criterion discussed, are supposed to be prototypical for adjuncts, and vice versa. Thus, there can be PP arguments, and there can be NP adjuncts, in VPs. Starting with the latter, bare NP adverbials in English include adjuncts such as the time adverbial in (78).

(78) *Harry met Sally* ***the other day***.

PP-arguments come in various guises. In copular sentences the subject can be a PP expressing location or time, for example, as in the following:

(79) a. ***Under the bed*** *is a good hiding place.*
b. ***After three o'clock*** *is not a good time for me.*

Some verbs have the idiosyncratic property that they select for a particular preposition to introduce their complement, instead of this complement being an NP. Examples of such PP-complements are the phrases in boldface in (80).

(80) a. *David counts* ***on Carol*** *to do that job.*
b. *Our firm strongly believes* ***in good customer service***.

That the PPs in (80) are really complements (that is, arguments), rather than modifying adjuncts, shows itself in a number of ways. For a start, it should be noted that the preposition in these cases is semantically bleached: it does not express a location, time, direction, or anything like that anymore, but is really meaningless. (The choice of preposition for a PP-complement with a particular verb is unpredictable and can vary idiosyncratically from language to language, even if the same verb takes a PP-complement in the different languages). Also, the tests introduced in section 1 show that these PPs are complements: they are obligatorily included in *do so* replacement and in V'-fronting:

(81) a. *David* ***counts on Carol****, and Harry* ***does so*** *too.*
b. **David* ***counts*** *on Carol and Harry* ***does so*** *on Jane.*

(82) a. *David said he would count on Carol, and count on Carol he did.*
b. **David said he would count on Carol, and count he did on Carol.*

Considering next arguments and adjuncts in NPs, it appears that here the distinction in terms of category disappears altogether in English, since complements must standardly be expressed by a PP, rather than NP, in this environment:

(83) a. *the collection of mushrooms*
a'. **the collection mushrooms*

Note, though, that as in PP-complements to verbs, the preposition introducing the complement in (83a) is meaningless. In older English, as in many other languages, complements to nouns could in fact be expressed by NPs, as long as these bore a particular type of case morphology (typically the genitive). It seems that the meaningless preposition has somehow taken over the role of the case morphology that was lost in the history of English (see for instance Weerman and De Wit 1999 for discussion).

All in all, distinguishing arguments and adjuncts on the basis of their lexical category is rather shaky. Another way in which arguments and adjuncts have been claimed to behave differently is rather more subtle than the ones discussed so far. This concerns their behaviour under movement.

Consider wh-movement in English. As is well-known, both arguments and adjuncts can undergo long-distance wh-movement (movement out of an embedded clause into the matrix clause).

(84) a. *[Which book]$_i$ do you think [that John read e$_i$ yesterday]?*
b. *[Why]$_i$ do you think [that John read that book e$_i$ yesterday]?*

But as is also well-known, such movement is degraded if the extracted element originates inside an island (Ross 1967), such as the wh-island in (85).

(85) *??[Which book]$_i$ do you wonder [whether John read e$_i$ yesterday]?*

Although moving a constituent out of an island is always bad, it seems that arguments and adjuncts differ in how bad it is to extract them in this way. Taking an adjunct out of an island appears to give a worse result than doing the same with an argument (Chomsky 1986; Rizzi 1990). Compare (85) with (86), in which an adjunct is extracted out of the wh-island.

(86) **[Why]$_i$ do you wonder [whether John read that book e$_i$ yesterday]?.*

While it is possible at least to assign (85) its intended meaning (despite its degraded status), in (86) it seems impossible altogether to associate *why* with the predicate of the embedded clause.

It is doubtful, however, that the difference between (85) and (86) really reflects an argument-adjunct distinction. The real distinction appears to be between phrases that are discourse-linked (d-linked) and phrases that are not. A d-linked phrase is a phrase that refers to something that has already been mentioned in the current discourse. Using a *which*-phrase such as *which book* in (85) usually implies that the hearer is already familiar with a particular set of books and is now asked to pick one of them as the answer to the question. Using a bare question phrase such as *why* in (86) has no similar implication, however, and for some reason this seems to make it more difficult to extract such a phrase from an island (for possible explanations of this see Pesetsky 1987; Rizzi 1990; Cinque 1990; Kluender 1998; Van Craenenbroeck 2010, among many others). Crucially, this also holds when the questioned phrase is an argument rather than an adjunct. Thus, at least in an out-of-the-blue context, where *what* cannot be d-linked, (87) seems to have the same, strongly ungrammatical, status as (86).

(87) **[What]$_i$ do you wonder [whether John read e$_i$]*

Conversely, replacing *why* in (86) by a d-linked phrase such as *for which of these reasons* gives a measurably better result (see for instance Kluender 1998). If so, the impression that this difference concerns a difference between arguments and adjuncts arises from the fact that it is less likely for modifiers to be d-linked than it is for arguments. (Incidentally, it should be noted that this discussion on extraction ignores a further distinction within the class of arguments themselves: while long-distance displacement of objects is fine as long as the object is not taken out of an island, displacement of subjects is degraded in English if the subject is taken from a clause that is introduced by a complementizer; on this so-called *that*-trace effect see Chomsky and Lasnik 1977; Rizzi 1990, 2006; Culicover 1993; Ackema and Neeleman 2004, among many others. Also ignored here is the distinction between weak islands, such as the wh-islands just discussed, and strong islands, out of which even extraction of any argument is prohibited; see for instance Huang 1982 and Szabolcsi and Den Dikken 2003 for discussion).

The final difference between arguments and adjuncts to be discussed here concerns some of the processes of argument structure manipulation discussed in section 1.4. In some of these processes, something that is not usually the subject of a verb becomes the subject when the process is applied. For example, a Theme argument or a Goal argument can become the subject when passivisation is applied, and Theme arguments can become subjects in middle sentences. Adjuncts, however, do not seem to be able to acquire subject status in this way, as the contrast between the passives in (88b) and (88b'), and the contrast between the middles in (89b) and in (89b'), show.

(88) a. *They built the houses in 1959.*
b. *The houses were built in 1959.*
b′. **In 1959 was built the houses. / *1959 was built the houses.*

(89) a. *They read the book on the train.*
b. *Such books read easily on the train.*
b′. **On the train reads such books easily. / *The train reads such books easily.*

This difference between arguments and adjuncts, too, is not entirely without apparent exceptions. In some instances of the so-called pseudo-passive, an active sentence containing a phrase that to all intents and purposes looks like an adjunct PP is turned into a passive in which the complement of the preposition in this PP is promoted to subject, leaving the preposition stranded with the verb; examples are given in (90) (cf. Hornstein and Weinberg 1981).

(90) a. *The author wrote the manuscript with a pen.* (active)
a′. *This pen has never been written with.* (pseudo-passive)
b. *Someone has slept in this bed.* (active)
b'. *This bed has been slept in.* (pseudo-passive)

In some languages other than English something similar is possible in middle sentences. Dutch, for example, allows adjunct middles as in (91a') and (91b').

(91) a. *Die club voetbalt op kunstgras.* (active) [Dutch]
that club footballs on artgrass
'That club plays football on artificial grass'

a′. *Kunstgras voetbalt niet zo lekker.* (middle)
artgrass footballs not so nicely
'Artificial grass is not so nice for playing football on'

b. *Ik zit altijd in deze stoel.* (active)
I sit always in this chair
'I always sit in this chair'

b′. *Deze stoel zit lekker.* (middle)
this chair sits nicely
'This chair is comfortable to sit in'

As the examples indicate, in these cases the preposition that appears in the adjunct PP in the active disappears altogether when its complement is promoted to subject in the middle (see Hoekstra and Roberts 1993 and Ackema and Schoorlemmer 1994 for discussion).

4. Conclusion

The distinction between semantic arguments and modifiers seems to have a correlate in syntax in that there seems to be a structural distinction between syntactic constituents that express an argument and those that express a modifier. The latter appear in the structure as adjuncts, the former as (syntactic) arguments. Several other syntactic distinctions have been argued to correlate with this basic distinction, though the further criteria by which the two are distinguished are not entirely clear-cut, and allow for some grey areas or exceptional cases.

9. Acknowledgements

I am indebted to two anonymous reviewers for their helpful comments on an earlier version of this chapter.

5. References (selected)

Ackema, Peter, and Ad Neeleman
2004 *Beyond Morphology*. Oxford: Oxford University Press.
Ackema, Peter, and Maaike Schoorlemmer
1994 The middle construction and the syntax-semantics interface. *Lingua* 93: 59–90.
Ackema, Peter, and Maaike Schoorlemmer
1995 Middles and non-movement. *Linguistic Inquiry* 26: 173–197.
Ackema, Peter, and Maaike Schoorlemmer
2005 Middles. In: M. Everaert and H. van Riemsdijk (eds.), *The Blackwell Companion to Syntax* vol. III, 131–203. Oxford: Basil Blackwell.
Alexiadou, Artemis
1997 *Adverb Placement*. Amsterdam: John Benjamins.
Alexiadou, Artemis, Elena Anagnostopoulou, and Martin Everaert (eds.)
2003 *The Unaccusativity Puzzle*. Oxford: Oxford University Press.
Alsina, Alex, and Sam Mchombo
1993 Object asymmetries and the Chichewa applicative construction. In: S. Mchombo (ed.), *Theoretical Aspects of Bantu Grammar 1*, 17–46. Stanford: CSLI Publications.
Aranovich, Raul, and Jeffrey Runner
2000 Diathesis alternations and rule interaction in the lexicon. In: K. Meegerdomian and L. A. Bar-el (eds.), *Proceedings of WCCFL 20*, 15–28. Somerville, MA: Cascadilla Press.
Authier, Jean-Marc, and Lisa Reed
1996 On the Canadian French middle. *Linguistic Inquiry* 27: 513–523.
Baker, Mark
1985 The mirror principle and morphosyntactic explanation. *Linguistic Inquiry* 16: 373–416.
Baker, Mark
1988a *Incorporation*. Chicago: University of Chicago Press.
Baker, Mark
1988b Theta theory and the syntax of applicatives in Chichewa. *Natural Language and Linguistic Theory* 6: 353–389.
Baker, Mark
1996 *The Polysynthesis Parameter*. Oxford: Oxford University Press.
Baker, Mark, Kyle Johnson, and Ian Roberts
1989 Passive arguments raised. *Linguistic Inquiry* 20: 219–251.
Bobaljik, Jonathan
1993 On ergativity and ergative unergatives. *MIT Working Papers in Linguistics* 19: 45–88.
Bok-Bennema, Reineke
1991 Case and agreement in Inuit. PhD dissertation, University of Tilburg.
Bouchard, Denis
1995 *The Semantics of Syntax*. Chicago: University of Chicago Press.
Chomsky, Noam
1970 Remarks on nominalization. In: R. Jacobs and P. Rosenbaum (eds.), *Readings in English Transformational Grammar*, 184–221. Waltham, MA: Ginn.
Chomsky, Noam
1981 *Lectures on Government and Binding*. Dordrecht: Foris.

Chomsky, Noam
1986 *Barriers*. Cambridge, MA: MIT Press.
Chomsky, Noam
1995 *The Minimalist Program*. Cambridge, MA: MIT Press.
Chomsky, Noam, and Howard Lasnik
1977 Filters and control. *Linguistic Inquiry* 8: 425–504.
Cinque, Guglielmo
1990 *Types of A'-Dependencies*. Cambridge, MA: MIT Press.
Cinque, Guglielmo
1999 *Adverbs and Functional Heads*. Oxford: Oxford University Press.
Culicover, Peter
1993 Evidence against ECP accounts of the that-t effect. *Linguistic Inquiry* 24: 557–561.
Culicover, Peter, and Ray Jackendoff
2005 *Simpler Syntax*. Oxford: Oxford University Press.
Den Dikken, Marcel
1995 *Particles*. Oxford: Oxford University Press.
Dixon, R. M. W.
1972 *The Dyirbal Language of North Queensland*. Cambridge: Cambridge University Press.
Ernst, Thomas
2002 *The Syntax of Adjuncts*. Cambridge, Cambridge University Press.
Ernst, Thomas
2007 On the role of semantics in a theory of adverb syntax. *Lingua* 117: 1008–1033.
Fagan, Sarah
1988 The English middle. *Linguistic Inquiry* 19: 181–203.
Fagan, Sarah
1992 *The Syntax and Semantics of Middle Constructions*. Cambridge: Cambridge University Press.
Gazdar, Gerald, Ewan Klein, Geoffrey Pullum, and Ivan Sag
1985 *Generalized Phrase Structure Grammar*. Cambridge, Mass.: Harvard University Press.
Grimshaw, Jane
1979 Complement selection and the lexicon. *Linguistic Inquiry* 10: 279–326.
Grimshaw, Jane
1990 *Argument Structure*. Cambridge, MA: MIT Press.
Grimshaw, Jane, and Sten Vikner
1993 Obligatory adjuncts and the structure of events. In: E. Reuland and W. Abraham (eds.), *Knowledge and Language* vol. II, 145–159. Dordrecht: Kluwer.
Hale, Ken
1983 Warlpiri and the grammar of non-configurational languages. *Natural Language and Linguistic Theory* 1: 5–47.
Hale, Ken, and Samuel J. Keyser
1993 On argument structure and the lexical expression of syntactic relations. In: K. Hale and S. J. Keyser, *The View from Building 20*, 53–109. Cambridge, MA: MIT Press.
Hoekstra, Teun, and Ian Roberts
1993 The mapping from the lexicon to syntax: null arguments. In: E. Reuland and W. Abraham (eds.), *Knowledge and Language* vol. II, 183–220. Dordrecht: Kluwer.
Hornstein, Norbert, and Amy Weinberg
1981 Case theory and preposition stranding. *Linguistic Inquiry* 12: 55–92.
Huang, C.-T. James
1982 Logical relations in Chinese and the theory of grammar. PhD dissertation, MIT.
Hyman, Larry
2003 Suffix ordering in Bantu: A Morphocentric Approach. In: G. Booij and J. van Marle (eds.), *Yearbook of Morphology 2002*, 245–281. Dordrecht: Kluwer.

Jackendoff, Ray
1977 *X-bar Syntax*. Cambridge, MA: MIT Press.
Jackendoff, Ray
1990a *Semantic Structures*. Cambridge, MA: MIT Press.
Jackendoff, Ray
1990b On Larson's treatment of the double object construction. *Linguistic Inquiry* 21: 427–456.
Jackendoff, Ray
1993 On the role of conceptual structure in argument selection: a reply to Emonds. *Natural Language and Linguistic Theory* 11: 279–312.
Jaeggli, Osvaldo
1986 Passive. *Linguistic Inquiry* 17: 587–622.
Jelinek, Eloise
1984 Empty categories, Case, and configurationality. *Natural Language and Linguistic Theory* 2: 39–76.
Jelinek, Eloise
2006 The pronominal argument parameter. In: P. Ackema, P. Brandt, M. Schoorlemmer and F. Weerman (eds.), *Arguments and Agreement*, 261–288. Oxford: Oxford University Press.
Johns, Alana
1987 Transitivity and grammatical relations in Inuktitut. PhD dissertation, University of Ottawa.
Kiss, Katalin É. (ed.)
1995 *Discourse Configurational Languages*. Oxford: Oxford university Press.
Kluender, Robert
1998 On the distinction between strong and weak islands: a processing perspective. In: P. Culicover and L. McNally (eds.), *The Limits of Syntax*, 241–279. San Diego: Academic Press.
Kozinsky, Isaac, Vladimir Nedjalkov, and Maria Polinskaja
1988 Antipassive in Chuckchee. In: M. Shibatani (ed.), *Passive and Voice*, 651–706. Amsterdam: John Benjamins.
Larson, Richard
1988 On the double object construction. *Linguistic Inquiry* 19: 335–92.
Lasnik, Howard, and Tim Stowell
1991 Weakest crossover. *Linguistic Inquiry* 22: 687–720.
Lekakou, Marika
2004 In the middle, somewhat elevated. Ph.D. dissertation, University College London.
Lekakou, Marika
2006 A comparative view of the requirement for adverbial modification in middles. In: B. Lyngfelt and T. Solstad (eds.), *Demoting the Agent*, 167–196. Amsterdam: John Benjamins.
Levin, Beth, and Malka Rappaport Hovav
1994 *Unaccusativity*. Cambridge, MA: MIT Press.
Marantz, Alec
1984 *On the Nature of Grammatical Relations*. Cambridge, Mass.: MIT Press.
Marelj, Marijana
2004 Middles and argument structure across languages. PhD dissertation, Utrecht University. LOT Dissertation Series 88.
Mchombo, Sam (ed.)
1993 *Theoretical Aspects of Bantu Grammar 1*. Stanford: CSLI Publications.
Neeleman, Ad, and Fred Weerman
1999 *Flexible Syntax*. Dordrecht: Kluwer.
Ngonyani, Deo, and Peter Githinji
2006 The asymmetric nature of Bantu applicative constructions. *Lingua* 116: 31–63.

Nilsen, Øystein
2003 Eliminating positions. PhD dissertation, Utrecht University. LOT Dissertation Series 73.
Pesetsky, David
1987 Wh-in-situ: movement and unselective binding. In: E. Reuland and A. ter Meulen (eds.), *The Representation of (In)definiteness*, 98–129. Cambridge, MA: MIT Press.
Pesetsky, David
1995 *Zero Syntax*. Cambridge, MA: MIT Press.
Polinsky, Maria
2005 Antipassive constructions. In: M. Haspelmath, M. Dryer, D. Gil and B. Comrie (eds.), *The World Atlas of Language Structures*, 438–441. Oxford: Oxford University Press.
Postal, Paul
1971 *Cross-over Phenomena*. New York: Holt, Rinehart and Winston.
Postal, Paul
1986 *Studies of Passive Clauses*. Albany: SUNY Press.
Postal, Paul
1993 Remarks on weak crossover effects. *Linguistic Inquiry* 24: 539–556.
Reinhart, Tanya
2002 The Theta System: an overview. *Theoretical Linguistics* 28: 229–290.
Reinhart, Tanya, and Eric Reuland
1993 Reflexivity. *Linguistic Inquiry* 24: 657–720.
Reinhart, Tanya, and Tal Siloni
2005 The lexicon-syntax parameter: reflexivization and other arity operations. *Linguistic Inquiry* 36: 389–436.
Rizzi, Luigi
1986 Null objects in Italian and the theory of pro. *Linguistic Inquiry* 17: 501–557.
Rizzi, Luigi
1990 *Relativized Minimality*. Cambridge, MA: MIT Press.
Rizzi, Luigi
2006 On the form of chains: criterial positions and ECP effects. In: L. Cheng and N. Corver (eds.), *Wh-Movement: Moving On*, 97–133. Cambridge, MA: MIT Press.
Ross, John Robert
1967 Constraints on variables in syntax. Ph.D. dissertation, MIT.
Ruys, E.G.
2000 Weak crossover as a scope phenomenon. *Linguistic Inquiry* 31: 513–540.
Schäfer, Florian
2009 The causative alternation. *Language and Linguistics Compass* 3: 641–681.
Siewierska, Anna
1984 *The Passive*. London: Croom Helm.
Spencer, Andrew, and Louisa Sadler
1998 Morphology and argument structure. In: A. Spencer and A. Zwicky (eds.), *The Handbook of Morphology*, 206–236. Oxford: Blackwell.
Steinbach, Markus
2002 *Middle Voice*. Amsterdam: John Benjamins.
Stroik, Thomas
1992 Middles and movement. *Linguistic Inquiry* 23: 127–137.
Szabolcsi, Anna, and Marcel den Dikken
2003 Islands. In: L. Cheng and R. Sybesma (eds.), *The Second* Glot International *State-of-the-Article Book*, 213–240. Berlin: Mouton de Gruyter.
Van Craenenbroeck, Jeroen
2010 Complex wh-phrases don't move. In: P. Panagiotidis (ed.). *The Complementizer Phase*, 236–260. Oxford: Oxford University Press.

Van de Visser, Mario
2006 The marked status of ergativity. PhD dissertation, Utrecht University. LOT Dissertation Series 141.
Weerman, Fred, and Petra de Wit
1999 The decline of the genitive in Dutch. *Linguistics* 37: 1155–1192.
Williams, Edwin
1981 Argument structure and morphology. *The Linguistic Review* 1: 81–114.

Peter Ackema, Edinburgh (UK)

10. The Morpho-Syntactic Realisation of Negation

Abstract

Every natural language has some lexical element at its disposal to reverse the truth-conditional content of a sentence. Sometimes, sentences are rendered negative by means of a negative marker, sometimes by means of a negative indefinite, and sometimes even by a combination of both of them. It turns out that the syntactic and semantic behaviour of these negative markers and indefinites is much more complex than may be initially thought. In this chapter, I discuss the general syntactic and semantic properties of both negative markers and negative indefinites and I focus on three particular phenomena that shed more light on these intricate syntactic and semantic properties: negative concord, split-scope readings, and the co-occurrence of multiple negative markers in a single clause.

1. Introduction

Every natural language has some device at its disposal to reverse the truth-conditional content of a sentence. Take, for instance, the examples in (1).

(1) a. *John walks*
    b. *John does not walk*

Sentence (1a) is true exactly when (1b) is false and vice versa. The semantic operation that reverses truth conditions is known as negation.

However, it is not the case that every negative sentence is equivalent to its positive counterpart preceded by *it is not the case that*. This depends on the position within the sentence from where negation takes scope. In (1b) the negation takes scope over the entire proposition *John walks*. This is due to the fact that no other scope-taking element surfaces above the negation in these examples. Now take the following sentences:

(2) a. *Somebody didn't walk*
 b. *Probably John didn't walk*
 c. *Not long ago John walked*

In all examples in (2) the meaning of the negative sentence is not the same as its positive counterpart preceded by *it is not the case that*. Clearly, (2a) does not mean *it is not the case that somebody walked* (which is equivalent to *nobody walked*) and the same applies to (2b), which states that it is probable that John didn't walk. This is due to the scopal position of the negation with respect to the position of a higher scope-taking element. In (2a), the negation is under the scope of *somebody*; therefore not the entire clause is negated, but only the predicate *walk*. In (2b), the negation takes scope below the modal adverb *probably*. In (2c), even the predicate *walk* is not under the scope of negation. Negation only applies to *long ago* and (2c) actually indicates that John did walk, in fact quite recently.

Even though in all examples in (2) negation does not take scope over the entire sentence, there is a difference between examples (2a–b) and (2c). In the first examples, the entire sentence is felt to be negative, even though negation does not necessarily outscope the full clause. However, in (2c), only a single constituent is negated; the sentence itself is felt to be positive. The distinction between (2a–b) and (2c), for that reason, is referred to as the distinction between *sentential negation* and *constituent negation*.

This distinction is grammatically reflected as well. An observation dating back to Klima (1964), for instance, is that sentences exhibiting sentential negation select *either*-modification, whereas sentences with constituent negation can only be modified by *too*, as is shown below.

(3) a. *Somebody didn't walk and somebody didn't talk either/*too*
 b. *Probably John didn't walk and probably Mary didn't walk either/*too*
 c. *Not long ago John walked and not long ago Mary walked too/*either*

Currently, it is assumed that the difference between sentential and constituent negation reduces to negative scope. Acquaviva (1996), building on Jackendoff (1972) and Krifka (1989), and followed upon by Herburger (2001), Weiss (2002) and Penka (2010), amongst others, argues that sentential negation involves negation of the quantifier that binds the event variable. According to Acquaviva, (2a–b) then differ from (2c), as no reference is made to any walking event in (2a–b), whereas in (2c) there is. The idea that the difference between sentential and constituent negation lies in their semantics, seems at first sight at odds with the fact that the distinction comes along with certain syntactic effects. However, as is well known since the work of Diesing (1992), Ladusaw (1992),

Herburger (2001) and others, the semantic locus where the event variable of the main predicate is bound, corresponds to the level of *v*P and is thus reflected syntactically. Consequently, the existence of syntactic effects related to the distinction between sentential vs constituent negation are therefore not unexpected (cf. Horn 1989; Zeijlstra 2004, 2013; Penka 2010 for an overview of the discussion).

2. Expressing negation

Although every language has some way to express sentential negation, languages differ to quite some extent in the way they do this. Following Dahl (1979), Horn (1989), Zanuttini (2001), various expression strategies for negation can be distinguished. The major distinction is between languages that use some designated verbs to express sentential negation and languages that use a negative marker instead. An example of the former (taken from Payne 1985; cited in Zanuttini 2001) is Evenki, an example of the latter is Dutch:

(4) a. *Bi ə-ə-w dukuwūn-ma duku-ra* [Evenki]
I NEG-PST-1SG letter-OBJ write-PTCP
'I didn't write a letter'

b. *Hans is niet thuis* [Dutch]
Hans is NEG at.home
'Hans isn't at home'

In (4a), the negative verb is (presumably) some auxiliary that takes the *v*P as its complement. In (4b), sentential negation is expressed by including a negative marker in the sentence.

However, not every language with a negative marker at its disposal must always use it in order to express sentential negation. Instead, some languages can also express sentential negation by means of a negative indefinite, as is shown for Dutch below. Here, the word *niemand* ('nobody') in object position is what yields sentential negation. The same applies to English, as the translation of (5) suggests.

(5) *Jan ziet niemand* [Dutch]
Jan sees nobody
'Jan sees nobody'

Most of the literature on negation has focused on the syntactic and semantic behaviour of negative markers and negative indefinites. In this section, therefore, I briefly discuss what their major syntactic and semantic properties are generally taken to be, and introduce the primary questions that have guided the research in this area over the past 15 years. Section 2.1 is about negative markers; section 2.2 is about negative indefinites. In section 2.3, the syntactic and semantic behaviour of negative markers and negative indefinites and the way they interact between themselves and other scope-taking elements is discussed, which turns out to be much more complex that what would be expected at first sight.

2.1. Negative markers

As has been addressed in section 1, in order to express sentential negation, negative markers should appear in a syntactic position from where they can take scope over the *v*P in order to outscope the quantifier that binds the event variable. Since Pollock's influential paper (Pollock 1989), it is generally assumed that such negative markers occupy a position in a designated functional projection NegP that is located somewhere in the clausal spine. For Pollock, focusing in particular on French, this NegP is located between TP and AgrP:

(6) $[_{TP}$ $[_{NegP}$ $[_{AgrP}$ $[_{VP}$ $]]]]$

The postulation of a NegP, consisting of a specifier and a head position in the clausal spine yields at least two questions. First, do negative markers occupy the head or specifier position of this NegP? Second, is the relative position of this NegP in the inflectional domain universally fixed, or do languages vary in this respect? Related to this second question is whether every language must actually have a NegP hosting its negative markers.

Concerning the first question, the postulation of a NegP in the clausal spine predicts that two types of negative markers should be attested: those that are phrasal and those that occupy Neg°. Indeed, both types of negative markers have been attested.

Negative markers come about in two kinds: negative affixes and negative particles. An example of negative affix is Turkish *me*, which is part of the verbal inflectional domain (example from Ouhalla 1991; also cited in Zanuttini 2001):

(7) *John elmalari ser-me-di* [Turkish]
John apples like.NEG-PST-3SG
'John doesn't like apples'

Traditionally, negative affixes have been seen as elements that are base-generated in the inflectional domain and picked up by the raising finite verb (cf. Baker 1985; Pollock 1989). Under such analyses, inflectional negative markers such as Turkish *me*, are then base-generated in Neg°.

Such a view (as has been proposed by Pollock 1989) is, however, currently disputed, and has been replaced by either lexicalist positions, where lexical items enter the derivation fully inflected (cf. Chomsky 1995 *et seq*), or positions based on Distributed Morphology, where the formal features in the verbal tree are post-syntactically spelled out as either inflectional morphemes or separate words (cf. Halle and Marantz 1993 and many subsequent works). Under lexicalist approaches, the negative inflectional affix should already be part of the lexically inserted finite verb, and either move to or agree with the abstract negative head. Under post-syntactic approaches, any negative marker is the spell-out of some negative feature (present in NegP), with languages differing with respect to the way these features are spelled-out exactly.

Negative particles, the other type of negative markers, also vary in terms of their morpho-syntactic behaviour. Czech *ne* and Italian *non* are negative particles that are left-attached to the finite verb (with the additional difference that in Czech the negative particle also phonologically attaches to the finite verb).

(8) a. *Milan ne-volá* [Czech]
Milan NEG-calls
'Milan doesn't call'

b. *Gianni non ha telefonato* [Italian]
Gianni NEG has called
'Gianni did not call'

Such negative particles are generally taken to be heads of NegP (cf. Zanuttini 1997, 2001; Zeijlstra 2004). Evidence for this comes from the fact that whenever the verb raises to a higher position than Neg°, for instance to C°, the negative particle accompanies it, as is shown for Italian in (9), taken from Rizzi (1982). This is a direct result of the Head Movement Constraint (after Travis 1984), which forbids head-to-head movement across intervening heads: the negative particle, therefore, must attach to the verb.

(9) [[$_{C°}$ *non avendo*] *Gianni fatto questo*] [Italian]
NEG having Gianni done this
'Gianni having not done this, …'

Another diagnostic test, introduced by Merchant (2006), concerns adjunction of the negative particle to a *Wh*-term like 'why'. Since 'why' is phrasal and head-to-phrase adjunction is forbidden, negative head particles should not be allowed to adjoin to 'why'. This is indeed the case in Italian:

(10) **Perche non*? [Italian]
why NEG
'Why not?'

Note, though, that in order to express something with the meaning 'why not' in these languages the expression 'why no' is used (with 'no' as in 'yes/no'). This means that in languages where the negative marker and the word for 'no' are homophonous, such as Czech, the test is inapplicable.

In other languages, however, the negative particle behaves as a specifier of a clausal functional projection rather than as a head of it. Dutch *niet* is such a negative particle. Contrary to Italian *non*, verbs may raise across *niet* (11) and *niet* may adjoin to *waarom* ('why') (12):

(11) a. *… dat Jan niet liep* [Dutch]
… that Jan NEG walked
… 'that Jan didn't walk'

b. *Jan liep niet*
Jan walked NEG
'Jan didn't walk'

(12) *Waarom niet*? [Dutch]
why NEG
'Why not?'

Although the postulation of NegP for languages like Italian and Czech is fairly uncontroversial, some controversy has arisen concerning its locus in the clausal spine (cf. Belletti 1990; Laka 1990; Zanuttini 1991; Pollock 1993; Haegeman 1995 among many others). Most of these proposals point out that nothing a priori forces the position of the negative projection to be universally fixed. Ouhalla (1991), for instance, argues that in Turkish negative affixes are in between the verb and tense affixes, whereas in Berber negation is in the outer layer of verbal morphology, as is shown in (13), taken from Ouhalla (1991).

(13) a. *Ur-ad-y-xdel* *Mohand dudsha* [Berber]
NEG-FUT-3M-arrive Mohand tomorrow
'Mohand will not arrive tomorrow'

b. *John elmalari ser-me-di* [Turkish]
John apples like.NEG-PST-3SG
'John didn't like apples'

Under the assumption that both inflectional negative markers are hosted at Neg°, Ouhalla argues that the position occupied by NegP in the clause is subject to parametric variation along the lines of what he referred to as the *NEG parameter* (14), which either puts NegP on top of TP or on top of VP.

(14) NEG Parameter
a. NEG selects TP
b. NEG selects VP

According to Ouhalla, the different values of this NEG parameter are also reflected by the differences in the expression of sentential negation in Romance languages and Germanic languages. In Ouhalla's analysis, NegP dominates TP in Romance languages, while in Germanic languages TP dominates NegP.

However, not only the universality of the locus of NegP has been disputed, but also its universal presence. Evidence for the existence of NegP comes from examples, as presented above, that show that some negative particles must occupy some designated head position in the extended verbal domain. At the same time, not every negative particle is a negative head. However, nothing forces these negative specifiers, such as Dutch *niet*, to occupy the specifier position of an abstract negative head. Zeijlstra (2004), inspired by Nilsen (2003), argues that this *niet* could also occupy a specifier position of *v*P. Most arguments for or against the position of the presence of universal NegP are based on more general conceptual arguments regarding the so-called cartographic approach (initiated by Rizzi 1997; Cinque 1999), or Kayne's (1995) claim that functional projections maximally allow for one specifier position. Both conjectures predict that NegP, at least in every sentence expressing sentential negation, is universally present.

Another prediction, coming from the NegP hypothesis is that since NegP has two positions at its disposal that could host negative markers, the possibility arises that (at least in those languages that have a NegP) both slots are filled.

This prediction seems to be born out: many languages allow more than one negative markers to appear in negative clauses. Catalan for example has, apart from its preverbal negative particle *no*, occupying Neg°, the possibility of including an additional phrasal negative particle *pas* in negative expressions. In Standard French, the negative particle *pas* must even be accompanied by a preverbal negative particle *ne* (though in colloquial French this negative marker *ne* is often dropped). In West Flemish, finally, the negative particle *nie*, may optionally be joined by a negative particle *en* that attaches to the finite verb (15) (cf. Haegeman 1995).

(15) a. *No sera (pas) facil* [Catalan]
NEG be.FUT.3SG NEG easy
'It won't be easy'

b. *Jean ne mange pas* [French]
Jean NEG eats NEG
'Jean doesn't eat'

c. *Valère (en) klaapt nie* [West Flemish]
Valère NEG talks NEG
'Valère doesn't talk'

Jespersen (1917) already observed that examples like the ones in (15) reflect a widespread diachronic development of languages. Languages like English, Dutch, German, Latin and many others all changed from languages with only a single negative marker through intermediate stages with an additional second negative marker, as in (15a–c), to a stage in which the first negative marker becomes obsolete. This process is known as Jespersen's Cycle (after Dahl 1979) and has been formulated by Jespersen as follows:

> The history of negative expressions in various languages makes us witness the following curious fluctuation; the original negative adverb is first weakened, then found insufficient and therefore strengthened, generally through some additional word, and in its turn may be felt as the negative proper and may then in course of time be subject to the same development as the original word. (Jespersen 1917: 4)

For a comprehensive overview of the Jespersen Cycle in the above-mentioned languages, see Breitbarth et al. (to appear). For a discussion of the Jespersen Cycle in English, the reader is referred, Van Kemenade (2000), Ingham (2007) Wallage (2008) and Van Gelderen (2009); for French, to Rowlett (1998) and Roberts and Roussou (2003); for German to Jäger (2008) and Breitbarth (2009) and for Dutch to Burridge (1993) and Hoeksema (1997).

At the same time, it is not always clear whether, in languages with two negative markers, these negative markers occupy both slots of NegP. Afrikaans, for instance, has a single negative particle that sometimes has to appear twice in the sentence. However, it is doubtful that these two negative particles *nie* occupy Neg° and SpecNegP, respectively (cf. Biberauer 2008).

(16) *Jan eet nie kaas nie* [Afrikaans]
Jan eat NEG cheese NEG
'Jan doesn't eat cheese'

Finally, note that even though syntactically there is space for two negative markers, semantically it is far from clear why it is that a single semantic negation is expressed by two morpho-syntactically negative elements.

2.2. Negative indefinites

As indicated in the beginning of this section, another way to express sentential negation is by using negative indefinites. This system surfaces in a number of languages. In Dutch, for instance, sentential negation can be expressed by including a negative indefinite, either in preverbal or postverbal position. The same applies to English, as the translations of the examples show.

(17) a. *Niemand ziet hem* [Dutch]
NEG.body sees him
'Nobody sees him'

b. *Hij ziet niemand*
he sees NEG.body
'He sees nobody'

These facts strongly suggest that negative indefinites are (semantically active) negative quantifiers (or indefinites in the Heimian sense, cf. Kamp 1981; Heim 1982). The assumption that negative indefinites are negative quantifiers is furthermore confirmed by the fact that negative indefinites in languages like Dutch may express sentential negation even from a *v*P-internal position: it is an independently established property of quantifiers that they may undergo LF-raising to a *v*P-external position.

However, the assumption that negative indefinites are negative quantifiers is disputed on two grounds: Negative Concord and split-scope readings. First, contrary to expectation, in many languages occurrences of a negative indefinite together with a negative marker yield one semantic negation only. Also, in most such languages combinations of two negative indefinites yield one semantic negation as well, as is illustrated in (18) below for Italian.

(18) a. *Non ha telefonato nesssuno* [Italian]
NEG has called NEG.body
'Nobody called'

b. *Nessuno ha telefonato a nessuno*
NEG.body has called to NEG.body
'Nobody called anybody'

This phenomenon is referred to as Negative Concord. As Negative Concord is a well-studied phenomenon that has lead to far-reaching conclusions with respect to the analysis of negative indefinites and negative markers, it will be discussed in section 3 in much more detail.

However, Negative Concord is not the only phenomenon that casts doubt on the idea that negative indefinites denote negative quantifiers. Take the following example from German:

(19) *Es braucht kein Arzt anwesend zu sein* [German]
There needs no physician present to be
'It is not the case that there must be a doctor present'

As the translation already indicates, this sentence only allows a reading where negation out-scopes the modal, whereas the indefinite 'a doctor' takes scope under it. The modal, so to speak, splits the scope of the negative and the indefinite part of the negative indefinite. For that reason, constructions like (19) are dubbed split-scope readings. Such split-scope readings are hard to explain if negative indefinites are taken to be plain negative quantifiers.

The remainder of this chapter consists of a discussion of the three addressed phenomena that pose a challenge for the standard syntactic and semantic analyses of negative markers and negative indefinites. In section 3, I discuss what Negative Concord may reveal about the syntax and semantics of negative indefinites. Section 4 continues challenging the conjecture that negative indefinites are negative quantifiers by discussing split-scope readings. Then, in section 5, the discussion shifts from negative indefinites back to negative markers again, where I discuss several problems that constructions consisting of multiple negative markers pose for the NegP hypothesis. Finally, section 6 concludes this chapter.

3. Negative Concord

In many languages, a clause-internal combination of two elements that can independently induce semantic negation does not yield a reading where each morpho-syntactically negative element corresponds to a semantic negation (a so-called Double Negation –DN– reading). Instead, it yields a Negative Concord (NC) reading, which contains only one semantic negation. This is illustrated for Italian below, where both *non* ('not') and *nessuno* ('nobody') receive a negative interpretation, as shown in (20), but jointly do not yield two semantic negations (21).

(20) a. *Gianni non ha telefonato* [Italian]
Gianni NEG has called
'Gianni didn't call'

b. *Nesssuno ha telefonato*
NEG.body has called
'Nobody called'

(21) a. *Non ha telefonato nesssuno* [Italian]
NEG has called NEG.body
'Nobody called'

b. *Nessuno ha telefonato a nessuno*
NEG.body has called to NEG.body
'Nobody called anybody'

At first sight, the readings in (21) seem to violate the principle of compositionality (cf. Frege 189; Janssen 1997). Why is it that these readings do not contain two semantic negations?

However, this essentially semantic question is not the only question to be addressed. First of all, not all languages exhibit NC. Dutch, for instance, is a language that lacks NC:

(22) *Jan belt niet niemand* [Dutch]
Jan calls NEG NEG.body
DN: 'Jan doesn't call nobody' = 'Jan calls somebody'

Thus, languages differ cross-linguistically with respect to whether they exhibit NC or not. Note that this is not as straightforward as it sounds. Several scholars (Weiss 2002; Sag and De Swart 2002) have argued that every language that exhibits negative markers and negative indefinites is underlyingly an NC language and only normative effects and/or other properties of language usage lead to the fact that people disapprove of NC interpretations of sentences with more than one negative element. However, research into the microvariation in Dutch (Barbiers 2005/2008) shows that people violating all kinds of normative effects still strongly assign DN readings to sentences containing multiple negative elements.

Second, the pattern in (21) only reflects properties of a number of NC languages; the variation that languages exhibit with respect to the expression/interpretation of sentences containing multiple negative elements is much richer. NC languages come about in two kinds: Strict NC and Non-strict NC languages (after Giannakidou 2000).

In Czech, which is a Strict NC language, *neg-words*, the name for negative indefinites in NC languages (sometimes also dubbed *n-words* after Laka 1990), always need to be accompanied by a negative marker, as shown in (23), regardless whether these neg-words are in preverbal or postverbal position. In a Non-strict NC language such as Italian, however, preverbal neg-words cannot precede the negative marker (5).

(23) a. *Dnes nikdo *(ne-)volá* [Czech]
today NEG.body NEG-calls
'Today nobody calls'

b. *Dnes *(ne-)vola nikdo*
today NEG-calls NEG.body
'Today nobody calls'

(24) a. *Ieri nessuno (*non) ha telefonato* [Italian]
Yesterday NEG.body NEG has called
'Yesterday nobody called'

b. *Ieri *(non) ha telefonato nessuno*
Yesterday NEG has called NEG.body
'Yesterday nobody called'

Another domain of variation amongst NC languages concerns optionality. In the NC languages discussed above, NC is obligatory. The negative markers in (23) and (24) may not simply be removed. In other languages this is however not the case. NC in West Flemish, for instance, is always optional (cf. Haegeman 1995; Haegeman and Zanuttini 1996).

(25) ... *da Valèren niemand (nie) ken* [West Flemish]
... that Valère NEG.body NEG knows
'... that Valère doesn't know anybody'

This introduces a second, equally important, question: how can the cross-linguistic variation that is attested with respect to the expression of multiple negation be explained?

The two issues that have to be addressed are (i) how to explain the compositionality problem, and (ii) how to account for the attested cross-linguistic variation. Most accounts of NC focus on (i) and either discuss only a subclass of NC languages, or leave the second question aside. In this chapter, I discuss various proposals that have been put forward to solve the compositionality problem and I will discuss to what extent they cover the attested variation. In short, there are four types of approaches.

A – *The Negative Quantifier Approach*: All neg-words are negative quantifiers; some kind of absorption mechanism then accounts for why two neg-words are interpreted as if there were only one single negation (Zanuttini 1991; Haegeman 1995; Haegeman and Zanuttini 1996; De Swart and Sag 2002; Watanabe 2004).

B – *The Lexical Ambiguity Approach*: Neg-words are contextually/lexically ambiguous between Negative Quantifiers and so-called Negative Polarity Items (NPIs) (like English *any*-indefinites). The question is then what determines which reading which neg-word may receive (Van der Wouden 1994; Herburger 2001).

C – *The NPI Approach*: All neg-words are NPIs; in cases where there is no negative marker, an abstract negative operator is assumed to be present; the question then is why plain NPIs are different from neg-words (Ladusaw 1992; Giannakidou 2000).

D – *The Agreement Approach*: NC is an instance of syntactic agreement, where neg-words carry uninterpretable formal negative features that need to be checked against a single interpretable negative feature (Ladusaw 1992; Brown 1999; Weiss 2002; Zeijlstra 2004).

In the next subsections, I consecutively discuss four recent accounts of NC, each representative for one of the approaches outlined, and describe to what extent they can account for the compositionality puzzle and the attested cross-linguistic variation.

However, before discussing the various proposals, it is important to emphasise that it is not necessary that NC in every language follows from one and the same mechanism. Nothing a priori demands that all different types of NC should receive the same explanation for the compositionality problem, a point repeatedly emphasized by Giannakidou (2000, 2010).

3.1. The Negative Quantifier Approach

De Swart and Sag (2002), basing themselves on ideas proposed by Zanuttini (1991, 1997, 2001), Haegeman (1995) and Haegeman and Zanuttini (1996) argue that NC is similar to the so-called pair-list readings of multiple *Wh*-questions. Take, for instance, (26):

(26) *Who bought what?*

The most salient reading of this sentence is not so much for which person is it the case that s/he bought which thing, but rather a reading where it is asked what pairs <x,y> there are, such that x bought y. An answer then could be:

(27) *John bought apples and Mary pears*

Apparently, (26) comes about with a reading where a single *Wh*-operator applies to pairs of variables. Such a reading is different from a reading that consists of a pair of *Wh*-operators each binding a single variable.

For De Swart and Sag, the exact same mechanism applies to sentences with multiple negative quantifiers. For instance, the French sentence (28) also has two readings: one where every negative quantifier binds a single variable and one where a single quantifier binds a pair of variables.

(28) *Personne (n') aime personne* [French]
NEG.body NEG loves NEG.body
1. DN: No one is such that they love no one
$\neg\exists x\neg\exists y$ Love(x, y)
'Nobody loves nobody'
2. NC: No pair of people is such that ones loves the other
$\neg\exists$<x,y> Love(x, y)
'No one loves anyone'

As the reader can see, the first reading amounts to a DN reading while the second reading is the NC reading. Thus, if the mechanism responsible for the creation of the pair-list readings in multiple *Wh*-questions, standardly referred to as *quantifier resumption* after May (1985), also applies to multiple negative indefinites, then it is predicted that every sentence containing two neg-words must have two readings as well: a DN and an NC reading. As De Swart and Sag show, this ambiguity for sentences like (28) is indeed attested amongst speakers of French.

The main advantage of this proposal is that the availability of NC readings does not have to be independently accounted for, but comes for free, once it is assumed that quantifier resumption applies to negative quantifiers. Also, it follows nicely for languages such as French that sentences containing multiple negative elements are felt to be ambiguous between a DN and an NC reading, although the NC reading is the one that is generally preferred.

At the same time, the strength of this proposal is also its weakness. The prediction that every sentence containing two or more negative quantifiers, and only those sentences, are always ambiguous between an NC and a DN reading is too strong. Although French reflects this kind of ambiguity, similar constructions in most other languages are clearly unambiguous. Therefore, the question arises as to why languages display cross-linguistic variation in this respect. For De Swart and Sag (2002: 390), this is "really a question about the relation between language system and language use." In principle, both interpretations are always available, but for De Swart and Sag it is a matter of preference which reading surfaces in the end. In later work, however, De Swart (2006, 2010) takes the cross-linguistic differences to be a result of independently applying constraints in a system based on Optimality Theory.

Another question that arises, concerns the role of negative markers in De Swart and Sag's system. Why are the sentences in (29) without the negative markers ruled out? If neg-words are negative quantifiers, why can they not stand by themselves, as they can in English?

(29) a. *Dnes nikdo *(ne)volá* [Czech]
Today NEG.body NEG.calls
'Today nobody calls'

b. *Ieri *(non) ha telefonato nessuno* [Italian]
Yesterday NEG has called NEG.body
'Yesterday nobody called'

Moreover, if negative markers (optionally or obligatorily) participate in NC constructions, how can this be accounted for in terms of quantifier resumption? De Swart and Sag argue that negative markers should be conceived as zero-quantifiers, i.e. quantifiers lacking an argument. This way they can participate in quantifier resumption, resulting in NC readings as well. Note, though, that this only explains why negative markers may participate in NC constructions, not why they quite often must participate in them, but see De Swart (2006, 2010) for an answer to this question.

Finally, the question remains open as to why neg-words may sometimes establish NC relations with elements that do not appear to be semantically negative. This is, for instance, the case in complement clauses of verbs expressing doubt or fear, prepositions as *without*, or in comparatives, as the following examples from another Non-strict NC language, Spanish, taken from Herburger (2001), illustrate (PRT stands for particle):

(30) a. *Dudo que vayan a encontar nada* [Spanish]
doubt.1SG that will.3PL.SBJ PRT find NEG.thing
'I doubt they will find anything'

b. *Juan ha llegado más tarde que nunca*
Juan has arrived more late than NEG.ever
'Juan has arrived later than ever'

For De Swart and Sag all these elements must be analysed as containing a true negation, something that they explicitly show for French *sans* ('without'). If *without* underlyingly means something like *not with*, then this *not* may undergo resumption again. Still, the question is open why some non-anti-additive elements may participate in NC relations and others cannot, and why languages differ with respect to this matter. Slavic languages, for instance, are more restrictive in this sense.

3.2. The Lexical Ambiguity Approach

The existence of examples such as the ones in (30) suggests that neg-words behave differently from plain negative quantifiers. In fact, the contexts (expressions of doubt or comparatives) in which the neg-words appear in (30) are all so-called downward entailing contexts, i.e. contexts that allow inferences from sets to their subsets. For instance, *to doubt*, is downward entailing since the entailment in (31a) valid; *to be sure*, by contrast, is not downward entailing, since this entailment is not valid, as shown in (31b).

(31) a. I doubt Mary has a car → I doubt Mary has a BMW
b. I am sure Mary has a car ↛ I am sure Mary has a BMW

In this sense, neg-words are similar to so-called Negative Polarity Items (NPIs), i.e. elements such as English *any* or *ever*, that may appear in exactly those contexts where a neg-word does not bring in a semantic negation of its own. This is shown in the examples in (32), which are the translations of the examples in (30), where *any* and *ever* are fine. Note that in non-downward-entailing contexts, such elements may not appear, as illustrated in (33).

(32) a. *I doubt they will find anything*
b. *Juan has arrived later than ever*
c. *No one loves anyone*

(33) a. **I know they will find anything*
b. **Juan has ever arrived*
c. **John loves anyone*

It is tempting to solve the problem regarding the examples in (30) by assuming that neg-words form a particular class of NPIs. However, neg-words that are not in downward entailing contexts do not exhibit any NPI-like behaviour. In such contexts, they rather behave like negative quantifiers. This is for instance the case in (34), also taken from Herburger (2001):

(34) a. *Nadie vino* [Spanish]
NEG.body came
'Nobody came'

b. Q: *A quién viste?* A: *A nadie!* / **A un alma*
to whom saw.2SG? to NEG.body / to a soul
'Who did you see? Nobody / a soul'

c. *Me caso contigo o con nadie.*
me marry.1SG with.you or with NEG.body
'I marry you or nobody.'

Herburger (2001), following ideas by Longobardi (1991) and Van der Wouden and Zwarts (1995), took the contrasts between the examples in (30) and (34) to suggest that neg-words are actually lexically ambiguous between negative quantifiers and NPIs. Since NPIs may only surface in downward-entailing contexts, this means that in all non-downward-entailing contexts neg-words must be interpreted as negative quantifiers, but in downward-entailing contexts they can either also be interpreted as a negative quantifier, or as a (semantically non-negative) NPI.

This analysis has several major advantages. Apart from the fact that it solves the compositionality problem (a sentence with a negative marker and an neg-word, for instance, may give rise to a reading where the neg-word is interpreted as an NPI and only one semantic negation is available at LF), it provides a solution to examples as (30): the parallel between the distribution of NPIs and neg-words in downward-entailing contexts is accounted for. Also, the source of the cross-linguistic variation with respect to NC now lies in the lexicon, which is generally taken to be the source of cross-linguistic variation (cf. Borer 1984; Chomsky 1995): in NC languages, neg-words are lexically ambiguous between negative quantifiers and NPIs; in DN languages such an ambiguity is absent: negative indefinites are always negative quantifiers.

The account by Herburger works nicely for those neg-words that induce a semantic negation. However, Herburger's claim that neg-words can always be interpreted as a negative quantifier appears to be too strong. This is manifested in the two following examples in (35).

(35) a. **Gianni ha telefonato a nessuno* [Italian]
Gianni has called to NEG.body
'Gianni didn't call anybody'

b. *Nessuno ha telefonato a nessuno*
Nobody has called to NEG.body
NC: 'Nobody called anybody'
*DN: 'Nobody called nobody'

First, why is (35a) ill-formed? If *nessuno* is a negative quantifier here, it should be able to appear in postverbal position, just as the English counterpart of (35a), *John called nobody.* Second, why does (35b) not receive a DN reading in addition to the NC one? If *nessuno* is ambiguous between a negative quantifier and an NPI in negative contexts, this reading should be possible as well.

Herburger argues that sometimes an neg-word in postverbal position does in fact receive a negative interpretation, but that the reading is different from general negative quantifiers. The examples she provides are in (36).

(36) a. *El bebé pasa el tiempo mirando a nadie* [Spanish]
The baby spends the time looking at NEG.thing
'The baby spends the time looking at nothing'

b. *El bebé no pasa el tiempo mirando a nadie*
The baby NEG spends the time looking at NEG.thing
NC: 'The baby does not spend the time looking at nothing'
DN: 'The baby does not spend the time looking at anything'

These examples show that neg-words in postverbal position can be interpreted as being semantically negative, but that they can never yield sentential negation in such cases. In (36), the negation induced by the postverbal neg-word is not allowed to outscope the existential quantifier that binds the event variable, yielding a reading in (36a) where the baby is looking, but where there is no object being looked at. The DN reading in (36b) then denies the claim made in (36a).

Herburger does not offer an answer to the question as to why this second negation may take narrow scope only. But if this mechanism is correct, then it is accounted for why (35a) is odd and why (35b) does not receive a plain DN reading. The semantics of (35a) and the semantics of (35b) under the DN readings can only be uttered in pragmatically very unusual situations, as a calling event naturally entails the presence of a callee. Thus, (35a), according to Herburger, is actually not ill-formed, but something that can hardly ever be felicitously uttered.

However, one might wonder to what extent an account of NC in terms of lexical ambiguity is attractive in the first place. As Herburger points out, if an analysis that takes neg-words to be negative quantifiers all the time, or NPI's, and such an analysis can successfully account for the facts, such an analysis is to be preferred on pretheoretical grounds. Herburger notes, however, that such analyses face serious problems as well and therefore her analysis in terms of lexical ambiguity should be seen as a last resort option.

3.3. The NPI Approach

The previous subsection showed that several problems concerning NC disappear once it is assumed that neg-words are not semantically negative. However, the analysis outlined above still faces some problems in the sense that neg-words sometimes at least seem to induce a semantic negation. Hence, the question is legitimate to what extent neg-words actually do induce a semantic negation. Or, put differently, how much evidence is there for the claim that neg-words are semantically negative and how much evidence is there the neg-words are semantically non-negative?

This question has already been addressed by Ladusaw (1992) and he concludes that there is ample evidence for the claim that neg-words are semantically non-negative: constructions with a negative marker and an neg-word, with multiple neg-words, or with an neg-word in a downward-entailing context, already provide evidence for this claim. On the other hand, there is actually not that much evidence that neg-words are semantically negative. As Ladusaw observes, at best there is evidence that every clause in which one or more neg-words surface must be interpreted negatively.

Ladusaw, for that reason, concludes that the hypothesis that all neg-words are NPIs can be entertained, as long as some mechanism is available that can license these NPIs in absence of an overt negation, i.e. neg-words that induce a semantic negation are nothing but NPIs, like the English *any*-terms, that are licensed by some covert negative operator.

Ladusaw's approach overcomes the problems that the previous approaches have been facing, but does do so at some price. It allows inclusion of abstract negative operators. However, inclusion of such abstract negative operators must be constrained to exactly those cases where neg-words appear overtly in the clause. To illustrate the problem: only in example (37a) may an abstract negative operator be assumed to be present; in (37b) an overt negation is already present and (37c) is intended as a positive sentence and should never be able to receive a negative interpretation.

(37) a. *Nessuno telefona* [Italian]
NEG.body calls
'Nobody calls'

b. *Non telefona nessuno*
NEG calls NEG.body
'Nobody calls'

c. *Gianni telefona*
Gianni calls
'Gianni calls'

Thus, the two following questions arise: (i) what is the exact mechanism that ensures that only neg-words in non-downward entailing contexts may trigger the presence of an abstract negative operator, and (ii) why is it that neg-words have this self-licensing property, whereas all other known NPIs do not? Only if these questions can be satisfactorily answered, can Ladusaw's hypothesis be successfully implied.

Ladusaw (1992) does not provide a full-fledged analysis of how this self-licensing mechanism can be implemented, although he does provide some suggestions. Others, however, have followed up on this idea. One such account, proposed by Giannakidou (2000), argues that, at least in Strict NC languages like Greek, the difference lies in the quantificational status of neg-words as opposed to plain NPIs. Another proposal, Zeijlstra (2004), states that neg-words are not NPIs but plain indefinites that must stand in a syntactic Agree relation with a negative operator.

Giannakidou (2001) strictly focuses on Strict NC languages, such as Greek. In these languages, the negative marker must always be present in sentences containing an neg-word, unless the neg-word constitutes a fragmentary answer or a disjunction, as in (39) and (40).

(38) *KANENAS *(dhen) ipe TIPOTA* [Greek]
NEG.body NEG saw NEG.thing
'Nobody saw anything'

(39) Q: *Ti idhes?* A: *TIPOTA* [Greek]
what saw.2SG? NEG.thing
'What did you see? Nothing.'

(40) *Elo na pandrefto ton Petro i KANENAN (alo)* [Greek]
want.1SG SBJ marry.1SG the Peter or NEG.person else
'I want to marry either Peter or nobody (else)'

In these languages, the neg-word is an NPI but deviates from plain NPIs in its quantificational force: a neg-word is a universal quantifier that must outscope the negation, whereas plain NPIs are existential quantifiers or indefinites that must be outscoped by a negative (or other downward-entailing) operator. This means that at the level of LF, all neg-words must precede the negative marker; postverbal neg-words only do so after spell-out.

By postulating this difference, Giannakidou avoids the self-licensing question by assuming that the only cases where neg-words appear in isolation, the negative marker is deleted under ellipsis. The underlying structure of (39) would then be something like (41).

(41) Q: *Ti idhes?* A: *TIPOTA ~~dhen ida~~* [Greek]
what saw.2SG? NEG.thing NEG saw.1SG
'What did you see? Nothing.'

Again, this analysis accounts for the compositionality problem and is able to reduce the cross-linguistic variation that is attested with respect to NC languages to different properties of lexical items. Nevertheless, this analysis can only account for one specific subtype of NC: Strict NC. Non-strict NC languages, such as Italian, where preverbal neg-words may not be followed by a negative marker, cannot be analysed along these lines.

Apart from that, the ellipsis analysis has met some criticism. For instance, Watanabe (2004) argues that the negative marker in (41) may not be assumed to be deleted under ellipsis if no semantic negation is present in the question, an argument that Giannakidou (2006) argues to be incorrect. Also, Zeijlstra (2004, 2008) argues that the negative marker in disjunctions like (40) may not be deleted under ellipsis.

3.4. The Agreement Approach

Another implementation of Ladusaw's conjecture that all neg-words are semantically non-negative, is proposed by Zeijlstra (2004, 2008). Zeijlstra points out that assuming that neg-words are semantically non-negative indefinites that must appear under negation, does not entail that such neg-words are NPIs. For Zeijlstra, NPIs, like the English *any*-terms, are indefinites that, due to some pragmatic and semantic properties, can only be felicitously uttered in downward entailing contexts. This proposal follows a line of research initiated by Kadmon & Landman (1992), Krifka (2005) and Chierchia (2006). By contrast, Zeijlstra proposes that neg-words are plain indefinites that carry some uninterpretable negative feature [uNEG] that must be checked against a higher, semantically negative element that carries an interpretable formal negative feature [iNEG]. NC, in his view, is then nothing but an instance of syntactic agreement. Since the Agree system, after Chomsky (1995, 2002), that Zeijlstra adopts allows for Multiple Agree (cf. Ura 1996; Haraiwa 2001), multiple neg-words can be checked against a single negative operator.

Zeijlstra further assumes that, just like in other cases of syntactic agreement, the element carrying the interpretable feature may be phonologically null. A good parallel are null-subjects. Whereas in some languages finite verbs do not agree with their subjects and every subject must be pronounced, other languages allow their finite verbs to agree with their subjects and allow the actual subject to be a phonological null-element. Null subject-hood and NC, for Zeijlstra, are two sides of the same coin, as illustrated in (42) for Italian. In both examples some element (the neg-word and the finite verb respectively) is equipped with some feature that requires that some other, possibly null element, must check it (the abstract negative operator and abstract *pro* respectively).

(42) a. $\text{Op}_{\text{NEG[iNEG]}}$ *nessuno*$_{[uNEG]}$ *telefona* [Italian]
b. $\text{pro}_{\text{[i3SG]}}$ *telefona*$_{[u3SG]}$

Zeijlstra's analysis thus accounts for NC in a compositional way as well, and it can account for the cross-linguistic variation that is attested with respect to NC. The difference between DN and NC languages reduces to whether neg-words are also semantically marked for negation, or only syntactically. Furthermore, Zeijlstra states that the difference between Strict versus Non-strict NC results from a similar treatment of negative markers. Since in Strict NC languages, neg-words may precede the negative marker, negative markers in those languages should be taken to carry a [uNEG] feature as well, while the semantically active negative operator, by contrast, is always phonologically null. In Non-strict NC languages, the negative marker may only appear to the left of neg-words (in an NC construction) and always corresponds to the locus of the interpretation of semantic negation. Therefore, in those languages the negative marker must carry [iNEG] as well.

The relevant structures for preverbal and postverbal neg-words are thus:

(43) a. $\text{Op}_{\text{NEG[iNEG]}}$ *nessuno*$_{[uNEG]}$ *telefona* [Italian]
b. $\text{Non}_{\text{[iNEG]}}$ *telefona nessuno*$_{[uNEG]}$

(44) a. $\text{Op}_{\text{NEG[iNEG]}}$ *nikdo*$_{[uNEG]}$ *nevolá*$_{[uNEG]}$ [Czech]
b. $\text{Op}_{\text{NEG[iNEG]}}$ *nevolá*$_{[uNEG]}$ *nikdo*$_{[uNEG]}$

The advantages of Zeijlstra's system are that it can allude to an independently motivated self-licensing principle (whose application is attested in other Agree domains as well) and that it takes neg-words to be different from both NPIs and negative quantifiers. Furthermore, the problems around the data in (36), repeated in (45) below, are overcome, since under Zeijlstra's system the role of the negative marker in example (44b) is to ensure that the abstract negative operator takes scope above *v*P, a requirement for the expression of sentential negation (see section 1).

(45) a. *El bébé no* [$_{vP}$ *está mirando a nadie*] [Spanish]
The baby NEG is looking at NEG.thing
'The baby isn't looking at anything'
$\neg\exists x \exists e[\textbf{look'}(e)\ \&\ \text{Agent}(e, \textbf{b})\ \&\ \textbf{thing}'(x)\ \&\ \text{Patient}(e, x)]$

b. *El bébé* [$_{vP}$ *está mirando Op*$_{\neg}$ *a nadie*]
The baby is looking at NEG.thing
'The baby is staring at nothing'
$\exists e[\textbf{look'}(e)\ \&\ \text{Agent}(e, \textbf{b})\ \&\ \neg\exists x[\textbf{thing}'(x)\ \&\ \text{Patient}(e, x)]]$

Less clear under this approach, is the question as to why neg-words may appear in non-negative downward entailing contexts as well. This cannot be explained in terms of the lexical properties of neg-words. Instead, they must follow from the properties of the licensers. Zeijlstra argues that language learners simply have to acquire that some non-negative elements carry an [iNEG] feature as well. The fact that this only applies to classical NPI licensing contexts is, for Zeijlstra, nothing but a historical accident: since most neg-words developed from plain NPIs, their licensers should also be reanalysed accordingly (cf. Jäger 2010).

Another question that emerges for Zeijlstra, concerns the ambiguity of examples that can receive both an NC and a DN interpretation, such as the French data in (28). Here, Zeijlstra has to assume that these sentences are structurally ambiguous with either one or two abstract negative operators being present.

Finally, the Agree mechanism that Zeijlstra adopts is one where [iNEG] features must c-command [uNEG] features. This is the opposite of standard Chomskyan Agree, although this system allows instances of reverse Agree too. In recent work, however, Zeijlstra (2012) argues that all instances of Agree should actually apply in this reversed fashion.

4. Negative indefinites and split-scope effects

In this section, a second phenomenon is introduced that challenges the view that negative indefinites in Dutch and German are negative quantifiers. Take, for instance, examples (46) and (47) from German and Dutch:

(46) *Du musst keine Krawatte anziehen* [German]
You must no tie wear
a. 'It is not required that you wear a tie' $\neg > \text{must} > \exists$
b. 'There is no tie that you are required to wear' $\neg > \exists > \text{must}$
c. 'It is required that you don't wear a tie' $\text{must} > \neg > \exists$

(47) *Ze mogen geen verpleegkundige ontslaan* [Dutch]
They may no nurse fire
a. 'They are not allowed to fire any nurse' $\neg > \text{may} > \exists$
b. 'There is no nurse who they are allowed to fire' $\neg > \exists > \text{may}$
c. 'They are allowed not to fire a nurse' $\text{may} > \neg > \exists$

In both examples, three readings are present, one where the entire negative indefinite takes wide scope with respect to the modal verb, a reading where it takes narrow scope, and a so-called split-scope reading where negation outscopes the modal but where the indefinite still scopes under the modal.

Independent evidence for the existence of these readings comes from examples such as (48). German *brauchen*, which, being an NPI, must scope under negation, whereas in the context of expletive *es* ('there'), an indefinite embedded under a modal can only take narrow scope. Consequently, both the wide-scope and the narrow-scope reading in (48) are ruled out. Still, the sentence is grammatical, yielding a split-scope reading only.

(48) *Es braucht kein Arzt anwesend zu sein* [German]
There needs no physician present to be
a. 'It is not required that there be a physician present' $\neg > \text{need} > \exists$
b. *'There is no physician who is required to be present' $\neg > \exists > \text{need}$
c. *'It is required that there be no physician present' $\text{need} > \neg > \exists$

It must be noted that split-scope effects do not only appear in combinations with modals and negative indefinites (NIs). Object-intensional verbs also invoke split-scope readings (although the narrow-scope reading is independently ruled out, cf. Zimmermann 1993), as is shown in (49) and (50).

(49) *Perikles schuldet Socrates kein Pferd* [German]
Perikles owes Socrates no horse
a. 'Perikles is not obliged to give Socrates a horse' $\neg > \text{owe} > \exists$
b. 'There is no horse that P. is obliged to give to Socrates' $\neg > \exists > \text{owe}$
c. *'Perikles is obliged not to give Socrates a horse' $\text{owe} > \neg > \exists$

(50) *Hans zoekt geen eenhoorn* [Dutch]
Hans seeks no unicorn
a. 'Hans does not try to find a unicorn' $\neg > \text{seek} > \exists$
b. 'There is no unicorn Hans tries to find' $\neg > \exists > \text{seek}$
c. *'Hans tries not to find a unicorn' $\text{seek} > \neg > \exists$

Also, for many, but (crucially) not all speakers of Dutch and German, combinations of universal quantifiers and NIs may also induce split-scope effects: in these cases the universal quantifier intervenes between the negation and the indefinite. Here, however, special intonation is required (with raising intonation on the universal and decreasing intonation on the negative indefinite).

(51) *Alle Ärzte haben kein Auto* [German]
all doctors have no car
'No doctor owns a car' $\forall > \neg > \exists$
*'Not every doctor owns a car' $\neg > \forall > \exists$

(52) *Iedereen is geen genie* [Dutch]
Everybody is no genius
'Nobody is a genius' $\forall > \neg > \exists$
*'Not everybody is a genius' $\neg > \forall > \exists$

Finally, De Swart (2000) has shown that scope-splitting is not restricted to negative indefinites but may apply to all kinds of downward entailing DPs, such as *few N*, as shown below (note that the third reading is unavailable because Dutch *hoeven* 'need' is a negative polarity item):

(53) *Ze hoeven weinig verpleegkundigen te ontslaan* [Dutch]
They need few nurses to fire
a. 'They are required to fire few nurses' $\neg > \text{need} > \exists$
b. 'There are few nurses who they are need to fire' $\neg > \exists > \text{need}$
c. *'They need to fire few nurses' $\text{need} > \neg > \exists$

In the literature, three types of approaches have been spelled out to account for the existence of split-scope readings. In the next three subsections, they will be discussed and evaluated in detail.

A – *The Negative Quantifier Approach*: All negative indefinites are negative quantifiers; split-scope effects arise if these quantifiers do not quantify over simple individuals as usually, but rather over kinds or properties (Geurts 1999; De Swart 2000; see also Abels and Marti 2010).

B – *The Decomposition Approach*: All negative indefinites spell out two PF-adjacent distinct features: a negation and an indefinite; split-scope readings arise when these features are adjacent at LF but are intervened by some third scope-taking element at LF (Jacobs 1980; Rullman 1995; Zeijlstra 2011).

C – *The Syntactic Agreement Approach*: All negative indefinites are semantically non-negative, but mark the presence of a covert abstract negation; under this approach split-scope readings are a special type of NC readings (Penka 2010).

It should be noted that the variety of different approaches to NC and split-scope is remarkably similar: either neg-words or negative indefinites are just negative quantifiers and some special interpretation mechanism is adopted to derive the unexpected readings (the null hypothesis), or these elements are taken to be lexically different from plain negative quantifiers, so that the NC or split-scope reading is no longer unexpected. In the remainder of this section, I briefly illustrate and evaluate each approach.

4.1. The Negative Quantifier Approach

Geurts (1996) argues that negative indefinites are negative quantifiers, but that these negative quantifiers do not necessarily quantify over individuals, but also over *kinds* in the sense of Carlson (1977). This is illustrated in (54), taken from Geurts (1996).

(54) *Ich suche keine Putzfrau* [German]
I seek no cleaning.lady
'I do not look for a cleaning lady'

Both the narrow and the wide scope reading of (54) involve quantification over individuals. The wide-scope reading, for instance, says that there are no cleaning ladies such that I am looking for them. Geurts argues, however, that the sentence may also have a reading where *cleaning lady* refers to a kind. Then the sentence means 'there is no kind-element *cleaning lady* such that I seek this kind' or, in other words, 'I am not a cleaning-lady-seeker'. That reading is equivalent to the split-scope reading: 'if I am not a cleaning-lady-seeker, it means that it is not the case that I am seeking any cleaning lady'.

If this line of reasoning is correct, no additional assumptions have to be made in order to account for the existence of split-scope readings, and the null-hypothesis that all negative indefinites should be interpreted as negative quantifiers can be maintained. However, the strength of this proposal may also be its weakness.

First, Geurts's account treats split-scope with modals or object-intensional verbs akin to split-scope readings with negative indefinites and universal quantifiers, as in (51). However, as we discussed before, many speakers (including the author of this chapter) do accept the former, but not the latter reading, suggesting the two phenomena should not be treated on a par.

Apart from that, in order to account for split readings, sometimes strange kinds would have to be assumed. For instance, to get the paraphrased reading of (55), Geurts would have to appeal to the kind 'student who attended Arnim's lecture yesterday'. The same applies to (56), where the negative indefinite contains a numeral ('two cars'), and so cannot be taken to denote a kind in the first place.

(55) *Ich suche keinen Student, der gestern in Arnims Vorlesung war.* [German]
I seek no student who yesterday in Arnim's lecture was
'I do not look for a student who attended Arnim's lecture yesterday.'

(56) *Wir müssen keine zwei Autos haben.* [German]
We must no two cars have
'We don't need to have two cars.'

Stronger yet, the Geurts type of approach must somehow allude to some kind of lexical ambiguity in order to enable negative quantifiers to quantify both over individuals and kinds. This argument does not only play a role for Geurts's particular analysis of split-scope readings. De Swart (2002), who proposes a modification of Geurts's account where split-scope readings are not the result of quantification over kinds but over properties, even postulates two different lexical entries of negative indefinites.

4.2. The Decomposition Approach

An alternative way of accounting for of split-scope effects is lexical decomposition, as has been proposed by Jacobs (1980) and Rullmann (1995). This states that a negative indefinite, such as German *kein* or Dutch *geen*, underlyingly consists of a plain negative marker and a plain indefinite. Only under PF adjacency can the two be jointly spelled out as a single morphological word, following a rule like (57).

(57) *nicht* + *ein* → *kein* [German]
nicht + *een* → *geen* [Dutch]

Now the split-scope reading can emerge if *nicht/niet* and *ein/een* are adjacent at PF while structurally intervened by some additional scope-taking element at LF. To illustrate this for Dutch, take the following example (after Rullmann 1995):

(58) *Ze mogen geen verpleegkundige ontslaan* [Dutch]
They may no nurse fire
a. 'They are not allowed to fire any nurse' ¬ > may > ∃
b. 'There is no nurse who they are allowed to fire' ¬ > ∃ > may
c. 'They are allowed not to fire a nurse' may > ¬ > ∃

The three different readings all have a different LF structure, as is shown in (59)–(61), the modal being interpreted in its trace position. However, regardless of the exact LF's of this sentence, *niet* and *een* are adjacent at PF, even in (61), where at LF the modal takes scope in between the two.

(59) [Zij mogen$_i$ [niet een verpleegster [ontslaan t$_i$]]] ¬ > ∃ > may

(60) *[Zij mogen [niet een verpleegster ontslaan] t$_i$]]* may > ¬ > ∃

(61) *[Zij mogen$_i$ niet [een verpleegster [ontslaan t$_i$]]]* ¬ > may > ∃

This lexical decomposition approach, in its various forms, circumvents the semantic problems of a split-scope effect by taking the spell-out of negative indefinites to be a PF phenomenon. A problem, though, with this type of approach is that not every indefinite is always phonologically realized. Plural indefinites in Dutch or German lack overt determiners, as shown for Dutch in (62), but plural negative indefinites may still give rise to a split-scope reading (63).

(62) *Ze mogen verpleegkundigen ontslaan* [Dutch]
They may nurses fire
'They may fire nurses'

(63) *Ze mogen geen verpleegkundigen ontslaan* [Dutch]
They may no nurses fire
a. 'There are no nurses who they are allowed to fire' $\neg > \exists >$ may
b. 'They are allowed not to fire nurses' may $> \neg > \exists$
c. 'They are not allowed to fire any nurses' $\neg >$ may $> \exists$

However, such criticisms can be easily overcome once these analyses are rephrased in terms of distributed morphology, where post-syntactic spell-out mechanisms can determine the phonological contexts of one (or more adjacent) features. The rule in (57) should then be rephrased along the lines of (64):

(64) [NEG] + [INDEF] → *kein* [German]
[NEG] + [INDEF] → *geen* [Dutch]

A stronger problem for these analyses, though, is that they only apply to OV languages, i.e. languages where a *v*P-external negative marker may appear to the direct left of a *v*P-internal object. In languages like English, however, the surface position of a negative indefinite is always lower than the position of the negative marker. Take for instance (65):

(65) *You have to do no homework.*

Even though (65) comes along with a split-scope reading, there is no way how this split-scope reading could have been derived from PF adjacency of the negative marker and the indefinite: the position of the negative marker must be structurally higher than the modal, whereas the modal must always appear to the left of its complement.

In order to solve this problem, Zeijlstra (2011) has proposed a mixture of the negative quantifier approach and the lexical decomposition approach. In short, he takes the negation and the indefinite to merge into a negative quantifier that can further undergo quantifier raising. This then leads to two copies of the [NEG] + [INDEF] treelet. Consequently, one of these copies may be spelled out at PF as a negative indefinite along the lines of (64), whereas at the level of LF, nothing forbids that the negation is interpreted in the higher copy and the indefinite in the lower copy. The underlying LF of (65) is then as in (66), whereas the lowest copy gets jointly spelled out as *no homework* at PF.

(66) *You* [[[NEG] [~~INDEF~~]] ~~homework~~] *have to do* [[[~~NEG~~] [INDEF]] *homework*]

Under Zeijlstra's (2011) account, the decomposition approach can be extended to all languages, instead of VO languages only. On the other hand, this account crucially relies on the availability of negative quantifiers to undergo quantifier raising. This assumption is not uncontroversial. Von Fintel & Iatridou (2002) have shown that negative indefinites cannot scope over other quantifiers, as the following examples show for English:

(67) *Everybody touched no desert.* $\forall > \neg\exists$; $*\neg\exists > \forall$

Thus, Zeijlstra's account can only be successful if some other mechanism is responsible for ruling out the possibility of the negative indefinite to outscope the universal quantifier in examples such as (67).

4.3. The Syntactic Agreement Approach

A recent approach that opposes Geurts's and De Swart's analyses and is in a way a radical extension of the lexical decomposition approach, is Penka's (2010) analysis that takes all negative indefinites to be semantically non-negative.

Penka (2010), following on Penka (2007), draws a parallel between Negative Concord and split-scope readings, and argues that the same process underlies both phenomena. Penka adopts Zeijlstra's (2004) analysis of NC, where neg-words (in NC languages) are taken to be semantically non-negative, and carry an uninterpretable negative feature ([uNEG]) that needs to be checked against a negative operator, which in turn may be phonologically abstract. For the sake of exposition, the relevant examples are included again below.

(68) a. *Non telefona nessuno* [Italian]
NEG calls NEG.body
'Nobody calls'
[Non$_{[\text{iNEG}]}$ telefona nessuno$_{[\text{uNEG}]}$]

b. *Nessuno dice niente*
NEG.body says NEG.thing
'Nobody says anything'
[$Op_{\text{NEG}[\text{iNEG}]}$ nessuno$_{[\text{uNEG}]}$ dice niente$_{[\text{uNEG}]}$]

Penka argues that in Dutch and German the same process is going on, the only difference being that multiple Agree is not allowed these languages. Hence, every negative indefinite is semantically non-negative and carries a [uNEG] feature, and needs have its feature checked against an abstract negative operator $Op_{\text{NEG}[\text{iNEG}]}$. In case two negative indefinites show up in the sentence, each negative indefinite must be licensed by a separate $Op_{\text{NEG}[\text{iNEG}]}$.

Penka then derives split-scope readings by having the abstract negative operator outscope the intervening operator, which in turn outscopes the indefinite DP, as illustrated in (69).

(69) ... *dass Du keine Krawatte anziehen musst* [German]
... that you no tie wear must
[dass Du [$Op_{\text{NEG}[\text{iNEG}]}$ [[keine$_{[\text{uNEG}]}$ Krawatte anziehen] musst]]]
'It is not required that you wear a tie' $\neg$ > must > $\exists$

The advantage of Penka's account is that it adopts an independently motivated mechanism to account for split-scope readings and she does not have to make any particular claims about the behaviour of negative indefinites in DN languages.

However, two problems show up for this analysis. First, it is not clear what determines the licensing conditions of the abstract negative operator. Zeijlstra (2004, 2008) explicitly states that the Op_{NEG} may only be introduced in a derivation, immediately dominating the highest element carrying [uNEG]. Hence, under this condition the split-scope reading cannot be derived. Penka (2010) states that adjacency at surface structure is the proper licensing domain for NI's. Otherwise, the other readings could not have been derived, as is demonstrated in (70).

(70) [*dass Du* [$Op_{\text{NEG[iNEG]}}$ [[$keine_{\text{[uNEG]}}$ *Krawatte anziehen*] *musst*]]] $\neg > \text{must} > \exists$
[*dass Du* [$Op_{\text{NEG[iNEG]}}$ [$keine_{\text{[uNEG]}}$ Krawatte [*anziehen musst*]]]] $\neg > \exists > \text{must}$
[*dass Du* [[$Op_{\text{NEG[iNEG]}}$ [$keine_{\text{[uNEG]}}$ *Krawatte anziehen*]] *musst*]] $\text{must} > \neg > \exists$

However, linear adjacency is not a notion that applies at the level of surface structure, but at the level of PF. Surface structure is not about linearization: it is a process that takes place at PF. For the derivation, it does not make any difference whether two elements precede or follow each other. Before Spell-out the two structures in (71) are identical:

(71) [A [B C]]
[A [C B]]

The two structures only diverge at PF. Consequently, Penka's licensing condition of NI's is a PF condition in disguise. This entails, however, that this claim cannot apply to other types of languages than OV languages.

Second, Penka (2010) takes every language to exhibit formal negative features and thus extends Zeijlstra's NC analysis to DN languages as well. However, Zeijlstra's analysis is not directly compatible with this extension. In his approach, the difference between NC and DN languages lies in the fact that negative indefinites in DN languages have no formal negative features at their disposal in (2004, 2008). According to Zeijlstra, in DN languages the negative feature does not have any syntactic status: it is a purely semantic feature. This leads to the prediction that non-Negative Concord languages do not exhibit a formal feature [NEG], which may project itself (Giorgi and Pianesi 1997), as illustrated in (72).

(72) a. NC: b. No NC:

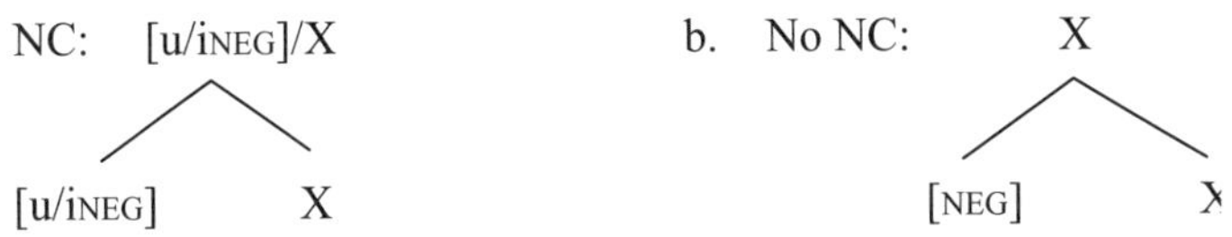

As a result, negative heads (X°) are predicted not to be available in non-Negative Concord languages. Zeijlstra claims that this prediction is born out (on the basis of an extensive cross-linguistic and language-internal survey, cf. Zeijlstra 2004): there is no language without NC that exhibits a negative marker that is a syntactic head. This prediction is unexpected, though, under Penka's analysis where every language has a formal negative feature.

5. Multiple negative particles

The third case study concerns occurrences of multiple negative markers, as is illustrated for a number of languages below:

(73) a. *Jean ne mange pas* [French]
Jean NEG eats NEG
'Jean does not eat'

b. *Ze en weet dat niet* [West Flemish]
She NEG knows that NEG
'She does not know that'

c. *No menjo pas* [Catalan]
NEG eat.1SG NEG
'I do not eat'

d. *Jan eet nie kaas nie* [Afrikaans]
Jan eat NEG cheese NEG
'Jan does not eat cheese'

e. *Ele não comprou a casa não* [Brazilian Portuguese]
He NEG bought the house NEG
'He has not bought the house'
(Schwenter 2005: 1441)

In all these languages, sentential negation is expressed by two negative markers instead of one. The two negative markers, however, are not always equally strong. Quite often, the weaker one of the two may be dropped, but not the stronger one, as is shown in (74)–(75). This shows that in all these languages one of the negative markers is a real negative particle while the other one is more like a dependent negative particle: it may or must show up in all kinds of negative constructions, but may not render a sentence negative by itself.

(74) a. *Jean (ne) mange pas* [French]
Jean NEG eats NEG
'Jean does not eat'

b. *Ze (en) weet dat niet* [West Flemish]
she NEG knows that NEG
'She does not know that'

c. *No menjo (pas)* [Catalan]
NEG eat.1SG NEG
'I do not eat'

d. *Jan eet nie kaas (nie)* [Afrikaans]
Jan eat NEG cheese NEG
'Jan does not eat cheese'

e. *Ele não comprou a casa (não)* [Brazilian Portuguese]
he NEG bought the house NEG
'He has not bought the house'
(Schwenter 2005: 1441)

(75) a. **Jean ne mange* [French]
Jean NEG eats
'Jean does not eat'

b. **Ze en weet dat* [West Flemish]
she NEG knows that
'She does not know that'

c. **Menjo pas* [Catalan]
eat.1SG NEG
'I do not eat'

d. **Jan eet kaas nie* [Afrikaans]
Jan eat cheese NEG
'Jan does not eat cheese'

e. **Ele comprou a casa não* [Br. Portuguese]
he bought the house NEG
'He has not bought the house'
(Schwenter 2005: 1441)

Also, in NC constructions, only one of these negative markers is generally present, not both.

(76) a. *Personne (ne) mange rien* [French]
NEG.body NEG eats NEG.thing
'Nobody eats anything'

b. *K' (en) een niets* [West Flemish]
I NEG have NEG.thing
'I have not seen anything'

c. *No menjo res* [Catalan]
NEG eat.1SG NEG.thing
'I eat nothing'

d. *Jan eet niks nie* [Afrikaans]
Jan eat NEG.thing NEG
'Jan ate nothing'

e. *La ninguem da festa não* [Br. Portuguese]
there NEG.body gives party NEG
'There no-one gives a party'
(Schwenter 2005: 1441)

However, most languages allow both of their negative markers to be present in NC constructions. One exception to this generalisation is French, where *pas* is never allowed to participate in NC constructions:

(77) *Personne (ne) mange *(pas) rien* [French]
NEG.body NEG eats NEG NEG.thing
'Nobody eats anything'

Hence, the two following questions arise. First, what are the *syntactic* differences between the different types of negative markers that are attested? Second, what are the *semantic* differences between the types of negative markers that are attested? The latter question reduces to two subquestions: why is it that some negative markers can render a sentence negative by themselves and others cannot? And why is it that most, but not all, negative markers may participate in NC constructions?

The most elaborate answer to this question is voiced in Zanuttini (1997). Zanuttini claims, basing herself particularly on various Italian dialect data, that different negative markers in Romance varieties occupy different positions in the sentential structure and that universally at least four different NegPs are available (see also Benincà 2006; Poletto 2000; 2007; Manzini and Savoia 2005 for a discussion of negation in various Italian dialects):

(78) [$_{\text{NegP1}}$ [$_{\text{TP1}}$ [$_{\text{NegP2}}$ [$_{\text{TP2}}$ [$_{\text{NegP3}}$ [$_{\text{AspPperf}}$ [$_{\text{Aspgen/prog}}$ [$_{\text{NegP4}}$]]]]]]]]

In Zanuttini's work, different types of negative markers have different syntactic and/or semantic properties, such as sensitivity to mood (in many dialects/languages a different negative marker appears if the sentence displays irrealis mood) or the ability to induce sentential negation without the support of other negative elements (which Italian *non* is able to, but French *ne* is not). Negative markers appearing in NegP1 are then said to be able to induce sentential negation by themselves; elements in NegP2, for instance, are not.

Zanuttini strengthens her proposal by arguing that quite often the two different semantic types of negative markers also share other syntactic properties: elements occurring in Neg1, for instance, are generally ruled out negative imperatives, whereas those in NegP2 are not. However, the question arises as to whether Zanuttini's system is fine-grained enough to cover all the differences, in particular to properly distinguish all semantic differences between negative markers.

It follows automatically that the negative markers that Zanuttini refers to as NegP2 markers should exhibit syntactically different behaviour than those in NegP1, as they occupy different positions in the syntactic structure of negative sentences. However, it is unclear to what extent they should be treated as two semantically distinct classes. For instance, within the class of negative elements where French *pas* shows up, which cannot participate in NC constructions, other negative markers appear that can. Moreover, again it is a question whether, cross-linguistically, all negative markers occupy a NegP1–4 position. Zeijlstra (2004) argues that negative elements in DN languages cannot be taken to carry/contain a syntactic negative feature but rather occupy a *v*P specifier or a DP argument position.

Although the consideration outlined above might actually call for an even more fine-grained distinction between types of NegP, Breitbarth (2009), followed by Haegeman and Lohndal (2010) and Zeijlstra (2010) pushes this discussion in a different direction. She argues that, at closer inspection, negative markers that cannot render a sentence negative by themselves, by definition, should not be taken to be negative markers and for that reason should be banned from NegP positions in the first place. For Breitbarth, these negative markers can never be said to carry a negative feature, as carrying negative features is what enables negative elements to induce a semantic negation. Instead, she argues that West Flemish *en* carries a weak polarity feature that constitutes a Polarity Phrase (PolP). Similar arguments have been proposed for the Afrikaans sentence-final negative marker *nie* (Oosthuizen 1998; Biberauer 2008).

Zeijlstra (2010) goes one step further. He argues that those negative markers that, like French *ne* or West Flemish *en*, may only survive in (semi-)negative contexts without contributing any semantic negation, should actually be considered plain NPIs. This seriously reduces the number of elements that can host a NegP, albeit it that those NPIs that are syntactic heads should then host some other head position. An argument in favour of his position is that such NPI markers appear in all kinds of downward-entailing contexts, even those where neg-words are quite often banned, as is illustrated for West Flemish below:

(79) a. *IJ is veel leper of datrij uit en ziet* [West Flemish]
He is much smarter if that.there.he out NEG looks
'He is much smarter than he looks'

b. *K en e maar drie pillen*
I NEG have only three tablets
'I have only three tablets'

c. *K en twijfele*
I NEG doubt
'I doubt (it)'

However, by assuming that negative markers can be NPIs as well, the class of possible NPIs is further enriched, though it is not clear how the NPI property of French *ne* or West Flemish *en* is semantically or formally encoded. As always, a possible solution to one problem, immediately introduces new questions.

6. Conclusions

In this chapter, I have argued that closer inspection of the syntactic and semantic behaviour of negative markers and negative indefinites shows the way that sentential negation is morpho-syntactically realized is much more complex than one might expect at first sight. Quite often, the appearance of a negative form does not straightforwardly correspond to a negative meaning. This leads to all kinds of questions and each question receives a number of different, quite often conflicting, answers.

In this chapter, I have not tried to pursue one particular view on the relation between negative form and negative meaning, but rather I have tried to show what kinds of solutions each approach may bring and what kinds of new problems subsequently emerge.

The debates have not been settled yet, but this no reason for disappointment: studying the various options for how to solve the discrepancies between negative form and negative meaning does not only increase our understanding of negation, but also of functional categories and the way their meaning is manifested in natural language in general.

10. Acknowledgements

Section 2.1 has been based on Zeijlstra (2013), where these issues are addressed in more detail.

7. References (selected)

Abels, Klaus, and Luisa Marti
2010 A unified approach to split scope. *Natural Language Semantics* 18: 435–47.

Acquaviva, Paolo
1997 *The Logical Form of Negation: A Study of Operator-Variable Structures in Syntax.* (Garland outstanding dissertations in linguistics.) New York: Garland.

Baker, Marc
1985 The mirror principle and morphosyntactic explanation. *Linguistic Inquiry* 16: 373–415.

Barbiers, Sjef, Hans Bennis, Gunther de Vogelaer, Magda Devos, and Margreet van der Ham
2005/2008 *Syntactische Atlas van de Nederlandse Dialecten / Syntactic Atlas of the Dutch Dialects. (Volume I/II.)* Amsterdam: Amsterdam University Press.

Belletti, Adriana
1990 *Generalized Verb Movement.* Torino: Rosenberg & Sellier.

Benincà, Paola
2006 A detailed map of the left periphery in medieval Romance. In: R. Zanuttini, H. Campos, E. Herburger, and P. Portner (eds), *Negation, Tense, and Clausal Architecture: Crosslinguistic Investigations*, 53–86. Washington, D.C.: Georgetown University Press.

Biberauer, Theresa
2008 Doubling vs. omission: insights from Afrikaans negation. In: S. Barbiers, O. Koeneman, M. Lekakou, and M. Van der Ham (eds.), *Microvariation in Syntactic Doubling*, 103–140. (Syntax and Semantics 36.) Bingley: Emerald Publishers.

Borer, Hagit
1984 *Parametric Syntax: Case Studies in Semitic and Romance Languages*. Dordrecht: Foris Publications.

Breitbarth, Anne
2009 A hybrid approach to Jespersen's cycle in West Germanic. *Journal of Comparative Germanic Linguistics* 12: 81–114.

Brown, Sue
1999 *The Syntax of Negation in Russian: A Minimalist Approach.* Stanford: CSLI Publications.

Burridge, Kate
1993 *Syntactic Change in Germanic. Aspects of Language Change in Germanic.* Amsterdam: Benjamins.

Carlson, Greg
1977 Reference to kinds in English. PhD Dissertation, University of Massachusetts at Amherst.

Chierchia, Gennaro
2006 Broaden your views. Implicatures of domain widening and the "logicality" of language. *Linguistic Inquiry* 37: 535–590.

Chomsky, Noam
1995 *The Minimalist Program*. Cambridge, MA: MIT Press.

Chomsky, Noam
2002 Derivation by phase', in M. Kenstowicz (ed.), *Ken Hale. A Life in Language*, 1–52. Cambridge, MA: MIT Press.

Cinque, Guglielmo
1999 *Adverbs and Functional Heads*. Oxford: Oxford University Press.

Dahl, Oystein
1979 Negation. In: J. Jacobs, A. von Stechow, W. Sternefeld, and Th. Vennemann (eds), *Syntax, ein Internationales Handbuch Zeitgenössischer Forschung*, 914–923. Berlin/ New York: De Gruyter.

De Swart, Henriette
2000 Scope ambiguities with negative quantifiers. In: K. von Heusinger and U. Egli (eds.), *Reference and Anaphoric Relations*. Dordrecht: Kluwer Academic Press.

De Swart, Henriette
2006 Marking and interpretation of negation: a bi-directional OT approach. In: R. Zanuttini, H. Campos, E. Herburger, and P. Portner (eds.), *Comparative and Cross-linguistic Research in Syntax, Semantics and Computational Linguistics, GURT 2004*, 199–218. Washington DC: Georgetown University Press.

De Swart, Henriette
2010 *Expression and Interpretation of Negation*. Dordrecht: Springer.

De Swart, Henriette, and Ivan Sag
2002 Negative concord in Romance. *Linguistics and Philosophy* 25: 373–417.

Diesing, Molly
1992 *Indefinites*. Cambridge, MA: MIT Press.

von Fintel, Kai, and Sabine Iatridou
2003 Epistemic containment. *Linguistic Inquiry* 34: 173–198.

Frege, Gottlob
1892 Über Sinn und Bedeutung. *Zeitschrift für Philosophie und Philosophische Kritik* 100: 25–50.

Geurts, Bart
1999 On no. *Journal of Semantics* 13: 67–86.

Giannakidou, Anastasia
2000 Negative … concord? *Natural Language and Linguistic Theory* 18: 457–523.

Giannakidou, Anastasia
2006 N-Words and negative concord. In: M. Everaert, H. van Riemsdijk, and R. Goedemans (eds.), *The Linguistics Companion*, 327–391. (Volume 3.) Oxford: Blackwell Publishing.

Giannakidou, Anastasia
2010a Negative and positive polarity items: licensing, compositionality and variation. In: C. Maienborn, K. von Heusinger, and P. Portner (eds.), *Semantics: An International Handbook of Natural Language Meaning*. Berlin: Mouton de Gruyter.

Giorgi, Alexandra, and Fabricio Pianesi
1997 *Tense and Aspect: From Semantics to Morphosyntax*. Oxford: Oxford University Press.

Haegeman, Liliane
1995 *The Syntax of Negation*. (Cambridge Studies in Linguistics 75.) Cambridge: Cambridge University Press.

Haegeman, Liliane, and Terje Lohndal
2010 Negative concord and (multiple) agree: A. Case Study of West Flemish. *Linguistic Inquiry* 41: 181–211.
Haegeman, Liliane, and Rafaella Zanuttini
1996 Negative concord in West Flemish. In A. Belletti, and L. Rizzi (eds.), *Parameters and Functional Heads. Essays in Comparative Syntax*, 117–179. Oxford: Oxford University Press.
Halle, Morris, and Alec Marantz
1993 Distributed morphology and the pieces of inflection. In: K. Hale, and S. Keyser (eds.), *The View from Building 20*, 111–176. Cambridge, MA: MIT Press.
Hiraiwa, Ken
2001 Multiple agreement and the defective intervention effect. In: O. Matsushansky (ed.), *The Proceedings of the MIT-Harvard Joint Conference (HUMIT 2000)*, 67–80. Cambridge, MA: MITWPL.
Heim, Irene
1982 The semantic of definite and indefinite Noun Phrases. PhD Dissertation, University of Massachusetts at Amherst.
Herburger, Elena
2001 The negative concord puzzle revisited *Journal of Semantics* 9: 289–333.
Hoeksema, Jack
2007 Negation and negative concord in Middle Dutch. In: D. Forget, F. Hirschbüller, F. Martineau, and M.-L. Rivera (eds.), *Negation and Polarity: Syntax and Semantics*. Amsterdam/Philadelphia: Benjamins.
Horn, Larry
1989 *A Natural History of Negation*. Chicago: The University of Chicago Press.
Ingham, Richard
2007 NegP and negated constituent movement in the history of English. *Transactions of the Philological Society* 105: 1–33.
Jackendoff, Ray
1972 *Semantic Interpretation in Generative Grammar*. Cambridge, MA: MIT Press.
Jacobs, Joachim
1980 Lexical decomposition in Montague grammar. *Theoretical Linguistics* 7: 121–136.
Jaeger, Agnes
2008 *History of German Negation*. Amsterdam: Benjamins.
Janssen, Theo
1997 Compositionality. (With an appendix by B. Partee.) In: J. Van Benthem, and A. Ter Meulen (eds.), *Handbook for Logic and Language*, 417–473. Amsterdam: Elsevier; Cambridge, MA: MIT Press.
Jespersen, Otto
1917 *Negation in English*. Copenhagen: A.F. Høst.
Kadmon, Nirit, and Fred Landman
1993 Any. *Linguistics and Philosophy* 16: 353–422.
Kamp, Hans
1981 A theory of truth and semantic representation. In: J. Groenendijk, Th. Janssen, and M. Stokhof (eds.), *Formal Methods in the Study of Language*. Amsterdam: Mathematical Centre.
Kayne, Richard
1995 *The Anti-symmetry of Syntax*. Cambridge, MA: MIT Press.
Klima, Edward
1964. Negation in English. In: J. Fodor and J. Katz (eds.), *The Structure of Language. Readings in the Philosophy of Language*. Englewoods Cliffs, NJ: Prentice-Hall.

Krifka, Manfred
1995 The semantics and pragmatics of polarity items in assertion. *Linguistic Analysis* 15: 209–257.
Ladusaw, Bill
1992 Expressing negation. In: C. Barker and D. Dowty, SALT II. Ithaca, NY: Cornell Linguistic Circle.
Laka, Itziar
1990 Negation in Syntax: On the nature of functional categories and projections. PhD Dissertation, MIT.
Longobardi, Pino
1991 Island effects and parasitic constructions. In: J-T. Huang, and R. May (eds.), *Logical Structure & Linguistic Structure*, 149–196 Dordrecht: Kluwer.
Manzini, Rita, and Leonardo Savoia
2005 *I Dialetti Italiani e Romanci*. Alessandria: Edizioni dell'Orso.
May, Robert
1985 *Logical Form*. Cambridge, MA: The MIT Press.
Merchant, Jason
2006 Why no(t)? *Style* 20: 20–23.
Nilsen, Oystein
2003 Eliminating positions: syntax and semantics of sentential modification. PhD Disseration. Universiteit Utrecht.
Oosthuizen, Johan
1998 The final nie in Afrikaans negative sentences. *Stellenbosch Papers in Linguistics* 31: 61–93.
Ouhalla, Jamal
1991 *Functional categories and parametric variation*. London/New York: Routledge.
Payne, John
1985 Negation. In: T. Shopen (ed.), *Language typology and syntactic description*, 197–242. (Vol. I: Clause structure.) Cambridge: Cambridge University Press.
Penka, Doris
2007 Negative indefinites. PhD Dissertation Tübingen University.
Penka, Doris
2010 *Negative Indefinites*. (Oxford Studies in Theoretical Linguistics 32.) Oxford: Oxford University Press.
Poletto, Cecilia
2000 *The Higher Functional Field in the Northern Italian Dialects*. Oxford University Press, New York, Oxford.
Poletto, Cecilia
2008 *On Negation Splitting and Doubling*. University of Venice – CNR Padua.
Pollock, Jean-Yves
1989 Verb movement, universal grammar, and the structure of IP. *Linguistic Inquiry* 20: 365–424.
Pollock, Jean-Yves
1993 Notes on clause structure. Ms. Université de Picardie, Amiens.
Rizzi, Luigi
1982 *Issues in Italian Syntax*. Dordrecht: Foris.
Rizzi, Luigi
1997 The fine structure of the left periphery. In: L. Haegeman (ed.), *Elements ofGgrammar: Handbook in Generative Syntax*, 281–337. Dordrecht: Kluwer.
Roberts, Ian, and Anna Roussou
2003 *Syntactic Change: A Minimalist Approach to Grammaticalization*. Cambridge: Cambridge University Press.

Rowlett, Paul
1998 Sentential *Negation in French*. Oxford/New York: Oxford University Press.
Rullman, Hotze
1995 Geen eenheid [No unity]. *Tabu* 25: 194–197
Schwenter, Scott
2005 The pragmatics of negation in Brazilian Portuguese. *Lingua* 115: 1427–1456.
Travis, Lisa
1984 Parameters and effects of word order variation. PhD Dissertation, MIT.
Ura, Hiroyuki
1996. Multiple feature-checking: A theory of grammatical function splitting. Ph.D. Dissertation, MIT.
Van Gelderen, Elly
2009 Cyclical Change. Amsterdam: Benjamins.
Van der Wouden, Ton
1994 Negative contexts. PhD Dissertation. University of Groningen.
Van der Wouden, Ton, and Frans Zwarts
1995 A semantic analysis of negative concord. In: U. Lahiri, and A. Wyner (eds.), *SALT III*. Ithaca, NY: Cornell.
Van Kemenade, Ans
2000 Jespersen's cycle revisited: formal properties of grammaticalisation. In: S. Pintzuk, G. Tsoulas, and A. Warner (eds.), *Papers from 5th Diachronic Generative Syntax Conference*. Oxford: Oxford University Press.
Wallage, Philip
2008 Jespersen's cycle in Middle English: parametric variation and grammatical competition. *Lingua* 118: 643–74.
Watanabe, Akira
2004 The genesis of negative concord. *Linguistic Inquiry* 35: 559–612.
Weiss, Helmut
2002 Three types of negation: a case study in Bavarian. In: S. Barbiers L. Cornips, and S. Van der Kleij (eds.), *Syntactic Microvariation*, 305–332. Meertens Institute Electronic Publications in Linguistics.
Zanuttini, Rafaella
1991 Syntactic properties of sentential negation. Ph.D. Dissertation, University of Pennsylvania.
Zanuttini, Rafaella
1997 *Negation and Clausal Structure. A Comparative Study of Romance languages*. (Oxford studies in comparative syntax.) New York, Oxford: Oxford University Press.
Zanuttini, Rafaella
2001 Sentential negation. In: M. Baltin, and C. Collins (eds.), *The Handbook of Contemporary Syntactic Theory*, 511–535. New York: Blackwell.
Zeijlstra, Hedde
2004 Sentential negation and negative concord. Ph.D. Dissertation, University of Amsterdam.
Zeijlstra, Hedde
2008 On the syntactic flexibility of formal features. In: Th. Biberauer (ed.), *TheLlimits of Syntactic Variation*, 143–173. Amsterdam: John Benjamins.
Zeijlstra, Hedde
2010 On French negation. In: I. Kwon. H. Pritchett and J. Spence (eds.), *Proceedings of the 35th annual meeting of the Berkely Linguistics Society*, 447–458. Berkely, CA: BLS.
Zeijlstra, Hedde
2011 On the syntactically complex status of negative indefinites. *Journal of Comparative Germanic Linguistics* 14: 111–138.

Zeijlstra, Hedde
2012 There is only one way to Agree. *The Linguistic Review* 29: 491–539.
Zeijlstra, Hedde
2013 *Negation and polarity*. In: M. Den Dikken (ed.), *The Cambridge handbook of generative syntax*. Cambridge, Cambridge University Press. 793–826.
Zimmermann, Ede
1993 On the proper treatment of opacity in certain verbs. *Natural Language Semantics* 1: 149–179.

Hedde Zeijlstra, Göttingen (Germany)

11. The Syntactic Role of Agreement

Abstract

Agreement, the grammatically determined systematic covariation between forms in syntax, functions to signal grammatical relations in a sentence. Person agreement morphemes resemble the incorporated affixal personal pronouns from which they historically derive, but the two are distinct. A number of factors influence the question of whether the form or meaning of an agreement trigger determines the target form. Coordination interacts with agreement in complex ways.

1. Introduction: triggers, targets, and features

Agreement has been defined as the "systematic covariance between a semantic or formal property of one element and a formal property of another." (from Steele 1978: 610; see also Pollard and Sag 1994: 60; and Corbett 2006: 4). This is illustrated in the simple English example in (1). As the subject varies between singular (*the girl*) and plural (*the girls*), the form of the verb likewise varies between singular (*is*) and plural (*are*):

(1) a. *The girl is/*are happy.*
b. *The girls are/*is happy.*

In this example the subject varies both in form (singular versus plural) and in meaning (denoting one versus multiple girls), so the question immediately arises as to whether the form of the verb is sensitive to the form or meaning of the subject (the "semantic or formal property" referred to in the quote above). That question is addressed in Section 4 below.

In example (1) above, the choice of singular versus plural for the subject is an independent variable, in the sense that these number values are available for a noun phrase (NP) regardless of whether that NP is a subject involved in an agreement relation, or instead appears as an object, a fragment, or elsewhere in the sentence, where no agreement relation is involved. This choice of number value is determined not by agreement but by the meaning the speaker wishes to express: in this case, whether the referent is one girl or more than one. In contrast with the subject, the verb form is dependent upon the subject. In an agreement relation the independent variable (here, the subject) is referred to as the agreement trigger or controller (I use the term *trigger* below), and the dependent one (here, the verb) as the agreement *target*. Languages like French with grammatical gender, where nouns are lexically classified into genders that need not have any semantic correlate, illustrate this trigger/target asymmetry even more clearly. Feminine gender is an inherent property of the French noun *table* 'table', hence the definite article (*la*) and predicate adjective (*vielle*) must appear in feminine form, and mutatis mutandis for the masculine noun *mur* 'wall':

(2) a. *La table est vielle.* [French]
the.F.SG table be.3SG old.F
'The table is old.'

b. *Le mur est vieux.*
the.M.SG wall be.3SG old.M
'The wall is old.'

In this case the speaker has no choice in the matter. The gender is fixed by the noun, which triggers the appropriate gender form on the agreement targets, here the determiner (*le/la*) and predicate adjective (*vieux/vielle*).

The three main dimensions of variation, or features, observed in agreement are person, number, and gender. Example (1) illustrates agreement in number, while example (2) illustrates gender (on the adjective) as well as person and number (on the verb). Features of person, number, and gender are called PNG features or else *phi-features* (*ϕ-features*); the latter term will be used here. They are formal grammatical categories with a close but complex relation to meaning (see Section 4). Number is related to the cardinality of the set of countable entities denoted by the trigger. Person relates to the role of a participant in the speech act, such as speaker (first person), hearer (second person), and others (third person) (see Section 7). In grammatical theory the term gender refers to categories of nouns (grammatical gender) or categories of the things nouns refer to (semantic gender). Typical semantic gender categories include human versus non-human and male versus female, but many others categories are attested.

A grammar specifies a fixed set of possible values for each phi-feature. For example, English distinguishes three genders in the (singular) pronoun system, masculine (*he, him, himself, his*), feminine (*she, her, herself, hers*), and neuter (*it, itself, its*). But grammatical agreement targets are sensitive to a subset of those phi-features. In general, targets are not necessarily specified for all of the phi-features, but often only for some subset of them. English demonstrative determiners agree with their head nouns in number only (*this girl* ~ *these girls*) while present tense finite verbs agree in person and number. Bound pronouns such as reflexives agree with their antecedents in all three features, but no other English agreement targets agree in gender. Similarly, Swedish distinguishes masculine, feminine, and neuter pronouns, but only two genders, neuter and non-neuter, are active in the grammatical agreement system. Other languages have more gender values, such as Bantu languages with up to seven genders.

In the following Serbian/Croatian two-sentence discourse, the noun *knjiga* 'book' is lexically feminine and appears in the unmarked singular form, and like all common nouns it is in third person. So it triggers third person feminine singular agreement. The pronoun *je* is marked for all three features, hence registers the third person feminine singular, but determiner and attributive adjective within the NP register only gender and number, and the finite verb shows only person and number:

(3) *Ov-a star-a knjig-a stalno pad-a.* [Serbian/Croatian]
this-NOM.F.SG old-NOM.F.SG book-NOM.SG always fall-3SG
Molim vas, podignite je.
please you pick.2PL it.3.F.SG
'This old book keeps falling. Please pick it up.'
(from Wechsler and Zlatić 2003: 49)

Cross-linguistically, person agreement on adjectives is relatively rare, in comparison to verbs which are often marked for person (Stassen 1997; Baker 2008; Wechsler 2011).

2. Agreement versus incorporated pronoun

Person agreement inflection on a target form is historically derived from incorporated pronouns (Bopp 1842; Givón 1976). As for how exactly pronouns become reanalyzed as agreement markers, several hypotheses have been offered. On the NP-detachment hypothesis (Givón 1976), pronouns were reanalyzed as affixes in topic-shifting constructions, a process depicted schematically in (4).

(4) Stage I. Analytic pronoun argument agrees with a dislocated NP.
(Marie$_i$,) she$_i$ like strawberries.
ADJUNCT SUBJECT VERB

Stage II. Incorporated pronoun agrees with a dislocated NP.
(Marie$_i$,) she$_i$-like strawberries.
ADJUNCT SUBJECT-VERB

Stage III. Grammatical agreement marker agrees with subject NP.
Marie 3SG.FEM-like strawberries.
SUBJECT AGR-VERB

At Stage I the subject argument is an analytic pronoun (i.e. an independent word), which may be coreferential with an adjunct NP in the same clause. At that stage the pronoun agrees with its NP antecedent, if there is one; such pronoun-antecedent agreement is sometimes called *anaphoric agreement.* At Stage II the pronoun, still serving as subject, is incorporated into the verb, retaining anaphoric agreement with a dislocated NP, if there is one. Finally, at Stage III the incorporated pronoun loses its referential properties and is reanalyzed as a formal marker of agreement (indicated as AGR in 4), while the dislocated NP is reanalyzed as the true subject argument. This new agreement relation at Stage III is sometimes called *grammatical agreement* to distinguish it from anaphoric agreement (this terminology is from Bresnan and Mchombo 1987).

An alternative hypothesis does not involve the floating topic. Instead, pronoun incorporation is seen as arising from reduced coding of those arguments that are more discourse-accessible. The affixal pronoun form then exists alongside the free form (Ariel 2000). On a third hypothesis, pronoun incorporation is seen as an instance of frequency-driven morphologization: according to this view frequently-occurring adjacent forms are likely to become fused for reasons of economy (see Siewierska 2004: 266). In any case, agreement results from the loss of referentiality of the affix.

However, the historical change from pronoun to agreement is more complex than the schematic depiction in (4) would suggest. With respect to the change in form from free word to affix, this schema omits intermediate stages of unstressed pronoun and clitic (see below regarding the hierarchy of pronoun forms from least to most reduced). With respect to the change in function from pronoun to agreement, it omits intermediate stages in which the form retains some pronoun-like semantic properties, imposing restrictions such as specific reference on the NP associate, but no longer functions anaphorically (Suñer 1988). Furthermore, as Corbett (2006: 265) notes, "The formal and functional changes do not necessarily run in parallel." As a consequence, whether a particular language or clause represents a Stage II structure (incorporated pronoun) or a Stage III structure (grammatical agreement) is often not immediately obvious.

Indeed, the question of whether specific verbal affixes are properly analyzed as grammatical agreement markers or incorporated pronouns, and the attendant theoretical implications, are matters of controversy (Bresnan and Mchombo 1987; Jelinek 1984; Baker 1996; Austin and Bresnan 1996; Legate 2002; Mithun 2003; Evans 1999). There are two fundamental theoretical differences between incorporated pronouns and grammatical agreement markers. First, they are distinguished by whether the verbal affix functions semantically as a pronoun or not. Second, they are distinguished by whether the associated NP functions grammatically as an adjunct or an argument of the verb. Thus the narrow issue of agreement interacts with a tangle of questions concerning pronominal reference, binding, and the argument/adjunct distinction, hence its complexity and importance to grammatical theory.

Bresnan and Mchombo (1987) address this issue for the Bantu language Chichewa (see also Bresnan 2001a, chapter 8). Chichewa verbs cross-reference both subject and object. The numbers in (5) and (6) refer to noun classes (genders).

(5) *Njûchi zi-ná-wá-lum-a a-lenje.* [Chichewa]
10.bee 10.SBJ-PST-2.OBJ-bite-FV 2-hunter
'The bees bit them, the hunters.'
(from Bresnan and Mchombo 1987: 744)

Bresnan and Mchombo argue that (i) the Chichewa object marker is an incorporated pronoun, as the translation of the sentence (5) is meant to suggest; and (ii) the subject marker alternatively functions as either an agreement marker, when cooccurring with an associated subject NP (*njûchi* 'bees' in 5), or an incorporated pronoun, when no subject NP appears. Hence either NP can be dropped from (5), yielding pronoun-like interpretations for subject and/or object, so that the one-word utterance *Zi-ná-wá-lum-a* means 'They bit them.'

Bresnan and Mchombo support their analysis by demonstrating a number of systematic differences between subject and object markers. First, the subject marker is obligatory but the object marker can be omitted. Moreover, the object marker can be omitted only when the object NP (*alenje* '2-hunter', in 5) is right-adjacent to the verb. This follows if that right-adjacent position is the object NP position: when the NP appears anywhere else, it must not be an object but rather a dislocated topic, hence the object marker is required to serve as the verb's true object argument. That argument illustrates how the agreement versus incorporated pronoun issue can interact with the word order constraints in a language.

Information structure also plays an important role in this issue. Bresnan and Mchombo (1987) further support the dislocated topic status of NP associates of the Chichewa object marker by showing that, while an NP object of an object marker-less verb can serve as contrastive focus (as in 'The bees bit *the sailors*, not the hunters.'), the presence of an object marker morpheme on the verb renders such sentences unacceptable. This follows, according to Bresnan and Mchombo, from the topic discourse function of dislocated NP associates. The *topic* discourse function is for old or presupposed information, which inherently clashes with the *focus* function, which is for newly introduced information.

In addition to the evidence from word order and discourse function, markedness considerations can be brought to bear on the identification of a morpheme as pronoun versus agreement marker. Incorporated pronouns typically alternate with analytic pronouns that appear in argument NP positions. Referring to the schemas in (4), the analytic pronoun from Stage I survives into Stage II, often retaining a fuller phonological form relative to the phonologically reduced or assimilated incorporated variant. When the two alternative pronoun forms are available, they are typically specialized for different discourse functions: the weak (incorporated) pronominal is anaphoric to a discourse topic, while the strong (analytic) pronominal introduces new discourse referents. This is part of a broader correlation between personal pronoun form and function: as we move down a hierarchy of pronominal forms, from most to least reduced – zero, bound (affixal), clitic, weak (unstressed, prosodically dependent), and finally full, stressed pronouns appearing in argument positions – pronominals are decreasingly likely to be employed for anaphora to a discourse-old topic (Bresnan 2001b). This specialization of weak and strong forms is illustrated for the Chichewa object marker and analytic pronoun in (6a) and (6b) respectively (1A is a subclass of noun class 1):

(6) a. *Fîsi* *a-na-dyá* *chí-manga.* *Á-tá-chí-dya,* [Chichewa]
1A.hyena 1A.SBJ-PST-eat 7-corn 1A.SBJ-SEQ-7.OBJ-eat
a-na-pítá *ku San Francîsco.*
1A.SBJ-PST-go to San Francisco
'The hyena ate the corn. Having eaten it, he went to San Francisco.'

b. *Fîsi* *a-na-dyá* *chí-manga.* *Á-tá-dyá* *icho,* *a-na-pítá* *ku*
1A.hyena 1A.SBJ-PST-eat 7-corn 1A.SBJ-SEQ-eat 7.it 1A.SBJ-PST-go to
San Francîsco.
San Francisco
'The hyena ate the corn. Having eaten it (something other than corn), he went to San Francisco.'

(from Bresnan and Mchombo 1987: 748–749)

The object marker in (5a) is anaphoric to the discourse topic but the analytic pronoun in (5b) cannot be topic-anaphoric. This serves as indirect evidence that the Chichewa object marker is a pronoun and not an agreement marker. On the other hand, if a language, or a particular verbal affix in a language, has progressed to Stage III, then the bound form has lost its semantic function as pronoun, so it is no longer in paradigmatic opposition with the analytic pronouns. The analytic pronoun is then the only option available and so it loses any specialization with regard to discourse function. Bresnan and Mchombo argue that this is the case for Chichewa analytic subject pronouns: they can either be anaphoric to discourse-old topics or introduce new ones, thus supporting the analysis of the subject marker as a true agreement marker.

That argument is based on a fundamental contrast between pronominals and agreement markers: the former are subject to discourse-related semantic restrictions that the latter lack. That observed contrast plays an important role in our understanding of this issue. Evans (1999: 256–7) observes that agreement morphemes are "non-committal about reference and discourse status," noting that a third person singular verb form in many languages like English is "compatible with any possible referential status of the subject":

(7) a. anaphoric pronouns: She come-**s**.
b. definite NPs: The old postman come-**s** every morning.
c. indefinites: A tall/different man come-**s** here every day.
d. negative quantifiers Noone civilized ring-**s** so early.
e. NPs under the scope of *again:* A new president lie-**s** again every term.

(Evans 1999: 256–7)

This flexibility suggests that English third person singular *-s* is an agreement marker and not a pronoun. In contrast, true pronominals, whether free or incorporated, have semantic restrictions. Let us consider some of those differences in turn.

Examples (7a, b, c) show that the agreement marker allows definite or indefinite triggers. In contrast, a key semantic property of pronouns is specificity. Except in certain situations such as when it is bound by a semantic operator such as a quantifier (e.g. *Every girl$_i$ thinks she$_i$ is pretty*), a pronoun normally refers to a specific entity or entities. Austin and Bresnan (1996) and Legate (2002) argue on that basis that the argument cross-referencing morphemes on verbs and auxiliaries in Warlpiri (Australian) are agreement markers and not incorporated pronouns. They note that NP arguments can be interpreted as either definite or indefinite depending on context (8); in example (9), the word order and context force an indefinite, existential interpretation. In contrast, the omission of an NP argument forces a specific interpretation, so that (10) cannot mean 'Someone is spearing someone or something.'

(8) *Ngarrka-ngku=ka wawirri panti-rni.* [Warlpiri]
man-ERG=PRS kangaroo.ABS spear-NPST
'The/a man is spearing the/a kangaroo.'
(Simpson 1991: 153)

(9) *Balgo Mission-rla ka-lu Warlpiri-ji.* [Warlpiri]
Balgo Mission-LOC IPFV-3PL Warlpiri-TOP
'At Balgo Mission there are Warlpiri people living.'
(Legate 2002: 71)

(10) *Panti-rni=ka.* [Warlpiri]
spear-NPST=PRS
'He/she is spearing him/her/it.'
(Simpson 1991: 153)

This contrast in interpretation follows if the omission of argument NPs is a case of null anaphora (pro-drop) of the type found also in agreement-poor languages like Japanese, Chinese, and many others, that is, languages lacking verb morphology to cross-reference the arguments of the verb. Null arguments of this kind have a pronoun-like interpretation, as seen in (10), while full NP arguments have a broader range of interpretations. But this contrast is mysterious if all of these sentences have incorporated pronominal arguments.

While pronouns typically encode specific reference, specificity does not necessarily entail that a verbal affix is an incorporated pronominal rather than an agreement marker. It is possible that an agreement marker could retain the restriction to specific reference as a semantic vestige of its pronominal pedigree. Indeed it has been observed that certain agreement markers appear only under a condition of specificity or animacy in various languages including Bantu languages (Givón 1976; Wald 1979) and some Spanish dialects (Suñer 1988). Regarding clitic doubling in some Spanish dialects, Suñer (1988) argues on the basis of extraction and other evidence that the NP associate of a clitic is an argument and not an adjunct, hence the clitic is an agreement marker. But she further notes that such clitic agreement markers, which are typically optional and often colloquial, require specific (and animate) reference, hence the contrast between the unacceptability of a clitic doubling the *non-specific* NP in (11a) and the acceptability of a *specific* one in (11b) (Suñer 1988: 396, ex. 6b and 7b):

(11) a. *(*La) buscaban a alguien que los ayudara.* [Spanish]
her 3PL.searched for somebody who them could.help.SBJ
'They were looking for somebody who could help them.'

b. *Diariamente, la escuchaba a una mujer que cantaba tangos.*
daily, her 3SG.listened to a woman who sang.IND tangos
'Every day he listened to a woman who sang tangos.'

In a related vein, agreement markers in some languages cross-reference only free pronouns, not common noun phrases. See Bresnan (2001a: 147) for discussion and references.

Negative quantifier NPs can trigger agreement just like any other NP, as shown in (7d). But while certain left-dislocated NPs can bind pronouns (*Mary, she always rings very early*), negative quantifiers cannot (**Noone civilized, he rings very early*). This was observed by Rizzi (1986) for Italian clitic pronouns:

(12) **Nessuno, lo conosco in questa citta.* [Italian]
nobody, him know.1SG in this city
'Nobody, I know him in this city.'
(Bresnan 2001a: 23, ex. 20a)

Another difference involves the scope of adverbs like *again* in (7e) (Evans 1999). The sentence *Mary caught a fish again today* presupposes that she caught a fish previously, but not (necessarily) the same fish. In contrast, a sentence with a pronoun such as *Mary caught it, a fish, again today*, has only the implausible reading in which she had caught the same fish previously. The reason is that the indefinite *a fish* introduces an existential quantifier, which can be under the scope of *again* in the former sentence, while the pronoun *it* in the latter sentence has specific reference, hence lacks scope. Evans (1999) uses this scopal property of words like *again* to argue that the Bininj Gun-Wok (Australian) third person subject / third person object portmanteau verbal prefix *bi-* is an agreement marker rather than an incorporated pronominal (example from Carroll 1995 cited in Evans 1999: 271):

(13) Referring to a cannibal who had already speared various people:
wanjh bi-yawoyh-yam-i na-buyika [Bininj Gun-Wok]
then 3 > 3.PST-again-spear-PST.IPFV M-other
'then he would (go again and) spear another'
(*not:* 'then he would spear it again')

This sentence clearly does not presuppose that the cannibal had the same victim before. That implausible interpretation would however be expected if the verb incorporated an object pronoun.

According to the influential but controversial Pronominal Argument Hypothesis, certain languages have the special property that all arguments of a verb are expressed within the morphology of the verb itself, either as incorporated pronouns or incorporated common nouns (Jelinek 1984; Baker 1996). This would be like the Stage II language schematized in (4), only instead of *(Marie$_i$,) she$_i$-likes strawberries*, we would find incorporated pronominal objects as well as subjects, as in *(Marie$_i$,) she$_i$-likes-them$_j$ (strawberries$_j$)*; or noun incorporation, as in *(Marie$_i$,) she$_i$-strawberry-likes*. Since all arguments are incorporated, any NP associates of the affixal pronouns (*Marie*; or *strawberries* when it is an NP and not an incorporated noun root) must necessarily be adjuncts. Baker (1996), who classifies such languages as *polysynthetic*, argues that Mohawk is polysynthetic. That argument is based on several pieces of evidence that the NP associates of the verbal affixes are always adjuncts, never true arguments.

Among Baker's many arguments, two are mentioned here. First, Baker reasons that a polysynthetic language is predicted to lack true NP anaphors such as (morphologically free) reflexive and reciprocal pronouns such as *himself* and *each other.* Briefly put, the reason is that a sentence like 'John likes himself,' in such a language, would be, in effect, 'John, he-likes-him, himself.' The object anaphor could never be in a position from which it could be bound by the subject. In a related argument, Baker reasons that such a language should lack true quantified NPs (QNPs) like *everybody*, which do not refer to a group but rather encode a quantifier (such a true QNP is singular, cp. *Everybody is/*are dancing.*) The reason is that QNPs normally cannot bind pronouns from adjunct positions: **Every man$_i$, he$_i$ left.* Indeed, Mohawk lacks both NP anaphors and true QNPs. However, Legate (2002: 58–9) disputes the cross-linguistic generalization that polysynthetic languages lack QNPs and challenges some of Baker's other arguments as well.

Another criterion for distinguishing pronominal affixes from agreement was proposed by Nevins (2008). Nevins observes that the form of a pronoun is not expected to depend upon tense, while that of an agreement marker could vary. Indeed, many forms that appear on independent grounds to be incorporated pronouns are tense-invariant, while agreement markers can vary across tenses. Nevins (2008) notes that Dutch second person *-t*, Latin first person *-am*, Russian first person *-u*, and English third person *-s* are all tense-sensitive: they have different allomorphs in different tenses and often are synthetic with the tense marker itself. This supports the view that they are agreement markers and not pronouns. In contrast, clitics like Romance *le*, Greek *mu*, Kashmiri *s*, Basque *g*, and Georgian *v* are tense-invariant: both past and present tense employ them, thus making possible a pronoun analysis. Coppock and Wechsler (2012: 8–9) apply this criterion to Hungarian, arguing that the definite inflection on verbs is a definite agreement marker and not an incorporated object pronoun. They contrast the definite verb forms, which vary across tense (e.g. *szeret-i* like-3SG.DEF vs. *szeret-t-e* like-PST-3SG.DEF), to the special extraparadigmatic verbal affix *lak/-lek*, which is used with a first person subject and second person object: the latter is invariant across all tenses and moods, suggesting that this second person object form, unlike the definite object inflection, could be a true incorporated object pronoun in Hungarian.

3. The function of agreement in grammar; locality

The fact that agreement morphemes are historical vestiges of incorporated pronouns does not entail that agreement itself lacks a practical function in grammar. On the contrary, grammatical agreement is one of the three main mechanisms employed by languages for signaling grammatical relations like subject and object: head-marking (agreement), dependent-marking (case), and word order (Nichols 1986). Matching of phi-features between the triggering dependent phrase and the target form aids syntactic coherence by helping the listener to pick out the dependent from among the other phrases in the sentence. Similarly, anaphoric agreement between a pronoun and its antecedent aids in discourse coherence. This function has been confirmed by numerous processing studies of language use in real-time which have shown that "Coherence in language relies in part on basic devices like number agreement." (Bock, Nicol, and Cutting 1999: 330).

The two main alignment systems for grammatical relations, nominative-accusative and ergative-absolutive systems, are most typically associated with case systems and are named for the cases found in the language: nominative, accusative, ergative, absolutive. But both systems are also well-represented among agreement systems in the world's languages. In a *nominative-accusative agreement* system, a verbal morpheme cross-references the subject regardless of whether the verb is transitive or intransitive, and if the language has object agreement then the object agreement marker on a transitive verb cross-references the object. Nominative-accusative systems are illustrated in several of the examples above, including the Chichewa example (5). In an *ergative-absolutive agreement* system the same verbal affix (the absolutive) cross-references the object of a transitive and the subject of an intransitive, with a distinct form (the ergative) to cross-reference the subject of a transitive. An example of ergative-absolutive agreement is in the Northwest Caucasian language Abaza (Tallerman 1998: 161–2). The third person singular absolutive marker *d-* cross-references subjects of intransitives (*d-θád* 'He/She has gone') and objects of transitives (*d-h-bád* 'We saw him/her'). The third person singular ergative marker, which cross-references subjects of transitives, is distinct and moreover distinguishes gender, *l-* for feminine (*h-l-bád*, 'She saw us') and *y-* for masculine (*h-y-bád* 'He saw us').

The fact that grammatical agreement signals grammatical relations such as subject and object explains certain observed locality conditions on the relation between the agreement trigger and target. Grammatical agreement, or at least a well-defined subcase of agreement, is expected to be syntactically local with respect to the structure of the sentence in the same way that the relation between a predicator and its dependents is local. On the other hand anaphoric agreement is not expected to be local in the same sense. Broadly speaking, anaphoric agreement relations are defined on discourse structure while grammatical agreement relations belong to the structural syntax. One theoretical consequence of this division is a difference in locality: "Our theory tells us that grammatical agreement relations (...) can be distinguished from anaphoric agreement relations by locality: only the anaphoric agreement relations can be non-local to the agreeing predicator." (Bresnan and Mchombo 1987: 752–3) In cases of grammatical agreement, a verb cannot specify agreement features for just any phrase, anywhere in a sentence, but rather is restricted to those with direct, or at least a very close, grammatical relationship to the verb. For example, a transitive verb selects its subject and object NPs but has nothing to say about whether there should be a PP embedded inside its subject. Hence the agreement on the verb does not register facts about a PP embedded in the subject either. However, some interesting cases of so-called Long-Distance Agreement appear to violate this strict locality (Polinsky and Potsdam 2001; Bhatt 2005).

4. Agreement in form versus meaning

Recall the disjunction between semantic and formal properties of the trigger in the definition of agreement provided at the beginning of this article: "systematic covariance between a semantic or formal property of one element and a formal property of another." (Steele 1978: 610). Now we address the question of whether the target is sensitive to a semantic or formal property of the trigger. As noted already, in example (1) above the subject varies both in form (singular versus plural) and in meaning (denoting one versus multiple girls), so it is not clear which property is responsible for the number feature of the verb. But in those cases where it is clear, we find a split between semantic and formal agreement.

Several factors influence whether agreement is governed by form or meaning. The main factors can be divided into syntactic properties of the trigger and syntactic properties of the target. First consider the trigger. Focusing for concreteness on the subject number agreement of an English verb, we can identify instances of both formal and semantic agreement. Some data clearly indicate that agreement is driven by the morphology of the subject trigger, ignoring the meaning of the subject if needed:

(14) a. *His clothes are/*is dirty but his hands are clean.*
b. *His clothing is/*are dirty but his hands are clean.*
c. *On average 1 quart of milk is/*are consumed per day in this household.*
d. *On average 1.0 quarts of milk are/*is consumed per day in this household.*

Plural nouns lacking a singular form, like the English nouns *clothes, scissors, pants*, and *leftovers*, are called *pluralia tantum* nouns. The classification of such nouns is not entirely arbitrary, that is, the denotation is typically related in some way to the semantic notion of plurality. Nouns like *scissors* and *pants* are inherent grammatical duals in the sense that they use the count classifier *pair*, as in *a pair of scissors/pants* (Copestake 1992; Copestake 1995), and they have a bipartite physical structure consisting of two legs or blades. But one blade of a pair of scissors is not called a *scissor*, nor is a pantleg referred to as a *pant* (**I got a mustard stain on my left pant*), and moreover, not every noun with similar meaning is a pluralia tantum noun, e.g. *brassiere* and *underwear* also have a bipartite structure but the former is an ordinary count noun, the latter a mass noun. Collective pluralia tantum nouns suggest semantic plurality, such as *clothes* which suggests more than one article of clothing. But semantic minimal pairs such as the nouns *clothes* and *clothing* in (14a, b) show that agreement is driven by the form, not the meaning of the subject. The contrast in (14c, d), based on (Krifka 1995: 407), shows that number assignment to the noun itself is subject to non-semantic conventions: in this case, the convention is that English numerals with decimal points select plural nouns. Verb agreement follows whatever morphological number value characterizes the noun trigger as a consequence of such conventions.

On the other hand, the examples in (15) point to the opposite conclusion, namely semantic agreement.

(15) a. *[My friend and colleague] is/are here.*
(is: 1 person / are: 2 people) (King and Dalrymple 2004: 75)
b. *To err is human, to forgive divine.* (Alexander Pope)
c. *To err and to forgive are/*is human and divine, respectively.*
d. *To err and to forgive are/*is equally human.*
e. *To start a war and to blame the enemy is/#are hypocritical.*

The conjoined subject in example (15a) refers to a single individual when the singular verb is used (the friend is the colleague), while it refers to two individuals when the plural verb is used. Conjoined verb phrases trigger plural agreement when the predicate has a distributive interpretation as in (15c, d), that is, when the predicate's meaning distributes over the individual conjuncts of the subject so that, for example, (15d) entails that to err is human and that to forgive is human. But a non-distributive predicate as in (15e) does not allow a plural verb under the intended interpretation: (15e) does not entail that to start a war is hypocritical, nor that to blame the enemy is hypocritical. Instead, hypocrisy is attributed precisely to the conjunction of the two. The semantics of number is a complex area (Link 1983; Krifka 1995). But the crucial point is that the syntax of the subjects in (15c–e) is essentially the same: a conjoined infinitive verb phrase. These subjects do not seem to differ appreciably in grammatical form. Apparently it is the meaning of the subject that determines the verb form, or rather, as suggested below, the number feature of the verb form affects the meaning.

The contrast between (14) and (15) depends upon the trigger. Broadly speaking, agreement is driven by a formal grammatical feature of the trigger, but only if the trigger has such a feature. If not, then the semantics takes over (Wechsler and Hahm 2011; Wechsler 2011). Specifically, each subject NP in (14) has a clear head noun, namely *clothes*, *clothing, quart,* and *quarts* in (14a–d) respectively. Being endocentric (headed), the NP simply inherits the formal phi features of its head noun, and this determines agreement on the verb. Thus a singular expletive subject triggers singular agreement, regardless of meaning. Contrast (15d) with *It is/*are equally human to err and to forgive* (McCloskey 1991). But the coordinate NP subject in (15a) lacks a (unique) head noun, hence the subject fails to supply a formal feature to its verb. Similarly, infinitive VPs, whether coordinate or not, lack number features entirely because their heads lack number features, so there again the meaning determines agreement.

A similar point can be illustrated with French gender agreement. The predicate adjectives in (16a, b) show grammatical gender agreement with the subject, masculine in (16a) since *mur* 'wall' is lexically masculine, feminine in (16b) since *table* 'table' is lexically feminine. But when the subject is unmarked for grammatical gender, as when it is the second person pronoun *tu*, the gender value of the predicate adjective becomes semantically potent:

(16) a. *La table est vielle.* (= 2a) [French]
the.F.SG table be.3SG old.F
'The table is old.'

b. *Le mur est vieux.* (= 2b)
the.M.SG wall be.3SG old.M
'The wall is old.'

c. *Tu es vielle.*
you.SG are.2SG old.F
'You (a female) are old.'

d. *Tu es vieux.*
you.SG are.2SG old.M
'You (a male) are old.'

This simple markedness principle, that the feature of the target is semantically interpreted whenever the trigger lacks marking for a formal feature, plays a role in some of the discussions below.

The markedness approach predicts that a formal grammatical feature of the trigger, if there is one, takes priority over a semantic feature. The question then is what determines whether a formal grammatical feature of the NP is available. The idea suggested above is that it is available if the NP has a head word that is marked for phi-features. That is, endocentricity and phi marking of the head of the trigger NP are necessary conditions for supplying grammatical phi-features to the target. But they are apparently not sufficient. There are several cases that meet those criteria but nevertheless ignore the head features, showing semantic agreement instead.

One such case arises in the phenomenon of *reference transfer* (Nunberg 1995). Suppose two restaurant servers are discussing various customers, using the customers' food orders to refer to them. One waiter might say that *The ham sandwich is sitting at table 20*, and so on. Nunberg (1995: 115) notes that verb agreement is driven by the *transferred* referent of the subject:

(17) *The french fries at table 7 is/*are getting impatient.*

The waiter uses a singular verb because he is referring not to the french fries per se but to the person who ordered them. The problem for the markedness approach is that the subject of (17) has the plural head noun *french fries* (cp. *The french fries at table 7 are/ *is greasy*), yet agreement follows the semantics.

A second problem arises with certain English NPs of the form [Det N of NP2]$_{NP1}$. An apparently endocentric NP fails to trigger the agreement feature of its head noun, showing semantic agreement instead. For example, in (18a) importance is attributed to the *variety*, while in (18b) it is the vegetables, not the variety, that are on sale. The problem is that the noun *variety* is apparently the syntactic head in both cases (Reid 2011, inter alia):

(18) a. *[A variety of fresh vegetables] is important for good health.*
b. *[A variety of fresh vegetables] are on sale at the market.*
c. *If you are interested in fresh vegetables, a variety are available.*

Such examples raise the question of why the target verbs in (18b, c) ignore the singular number feature on the noun *variety*. Apparently such nouns are too weak semantically to force the number feature to project to the NP, behaving instead like classifiers or quantifiers (cp. *a number of*, *a set of*, *a lot of*, and so on). Semantic agreement is the result. A similar phenomenon occurs with quantified NPs in many languages, including Serbian/Croatian (Wechsler and Zlatić, 2003: 121).

Scandinavian *pancake sentences*, illustrated by the Swedish example (19b), pose a related problem (Faarlund 1977; Enger 2004; Wechsler 2013):

(19) a. *Pankak-er är goda.* [Swedish]
pancake-PL be.PERS good.PL
'Pancakes are good.'

b. *Pankak-er är gott.*
pancake-PL be.PERS good.N.SG
Roughly, 'Eating pancakes is good.'
(Wellander 1955: 379)

Sentence (19a) illustrates normal plural agreement of the adjective with the plural noun *pankaker* 'pancakes'. But the adjective in (19b) appears in neuter singular, which is the default form that appears with subjects lacking formal phi-features, such as infinitival subjects, for example. As suggested by the English translation of (19b), such sentences are appropriate for expressing a predication on some sort of situation related to the referent of the subject NP, in this case a situation related to pancakes, such as eating them. The following attested sentence contains an English pancake sentence, with a plural subject (*steroids*) and singular verb (*is*): *Crack is a cop-out, this reasoning goes; steroids is a business decision* (example from Reid 2011). Once again, the lexical phi-features of the head noun are somehow blocked from triggering agreement.

Having reviewed some ways in which the choice between formal and semantic agreement is influenced by properties of the trigger, let us consider the influence of the target. Comrie (1975) and Corbett (1979, 1983, 2006) surveyed agreement processes across different target types in many typologically diverse languages with respect to whether a given agreement type is more likely to involve grammatical agreement (which he called syntactic agreement) or semantic agreement. Corbett summarized his rather striking crosslinguistic findings in the following Agreement Hierarchy (Corbett 1979, 2006):

(20) The Agreement Hierarchy (Corbett 2006: 207)
attributive < predicate < relative pronoun < personal pronoun
⟵ syntactic agreement ——— semantic agreement ⟶
As we move rightwards along the hierarchy, the likelihood of semantic agreement will increase monotonically (that is, with no intervening decrease).

The Agreement Hierarchy entails, for example, that if a given noun shows a split between the features determined on personal pronouns and relative pronouns, then the relative pronouns will show syntactic agreement and the personal pronouns semantic agreement, rather than the other way around. If there is a split between all pronouns and predicates, then the predicate shows syntactic agreement and the pronouns semantic agreement; and so on.

Evidence for the Agreement Hierarchy comes from agreement *mismatches*, also called *hybrid* agreement. In an agreement mismatch, a single trigger determines different features on different targets. Agreement mismatches provide clues about the operation of normal, non-mismatched agreement (Corbett 1983, 1991, 2006). One example discussed by Corbett (1983) involves Serbian/Croatian collective common nouns such as *deca* 'children', which triggers feminine singular on modifiers, here *ta* ('that.F.SG') and *dobra* ('good.F.SG'), but neuter plural on coreferential pronouns (*ona* in 21):

(21) *Posmatrali smo ovu dobru decu*$_i$. [Serbian/Croatian]
watched.1PL AUX this.F.SG good.F.SG children.ACC
'We watched these good children$_i$.'

Ona$_i$ *su se lepo igrala.*
they.N.PL AUX.3PL REFL nicely played.N.PL
'They$_i$ played well.'

(Wechsler and Zlatić 2003: 6)

The neuter plural found on the pronoun is not the normal semantically motivated form for groups of mixed or unknown sex in Serbian/Croatian. Masculine plural is used for that, and indeed a masculine plural pronoun is a possible alternative to the neuter plural pronoun in the second sentence of (21), as discussed in Section 5 below. Example (21) shows that both {*feminine, singular*} and {*neuter, plural*} are grammatical (i.e., formal) feature sets lexically associated with the noun lexeme *deca* 'children'.

Formal accounts of mixed agreement assume two distinct though related phi feature sets for nouns (Pollard and Sag 1994; Kathol 1999; Wechsler and Zlatić 2000; Wechsler and Zlatić 2003; King and Dalrymple 2004). Pollard and Sag (1994) proposed that one of those two feature sets, the elements of which are called *Index features*, is tied to the referential index of the noun. Anaphoric binding involves sharing of the index of the binder and the index of the pronoun that it binds, which explains anaphoric agreement. Regardless of the exact formal account, the point is that anaphoric agreement between a pronoun and its antecedent involves a certain set of phi-features of the antecedent NP, a set called Index features. The neuter plural pronoun in the second sentence of (21) above reflects the neuter plural Index features of its antecedent, the noun *deca* 'children' (see Section 5 below). In contrast, NP-internal modifers of the noun *deca* 'children' appear in the feminine singular, as illustrated in the first sentence of (21). Thus in addition to the neuter plural Index features, the noun *deca* is also lexically associated with feminine singular features. Features in this latter set Wechsler and Zlatić (2000, 2003) dubbed *Concord features*.

The lexical Concord features of a given noun lexeme are closely related to that noun's inflected form, while the Index features are closely related to the noun's meaning. The Index-meaning correlation can be seen in the plural Index feature of *deca* 'children', which also has plural semantics: more than one child. The Concord-form correlation has several facets. To the extent that declension class correlates with gender, it is the Concord (not Index) gender that is relevant, hence the noun *deca* belongs to the second declension class, which is typical of feminine (not neuter) nouns. Also, the inflected forms are determined by the Concord (not Index) number, hence the noun *deca* not only determines singular number agreement on its NP-internal modifiers but it also is itself declined as a singular noun. These correlations can be summarized in a chain of defeasible constraints applying to the lexical representations of nouns (from Wechsler and Zlatić 2000: 800, 2003: 83):

(22) morphology ⇔ Concord ⇔ Index ⇔ semantics

In essence, the Concord features reflect the noun's morphological properties (captured by the constraint morphology ⇔ Concord), while the Index features reflect its semantic properties (captured by the constraint Index ⇔ semantics).

The relation between the Concord and Index phi feature sets for a given noun (captured by the constraint Concord ⇔ Index) is usually identity. Lexically encoded Concord/Index mismatches with double marking, as is found with the Serbian/Croatian collective nouns that trigger feminine on some targets and neuter on others, are rare. Looking across languages, the bifurcation between a nominal trigger's Concord and Index features is more often seen in situations where the noun is marked for a feature of one type and unmarked for the other, e.g. marked for Index number but not Concord number.

Due to the markedness principle illustrated above with examples (14) and (15), agreement targets default to the semantics when the trigger is unmarked for a feature.

For example, consider the question of how French finite verbs and predicate adjectives, respectively, agree with a subject, in light of examples (23)–(24) below. Are these targets sensitive to the meaning or the form of the subject NP?

(23) a. *Vous êtes loyal.* [French]
you.PL be.2PL loyal.M.SG
'You (formal; one male addressee) are loyal.'

b. *Vous êtes loyaux.* [French]
you.PL be.2PL loyal.PL [French]
'You (multiple addressees) are loyal.'

(24) *Ces ciseaux sont géniaux!* [French]
this.PL scissors are.3PL brilliant.M.PL
'These scissors are cool!'

(Wechsler 2012: 1016)

The French second person plural pronoun *vous* refers to multiple addressees, and also has an honorific or polite use for a single (or multiple) addressee. When used to refer politely to one addressee, *vous* triggers mixed agreement: singular on a predicate adjective but plural on the verb, as seen in (23a). Similar facts are observed for honorific second person pronouns in Romanian, Czech, Bulgarian, and many other languages (Comrie 1975; Corbett 1983, 2006). When *vous* 'you.PL' is the trigger, any bound anaphors, as well as the finite verb, must show second person plural agreement, irrespective of whether the referent is semantically singular (in the honorific usage) or plural. But predicate adjectives indicate semantic cardinality, showing singular or plural depending on whether *vous* refers to one addressee (23a) or more than one (23b). Like the number, the gender of the adjective inflection is also semantically potent, as seen in (23a), where the addressee is understood as male due to the masculine form of the adjective.

However, when the trigger is a pluralia tantum noun like French *ciseaux* 'scissors' then both the verb and the adjective invariably show grammatical number and gender agreement, hence a plural verb and masculine plural adjective (see 24). This variable behavior of predicate adjective targets across these two types of triggers suggests a markedness account, as in (14)–(16) above. Adjectives agree with the Concord features of the trigger. But suppose the triggers differ in their markedness properties: the local pronouns lack Concord features while the pluralia tantum common nouns have them. Failing to find a Concord number or gender feature on the subject pronoun *vous*, the adjective's agreement features are semantically potent (see 23). But verb agreement depends on the Index features, for which triggers of both types are marked:

(25) a. *vous*: [Index: {2^{nd}, *pl*}] (n.b.: unmarked for Concord phi-features)
b. *ciseaux*: [Index/Concord: {3^{rd}, *pl, masc*}]

As far as the syntax of agreement is concerned, the common noun *ciseaux* 'scissors' is an ordinary common noun: the Concord and Index are both marked, and for the same features, namely {third person, masculine, plural}. Such pluralia tantum nouns are special only with regard to interpretation. Hence all agreement is masculine plural, although the scissors are semantically neither plural nor male. But assuming that *vous* is unmarked for Concord features, we predict that Concord targets are semantically interpreted, thus explaining (23). Even attributive adjectives, which are at the extreme syntactic agreement end of the Agreement Hierarchy (20), have semantically interpreted phi-features when the trigger is *vous*, as shown by the contrast between *Pauvre vous!* 'Poor.SG you' (one addressee) and *Pauvres vous!* 'Poor.PL you' (more than one addressee).

Some dialects of English have agreement mismatches with collective nouns like *band, committee*, and *team*:

(26) *%You can usually tell when a[SG] band are[PL] enjoying themselves.*
(dialectal, primarily British)

In some dialects of English, especially British variants, collective nouns like *committee* and *team* can trigger plural agreement on a verb even though they are morphologically singular and alternate with plurals (*committees, teams*), and morever take a singular determiner (Copestake 1992). Internally the NP *a band* is singular, but it nonetheless can take either singular or plural agreement on the verb, with an effect on the semantic interpretation. Copestake (1992) shows that plural agreement produces a plural sum interpretation virtually equivalent to a normal plural NP denoting the members of the group, such as *the members of the band*. She noted that, as with normal plurals, individual members can be referred to using phrases like *one of NP* (cp. *one of the members of the band*), as in (27a). Also, for human-denoting group nouns, a relative clause is introduced by *who* if plural agreement is used, and by *which* if it is not (27b, c). This follows since the members are human, while the group is an abstract institutional entity, hence the non-human relative pronoun is appropriate (examples from Copestake 1992: 101–102).

(27) a. *One of the band smashed her guitar.*
b. *The band who get (/*gets) top billing at the festival receive (/*receives) a prize.*
c. *The band which gets (/*get) top billing at the festival receives (/*receive) a prize.*

These group plurals have attracted the attention of linguists from a variety of perspectives. Bock, Nicol, and Cutting (1999) used them in psycholinguistic experiments designed to assess meaning- versus form-based number agreement. They compared the behavior of different agreement targets, namely verbs and two types of pronouns, in a sentence-completion task, and found that verbs tended to reflect the morphological number of the collective controller, whereas pronouns were more likely to reflect the notional number. Bock, Nicol, and Cutting conclude that the number features of pronouns may be retrieved under control from the speaker's meaning, while the number features of verbs are more likely to be retrieved under control from the utterance's form. This observation is consistent with Corbett's Agreement Hierarchy in (20) above.

If we further distinguish among the different part-of-speech categories of predicates then the following Predicate Hierarchy emerges (Comrie 1975; Corbett 2006).

(28) The Predicate Hierarchy
verb > participle > adjective > noun
← syntactic agreement semantic agreement →
(Corbett 2006: 231)

The Predicate Hierarchy is considered to be a stable cross-linguistic generalization, confirmed by typological study of diverse languages.

However, Wechsler and Hahm (2011) argue that verbs and adjectives are reversed, that is, that adjectives should precede verbs on the Predicate Hierarchy depicted in (28). Comrie supported his Predicate Hierarchy entirely on the basis of polite plural pronoun triggers, and Corbett expanded the empirical base, adding coordinate subject triggers. But it was suggested above that triggers of both types lack Concord phi-features, thus forcing semantic interpretation of the target features. This suggests that predicate adjectives only appear to favor semantic agreement; the real cause of the semantic agreement is the trigger. When the trigger is a noun phrase headed by a hybrid common nouns, which are marked for those phi-features, then we see the real effect of the target type. For example, Serbian/Croatian *deca* 'children' discussed above, is notionally plural, referring to an aggregate of children, and marked with feminine singular formal Concord features (Corbett 1983; Wechsler and Zlatić 2003). Interestingly, this noun triggers plural on verbs but feminine singular on secondary predicate adjectives:

(29) a. *Ta dobra deca dolaze* [Serbian/Croatian]
that.F.SG good.F.SG children come.3PL
'Those good children came.'

b. *Ja smatram decu gladnom.*
I consider children hungry.INS.F.SG
'I consider the children hungry.'
(Wechsler and Zlatić, 2003: 53)

The instrumental plural form *gladnim* cannot replace *gladnom* in (29b). Thus with a fully marked trigger such as the hybrid noun *deca*, verb agreement is more, not less, semantic than predicate adjective agreement. Whether agreement is syntactic or semantic depends on both the target type and the trigger type, and it is important to control for each factor in assessing the other.

5. Anaphoric agreement in form versus meaning

Pronoun-antecedent agreement is subject to grammatical constraints, but also extends beyond the scope of sentence grammar and into the discourse. As such, pronoun agreement provides us with a tool for exploring the limits of grammar and the nature of discourse processes. Semantic agreement is typical of coreferential elements since they must have semantically compatible anchoring conditions in order to corefer. In a natural gender language like English, the antecedent of the feminine pronouns *she* or *her* normally must be female, because the pronouns themselves are semantically restricted to female referents, as shown by the interpretation of deictic locutions like *Who is she?* (pointing to a female). Thus some cases of covariation of form between a pronoun and its antecedent follow simply from coreference itself, together with the meanings of the pronoun and antecedent.

In addition, the formal phi-features of the agreement trigger can survive into the discourse, even beyond the end of the sentence containing the trigger. For example, the feminine pronoun *elle* in the following French two-sentence discourse appears to show inter-sentential agreement with the grammatical gender of the antecedent *une chaise* 'a chair':

(30) *Pierre a une chaise Louis XV. Elle est belle.* [French]
Pierre has a.F chair Louis XV PRON.3SG.F is beautiful.F
'Pierre has a Louis the 15th chair$_i$. It$_i$ (Fem.) is beautiful.'

A pronoun's gender sometimes matches an unspoken common noun, a well-attested and well-known phenomenon in grammatical gender languages, as in the following French examples of *deixis*, where the referent is physically present (31), and *exophora*, where it is not (32):

(31) Speaker gestures towards a car:
Elle est sale. (*l'auto* or *la voiture*, 'the car', both FEM) [French]
it.F.SG is dirty
'It is dirty.'
(Cornish 1999: 118, citing Kleiber 1994)

(32) At an open-air swimming pool in southwest France. A customer, on entering the reception area, to myself, who was just leaving:
Elle est froide? (*l'eau* 'water', FEM) [French]
it.F.SG is cold.F
'Is it cold?'
(Cornish 1999: 131)

There has been a great deal of discussion of pronoun agreement vis-à-vis these two sources for the pronoun interpretation, namely the linguistic antecedent (in anaphora) and the referent made available in the speech context (Dowty and Jacobson 1988; Cornish 1999; Pollard and Sag 1994; Bosch 1989; Tasmowski-DeRijk and Verluyten 1982; Tasmowski and Verluyten 1985).

When the antecedent of a pronoun has clashing grammatical and semantic features, then the pronoun often allows either formal or semantic agreement. For example, in Serbian/Croatian, masculine plural is the default form for pronouns referring to collections of mixed or unknown sex or gender. Recall that *deca* 'children' has neuter plural (Index) features. Hence when the antecedent of a pronoun is *deca* 'children', we find variation between neuter plural and masculine plural:

(33) *Posmatrali smo ovu dobru decu$_i$.* [Serbian/Croatian]
watched.1PL aux this.F.SG good.F.SG children.ACC

(i) *Ona$_i$ su se lepo igrala.* (formal agreement)
they.N.PL AUX.3PL REFL nicely played.N.PL

(ii) *Oni$_i$ su se lepo igrali.* (semantic agreement)
they.M.PL AUX.3PL REFL nicely played.M.PL
'We watched these good children$_i$. They$_i$ played well.'
(Wechsler and Zlatić 2003: 6)

In general pronouns closer to the antecedent within the discourse are more likely to show formal agreement while those further away are more likely to show semantic agreement (Corbett 1983, 1988, 1991). Moreover, when multiple coreferential pronoun targets appear in a discourse, it is rare for a semantically agreeing pronoun to precede a formally agreeing one. Corbett (1991) cites supporting evidence from Old English (p. 242) and Chichewa (p. 250).

Wechsler and Zlatić (1998, 2003) explored the question of how this alternation between formal and semantic agreement on pronouns is affected by the mode of pronoun construal: coreference, bound variable, e-type, paycheck (or lazy pronoun), etc., in Serbian/Croatian. (Kratzer 2009 later carried out a similar study of German and English pronoun agreement.) A Serbian/Croatian coreferential pronoun in a separate sentence from its antecedent alternates between grammatical and semantic agreement, as shown already in (33). However, if the antecedent is in the same sentence, semantic agreement is strongly preferred, as illustrated with the neuter diminutive *devojče* 'girl' in (34).

(34) a. *(Svako) devojče$_i$ misli da je$_i$/*ga$_i$* [Serbian/Croatian]
every.NOM.N.SG girl.N.SG thinks that PRON.ACC.SG.F/*N
Jovan voli.
John likes
'Every/The girl thinks that John loves her.'

b. *Jovan je rekao (svakom) devojčetu da je$_i$/*ga$_i$ voli.*
John AUX told every girl.DAT.N.SG that PRON.ACC.SG.F/*N likes
'John told every/the girl that he loves her.'

(Wechsler and Zlatić 2003: 224)

Semantic gender is observed regardless of whether the antecedent is the subject (34a) or object (34b) and regardless of whether it is a definite NP (*devojče* 'the girl') or a quantifier (*svako devojče* 'every girl').

In contrast, bound reflexive pronouns are split: those with nominative case antecedents require grammatical (Index) agreement, while those with non-nominative antecedents require semantic agreement. Whether the antecedent is a quantifier or referential NP does not appear to affect this pattern:

(35) a. *(Svako) devojče je volelo* [Serbian/Croatian]
every.N.SG girl.NOM.N.SG AUX liked.N.SG
*samo/?*samu sebe.*
own.ACC.N.SG/?*F.SG self.ACC
'Every/The girl liked herself.'

b. *(Svakom) devojčetu je bilo žao same/*samog sebe.*
every.DAT.N.SG girl.DAT.N.SG AUX be.N.SG sorry own.GEN.F.SG/*N.SG self
'Every/The girl felt pity for herself.'

(Wechsler and Zlatić 2003: 209)

Next we turn to e-type or donkey pronouns, pronouns that have a quantifier as antecedent, but are not semantically bound by that quantifier, at least under some analyses (see

Geach 1962; Evans 1980, 1977). Serbian/Croatian donkey pronouns allow either index or pragmatic agreement:

(36) a. *Svaki čovek koji ima decu misli da su* [Serbian/Croatian]
every man who has children thinks that AUX.3PL
ona najpametnija.
they.N.PL smartest.N.PL

b. *Svaki čovek koji ima decu misli da su oni najpametniji.*
every man who has children thinks that AUX.3PL they.M.PL smartest.M.PL
'Every man who has children$_i$ thinks they$_i$ are the smartest.'
(Wechsler and Zlatić 2003: 210)

As shown here, either neuter plural or masculine plural is permitted.

The pronouns Evans (1977) called "genuine pronouns of laziness" (later called *paycheck pronouns*) are not coreferential with their antecedents, but can usually be interpreted by substituting the antecedent noun phrase for the pronoun. Let us now consider paycheck pronouns:

(37) *Otac koji je insistirao da mu deca idu na studije* [Serbian/Croatian]
father who aux insisted that his children go to college
je bio pametniji od onog oca koji je insistirao da se
AUX was smarter from that father who aux insisted that REFL
ona/oni odmah zaposle.
they.N.PL/they.M.PL immediately employed
'The father who insisted that his children go to college was smarter than the father who insisted that they immediately get a job.'

ona (they.N.PL) → *strict or sloppy reading*
oni (they.M.PL) → *only strict reading*
(Wechsler and Zlatić 2003: 206)

Interestingly, in order to yield the pragmatically plausible sloppy interpretation, the pronoun must appear in neuter plural form, showing grammatical agreement with the antecedent *mu deca* 'his children'. The masculine plural pronoun forces the rather implausible strict reading in which the second (less smart) father has the audacity to insist that the children of the first (smarter) father get a job.

To summarize the results of this study of pronoun construal and agreement: Semantic versus grammatical agreement depends on locality and other factors. Grammatical agreement is required for nominative-bound reflexives and genuine pronouns of laziness, while local domains favor semantic agreement for ordinary pronouns. Outside of the local domain, pronouns alternate. Otherwise agreement does not depend on the mode of construal per se, such as bound variable, e-type, or coreference.

6. Coordination and agreement

As Corbett (2006: 263) observes, "Conjoined structures are in a way marginal, and yet they are of key importance for understanding agreement." How do languages handle gender agreement with a coordinate NP when we conjoin NPs with different values for the gender feature? Languages follow two strategies to handle coordination of unlike conjuncts, either *partial agreement* or *resolution* (this terminology follows Corbett 1991). In partial agreement, agreement consults one conjunct and ignores the other(s), as in this example from Ndebele (Bantu) taken from Moosally (1998: 88):

(38) *In-khezo lemi-ganu i-qamukila.* [Ndebele]
12-spoon and.4-plate 4-broke
'The spoons and plates broke.'
(Moosally 1998: 88)

The verb appears with the Noun Class 4 agreement prefix in agreement with the closer conjunct, ignoring the more distant one. The phenomenon of agreement with the nearest conjunct is well attested across many languages. For references, see Corbett (2006: 170).

A resolution rule derives the agreement features of a coordinate NP on the basis of the features of all the individual conjuncts. Example (39) illustrates the purported French resolution rule dictating that mixes of genders are resolved to the masculine.

(39) *Le garçon et sa soeur sont compétents / *compétentes.* [French]
the.M boy and his.F sister are competent.M.PL / competent.F.PL
'The boy and his sister are competent.'
(Wechsler 2008: 568)

If the subject is a conjoined masculine and feminine NP, the predicate adjective appears in masculine plural. Masculine is the unmarked or resolution gender for French.

The question of formal versus semantic agreement (Section 4 above) arises in gender resolution. In French feminine plural is used for a group of females, while masculine (plural) agreement indicates a group of males or a mixed-sex group. According to a long-noted cross-linguistic generalization (Greenberg 1966), the gender used for mixed sex groups in a given language is a constant across different forms of grammatical expression. For example, French uses masculine plural for mixed groups whether in expressions involving coordinate structures (39), plural pronouns, sex-differentiated plural common nouns, non-sex-differentiated plural common nouns, and proper nouns (examples from Wechsler and Zlatić 2003: 181):

(40) *Ils / Elles parlent dans la cuisine.* [French]
they.M.PL / they.F.PL speak.3PL in the kitchen
'They (a male or mixed-sex group / a female group) are talking in the kitchen.'

(41) a. *les Americain-s* [French]
the.PL American-PL
'the male or mixed sex Americans'

b. *les Americain-e-s*
the.PL American-F-PL
'the female Americans'

(42) a. *Les journalistes sont compétents.* [French]
the.PL journalists are competent.M.PL
'The male or mixed sex journalists are competent.'

b. *Les journalistes sont compétentes.*
the.PL journalists are competent.F.PL
'The female journalists are competent.'

(43) a. *Les Dupont sont compétents.* [French]
the.PL name are competent.M.PL
'The Duponts (all male or mixed sex) are competent.'

b. *Les Dupont sont compétentes.*
the.PL name are competent.F.PL
'The Duponts (all female) are competent.'

The simplest explanation for this correlation is that the target gender feature itself has semantic content: feminine is interpreted as '(all) female', and masculine is unmarked. That semantic content is ignored when the trigger bears an inherent grammatical gender feature as in (2) above, but it surfaces when the trigger lacks one. Since a coordinate NP lacks a unique head noun, the agreement feature of the target is semantically interpreted, as suggested already in connection with (15a) above.

Interesting evidence for this view comes from cases where one of the conjunct nouns is a hybrid, lexically specifying feminine grammatical gender despite lacking a semantic restriction to females. An example is the French noun *sentinelle* 'sentry', which triggers feminine agreement on all targets: *la/*le sentinelle* 'the.FEM/*the.MASC sentry'. Assuming that a coordinate structure like the subject of (44) lacks a grammatical gender feature due to its exocentricity, we predict the semantic interpretation of the target feature: masculine, the French gender for a mixed-sex group, and crucially not feminine plural as one would expect if it depended on the grammatical feature, since both conjuncts are grammatically feminine (Wechsler 2008; Farkas and Zec 1995):

(44) *La sentinelle et sa femme ont été pris /*prises* [French]
the.F sentry and his.F wife have been taken.M /*taken.F.PL
en otage.
hostage
'The sentry and his wife were taken hostage.'
(Wechsler 2008: 572)

This suggests that at least some cases of gender agreement with coordinate NPs are not determined by special resolution rules, but rather by consulting the meaning of the coordinate NP.

Bantu languages illustrate the same phenomenon. Bantu coordination resolution is based on meaning and not morphological Noun Class, even though agreement with simple, non-coordinate NPs is based on Noun Class. In Luganda, conjuncts of the same noun class in Luganda can be conjoined, yielding plural agreement of that class (Givón 1970: 252). This property is called distributivity-based resolution below, since the noun class of the coordinate NP distributes over the individual conjuncts. Givón observes that all Bantu languages allow this. But when the conjuncts differ in noun class, then the semantic value of the target Noun Class is activated. In Luganda human-denoting nouns typically fall into class 1/2 (class 1 in singular, class 2 in plural), although there are exceptions. (Following the Bantuist tradition, a noun is lexically associated with a representation of the form *x/y*, where *x* is the noun's singular Noun Class and *y* is its plural Noun Class.) Noun Class 1/2 is the resolution class for humans, while NC 7/8 is used for non-humans, irrespective of the Noun Classes of the conjuncts (Corbett 1991):

(45) *Ek-kazi, aka-ana ne olu-sajja ba-alabwa.* [Luganda]
5-fat.woman 12-small.child and 11-tall.man **2**-were.seen
'The fat woman, small child, and tall man were seen.'

(46) *En-te, omu-su, eki-be ne ely-ato bi-alabwa.*
9-cow 3-wildcat 7-jackal and 5-canoe **8**-were.seen
'The cow, the wildcat, the jackal, and the canoe were seen.'
(Givón 1970: 253)

Of course, with a normal non-coordinate subject the predicate must agree in Noun Class: *ek-kazi* 'fat woman' normally triggers class 5 agreement, and so on. But in coordination resolution the meaning is what matters.

The neat picture of resolution presented thus far encounters a serious empirical shortcoming. It does not extend to resolution of grammatical gender that lacks a semantic correlate, as for example with French inanimates. Corbett (1991: 279) notes that inanimates follow the same rule as animates:

(47) a. *Le livre et le cahier sont neufs / *neuves.* [French]
the.M book(M) and the.M notebook(M) are new.M.PL / *new.F.PL
'The book and the notebook are new.'

b. *La misère et la ruine sont désastreuses / *désastreux.*
the.F misery(F) and the.F ruin(F) are disastrous.F.PL / disastrous.M.PL
'The misery and the ruin are disastrous.'

c. *Ce savoir et cette adresse sont merveilleux / *merveilleuses.*
this.M knowledge(M) and this.F skill(F) are marvellous.M / marvellous.F.PL
'This knowledge and this skill are marvelous.'
(Corbett 1991: 279)

A mix of genders, as in (47c), yields masculine plural agreement. The descriptive generalization is as follows:

(48) French rule:
1. Fem + Fem: use F.PL
2. Elsewhere: use M.PL

The problem is that the gender features of these adjectives are not semantically interpreted, so something else is responsible for resolution in such instances. We return to this issue below after first considering resolution in three-gender systems.

Three-gender systems yield further insights into gender resolution. Two basic patterns emerge, depending on whether markedness or distributivity is primary. Examples of markedness-based systems are Serbian/Croatian and Slovene, which have three genders: masculine, feminine, and neuter. The resolution rule is the same as for the two-gender language French: a group of feminine conjuncts yields feminine plural agreement, and all other combinations result in masculine plural agreement, as shown in the Serbian/ Croatian examples in (49). Perhaps most surprisingly, a coordinate structure with all neuter gender conjuncts triggers, not neuter plural, but masculine plural agreement, as shown in (49c).

(49) a. *Sve snage i sva pažnja biće posvećene toj borbi*
all power.PL(F) and all attention(F) will.be dedicated.**F.PL** this.DAT.SG struggle.DAT.SG
(Corbett 1983: 188)

b. *Ogledalo i cetka za kosu su bili na stolu.*
mirror(N) and brush(F) for hair AUX were.**M.PL** on table
'The mirror and the hair brush were on the table.'
(Wechsler 2008: 569)

c. *Ogledalo i nalivpero su bili / *bila na stolu.*
mirror(N) and fountain.pen(N) AUX were.M.PL/*N.PL on table
'The mirror and the fountain pen were on the table.'
(Wechsler 2008: 569)

The Serbian/Croatian rule is actually identical to the French rule above, but has a different effect because the language has three rather than two genders.

(50) Serbian/Croatian rule:
1. Fem + Fem: use F.PL
2. Elsewhere: use M.PL

The masculine serves as the elsewhere or default gender, serving whenever the conditions for the feminine plural are not met.

However, the Serbian/Croatian type resolution appears to be relatively rare. In most three-gender languages *distributivity* is primary: gender is a distributive feature (Dalrymple 2001: 155), that is, the gender value of a coordinate NP distributes over the conjuncts so that when all conjuncts bear the same gender, then the target must appear in that gender as well. Examples include the Bantu languages (as noted above), as well as Icelandic, Latin, and many others. In Icelandic, when gender is homogeneous across all conjuncts then that gender is inherited by the coordinate structure. Any heterogeneity of gender is resolved with the neuter plural form, as in (51). The Icelandic pattern is summarized in (52).

(51) a. *Drengurinn og telpan eru þreytt.* [Icelandic]
the.boy and the.girl are tired.N.PL
'The boy and the girl are tired.'

b. *ég sá á og lamb, boeði svort.*
I saw ewe(F) and lamb(N), both.N.PL black.N.PL
'I saw a ewe and a lamb, both black.'

(Corbett 1991: 283)

(52) Icelandic rule:
1. Gender α on all conjuncts: use α.PL (α ∈ {M, F, N})
2. Elsewhere: use N.PL

Various feature computation systems have been proposed for calculating the phi-features of conjoined nominals. Dalrymple and Kaplan (2000) propose a theory of feature resolution using closed set descriptions (Dalrymple 2001). Phi feature values are represented with sets of abstract features, and the sets corresponding to the conjuncts are unioned to derive the value for the conjoined NP as a whole. Vincent and Börjars (2000) propose a similar system that uses set intersection instead of union. Both set union and intersection are idempotent (for any set X, $X \cup X = X$ and $X \cap X = X$), which captures the common distributivity property but wrongly disallows the markedness-based type illustrated by Serbian/Croatian above. Recall that in that language, coordinated neuter NPs yield masculine plural agreement. Whether union or intersection is employed, any feature set assigned to neuter will incorrectly yield neuter and not masculine agreement. Wechsler's (2008) system uses intersection but solves this problem by positing that genders lacking a semantic correlate, such as neuter, are ignored by this computation in some languages (such as Serbian/Croatian) but not others (such as Icelandic).

When we coordinate nouns (rather than NPs) under a single determiner, we usually find a rather different situation. Determiner agreement distributes over each of the conjuncts (53d is from King and Dalrymple 2004: 70):

(53) a. *this boy and girl / a boy and girl*
b. **these boy and girl*
c. *these boys and girls*
d. ***This** boy and girl **have** become skilled at setting the places for **their** classmates at snacktime.*

Although *boy and girl* is clearly semantically plural, it allows only a singular determiner (*this, a*). Apparently this is distributive agreement, reflecting the singular form of each conjunct noun, since with plural nouns as in (53c) we get a plural determiner. As shown in (53d), a verb or anaphoric pronoun agreeing with the NP as a whole shows plural agreement, hence semantic agreement, which is consistent with our assumptions above about coordination. King and Dalrymple (2004) survey a number of languages and show that determiner agreement is usually distributive as in English. A rare exception is Russian, which takes a plural determiner with conjoined singulars:

(54) *èti* *mužčina* *i* *ženščina* [Russian]
these.PL man.SG and woman.SG
'this man and woman' (literally 'these man and woman')
(King and Dalrymple 2004: 95)

See King and Dalrymple 2004 for discussion.

7. Person paradigms and person resolution

Next we introduce person marking paradigms before turning to person resolution in coordinate structures. Person marking paradigms vary greatly across languages in their homophony (syncretism) patterns (Cysouw 2003). For example, in standard English, the second person pronoun *you* is not distinguished by number; and present tense verbs (except *be*) distinguish only the third person singular from all other person and number value combinations. The English pattern is not typical, however, and is only one among many different patterns attested in the world's languages. Indeed, both pronouns and agreement targets in other languages vary greatly, splitting up the paradigm in many different ways.

Person paradigms for triggers (personal pronoun systems) and targets maximally distinguish the four person values shown in Table 11.1.

(55) Tab. 11.1: The four attested person values in a maximal person system

Reference set	Person value	Closed set description

speaker(s);
hearer(s);
possibly other(s)
	'inclusive'	{S, H}

speaker(s); possibly other(s) (hearer(s) excluded)	'exclusive'	{S}
hearer(s); possibly other(s) (speaker(s) excluded)	'second person'	{H}
other(s) only	'third person'	{ }

Many languages, including English, collapse inclusive and exclusive into a single first person category, meaning speaker(s), possibly hearer(s), and possibly other(s). Note that the first three rows of Table 11.1 all indicate a meaning that can include other(s). In other words, first and second person plural forms denote a reference set that allows for the inclusion of persons outside the speech act. For example, the Swedish nominative pronoun *ni* 'you.PL' refers to a group that includes at least one hearer; the others in the reference set can be other hearers or any non-hearers other than the speaker. This optional inclusion of non-speech act participants in the denotation of plural first and second person pronouns appears to be a universal property of language (Cysouw 2003; Bobaljik 2008; Wechsler 2010).

Person resolution in coordinate structures will be illustrated with data from NP fronting in Fula (examples from Dalrymple and Kaplan 2000: 782). When an NP is fronted for focus, it triggers anaphoric agreement on an incorporated pronoun on the verb. Fula has the four-value system represented in Table 11.1. Fronted coordinate phrases containing a first person and second person conjunct cooccur with the first person inclusive (1INCL) incorporated pronoun (56a, b); those containing a first person but no second person occur with first person exclusive (1EXCL) (56c, d); those containing a second person conjunct but lacking a first person conjunct occur with second person agreement (56e); and those lacking a first or second person conjunct determine third person (56f):

(56) a. *an e min kö Afriki djodu-dèn.* [Fula]
you and I in Afrika live-1INCL
'You and I, we live in Africa.'

b. *an e Bill e min kö Afriki djodu-dèn.*
you and Bill and I in Afrika live-1INCL
'You and Bill and I, we live in Africa.'

c. *Bill e min kö Afriki mèn-djodi.*
Bill and I in Afrika 1EXCL-live
'Bill and I, we live in Africa.'

d. *Bill e mènèn kö Afriki mèn-djodi.*
Bill and we.EXCL in Afrika 1EXCL-live
'Bill and us, we live in Africa.'

e. *an e Bill kö Afriki djodu-don.*
you and Bill in Afrika live-2
'You and Bill, you live in Africa.'

f. *Bill e George kö Afriki bè-djodi.*
Bill and George in Afrika 3-live
(Dalrymple and Kaplan 2000: 782)

In effect, the following priority hierarchy operates to resolve combinations of person values: first > second > third (Silverstein 1976). In any combination that includes first person, the first person takes priority over second and third; otherwise, in a combination that lacks first person but includes second person, the second person takes priority over third. The primacy of first person is sometimes attributed to egocentricity in language. That may be a factor, but it should be noted that there is a simple functional explanation for why combinations of first and second resolve to first rather than second, that does not involve egocentricity. Speech acts with multiple speakers speaking in unison, as in a Greek chorus or athletes chanting *We are the champions!*, are very rare, in contrast to speech acts with multiple hearers, which are relatively common. The rarity of speech acts with multiple speakers means that the first person plural forms are available for other uses, with relatively little risk of confusion or ambiguity. On the other hand, if, contrary to fact, reference sets including both the speaker and hearer were expressed in the same way as those denoting multiple hearers, then such forms would very often be ambiguous as to whether the speaker meant to include herself or not. Instead, reference sets including both the speaker and hearer are typically expressed by the same form used for reference sets including multiple speakers, which as noted is so rare that confusion rarely results.

Formal accounts of person paradigms typically involve boolean features [±Speaker], [±Hearer], which encode the inclusion versus exclusion of the speaker and hearer (Silverstein 1976; Noyer 1997; Bobaljik 2008). Similarly, in Dalrymple and Kaplan's (2000) system the symbols S (for speaker) and H (for hearer) are elements of closed sets representing the different feature values. See the rightmost column of Table 11.1. The sets for a coordinate NP is calculated by unioning of the sets for the conjuncts. For example the conjuncts in (56b) have the follwing set representations: *an* 'you', {H}; *Bill* { }; and *min* 'I' {S}. The union of these sets is $\{H\} \cup \{\ \} \cup \{S\} = \{S, H\}$. The first person inclusive form *-den* encodes the set {S, H}, so that form is used here.

8. Summary and conclusion

Agreement plays an important role in syntax. Agreement is one of the key syntactic mechanisms, along with case and word order, for linking a predicate to one or more of its dependents. Moreover, agreement interacts deeply with many other aspects of grammar, and as a consequence the study of agreement sheds light on those other aspects. Agreement morphology typically derives historically from incorporated pronouns and studying the contrasts between agreement and pronouns aids our understanding of the semantics of pronouns and of grammatical functions like subject, object, and adjunct. The observed locality conditions on grammatical agreement reflect the function of agreement as a marker of grammatical function.

The person, number, and gender features of agreement lead a double life as semantic features and formal grammatical features, and the attempt to understand how the grammar negotiates between these two aspects of those features leads to a better understanding of the complex connection between them. The array of different agreement targets, classified by part of speech (verbs, adjectives, determiners, etc.) and grammatical function (modifier, predicate, etc.), fall into systematic typological patterns with respect to the range of agreement features they register and whether they register formal or semantic agreement. In addition to their relevance to semantic interpretation, agreement features are also related to declension class and other determinants of word morphology. Anaphoric agreement between pronouns and their antecedents provides clues to discourse structure and to the operation of anaphora. Finally, agreement sheds light on the nature of coordination, because agreement targets sometimes peak inside the structure of a coordinate phrase to see the individual conjuncts, while in other cases they fail to do so. Because agreement is so intimately related to all of these aspects of grammar, the study of agreement is important to our understanding of morphology, syntax, semantics, and discourse pragmatics more generally.

9. Abbreviations

FV	final vowel
PRON	pronoun
SEQ	sequential perfective aspect

10. References (selected)

Ariel, Mira
2000 The development of person agreement markers: from pronouns to higher accessibility markers. In: Suzanne Kemmer and Michael Barlow (eds.) *Usage-Based Models of Language*, 197–260. Stanford: CSLI Publications.

Austin, Peter, and Joan Bresnan
1996 Non-configurationality in Australian aboriginal languages. *Natural Language and Linguistic Theory* 14, no. 2: 215–268.

Baker, Mark C.
1996 *The Polysynthesis Parameter*. Oxford: Oxford University Press.

Baker, Mark C.
2008 *The Syntax of Agreement and Concord*. Cambridge: Cambridge University Press.

Bhatt, Rajesh
2005 Long distance agreement in Hindi-Urdu. *Natural Language and Linguistic Theory* 23, no. 4: 757–807.

Bobaljik, Jonathan David
2008 Missing persons: A case study in morphological universals. *The Linguistic Review* 25: 203–230.

Bock, Kathryn, Janet Nicol, and J. Cooper Cutting
1999 The ties that bind: creating number agreement in speech. *Journal of Memory and Language* 40, no. 3: 330–346.

Bopp, Franz
1842 *Vergleichende Grammatik des Sanskrit, Zend, griechischen, lateinischen, litthauischen, gothischen und deutschen*. Berlin: F. Dümmler.

Bosch, Peter
1989 Coherence and cohesion: Comments on Roger G. van de Velde's Paper "Man, Verbal Text, Inferencing, and Coherence". In: W. Heydrich, F. Neubauer, J. S Petofi, and E. Sozer (eds.), *Connexity and Coherence – Analysis of Text and Discourse*, 218–227. Berlin: Walter de Gruyter.

Bresnan, Joan
2001a *Lexical-Functional Syntax*. Oxford: Blackwell.

Bresnan, Joan
2001b The emergence of the unmarked pronoun. In: Géraldine Legendre, Jane Grimshaw, and Sten Vikner (eds.), *Optimality-Theoretic Syntax*, 113–42. Cambridge, MA: MIT Press.

Bresnan, Joan, and Sam A. Mchombo
1987 Topic, pronoun, and agreement in Chichewa. *Language* 63, no. 4: 741–782.

Carroll, Peter J.
1995 *The Old People Told Us: Verbal Art In Western Arnhem Land*. University of Queensland.

Comrie, Bernard
1975 Polite plurals and predicate agreement. *Language* 51, no. 2: 406–418.

Copestake, Ann
1992 The representation of lexical semantic information. PhD dissertation, University of Sussex.

Copestake, Ann
1995 The representation of group denoting nouns in a lexical knowledge base. In: P. Saint-Dizier and E. Viegas (eds.), *Computational Lexical Semantics*, 207–231. Cambridge: Cambridge University Press.

Coppock, Elizabeth, and Stephen Wechsler
2012 The objective conjugation in Hungarian: agreement without phi features. *Natural Language and Linguistic Theory* 30, no. 3: 699–740

Corbett, Greville
1979 The agreement hierarchy. *Journal of Linguistics* 15: 203–224.
Corbett, Greville
1983 *Hierarchies, Targets and Controllers: Agreement Patterns in Slavic*. London: Croom Helm.
Corbett, Greville
1991 *Gender*. Cambridge: Cambridge University Press.
Corbett, Greville
2006 *Agreement*. Cambridge: Cambridge University Press.
Cornish, Francis
1999 *Anaphora, Discourse, and Understanding. Evidence from English and French*. Oxford: Oxford University Press.
Cysouw, Michael
2003 *The Paradigmatic Structure of Person Marking*. Oxford: Oxford University Press.
Dalrymple, Mary
2001 *Lexical Functional Grammar*. San Diego, CA: Academic Press.
Dalrymple, Mary, and Ronald M. Kaplan
2000 Feature indeterminacy and feature resolution. *Language* 76: 759–798.
Dowty, David, and Pauline Jacobson
1988 Agreement as a semantic phenomenon. In: Joyce Powers and Kenneth de Jong (eds.), *Eastern States Conference on Linguistics*. Vol. 5. Ohio State University, Columbus: Ohio State University.
Enger, Hans-Olav
2004 Scandinavian pancake sentences as semantic agreement. *Nordic Journal of Linguistics* 27, no. 01: 5–34.
Evans, Gareth
1977 Pronouns, quantifiers and relative clauses (I). *Canadian Journal of Philosophy* 7, no. 3: 467–536.
Evans, Gareth
1980 Pronouns. *Linguistic Inquiry*: 337–362.
Evans, Nicholas
1999 Why argument affixes in polysynthetic languages are not pronouns: evidence from Bininj Gun-wok. *Sprachtypologie und Universalienforschung* 52, no. 3: 255–281.
Faarlund, Jan Terje
1977 Embedded clause reduction and Scandinavian gender agreement. *Journal of Linguistics*: 239–257.
Farkas, Donka F., and Draga Zec
1995 Agreement and pronominal reference. In: Guglielmo Cinque and Giuliana Giusti (eds.), *Advances in Roumanian Linguistics*, 83–101. Philadelphia: John Benjamins.
Geach, Peter T.
1962 *Reference and generality: An Examination Of Some Medieval and Modern Theories*. Ithaca, NY: Cornell University Press.
Givón, Talmy
1970 The resolution of gender conflicts in Bantu conjunction: when syntax and semantics clash. In: *Papers from the Sixth Regional Meeting, Chicago Linguistic Society, April 16–18, 1970*, 250–261. Chicago: Chicago Linguistic Society.
Givón, Talmy
1976 Topic, pronoun and grammatical agreement. In: Charles N. Li (ed.), *Subject and Topic*, 149–188. New York: Academic Press.
Greenberg, Joseph H.
1966 *Language Universals With Special Reference To Feature Hierarchies (Janua Linguarum Series Minor 59)*. The Hague: Mouton.

Jelinek, Eloise
1984 Empty categories and non-configurational languages. *Natural Language and Linguistic Theory* 2: 39–76.
Kathol, Andreas
1999 Agreement and the syntax-morphology interface in HPSG. In: Robert Levine and Georgia Green (eds.) *Studies in Contemporary Phrase Structure Grammar*, 223–274. New York: Cambridge University Press.
King, Tracy H., and Mary Dalrymple
2004 Determiner agreement and noun conjunction. *Journal of Linguistics* 40, no. 01: 69–104.
Kleiber, Georges
1994 *Anaphores et pronoms*. Paris: Duculot.
Kratzer, Angelika
2009 Building a pronoun: fake indexicals as windows into the properties of bound variable pronouns. *Linguistic Inquiry* 40: 187–237.
Krifka, Manfred
1995 Common nouns: a contrastive analysis of Chinese and English. In: Greg N. Carlson and Francis Jeffry Pelletier (eds.), *The Generic Book*, 398–411.
Legate, Julie A
2002 Warlpiri: theoretical implications. PhD Dissertation, Massachusetts Institute of Technology.
Link, Godehard
1983 The logical analysis of plurals and mass terms: A lattice-theoretical approach. In: Bäerle, Schwarze, and von Stechow (eds.), *Meaning, Use and Interpretation of Language*, 302–323. Berlin: de Gruyter.
McCloskey, James
1991 There, it, and agreement. *Linguistic Inquiry* 22, no. 3: 563–567.
Mithun, Marianne
2003 Pronouns and agreement: the information status of pronominal affixes. *Transactions of the Philological Society* 101, no. 2: 235–278.
Moosally, Michelle
1998 Noun phrase coordination: Ndebele agreement patterns and cross-linguistic variation. PhD dissertation, University of Texas.
Nevins, Andrew
2008 Phi-interactions between subject and object clitics. Paper presented at the Linguistic Society of America Annual Meeting, Chicago, Illinois.
Nichols, Johanna
1986 Head-marking and dependent-marking grammar. *Language* 62.1: 56–119.
Noyer, Rolf
1997 *Features, Positions and Affixes in Autonomous Morphological Structure*. New York: Garland Press.
Nunberg, Geoffrey
1995 Transfers of meaning. *Journal of Semantics* 12, no. 2: 109.
Polinsky, Maria, and Eric Potsdam
2001 Long-distance agreement and topic in Tsez. *Natural Language & Linguistic Theory* 19, no. 3: 583–646.
Pollard, Carl, and Ivan Sag
1994 *Head Driven Phrase Structure Grammar*. Stanford and Chicago: CSLI Publications and University of Chicago Press.
Reid, Wallis
2011 The communicative function of English verb number. *Natural Language and Linguistic Theory* 29, no. 4: 1087–1146.

Rizzi, Luigi
1986 On the status of subject clitics in Romance. In: Osvaldo Jaeggli and Carmen Silva-Corvalan (eds.), *Studies in Romance linguistics*, 24:391–419. Dordrecht: Foris.
Siewierska, Anna
2004 *Person* Cambridge: Cambridge University Press.
Silverstein, Michael
1976 Hierarchy of features and ergativity. In: Pieter Muysken, and Henk C. van Riemsdijk (eds.), *Features and Projections*, 163–232. Dordrecht: Foris.
Simpson, Jane H.
1991 *Warlpiri Morpho-Syntax: A Lexicalist Approach*. Dordrecht: Kluwer Academic Publishers.
Stassen, Leon
1997 *Intransitive Predication*. NY and Oxford: Oxford University Press.
Steele, Susan
1978 Word order variation: A typological study. In: Joseph H Greenberg, Charles A Ferguson, and Edith A Moravcsik (eds.), *Universals of Human Language IV: Syntax*, 4: 585–624. Stanford: Stanford University Press.
Suñer, Margarita
1988 The role of agreement in clitic-doubled constructions. *Natural Language and Linguistic Theory* 6, no. 3: 391–434.
Tallerman, Maggie
1998 *Understanding Syntax*. London: Arnold.
Tasmowski, Liliane, and S. Paul Verluyten
1985 Control mechanisms of anaphora. *Journal of Semantics* 4: 341–370.
Tasmowski-DeRijk, Liliane, and S. Paul Verluyten
1982 Linguistic control of pronouns. *Journal of Semantics* 1: 323–346.
Vincent, Nigel, and Kersti Borjars
2000 Feature resolution and the content of features. In: *Online Proceedings of the LFG2000 Conference*. CSLI On-line Publications.
Wald, Benji
1979 The development of the Swahili object marker: A study of the interaction of syntax and discourse. In: Talmy Givón (ed.), *Discourse and syntax*, 12: 505–524.
Wechsler, Stephen
2008 Elsewhere in gender resolution. In: Kristin Hanson and Sharon Inkelas (eds.), *The Nature of the Word – Essays in Honor of Paul Kiparsky*, 567–586. Cambridge: MIT Press.
Wechsler, Stephen
2010 What 'you' and 'I' mean to each other: person indexicals, self-ascription, and theory of mind. *Language* 86 no. 2: 332–365.
Wechsler, Stephen
2011 Mixed agreement, the person feature, and the index/concord distinction. *Natural Language and Linguistic Theory* 29, no. 4: 999–1031.
Wechsler, Stephen
2013 The structure of Swedish pancakes. In: Philip Hofmeister and Elisabeth Norcliffe (eds.) *The Core and the Periphery: Data-Driven Perspectives on Syntax Inspired by Ivan A. Sag*, 71–98. Stanford: CSLI Publications.
Wechsler, Stephen, and Hyun-Jong Hahm
2011 Polite plurals and adjective agreement. *Morphology* 21: 247–281.
Wechsler, Stephen, and Larisa Zlatić
1998 Agreement in discourse. In: *Proceedings of the Conference on the Structure of Non-narrative Texts*. University of Texas, Austin, February 13, 1998.
Wechsler, Stephen, and Larisa Zlatić
2000 A theory of agreement and its application to Serbo-Croatian. *Language* 76, no. 4: 799–832.

Wechsler, Stephen, and Larisa Zlatić
2003 *The Many Faces of Agreement*. Stanford, California: CSLI Publications.
Wellander, Erik
1955 *Riktig Svenska: En Handledning i Svenska Språkets Vård*. 3rd ed. Stockholm: Svenska bokförlaget, P. A. Norstedt & Söner.

Stephen Wechsler, Austin (USA)

12. Verb Second

Abstract

This is an overview of the verb-second phenomenon and theories of it. Issues taken up include: differences between real and apparent verb second, which categories can be first constituents, (apparent) exceptions to V2, the two types of V2 languages (I-V2 and C-V2), embedded V2 in C-V2 languages. Among theories of V2 the following are considered specially: den Besten (1983/1989), Travis (1984, 1991), V2 as remnant VP movement, V2 in Optimality Theory, V2 in the framework of an articulated CP. The question whether V2 is narrow syntax or PF is discussed, including the question whether V-to-C has semantic effects, and the variety of meanings/functions the constituent preceding the verb may have. A key question which the paper endeavours to answer is whether "V2 language" is a meaningful, well-defined notion. The answer is that it is. It is a language that has the following property: A functional head in the left periphery attracts the finite verb and (separately) a phrasal constituent without categorial restrictions. This doesn't exclude the possibility of more than one constituent preceding the finite verb, provided that it has not been moved there – which there are examples of in most (or all) of the known V2 languages.

The V2 languages which are considered specially include the Germanic ones, Breton, and Kashmiri. The system in Breton differs from that in the other languages in that even an externally merged (non-expletive) constituent can satisfy V2.

1. Introduction

A language is called a verb-second (V2) language when the finite verb is obligatorily the second constituent, either specifically in main clauses or in all finite clauses.

(1) a. *Jag* ***har*** *ärligt talat aldri sett huggormar i den här skogen* [Swedish]
I have honestly speaking never seen adders in this here forest

b. *Huggormar* ***har*** *jag ärligt talat aldrig sett i den här skogen.*
adders have I honestly speaking never seen in this here forest

c. *I den här skogen* ***har*** *jag ärligt talat aldrig sett huggormar.*
in this here forest have I honestly speaking never seen adders

d. *Ärligt talat* ***har*** *jag aldrig sett huggormar i den här skogen.*
honestly speaking have I never seen adders in this here forest
'To be honest I've never seen adders in this forest.'

The examples illustrate the fact that the finite verb (in this case an auxiliary verb) is the second constituent in main clauses in Swedish, regardless what the first constituent is. V2 is characteristic of the Germanic languages, with Modern English as the only exception. Among the modern Romance languages, only some of the Rhaetoromance languages/dialects have the V2 property (Poletto 2002; Anderson 2006) but, according to Beninca (1983/1984, 2006) it was characteristic of many, or even all Medieval Romance languages (see Roberts 1993 on Old French; Fontana 1993, 1997 on Old Spanish). Among the modern Celtic languages, Breton has V2, but it was earlier more wide-spread at least among the Brythonic Celtic languages (Willis 1998). Among the Finno-Ugric languages, Estonian has V2. Among the Slavic languages, Sorbian is reported to have V2 (Plank 2003). Outside Europe, Kashmiri, an Indo-Aryan language, is a V2 language (Bhatt 1999), as are two dialects of Himachali (also Indo-Aryan and adjacent to Kashmiri), according to Hendriksen (1986, 1990). Karitiana, a Tupi language of Brazil, has also been characterised, by Storto (1999, 2003) as a V2 language (although this characterisation can be questioned, as will be discussed below). This is still a very small percentage of the languages of the world. In fact, one interesting question regarding V2 is why it appears to be so rare, globally.

In the history of generative linguistics V2 has played a particularly important part, in that it was the first well-studied and widely known case of head-movement, and also one of the first well-studied cases where a functional category, namely C (or COMP), was successfully analysed as a head in X-bar-based phrase structure theory.

The V2 languages are traditionally divided into two types, those that have V2 in main clauses only, and those that have V2 in all finite clauses. The former, which include the Mainland Scandinavian languages and all the Continental Germanic languages except Yiddish, will be referred to as C-V2 languages, for reasons to be made clear below in section 3.4. The latter, which include Icelandic, Yiddish, and (with some provisos) Breton are I-V2 languages. Some of the V2 languages have OV order (Continental Germanic, Kashmiri), others VO order (Breton, Rhaetoromance, the Scandinavian languages).

In the following I will first characterise and delineate V2, distinguishing it from some partly similar syntactic rule systems; not a trivial issue, as we shall see. I will then describe the basic facts, the generalisations and exceptions, in the various languages where V2 occurs. Thereafter I will present and discuss the theories that have been proposed in the literature, within generative grammar. Finally I will discuss what the fundamental nature is of V2, including whether it is a matter of Narrow Syntax or a postsyntactic "PF" matter.

For reasons of space I leave some important aspects of the V2 phenomenon aside in this overview paper, such as the history of V2 and L1 acquisition of V2 (on the acquisition of V2, see Westergaard 2008, 2009).

2. Real and apparent V2

2.1. Residual V2

So called residual V2 is when the finite verb is in second position in wh-questions and perhaps certain other constructions, but not across the board. The term is due to Rizzi (1990b), and the implication is that this is a residue of a more general V2 system. English is an example:

(2) a. *Which battery type (**would**) you (***would**) recommend?*
 b. *This battery type (***would**) I (**would**) not recommend.*
 c. *None of them (**would**) I (***would**) recommend.*
 d. *So good (**was**) his performance (***was**), that he got a standing ovation.*
 e. *In the sink (***found**) John (**found**) a spider.*

As shown, English has "V2" when the initial constituent is a wh-phrase or a negated phrase, and in a few other cases where an operator-like constituents is fronted, but not when it is a topicalised non-negative object or adverbial; see Vikner (1995: 48–50), Haegeman (2002). Even in the cases where English has inversion, only auxiliaries ever undergo it, which is another, presumably independent, difference between (Modern) English and the other Germanic languages.

Spanish is another language with residual V2:

(3) *Con quien (**vendrá**) Juan (***vendrá**) hoy?* [Spanish]
 With who will.come Juan will.come today
 'With who will Juan come today?'

In the case of English and Spanish this system may be rightly characterised as a historical residue of an earlier general V2 system, since Old English and Old Spanish were both V2 languages (see Fischer et al. 2000; Fontana 1993, 1997). This may not be the case for residual V2 effects in general, though, as will be discussed below.

2.2. Other apparent and borderline cases of V2

Some languages derive word orders that are descriptively speaking verb-second, yet are arguably different from "real V2". If a language has movement of the finite verb to T/

INFL, as very many languages do, and allows the subject to remain in a low position, and place a non-subject constituent in initial position, then the word order will be verb-second. Some languages generally classified as VSO have this property, for example Standard Arabic.

(4) a. ***Kataba*** *Zaydun r-risaalata.* [Standard Arabic]
wrote Zayd.NOM the-letter.ACC
'Zayd wrote the letter.'

b. *Zaydun* ***kataba*** *r-risaalata.*
Zayd.NOM wrote the-letter.ACC
'Zayd wrote the letter.'

c. *R-risaalata* ***kataba*** *Zaydun.*
the-letter.ACC wrote Zayd.NOM
'The letter, Zayd wrote.'

d. *Maadaa* ***kataba*** *Zaydun?*
what wrote Zayd.NOM
'What did Zayd write?'

e. **Maadaa Zaydun* ***kataba****?*
what Zayd.NOM wrote

See Fassi Fehri (1993: 19–33). (4d, e), in particular, looks like a V2 effect, or at least, like a residual V2 effect (indicating that this is not necessarily always a historical residue of general V2). However, what makes Standard Arabic clearly different from V2 languages is the fact that V-initial order is unmarked, in declarative sentences; see Fassi Fehri (1993: 19–33).

Another non-V2-like property of Arabic is that in wh-questions the fronted whP may be, and often is, preceded by a topicalised phrase, giving verb-third order.

(5) *Zaydun maadaa kataba?* [Standard Arabic]
Zayd.NOM what wrote
'What did Zayd write?/As for Zayd, what did he write?'

On the other hand, this is also characteristic of Kashmiri (Bhatt 1999: 107–109) a language which in other respects is a well-behaved V2 language (see below section 3.1), and also of Rhaetoromance (Poletto 2002). This, too, indicates that the V2 property involves more than one parameter, maybe more than two.

Estonian exhibits, in a sense, the opposite situation to remnant V2: In the case of fronted arguments or adverbials it is robustly V2 (Ehala 1998, 2006).

(6) a. *Lapsed* ***söövad*** *täna suppi.* [Estonian]
children eat today soup

b. *Täna* ***söövad*** *lapsed suppi.*
today eat children soup

c. *Suppi* ***söövad*** *lapsed täna.*
soup eat children today
'Today the children will eat soup.'
(Ehala 2006: 59)

But V2 is not obligatory in wh-questions.

(7) *Miks* ***(on)*** *külalised* ***(on)*** *saabunud?* [Estonian]
why are guests are arrive.PTCP
'Why have the guests arrived?'
(Anne Tamm, personal communication.)

Karitiana, as reported in Storto (1999, 2003), exhibits V2 order quite generally, as exemplified in (8):

(8) a. *Taso Ø-naka-'y-j ohy* [Karitiana]
man 3-DECL-eat-IRR potatoe
'The man will eat potatoe.'

b. *Ohy a-taka-'y-j taso*
potatoe PASS-DCL-eat-IRR man
'Potatoe, the man will eat.'
(Storto 1999: 151)

c. *Mynda taso na-m-potpora-j ese*
slowly man DCL-CAUS-boil-IRR water
'The man boiled the water slowly.'
(Storto 1999: 155)

However, (8c) shows that there is no prohibition as such against more than one XP preceding the verb. Storto also acknowledges that V-initial order is an option in declarative clauses. So why do we even consider calling it a V2 language, then? As we shall see below, all the V2 languages allow certain deviations from the strict V2 model, raising the question whether "V2 language" is actually a well-defined notion. For example, various dialects of Norwegian, otherwise a strict V2 language, allow non-V2 order in certain subtypes of wh-questions, not unlike Estonian (see Westergaard 2007, 2008, 2009):

(9) *Kem du like best?* [Norwegian, Tromsø dialect]
who you like best
'Who do you like best?'
(Westergaard 2009: 43)

Thus one of the aims of this paper is to investigate whether V2 language is a well-defined notion or not.

Almost all the examples of V2 order in the following will be from a set of core V2 languages, comprising a subset of the Germanic V2 languages, Kashmiri, and Breton. The data and analyses of Kashmiri are all based on Bhatt (1999).

3. V2 facts

3.1. Categories that can be "the first constituent"

All the V2 languages allow preposing/fronting of a very wide variety of categories: NPs (subjects, objects), PPs, embedded clauses, adverbs, predicative APs, etc., with some variation across the languages regarding which categories are frontable, and what information-structural or other effects the fronting has. The rough generalisation is, however, that whatever category is moved to the left periphery (the C-domain) will count as the first constituent for V2, while categories which are externally merged (first-merged, base-generated) in the left periphery, including conjunctions and question particles, do not count as first constituents for V2 (but see below section 3.1.7 on Breton). Likewise, clearly left-dislocated phrases, which are also plausibly analysed as externally merged in the left-periphery of the clause, do not count for V2. The structural position of the subject in V2 clauses (whether it is in the C-domain or not) is a controversial issue which I will return to below in sections 3.3 and 4.2. The following is an overview of the categories that are fronted.

3.1.1. The subject

In all the V2 languages the subject can precede the finite verb, counting as the first constituent of V2 order. In all the V2 languages this is the order typically found in sentences with wide focus (or sentence focus), that is information-structurally unmarked sentences (possible answers to the question *What happened?*). Breton is a special case, though: SVO in Breton can be unmarked, but is only one of many unmarked V2 orders; see Timm (1989, 1991), Schafer (1995), and especially Jouitteau (2005: 168, 2008).As for Kashmiri, most of the subject-first examples in Bhatt (1999) are translated into English as clefts, hence have a focused subject. Yet there are some examples, including (10b), where the subject is apparently unmarked in information-structural terms.

(10) a. *André het gister die storie geskryf.* [Afrikaans]
André has yesterday the story written
'André wrote the story yesterday.'

b. *Rameshas cha azkal shiilaa khosh karaan* [Kashmiri]
Ramesh these days Sheila happy do.NPRF
'Ramesh likes Sheila these days.'
(Bhatt 1999: 88)

c. *Azenor a redas d 'ar gêr.* [Breton]
Azenor PRT ran to the home
'Azenor ran home.'
(Jouitteau 2005: 35, 436)

PRT in the Breton examples is the particle called *rannig* in traditional Breton grammar, analysed by Jouitteau (2005) as a realisation of Fin(iteness). According to Jouitteau, the verb moves and adjoins to the right of PRT.

3.1.2. Objects

All of the V2 languages allow preposing of an object as a marked option.

(11) a. *Tidningar läser barnen inte.* [Swedish]
Newspapers read the.children not
'Newspapers, the children don't read.'

b. *Darvaaz mutsroov Ramesh-an.* [Kashmiri]
door opened Ramesh-ERG
'It was the door that Ramesh opened.'
(Bhatt 1999: 85)

c. *Ur marc'h a brenas an den.* [Breton]
a horse PRT bought the man
'It was a horse that the man bought.'
(Jouitteau 2005: 36)

There is variation across the languages regarding the information-structural import of a preposed object. In the Swedish example, the preposed object can be (contrastive) topic, but not focus (hence is not translatable into English as a cleft), while this is a possible reading of the Breton example, and, according to Bhatt (1999), the only reading of the Kashmiri example. See below section 5.2.

3.1.3. Adverbials

All of the V2 languages allow preposing of adverbs and any kind of adverbial phrases and clauses.

(12) a. *Vandag het 'n nuwe blogger by ons aangesluit.* [Afrikaans]
today has a new blogger with us joined
'Today a new blogger has joined us.'

b. *Heldigvis er den politiske kunst på vej tilbage.* [Danish]
luckily is the political art on way back
'Luckily, political art is making a come-back.'

c. [*Wenn man keine Träume mehr hat*] *ist man leer.* [German]
if one no dreams anymore has is one empty
'If you have no dreams anymore, you're empty.'

d. [*E brezhoneg*] *e vez lakaet ar verb d' an* [Breton]
in Breton PRT is.habitual put the verb to the
eil plas.
second position
'IN BRETON, the verb is in second position.'
(Jouitteau 2005)

In all the V2 languages preposing of adverbs is common and, at least for many types of adverbs (including scene-setting ones, as in [12a] and epistemic adverbs, as in [12b]), not necessarily associated with a marked pragmatic value.

3.1.4. Wh-phrases

All the V2 languages have wh-movement, not wh-in-situ, so a wh-phrase can be the first constituent in V2 clauses.

(13) a. *Wat hebben jullie besteld?* [Dutch]
what have you ordered
'What have you ordered?'

b. *Varför blir löv gula på hösten?* [Swedish]
why become leaves yellow in autumn
'Why do leaves become yellow in the autumn?'

c. *Hvers vegna hefur kreditkortinu mínu verið hafnað?* [Icelandic]
why has credit .card my been rejected
'Why has my credit card been rejected?'

Kashmiri differs from the other V2 languages in that wh-initial order is marked. The unmarked order has a topic preceding the wh-phrase (Bhatt 1999: 107–109). That is to say, wh-questions are generally V3.

(14) a. *rameshan kyaa dyutnay tse* [Kashmiri]
Ramesh.ERG what gave you.DAT
'As for Ramesh , what is it that he gave you?'

b. *tse kyaa dyutnay rameshan*
you.DAT what gave Ramesh.ERG
'As for you, what was it that Ramesh gave you?'

3.1.5. Predicates

Predicates such as predicative adjectives or nouns can be preposed in all the V2 languages. Some, but not all, of the V2 languages allow preposing of VP (Yiddish and Icelandic do not; see Källgren and Prince 1989; Holmberg and Platzack 1995: 223).

(15) a. *Sint er jeg ikke, bare veldig skuffet.* [Norwegian]
angry am I not only very disappointed
'I'm not angry, just very disappointed.'

b. [*Gelesen het boek*] *heeft hij niet.* [Dutch]
read the book has he not
'Read the book, he hasn't.'

3.1.6. Heads, the negation

With regard to preposing of heads, there is variation across the V2 languages. In Breton a non-finite verb can be preposed. This is also possible in Icelandic and Yiddish.

(16) a. *Skrivet em eus ar frasenn a-benn.* [Breton]
written PRT.1SG have the sentence entirely
'I've written the entire sentence.'
(Jouitteau 2005: 439)

b. *Komið hafa margir stúdentar.* [Icelandic]
come have many students
'Many students have come.'

c. *Leyenen leyent er dos bukh yetst.* [Yiddish]
read.INF reads he the book now
'As for reading, he's reading the book now.'
(Källgren and Prince 1989)

In Icelandic this movement falls under the fronting operation called Stylistic Fronting, characterised by absence of any semantic or pragmatic effect (see Holmberg 2000, 2005). It has the character of a last resort operation to satisfy V2 (an alternative to fronting the verb in [16b] is merge of an expletive pronoun in initial position). See Jouitteau (2005: 450–465, passim, 2008) for arguments that V-fronting in Breton has this character as well. More precisely, in Breton a constituent may be fronted for pragmatic effect, such as a subject, object, or adverbial, but in the absence of this, some other constituent, which may even be a head, is fronted as a last resort. In Yiddish, on the other hand, verb copying and fronting, as in (16c), is a topicalisation device.

Some of the V2 languages allow preposing of the negation. Breton does, as does Icelandic, Swedish, and Norwegian. In the case of Breton, Jouitteau (2005: 418–420) argues that the negation can satisfy V2 as a C-element (see section 3.1.7; Schafer 1995; Borsley and Kathol 1995). In Icelandic, Norwegian, and Swedish the negation is a sentence adverb, frontable on a par with other sentence adverbs; see Holmberg and Platzack (1995).

(17) a. *N' em eus ket kousket un dakenn gant Pouchka.* [Breton]
NEG PRT have NEG slept a drop with Pouchka
'I haven't slept at all because of Pouchka.'
(Jouitteau 2005: 98)

b. *Ekki veit ég hvað ætlar úr þér að verða.* [Icelandic]
not know I what will of you to become
'I don't know what will become of you.'

3.1.7. Particles

As for various polarity-related or modal particles such as German *doch*, *eben*, *ja*, *schon,* which are typically found in the IP-domain (the *Mittelfeld*) in the Germanic V2 languages, insofar as they can be initial, they will typically count as first constituent for V2. Particles that have a conjunctive function, such as 'yet', 'even so', 'however', etc. are particularly natural in clause-initial position, counting as first constituents (although they can also occur in the IP-domain).

(18) a. ***Emellertid** kan du inte använda en DVD-RAM skiva som* [Swedish]
however can you not use a DVD.RAM disc as
startskiva.
start.disc
'However, you cannot use a DVD-RAM disc as start-up disc.'

b. *Es war kein optimales Spiel, **trotzdem** haben wir gewonnen.* [German]
it was no optimal game yet have we won
'It wasn't an optimal game, yet we won.'

True conjunctions, i.e. counterparts of *and*, *but* and *or* generally do not count as first constituent for V2, although some exceptions exist (thus Swedish *eller* 'or' can function as first constituent; see also Jouitteau 2005: 68). The question particle counts as first constituent in Breton, but the question particle *mon* in Danish does not, nor does the desiderative particle *bara* in Swedish (another example of a "force-particle"; see below section 5.2).

(19) *... og (***tok***) de* ***tok*** *bussen til sentrum.* [Norwegian]
and took they took the.bus to centre
'... and they took the bus to the town centre.'

(20) a. *Hag* ***eo*** *gwir an dra-se* [Breton]
Q is true the thing-here
'Is that true?'
(Jouitteau 2005: 61)

b. *Mon (***er**) han (**er**) syg?* [Danish]
Q is he is ill
'I wonder if he's ill?'

c. *Bara (***kommer**) han (**kommer**) snart!* [Swedish]
only comes he comes soon
'If only he'd be here soon.'

As for complementisers, including adverbial clausal subordinators like 'because', 'although', etc., they are irrelevant for V2 in C-V2 languages (as they have V2 in main clauses only). Among the I-V2 languages they do count for V2 in Breton, at least in the case of some complementisers, including the main clause C-element *e-* exemplified in (21a), but not in the Germanic I-V2 languages Icelandic and Yiddish.

(21) a. ***Emañ*** *Maijo el levraoueg.* [Breton]
COMP.is Maijo in.the library
'Maijo is in the library.'
(Jouitteau 2008)

b. *Ég veit* [***að*** *(*kemur) hann (kemur) ekki*]. [Icelandic]
I know that comes he comes not
'I know that he's not coming.'

See Jouitteau (1995: 240–241, 407–431, 2008) for arguments that (21a) is an instance of V2 with a complementiser as first element (see below section 3.4).

For the latter languages the following generalisation seems to hold: If a particle can occur anywhere but in initial position, then it will count as first constituent when it does occur initially. This suggests that V2 is an accompaniment specifically to movement to the C-domain, in the languages in question (see section 5.2).

3.2. Only one category can precede the verb

One of the defining characteristics of V2 languages is that only one category can ever be fronted, to preverbal position.

(22) a. **Vandag die koerant lees hy. / *Die koerant vandag lees hy.* [Afrikaans]
today the newspaper read he / the newspaper today read he

b. **Varför ensam vill du inte vara? / *Ensam varför vill du inte vara?* [Swedish]
why alone want you not be / alone why want you not be

This distinguishes V2 languages from many other languages, where the left periphery preceding the finite verb may contain a string of sentential constituents, including, in addition to the subject, a fronted focus, or topic, and scene-setting adverbials. The following example is from Italian (Rizzi 2002):

(23) *Il mio libro, perchè, a Gianni, non glielo avete anchora dato.* [Italian]
The my book why to Gianni not to.him.it have.2PL still given
'Why have you still not given my book to Gianni?'

This generalisation has exceptions, though, discussed in the next section.

3.3. Exceptions

3.3.1. V1 order

There is a variety of (apparent) exceptions to the V2 rule in V2 languages. To begin with, V1 is the unmarked order in yes/no-questions; see (24a). It is also the order in imperatives, which is apparent when the subject is overt; see (24b). In some of the V2 languages it occurs in declaratives as well, as a marked alternative, for example in Icelandic (so called Narrative Inversion); see (24c), Sigurdsson (1990). Finally, it is also not uncommon as a result of ellipsis of a topicalised subject or object pronoun.

(24) a. *Lees hy vandaag die koerant?* [Afrikaans]
Read he today the newspaper
'Did he read the newspaper today?'

b. *Var du tyst!* [Swedish]
be you quiet
'You be quiet!'

c. *Kom Ólafur seint heim.* [Icelandic]
came Ólafur late home
'Olafur came home late.'
(Sigurðsson 1990)

d. *Weiss ich nicht.* [German]
know I not
'I don't know.'

(24d) is plausibly covertly V2, in that the initial position contains a fronted pronoun (here *dass* 'that'), which is optionally deleted in spoken German by topic drop (or "pronoun zap"); see Cardinaletti (1990), Mörnsjö (2001). The interrogative case has been analysed as also being covertly V2, the initial position occupied by an abstract question operator (as originally proposed by Katz and Postal 1964). The imperative may likewise be analysed as having an imperative operator in initial position (again following Katz and Postal 1964). In the case of Narrative Inversion, it is not inconceivable that the initial position is filled by a covert temporal adverbial particle 'then'.

3.3.2. Stacked adverbials

In the Germanic languages, and possibly generally in V2 languages, circumstantial adverbials can be stacked in initial position.

(25) *I går, vid femtiden, utanför stationen, när jag kom från* [Swedish]
yesterday at about.five outside the.station, when I came from
jobbet, mötte jag en gammal skolkamrat.
work, met I an old schoolmate
'Yesterday, at about five, outside the station, when I came home from work, I met an old schoolmate of mine.'

Typically it is a cluster of time or place adverbials which specify the time and/or place with increasing specificity. If these adverbials form a complex constituent, each adverbial adjoined to the next one, these constructions do conform to the V2 rule. I am not familiar with any other evidence that this is the right analysis, though. The stacked adverbials do not make up a single prosodic phrase, but instead, typically, each adverbial makes up an independent prosodic phrase (reflected in spelling by the commas).

Not any adverbial can be part of an initial cluster. For instance, sentence adverbs or aspectual adverbs ('often', 'rarely', 'never', etc.) apparently cannot.

(26) *Nede vid ån, under bron, (*tydligen) (*aldrig) har det* [Swedish]
down by the.river, under the.bridge, apparently never has there
bott en bisamråtta.
lived a muskrat
Intended reading: 'Apparently there has never lived a muskrat down by the river, under the bridge.'

3.3.3. Left dislocation

In the Germanic V2 languages there are two left-dislocation constructions, both of which violate the V2 rule, on a descriptive level (see Anagnostopoulou et al. 1997; Frey 2004). The first one is the Hanging Topic Left Dislocation (HTLD) construction in (27): An argument or adverbial is merged with a subject-initial main clause containing a resumptive pronoun.

(27) *Peter, ich werde ihn morgen sehen.* [German]
Peter I will him tomorrow see
'I will see Peter tomorrow.'

In the other dislocation construction the dislocated constituent is, in a sense, more closely integrated with the clause.

(28) a. *Die man,* ***die*** *ken ik niet.* [Dutch]
that man him know I not
'That man, I don't know.'

b. *För två veckor sen,* ***då*** *köpte Johan sin första bil.* [Swedish]
for two weeks ago then bought Johan his first car
'Two weeks ago Johan bought his first car.'

In this construction, a left-dislocated phrase is merged with a sentence in which a pronoun or other adequate proform cross-referenced with the dislocated phrase is fronted, functioning as first constituent for V2. This is, for some reason, traditionally called Contrastive Left Dislocation (CLD), even though it need not actually be contrastive. That CLD is different, and "more integrated" than HTLD, is shown, for example, by the fact that it may occur in so called embedded root clauses (see section 3.4), which HTLD cannot do.

(29) a. *Jag har hört [att för två veckor sen,* ***då*** *köpte Johan* [Swedish]
I have heard that for two weeks ago then bought Johan
sin första bil].
his first car
'I've heard that Johan bought his first car two weeks ago.'

b. **Jag har hört [att för två veckor sen, Johan köpte sin första bil* ***då****].*
I have heard that for two weeks ago Johan bought his first car then

The derivation of CLD remains controversial. The question is whether the left-dislocated phrase is derived by movement (specifically a two step-movement which leaves a pro-form in the first landing site), or by external merge of the dislocated phrase with the clause, and movement of only the resumptive pronoun; see Vat (1981); Grohmann (2000); Anagnostopoulou et al. (1997); Frey (2004). There is also a time-honoured analysis according to which topicalisation of NPs, clauses, PPs, VPs, etc. in the Germanic V2 languages is derived by CLD followed by deletion of the moved pronoun (see Koster 1978). See, however, Frey (2004) for arguments that at least the German variety of CLD is not information-structurally identical to topicalisation (see also Müller 2005 for a wide variety of V3, and V-more, sentences extracted from German corpora).

3.3.4. Exceptional adverbs

There is a set of focus adverbs in Scandinavian, including (in Swedish) *bara* 'only', *nästan* 'nearly', *till och med* 'even', *helt enkelt* 'simply', which systematically cause violation of V2 order (see Egerland 1998; Nilsen 2003).

(30) a. *Han bara hló að mér.* [Icelandic]
he just laughed at me
'He just laughed at me.'
(Sigurðsson 1990: 63)

b. *Han nesten brølte hurra.* [Norwegian]
he almost roared hooray
'He almost roared hooray.'
(Nilsen 2002: 79)

Nilsen (2003) takes these adverbs to provide evidence that V2 is not derived by V-movement, but VP movement (see below section 4.3), where this class of adverbs move along with the VP to the C-domain.

Another exceptional adverb discussed in the literature is the Swedish adverb *kanske* 'maybe', which optionally does not trigger V2 (see Platzack 1986).

(31) *Kanske* ***(kommer)*** *han inte* ***(kommer)****.* [Swedish]
maybe comes he not comes
'Maybe he's not coming.'

Plausibly this has to do with the historical origin of *kanske* as a predicate meaning 'may happen', taking a clausal complement. In fact, a complementiser *att* 'that' may be inserted after *kanske*: *Kanske* ***att*** *han inte kommer.*

3.4. I-V2 and C-V2 languages

Of the modern Germanic V2 languages Icelandic, some dialects of Faroese, and Yiddish have V2 in all finite clauses, main and embedded (but see reservations below). Modern spoken Afrikaans is, apparently, in the process of developing into such a language (see Biberauer 2002). The rest of the languages have V2 in main clauses only; see Thráinsson et al. (2004) (on Faroese); Diesing (1990), Santorini (1989); Vikner (1995). There are exceptions both ways, though, as will be discussed below. I have used *I-V2* and *C-V2* for the two types, reflecting the hypothesis according to which the former languages are V2 by virtue of V-to-I movement (at least in embedded clauses), the latter by virtue of V-to-C movement. The names do not imply a commitment to a particular analysis, in the present context. Another pair of terms in use is *asymmetrical* and *symmetrical* V2 languages. Yet another one is *restricted* and *general* V2 languages. As will be discussed below, the supposedly symmetrical or general V2 languages are not so symmetrical or general after all (at least not Icelandic).

In (32) and (33) a Scandinavian I-V2 language and C-V2 language are contrasted. Since these languages are SVO languages, the difference only appears in the presence of a negation or sentence adverb or other category placed between the subject and the VP. The finite verb will then precede the negation/adverb in embedded clauses in Icelandic, an I-V2 language, but follow it in Norwegian, a C-V2 language (data from Wiklund et al. 2007).

(32) *Hann efast um [að hun* ***(hafi)*** *ekki* ***(*hafi)*** *hitt þennan mann].* [Icelandic]
he doubts about that she has not has met this man
'He doubts that she has not met this man.'

(33) *Han tvilte på [at hun* ***(*hadde)*** *ikke* ***(hadde)*** *møtt denne* [Norwegian]
he doubted on that she had not had met this
mannen].
man
'She doubted that she hadn't met this man.'

In (34) and (35) a Continental I-V2 language (Yiddish) is contrasted with a Continental C-V2 language (German); examples from Diesing (1990) (with translations added).

(34) *Avrom gloybt az Max* ***shikt*** *avek dos bukh.* [Yiddish]
Avrom believes that Max sends away the book
'Avrom believes that Max will send away the book.'

(35) *Sigrid glaubt dass Waltraud wahrscheinlich das Buch gekauft* ***hat.*** [German]
Sigrid thinks that Waltraud probably the book bought has
'Sigrid thinks that Waltraud has probably bought the book.'

Of the non-Germanic V2 languages, Kashmiri has V2 in main clauses and complement clauses, but not in relative clauses and adverbial clauses.

(36) a. *me buuz [ki rameshan* ***vuch*** *raath shiila]* [Kashmiri]
I heard that Ramesh.ERG saw yesterday Sheila

b. *me buuz [ki raath* ***vuch*** *rameshan shiila]*
I heard that yesterday saw Ramesh.ERG Sheila
'I heard that Ramesh saw Sheila yesterday.'
(Bhatt 2002: 98)

(37) a. *su LaRk [yus raath yath karmas manz batI khyvaan oos]* [Kashmiri]
that boy who yesterday this room in food eat **was**
'the boy who was eating food in this room yesterday'
(Bhatt 2002: 122)

b. *yodivay su Daak-as khat* ***traav-yi*** [Kashmiri]
if he.NOM mail-DAT letter put-FUT
'if he will put the letter in the mail'
(Bhatt 2002: 123)

Interestingly, this is not that different from the situation in Icelandic. Although V2 is found in all embedded finite clauses in Icelandic, and even some non-finite ones (control infinitivals), it is in fact obligatory only in complement clauses, being optional in relatives and adverbial clauses, as pointed out in Sigurðsson (1992), and more recently discussed by Angantýsson (2001) and Wiklund et al. (2007) (who also add indirect questions to the list of possible non-V2 clauses in Icelandic).

(38) *Ég veit um ena bók sem Jón* ***(hefur)*** *ekki* ***(hefur)*** *lesið.* [Icelandic]
I know of one book that Jon has not has read
'I know about one book that Jon has not read.'
(Wiklund et al. 2007)

(39) *...fyrst einhverjir stúdentar* ***(skiluðu)*** *ekki* ***(skiluðu)*** *verkefnum.* [Icelandic]
as some students handed.in not handed.in assignments
'... as some students didn't hand in assignments.'

The difference between the I-V2 language Icelandic and the C-V2 languages is, therefore, smaller than it is made out to be in much of the literature (e.g. Vikner 1995). As will be discussed in the next section, the C-V2 languages all allow V2 order in some embedded clauses, and, correspondingly, the I-V2 languages allow non-V2 order in some embedded clauses. As a rough generalisation, V2 in embedded clauses in Icelandic is obligatory in clauses/contexts that allow optional embedded V2 in Mainland Scandinavian, and is optional in embedded clauses/contexts that do not allow embedded V2 in Mainland Scandinavian.

As for Breton, it is VSO in embedded clauses, which, according to Jouitteau (1995), is because C satisfies the requirement that the finite verb be preceded by a syntactically specified category. Arguably, whether or not the order C-VSO is permitted is a more fundamental typological distinction among the V2 languages than the C-V2/I-V2 distinction (see Jouitteau 2010).

3.5. V2 in embedded clauses in C-V2 languages

All the Germanic C-V2 languages have V2 order in some embedded clauses, as an alternative to the usual V-final (Continental Germanic) or "V3" order (Mainland Scandinavian). For some reason embedded V2 is rare in Dutch, though (but see Hoekstra 1993: 168–169 on Northern Dutch), while Frisian has embedded V2 with, as well as without, a complementiser, as will be discussed below. Embedded V2 word order is associated with specific semantic-pragmatic and syntactic effects.

(40) a. *Maria glaubt [Peter* ***geht*** *nach Hause].* [German]
Maria thinks Peter goes to home
'Maria thinks that Peter is going home.'

a′. *Maria glaubt [dass Peter nach Hause* ***geht****].*
Maria thinks that Peter to home goes
'Maria thinks that Peter is going home.'

b. *Eva säger [att hon* ***(ser)*** *aldrig* ***(ser)*** *på TV].* [Swedish]
Eva says that she watches never watches at TV
'Eva says that she never watches TV.'

c. *Watson påstod att disse penge* ***havde*** *Moriarty stjålet.* [Danish]
Watson claimed that this money had Moriarty stolen
'Watson claimed that Moriarty had stolen this money.'
(Vikner 1995: 71)

(40a, b) exemplify subject-initial embedded V2 clauses. (40c) shows that topicalisation of, for example, an object with concomitant V2 is also possible in embedded clauses, in C-V2 languages.

In all the Germanic C-V2 languages embedded V2 is particularly common in complements of verbs of saying and thinking, as in (40), but actually occurs in a wider range of embedded clauses, including complements of "predicates of certainty" (41) and semifactive predicates (42).

(41) *Det är uppenbart [att Eva* ***(ser)*** *aldrig* ***(ser)*** *på TV].* [Swedish]
it is obvious that Eva watches never watches at TV
'It's obvious that Eva never watches TV.'

(42) *Jeg oppdaget [at jeg* ***(hadde)*** *ikke* ***(hadde)*** *lest den].* [Norwegian]
I discovered that I had not had read it
'I discovered that I hadn't read it.'
(Wiklund et al. 2007)

See Truckenbrodt (2006: 297) on German. Semi-factive predicates include *know*, *understand*, *discover*, *realise*, to be distinguished from true factives like *regret*, *be sad*, *be surprised*, etc., which never allow embedded V2.

Embedded V2 also occurs in the complement of certain nouns.

(43) a. *der Glaube, die Erde* ***sei*** *flach* [German]
The belief the earth is.SBJV flat
'the belief that the world is flat'
(Heycock 2005)

b. *Pyt hie my in boadskip stjoerd, dat hy* ***(koe)*** *moarn* [Frisian]
Pyt had me a message sent that he could tomorrow
net komme ***(koe)***.
not come could
'Pyt had sent me a message that he couldn't come tomorrow.'
(de Haan 2001)

Some of the Germanic V2 languages allow V2 in "extent clauses" (for instance Frisian and Swedish do, but not Danish, according to Iatridou and Kroch 1992: fn. 4).

(44) a. *Hy is sa siik [dat hy* ***(kin)*** *dy hjoed net helpe* ***(kin)****]*. [Frisian]
he is so sick that he can you today not help can
(de Haan 2001)

b. *Han er så sjuk [så/att han* ***(kan)*** *inte* ***(kan)*** *hjälpa dej]*. [Swedish]
he is so sick so/that he can not can help you
'He is so sick that he can't help you.'

Embedded V2 is also found in adjunct clauses denoting cause, in German, Frisian, and at least some varieties of Scandinavian (see de Haan 2001; Andersson 1975), and, in German only, in relative clauses; see Reis (1997); Gärtner (2001, 2002).

(45) *He koe net kommer omdat hy* ***(moast)*** *Teake helpe* ***(moast)***. [Frisian]
he could not come because he must Teake help must
'He couldn't come because he had to help Teake.'
(de Haan 2001)

(46) *Das Blatt hat eine Seite, die* ***(ist)*** *ganz schwarz* ***(ist)***. [German]
the sheet has one side that is entirely black is
'The sheet has one side that is entirely black.'
(Gärtner 2001)

As for the meaning of embedded V2 the received view, which goes back to Hooper and Thompson's (1973) study of embedded root phenomena in English, is that they have, in some sense, the force of assertions, albeit of a weaker kind than in main clauses. This will be further discussed in section 5.

Considering V2 in complement clauses, there are two types, one without an overt complementiser, the other with an obligatory complementiser. The first type is characteristic of Continental Germanic, the other of Scandinavian, with Frisian straddling the boundary, having embedded V2 with or without a complementiser (see de Haan and Weermann 1986; de Haan 2001). Note that Mainland Scandinavian allows a null or deleted complementiser heading complement clauses with V3 order in clauses which are complements of so called bridge verbs, but does not allow a null or deleted complementiser in the corresponding V2 clauses embedded under the very same matrix verbs (see Iatridou and Kroch 1993; Vikner 1995; Heycock 2005).

(47) a. *Maria glaubt (*dass) Peter geht nach Hause.* [German]
Maria thinks that Peter goes to home
'Maria thinks that Peter is going home.'

b. *Eva säger *(att) hon* ***ser*** *aldrig på TV.* [Swedish]
Eva says that she watches never at TV
'Eva says that she never watches TV.'

b′. *Eva säger (att) hon aldrig* ***ser*** *på TV.*
Eva says that she never watches at TV
'Eva says that she never watches TV.'

As regards syntactic as well as semantic-pragmatic properties, embedded V2 clauses are very similar across the two types, and across different languages. Very broadly, embedded V2 clauses exhibit a lesser degree of syntactic dependence on the matrix predicate than embedded non-V2 clauses, corresponding to their lesser degree of semantic dependence (consider the notion that they have their own illocutionary force). One consequence of this is that extraction out of embedded V2 clauses is prohibited, or much more restricted than in the case of embedded non-V2 clauses (Holmberg 1986: 109–115; Vikner 1995: 108–110). See Wiklund et al. (2009) on variation regarding extraction from V2 clauses among varieties of Scandinavian.

(48) *Vilken fest$_i$ sa hon [att vi (****behöver***) *inte (****behöver***) *köpa roliga* [Swedish]
which party said she that we need not need buy funny
hattar till t_i]?
hats for
'Which party did she say that we don't need to buy funny hats for?'
(Holmberg 1986: 111)

This is, in fact, controversial in the case of German, in view of sentences such as (49):

(49) *Welchen Film hat sie gesagt haben die Kinder gesehen?* [German]
which film has she said have the children seen
'Which film did she say that the children have seen?'
(Vikner 1995: 114)

However, if Reis (1997, 2002) is right, (49) does not exemplify extraction in a biclausal construction, but interpolation of a parenthetical, here *hat sie gesagt* 'did she say', in a monoclausal wh-question.

Other effects of the relative independence of the embedded V2 clauses include the fact that they cannot be topicalised (see Reis 1997; Heycock 2005; the quantifier and the pronoun are included in the example to control for the possibility that the string in [45b] is parsed as a main clause followed by a parenthetical).

(50) a. *Dass er$_i$ unheimlich beliebt sei, möchte jeder$_i$ gern* [German]
that he extremely popular is.SBJV would everyone gladly
glauben.
believe
'Everyone would gladly believe that he is popular.'

b. **Er sei unheimlich beliebt, möchte jeder$_i$ gern glauben.*
he is.SBJV extremely popular would everyone gladly believe

c. [*Att fett (*är) inte (är) bra för hjärtat*] *vet jag.* [Swedish]
that fat is not is good for the.heart know I
'I know that fat is not good for the heart.'

This can be understood if the V2 clause is not a proper complement of the verb, but is rather in a relation which Reis (1997) refers to as "relatively unintegrated", characterized in some work as "paratactic" rather than "hypotactic" (see Gärtner 2001; de Haan 2001; Truckenbrodt 2006).

Yet another effect of the independence of V2 clauses, pertaining to cause clauses, is that a negation in the matrix clause cannot scope over a cause clause with V2 order.

(51) *Er kommt nicht, weil er (ist) faul (ist).* [German]
he comes not because he is lazy is
'He is not coming, because he is lazy.'

While the V-final alternative is ambiguous, the V2 alternative lacks the reading where the reason why is coming is not that he is lazy (predicted if the relation between the clauses is paratactic, i.e. coordination, rather than hypotactic/subordination). See de Haan (2001); Heycock (2005).

As far as the structure of embedded V2 clauses is concerned, the analysis of the continental, complementiserless type seems relatively straightforward: V2 order is derived in the same way as in main clauses; I return to the details in the next section. As for the Scandinavian/Frisian type, where a complementiser combines with V2 order, the majority view is that it is a case of CP-recursion: The complementiser corresponding to 'that', which normally takes an IP complement, can alternatively take a full CP complement, which makes possible the syntax of a main clause, including V2, and at least to some extent the semantics of a main clause, including illocutionary force, in the embedded clause (see Holmberg 1986; Holmberg and Platzack 1995; de Haan et Weermann 1989; Iatridou and Kroch 1993; Vikner 1995; Heycock 2005; Wiklund et al. 2007, 2009). The prohibition against extraction could then be essentially a Subjacency effect: There is one more CP-boundary to cross for an extracted element. This explanation does not carry over to Continental Germanic, though. Instead, whatever special properties the embedded V2 clauses have in these languages would be the effect of the special attachment, the lack of "integration" of these clauses in the main clause. (50) suggests that the attachment/integration of embedded V2 clauses in Mainland Scandinavian may be more or less the same as in Continental Germanic. See de Haan (2001) for arguments that the embedded main clauses in Frisian are essentially coordinated rather than subordinated to the matrix clauses. See Vikner (1995: 80–82) for discussion of the issue whether the I-V2 languages Icelandic and Yiddish also have general CP-recursion, deriving general V2. For a more recent discussion and reappraisal of the issue, see Wiklund et al. (2007, 2009), who argue that embedded V2 in Icelandic is not derived by V-to-I, but by V-to-C, same as in main clauses. The issue is put in a different light in the framework of a theory with an articulated left periphery; see section 5.2

4. Theories of V2

4.1. Den Besten 1983/89

Den Besten's paper was first circulated in 1977, was eventually published in 1983, with an added appendix updating the theory, and was later made part of den Besten's PhD thesis, with an added commentary further updating the theory. Den Besten takes as his starting point the observation that V2 is a root phenomenon, in German, Dutch, and Swedish. But importantly, he notes that this is part of a broader generalisation, which is that complementisers and V-fronting have complementary distribution in these languages, a fact which was noted for French in Dubuisson and Goldsmith (1976) and further discussed in Goldsmith (1981). Thus we find, for example the alternations in (52) and (53).

(52) a. *Er sagte, **dass** er morgen **komme**.* [German]
he said that he tomorrow comes.SBJV

b. *Er sagte, er **komme** morgen.*
he said he comes.SBJV tomorrow

c. **Er sagte, **dass** er **komme** morgen.*
he said that he come.SBJV tomorrow
'He said that he would come tomorrow.'
(after den Besten 1989: 82)

(53) a. –, *als **ob** er es nicht gesehen **hätte**.* [German]
as if he it not seen had.SBJV

b. –, *als **hätte** er es nicht gesehen.*
as had.SBJV he it not seen

c. *–, *als **ob hätte** er es nicht gesehen.*
as if had.SBJV he it not seen
'as if he hadn't seen it.'
(after den Besten 1989: 91)

Den Besten's great contribution was to propose an explanation of this generalisation, which was that the complementiser and the verb compete for the same position, namely C. The generalisation is that C must be lexicalised in these languages, which is accomplished by V-movement (later re-defined as I-to-C movement, with I containing V), in the absence of a complementiser.

This idea was further developed in a host of works during the eighties and early nineties, including the papers in Haider and Prinzhorn (1986); Platzack (1986); Holmberg (1986); Diesing (1990); Sigurðsson (1990); Rögnvaldsson and Thráinsson (1990); Vikner (1995); Platzack and Holmberg (1995). This was, arguably, the first time head movement was proposed as a transformation in generative grammar, with the properties which have since become familiar, in particular the idea that head movement is movement to a head-position (first formalised by den Besten 1983 as head-substitution, and later reanalysed as head-adjunction). It also became an important link in the argument for the analysis, which soon became near-universally accepted, that C is a clausal head (Stowell 1983; Holmberg 1986; Chomsky 1986).

In relation to V2, it provided a starting point for the analysis where V2 is a consequence of two independent operations: V-to-C, or more correctly, V-to-I-to-C, and A'-movement to SpecCP. V2 languages, or at least the Germanic C-V2 languages, would be languages that have generalised V-(to-I)-to-C in complementiserless clauses, and generalised XP-movement to SpecCP, with, crucially, only one SpecCP available (in the languages in question, or perhaps universally, as a consequence of X'- theory).

4.2. Travis (1984, 1991): asymmetrical V2

Den Besten's theory, and a number of its successors, including Platzack (1986), Holmberg (1986), Holmberg and Platzack (1995), Vikner (1995), adopted den Besten's "symmetrical analysis" (Vikner 1995: 81) of V2, according to which subject-initial main clauses have the finite verb in C and the subject in SpecCP. Only embedded clauses with non-V2 order would have the subject in SpecIP. Travis (1984) articulates an alternative analysis, according to which the subject is in SpecIP in main and embedded clauses, and the verb moves to C only in connection with movement of a non-subject phrase to SpecCP, or else when a verb-first structure is called for. This theory is further developed in Travis (1994), and notably in Zwart (1993, 1996) within a Chomskyan minimalist theory (Chomsky 1993, 1995). It is also supported by Rögnvaldsson and Thráinsson (1990) for Icelandic and Diesing (1990) for Yiddish. The matter is partly different in these two I-V2 languages, though.

In the case of the Continental Germanic OV languages, Travis (1984, 1991) argued, controversially at the time, that they have I-VP order. Hence V-to-I and subject placement in SpecIP derives SVO order, in main clauses. In the Scandinavian languages, too, V moves to I in main clauses, according to Travis (1991). In this perspective, the symmetrical theory of V2 has the disadvantage that it must assume that finite I and the subject both undergo a movement (I-to-C and A'-movement to SpecCP, respectively) which has the effect that they end up in the same specifier-head configuration and order that they had before movement. In GB theory, where movement is in principle always optional and not subject to any cost-calculus, this is not necessarily a problem from the point of view of the architecture of the grammar. However, it makes it harder to detect the effects of the movement in the Phonetic Form (PF), and is therefore predicted to pose an acquisition problem. In the I-V2 languages it poses what would seem to be an insurmountable problem: There would be no surface (PF) difference ever between a structure before and after the putative movements to C and SpecCP. In a minimalist framework, where the form and functioning of grammar is assumed to be subject to economy of derivation (following Chomsky 1993 and much subsequent work), the superfluous movement from I to C and SpecIP to SpecCP is obviously anathema. Travis's theory is further developed by Zwart (1993, 1998) and Koster (1994), among others. They provide a new range of arguments that I is "on the left" in Dutch (and OV languages in general), based on Kayne's (1994) Linear Correspondence Axiom, with the consequence that head-final order is always derived by movement of complements leftwards.

The symmetrical analysis thus relies on what is arguably a violation of a straightforward economy condition, and may even be unlearnable, at least in the case of I-V2 languages. The asymmetrical analysis of Travis (1984, 1991) and Zwart (1993, 1996), on the other hand, has the empirical disadvantage of predicting similarity between subject-first main clauses and embedded clauses, and not predicting similarity between subject-first main clauses and non-subject-first main clauses. Consider, for example, the extraction facts illustrated in (47): Movement out of embedded V2 clause is prohibited in the C-V2 languages, even when the subject is the first constituent. According to the symmetrical theory, this is explained since SpecCP, the escape-hatch for extraction out of clauses, is always occupied in embedded V2 clauses (by the subject or a non-subject). Under the asymmetrical theory SpecCP is filled in non-subject-first but not in subject-first embedded V2 clauses, predicting that extraction should be possible out of the latter, contrary to fact (note, however, that Norwegian behaves rather as predicted by the asymmetrical theory, according to Wiklund et al. 2007, as mentioned in section 3.5).

Branigan (1996) has articulated a theory which aims to combine the advantages of each theory, while avoiding their drawbacks. The theory is based on the idea that the subject in V2 clauses is neither in SpecIP nor in SpecCP, but in an A-bar position in between. This analysis is, in fact, commonplace today, within cartography-oriented theory, following Rizzi (1997); see below section 5.2. See Craenenbroeck and Haegeman (2007) for some (very convincing) evidence that a symmetrical analysis of V2 is correct at least for some Flemish dialects.

4.3. V2 as remnant vP fronting

An idea that has been developed in recent years, starting with Kayne (1998), is that what has traditionally been analysed as head-movement is, in fact, movement of a phrase, out of which the complement and the specifier(s) have been moved, leaving only the head behind. When this remnant phrase moves, it has the effect of head movement. An obvious advantage, if all head movement can be reduced to remnant XP movement, is that movement theory is simplified: Only maximal categories ever move. V2 as derived by remnant VP movement is pioneered in Mahajan (2001). A version of this idea, applied to German, is proposed by Müller (2004), whose theory is summarised here (see also Nilsen 2002; Wiklund et al. 2007, 2009).

The gist of Müller's theory is that V2 in German is the effect of movement of a remnant vP to SpecCP, where the moving vP consists of just the finite verb and the edge of vP, which crucially contains only one phrase. This vP has V2 order, so when it is moved to SpecCP, the result is a clause with V2 order. In the unmarked case of a transitive sentence the edge of vP contains the subject and nothing else, as the subject is the one category which is externally merged in that position. As noted in section 3.1.1 above, subject-initial root clauses are the unmarked case in German (and the other Germanic V2 languages), which fact is thus explained in Müller's theory. The derivation of (54) is shown in (55), where (55a) represents the complete vP.

(54) *Die Maria hat den Fritz geküsst.* [German]
the Maria.NOM has the Fritz.ACC kissed
'Maria kissed Fritz.'

(55) a. $[_{vP}$ die Maria $[_{v'}$ $[_{VP}$ den Fritz geküsst] hat]]] → Merge T, Move VP to SpecTP
b. $[_{TP}$ $[_{VP}$ den Fritz geküsst]$_i$ T $[_{vP}$ die Maria $[_{v'}$ t_i hat]]] → Move vP to SpecCP
c. $[_{CP}$ $[_{vP}$ die Maria $[_{v'}$ t_i hat]]$_k$ C $[_{TP}$ $[_{VP}$ den Fritz geküsst]$_i$ T t_k]]]

A V2 clause with a non-subject constituent such as an object or an adverbial in initial position is derived by movement of the constituent in question to the edge of vP; such movement is standardly assumed anyway within theories assuming that derivation proceeds in phases, in the sense of Chomsky (2000, 2001). In this case, to leave only one constituent in the edge of vP, the subject has to move to SpecTP (an outer SpecTP, with VP occupying the inner SpecTP).

The theory needs to be constructed so that a root clause vP will, in every case, be evacuated, leaving only one constituent in the edge of vP. Movement of VP to SpecTP is one important component of this theory; see also Hinterhölzl (2006), Biberauer and Roberts (2006) for other theories which assume VP movement to SpecTP as part of the derivation of V-final order.

This theory (or family of theories) predicts that the same constraints that are found at the edge of vP will recur at the edge of CP in V2 clauses. Thus Müller points out that the theory can explain why two categories that do not undergo scrambling in German also do not occur in initial position in V2 clauses: weak object pronouns and finite clauses. Assuming that scrambling is movement to the edge of vP, and assuming that, for whatever reason (presumably different reasons) weak pronouns and finite clauses cannot be accommodated in the edge of vP, it follows under Müller's theory, that they will also not occur initially in V2 clauses. (56) exemplifies the weak pronoun restriction; (56a) shows that the unstressed object pronoun *sie* must move to SpecTP, and cannot occur scrambled in the *Mittelfeld*. (56b) exemplifies the observation that the weak object pronoun cannot be clause-initial in a V2 clause.

(56) a. *dass gestern (sie) der Fritz (*sie) der Maria (*sie)* [German]
that yesterday her.ACC the Fritz her.ACC the Maria her.ACC
empfohlen hat.
recommended has
'that yesterday Fritz recommended her to Maria'

b. *Es hat Maria gelesen.*
it has Maria.NOM read
Intended reading: 'Maria has read it.'

However, the prediction goes wrong in the case of the German Infinitivus pro participio (IPP). In a sequence of verbs, a modal cannot be followed by an auxiliary that requires a participial form on the preceding verb. The finite verb must be fronted instead, as in (57c, d).

(57) a. **dass er es lesen gemusst hätte* [German]
that he it read.INF must.PTCP had.SBJV

b. **dass er es lesen müssen hätte*
that he it read.INF must.INF had.SBJV

c. *dass er es lesen hätte müssen*
that he it read.INF had.SBJV must.INF

d. *dass er es hätte lesen müssen*
that he it had.SBJV read.INF must.INF
'that he had to read it'

However, (57b) contrasts with (58): the CP-edge can accommodate the word order ruled out in the vP-edge, unremarkable under the standard V-movement analysis of V2, but unexpected under the remnant movement theory of V2.

(58) *Lesen müssen hätte er es.* [German]
read.INF must.INF had.SBJV he it
'Read it, he had to.'

A problem of a conceptual nature is that the remnant vP-movement theory requires two V2-related stipulations: First, the edge of the vP undergoing movement to SpecCP in main clauses (the movement itself is triggered by a feature of C, which is the crucial parametrised property of V2 languages) must only contain one constituent. Second, the CP-edge must also be restricted to containing only one constituent. The theory is constructed so that the first condition is derived (for the cases Müller discusses), but, needless to say, the required theoretical assumptions can be questioned. The second condition is not even discussed, although it is explicitly mentioned in connection with the islandhood of embedded V2 clauses (Müller 2004: 213).

4.4. V2 in Optimality Theory

The main idea in Anderson's (2000) theory of V2, couched within Optimality Theory (OT), is that second-position placement in general, including V2, is the effect of the interplay of two constraints: One is a member of a family of EDGEMOST(e,E,D) constraints. These constraints say that an element e should appear as close to the edge E (Left or Right) of the domain D as possible. Thus there is a constraint (universal, as are all OT constraints) EDGEMOST(V_{fin},L,S). The constraint says that the finite verb should be as close to the left edge of the sentence as possible. This constraint is highly ranked in the V2 languages, less highly ranked in other languages (meaning that it will not necessarily have any visible effects). The constraint is, however, in competition with a member of another family of constraints NON-INITIAL(e,D), saying that an element e should not be initial in a given domain. In V2 languages a member of this family, NON-INITIAL(V_{fin},S) is ranked higher than EDGEMOST(V_{fin},L,S). The effect of this ranking is that the finite verb will be as close to the left edge of the sentence (that is CP) as possible without being initial. That is to say, it will be the second constituent of CP. Anderson's theory is assumed, and developed further, in Legendre (2001).

Anderson (2000) assumes, following the tradition of den Besten (1983), that the finite verb ends up in second position by movement of V-to-I-to-C (while stressing that this is not crucial to the theory), and that the first position is then filled by movement of some category to SpecCP. A consequence of the OT perspective is, however, that the movement of I to C is not triggered (necessarily) by any feature of C, but rather

> [t]he verb moves from I to C (or whatever positions are involved) because (a) this movement is syntactically possible, and violates no constraints of the syntactic computational system; and (b) the structures that result have fewer violations of the constraints [EDGEMOST(V_{fin},L,S) and NON-INITIAL(V_{fin},S)] than structures in which the movement has not taken place, and in which the verb is thus farther from the left edge of the sentence. (Anderson 2000: 325–326)

Anderson points out that proposals made in the literature for features driving I to C in V2 sentences, typically in terms of feature-checking "amount to camouflaged language-particular stipulations of the requirement 'Move I to C'." (Anderson 2000: 325). It is, for example, a well-known fact that there is no particular morphology associated with I-to-C, and arguably there is no semantic effect either, given (a) that it is a requirement in all main clauses, and (b) synonymous sentences in other languages do not have I-to-C (although this view can be, and has been, challenged; see next section). The OT view implies that V2 is a fact purely about linearization, forced by the accidental ranking of two constraints. A prediction which the theory makes is that there might be structures where V2 holds but not as a result of I-to-C and XP-movement to SpecCP. The case Anderson brings up is Stylistic Fronting in Icelandic (Maling 1980; Holmberg 2000, 2005). In this construction a category is moved to pre-finite-verb position in embedded clauses where the subject is not available for filling this position, for example subject relatives.

(59) *sá sem fyrstur er að skora mark* [Icelandic]
he that first is to score goal
'he who is first to score a goal'

The finite verb, in this construction, is not in C, and the category preceding it is not in SpecCP. Furthermore, that category can be a head (as would seem to be the case in [53]); see Holmberg (2000, 2005). Yet, in the OT framework of Anderson (2000), Stylistic Fronting would be the result of exactly the same constraint ranking as "standard V2" – as is also consistent with the observation that the movement has no semantic effect. Another pertinent example is V2 in Breton, as discussed in Legendre (2001), if

V2 in Breton is not a matter of the C-domain; see also Borsley and Kathol (2000). See, however, Jouitteau (2005, 2008) for arguments that V2 in Breton is a matter of the C-domain, insofar as the finite verb always moves to Fin, the lowest head in the C-domain.

An interesting property of the theory of Anderson (2000) and Legendre (2001) is that V2 can be united with other second position phenomena. The case they both discuss in great detail is clitic-second position effects, as found in many languages. Clitic second position placement would be the effect of versions of the same constraints, specified to apply to (some subcategory of) clitics instead of the finite verb. This connection is not made in work on V2 in the tradition emanating from den Besten (1983/89) and Travis (1984).

5. The nature of V2: PF or Narrow Syntax?

The title question has already been broached in the previous section. The question is whether V2 order is an effect of a language-particular linearization requirement, or whether it is an effect of movements that are triggered by features operative in the Narrow Syntax, with effects at the LF-interface, as well as, accidentally as it were, at PF.

There is no question that the movement of various constituents to SpecCP has semantic, particularly information-structural, effects. Thus, for instance, a fronted object is typically interpreted as topic in the Germanic V2 languages, but typically as focus in Kashmiri. This is not an effect of V2 as such, however, but an effect of movement to the CP-domain; non-V2 languages, too, employ movement to the left periphery for information-structural effects. What makes the V2 languages special in this connection is that they only want exactly one constituent to be moved to the CP-domain (in the general case, or even strictly, if the V3 orders discussed in section 3.3 are not derived by movement). The question posed here is rather (a) whether fronting the verb to the second position, in connection with fronting some other category to initial position, has a semantic effect, and (b) whether fronting/placing a category in sentence-first position always has some particular semantic/pragmatic effect?

Consider first question (a).

5.1. The meaning of V-to-C

The most detailed study of the semantic effect of V-to-C in a V2 language is Truckenbrodt's (2006) study of German, building on Wechsler (1990) and Lohnstein (2000), among others. Truckenbrodt elucidates the effect of V-to-I by comparing (a) the semantics of main clauses with and without V-to-C and (b) the semantics of embedded clauses with and without V-to-C.

Some main clauses without V-to-C, all German, are exemplified in (60), to be compared with a main clause with V-to-C in (61).

(60) a. *Dass du (ja) das Fenster öffnest!* [German]
that you PRT the window open
'Don't forget to open the window.'

b. *Dass ich noch einmal Venedig sehen könnte!*
That I still once Venice see could
'I would like to see Venice once more.'

c. *Das Fenster öffnen!*
The window open.INF
'Open the window.'

d. *Dass die immer nur Turnschuhe anzieht!*
that she.DEM always only trainers wears
'Why does she always wear trainers!'
(Rosengren 1992)

(61) *Du öffnest das Fenster.* [German]
you open.PERS.2SG the window
'You're opening the window.'

As Truckenbrodt points out, (60a) has the same morphological properties as its V2 counterpart (61), and denotes a proposition, like (61), but the non-V2 sentence cannot be used as an assertion. Instead, the non-V2 root clauses can be used as directives, desideratives, or as exclamatives. The basis of Truckenbrodt's account is the claim that

> all sentential speech acts (with the exception of some pure exclamations) are volitional on the part of the speaker ('deontic' in the following): S wants something, wishes for something, invites A [the addressee: AH] to do something etc. I paraphrase this as '*S wants (from A)...*'. (...) Also as a starting point I assume that the interpretation that is inherent to declaratives and interrogatives always has the common ground as the epistemic desideratum. (Truckenbrodt 2006: 259–260)

The meaning of the declarative (62a) and the interrogative (62b) can therefore be paraphrased as shown:

(62) a. *Der Peter hat das gemacht.* [German]
the Peter has this done
'S wants from A that it is common ground that Peter has done this.'

b. *Hat der Peter das gemacht?*
has the Peter this done
'S wants from A that it is common ground whether Peter has done this.'

More formally, T proposes that C has a set of features making up what is called a *context index*, as follows:

(63) In a context index <Deont$_S$ (,x) (,<Epist>)> in C
a. Epist is present iff
(i) C contains a finite verb with indicative or subjunctive II, or
(ii) C/CP is marked [+WH];
b. x = A iff C contains a finite verb with person inflection.

The feature $Deont_S$ yields the meaning component 'S wants ...', $Deont_S$ (A) is then 'S wants from A that ...', while Epist is 'it is common ground that/whether ...'. The feature values A and Epist are the result of V-to-C, as only V-to-C provides the indicative/subjunctive and person features required. Thus x and Epist in the context index of C can be seen as unvalued features triggering V-to-C (Truckenbrodt 2006: 262). There are sentence types which have [$Deont_S$] without A or Epist, among them the directive and desiderative type exemplified in (58) above, and one type which has neither $Deont_S$, A, nor Epist, that is exclamatives. These sentence types do not (necessarily) have V-to-C.

A complication, which Truckenbrodt deals with in some detail (see also Truckenbrodt 2004), is that non-V2 root interrogatives do have the epistemic interpretation.

(64) *Ob er immer noch kubanische Zigarren mag?* [German]
Whether he always still Cuban cigars likes
'I wonder whether he still likes Cuban cigars.'
'S wants it to be common ground whether he still likes Cuban cigars.'

This is why (aii) is included in (63): [+WH] can value Epist even in the absence of V-to-T. As indicated by the paraphrase in (64), this question lacks the component 'from A', though (compare [62b]). The non-V2 question form is typically used when the speaker does not expect the addressee to know the answer. The context Truckenbrodt gives for (64) is that interlocutor 1 says (in German) 'I haven't heard from Peter in years'. Interlocutor 2 replies 'Me neither', whereupon interlocutor 1 utters (64), obviously with no hope of an answer from interlocutor 2 (call them *speculative questions*). The conclusion Truckenbrodt draws is that [+WH] cannot provide the value A for x in the context index of C; only V-to-C can do that.

Truckenbrodt then goes on to discuss embedded V2. There is a long tradition of work on the meaning of embedded V2, alluded to in section 3.5 (Hooper and Thompson 1973; Andersson 1975; Wechsler 1990; Iatridou and Kroch 1992; Heycock 2005). The consensus is that embedded V2 has assertive force, in some sense: Thus, while the standard, non-V2 embedded clause in (65a) merely reports what Eva says, (65b) in some sense also asserts it (although, as Heycock 2005 notes, unlike main clauses, it does not actually convey an assertion on the part of the speaker, but of the matrix subject).

(65) a. *Eva säger [att hon aldrig ser på TV].* [Swedish]
Eva says that she never watches at TV

b. *Eva säger [att hon ser aldrig på TV].*
Eva says that she watches never at TV
'Eva says that she never watches TV.'

In terms of the theory Truckenbrodt develops, C in embedded clauses lacks [$Deont_S$ (A)], but may have, in the context of predicates of the right type, [Epist], triggering V-to-C.

It seems clear enough that V-to-C in German has semantic effects of the sort Truckenbrodt discusses. Similar word order phenomena can be observed in other Germanic V2 languages (for instance the question headed by a question particle in [20b] is a speculative question, as predicted by Truckenbrodt 2006 applied to Danish, while [20c] is a desiderative without V-to-C). This would seem to entail that V-(to-I)-to-C movement takes place in Narrow Syntax, with effects at both interfaces, LF and PF – contradicting Anderson (2000) (see section 4.4).

The question is, why don't all languages have V-to-C of the German type, then? Apparently there are other ways to check [Deont$_S$ (A)] and [Epist], not made use of in German or the other Germanic V2 languages (in fact, Reis 2006 argues that there are other ways, even in German, in certain constructions). On the assumption that these features are universally located in C, it would seem to be the case, then, in languages which do not have V-to-C, nor any other visible C-element in declarative main clauses, that the relevant features are checked by a null C. The "exceptional sentence types" (speculative questions, desideratives, etc.) would then, presumably, be marked by overt C-elements, such as particles of some kind.

Thus, on a very "narrow interpretation of Narrow Syntax" one might still claim that the checking of Truckenbrodt's (2006) features in C is a postsyntactic matter, dependent on vocabulary insertion (in a Distributive Morphology framework), which provides a form of particle, one that has null realisation and checks the relevant C-features, in some languages, where the V2 languages instead rely on V-to-C.

Truckenbrodt's theory of German appears to generalise to Germanic V2 languages. It does not generalise to Breton, though. Verb fronting is quite simply compulsory in finite clauses in Breton, so verb fronting cannot have the sort of distinctive semantic function it has in Germanic. The minor sentence types are, therefore, not distinguished by absence of verb fronting, the way they are in Germanic (Mélanie Jouitteau, personal communication).

5.2. The meaning of XP-fronting and the articulated left periphery

V-movement is only half of the V2 phenomenon. The other half is the restriction to one constituent preceding the fronted finite verb. The question whether V-to-C has a semantic effect, and thus belongs in Narrow Syntax was answered in the affirmative (although possible objections were noted). The complementary question is whether fronting/placing a category in sentence-first position always has some particular semantic/pragmatic effect? The answer would seem to be no. The fronted category can have a variety of information-structural functions, with some variation across the different V2 languages. For example in Swedish, a fronted object can be aboutness topic (Frey 2004; Frascarelli and Hinterhölzl 2007), as in (66), seen as a continuation of the statement *Slumdog Millionaire is wonderful.*

(66) *Den filmen får du bara inte missa.* [Swedish]
that film must you just not miss
'You simply mustn't miss that film.'

Or it can be contrastive topic, as in (67), uttered as a reply to the question *Do you see a lot of film and theatre?*.

(67) *Film går jag mycket på, men inte teater.* [Swedish]
film go I much on, but not theatre
'I go to a lot of films, but not theatre.'

It is definitely less natural with contrastive focus, as in (68a), uttered as a correction of the claim *I hear you like theatre a lot.*, and it cannot be new information focus, as in (68b) taken as a reply to the question *What book are you reading?*.

(68) a. *#Film gillar jag, inte teater.* [Swedish]
film like I not theatre
Intended reading: 'It's film I like, not theatre.'

b. *#Harry Potter läser jag.*
Harry Potter read I
Intended reading: 'I'm reading Harry Potter.'

Thus, there are definite restrictions on the interpretation of an object fronted to SpecCP. On the other hand the subject can be the first constituent apparently regardless of its semantic import: Anything from an expletive pronoun to a contrastively focused, complex, quantified DP can be subject, preceding the finite verb. Thus if V2 involves fronting of the subject to some position higher than SpecIP/TP (not an uncontroversial assumption; see sections 4.2, 4.3), then this movement cannot always be triggered by a semantically interpretable feature. Sentences with an initial sentence adverb may also be virtually identical in terms of semantics and pragmatics to the counterpart where the adverb is in post-V2 position.

(69) a. *Antagligen är han mycket rik.* [Swedish]
probably is he very rich

b. *Han är antagligen mycket rik.*
he is probably very rich
'He is probably very rich.'

The syntax of the Icelandic expletive pronoun also indicates that filling the pre-C position is a purely formal requirement, similar to the classical EPP. The pronoun must be sentence–initial:

(70) a. *Það rignir.* [Icelandic]
it rains
'It's raining.'

b. *Rignir (*það)?*
rains it
'Is it raining.'

c. *Nú rignir (*það).*
now rains it
'It's raining now.'

(70b, c) show that the expletive cannot occupy SpecIP. If so, it must be in SpecCP in (70a). If so, then V2 must be a purely formal requirement.

The effects of fronting are different across the V2 languages, though. Thus, a fronted object in Kashmiri can only be a focus (according to Bhatt 1999).

(71) *darvaaz mutsroov rameshan* [Kashmiri]
door opened Ramesh
'Ramesh opened the door/It was the door that Ramesh opened'
(Bhatt 1999: 85)

An observation (among several) which Bhatt (1999) mentions in support of the generalisation that a fronted object in Kashmiri is focus, not topic, is that universal quantifiers, notoriously not good topics, can be fronted as objects in Kashmiri. This is not an option in Swedish, where a fronted object can only be a topic.

(72) a. *sooruyikeNh khyav rameshan* [Kashmiri]
everything ate Ramesh
'Ramesh ate everything.'

b. **?Allt åt Johan.* [Swedish]
everything ate Johan
Intended reading: 'Johan ate EVERYTHING.'

An interesting and topical question is how to account for V2 within a theory postulating an articulated left periphery, along the lines of Rizzi (1997, 2001, 2004) and related work. According to this theory the left periphery of sentences is made up of a hierarchy of heads and/or corresponding "positions" which encode sentential and information-structural functions such as Force, Focus, Topic, and Finiteness, and which is at least in part determined by Universal Grammar. The following hierarchy is based on Poletto (2002).

(73) [HT [Scene-setting [Force [Topic [Focus [WH [Fin]]]]]]]

The hierarchy should be seen as a hierarchy of fields or sub-hierarchies, which each consists of a fixed number of defined projections (Beninca and Poletto 2004; see also Frascarelli and Hinterhölzl 2007 for arguments that there is a hierarchy of different types of Topics and Foci). HT is the head/projection of the Hanging Topic, followed by a sub-hierarchy of projections for scene-setting adverbials, followed by a clause-typing functional head Force, followed by a sub-hierarchy of Topic projections, followed by projections of Focus, WH (interrogative force), and Fin(iteness) (Fin is discussed but not explicitly included in Poletto's 2000 representation of the hierarchy).

The empirical support for this theory comes primarily from the possibility of stacking constituents with definable sentential/information-structural functions in the left periphery in some languages (see [23] above for an example from Italian). In V2 languages this possibility is, obviously, highly restricted: typically only one XP can occur in the left periphery. Poletto (2002) discusses two alternative ways to account for V2 within this type of framework. One is that languages may differ with respect to whether the relevant left-peripheral functional features are distributed over a hierarchy of distinct heads, each with their own spec-position (for example Standard Italian), or whether they are encoded in one head, with one spec-position (V2 languages). In the latter case, the constituent in the spec of that head can have a variety of functions. The alternative, advocated by Poletto (2002) and Beninca and Poletto (2004), is that all languages have the full hierarchy of left-peripheral heads/projections. The V2 constraint would then be an effect of a requirement to "check a low CP", i.e. lexically fill the spec of a head low in the hierarchy, where this filled spec will then block movement of any other category to a higher position.

Another theory of V2 in the framework of an articulated CP is developed by Westergaard (2007, 2008, 2009). She shows that V2 languages exhibit considerable variation with regard to which sentence types require V2. A favourite example of hers is the variety of Norwegian where certain subtypes of wh-interrogatives do not have V2 (see [9]). She argues that this is due to micro-parametric variation regarding which heads in the articulated C-domain trigger verb-movement and XP-movement to their specifier position.

An interesting prediction that Poletto's (2002) and Beninca and Poletto's (2004) hypothesis makes is that V3 orders should be possible in V2 languages provided that the first constituent is not moved to that position, but externally merged (base-generated) there. We have seen some evidence of this in the course of this paper: The Hanging Topic in (27) is a clear example. The CLD constructions in (28) are also potentially examples, although more controversially, as CLD has also been analysed as derived by movement. In Kashmiri V3 order appears to be particularly common, with a left-dislocated topic phrase, followed by a focused phrase, followed by the finite verb.

(74) *su laRk*$_i$, *rameshan vuch temis*$_i$ *tsuur karaan* [Kashmiri]
that boy.NOM Ramesh.ERG saw he.DAT theft do.NPRF
'As for that boy, it is Ramesh who saw him stealing.'
(Bhatt 1999: 102)

Bhatt analyses the initial phrase as base-generated in initial position (note that the case of the initial NP is different from that of the resumptive pronoun, ruling out a movement analysis). Poletto's (2002) theory is, indeed, based on the observation that Rhaetoromance languages exhibit V3 order as an alternative to V2, but the V3 order is constrained in a way which is predicted if (a) the hierarchy in (73) is assumed, and (b) there is a division in this hierarchy between a lower domain (from Focus down) where spec-positions are filled by movement/internal merge, and a higher domain (the Topic domain), where they are filled by external merge, and (c) only one spec-position higher than the head hosting the finite verb is ever filled by movement (wh-questions in Kashmiri, shown in [14], are a possible counterexample, though; see also Müller 2005 for some German V3 constructions which appear not to conform to Poletto's generalisation).

The conceptual reason for the movement-blocking effect in V2 languages which Poletto (2002) draws on is articulated in Roberts (2004). The idea is that it is fundamentally due to Relativised Minimality (Rizzi 1990a), according to which "like repels like", so that A'-movement is blocked across a filled A'-position, A-movement across a filled A-position, and head-movement across a filled head. Roberts adopts the formalisation proposed by Chomsky (2000, 2001), according to which (phrasal) movement is triggered by an EPP-feature, an essentially arbitrary property of certain heads, subject to cross-linguistic variation. Characteristic of V2 languages, according to Roberts, is that they have a generalised EPP feature in Fin which requires filling SpecFinP with "something", any phrase or particle, regardless of its feature composition and syntactic function (if no other category is available, it can be an expletive). This position filled with "anything" will then have the effect of blocking movement of "anything", by Relativised Minimality.

We have seen evidence above that "anything" can satisfy the V2 requirement as long as it is moved to (not externally merged in) initial position. This explained the contrast between, for example, (75a = 18b) and (75b):

(75) a. ... *trotzdem haben wir gewonnen.* [German]
yet have we won
'... yet we won.'

b. *... *und haben wir gewonnen.*
and have we won

The particle *trotzdem* has an alternative position in the IP-domain, which the conjunction *und* does not. Thus *trotzdem* is, not implausibly, moved to initial position in (75a), while *und* is externally merged there.

(76) *Wir haben trotzdem/* und gewonnen.* [German]
we have yet and won
'Yet we won.'

We also saw examples that pure force particles, presumably merged in initial position, do not satisfy V2 (hence do not violate V2), in Danish and Swedish. Whether or not we accept the explanation based on Relativised Minimality, this is support for the hypothesis that prohibition against more than one constituent preceding the finite verb in V2 languages is, indeed, a prohibition against movement.

On the other hand we also saw that the generalisation that only moved constituents can satisfy V2 does not apply to Breton, where, if Jouitteau (2005, 2008) is right, even an externally merged category, such as (certain types of) C can satisfy V2. No doubt there are other potential counterexamples, when a wider range of data is considered. Even so, a theory of V2 along the lines of Poletto (2002) seems promising enough to be worth exploring in more detail, applied to a wider range of languages.

6. Conclusions

The V2 property is made up of the two components (77a, b).

(77) a. A functional head in the left periphery attracts the finite verb.
b. This functional head wants a constituent moved to its specifier position.

Property (77b) may be formalised as a generalised EPP-feature, along the lines of Roberts (2004), that is a feature which triggers movement and re-merge of a constituent virtually of any kind (NP, PP, AP, adverbs, particles, etc.) with the projection of the head (if verb movement is actually movement of a remnant phrase headed by the finite verb, the two properties will have to be reformulated accordingly).

The two properties/parameters are, arguably, independent. It may thus be the case that, for example, certain VSO languages have property (77a) without having property (77b). Or a language may have, say, a finiteness particle or a null C with the generalised EPP property without any need for verb movement.

The generalised EPP feature has the effect of blocking movement of any other category, across the constituent which satisfies the EPP feature, as an effect of Relativised Minimality (following Roberts 2004). This yields V2 order.

If Truckenbrodt (2006) is right, in the C-V2 languages (or at least a subset of them) the verb movement has the effect of checking/valueing features in C which determine the illocutionary force of the sentence, and would as such be part of Narrow Syntax. This is not the case in C-VSO languages like Breton, though. For these languages, the movement could, on that account, be a postsyntactic linearization rule (which would be consistent with Anderson 2000; Legendre 2002; Kathol and Borsley 2000; but see Jouitteau 2008).

The constituent which satisfies the EPP feature may have a variety of syntactic and information-structural functions, with variation across the V2 languages, some allowing topics and disallowing focused phrases, others vice versa. But crucially, the constituent may be information-structurally neutral, most clearly in the case of expletives, but also in the case of an initial subject in wide focus sentences, or an initial epistemic adverb, or a conjunctive particle. This is the effect of the generalised EPP feature. Regardless of its interpretation, the moved constituent blocks movement of any other constituent to a higher position.

The question was posed in section 2.2 whether "V2 language" is a meaningful, well-defined notion. The answer is: yes it is. It is a language which has the two properties (77a, b). Property (a) accounts for the fronted verb, property (b), the generalised EPP feature, for the requirement that the verb be preceded by one and only one constituent. However, the EPP feature can only prevent V3 (V4, V5, etc.) order derived by movement. It does not prevent V3 order derived by external merge.

There is variation among the V2 languages regarding the interpretation of the constituent preceding the fronted verb; in some languages a moved non-subject argument can only be a topic, in other languages it can only be focus. There is also variation among the V2 languages regarding the V3 orders they "exceptionally" allow. In terms of a theory assuming a Rizzian articulated left periphery, this can be described as variation concerning which head in the left periphery has the properties (77a, b), hence how high in the left periphery a constituent may move. If it cannot move higher than SpecFocus, then a moved constituent could never be a topic (given the hierarchy [73]), meaning that a sentence-initial topic would have to be externally merged. On the other hand, in such a grammar, there is a wider variety of functions that can precede the moved constituent: it can be a topic (of any kind), or a scene-setting adverbial, or a HT (or conceivably a combination of these). If a moved constituent can be (or must be) a topic, thus move higher up the hierarchy, the functions that may precede it are correspondingly reduced.

The theory makes the prediction that V2 languages in which a moved constituent can be focus but not topic (as is the case in Kashmiri), should allow a wider variety of constituents in the "V3 position", which appears to be the case, as Kashmiri exhibits not only what appears to be quite general left-dislocation, but also certain adverbs in V3 position (Bhatt 1999: 104), and even (marginally) more than one topic preceding a fronted focus (Bhatt 1999: 110).

The question was posed in the introduction why the V2 property appears to be so rare, among the languages of the world. The idea that V2 is the result of properties (77a, b), has consequences for this question. To begin with, if the properties are independent of each other, V2 will only be found where the properties happen to co-occur. Second, V2 may not be quite as rare as we have been wont to think. In a V2 language where the generalised EPP feature is low, the finite verb may be quite regularly preceded by more than one constituent, even though only the innermost one is moved there, which will make it less obvious to an unsuspecting observer that it has the properties (77a, b) (see Beninca's 2004 description of the Medieval Romance languages). For instance, topic-prominent languages of the Chinese type, which quite regularly have one or more topics externally merged with CP, may have the properties (77a, b), yet the finite verb will much of the time be preceded by more than one constituent. And in languages of the head-marking type, as analysed in Jelinek (1984) and Baker (1996), where all lexical (non-pronominal) arguments are externally merged as adjuncts to CP, linked to null proforms in argument positions within IP, any effects of (77a, b), insofar as these properties could ever (co-) occur in such languages, would be very hard, indeed, to detect.

12. Acknowledgements

Thanks to Theresa Biberauer, Abdelkader Fassi Fehri, Anne Tamm, and Sten Vikner for comments and data on Afrikaans, Arabic, Estonian, and Danish, respectively. Special thanks to Mélanie Jouitteau for her advice and help with the Breton data and generally. Thanks finally to two anonymous referees.

7. References (selected)

Anagnostopoulou, Elena, Henk van Riemsdijk, and Frans Zwarts (eds.)
1997 *Materials on Left Dislocation.* Amsterdam: John Benjamins.

Anderson, Stephen R.
2000 Towards an optimal account of second position phenomena. In: J. Dekkers, F. van der Leeuw and J. van de Weijer (eds.), *Optimality Theory: Phonology, Syntax and Acquisition*, 302–333. Oxford: Oxford University Press.

Anderson, Stephen R.
2006 Verb second, subject clitics and impersonals in Surmiran (Rumantsch). To appear in *Proceedings of the Berkeley Linguistics Society* 32.

Andersson, Lars-Gunnar
1975 *Form and Function of Subordinate Clauses.* (Monographs in Linguistics 1.) Department of Linguistics, University of Gothenburg.

Angantýsson, Asgrimur
2001 Skandinavísk orðaröð í islenskum aukasetningum. [Scandinavian word order in Icelandic embedded clauses] *Íslenskt Mál* 23: 93–122.

Baker, Mark
1996 *The Polysynthesis Parameter.* New York: Oxford University Press.

Beninca, Paola
1993/8 Un 'ipotesi sulla sintassi delle lingue romanze medievali. *Quaderni Patavini di Linguistica* 4: 3–19. Reprinted in Beninca, P. 1994 *La Variazione Sintattica. Studi di Dialettologia Romanza*, 177–194. Bologna: Il Mulino.

Beninca, Paola
2006 A detailed map of the left periphery of Medieval Romance. In: Raffaella Zanuttini, Hector Campos and Elena Herburger (eds.), *Crosslinguistic Research in Syntax and Semantics: Negation, Tense, and Clausal Architecture*, 53–86. Washington DC: Georgetown University Press.

Beninca, Paola , and Cecilia Poletto
2004 Topic, focus, and V2: Defining the sublayers. In: Luigi Rizzi (ed.), *The Cartography of Syntactic Structures, vol. 2: The Structure of CP and IP*, 52–75. New York and Oxford: Oxford University Press.

den Besten, Hans
1983/89 On the interaction of root transformations and lexical deletive rules. In: Werner Abrahams (ed.), *On the Formal Syntax of the Westgermania*, 47–131. Amsterdam: John Benjamins. Reprinted in Hans den Besten 1989 *Studies in Westgermanic Syntax*. Doctoral dissertation, Katholieke Universiteit Brabant. Amsterdam+Atlanta, GA: Rodopi.

Bhatt, Rakesh M.
1999 *Verb Movement and the Syntax of Kashmiri*. Dordrecht: Kluwer.

Biberauer, Theresa
2002 Verb second in Afrikaans: Is this a unitary phenomenon? *Stellenbosch Papers in Linguistics* 34 (SPIL 34): 19–68.

Biberauer, Theresa, and Ian Roberts
2006 Loss of residual 'head final' orders and remnant fronting in Late Middle English: causes and consequences. In: Jutta Haartmann and Laszlo Molnarfi (eds.), *Comparative Studies in Germanic Syntax*, 263–297. Amsterdam: John Benjamins.

Borsley, Robert, and Andreas Kathol
2000 Breton as a V2 language. *Linguistics* 38: 665–710.

Branigan, Philip
1996 Verb-second and the A-bar status of subjects. *Studia Linguistica* 50: 50–79.

Cinque, Guglielmo
1990 *Types of A-bar Dependencies*. Cambridge MA: MIT Press.

Cardinaletti, Anna
1990 Subject-object asymmetries in German null-topic constructions and the status of specCP. In: Joan Mascaró and Marina Nespor (eds.), *Grammar in Progress: Essays in Honour of Henk van Riemsdijk*, 75–84. Groningen: Foris.

Chomsky, Noam
1986 *Barriers*. Cambridge MA: MIT Press.

Chomsky, Noam
1993 A minimalist program for linguistic theory. In: Kenneth Hale, Samuel J. Keyser (eds.), *The View from Building 20*, 1–52. Cambridge MA: MIT Press.

Chomsky, Noam
1995 *The Minimalist Program*. Cambridge MA: MIT Press.

Chomsky, Noam
2000 Minimalist inquiries: the framework. In: Roger Martin, D. Michaels and Juan Uriagereka (eds.), *Step by Step. Essays on Minimalist Syntax in Honor of Howard Lasnik*, 83–155. Cambridge, MA: MIT Press.

Chomsky, Noam
2001 Derivation by phase. In: Michael Kenstowicz (ed.) *Ken Hale: A Life in Language*, 1–59. Cambridge MA.: MIT Press.

Craenenbroeck, Jeroen, and Liliane Haegeman
2007 The derivation of subject-initial V2. *Linguistic Inquiry* 38: 167–178.
Diesing, Molly
1990 Verb movement and subject position in Yiddish. *Natural Language and Linguistic Theory* 8: 41–79.
Dubuisson, Colette, and John Goldsmith
1976 A propos de l'inversion du clitique sujet en francais. *Proceedings of the Sixth Meeting of the North East Linguistic Society (NELS 6):* 103–112. Montreal: Université de Montréal.
Ehala, Martin
1998 How a man changed a parameter value: the loss of SOV in Estonian subclauses. In: Richard M. Hogg and Linda van Bergen (eds.), Historical Linguistics 1995, 73–88. Amsterdam: John Benjamins.
Ehala, Martin
2006 The word order of Estonian: Implications to universal language. *Journal of Universal Language* 7: 49–89.
Egerland, Verner
1998 On verb-second violations in Swedish and the hierarchical ordering of adverbs. *Working Papers in Scandinavian Syntax* 61, 1–22. Lund University.
Fassi Fehri, Abdelkader
1993 *Issues in the Structure of Arabic Clauses and Words*. Dordrecht: Kluwer.
Fischer, Olga, Ans van Kemenade, Willem Koopman, and Wim van der Wurff
2000 *The Syntax of Early English.* Cambridge University Press.
Fontana, Josep M.
1993 Phrase structure and the syntax of clitics in the history of Spanish. Doctoral dissertation, University of Pennsylvania.
Fontana, Josep M.
1997 On the integration of second position phenomena. In: Ans van Kemenade and Nigel Vincent (eds.), *Parameters of Morphosyntactic Change*, 207–250. Cambridge: Cambridge University Press.
Frascarelli, Mara, and Roland Hinterhölzl
2007 Types of topics in German and Italian. In: Susanne Winkler and Kerstin Schwabe (eds.), *On Information Structure, Meaning, and Form*, 87–116. Amsterdam/Philadelphia: John Benjamins.
Frey, Werner
2004 Notes on the syntax and the pragmatics of German left dislocation. In: Horst Lohnstein and Susanne Trissler (eds.), *The Syntax and Semantics of the Left Periphery*, 203–233. Berlin: Mouton de Gruyter.
Goldsmith, John
1981 Complementizers and root sentences. *Linguistic Inquiry* 12: 541–574.
de Haan, Germen, and Fred Weerman
1986 Finiteness and verb fronting in Frisian. In: Hubert Haider and Martin Prinzhorn (eds.), *Verb Second Phenomena in Germanic Languages*, 77–110. Dordrecht: Foris.
Haider, Hubert, and Martin Prinzhorn (eds.)
1986 *Verb Second Phenomena in Germanic Languages*. Dordrecht: Foris.
Heycock, Caroline
2005 Embedded root phenomena. In: Martin Everaert and Henk Van Riemsdijk (eds.), *The Blackwell Companion to Syntax*, vol. 5. Oxford: Blackwell.
Also online: http://www.blackwellreference.com/public/tocnode?id=g9781405114851_chunk_g97814051148511

Hoekstra, Eric
1993 Parametric variation inside CP as parametric variation. In: Werner Abraham and Josef Bayer (eds.), *Dialektsyntax*, 246–270 (Linguistische Berichte Sonderheft 5.) Opladen: Westdeutscher Verlag.

Holmberg, Anders
1986 Word order and syntactic features in the Scandinavian languages and English. Doctoral dissertation, Stockholm University.

Holmberg, Anders
2000 Scandinavian stylistic fronting: how any category can become an expletive. *Linguistic Inquiry* 31: 445–484.

Holmberg, Anders
2005 Stylistic fronting. In: Martin Everaert and Henk Van Riemsdijk (eds.), *The Blackwell Companion to Syntax*, vol. 5, 532–565. Oxford: Blackwell.
Also online: http://www.blackwellreference.com/public/tocnode?id=g9781405114851_chunk_g978140511485168

Hooper, Joan, and Sandra Thompson
1973 On the applicability of root transformations. *Linguistic Inquiry* 4: 465–497.

Iatridou, Sabine, and Anthony Kroch
1992 The licensing of CP-recursion and its relevance to the Germanic verb-second phenomenon. *Working Papers in Scandinavian Syntax* 50: 1–25. Lund University.

Jelinek, Eloise
1984 Empty categories, case and configurationality. *Natural Language and Linguistic Theory* 2: 39–76.

Jouitteau, Mélanie
2005 La syntaxe comparée du breton. Doctoral dissertation, University of Nantes.

Jouitteau, Mélanie
2008 The Brythonic reconciliation. In: Jeroen van Craenenbroeck (ed.), *Linguistic Variation Yearbook*, 163–200. Amsterdam: John Benjamins.

Jouitteau, Mélanie
2010 A typology of V2 with regard to V1 and second position phenomena: An introduction to the V1/V2 volume. *Lingua* 120: 197–209.

Katz, Jerrold, and Paul Postal
1964 *An Integrated Theory of Linguistic Descriptions*. Cambridge MA: MIT Press.

Källgren, Gunnel, and Ellen Prince
1989 Swedish VP-topicalization and Yiddish verb-topicalization. *Nordic Journal of Linguistics* 12: 47–58.

Kayne, Richard
1994 *The Antisymmetry of Syntax*. Cambridge MA: MIT Press.

Kayne, Richard
1998 Overt vs. covert movements. *Syntax* 1: 128–191.

Koster, Jan
1994 Predicate incorporation and the word order of Dutch. In: Guglielmo Cinque, Jan Koster, Jean-Yves Pollock, Luigi Rizzi and Raffaella Zanuttini (eds.), *Paths towards Universal Grammar: Studies in Honor of Richard S. Kayne*, 255–276. Washington DC: Georgetown University Press.

Legendre, Geraldine
2001 Masked second-position effects and the linearization of functional features. In: Geraldine Legendre, Jane Grimshaw and Sten Vikner (eds.), *Optimality-Theoretic Syntax*, 241–278. Cambridge MA: MIT Press.

Lohnstein, Horst
2000 *Satzmodus-Kompositionell. Zur Parametrisierung der Modusphrase im Deutschen*. Berlin: Akademie Verlag.

Maling, Joan
1980 Inversion in embedded clauses in Modern Icelandic. *Íslenskt Mál og Almenn Málfræði* 2: 175–193.
Mörnsjö, Maria
2001 V1 declaratives in spoken Swedish. Doctoral dissertation, Lund University.
Müller, Gereon
2004 Verb-second as vP-first. *Journal of Comparative Germanic Linguistics* 7: 179–234.
Müller, Stefan
2005 Zur Analyse der scheinbar mehrfachen Vorfeldbesetzung. *Linguistische Berichte* 203: 297–330.
Nilsen, Øystein
2003 *Eliminating Positions*. Doctoral dissertation, University of Utrecht [published by LOT].
Plank, Frans (ed.)
2003 Des grammatische Raritätenkabinett. http://typo.uni-konstanz.de/rara/intro/
Platzack, Christer
1986 COMP, INFL, and Germanic word order. In: Lars Hellan and Kirsti Koch Christensen (eds.), *Topics in Scandinavian Syntax*, 185–234. Dordrecht: Kluwer.
Poletto, Cecilia
2002 The left-periphery of V2-Rhaetoromance dialects: a new view on V2 and V3. In: Sjef Barbiers, Leonie Cornips and Susanne van der Kleij (eds.), *Syntactic Microvariation*. Electronic publications of Meertens Instituut. www.meertens.knaw.nl/projecten/sand/sandeng.html
Reis, Marga
1997 Zum syntaktischen Status unselbständiger Verbzweit-Sätze. In: C. Dürscheid, K.H. Ramers and M. Schwarz (eds.), *Sprache im Fokus. Festschrift für Heinz Vater zum 65. Geburtstag*, 121–144. Tübingen: Niemeyer.
Reis, Marga
2002 Wh-movement and integrated parenthetical constructions. In: Jan Wouter Zwart and Werner Abraham (eds.), *Proceedings of the 15th Germanic Syntax Workshop,* 3–40. Amsterdam: Benjamins.
Reis, Marga
2006 Is German V-to-C movement really semantically motivated? Some empirical problems. *Theoretical Linguistics* 32(3): 369–380.
Rizzi, Luigi
1990a *Relativized Minimality*. Cambridge MA: MIT Press.
Rizzi, Luigi
1990b Speculations on verb-second. In: Joan Mascaró and Marina Nespor (eds.), *Grammar in Progress: Essays in Honour of Henk van Riemsdijk*, 375–386. Groningen: Foris.
Rizzi, Luigi
2002 On the position "(Int)errogative" in the left periphery of the clause. In: Guglielmo Cinque and Gianpaolo Salvi (eds.), *Current Studies in Italian Syntax. Essays Offered to Lorenzo Renzi*. Amsterdam: North Holland.
Rizzi, Luigi (ed.)
2004 *The Cartography of Syntactic Structures*, volume 2. New York and Oxford: Oxford University Press.
Roberts, Ian
1993 *Verbs and Diachronic Syntax: A Comparative History of English and French*. Dordrecht: Kluwer.
Roberts, Ian
2004 The C-system in Brythonic Celtic languages, V2, and the EPP. In: Luigi Rizzi (ed.), *The Cartography of Syntactic Structures*, volume 2, 297–327. New York and Oxford: Oxford University Press.

Roberts, Ian
2005 *Principles and Parameters in a VSO Language, a Case Study in Welsh*. New York and Oxford: Oxford University Press.
Rögnvaldsson, Eirikur, and Höskuldur Thráinsson
1990 On Icelandic word order once more. In: Joan Maling and Annie Zaenen (eds.), *Syntax and Semantics 24: Modern Icelandic Syntax*, 3–40. New York: Academic Press.
Santorini, Beatrice.
1989 The generalization of the verb-second constraint in the history of Yiddish. Doctoral dissertation, University of Pennsylvania.
Schafer, Robin
1995 Negation and verb second in Breton. *Natural Language and Linguistic Theory* 13: 135–172.
Sigurðsson, Halldor A.
1990 V1 declaratives and verb raising in Icelandic. In: Joan Maling and Annie Zaenen (eds.), *Syntax and Semantics 24: Modern Icelandic Syntax*, 41–69. New York: Academic Press.
Storto, Luciana
1999 Aspects of Karitiana grammar. Doctoral dissertation, MIT.
Storto, Luciana
2003 Interactions between verb movement and agreement in Karitiana (Tupi stock). *Revista Letras, Curitiba* 60: 411–433.
Stowell, Tim
1983 Origins of phrase structure. Doctoral dissertation, MIT.
Thráinsson, Höskuldur, Hjalmar P. Petersen, Jogvan i Lon Jacobsen, and Zakaris Svabo Hansen
2004 *Faroese: An Overview and Reference Grammar.* Torshavn: Føroya Frodskaparfelag.
Timm, Lenora
1989 Word order in 20th century Breton. *Natural Language and Linguistic Theory* 6: 361–378.
Timm, Lenora
1991 The discourse pragmatics of NP-initial sentences in Breton. In: J. Fife and E. Pope (eds.), *Studies in Brythonic Word Order*, 275–310. Amsterdam: Benjamins.
Travis, Lisa
1984 Parameters and effects of word order variation. Doctoral dissertation, MIT.
Travis, Lisa
1991 Parameters of phrase structure and verb-second phenomena. In: Robert Freidin (ed.), *Principles and Parameters in Comparative Grammar*, 339–364. Cambridge MA: MIT Press.
Truckenbrodt, Hubert
2006 On the semantic motivation of syntactic verb movement to C in German. *Theoretical Linguistics* 32(3): 257–306.
Vikner, Sten
1995 *Verb Movement and Expletive Subjects in the Germanic Languages*. New York and Oxford: Oxford University Press.
Wechsler, Stephen
1990 Verb second and illocutionary force in Swedish. In: Elisabet Engdahl, Mike Reape, Martin Mellor and Richard Cooper (eds.), *Parametric Variation in Germanic and Romance: Proceedings from a DYANA Workshop*, September 1989, Edinburgh *Working Papers in Cognitive Science* 6: 229–244.
Westergaard, Marit
2007 English as a mixed V2 grammar: Synchronic word order inconsistences from the perspective of first language acquisition. *Poznan Studies in Contemporary Linguistics* 43: 107–131.
Westergaard, Marit
2008 Acquisition and change: On the robustness of the triggering experience for word order cues. *Lingua* 118: 1841–1863.

Westergaard, Marit
2009 *The Acquisition of Word Order. Micro-Cues, Information Structure and Economy.* Amsterdam/Philadelphia: John Benjamins.
Wiklund, Anna-Lena, Gunnar H. Hrafnbjargarsson, Thorbjörg Hróarsdóttir, and Kristine Bentzen
2007 Rethinking Scandinavian verb movement. *Journal of Comparative Germanic Linguistics* 10: 203–233.
Wiklund, Anna-Lena, Kristine Bentzen, Gunnar H. Hrafnbjargarsson, and Thorbjörg Hróarsdóttir
2009 On the distribution and illocution of V2 in Scandinavian *that*-clauses. Lingua 119: 1914–1938.
Willis, David
1998 *Syntactic Change in Welsh: A Study of the Loss of Verb-Second.* Oxford: Clarendon Press.
Zwart, Jan Wouter
1993 Dutch syntax: a minimalist approach. Doctoral dissertation, University of Groningen.
Zwart, Jan Wouter
1996 *Morphosyntax of Verb Movement. A Minimalist Approach to the Syntax of Dutch.* Dordrecht and Boston: Kluwer.

Anders Holmberg, Newcastle (UK)

13. Discourse Configurationality

Abstract

Discourse-configurationality means the encoding of information structure, i.e., the topic–predicate and focus–background articulations, in syntactic structure. Though all languages encode information structure in grammar, they rely on syntax – as opposed to phonology and morphology – to varying degrees. This article first surveys the family of topic notions playing a role in syntax, involving givenness, the subject-of-predication role, and frame setting. A type of contrastive topics is shown to assume the topic function owing to its contrastive intonation, individuating also non-individual-denoting expressions. It is discussed how the topic function (and its subtypes) are realized across languages; along which parameters languages may differ in this respect. Most languages traditionally analyzed as subject-prominent are shown to represent a constrained subtype of topic-prominent languages where only the grammatical subject can be topicalized, provided it satisfies the criteria of topichood.

The focus induces the partitioning of the sentence into a focus and a background, or a focus, and a focus-frame. The focus-frame is derived by replacing the focus by a variable – hence the focus introduces a set of alternatives. In the case of a prosodically encoded focus, the focus constituent corresponds to the wh-part of the explicit or implicit constituent question eliciting the sentence, i.e., it is the constituent conveying new information. A syntactically encoded focus, derived by focus movement into an A-bar position, not only elicits alternatives, but also excludes them except the one identified by the focus.

1. What is discourse-configurality?

Natural languages can organize, or package, the information conveyed in an utterance in many different ways – depending on how it relates to the preceding context, and, more generally, to the shared knowledge base of the interlocutors. Thus an event can be presented as an out-of-the-blue statement; or it can be formulated as a statement about an event participant that has already been introduced into the discourse. In English, the two types of sentences only seem to differ with respect to prosody (but see section 2.6. below). The sentence *My car broke down* (an example of Lambrecht 1994), for instance, can either be an all-new sentence, answering the question in (1a), or it can involve predication about the speaker's car, answering (1b). In the out-of-the-blue sentence, only *my car* carries a pitch accent; in the latter case, there is a pitch accent both on *my car*, and on the particle verb.

(1) a. *What is the matter?*
My CAR broke down.
b. *What is the matter with your car?*
My CAR broke DOWN.

In many languages, for example, in Hungarian, the sentence variants matching different contexts and situations are clearly different also syntactically:

(2) a. *Le győz-t-e a svédek-et a holland csapat.* [Hungarian]
PRT beat-PST-3SG the Swedes-ACC the Dutch team.NOM
'The Dutch team beat the Swedes.'

b. *A holland csapat le győz-t-e a svédek-et.*
the Dutch team.NOM PRT beat-PST-3SG the Swedes-ACC

c. *A svédek-et le győz-t-e a holland csapat.*
the Swedes-ACC PRT beat-PST-3SG the Dutch team.NOM

(In the glosses, PRT stands for *verbal particle.*) (2a) is an out-of-the-blue sentence, felicitous as the first sentence of a newspaper article, or as an answer to the the question *What happened at the Olympics*. (2b) involves predication about the Dutch team, answering the question *How did the Dutch team do?* (2c) predicates about the Swedes, answering a question like *What is new about the Swedes*?

The answers in (1a) and (1b), and the sentences in (2a), (2b), and (2c) have identical propositional contents but different information structures. (1b) and (2b, c) display a partitioning that is absent in (1a) and (2a): their first unit presents an entity that is presupposed to exist by the interlocutors, and the second unit predicates something new about it. This is the so-called topic–comment, or topic-predicate articulation.

If it is part of the shared knowledge base of the speaker and the listener that someone beat the Swedes, and the explicit or implicit question eliciting the sentence is the constituent question *Who beat them?*, the proposition that also underlies (2a), (2b), and (2c) will be formulated somewhat differently:

(3) *A* ***HOLLAND CSAPAT*** *győz-t-e le a svédek-et.* [Hungarian]
the Dutch team beat-PST-3SG PRT the Swedes-ACC
a. 'The DUTCH team beat the Swedes.'
b. 'It was the DUTCH team that beat the Swedes.'

(3a) consists of two units: the first one: *a holland csapat*, answering the wh-part of the corresponding constituent question, is the focus of the sentence, whereas the second one, identical with the presupposed part of the corresponding question, is the so-called background, or focus-frame, or presupposition. The information-structural function of the focus is, according to some approaches, the highlighting of new information; according to other theories, the indication of the presence of alternatives, and – in the case of certain types of focus, e.g., the Hungarian preverbal focus illustrated in (3), and its English translation involving a cleft focus (3b) – the exclusion of them. The Hungarian (3) and the English (3b) are true if and only if the Dutch team was the only one of the relevant alternatives, i.e., the participants of the tournament, that beat the Swedes.

A much discussed question is how the topic–comment and the focus–background articulation relate to each other; whether they can be conflated, with the topic corresponding to a narrow presupposition, and the comment corresponding to a wide focus; or they are two independent ways of organizing information; or they represent different levels of a hierarchical information structure. Data from more and more languages – see, e.g., Vallduví (1992) on Catalan, Ortiz de Urbina (1995) on Basque, Benincá (2001) on Italian, Enrico (2003) on Haida, etc. – support the latter view. In Hungarian, too, the focus-background partitioning is internal to the comment in sentences with a topic-comment articulation, as shown in (4). (4) answers the question *Who beat the Swedes* in the form of a statement about the Swedes:

(4) [$_{\text{Topic}}$ *A svédek-et*] [$_{\text{Comment}}$ [$_{\text{Focus}}$ *A HOLLAND CSAPAT*] [Hungarian]
the Swedes-ACC the Dutch team.NOM
győz-t-e le]
beat-PST-3SG PRT
'The Swedes were beaten by the Dutch team.'

Information structure, i.e., the topic–comment, and focus–background articulation can be encoded in many different ways across languages and also in one and the same language: syntactically, morphologically, prosodically, or by a combination of these means. The English examples (1) and (3b) illustrate prosodic encoding, and the Hungarian (2a–c), (3), and (4) illustrate syntactic encoding. The syntactic marking of information structure often goes together with prosodic marking, which raises the question which of them is primary; whether information-structure-related syntactic movements are triggered by prosodic requirements, as claimed by Zubizarreta (1998) and Szendrői (2003), or information-structure-related prosodic patterns are consequences of syntactic operations (cf. Horvath 2005). The syntactically encoded topic and focus is also marked morphologically in various languages.

The term *discourse-configurationality* means the syntactic encoding of information structure. In the first decades of generative theory, discourse configurationality was regarded as an exotic property characterizing only a subset of languages (cf. Li and Thompson 1976). Since the nineteen eighties, however, more and more constructions of more and more languages have turned out to instantiate a topic–comment or a focus-background articulation. For most current versions of generative syntactic theory, the question is not whether a language is discourse-configurational or not, but to what extent it is discourse-configurational; what is the division of labor among the syntactic, morphological, and phonological components of its grammar in the encoding of information structure.

Assuming that the topic–predicate and the focus–background articulation represent independent levels of information structure, this chapter will discuss their syntactic realizations separately.

2. The topic–predicate (or topic–comment) articulation

2.1. The topic function

The idea that sentences across languages tend to proceed from the given to the new, first presenting a familiar object, that which the sentence is about, and then saying something new about it, emerged in the middle of the 19th century. It was first raised by Weil (1844), and was first elaborated in detail by Brassai in a series of studies written in Hungarian (Brassai 1860, 1863–65, etc.). (For an English summary of Brassai's ideas, see É. Kiss 2008b). Brassai was looking for universal features in the various sentence types of a number of languages from different language families. He found that both fixed and free word order languages share a sentence structure which begins with one or more complements conveying already known information. These complements „practically lay a basis for the meaning of the sentence in the listener's mind, i.e., they are calling attention, and pointing forward (…)" (Brassai1860: 341). He first called this initial part of the sentence *subject in a different sense of the word* (Brassai 1852); then he borrowed the term *inchoativum* from Arab linguistics (Brassai 1860). The second part of the sentence, including the verb, is the *predicate* (Brassai 1852), or *bulk* (Brassai 1860). The function of this second part is the communication of an action, or a circumstance of an action that the speaker supposes to be unknown to the listener. Besides the new ideas, the known ones that are not set off as an introduction are also to be found in the bulk. The bulk, which is more important than the inchoativum by virtue of its informative value, is present in every sentence; the inchoativum, on the other hand, may also be missing. The sentence structure consisting of an inchoativum and a bulk can be found in all languages. Which complements can serve as an inchoativum, on the other hand, is specific to a given language. E.g. in the Semitic languages and in Hungarian every kind of complement can function as an inchoativum, while in the Romance languages the inchoativum is usually the nominative. In German the inchoativum always consists of a single complement, while in Hungarian it can also consist of two or more complements. It might also be characteristic of a language if its sentences necessarily, often, or rarely begin with an inchoativum.

Gabelentz (1869) put forth similar ideas in his theory of psychological subject–psychological predicate articulation, which was further developed by Paul (1880) and Wundt (1912). Information structure as a key factor of determining word order assumed a central role in the work of the Prague School, especially Mathesius (1928, 1929), then Sgall (1967), Sgall Hajičová and Benesová (1973), etc. Whereas Mathesius used the terms *theme* and *rheme*, since Hockett (1963) and the studies in Li (1976), the terms *topic–comment* have become prevalent. The term *topic-predicate articulation* also occurs – cf. Sasse (1987), Erteschik-Shir (1997), and É. Kiss (1994, 2002). A further alternative term in use is Valduví's (1992) *link*.

Not only the terminology but the interpretation of these terms has also displayed great variation. Some of the definitions are built on the features *given* and *new*: the topic (theme) is the sentence part carrying old information, and the comment (rheme) is the sentence part carrying new information. This is the topic notion that can be traced back to the work of Weil (1844) and Brassai (1860). Other definitions are built on the notion of aboutness: the topic is what the sentence is about, and the comment is what is said about the topic. There are also authors who regard both notions relevant, and distinguish them as theme and topic (Halliday 1967; cf. also Frey 2005), or as familiarity topic and aboutness topic (Frascarelli and Hinterhölz 2007). A family of topic definitions regards both givenness and aboutness necessary features of topics (Strawson 1964; Reinhart 1981; Erteschik-Shir 1997, and many others).

Those who identify topicality with givenness have to interpret givenness in a very broad sense. Not only contextually given noun phrases, e.g., pronouns (5a), definite noun phrases (5b), and specific indefinites, denoting a subset of a contextually given referent (5c), can function as topics, but also noun phrases that are discourse-new but whose referent can be accommodated as an element of a previously mentioned situation (5d), as well as discourse-new topics whose referent is present in the shared knowledge base of the interlocutors, e.g., names of kinds/generics, and proper names (6a–c).

(5) a. *Jól ismer-em János-t.* ***Benne*** *meg bíz-hat-sz.* [Hungarian]
well know-I John-ACC he.in PRT trust-can-2SG
'I know John well. You can trust him. / He can be trusted.'

b. *Jól ismer-em a város-t.* ***A 2. kerület-ben*** *a gazdag-ok lak-nak.*
well know-I the city-ACC the 2nd district-in the rich-PL live-3P
'I know the city well. In the 2nd district, the rich live. / The 2nd district is inhabited by the rich.'

c. *Le vizsgáztatt-am az elsőévesek-et.* ***Egy lány-t*** *meg buktatt-am.*
PRT examined-1SG the first.year.students-ACC a girl-ACC PRT failed-I
'I examined the first-year students. A girl, I failed. / A girl was failed by me.'

d. *Tegnap volt a szintaxis-vizsga.* ***Egy lány-t*** *meg buktatt-am.*
yesterday was the syntax-exam.NOM a girl-ACC PRT failed-I
'The syntax exam was yesterday. A girl, I failed. / A girl was failed by me.'

(6) a. ***A macska*** *nem szereti a víz-et.* [Hungarian]
cat.NOM not likes the the water-ACC
'Cats don't like water.'

b. ***A jó*** *el nyeri jutalm-á-t.*
the good PRT wins reward-its-ACC
'The good is reaping its reward.'

c. ***Michael Phelps*** *nyolc arany-érm-et nyert az Olimpiá-n.*
Michael Phelps eight gold-medal-ACC won the Olympics-at
'Michael Phelps won eight gold medals at the Olympics.'

The identification of the topic–comment articulation with the the given–new partitioning of the sentence, however, faces at least two problems even under the most liberal interpretation of givenness. First, there are types of constituents that clearly share the behaviour of topics but whose referent is not given in any sense. Observe the following Hungarian examples:

(7) a. ***Valami*** *le esett a tető-ről.* [Hungarian]
something off fell the roof-from
'Something fell off the roof.'

b. ***Egy kutya*** *meg harapott egy postás-t.*
a dog PRT bit a postman-ACC
'A dog bit a postman.'

Valami 'something' and *egy kutya* 'a dog' appear in topic position, and they have the prosody of prototypical topics; at the same time, they introduce new referents.

The second problem with the interpretation of the topic–comment articulation as a given–new partitioning is that the comment can also contain old referents, as illustrated in (8):

(8) a. *Do you know what Mary did with the book?*
b. [$_{\text{Topic}}$ *She*] [$_{\text{Comment}}$ *gave it to John*]

In (8b), the distribution of given and new elements is [$_{\text{Topic}}$ *Given*] [$_{\text{Comment}}$ *New Given New*].

Within the *aboutness topic* approach, a line of reseach explicitly identifies the topic with the constituent that is predicated about. In the terminology of Kuroda (1972), the topic is subject in the logical sense, in the terminology of Sasse (1987), it is the predication base, in the terminology of É. Kiss (1994), it is the logical subject of predication. The function *logical subject* is different from the function *grammatical subject*, associated with the constituent bearing the most prominent theta-role – even if the two functions are often carried by the same constituent. In (2c), (5c), and (5d), the topic/logical subject of predication is the object, whereas in (5b), it is the locative.

Kuroda (1972) based his analysis of the Japanese sentence on the logical theory of Marty (1918, 1965), who distinguished two types of judgments, one conforming to the traditional (Aristotelian) subject-predicate articulation, the other lacking such a partitioning. Kuroda discovered that these two types of judgments exactly correspond to the two basic sentence structures of Japanese, one displaying a topic–comment articulation, the other lacking a topic. Marty called the former type of judgments categorical, the latter type, thetic. The categorical judgment is assumed to consist of two separate acts: the act of recognition of that which is to be made the subject, and the act of affirming or denying what is expressed by the predicate about the subject. The thetic judgment represents the recognition or rejection of the material of a judgment. The logical subject need not coincide with the grammatical subject in Marty's theory, either; e.g., (9) is a thetic judgment containing a grammatical subject but no logical subject:

(9) *A new guest has arrived.*

Kuroda claims that in Japanese, categorical judgments are those whose initial constituent is marked by *wa*, e.g.:

(10) a. *Inu wa niwa de neko o oikakete iru.* [Japanese]
dog TOP garden in cat ACC chasing is
'The dog is chasing a cat in the garden.'

b. *Neko wa inu ga niwa de oikatete iru.*
cat TOP dog ACC garden in chasing is
'The cat is being chased by a dog in the garden.'

c. *Niwa de wa inu ga neko o oikakete iru.*
garden in TOP dog NOM cat ACC chasing is
'In the garden, a dog is chasing a cat.'

In (10a–c), the initial topic constituent, marked by *wa*, is presupposed ("recognized") to exist. It is this constituent (whether represented by the grammatical subject, object, or a locative) that the subsequent sentence part, the comment, predicates about.

Japanese sentences with no *wa*-marked constituent function as thetic judgments, lacking a logical subject–predicate articulation, e.g.:

(11) *Inu ga niwa de neko o oikakete iru.* [Japanese]
dog NOM garden in cat ACC chasing is
'There is a dog chasing a cat in the garden.'

The approach identifying the topic with the logical subject of predication does not directly associate topichood with givenness; it only requires that the identity of the referent of the topic be established in the speaker's mind prior to, and independent of the predication act. Consequently, this approach can, in principle, also handle the subjects of (8a, b), analyzing *valami* 'something' as the equivalent of 'a certain thing'. Definite generics, which can function as topics across languages, see, e.g. (6a), have to be regarded as names of kinds in this framework. This definition of topic excludes the theme argument of verbs of existence, coming into being, and creation from the set of possible topics, as their existence is the result of the event described by the predicate. Indeed, as will be shown in section 2.4, these types of elements remain in the predicate phrase.

(12) a. *There is* ***a book*** *on the table.*
b. *Született* ***egy gyerek****.* [Hungarian]
was.born a child
'A child was born.'

Adapting the definition of Geach (1985), the logical predicate of a sentence can be obtained if we extract a referring expression from it. The referring expression extracted from the sentence in a predication structure is the logical subject itself. This leads us to the following definition of the topic:

(13) The topic is an expression with a referent existing independently of the predicate phrase, occupying a position external to the predicate phrase, and binding an argument position in it.

The aboutness relation between the topic and the predicate phrase follows from this definition.

Sentence adverbials are also external to the predicate phrase, hence referential sentence adverbials, e.g., locatives and temporals, share at least two criteria of topichood. The aboutness relation between the adverbial and the predicate phrase, indicative of a logical subject–predicate structure, is felt to be optional in many cases. The optionality of the topic interpretation of referential sentence adverbials can be derived from the optionality of their argument status (cf. É. Kiss 1994). Other aproaches, e.g., Erteschik-Shir (1997) and Krifka (2008), distinguish aboutness topics and stage/frame topics. Locatives and temporals belong to the latter type.

The topic definition of Strawson (1964), Reinhart (1981), and Erteschik-Shir (1997), according to which the topic is the expression with respect to which the predicate is evaluated as true or false, extends to aboutness topics and stage topics alike. Reinhart (1981) and Erteschik-Shir (1997) describe information structure in the framework of a filing system metaphor. They assume that the information constituting the knowledge base of the interlocutors, the so-called common ground, is stored on file cards, each of which is associated with an entity, its heading. The topic constituent identifies the entity or set of entities under which the information expressed in the comment constituent should be stored in the common ground content. In this framework, topics are headings on existing file cards – i.e., in this approach, both aboutness and givenness are properties of topics.

According to Jacobs (2001), the topic has four prototypical attributes: informational separation (with the topic processed separately from the comment), predication (with X specifying a variable in the semantic valency of an element in Y), addressation (with X marking the point in the speaker-hearer knowledge where the information carried by Y has to be stored), and frame-setting (with X specifying a domain of reality to which the proposition expressed by Y is restricted). He shows for German constructions traditionally analyzed as topic-comment structures (left dislocation, contrastive topicalization, free topics) that they all sufficiently resemble the prototypical examples of topic-comment articulation, i.e., their topic has more than one of these prototypical properties.

2.2. Topic prominence and subject prominence

Li and Thompson (1976) suggested that some languages organize their sentences into a topic–comment structure, whereas in other languages the subject–predicate articulation represents the unmarked sentence pattern. They called the former type topic-prominent, the latter type subject-prominent. Their proposal could be reformulated in a more up-to-date and more precise terminology as follows: in some languages any argument satisfying the functional criteria of topichood can be extracted from the predicate in order to establish a (logical) predication structure, whereas in other languages it is always the grammatical subject that is externalized. The former, topic-prominent language type would be the discourse configurational type; the latter, subject-prominent type would represent grammatical-function configurationality instead. Brassai (1860) held a different view: he claimed that the topic-predicate articulation is universal. Languages like English are also „topic-prominent", i.e., discourse-configurational, in this sense; but they constrain topic-selection; only the subject can be topicalized in them. The two theories make different predictions. In a topic-prominent language in which only the subject can be topicalized, only subjects satisfying the criteria of topichood can be externalized. In a truly subject-prominent language, every type of subject can be extracted from the predicate phrase.

Before testing these predictions, the syntactic encoding of the topic–predicate articulation will be examined in languages generally acknowledged to be topic-prominent, primarily in Hungarian.

2.3. Topic–predicate articulation in the sentence structure of topic-prominent languages

In the neutral Hungarian sentence, the predicate phrase is an IP, with the V raised to I, and a predicative element, usually the verbal particle, raised to SpecIP. In non-neutral sentences, IP is subsumed by a FocP and/or a NegP, and verb movement takes place across the verbal particle into a functional head F. (F is assumed to be different from Foc, i.e., the V-initial section of a FocP is assumed to represent a maximal projection, because it is a possible target of such syntactic operations as coordination and deletion.) IP, FocP, and NegP are all potential adjunction sites for overt quantifier-raising and for certain types of adverbials.

(14)

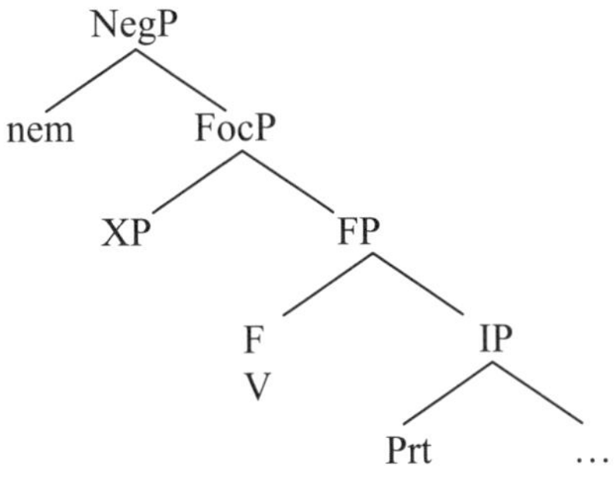

(15)

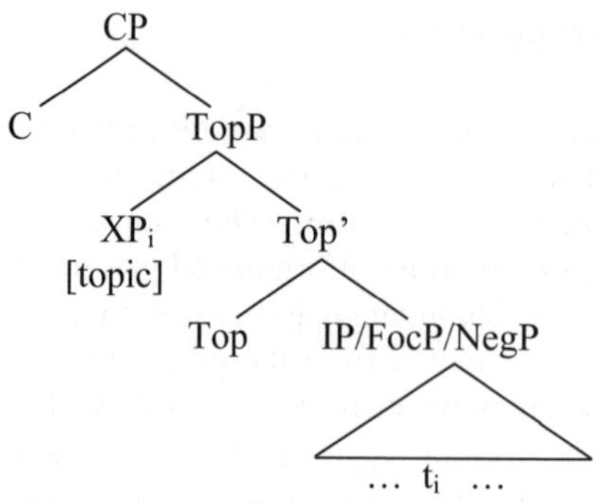

A topic/logical subject is, by definition, external to the predicate phrase. In most current generative grammars, the topic–predicate relation is mediated by an abstract functional head called Top; the topic phrase is its specifier, the predicate phrase is its complement.

In most known languages, the topic constituent not only c-commands but also precedes the predicate phrase, but predicate–topic constructions have also been reported from VSO languages like Malagasy (Pearson 2005).

In Germanic main clauses, the filler of SpecTopP is moved on into SpecCP in the unmarked case (but, alternatively, SpecCP can also be filled by a contrastive focus (cf. Frey 2006).

In many languages, the TopP projection can be iterated. Some languages, e.g., Italian (Rizzi 1997), Somali (Svolacchia, Mereu and Puglielli 1995), and Russian (King 1995), have been claimed to allow topics not only before but also after the focus, as representd in (16), proposed by Rizzi (1997). Benincá (2001), however, argues that a post-focus constituent is preposed via scrambling; it lacks topic properties.

(16)

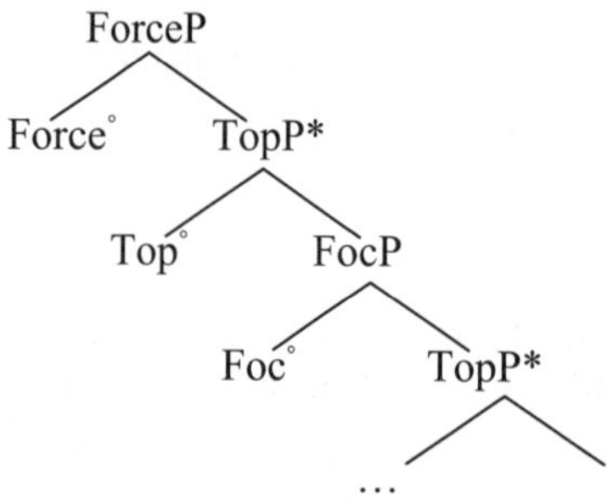

Frascarelli and Hinterhölz (2007) argue that multiple topic constructions involve topics of different kinds. The highest topic projection, called AboutP, harbors an aboutness topic, which can be followed by a contrastive topic, occupying the specifier of a ContrP. The lowest topic projection, called FamP, which can be subsumed by FocP in some languages, is reserved for familiarity topics. FamP can be iterated.

In English, unlike in Romance languages, topics are restricted to main clauses and a subset of embedded clauses, those having root properties. Haegeman (2006) derives this fact from the assumption that the landing site of English topicalization is the specifier of a higher TopP, which is absent in embedded clause types with a restricted left periphery, among them central adverbial clauses, factive complements, subject clauses and infinitival complements. The position occupied by a Romance topic, on the other hand, is the specifier of a lower TopP, which is available in all kinds of embedded clauses.

In accordance with the fact that a logical predication relation is derived by the extraction of a referring expression from the predicate, the topic constituent binds an argument position in the predicate phrase. In languages like Hungarian and Japanese, the argument position coindexed with, and c-commanded by, the topic is phonologically empty (in Minimalist terminology, it is occupied by a silent copy of the topic), which suggests that topicalization is a movement transformation. Long topic movement is also possible in many languages:

(17) [$_{\text{TopP}}$ *János-t*$_i$ [$_{\text{FocP}}$ *PÉTER* *akarta* [$_{\text{CP}}$ t_i *hogy* [$_{\text{IP}}$ *be* [Hungarian]
John-ACC Peter.NOM wanted that PRT
muta-ss-am t_i *Mari-nak*]]]]
introduce-SBJV-1SG Mary-DAT
'John, it was Peter who wanted me to introduce to Mary.'

In a large group of topic-prominent languages, among them Romance (Cinque 1990), Greek (Tsimpli 1995), and Haida (Enrico 2003), the topic is coindexed with a predicate-phrase-internal resumptive pronoun. Cinque (1990) calls this construction Clitic Left Dislocation. Observe the following Greek example of Tsimpli (1995):

(18) *Tus fitites oli i kathigites tus-ipostirizun.* [Greek]
the.ACC students all the lecturers them-support.3PL
'The students, all the lecturers support them.'

In the so-called hanging topic construction, the topicalized element does not agree in case with the resumptive pronoun.

Some languages, e.g., Chinese (Huang 1984), allow a contextually determined topic to be phonologically empty. Cf.

(19) 0_i [*Zhangsan shou* [*Lisi bu enshi* e_i]. [Chinese]
Zhangsan say Lisi not know
'Zhangsan says Lisi does not know [him].'

The empty embedded object in (19) is referentially disjoint from both the embedded subject and the matrix subject, which follows if it is a variable bound by an empty topic c-commanding both subjects.

Various Asian topic-prominent languages, among them Japanese, also have a topic–predicate construction in which the topic constituent is coindexed with a predicate-phrase-internal lexical element such that its referent and the topic referent have a non-empty intersection, e.g.:

(20) *Sakana wa taiga oisii.* [Japanese]
fish TOP red.snapper delicious.is
'Speaking of fish, red snapper is the most delicious.'

In (20), the topic–predicate construction is obviously base-generated. Base-generation has also been proposed for topic–predicate constructions involving a resumptive pronoun, e.g., for Italian (Cinque 1990), and for Haida (Enrico 2003).

2.4. Constraints on topic selection

Topic selection is, in principle, free; however, topic constituents must satisfy the semantic-pragmatic criteria of topichood, i.e., they must be referring expressions, whose existence is independent of the event described in the predicate. Thus quantified expressions with no referential reading, for example, universals and noun phrases modified by *kevés* 'few', cannot be topicalized – see (21) and (22). Their comment-internal position is shown by two criteria: they bear main stress, which is assigned to the leftmost element of the comment in Hungarian, and – as shown by the (b) examples – they cannot precede a topic, even though Hungarian allows multiple topics.

(21) a. *János-t KEVÉS LÁNY-NAK mutatta be Péter.* [Hungarian]
John-ACC few girl-DAT introduced PRT Peter.NOM
'John was introduced to few girls by Peter.'

b. **Kevés lány-nak János-t BE mutatta Péter.*
few girl-DAT John-ACC PRT introduced Peter.NOM

(22) a. *János-t MINDEN LÁNY-NAK be mutatta Péter.* [Hungarian]
John-ACC every girl-DAT PRT introduced Peter.NOM
'John was introduced to every girl by Peter.'

cf. b. **Minden lány-nak János-t BE mutatta Péter.*
every girl-DAT John-ACC PRT introduced Peter.NOM

Phrases involving a monoton decreasing quantifier like *kevés* must be focused, whereas universal quantifiers like that in (22) undergo quantifier raising (i.e., adjunction to IP). Indefinites, on the other hand, can function as topics if they have a referent that can be associated with an existential presupposition:

(23) *Két lány MEG bukott a vizsgá-n.* [Hungarian]
two girl PRT failed the exam-at
'Two girls failed the exam.'

The theme argument of a verb of existence, coming into being, appearance, or creation, whose existence the predicate asserts, is predicted not to be topicalizable. This is, indeed, the case: in Hungarian, it must follow the verb, or must appear as a predicative bare nominal in the specifier of IP:

(24) a. *Van* ***egy könyv*** *az asztal-on.* [Hungarian]
is a book.NOM the table-on
'There is a book on the table.'

b. *Érkezett* ***egy vendég***.
arrived a guest
'There arrived a guest. / A guest arrived.'

c. *János épített* ***egy ház-at***.
John built a house-ACC
'John built a house.'

(25) a. ***Könyv*** *van az asztal-on.* [Hungarian]
book is the table-on
'There is a book on the table.'

b. ***Vendég*** *érkezett.*
guest arrived
'A guest/Guests arrived.'

c. *János* ***ház-at*** *épített.*
John house-ACC built
'John built a house.'

Sentences with no topicalizable constituent such as (24a, b), and (25a, b) are thetic judgments realized as topicless sentences. Some authors, e.g., Kratzer (1995), Erteschik-Shir (1997), and Maleczki (2004), however, claim that apparently topicless sentences also display a predication structure; they predicate about the given situation represented by a phonologically empty spaciotemporal argument in SpecTopP.

2.5. Contrastive topics

If a topic constituent is pronounced with a particular, contrastive fall-rise contour (to be marked by the symbol √), it is understood to be contrasted with either an explicit or an implied alternative topic, for which an alternative predicate holds (cf. Büring 1997, 2003; Gyuris 2009). For example:

(26) *√Évá-nak NEM mutatta be Péter János-t.* [Hungarian]
Eve-DAT not introduced PRT Peter.NOM John-ACC
'To Eve, Peter didn't introduce John.'

(26) implies that, as opposed to Eve, to whom Peter did not introduce John, there is at least one other person to whom Peter did introduce John.

What makes contrastive topics interesting is that non-referring expressions, for example, adjectival and adverbial phrases and quantified expressions, which are barred from SpecTopP as ordinary topics, are licensed in SpecTopP if pronounced with a contrastive intonation. A further mystery is that, whereas ordinary topics as referring expressions have maximal scope, quantifiers functioning as contrastive topics appear to have narrow scope:

(27) a. *Gazdag nem vagy-ok.* [Hungarian]
rich not am-I
'Rich, I am not.'

b. *Fel csak ÉVA ment gyalog.*
up only Eve went on.foot
'Up(stairs), only Eve went on foot.'

c. *Minden kötelező olvasmány-t KEVÉS diák olvasott el a*
every compulsory reading-ACC few student read PRT the
vizsgá-ra.
exam-for
'Every compulsory reading, few students read for the exam.'

According Krifka (1998), a clause-initial constituent pronounced with a fall-rise is a focus in topic (the fall encodes its topic function, the rise its focus function); according to Molnár (1998), it is a topic in focus. Gyuris and É. Kiss (2003) analyze the contrastive topic as a constituent in SpecTopP, whose contrastive intonation serves the purpose of individuating a non-individual-denoting expression, thereby making it suitable for the topic role. Individuation by contrast is claimed to enable non-individual-denoting expressions to be interpreted as semantic objects (properties) which the rest of the sentence predicates a (higher-order) property about. A quantifier functioning as a contrastive topic, e.g., that in (27c), denotes a property of plural individuals, and its apparent narrow scope arises from the fact that it is considered to be a predicate over a variable inherent in the lexical representation of the verb.

2.6. Topic–predicate articulation in the sentence structure of subject-prominent languages

The question whether English-type languages display a grammatical subject–grammatical predicate articulation, as claimed by Li and Thompson (1976), or they are also of the topic-prominent type with constrained topic selection, as claimed by Brassai (1860), can be decided by examining how subjects unsuitable for the topic role behave in them. The non-specific subjects of verbs of existence, appearence, and coming into being cannot be topicalized because their referent does not exist independently of, and prior to, the event described in the predicate. In a truly subject-prominent language, specific and non-specific subjects occupy the same subject position, i.e., categorical and thetic judgments are realized by the same syntactic structure. In a topic-prominent language in which topicalization can only target the subject, on the other hand, only specific subjects are external to the predicate phrase; non-specific subjects are internal to it.

A survey of 35 European languages in the EUROTYP project (É. Kiss 1998b) provided no evidence of the subject-prominent language type: non-specific subjects turned out to be systematically internal to the predicate phrase in practically all of the languages. The questionnaire asked the informants, for example, to translate the following minimal pair. In (28a), the context licences the specific reading of the noun phrase *a girl*. In (28b), on the other hand, the context makes it clear that the referent of *a girl* is introduced by the predicate of the second sentence; i.e., its existence cannot be presupposed.

(28) a. (Several girl-friends of yours were waiting for the bus. The bus arrived.)
A girl got on the bus.
b. (You were sitting in a bus alone at night, frightened. Luckily,) *a girl got on the bus.*

The specific indefinite subject of (28a) occupies a more external position than the non-specific indefinite subject of (28b) in practically every language tested, e.g.

(29) a. *Bir kiz otobüs-e bin-di.* [Turkish]
a girl bus-DAT board-PST
'A girl boarded the bus.'

b. *Otobüs-e bir kiz bin-di.*
bus-DAT a girl board-PST

(30) a. *Una ragazza è salita sull' autobus.* [Italian]
a girl be.PRES.3SG got on.the bus
'A girl got on the bus.'

b. *È salita sull' autobus una ragazza.*
be.PRES.3SG got on.the bus a girl

(31) a. *En flicka steg på bussen.* [Swedish]
a girl got on.the bus
'A girl got on the bus.'

b. *Det steg en flicka på bussen.*
there got a girl on.the bus

The language which came closest to representing the subject-prominent type was English. However, there is distributional evidence even in English indicating that specific and nonspecific subjects occupy different structural positions (see É. Kiss 1996). Namely,

(i) Whereas the specific subject of a categorical sentence can be followed by a sentence adverbial (without any comma-intonation), the non-specific subject of a thetic sentence cannot:

(32) a. *John fortunately has been born on time.*
b. **A baby fortunately has been born.*

(ii) The negative particle follows the specific subject of a categorical sentence, and precedes the non-specific subject of a thetic sentence:

(33) a. *John was not born on time.*
b. **A baby was not born.*

(34) a. *Not a baby was born.*
b. **Not John was born on time.*

If the sentence adverbial in (32) and the negative particle in (33)–(34) are located between the (logical) subject of predication and the predicate phrase (as is attested across languages), then English non-specific subjects are internal to the predicate phrase (IP), and specific subjects are external to it.

(iii) The VP of a thetic sentence cannot undergo VP-deletion, as was observed by Guéron (1980):

(35) **A riot occurred and then a flood did.*

On the basis of the evidence in (i) and (ii), let us assume that specific subjects occupy SpecTopP in English, too, whereas non-specific subjects raise only as far as SpecIP, where they must move in order to check their nominative case. Then the ungrammaticality of (35) follows if verb phrase deletion is, in fact, predicate phrase (i.e., IP-) deletion. In (35), deletion is illicit because the deleted phrase constitutes merely a subpart of the predicate phrase (IP).

(iv) A sentence-initial *only* (as well as as a sentence-initial *also* or *even*) can only have sentential scope when it is followed by a non-specific subject, as in (36b). A sentence-initial *only* followed by a specific subject, e.g. that in (36a), can only have scope over the subject:

(36) a. *%Only John was born on time, nothing else happened.*
b. *Only a baby was born, nothing else happened.*

The grammaticality difference between (36a) and (36b) follows if the maximal scope of *only* (as well as *also* and *even*) is the predicate phrase (IP), which includes the subject in thetic sentences but does not include it in categorical sentences.

The data in (32)–(36) indicate that the subject of a thetic sentence and that of a categorical sentence occupy different positions in English, too, i.e., not even English is a subject-prominent language. It is a special type of topic-prominent language, in which the subject satisfying the criteria of topichood must be topicalized. Additional topic movement is also possible:

(37) *[$_{TopP}$ John [$_{TopP}$ Peter introduced to Eve]]*

Written French also might appear to be a potential example of subject-prominence. Spoken French, on the other hand, employing a great a variety of dislocation rules, has been shown by Lambrecht (1986) and de Cat (2007) to be clearly discourse-configurational.

3. The focus–background articulation

The interpretation of the notion *focus* is at least as diffuse as that of the notion *topic*. A linguistic tradition (traced back to Paul 1880) identifies focus with new information. In this framework, every sentence has a focus, and there are all-focus sentences (those answering the question *What happened?*). According to another definition (which can be traced back to Brassai 1860), the focus of a sentence is the constituent which corresponds to the wh-part of the explicit or implicit constituent question eliciting the sentence. Sentences answering non-constituent questions like *What happened?* involve no focus – because a focus always induces the partitioning of the sentence into a focus and a background, or a focus, and a focus-frame. The focus-frame is derived by replacing the focus by a variable – hence the focus introduces a set of alternatives. In a third view of focus, focusing not only elicits alternatives, but also excludes them except the one identified by the focus. These – partially overlapping – notions of focus are often based on different languages. Here, two major focus notions will be distinguished: information focus, encoded prosodically, and identificational focus, encoded configurationally.

3.1. Prosodically encoded (information) focus

In the literature on English, focus is mostly a prosodic notion with pragmatic import. Since in mainstream generative grammar the relation between prosody and semantic-pragmatic interpretation is mediated by syntax, a constituent to be assigned metrical prominence in phonology, and to be interpreted as new information must be marked as [+F(ocus)] in syntactic structure.

This type of focus, often referred to as information focus, can be of any size, extending over a mere head, a phrase, or the whole sentence. It is a much discussed research question how the [+F] feature can project in syntactic structure; what licences, and what blocks, its projection; i.e., how the size of semantic focus can be derived from the locus of intonation center. Compare (38a) and (38b) (adapted from Chomsky 1971). In the former, focus projection is free, i.e., the [+F] feature of the noun *shirt* can be extended to any of the subsuming NP, PP, higher NP, higher PP, embedded VP, embedded IP, matrix VP, and matrix IP nodes. In (38b) focus projection is blocked.

(38) a. *He was warned to look out for an ex-convict with a red SHIRT.*
b. *He was warned to look out for an ex-convict with a RED shirt.*

Whereas (38a) can be a response to any of the questions in (39), (38b) can only be an answer to (40):

(39) a. *Was he warned to look out for an ex-convict with a red cap?*
b. *Was he warned to look out for an ex-convict with a blue jacket?*
c. *Who was he warned to look out for?*
d. *What was he warned to do?*
etc.

(40) *Was he warned to look out for an ex-convict with a blue shirt?*

The rules of focus projection were formulated by Selkirk (1984: 207) as follows:

(41) a. Basic Focus Rule
A constituent to which a pitch accent is assigned is a focus.

b. Phrasal Focus Rule
A constituent may be a focus if (i) or (ii) (or both) are true:
(i) The constituent that is its *head* is a focus.
(ii) A constituent contained within it that is an *argument* of the head is a focus.

In (38b), the constituent bearing pitch accent is neither a head, nor an argument, that is why the phrases containing it cannot function as foci.

The Phrasal Focus Rule as formulated in (41b) is actually not universal. In Hungarian, for example, a noun phrase cannot be information focus unless its modifier is a focus; thus focus projection is allowed in (42a), and is blocked in (42b). (42a) – with secondary stress on *fegyencet* 'convict.ACC' – can answer (43a, b, and c) alike, whereas (42b) can only be a response to (44).

(42) a. *A rendőrség egy PIROS inges volt fegyenc-et keres.* [Hungarian]
the police a red shirted former convict-ACC seeks
'The police look for an ex-convict with a red shirt.'

b. A rendőrség egy piros inges volt FEGYENCET keres.

(43) a. *A rendőrség egy MILYEN inges volt fegyenc-et keres?* [Hungarian]
the police a what shirted former convict-ACC seeks
'An ex-convict in what shirt are the police looking for?'

b. *A rendőrség MILYEN volt fegyenc-et keres?*
the police what former convict-ACC seeks
'What kind of ex-convict do the police look for?'

c. *A rendőrség KIT keres?*
the police whom seeks
'Who do the police look for?'

(44) *A rendőrség egy piros inges volt KATONÁ-T keres?* [Hungarian]
the police a red shirted former soldier-ACC seeks
'Do the police look for an ex-soldier with a red shirt?'

The Phrasal Focus Rule seems to be sensitive to where phrasal stress is assigned in the given language. The differences between the focus-interpretation possibilities of (38a, b) and (42a, b) derive from the fact that the Hungarian Nuclear Stress Rule assigns phrasal stress to the left branch of phrases, i.e., to modifiers instead of arguments (its direction is the opposite of the direction of the English Nuclear Stress Rule – cf. Varga 2002).

Reinhart's (1995) Stress–Focus Correspondence Principle offers the following solution to the stress–focus correspondence problem: the [+F] feature can project to any constituent within which the [+F] marked constituent would receive the highest stress by the regular stress rules of the language. In (38a), the main stress on *shirt* is the neutral stress of the clause, i.e., the N *shirt* is the most highly stressed constituent of each of the NP, PP, higher NP, higher PP, embedded VP, embedded IP, matrix VP, and matrix IP projections subsuming it; hence all these phrases are potential foci. In (38b), the most highly stressed constituent is an adjective on the left branch, which is not assigned highest stress by the Nuclear Stress Rule in any of the phrases dominating it. Hence none of those phrases are possible foci; the adjective is the only possible focus of the clause. In Hungarian, it is the other way round. In (42a), the adjective *piros* 'red' bears the nuclear stress of the sentence; it receives phrasal stress in each of the AdjP, NP and FocP projections dominating it; therefore, all of these phrases can be interpreted as information foci. In (42b), the most highly stressed *fegyencet* 'convict.ACC', being on the right branch, is not assigned phrasal stress in any cycle; therefore it is information focus in itself.

If the feature [+F] marks new information in semantics, and highest metrical prominence in phonology, then a focus is not always [+F]. As shown in (45a), a contrastive focus can be discourse-given, and, as shown in (45b), a second occurrence focus (*Mrs Clinton* in sentence B) can bear the lowest possible degree of phrase stress:

(45) a. A: *Good morning. I am here to see Mrs Clinton again.*
B: *Sure, Mr. Smith. Let's see ... One of her assistants will be with you in a second.*
A: *I'd like to see [$_F$ HER] today. I'm always talking to her assistants.*
(Vallduví and Engdahl 1996)

b. A: *Mary would only like to see [$_F$ MRS CLINTON].*
B: *Also [$_F$ JOHN] would only like to see [$_F$ MRS CLINTON].*

Selkirk (2008) has demonstrated the necessity of a three-way distinction instead of [+/– F]. In her theory an F-feature marks just contrastive focus (as proposed by Truckenbrodt 1995 and Rooth 1996), and a G-feature (proposed by Féry and Samek-Lodovici 2006) marks discourse-given constituents, while discourse-new is unmarked. A second occurrence focus is both F-marked and G-marked.

Theories interpreting the [+F] feature as [+new] cannot predict that focus placement – e.g, in its interaction with negation and with such focus-sensitive particles as *only, also*, and *even* – can affect truth conditions. Cf.

(46) a. *John only introduced Mary to BILL.*
b. *John only introduced MARY to Bill.*

More sophisticated semantic approaches to focus include the *structured meaning* theory of focus, elaborated by von Stechow (1990, 1991), Jacobs (1983, 1986), Krifka (1991, 1992), etc. In this theory, the focus feature of a constituent induces the partitioning of the semantic representation of a sentence into a focus part and a background part. Consider the semantic structure of (47a):

(47) a. *John loves MARY.*
b. $<\lambda$ x [loves John x], Mary$>$

(47) expresses that the individual who has the property of being loved by John is Mary. Particles like *only* require a focus–background partitioning, and bind the focus (cf. Jacobs 1986; and Krifka 1992):

(48) a. *Peter met only Luise's YOUNGEST sister.*
b. ONLY (λ A [Peter met Luise's A sister], youngest)

The most influential semantic theory of focus is Rooth's (1985, 1992) Alternative Semantics. In this approach, the focus introduces a set of alternatives comparable to the referent of the focus, which yield alternative propositions. Thus in a situation involving five girls: Mary, Susan, Eve, Sarah, and Elisabeth, the sentence in (49a) has the ordinary meaning in (49b), and induces the alternatives in (49c). Crucially, an information focus is not predicted to exclude the alternatives; this can be done by a focus-sensitive operator like *only*. That is why contrastive topics, cf. (27), involving no exclusion, are also analyzed as (topicalized) foci in this framework.

(49) a. *John invited MARY*
b. Meaning: INVITED (John) (Mary)
c. Alternatives: John invited Susan,
John invited Eve,
John invited Sarah,
John invited Elisabeth.

Information focus is typically not a discourse-configurational phenomenon; it is only encoded prosodically. It can, nevertheless, trigger syntactic movement operations. English transformations like dative shift, locative inversion, or passive, have been claimed to often serve the purpose of realizing the [+F] constituent in the rightmost position of the clause, the unmarked locus of intonation center (cf. Rochemont and Culicover 1990; Reinhart 1995; Zubizarreta 1998). For example:

(50) a. *I gave John a BOOK.* cf. *I gave the book to JOHN.*
b. *Into the room came JOHN.*
c. *This was written by JOHN.*

In German, the focus is left-adjacent to the clause-final verb in the unmarked prosodic structure, which can be achieved by scrambling the material from between the clause-final verb and the [+F]-marked constituent:

(51) *dass ich dem Johann$_i$ ZWEI BÜCHER t_i geschenkt habe* [German]
that I the.DAT John.DAT two books given have
'that I gave to John TWO BOOKS'

3.2. Structurally encoded (identificational) focus

In a subset of languages (in about half of the European languages examined in the framework of the EUROTYP project, see É. Kiss 1998b), there is a designated focus position in syntactic structure. It is a non-argument (A-bar) position in the left periphery of sentence structure. Since Choe (1989) and Brody (1990), it has usually been identified as the specifier of a designated functional projection called Foc(us)P. In Rizzi's (1997) sentence structure, see (16) above, FocP is part of the C-domain; it is essentially a layer of CP. The focus position is filled by a transformation called focus movement. The fact that structural focus is established via movement determines its size: it must be a maximal projection; furthermore, it must be available for movement without the violation of Subjacency. Compare the following focus constructions:

(52) a. *A rendőrség EGY PIROS INGES FEGYENCET keres.* [Hungarian]
the police a red shirted convict.ACC seeks
'The police look for a convict in a red shirt.'
b. *A rendőrség EGY piros inges fegyencet keres.*
c. *A rendőrség egy PIROS inges fegyencet keres.*
d. *A rendőrség egy piros inges FEGYENCET keres.*

The constituent undergoing focus movement and landing in SpecFocP, i.e., the structural focus, is the same noun phrase in each of these sentences: *egy piros inges fegyencet*; it is the referent of *egy piros inges fegyencet* that is identified as that being looked for by the police in each case. If (52a–d) were pronounced with the intonation countour of a *yes-no* question, each of them coud be answered as *Igen. Ronnie Biggset.* 'Yes, Ronnie Biggs' (cf. É. Kiss 1998).

In the analysis of Aboh (2004), and Aboh, Corver, Dyakonova and van Koppen (2010), on the other hand, sentences like (52b–d) contain a focussed subconstituent whose focus movement induces DP-piedpiping. Aboh's theory is based on Gungbe, in which a focused subconstituent is moved to the left periphery of the noun phrase, where it is marked by the same focus marker as a clausal focus. The topic and focus heads within the DP are claimed to represent active goals for the corresponding functional heads within the C domain, eliciting generalized piedpiping of the whole DP embedding the goal.

In Hungarian, focus movement also triggers V-movement; the V crosses the verbal particle and the adverbials and quantifiers adjoined to IP, landing in a position left-adjacent to the V:

(53) [$_{\text{FocP}}$ XP [V$_i$ [$_{\text{IP}}$ PRT [$_{\text{I'}}$ t$_i$ …

In some approaches, e.g., Brody (1995), the tensed V lands in the Foc head, where it participates in feature-checking. Horvath (2005), however, convincingly argues that the V-initial sentence part acts as a maximal projection, hence the V must have landed in a lower functional head.

The FocP projection can be iterated, as shown in (54a), containing two *csak* 'only' phrases, which are obligatorily focused. Long focus movement across SpecCP is also possible, see (54b).

(54) a. [$_{\text{FocP}}$ *Csak két diák-ot* [$_{\text{XP}}$ *buktatott*$_i$ [$_{\text{FocP}}$ *csak egy* [Hungarian]
only two student-ACC failed only one
tárgy-ból [$_{\text{XP}}$ t$_i$ [$_{\text{IP}}$ *meg* t_i [$_{\text{vP}}$ *a professzor*]]]]]]
subject-from PRT the professor.NOM
'It was only two students that the professor failed only in one subject.'

b. [$_{\text{FocP}}$ *Mikor*$_i$ [$_{\text{XP}}$ *szeretné János* [$_{\text{CP}}$ t_i *hogy* [$_{\text{IP}}$ *el indul-j-unk* t_i]]]]
when would.like John.NOM that off go-SBJV-1PL
'When would John like us to leave?'

Structurally encoded focus differs from prosodically marked focus in several respects (cf. É. Kiss 1998a; Vallduví and Vilkuna 1998).

(i) Structural focus expresses exhaustive identification (that is why this type of focus is called identificational). Observe the following Hungarian minimal pair. The English equivalents, with the structural focus translated as a cleft constituent, and the prosodic focus translated as a focus in situ, illustrate the same point.

(55) a. *Kit hívott meg János?* [Hungarian]
whom invited PRT John
'Who did John invite?'

b. *János MARI-T hívta meg.*
John Mary-ACC invited PRT
'It was Mary that John invited.'

cf. c. *János meg hívta MARI-T.*
John PRT invited Mary-ACC
'John invited MARY.'

(55b) expresses that there is a set of persons such that John invited them, and the referent that exhausts this set is the referent of *Mary*. Thus exhaustivity is a crucial feature of structural focus, which is absent in the case of the prosodic focus in (55c). Szabolcsi (1981) pointed out the exhaustivity of structural focus by various tests. For example, in the case of a sentence with a constituent represented by a coordinate expression, the omission of one of the conjuncts yields a sentence that is a logical consequence of the original one:

(56) *János meg hívta Mari-t és Évá-t.* → *János meg hívta Mari-t.* [Hungarian]
John PRT invited Mary-ACC and Eve-ACC   John PRT invited Mary-ACC
'John invited Mary and Eve.'   'John invited Mary.'

If, however, the coordinate expression is an exhaustive focus, the omission of one of the conjuncts results in a sentence that contradicts the corresponding sentence with the coordinate focus:

(57) a. *János MARIT ÉS ÉVÁT hívta meg.* ↛ *János MARIT hívta meg.* [Hungarian]
'It was Mary and Eve that John invited.'   'It was Mary that John invited.'

cf. b. *János nem MARI-T ÉS ÉVÁ-T hívta meg, hanem MARI-T.*
John not Mary-ACC and Eve-ACC invited PRT but Mary-ACC
'It wasn't Mary and Eve that John invited, but it was Mary.'

(ii) Another specific feature of structural focus is the existential presupposition associated with the background. Compare:

(58) a. *János nem hívta meg Mari-t a születésnap-já-ra.* [Hungarian]
John not invited PRT Mary-ACC the birthday-his-for
'John didn't invite Mary for his birthday.'

b. *János nem MARI-T hívta meg a születésnap-já-ra.*
John not Mary-ACC invited PRT the birthday-his-for
'It wasn't Mary that John invited for his birthday.'

(58b), with *Marit* in focus position, expresses that there is a person – other than Mary – that John invited for his birthday. In the case of (58a), involving a mere prosodic focus, there is no such presupposition.

(iii) Identificational focus involves distributional restrictions; for example, universal quantifiers cannot function as identificational foci.

(59) a. **János* [$_{\text{FocP}}$ *mindenki-t* [*hívott*$_i$ [$_{\text{IP}}$ *meg* t_i]]] [Hungarian]
John everybody-ACC invited PRT
'John invited everybody.'

b. *János* [$_{\text{IP}}$ *mindenkit* [$_{\text{IP}}$ *meg-hívott*]]

(iv) Identificational focus enters into a scope relation with negation and with quantifiers.
In (60a), focus has scope over negation; in (60b), negation has scope over focus; and in (61a), focus has scope over a universal quantifier, and in (61b), the universal quantifier has scope over the focus.

(60) a. *JÁNOS nem bukott meg szintaxis-ból.* [Hungarian]
John not failed PRT syntax-from
'It was John who did not fail in syntax.'

b. *Nem JÁNOS bukott meg szintaxis-ból.*
not John failed PRT syntax-from
'It wasn't John who failed in syntax.'

(61) a. *A PROFESSZOR buktatott mindenki-t meg szintaxis-ból.* [Hungarian]
the professor.NOM failed everybody-ACC PRT syntax-from
'It was the professor who failed everybody in syntax.'

b. *Mindenki-t A PROFESSZOR buktatott meg szintaxis-ból.*
everybody-ACC the professor.NOM failed PRT syntax-from
'Everybody was failed in syntax by the professor.'

In languages like Hungarian, structurally encoded focus is an unmarked phenomenon, present in a large percentage of sentences. Structural foci exists also in languages which express focus prosodically in the unmarked case; in English, they are represented by the cleft focus and the pseudo-cleft focus. Cleft and pseudo-cleft foci share all the relevant properties of Hungarian structural focus.

An important question is what is the source of the specific properties of structurally encoded foci; what is the explanation of their exhaustivity, the existential presupposition associated with their background, the impossibility of the focusing of universal quantifiers, and the scope interactions attested.

The theory which can account for all these properties is Higgins's (1973) theory of the English pseudo-cleft construction, adopted to the German and Swedish cleft construction by Huber (2000). According to this theory, structural focus is a derived predicate, bearing a specificational predication relation to its subject, the open sentence represented by the background. Focus movement serves the purpose of encoding this predicate–subject relation syntactically, by creating the appropriate partitioning, and establishing an m-command relation between the two parts.

The English cleft and pseudo-cleft focus clearly occupies the position of a predicate complement. In Hungarian, the predicate status of structural focus can be proven indirectly; e.g., it can be represented by a bare nominal (62a); and in examples like (62b), it can have a predicative, non-referential interpretation:

(62) a. *Évá-t HELYES FIÚ kérte fel táncolni.* [Hungarian]
Eve-ACC nice boy asked PRT to.dance
'It was a nice boy who asked Eve for a dance.'

b. *Nem A PROFESSZOR-NAK adta-m át a hely-em, hanem AZ ÖREGEMBER-NEK.*
not the professor-to gave-I PRT the seat-1SG.ACC but the old.man-to
'It was not the professor but the old man to whom I gave my seat.'

Higgins (1973) and Huber (2000) claim that in a specificational predication construction neither the subject, nor the predicate is referential; the subject (the open sentence) determines a set, and the predicate (the focus) specifies the referential content of this set by (exhaustively) listing its members. The exhaustivity of structural focus is entailed by its specifying function. The subject of predication, i.e., the background, is associated with an existential presupposition because only an existing set can be specified referentially. A universal quantifier cannot be focused because it cannot be used as a predicative nominal (cf. Giannakidou and Quer 1995). What were interpreted as scope interactions in (60) and (61) illustrate the fact that in focus constructions both the lower predicate (IP), and the higher predicate (FocP) can be negated, and can serve as adjunction sites of universal quantifiers. A negative particle or universal quantifier adjoined to the lower predicate only has scope over the open sentence functioning as the subject of specificational predication; a negative particle or universal quantifier adjoined to FocP, on the other hand, has scope over exhaustive identification.

4. References (selected)

Aboh, Enoch O.
2004 Snowballing movement and generalized pied-piping. In: Anne Breitbath, and Henk van Riemsdijk (eds.), *Trigger*, 15–47. Berlin: Mouton.
Aboh, Enoch O., Norbert Corver, Marina Dyakonova, and Michel van Koppen
2010 DP-internal information structure: some introductory remarks. *Lingua* 120: 782–801.
Benincá, Paola
2001 The position of topic and focus in the left periphery. In: *Current Studies in Italian Syntax, Essays Offered to Lorenzo Renzi*, 39–64. Amsterdam: Elsevier.
Brassai, Sámuel
1852–53 Tapogatódzások a magyar nyelv körül [Exploring the Hungarian language]. In: *Pesti Napló*, 802–885.
Brassai, Sámuel
1860 A magyar mondat [The Hungarian sentence]. In: *Magyar Akadémiai Értesítő. A Nyelv- és Széptudományi Osztály Közlönye* 1: 279–399.
Brody, Michael
1990 Some remarks on the focus field in Hungarian. *UCL Working Papers in Linguistics* 2: 201–225. University College London.
Brody, Michael
1995 Focus and checking theory. In: István Kenesei (ed.), *Approaches to Hungarian* 5, 29–44. Szeged: JATE.
Büring, Daniel
1997 The great scope inversion conspiracy. *Linguistics and Philosophy* 20: 175–194.
Büring, Daniel
2003 On d-trees, beans, and B-accents. *Linguistics and Philosophy* 26: 511–545.
Cat, Cécile de
2007 French dislocation without movement. *Natural Language and Linguistic Theory* 25: 1–53.
Choe, Hyon-Sook
1989 Restructuring parameters and scrambling in Korean and Hungarian. In: László Marácz,and Pieter Muysken (eds.), *Configurationality*, 267–292. Dordrecht: Foris.
Chomsky, Noam
1971 Deep structure, surface structre, and semantic interpretation. In: Danny D. Steinberg, and Leon A. Jakobovits (eds.), *Semantics*. London: Cambridge University Press.
Cinque, Guglielmo
1990 *Types of A' Dependencies*. Cambridge, Mass.: MIT Press.
É. Kiss, Katalin
1994 Sentence structure and word order. In: Ferenc Kiefer, and Katalin É. Kiss (eds), *The Syntactic Structure of Hungarian,* 1–90. New York/San Diego: Academic Press.
É. Kiss, Katalin
1995 *Discourse Configurational Languages*. Oxford: Oxford University Press.
É. Kiss, Katalin
1996 Two subject positions in English. *The Linguistic Review* 13: 119–142.
É. Kiss, Katalin
1998a Identificational focus versus information focus. *Language* 74: 245–273.
É. Kiss, Katalin
1998b Discourse-configurationality in the languages of Europe. In: Anna Siewierska (ed.), *Constituent Order in the Languages of Europe*, 681–727. Berlin: Mouton de Gruyter.
É. Kiss, Katalin
2002 *The Syntax of Hungarian*. Cambridge: Cambridge University Press.

É. Kiss, Katalin
2006 Focussing as Predication. In: Valéria Molnár, and Susanne Winkler (eds.), *Architecture of Focus*, 169–196. Berlin: Mouton de Gruyter.
É. Kiss, Katalin
2008a Free word order, (non-)configurationality and phases. *Linguistic Inquiry* 39: 441–474.
É. Kiss, Katalin
2008b A pioneering theory of information structure. *Acta Linguistica Hungarica* 55: 23–40.
É. Kiss, Katalin, and Beáta Gyuris
2003 Apparent scope inversion under the rise fall contour. *Acta Linguistica Hungarica* 50: 371–404.
Enrico, John
2003 *Haida Syntax*. Lincoln, Nebraska: University of Nebraska Press.
Erteschik-Shir, Nomi
1997 *The Dynamics of Focus Structure*. Cambridge: Cambridge University Press.
Féry, Caroline, and Vieri Samek-Lodovici
2006 Focus projection and prosodic prominence in nested foci. *Language* 82: 131–150.
Frey, Werner
2005 Pragmatic properties of certain German and English left peripheral constructions. *Linguistics* 43: 89–129.
Frey, Werner
2006 Contrast and movement to the German prefield. In: Valéria Molnár, and Susanne Winkler (eds.), *Architecture of Focus*, 235–264. Berlin: Mouton de Gruyter.
Gabelentz, Georg von der
1869 Ideen zu einer vergleichenden Syntax. *Zeitschrift für Völkerpsychologie und Sprachwissenschaft* 6: 376–84.
Geach, Peter
1985 Subject and predicate. In: Peter Martinich (ed.), *The Philosophy of Language*, 189–199. Oxford: Oxford University Press.
Giannakidou, Anastasia, and Josep Quer
1995 Two mechanisms for the licensing of indefinites. In: L. Gabriele, D. Hardison, and R. Westmoreland (eds.), *Formal Linguistics Society of Mid-America (FLSM 6)*, 103–114. Bloomington: Indiana University Linguistics Club.
Guéron, Jacquéline
1980 On the syntax and semantics of PP extraposition. *Linguistic Inquiry* 11: 637–678.
Gyuris, Beáta
2009 The semantics and pragmatics of the contrastive topic in Hungarian. Budapest: Lexica.
Halliday, M. A. K.
1967 *Intonation and Grammar in British English*. The Hague: Mouton.
Higgins, Roger F.
1973 The pseudo-cleft construction in English. Ph.D. dissertation, MIT, Cambridge, Mass.
Hockett, Charles F.
1963 The problem of universals in language. In: Joseph H. Greenberg (ed.), *Universals of Language*. Cambridge, Mass.: MIT Press.
Horvath, Julia
2000 Interfaces vs. the computational system in the syntax of focus. In: Hans Bennis, Martin Everaert, and Eric Reuland (eds.), *Interface Strategies*, 183–206. Amsterdam: Royal Netherlands Academy of Arts and Sciences.
Horvath, Julia
2005 Is „focus movement" driven by stress? In: Christopher Piñon, and Péter Siptár (eds.), *Approaches to Hungarian 9*, 131–158. Budapest: Kluwer Akadémiai Kiadó.
Huang, James C.-T.
1984 On the distribution and reference of empty pronouns. *Linguistic Inquiry* 15: 531–574.

Huber, Stefan
2000 *Es-Clefts und det-Clefts. Zur Syntax, Semantik und Informationsstruktur von Spaltsätzen im Deutschen und Schwedischen*. Stockholm: Almquist and Wiksell International.

Jackendoff, Ray
1972 *Semantic Interpretation in Generative Grammar*. Cambridge, Mass.: MIT Press.

Jacobs, Joachim
1983 *Fokus und Skalen*. Tübingen: Niemeyer.

Jacobs, Joachim
1986 The syntax of focus and adverbials in German. In: Werner Abraham, and Sjaak de Meij (eds.), *Topic, Focus, and Configurationality*, 103–128. Amsterdam: John Benjamins.

Jacobs, Joachim
2001 The dimensions of topic-comment. *Linguistics* 39: 641–681.

King, Tracy Holloway
1995 *Configuring Topic and Focus in Russian*. Stanford: CSLI.

Kratzer, Angelika
1995 Stage level and individual level predicates. In: Gregory Carlson, and Francis Jeffry Pelletier (eds.), *The Generic Book*. Chicago: University of Chicago Press.

Krifka, Manfred
1991 A compositional semantics for multiple focus constructions. In: Joachim Jacobs (ed.), *Informationsstruktur und Grammatik*, 17–53. (Sonderheft der Linguistischen Berichte) Opladen: Westdeutscher Verlag.

Krifka, Manfred
1992 A framework for focus-sensitive quantification. In: C. Barker and David Dowty (ed.), *SALT II. Proceedings from the Second Conference on Semantics and Linguistic Theory*, 215–336. (Working Papers in Linguistics 40) Columbus: Ohio State University.

Krifka, Manfred
1998 Scope inversion under the rise fall contour in German. *Linguistic Inquiry* 29: 75–112.

Krifka, Manfred
2008 Basic notions of information structure. *Acta Linguistica Hungarica* 55: 243–276.

Kuroda, Sige-Yuki
1972 The categorical and the thetic judgment. *Foundations of Language* 9: 153–185.

Lambrecht, Knud
1986 Topic, focus, and spoken French. PhD dissertation, University of California.

Lambrecht, Knud
1994 *Information Structure and Sentence Form. Topic, Focus and the Mental Representations of Discourse Referents*. Cambridge: Cambridge University Press.

Li, Charles, and Sandra Thompson
1976 Subject and topic. A new typology of language. In: Charles Li (ed.), *Subject and topic*, 457–490. New York: Academic Press.

Li, Charles (ed.)
1976 *Subject and topic*. New York: Academic Press.

Maleczki, Márta
2004 The semantic analysis of thetic judgments. In: László Hunyadi, György Rákosi, and Enikő Tóth (eds.), *The Eighth Symposium on Logic and Language. Preliminary Papers*, 107–118. Debrecen: University of Debrecen.

Marty, Anton
1918 *Gesammelte Schriften* II/1. Edited by Josef Eisenmeier. Halle: Max Niemeyer.

Marty, Anton
1965 *Psyche und Sprachstruktur*. Edited by Otto Funke. Bern: Verlag A. Francke.

Mathesius, Vilém
1928 On linguisitic characterology. *Actes du Premiere Congrès International de Linguists a La Haye*. Leiden.

Mathesius, Vilém
1929 Zur Satzperspektive im modernen Englisch. *Archiv für das Studium der neueren Sprachen und Literaturen* 155: 202–210.
Molnár, Valéria
1998 Topic in focus: the syntax, phonology, semantics, and pragmatics of the so-called “contrastive topic” in Hungarian and German. *Acta Linguistic Hungarica* 45: 389–166.
Ortiz de Urbina, Jon
1995 Residual verb second and verb first in Basque. In: Katalin É. Kiss (ed.), *Discourse Configurational Languages*, 99–121. Oxford: Oxford University Press.
Paul, Herman
1880 *Prinzipien der Sprachgeschichte*. Halle: Max Niemeyer.
Pearson, Matthew
2005 The Malagasy subject/topic as an A’-element. *Natural Language and Linguistic Theory* 23: 381–457.
Reinhart, Tanya
1981 Pragmatics and linguistics. An analysis of sentence topics. *Philosophica* 27: 53–94.
Reinhart, Tanya
1995 Interface strategies. OTS Working Papers OTS-WP-TL-95002. Utrecht.
Rizzi, Luigi
1997 The fine structure of the left periphery. In: Liliane Haegeman (ed.), *Elements of Grammar,* 281–337. Dordrecht: Kluwer.
Rochemont, Michael S., and Peter W. Culicover
1990 *English Focus Constructions and the Theory of Grammar.* Cambridge: Cambridge University Press.
Rooth, Mats
1985 Association with Focus. PhD dissertation, University of Massachusetts, Amherst.
Rooth, Mats
1992 A theory of focus interpretation. *Natural Language Semantics* 1: 75–16.
Rooth, Mats
1996 On the interface principles for intonational focus. In: T. Galloway, and J. Spence (eds.), *Proceedings of SALT VI*, 202–226. Ithaca, NY: Cornell University.
Sasse, Hans-Jürgen
1987 The thetic/categorical distinction revisited. *Linguistics* 25: 511–580.
Selkirk, Elisabeth
1984 *Phonology and Syntax. The Relation between Sound and Structure.* Cambridge, Mass.: MIT Press.
Selkirk, Elisabeth
2008 Contrastive focus, givenness and the unmarked status of ‘discourse-new’, *Acta Hungarica Linguistica* 55: 331–346. Special issue on information structure ed. by C. Féry, and Gisebert Fanselow.
Sgall, Petr
1967 Functional sentence perspective in a generative description. *Prague Studies in Mathematical Linguistics* 2: 203–225.
Sgall, Petr, Eva Hajičová, and Eva Benesová
1973 *Topic/Focus and Generative Semantics*. Kronberg, Taunus: Scriptor Verlag.
Stechow, Arnim von
1990 Focusing ad backgrounding operators. In: Werner Abraham (ed.), *Discourse Particles*, 37–84. Amsterdam: John Benjamins.
Stechow, Arnim von
1991 Current issues in the theory of focus. In: Arnim von Stechow and Dieter Wunderlich (eds.), *Semantics. An International Handbook of Contemporary Research*, 804–835. Berlin: De Gruyter.

Strawson, P. F.
1971 Identifying reference and truth-values. In: Danny D. Steinberg and Leon A. Jakobovits (eds.), *Semantics*, 86–99. London: Cambridge University Press.
Svolacchia, Marco, Lunella Mereu, and Annarita Puglielli
1995 Aspects of discourse configurationality in Somali. In: Katalin É. Kiss (ed.), *Discourse Configurational Languages*, 65–98. Oxford: Oxford University Press.
Szabolcsi, Anna
1981 The semantics of Topic-Focus articulation. In: J. Groenendijk et al. (eds.), *Formal Methods in the Study of Language*. Amsterdam: Matematisch Centrum.
Szendrői, Kriszta
2003 A stressed-based approach to the syntax of Hungarian focus. *The Linguistic Review* 20: 37–78.
Tsimpli, Ianthi Maria
1995 Focusing in modern Greek. In: Katalin É. Kiss (ed.), *Discourse Configurational Languages*, 176–206. Oxford: Oxford University Press.
Truckenbrodt, Hubert
1995 Phonological Phrases: Their relation to syntax, focus, and prominence. PhD dissertation, MIT.
Vallduví, Enric
1992 *The Informational Component*. New York: Garland.
Vallduví, Enric, and Elisabeth Engdahl
1996 The linguistic realization of information packaging. *Linguistics* 34: 53–78.
Vallduví, Enric, and Maria Vilkuna
1998 On rheme and kontrast. In: Peter W. Culicover, and Louise McNally (eds.), *The Limits of Syntax*, 79–108. (Syntax and Semantics volume 29) San Diego: Academic Press.
Varga, László
2002 *Intonation and Stress. Evidence from Hungarian*. Basingstoke: Palgrave Macmillan.
Zubizarreta, Maria Luisa
1998 *Prosody, Focus, and Word Order*. Cambridge, Mass.: MIT Press.
Wedgwood, David
2006 *Shifting the Focus from Static Structures to the Dynamics of Interpretation*. Amsterdam: Elsevier.
Weil, Henri
1844 *De l'ordre des mots dans les languages anciennes comparées aux langues modernes*. Paris: Joubert.
Wundt, Wilhelm
1912 *Völkerpsychologie*. Leipzig: Engelmann.

Katalin É. Kiss, Budapest (Hungary)

14. Control

Abstract

Certain types of clausal complements and clausal adjuncts show an identification of its subject with a DP in the matrix clause, which is subsumed under the notion of control. The ingredients of control involve the controller, i.e., the matrix DP, the controllee, i.e., the subject of the complement/adjunct clause, and the structural properties of the complement/adjunct clause. For the latter, the classification of control-inducing vs. control-neutral structures will be introduced. On the basis of this distinction, control appears in two guises: as structural control, i.e., bound to specific structures, and as inherent control, i.e., as invariant property of certain clause-embedding predicates. Whereas the properties of the controller (e.g., fixed vs. variable choice of the subject or object as controller and the various control readings) are strongly associated with the matrix predicate in most languages, the properties of the controllee are usually determined by the syntax of the respective language. The main focus of this chapter lies on complement control; basic properties of adjunct control are presented as well. This chapter also introduces the diagnostics for distinguishing control structures from raising structures.

1. Introduction

Control (also known as *Equi-NP Deletion*, see Rosenbaum 1967) is an exemplary test case for the interaction of lexicon and syntax. It is a syntactic phenomenon in that it is confined to certain syntactic configurations, and it is a lexical phenomenon in that its properties are heavily influenced by the predicates embedding the respective syntactic configuration – at least in the case of complement control, i.e., control into clausal complements.

Control, which is a specific instance of argument identification, has been mainly discussed with infinite, mostly infinitival complements. The following two examples represent the canonical case discussed most in the literature: the non-overt subject of the infinitival complement (indicated in the following by _) has to be identified with the subject of the matrix predicate *hoffen* 'hope' (subject control) or with the object of *ermutigen* 'encourage' (object control); the readings are indicated by the subscripts. Disjoint readings are excluded.

(1) a. *Maria$_i$ hofft, [_$_{i/*j}$ beim Rennen zu siegen].* [German]
Mary hopes at.the race to win.INF
'Mary hopes to win the race'

b. *Maria$_i$ ermutigt ihren Sohn$_j$ [_$_{j/*i/*k}$ am Rennen teil-zu-nehmen].*
Mary encourages her son at.the race PT-to-participate.INF
'Mary encourages her son to participate in the race'

The situation changes if the clausal argument is realized as a finite clause. Then argument identification becomes optional with *hoffen*, but remains obligatory with *ermutigen:*

(2) a. *Maria$_i$ hofft, [dass sie$_{i/j}$ / Peter beim Rennen siegt].* [German]
Mary hopes that she/ Peter at.the race wins
'Mary hopes that she/Peter will win the race'

b. *Maria$_i$ ermutigt ihren Sohn$_j$ (da-zu) [dass er$_{j/*k}$ am Rennen teilnimmt].*
Mary encourages her son (there-to) that he at.the race participates
lit. 'Mary encourages her son that he participates in the race'

The same situation holds with nominalized clausal arguments:

(3) a. *Maria$_i$ hofft auf ihren$_{i/j}$ / Peters Sieg.* [German]
Mary hopes on her/ Peter.GEN win.NMLZ
'Mary hopes for her/Peter's victory'

b. *Maria$_i$ ermutigt ihren Sohn$_j$ [zur _$_{j/*i/*k}$ Teilnahme am Rennen].*
Mary encourages her son to.the participation at.the race
'Mary encourages her son in participating in the race'

Thus, *hoffen* is a predicate that shows control only with infinitival complements, whereas *ermutigen* shows control as a lexically inherent property. Thus, control arises in certain syntactic configurations (*structural control*) or with certain predicates (*inherent control*). This distinction is often blurred by the fact mainly infinitival complements have been taken into account; in order to determine the control properties of clause-embedding predicates, all potential clausal complementation structures must be considered.

I will begin the discussion with the following preliminary definition of (complement) control, which extends the notion of control to structures other than the canonical subjectless infinitival complements of Indo-European languages. Note that I use *argument* in semantic terms.

(4) Definition of control (first version)
Control applies to structures in which a predicate P_1 selects a clausal argument (state of affairs argument = SOA-argument) and one of the arguments of the em-

bedded predicate P_2 heading the clausal argument has to be identified with an argument of the matrix predicate.
$[X_i\ P_1\ (Y_j)\ [_{SOA}\ Z_k\ P_2\ ...]]$

X and Y denote potential controllers, Z denotes the controlled argument (controllee). What has to be understood by identification will be discussed in section 3. The schema in (4) raises the following questions:

- Which structures of complementation induce control (see section 2)
- Which argument (X or Y) is selected as controller? (see 3.1)
- Is control invariant, i.e., fixed to either X or Y as controller? (see 3.2)
- Which referential relations between controller and controllee can be observed? (see 3.3)
- Does the controller have to be overt? (see 3.4)
- Which properties does the controllee display? Does it have to remain covert? (see section 4)
- Which predicates instantiate inherent control? (see section 5)

I will also deal with two further issues: the delimitation of control vs. raising (section 6) and control in clausal adjuncts (section 7). Note that this chapter is concerned with the descriptive properties of control; the various theoretical approaches to control are discussed in chapter 38.

2. Structures of control

If one takes into account the various possible types of subordination cross-linguistically available, one has to distinguish structures that induce control (due to their need for argument identification) from those that do not. The need for argument identification is either motivated structurally, due to the deficiencies of argument realization (e.g., with infinitival or other infinite complements), i.e., not all arguments may be realized within the linking domain of the clausal head, or semantically, due to the requirement of denoting coherent events; situational coherence is commonly established by shared participants in the various subevents of a complex event (e.g., with serial verbs). In the case of structurally motivated argument identification, argument raising is an alternative to control, which is already reflected in the predicates that serve a double function as control and raising predicates (see section 6). Generally, infinitival/infinite complements, serial verb constructions, and verb incorporation are structures of argument identification; they are control-inducing. In contrast, nominalizations and finite clauses do not require argument identification in most languages; all arguments may be realized overtly within the linking domain of the nominalized or finite head; they are control-neutral.

In the traditional syntactic view, control is a property of biclausal structures (see, for instance, the distinction of syntactic vs. semantic control by Wurmbrand 2002). However, I will include also monoclausal structures (including restructuring infinitival complements, verb incorporation and serial verb constructions) in my presentation.

2.1. Infinite/infinitival complements

In many languages, infinitives/infinite verb forms are not able to license the realization of all arguments. Typically, the unmarked structural linker (nominative/absolutive) cannot be assigned in an infinitival complement, although there are well-known counterexamples from Romance (Raposo 1987; Mensching 2000) and other languages (Szabolcsi 2009). The Romance languages show an intricate variation concerning lexical subjects with infinitives: in Portuguese, lexical subjects are possible with inflected infinitives (see [5a]), whereas in Spanish adverbial PPs and certain subject clauses (see [5b]) may show lexical subjects with infinitival heads.

(5) a. *para as mulheres chegar-*(em)* [Portuguese]
for the women arrive.INF-3PL
'for the women to arrive'
(Mensching 2000: 7)

b. [*Haber=se Julia presentado a las elecciones*] *fue un error.* [Spanish]
have.INF=REFL Julia present.PTCP at the elections] was a mistake
'the fact that Julia presented herself at the elections was a mistake'
(Mensching 2000: 6)

(5a/b) do not represent structures of complement control; there seem to be certain limitations regarding overt subjects in infinitival complements (Szabolcsi 2009): they are much more restricted in infinitival control complements (possible in Hungarian and Italian) than in raising complements.

Besides the infinitive there are other types of infinite complements, e.g., supine complements, which do not allow the use of the default linker in their linking domain. In Kolma Yukaghir, for example, predicates selecting supine complements are restricted to structures of subject control (including split control) and to cases in which the situation denoted by the clausal argument is not implied (see Maslova 2003: 415).

2.2. Verb incorporation

In structures of verb incorporation a verb is morphologically integrated into another verb. The incorporated verb must share at least one argument with the incorporating verb, either semantically and/or structurally. In the following example from the Uto-Aztecan language Yaqui (Guerrero 2006: 88), the matrix verb *su'utoja* 'allow' incorporates a transitive verb whose highest argument is identified with the internal argument of the higher predicate.

(6) *U tata^paare ili uusi-ta teopo-ta tu'ute-ne-su'utoja-k.* [Yaqui]
the priest.NOM little child-ACC church-ACC fix-EXPE-allow-PFV
'the priest allowed the child to clean the church.'

The only alternative to control in case of verb incorporation is raising, as shown in the following example (Guerrero 2006: 170):

(7) a. *Ne* *Peo-ta* *kaba'i-ta* *jinu-maachia* [Yaqui]
1SG.NOM Pedro-ACC horse-ACC buy-believe.PRS
'I believe Pedro to be buying a horse'

b. *Peo* *kaba'i-ta* *jinu-maachia-wa*
Pedro.NOM horse-ACC buy-believe-PASS.PRS
'Pedro is believed to be buying a horse'

Both accusative DPs in (7a) are semantic arguments of *jinu* 'buy', but not of the matrix verb *maachia* 'believe'. However, in the process of semantic composition the embedded agent argument *Peo* becomes a structural argument of the resulting complex verb. If the complex is passivized as in (7b), this DP is realized as subject.

2.3. Serial verb constructions

Among the various patterns of serial verb constructions (SVC) one can also find structures of complement control – at least in some languages (see Aikhenvald 2006; Muysken and Veenstra 2006 for an overview of serial verb structures). Besides the typical SVC patterns such as resultatives (e.g., *hit-die*, *hit-kill*), directionals (e.g., V-*go*), argument-extending SVCs (e.g., instrumental *take*-V, beneficiary V-*give*), one also finds types in which a clause-embedding predicate is the main functor of a SVC. Generally, SVCs require argument sharing between the predicates involved due to situational coherence of the subevents denoted by the predicates of the SVC. Apart from the more marginal cases of *ambient serialization* (Crowley 1987), which involve identification of event variables, argument sharing may concern the subject, or both subject and object, or the object of one verb and the subject of the other. The required argument identification qualifies SVCs as control-inducing structures. Let me show this with data from the Amazonian language Tariana (Aikhenvald 2003: 432, 433, 439), which exhibits a great variety of SVCs: like regular SVCs, structures of complement control are monoclausal; the predicates exhibit the same subject agreement, even if the object of the first verb and not its subject is the shared argument as in (8c); here, the subject of the control verb is third person non-female, whereas the subject of the embedded predicate is first person, which does not surface in verbal agreement.

(8) a. *nese-pida* [*dhipa* *di-keta*] *diha* *malie-tiki-nuku* [Tariana]
then-REP 3SG.NF.grab 3SG.NF-meet DET knife-DIM-TOP
'then he managed to grab the little knife'

b. [*di-ni* *di-mataRa-pidana*] *diha*
3SG.NF-do 3SG.NF-leave-REM.PST.REP he
'he stopped doing (this)'

c. *emite-tiki* *nu-na* [*dihpani* *di-adeta-naka*]
child-DIM 1SG-OBJC 3SG.NF.work 3SG.NF-prevent-PRS.VIS
'the little boy is preventing me from working'

Languages differ as to which predicates may instantiate SVCs and whether they include clause-embedding predicates.

2.4. Nominalized complements

Nominalization is a major means of subordination in many languages or at least an important structural alternative to other structures of complementation (Noonan 1985). Depending on the linking potential of nominalized verbs, all arguments may be realized in the domain of the nominalized head. Therefore, argument identification is not required, at least in those languages without restrictions on the linking of the arguments of the nominalized verb. The German example in (3b) is illustrative in this regard; a similar point can be made with Turkish, whose primary structure of complementation is based on nominalized clauses. Here, argument linking is that of a mixed category, i.e., the highest argument is realized nominally (marked by genitive), the other arguments are realized verbally (marked by the usual verbal cases). Therefore, argument identification is not required. Turkish distinguishes three types of nominals: factive nominals (*-dIK*) as in (9a), event nominals with possessor agreement (*-mE*) as in (9b), and event nominals without possessor agreement (*-mEK*) as in (9c/d), the latter often being called "infinitive".

(9) a. *(ben) [Ahmed-in öl-**düğ**-ün]-ü duy-du-m* [Turkish]
I Ahmed-GEN die-NMLZ-3SG.PA-ACC hear-PST-1SG
'I heard that Ahmet died'

b. *(ben) [Ahmed-in öl-**me**-sin]-den kork-uyor-du-m*
I Ahmed-GEN die-NMLZ-3SG.PA-ABL fear-PROG-PST-1SG
'I was afraid that Ahmet would die'

c. *lütfen [_ pencere-yi aç-**mağ**]-ı unut-ma!*
please window-ACC open-NMLZ-ACC forget-NEG
'please don't forget to open the window'

d. *(ben) Ahmed-i [_ kaç-**mağ**]-a zorla-dı-m*
1SG Ahmed-ACC flee-NMLZ-DAT force-PST-1SG
'I forced Ahmet to flee'

(Kornfilt 1997: 50, 51, 53)

Control predicates typically instantiate the infinitival construction shown in (9c/d). Clausal arguments realized with agreeing deverbal nouns as in (9b) as well as factive nominals as in (9a) do not induce control readings (Słodowicz 2007). Gamerschlag (2007) demonstrates the control-neutral character of Korean nominalized complements.

Restrictions on the realization of the arguments inherited from the underlying verb may lead to structures which show parallels to infinitival complements: the argument that cannot be realized overtly survives by control through a matrix argument. K'ekchí and possibly other Mayan languages exhibit nominalized clausal complements that do not allow all inherited verbal arguments to be overtly realized because structural linking is restricted here to possessor (ergative) agreement; hence, they are control-inducing with polyvalent matrix predicates. In the following example taken from Kockelman (2003: 32), the ergative possessor agreement (EA) indexes the lower argument, i.e., the theme *li kabl* 'the house'; the higher argument has to be controlled by the matrix subject, here realized as pronominal affix.

(10) *n-in$_i$-lub* [*chi* _$_j$ *x-mesunk-il* *li* *kabl*] [K'ekchí]
PRS-1SG.NA-tire OBL.COMP 3SG.EA-sweep-NMLZ the house
'I'm tired of sweeping the house'

2.5. Finite complements

Finite complements are generally control-neutral, although there may be exceptions (see below). They do not require argument identification in structural or semantic terms. A rather common finite structure instantiated by control verbs are so-called subjunctive complements, already discussed by Noonan (1985). The notion *subjunctive* covers non-indicative verbal categories (e.g., in Spanish, Hungarian or Persian) or specific complementizer forms (e.g., in some Balkan languages, where the verbs do not display a distinct subjunctive mood).

Generally, subjunctive complements do not induce control, which I will show with data from Albanian (Noonan 1985: 67), in which the subjunctive has replaced the infinitive completely. (11a) illustrates the use of the subjunctive with the desiderative verb *dua* 'want'; the embedded subject does not need to be co-referential with the matrix-subject. Directive/causative predicates such as *detyroj* 'force' induce a control reading as shown in (11b).

(11) a. *Njeriu$_i$ deshi* [*ta* _$_{i/j}$ *vjedhë* *pulën*] [Albanian]
man wanted.3SG COMP steal.3SG.SBJV chicken
'the man wanted to steal the chicken' / 'the man wanted him to steal the chicken'

b. *Gruaja$_i$ e* *detyroi njeriun$_j$* [*ta* _$_j$ *vjedhë* *pulën*]
woman PRO forced man.ACC COMP steal.3SG.SBJV chicken
'the woman forced the man to steal the chicken'

Patterns such as (11b) fall under the notion of finite control (Comorovski 1985; Varlokosta and Hornstein 1993; Landau 2004), which occurs with inherent control predicates. I will return to these cases in section 5, where I will discuss the properties of inherent control.

Sometimes mood markers may restrict the readings of finite clauses. In Korean an embedded imperative marker enforces a directive reading in *verba dicendi*, thus yielding obligatory object control. Compare (12a) with a free reading for the embedded subject and (12b) with an object control reading (see Gamerschlag 2007: 91).

(12) a. *Chelswu-nun$_i$ Yenghi-eykey$_j$* [_$_{i/j/k}$ *caknyen-ey safari-yehayng-ul* [Korean]
Chelswu-TOP Yenghi-DAT last.year-in safari-trip-ACC
hay-ss-ta-ko] *malhay-ss-ta.*
do-PST-DECL-COMP say-PST-DECL
'Chelswu told Yenghi that he/she/s.o. did a safari trip last year.'

b. *Chelswu-nun$_i$ Yenghi-eykey$_j$* [*_$_{j/*i/*k}$ naynyen-ey safari-yehayng-ul*
Chelswu-TOP Yenghi-DAT next.year-in safari-trip-ACC
*ha-**la**-ko*] *malhay-ss-ta.*
do-IMP-COMP say-PST-DECL
'Chelswu told Yenghi to go on a safari trip next year.'

That finite clauses are not control-neutral per se is evidenced by K'ekchí and some other Mayan languages. Here, a complementizerless finite clause induces a control reading (see [13a]); a disjoint reading becomes obligatory if the complementizer *naq* is added as in (13b). Note that the matrix predicate may alternatively select an infinitival complement as in (13c), which only allows a control reading.

(13) a. *n-inw$_i$-aj* [*t-in$_i$-xik sa' li k'ayil*] [K'ekchí]
PRS-1SG.EA-want FUT-1SG.NA-go inside the market
'I want to go to the market'
(Kockelman 2003: 28)

b. *ta-cu-aj* [*naq t-at-xik /*t-in-xik*]
TNS-1.EA-want COMP FUT-2.NA-go FUT-1SG.NA-go
'I want you to go'/*'I want to go'
(Berinstein 1985: 257)

c. *n-inw-aj* [*xik sa' li k'ayil*]
PRS-1SG.EA-want go into the market
'I want to go to the market'
(Kockelman 2003: 30)

2.6. Interrogative complements

Since languages often use parallel complementation structures in embedded declaratives and interrogatives, one can also find control-inducing interrogatives. *Wh*-infinitives represent a well-known case. Their occurrence is language-specific, as the following contrast between English and Standard German shows: (14a/b) illustrate *wh*-infinitives with extensional and intensional interrogatives in English, (14c/d) their German translations, which are ungrammatical. Since the controllee has to be covert in English, subject questions are ungrammatical as in (14e).

(14) a. *She cabled Helen* [*when _ to send the package*].
b. *He wondered* [*how _ to reach the summit*].
c. **Sie telegraphierte Helen* [*wann _ das Paket zu schicken*].
she cabled Helen when the package to send.INF
'she cabled Helen when to send the package'
d. **Er fragte sich* [*wie _ den Gipfel zu erreichen*].
he asked 3.REFL how the summit to reach.INF
'he wondered how to reach the summit'
e. **I don't know* [*who to go first*].

In the literature this parameterization has been attributed, for instance, to the option of filling the infinitival C-system with a base-generated overt element (e.g., *for* in English; see Sabel 1996) or to the potential ambiguity of the *wh*-element as indefinite pronoun (Gärtner 2010), which is true for German but not for English. As shown by Huddleston (2002: 985), *wh*-infinitives are more restricted than their finite counterparts; they occur only with a subset of the predicates that embed finite interrogative structures.

2.7. Subject vs. object clauses

Many linguists who have dealt with control in subject clauses (e.g., Williams 1980; Manzini 1983) have assumed that there is no true control in subject clauses, which, however, is false as a general claim. The predicates that impose a control reading on a clausal subject belong to Belletti and Rizzi's (1988) *preoccupare*-class or Levin's (1993) *amuse*-class, which denote the causation of an experience, hence, exhibit an internal experiencer argument; the higher clausal argument denotes the stimulus. As (15a/b) show, *thrill* requires its internal argument to be identified with the controllee in the subject clause, independent of the position of the subject clause.

(15) a. *[$\_{i/*j}$ to win the prize] would thrill me$_i$.*
b. *It would thrill me$_i$ [$\_{i/*j}$ to win the prize].*

The same applies to German *ärgern* 'annoy, make angry'. Its internal argument must control the covert subject of the subject clause, shown in (16a). It is not possible to interpret the controllee generically, as shown in (16b).

(16) a. [$\_{i}$ *bei der Stellen-planung nicht berücksichtigt worden zu sein*] [German]
at the job-planning not consider.PTCP AUX.PTCP to be.INF
ärgert Peter$_i$.
annoy.3SG Peter
'it annoys Peter not to have been considered in the staff planning'

b. *[$\_{arb=gen}$ *die Wände mit Graffiti zu besprühen*] *ärgert Peter.*
the walls with graffiti to spray.INF annoy.3SG Peter
intended reading: 'it annoys Peter that people spray graffiti on the walls'

In general terms, these predicates have the simplified Semantic Form in (17): regarding the experiencer argument x, the clausal stimulus argument p is both higher – in terms of CAUSE – and lower – in terms of the EXPERIENCE-relation.

(17) $\lambda x\ \lambda p$ CAUSE(p, EXPERIENCE(x, p))

That the clausal argument is lower than the experiencer argument in terms of the experience relation may explain the unexpected obligatory control because this is the semantic structure found with clausal objects. Systematic studies are needed to exhaustively determine the class of predicates that show obligatory control in subject clauses.

2.8. The interaction between control-inducing and control-neutral structures

The parallel presence of control-inducing and control-neutral structures in a language may lead to a division of labor between the two structure types – at least with some predicate classes. In these cases the control-neutral structure encompasses readings not subsumed by the control-inducing structure, namely disjoint reference or *obviative* readings (see, for instance, Comorovski 1985; Kempchinsky 1987; Zec 1987). In Spanish (Kempchinsky 1987: 123) as well as most other Romance languages, control readings are realized with infinitival complements as in (18a). The control reading is blocked in the subjunctive, which, then, has the disjoint reference reading only (see [18b]).

(18) a. *Reagan$_i$ desea [_$_{i/*j}$ derrotar a los Sandinistas]* [Spanish]
Reagan desire.3SG defeat.INF ACC DET.PL Sandinistas
'Reagan wants to defeat the Sandinistas'

b. *Reagan$_i$ desea [que _$_{j/*i}$ derrote a los Sandinistas]*
Reagan desire.3SG COMP defeat.SBJV.3SG ACC DET.PL Sandinistas
'Reagan desires that they defeat the Sandinistas'

Of course, this division of labor only makes sense for predicates that are not inherently bound to control readings; inherent control predicates are incompatible with disjoint reference readings.

The disjoint reference effect can also be found with certain clausal subjects in the subjunctive, as shown in (19) for Spanish (Bosque and Demonte 1999: 3247).

(19) a. *Me$_i$ molesta [_$_i$ venir tan tarde]* [Spanish]
1SG.ACC disturb.3SG come.INF so late
'it disturbs me to come so late'

b. **Me$_i$ molesta [que yo$_i$ haya venido tan tarde]*
1SG.ACC disturb.3SG COMP 1SG AUX.SBJV come.PTCP so late
'it disturbs me that I have come so late'

This blocking effect is only explained under the assumption that subject clauses of causative experiencer predicates exhibit obligatory control.

3. The controller

The predicate-specific nature of complement control manifests itself most clearly in the role of the controller, i.e., whether it corresponds to the subject, object or some other entity in the matrix clause and whether it is fixed as such or variable. Moreover, the more complex cases of argument identification are restricted to certain classes of control predicates (see 3.3).

3.1. Subject vs. object control

The distinction of subject vs. object control is one of the earliest in the research on complement control. Predicates that have only one individual argument besides the clausal argument do not pose a challenge for any theory of control. Polyvalent predicates are more interesting because they may show either subject or object control. Verbs with a causative semantic structure belong to the canonical class of object control predicates. Predicates denoting directive speech acts (e.g., *ask*, *request*) or predicates that ascribe an activity or property to an object referent (e.g., *ankreiden* 'fault s.o.', *anlasten* 'blame', *anzeigen* 'bring charge against') are likewise object control predicates. Predicates that refer to commissive speech acts (e.g., *versprechen* 'promise', *geloben* 'vow') and verbs of communication with an implied addressee (e.g., *verkünden* 'announce') are typical subject control predicates.

Many syntactic approaches (since Rosenbaum 1967) have assumed that polyvalent control verbs should exhibit object control (see Rosenbaum's *Minimal Distance Principle* or the *Minimal Link Condition* between controller and controllee used by Hornstein 1999); subject control verbs such as *promise* are considered to be highly marked exceptions – an assumption that ignores the systematic pattern of subject control with commissive predicates. The impression that polyvalent subject control verbs are exceptional may arise from the observation that in quantitative terms, languages such as English or German display more object control verbs than (polyvalent) subject control verbs: on the one hand, directive/manipulative verbs show more lexical differentiation in these languages than commissive verbs. On the other hand, verbs of communication are often not used as control verbs; moreover, they are not confined to subject control. However, it has not been acknowledged so far that many object control predicates are inherent control predicates and thus also exhibit finite control (see Stiebels 2010).

In the well-known Indo-European languages controller choice does not depend on the syntactic realization of the controller (see, for instance, Jackendoff and Culicover 2003 for English, Siebert-Ott 1983 and Stiebels 2007 for German); one and the same case frame (e.g., a nominative-dative pattern) may occur with a subject control verb (*versprechen* 'promise') or an object control verb (*nahelegen* 'suggest to sb').

However, one can find (sparse) evidence for a syntactic organization of control. Syntactic controller choice has been claimed for the Austronesian language Kavalan and some closely related languages (Chang and Tsai 2001). Here, the controller must always be the actor subject, which implies that canonical object control verbs cannot surface as such. According to Chang and Tsai, Kavalan chooses a strategy of causativization of the embedded predicate to maintain actor subject control with predicates that behave as object control verbs in other languages. (20a) shows the respective pattern, in which the actor subject is identified with the newly added causer argument in the embedded clause; (20b) shows the pattern that would correspond to the familiar pattern of object control (Chang and Tsai 2001: 3).

(20) a. *pawRat a tina-na$_i$ tu suni$_j$* [_$_i$ *pa-qaynəp*] [Kavalan]
force NOM mother-3SG.PA ACC child CAUS.AV-sleep
'his mother forces her child such that she causes him/her to sleep'

b. ??*pawRat a tina-na*$_i$ *tu suni*$_j$ [_$_j$ *m-aynəp*].
force NOM mother-3SG.PA ACC child AV-sleep
'his mother forces her child to sleep'

Unfortunately, the authors do not discuss cases in which causativization of the embedded predicate would be semantically inadequate: a) with negation of the matrix predicate, b) with non-implicative directive verbs such as *ask*. In these cases, Kavalan should resort to some other strategy.

A further case for a syntactic restriction on controllers is attested in the Mayan language Mam (England 1989): with matrix predicates that select an infinitival complement, control is restricted to controllers in the absolutive case; this restriction does not apply to finite clausal complements. In (21a) the controller is an internal argument, indexed by default NOM-agreement (NA). With a controller indexed by ERG-agreement, only a finite clausal complement is possible as in (21b); an infinitival complement is excluded as in (21c).

(21) a. *ma tz'-ok t-laj-o-'n Kyel [tx'eem-al sii']* [Mam]
REC.PST 3SG.NA-DIR 3SG.EA-oblige-TH-DIR Miguel cut-INF wood
'Miguel obliged him to cut wood'

b. *w-ajb'el-a [chin aq'n-a-an-a]*
1SG.EA-want-1SG 1SG.NOM work-TH-ANTIP-1SG
'I want to work'

c. **w-ajb'el-a [aq'n-a-al]*
1SG.EA-want-1SG work-TH-INF
(England 1989: 291–292)

The literature on complement control does not reveal how widespread syntactic restrictions on controllers may be. There is no systematic evidence for such a pattern. The Kavalan case, however, already indicates the expenses of syntactic control: in order to maintain certain structural configurations for control, lexical predicates have to be accommodated in order to exhibit the adequate syntactic potential. It is also likely that in languages with a purely syntactic control pattern, lexical control predicates are more homogeneous than in languages with semantically based control because in the latter no syntactic requirements restrict possible control predicate classes.

3.2. Variable control and control shift

Whereas many predicates exhibit invariant subject or object control, some predicates do not show a preference in this regard; they allow control with either argument, thus being instances of *variable control*. Typically, these are verbs of joint intentions/plans/arrangements, e.g., *vorschlagen* 'propose'.

(22) *Maria*$_i$ *schlug Peter*$_j$ *vor* [_$_{i/j/i+j}$ *einen Tisch im Restaurant* [German]
Mary proposed Peter pt a table in.the restaurant
zu bestellen].
to order.INF
'Mary proposed to Peter to reserve a table in the restaurant'

Usually, the context triggers a preferred reading as subject or object control.

Related to the phenomenon of variable control is the phenomenon of *control shift* (Růžička 1983, 1999; Comrie 1985; Farkas 1988; Sag and Pollard 1991; Panther 1993): the controller of polyvalent control verbs shifts from subject to object control (e.g., with *versprechen* 'promise') or vice versa (e.g., *bitten* 'ask'). Unlike variable control, control shift is generally triggered in specific environments, i.e., the shift is typically induced by modal predicates such as *be allowed*, by passivization of the embedded verb or by the embedding of non-agentive, i.e., recipient-oriented verbs. In (23a) the shift from object to subject control is triggered by passive, in (23b) by the context, which renders the subject referent the more likely candidate for control. In German the modal *dürfen* 'be allowed to' is the strongest trigger for control shift. (23c) shows that *bitten* 'ask' may shift, whereas this shift is not plausible for *raten* 'advise' (see [23d]).

(23) a. *Mary*$_i$ *asked Peter*$_j$ [_$_i$ *to be invited to the party*].
b. *The pupil*$_i$ *asked the teacher*$_j$ [_$_i$ *to leave early*].
c. *Maria*$_i$ *bat Peter*$_j$ [_$_i$ *zur Party gehen zu dürfen*]. [German]
Mary asked Peter to.the party go.INF to be.allowed.INF
'Mary asked Peter to be allowed to go to the party'
d. *??Maria*$_i$ *riet Peter*$_j$ [_$_{i/j}$ *zur Party gehen zu dürfen*].
Mary advised Peter to.the party go.INF to be.allowed.INF
'Mary advised Peter to be allowed to go to the party.'

The shift is actually not a simple change of the controller on the syntactic surface; as argued by Farkas (1988), Sag and Pollard (1991), and Jackendoff and Culicover (2003), the embedded predicate undergoes semantic coercion, i.e., it is enriched with a causative-like component, either implicitly or explicitly. In (23c), for instance, the matrix object is identified with the implicit deontic authority of *dürfen*.

The availability of control shift is language-specific (Růžička 1983, 1999; Comrie 1985). Germanic languages seem to be more prone to control shift than other languages. Comrie's observation that English displays less control shift than German has been studied by Panther (1993) in more detail, who tested several control predicates with native speakers of English and German and found out that German control predicates are more likely to shift than their English equivalents. Since control shift seems to depend on the (implicit) coercion mechanisms, languages that avoid such operations are expected to avoid control shift as well.

In control shift languages such as German one may find predicates that admit infinitival complements only with control shift structures (Stiebels 2010). This is due to a syntax-semantics mismatch: semantically, the verb requires a control pattern that cannot be realized on the syntactic surface. The German verb *verhindern* 'prevent', for instance, which is derived from the object control verb *hindern* 'prevent s.o. from', preserves the causative-implicative meaning but undergoes argument reduction; the internal argument is eliminated. The control requirement can only be fulfilled via a shift to subject control; in (24) the shift is triggered by passivization.

(24) *Der Lehrer verhinderte (es) [_ von seinen Schülern lächerlich* [German]
the teacher prevented it by his students ridiculous
gemacht zu werden].
make.PTCP to AUX.INF
'the teacher prevented his students to make him look silly'

3.3. Control readings

Independent of the simple contrast of subject vs. object control further dimensions of control relations have to be taken into account. Whereas in the simple case controller and controllee overlap completely in terms of their reference (= exhaustive control), other control readings occur as well, namely *split control* and *partial control.* Split control occurs if the two individual arguments of a polyvalent matrix predicate jointly control the controllee, which is indicated by +:

(25) *Peter$_i$ vereinbarte mit Maria$_j$ [_$_{i+j}$ am Abend (gemeinsam)* [German]
Peter agreed with Mary at.the evening together
ins Kino zu gehen]
in.the cinema to go.INF
'Peter and Mary agreed on going to the cinema together'

Predicates that denote a cooperative behavior typically allow split control, but other predicates may do as well, especially if modifiers such as *together* support the split control reading. In general, split control is not the only reading available with the respective matrix predicate, although it may be the preferred reading.

Another control pattern, which has been highlighted by Landau (2000) and since then has been a matter of dispute between the various theoretical approaches to control is the so-called partial control, in which the controllee refers to an entity that includes the referent of an argument of the matrix verb and a further participant (i+v) not included in the referents of the arguments of the matrix predicate. As the examples in (26) show, the admissibility of partial control is a lexical property of the matrix verb: *manage* excludes it, *want* allows it.

(26) a. **John$_i$ managed [_$_{i+v}$ to meet at six].*
b. *John$_i$ wanted [_$_{i+v}$ to meet at six].*

Partial control involves a semantic plural in the controllee, which is enforced by the embedding of a collective predicate or by modification of the embedded verb with the adverb *together.* Collective predicates typically come in two patterns: they either select a plural subject (*they meet at six*) or a comitative structure (*John met with Mary*); the former structure is used as a test for partial control. Split control, in contrast, involves a syntactic plural in the controllee, as has been pointed out by Landau (2000).

According to Landau partial control is possible with predicates that allow tensed complements (i.e, factive, propositional, desiderative and interrogative predicates), which is evidenced by the mismatching temporal modifiers test, i.e., the use of incompatible temporal modifiers in matrix and embedded clause (*yesterday, Mary wanted/*tried to clean up her room tomorrow*). However, the overall picture is more intricate, as shown by Pearson (2012); certain predicates do not correlate in the predicted way: *enjoy* and *like*, for instance, do not pass the test but allow partial control, whereas *deserve* passes the test without allowing partial control. I refer the reader to Pearson's elaborate semantic analysis of partial control.

Despite its current significance for theories of control one has to concede that the analyses of partial control mostly refer to introspective data; naturally occurring data of partial control are rare. It is also unclear to what extent partial control is cross-linguistically available (see Słodowicz 2008 for Polish). Partial control is less common in German than in English: the German equivalents of the collective predicates *meet* and *gather* (*sich treffen* and *sich versammeln*) are inherently reflexive verbs; many speakers do not tolerate the feature clashes that arise in a partial control reading with respect to person/number. The German equivalent of (26b) is not really acceptable: a sentence with the third person reflexive, which is underspecified in terms of number, is already hardly acceptable (see [27a]); in case of a person/number clash as in (27b) it is completely ungrammatical.

(27) a. *??Jan$_i$ will [_$_{i+v}$ sich um 6 Uhr versammeln].* [German]
John wants 3.REFL at 6 o'clock gather.INF
'John wants to gather at six'.

b. **Ich will [_ mich/uns/sich um 6 Uhr versammeln].*
I want 1SG.REFL/1PL.REFL/3.REFL at 6 o'clock gather.INF

Likewise, partial control readings with the German adverb *zusammen* 'together' are hard to obtain. The class of German predicates that allow partial control seems to be restricted to propositional attitude predicates such as *befürworten* 'approve', *ablehnen* 'decline', *dagegen/dafür sein* 'to be against/for it', *bereit sein* 'be ready', though one can observe inter-individual variation.

3.4. Implicit control

The controller does not necessarily have to be overt; in some cases it can or must remain implicit. Generally, the control relation is not affected if the potential controller is left implicit (see [28a/b]). However, predicates such as *ask* show a control shift if the potential controller argument is left implicit (Jackendoff and Culicover 2003); see (28c/d).

(28) a. *John$_i$ shouted to Sally$_j$ [_$_{j/*i}$ to take care of herself].*
b. *John$_i$ just shouted [_$_{j/*i}$ to look out for him$_i$].*
c. *John$_i$ asked Sally$_j$ [_$_{j/*i}$ to take care of herself$_j$].*
d. *John$_i$ asked [_$_i$ to take care of himself$_i$/*him$_i$].*

Jackendoff and Culicover (2003: 541–544) attribute the difference between these two verbs to the admissibility of a "bring about coercion", which is compatible with *ask*, but not with *shout*.

Implicit control has often been mistaken as generic or arbitrary control (see also Landau 2000). Superficially, (29a) seems to involve arbitrary control, i.e., non-control (indicated by the index $_{\text{arb}}$) due to the lack of a controller. However, (29b) reveals that the predicate has an implicit controller, which may surface as PP.

(29) a. *Es ist leicht [_$_{arb}$ das Fahrrad-fahren zu erlernen].* [German]
it is easy the bicycle-ride.NMLZ to learn.INF
'it is easy to learn to ride a bike'

b. *Es ist leicht für Kinder$_i$, [_$_i$ das Fahrrad-fahren zu erlernen].*
it is easy for children the bicycle-ride.NMLZ to learn.INF
'it is easy for children to learn to ride a bike'

Therefore, (29a) has to be interpreted as to involve an implicit generic controller (i.e., *Es ist leicht* _$_{j=gen}$ [_$_j$ *das Fahrradfahren zu erlernen*]). In the following I will use *generic control* as the label for control by a generically understood argument and *arbitrary control* as the label for non-control; in the latter case, the referent of the controllee must be determined otherwise.

Another pattern of implicit control can be found with passivized subject control predicates in German and other languages. Since German allows impersonal passives, intransitive subject control predicates can be passivized, as shown in (30); the implicit agent controls the embedded subject.

(30) *Es wurde _$_i$ versucht, [_$_i$ das Auto zu reparieren].* [German]
it AUX try.PTCP the car to repair.INF
'someone tried to repair the car' (lit. 'it was tried (by someone) to repair the car')

The structure in (30) does not fall under the restriction known as Visser's generalization (see Bresnan 1982 and van Urk 2013 for a recent re-evaluation), which states that subject control verbs cannot be passivized. This restriction is only valid for personal passives in contexts that do not exhibit control shift, as the following examples from Bresnan (1982: 355) demonstrate. (31a) illustrates a the use of passivized *promise* with a non-shifted complement, (31b) with a shifted one; here, the derived matrix subject functions as controller.

(31) a. **Frank was promised to leave (by Mary).*
b. *Mary was never promised to be allowed to leave.*

Implicit control is also frequently found in nominals derived from control verbs (e.g., *the refusal [_ to learn Arabic]*; see Sichel 2010), which results from the fact that nominal arguments are optional in most cases; there is often no requirement to realize the controller in the DP domain.

3.5. Local vs. non-local control

If the controller is an argument of the matrix clause, control is local. Non-local control involves discourse or speech act participants or controllers in a clause higher than the respective clause-embedding predicate (= *long-distance control*; alternatively *Super-Equi*, Grinder 1970). Typically, clausal subjects of predicates allow for non-local control; there are certain exceptions to this generalization, as discussed in 2.6. The controller of the example in (32) can be the subject of the highest clause, the object of *intrigue*, a joint controller or a generically interpreted controller.

(32) *Amy$_i$ thinks that [_$_{i/j/i+j/gen}$ dancing with Dan] intrigues Tom$_j$.*

The following examples from Jackendoff and Culicover (2003: 522) illustrate control by a discourse participant (see [33a]) or the speaker/hearer (see [33b]).

(33) a. *Brandeis$_i$ is in a lot of trouble, according to today's newspaper. Apparently, [_$_i$ firing the football coach] has turned off a lot of potential donors.*

b. *Here's the thing: [_$_{\text{speaker/hearer/speaker+hearer}}$ undressing myself/yourself/ourselves in public] could cause a scandal.*

According to Jackendoff and Culicover, some predicates with clausal objects may also show non-local control (*beat*, *outranks*, *entails*, *be as good as*).

3.6. The notion of obligatory control

For the sake of illustration, I will take the locality condition as the decisive criterion for obligatory control in the rest of the paper; Landau (2000) likewise restricts obligatory control to local control. Most syntacticians follow Williams (1980) in that they restrict obligatory control to invariant exhaustive control, thus ignoring the locality restrictions for many cases of non-exhaustive control.

(34) Definition of obligatory control (OC) OC applies to structures in which a predicate P_1 selects a clausal argument (SOA) and requires one of its (individual) arguments to be (improperly) included in the set of referents of an argument of the embedded predicate P_2 heading the clausal argument.
$[\mathbf{X}_i\ \mathbf{P}_1\ (\mathbf{Y}_j)\ [_{SOA}\ \mathbf{Z}_k\ \mathbf{P}_2 \ldots]]$ with $k \cap \{i, j\} \neq \emptyset$

This definition thus subsumes exhaustive as well as non-exhaustive control, invariant vs. variant control, overt vs. implicit control (both regarding the controller and the controllee) and control in subject as well as object clauses under obligatory control. It does not confine control to certain types of clausal complements and it admits pronominal controllees.

3.7. Possessors as controllers

According to the standard assumption that the controller should c-command the controllee (Williams 1980; Hornstein 1999), control by possessor arguments is ruled out:

(35) *[John$_i$'s aunt]$_j$ promised [_$_{j/*i}$ to come].*

The definition of (obligatory) control in (34) likewise precludes control by possessor arguments. However, in some languages one can find structures of possessor control; here, the possessor argument is part of a complex predicate based on body part expressions. Mesoamerican languages, for instance, display a range of such constructions. Consider the following example from the Mayan language K'ekchí (Kockelman 2003: 30). 'Remember' is expressed as 'someone's heart drops'; the possessor, which is marked by ergative agreement, controls the covert subject of the embedded clause.

(36) *x-naq sa' in$_i$-ch'ool* [_$_i$ *chalk*]. [K'ekchí]
PFV-drop inside 1SG.EA-heart come
'I remembered to come' (lit. 'it has dropped into my heart to come')

Since body part expressions are inherently relational, their possessor argument is automatically activated in the interpretation of the respective predicates, which then allows the interpretational shift from the body part noun, which could not function as controller, to the respective possessor. The conditions under which possessor control is possible are thus semantic in nature.

4. The controllee

In canonical cases of complement control the controller corresponds to an overt DP in the matrix clause whereas the controllee in the embedded clause remains covert. However, the controllee may also be realized overtly, for instance as lexical subject in infinitives (see Szabolcsi 2009):

(37) *Szeretnék/ utálok* [*én is magas lenni*]. [Hungarian]
like.COND.1SG/ hate.1SG 1SG too tall be.INF
'I want/hate it to be the case that I too am tall'

Note that condition C of the binding theory (see chapter 39) precludes overt referential expressions in the position of the controllee; only pronominal controllees are possible in these cases. However, there are two further scenarios, albeit less common cross-linguistically: *backward control* (Polinsky and Potsdam 2002) and *copy control* (Polinsky and Potsdam 2006; Haddad 2009, 2011). Backward or inverse control is characterized by argument identification of a covert argument in the matrix clause and an overt element in the embedded clause; here, the embedded overt DP may surface as referential expression – like regular controllers. Further properties and theoretical accounts of backward control are treated in chapter 38. In the third scenario, copy (or resumptive) control, both controller and controllee are overt.

4.1. Pivot property of the controllee

Since Keenan's (1976) seminal paper on subject properties, controllee choice has been taken as one of the central subject properties, i.e., the argument that is controlled in complement control is considered to be the subject (or the *pivot*). Languages mainly follow two patterns: the controllee corresponds to the highest-ranked argument of the embedded predicate (*logical subject*) or to the argument that would receive the default linker (usually nominative/absolutive case/agreement). This distinction does not play such an important role in languages in which all highest-ranked arguments receive the default linker. However, languages that exhibit quirky case, i.e., lexically induced oblique/non-canonical case, either show sensitivity to the argument role of the embedded predicate or to its argument realization. Whereas German only allows arguments to be controlled that would receive the default linker (NOM), Icelandic (Andrews 1990) seems to allow quirky subjects to be controlled. (38b) shows that it is impossible in German to embed a verb with a dative-marked highest argument (e.g., *grauen* 'dread'; see [38a]) under a control verb. Note that *hoffen* 'hope' does not require the embedded verb to be agentive; therefore, semantic inconsistencies between matrix and embedded predicate are ruled out as the explanation for the unacceptability of the example.

(38) a. *Mir graut vor der nächsten Prüfung.* [German]
I.DAT dread.3SG before the next exam
'I'm dreading the next exam'

b. **Ich hoffe* [_ *nicht vor der nächsten Prüfung zu grauen*].
I hope.1SG Ø.DAT not before the next exam to dread.INF
'I hope not to be dreading the next exam'

(39b) shows that an Icelandic verb with an ACC-subject can be embedded under a control verb (Andrews 1990: 198); it is the ACC-subject that is controlled.

(39) a. *stelpuna vantar efni í ritgerðina* [Icelandic]
girl.DEF.ACC lacks material in paper.DEF
'the girl lacks material for the paper'

b. *stelpun/ *stelpuna vonast [til að _ vanta ekki*
girl.DEF.NOM/ girl.DEF.ACC hopes toward to Ø.ACC lack not
efni í ritgerðina]
material in paper.DEF
'the girl hopes not to lack material for the paper'

The syntactic selection of the controllee argument is not strictly parameterized such that languages either only select the highest argument or the default linker argument. In a few languages, e.g., Tagalog (Kroeger 1993), both options are available in principle. In Tagalog, usually the highest (actor) argument is controlled – independent of the verbal voice morphology. The Tagalog voice system, which can be found in other West-Austronesian languages as well, is based on an inventory of voice markers that render specific verbal arguments as most prominent; each voice marker is designated for a specific argument role. The argument targeted by the voice marker receives the default linker: in (40a) the actor, in (40b) the theme and in (40c) the recipient. The examples (Kroeger 1993: 39) demonstrate that the actor argument may be controlled in the actor voice (AV) as in (40a), corresponding to an overt NOM-argument, or it may be controlled in the instrumental (IV) or dative voice (DV) as in (40b)/(40c), corresponding to an overt GEN-argument.

(40) a. *binalak* *niya=ng* [*mag-bigay* *ng=pera* *sa=nanay* [Tagalog]
PFV.plan.OV 3SG.GEN=COMP AV-give GEN=money DAT=mother
_]
Ø.NOM
'he planned to give money to Mother'

b. *binalak* *niya=ng* [*i-bigay* _ *sa=Nanay* *ang=pera*]
PFV.plan.OV 3SG.GEN=COMP IV-give Ø.GEN DAT=mother NOM=money
'he planned to give money to Mother'

c. *binalak* *niya=ng* [*bigy-an* _ *ng=pera* *ang=nanay*]
PFV.plan.OV 3SG.GEN=COMP give-DV Ø.GEN GEN=money NOM=mother
'he planned to give money to Mother'

Control of the NOM-argument is obligatory in the non-volitive mood, which is marked by *ma-* (Kroeger 1993: 95):

(41) a. **in-utus-an* *ko* *si=Maria=ng* [*ma-halik-an* _ [Tagalog]
PFV-order-DV 1SG.GEN NOM=Maria=COMP NVOL-kiss-DV Ø.GEN
si=Pedro]
NOM=Pedro
'I ordered Maria to kiss Pedro'

b. *in-utus-an* *ko* *si=Maria=ng* [*ma-halik-an* *ni=Pedro* _]
PFV-order-DV 1SG.GEN NOM=Maria=COMP NVOL-kiss-DV GEN=Pedro Ø.NOM
'I ordered Maria (to allow herself) to be kissed by Pedro'

As (41a) shows, it is not possible in the non-volitive mood to control a genitive argument; only control of NOM-arguments as in (41b) is possible; the dative voice renders the patient argument accessible to the default linker. However, a small set of predicates allows both actor control and NOM control – the latter not being restricted to the non-volitive mood (see Kroeger 1993: 97 f. for further details). Balinese, another Austronesian language, shows consistent NOM control (Wechsler and Arka 1998), whereas Madurese (Davies 2005a) instantiates both actor and NOM control.

In languages that lack quirky or lexical case, voice operations may reveal the nature of the controllee: does passivization, for instance, shift the controllee (the argument that would be realized with the default linker) or does it leave the controllee unchanged (e.g., the agent argument)? In the first case, there is NOM control, in the second actor control. The Mayan language Tojolabal (Robertson 1980: 226) provides a case for actor control: in the passivized complement shown in (42) the actor argument is controlled, not the patient argument of 'cure', which is indexed by the ergative affix.

(42) *ha-kol-t-ay-on* [_ *y-ahn-a-he-el*] [Tojolabal]
2SG.EA-help-TR-TH-1SG.NA 3SG.EA-cure-TH-PASS-NMLZ
'you helped me cure him'

4.2. Readings of the controllee

The research on the interpretation of the controllee has revealed three interesting properties, which are taken as definitional for obligatory control by many syntacticians (e.g., Hornstein 1999).

First, as observed by Chierchia (1989a), infinitival complements only allow sloppy readings in VP-ellipsis; strict readings are excluded. (43a) only exhibits the sloppy reading indicated in (43b); the strict reading in (43c) is ruled out.

(43) a. *Maria liebt es,* [*Klavier zu spielen*], *aber Petra (liebt es) nicht.*
Mary love.3SG it piano to play.INF but Petra love.3SG it NEG
'Mary loves to play piano, but Petra doesn't'

b. = 'Petra does not love to play piano.' [sloppy reading]

c. ≠ 'Petra does not love it when Maria plays piano.' [strict reading]

Secondly, as observed by Higginbotham (1980), controllees exhibit bound variable readings with respect to a controller modified by *only*; this does not apply to pronominal subjects in finite complements (compare [44a/c]).

(44) a. *Only John expects [_ to win].*
b. = 'Only John is an x such that x expects that x will win.'
c. *Only John$_i$ expects [that he$_i$ will win].*
d. = 'Only John is an x such that x expects that John will win.'

Thirdly, controllees of infinitival complements must be interpreted *de se* (Chierchia 1989b). Attitudinal predicates such as *believe* allow readings in which the attitude holder has certain beliefs about an individual without being aware that he or she is that respective person. For instance, even if the attitude holder does not recognize himself/herself in a video that shows a car accident, the following statement may be true:

(45) *Mary$_i$ believes that she$_i$ caused the accident.*

However, if the verb selects an infinitival complement, the awareness condition applies. (46) is only true if Mary is aware of the fact that she caused the accident.

(46) *Mary$_i$ believes [_$_i$ to have caused the accident].*

5. Inherent control

Since most studies of control focus on infinitival/infinite complements, the role of inherent control has often been ignored or only received marginal attention. Its significance becomes obvious if one takes complementation structures other than infinite complements into account.

Control-neutral structures present the test case for the control property of the matrix predicate: if a control reading is obligatory even in this case, the matrix predicate must be an inherent control predicate. If there is no obligatory control reading but free reference of the embedded subject, the matrix predicate does not show any inherent control. Languages that lack control-inducing structures only distinguish between inherent control predicates and non-control predicates.

Verbs/predicates are usually not restricted to one pattern of subordination but may allow for various subordination patterns (e.g., allowing a control-inducing structure such as an infinitival clause and a control-neutral structure such as a nominalized complement). If a language has control-inducing structures, these are expected to occur with inherent control predicates. Surprisingly, some languages do not consistently realize such a perfect match: certain predicates only select control-neutral structures although control-inducing structures are available (= marked inherent control; see Stiebels 2007). In Hungarian (see also Noonan 1985 for Lango) directive/manipulative verbs with an inherent control reading (e.g., *meg-kér* 'ask', *kényszerít* 'force', *meg-győz* 'convince') select a subjunctive complement even though Hungarian has a regular infinitive:

(47) a. *János$_i$ meg-győz-te Mariá-t$_j$ [hogy _$_{j/*i/*k}$* [Hungarian]
János PV-convince-PST.3SG Mary-ACC COMP
*men-jen/ *men-ni vel-e*]
go-3SG.SBJV/ go-INF with-3SG
'János convinced Mary to go with him'
(Farkas 1992: 91)

b. *Péter$_i$ meg-kér-te Mariá-t$_j$ [hogy _$_{j/*i/*k}$ vegye meg*
Peter PV-ask-PST.3SG Mary-ACC COMP buy.SBJV.3SG PV
az ennivaló-t]
the food-ACC
'Peter asked Mary to buy the food'
(Beata Gyuris, p.c.)

Interestingly, inherent control predicates show the interpretational effects described for infinitival complements: a) sloppy readings, b) *de se* readings and c) bound variable readings. This can be nicely demonstrated with the lexical contrast of the two German factive verbs *bereuen/bedauern* 'regret', which are almost synonymous. Whereas *bedauern* can refer to attitudes that are not subject-directed, *bereuen* (which is reminiscent of *repent*, though without a religious undertone) is confined to attitudes that refer to the subject referent's convictions and deeds. Consider the following example:

(48) *Peter bereut, /bedauert [dass er sich für die Tagung* [German]
Peter repent.3SG regret.3SG that he 3.REFL for the conference
angemeldet hat]$_i$, *und Norbert tut es$_i$ auch.*
register.PTCP AUX.3SG and Norbert do.3SG it too
'Peter repents/regrets that he registered for the conference,
and Norbert does it, too'

i. *bereuen*: 'Norbert repents/regrets that he registered for the conference, too'
ii. *bedauern*: reading (i) + 'Norbert regrets that Peter registered for the conference'

Whereas *bedauern* exhibits a strict and a sloppy reading for the elided/pronominalized complement, *bereuen* is confined to the sloppy reading. *Bereuen* also requires a *de se* reading with finite complements, whereas *bedauern* does not. Likewise, *bereuen* shows a bound variable reading with *nur* 'only' – in contrast to *bedauern* (see Stiebels 2010).

Which predicates belong to the class of inherent control predicates? As demonstrated in Stiebels (2010), the class of inherent control predicates cannot be characterized in syntactic terms. There is no syntactic feature that would single out inherent control predicates – in contrast to other clause-embedding predicates. One could speculate that the class of inherent control is to be equated with the class of predicates that are confined to invariant exhaustive control. However, certain predicates, namely variable control verbs such as *drohen* 'threaten' or partial control predicates such as *bereit sein* 'be ready' falsify this assumption. Likewise, not all inherent control predicates select for actional clausal complements (see Jackendoff and Culicover's 2003 characterization of *unique control*); predicates that ascribe an activity or property to some object referent (e.g., *unterstellen* 'imply', *nachsagen* 'say sth. of sb.') occur with non-actional complements.

In general one can observe two major classes of inherent control predicates: predicates with event coherence and predicates that lack this semantic property. Event coherence is given if two subevents have to show temporal and local overlap in order to be conceivable as a coherent complex event (see the mismatching temporal modifiers test mentioned above). Event coherence implies the (partial) overlap of actants in the respective subevents; two subevents with disjoint participants will never be integrated as a coherent complex event. Therefore, control, which is a specific instance of argument sharing, follows automatically from the property of event coherence. Typical event-coherent or single-event predicates are aspectual (e.g., *beginnen* 'begin', *aufhören* 'stop', *fortfahren* 'continue', *pflegen* 'use to'), modal (*freistehen* 'to be free to do', *obliegen* 'to be in sb.'s responsibility', *vergönnt sein* 'to be granted to do') and implicative predicates (e.g., *zwingen* 'force', *gelingen* 'manage', *meiden* 'avoid', *versäumen* 'miss'; see also Karttunen's 1971 characterization of implicative predicates). Some intentional predicates are likewise event-coherent (e.g., *versuchen* 'try', *wagen* 'dare').

Inherent control predicates that lack event coherence include several subclasses with different triggering factors for inherent control (see Stiebels 2010 for details): with certain speech act verbs, the inherent control reading results from felicity conditions of the denoted speech act; this is true for commissive predicates and directive predicates. A second subclass includes predicates of direct predication, i.e., the clausal argument is integrated as a predicate over the internal argument of the matrix predicate, for instance with verbs that ascribe activities or properties to the object referent (e.g., *verdächtigen* 'suspect', *vorhalten* 'reproach', *bezichtigen* 'accuse', *attestieren* 'certify'). The third subclass consists of verbs like *bereuen*, which have acquired a very specific reading in lexical contrast with almost synonymous predicates. Whereas the other classes have a systematic and class-defining meaning component that may show up in other languages, the last subclass is very language-specific and idiosyncratic.

There is a pattern of argument extension in which predicates are turned into inherent control predicates. As noted by Siebert-Ott (1983) and Farkas (1988), verbs of speech/

evaluation allow the integration of a DP that functions as the topic to be elaborated on in the complement clause. If this DP is animate, it induces a control relation. Consider the following examples from Farkas (1988: 54):

(49) *John said/thinks of Peter$_i$ that ...*
  a. *he$_i$ was seen by Mary*
  b. *Mary saw him$_i$*
  c. *he$_i$ saw Mary*
  d. *his$_i$ grades are bad*
  e. *#Bill kissed Mary.*

The clausal complements are well-formed as long as there is some kind of argument identification between the prepositional object in the matrix clause and a DP in the embedded clause; (49e), which shows no co-reference, is thus ungrammatical. These examples illustrate in addition that finite complements of inherent control predicates allow the controllee to surface in any position (even as possessor DP). Whereas the argument extension of *say/think* is not marked in the verbs, some languages use applicative-like structures in this case. The Austronesian language Madurese (and some of its relatives) uses a verbal marker to encode such proleptic structures. In (50a) the respective DP is realized within the embedded clause; in (50b) it has become the object of the matrix verb via applicative derivation (Davies 2005b: 648).

(50) a. *Guru-na yaken [**Bambang** bakal lolos tes-sa].* [Madurese]
  teacher-DEF sure Bambang will pass test-DEF
  'the teacher is sure that Bambang will pass the exam'

  b. *Guru-na ng-yaken-**ne** **Bambang** [ja' bakal lolos tes-sa].*
  teacher-DEF AV-sure-APPL Bambang COMP will pass test-DEF
  'the teacher is sure about Bambang that he will pass the exam'

As Davies shows, these structures cannot be analyzed as instances of subject-to-object raising.

6. Control vs. raising

One cannot deal with control predicates without taking raising predicates into account (see also the comprehensive discussion of raising in Davies and Dubinsky 2004). Often, both predicate types select for the same type of syntactic subordination structure (typically, infinitival complements). Raising predicates such as *scheinen/seem* (e.g., *the lake seems to be frozen*) allow an argument of the embedded predicate to be realized as its own subject, yielding a semantics-syntax mismatch: semantically, the respective argument belongs exclusively to the embedded predicate, syntactically to the matrix predicate.

Besides subject raising there are also structures that have been dubbed *Subject-to-object Raising*, the latter also being called *Exceptional Case Marking* or, traditionally, *Accusativus cum Infinitivo*; here the subject of the embedded predicate is realized as the matrix predicate's object. English has quite a number of such raising predicates, some of which are shown in (51), whereas in many other languages only perception verbs and/or a general causative verb (e.g., German *lassen* 'let') exhibit this syntactic pattern.

(51) a. *Mary* ***wants*** *John to mow the lawn.*
b. *John* ***expects*** *Mary to arrive late.*
c. *Mary* ***believes*** *John to not have told her the truth.*

In the literature various diagnostics have been discussed for distinguishing raising predicates from control predicates; these diagnostics reflect the semantic differences between these two predicate types. Quite a number of predicates may function both as raising and control predicates; typically, these are aspectual predicates such as *begin* or *stop* (subject control/subject raising) or desiderative predicates such as *want* (subject control/subject-to-object raising). *Promise* and *threaten* also have a double function in some languages (e.g., German, English, French). Certain directive/mandative predicates in English (e.g., *order, command*) also exhibit properties of raising verbs, as shown by Barrie and Pittman (2010).

One distinctive feature of raising predicates is that they allow the raising of expletives as in (52a), whereas control predicates cannot embed structures/predicates in which the controllee would be a semantically uninterpretable element as in (52b). Therefore, the admissibility of weather verbs or other impersonal verbs is an indication of a raising structure.

(52) a. *It seems [to rain].*
b. **John tries [_ to rain].*

Parallel to the admissibility of pleonastic elements raising predicates do not impose selectional restrictions on the raised argument; however, control predicates preclude the embedding of predicates that would yield a conflict in terms of the sortal features of the controlled argument (*#Peter tried to be frozen / #the lake tried to be frozen.*).

Furthermore, the truth conditions of sentences with raising verbs do not change if the embedded verb is passivized (voice transparency):

(53) a. *She seems [to prefer red roses].*
b. *Red roses seem [to be preferred by her].*

In contrast, control relations are affected by passivization of the embedded predicate, as different buletic situations are characterized by the following sentences:

(54) a. *I want [_ to praise them].*
b. *They want [_ to be praised by me].*

A further test concerns the embedding of idiomatic expressions in which the subject is also idiomatic (e.g., German *die Katze ist aus dem Sack* = *the cat is out of the bag*). The idiomatic reading is retained with embedding under raising verbs (*the cat seems to be out of the bag*), but lost with embedding under a control verb (?*the cat wanted to be out of the bag*).

There are also language-specific diagnostics for the distinction of control and raising predicates. In German, for instance, subject control predicates are distinguished from subject raising predicates by their potential to be passivized. In its use as raising verb, *beginnen* 'begin' cannot be passivized (see [55a]), which, however, is possible in its use as control verb (see [55b]). This is due to the fact that German allows impersonal passives.

(55) a. * *Es wurde begonnen [zu regnen].* [German]
it AUX.PRET begin.PTCP to rain.INF
lit. 'it was begun to rain'

b. *Es wurde begonnen [_ die Tische ab-zu-räumen].*
P AUX.PRET begin.PTCP the table PT-to-clear.INF
lit. 'it was begun to clear the tables'

Other properties that are claimed to distinguish control and raising predicates cannot be operationalized in the same way as the previous tests (e.g., the claim that languages may display control nominals but no raising nominals; see the discussion in Hornstein and Polinsky 2010).

7. Adjunct control

Control is not confined to selected clausal complements but also occurs with clausal adjuncts. Due to the fact that the clause is not selected by a matrix predicate, control arises mainly as a property of the syntactic structure of the adjunct clause, which is generally control-inducing. Typically, infinite purpose clauses, co-predicative participles or converbs instantiate adjunct control. I consider only those instances of adjunct control as control proper that obey the locality constraint that the controller must be an (explicit/implicit) argument in the matrix clause.

Purpose clauses, which due to their semantics can only be adjoined to clauses that contain an agentive predicate, have been studied most (e.g., Bach 1982; Chierchia 1989a; Jones 1991). Languages may display purpose clauses that are confined to subject control, as the English clauses headed by *in order to* (compare [56a/b]). Complementizerless infinitival purpose clauses such as (56c) allow both a subject and an object control reading; the pronoun *her* in (56d) then excludes the subject control reading due to binding restrictions.

(56) a. *Mary$_i$ brought John$_j$ along [_$_i$ in order to talk to him].*
b. **Mary$_i$ brought John$_j$ along [_$_j$ in order to talk to her].*
c. *Mary$_i$ brought John$_j$ along [_$_{i/j}$ to talk].*
d. *Mary$_i$ brought John$_j$ along [_$_j$ to talk to her].*

Converbs are nonfinite verbal adverbs (Haspelmath 1995), i.e., they modify clauses. They differ cross-linguistically and language-internally in terms of the realization of their subject. The interesting cases are those in which the subject may not surface like in the following Russian example (Haspelmath 1995: 10):

(57) *(*Ona) prigotoviv zavtrak, Zamira razbudila detej* [Russian]
she prepare.PFV.CVB breakfast Zamira woke.up children
'having prepared breakfast, Zamira woke up the children'

As Haspelmath points out, converbs that do not allow the overt realization of the subject usually show subject control, hence, are control-inducing, whereas converbs that require the subject to be overtly realized exhibit a different-subject pattern (i.e., non-control). Converbs whose subject may be optionally realized allow a co-referential reading but do not require it. If two or more converbs express roughly the same adverbial relation, a division of labor is likely to occur such that one converb is control-inducing whereas the other is not. An illustrative case can be found in the Tungusic language Evenki (Nedjalkov 1995: 450), which has both control-neutral and control-inducing converbs among the set of converbs expressing simultaneity: *-d'ana*, *-ŋasi*, *-d'anma*. *-D'ana* is control-inducing, requiring subject control, *-ŋasi* is control-neutral, allowing both co-referential and disjoint readings, whereas the archaic *-d'anma* only allows disjoint readings. Not that control-inducing converb structures do not take possessive markers:

(58) *bejumimni-l$_i$* [_$_i$ *bira-li d'avra-**d'ana**-l*] *moti-va iče-če-tin* [Evenki]
hunter-PL river-PROL boat-CVB-PL elk-ACC see-PST-3PL
'boating along the river, the hunters saw the elk'

In contrast, control-neutral converbs allow possessive inflection (Nedjalkov 1995: 445, 446). Here, the type of possessive marker distinguishes between a co-referential and a disjoint reading. Co-reference with the matrix subject is marked by the reflexive possessive (see [59a]), whereas disjoint readings are marked by regular possessive inflection (see [59b]).

(59) a. [_$_i$ *Turu-du bi-ŋesi-**vi***] *tara-ve sa-ča-v$_i$* [Evenki]
Turu-LOC be-CVB-REFL.SG that-ACC know-PST-1SG
'I knew that when I was/lived in Tura'

b. [_$_j$ *Turu-du bi-ŋesi-**n***] *tara-ve sa-ča-v$_i$*
Turu-LOC be-CVB-3SG.PA that-ACC know-PST-1SG
'I knew that when he/she was/lived in Tura'

According to Haspelmath (1995: 29–37), converbs display subject control in the unmarked case. Control by non-subjects is, however, possible; Haspelmath lists quite a number of cases for non-subject control; here, the control readings are typically pragmatically induced.

Interestingly, languages tend to develop formal means for encoding control relations in adjunct control but far less so in complement control; in the latter, languages seem to rely on the selection relation between the matrix predicate and its clausal complement: the control reading is lexically induced by the matrix predicate. There are two typical strategies for specifying the control relation in adjunct control: switch-reference markers or case concord with the controller NP/DP. The strategy of Evenki is not that common.

Switch-reference markers are important means of reference tracking in verbal chains/ sequences or in the integration of verbal adjuncts (Haiman and Munro 1983; Stirling

1993). Usually, they indicate whether the subject of the respective predicate is co-referential with the subject of some other predicate higher in the clause or in a verbal chain. Therefore, the same subject marker (SS) is used with subject control, whereas the different subject marker (DS) is used with control by some other argument of the matrix predicate or with arbitrary control. The Australian language Warlpiri uses a kind of switch-reference system as well as (optional) case concord. *-karra* is used in cases of subject control, either with ergative-marked subjects as in (60a) or with absolutive-marked subjects as in (60b). *-kurra* is used with object control, again independent of the case concord pattern: an absolutive-marked object in (60c) and a dative-marked object in (60d).

(60) a. *Ngarrka$_i$-ngku ka purlapa$_j$ yunpa-mi [_$_i$ karli* [Warlpiri]
man-ERG PRS corroboree sing-NPST boomerang
jarnti-rninja-karra-rlu].
trim-INF-SS-ERG
'the man is singing a corroboree song while trimming the boomerang'

b. *Karnta$_i$ ka-ju$_j$ wangka-mi [_$_i$ yarla karla-nja-karra*].
woman PRS-1SG.ACC speak-NPST yam dig-INF-SS
'the woman is speaking to me while digging yams'

c. *Ngarrka-patu$_i$ ka-rna$_j$-jana nya-nyi [_$_i$ wawirri*
man-PL PRS-1SG.NOM-3PL.ACC see-NPST kangaroo
panti-rninja- kurra].
spear-INF-DS
'I see the several men spearing a kangaroo'

d. *Marlu$_i$-ku ka-rna$_j$-rla wurruka-nyi [_$_j$ marna*
kangaroo-DAT PRS-1.NOM-NG stalk-NPST grass
nga-rninja-kurra-(ku)].
eat-INF-DS-DAT
'I am sneaking up on the kangaroo (while it is) eating grass'
(Hale 1983: 20, 21)

This degree of redundancy in marking the co-reference relation is not very common cross-linguistically. But whereas switch-reference systems are well attested for structures of adjunct control, there seem to be only few languages that instantiate switch-reference systems in cases of complement control (see, for instance, Hale 1992 for Hopi).

The conjunctive participle found in many South Asian languages is another control-inducing adverbial structure (see Haddad 2009, 2011 for data on Assamese and Telugu), which is confined to subject control. As Haddad shows, Telugu conjunctive participles may occur with structures of backward and copy control besides the canonical forward control, whereas Assamese excludes backward control but allows copy control.

There is also evidence that even control-neutral adjunct structures may require a control reading. An illustrative case would be finite adverbial clauses in German headed by the complementizer *indem* 'by' (e.g., *die Mutter beruhigte das Baby, indem sie* ... 'the mother pacified the baby by V-ing ...'). These adjunct clauses specify the manner of the activity denoted by the matrix predicate; if the latter corresponds to an agentive predicate, control is obligatory. Converbs with an equivalent semantics show the same behavior.

8. Open issues

Some control phenomena deserve further research. As mentioned in 2.7, the control properties of subject clauses should be systematically re-evaluated with respect to the role of the selecting predicates.

The next issue concerns the control readings in *wh*-infinitives, for which no consensus has been reached so far. In the syntactic literature, *wh*-infinitives have been assumed to show arbitrary control, typically illustrated by examples like the following, in which the anaphor *oneself* is taken as an indication for arbitrary control.

(61) *John$_i$ asked [how _$_j$ to behave oneself$_j$].*

In contrast, Landau (2000) assumes obligatory control for *wh*-infinitives. Barrie (2010) argues that obligatory as well as generic control occurs and that the corresponding structures differ in their extraction properties. Jackendoff and Culicover (2003) show that generic readings are excluded for embedded infinitival polar questions:

(62) *Harry$_i$ asked Sally$_j$ [whether _$_{i/*gen/*j}$ to take care of himself/*oneself/*herself].*

Split control readings are also possible, as the following Spanish example (Bosque and Demonte 1999: 2186) illustrates:

(63) *Mi novia$_i$ no me$_j$ especificó [dónde _$_{i+j}$ encontrar=nos]* [Spanish]
my girl.friend NEG 1SG.ACC tell.PRET.3SG where meet.INF=1PL.ACC]
'my girl-friend didn't tell me where to meet'

In order to get a clear picture of the admissible control readings in *wh*-infinitives an exhaustive study of interrogative predicates selecting *wh*-infinitives, has to be carried out. This may answer the question whether interrogative predicates display less lexical variation in their control properties than other clause-embedding predicates.

Another issue that deserves further research is the potential correlation between control and restructuring. According to Wurmbrand (2002) restructuring predicates do not allow partial control. In a similar spirit Grano (2012) equates exhaustive control with restructuring and partial control with non-restructuring structures. Given that languages show different restructuring properties (e.g., clitic climbing, long passive, genitive of negation, licensing of polarity items) and that these properties do not necessarily converge in the respective set of clause-embedding predicates, the question arises whether this claim can be maintained for a larger set of languages (and predicates) or whether it needs further refinements. In view of the highly marked status of partial control, *non-exhaustive control* may be a better characterization of the control properties of non-restructuring cases.

Finally, taking up an observation by Szabolcsi (2009), I want to mention that the scopal properties of control verbs may also show more variation than expected. (64) illustrates an interesting contrast between *want* and *hate*. *Want* allows reconstruction with the scope-taking particle *too* (see [64b]); *hate* does not (see [64d]).

(64) a. *Mary wants to be tall. I too want to be tall.*
= 'I too want it to be the case that I am tall'

b. *Mary is tall. I too want to be tall.*
= 'I want it to be the case that I too am tall'

c. *Mary hates to be tall. I too hate to be tall.*
= 'I too hate it that I am tall'

d. *Mary is tall. #I too hate to be tall.*
Intended: 'I hate it that I too am tall'

Although it is generally assumed that control verbs – unlike raising predicates – do not exhibit scope reconstruction, the particle *too* points to a more complex picture, which is worth being pursued further.

9. Summary

The previous sections have shown that control structures result from an intricate interaction of syntax and lexicon. In many, if not most languages the choice of the controller (subject vs. object control, fixed, vs. variable vs. shift control) and the control readings (exhaustive vs. split vs. partial control) are associated with specific control predicates or predicate classes. Only few languages generalize controller choice syntactically. In addition, the class of inherent control predicates can only be characterized in lexical-semantic terms. The lexical nature is further corroborated by the fact that the control properties are preserved under a category shift of the respective predicate, i.e., with control nominals derived from verbs. The syntactic nature of control manifests itself in the presence or absence of control-inducing structures (e.g. control-neutral vs. control-inducing nominalized or finite clauses) and in the properties of the latter. Moreover, the pivot properties of the controllee, i.e., whether a language displays control of NOM or actor arguments, are also a matter of syntax.

Any theoretical account of control will depend on the control structures and properties to be included in the domain of control proper. Exhaustive (structural) control can be modeled more easily than the complex cases of partial or variable control. Therefore, many theories focus on this aspect of control (see chapter 38). Inherent control, which surfaces in all types of complement structures and also shows more variability concerning the position of the controllee, is usually disregarded in syntactic accounts of control.

10. Abbreviations

#	semantic deviance
^	phonological word boundary
AV	actor voice
DIM	diminutive
DIR	directional
DS	different subject
DV	dative voice
EA	ergative agreement
EXPE	expected
IV	instrumental voice
NA	nominative agreement
NG	not glossed by author
NVOL	non-volitive
OBJC	object case
OV	object voice
PA	possessor agreement

PRET	preterite	REM.PST	remote past
PRO	pronominal form	REP	reported evidential
PROL	prolative	SS	same subject
PT	(verbal) particle	TH	thematic element
PV	preverb	TNS	tense marker
REC.PST	recent past	VIS	visual (evidential)

11. References (selected)

Aikhenvald, Alexandra Y.
2003 *A Grammar of Tariana, from Northwest Amazonia*. Cambridge: Cambridge University Press.

Aikhenvald, Alexandra Y.
2006 Serial verb constructions in typological perspective. In: Alexandra Y. Aikhenvald and R. M. W. Dixon (eds.), *Serial Verb Constructions: A Cross-Linguistic Typology*, 1–68. Oxford: Oxford University Press.

Andrews, Avery
1990 Case structures and control in Modern Icelandic. In: Joan Maling and Annie Zaenen (eds.), *Modern Icelandic Syntax. Syntax and Semantics* 24, 187–234. San Diego: Academic Press.

Bach, Emmon
1982 Purpose clauses and control. In: Pauline Jacobson and Geoffrey K. Pullum (eds.), *The Nature of Syntactic Representation*, 35–57. Dordrecht: Reidel.

Barrie, Michael
2007 Control and *wh*-infinitivals. In: William D. Davies and Stanley Dubinsky (eds.), *New Horizons in the Analysis of Control and Raising*, 263–279. Dordrecht: Springer.

Barrie, Michael, and Christine Pittman
2010 Mandatives: lessons on raising/control diagnostics. *Canadian Journal of Linguistics* 55: 131–138.

Belletti, Adriana, and Luigi Rizzi
1988 Psych-verbs and Θ-theory. *Natural Language and Linguistic Theory* 6: 291–352.

Berinstein, Anne
1985 *Evidence for Multiattachment in K'ekchi Mayan*. New York: Garland.

Bosque, Ignacio, and Violeta Demonte (eds.).
Gramática Descriptiva de la Lengua Española. [Descriptive grammar of Spanish] Vol. 2. Madrid: Espasa.

Bresnan, Joan
1982 Control and complementation. In: Joan Bresnan (ed.), *The Mental Representation of Grammatical Relations*, 282–390. Cambridge, MA: MIT Press.

Chang, Yung-Li, and Wei-tien DylanTsai
2001 Actor-sensitivity and obligatory control in Kavala and some other Formosan languages. *Language and Linguistics* 2: 1–20.

Chierchia, Gennaro
1989a Structured meanings, thematic roles and control. In: Gennaro Chierchia, Barbara H. Partee, and Raymond Turner (eds.), *Properties, Types and Meaning. Volume II: Semantic Issues,* 131–166. Dordrecht: Kluwer.

Chierchia, Gennaro
1989b Anaphora and attitudes de se. In: Renate Bartsch, Johan van Benthem, and P. van Emde Boas (eds.), *Semantics and Contextual Expression*, 1–32. Dordrecht: Foris.

Comorovski, Ileana
1985 Control and obviation in Romanian. *Proceedings of Eastern States Conference on Linguistics* 2: 47–56.
Comrie, Bernard
1985 Reflections on subject and object control. *Journal of Semantics* 4: 47–65.
Crowley, Terry
1987 Serial verbs in Paamese. *Studies in Language* 11: 35–84.
Davies, William D., and Stanley Dubinsky
2004 *The Grammar of Raising and Control: A Course in Syntactic Argumentation*. Oxford: Blackwell.
Davies, William
2005a Madurese control. *Kata* 7: 48–63.
Davies, William D.
2005b Madurese prolepsis and its implications for a typology of raising. *Language* 81: 645–665.
England, Nora C.
1989 Comparing Mam (Mayan) clause structures: subordinate vs. main clauses. *International Journal of American Linguistics* 55: 283–308.
Farkas, Donka F.
1988 On obligatory control. *Linguistics and Philosophy* 11: 27–58.
Farkas, Donka F.
1992 On obviation. In: Ivan A. Sag and Anna Szabolcsi (eds.), *Lexical Matters*, 85–110. Stanford: CSLI Publications.
Gärtner, Hans-Martin
2010 More on the indefinite-interrogative affinity: The view from embedded non-finite interrogatives. *Linguistic Typology* 13: 1–37.
Gamerschlag, Thomas
2007 Semantic and structural aspects of complement control in Korean. In: Barbara Stiebels (ed.), *Studies in Complement Control. ZAS Papers in Linguistics* 47: 81–123.
Grano, Thomas Angelo
2012 Control and restructuring at the syntax-semantics interface. Unpublished PhD thesis, University of Chicago.
Grinder, John
1970 Super equi-NP deletion. *Chicago Linguistic Society* 6: 297–317.
Guerrero, Lilian
2006 *The Structure and Function on Yaqui Complementation*. München: Lincom Europa.
Haddad, Youssef A.
2009 Adjunct control in Telugu: exceptions as non-exceptions. *Journal of South-Asian Linguistics* 2: 35–51.
Haddad, Youssef A.
2011 *Control into Conjunctive Participle clauses: the case of Assamese*. Berlin: De Gruyter Mouton.
Haiman, John, and Pamela Munro (eds.)
1983 *Switch-Reference and Universal Grammar*. Amsterdam: Benjamins.
Hale, Ken
1983 Warlpiri and the grammar of non-configurational languages. *Natural Language and Linguistic Theory* 1: 5–47.
Hale, Ken
1992 Subject obviation, switch reference, and control. In: Richard K. Larson, Sabine Iatridou, Utpal Lahiri, and James Higginbotham (eds.), *Control and Grammar*, 51–77. Dordrecht: Kluwer.

Haspelmath, Martin
1995 The converb as a cross-linguistically valid category. In: Martin Haspelmath and Ekkehard König (eds.), *Converbs in Cross-linguistic Perspective*, 1–55. Berlin: Mouton de Gruyter.
Hornstein, Norbert
1999 Movement and Control. *Linguistic Inquiry* 30: 69–96.
Hornstein, Norbert, and Maria Polinsky
2010 Control as movement: Across languages and constructions. In: Norbert Hornstein and Maria Polinsky (eds.), *Movement Theory of Control*, 1–41. Amsterdam: John Benjamins.
Huddleston, Rodney
2002 Content clauses and reported speech. In: Rodney Huddleston and Geoffrey K. Pullum (eds.), *The Cambridge Grammar of the English Language*, 947–1030. Cambridge University Press.
Jackendoff, Ray, and Peter W. Culicover
2003 The semantic basis of control in English. *Language* 79: 517–556.
Jones , Charles
1991 *Purpose Clauses: Syntax, Thematics, and Semantics of English Purpose Constructions*. Dordrecht: Kluwer.
Karttunen, Lauri
1971 Implicative verbs. *Language* 47: 340–358.
Keenan, Edward L.
1976 Towards a universal definition of 'subject'. In: Charles N. Li (ed.), *Subject and Topic*, 303–333. New York: Academic Press.
Kempchinsky, Paula
1987 The subjunctive disjoint reference effect. In: Carol Neidle and Rafael A. Nuñez-Cedeño (eds.), *Studies in Romance Languages*, 123–140. Foris: Dordrecht.
Kockelman, Paul
2003 The interclausal relations hierarchy in Q'eqchi' Maya. *International Journal of American Linguistics* 69: 25–48.
Kornfilt, Jaklin
1997 *Turkish*. London: Routledge.
Kroeger, Paul
1993 *Phrase Structure and Grammatical Relations in Tagalog*. Stanford: CSLI publications.
Landau, Idan
2000 *Elements of Control: Structure and Meaning in Infinitival Constructions*. Dordrecht: Kluwer.
Landau, Idan
2004 The scale of finiteness and the calculus of control. *Natural Language and Linguistic Theory* 22: 811–877.
Levin, Beth
1993 *English Verb Classes and Alternations: A Preliminary Investigation*. Chicago: The University of Chicago Press.
Manzini, Rita
1983 On control and control theory. *Linguistic Inquiry* 14: 421–446.
Maslova, Elena
2003 *A Grammar of Kolyma Yukaghir*. Berlin: Mouton de Gruyter.
Mensching, Guido
2000 *Infinitive Constructions with Specified Subjects: A Syntactic Analysis of the Romance Languages*. Oxford: Oxford University Press.
Muysken, Pieter, and Tonjes Veenstra
2006 Serial verbs. In: Martin Everaert and Henk van Riemsdijk (eds), *The Blackwell Companion to Syntax*. Volume IV, 234–270. Oxford: Blackwell.

Nedjalkov, Vladimir P.
1995 Converbs in Evenki. In: Martin Haspelmath and Ekkehard König (eds.), *Converbs in Cross-linguistic Perspective*, 441–464. Berlin: Mouton de Gruyter.

Noonan, Michael
1985 Complementation. In: Timothy Shopen (ed.). *Language Typology and Syntactic Description: Complex Constructions,* Volume II, 42–140. Cambridge: Cambridge University Press.

Panther, Klaus-Uwe
1993 *Kontrollphänomene im Englischen und Deutschen aus semantisch-pragmatischer Perspektive*. Tübingen: Narr.

Pearson, Hazel
2012 The sense of self: topics in the semantics of de se expressions. PhD thesis, Harvard University. [Slightly revised version: http://semanticsarchive.net/Archive/WNhNjVjO/; accessed 19. 2. 2013].

Polinsky, Maria, and Eric Potsdam
2002 Backward control. *Linguistic Inquiry* 33: 245–282.

Polinsky, Maria, and Eric Potsdam
2006 Expanding the scope of control and raising. *Syntax* 9: 171–192.

Raposo, Eduardo
1987 Case theory and Infl-to-Comp: the inflected infinitive in European Portuguese. *Linguistic Inquiry* 18: 85–109.

Robertson, John S.
1980 *The Structure of Pronoun Incorporation in the Mayan Verbal Complex*. New York: Garland.

Rosenbaum, Peter
1967 *The Grammar of English Predicate Complement Constructions*. Cambridge, MA: MIT Press.

Růžička, Rudolf
1983 Remarks on control. *Linguistic Inquiry* 18: 309–324.

Růžička, Rudolf
1999 *Control in Grammar and Pragmatics: A Cross-linguistic Study*. Amsterdam: Benjamins.

Sabel, Joachim
1996 *Restrukturierung und Lokalität: Universelle Beschränkungen für Wortstellungsvarianten*. Berlin: Akademie Verlag.

Sag, Ivan A., and Carl Pollard
1991 An integrated theory of complement control. *Language* 67: 63–113.

Sichel, Ivy
2010 Towards a typology of control in DP. In: Norbert Hornstein and Maria Polinsky (eds.), *Movement Theory of Control*, 245–266. Amsterdam: John Benjamins.

Siebert-Ott, Gesa Maren
1983 *Kontroll-Probleme in infiniten Komplementkonstruktionen*. Tübingen: Gunter Narr.

Słodowicz, Szymon
2007 Complement control in Turkish. In: Barbara Stiebels (ed.), *Studies in Complement Control. ZAS Papers in Linguistics* 47: 125–157.

Słodowicz, Szymon
2008 *Control in Polish Complement Clauses*. München: Sagner.

Stiebels, Barbara
2007 Towards a typology of complement control. In: Barbara Stiebels (ed.), *Studies in Complement Control. ZAS Papers in Linguistics* 47, 1–80.

Stiebels, Barbara
2010 Inhärente Kontrollprädikate im Deutschen. *Linguistische Berichte* 224: 391–440.

Szabolcsi, Anna
2009 Overt nominative subjects in infinitival complements cross-linguistically: data, diagnostics, and preliminary analyses. *NYU Working Papers in Linguistics* 2: 1–55.
Stirling, Lesley
1993 *Switch-Reference and Discourse Representation*. Cambridge: Cambridge University Press.
Urk, Coppe van
2013 Visser's generalization: the syntax of control and the passive. *Linguistic Inquiry* 44: 168–178.
Varlokosta, Spyridoula, and Norbert Hornstein
1993 Control in Modern Greek. In: A. Schafer (ed.), *North Eastern Linguistics Society (NELS) 23*, 507–521. Amherst, MA: GLSA Publications.
Wechsler, Stephen, and I Wayan Arka
1998 Syntactic ergativity in Balinese: An argument structure based theory. *Natural Language and Linguistic Theory* 16: 387–441.
Williams, Edwin
1980 Predication. *Linguistic Inquiry* 11: 203–238.
Wurmbrand, Susi
2002. Syntactic vs. semantic control. In: Jan-Wouter Zwart and Werner Abraham (eds.), *Studies in Comparative Germanic Syntax,* 95–129. Amsterdam: Benjamins.
Zec, Draga
1987 On obligatory control in clausal complements. In: Masayo Iida, Stephen Wechsler and Draga Zec (eds.), *Working Papers in Grammatical Theory and Discourse Structure*, 139–168. Stanford: CSLI Publications.

Barbara Stiebels, Leipzig (Germany)

15. Pronominal Anaphora

Abstract

This chapter aims to provide an overview of the general patterning and distribution of pronominal anaphora. After a brief introduction in which the object of study is defined, the basic properties of pronominal and anaphoric binding are discussed – first, with a focus on the English language, then considering both crosslinguistic variation and underlying universal tendencies that seem to hold.

In this context it is also observed that binding is sensitive to domains of different size and that reflexives can even be bound across clause boundaries. These so-called long-distance reflexives are again considered crosslinguistically, and also non-syntactic factors that influence their distribution (like logophoric aspects) are considered.

Another issue which is again subject to crosslinguistic variation concerns the observable subject-object asymmetries as regards the licit forms of bound elements. Finally, the occurrence of locally free reflexives is scrutinized, which are not restricted to languages that allow long-distance binding but emerge also in languages like English. Apart from the syntactic configurations in which these types of reflexives occur, typical constructions in which they appear (like picture noun phrases) are taken into account. Moreover, different approaches as to how these reflexives can be dealt with are briefly discussed.

1. Introduction

The goal of this chapter is to shed light on the notion of pronominal anaphora and to take a closer look at their syntactic behaviour. After a brief definition of the term itself, we will investigate in which contexts they occur. Of course, one question that arises is whether some general patterns can be observed – how do pronominal anaphora generally behave, and do we find exceptions? Moreover, the issue of crosslinguistic variation has to be addressed, and there are also some universal tendencies that can be identified.

However, before turning to the syntactic structures in which pronominal anaphora occur and the peculiarities that show up in connection with them, the term itself has to be scrutinized more closely, since both parts of it can be understood in different ways. If we abstract away from recent syntactic theory, the term anaphora is generally used for expressions that receive interpretation by something mentioned before in the discourse, the so-called antecedent. In literary theory, the term denotes a rhetoric device which involves the repetition of a (group of) word(s) in successive clauses (cf. Cuddon ^{3}1992). Hence, we can conclude that the term generally implies that something mentioned before is resumed in one way or the other.

Following this definition, an anaphoric expression might be a reflexive, as in (1a), or a personal pronoun, as in (1b). In this sense, *herself* and *she* in (1) are anaphoric because they both refer to *Anna* (which is indicated by coindexation); so *Anna* functions in both examples as antecedent for the anaphoric expressions.

(1) a. *Anna*$_1$ *recognized herself*$_1$ *in the picture.*
    b. *Paul invited Anna*$_1$ *for a drink, and she*$_1$ *accepted.*

In a stricter sense, the term anaphora refers exclusively to reflexives and reciprocals, whereas personal pronouns are referred to as pronouns, independent of whether there is a syntactic antecedent or not.

Following this definition, only (1a) contains an anaphor, while *she* in (1b) is a pronoun. This classification has been adopted in particular in literature on binding and reflexivity in generative grammar (cf. in particular Chomsky 1981 and subsequent work, among many others).

(2) a. Definition 1:
Anaphora = Expressions which receive interpretation by an antecedent.

b. Definition 2:
Anaphora = Reflexives and reciprocals (= subset of [2a]).

Against this background it might sound contradictory to talk about pronominal anaphora if we stick to definition (2b) and interpret the term pronominal in a strict way as referring to personal pronouns (which contrast with anaphora). However, what is meant is that we will focus on non-clitic proforms and ignore anaphoricity expressed by clitics or other devices (cf., for instance, Everaert 2012 as regards different means to express anaphoricity).

In the following, I will adhere to the stricter definition in (2b) when talking about anaphors, and I will use the term pronoun instead when talking about personal pronouns. In section 2, I will take a closer look at both types of expressions and briefly consider their general binding behaviour. Section 3 focuses on crosslinguistic variation and universal tendencies and offers some means to describe different binding patterns by measuring the distance between anaphor and antecedent. In section 4, long-distance binding and its characteristics will be discussed, before we then turn to locally free reflexives in section 5, where we distinguish different occurrences of locally free reflexives and consider different accounts of them. Finally, section 6 offers a brief conclusion.

2. Basic properties of pronominal and anaphoric binding

There are good reasons why anaphors are generally contrasted with pronouns: They behave completely differently as far as the potential syntactic position of their antecedent is concerned. In this section, I will therefore take a closer look at the relation between anaphors/pronouns and their antecedents before turning to less expected patterns of behaviour of anaphors in the following sections. What I will neglect is the analysis of reciprocals; thus, the notion anaphor will basically refer to reflexives. Note, however, that although reciprocals and reflexives seem to have a very similar distribution (cf. [3] vs. [6]), it is not completely identical (cf., for example, the contrasts in [4a] vs. [4b] and [5a] vs. [5b]) (cf. also Fischer 2004b: 18, 19).

(3) a. *[Anna and Paul]$_1$ recognized each other$_1$ in the picture.*
b. **Each other laugh in the picture.*
c. **Their$_1$ brothers recognized each other$_1$ in the picture.*
d. **[Anna and Sally]$_1$ said that Paul and John recognized each other$_1$ in the picture.*

(4) a. *It would please [the boys]$_1$ very much for each other$_1$ to win.*
b. *??It would please John$_1$ very much for himself$_1$ to win.*
(cf. Lebeaux 1983: 723)

(5) Long-distance binding into an infinitival clause in Russian:
a. *My poprosili ix [nalit' drug drug-u čajku].* [Russian]
we asked them to.pour each other tea
'We$_1$ asked them$_2$ [to pour each other$_{*1/2}$ tea].'
b. *On ne razrešaet mne [proizvodit' opyty nad soboj].*
He not permit me to.perform experiments on self
'He$_1$ does not allow me$_2$ [to perform experiments on himself$_1$/myself$_2$].'
(cf. Rappaport 1986: 104)

2.1. Anaphors

The sentences in (6) allow us to draw first conclusions concerning the behaviour of anaphors. Obviously, (6a) is the only sentence that provides a configuration in which the anaphor is grammatical. Thus the question arises as to what the decisive difference between (6a) and the remaining examples is.

(6) a. *Anna$_1$ recognized herself$_1$ in the picture.*
b. **Herself/*Sheself likes the picture.*
c. **Anna$_1$'s brother recognized herself$_1$ in the picture.*
d. **Anna$_1$ said that Paul recognized herself$_1$ in the picture.*

At first sight, the most striking characteristic of (6a) is that it contains an antecedent for the anaphor *herself*, namely *Anna*. On this antecedent the anaphor depends for its interpretation, thus it must agree with it with respect to person, number, and gender. If we assume that the presence of this antecedent is obligatory, we can account for the ungrammaticality of sentence (6b), which does not contain an antecedent for the anaphor.

However, as (6c) and (6d) show, this restriction alone does not suffice to account for the distribution of anaphors. As far as (6c) is concerned, it differs from (6a) with respect to the syntactic configuration that holds between the antecedent and the anaphor. According to the definition in (7), *Anna* c-commands the anaphor in (6a) (cf. also [8a]), whereas in (6c), the antecedent *Anna* does not c-command *herself*, as (8b) illustrates. Note that the relevant branching nodes are boldfaced in (8). However, the concrete labelling of the nodes does not play a role.

(7) C-command: (following Reinhart 1976)
X c-commands Y iff the first branching node dominating X dominates Y, X does not dominate Y, and X ≠ Y.

(8) a. *[$_{\mathbf{TP}}$ [$_{DP}$ Anna$_1$] recognized herself$_1$ in the picture]*
b. *[$_{\mathbf{TP}}$ [$_{\mathbf{DP}}$ [Anna$_1$]'s brother] recognized herself$_1$ in the picture]*

Based on the observation that c-command plays such a crucial role, the notion of syntactic binding has been introduced and defined as follows.

(9) Syntactic binding:
X binds Y iff X c-commands Y and X and Y are coindexed.

Thus we can say that there are good grounds for the assumption that anaphors must be bound. However, example (6d) (**Anna*$_1$ *said that Paul recognized herself*$_1$ *in the picture*) shows that binding as such is not a sufficient restriction on the occurrence of anaphors: In (6d), *herself* is bound by *Anna*, but still the sentence is ungrammatical. Hence, the following question remains open: In which respect does (6d) differ from (6a)? The most obvious answer is that the distance between the antecedent and the anaphor is much smaller in the latter example. Informally it can thus be concluded that the distribution of anaphors is regulated as follows:

(10) Anaphors must be bound in a relatively local domain.

Of course, the crucial question is how this domain is properly defined. A first step into this direction was taken by Chomsky (1973). On the basis of examples like (11), he made the following observations: As (11a) illustrates, binding into a tensed clause is illicit; the antecedent *Anna* in the matrix clause seems to be too far away for the reflexive in the finite embedded clause. Moreover, an intervening subject between anaphor and antecedent (like *Paul* in [11b]) blocks anaphoric binding as well.

(11) a. **Anna*$_1$ *confirmed [*$_{CP}$ *that herself*$_1$*/sheself*$_1$ *was in the picture].*
b. **Anna*$_1$ *believes [Paul to like herself*$_1$*].*

As a first approach towards the definition of the syntactic domain in which anaphoric binding has to take place, these two observations have been summarized in the so-called Tensed-S Condition and the Specified Subject Condition, cf. (12) (cf., for instance, Roberts 1997: 127, 128). (Note that both conditions are also violated in example [6d] and thus account for its ungrammaticality.)

(12) a. Tensed-S Condition:
No binding into a tensed clause.

b. Specified Subject Condition:
No binding across an intervening subject.

A lot more would have to be said on the precise definition of this domain which restricts anaphoric binding (usually termed binding domain). However, for the time being we will ignore this issue here and just keep in mind the basic observation in (10), namely that we expect anaphors to be locally bound. In fact, following Chomsky (1981) and subsequent work, refined versions of the constraint in (10) have become known as binding principle A. For a more detailed discussion of Chomsky's and other binding theories see Fischer (this volume).

2.2. Pronouns

Let us now take a look at the distribution of pronouns and consider the examples in (13), the counterparts of the anaphoric examples in (6).

(13) a. *$Anna_1$ recognized her_1 in the picture.*
b. *She likes the picture.*
c. *$Anna_1$'s brother recognized her_1 in the picture.*
d. *$Anna_1$ said that Paul recognized her_1 in the picture.*

Here, only the first sentence is ungrammatical, in which the pronoun and its antecedent establish a relatively local binding relation. By contrast, the pronoun is licit in (13b)–(13d).

As (13c) and (13d) show, pronouns can have an antecedent, but this is not a necessary condition (cf. [13b]). So unlike anaphors, pronouns do not need an antecedent. As far as the role of c-command is concerned, the potential lacking of an antecedent in general already suggests that a pronoun need not be c-commanded by its antecedent. This is confirmed by (13c), where the antecedent is embedded inside a larger subject and therefore does not c-command the pronoun it is coindexed with. To sum up, there is no binding relation at all in (13b) and (13c). In (13d), *Anna* binds the pronoun, but not as locally as in (13a).

If this situation is compared with the sentences in (6), it can be concluded that anaphors and pronouns seem to be in complementary distribution – at least as far as the syntactic environments given in (6) and (13) are concerned. Hence, the distribution of pronouns may roughly be described as in (14). (Following Chomsky 1981 and subsequent work, refined versions of this constraint have become known as binding principle B.)

(14) Pronouns must not be locally bound.

Considering the examples we have mentioned so far, the relevant domain seems to be the same as the one in (10). Hence, we also expect that pronouns can be bound across intervening subjects and tensed clauses, i.e., technically speaking, that pronouns are neither subject to the Tensed-S Condition nor to the Specified Subject Condition, a prediction which is indeed borne out (cf. [15], which contrasts with the anaphoric examples in [11]).

(15) a. *$Anna_1$ confirmed [$_{CP}$ that she_1 was in the picture].*
b. *$Anna_1$ believes [Paul to like her_1].*

Note, however, that examples like (19) and (21) in section 3.1 (and many more in the following sections) will reveal that pronouns and anaphors are not always in complementary distribution.

3. English and beyond: variation and generalizations

3.1. Crosslinguistic variation

In the previous sections, exclusively English data have been considered. However, if we take into account other languages as well, a broad range of crosslinguistic variation can be observed. First, it is a well-known fact that English is rather the exception than the rule as far as the morphological inventory of reflexives is concerned. In English, we only find one type of reflexive, namely the morphologically complex SELF variant (like *himself, herself, themselves* etc.). In most other languages which use pronominal anaphora in local anaphoric dependencies, two different types of anaphors can be found. Apart from SELF anaphors these languages also exhibit morphologically simple anaphors. I will follow Reinhart and Reuland's (1991, 1993) terminology in referring to the morphologically complex anaphors as SELF anaphors and to the morphologically simple anaphors as SE anaphors (= simplex expressions). (Note that the term SE will also be used in the glosses since the English equivalent does not exist.) These two types of anaphors are not only different with respect to their morphological make-up, they also behave differently as far as their syntactic distribution is concerned. This is illustrated by the Dutch data in (16)–(18). Although there are constructions in which both types of anaphors are admissible (cf. [16] or [24]), there are also contexts, in which only one of the anaphors is licit, like the SELF anaphor in (17) or the SE anaphor in (18). As to the difference between examples like (16) and (17), it has been argued that additional semantic factors play a role depending on the semantics of the verb. As pointed out, for instance, by Kemmer (1993) and Schäfer (2012), *wash* can be classified as naturally reflexive verb, since a reflexive interpretation is the preferred option; this is not the case with *hate*, which is therefore classified as naturally disjoint verb.

(16) *Max*$_1$ *wast zich*$_1$/*zichzelf*$_1$. [Dutch]
Max washes SE/ himself
'Max$_1$ washes himself$_1$.'
(cf. Koster 1984: 141; Reuland and Reinhart 1995: 242)

(17) *Max*$_1$ *haat zichzelf*$_1$/ **zich*$_1$. [Dutch]
Max hates himself/ SE
'Max$_1$ hates himself$_1$.'
(cf. Koster 1984: 141; Reuland and Reinhart 1995: 242)

(18) *Max*$_1$ *keek achter zich*$_1$/ **zichzelf*$_1$. [Dutch]
Max glanced behind SE/ himself
'Max$_1$ glanced behind himself$_1$.'
(cf. Koster 1986: 334, 335)

However, not only the types of anaphors that are involved might differ from the English scenario; there are also differences across languages as far as the choice of the bound element in the same syntactic context is concerned. For instance, if we compare the English, German, and Dutch examples in (19)–(21), it can be observed that English allows the complex anaphor and the pronoun, German must use the SE anaphor, and Dutch can use either the SE anaphor or the pronoun. Hence, the data in (19)–(21) do not only serve as an example of the broad range of crosslinguistic variation we find with respect to anaphoric binding; they also show that anaphors and pronouns are not always in complementary distribution – not even in English (cf. [19] and also [21]). (Note that some Dutch native speakers prefer the weak pronoun *'m* instead of the strong pronoun *hem* in [21]). As to the German anaphors *sich* and *sich selbst*, they are more interchangeable than Dutch *zich* and *zichzelf*. It has therefore often been argued that German *sich selbst* is not a SELF anaphor like Dutch *zichzelf* but rather an intensified SE anaphor.

(19) *Max*$_1$ *glanced behind himself*$_1$*/him*$_1$.
(cf. Reuland and Everaert 2001: 642)

(20) *Max*$_1$ *blickte hinter sich*$_1$*/ ??sich selbst*$_1$*/ *ihn*$_1$. [German]
Max glanced behind SE/ himself/ him
'Max$_1$ glanced behind himself$_1$.'
(cf. Fischer 2004a: 490)

(21) *Max*$_1$ *keek achter zich*$_1$*/ *zichzelf*$_1$*/ hem*$_1$. [Dutch]
Max glanced behind SE/ himself/ him
'Max$_1$ glanced behind himself$_1$.'
(cf. Koster 1986: 334, 335)

Another peculiarity we find in some languages other than English is long-distance binding (cf. section 4 for a more detailed discussion). As the Icelandic example in (22) illustrates, the exact degree of the locality restriction on anaphoric binding relations can also vary from language to language: While anaphoric binding would be ruled out in this context in English, the Icelandic SE anaphor *sig* in the infinitival complement clause in (22) can be bound by the matrix subject *Jón*. Moreover, it can be observed that pronominal binding is a licit option here as well, so again anaphoric and pronominal binding do not necessarily exclude each other.

(22) *Jón*$_1$ *skipaði Pétri að raka ??sjálfan sig*$_1$*/ sig*$_1$*/ hann*$_1$ *á* [Icelandic]
John ordered Peter to shave-INF himself/ SE/ him on
hverjum degi.
every day
'John$_1$ ordered Peter to shave him$_1$ every day.'
(cf. Reuland and Everaert 2001: 649; Fischer 2004a: 504)

Note that in older literature on Icelandic (cf., e.g., Thráinsson 1979, 1991; Anderson 1986; Everaert 1986), the pronoun is usually ruled out in examples like (22) and the simple anaphor is assumed to be the only admissible bound element. I leave it open as to whether these different judgements are due to generational differences, as suggested by Gunnar Hrafn Hrafnbjargarson, or whether this is some general variation among speakers of Icelandic, as Joan Maling proposes.

3.2. Universal tendencies

But despite all the differences as regards the binding behaviour of pronouns and anaphors in different languages, we can still identify a general underlying pattern. Thus, it seems to be the case that all languages choose the SELF anaphor in the most local binding scenarios. When the distance between antecedent and anaphor increases, every language reaches a point where it opts for the SE anaphor (if SE anaphors are available in the given language), and for the least local binding relations, the pronoun is selected. In the transition zones from SELF to SE anaphors as chosen anaphoric forms, it might be the case (depending on the language) that both forms can occur and we get optionality, and the same holds for the transition from SE anaphors to pronouns. The latter can be observed, for instance, in the Dutch example in (21), or the Icelandic example in (22). Optionality between SELF and SE anaphor arises, for instance, in the Dutch and German examples in (24) and (25), respectively.

(23) *Jan₁ heard himself₁/*him₁ sing.*
(cf. Reinhart and Reuland 1993: 699)

(24) *Jan_1 hoorde zichzelf$_1$/ zich$_1$/ *hem$_1$ zingen.* [Dutch]
Jan heard himself/ SE/ him sing
'Jan_1 heard himself$_1$ sing.'
(cf. Reinhart and Reuland 1993: 691, 710)

(25) *Jan_1 hörte sich selbst$_1$/ sich$_1$/ *ihn$_1$ singen.* [German]
Jan heard himself/ SE/ him sing
'Jan_1 heard himself$_1$ sing.'
(cf. Fischer 2004a: 502)

So languages can vary from each other in two respects. First, they might differ with regard to the exact size of the domains where we can observe a transition from SELF to SE anaphor or SE anaphor to pronoun as chosen form of the bound element. Obviously, Icelandic (and any other language with long-distance binding) reaches the point when a pronominal realization must be chosen later than languages without long-distance binding. In languages of the latter type, the distance between antecedent and (SE) anaphor cannot become so big. The second difference concerns optionality. Thus, the transition from one realization form to another (from SELF anaphor to SE anaphor to pronoun, as the domain increases) might be abrupt and not give rise to optionality, or, as mentioned before, a certain size of the domain in which binding takes place might allow two realization forms: SELF and SE anaphor, or SE anaphor and pronoun.

What we do not find, however, are patterns of the following type, namely that anaphoric binding is licit if it takes place in domain D_1, but illicit if it takes place in domain D_2, where D_2 is smaller than D_1. Similarly, if pronominal binding is licit in domain D_1, it will also be licit in domain D_2, if D_2 is bigger than D_1. The fact that we turn from SELF anaphors to SE anaphors and finally to pronouns as the distance between antecedent and bound element increases has also consequences for the transition zones, and we will not find optionality between SELF anaphors and pronouns (if SE anaphors are available in the language under consideration). The general pattern can thus be summarized as follows:

(26) General patterns:

a. If anaphoric binding is licit in domain D_1, it is also licit in domain D_2, if D_2 is smaller than D_1.

b. If pronominal binding is licit in domain D_1, it is also licit in domain D_2, if D_2 is bigger than D_1.

c. As the distance between antecedent and bound element increases, the realization form of the bound element changes from SELF anaphor to SE anaphor and then to pronoun.

d. Optionality between SELF anaphors and pronouns cannot arise if SE anaphors are also available.

(27) Crosslinguistic variation:
a. The size of the domains (i.e. the degree of locality) when the realization form changes from SELF to SE anaphor and from SE anaphor to pronoun can vary.
b. Whether optionality occurs at all and in which domains also depends on the language under consideration.

3.3. Binding-sensitive domains

As far as the domains are concerned, Fischer (2004a, b, 2006) distinguishes six domains of different size to which binding seems to be sensitive. (The general idea that domains of different size might play a role for binding has also been considered by Manzini and Wexler 1987; Dalrymple 1993; Büring 2005, among others.) This is motivated by the observation that the choice of the bound element (= α), i.e. its realization as SELF anaphor, SE anaphor, or pronoun, depends on the question in which of these domains binding takes place. On the basis of the English, Dutch, and German data below in (33)–(35), we can thus identify already four different domains, which are defined in (28)–(31).

(28) The θ-domain of α is the smallest XP containing the head that θ-marks α plus its argument positions.

(29) The case domain of α is the smallest XP containing α and the head that case-marks α.

(30) The subject domain of α is the smallest XP containing α and a subject distinct from α.

(31) The root domain of α is the XP that forms the root of the sentence containing α.

If the domains in (28)–(31) are interpreted as the sets of nodes that constitute the respective domain, we can conclude that the subset relations indicated in (32) hold.

(32) θ-domain $\subseteq$ case domain $\subseteq$ subject domain $\subseteq$ root domain

Considering now the examples below, we can observe that the predictions in (26) and (27) are indeed confirmed (the boldfaced marking of the bound elements in [33]–[35] shows this visually). The realization form of α depends on two factors – the domain in which binding takes place (which increases from example [a] to [d]), and the language under consideration, since different parametric settings determine at which point the realization form changes from SELF to SE anaphor and from SE anaphor to pronoun (cf. [27a]).

Hence, we can observe that English chooses the SELF anaphor if the binding relation is very local, i.e., if it takes place within the θ-domain. This is illustrated in (33a), because the domain comprising the θ-marking head (= *hates*) and its argument positions also contains the antecedent (which is a coargument of α); hence we have binding inside the θ-domain (which implies of course that binding also takes place within the case, subject, and root domain in [33a]; however, the θ-domain is the smallest binding domain in this example).

In (33b), the θ-domain of the bound element does not contain the antecedent *Max* (or a trace of it), because *Max* is not θ-marked by the same predicate as α (*heard* vs. *sing*). Instead, the smallest domain in which binding takes place in this example is the case domain: α is case-marked by the matrix verb *heard*, and on the assumption that the matrix subject *Max* is base-generated in the matrix VP (following the VP-Internal Subject Hypothesis), binding takes place within the case domain. Here, the SELF anaphor is still the only grammatical choice (cf. [33b]); however, in (33c), where the smallest domain which contains antecedent and bound element is the subject domain (since α is θ- and case-marked inside the PP, in contrast to its antecedent), both the SELF anaphor and the pronoun are licit.

Finally, in (33d), we only have binding in the root domain; the intervening subject *Mary* restricts the subject domain to the embedded clause, and also θ- and case marking of α take place inside the embedded clause, whereas the antecedent *Max* is θ- and case-marked in the matrix clause. In this binding scenario, the anaphor is ruled out and the pronoun is the only licit option.

(33) a. *Max$_1$ hates **himself$_1$**/*him$_1$.*
b. *Max$_1$ heard **himself$_1$**/*him$_1$ sing.*
c. *Max$_1$ glanced behind **himself$_1$**/him$_1$.*
d. *Max$_1$ knows that Mary likes *himself$_1$/**him$_1$**.*
(cf. Fischer 2004b: 219)

The sentences in (34) and (35) are the Dutch and German counterparts of (33). Hence, the domains in which binding takes place are the same. What can be seen at first sight is that the prediction from (26c) is again borne out – as the distance between antecedent and bound element increases, the realization form of α changes from SELF anaphor to SE anaphor and then to pronoun, and in some domains, optionality among adjacent realization forms (SELF/SE anaphor or SE anaphor/pronoun) may arise.

If we consider the Dutch data, it is again the SELF anaphor which is chosen in the most local binding scenario (binding in the θ-domain; cf. [34a]). If we consider binding in the case domain, the SELF anaphor or the SE anaphor can be used (cf. [34b]). In (34c), where we have binding within the subject domain, the SE anaphor and the pronoun are licit, and in (34d), finally, when binding takes place within the root domain, it is again the pronoun which must be used.

(34) a. *Max$_1$ haat **zichzelf$_1$**/ *zich$_1$/ *hem$_1$.* [Dutch]
Max hates himself/ SE/ him
'Max$_1$ hates himself$_1$.'

b. *Max$_1$ hoorde **zichzelf$_1$**/ **zich$_1$**/ *hem$_1$ zingen.*
Max heard himself/ SE/ him sing
'Max$_1$ heard himself$_1$ sing.'

c. *Max$_1$ keek achter *zichzelf$_1$/ **zich$_1$**/ **hem$_1$**.*
Max looked after himself/ SE/ him
'Max$_1$ glanced behind him$_1$/himself$_1$.'

d. *Max*$_1$ *weet dat Mary *zichzelf*$_1$/ **zich*$_1$/ ***hem***$_1$ *leuk vindt.*
Max knows that Mary himself/ SE/ him nice finds
'Max$_1$ knows that Mary likes him$_1$.'
(cf. Fischer 2004b: 225)

As expected, German also uses anaphors in the local binding scenarios. In (35a) and (35b), where binding takes place in the θ- and case domain, respectively, both anaphoric forms are licit. If the smallest domain in which binding takes place is the subject domain (cf. [35c]), the SELF anaphor is ruled out; and if binding occurs only in the root domain (as in [35d]), the bound element has to be realized as pronoun.

(35) a. *Max*$_1$ *hasst* ***sich selbst***$_1$/ ***sich***$_1$/ **ihn*$_1$. [German]
Max hates himself/ SE/ him
'Max$_1$ hates himself$_1$.'

b. *Max*$_1$ *hört* ***sich selbst***$_1$/ ***sich***$_1$/ **ihn*$_1$ *singen.*
Max hears himself/ SE/ him sing
'Max$_1$ hears himself$_1$ sing.'

c. *Max*$_1$ *schaut hinter ??sich selbst*$_1$/ ***sich***$_1$/ **ihn*$_1$.
Max glanced behind himself/ SE/ him
'Max$_1$ glanced behind him$_1$/himself$_1$.'

d. *Max*$_1$ *weiß, dass Maria *sich selbst*$_1$/ **sich*$_1$/ ***ihn***$_1$ *mag.*
Max knows that Mary himself/ SE/ him likes
'Max$_1$ knows that Mary likes him$_1$.'
(cf. Fischer 2004b: 210)

So what all three languages have in common is that anaphoric binding becomes illicit if the antecedent is outside the subject domain (cf. [33d]–[35d]). However, this pattern does not hold universally, as the next section reveals.

4. Long-distance reflexives

Recall what we have said about reflexives so far: They must be bound in a relatively local domain (cf. [10]). Against this background, there are in particular two environments in which we do not expect to find reflexives. First, (10) explicitly rules out non-local binding relations (whatever locality means in this context; cf. the variation we have encountered in the previous section); and second, it implies that reflexives cannot occur without a(n) (c-commanding) antecedent. In section 4 and 5, however, we will see that occurrences of exactly these types do exist, and we will take a closer look at these (at least at first sight) unexpected scenarios. In this and the following section, I will use the terms anaphor vs. reflexive in a more careful way. Although the difference is often neglected in the literature (this is why I followed standard terminology in the previous sections), Kiss (2012) points out that we have to distinguish between the lexical form and its role in specific syntactic contexts. Following Kiss (2012), I will therefore call the forms reflexives and use the notions anaphor/anaphoric only if used to indicate an anaphoric dependency in a given syntactic context.

4.1. Long-distance reflexives and crosslinguistic variation

Let us first turn to the phenomenon of long-distance binding (= LD binding), which we have already come across before when talking about crosslinguistic variation in section 3. If we reconsider the Icelandic example from (22), repeated in (36), we can observe that the sentence violates one of the locality constraints we have mentioned in section 2.1. On the standard assumption that there is a covert subject in the embedded clause which is coreferent with the matrix object, (36) violates the Specified Subject Condition (cf. [12b]), because the covert subject intervenes between the bound element and its antecedent.

(36) *Jón$_1$ skipaði Pétri að raka ??sjálfan sig$_1$/ sig$_1$/ hann$_1$ á* [Icelandic]
John ordered Peter to shave.INF himself/ SE/ him on
hverjum degi.
every day
'John$_1$ ordered Peter to shave him$_1$ every day.'
(cf. Reuland and Everaert 2001: 649; Fischer 2004a: 504)

Moreover, the Tensed-S Condition can also be violated by LD binding, since the latter can also occur into subjunctive complement clauses, as the Icelandic example in (37) shows.

(37) *Jón$_1$ segir að Pétur raki ??sjálfan sig$_1$/ sig$_1$/ hann$_1$ á* [Icelandic]
John says that Peter shave.SBJV himself/ SE/ him on
hverjum degi.
every day
'John$_1$ says that Peter shaves him$_1$ every day.'
(cf. Reuland and Everaert 2001: 649; Fischer 2004a: 506)

This means that LD binding can be observed with different types of complement clauses, and we can conclude that it generally refers to binding relations which are nonlocal in the sense that they are not restricted to one clause; instead, the domain in which binding takes place stretches across (at least) two clauses: The bound element is embedded in a complement clause, while its antecedent is part of the matrix or another embedding clause. In terms of the domains defined in the previous section, we are dealing with LD binding if binding takes place outside the subject domain.

Since the option of LD binding is not available in every language, it is obviously subject to crosslinguistic variation. In fact, the system is even more fine-grained than it might seem at first sight, because we can find further differences among those languages which allow LD binding. So it can be observed that LD binding is sensitive to the type of complement clause in which the bound element occurs. In Icelandic, we have already seen that anaphoric binding might take place into an infinitival or subjunctive embedded clause; cf. (36) and (37), respectively. But as (38) illustrates, LD binding is ruled out if the anaphor is part of an indicative clause.

(38) *Jón$_1$ veit að Pétur rakar *sjálfan sig$_1$/ ??sig$_1$/ hann$_1$ á* [Icelandic]
John knows that Peter shaves.IND himself/ SE/ him on
hverjum degi.
every day
'John$_1$ knows that Peter shaves him$_1$ every day.'
(cf. Reuland and Everaert 2001: 649; Fischer 2004a: 506)

However, this is not universally the case. Faroese, for instance, is a language in which LD binding can also be observed into indicative clause boundaries, as shown in (39). (Note that in Faroese there is no subjunctive, but both infinitive and indicative clause boundaries may intervene between Faroese LD reflexives and their antecedents; cf. Petersen et al. 1998).

(39) a. *Jógvan$_1$ bað meg raka *sær sjálvum$_1$/ sær$_1$/ honum$_1$.* [Faroese]
Jógvan asked me shave.INF himself.DAT/ SE.DAT/ him.DAT
'Jógvan$_1$ asked me to shave him$_1$.'

b. *Jógvan$_1$ sigur at eg havi sligið *seg sjálvan$_1$/ seg$_1$/ hann$_1$.*
Jógvan says that I have.IND hit himself.ACC/ SE.ACC/ him.ACC
'Jógvan$_1$ says that I hit him$_1$.'
(cf. Petersen et. al. 1998: 242, 243, 244)

In general, it can be concluded that LD binding occurs most likely into infinitival complements, and least likely into indicative complements. The underlying pattern can be summarized as follows: If a language can have LD reflexives in subjunctive complements, they are also licit in infinitival complements, and if LD reflexives can occur in indicative complements, they are also licit in subjunctive complements (cf. also Burzio 1998; Fischer 2004a, b, among others). The possibilities which result from this generalization are summarized in (40). As we have seen before, English, Dutch, and German, for instance, are languages of type 1 (cf. section 3). A language which only allows LD reflexives in infinitival complements (= type 2) is Russian (cf., for instance, Rappaport 1986 and example [5]). Icelandic, finally, corresponds to language type 3, cf. (37)–(38), and Faroese exemplifies language type 4, cf. (39).

(40) Crosslinguistic variation with respect to LD binding:
a. Type 1: LD binding is generally ruled out.
b. Type 2: LD binding is only allowed into infinitival complement clauses.
c. Type 3: LD binding is allowed into infinitival and subjunctive complement clauses.
d. Type 4: LD binding is allowed into infinitival, subjunctive, and indicative complement clauses.

In fact, this pattern follows straightforwardly from the generalization in (26a) if it is assumed that the type of domain in which binding takes place gets bigger when we replace an infinitival with a subjunctive complement clause or a subjunctive with an indicative complement clause.

This view is not unreasonable if we extend the set of relevant binding domains in the following way: As the crosslinguistic differences with respect to LD binding show, we do not find a uniform scenario if binding takes place outside the subject domain; in fact, three different patterns have been distinguished (cf. [40b]–[40d]). In order to describe this scenario adequately in terms of domains, the following two additional domains can be defined.

(41) The finite domain of α is the smallest XP that contains α and a finite verb.

(42) The indicative domain of α is the smallest XP that contains α and an indicative verb.

Taking into account these definitions, the different options of LD binding can be described as follows (cf. Rappaport 1986; Fischer 2004a, b): If only an infinitival clause boundary intervenes between α and its antecedent, the only finite verb of the sentence occurs in the matrix clause, and the finite domain will therefore also contain the matrix subject, i.e. the antecedent. Hence, binding takes place in the finite domain, the indicative domain (which is in this case identical with the finite domain), and the root domain. If a subjunctive clause boundary intervenes, the finite domain is smaller than in the infinitival case – in this scenario, the complement clause contains a finite verb (the subjunctive), and hence, binding does not take place inside the finite domain. However, the indicative domain must contain the matrix verb, so the indicative domain stretches across the matrix clause and also comprises the antecedent, which means that binding takes place inside the indicative (and root) domain.

The last scenario refers to indicative complement clauses. Here, the embedded verb is not only finite but also an indicative; therefore the finite domain equals the indicative domain and comprises only the embedded clause. Thus, it does not contain the antecedent, which is part of the matrix clause. The smallest domain in which binding takes place is therefore the root domain.

Obviously, the finite domain can never be bigger than the indicative domain, since an XP that fulfils the definition in (42) automatically contains a finite verb. Hence, the following subset relations hold among the six domains that have been defined.

(43) θ-domain $\subseteq$ case domain $\subseteq$ subject domain $\subseteq$ finite domain $\subseteq$ indicative domain $\subseteq$ root domain

As further illustration as to how the realization of α changes if the binding domain gets bigger, consider the following Icelandic examples, which display binding inside the θ-domain, the case domain, the subject domain, the finite domain, the indicative domain, and finally the root domain, respectively.

(44) a. *Max*$_1$ *hatar* ***sjálfan sig***$_1$/ ***sig***$_1$/ **hann*$_1$ [Icelandic]
Max hates himself/ SE/ him
'Max$_1$ hates himself$_1$.'

b. *Max*$_1$ *heyrði* ***sjálfan sig***$_1$/ ***sig***$_1$/ **hann*$_1$ *syngja.*
Max heard himself/ SE/ him sing
'Max$_1$ heard himself$_1$ sing.'

c. Max$_1$ *leit aftur fyrir* ***sjálfan sig***$_1$/ ***sig***$_1$/ **hann*$_1$.
Max glanced behind himself/ SE/ him
'Max$_1$ glanced behind himself$_1$/him$_1$.'

d. *Jón*$_1$ *skipaði Pétri að raka ??sjálfan sig*$_1$/ ***sig***$_1$/ ***hann***$_1$ *á*
John ordered Peter to shave.INF himself/ SE/ him on
hverjum degi.
every day
'John$_1$ ordered Peter to shave him$_1$ every day.'

e. *Jón*$_1$ *segir að Pétur raki ??sjálfan sig*$_1$/ ***sig***$_1$/ ***hann***$_1$ *á*
John says that Peter shave.SBJV himself/ SE/ him on
hverjum degi.
every day
'John$_1$ says that Peter shaves him$_1$ every day.'

f. *Jón*$_1$ *veit að Pétur rakar *sjálfan sig*$_1$/ *??sig*$_1$/ ***hann***$_1$ *á*
John knows that Peter shaves.IND himself/ SE/ him on
hverjum degi.
every day
'John$_1$ knows that Peter shaves him$_1$ every day.'
(cf. Fischer 2004b: 239, 240)

Another generalization which has widely been observed (starting with Pica 1987) is that LD reflexives typically are of the SE type. Considering the generalization in (26a), this is expected. If the complex anaphor were used in LD binding relations, this would imply that it should also be licit in any binding relation that is more local; hence, the SELF anaphor should be possible in almost all binding scenarios. Moreover, we would not expect SELF anaphors to be exchangeable with pronouns in languages with SE anaphors in the inventory (cf. [26d]); however, contrary to these hypothetical predictions, pronouns generally are a licit option in LD binding contexts as well.

4.2. Logophoric aspects

In the previous section, only syntactic aspects of LD binding have been taken into account. However, it has widely been observed that discourse factors also play an important role for LD reflexives. What has often been proposed is that at least in some languages and certain contexts the SE form in apparent LD binding scenarios does not really function as an anaphor but rather as a logophor. This means that it is "restricted to reportive contexts transmitting the words or thought of an individual (...) other than the speaker narrator" (cf. Reuland and Everaert 2001: 650 following Clements 1975); the logophor thus "refers to the person whose point of view is being represented or who serves as the 'subject of consciousness'" (cf. Baker 1995: 65).

As to Icelandic, one of the most discussed languages in this respect (cf., for example, Maling 1984; Thráinsson 1991; Reuland and Everaert 2001), it has frequently been suggested that logophoricity plays a central role in LD binding contexts containing a subjunctive complement clause. This assumption is supported by the following example.

(45) a. *Jón$_1$ sagði Pétri að ég elskaði sig$_1$.* [Icelandic]
John told Peter that I loved.SBJV SE
'John$_1$ told Peter that I loved him$_1$.'

b. **Pétri$_1$ var sagt að ég elskaði sig$_1$*
Peter was told that I loved.SBJV SE
'Peter$_1$ was told that I loved him$_1$.'
(cf. Reuland and Everaert 2001: 651)

While *Jón* can function as an adequate discourse antecedent in (45a), this is not possible for *Pétri* in the passivized counterpart in (45b), because the latter subject does not qualify as antecedent for a logophor – it is not *Pétri* whose point of view is being represented.

Since a logophor is subject to discourse rather than syntactic requirements, we also expect it not to be restricted by the c-command requirement and the need to have a syntactic antecedent. In fact, we find examples of this type in Icelandic, for instance in (46), where the antecedent is in a non-c-commanding position. (Cf. also section 5 as regards instances of free reflexives. Note also that this does not necessarily imply that syntactic constraints do not play a role at all for LD binding into subjunctive clauses – cf. the discussion of Faroese below.)

(46) *[Skoðun Jóns$_1$] er að sig$_1$ vanti hæfileika.* [Icelandic]
Opinion John's is that SE.ACC lacks.SBJV talent
'John$_1$'s opinion is that he$_1$ lacks talent.'
(cf. Reuland and Everaert 2001: 650)

Another test to find out whether reflexives function as anaphora or not involves VP ellipsis. As Cole et al. (2001) (among many others) point out, only the sloppy reading is available in the former case, whereas both the strict and sloppy reading are possible otherwise. Thráinsson (1991) and Reuland and Everaert (2001) show that in the Icelandic subjunctive case of LD binding both the strict and sloppy reading are available. (Note, however, that the sloppy reading requires a c-commanding antecedent.) Cole et al. (2001) illustrate this in the following two (local) examples. (47) displays an example from Hindi-Urdu in which only the sloppy reading is available, which suggests that this reflexive really functions as an anaphor.

(47) *Guatam$_1$ [apnee (aap$_1$)-koo caalaak] samajhtaa hai, aur* [Hindi-Urdu]
Guatam self's self-DAT smart consider.IPFV is and
vikram$_2$ bhii Φ.
Vikram also
'Guatam considers himself smart, and so does Vikram'
(= V. considers Vikram smart / *V. considers Guatam smart)
(cf. Cole et al. 2001: xvii, xviii)

In the Malay example in (48), by contrast, both readings are available, which suggests that the reflexive *dirinya* (a form which also occurs as LD reflexive) is not used as an anaphor here. In fact, Cole et al. (2001) argue that it is not a logophor either, since it does not have to fulfil the typical discourse conditions constraining the use of logophors; hence they argue that it is a pronominal expression which takes the form of the reflexive that we also find in local binding contexts. Following Cole et al. (2001), we would therefore get a tripartite distinction among LD reflexives: those functioning as anaphors; those functioning as pronominals (using the form of a local reflexive); and those forms functioning mainly as locally bound anaphors but which can non-locally be used logophorically, depending on the discourse conditions and the syntactic structure.

(48) *John nampak dirinya di dalam cermin; Frank pun.* [Malay]
John see self.3SG at inside mirror Frank also
'John saw himself/him in the mirror and Frank did too.'
(= F. saw Frank in the mirror / F. saw John in the mirror)
(cf. Cole et al. 2001: xvii)

However, LD reflexives cannot exclusively be analyzed in terms of logophoricity, as in particular those examples involving LD binding into infinitival or indicative clauses show. As Reuland and Everaert (2001) point out, constructions analogous to (45b) turn out to be grammatical when used with an infinitival, and disregarding the c-command requirement as in (46) does not work in these constructions either; cf. (49a) and (49b), respectively.

(49) a. *María*$_1$ *var sögð [t*$_1$ *hafa látið [mig þvo sér*$_1$*]].* [Icelandic]
Mary was said have.INF made me wash.INF SE
'Mary$_1$ was said to have made me wash her$_1$.'

b. *[*Skoðun Jóns*$_1$] *virðist vera hættuleg fyrir sig*$_1$.
Opinion John's seems be.INF dangerous for SE
'John$_1$'s opinion seems to be dangerous for him$_1$.'
(cf. Reuland and Everaert 2001: 651)

As far as binding into indicative clauses is concerned, the contrast between the nongrammatical Icelandic example in (51) and the grammatical Faroese example in (50) (cf. Barnes 1986; Anderson 1986) also indicates that here rather syntactic than logophoric conditions are involved (at least additionally): The two examples have exactly the same meaning, and it does not seem reasonable to assume crosslinguistic variation with respect to discourse factors, whereas this is a common assumption for syntactic constraints. So crosslinguistic variation might be a general problem for accounts in terms of logophoricity (cf. also section 5.3).

(50) *Gunnvør visti, at tey hildu lítið um seg.* [Faroese]
Gunnvør knew that they held little of SE
'Gunnvør knew that they had a poor opinion of her.'
(cf. Anderson 1986: 78; Barnes 1986: 96)

(51) *Gunnvör vissi að þau höfðu lítið álit á henni/ *sér.* [Icelandic]
Gunnvör knew that they had little opinion on her/ SE
'Gunnvör knew that they had a poor opinion of her.'
(cf. Fischer 2004a: 508)

However, it is worth mentioning that we also find occurrences of LD reflexives in Faroese which do not have a syntactic antecedent "although there is one implied by the preceding discourse" (cf. Petersen et al. 1998: 245). This suggests that discourse factors also play a role for LD binding into indicative clauses, at least in certain cases, which means that we probably do not get a clear-cut division between syntactically constrained and discourse-constrained instances of LD binding; instead, both types of requirements seem to interact.

This is also suggested by Cole et al. (2001) in the case of Mandarin Chinese, where LD reflexives generally seem to behave like bound anaphors (a simple example of Mandarin LD binding is given in [52]). Thus, they typically require a c-commanding antecedent, and under VP ellipsis only the sloppy reading is available. However, in "limited discourse contexts" (Cole et al. 2001: xviii), as they put it, we also find examples of *ziji* without syntactic antecedent; cf. (53). So Mandarin also supports the assumption that the labour between syntactic and discourse constraints can probably not be separated completely.

(52) *Zhangsan$_1$ renwei Lisi$_2$ zhidao Wangwu$_3$ xihuan ziji$_{1/2/3}$.* [Mandarin]
Zhangsan think Lisi know Wangwu like SE
'Zhangsan$_1$ thinks that Lisi$_2$ knows that Wangwu$_3$ likes him$_{1/2}$/ himself$_3$.'
(cf. Cole et al. 2001: xiv)

(53) *Zhangsan$_1$ zhidao neijian shi yihou hen qifen; Lisi$_2$ shuo neixie* [Mandarin]
Zhangsan know that.CLF thing after very angy Lisi say those
hua mingming shi zai he ziji$_{1/2}$ zuodui.
word obviously is being with SE against
'Zhangsan$_1$ was very angry when he learned that. By saying those words, Lisi$_2$ was obviously acting against himself$_2$/him$_1$.'
(cf. Cole et al. 2001: xviii)

4.3. Subject-object asymmetries

What has been excluded from the discussion so far is another typical property of LD reflexives: They tend to be subject-oriented. As (54) shows, LD reflexives in Icelandic, for instance, cannot have object antecedents, irrespective of the type of complement clause.

(54) *Ég$_1$ lofaði Önnu$_2$ [að kyssa *sjálfa sig$_2$/ *sig$_2$/ hana$_2$]* [Icelandic]
I promised Anna to kiss.INF herself/ SE/ her
'I promised Anna$_2$ to kiss her$_2$.'
(cf. Thrainsson 1991: 52; Fischer 2004b: 109)

This subject–object asymmetry with respect to anaphoric binding can also be found if binding is more local; in Norwegian, for example, it can even be observed if binding takes place within the θ-domain (cf. Richards 1997; Safir 1997). Note also that the subject–object asymmetry can affect either type of reflexive, the SE form or the SELF form, as the two examples in (54) and (55) show. According to Safir (1997), only the intensified pronoun is grammatical in sentences like (55b). As to the corresponding Danish data, cf. Vikner (1985: 10, 16); with respect to the observed subject-object asymmetry, Danish patterns exactly like Norwegian.

(55) a. *Karl$_1$ fortalte Jon om seg selv$_1$.* [Norwegian]
Karl told Jon about himself
'Karl$_1$ told John about himself$_1$.'

b. **Karl fortalte Jon$_2$ om seg selv$_2$.*
Karl told Jon about himself
'Karl told John$_2$ about himself$_2$.'
(cf. Safir 1997: 351)

Moreover, it is possible that a language which does not show a subject-object asymmetry in relatively local binding relations is subject-oriented if binding is less local. This seems to be the case in German. In (56b), where binding takes place within the θ-domain, the object can bind either type of anaphor (unlike the Norwegian object in [55b]). The reason why the SELF anaphor sounds slightly better than the SE anaphor in sentences like (56b) is that an intensifier is desirable for pragmatic reasons, since it is less expected that the object should function as antecedent (cf. also König and Siemund 2000). In (57), on the other hand, where binding takes place within the subject domain but not within the θ-domain, a subject-object asymmetry arises.

As regards German double object constructions, note moreover that I have restricted myself to examples where the bound element is embedded in a PP and does not function as object on its own, because data of the former type are easier to judge, whereas judgements vary considerably with respect to the latter configuration; cf. Featherston and Sternefeld (2003) and Sternefeld and Featherston (2003) for a detailed discussion of data like these.

(56) a. *Peter$_1$ erzählte uns von sich selbst$_1$/ sich$_1$/ *ihm$_1$.* [German]
Peter told us.DAT of himself/ SE/ him
'Peter$_1$ told us about himself$_1$.'

b. *Wir erzählten Peter$_2$ von sich selbst$_2$/ ?sich$_2$/ *ihm$_2$.*
we told Peter.DAT of himself/ SE/ him
'We told Peter$_2$ about himself$_2$.'
(cf. Fischer 2004b: 111)

(57) a. *Peter$_1$ zeigte mir die Schlange neben ??sich selbst$_1$/* [German]
Peter showed me.DAT [the snake near himself/
*sich$_1$/ *ihm$_1$.*
SE/ him].ACC
'Peter$_1$ showed me the snake near him$_1$.'

b. *Ich zeigte Peter$_2$ die Schlange neben *sich selbst$_2$/ ??sich$_2$/ ihm$_2$.*
I showed Peter.DAT [the [snake near himself/ SE/ him].ACC
'I showed Peter$_2$ the snake near him$_2$.'
(cf. Fischer 2004b: 111)

Generally, we might draw the following conclusion: If a subject-object asymmetry can be observed in domain D_1 in a given language, it will also surface in any domain bigger than D_1. What is again subject to crosslinguistic variation is the question of which the smallest domain is in which a subject-object asymmetry arises.

5. Locally free reflexives

In section 2.1, we have concluded that reflexives must be bound in a (more or less) local domain; but already in section 3 and in particular in section 4 we have come across many counterexamples: We have considered data in which binding takes place across more than one clause (LD binding); we have seen examples with non-c-commanding antecedents; and we have talked about occurrences of reflexives without any syntactic antecedent at all. The languages we have mentioned in this context were in particular Icelandic, Faroese, Russian, Malay, and Mandarin Chinese – these are all languages with LD reflexives. However, the occurrence of locally free reflexives (LFRs) is by no means restricted to languages with LD binding. In English, for instance, where LD binding is generally ruled out, we also find many examples in which the SELF reflexive is not (locally) bound, contrary to what we would expect.

In this section we will take a closer look at typical constructions in which LFRs arise and possible accounts of them. As noted before, the basic observation concerning LFRs is that they violate the standard assumption on anaphora, namely that they must be locally bound. This is why Pollard and Sag (1992, 1994) coined the term exempt anaphora for locally free reflexives, since they seem to be exempt from Principle A of the standard binding theory. However, I will stick to the more neutral term of locally free reflexives (LFRs) in this section.

5.1. An overview of locally free reflexives

As regards the syntactic configurations in which LFRs occur, we can basically distinguish four different scenarios: LFRs with non-local antecedents (cf. [58]), LFRs with non-c-commanding antecedents (cf. [59]), LFRs with split antecedents (cf. [60]), and LFRs with no syntactic antecedent at all (cf. [61]). Examples of all types are given below.

(58) a. *Max$_1$ boasted that the queen invited Lucie and himself$_1$ for a drink.*
(cf. Reinhart and Reuland 1993: 670)
b. *John$_1$ knows that there is a picture of himself$_1$ in the morning paper.*
(cf. Runner et al. 2002: 402)

(59) a. *As for himself*$_1$*, John*$_1$ *said that he would not need to move.* (cf. König and Siemund 2000: 52)

b. *John*$_1$*'s campaign requires that pictures of himself*$_1$ *be placed all over town.* (cf. Pollard and Sag 1992: 264; Lebeaux 1984: 358)

(60) a. *John*$_1$ *asked Mary*$_2$ *to send reminders about the meeting to everyone on the distribution list except themselves*$_{1+2}$. (cf. Pollard and Sag 1992: 269)

b. *John*$_1$ *told Mary*$_2$ *that pictures of themselves*$_{1+2}$ *were on sale.* (cf. Kiss 2012: 158)

(61) a. *There were three students in the room apart from himself.* (cf. Fischer 2004b: 117)

b. *Mary*$_1$ *was extremely upset. That picture of herself*$_1$ *on the front page of the Times would circulate all over the world.* (cf. Pollard and Sag 1992: 268)

Apart from the different syntactic structures considered above, we can moreover identify certain constructions in which LFRs are likely to occur. As the (b)-examples in (58)–(61) illlustrate, picture noun phrases are a case in point, where picture noun phrases (picture NPs) are "NPs headed by a "representational" noun, such as *picture*, *photograph*, *story*, *opinion*, and so on" (cf. Runner et al. 2006: 195). As the examples show, picture NPs with LFRs can be found in all syntactic contexts mentioned above. Moreover, it has often been observed that these picture NPs containing LFRs frequently occur in psych verb constructions; cf. (62).

(62) a. *The picture of himself*$_1$ *in the museum bothered John*$_1$. (cf. Pollard and Sag 1992: 264)

b. *The picture of himself*$_1$ *in Newsweek made John*$_1$*'s day.* (cf. Pollard and Sag 1992: 278)

We will briefly come back to these two constructions in the following two sections. For a more detailed discussion of reflexives in psych verb constructions, cf., for instance, Kiss (2012) (which is also discussed in Fischer, this volume).

5.2. Different accounts of locally free reflexives

Considering the different accounts of LFRs that have been proposed, three main lines of thought can be distinguished: analyses in terms of logophoricity, analyses in terms of intensification, and structural accounts.

The former two have in common that they assume that LFRs, in contrast to bound anaphora, cannot be analyzed (purely) structurally but depend on pragmatic or discourse factors in one way or the other.

The logophoricity approach is presumably most widely spread. This approach has already been mentioned in section 4.2 in connection with LD reflexives. In the following, a more detailed classification will be presented as to which discourse factors can license the use of logophors (cf. Kuno 1987; Runner et al. 2002, 2006).

There are basically four relevant factors that can be identified; they comprise point of view (cf. [63]), awareness (cf. [64]), focus (cf. [65]), and indirect agenthood (cf. [66]).

In (63), the difference between the acceptable and the unacceptable version relates to the question of whose point of view is being represented. If the free reflexive refers to this person, the construction is grammatical (cf. [63a]), otherwise it is not (cf. [63b]). A similar contrast in grammaticality arises in (64), where it is crucial that the discourse antecedent of the reflexive knows about the entity which formally contains the reflexive. As (65) shows, it might also play a role which arguments are focused; and as (66) illustrates, it can moreover make a difference whether the discourse antecedent (which does not bind the reflexive in this example) is an Agent or not.

(63) a. *John$_1$ was going to get even with Mary. That picture of himself$_1$ in the paper would really annoy her, as would the other stunts he had planned.*
b. **Mary was quite taken aback by the publicity John$_1$ was receiving. That picture of himself$_1$ in the paper had really annoyed her, and there was not much she could do about it.* (cf. Pollard and Sag 1992: 274)

(64) a. *John$_1$ knows that there is a picture of himself$_1$ in the morning paper.*
b. **John$_1$ still doesn't know that there is a picture of himself$_1$ in the morning paper.* (cf. Runner et al. 2002: 402)

(65) a. *John$_1$ didn't tell MARY that there was a picture of himself$_1$ in the post office; he told SAM.*
b. **JOHN$_1$ didn't tell Mary that there was a picture of himself$_1$ in the post office; SAM did.* (cf. Runner et al. 2002: 403)

(66) a. *I hate the story about himself$_1$ that John$_1$ always tells.*
b. **I hate the story about himself$_1$ that John$_1$ likes to hear.*
(cf. Runner et al. 2002: 402)

As, for instance, Baker (1995) and König and Siemund (2000) argue, another way of interpreting the occurrences of LFRs is to assume that these locally free SELF forms in English are no reflexives at all but should rather be analyzed as intensified pronouns, which are "identical in form, though not in distribution" (cf. König and Siemund 2000: 41). This point of view is supported by data which lack the typical discourse factors that usually license logophoricity (cf. above). In fact, LFRs of this type are also mentioned by Cole et al. (2001: xx), who point out that the Malay LD reflexive *dirinya* "does not require any special perspective or self-awareness (...). Rather, it has the same discourse properties as a personal pronoun". Baker (1995) presents in particular literary examples as, for instance, (67), in which the subject of consciousness corresponds to the outside narrator.

(67) *Sir William Lucas$_1$, and his daughter Maria, a good humoured girl, but as empty-headed as himself$_1$, had nothing to say that could be worth hearing, and were listened to with about as much delight as the rattle of the chaise.*
(cf. Baker 1995: 67, citing Jane Austen: *Pride and Prejudice*)

Notwithstanding the fact that non-logophoric occurrences of LFR might well exist (cf. also Cole et al. 2001), the previous example might not suffice to show this because literary examples may reflect a poetic language which can differ also in grammatical aspects from the standard language; cf. also Pollard and Sag (1992: 279), who point out that "grammatical constraints can sometimes be relaxed by writers who exercise certain license with their language". Of course, apart from this the English language might have undergone further changes since the publication of the novel in 1813. So the question might arise as to whether LFRs still behave the same nowadays.

However, the assumption that some instances of *himself* should rather be analyzed as intensified pronoun might also be supported by the fact that in a language like German, where intensified and reflexive pronouns differ in form, only the (intensified) pronoun is grammatical in many of these examples (cf. also Kiss 2012 as to the observation that German generally lacks exempt reflexives); cf., for instance, (68)–(70): In the German examples below, reflexive forms are generally excluded, and only the pronoun or the intensified version (= the form pronoun plus intensifier *selbst*) is licit.

(68) a. *There were three students in the room apart from himself.*

b. *Außer ihm selbst/ ihm/ *sich/ *sich selbst waren drei* [German]
Apart.from him INTENSIFIER/ him/ SE/ himself.REFL were three
Studenten im Raum.
students in.the room
'There were three students in the room apart from himself.'
(cf. Fischer 2004b: 117, 118)

(69) a. *Max$_1$ boasted that the queen invited Lucie and himself$_1$ for a drink.*
(cf. Reinhart and Reuland 1993: 670)

b. *Max$_1$ prahlte damit, dass die Königin Lucie und ihn selbst$_1$/* [German]
Max boasted with.it that the queen Lucie and him INTENSIFIER/
*ihn$_1$/ *sich$_1$/ *sich selbst$_1$ auf einen Drink eingeladen hätte.*
him/ SE/ himself.REFL on a drink invited have.SBJV
'Max$_1$ boasted that the queen invited Lucie and himself$_1$ for a drink.'
(cf. Fischer 2004b: 118)

(70) a. *As for himself$_1$, John$_1$ said that he would not need to move.*
(cf. König and Siemund 2000: 52)

b. *Was ihn selbst$_1$/ ihn$_1$/ *sich$_1$/* sich selbst$_1$ anginge,* [German]
What him INTENSIFIER/ him/ SE/ himself.REFL concern.SBJV
so würde er nicht umziehen müssen, sagte John$_1$.
so would he not move must said John
'As for himself$_1$, John$_1$ said that he would not need to move.'
(cf. Fischer 2004b: 118)

Following the intensification approach, data as in (68)–(70) do therefore not contradict standard assumptions on the behaviour of reflexives, because – as the German counterparts suggest – the English SELF forms here are in fact pronominal expressions; this means that they are not expected to be locally bound. Keep in mind, however, that the intensification approach also assumes that discourse factors determine the occurrence of LFRs. In Baker's (1995) analysis, intensification is regulated by the so-called Contrastiveness Condition and the Condition of Relative Discourse Prominence (cf. Baker 1995: 77, 80).

(71) Contrastiveness Condition:
Intensive NPs are appropriate only in contexts in which emphasis or contrast is desired.

(72) Condition of Relative Discourse Prominence:
Intensive NPs can only be used to mark a character in a sentence or discourse who is relatively more prominent or central than other characters.

Finally, as regards the structural approaches to LFRs, they attempt to show that these examples are not exempt from the standard way of dealing with reflexives; hence, they try to subsume them under the standard restrictions on anaphora. The first attempts along this line have been proposed by Chomsky (1981, 1986). I will not present any details of these accounts, but just sketch the main line of reasoning. The general strategy looks as follows: The examples are associated with a syntactic structure which meets the syntactic requirements for anaphora at least at some point in the derivation.

The first kind of construction which had been considered was of type (73a) (repeated from [58b]/[64a]). The proposed analysis is sketched in (73b), in which a local antecedent for the reflexive has been inserted – the phonetically silent pronoun PRO, functioning here as a possessive pronoun.

(73) a. *John$_1$ knows that there is a picture of himself$_1$ in the morning paper.*
(cf. Runner et al. 2002: 402)

b. *John$_1$ knows that there is [PRO$_1$'s picture of himself$_1$ in the morning paper].*

Instead of inserting an adequate syntactic antecedent, an alternative way to rescue the standard binding account in other examples has been reconstruction. Considering examples like (74a) (repeated from [62a]), it has been proposed (following the unaccusativity analysis of psych verbs suggested by Belletti and Rizzi 1988) that the reflexive is locally bound in its base position. The local binding requirement can thus be met on the assumption that it must be fulfilled only at some point in the derivation (for instance, before movement takes place) or by assuming reconstruction at the appropriate level. However, example (74b) (repeated from [62b]) shows how vulnerable the whole enterprise is: By changing the position of *John* only slightly with the effect that it no longer c-commands the base position of the reflexive, the analysis sketched before no longer works, although the sentence remains grammatical (leaving aside the fact that there are also counterarguments against the unaccusativity hypothesis as such, which is crucial for this analysis of [74a]).

(74) a. *The picture of himself$_1$ in the museum bothered John$_1$.*
(cf. Pollard and Sag 1992: 264)

b. *The picture of himself$_1$ in Newsweek made John$_1$'s day.*
(cf. Pollard and Sag 1992: 278)

So it can be concluded that – considering the vast variety of exempt examples we have already come across – the structural approach is definitely the trickiest one. Among the problems such an approach encounters are, for instance, the question of how to deal with split antecedents (cf. [60]), examples in which the antecedent does not c-command the reflexive at any point in the derivation (as in [74b]), or the analysis of free reflexives without picture NPs or psych verb constructions; notwithstanding theory-internal problems like the interpretation or positioning of the inserted PRO (cf. also Pollard and Sag 1992 and Runner et al. 2006 for some critical remarks on purely structural accounts along these lines).

5.3. Picture NPs revisited

Coming back to the issue of picture NPs, it has often been observed that an overt possessor triggers a blocking effect of the following type: A reflexive inside the picture NP which is not coindexed with the possessor renders the construction ungrammatical; if there is no possessor NP in the picture NP's specifier, a reflexive form is licit. This is what we expect in examples like (75) (cf. Büring 2005) under standard assumptions on anaphoric binding. In (75a), the anaphor is locally bound, in (75b), the intervening NP *Mary* blocks local binding (cf. the Specified Subject Condition).

(75) a. *John$_1$ saw a picture of himself$_1$/*him$_1$.*
b. *John$_1$ saw Mary's picture of ??himself$_1$/him$_1$.*
(cf. Büring 2005: 50)

However, as discussed before (cf. section 5.1), we often find locally free reflexives inside picture NPs, and on the assumption that LFRs are not restricted by structural but rather by pragmatic or discourse factors (cf. section 5.2), it is unexpected that a possessor inside the picture NP should make a difference and rule the reflexive out. But this exactly seems to be the case, as the contrast between (76a) and (76b) illustrates.

(76) a. *The picture of himself$_1$ that John$_1$ saw in the post office was ugly.*
b. **Your picture of himself$_1$ that John$_1$ saw in the post office was ugly.*
(cf. Reinhart and Reuland 1993: 682, 683; Kiss 2012: 183)

This observation led linguists pursuing the logophoric approach to LFRs (cf., for example, Pollard and Sag 1992; Reinhart and Reuland 1993) to propose the following distinction: Reflexives in picture NPs without possessor are analyzed as logophors, whereas reflexives in picture NPs with a possessor are considered to be anaphors, which are restricted by structural conditions. This distinction follows as a consequence from their syntactic constraint on anaphors. Pollard and Sag (1992: 266), for instance, put it this way:

(77) An anaphor must be coindexed with a less oblique coargument, if there is one.

In cases like (76b), the possessor qualifies as such a less oblique coargument and thereby turns the reflexive into an anaphor requiring local binding (by the possessor).

However, the status of picture NPs with possessors is not as clear as the examples in (75) and (76) might suggest. As experiments described by Keller and Asudeh (2001) and Runner et al. (2002, 2006) have shown, speakers accept reflexives in picture NPs with possessor more readily than expected. Hence, a reflexive inside picture NPs of this type need not necessarily take the possessor as antecedent, but can also refer to the matrix subject; cf. (78). Keller and Asudeh (2001) (using the magnitude estimation technique) point out that native speakers find the reflexive and the pronominal form equally acceptable in sentences like (78a). Runner et al. (2002, 2006) also conclude on the basis of their eye-tracking experiment that reflexives and pronominals are not in complementary distribution in these examples; however, they observe a preference for interpreting the possessor as antecedent in sentences like (78b).

(78) a. *Hanna$_1$ found Peter's picture of her$_1$/herself$_1$.*

(cf. Runner et al. 2002: 403; 2006: 198)

b. *Have Joe$_1$ touch Harry$_2$'s picture of himself$_{1/2}$.*

(cf. Runner et al. 2002: 404)

As a result, Runner et al. (2002, 2006) propose that the reflexive in picture NPs might generally have to be analyzed as a logophor. Otherwise, they argue, it might also be problematic to account for contrasts like the one in (79):

(79) a. *John$_1$ *said that Bill likes himself$_1$.*

b ?John$_1$ *liked Bill's photograph of himself$_1$.*

(cf. Runner et al. 2006: 199)

But although the subject *Bill* intervenes in both examples, note that there is also a crucial structural difference between the two examples: The domain in which binding takes place is much smaller in (79b) than in (79a); in (79a), the smallest domain in which the binding relation holds is the root domain, whereas in (79b) it is the finite domain.

Apart from the unclear role of possessors in picture NPs, a second type of intervention effect has been described. Hence, it can be observed that in the case of two potential c-commanding antecedents, only the lower one can license a reflexive inside a picture NP; cf. (80). This is another reason why people have assumed that syntactic factors might play a role in these constructions, after all.

(80) *Bill$_1$ remembered that Tom$_2$ saw [a picture of himself$_{*1/2}$] in the post office.*

(cf. Pollard and Sag 1992: 271)

As Pollard and Sag (1992) point out, the acceptability of the reflexive in (80) increases if the intervening subject is inanimate, a quantifier, or an expletive; cf. (81).

(81) a. *?Bill$_1$ remembered that The Times had printed [a picture of himself$_1$] in the Sunday edition.*

b. *Bill$_1$ thought that nothing could make [a picture of himself$_1$ in the Times] acceptable to Sandy.*

c. *Bill$_1$ suspected that there would soon be [a picture of himself$_1$] on the post office wall.*

(cf. Pollard and Sag 1992: 272)

However, in the examples that are mentioned, no intervenor bears the same φ-features as the matrix subject (in contrast to the situation in [80]), and the question might arise as to whether (80) generally improves if the intervenor does not qualify as potential antecedent. If this were true, the examples in (81) are not necessarily counterexamples to a syntactic approach.

Another remarkable observation concerns the fact that the situation changes if the picture NP is moved to a position in between the two potential antecedents. If this happens, both NPs can function as antecedent for the reflexive inside the picture NP, as (82) illustrates (cf., for instance, Barss 1986; Epstein et al. 1998). So if moving the picture NP makes a difference, the assumption is again suggested that syntactic factors cannot be completely ignored.

(82) *John$_1$ wondered [which picture of himself$_{1,2}$]$_3$ Bill$_2$ saw t_3.*
(cf. Epstein et al. 1998: 48)

Another aspect which should not be neglected in this discussion concerns once more crosslinguistic variation. Since many analyses of LFRs focus on English in the first place, it is not immediately clear how much variation we encounter in these constructions. However, as mentioned already in section 5.2, German patterns slightly differently from English, which is illustrated in (83) and (84) (cf. Fischer 2004b).

(83) a. *I wonder which pictures of her$_1$/herself$_1$ Mary$_1$ has found.*

b. *Ich frage mich, welche Bilder von *ihr$_1$/ sich$_1$/ sich selbst$_1$* [German]
I ask myself which pictures of her/ SE/ herself
Maria$_1$ gefunden hat.
Mary found has
'I wonder which pictures of her$_1$/herself$_1$ Mary$_1$ has found.'
(cf. Fischer 2004b: 310)

(84) a. *Mary$_1$ wonders which pictures of her$_1$/herself$_1$ I have found.*

b. *Maria$_1$ fragt sich, welche Bilder von ihr$_1$/ *sich$_1$/ *sich selbst$_1$* [German]
Mary asks SE which pictures of her/ SE/ herself
ich gefunden habe.
I found have
'Mary$_1$ wonders which pictures of her$_1$/herself$_1$ I have found.'
(cf. Fischer 2004b: 310)

In German, we find the following scenario: If the embedded subject functions as antecedent, a SELF or SE form must be used in the picture NP (cf. [83b]), and if the antecedent corresponds to the matrix subject, it cannot be a reflexive but must be a pronominal (cf. [84b]). This pattern is what we expect if we assume a standard syntactic analysis, but it is, in fact, also compatible with the accounts in terms of logophoricity or intensification. This is the case because (as already mentioned in section 5.2) (i) there are no logophoric reflexives in German (cf. Kiss 2001, 2012) – hence the use of a logophoric reflexive is excluded in (84b) – and (ii) German has different forms for intensified pronominals and

SELF anaphors – so the ambiguity we find in English (where the SELF form in [84a] can be analyzed as an intensified pronoun though it looks like a reflexive) does not arise in German.

6. Conclusion

In this chapter we have seen that pronominal anaphora (in the broad sense of the definition) occur in a wide range of different syntactic environments. Starting with the best-known variants, locally bound anaphora and personal pronouns in English, we then turned to other languages, where a lot of crosslinguistic variation can be observed with respect to the chosen realization form of bound elements in a given context. On the other hand, however, there are also universal patterns that can clearly be identified.

In connection with crosslinguistic variation, the manifestation and patterning of long-distance reflexives then had to be considered, and it became clear that the occurrence of reflexive forms does not always imply that we are dealing with a binding relation. (And of course, this restriction also holds the other way round: If we have an anaphoric dependency, it need not necessarily be expressed by pronominal anaphora. As regards languages choosing different strategies, cf., for instance, Everaert 2012 and references cited there.) Consequently, it is crucial to distinguish between the two notions anaphor and reflexive, even more since the former can be used in different ways independently, as discussed in the introduction.

In any case, both the discussion of LD reflexives and of locally free reflexives have shown that the distribution of reflexives cannot always be accounted for purely structurally; in many examples, discourse and pragmatic factors also play a role. However, we have also seen that it does not seem to be a clear-cut distinction, which means that those accounts are probably on the right track that allow for an interaction of both types of factors.

7. References (selected)

Anderson, Stephen
1986 The typology of anaphoric dependencies: Icelandic (and other) reflexives. In: Lars Hellan and Kirsti Koch Christensen (eds.), *Topics in Scandinavian Syntax*, 65–88. Dordrecht: Reidel.

Baker, Carl
1995 Contrast, discourse prominence, and intensification, with special reference to locally free reflexives in British English. *Language* 71: 63–101.

Barnes, Michael
1986 Reflexivisation in Faroese: a preliminary survey. *Arkiv för Nordisk Filologie* 101: 95–126.

Barss, Andrew
1986 Chains and anaphoric dependence. Doctoral dissertation, MIT, Cambridge, MA.

Belletti, Adriana, and Luigi Rizzi
1988 Psych-verbs and θ-theory. *Natural Language and Linguistic Theory* 6: 291–352.

Büring, Daniel
2005 *Binding Theory.* Cambridge: Cambridge University Press.

Burzio, Luigi
1998 Anaphora and soft constraints. In: Pilar Barbosa, Danny Fox, Paul Hagstrom, Martha McGinnis, and David Pesetsky (eds.), *Is the Best Good Enough?*, 93–113. Cambridge, MA: MIT Press.
Chomsky, Noam
1973 Conditions on transformations. In: Stephen Anderson and Paul Kiparsky (eds.), *A Festschrift for Morris Halle*, 232–286. New York: Holt, Rinehart and Winston.
Chomsky, Noam
1981 *Lectures on Government and Binding.* Dordrecht: Foris.
Chomsky, Noam
1986 *Knowledge of Language.* New York: Praeger.
Clements, George
1975 The logophoric pronoun in Ewe: its role in discourse. *Journal of West African Languages* 10: 141–177.
Cole, Peter, Gabriella Hermon, and Li-May Sung
1990 Principles and parameters of long-distance reflexives. *Linguistic Inquiry* 21: 1–22.
Cole, Peter, Gabriella Hermon, and C.-T. James Huang
2001 Long-distance reflexives: the state of the art. In: Peter Cole, Gabriella Hermon, and C.-T. James Huang (eds.), *Syntax and Semantics 33: Long-Distance Reflexives*, xiii–xlv. San Diego: Academic Press.
Cuddon, John Anthony
^{3}1992 *Dictionary of Literary Terms and Literary Theory.* Harmondsworth: Penguin Books.
Dalrymple, Mary
1993 *The Syntax of Anaphoric Binding.* Stanford: CSLI Publications.
Epstein, Samuel, Erich Groat, Ruriko Kawashima, and Hisatsugu Kitahara
1998 *A Derivational Approach to Syntactic Relations.* Oxford: Oxford University Press.
Everaert, Martin
1986 *The Syntax of Reflexivization.* Dordrecht: Foris.
Everaert, Martin
2012 The criteria for reflexivization. In: Dunstan Brown, Marina Chumakina, and Greville G. Corbett (eds.), *Canonical Morphology and Syntax*, 190–206. Oxford: Oxford University Press.
Featherston, Sam, and Wolfgang Sternefeld
2003 The interaction of factors in judgements of reflexive structures: data from object coreference in German. In: Lutz Gunkel, Gereon Müller, and Gisela Zifonun (eds.), *Arbeiten zur Reflexivierung*, 25–50. Tübingen: Niemeyer.
Fischer, Silke
2004a Optimal binding. *Natural Language and Linguistic Theory 22: 481–526.*
Fischer, Silke
2004b Towards an optimal theory of reflexivization. Doctoral dissertation, University of Tübingen.
Fischer, Silke
2006 Matrix unloaded: binding in a local derivational approach. *Linguistics* 44: 913–935.
Keller, Frank, and Ash Asudeh
2001 Constraints on linguistic coreference: structural vs. pragmatic factors. In: Johanna D. Moore and Keith Stenning (eds.), *Proceedings of the 23rd Annual Conference of the Cognitive Science Society*, 483–488. Mahwah, NJ: Lawrence Erlbaum Associates.
Kemmer, Suzanne
1993 *The Middle Voice.* Amsterdam: Benjamins.
Kiss, Tibor
2001 Anaphora and exemptness. A comparative treatment of anaphoric binding in German and English. In: Dan Flickinger and Andreas Kathol (eds.), *Proceedings of the 7th Inter-*

national Conference on Head-Driven Phrase Structure Grammar, 182–197. CSLI Publications, http://csli-publications.stanford.edu/HPSG/1/hpsg00kiss.pdf.

Kiss, Tibor
2012 Reflexivity and dependency. In: Artemis Alexiadou, Tibor Kiss, and Gereon Müller (eds.), *Local Modelling of Non-Local Dependencies in Syntax*, 155–185. Berlin: de Gruyter.

König, Ekkehard, and Peter Siemund
2000 Intensifiers and reflexives: a typological perspective. In: Zygmunt Frajzyngier and Traci Curl (eds.), *Reflexives. Forms and Functions*, 41–74. Amsterdam: Benjamins.

Koster, Jan
1984 Reflexives in Dutch. In: Jacqueline Guéron, Hans-Georg Obenauer, and Jean-Yves Pollock (eds.), *Grammatical Representation*, 141–167. Dordrecht: Foris.

Koster, Jan
1986 *Domains and Dynasties*. Dordrecht: Foris.

Kuno, Susumu
1987 *Functional Syntax*. Chicago: University of Chicago Press.

Lebeaux, David
1983 A distributional difference between reciprocals and reflexives. *Linguistic Inquiry* 14: 723–730.

Lebeaux, David
1984 Locality and anaphoric binding. *The Linguistic Review* 4: 343–363.

Maling, Joan
1984 Non-clause-bounded reflexives in Modern Icelandic. *Linguistics and Philosophy* 7: 211–241.

Manzini, Rita, and Kenneth Wexler
1987 Parameters, binding theory, and learnability. *Linguistic Inquiry* 18: 413–444.

Petersen, Hjalmar P., Jógvan í Lon Jacobsen, Zakaris Svabo Hansen, and Höskuldur Thráinsson
1998 Faroese: an overview for students and researchers. Ms., University of Iceland and Academy of the Faroes. Appeared as: Thráinsson, Höskuldur et al. 2003. *Faroese. An Overview and Reference Grammar.* Tórshavn: Fróðskaparfelag Föroya.

Pica, Pierre
1987 On the nature of the reflexive cycle. In: Joyce McDonough and Bernadette Plunkett (eds.), *Proceedings of NELS 17, 2*, 483–499. Amherst, MA: GSLA.

Pollard, Carl, and Ivan Sag
1992 Anaphors in English and the scope of binding theory. *Linguistic Inquiry* 23: 261–303.

Pollard, Carl, and Ivan Sag
1994 *Head-Driven Phrase Structure Grammar.* Chicago: University of Chicago Press.

Rappaport, Gilbert
1986 On anaphor binding in Russian. *Natural Language and Linguistic Theory* 4: 97–120.

Reinhart, Tanya
1976 The syntactic domain of anaphora. Doctoral dissertation, MIT, Cambridge, MA.

Reinhart, Tanya, and Eric Reuland
1991 Anaphors and logophors: an argument structure perspective. In: Jan Koster and Eric Reuland (eds.), *Long-Distance Anaphora*, 283–321. Cambridge: Cambridge University Press.

Reinhart, Tanya, and Eric Reuland
1993 Reflexivity. *Linguistic Inquiry* 24: 657–720.

Reuland, Eric, and Martin Everaert
2001 Deconstructing binding. In: Mark Baltin and Chris Collins (eds.), *The Handbook of Contemporary Syntactic Theory*, 634–669. Oxford: Blackwell.

Reuland, Eric, and Tanya Reinhart
1995 Pronouns, anaphors and case. In: Hubert Haider, Susan Olsen, and Sten Vikner (eds.), *Studies in Comparative Germanic Syntax*, 241–268. Dordrecht: Kluwer.

Richards, Norvin
1997 Competition and disjoint reference. *Linguistic Inquiry* 28: 178–187.
Roberts, Ian
1997 *Comparative Syntax.* London: Arnold.
Runner, Jeffrey T., Rachel S. Sussman, and Michael K. Tanenhaus
2002 Logophors in possessed picture noun phrases. In: Line Mikkelsen and Christopher Potts (eds.), *WCCFL 21 Proceedings*, 401–414. Somerville, MA: Cascadilla Press.
Runner, Jeffrey T., Rachel S. Sussman, and Michael K. Tanenhaus
2006 Processing reflexives and pronouns in picture noun phrases. *Cognitive Science* 30: 193–241.
Safir, Ken
1997 Symmetry and unity in the theory of anaphora. In: Hans Bennis, Pierre Pica, and Johan Rooryck (eds.), *Atomism and Binding*, 341–379. Dordrecht: Foris.
Schäfer, Florian
2012 The passive of reflexive verbs and its implications for theories of binding and case. *The Journal of Comparative Germanic Linguistics* 15: 213–268.
Sternefeld, Wolfgang, and Sam Featherston
2003 The German reciprocal *einander* in double object constructions. In: Lutz Gunkel, Gereon Müller, and Gisela Zifonun (eds.), *Arbeiten zur Reflexivierung*, 239–265. Tübingen: Niemeyer.
Thráinsson, Höskuldur
1979 *On Complementation in Icelandic.* New York: Garland.
Thráinsson, Höskuldur
1991 Long-distance reflexives and the typology of NPs. In: Jan Koster and Eric Reuland (eds.), *Long-Distance Anaphora*, 49–75. Cambridge: Cambridge University Press.
Vikner, Sten
1985 Parameters of binder and of binding category in Danish. *Working Papers in Scandinavian Syntax* 23: 1–61.

Silke Fischer, Stuttgart (Germany)

16. Coordination

Abstract

This article gives an overview over the basic concepts and notions of coordination. In defining the formal properties of coordination the article discusses the typological variation of the coordinator, the order of the conjuncts, the functions of coordination and its syntactic structure. Coordination shows properties of a symmetric structure which is analysed with respect to semantic symmetry, symmetric contrast, and the Coordinate Structure Constraint. At the same time, coordination may exhibit asymmetries, which concern the categories and feature specification of the conjuncts, or, in cases of so-called asymmetric coordination, the collocation of the conjuncts. The article also addresses nominal coordination without a determiner. It investigates ellipsis in coordination and finally discusses the influence of information structure on the syntax and intonation of the conjuncts.

1. Introduction

Coordination is one of the major structure building operations in language. In contrast to subordination, which creates embedding structures, coordination leads to complexity at one and the same syntactic level. Coordination exists in all languages of the world. It is thus a universally available means of structuring and ordering language.

The main objective of the present article is to discuss the fundamental syntactic properties of coordination. It considers the characteristic symmetric collocation of conjuncts, but it also adduces evidence for asymmetric coordination structures. In addition, the article discusses a number of empirically interesting aspects of coordination, some of which have not yet been treated much in the literature. The article does not present analyses of coordination in different theoretical frameworks. For an overview on different theories of the phrase structure of coordination, see van Oirsouw (1993), Wesche (1995), Progovac (1998), and Crysmann (2006).

The main object language of the article is German. The English translations of the examples show the strong relationship between these two languages with respect to coordination. Chapter 2.2 has a broader empirical basis. It discusses the different forms of the coordinators in a variety of languages (see also Haspelmath 2004, 2007).

2. Definition and formal properties

2.1. The conjuncts and the coordinators

Coordination is a term describing the concatenation of at least two words (1) or phrases (2) (the *conjuncts*) with an identical semantic function at the same syntactic projection level. The conjuncts form a complex constituent that has the same syntactic category as the conjuncts, see (3).

(1) a. [$_{N}$ [$_{N}$ *Birken*] *und* [$_{N}$ *Buchen*]] [German]
birches and beeches
'birches and beeches'

b. *Sie* [$_{V}$ [$_{V}$ *hüpften*] *und* [$_{V}$ *rannten*]] *im Hof.*
they jumped and ran in.the yard
'They jumped and ran in the yard.'

c. [$_{PP}$ [$_{P}$ [$_{P}$ *neben*] *oder* [$_{P}$ *hinter*]] *dem Sofa*]
besides or behind the sofa
'besides or behind the sofa'

(2) a. [$_{NP}$ [$_{NP}$ *spielende Kinder*] *und* [$_{NP}$ *bellende Hunde*]] [German]
playing children and barking dogs
'playing children and barking dogs'

b. *Sie haben* [$_{VP}$ [$_{VP}$ *die Alleen abgeholzt*] *und* [$_{VP}$ *die Straßen verbreitert*]].
they have the alleys lumbered and the streets broadened
'They lumbered the alleys and broadened the streets.'

c. [$_{CP}$ [$_{CP}$ *Sie haben die Alleen abgeholzt*] *und* [$_{CP}$ *sie haben die Straßen*
they have the alleys lumbered and they have the streets
verbreitert]].
broadened
'They lumbered the alleys and they broadened the streets.'

(3) [$_{X(P)}$ X(P) and X(P)]

Coordination is also a structure building device below the word level. It can coordinate prefixes that then combine with a stem (4a, b). In addition, the coordinator *und* 'and' concatenates numbers which are added to form higher numbers (4c) (see section 2.4).

(4) a. *be- und entladen* [German]
be- and unload
'load and unload'

b. *über- oder unterordnen*
over- or underestimate
'to place over or under '

c. *vier-und-vierzig*
four-and-fourty
'fourty-four'

The conjoined conjuncts may be combined with a *coordinator*. Coordination with *and/und* is called *conjunctive coordination*, see examples (1) and (2). Coordination with *or/oder* is called *disjunctive coordination*, and coordination with *but/aber* is called *adversative coordination.* The disjunctive and adversative coordinators show the same flexibility as the conjunctive coordinators with respect to the category of the conjuncts. Coordination is a recursive operation; that is it may conjoin two or more conjuncts.

Coordination is *syndetic* if the conjuncts are concatenated by an overt coordinator. If the coordinator is missing, the coordination is *asyndetic*. German (and English) has both, the syndetic and the asyndetic pattern. Asyndetic coordination is common with adjectival modifiers (5a) and marginally possible with some adverbials (5b). It may also occur with sentential conjuncts, see (2c) without the coordinator. Asyndetic coordination is finally used to replace a number of indefinite pronouns such as *alles* 'all' in (6a) or *überall* 'everywhere' in (6b); the English translation in (6b) is from Grover (1994: 763). The indefinite pronouns are correlates of the exhaustively interpreted juxtaposed elements, which do not form part of the main clause. Note that even strict syndetic coordination such as N/NP coordination (Haspelmath 2004) allows the asyndetic pattern in the replacive construction, see (6c).

(5) a. *ein* [$_A$ [$_A$ *langes*] [$_A$ *seidenes*]] *Kleid* [German]
a long silky dress
'a long silky dress'

b. *Er zog sich* [$_{PP}$ [$_{PP}$ *in der Küche*] [$_{PP}$ *im Dunkeln*]] *an.*
he dressed REFL in the kitchen in.the dark on
'He dressed in the kitchen in the dark.'

(6) a. *Ewa hatte alles gemacht: geputzt, gebügelt, gespült.* [German]
Ewa had all done cleaned ironed washed.the.dishes
'Ewa did it all: she cleaned, ironed, and washed the dishes.'

b. *Sie haben überall gesucht: auf dem Speicher, unter den Dielen,*
they have everywhere searched on the attic under the floorboards
unten im Keller.
down in.the cellar
'They searched everywhere: in the attic, under the floorboards, down in the cellar.'

c. *Michael hat die meisten seiner Ex-Freundinnen eingeladen:* [German]
Michael has the most his.GEN ex-girlfriends invited
Joyce, Jolene, Joëlle.
Joyce, Jolene, Joëlle
'Michael invited most of his ex-girlfriends: Joyce, Jolene, Joëlle.'

Asyndetic coordination is not possible for all other categories in German, which require an overt coordinator if two conjuncts are conjoined. In coordinated structures with more than two conjuncts, only the last two have to be combined with a coordinator.

(7) a. *Birken (und) Buchen *(und) Eichen* [German]
birches and beeches and oaks
'birches, beeches, and oaks'

b. *Sie haben* [$_{VP}$ [$_{VP}$ *die Alleen abgeholzt*] *(und)* [$_{VP}$ *die Straßen verbreitert*]
they have the alleys lumbered and the streets broadened
**(und)* [$_{VP}$ *den Belag erneuert*]].
and the pavement renewed
'They lumbered the alleys, broadened the streets and renewed the pavement.'

The presence of a coordinator between two sentential conjuncts may extend the semantic scope of certain operators to the left showing that syndetic and asyndetic coordination differ structurally. Example (8) illustrates scope extension with a negative operator. In (8a) the scope of negation is restricted to the second conjunct. In contrast, (8b) has a reading with the negation taking scope over both conjuncts. Similarly in (9) where the scope of the modal adverbial *immer wieder* 'again and again' is restricted to the second conjunct in (9a), but can extend over the whole coordination in (9b).

(8) a. *Die Sonne scheint. Die Vögel singen nicht.* [German]
the sun shines the birds sing NEG
'The sun shines. The birds don't sing.'

b. *Die Sonne scheint und die Vögel singen nicht.*
the sun shines and the birds sing NEG
'It is not the case that the sun is shining and the birds are singing.'

(9) a. *Der Vorhang öffnete sich. Die Tänzer verbeugten sich immer* [German]
the curtain opened REFL the dancers bowed REFL always
wieder.
again
'The curtain opened. The dancers bowed again and again.'

b. *Der Vorhang öffnete sich und die Tänzer verbeugten sich immer wieder.*
the curtain opened REFL and the dancers bowed REFL always again
'The curtain opened and the dancers bowed, again and again.'

Syntactically, the wide scope readings of the operators can be achieved by assuming a Right Node Raising structure as discussed in section 6.2. Note that not all coordinators allow for scope extensions. While *und/and* let scope go through, the adversatives *aber/but* do not. This is shown in (10) where the scope of the negation is necessarily restricted to the second conjunct.

(10) *Der Vorhang öffnete sich, aber die Tänzer verbeugten sich nicht.* [German]
the curtain opened REFL but the dancers bowed REFL NEG
'The curtain opened, but the dancers didn't bow.'

Apart from the simple coordinators *und*, *oder* and *aber*, German has a set of *correlative* coordinators, such as *entweder ... oder* 'either … or', *sowohl ... als auch* 'both … and', *nicht nur … sondern auch* 'not only … but' and *weder … noch* 'neither … nor', each part introducing one conjunct. The challenges for a syntactic analysis of correlative coordinations will be addressed in section 2.5.

2.2. Typological variation of the coordinator

This section presents two types of typological variation both concerning the nature of the coordinator. The first type discusses the form of the coordinator across languages. Three degrees of variation will be considered: (i) languages that use the same element to coordinate nouns and NPs (henceforth *nominal coordination*) and VP/sentences (henceforth *event coordination*), (ii) languages that have an element for nominal but not for event coordination, and (iii) languages that use different elements. The second type of variation addresses the distinction between languages using the preposition *with* to coordinate NPs and those that use different elements.

2.2.1. Nominal and event coordination

In German (and English), coordinators are binary functors with hardly restricted syntactic selection properties. They combine with all major lexical and phrasal categories, cf. Grover (1994). As discussed in section 2.1, NPs and events are coordinated by the same element in German. In other languages, coordinators have c-selectional properties to the effect that nominal and event coordination is differentiated. Such differentiation comes in two forms. Coordinators may serve to concatenate conjuncts of specific syntactic categories. This is the case in Hausa (Chadic, Afroasiatic). Hausa has the coordinators *dà* 'and, with' and *kóo* 'or' selecting conjuncts with a [+N] specification, thus, nouns (11a), adjectives (11b), or nominalized verbs (11c). VPs and sentences must be coordinated asyndetically, they cannot be combined by an overt coordinator, see (12) for VP and (13) for sentential conjuncts.

(11) a. *Àbêokùtá dà/kóo Àbúujáa dà/kóo Ìlòoři dà/kóo Ìbàadàn* [Hausa]
Abeokuta and/or Abuja and/or Ilorin and/or Ibadan
'Abeokuta and/or Abuja and/or Ilorin and/or Ibadan'

b. *Wánnàn rìigáa tánàa dà káláa jáa dà/kóo kóořèe.*
this dress 3SG.F.PROG with colour red and green
'This dress has red and green colour.'

c. *cîn náamà-n àládèe dà shân gíyàa*
eating meat-of pig and drinking beer
'eating pork and drinking beer' (Newman 2000: 135)

(12) *Hàbîb yáa háu Mount Patti, (*dà/*kóo) yáa núunàa* [Hausa]
Habib 3SG.M.PFV climb Mount Patti and/or 3SG.M.PFV show
*mánà kòogí-n Íisà, (*dà/*kóo) yáa gyáarà móotà-r-sà.*
us river-GEN Niger and/or 3SG.M.PFV repair car-GEN-his

'Habib has climbed Mount Patti, has showed us the river Niger, has repaired his car.'

(13) *Júmmáí táa kíráa 'yá-r-tà, (*dà/*kóo) Màimúnà* [Hausa]
Jummai 3SG.F.PFV call daughter-GEN-her and/or Maimuna
*tánàa yîn wàasáa, (*dà/*kóo) Hàlíimà tánàa shân rúwáa.*
3SG.F.PROG do play and/or Halima 3SG.F.PROG drink water
'Jummai called her daughter, Maimuna is playing, Halima is drinking water.'

The disjunctive coordinator *kóo* 'or' may appear between two events only in correlative coordination. Like in German, both conjuncts of a correlative coordination are introduced by a coordinator, e.g. *kóo ... kóo* 'either or' in (14).

(14) *Kóo Hàbîb yáa tàfí Lákwájà kóo yáa tàfí Sákkwátó.* [Hausa]
either Habib 3SG.M.PFV travel Lokoja or 3SG.M.PFV travel Sokoto
'Either Habib went to Lokoja or he went to Sokoto.'

Given this, the occurrence of *kóo* 'or' between the first and second conjunct, and the second and third conjunct in (15) is possible in the *either ... or*-interpretation.

(15) *Hàbîb yà háu Mount Patti, kóo yáa núunàa* [Hausa]
Habib 3SG.M.PFV.SBJV climb Mount Patti or 3SG.M.PFV show
mána kòogí-n Íisà, kóo yáa gyáarà móotà-r-sà.
us river-GEN Niger or 3SG.M.PFV repair car-GEN-his
'Habib climbed Mount Patti either to show us river Niger or to repair his car.'

The third type of variation concerns languages that differentiate between nominal and event coordination using different coordinators for the two types of coordination. An example is Dagbani (Gur, Niger-Congo), see Olawsky (1999), cited in Haspelmath (2008). Dagbani has the coordinators *mini* 'and' to coordinate NPs (16a) and *ka* 'and' to coordinate events (16b).

(16) a. *doo ŋɔ mini m ba* [Dagbani]
man this and my father
'this man and my father'

b. *Gbuɣima ŋubiri nimdi ka jansi diri kɔdu.*
lion.PL chew.IPFV meat and monkey.PL eat.IPFV banana
'Lions eat meat and monkeys eat bananas.'

The same kind of differentiation is found in Turkish, which uses the suffix *-la* to coordinate nominals (17a), and the suffix *-ıp* 'and' to coordinate events (17b), from Haspelmath (2007: 20).

(17) a. *Hasan-la Amine* [Turkish]
Hasan-and Amine
'Hasan and Amine'

b. *Çocuk bir kasık çorba al-ıp içer.*
child one spoon soup take-and eat
'The child takes a spoon of soup and eats.'

2.2.2. *And/with*-languages

Languages also show cross-linguistic variation with respect to the nature of the nominal coordinator (see Stassen 2000, 2001, 2008). Apart from using prototypical coordinators, languages may also express the simultaneous predication of an event to several participants by employing the comitative marker *with*. The coordinate and the comitative strategy are semantically equivalent (they share at least one reading), but they differ syntactically: the coordinated NPs form a complex constituent which triggers plural agreement on the verb (18a) and represent an island for extraction (19a), see also section 3.3. The comitative phrase is an independent constituent, which neither forms a constituent with nor is coordinated with the noun. It does not have an impact on verbal agreement (18b) and may be extracted (19b). Semantically, the symmetric-comitative interpretation is obtained by inference: if A is doing X with B, then B is also doing X with A; it may then be inferred that A and B are doing X.

(18) a. *Peter und Carlo sind nach Kassel gefahren.* [German]
Peter and Carlo are to Kassel driven
'Peter and Carlo went to Kassel.'

b. *Peter ist mit Carlo nach Kassel gefahren.*
Peter is with Carlo to Kassel driven
'Peter went to Kassel with Carlo.'

(19) a. *[*Und Carlo*]$_i$ *sind* [$_{DP}$ *Peter* t_i] *nach Kassel gefahren.* [German]
and Carlo are Peter to Kassel driven

b. *Mit Carlo ist Peter nach Kassel gefahren.*
with Carlo is Peter to Kassel driven
'Peter went to Kassel with Carlo.'

In many languages the comitative strategy exists in addition to syntactic coordination (German, English etc.). In a number of languages, however, comitative constructions represent the only means of semantic concatenation. These languages do not have nominal coordination structures in the sense of the definition given in section 2.1. An example is Samoan (Austronesian, Polynesian), see Marsack (1975: 119), cited in Stassen (2001: 1109).

(20) *o io'o 'a'ai Mana ma Ioane i fa'i.* [Samoan]
PROG eat Mana and/with Ioane at banana
'Mary and John are eating bananas/Mary is eating bananas with John.'

2.3. Order of the conjuncts

Two conjuncts *A* and *B* can often occur in either order without decrease in grammaticality. The order may vary if the conjuncts are semantically and pragmatically independent from each other and at the same time structurally similar, see the predicate coordination in (21).

(21) a. *Sie trennte die Eier und schlug die Sahne.* [German]
she separated the eggs and whipped the cream
'She separated the eggs and whipped the cream.'

b. *Sie schlug die Sahne und trennte die Eier.*
she whipped the cream and separated the eggs
'She whipped the cream and separated the eggs.'

The sequencing of conjuncts may be subject to a number of restrictions. Ordering effects result from pragmatic and formal requirements. Thus, the order of mentioning may indicate, among others (see Müller 1997), the order of events (22a) (Posner 1980), social rank (22b), relevance (22c), natural or world order (22d) (Behaghel 1909: 111; Cooper and Ross 1975). In these cases, the ordering effect results from a conversational implicature. (22e), see Cooper and Ross (1975, fn 6), exemplifies a special instance of world order which shows that in compounds denoting mixed drinks, the alcoholic drink tends to be mentioned first.

(22) a. *Sie machte das Licht aus und schlief sofort ein.* [German]
she do.PST the light PRT and sleep.PST immediately PRT
'She switched the light off and fell immediately asleep.'

b. *Sehr geehrter Herr Präsident, sehr geehrter Herr Dekan, liebe*
very honored mister president very honored mister dean dear
Kollegen und Kolleginnen, liebe Freunde ...
colleagues and colleagues.F dear friends
'Dear Mr. President, dear Mr. Dean, dear colleagues, dear friends …'

c. *Der Pilot, die Stewardessen und die Passagiere gingen von Bord.*
the pilot the stewardesses and the passengers go.PST from board
'The pilot, the stewardesses and the passengers deboarded.'

d. *Tag und Nacht (#Nacht und Tag); Aufgang und Untergang (#Untergang*
day and night night and day rise and set set
und Aufgang)
and rise
'day and night; rise and set'

e. *Gin Tonic, Wodka Soda, Whiskey Cola, Campari Orange*

Apart from pragmatic restrictions, the order of the conjuncts is also formally restricted. The length of the conjuncts may have an ordering effect in that longer conjuncts tend to follow shorter ones (*Gesetz der wachsenden Glieder,* Behaghel 1909: 139). The examples in (23) are taken from Behaghel's seminal article. They all illustrate coordination where the second conjunct is structurally more complex than the first one. (23a) is an Old High German example from Hartmann von der Aue (*Der arme Heinrich*, V. 1–1000). (23b) is from Goethe's *Faust*, and (23c) from Gustav Roethe, *Vom literarischen Publikum in Deutschland* (1902).

(23) a. *gürtel und vingerlin Und swaz kinden liep solde sin* [Old High German]
belt and little.ring and what children dear should be
'belt and little ring and what children should like'

b. *viel Irrtum und ein Fünkchen Wahrheit* [German]
much error and a spark truth
'much error and a grain of truth'

c. *der geschichtliche Geist Herder-s und der neuen Zeit* [German]
the historical spirit Herder-GEN and the new time
'the historical spirit of Herder and the new time'

Length effects are also observed in idiomatic coordinated binomials. As argued in Müller (1997: 19), the conjunct that is longer in terms of syllable number follows the shorter one.

(24) a. *Kind und Kegel (*Kegel und Kind)* [German]
child and cone
'everybody'

b. *Pauken und Trompeten (*Trompeten und Pauken)*
timbal and trumpet
'totally'

Coordinated binomials are also ordered according to syllabic prominence see Cooper and Ross (1975, section 3) and Müller (1997: 33). Thus, shorter syllable onsets precede longer ones (25a), shorter nuclei precede longer ones (25b). The vowel quality also influences the order of the binomials in that high vowels precede low vowels. If the vowels have the same height, front vowels precede back vowels (25c). Finally, the onset of the first conjunct tends to be more sonorant than the onset of the second one (25d). The following examples are Müller's:

(25) a. *(sich) [r]ecken und [str]ecken (*[str]ecken und [r]ecken)* [German]
REFL strain and stretch strech and strain
'to stretch'

b. *k[u]rz und g[u:t] (*gut und kurz)*
short and good good and short
'in short'

c. *h[ie]r und d[a] (*da und hier) / d[i]ck und d[ü]nn (*dünn und dick)*
here and there there and here thick and thin thin and thick
'here and there / thick and thin'

d. *(mit [R]at und [T]at (*Tat und Rat)*
with advice and deed deed and advice
'(with) words and deeds'

2.4. Functions of coordination

The primary function of coordination is enumeration, i.e. listing of semantically different elements that are instances of some "common integrator" (Lang 1984: 69–79), i.e. a superordinate semantic category. In (26) the common integrator is food that can be ordered in a restaurant.

(26) *Er bestellte eine Suppe und einen gemischten Salat.* [German]
he ordered a soup and a mixed salad
'He ordered a soup and a mixed salad.'

Coordination is a common strategy to form numbers with two or more digits. The coordinative function of number formation is addition or multiplication or a combination of both. In German, two-digit numbers such as *vier-und-zwanzig* (= 4-and-20 '24') are formed by syndetic addition, whereas three-digit numbers show a mixed system of syndetic multiplication and syndetic/asyndetic addition. Thus, the number *zwei-hundert-vier-und-zwanzig* (= 2-100-4-and-20 '224') results from three different morpho-mathematical operations: the two first numbers are multiplied (·), the last two numbers are syndetically added ($+_s$), and finally the two numbers are asyndetically added ($+_a$): *[zwei · hundert]* $+_a$ *[vier* $+_s$ *zwanzig]*. French also uses a mixed system which is – in contrast to German – almost always asyndetic. Usually, the numbers below 100 are asyndetically added, cf. *cinquante-cinque* (= fifty-five '55'). There is one interesting exception to this. Depending on the order of the numbers, the conjuncts *twenty* and *four* are either added: *vingt-quatre* (= 20-4 '24' – higher number precedes smaller number), or multiplied: *quatre-vingt* (= 4-20 '80' – smaller number precedes higher number), reflecting the French vigesimal system. The complex number *deux-cent-quatre-vingt-dix-huit* (= 2-100-4-20-10-8 '298') involves the following operations: *[deux · cent]* $+_a$ *[quatre · vingt]* $+_a$ *[dix* $+_a$ *huit]*. Syndetic addition only occurs if *one* is added, compare *vingt-et-un* (= 20-and-1 '21') with *vingt-deux* (= 20-2 '22'), *vingt-trois* (= 20-3 '23') etc.

It is also possible to coordinate identical conjuncts. The coordination of identical conjuncts gives rise to conversational implicatures since the listing of identical elements always violates the maxime of quantity (Grice 1989). The implicature can be the intensification of the event expressed by one conjunct, or an emphasis on it. In (27a), coordination of the verb *aß* 'ate' gives rise to the interpretation that the subject ate a lot (intensity). The coordination of identical verbs in the scope of negation (27b) results in an emphatic reading. Note that (27b) has a second reading where the negation takes scope only over the second conjunct ('He left and he didn't leave.'). Finally, coordination of a lexeme also serves to express continuation, see (27c), where the coordination expresses the repetition of a single event.

(27) a. *Er aß und aß und aß.* [German]
he ate and ate and ate
'He ate and ate and ate.' (= He ate a lot.)

b. *Er ging und ging nicht.*
he left and left NEG
'He did not leave (although he was expected to leave).'

c. *Er tat es wieder und wieder.*
he did it again and again
'He did it again and again.'

Coordination of identical constituents is only possible with syntactic heads as in (27). At the phrasal level, identical conjuncts cannot be coordinated, see (28). The ungrammaticality of (28) follows from a cumulativity effect (*horror aequi*). It is impossible to neutralize this effect by a conversational implicature.

(28) a. **Er aß Kuchen und (er) aß Kuchen und (er) aß Kuchen.* [German]
he ate cake and he ate cake and he ate cake
'He ate cake and he ate cake and he ate cake.'

b. **Er beging das Verbrechen wieder und (er) beging das Verbrechen wieder.*
he committed the crime again and he committed the crime again
'He committed the crime again and he committed the crime again.'

To my knowledge, the contrast between (27) and (28) remains unaccounted in the literature on coordination.

2.5. Syntactic structure

Chomsky (1957: 36) introduces a phrase structure rule for coordination which extends a category to two categories of the same type and optionally combines them by a coordinator.

(29) X → X (and) X

This rule yields a tripartite structure, which seems to be reserved for coordination only, see also Jackendoff (1977: 51), Gazdar et al. (1985: 171), Steedman (1990: 214), among many others. However, there are three good arguments for the assumption of a binary branching coordination structure (Kayne 1984). The first is a prosodic one and goes back to Ross (1967). Ross argues that there is an intonational break before the coordinator, but not after it, showing that the coordinator is prosodically integrated into the following conjunct. This is taken to be a consequence of the syntactic structure, which groups the coordinator together with the following conjunct, see (30) from Ross (1967: 91), and also Dik (1968).

(30) *((Tom) (and Dick) (and Harry)) all love watermelon.*

The second argument for a binary branching coordination structure comes from structural asymmetries, which will be discussed in section 4. Anticipating this discussion, it often appears that not both of the conjuncts are selected with respect to case and agreement features. An example is given in (31) (from Bergen Norwegian, see Johannessen 1998: 8) where only the first conjunct realizes the nominative case assigned to the position of the whole coordination. A tripartite structure would predict a symmetric distribution of case.

(31) *Det sku' bare mangle at [eg og deg] ikkje* [Bergen Norwegian]
it should only lack that I.NOM and you.ACC should
sku' gjere det.
do it
'Of course, I and you should do it.'

The third argument is a structural one. It can be shown that the first conjunct has scope over the second conjunct. Thus, a quantifier in the first conjunct can bind a pronoun in the second, see (32). Pronoun binding is only possible assuming an asymmetric structure of the coordinated DPs.

(32) *The host welcomed [$_{DP}$ every woman$_i$ and her$_i$ companion].*

Asymmetric coordination can be structurally encoded in two ways. The first involves adjunction of the second conjunct (including the coordinator) to the first conjunct. The structure in (33a) presents a schematic representation of this idea; see Schachter (1977: 88). The second option is to assume a functional projection whose head is the coordinator. Such projections have been called BP (= boolean phrase, Munn 1993), CoP (= coordination phrase, Johannessen 1998), CoordP (Camacho 2003), or simply &P (Wilder 1997) in the literature. The conjuncts are located in the specifier of this functional projection and the complement position of its head, respectively, see (33b).

(33) a.
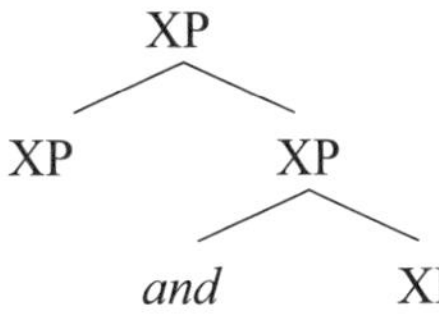

b.
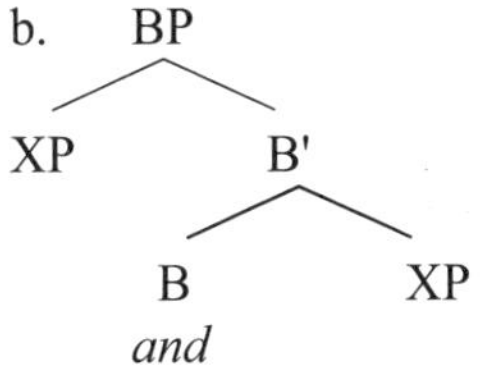

The structure in (34) mixes aspects of the coordination in (33a, b). The BP is represented only by the second conjunct, which is adjoined to the first. An advantage of this structure over the one in (33b) for categorial selection is that the conjuncts have the same syntactic category as the whole coordination.

(34)
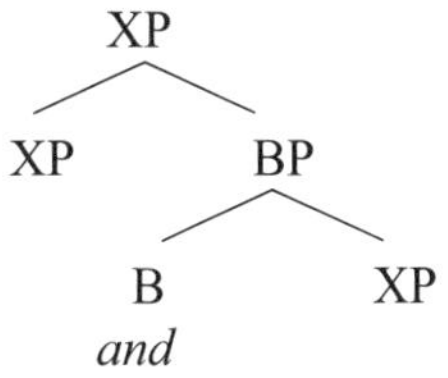

The endocentric structures in (33) to (34) have to be extended in order to account for correlative coordinations such as *entweder ... oder* 'either … or', *sowohl ... als auch*

'both … and' etc., which contain split coordinators. Correlative coordinations appear to fall into two classes depending on the status of the conjoining elements. In the first group, the initial conjunct is taken to be an adverbial with focus properties, which selects for a simple coordination structure (e.g. Hendriks 2004; Johannessen 2005). This is expressed by an asymmetric structure as sketched in (35a). The second group does not provide evidence for asymmetric structure and can be represented by a symmetric tree as given in (35b). Such structures have been proposed e.g. for French correlatives like *et* ... *et* 'both … and' (e.g. Piot 2000; Mouret 2005).

(35) a.

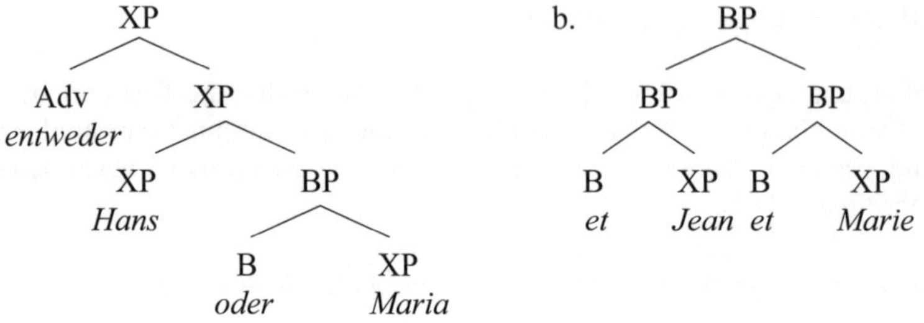

3. Symmetries

Coordination is one of the major structure building operations, which, in contrast to embedding, results in paratactic complexity. The conjuncts usually require a syntactically and semantically symmetric (i.e. parallel) structure. Section 2 discussed the requirement of categorial identity of the conjuncts. The following subsections discuss several semantic symmetry conditions of the conjuncts. Section 3.1 addresses the requirement that the conjuncts must have the same thematic role (thematic identity requirement) and show the same degree of semantic saturation. Section 3.2 analyzes the contrastive potential of the two conjuncts. Section 3.3 discusses the Coordinate Structure Constraint, a structural parallelism requirement, which disallows asymmetric extraction out of only one conjunct.

3.1. Semantic symmetry

Conjuncts are semantically parallel in that they (i) realize the same thematic role, and (ii) show the same degree of semantic saturation (see Crysmann 2006: 184). The coordination of two DPs realizing different thematic roles is impossible as shown for instance by the ungrammatical coordination of an agent role (*Gerda*) and a recipient (*ihrem Enkelkind* 'her grandchild) in (36).

(36) *Das Kostüm hat* [$_{\text{DP}}$ *Gerda*] *(*und)* [$_{\text{DP}}$ *ihrem Enkelkind*] [German]
the costume has Gerda and her grandchild
geschenkt.
given
'As for the costume, Gerda gave it to her grandchild.'

This thematic identity requirement is violated in (37) where the coordination of constituents with different thematic roles appears to be only marginally possible. Example (37a) contains a coordination of an instrumental and a directional role. In (37b), a theme is coordinated with an instrument. Such coordination structures are not ungrammatical but they have a funny interpretation, which is referred to as a *zeugmatic effect.*

(37) a. *?Hauke ging am Stock und nach Hause.* [German]
Hauke walked at.DAT cane and to home
'Hauke walked with a cane and home.'

b. *?Er zeichnete ein Portrait und mit dem Bleistift.*
he drew a portrait and with a pencil
'He drew a portrait and with a pencil.'

A reason for the marginal availability of the examples in (37) could be that they are underlyingly bisentential. As a result of leftperipheral deletion (Wilder 1997), the two conjuncts appear to be coordinated only at the surface, see section 6 for further discussion of ellipsis in coordination. Coordination reduction is represented by doubly striking out the elided constituents.

(38) a. ?[$_{\text{CP}}$ *Hauke ging am Stock*] *und* [German]
Hauke walked at.DAT cane and
[$_{\text{CP}}$ ~~*Hauke ging*~~ *nach Hause*].
to home
'Hauke walked with a cane and home.'

b. ?[$_{\text{CP}}$ *Er zeichnete ein Portrait*] *und*
he drew a portrait and
[$_{\text{CP}}$ ~~*er zeichnete*~~ *mit dem Bleistift*].
with a pencil
'He drew a portrait and with a pencil.'

Such an analysis is not available in (36) since a bisentential structural basis as in (39) would be a coordination of two identical conjuncts, which is excluded at least for phrasal conjuncts (see section 2.4).

(39) #[$_{\text{CP}}$ *Das Kostüm hat Gerda ihrem Enkelkind geschenkt*] *und* [German]
the costume has Gerda her grandchild given and
[$_{\text{CP}}$ *das Kostüm hat Gerda ihrem Enkelkind geschenkt*].
the costume has Gerda her grandchild given
'Gerda gave the costume to her grandchild and Gerda gave the costume to her grandchild.'

A second semantic condition on the conjuncts is that they must show the same degree of semantic saturation (Crysmann 2006: 184). This is illustrated in example (40a), whose ungrammaticality results from the fact that the verb *beat* is lacking a direct object, compare (40a) to the grammatical (40b). (41a) shows that it is possible to coordinate fully saturated intransitive and transitive predicates. (41b) shows that this is also possible if one of the predicates realizes its argument only optionally. The two realizations of (41b) slightly differ in meaning. With the intransitive *aßen* 'ate', it is implied that strawberries were eaten, whereas the pronoun in *aßen sie* 'ate them' can only refer back to the parallel direct object introduced in the first conjunct.

(40) a. **We will [$_{VP}$ [$_{VP}$ attack the enemy] and [$_{V}$ beat]].*
b. *We will [$_{V}$ [$_{V}$ attack] and [$_{V}$ beat]] the enemy.*

(41) a. *Wir rannten und warfen uns in den Schnee.* [German]
we ran and threw ourselves in the snow
'We ran and threw ourselves in the snow.'

b. *Wir kauften ein Kilo Erdbeeren und aßen / aßen sie.*
we bought a kilo strawberries and ate ate them
'We bought a kilo of strawberries and ate / ate them.'

Not every phrase preceded by a coordinator is necessarily a conjunct. Coordinators may also introduce a syntactic parenthesis, see (42). Parentheses and conjuncts share the two properties that they are not embedded, and that they may be introduced by a coordinator.

(42) *Peter hat – und das sage ich dir ganz unter uns – noch nicht* [German]
Peter has and this say I you just between us not yet
bezahlt.
paid
'Peter has – and this is just between us – not yet paid.'

Notwithstanding the similarities between syntactic parentheses and syndetic conjuncts, they can be also differentiated. Parentheses are not coordinated with any constituent of the clause, thus they do not form part of the clause. Observe that a parenthetical interpretation becomes available in (36) if the particle *zwar* with the approximate meaning 'namely' or 'that is' follows the coordinator, see (43):

(43) *Das Kostüm hat Gerda, und zwar ihrem Enkelkind, geschenkt.* [German]
the costume has Gerda and that.is her grandchild given
'Gerda gave the costume, to her grandchild, to be precise.'

In (43) the alleged second conjunct is a parenthesis rather than a nominal conjunct. The *und zwar*-phrase cannot be a DP since it can be extraposed, which is impossible for simple DPs in German:

(44) *Das Kostüm hat Gerda geschenkt, *(und zwar) ihrem Enkelkind.* [German]
the costume has Gerda given and that.is her grandchild
'Gerda gave the costume, to her grandchild, to be precise.'

The *und zwar*-clause in (43) and (44) identifies the recipient of the verb *schenken* 'give as a present'. The general semantic function of the *und zwar*-clause is to sub-specify an introduced event or entity. In (43), the sub-specification of the costume giving event consists in the addition of the recipient. Further examples are given in (45). In (45a), the entity *Blumen* 'flowers' is specified by identification with a meteronyme. In (45b), the event of wanting a glass of water is sub-specified by the addition of an adverbial.

(45) a. *Ich habe Blumen, und zwar Tulpen, gekauft.* [German]
I have flower and that.is tulips bought
'I bought flowers, that is tulips.'
(≠ I bought flowers and tulips.)

b. *Ich möchte ein Glas Wasser, und zwar schnell.*
I want a glass water and that.is quickly
'I want a glass of water, and quickly.'

3.2. Symmetric contrast

As discussed in the preceding section, conjuncts are subject to a number of identity conditions. At the same time, they have to differ semantically. It is often claimed that the conjuncts of a coordinated structure involve a contrast (Féry and Hartmann 2005; Repp 2009). Two linguistic expressions are said to be in a relation of contrast if they belong to the same semantic field (the common integrator, see section 2.4) without being identical. An example is given in (46). The common integrator of the conjuncts is the profession of the (unsatisfied) civil servants.

(46) [$_{DP}$ *Die Lehrer*] *und* [$_{DP}$ *die Busfahrer*] *(sind in den Streik getreten).* [German]
the teachers and the bus.drivers are in the strike stepped
'The teachers and the bus drivers have gone on strike.'

The contrasting constituents may be phrases as in (46) or heads. In (47a) the two coordinated prepositions contrast. In (47b), the contrast is temporal: a past tense and a future tense auxiliary are coordinated. (47c) shows that conjuncts may also be homophonous if they contrast referentially.

(47) a. *Der Zement liegt entweder* [$_{P}$ *hinter*] *oder* [$_{P}$ *neben*] *dem* [German]
the cement lies either behind or besides the
Holzstapel.
wood.stack
'The cement is either behind or beside of the wood stack.'

b. *Sie* [$_{C}$ *war*] *und* [$_{C}$ *wird*] *immer glücklich sein.*
she was and will always happy be
'She was and will be always happy.'

c. *Ich möchte* [$_{DP}$ *dich$_1$*] *und* [$_{DP}$ *dich$_2$*] *einladen.*
I want you$_1$ and you$_2$ invite
'I want to invite you and you.'

It is not always the whole conjunct that is contrasting but only some part of it. In (48) (adopted from Artstein 2002: 13), the semantic contrast between the two entities is formally expressed only by the different onsets of the final syllables.

(48) *I saw stalag**m**ites and stalag**t**ites.*

In clausal coordination, sentence parts of the first conjunct form contrastive pairs with those of the second conjunct. Constituents that are identical in the first and second conjuncts may be elided either at the right edge of the first conjunct (Right Node Raising), at the left edge of the second conjunct (Left Peripheral Deletion), the right edge of the second conjunct (VP-deletion, Sluicing) or within the second conjunct (Gapping), see section 6 and Aelbrecht (this volume) for detailed discussion. (49) is an example illustrating Gapping. The subjects (underlined) as well as the prepositional objects (underlined with a broken line) in both conjuncts are contrastive in the sense given above. The finite verb is identical and elided in the second conjunct.

(49) *Claus geht in eine Privatschule und sein Freund ~~geht~~ in eine* [German]
Claus goes in a private.school and his friend goes in a
öffentliche Schule.
public school
'Claus goes to a private school and his friend to a public school.'

3.3. The Coordinate Structure Constraint

It is well-known that extractions from coordinated structures are subject to strict symmetry requirements. This insight is encoded in Ross' famous *Coordinate Structure Constraint* (Ross 1967). The CSC states that it is neither possible to extract a constituent out of a coordinated structure (50a) nor to extract a conjunct alone (50b). The examples are from Ross (1967: 88, 89). The deleted copies of the extracted elements are crossed out.

(50) a. **The lute which Henry [plays ~~the lute~~] and [sings madrigals] is warped.*
b. **What sofa will be put the chair between some table and ~~what sofa~~?*

The CSC holds across all languages showing that coordinated structures represent true islands for extraction. A constituent may only be extracted out of a coordinated structure if it leaves a gap in all the conjuncts. Such simultaneous extraction is called *Across-The-Board extraction* (ATB-extraction, see Ross 1967; Williams 1978). ATB-extraction results in a strictly symmetric structure. It applies to all types of extraction, i.e. *wh*-question formation (51a), topicalization (51b), and head movement (51ab).

(51) a. *Welches Verbrechen hat* [$_{TP}$ *der BND* ~~*welches Verbrechen*~~ [German]
which crime has the BND
verheimlicht ~~*hat*~~] *und* [$_{TP}$ *der* Spiegel ~~*welches Verbrechen*~~ *aufgeklärt* ~~*hat*~~]?
kept.secret and the Spiegel uncovered
'Which crime did the BND keep secret and the *Spiegel* uncover?'

b. *Im Tischtennis* ~~*hat*~~ [$_{TP}$ *Malta* ~~*im Tischtennis*~~ *verloren* ~~*hat*~~] *und*
in.DAT table.tennis has Malta lost and
[$_{TP}$ *Mexiko* ~~*im Tischtennis*~~ *gewonnen* ~~*hat*~~].
Mexiko won
'Malta lost and Mexico won in table tennis.'

Although the CSC systematically restricts asymmetric extraction out of coordinated structures across languages, there are notorious exceptions to it. The following examples are from Lakoff (1986), see also Goldsmith (1985), and Postal (1998).

(52) a. *Who did you [$_{VP}$ turn around] and [$_{VP}$ say hello to* ~~*who*~~*]?*
b. *the stuff which [OP Arthur [$_{VP}$ sneaked in] and [$_{VP}$ stole* ~~*OP*~~*]]*
c. *How many dogs can a person [$_{VP}$ have* ~~*how many dogs*~~*] and [$_{VP}$ still stay sane]?*

In all three examples in (52), an operator is moved out of only one conjunct in obvious violation of the CSC. Examples such as (52) have been used in the literature to question the universality of the CSC. But note that coordination that seems to allow for a violation of the CSC has a special format. First one of the conjuncts must be an intransitive verb. Second, the coordination requires the coordinator *and*. Note that *or*, which is truth-conditionally equivalent to *and*, but requires a semantic contrast, is ruled out. And third, the extensions of the predicates of the two conjuncts denote events that are in immediate succession (52ab), or stand in a close semantic connection (52c). If these conditions are not met, asymmetric extraction is ruled out.

(53) a. **Who did you [$_{VP}$ call Mary] and [$_{VP}$ say hello to* ~~*who*~~*]?*
b. **the stuff which [OP Arthur [$_{VP}$ saw a pharmacy] and [$_{VP}$ stole* ~~*OP*~~*]]*

How can we account for the violations of the CSC in (52) then? The close semantic dependency between the coordinated predicates in (52ab) could be due to the fact that the examples do not involve VP-coordination but coordination of the verbs, which thus form semantically complex predicates, see de Vos (2005). Under this assumption, the *wh*-object in (52a) and the empty operator in (52b) would be the objects of the coordinated complex verbs, and no CSC-violation would occur, see (54). The challenge posed by such structures is to define a formalism which allows the composition of predicates of different valencies resulting in a complex transitive predicate.

(54) a. *Who did you [$_{V}$ [$_{V}$ turn around] and [$_{V}$ say hello]] to* ~~*who*~~*?*
b. *the stuff which [OP Arthur [$_{V}$[$_{V}$ sneaked in] and [$_{V}$ stole]]* ~~*OP*~~*]*

The example in (52c) cannot be reanalysed along these lines since the gap is contained in the first conjunct. Instead, the example involves *asymmetric coordination*, which will be discussed in section 4.2.

The following German example (55b) seems to represent a further exception to the CSC. (55a) is an example with a coordinated subject. In (55b) the second conjunct is extraposed, it appears in the right periphery of the clause.

(55) a. *Antje und Ellen demonstrierte-n gegen die Schließung des* [German]
Antje and Ellen demonstrated-3PL against the closing the.GEN
Schillertheaters.
Schiller.theatre
'Antje and Ellen demonstrated against the closing of the Schiller theatre.'

b. *Antje demonstrier-te/*ten gegen die Schließung des*
Antje demonstrate-PST.3SG/PST.3PL against the closing the.GEN
Schillertheaters, und Ellen.
Schiller.theater and Ellen
'Antje demonstrated against the closing of the Schiller theatre, and Ellen.'

The verb *demonstrierten* 'demonstrated' in (55a) shows plural agreement with the coordinated subject. In (55b), however, subject agreement is singular. This is evidence against a rightward movement analysis of the second nominal conjunct. Instead, the DP in the right periphery represents an afterthought, see Averintseva-Klisch (2008), and Prinzhorn and Schmitt (2010) for a detailed analysis of discontinuous DP-conjuncts. In (56) (Sternefeld 2007: 410), the second conjunct is semantically in the scope of the participle *gehört* 'heard'. Syntactically, however, it appears extraposed, again violating the CSC, see the analysis in (57a). As an alternative, (56) could be derived by coordination of larger conjuncts and Gapping, i.e. ellipsis of the predicate and possibly other constituents in the second conjunct, see (57b). The advantage of the Gapping analysis is that it circumvents a violation of the CSC.

(56) *Ich selbst habe ihn schreien gehört und nach dem Schaffner* [German]
I REFL have him scream heard and for the conductor
klingeln.
call
'I myself heard him scream and call for the conductor.'

(57) a. Extraposition analysis
Ich selbst habe [$_{VP}$ [$_{VP}$ ihn schreien] [$_{VP}$ ~~und nach dem Schaffner klingeln~~] gehört] und nach dem Schaffner klingeln.

b. Gapping analysis
Ich selbst [$_{C'}$ habe ihn schreien gehört] und [$_{C'}$ ~~habe ihn~~ nach dem Schaffner klingeln ~~gehört~~].

4. Asymmetries

The standard assumption that coordination is a concatenation of two or more balanced, symmetric conjuncts is challenged by coordinated structures that show asymmetries between the first and the second conjunct. This section presents two types of asymmetries.

Section 4.1 discusses cross-linguistic examples of unbalanced coordination, i.e. coordination of conjuncts that differ with respect to their feature specification. Section 4.2 addresses an interesting structural asymmetry in German in which the subject of the second conjunct is unexpressed.

4.1. Categorial and feature asymmetries

Conjuncts do not necessarily have the same syntactic category. This fact has been acknowledged in the literature on coordination ever since, see e.g. Schmerling (1975), Gazdar (1981), Sag et al. (1985), Goodall (1987), Munn (1993), Johannessen (1998). The following examples show conjuncts of different category in English. In (58a), the coordinated conjuncts are a DP and an AP, respectively. Both conjuncts are selected by the copula verb, see (58b, c).

(58) a. *He is [$_{DP}$ a republican] and [$_{AP}$ proud of it].*
b. *He is a republican.*
c. *He is proud of it.*

(59a) (Munn 1993: 80) differs from (58) in that only the first conjunct (PP) is selected by the matrix verb, but not the second (CP), see (59b, c).

(59) a. *You can depend [$_{PP}$ on my assistant] and [$_{CP}$ that he will be on time].*
b. *You can depend on my assistant.*
c. **You can depend on that he will be on time.*

The coordination of conjuncts of unlike categories poses two problems for a theory that takes conjuncts to be fully symmetric. First, the categorial specification of the coordinated structures in (58a) and (59a) cannot represent the category of both conjuncts. Second, (59a) contradicts the view that a coordinated structure is selected as a whole. Such examples represent further evidence of an asymmetric structure of coordination as proposed in section 2.5.

The second type of asymmetry in coordination concerns conjuncts that differ in their feature specification. All examples illustrating unbalanced constituent coordination are taken from Johannessen (1998) who also gives the original references; see also Camacho (2003). In an unbalanced coordination, the conjuncts have a fixed order. Only one of the conjuncts seems to be selected and the question which one is systematically correlated to the word order facts of the language investigated. In (60) from Bergen Norwegian, repeated from (31), see Johannessen (1998: 8), the pronominal coordination is in the nominative case position, but only the first conjunct is overtly marked for it. The coordinated second pronoun *deg* 'it' carries (unlicensed!) accusative case.

(60) *Det sku' bare mangle at [eg og deg] ikkje* [Bergen Norwegian]
it should only lack that I.NOM and you.ACC should
sku'gjere det.
do it
'Of course, I and you should do it.'

(61a) shows an example of the verb-final language Eastern Mari (Uralic, see Johannessen 1998: 11) where only the second conjunct of a nominal coordination is marked for accusative case. The first conjunct may not be case-marked, see (61b).

(61) a. *Məj Annan [ydəržö den ergəžəm]* [Eastern Mari]
I Annan.GEN daughter.3SG.POSS and son.3SG.POSS.ACC
palem
know.1SG
'I know Anna's daughter and son.'

b. **Məj Annan [ydəržöm den ergəžəm] palem*
I Annan.GEN daughter.3SG.POSS.ACC and son.3SG.POSS.ACC know.1SG

It could be assumed that the case-marker is in a postposition marking the whole coordination in (61a) for accusative. But note that vowels in Eastern Mari are reduced when followed by a clitic (Johannessen 1998: 12). Thus, *ergəžəm* 'son' is derived from *ergeže-m* 'son.3SG-ACC'. If the case marker would be a postposition, the full form [e] on the possessive marker *že* would be expected. This shows that the case-marker in Eastern Mari should be analysed as a clitic on the second conjunct instead.

The following German example shows unbalanced coordination with respect to number (Johannessen 1989: 29). The first nominal conjunct is singular and agrees with the singular copula *war*, whereas the second conjunct is plural.

(62) *Aber links war die Binnenalster und die weißen Lichtreklamen.* [German]
but left was the inner.Alster.SG and the white.PL light.advert.PL
'But to the left were the Inner Alster and the white light adverts.'

Agreement with only one conjunct is also observed in Czech (cf. Johannessen 1998: 8). In (63), only the first conjunct agrees in number with the matrix predicate.

(63) *Půjdu tam [já a ty].* [Czech]
will.go.1SG there I and you
'You and I will go there.'

To summarize, asymmetric coordination exists cross-linguistically. There is a close connection to word order: The selecting predicate must be adjacent to the conjunct it agrees with. The German example in (62) suggests that it cannot be the verb's base-position that licenses unbalanced coordination: The copula in (62) appears in the derived verb second position. If the singular copula is in its final base-position, it cannot license unbalanced coordination with a second plural subject. This is illustrated in (64), which shows that the final copula must agree with the adjacent plural conjunct.

(64) *weil links [die Binnenalster]*$_{SG}$ *und [die weißen Lichtreklamen]*$_{PL}$ [German]
because left the inner.Alster.SG and the white.PL light.advert.PL
waren$_{PL}$*/* war*$_{SG}$
were / was
'because the Inner Alster and the white light adverts were to the left.'

The result of the present discussion is that only the verb-adjacent conjunct seems to be selected with respect to case and agreement features. This shows that – at least in cases of unbalanced coordination – the coordinated structure cannot be symmetric. Thus, only one conjunct appears to be selected, and the other adjoined to it. The selected conjunct satisfies the verb's case requirement and shows agreement, whereas the adjoined conjunct does not. A structure that reflects these facts is proposed in (65) for asymmetric number agreement in German (see also section 2.3). The BP is right-adjoined to the nominal predicate *die Binnenalster* 'the Inner Alster'. As an adjunct, it is free to take any number specification. The structure in (65) does not necessarily carry over to instances of symmetric coordination such as (64), where the feature specification of the coordination is specified by grammatical features of both conjuncts.

(65)

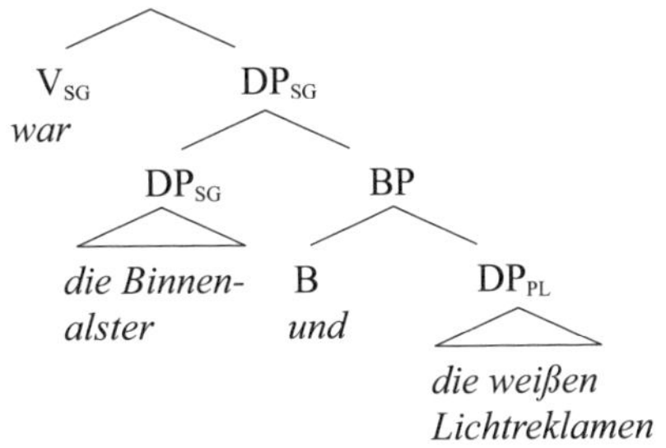

The following section discusses another instance of asymmetric coordination and comes to the same conclusion that the second conjunct may sometimes be adjoined to the matrix clause rather than being symmetrically coordinated with the first conjunct.

4.2. A structural asymmetry

This section discusses so called asymmetric coordination (AC) in German (Höhle 1983, 1990; Heycock and Kroch 1993; Büring and Hartmann 1998; Johnson 2002; Reich 2007). This construction is asymmetric in two respects. First, the *Vorfeld* is overt only in the first conjunct, but it must be empty in the second. The result is a coordination of a verb second and a verb first clause, see (66a) for illustration. (66b, c) show that topicalization is ruled out in the second conjunct. In (66b) the prepositional object is topicalized, in (66c) it is a modified participle.

(66) a. *Auf deinem Teller liegt ein Schnitzel und wartet auf dich.* [German]
on your plate lies a schnitzel and waits for you
'There is a schnitzel on your plate waiting for you.'

b. **Auf deinem Teller liegt ein Schnitzel und* [*auf dich*] *wartet.*
on your plate lies a schnitzel and for you waits

c. **Auf deinem Teller liegt ein Schnitzel und* [*kalt werdend*] *wartet auf dich.*
on your plate lies a schnitzel and cold becoming waits for you

It could be assumed that the fronted PP in (66a) *auf deinem Teller* 'on your plate' is moved across-the-board (ATB) from both conjuncts. However, the following examples (Büring and Hartmann 1998: 178) clearly illustrate that the fronted constituent belongs to the first conjunct only. While ATB-topicalization appears to be possible in symmetric coordination, see (67a), the topicalized object in AC cannot have a trace in the second conjunct where an object pronoun is obligatory, see (67b) (PRT = particle).

(67) a. *In Italien kaufte Hans einen Wagen ~~in Italien~~ und* [German]
in Italy bought Hans a car and
meldete ihn ~~in Italien~~ an.
registered it PRT
'Hans bought a car in Italy and registered it.'

b. *Einen Wagen kaufte Hans ~~einen Wagen~~ und meldete *~~einen Wagen~~ /*
a car bought Hans and registered
ihn sofort an.
it immediately PRT
'Hans bought a car and registered it immediately.'

The second characteristic trait of AC is the empty subject in the second conjunct, which cannot be a trace for syntactic and semantic reasons. An ATB-analysis of the subject would result in a combination of asymmetric topicalization of *einen Wagen* 'a car' in the first conjunct, see (67b), and symmetric ATB-movement of *Hans*. (68) gives a hypothetical structure for (67b), which should be ruled out for various theoretical reasons (but see Johnson 2002).

(68) *[$_{CP}$ [$_{DP}$ einen Wagen] kaufte [Hans [$_{IP}$ ~~Hans einen Wagen~~] und [$_{CP}$ meldete [$_{IP}$ ~~Hans~~ ihn sofort an]]*

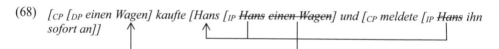

The assumption of an ATB-trace in the second conjunct also faces semantic problems. Büring and Hartmann (1998, section 5) argue that the fronted constituent in AC does not show reconstruction effects, which would be expected in an ATB-derivation. This is shown in (69) (Büring and Hartmann 1998: 188). In the symmetric coordination (69a), the subject is ATB-moved to a shared *Vorfeld* position. Reconstruction allows an interpretation where the indefinite subjects are in the scope of the quantified locative phrases in both conjuncts. This reading is excluded in the AC-construction in (69b), which has the contradictory interpretation that the same crucifix is in every living room and in every stairwell. Hence, the empty subject in the second conjunct is unlikely to be a trace (but see Heycock and Kroch 1993 and Johnson 2002 for different views).

(69) a. *Ein Kruzifix steht in Italien in jedem Wohnzimmer* [German]
a crucifix stands in Italy in every living.room
~~ein Kruzifix~~ und hängt in jedem Treppenhaus ~~ein Kruzifix~~.
and hangs in every stairwell
'In Italy there is a crucifix in every living room and in every stairwell.'

b. *#In Italien steht in jedem Wohnzimmer ein Kruzifix und hängt in*
in Italy stands in every living.room a crucifix and hangs in
jedem Treppenhaus.
every stairwell
'In Italy one and the same crucifix is in every living room and in every stairwell.'

Höhle (1990) assumes that the second conjunct is a semantically unsatisfied predicate which can be coordinated with another predicate. The problem of this analysis is to account for the obligatory verb-initial order in the second conjunct, which is generally expressed by head movement to a higher functional projection of the clause. Büring and Hartmann (1998) assume that the empty subject is a base generated empty variable, which is bound by the overt subject in the first conjunct (see also Reich 2007 who takes the empty subject to be *pro*). As for the structure of AC, Büring and Hartmann (1998) provide strong evidence for an analysis that takes the second conjunct to be a sentential adjunct which flexibly adjoins to the verbal projection line of the matrix clause (see also Reich 2007). This theory accounts for a number of subordination effects observed with AC.

The assumption of asymmetric coordination is also able to account for some alleged cases of CSC-violations, which were discussed in section 4.1. (70) repeats (52c) from section 4.1. Such examples are claimed to violate the CSC since extraction takes place only out of one conjunct.

(70) *How many dogs can a person have ~~how many dogs~~ and still stay sane?*

The assumption of asymmetrically structured coordination is able to account for these cases as well. Assuming that the "second conjunct" is in fact adjoined to the "first conjunct", ATB-extraction is not even expected to occur. The *wh*-phrase is extracted in the matrix clause just as the PPs *auf deinem Teller* 'on your plate' and *in Italien* 'in Italy' are extracted in the examples (66a) and (67a), respectively.

5. Bare Nominal Coordination

In German and English, count nouns may be coordinated without overt determiners. In so-called bare nominal coordination (BNC) the conjuncts look like bare nouns. BNC often occurs in idioms (71), but it is also attested in non-idiomatic clauses (72).

(71) a. *Er riskierte Kopf und Kragen.* [German]
he risked head and collar
'He risked life and limb.'

b. *Hier sagen sich Fuchs und Hase gute Nacht.*
here say REFL fox and hare good night
'This is the middle of nowhere.'

(72) a. *Er hat sich an Daumen und Zeigefinger verletzt.* [German]
he has REFL on thumb and forefinger injured
'He injured his thumb and forefinger.'

a′. **Er hat sich an Daumen verletzt.*
he has REFL on thumb injured

b. *Ich packe Kleid und Pullover ein.*
I pack dress and sweater PRT
'I am packing my dress and sweater.'

b′. **Ich packe Kleid ein.*
I pack dress PRT

c. *He gave me a key, a letter for the landlord, and some instructions. I have to give key and letter to the tenant, and read the instructions myself.*
(Heycock and Zamparelli 2003: 439)

According to Heycock and Zamparelli (2003: 451) BNC has a definite meaning because it can be used anaphorically, see (72c) and (73a) (Heycock and Zamparelli 2003: 448). This sets BNC apart from bare plurals, see (73b).

(73) *We had to set the table for the queen. We arranged one crystal goblet, one silver spoon, two antique gold forks, and two platinum knives.*
a. *Forks and knives were equally dirty.*
b. **Forks were very dirty.*

The BNC in (72) and (73) are semantically equivalent to coordination of definite NPs. This is shown in (74a) where the form *am* is an amalgamation of the preposition *an* and the definite dative determiner *dem*, and (74bc).

(74) a. *Ich habe mich am Daumen und am Zeigefinger verletzt.* [German]
I have REFL on thumb and on forefinger injured
'I injured my thumb and forefinger.'

b. *... I have to give the key and the letter to the tenant.*

c. *The forks and the knives were equally dirty.*

Following Heycock and Zamparelli (2003), the definiteness of BNC is an effect of moving the coordinated nouns to the specifier of DP, which applies in order to identify the empty determiner. Identification may be satisfied by attraction of a feature [+Q]. Since BNC participates in scope interactions (Heycock and Zamparelli 2003: 460), the coordinator *and* is assumed to bear such a [+Q] feature, which triggers raising of the coordination. Their analysis is sketched in (75).

(75) $[_{DP}\ [_{CoordP}\ [_{NP}\ \textit{key}]\ \textit{and}\ [_{NP}\ \textit{letter}]]\ [_{D'}\ D^{e}\ [_{CoordP}\ [_{NP}\ \sout{\textit{key}}]\ \sout{\textit{and}}\ [_{NP}\ \sout{\textit{letter}}]]\ ]]$

The raising analysis predicts that BNC generally behave alike with respect to definiteness. However, the nouns in BNC may also receive indefinite interpretations, at least in German. In (76), it is understood that the addressee should wear some cap and scarf (76a), and that the speaker wants to eat with some knife and fork (76b). Thus, the interpretation of the BNC in these examples is clearly not definite.

(76) a. *Du musst heute Mütze und Schal anziehen.* [German]
you must today cap and scarf wear
'You must wear a cap and scarf today.'

b. *Ich möchte mit Messer und Gabel essen.*
I want with knife and fork eat
'Knife and fork is what I want to eat with.'

The following examples show that one and the same BNC can be anaphoric (quasi definite in Heycock and Zamparelli's terms) (77a), indefinite (77b) or non-referential at all (77c).

(77) a. *Ich habe mir ein hübsches Anwesen gekauft. Haus und Hof* [German]
I have REFL a nice estate bought house and yard
sind von einem großen Garten umgeben.
are by a big garden surrounded
'I bought a nice estate. (The) house and (the) yard are surrounded by a big garden.'

b. *Später wirst du sicher einmal Haus und Hof besitzen.*
later will.2SG you surely once house and yard own
'Later you will certainly own (a) house and (a) yard.'

c. *Er hat Haus und Hof verspielt.*
he has house and yard gambled.away
'He lost it all.'

Examples such as (76) and (77) suggest that the empty determiner is not specified with respect to definiteness (against Heycock and Zamparelli). BNC can be used anaphorically, but it can also introduce a new referent.

6. Ellipsis in coordination

In section 3.2 it was argued that conjuncts always contain a contrastive element, which is marked by a pitch accent. The non-contrastive parts are prosodically deaccented (see section 7) or sometimes even omitted. The phenomenon of leaving out constituents is called *ellipsis*. Since ellipsis is described in detail in Lobke Aelbrecht's article in this handbook, especially VP-ellipsis and Sluicing, the present section is restricted to Gapping and Right Node Raising.

Ellipsis very commonly occurs in coordinated structures since conjuncts often contain non-contrastive, identical parts. It is often assumed that ellipsis targets the phonological form of a linguistic expression. Theories vary as to the question whether the ellipsis contains an intact syntactic structure, or not. In the first case, it is only the phonetic form that is missing; in the second case, the ellipsis is an empty pronominal without internal structure. For an in-depth discussion of these different theories and for bibliographic information, see Aelbrecht (this volume). In another tradition of theories, ellipsis is taken to be a process with a direct impact on phrase structure; see e.g. Chao (1988) and especially Steedman (1996, 2000). The present section adopts a deletion analysis of ellipsis. Section 6.1 discusses left peripheral ellipsis, i.e. ellipsis at the left periphery of the second conjunct. It compares two possible analyses for these coordinated structures, a large and a small conjunct analysis. Section 6.2 presents an exemplary discussion of two kinds of ellipsis: *Gapping* (anaphorical, or forward ellipsis) and *Right Node Raising* (cataphorical, or backward ellipsis).

6.1. Large conjuncts versus small conjuncts

Left peripheral deletion (LPD) is ellipsis of repeated material at the left periphery of the second conjunct. It can involve one (78a) or more (78b) constituents and even subconstituents (78c).

(78) a. *Obama ist erst nach London geflogen und ~~Obama~~ wird dann* [German]
Obama is first to London flown and will then
nach Prag weiter reisen.
to Prague further travel
'Obama first flew to London and will then continue to travel to Prague.'

b. *Obama ist erst nach London geflogen und ~~Obama ist~~ dann nach Prag*
Obama is first to London flown and then to Prague
weiter gereist.
further traveled
'Obama first flew to London and then continued to travel to Prague.'

c. *Obama fliegt im April nach London und ~~Obama fliegt im April nach~~*
Obama flies in.DAT April to London and
Prag.
Prag
'Obama flies to London and Prague in April.'

Instead of analysing (78) as underlyingly bi-sentential (large conjunct hypothesis, see Gleitmann 1965; Wilder 1997), the sentences in (78) could alternatively have a mono-clausal structure with constituent coordination (small conjunct hypothesis). The representations in (79) do not involve ellipsis.

(79) a. *Obama [$_{C'}$ ist erst nach London geflogen] und [$_{C'}$ wird dann nach Prag weiter reisen].* [German]

b. *Obama ist [$_{VP}$ erst nach London geflogen] und [$_{VP}$ dann nach Prag weiter gereist].*

c. *Obama fliegt im April [$_{PP}$ nach [$_{DP}$ London] und [$_{DP}$ Prag]].*

There is no principled way of preferring a large conjunct over a small conjunct analysis. Thus, any coordination can be bi-sentential, even coordination below the word level as illustrated in (80), see Wilder (1997) for a proposal.

(80) *Manon presste Frühlings~~blumen~~ und ~~Manon presste~~ Herbstblumen.* [German]
Manon pressed spring and autumn.flowers
'Manon pressed spring- and autumn flowers.'

Example (80) involves forward ellipsis in the first conjunct, and backwards ellipsis in the second conjunct. Both kinds of ellipsis are independently motivated, see the following subsection. There is one type of data which seems to be incompatible with a large conjunct hypothesis, though. It was claimed in section 4.1 that only one conjunct is selected in asymmetric coordination structures. In the following example (example [62] in section 4.1) a singular and a plural conjunct are coordinated. Recall that the second plural subject does not agree with the singular copula verb *war* 'was'. Hence, it cannot be derived from a sentential conjunct as shown in (81b).

(81) a. *Aber links war die Binnenalster und die weißen Lichtreklamen.* [German]
but left was the inner.alster.SG and the white.PL light.advert.PL
'But to the left were the Inner Alster and the white light adverts.'

b. *... *und links war die weißen Lichtreklame-n*
and left be.3SG.PST the white light.advert-PL

6.2. Gapping and Right Node Raising

Gapping is the name of a coordinated structure with an omitted finite verb in the second conjunct (82a). In addition to the finite verb, further constituents can be elided (82b).

(82) a. *Sarah isst ein Käsebrot und Luise ~~isst~~ Müsli.* [German]
Sarah eats a cheese.bread and Luise muesli
'Sarah eats cheese bread and Luise muesli.'

b. *Sarah isst am liebsten ein Käsebrot und Luise ~~isst am liebsten~~*
Sarah eats at most.favourite a cheese.bread and Luise
Müsli.
muesli
'Sarah likes cheese bread most and Luise muesli.'

Ellipsis in Gapping is not unrestricted. Thus, the elements left behind after ellipsis must be major constituents, that is they must be "either immediately dominated by S_0 or immediately dominated by VP, which is immediately dominated by S_0" (Hankamer 1973, fn 3). The Major Constituent Condition accounts for the ungrammaticality of the examples in (83), taken from Hartmann (2000: 147–148).

(83) a. **John spoke to Fred and Mark ~~spoke to~~ Peter.*

b. **Karl versteckt sich hinter einer Mülltonne und Peter* [German]
Karl hides REFL behind a garbage.can and Peter
~~versteckt sich hinter~~ einem Auto.
a car
intended: 'Karl hides behind a garbage can and Peter behind a car.'

Gapping is sensitive to locality conditions. It is widely acknowledged that the Gapping string may not contain a syntactic barrier (Hankamer 1973; Neijt 1979; Chao 1988; Gardent 1991). Thus (84) (Neijt 1979: 153) shows that Gapping may not violate the Complex NP Constraint.

(84) **John discussed the question of which roses are to be planted and Peter ~~discussed~~ [$_{DP}$ ~~the question~~ (of) which apple trees ~~are to be planted~~].*

Although Gapping is clearly restricted by syntactic conditions, it is often analysed as phonological deletion. Such analyses assume that Gapping is deletion of the phonological matrix of the repeated verb (and optionally further constituents) in the second conjunct (e.g. Jackendoff 1971; Hankamer 1973; Sag 1976; Neijt 1979; van Oirsouw 1987; Hartmann 2000; Repp 2009). The theories of Gapping are manifold and have developed hand in hand with the evolution of linguistic theory. For an excellent literature review, see Repp (2009).

Right Node Raising (RNR) is the name of a coordination containing a shared constituent at the end of the second conjunct. The name of the construction was coined by Postal (1974: 125) and was originally due to the assumption that an element is raised from both conjuncts to the right periphery of the coordinated structure (see also Williams 1990; Larson 1990; Sabbagh 2007 for a recent movement approach to RNR). The movement theory has been challenged by the fact that the assumed derivation contradicts well established conditions of syntactic movement. Hartmann (2000) proposes that RNR contains an ellipsis at the right edge of the first conjunct (85a). In contradistinction to Gapping, RNR does not have to leave major constituent remnants (85b). Moreover, the RNR target does not have to be a constituent itself (85c).

(85) a. *Peter jagte ~~einen schwarzen Elch~~ und Martin schoss einen* [German]
Peter hunted and Martin shot a
schwarzen Elch.
black moose
'Peter hunted and Martin shot a black moose.'

b. *Karl versteckt sich hinter ~~einer Mülltonne~~ und Peter versteckt sich*
Karl hides REFL behind and Peter hides REFL
vor einer Mülltonne.
in.front.of a garbage.can
'Karl hides behind and Peter hides in front of a garbage can.'

c. *Claudia hat uns ~~versprochen, bald zu kommen~~ und Petra hat euch*
Claudia has us and Petra has you.PL
versprochen, bald zu kommen.
promised soon to come
'Claudia has promised us and Petra has promised you to come soon.'

RNR is also not restricted by locality constraints. As (86) (Hartmann 2000: 64) shows, it can cross the border of a coordination, thus violating the CSC (see section 3.3).

(86) *Maria hat ein [$_{DP}$ Zebra und zwei ~~Giraffen] gesehen~~, aber Petra* [German]
Maria has a zebra and two but Petra
hat [$_{DP}$ ein Kamel und fünf Giraffen] gesehen.
has a camel and five giraffes seen
'Maria has seen a zebra and two giraffes, but Petra has seen a camel and five giraffes.'

This strongly suggests that RNR is the result of a phonologically triggered reduction (Hartmann 2000: 55). The influence of prosody on ellipsis in RNR is also manifested in the peculiar prosodic shape of the construction: In German, a strong rising accent on the last word of the first conjunct is obligatory (see Féry and Hartmann 2005). The resulting progredient intonation signals the non-finality of the sentence at the end of the first conjunct. The sentence is completed only at the end of the second conjunct when the shared constituents appear. Féry and Hartmann (2005) argue that this rising accent is the main indication of cataphorical (or backward) ellipsis. Phonologically, it is a contour tone consisting of a low tone (L*), and a high tone (H), which is extraordinarily high, due to its function to demarcate a prosodic phrase boundary (H_P for the phonological phrase, and H_I for the intonational phrase boundary). The prosodic structure of a RNR sentence is illustrated in (87).

(87) L*H L*H$H_P$$H_I$ L*H H*L $L_P$$L_I$ [German]
HANna SUMMte und Erika SANG eine Melodie.
Hanna hummed and Erika sang a melody
'Hanna hummed and Erika sang a melody.'

7. Coordination and information structure

The conjuncts of a coordinated structure are subject to a number of parallelism requirements. In section 3 we observed that conjuncts usually belong to the same syntactic category and satisfy the same degree of semantic saturation. In addition, the conjuncts must have a parallel prosodic structure. This is shown in (88) where the capital letters indicate the positions of the nuclear accents. In (88a), the nuclear accents are associated with the objects of the two predicate conjuncts. In (88b), the nuclear accents are asymmetrically distributed across the conjuncts. The coordination is clearly degraded. It only has a very restricted use which requires a correction of the verb in the second conjunct.

(88) a. *Der Abgeordnete verließ die SITZung und rauchte eine* [German]
the deputy left the meeting and smoked a
ZigaRETte.
cigarette
'The deputy left the meeting and smoked a cigarette.'

b. *#Der Abgeordente verließ die SITZung und RAUCHte eine Zigarette.*
the deputy left the meeting and smoked a cigarette
'The deputy left the meeting and SMOKED a cigarette.'

The same category restriction could be taken to follow from a selection requirement of the coordinator, which presumably has the same subcategorization feature for both conjuncts. However, the parallel distribution of accents cannot be derived from the properties of the coordinator. Instead it is an expression of a higher ordering principle of the clause, which is its information structure (IS). IS determines the level of familiarity of each constituent with respect to the preceding context and partitions a sentence into new, unexpected or unfamiliar parts (the focus) and familiar ones (the background). In German (and English), the focus-background distinction is marked prosodically: The focus constituent is associated with the nuclear accent of the clause whereas the background is usually unaccented.

In coordinated structures, the conjuncts must share the same IS-status as argued for in Hartmann (2000), Lang (2004), Winkler (2005), and Repp (2009), for instance. This IS-identity requirement is responsible for the degraded acceptability of (88b) in contrast to (88a). In (88a), the nuclear accents on the objects indicate focus on the VPs. Hence (88a) could be taken as an answer to the question 'What did the deputy do?', which is the question under discussion (QUD), see Büring (1997). Each of the VPs represents a well-formed answer to the QUD. Thus, the conjuncts have an identical focus semantic value (see Roth 1985, 1992). This is not the case in (88b). The nuclear accent on the verb in the second conjunct can only mark a narrow verb focus. The conjunct is partitioned into a focus (*RAUCHte* 'smoked') and a background (*eine Zigarette* 'a cigarette'). The conjuncts in (88b) express different information structures, which causes the marked grammaticality of the coordinated structure.

A varying IS-status of the conjuncts is only licensed in restricted pragmatic contexts such as the correction of a preceding utterance. (89c) is well-formed in the contexts of the yes/no question in (89a) or the echo question in (89c). Since only one conjunct is corrected, the coordination consists of a focus (*CLAUdia*) and a background conjunct (*Luise*).

(89) a. *Hast du Luise und Charlotte eingeladen?* [German]
have you Luise and Charlotte invited
'Did you invite Luise and Charlotte?'

b. *Du hast Luise und WEN eingeladen?*
you have Luise and whom invited
'You invited Luise and whom?'

c. *Ich habe Luise und CLAUdia eingeladen.*
I have Luise and Claudia invited
'I invited Luise and Claudia.'

IS also has an impact on ellipsis in coordination. In a nutshell, only background constituents can be elided. This is shown in (90). In both constructions, Right Node Raising (90b) and Gapping (90c), the verb is a background constituent due to the preceding *wh*-question in (90a). In (90b) it is deleted in the first and in (90c) in the second conjunct (see Hartmann 2000). A focus constituent cannot be deleted as the ungrammatical RNR example in (91) shows.

(90) a. *Was hast du auf dem Markt gekauft* [German]
('What did you buy at the market?')

b. *Klaus hat eine MeLOne ~~gekauft~~ und ich habe eine PampelMUse gekauft.*
Klaus has a melon and I have a grapefruit bought
'Klaus bought a melon and I bought a grapefruit.'

c. *Klaus hat eine MeLOne gekauft und ich ~~habe~~ eine PampelMUse ~~gekauft~~.*
Klaus has a melon bought and I a grapefruit
'Klaus bought a melon and I a grapefruit.'

(91) a. *Was hast du auf dem Markt gekauft?* [German]
('What did you buy at the market?')

b. * *Klaus kaufte ~~eine PampelMUse~~ und ich kaufte eine PampelMUse.*
Klaus bought and I bought a grapefruit

Many properties of symmetric coordination can be derived from restrictions on the focus denotation of the conjuncts. According to Rooth (1985, 1992) focus denotes a set of pragmatically plausible alternatives to the expression marked for focus. The alternatives have to belong to the same semantic domain. This requirement could be responsible for the same category restriction discussed in section 3. It is trivially fulfilled if the conjuncts have the same syntactic category. It also predicts that coordination of constituents with unlike syntactic categories is well-formed if the conjuncts have the same semantic type. This prediction seems to be borne out as shown in (92) (= [58a]) where a DP is coordinated with an AP. Since both conjuncts are predicates, they are both of type <e,t>.

(92) *He is [$_{DP}$ a republican] and [$_{AP}$ proud of it].*

The semantic restrictions on the conjuncts appear to be stronger than those on focus alternatives, which only have to belong to the same semantic domain. Thus, the alternative set of the *wh*-constituent in *Who did he visit?* is the set of $x \in D_{<e>}$ such that somebody visited x. In addition, focus alternatives may be contextually constrained, as for instance in contexts of selective focus where the alternatives under debate are overtly given. The conjuncts of a coordinated structure have to belong to the same semantic field (see section 3.2). This is not a necessary requirement of focus alternatives.

16. Acknowledgements

This article is dedicated to the memory of Ewald Lang who passed away during the process of accomplishing this book. Ewald Lang contributed considerably to a deeper understanding of the syntax and semantics of coordination. I am grateful that he always shared his ideas on this topic with me. Thanks also go to Tibor Kiss for detailed comments on this article and to Philip Jaggar for assistance with the Hausa examples.

8. References (selected)

Artstein, Ron
2002 Parts of words: Compositional semantics for prosodic constituents. Ph.D. dissertation, Rutgers University.
Averintseva-Klisch, Maria
2008 To the right of the clause: Right dislocation vs. afterthought. In: Cathrine Fabricius-Hansen, and Wiebke Ramm (eds.) *'Subordination' versus 'Coordination' in Sentence and Text. A Cross-linguistic Perspective*, 217–240. Amsterdam: John Benjamins.
Behaghel, Otto
1909 Beziehungen zwischen Umfang und Reihenfolge von Satzgliedern. *Indogermanische Forschungen* 25: 110–142.
Büring, Daniel
1997 The Meaning of Topic and Focus – The 59th Street Bridge Accent. London: Routledge.
Büring, Daniel, and Katharina Hartmann
1998 Asymmetrische Koordination. *Linguistische Berichte* 174: 172–201.
Camacho, José
2003 *The Structure of Coordination*. Dordrecht: Kluwer.
Chao, Wynn
1988 *On Ellipsis*. New York: Garland.
Chomsky, Noam
1957 *Syntactic Structures*. Den Haag: Mouton.
Cooper, William E., and John Robert Ross
1975 World order. In: Robin E. Grossman et al. (eds.), *Papers from the Parasession on Functionalism*, 63–111. Chicago: Chicago Linguistic Society.
Crysmann, Berthold
2006 Coordination. In: Keith Brown (ed.), *Encyclopedia of Language and Linguistics, 2nd Edition*, 183–195. Amsterdam: Elsevier.
de Vos, Mark Andrew
2005 *The syntax of verbal pseudo-coordination in English and Afrikaans*. Utrecht: LOT.
Dik, Simon
1968 *Coordination*. Amsterdam: North Holland.
Féry, Caroline, and Katharina Hartmann
2005 Focus and prosodic structures of German Gapping and Right Node Raising. *The Linguistic Review* 22: 67–114.
Gardent, Claire
1991 Gapping and VP-ellipsis in unification-based grammar. Ph.D. dissertation, University of Edinburgh.
Gazdar, Gerald
1981 Unbounded dependencies and coordinate structures. *Linguistic Inquiry* 12: 155–184.
Gazdar, Gerald, Ewan Klein, Geoffrey Pullum, and Ivan Sag
1985 *Generalized Phrase Structure Grammar*. Oxford: Blackwell.
Gleitmann, Lisa
1965 Coordinating conjunctions in English. *Language* 41: 260–293.
Goldsmith, John
1985 A principled exception to the Coordinate Structure Constraint. *Papers from the Chicago Linguistics Society* 21: 133–143.

Goodall, Grant
1997 *Parallel Structure in Syntax.* Cambridge: Cambridge University Press.
Grice, Paul
1989 Logic and Conversation. In: Paul Grice, *Studies in the Way of Words*, 22–40. Cambridge, Mass: Harvard University Press.
Grover, Claire
1994 Coordination. In: Ronald E. Asher and J. M. Y. Simpson (eds.), *Encyclopedia of Language and Linguistics Vol. 2*, 762–768. Oxford: Pergamon Press.
Hankamer, Jorge
1973 Unacceptable ambiguity. *Linguistic Inquiry* 4: 17–68.
Hartmann, Katharina
2000 *Right Node Raising and Gapping. Interface Conditions on Prosodic Deletion.* Amsterdam: John Benjamins.
Haspelmath, Martin (ed.)
2004 *Coordinating Constructions.* (Typological Studies in Language 58.) Amsterdam: John Benjamins.
Haspelmath, Martin
2007 Coordination. In: Timothy Shopen (ed.), *Language Typology and Syntactic Description, Vol. II: Complex Constructions,* 1–51. 2nd ed. Cambridge: Cambridge University Press.
Haspelmath, Martin
2008 Nominal and verbal conjunction. In: Martin Haspelmath, Matthew S. Dryer, David Gil, and Bernard Comrie (eds.), *The World Atlas of Language Structures Online*, chapter 64. Munich: Max Planck Digital Library. Available online at http://wals.info/feature/64, accessed on 2009-03-26.
Hendriks, Petra
2004 *Either, both* and *neither* in coordinate structure. In: Alice ter Meulen, and Werner Abraham (eds.), *The Composition of Meaning: from Lexeme to Discourse*, 115–138. Amsterdam: John Benjamins.
Heycock, Caroline, and Anthony Kroch
1993 Verb movement and the status of subjects: implications for the theory of licensing. *Groninger Arbeiten zur Germanistischen Linguistik* 36: 75–102.
Heycock, Caroline, and Roberto Zamparelli
2003 Coordinated bare definites. *Linguistic Inquiry* 34: 443–469.
Höhle, Tilman
1983 Subjektlücken in Koordinationen. Unpublished manuscript, University of Tübingen.
Höhle, Tilman
1990 Assumptions about asymmetric coordination in German. In: Joao Mascaró, and Marina Nespor (eds.), *Grammar in Progress. Glow Essays for Henk van Riemsdijk*, 221–235. Dordrecht: Foris.
Jackendoff, Ray
1971 Gapping and related rules. *Linguistic Inquiry* 2: 21–35.
Jackendoff, Ray
1977 *X-Bar Syntax. A Study of Phrase Structure.* Cambridge, Mass.: MIT Press.
Johannessen, Janne B.
1998 *Coordination.* Oxford: Oxford University Press.
Johannessen, Janne B.
2005 The syntax of the correlative adverbs. *Lingua* 115–4: 419–433.
Johnson, Kyle
2002 Restoring exotic coordinations to normalcy. *Linguistic Inquiry* 33: 97–156.
Kayne, Richard
1984 *Connectedness and Binary Branching.* Dordrecht: Foris.

Lakoff, George
1986 Frame semantic control of the coordinate structure constraint. In: Anne Farley, Peter Farley, and Karl Eric McCullogh (eds.), *Papers from the parasession on pragmatics and grammatical theory at the 22nd Regional Meeting, Chicago Linguistics Society.* 152–167.
Lang, Ewald
1984 *The Semantics of Coordination*. Amsterdam: John Benjamins.
Lang, Ewald
2004 Schnittstellen bei der Konnektoren-Beschreibung. In: Hardarik Blühdorn, Eva Breindl, and Ulrich Hermann (eds.), *Brücken schlagen. Grundlagen der Konnektorensemantik,* 45–92. Berlin: Walter de Gruyter.
Larson, Richard
1990 Double objects revisited: reply to Jackendoff. *Linguistic Inquiry* 19: 335–391.
Marsack, C. C.
1975 *Teach yourself Samoan*. London: Hodder and Stoughton.
Mouret, François
2005 La syntaxe des coordinations corrélatives du français. *Langages* 160: 67–92.
Müller, Gereon
1997 Beschränkungen für Binomialbildungen im Deutschen. *Zeitschrift für Sprachwissenschaft* 16: 5–51.
Munn, Alan
1993 Topics in the syntax and semantics of coordinate structures. Ph.D. dissertation, University of Maryland.
Neijt, Anneke
1997 *Gapping*. Dordrecht: Foris.
Newman, Paul
2000 *The Hausa Language*. New Haven and London: Yale University Press.
Olawsky, Knut
1999 *Aspects of Dagbani Grammar.* München: Lincom Europa.
Piot, Mireille
2000 Les conjonctions doubles: Coordination-subordination. *Linguisticae Investigationes* XXIII-1: 45–76.
Posner, Roland
1980 Semantics and pragmatics of sentence connectives and natural language. In: John Searle, Ferenc Kiefer, and Manfred Bierwisch (eds.), *Speech Act Theory and Pragmatics*, 168–203. Dordrecht: Reidel.
Postal, Paul
1974 *On Raising*. Cambridge, Mass.: MIT Press.
Postal, Paul
1998 *Three Investigations of Extraction*. Cambridge, Mass.: MIT Press.
Prinzhorn, Martin, and Viola Schmitt
2010 Discontinuous DP-coordination in German. *Linguistic Variation Yearbook* 10: 161–200.
Progovac, Ljiljana
1998 Structure for coordination. Part I and II. *Glot International* 3/7: 3–6 and 3/8: 3–9.
Reich, Ingo
2007 *„Asymmetrische Koordination" im Deutschen*. Habilitationsschrift, Universität Tübingen.
Repp, Sophie
2009 *Negation in Gapping.* Oxford: Oxford University Press.
Rooth, Mats
1985 Association with focus. Ph.D. dissertation, University of Massachusetts, Amherst.

Rooth, Mats
1992 A theory of focus interpretations. *Natural Language Semantics* 1: 75–116.
Ross, John R.
1967 Constraints on variables in syntax. Ph.D. dissertation, MIT.
Sabbagh, Joseph
2007 Ordering and linearizing rightward movement. *Natural Language and Linguistic Theory* 25: 349–401.
Sag, Ivan
1976 *Deletion and logical form*. Ph.D. dissertation, MIT.
Sag, Ivan, Gerald Gazdar, Thomas Wasow, and Steven Weisler
1985 Coordination and how to distinguish categories. *Natural Language and Linguistic Theory* 3: 117–171.
Schachter, Paul
1977 Constraints on coördination. *Language* 53: 86–103.
Schmerling, Susan
1975 Asymmetric conjunction and rules of conversation. In: Peter Cole, and Jerry L. Morgan (eds.), *Syntax and Semantics 3: Speech Acts*, 221–231. New York: Academic Press.
Stassen, Leon
2000 AND-languages and WITH-languages. *Linguistic Typology* 4.1: 1–54.
Stassen, Leon
2001 Noun phrase coordination. In: Martin Haspelmath, Ekkehard König, Wulf Oesterreicher, and Wolfgang Raible (eds.), *Language Typology and Language Universals. An International Handbook*, 1105–1111. Berlin: Walter de Gruyter.
Stassen, Leon
2008 Noun phrase conjunction. In: Martin Haspelmath, Matthew S. Dryer, David Gil, and Bernard Comrie (eds.), *The World Atlas of Language Structures Online*, chapter 63. Munich: Max Planck Digital Library. Available online at http://wals.info/feature/63, accessed on 2009-04–04.
Steedman, Mark
1990 Gapping as constituent coordination. *Linguistics and Philosophy* 13: 207–264.
Steedman, Mark
1996 *Surface Structure and Interpretation*. Boston, Mass.: MIT Press.
Steedman, Mark
2000 *The Syntactic Process*. Boston, Mass.: MIT Press.
Sternefeld, Wolfgang
2007 *Syntax. Eine morphologisch motivierte generative Beschreibung des Deutschen*. 2 volumes. Tübingen: Stauffenburg.
van Oirsouw, Robert
1987 *The Syntax of Coordination*. London: Croom Helm.
van Oirsouw, Robert
1993 Coordination. In: Joachim Jacobs, Arnim von Stechow, Wolfgang Sternefeld, and Theo Vennemann (eds.), *Syntax – Ein internationals Handbuch zeitgenössischer Forschung*, 748–763. Berlin: Walter de Gruyter.
Wesche, Birgit
1995 *Symmetric Coordination. An Alternative Theory of Phrase Structure*. Tübingen: Niemeyer.
Wilder, Chris
1997 Some properties of ellipsis in coordination, In: Artemis Alexiadou, and Tracy Hall (eds.) *Studies on Universal Grammar and Typological Variation*, 59–107. Amsterdam: John Benjamins.
Williams, Edwin
1978 Across-the-board rule application. *Linguistic Inquiry* 9: 31–43.

Williams, Edwin
1990 The ATB theory of parasitic gaps. *The Linguistic Review* 6: 265–279.
Winkler, Susanne
2005 *Ellipsis and Focus in Generative Grammar.* Berlin: Mouton de Gruyter.

Katharina Hartmann, Wien (Austria)

17. Word Order

Abstract

The focus of this article will be on the behaviour of clause-level constituents, arguments and adverbials in the so-called middle field of German. German's middle field is a good object for studying clausal word order. Here, the number of word order alternatives is very high; nevertheless, there seems to be a basic word order. The main topics are the means to determine this basic order and a discussion of the factors which (presumably) cause abandonment of the basic order.

1. Introduction

How the units of a linguistic expression are linearly ordered is one of the central issues in syntax. In this chapter, only a very small area of this extremely broad topic can be tackled. The chapter is organised as follows. The second section reviews some basic typological patterns of word order of clause-level constituents. It will be shown that less surface-oriented approaches could lead to very different results compared to more surface-oriented typological work, especially because the former are willing to postulate movement rules. Section 3 introduces some basic notions necessary for the following discussions. In Section 4, first different tests for the determination of the basic word order in German are introduced, some of which are applicable to other languages. After having applied these tests to arguments, the question is asked whether they can also be fruitfully applied to adverbials. Next, data are discussed which indicate that certain constituents, though they are maximal projections, form a complex predicate with the verb and therefore show a different behaviour compared to regular sentence constituents. The section about sentence negation in German presents some data which raise doubts about the standard assumption about the position of negation in universal grammar. Section 4 is closed by showing that in German and other languages base order is determined by the thematic roles of the sentence constituents. Section 5 is concerned with non-basic word order inside the core of the clause and the presumed triggers for the reordering of sentence constituents. The remarks on focus scrambling serve to isolate standard reordering.

2. Word order universals in the clausal domain

It was Greenberg (1963) who started the systematic search for word order universals. Based primarily on a sample of 30 languages, he tried to find overall properties of word order regularities, which are interpreted as being founded in the human being's faculty of speech. Hereby, the concept of a basic word order of a given language is central. Basic word orders are formulated with respect to declarative clauses in terms of the position of subject, object, and (finite or non-finite) main verb, and with respect to sentence constituents in terms of the position of noun, adjective, preposition, etc. Thus, for example, languages are classified by whether they are SOV (e.g. Japanese), SVO (e.g. English), VSO (e.g. Welsh), etc. The main groups are SOV- and SVO-languages. A much smaller proportion of languages has VSO-order. Even fewer languages are VOS, OVS, or OSV. Note that if one talks about the basic order of a language, one refers to clauses with full noun phrases. For example, Romance languages are classified as SVO, although the order is SOV if the object is a weak pronominal.

Obviously, this approach presupposes that subjects, objects, nouns, adjectives, etc. can be identified across languages. It is not immediately clear that this should always be possible. For example, it is not evident how to decide in theoretic terms whether in an ergative language the argument with the absolutive or the argument with the ergative case should count as the subject. In practice, this problem is circumvented by taking as the subject the single lexical argument in an intransitive verbal clause, and the more agent-like argument in a transitive clause (Comrie 1981; Dryer 2011a, 2011b). Furthermore, the search for word order universals presupposes that a basic word order can be determined for any language. This is more or less straightforward for languages that have relatively restrictive word orders. However, a basic word order also has to be determined for languages with seemingly free word orders (like Latin, Finnish, Polish, etc.), for languages with varying word orders (like e.g. German with regard to the position of the finite verb in verb-second and verb-final clauses, or like French with regard to the ordering of adjectives and nouns), and for languages showing discontinuous constituents (like Latin).

In practice, this problem is approached by considering the frequency with which a certain order appears in a language and by taking the order with the significantly highest frequency as the basic word order (Dryer 2011e). Using this procedure, Finnish and Polish, for example, are categorised as SVO-languages. However, if only intransitive clauses are considered, Finnish is categorised as SV whereas Polish is said to have no dominant order. Presumably, many linguists would prefer an approach which at least also considers pragmatic unmarkedness or contextual independence as an important sign of basic word order, even though the notion of pragmatic unmarkedness is not trivial.

For example, Dryer (2011c) states that in the Austronesian language Boumaa Fijian, both VSO- and VOS-order are common but neither can be considered dominant and that the context determines which NP is the subject in a clause of the form V NP NP. In contrast, opponents of the frequency approach would try to find out whether there is a preference if no element of the clause is given and the NPs are of equal status in terms of definiteness, genericity, contrastiveness and so on. Yet, proponents of the frequency approach would argue that a pragmatically unmarked order will also be the order with the highest frequency. However, be that as it may, the frequency approach cannot distinguish word orders which reflect grammatical properties from orders which reflect the frequency of communicative circumstances.

As can be expected, the surface-oriented frequency strategy yields results which are quite different to the claims made in more theoretically oriented approaches. For example, Dryer (2011a: section1) states that "in German and in Dutch, the dominant order is SVO in main clauses lacking an auxiliary and SOV in subordinate clauses and clauses containing an auxiliary. Because this results in both orders being common, neither order is considered dominant here." Thus, the two languages are treated as lacking a dominant word order with regard to object and verb. In contrast, as is well known, theories in the tradition of generative syntax assume for German and Dutch that the base position of verbs is clause-final and that in a verb-second clause the finite verb is in a derived position. Thus, these theories classify German and Dutch as unambiguously SOV. Similarly, there are a number of Central Sudanic languages in eastern Africa which are SVO or SOV depending on the featural equipment of the verb. Typologists tend to assume that such languages are neither OV nor VO whereas generative syntacticians are likely to apply the tool of head movement and try to classify these languages as OV. (Similar considerations apply to the typologists' generalisations about the positions of sentence negation. Again, the picture can change significantly if the possibility of verb-movement is taken into account.)

Some still famous universals for word order are formulated by Greenberg (1963). According to his universal 1, in declarative clauses the subject usually precedes the object. By using a much more comprehensive sample than Greenberg's, Dryer (2011a) has confirmed this finding: out of 1228 languages, 1017 languages are classified as SOV, SVO, or VSO (whereby VSO is much rarer than SOV and SVO). For language typology, correlations between orders found in different syntactic subdomains are of great interest. The implicative universals 3 and 4 concern the correlation between the placement of the verb and the placement of adpositions (cf. [1b,c]). VSO-languages usually have prepositions, i.e. VSO ⇒ P NP, while SOV-languages usually have postpositions, i.e. SOV ⇒ NP P. With a bigger sample of languages and based on the broader classification into OV- and VO-languages, Greenberg's findings have been confirmed by more recent studies (Dryer 2011 f.). In (1d–g), some more of Greenberg's implicative universals are listed:

(1) a. In declarative clauses, the subject usually precedes the object (Universal 1).
 b. VSO-languages usually have prepositions, i.e. VSO ⇒ P NP (Universal 3).
 c. SOV-languages usually have postpositions, i.e. SOV ⇒ NP P (Universal 4).
 d. In VSO-languages, adjectives usually follow nouns, i.e. VSO ⇒ NA (Universal 17).

e. In languages with prepositions, a genitive noun phrase usually follows the noun, i.e. P NP ⇒ N GenNP, and in languages with postpositions a genitive noun phrase usually precedes the noun, i.e. NP P ⇒ GenNP N (Universal 2).
f. Languages with clause-initial question particles usually have prepositions, i.e. Q S ⇒ P NP, and languages with clause-final question particles usually have postpositions, i.e. S Q ⇒ NP P (Universal 9).
g. In VSO-languages, an auxiliary precedes the main verb, i.e. VSO ⇒ AUX V, and in SOV-languages, an auxiliary follows the main verb, i.e. SOV ⇒ V AUX (Universal 16).

Interestingly, Dryer (1988) has shown that no correlation exists between the order of object and verb and the orders of adjective and noun, i.e. it is not true that OV-languages tend to be AdjN, while VO-languages tend to be NAdj.

As a rationale for universal 1, it could be assumed that subjects often denote that entity about which the speaker is talking, i.e. that subjects usually are the topic of the clause (Tomlin 1986). For reasons of efficient processing, it is advantageous to present the topic first and then to predicate something about it. A possible rationale for the fact that VSO is much rarer than SOV and SVO could be that O and V should build a constituent, which is not possible in the base order of a VSO-language. Finally, it is tempting to relate the universals in (1b–g) to the head parameter: languages tend to order their heads consistently with respect to their dependents (arguments and modifiers) (Venneman 1973; Lehmann 1978). Obviously, this presupposes that question particles and auxiliaries can reasonably be considered heads, which in fact they are in generative grammar. However, the fact that at least on the surface, there is no correlation between the order of noun and adjective or numeral on the one hand and of verb and object on the other does not fit. Other exceptions to the generalisation can be found. For example, Chinese has both prepositions and postpositions. Although German and Dutch are OV, they have prepositions and complementisers precede their clauses. That German and Dutch are of a mixed type becomes even clearer if one considers arguments and adjuncts of nouns. Arguments and relative clauses follow the noun, whereas adjectives and participle constructions precede it, (2). (Note, however, that the reasoning could be quite different. Dryer 1996 takes the fact that Dutch places the adjective before the noun and the genitive after the noun as evidence that it is not SOV, since SOV-languages do not usually show this distribution of elements inside the NP.) A large sample of languages shows that it is not true that OV-languages are usually RelN. However, it is true that VO-languages are usually NRel, cf. Dryer (2011d).

(2) a. *das Unterstützen der Kandidatin* [German]
the supporting of.the candidate
'The supporting of the candidate'

b. *die von vielen unterstützte Kandidatin*
the by many supported candidate
'The candidate who is supported by many'

c. *die Kandidatin, die von vielen unterstützt wird*
the candidate who by many supported is
'The candidate who is supported by many'

Despite the many exceptions, it is certainly true that languages have a tendency to be consistently prespecificational, i.e. right headed, or consistently postspecificational, i.e. left headed. Different proposals for the interpretation of this tendency have been made. The semantic one assumes that semantically similar relations, here the dependent-head relations, are formally expressed in a similar way. Others point to the fact that unidirectional specification yields uniform trees: the expanding nodes always appear on the same side. Furthermore, there are efforts to explain the correlations in word order with historical developments. For example, it can be argued that adpositions have evolved from verbs and nouns. A very influential processing account has been developed by Hawkins (1998). According to Hawkins, conventions of ordering have emerged out of performance preferences. The parsing window that captures all heads is much smaller when a language is unispecificational. Thus, in such a language the human processor typically can recognise a mother phrase and its immediate constituent daughters much faster than in a language in which heads occur on different sides, cf. e.g. (3):

(3) a. [$_{VP}$ V [$_{PP}$ P NP]] b. [$_{VP}$ [$_{PP}$ NP P] V]
c. [$_{VP}$ V [$_{PP}$ NP P]] d. [$_{VP}$ [$_{PP}$ P NP] V]

3. Some basic notions

3.1. Head movement

Approaches in typology take the most frequent order of given elements occurring in a language as the base order and consider other possible orders as generated independently. In contrast, as is well known, generatively oriented approaches usually assume that the base order of given elements can be determined by different syntactic, semantic or even pragmatic criteria and that other orders are derived from the base order by movement operations or equivalent mechanisms. Consider the V2-clause in (4a) and the verb-final clause in (4b) (PRT abbreviates "particle".). Both clauses can be considered as pragmatically neutral, i.e. they can be uttered in an out-of-the-blue context, and no element is highlighted.

(4) a. *Laut Maria rempelte leider wer im* [German]
according.to Maria jostled unfortunately someone in.the
Hörsaal wen unsanft an.
lecture.hall someone.ACC ruggedly PRT
'According to Maria unfortunately someone ruggedly jostled someone in the lecture hall.'

b. *(Maria sagte,) dass leider wer im Hörsaal wen*
Maria said that unfortunately someone in.the lecture.hall someone.ACC
unsanft anrempelte
ruggedly PRT.jostled
'(Maria said) that unfortunately someone ruggedly jostled someone in the lecture hall.'

There are different reasons to consider the two clauses (4a, b) as being related. First, the constituents preceding the clause-final verbal prefix in (4a) are ordered in the same way as the constituents preceding the verb in (4b). This would be surprising if the two clauses were independent of each other since on the surface, the most central element of the clause, the verb, occupies very different positions. Second, the prefix of the verb *anrempeln*, which in (4a) is separated from the verb, occurs in the same position in the two sentences. Third, in both clauses the sentence adverbial *leider* has scope over the verb. Scope is subject to structural conditions. Thus, in (4a, b) the same structural conditions must be satisfied, which would be implausible if the clauses were generated independently. These three observations immediately become understandable if it is assumed that the two clauses are related by movement of the verb. Since all non-finite verbs in German always occur clause finally, an economical description is achieved if it is assumed that all verb forms are generated clause finally and the finite verb may move to the left leaving a trace (or a copy as in current generative theories) in its original position (Bierwisch 1963). (In the remainder of the text the term "trace" is used. This term is meant to be maximally theory neutral. Different theories employ different mechanisms to make the base position of a moved item part of the syntactic representation.) The observed scope fact can be immediately accounted for because in German scope is usually from left to right, i.e. a scopal element occurring to the left may have scope over a scope sensitive element occurring to the right, and a trace counts for the computation of scope. Another piece of evidence that in German the base position of verbs is clause final is given by the fact that German-learning children who have not fully mastered the finite/non-finite distinction systematically produce utterances of the form *Milch trinken* (milk drink.INF). Children learning the VO-languages English and Swedish, for example, do not produce the corresponding forms systematically.

Given the existence of verb movement, some linguists assume that canonical VSO-languages are underlyingly SVO or SOV. For example, Sproat (1985) argues that in Welsh, the base first generates SVO and afterwards the verb is moved to the left. The reasons for this assumption are that non-finite verbs typically appear in SVO-orders, and that a non-finite verbal projection can be fronted along with its complements, stranding the subject. Similar arguments apply to Irish. Note that Greenberg (1963: 79) already mentions that all VSO-languages sometimes show SVO-order.

3.2. Phrasal movement

As is well known, in addition to head movement generatively oriented syntactic theories also employ movement (or a technical variant thereof) of maximal phrases. In many theories, a distinction is made among phrasal movements between Ā-movement and A-movement. Standardly, Ā-movement concerns movement out of the core of the clause (the TP-domain) to the left periphery (and in some approaches, also movement to the right of the core clause). A-movement concerns movement inside the core of the clause. In (5), this is illustrated by an English passive and an English raising construction:

(5) a. *Today, the introduction will be given by Max.*
  b. *According to Mary, John seems to be nice.*

The majority of generative syntactic analyses have treated the different linearizations of the arguments inside the TP in (semi-)free word order languages as the result of A-movement.

The landing site of movement has to be higher in the structure than its starting point, i.e. the target position of movement has to c-command the base position. (Since inside the TP-domain of a language like German, surface c-command is mirrored by left-right ordering, in a linear syntax this corresponds to the claim that inside TP the moved element has to be to the left of its base position.)

3.3. The basic skeleton of the Germanic clause

All Germanic languages except English are so-called V2-languages. V2-clauses have the form in (6):

(6) XP V_{fin} ... V_{inf}* ...

In (6), XP occupies a position which is often called *Vorfeld* 'prefield'. Standardly, it is assumed that XP gets to its position by Ā-movement. Among the V2-languages, Dutch and German are the only languages for which V_{inf}* in (6) marks the end of the core clause, i.e. they are OV-languages; all elements following V_{inf}* are extraposed. In the other V2-languages, V_{inf}* precedes all objects unless an object is in the *Vorfeld*, i.e. they are VO-languages.

German and Dutch clause topology is characterised by the so-called *Satzklammer*-structure 'sentence bracket structure', i.e. there are two fixed positions, called *Satzklammer* positions. The left one is occupied by the finite verb in a V2-clause or by a complementiser, while the right one is occupied by the (remaining) elements of the verbal group constituting the verbal complex. It is assumed that the filling of the left *Satzklammer* with the finite verb is accomplished by head movement. The two fixed *Satzklammer*-positions subdivide the clause into three main fields. The field between them, called the *Mittelfeld* 'middle field', can contain multiple constituents, which may occur in different orders – the freedom of serialisation being much higher in German than in Dutch. Often, the *Mittelfeld* together with the right *Satzklammer* is referred to as the TP-domain. The *Vorfeld* together with the left *Satzklammer* is referred to as the C-domain. Finally, the region following the right *Satzklammer* is often called the extraposition domain. Many linguists assume that at the very left of the *Mittelfeld* (i.e. of the TP-domain) there is a special position, called the *Wackernagel-Position*, which hosts (clitic) pronouns.

With regard to word order, some rules are called strong (grammatical) rules. In the case at hand, strong rules are, for example, the positioning of the verbs and the filling of the *Vorfeld* in a V2-clause as well as some alleged obligatory instances of extraposition. Under well-defined circumstances, these rules have to apply, otherwise ungrammaticality results. Often, the filling of the *Wackernagel-Position* is also considered to be regulated by a strong rule. Commonly, linguists working on word order in German assume that most of the rules which regulate the ordering of *Mittelfeld* constituents are weak rules, the reason being that the application of these rules is thought to be determined by pragmatic factors with the result that non-application does not result in plain ungrammaticality but in a certain degree of markedness. In Russian, for example, the position of the verb inside a simple clause is also subject to a weak rule, since any permutation of DPs and the verb diverging from the unmarked order, often assumed to be SVO, is in principle possible and the positioning of the verb is contextually and not grammatically determined.

4. Base positions

4.1. TP-internal unmarked word order

In section 2, it was mentioned that often frequency of occurrence is used as a means to determine the unmarked or base order of elements. However, this method is certainly not without problems. For example, in German, the frequency of V2-clauses is much higher than the frequency of verb-final clauses. Nevertheless, there are good reasons to believe that the verb-final order is the base order (section 3.1).

As is well known, German allows a great freedom in the serialisation of constituents inside the *Mittelfeld*. In principle, all clause-level constituents can appear in any order. Thus, the *Mittelfeld* elements of (7) could appear in 23 other variants in addition to the given one, all orders being truth-conditionally equivalent.

(7) *Wahrscheinlich wird Max an Weihnachten eine Opernkarte der* [German]
probably will Max at Christmas an opera.ticket the
Chefin schenken.
boss.DAT.F give
'Max will probably give the boss an opera ticket at Christmas.'

The following questions immediately arise: what are the determinants of the different orders and is one of them to be characterised as more basic than the others? The rules which govern the serialisation in the German *Mittelfeld* have always been believed to be highly complex (Blümel 1914: 530; Kromann 1974; Engel 1972; Lötscher 1981; Abraham 1986; Reis 1987). Some authors assume that the word order is regulated by different principles which can be violated to a certain degree. As a result, the different orders exhibit different degrees of markedness, rather than complete wellformedness or ill-formedness (e.g. Uszkoreit 1986; Jacobs 1988; Müller 1999; Pafel 2009).

For the account of the serialisation of sentence constituents in the TP-domain, two main groups of approaches can be distinguished. The first group does not assume that there is a grammatically encoded basic serialisation of the sentence constituents. Rather, the surface serialisation is directly generated out of the unordered set of the given constituents. It is assumed that the serialisation is solely determined by certain properties of the constituents (e.g. Uszkoreit 1986; Jacobs 1988; Pafel 2009). These properties determine different principles for linearisation, which potentially conflict with each other. (8) lists the ones which have been proposed most often (< stands for "precedes"). Often, the principles are weighted to reflect the strength with which they are supposed to influence the grammaticality status of a given linearisation. Since not all constraints are necessarily satisfiable in a given linguistic structure, grammaticality becomes a gradient notion; the degree of grammaticality of a linguistic structure is computed as the sum of the weights of the constraint violations the structure incurs.

(8) a.	subject < indirect object < direct object	grammatical function
b.	agent < other roles	thematic role
c.	recipient/goal < theme	thematic role
d.	definite DP < indefinite DP	definiteness
e.	pronominal < non-pronominal	pronominal status
f.	topic < non-topic	information structure
g.	non-focal < focal	information structure
h.	given < new	discourse status
i.	animate < non-animate	animacy
j.	non-heavy < heavy	formal complexity
k.	scope bearer < scope taker	scope

Different authors consider different principles to be relevant. For German, for example, Jacobs (1988) assumes the following principles from (8) with decreasing importance: k − (b,e) − (c,d) − g for the order of personal pronouns he assumes: subject < direct object < indirect object. Uszkoreit (1986) adopts e − (b,c) − g − j. According to Pafel (2009), (variants of) a to g are relevant. He uses an additive model, i.e. the different constituents cumulate values according to their properties. (The weighting is as follows: a: SMOD: 15, SUBJECT: 10; b: STRONG PAT: 10, WEAK PAT: 2.5, AGENT: 2.5; d: DEF: 5; e: PRON^{ACC}: 15, PRON: 10; f, g: TOPIC: 15, FOCUS: −7.5. SMOD stands for higher adverbials and modal particles; a STRONG PAT is, for example, the experiencer of a psych verb, while a WEAK PAT is, for example, the recipient of a verb of transfer. A personal or reflexive pronoun which is in the accusative is a PRON^{ACC}; the others are a PRON.)

The approaches of the other group postulate that there exists a grammatically encoded basic word order. Following Daneš (1967), this word order is often considered the unmarked one; any deviation from the basic order which is motivated by non-grammatical conditions is usually considered marked or non-neutral. Occasionally, non-basic TP-internal serialisations are called scrambled orders. In modern syntactic theories, more often than not it is assumed that scrambled orders are the result of a movement operation which leaves a trace in the base position of the moved element, cf. section 4.2. In the literature, many of the factors listed in (8) have been proposed as triggers for scrambling, cf. section 5. Müller (1999) assumes that scrambling is induced by different triggers, which are ordered based on their strength.

The examination of scrambling within modern syntactic theory goes back to Ross (1967). Ross proposed the rule of scrambling as an operation of the stylistic component without semantic effects, i.e. as an operation which does not belong to core syntax. However, in the meantime it has become clear that in many languages, scrambling is not interpretatively vacuous. Different orders may even bring out readings that differ in regard to their truth conditions, cf. (9). Therefore, most researchers now assume that scrambling belongs to core syntax (cf. Abels, this volume).

(9) a. *dass Paul einen Vortrag auf verschiedenen Konferenzen hält* [German]
that Paul a.ACC talk.ACC at different conferences gives

b. *dass Paul auf verschiedenen Konferenzen einen Vortrag hält*
that Paul at different conferences a.ACC talk.ACC gives
'that Paul gives a talk at different conferences'

c. *weil jeden Autor$_1$ sein$_1$ erstes Werk entzückt*
since every author.ACC his first creation delights
'since every author is delighted by his first creation'

d. **weil sein$_1$ erstes Werk jeden Autor$_1$ entzückt*
since his first creation every author.ACC delights

In one of its readings, (9a) claims that there is one talk which is given at different conferences; this reading is absent in (9b). (9c) has a reading according to which the interpretation of the pronoun is dependent on the object; with standard intonation (9d) lacks this reading.

For a long time, individual grammatical judgements built the empirical basis for the study of word order in German and other languages. In recent years though, new different empirical studies have been undertaken: psycholinguistic experiments based on processing time differences (e.g. Poncin 2001), studies of corpus material (e.g. Primus 1994; Heylen 2005; Kempen and Harbusch 2005), and sophisticated methods of collecting grammaticality judgements, taken from multiple subjects and analysed with advanced statistical techniques (Keller 2000). However, it seems fair to say that these empirical studies have not given rise to a drastic change in the data that fundamental studies of word order have to account for (cf. Pafel 2009).

4.2. How to determine base positions of arguments

As stated in the preceding sections, not all linguists assume that there exists a basic word order in so-called free word order languages. Furthermore, when in the literature for a given language the existence of a basic order is assumed, the criteria given as to how to determine this order are not always clear. In this section some phenomena are presented which can be used to detect the basic word order of arguments inside TP in German. Some of these criteria are applicable to other free word order languages.

In German, there exist phrases which do not allow any reordering:

(10) a. *dass wer was lesen will* [German]
that someone something read.INF wants
'that someone wants to read something'

b. **dass was wer lesen will*
that something someone read.INF wants

c. **dass was wen empörte*
that something someone.ACC shocked

d. *dass wen was empörte*
that someone.ACC something shocked
'that something shocked someone'

e. *dass sie wem was gezeigt hat*
that she someone.DAT something shown has
'that she has shown someone something'

f. **dass sie was wem gezeigt hat*
that she something someone.DAT shown has

g. **dass er was wen aussetzte*
that he something.DAT someone.ACC exposed

h. *dass er wen was aussetzte*
that he someone.ACC something.DAT exposed
'that he exposed someone to something'

The data in (10) show that in German, the regularities of serialisation cannot be captured by only employing grammatical functions or case. For a verb like *lesen* the nominative *w*-indefinite has to precede the accusative *w*-indefinite, while for the verb *empören* it is the other way round, (10a–d). For a verb like *zeigen* the accusative *w*-indefinite has to follow the dative *w*-indefinite, but for *aussetzen* it is the other way round, (10e–h).

Other phrases which have to obey strict ordering restrictions are phrases carrying information focus. It was Lenerz (1977) who found out that in German, the positioning of the answering term to a *wh*-question is constrained absolutely. This is illustrated in (12b), which shows that the accusative object of *zeigen* has to follow the dative argument if it carries information focus. The procedure of Lenerz (1977) is somewhat different. He first defines the unmarked order (1977: 26): If two constituents can occur in the order AB as well as in the order BA and BA is only possible under certain testable conditions which do not apply to AB, then AB represents the unmarked order and BA constitutes a marked order. Then, he checks what happens if, for example, either the indirect or the direct object carries information focus. The result is taken to show that indirect object < direct object is the unmarked order. Note, however, that with the same kind of reasoning it could be established that a non-focussed constituent < focussed constituent is the unmarked order. Given observations like the ones in (10e, f), the contrast between (11) and (12) can be interpreted as showing that focussed phrases cannot be preposed.

(11) *Wem hast du das Bild gezeigt?* [German]
whom.DAT have you the painting shown
'Whom have you shown the painting?'

a. *Ich habe dem MilliarDÄR das Bild gezeigt.*
I have the billionaire.DAT the painting shown

b. *Ich habe das Bild dem MilliarDÄR gezeigt.*
I have the painting the billionaire.DAT shown
'I have shown the billionaire the painting.'

(12) *Was hast du dem Milliardär gezeigt?* [German]
what have you the billionaire.DAT shown
'What did you show the billionaire?'

a. *Ich habe dem Milliardär das BILD gezeigt.*
I have the billionaire.DAT the painting shown
'I have shown the billionaire the painting.'

b. *?*Ich habe das BILD dem Milliardär gezeigt.*
I have the painting the billionaire.DAT shown

A prohibition against preposing a direct object carrying information focus has also been shown to hold in Russian and Dutch (Sekerina 1997; Neeleman and Reinhart 1998). Note, however, that so-called contrastive focus may be reordered:

(13) *Man hat das BILD dem Milliardär gezeigt, nicht den DiaMANten.* [German]
they have the picture the billionaire.DAT shown not the diamond.ACC
'They have shown the picture to the billionaire, not the diamond.'

The data in (10)–(12) do not establish whether there is a designated base order of clause-level constituents. The data in (10) could be accounted for by an appeal to the hierarchy of thematic roles, (8b) and (8c), or to the animacy condition, (8i), the relevance of grammatical functions, (8a), being rejected. The remaining conditions of (8) do not discriminate between the argumental phrases in (10). With regard to (11) and (12) it could be claimed that the linearisation of the objects is fine as long as at least one of the conditions (8c) and (g) is satisfied. However, this reasoning presupposes that the animacy condition (8i) does not belong to the list of operative ordering constraints. That this condition can be suspended is also suggested by the following data, about which the animacy condition has nothing to say:

(14) a. *Er wollte jemandem wen zeigen.* [German]
he wanted someone.DAT someone.ACC show.INF
'He wanted to show someone to someone.'

b. *??Er wollte wen jemandem zeigen.*
he wanted someone.ACC someone.DAT show.INF

c. *weil er unvorsichtigerweise das Kind wem aussetzte*
since he carelessly the child someone.DAT exposed
'since he carelessly exposed the child to someone'

d. **weil er unvorsichtigerweise wem das Kind aussetzte*
since he carelessly someone.DAT the child exposed

Another of Lenerz's (1977) claims states that DPs with a non-definite article have to obey the same ordering restrictions as focussed DPs. In the following literature this claim is narrowed down to an ordering restriction on existentially interpreted indefinite DPs (cf. e.g. Lenerz 2001). However, it is doubtful that even the weaker formulation represents a robust generalisation. Lenerz judges an example like the answer in (15a) as deviant, a judgement which is not generally shared. Note that it also seems quite possible to prepose an indefinite direct object which is not given, (15b):

(15) a. *Wem hast du einen Diamanten gezeigt?* [German]
who.DAT have you a diamond.ACC shown
'To whom did you show a diamond?'

Ich habe einen Diamanten einer NACHbarin gezeigt.
I have a diamond.ACC a neighbor.DAT.F shown
'I have shown a neighbour a diamant.'

b. *Damals hat ja doch einer Geheimdokumente Journalisten gezeigt.*
then has PRT PRT someone secret.files.ACC journalists.DAT shown
'In those days, someone showed secret files to journalists.'
(cf. Haider 2010: 179, fn. 47)

The following data are more robust. These data are of special interest since they in fact give evidence for a neutral or basic word order, and, what is more, they signal that if a phrase leaves its base position, it leaves a trace. The first phenomenon concerns focus projection (Höhle 1982). To begin with, it can be observed that a whole utterance can only be in focus if the constituent carrying the nuclear accent (i.e. the element with the highest prominence in the sentence) is left-adjacent to the verb-final position:

(16) *Was ist passiert?* [German]
what is happened
'What has happened?'

a. *Gerade hat Maria dem Milliardär das BILD gezeigt.*
just.now has Maria the billionaire.DAT the painting.ACC shown
'Just now Maria has shown the billionaire the painting.'

b. *#Gerade hat Maria dem MilliarDÄR das Bild gezeigt.*

c. *#Gerade hat Maria das Bild dem MilliarDÄR gezeigt.*

d. *#Gerade hat Maria das BILD dem Milliardär gezeigt.*

In (16b, d), the stress falls on a constituent which is not adjacent to the verb, and the focus does not project. The crucial observation is that in (16c), in which the arguments of a regular ditransitive verb occur in the order ACC < DAT, the focus does not project either although the main accent falls on a verb-adjacent constituent. This suggests that for the focus on an element to project it is not enough that the element is phonetically adjacent to the verb-final position on the surface, but it must also be adjacent in the base serialisation (e.g. Haider and Rosengren 2003). Thus, if it is assumed that scrambling leaves a trace, the difference between (16a, c) is explained. The element which is, in fact, adjacent to the main verb in (16c) is not the accented dative but the trace of the scrambled accusative object.

Given this reasoning, (16a, c) shows that the base position of the accusative object of a verb like *zeigen* is structurally adjacent to the main verb, but not the base position of the dative object. Hence, with the help of the criterion of focus projection it can be determined whether the base position of an argument is adjacent to the base position of the verbal elements. In (17) and (18), this criterion is applied to some other verbs and their arguments (Haider 1993):

(17) a. *Es freut mich, dass Linguisten BalLADen interpretieren.* [German]
it pleases me that linguists.NOM ballads.ACC interpret (wide focus)

b. *Es freut mich, dass Balladen LinguISTen interpretieren.*
it pleases me that ballads.ACC linguists.NOM interpret (narrow focus)
'It pleases me that linguists interpret ballads.'

c. *Es freut mich, dass Linguisten BalLADen interessieren.*
it pleases me that linguists.ACC ballads.NOM interest (wide focus)

d. *Es freut mich, dass Balladen LinguISTen interessieren.*
it pleases me that ballads.NOM linguists.ACC interest (narrow focus)
'It pleases me that ballads interest linguists.'

(18) a. *Max vertraute einem Kind eine wichtige AUFgabe an.* [German]
Max entrusted a child.DAT an important task.ACC PRT (wide focus)

b. *Max vertraute eine wichtige Aufgabe einem KIND an.*
Max entrusted an important task.ACC a child.DAT PRT (narrow focus)
'Max entrusted a child with an important task.'

c. *Paul setzte einen Schüler einer großen GeFAHR aus.*
Paul exposed a pupil.ACC a great danger.DAT PRT (wide focus)
'Paul exposed a pupil to great danger.'

The following classification of verbs regarding their final argument in the basic order can be arrived at with the help of focus projection, cf. Haider (1993):

(19) a. NOM < ACC: *lesen, bedauern, interpretieren*
read regret interpret

b. ACC < NOM: *ängstigen, beeindrucken, interessieren*
frighten impress interest

c. NOM < DAT: *helfen, gratulieren, widersprechen*
help congratulate contradict

d. DAT < NOM: *einfallen, fehlen, imponieren*
occur.to, miss impress

e. NOM < DAT < ACC: *anvertrauen, schicken, verbieten, zeigen*
entrust send forbid show

f. NOM < ACC < DAT: *aussetzen, unterziehen, unterordnen*
expose.to subject.to subordinate

g. NOM < ACC < PP: *stellen, mitnehmen, schicken*
put take send

In the literature, just intuition as to which serialisation would be most appropriate at the beginning of a discourse is sometimes used as the means to determine the neutral order of arguments in a given language, cf. e.g. Dyakonova (2009) for Russian. Dyakonova (2009) considers the Russian equivalents of *read*, *occur to*, *show*, and *put* and arrives at the same serialisations of the arguments as in (19a, d, e, g).

The next phenomenon which gives evidence for base positions and for the existence of traces in the case of scrambling concerns scope effects. If one considers the examples in (20), one notices that (20a, c) have only one reading – the scope of the operators corresponds to their surface order – whereas (20b, d), at least for the majority of speakers, have two readings – the scope of the operators may correspond to their surface order or may be reversed (Frey 1993):

(20) *Peter denkt, DASS* [German]
'Peter thinks that'

a. *mindestens einer fast jeden Artikel gelesen hat*
at.least one nearly every article.ACC read has (only: ∃∀)
'that at least one has read nearly every article'

b. *mindestens einen Artikel fast jeder gelesen hat.*
at.least one article.ACC nearly everyone read has (∃∀ or ∀∃)
'that nearly everyone has read at least one article'

c. *man mindestens einem Experten fast jedes Bild zeigte.*
they at.least one expert.DAT nearly every picture showed (only: ∃∀)
'they showed at least one expert nearly every picture.'

d. *man mindestens ein Bild fast jedem Experten zeigte.*
they at.least one picture nearly every expert.DAT showed (∃∀ or ∀∃)
'they showed nearly every expert at least one picture.'

It is easy to explain these observations if again it is assumed that in (20a, c), the constituents occur in their base positions, whereas in (20b, d) scrambling has occurred. The fact that in (20b, d) we not only get the scope options corresponding to the surface order, but also the scope options of (20a, c), yields evidence that a reflex of a phrase's base position is present if the phrase is permuted to another position, i.e. that a trace is generated in its base position. It is a widely held assumption that an element α can only have scope over an element β if α c-commands β. If it is assumed that the direct objects in (20b, d) are base generated in the c-command domain (to the right) of the nominative and the dative argument, respectively, and that scrambling leaves a trace, the condition for the ∀∃-readings is fulfilled since the universally quantified DP c-commands the trace of the existentially quantified DP, cf. e.g. (20) d′:

(20) d′ *dass man mindestens ein Bild$_1$ fast jedem Experten t_1 zeigte*
that they at.least one picture nearly every.DAT expert.DAT showed

The alternative readings of (20b, d), i.e. the ∃∀-readings, are possible because on the surface the scrambled existentially quantified DP c-commands the universally quantified DP. Sentences like (20a, c), in which all quantified phrases are sitting in their base positions, only have the reading corresponding to the surface order of these phrases, since there are no traces which could give rise to an alternative reading.

The scope criterion confirms the results obtained by the other tests. For example, according to (19b), *interessieren* induces the base serialisation EXP < THEME/CAUSE, i.e. ACC < NOM. Thus, the order ACC < NOM is expected to yield non-ambiguity, and the order NOM < ACC to yield ambiguity. (21a, b) show that the expectations are fulfilled.

(21) a. *DASS mindestens einen Linguisten fast jeder Vortrag interessierte* [German]
that at.least one.ACC linguist.ACC nearly every talk interested (only: ∃∀)
'that nearly every talk interests at least one linguist'

b. *DASS [mindestens ein Vortrag]$_1$ fast jeden Linguisten t$_1$ interessierte* (∃∀ or ∀∃)
that at.least one talk nearly every.ACC linguist.ACC interested
'that at least one talk interests nearly every linguist'

Principle-C effects may also be used to determine base orders. According to Principle-C a non-pronominal DP (R-expression) must not be coindexed with a c-commanding element, cf. (22b, d):

(22) a. *weil Peters$_1$ Mutter ihm$_1$ sehr geholfen hat* [German]
because Peter's mother.NOM him a.lot helped has
'because Peter's mother helped him a lot'

b. **weil er$_1$ Peters$_1$ Mutter sehr geholfen hat*
because he Peter's mother.DAT a.lot helped has

c. *Sąsiad Janka$_1$ powiedział mu$_1$, że* [Polish]
neighbour Janka.GEN told.3SG.M him.DAT that
'Janka's neighbour told him that …'

d. **On$_1$ powiedział sąsiadowi Janka$_1$, że*
he told neighbour John's that
(Willim 1998: 41)

That Principle-C effects are not just due to a serialisation constraint disallowing a pronoun to precede a coreferential phrase is shown in (23):

(23) a. *[Peters$_1$ Mutter]$_2$ hat t$_2$ ihm$_1$ sehr geholfen.* [German]
Peter's mother has him.DAT a.lot helped
'Peter's mother has helped him a lot.'

b. *[*Peters$_1$ Mutter*]$_2$ *hat er$_1$ t$_2$ sehr geholfen.*
Peter's mother.DAT has he a.lot helped

(23b) contains a Principle-C violation. This can be accounted for under the assumption that a trace marks the base position of the moved constituent and that a coindexed item in the *Mittelfeld* may induce a Principle-C violation of an element in the *Vorfeld* via the trace (i.e., via reconstruction). In (23b), the trace is in the c-command domain of the *Mittelfeld* element coindexed with the R-expression. In contrast, in (23a), the trace of the *Vorfeld* constituent is not in the c-command domain of the pronoun and therefore no Principle-C violation arises.

It follows that Principle-C effects can be used to determine base positions. For example, with Principle-C it can be confirmed that psych verbs induce a different base order than transitive verbs, cf. (19a, b, d):

(24) a. [*Der Chef von Peter*$_1$]$_2$ *hat* t_2 *ihn*$_1$ *beleidigt.* [German]
the boss of Peter has him.ACC insulted
'The boss of Peter has insulted him.'

b. *[*Die Besprechung von Peters*$_1$ *Buch*]$_2$ *hat ihn*$_1$ t_2 *entsetzt.*
the review of Peter's book has him.ACC horrified

c. *[*Die Inszenierung von Walsers*$_1$ *Stück*]$_2$ *hat ihm*$_1$ t_2 *imponiert.*
the production of Walser's play has him.DAT impressed

Note that we also find Principle-C effects with TP-internal movement, i.e. with scrambling. Thus, for Principle-C scrambling is reconstructed:

(25) a. **Ich wollte* [*die Bilder von Maria*$_1$]$_2$ *ihr*$_1$ t_2 *schon immer* [German]
I wanted the picture of Maria her.DAT PRT always
zeigen.
show

b. **∅ Dałam stare zdjęcia Marii*$_1$]$_2$ *jej*$_1$ t_2 [Polish]
I gave.F old pictures.ACC Mary.GEN her.DAT
Intended: 'I gave Mary old pictures of her's.'
(Willim 1998: 83)

Some syntacticians would take this observation as an indication that scrambling is an instance of Ā-movement (Frey 1993, however, argues for a different interpretation). Yet, there are many phenomena which suggest considering scrambling as A-movement. For example, to check the condition operator binding, scrambling is not reconstructed. Often, this important difference between Principle-C and operator binding regarding the reconstruction of scrambling is not appreciated.

(26) **Ich habe seine*$_1$ *Bilder jedem Kollegen*$_1$ *zurückgegeben.* [German]
I have his pictures every colleague back.give

For the debate on whether scrambling is A- or Ā-movement, see Abels (this volume).

At this point, it should be noted that the data with focus projection, the scope data and the Principle-C effects cast doubt on approaches which assume that scrambling orders are base generated (e.g. Neeleman 1994b; Bayer and Kornfilt 1994; Fanselow 2001).

An important result of applying these tests has to be pointed out. As for example the scope test and the Principle-C test show, there are verbs which induce different base orders depending on the semantics of the arguments they take (see also Lenerz 1977).

(27) a. *DASS mindestens ein Medikament fast jedem Asthmatiker helfen kann* [German]
that at.least one medicine nearly every asthmatic.DAT help.INF can (∃∀ or ∀∃)
'that at least one medicine can help nearly every asthmatic'

b. *DASS mindestens ein Arzt fast jedem Asthmatiker helfen kann.*
that at.least one doctor nearly every asthmatic help.INF can (∃∀)
'that at least one doctor can help nearly every asthmatic'

c. **Peters₁ neues Medikament wird ihm₁ helfen.*
Peter's new medicine will him.DAT help.INF

d. *Peters₁ neue Chefin wird ihm₁ helfen.*
Peter's new boss.F will him.DAT help.INF
'Peter's new boss will help him.'

According to (27a), which has an inanimate subject, *helfen* belongs to the class (19d), while according to (27b), which has an animate subject, it belongs to (19c). Müller (1999) considers it as highly implausible that a predicate should induce different base orders depending on the animacy status of its indirect object. Note, however, that it might be assumed that an item like *helfen* has two lexical entries, which assign different thematic roles and different base positions to their subjects.

As noted, many linguists take the unmarked order of the arguments as their base order. However, there is an influential exception. Müller (1999) argues that the base order of arguments is always subject < direct object < indirect object notwithstanding the fact that for the majority of ditransitive verbs the unmarked order is indirect object < direct object. Müller's main argument concerns binding data with a reciprocal:

(28) a. *dass man die Gäste₁ einander₁ vorstellte* [German]
that they the guests.ACC each.other.DAT introduced
'that they introduced the guests to each other'

b. **dass man den Gästen₁ einander₁ vorstellte*
that they the guests.DAT each.other.ACC introduced

However, the scope test, for example, would yield the base order indirect object < direct object for a verb like *vorstellen*:

(29) a. *Man HAT mindestens einem Professor fast jeden Doktoranden vorgestellt.* [German]
they have at.least one professor.DAT nearly every doctoral.candidate.ACC introduced (only: ∃∀)
'They have introduced nearly every doctoral candidate to at least one professor.'

b. *Man HAT mindestens einen Doktoranden fast jedem Professor vorgestellt.*
they have at.least one doctoral.candidate.ACC nearly every professor.DAT introduced (∃∀ or ∀∃)
'They have introduced at least one doctoral candidate to nearly every professor.'

Since scrambling gives rise to new binding possibilities, (28a) is expected under the assumption of the base order indirect object < direct object, too. However, the ungrammaticality of (28b) is unexplained and must be attributed to an idiosyncratic property of the reciprocal forbidding its being bound by a dative co-argument.

4.3. Do adverbial phrases have base positions?

The positions of adverbial phrases play a crucial role in syntactic theory insofar as, starting with Emonds (1978), adverbials have often been taken as diagnostics for movement of arguments (and of verbs, cf. e.g. Pollock 1989). Nowadays, there are two extreme positions besides the standard assumption: (i) There are authors who reject any specific base positions for adverbials, cf. e.g. Neeleman and Reinhart (1998) and Haider (2010) with regard to Dutch and German. If there are ordering restrictions or preferences with regard to adverbials, they are assumed to be solely due to semantic scope and do not have to be accounted for in syntax. (ii) An author like Cinque (1999) assumes different base positions for 30 different adverbial types. (iii) In between the two extremes is the standard position (e.g. Jackendoff 1972; Kayne 1994; Karimi 2003), according to which all event-related adverbials (VP-adverbials) are base generated immediately above the VP (or rather above vP, which nowadays is assumed to be the projection directly above VP and in whose specifier position the verb's external argument is base generated). Proposition-related adverbials are base generated higher (S-adverbials), it often being assumed that they attach to TP. The positions (i)–(iii) of course each have several variants.

The following examples suggest that finer distinctions are needed than assumed in the first and third approaches.

(30) a. *Maria hat einige Bücher / was schnell weggeräumt.* [German]
Maria has several books something fast put.away
'Maria put away several books / something quickly.'

b. *Maria hat schnell einige Bücher / was weggeräumt.*
Maria has fast several books something put.away
'Maria quickly put away several books / something.'

The two sentences have distinct meanings. In (30a), the adverbial specifies that the manner in which the action was carried out was fast. In (30b), the adverbial relates to the whole event. It specifies the time span of the whole event or the time span between its beginning and some previous reference point as being short. Since it is very hard to see how the meaning difference between (30a, b) could be related to scrambling of the object in (30a), the two readings give evidence for different positions of the adverbials in (30a, b). Note that this simple observation has the far-reaching consequence that the fundamental assumption of generative grammar that the vP is a pure domain of theta-assignment does not seem to be right. The manner adverbial in (30) needs to be base generated between the object and the verb. Note furthermore that for the "adverbials can be base generated everywhere" theory, (30) is not easy to explain since it is not clear how different scope relations between the object and the adverbial in the two sentences could be made responsible for the different readings.

In this chapter, it is not possible to do any justice to the highly complex phenomenon of adverbials and to the vast literature on the topic. However, since it is impossible to avoid taking up a certain position anyway, following Frey and Pittner (1999) and Frey (2003), just a bit more German data will be presented which suggest that different adverbial classes in fact may have different base positions, thereby casting further doubt on the correctness of approach (i). These data also suggest that the standard account (iii) provides too few positions for adverbials. However, the observations in Frey and Pittner (1999) and Frey (2003) only give evidence for five different base positions, in sharp contrast to approaches like in (ii); that is, the data suggest that there are five syntactic zones which are hierarchically ordered, but within each zone semantic scope restrictions are responsible for any possible ordering restrictions between the adverbials base generated in that zone. Thus, with regard to base positions only five types of adverbial classes are distinguished:

(31) a. Sentence adverbials like *glücklicherweise* 'fortunately', *anscheinend* 'apparently', vermutlich 'presumably':
The base position of a sentence adverbial c-commands the finite verbal form, the base positions of the arguments and the base positions of the remaining adverbial classes.

b. Frame and domain adverbials (e.g. reference time related temporals):
The base position of a frame or of a domain adverbial c-commands the base positions of the arguments and the base positions of the remaining adverbial classes except for sentence adverbials.

c. Event-external adverbials (e.g. causals):
The base position of an event-external adverbial c-commands the base position of the highest ranked argument.

d. Event-internal adverbials (e.g. event-related temporals or locatives, instrumentals):
The base position of an event-internal adverbial is minimally c-commanded by the base position of the highest ranked argument.

e. Process-related adverbials (e.g. manner adverbials):
The base position of a process-related adverbial minimally c-commands the base position of the main predicate.

In the following, some of the data will be presented by which the claims in (31) can be verified. Besides the phenomena which are introduced above for the determination of base positions, Diesing's (1992) theory provides another means. Diesing (1992) argues that scrambled indefinite DPs cannot get non-specific existential interpretation, (32b, c). However (32a) suggests that it is more appropriate to say that existential indefinites must remain vP-internal.

(32) a. *weil heute wer Gedichte$_1$ den Kollegen t_1* [German]
since today someone poems the colleagues.DAT
vorgetragen hat
recited has (existential)
'since someone has recited poems to the colleagues today'

b. **weil heute Gedichte$_1$ wer den Kollegen t_1 vorgetragen*
since today poems someone the colleagues.DAT recited
hat
has (existential)

c. *weil Gedichte$_1$ ein Kollege t_1 aufbewahrt*
since poems a colleague stores (generic)
'since a colleague stores poems'

Let us see how Diesing's observation can be used to determine base positions of adverbials. Consider (33). If an indefinite object occurs to the left of a causal adverbial, the existential reading is cancelled, (33b). Note that there is no scopal interaction between the adverbial and the argument. However, the existential reading is still possible if the object occurs to the left of an event-related temporal, (33c). Furthermore, if an indefinite subject occurs to the left of a causal adverbial, it can only be interpreted generically, (33d); to the left of an event-related temporal, it can have an existential reading, (33e).

(33) a. *Der Verfassungsschutz hat wegen Pauls Hinweises im* [German]
the constitution.protection has due.to Paul's tip in.the
letzten Jahr Linguisten einer Überprüfung unterzogen.
last year linguists.ACC an examination submitted

b. *Der Verfassungsschutz hat Linguisten$_1$ wegen Pauls Hinweises*
the constitution.protection has linguists.ACC due.to Paul's tip
im letzten Jahr t_1 einer Überprüfung unterzogen.
in.the last year an examination submitted (only generic)

c. *Der Verfassungsschutz hat wegen Pauls Hinweises Linguisten$_1$*
the constitution.protection has due.to Paul's tip linguists.ACC
im letzten Jahr t_1 einer Überprüfung unterzogen.
in.the last year an examination submitted
(existential reading possible)
'Last year the constitutional protection agency checked up on linguists due to Paul's tip.'

d. *Laut Verfassungsschutz haben Linguisten$_1$ wegen der*
according.to constitution.protection have linguists.NOM because.of the
Sparmaßnahmen t_1 die Arbeit eingestellt.
austerity.measures the work stopped (only generic)
'According to the constitutional protection agency, linguists have stopped working because of the austerity measures.'

e. *Laut Verfassungsschutz haben Linguisten im letzten*
according.to constitution.protection have linguists.NOM in.the last
Jahr die Arbeit eingestellt.
year the work stopped (existential reading possible)
'According to the constitution protection agency, linguists stopped working last year.'

Thus, data like that in (33) give some evidence for (31c, d). That a causal is base generated higher than the highest argument is confirmed by (34): the lack of a Principle-C effect shows that the base position of the subject pronoun is below the base position of the causal adverbial.

(34) *Wegen Peters$_1$ hervorragenden Beziehungen hat er$_1$ gute* [German]
because.of Peter's excellent connections has he good
Chancen auf den Auftrag.
chances at the job
'Because of Peter's excellent connections, he has good shots at the job.'

The following examples contain a quantified frame adverbial and a quantified causal adverbial. The adverbial *in mindestens einem Land* gives the frame to which the truth claim of the assertion is restricted (Maienborn 2001). The order frame < causal is non-ambiguous; the order causal < frame is ambiguous. Thus, the judgements indicate that the base position of a frame adverbial is higher than the base position of a causal adverbial.

(35) a. *Sie IST in mindestens einem Land wegen fast jedem Lied* [German]
she is in at.least one country for nearly every song
weltberühmt.
world.famous (only: $\exists\forall$)
'In at least one country she is world-famous for nearly every song.'

b. *Sie IST wegen mindestens einem Lied in fast jedem Land*
she is for at.least one song in nearly every country
weltberühmt.
world.famous ($\exists\forall$ or $\forall\exists$)
'In nearly every country she is world-famous for at least one song.'

According to (31), semantics orders adverbial types belonging to the same class. If semantics allows, adverbials of the same class can be freely ordered. Thus, the ungrammaticality of (36b) suggests that causals do not belong to the class of frames.

(36) a. *weil wo wegen was ein Kollege weltberühmt ist* [German]
since somewhere for something a colleague world.famous is
'since somewhere a colleague is world-famous for something'

b. **weil wegen was wo ein Kollege weltberühmt ist*
since for something somewhere a colleague world.famous is

In sum, the data in (35) and (36) give some justification for a part of the claim in (31b).

That temporal and locative frame adverbials on the one hand, (37a, d), and event-related temporal and locatives on the other, (37b, c, e), indeed have different base positions can, for example, be shown by Principle-C effects:

(37) a. [*An Peters*$_1$ *18. Geburtstag*]$_2$ *hatte* t_2 *er*$_1$ *bereits zwei Romane geschrieben.* [German]
on Peter's 18th birthday had he already two novels written
'On Peter's 18th birthday he had already written two novels.'

b. *[*An Peters*$_1$ *18. Geburtstag*]$_2$ *hat er*$_1$ t_2 *Maria umarmt.*
on Peter's 18th birthday has he Mary embraced

c. *An Peters*$_1$ *18. Geburtstag hat Maria ihn*$_1$ *umarmt.*
on Peter's 18th birthday has Maria him embraced
'On Peter's 18th birthday Maria has embraced him.'

d. [*In Peters*$_1$ *Firma*]$_2$ *ist* t_2 *er*$_1$ *der Schwarm aller reiferen Damen.*
in Peter's company is he the heartthrob all mature women.GEN
'In Peter's company he is the heartthrob of all mature women.'

e. *[*In Peters*$_1$ *Büro*]$_2$ *las er*$_1$ t_2 *den Artikel durch.*
in Peter's office read he the article through

The next examples confirm parts of (31d). Event-related locatives are base generated below the highest argument (cf. also [37e]).

(38) a. *weil wer wo das Buch verloren hat* [German]
since someone somewhere the book lost has
'since someone has lost the book somewhere'

b. **weil wo wer das Buch verloren hat*
since somewhere someone the book lost has

c. *Peter hat heute im Hörsaal wen beleidigt.*
Peter has today in.the lecture.hall someone offended
'Today Peter offended someone in the lecture hall.'

d. *??Peter hat heute wen im Hörsaal beleidigt.*
Peter has today someone in.the lecture.hall offended

Data like the following are taken in Frey and Pittner (1999) and Frey (2003) as evidence that members of one and the same class in (31) are syntactically not ordered with respect to each other. In (39), this is illustrated with a quantified event-related locative and a quantified instrumental. Both orders of these adverbials yield an unambiguous reading showing that no trace is generated by syntactic movement.

(39) a. *Er HAT mit mindestens einer Maschine in fast jedem Haus* [German]
he has with at.least one machine in almost every house
gearbeitet.
worked (only: ∃∀)

b. *Er HAT in fast jedem Haus mit mindestens einer Maschine*
he has in almost every house with at.least one machine
gearbeitet.
worked (only: ∀∃)
'He has worked with at least one machine in almost every house.'

Let us now consider sentence adverbials. The following example gives a partial justification of (31a).

(40) a. [*In Marias$_1$ Firma*]$_2$ *sind anscheinend* t_2 *ihr$_1$* [German]
in Maria's company has apparently her.DAT
Machtbefugnisse entzogen worden.
authority.NOM deprived.INF been
'In Maria's company they apparently deprived her of authority.'

b. *[*In Marias$_1$ Firma*]$_2$ *sind ihr$_1$ anscheinend* t_2 *Machtbefugnisse*
in Maria's company are her apparently authority
entzogen worden.
deprived.INF been

Only if in (40) the base position of the frame adverbial *in Marias Firma* is below the base position of the sentence adverbial *anscheinend* do the indicated grammaticality judgements with regard to Principle-C follow.

Let us move next to manner adverbials. The standard position assumes that manner adverbials are positioned higher than the arguments. However, (30a) suggests that manner adverbials are base generated right above the verbal complex. This is expressed in (31e) and is confirmed by (41):

(41) a. *Er HAT mindestens eine Kollegin auf fast jede Art* [German]
he has at.least one colleague.F in nearly every way
und Weise umworben
and manner courted (only: ∃∀)
'He has courted at least one colleague in nearly every way.'

b. *Er HAT auf mindestens eine Art und Weise fast jede Kollegin*
he ha in at.least one way and manner nearly every colleague.F
umworben
courted (∃∀ or ∀∃)
'He has courted nearly every colleague in at least one way.'

The last type of adverbial to be considered is frequency adverbials. Interestingly what are called frequency adverbials do not seem to constitute their own adverbial type belonging to one of the classes in (31). Rather, frequency adverbials belong to different adverbial types. In the following German examples, the frequency adverbials occur in three different positions. All examples have only the reading corresponding to the surface order:

(42) a. *DASS Max fast alle Anwesenden oft beleidigte* [German]
that Max nearly all attendees often offended (unambiguous)
'that Max often offended nearly all attendees'

b. *DASS Max oft fast alle Anwesenden beleidigte*
that Max often nearly all attendees offended (unambiguous)
'that Max often offended nearly all attendees'

c. *DASS oft mindestens ein Teilnehmer protestierte*
that often at.least one participant protested (unambiguous)
'that at least one participant protested often'

This demonstrates that frequency adverbials may be base generated next to the predicate, between subject and object, or higher than the arguments. Note that the non-ambiguity of the examples in (42) also shows that the parser prefers to assign base structures to the input string if possible instead of assigning scrambling structures. The different possible positions of frequency adverbials correspond to different semantic domains of the base-generated items. Therefore, it makes perfect sense to have several frequency adverbials in one clause:

(43) *weil häufig wer mehrmals diese Schraube zu oft* [German]
since frequently someone several.times this screw too often
anzog
tightened
'since someone tightened this screw too often several times on several occasions'

4.4. Integration phenomena at the right periphery of the *Mittelfeld*: Complex predicate formation

As is well known, German is rather tolerant in allowing scrambling of the sentence constituents. However, in German there are also certain constituents that resist scrambling:

(44) a. *Max hat den Wagen in die Garage gefahren.* [German]
Max has the car into the garage driven
'Max has driven the car into the garage.'

b. **Max hat den Wagen in die Garage soeben gefahren.*
Max has the car into the garage just driven

c. *Paul hat alles unter das Klavier gelegt.*
Paul has everything under the piano laid
'Paul has laid everything under the piano.'

d. **Paul hat unter das Klavier alles hat gelegt.*
Paul has under the piano everything laid

The scrambling resistance of these directional PPs is not due to their status as PPs. The examples in (45) contain mobile PPs:

(45) a. *Max hat erst gestern über dieses Thema gesprochen.* [German]
Max has only yesterday about this topic talked

b. *Max hat über dieses Thema erst gestern gesprochen.*
Max has about this topic only yesterday talked
'Max has talked about this topic only yesterday.'

c. *Maria sollte jeden auf dieses Problem hinweisen.*
Maria should everyone.ACC to this problem point

d. *Maria sollte auf dieses Problem jeden hinweisen.*
Maria should at this problem everyone.ACC point
'Maria should point this problem out to everyone.'

For understanding these data a semantic difference between the PPs in (44) and (45) is likely to be relevant. The directional PPs in (44) express a predication on the direct object, which becomes true as a result of the event denoted by the main verb. This does not hold for the PPs in (45). Thus, it can be said that in the examples in (44), the main verb and the preposition together express a predication on the direct object. Therefore, the idea comes to mind that in (44) the PPs and the verbs together take the object as an argument, i.e. that they form a complex predicate (Helbig and Buscha 1986; Abraham 1986; Frey and Tappe 1992; Neeleman 1994a).

Under the assumption that manner adverbials are base generated inside the vP next to the predicate (cf. section 4.3), evidence for this assumption is constituted by the fact that manner adverbials have to be left-adjacent to these PPs, (46b), in contrast to the PPs of the type in (45), (46c):

(46) a. *Paul hat alles behutsam unter das Klavier gelegt.* [German]
Paul has everything with.caution under the piano laid
'Paul has laid everything under the piano with caution.'

b. **Paul hat alles unter das Klavier behutsam gelegt.*
Paul has everything under the piano with.caution laid

c. *Maria wird jeden auf dieses Problem nachdrücklich hinweisen.*
Maria will everyone.ACC at this problem emphatically point
'Maria will emphatically point this problem out to everyone.'

Further evidence can be seen in the fact that if a main predicate is moved to the *Vorfeld* without its directional PP the result is not well formed, (47b), in contrast to the situation with a standard prepositional object, (47c). The grammaticality of (47a) with a non-portable *w*-indefinite object in the middle field shows that the ungrammaticality of (47b) is not due to the scrambling resistance of the directional PP. In German, left branches of the verbal complex may undergo movement to the *Vorfeld*.

(47) a. *Zeigen will Otto ihr was.* [German]
show.INF wants Otto her something

b. **Gelegt hat Paul alles unter das Klavier.*
put has Paul everything under the piano

c. *Gesprochen hat Max erst gestern über dieses Thema.*
spoken has Max only yesterday about this topic
'Only yesterday did Max speak about this topic.'

The same pattern of data can be observed with other predicative elements. For example, a resultative predicate also cannot be scrambled (Reis 1985), (48b), it has to follow a manner adverbial, (48c), and it cannot be stranded when the main predicate is moved to the *Vorfeld*, (48d):

(48) a. *Otto hat den Tisch vorher sauber gewischt.* [German]
Otto has the table before clean wiped
'Otto wiped the table clean beforehand.'

b. **Otto hat den Tisch sauber vorher gewischt.*
Otto has the table clean before wiped

c. *Otto hat den Tisch (kräftig) sauber (*kräftig) gewischt.*
Otto has the table forcefully clean forcefully wiped
'Otto forcefully wiped the table clean.'

d. **Gewischt hat Otto den Tisch vorher sauber.*
wiped has Otto the table before clean

Again, these data make sense if one assumes that the resultative and the main predicate form a complex predicate and jointly provide one argument grid (cf. also Müller 2002).

In German, the phenomenon of complex predicate formation seems to be more widespread than usually assumed. If, as argued in section 4.3, manner adverbials are base generated adjacent to the verbal complex, the examples in (49) indicate that indefinites, in contrast to non-indefinites, may be part of a complex predicate (cf. also van Geenhoven 1998). Furthermore, (50) demonstrates that if the indefinite follows a manner adverbial, it cannot be left behind by movement of the predicate to the *Vorfeld*. Since unstressed "light" manner adverbials do not like to scramble, cf. (49b), this too indicates than an indefinite following a manner adverbial belongs to the complex predicate:

(49) a. *Sie hat heute wunderbar Mozartsonaten gespielt.* [German]
She has today marvellously Mozart.sonatas played

b. *??Sie hat heute wunderbar die letzten Mozartsonaten gespielt.*
she has today marvellously the last Mozart.sonata s played

(50) **Gespielt hat sie heute wunderbar Mozartsonaten.* [German]
played has she today marvellously Mozart.sonatas

Note that there are indefinites which obligatorily build a complex with their predicate; thus they cannot be scrambled and cannot be left behind by movement of the predicate to the *Vorfeld*:

(51) a. *weil er niemals Butter nimmt* [German]
because he never butter.ACC takes
'because he never takes butter'

b. **weil er Butter niemals nimmt*
because he butter.ACC never takes

c. **Genommen hat er niemals Butter.*
taken has he never butter
(cf. Meinunger 2000: 72)

The phenomena exhibited in (49)–(51) remind us of what is nowadays discussed under the name pseudo-incorporation, which has been reported to exist for a number of languages (for example, Dutch, Booij 2008; and Niuean, an Oceanic language, Massam 2001): the combination of an NP and a verb which forms a verbal predicate that does not have the status of a (complex) word, but is different from a regular VP in that the pseudo-incorporated NP constituent does not project to a regular sentence constituent of its own. It seems that in German, indefinite NPs even can be incorporated into the complex predicate, which is in the right *Satzklammer.*

Let us next consider the dative arguments of the few verbs which induce the base order NOM < ACC < DAT, cf. (19f) in 4.2. In the literature, it is occasionally observed that these datives do not like to be scrambled, (52a) (the same holds for the genitive of the very few verbs which induce the order NOM < ACC < GEN, *bezichtigen* 'accuse' being an example of such a verb). The question arises as to whether these arguments belong to the verbal complex, too. It is interesting to observe that the answer seems to be positive. (52b) shows that it is not possible to move the predicate without the dative to the *Vorfeld*; (52c) demonstrates that a manner adverbial cannot follow the dative. Thus, the dative arguments of these special verbs behave like the other phrases which seem to participate in the complex predicate. The reason why these dative arguments belong to the verbal complex might be that they historically have developed from directional PPs.

(52) a. *??Er will der Strahlung$_1$ die Probe t_1 aussetzen.* [German]
he wants the radiation.DAT the sample expose.INF
Intended: 'He wants to expose the sample to the radiation.'

b. **Aussetzen will er die Probe der Strahlung.*
expose.INF wants he the sample the radiation.DAT

c. *??Er hat die Probe der Strahlung geschickt ausgesetzt.*
he has the sample the radiation.DAT adroitly exposed

Finally, note that the well-known phenomenon of particle verbs in German and Dutch could be seen as complex predicate formation. The particle is separated from the verb if the verb undergoes V2-movement. Hence it must have phrasal status. On the other hand, the particle clearly cannot scramble, it has to follow a manner adverbial, and it cannot be left behind if the verb undergoes phrasal movement to the *Vorfeld*.

Other elements which cannot be scrambled and which fulfil the criteria for belonging to the verbal complex are selected adverbials like the ones in *freundlich behandeln* 'to treat in a friendly manner' or *zwei Stunden dauern* 'to last two hours', and predicative NPs like the ones in *eine erfolgreiche Geschäftsfrau sein* 'to be a successful business-woman' or *einen Idioten nennen* 'to call an idiot'.

The syntactic analysis of complex predicates involving XPs is still an open question. Booij (2008) suggests that pseudo-incorporation is assigned the category V'. Massam (2001) considers pseudo-incorporation to be a semantic phenomenon with a quite regular syntactic structure. Since in German, as indicated above, syntactic incorporation into the complex predicate seems involved, Frey and Tappe (1992) assume that the verbal complex in German may contain predicative XP-projections.

4.5. The position of sentence negation

According to the standard view in generative grammar, the universal base position of sentence negation is above the vP projected by the main predicate (Haegeman and Zanuttini 1991). However, the adoption of this view for German would have some unwanted consequences (Haider and Rosengren 2003). First, since (53a) in contrast to (53b) is unmarked, one would have to assume that scrambling of the object is necessary to arrive at an unmarked reading. In the literature, syntacticians often try to capture the presumed obligatory scrambling of the object in a sentence like (53a) by the claim that definites in German have to scramble out of the vP. However, (53c) shows that this claim is hard to maintain, since the *w*-indefinite subject, which cannot scramble, marks the boundary of vP. A second serious problem for the standard view is that it has to be assumed that these non-portable *w*-indefinites obligatorily have to be scrambled out of the domain of sentence negation in German, cf. (53d, e). Furthermore, one would have to assume that focussed phrases scramble, in contradiction to Lenerz's results, cf. (53f).

(53) a. *Hans hat das Buch über Weine nicht gelesen.* [German]
Hans has the book on wines not read
'Hans has not read the book on wines.'

b. *Hans hat nicht das Buch über Weine gelesen (sondern das Buch über Whiskeys).*
Hans has not the book on wines read but the book on whiskeys
'Hans has not read the book on wines, but the book on whiskeys.'

c. *Heute hat wer das Buch über Weine weggenommen.*
today has someone the book on wines taken.away
'Today someone has taken away the book on wines.'

d. *Maria hat heute wen nicht gegrüßt.*
Maria has today someone not greeted
'Today Maria has not greeted someone.'

e. **Maria hat heute nicht wen gegrüßt.*
Maria has today not someone greeted

f. *Wen hat Maria nicht eingeladen?*
who has Maria not invited
'Who did Mary not invite?'

Sie hat PAUL nicht eingeladen.
she has Paul not invited
'She has not invited Paul.'

g. *Otto hat (nicht) genau (*nicht) zugehört.*
Otto has not closely not listened
'Otto has not listened closely.'

Therefore, the standard view has been questioned (cf. e.g. Bayer and Kornfilt 1994; Haider 1993, 2010; Pafel 2009). For example, Haider argues that the alleged evidence for the received view comes from head-initial languages only. A better universal generalisation would be that sentence negation has to c-command the main predicate and is generated very close to it. Thus, in VO-languages, the negation particle precedes the vP. In OV-languages, it is generated below the arguments, still c-commanding the verbal complex and potentially occurring manner adverbials, (53g). Since sentence negation is generated very low, a negation particle in front of a sentence constituent can only be the so-called constituent negation, (53b), or an instance of so-called light negation (Schwarz and Bhatt 2006, Krifka 2010), which can only appear in certain environments (according to Schwarz and Bhatt 2006, these environments are similar but not quite identical to the environments which license negative polarity items). Light negation can be semantically contentful, (54a), or without an obvious semantic contribution, (54b).

(54) a. *Wenn nicht Max den Chef angerufen hätte, wäre alles einfacher.* [German]
if not Max the boss called had would.be everything easier
'If Max had not called the boss, everything would be easier.'

b. *Ich gehe nicht, bevor Max nicht einen Apfel gegessen hat.*
I leave not until Max not an apple eaten has
'I won't leave until Max has eaten an apple.'

Consider next the examples in (55). (55a, b) both contain an argumental PP and sentence negation. The observed different orders follow if one assumes that a directional PP-complement, (55a), in contrast to a prepositional object, (55b), belongs to the verbal complex (cf. section 4.4). Furthermore, the positioning of the indefinite object in (55c) confirms the observation in 4.4 that an indefinite NP (in contrast to any regular DP containing a quantifier) may belong to the verbal complex. Finally, (55d) shows that the special dative arguments of some verbs, which are base generated following the accusative, occur after sentence negation, confirming the above-stated suggestion that they too belong to the verbal complex. Note the contrast to the behaviour of the accusative argument of a regular ditransitive verb, (55e).

(55) a. *Hans hat den Wagen nicht in die Garage gefahren.* [German]
Hans has the car not into the garage driven
'Hans has not driven the car into the garage.'

b. *Max hat über dieses Thema nicht gesprochen.*
Max has about this topic not spoken
'Max has not spoken about this topic.'

c. *Otto will heute nicht schwierige Sonaten spielen.*
Otto want today not difficult sonatas play
'Otto does not want to play any difficult sonatas today.'

d. *Man hat die Kinder nicht dieser Gefahr ausgesetzt.*
one has the children not this danger.DAT exposed
'One has not exposed the children to this danger.'

e. **Max hat den Kindern nicht diese Geschichte erzählt.*
Max has the children not this story told
(under sentence negation)

Let us conclude this section with one of the great puzzles of German clausal syntax. It concerns the interaction of so-called VP-topicalisation and material in the *Mittelfeld*:

(56) a. *Das Buch über Weine gelesen hat Hans nicht (t).* [German]
the book on wines read has Hans not
'The books on wines Hans has not read.'

b. *Wen gegrüßt hat Maria nicht (t).*
who greeted has Maria not
'Maria has not greeted anyone.'

If the constituents in the *Vorfeld* were reconstructed to their supposed base positions, a different meaning or ungrammaticality would result, cf. (53b, e). To account for (56), proponents of the view that sentence negation is positioned outside of vP would have to assume that on the surface, the object of a transitive verb cannot appear in the c-command domain of sentence negation, but a trace representing a verbal projection containing an object can. Proponents of the minority view that sentence negation is generated very close to the verbal complex have to make the heretical assumption that the trace of a *Vorfeld* constituent containing the main predicate belongs to the verbal complex although this *Vorfeld* constituent itself cannot appear there (e.g. Haider 2010).

4.6. What determines base order?

In 4.2, evidence was given that in German the base position of an argument is not dependent on its case or on its grammatical function. Rather, the data show it is determined by its thematic properties (Uszkoreit 1986), confirming the common assumption that the syntactic projection of the arguments of a verb is conditioned by some – possibly universal – thematic hierarchy, (57). There is evidence that this holds for OV- and for VO-languages. The Uniformity of Theta Assignment Hypothesis (UTAH) of Baker (1988) states that identical thematic relationships between items must be represented by identical structural relationships between those items in base structure.

(57) Thematic Hierarchy (cf. Grimshaw 1990; Jackendoff 1990)
Agent < Experiencer/Recipient < Theme < Goal/Source/Location

It is a natural assumption that the base order of arguments reflects the order in which the arguments are discharged. Their relative order reflects their ranking in the lexical argument structure; a higher ranked argument ends up in a higher position in the syntactic structure (ordered merge). For example, in the base order a nominative DP which is a theme follows a dative DP which is an experiencer, (58a), or a recipient, (58b):

(58) a. *dass einigen Kritikern etliche Vorstellungen* [German]
that some.DAT critics.DAT several performances.NOM
gefallen haben
pleased have
'that several performances have pleased some critics'

b. *weil wem was erklärt wurde*
since whom.DAT what.NOM explained was
'since something was explained to someone'

Note that a nominative following an object in the base order can also be found on the surface in Dutch and in the VO-languages Icelandic (Yip, Maling and Jackendoff 1987) and Russian (Dyakonova 2009). Some Italian psych verbs (the *piacare*-class) also allow a nominative to follow the object on the surface optionally.

Let us next compare the verbs in (19e) and (19f) of section 4.2. The dative argument of the former is typically a recipient, and the dative of the latter typically a goal. Again, the difference in the base positions with respect to the accusative is a reflection of the difference in the argument ranking. Note that in English and Dutch, the verbs corresponding to the ones in (19f) code the DAT with a prepositional object.

A verb like *schicken* may induce NOM < DAT < ACC or NOM < ACC < PP. The associated thematic roles are Agent, Recipient, Theme and Agent, Theme, Goal, respectively. Hence, it resembles the famous dative-alternation verbs in English like *give* or *send*. Note that also in Japanese, one finds the following pair:

(59) a. *Taroo-ga kinoo Hakano-ni nimotu-o okutta.* [Japanese]
Taro-NOM yesterday Hakano-DAT package-ACC sent
'Taro sent Hakano a/the package.'

b. *Taroo-ga kinoo nimotu-o Hakano-ni okutta.*
Taro-NOM yesterday package-ACC Hakano-DAT sent
'Taro sent a/the package to Hakano.'

Miyagawa and Tsujioka (2004) argue that in (59a), the dative is interpreted as a possessor, while in (59b), the dative is interpreted as a locative. Thus, according to Miyagawa and Tsujioka (2004), the structure in (59b), conventionally analysed as a scrambled variant of (59a), is in fact a base-generated structure with an interpretation that differs from that of (59a).

It is worth pointing out once more that in fact the thematic roles are relevant for the base ordering and not just animacy. In the following example, the animacy status of DAT and ACC is the same (cf. also [14]).

(60) a. *dass man dem Chef den FRITZ empfahl* [German]
that they the boss.DAT the Fritz.ACC recommended (wide focus possible)

b. *dass man den Fritz dem CHEF empfahl*
that they the Fritz.ACC the boss.DAT recommended (only narrow focus)
'that they recommended Fritz to the boss'

c. *dass man mindestens einem Personalchef fast jeden Absolventen empfahl*
that they at.least one staff.manager.DAT nearly every graduate.ACC recommended (only ∃∀)
'that they recommended nearly every graduate to at least one staff manager'

While in German (and in other languages) the thematic hierarchy is realized as the base ordering on the surface, there are many languages which on the surface have to fulfil additional conditions. The most prominent example is the necessity to have a nominative DP in a special position. It is a plausible assumption that, for example, the English (61b) underlyingly has the same order as (61a), but that in English, the nominative has to be moved out of the VP for case reasons.

(61) a. *weil den Mann der Sturm erschreckt* [German]
since the man the storm scares
'since the storm scares the man'

b. *since the storm scares the man*

5. Non-base positions in the TP-domain

5.1. A note on "focus scrambling"

In the context of a discussion on non-base positions inside the German *Mittelfeld* a phenomenon has to be mentioned which, if it is not taken into consideration, might lead to incorrect claims about regular scrambling of constituents. It was Neeleman (1994a) who called attention to the fact that reordered sequences in the *Mittelfeld* of Dutch (and German) are not uniformly derived, and that one has to differentiate between at least two different syntactic processes: regular scrambling and what Neeleman calls "focus scrambling", which necessarily comes along with a contrastive interpretation of the reordered constituent. Neeleman found that for focus scrambling, but not for scrambling, the following properties hold: (i) it applies to all kinds of phrasal constituents; (ii) it is not restricted to the limits of a single clause, i.e. focus scrambling may target the *Mittelfeld* of a superordinated clause; (iii) it is not iterative (i.e. in a given domain it may only target one element); and (iv) it induces freezing, i.e. it does not allow further displacement out of the scrambled phrase. In (62), the properties (i), (ii), and (iv) are exemplified.

(62) a. **dass Peter grün$_1$ den Zaun nicht t_1 gestrichen hat* [German]
that Peter green the fence not painted has

b. *dass SO GRÜN$_1$ Peter den Zaun nicht t_1 streichen will*
that so green Peter the fence not paint.INF wants
'that Peter does not want to paint the fence that green'

c. **dass niemand die LÖsung$_1$ geglaubt hat, dass einer t_1 gefunden hätte*
that no.one the solution believed has that one found has

d. *dass [SO eine Lösung]$_1$ niemand geglaubt hat, dass einer t_1 finden könnte*
that such a solution no.one believed has that one find could
'that no one believed that anyone could find such a solution'

e. *Was$_1$ hat sich [t_1 ihr anzuvertrauen]$_2$ keiner t_2 vorgenommen?*
what has REFL her to.entrust no.one intended
'What has no one intended to entrust her with?'

f. **Was$_1$ hat [t_1 ihr anzuvertrauen]$_2$ Maria angenommen dass er t_2 geplant habe?*
what has her to.entrust Maria assumed that he intended has
'What has Maria assumed that he had intended to entrust her with?'

(62a, b) relate to the first property, illustrated with a resultative predicate. Such a predicate may appear preceding the subject if it is contrastive, (62b), but it cannot undergo standard scrambling, i.e. preposing in the *Mittelfeld* of such an item results in an ungrammatical structure if contrastive focus is absent (62a). (62c, d) relate to clause-boundedness. The DP *die Lösung* must remain within its clause if it is non-contrastive, but the contrastively focalised *so eine Lösung* may leave it. Finally, the structures in (62e, f) show the differences in opacity for regular and focus scrambling in German: regular scrambling of an infinitival clause (*was ihr anzuvertrauen*) is fully compatible with extraction of one of its arguments (here of *was*). But, as (62f) shows, a focus scrambled phrase is not transparent for extraction: if the infinitival clause headed by *anzuvertrauen* appears displaced to a position within the matrix clause, *was* cannot be extracted out of it.

Given these observations, what was stated in section 4.4 remains true: phrasal elements belonging to the complex predicate cannot undergo scrambling. However, they can undergo focus scrambling.

5.2. What determines non-base positions?

A potential formal candidate for triggering non-base word orders can be ruled out quickly. The trigger cannot be case (as e.g. proposed by Mahajan 1994). Scrambling is not restricted to cased elements. In German, PPs and clauses, both finite and infinitival ones, scramble as well, and they are not case-marked. In Dutch, PPs but not DPs may undergo regular scrambling.

In recent years another proposal for a kind of formal account of scrambling has gained some popularity. It is the claim that scrambling is prosodically motivated (e.g. Reinhart 1996; Sekerina 1997). In languages like German or Dutch, the rightmost XP in a clause receives the most prominent stress, the nuclear accent, by default if this XP is not an adjunct. According to the prosody approach to scrambling, the motivation for scrambling a phrase is to make it escape the default stress and to leave its left-adjacent sister constituent in the rightmost XP-position, where the latter can receive the nuclear accent by default. Thus, a phrase does not scramble to realise its own needs; rather, it moves for the benefit of another constituent.

This proposal does not appear to be satisfying either because of two basic observations. First, as to the example (11) of section 4.2, it would us lead to expect that the answer (11a) should be less appropriate than (11b), since if the trigger for scrambling is the need to direct default sentence stress to another constituent, it should apply if the indirect object needs to receive stress. However, (11a, b) are considered to be equally grammatical. Second, there is scrambling independent of the assignment of default sentence stress. The preposing of the dative in (63b) does not happen in order for default sentence stress to fall on its left-adjacent constituent.

(63) a. *Heute wird jemand dem Milliardär das BILD zeigen.* [German]
today will someone the billionaire.DAT the painting show.INF

b. *Heute wird dem Milliardär$_1$ jemand t_1 das BILD zeigen.*
today will the billionaire.DAT someone the painting show.INF
'Today someone will show the billionaire the picture.'

Hawkins (1998) makes another proposal for the motivation of scrambling which refers to a formal property. Hawkins assumes that constituent order is determined by the syntactic weight of the constituents, a notion that is supposed to reflect how easily the constituents can be recognised by the human parser. Constituents containing more words should follow constituents containing fewer. According to Hawkins, relative syntactic weight explains word order frequencies in corpora, as well as the relative acceptability of different orders in native speakers' judgements.

Hawkins does not assume a base-generated order. However, without that assumption the proposal cannot be right for the simple reason that for a regular transitive verb, SOV is less marked than OSV, even though the subject and the object both contain the same number of words. Furthermore, Hawkins's account predicts that pronouns have to precede full DPs (if the latter are longer than a single word), and if both the subject and the object are pronouns, then both SO and OS should be equally acceptable. Obviously, neither prediction is correct: (64a, b) are equally acceptable, and (64c) is strongly ungrammatical.

(64) a. *weil ihm der Chef misstraut* [German]
since him.DAT the boss mistrusts

b. *weil der Chef ihm misstraut*
since the boss him.DAT mistrusts
'since the boss mistrusts him'

c. **weil ihm sie misstraut*
since him.DAT she.NOM mistrusts

Note furthermore that since Hawkins predicts that information structure should not play a role in determining word order, the system does not account for data like (12b) of section 4.2.

It seems more promising to look for semantic and/or pragmatic effects of scrambling. In the literature, two very different views are argued for. According to the first one, semantic/pragmatic meaning is responsible for non-base word order. Thus, scrambling is seen as semantically/pragmatically driven; it is envisaged as a syntactic operation that is implemented only if required in order to obtain a new semantic/pragmatic meaning that cannot be obtained otherwise (among many others, Diesing 1992; Meinunger 2000; Kučerová 2007). The other view supposes that semantic/pragmatic meaning effects are merely a by-product of scrambling. That is, scrambling is not triggered to satisfy semantic/pragmatic needs, but scrambling is just an option which the grammar of a given scrambling language allows. That scrambled constituents sometimes are interpreted differently from non-scrambled ones is, according to this analysis, principally due to the way alternative orderings are exploited at the phonological and semantic/pragmatic interfaces (Neeleman and Reinhart 1998; Haider and Rosengren 2003).

A prominent example of the first view is the claim that it is given elements that scramble (e.g. Diesing 1997; Delfitto and Corver 1998). Note also that some authors conceive of any given element as a topic (e.g. Meinunger 2000; Grewendorf 2005). At first glance an example like the following seems to support this claim:

(65) *Peter traf neulich wieder Maria.* [German]
Peter met the.other.day again Maria
'The other day Peter met Maria again.'

a. *Er hat seine Freundin sofort umarmt.*
he has his girlfriend immediately embraced

b. *Er hat sofort seine Freundin umarmt.*
he has immediately his girlfriend embraced
'He immediately embraced his girlfriend.'

The reasoning goes as follows. (65a) is understood such that Maria is Peter's girlfriend, whereas (65b) is understood in the way that Maria and Peter's girlfriend are different persons. It is concluded that this interpretative difference proves that given elements scramble.

However, this reasoning is not compelling. By default, (65a) will be pronounced with the nuclear accent on *umarmt,* since the last occurring XP of the clause, *sofort*, is an adjunct. In contrast, the standard intonation of (65b) has the nuclear accent on *seine Freundin*. Normally, a given constituent is deaccented. Therefore, if *seine Freundin* gets an accent as in (65b), it will be interpreted as non-given; if it is deaccented as in (65a), it is interpreted as given. Under this perspective, (65) does not show first and foremost that a given constituent has to scramble but rather it shows the interpretative effects standard intonation may induce. This is verified by the fact that the interpretations of the very sentences (65a, b) can be exchanged if they receive a different intonation. If in (65b) *umarmt* receives the nuclear accent, (65b) is understood as Peter embraces Maria. If in (65a) *seine Freundin* receives the nuclear accent, it will be interpreted as being non-coreferent with *Maria*.

Let's move to the examples in (66). Neeleman and Reinhart (1998) and Abraham and Molnárfi (2001), among others, argue that the form of (66a) is the only possible way to answer a question in which the accusative object has been previously introduced in the discourse, since both (66b) and (66c), in which *das Bild* occupies the lower position, stressed and unstressed, respectively, are pragmatically ill formed. The far-reaching conclusion these authors draw is that the word order in a language like German is, in fact, constrained with respect to focussed/unfocussed material: an accusative object following vP-adjoined material is obligatorily interpreted as focal.

(66) *Was ist mit dem Bild geschehen?* [German]
what is with the picture happened
'What happened to the painting?'

a. *Paul hat das Bild gestern verKAUFT.*
Paul has the painting yesterday sold
'Paul sold the painting yesterday.'

b. *#Paul hat gestern das BILD verkauft.*
Paul has yesterday the painting sold

c. *#Paul hat gestern das Bild verKAUFT.*
Paul has yesterday the painting sold

However, remember that (11a) has already shown that a vP-internal constituent does not have to be focussed. The introductory question in (11) displays two discourse participants (the referents of *you, the picture*) as given, and asks for the identification of a new, third one, namely the recipient. Scrambling may be applied in the answer thereby achieving a given-before-new order, (11b), but, crucially, it does not have to, (11a).

So one has to ask what the difference between (11a) and (66c) is. It seems the crucial difference lies in the way in which the picture figures in the introductory questions. In (66), the content of the question necessarily has the consequence that in the answer, the term denoting the painting will be an aboutness topic. The answer has to be about the painting. There is evidence that in German, aboutness topics have to be scrambled to the left periphery of the *Mittelfeld* (Frey 2004). In (11), on the other hand, *das Bild* does not have to be treated as an aboutness topic in the answer. The picture is just some already introduced referent, but it does not have to be the object the answer is about.

The difference between (11a) and (66c) shows that a given element does not have to scramble – it may happily stay in situ; however, an element whose referent the proposition essentially concerns is positioned in the left periphery of the *Mittelfeld* (or, for that matter, in the *Vorfeld*). That the answer in (67) is deviant shows that for an aboutness topic it is not enough to just be scrambled across some elements, but rather it has to be scrambled to the beginning of the *Mittelfeld.*

(67) *Was ist mit dem Bild geschehen?* [German]
what is with the painting happend
'What happened with the painting?'

#Paul hat leider das Bild gestern verkauft.
Paul has unfortunately the painting yesterday sold

This analytic inspection of given elements is confirmed by experimental ones. Studies like Skopeteas and Fanselow (2009) and Bader and Häussler (2010) confirm that mere givenness is not a trigger for scrambling. Skopeteas and Fanselow (2009) report that the test subjects scrambled a given object across an agentive new subject in only one out of 64 cases. In seven out of 64 cases, the given object was positioned in the *Vorfeld.*

Let us now move to another presumed semantic trigger. It was proposed by Diesing (1992) for scrambling of indefinites and has been adopted by several linguists for scrambling in general (e.g. Hinterhölzl 2004; Putnam 2007). Diesing assumes that definites scramble without any change in interpretation, but in order to receive a so-called "strong" interpretation an indefinite DP has to be scrambled out of vP. The generic, the specific/referential, and the partitive reading of an indefinite count as strong interpretations. Definite DPs are in most cases specific/referential by definition. Although this proposal has received a lot of attention, it is hard to maintain, the reason simply being that an indefinite may very well receive a strong reading in its base position.

(68) a. *weil hier ja doch wer Fußballübertragungen anschaut* [German]
since here PRT PRT someone soccer.broadcasts watches
'since someone is watching soccer broadcasts here after all'

b. *Heute hat irgendein Hinterbänkler ein wichtiges Förderprogramm zu*
today has some backbencher an important support.programme to
Fall gebracht, nämlich ...
fall brought namely
'Today some backbencher brought down an important support programme, namely …'

c. *Viele Wissenschaftler sind in der Stadt. Es wäre gut, wenn wer*
many scientists are in the city it would.be good if someone
zwei Linguisten beherbergen könnte.
two linguists house.INF could
'Many scientists are in town. It would be good if someone could house two linguists.'

The objects in (68) all follow a non-specific existentially interpreted subject. Thus, they stay in situ. Nevertheless, in (68a, b) the object preferably has a generic and a specific interpretation, respectively, and in (68c), the object is partitively interpreted.

So, what remains is that indefinites cannot get a non-specific existential interpretation if they are positioned outside of vP, cf. (32b, c) in section 4.3. Scrambling of indefinites out of a certain domain cancels the "weak" reading, and just the "strong" reading remains. Thus, with regard to the semantics of indefinite DPs there is no scrambling trigger in sight.

Weak, existential DPs may not leave the vP, the domain of existential closure. However, in the literature with only very few exceptions, it is claimed that weak, existential DPs may not undergo any scrambling (e.g. Diesing 1992; de Hoop 1992; Büring 2001; Lenerz 2001). For example, Lenerz (2001) gives the judgements in (69).

(69) a. *Ich habe dem Studenten ein Buch gegeben.* [German]
I have the student.DAT a book.ACC given
'I have given the student a book.'

b. **Ich habe ein Buch dem Studenten gegeben.*
I have a book.ACC the student.DAT given

Note, however, that the judgement given for (69b) is highly problematic. As already mentioned with regard to the examples in (15) in section 4.2, informants do not disallow scrambling of a non-specific existential DP inside vP.

In section 4, it was already mentioned that according to various influential accounts scrambling has many different, potentially conflicting triggers. These approaches usually assume that the different triggers are not mandatory, i.e. the sentence in question does not become ungrammatical but rather marked if the triggers are not respected. As for the approaches which directly base generate all serialisations (cf. section 4.1), the different triggering factors are often ordered, i.e. it is assumed that the disregard of a given trigger may cause stronger markedness than the disregard of another. Thus, the (scrambled and unscrambled) orders exhibit different degrees of markedness or gradient wellformedness. A prominent example of this kind of approach is Müller (1999). He proposes a ranked set of violable surface linearisation constraints which may trigger scrambling. In (70), these constraints are listed according to decreasing strength.

(70) a. a nominative precedes a non-nominative
b. a DP with a definite article precedes a DP with a non-definite one
c. an animate precedes a non-animate
d. a non-stressed phrase precedes a stressed one
e. a dative precedes an accusative
f. a DP precedes an adverb

Obviously, these constraints are of highly varying nature. They concern grammatical functions, the form of a DP, semantics, accent, and syntactic category. Müller's (1999) examples are discussed without context; the degree of markedness is assigned to them on an intuitive level. With respect to degrees of markedness, the reliability of intuitive judgements is certainly not that obvious. Furthermore, it might be considered as problematic that it does not become clear why exactly the factors in (70) should be the triggers of scrambling, why the order of the constraints should be as it is claimed, and how factors stemming from various cognitive fields interact in grammar. Corresponding comments apply to proposals according to which the surface realisation is directly generated from the unordered set of the constituents in compliance with weighted linearisation principles, cf. section 4.1 (e.g. Uszkoreit 1986; Jacobs 1988; Pafel 2009). Like Müller's approach, so far these proposals have not as a whole been submitted to extensive empirical tests. As far as what intuition can tell us, all these systems achieve a certain degree of empirical correctness. However, they do not explain the observed patterns, and they do not intend to do so.

Since the standard proposals for a semantic trigger or effect of scrambling do not seem to work, one might conclude that scrambling is just an option of the grammar of certain languages which only sometimes – by accident, so to speak – might have semantic/pragmatic effects. Notably Haider propagates this view in his works. For this approach, the most natural thing would be cases of scrambling without any interpretative effect. As a case in point consider (11b) from above, here repeated in (71b):

(71) *Wem hast du das Bild gezeigt?* [German]
whom.DAT have you the painting shown

a. *Ich habe dem MilliarDÄR das Bild gezeigt.*
I have the billionaire.DAT the painting shown

b. *Ich habe das Bild dem MilliarDÄR gezeigt.*
I have the painting the billionaire.DAT shown
'I have shown the billionaire the painting.'

Many linguists assume that definites scramble without any change in interpretation (e.g. Büring 2001; Diesing 1992; Lenerz 2001). With regard to sentences like (71a, b), Lenerz (2001: 271) notes: "There should be a difference in meaning (…) Such a difference in meaning is, however, hard to establish."

Yet, perhaps such a difference can be established. It might be that the conclusion that there is no semantic effect of scrambling in (71b) is drawn too fast. Consider (72a, b). These contain the unstressed main verb *geschenkt*, which is not given by the introductory question in the strict sense. In (72a), the objects are in their base positions. In (72b), the given accusative object is scrambled. Interestingly, the variant with the objects in their base positions is deviant; the variant with scrambling is contextually appropriate (Manfred Krifka, p.c.).

(72) *Wem hast du das Buch gegeben?* [German]
whom have you the book given
'Whom have you given the book?'

a. *#Ich habe dem / einem StuDENten das Buch geschenkt.*
I have the a student the book presented

b. *Ich habe das Buch dem / einem StuDENten geschenkt.*
I have the book the a student presented
'I gave the book to the / a student.'

Perhaps an explanation for this difference could be sought in the fact that the event is described somewhat differently in (72a, b). In (72b), by means of scrambling of *das*

Buch, a perspective emphasis and a higher degree of salience is put on the referent of *das Buch*. Because the point of view is from the book, the difference in the predicates in the question and in the answer in (72b) is not considered as central, and therefore the predicate in (72b) can be considered as given despite the slight meaning change in the predicate between the question and answer. By contrast, the perspective under which the event is presented using the basic word order in (72a) is just the neutral one. All non-given elements need to be marked by accent. This is not fulfilled for the predicate, and therefore the sentence is not appropriate in the given context. If the predicate is stressed too, the word order of (72a) becomes possible in the given context:

(73) *Wem hast du das Buch gegeben?* [German]
whom have you the book given

Ich habe dem / einem StuDENten das Buch geSCHENKT.
I have the a student the book gave

So, after all scrambling is perhaps never without any interpretative effect. If scrambling is the expression of certain facets of the point of view of the speaker, scrambling will only induce subtle interpretative effects but nevertheless real ones. Any scrambling will have a slight effect on interpretation. Scrambling will belong to the movements which are triggered by certain needs of the moved item.

Lötscher (1981) also sees a connection between word order in the *Mittelfeld* and point of view and empathy in the sense of Kuno (1975). He observes that (74b, c) sound somehow strange. The fact that the term which denotes an animal precedes the term which denotes a human being gives the impression that the animal should be the speaker's/hearer's point of view for comprehending the event and that the speaker/hearer should empathise with the animal. However, this is not what we do in standard situations. This explains the judgements for the sentences in (74) if they occur in isolation. According to Lötscher, the term denoting the object of the hearer's empathy has to precede the other constituents.

(74) a. *Auf dem schottischen Hochland begegnete ein Hirte* [German]
in the Scottish highlands met a shepherd.NOM
einem Hund.
a dog.DAT
'In the Scottish highlands a shepherd met a dog.'

b. *#Auf dem schottischen Hochland begegnete einem Hund ein*
in the Scottish highlands met a dog.DAT a
Hirte.
shepherd.NOM

c. *#Auf dem schottischen Hochland begegnete ein Hund einem*
in the Scottish highlands met a dog.NOM a
Hirten.
shepherd.DAT

d. *Auf dem schottischen Hochland begegnete einem Hirten ein*
in the Scottish highlands met a shepherd.DAT a
Hund.
dog.NOM
'In the Scottish highlands a shepherd encountered a dog.'

That the order of the constituents in the *Mittelfeld* should affect their saliency might also help to explain the patterns in (75) and (76). These examples show that in cases where more than one possible antecedent is available, a personal pronoun and an anaphorically used demonstrative like *der* may differ in the preferences regarding which antecedent they relate to.

(75) *Heute habe ich dem Chef$_1$ Paul$_2$ vorgestellt.* [German]
today have I the boss.DAT Paul.ACC introduced
'Today I have introduced Paul to the boss.'

a. *Er hat sich sehr darüber gefreut.* *Er* = 1
he has REFL much in.that rejoiced
'He was very pleased about that.'

b. *Der hat sich sehr darüber gefreut.* *Der* = 2
this.one has REFL much in.that rejoiced
'He was very pleased about that.'

(76) *Heute habe ich Paul$_2$ dem Chef$_1$ vorgestellt.* [German]
today have I Paul.ACC the boss.DAT introduced
'Today I have introduced Paul to the boss.'

a. *Er hat sich sehr darüber gefreut.* *Er* = 2
'He was very pleased about that.'

b. *Der hat sich sehr darüber gefreut.* *Der* = 1
'He was very pleased about that.'

According to, for example, Bosch, Rozario and Zhao (2003), an anaphorically used demonstrative like *der* relates to the referent who has a lower degree of saliency, whereas a personal pronoun relates to the referent with the higher degree of saliency.

Let us now briefly turn to the impossibility of scrambling an element which is the information focus of the sentence, cf. (12b). Given the conjecture about the connection between scrambling and the allocation of a point of view, one may assume that there is a tension between being the only new information of a clause and being the locus of the point of view. Quite another way of seeing it is offered by Hopp (2007) with his reinterpretation of Lenerz's condition against scrambling of focussed elements. According to Hopp, (12b) is bad because it involves too many economy violations: it involves scrambling, which violates syntactic economy, and it violates optimal prosodic phrasing. Note, however, that scrambling of a focussed constituent is bad even if it is not scrambled out of the default accent position. (77) just contains scrambling; it does not violate optimal prosodic phrasing. Therefore, according to Hopp (2007), the answer in (77) should be as good as (63b); however, it is bad.

(77) a. *Wem hat heute ein Kollege den Kaffee weggenommen?* [German]
whom has today a colleague the coffee taken.away
'From whom did a colleague take the coffee away today?'

b. **Heute hat dem CHEF ein Kollege den Kaffee weggenommen.*
today has the boss.DAT a colleague the coffee taken.away
Intended: 'Today a colleague took the coffee away from the boss.'

Finally, let us address the question of scrambling of adverbials. Adverbial scrambling is directly ruled out by Neeleman and Reinhart's (1998) and Haider's (2010) analysis. These authors have adverbials base generated in every TP-internal position they may occupy. A theory like Cinque (1999) does not envisage TP-internal scrambling of adverbials either. An adverbial is base generated in the Spec-position of a designated functional projection with a fixed position in the hierarchy of functional projections. If a given adverbial seems to occupy different positions, this may be for two reasons. Either the adverbial belongs to different adverbial classes and, in fact, is a homonym, like *schnell* in (30a, b), or an argument has moved around it. In the proposal which was sketched in 4.3, adverbials have a certain base position, and they may scramble.

Authors who assume that there are no base positions for adverbials take it that syntax is just not concerned with adverbials. Because adverbials are not related to theta-grids, syntax is not able to assign base positions to adverbials, and, as a consequence, syntax is not able to manage scrambling of adverbials. In a theory in which an adverbial occupies the Spec-position of a designated functional projection, scrambling of an adverbial is not expected since the adverbial would have to move to a functional projection which is not compatible with its (semantic) properties. Thus, the variable positioning (or transportability) of an adverbial like *im Hörsaal* in (78) is a common objection to the Cinquean treatment of adverbial syntax: one and the same adverbial can apparently occur in different positions within a clause optionally, which seems diametrically opposed to a fixed hierarchy.

(78) a. *Hans hat heute ungeschickterweise im Hörsaal die* [German]
Hans has today blunderingly in.the lecture.hall the
Apparatur umgestoßen.
equipment *Knocked.over*

b. *Hans hat im Hörsaal heute ungeschickterweise die Apparatur*
Hans has in.the lecture.hall today blunderingly the equipment
umgestoßen.
knocked.over

c. *Hans hat heute im Hörsaal ungeschickterweise die Apparatur*
Hans has today in.the lecture.hall blunderingly the equipment
umgestoßen.
knocked.over
'Today in the lecture hall Hans blunderingly knocked over the equipment.'

It is obvious that the proposal sketched in 4.3 assumes the possibility of scrambling of adverbials. This is an immediate consequence of the scope data like (35b) and (41b). That these sentences are ambiguous is taken as evidence that the adverbials have undergone scrambling leaving a trace in their base position.

6. References (selected)

Abraham, W.
1986 Word order in the middle field of the German sentence. In: W. Abraham, and S. de Meij (eds.), *Topic, Focus and Configurationality*, 1–38. Amsterdam: Benjamins.

Abraham, W., and L. Molnárfi
2001 German clause structure under discourse functional weight: Focus and antifocus. In: W. Abraham, and C. J. W. Zwart (eds.), *Issues in Formal German(ic) Typology*, 1–43. Amsterdam: John Benjamins.

Bader, M., and J. Häussler
2010 Word order in German: A corpus study. *Lingua* 120(3): 717–762.

Baker, M. C.
1988 *Incorporation: A Theory of Grammatical Function Changing*. Chicago: University of Chicago Press.

Bayer, J., and J. Kornfilt
1994 Against scrambling as an instance of move-alpha. In: N. Corver, and H. van Riemsdijk (eds.), *Studies on Scrambling: Movement and Non-Movement Approaches to Free Word-Order Phenomena*, 17–60. Berlin: Mouton de Gruyter.

Bierwisch, M.
1963 *Grammatik des deutschen Verbs*. Studia Grammatica II. Berlin: Akademie Verlag.

Blümel, R.
1914 *Die Haupttypen der Heutigen Neuhochdeutschen Wortstellung im Hauptsatz.*Strassburg: K. J. Trübner.

Booij, G.
2008 Pseudo-incorporation in Dutch. *Groninger Arbeiten zur Germanistischen Linguistik* (GAGL) 46: 3–26.

Bosch, P., T. Rozario, and Y. Zhao
2003 Demonstrative Pronouns and Personal Pronouns. German *der* vs. *er*. In: Proceedings of the EACL 2003, Budapest. *Workshop on the Computational Treatment of Anaphora.*

Büring, D.
2001 Let's phrase it! Focus, word order, and prosodic phrasing in German double object constructions. In: G. Müller, and W. Sternefeld (eds.), *Competition in Syntax*, 69–105. Berlin: Mouton de Gruyter.

Cinque, G.
1999 *Adverbs and Functional Heads: A Cross-Linguistic Perspective.* Oxford: Oxford University Press.

Comrie, B.
1981 *Language Universals and Linguistic Typology: Syntax and Morphology.* Chicago: University of Chicago Press.

Daneš, F.
1967 Order of elements and sentence intonation. In: *To Honor Roman Jakobson. Essays on the Occasion of His Seventieth Birthday 11 October 1966.* Volume I, 499–512. (Janua Linguarum, Series Maior, 31.) The Hague, Paris: Mouton.

Delfitto, D., and N. Corver
1998 Feature primitives and the syntax of specificity. *Rivista di Linguistica* 10(2): 281–334.

Diesing, M.
1992 *Indefinites*. Cambridge, MA: MIT Press.

Diesing, M.
1997 Yiddish VP order and the typology of object movement in Germanic. *Natural Language and Linguistic Theory* 15: 369–427.

Dryer, M. S.
1988 Object-verb order and adjective-noun order: Dispelling a myth. *Lingua* 74: 77–109.

Dryer, M. S.
1996 Word order typology. In: J. Jacobs (ed.): *Handbook on Syntax, Vol. 2*, 1050–1065. Berlin: Walter de Gruyter.
Dryer, M. S.
2011a Order of subject, object and verb. In: M. S. Dryer, and M. Haspelmath (eds.), *The World Atlas of Language Structures Online,* chapter 81. Munich: Max Planck Digital Library. http://wals.info/chapter/81.
Dryer, M. S.
2011b Order of subject and verb. In: M. S. Dryer, and M. Haspelmath (eds.), *The World Atlas of Language Structures Online*, chapter 82. Munich: Max Planck Digital Library. http://wals.info/chapter/82.
Dryer, M. S.
2011c Order of object and verb. In: M. S. Dryer, and M. Haspelmath (eds.), *The World Atlas of Language Structures Online*, chapter 83. Munich: Max Planck Digital Library. http://wals.info/chapter/83.
Dryer, M. S.
2011d Order of relative clause and noun. In: M. S. Dryer, and M. Haspelmath (eds.), *The World Atlas of Language Structures Online*, chapter 90. Munich: Max Planck Digital Library. http://wals.info/chapter/90.
Dryer, M. S.
2011e Order of degree word and adjective. In: M. S. Dryer, and M. Haspelmath (eds.), *The World Atlas of Language Structures Online*, chapter 91. Munich: Max Planck Digital Library. http://wals.info/chapter/91.
Dryer, M. S.
2011 f. Relationship between the Order of Object and Verb and the Order of Adposition and Noun Phrase. In: M. S. Dryer, and M. Haspelmath (eds.), *The World Atlas of Language Structures Online*, chapter 95. Munich: Max Planck Digital Library. http://wals.info/chapter/95.
Dyakonova, M.
2009 A phase-based approach to Russian free word order. Ph.D. thesis, University of Amsterdam.
Emonds, J.
1978 The verbal complex V'-V in French. *Linguistic Inquiry* 9: 151–175.
Engel, U.
1972 Regeln zur "Satzgliedfolge". Zur Stellung der Elemente im einfachen Verbalsatz. In: H. Moser et al. (eds.), *Sprache der Gegenwart Bd. 19,* 17–75. (Linguistische Studien I.) Düsseldorf.
Fanselow, G.
2001 Features, θ-roles, and free constituent order. *Linguistic Inquiry* 32(3): 405–437.
Frey, W.
1993 *Syntaktische Bedingungen für die Semantische Interpretation.* (Studia Grammatica 35.) Berlin: Akademie Verlag.
Frey, W.
2003 Syntactic conditions on adjunct classes. In: Ewald Lang et al. (eds): *Modifying Adjuncts*, 163–209. Berlin: de Gruyter.
Frey, W.
2004 A medial topic position for German. *Linguistische Berichte* 198: 153–190.
Frey, W., and K. Pittner
1999 Adverbialpositionen im deutsch-englischen Vergleich. In: Monika Doherty (ed.), *Sprachspezifische Aspekte der Informationsverteilung*, 14–40. (Studia Grammatica 47.) Berlin: Akademie Verlag.

Frey, W., and H. T. Tappe
1992 Zur Interpretation der X-bar-Theorie und zur Syntax des Mittelfeldes – Grundlagen eines GB-Fragments. Ms. des SFB 340, Universität Stuttgart.

van Geenhoven, V.
1998 *Semantic Incorporation and Indefinite Descriptions.* Stanford: CSLI Publications.

Greenberg, J.
1963 Some universals of grammar with particular reference to the order of meaningful elements. In: J. Greenberg (ed.): *Universals of Language*, 2nd edition, 73–113. Cambridge, MA: MIT Press, 1966 (1st ed. 1963).

Grewendorf, G.
2005 The discourse configurationality of scrambling. In: J. Sabel, and M. Saito (eds.), *The Free Order Phenomenon: Its Syntactic Sources and Diversity*, 75–135. Berlin: Mouton de Gruyter.

Grimshaw, J.
1990 *Argument Structure.* Cambridge, MA: MIT Press.

Haegeman, L., and R. Zanuttini
1991 Negative heads and the Neg Criterion. *The Linguistic Review* 8: 233–251.

Haider, H.
1993 *Deutsche Syntax – Generativ.* Tübingen: Narr.

Haider, H.
2010 *The Syntax of German.* Cambridge: Cambridge University Press.

Haider, H., and I. Rosengren
2003 Scrambling: Nontriggered chain formation in OV languages. *Journal of Germanic Linguistics* 15: 203–267.

Hawkins, J. A.
1998 Some issues in a performance theory of word order. In: A. Siewierska (ed.), *Constituent Order in the Languages of Europe*, 729–780. Berlin: Mouton de Gruyter.

Helbig, G., and J. Buscha
1986 *Deutsche Grammatik: Ein Handbuch für den Ausländerunterricht.* Berlin: Langenscheidt, 9th edition.

Heylen, K.
2005 A quantitative corpus study of German word order variation. In: S. Kepser, and M. Reis (eds.), *Linguistic Evidence: Empirical, Theoretical and Computational Perspectives*, 241–264. Berlin: Mouton de Gruyter.

Hinterhölzl, R.
2004 Scrambling, optionality and non-lexical triggers. In: A. Breitbarth, and H. van Riemsdijk (eds.), *Triggers*, 173–203. (Studies in Generative Grammar 75.) Berlin, New York: Mouton de Gruyter.

Höhle, T.
1982 Explikation für "normale Betonung" und "normale Wortstellung". In: W. Abraham (ed.), *Satzglieder im Deutschen*, 75–153. Tübingen: Narr.

de Hoop, H.
1992 Case configuration and noun phrase interpretation. Ph.D. thesis, Groningen.

Hopp, H.
2007 *Ultimate Attainment at the Interfaces in Second Language Acquisition: Grammar and Processing.* Groningen: Grodil Press.

Jackendoff, R.
1972 *Semantic Interpretation in Generative Grammar.* Cambridge, MA: MIT Press.

Jackendoff, R.
1990 *Semantic Structures.* Cambridge, MA: MIT Press.

Jacobs, J.
1988 Probleme der freien Wortstellung im Deutschen. *Sprache und Pragmatik* 5: 8–37.

Karimi, S.
2003 On object positions, specificity, and scrambling in Persian. In: S. Karimi (ed), *Word Order and Scrambling*, 91–124. Malden, MA/Oxford: Blackwell.

Kayne, R.
1994 *The Antisymmetry of Syntax*. Cambridge, MA: MIT Press.

Keller, F.
2000 Gradience in grammar. Experimental and computational aspects of degrees of grammaticality. Unpubl. Ph.D. thesis, University of Edinburgh.

Kempen, G., and K. Harbusch
2005 The relationship between grammaticality ratings and corpus frequencies: A case study into word order variability in the midfield of German clauses. In: S. Kepser, and M. Reis (eds.), Linguistic Evidence: Empirical, Theoretical, and Computational Perspectives, 329–349. Berlin: Mouton de Gruyter.

Krifka, M.
2010 How to interpret "expletive" negation under *bevor* in German. In: Thomas Hanneforth, and Gisbert Fanselow (eds.), *Language and Logos. Studies in Theoretical and Computational Linguistics*, 214–236. Berlin: Akademie Verlag.

Kromann, H. P.
1974 *Satz, Satzklammer und Ausklammerung*. Kopenhagen: Akademisk.

Kučerová, I.
2007 The syntax of givenness. Ph.D. thesis, MIT.

Kuno, S.
1975 Three perspectives in the functional approach to syntax. In: *Papers from the Functionalism Parasession, 11th Meeting of the Chicago Linguistic Society*, 276–336.

Lehmann, C.
1978 *Der Relativsatz im Persischen und Deutschen. Ein funktionell-kontrastiver Vergleich.* Köln: Institut für Sprachwissenschaft der Universität (Arbeitspapier 35).

Lenerz, J.
1977 *Zur Abfolge Nominaler Satzglieder im Deutschen.* (Studien zur deutschen Grammatik 5.) Tübingen: Narr.

Lenerz, J.
2001 Word order variation: Competition or co-operation. In: G. Müller, and W. Sternefeld (eds.), *Competition in Syntax*, 249–281. Berlin: Mouton de Gruyter.

Lötscher, A.
1981 Abfolgeregeln für Ergänzungen im Mittelfeld. *Deutsche Sprache* 9: 44–60.

Mahajan, A.
1994 Toward a unified theory of scrambling. In: Norbert Corver, and Henk van Riemsdijk (eds.), *Studies on Scrambling: Movement and Non-Movement Approaches to Free Word-Order Phenomena*, 301–330. Berlin: Mouton de Gruyter.

Maienborn, C.
2001 On the position and interpretation of locative modifiers. *Natural Language Semantics* 9: 191–240.

Massam, D.
2001 Pseudo noun incorporation. *Natural Language and Linguistic Theory* 19: 153–197.

Meinunger, A.
2000 *Syntactic Aspects of Topic and Comment.* Amsterdam: Benjamins.

Miyagawa, S., and T. Tsujioka
2004 Argument structure and ditransitive verbs in Japanese. *Journal of East Asian Linguistics* 13(1): 1–38.

Müller, G.
1998 *Incomplete Category Fronting*. Dordrecht: Kluwer.

Müller, G.
1999 Optimality, markedness, and word order in German. *Linguistics* 37: 777–818.
Müller, S.
2002 *Complex predicates: Verbal Complexes, Resultative Constructions and Particle Verbs in German*. Stanford, CA: CSLI.
Neeleman, A.
1994a Complex predicates. Ph.D. thesis, Utrecht University.
Neeleman, A.
1994b Scrambling as a D-structure phenomenon. In: N. Corver, and H. van Riemsdijk (eds.), *Studies on Scrambling: Movement and Non-Movement Approaches to Free Word-Order Phenomena*, 387–429. Berlin: Mouton de Gruyter.
Neeleman, A., and T. Reinhart
1998 Scrambling and the PF interface. In: Miriam Butt, and Wilhelm Geuder (eds.), *The Projection of Arguments: Lexical and Compositional Factors*, 309–353. Stanford: CSLI.
Pafel, J.
2009 Zur linearen Syntax des deutschen Satzes. *Linguistische Berichte* 217: 37–79.
Pollock, J.-Y.
1989 Verb movement, universal grammar, and the structure of IP. *Linguistic Inquiry* 20(3): 365–424.
Poncin, K.
2001 Präferierte Satzgliedfolge im Deutschen: Modell und experimentelle Evaluation. *Linguistische Berichte* 186: 175–203.
Primus, B.
1994 Grammatik und Performanz: Faktoren der Wortstellungsvariation im Mittelfeld. *Sprache und Pragmatik* 32: 39–86.
Putnam, M.
2007 *Scrambling and the Survive Principle*. Amsterdam: Benjamins.
Reinhart, T.
1996 Interface economy: Focus and markedness. In: C. Wilder, H.-M. Gärtner, and M. Bierwisch (eds.), *The Role of Economy Principles in Linguistic Theory*, 146–169. (Studia Grammatica 40.) Berlin: Akademie Verlag.
Reis, M.
1985 Mona Lisa kriegt zuviel – Vom sogenannten ‚Rezipintenpassiv' im Deutschen. *Linguistische Berichte* 96: 140–155.
Reis, M.
1987 Die Stellung der Verbargumente im Deutschen – Stilübungen zum Grammatik:Pragmatik-Verhältnis. In: I. Rosengren (ed.), *Sprache und Pragmatik – Lunder Symposium 1986*, 139–178. Stockholm: Almquist & Wiksell.
Ross, J.
1967 Constraints on variables in syntax. Ph.D. thesis, MIT. Appeared in 1986 as *Infinite Syntax*. Norwood, New Jersey: Ablex Publishing Corporation.
Schwarz, B., and R. Bhatt
2006 Light negation and polarity. In: R. Zanuttini, H. Campos, E. Herburger, and P. Portner (eds.), *Cross-Linguistic Research in Syntax and Semantics: Negation, Tense and Clausal Architecture*, 175–198. Washington, DC: Georgetown University Press.
Sekerina, I. A.
1997 Split scrambling in Russian and focus: Syntax and sentence processing. In: B. Bruening (ed.): *MIT Working Papers in Linguistics* 31, 377–392. Cambridge, MA: MIT Press.
Skopeteas, S., and G. Fanselow
2009 Effects of givenness and constraint on free word order. In: C. Féry, and M. Zimmermann (eds.), *Information Structure. Theoretical, Typological, and Experimental Perspectives*, 307–332. Oxford: Oxford University Press.

Sproat, R.
1985 Welsh syntax and VSO structure. *Natural Language and Linguistic Theory* 3: 173–216.
Tomlin, R. S.
1986 *Basic Word Order: Functional Principles.* London: Croom Helm.
Uszkoreit, H.
1986 Constraints on order. *Linguistics* 24: 883–906.
Venneman, T.
1973 Explanation in syntax. In: J. Kimball (ed.): *Syntax and Semantics* 2: 1–50. New York: Seminar Press.
Willim, E.
1989 *On Word Order: A Government-Binding Study of English and Polish.* Kraków: Zeszyty Naukowe Uniwersytetu Jagiellońskiego [Jagellonian University Cracow].
Yip, M., J. Maling, and R. Jackendoff
1987 Case in tiers. *Language* 63(2): 217–250.

Werner Frey, Berlin (Germany)

18. Ellipsis

Abstract

Ellipsis is hot in syntactic research these days, even though it is sometimes hard to consider it one single topic. There is a whole range of elliptical phenomena, with differences in distribution, eliding different parts of the sentence or phrase, and it is unclear whether these should receive a uniform analysis. Apart from the phenomena themselves, there are several approaches to ellipsis, focussing on three main questions. The first question involves the nature of the ellipsis site: if ellipsis is a mismatch between form and meaning, does the syntax match up with the form or the meaning? In other words, is there syntactic structure in the ellipsis site or not? Another question deals with the identity relationship between the ellipsis site and the antecedent and explores whether the identity needs to be syntactic or semantic, or whether a more hybrid approach is necessary. A last question involves the syntactic licensing of ellipsis. This chapter gives an overview of these issues and presents the different answers these questions have received in the ellipsis literature.

1. Introduction: What is ellipsis?

Natural language allows us to communicate through utterances which consist of strings of sounds that correspond to a certain meaning. Because of this match between sound and meaning, the hearer can interpret the utterances. In the case of ellipsis, however, the usual pattern of form-to-meaning mapping is disturbed. Ellipsis is the omission of elements that are inferable from the context, and therefore crucially constitutes a mismatch between form and meaning: there is no form, but the meaning is understood nevertheless.

When a speaker utters an elliptical sentence, its interpretation is richer that what is actually pronounced. This is illustrated in the example in (1): the second conjunct, which is called the ellipsis clause, can be interpreted by the hearer as meaning that Ryan has not seen *The Hobbit*, but that is not what is realised in form. Instead this meaning can be recovered from the interpretation of the first conjunct, the antecedent clause. The underscore marks the position of where the missing material, here the verb phrase *seen The Hobbit*, would be.

(1) *Jasmin has seen* The Hobbit, *but Ryan hasn't _.*

There are various ways in which something can be missing from an utterance, and different portions of the clause can be left unpronounced, and these different types of ellipsis have received different names to distinguish them from one another. The particular kind of ellipsis in (1) is called VP-ellipsis (VPE), and it is in fact one of the best studied types of ellipsis in the generative literature. The next section of this chapter discusses the various types and their differences.

The study of ellipsis has given rise to several big questions, or rather domains of investigation, the answers to which have far-reaching consequences for our understanding of grammar in general. A first question involves the *nature of the ellipsis site*. When the phonological realization and the semantics of a phrase do not match, the question to ask is how form and meaning are linked to one another, and where to situate the syntax. In other words: does the ellipsis site contain syntactic structure that is simply not pronounced, or is there no syntax present in the ellipsis site? Does the syntax go with the LF side or with the PF side of the utterance?

Roughly speaking, one could say that there are three prominent answers to this question. A first line of approaches are the non-structural ones, which argue that the syntax matches the phonetic realisation: there is no more structure to the sentence than what you can actually hear ("what you see – or rather, 'hear' – is what you get", cf. Ginzburg and Sag 2000; Culicover and Jackendoff 2005). On the other hand, there are the structural approaches, which take there to be something else present in the syntax than what you hear. There are two distinct ways to approach this 'something else' still, however. One way is implemented by the null element analyses. These assume that there is an empty element present in the syntax, a null proform replacing the elided material, but which does not contain any syntactic structure itself. The meaning of the ellipsis site is derived from the antecedent, either by LF-copy, i.e., copying its LF representation into the ellipsis site, as argued by Fiengo and May (1994), Chung et al. (1995), Wilder (1997), Beavers and Sag (2004) and Fortin (2007), or by interpreting it the way regular pronouns are understood, as in Wasow (1972); Shopen (1972); Hardt (1993, 1999); Lobeck (1995) and Depiante (2000). A third strand of accounts, also structural, involves

PF-deletion (cf. Johnson 2001; Merchant 2001; Aelbrecht 2010; see also Ross 1969 for an early deletion analysis; Hankamer and Sag 1976). These authors argue that there is no syntactic structure missing, but that the phonological content is deleted at the PF level because the antecedent renders the interpretation of the unpronounced part recoverable. In this sense, the syntax follows the semantics, the meaning of the utterance, and not the form. Section 3 will be presenting these different approaches in more detail, and section 4 deals with the diagnostics that have been proposed to determine whether an ellipsis site hosts unpronounced syntactic structure or not.

A second important question that has dominated the literature on the topic, has to do with one of the principal conditions on ellipsis. Ellipsis is subject to two main constraints, namely recoverability and syntactic licensing (parallel to the conditions on empty elements such as *pro*, traces and PRO, see Rizzi 1986). It is clear that a constituent can only be elided when there is an antecedent present, but there has been quite some debate about the restrictions on this antecedent. What counts as an antecedent? How local or salient does it have to be? And most importantly, what is the *relationship of identity* between the antecedent and the ellipsis site? Do they have to be syntactically identical? Or only semantically? Or a certain combination of both? This question has given rise to quite some debate, and authors are divided in their answers, with among many others Sag (1976), Williams (1977), Fiengo and May (1994), Chung et al. (1995), Lasnik (1995), Kehler (2002), Merchant (2008a) and Johnson (2012) on the syntactic identity side, and Keenan (1971), Hankamer and Sag (1984), Hardt (1993), Ginzburg and Sag (2000), Merchant (2001), Culicover and Jackendoff (2005) and van Craenenbroeck (2010) representing the semantic identity view. A central role is being played by phenomena involving mismatches in syntactic structure between the antecedent and the ellipsis site, and the idea of syntactic identity combined with an *accommodated* antecedent has been pursued more recently (see for instance, Fox 1999, 2000; Nevins, Rodriguez, and Vicente 2007; van Craenenbroeck 2012; Johnson 2012). The identity issue will be treated in section 5.

Section 6 then deals with the second condition on ellipsis: *syntactic licensing*. Apparently, it is not enough to have an identical antecedent for the ellipsis site to be left unpronounced. This is indicated by the contrast between the English examples in (2): the first sentence displays a grammatical case of VP ellipsis, while the second occurrence, with a similar antecedent and ellipsis site, is unacceptable. Another example is shown in (3), where a cross-linguistic comparison illustrates that VP-ellipsis is fine in English, but not in Dutch or French, for instance, even though the antecedents are equally local and salient.

(2) a. *Lola should eat grapes, but Simon shouldn't.*
b. **Lola started to eat grapes, but Simon didn't start.*

(3) a. *Mark had played that game today, and Lia had too.*
b. **Mark had dat spel gespeeld vandaag, en Lia had ook.* [Dutch]
c. **Mark avait joué ce jeu aujourd'hui, et Lia avait aussi.* [French]

This indicates that recoverability of the ellipsis site is a necessary but not a sufficient condition for ellipsis, and that the syntactic context itself plays a role as well. Apparently, the ellipsis of the verb phrase is licensed in (2a), but not in (2b), nor in the Dutch or

French examples in (3), even though the recoverability condition is fulfilled to the same extent in all these languages. In other words, there must be something in the syntax of these languages that determines whether or not a certain (recoverable) constituent can be elided. The question of what licenses ellipsis syntactically is a long-standing one as well, starting with Sag (1976), Williams (1977) and Zagona's (1982, 1988a, b) concept of an ellipsis-licensing head. Lobeck's (1995) approach works out the idea that ellipsis is licensed in the same way as other (in her view) null *pro*'s by the Empty Category Principle (ECP, Chomsky 1981). Merchant (2001) later introduces the E-feature for ellipsis on the licensor, which has since been used and modified by many researchers (Aelbrecht 2010; van Craenenbroeck 2010; Gengel 2007a, 2008; among many others), and Thoms (2011) argues away from the notion of licensing heads and instead claims that ellipsis is licensed by movement. Some of these developments are explored in section 6.

2. Elliptical phenomena: a quick overview

As mentioned above, the term "ellipsis" covers several phenomena in which there is a mismatch between sound and meaning. Before I go into the various analyses that are available for ellipsis, I first illustrate some of the most common types with prototypical examples. Research on ellipsis tends to name the different phenomena in a rather creative way, which can become confusing if one is not familiar with these names. The list I present is by no means exhaustive, and some types might very well be taken together, representing one and the same type, but it gives the interested reader a starting-point.

2.1. VP-ellipsis

One of the most commonly studied elliptical phenomena, even though its distribution is notoriously restricted among the Western languages that have received most attention up till now, is VP-ellipsis (VPE). Typically, English VPE leaves the main (non-finite verbal) predicate and its arguments unpronounced, as in (4).

(4) a. *Roy likes strawberries, but Jen doesn't.*
 b. *Roy has bought cream, and Jen has, too.*

These sentences are interpreted by the hearer as if the predicate and its arguments (here indicated between squared brackets) were present:

(5) a. *Roy likes strawberries, but Jen doesn't [~~like strawberries~~].*
 b. *Roy has bought cream, and Jen has [~~bought cream~~], too.*

Unlike in the typical English cases, other languages which display VPE usually allow the main verb to remain overt as well when it is finite, as the Brazilian Portuguese example in (6) shows (see Raposo 1986; Cyrino and Matos 2002, 2005; Tescari 2013).

(6) *A Ana não leva o computador para as aulas,* [Brazilian Potuguese]
the Ana not brings the computer to the classes
porque os amigos também não ***levam****.*
because the friends too not bring
'Ana does not bring her computer to the classes because her friends don't either.'
(Cyrino and Matos 2002: 180)

This is what Goldberg (2005) calls "V-stranding VPE": in languages in which the main verb moves to IP to receive its finite inflection – unlike in English (see Emonds 1976, 1978; Pollock 1989; see also Lasnik 1995) – this verb has vacated the VP when VPE occurs, and consequently, is not included in the ellipsis site.

"VP-ellipsis" is not in fact ellipsis of just the VP. As has already been argued by Johnson (2001, 2004), Merchant (2001, 2008a, 2013) and Aelbrecht (2010), VPE elides at least as much as vP. More recently, a series of articles has been written which argue that VPE targets even more than this, based on arguments involving the deletion of non-finite auxiliary verbs: according to these works VPE targets the progressive layer or more (Sailor and Kuo 2010; Bošković *to appear*; Aelbrecht and Harwood 2013; Harwood 2013, among others).

2.2. Sluicing

In his seminal (1969) work, Ross examined a phenomenon he named sluicing: in a clause with a *wh*-element, the whole clause following this element can be left out if it has an antecedent, as in (7). The interpretation of the sentence includes this missing clause, however.

(7) a. *Roy invited someone, but I don't know who.*
b. *Roy invited someone, but I don't know who [~~Roy invited~~].*

Since it is the whole clause that is elided, sluicing is considered a kind of IP-ellipsis or clausal ellipsis. We will see later on that there are other kinds of clausal ellipsis as well, that do not involve a *wh*-element.

There are several phenomena which could be considered a subtype of sluicing. A first case is Relative Deletion in Hungarian (see Van Craenenbroeck and Lipták 2006: [1]), where ellipsis takes place in a relative clause, leaving the relative pronoun and a focused remnant (see also Hoyt and Theodorescu 2004 for what is called focus sluicing in Romanian):

(8) *Kornél AZT A LÁNYT hívta meg, akit ZOLTÁN* [Hungarian]
Kornél that.ACC the girl.ACC invited PV REL.who.ACC Zoltán
[~~*hívott meg*~~].
invited PV
'The girl who Kornél invited was the one who Zoltán did.'

Another subtype is known as *swiping*, Sluiced *Wh*-word Inversion with Prepositions in Northern Germanic (a term proposed by Merchant 2002), which looks like sluicing, but with an inversed preposition as extra remnant:

(9) a. *He was going to give a lecture, but I don't know what about.*
b. *He was going to give a lecture, but I don't know what [~~he was going to give a lecture~~] about.*

A third sluicing subtype is found in Dutch, for instance, and it is termed *spading* by Van Craenenbroeck (2010). Dutch has sluicing, similar to English, as in (10a), but it can also have an extra remnant in the form of a demonstrative pronoun *da* 'that', as is illustrated in (10b), with the elided material shown in (10c) (see Van Craenenbroeck 2004, 2010 for the details of the analysis).

(10) a. *Maaike heeft iemand uitgenodigd, maar ik weet niet wie.* [Dutch]
Maaike has someone invited but I know not who
'Maaike invited someone, but I don't know who.'

b. *Maaike heeft iemand uitgenodigd, maar ik weet niet wie da.*
Maaike has someone invited but I know not who that.DEM
'Maaike invited someone, but I don't know who.'

c. *Maaike heeft iemand uitgenodigd, maar ik weet niet wie ~~dat~~*
Maaike has someone invited but I know not who that.COMPL
da ~~is da~~ ~~Maaike uitgenodigd heeft~~
that.DEM is that.COMPL Maaike invited has

2.3. NP-ellipsis

Ellipsis does not always target a smaller or larger portion of the clausal spine; it can also apply within nominal phrases. Examples of this NP-ellipsis are given in (11), with the interpreted missing elements between square brackets.

(11) a. *Roy's older brother is taller than Jeff's [~~older brother~~].*
b. *Steve bought these pants and Jeff bought those [~~pants~~].*
c. *Jen wanted three balloons with pink ribbons and Jane wanted two [~~balloons with pink ribbons~~].*
d. *Jen wanted three balloons with pink ribbons and Jane wanted two [~~balloons~~] with blue ribbons.*

What is missing in this case is the head noun and sometimes also its adjectival modifiers and complement.

Next, I turn to several commonly discussed kinds of ellipses which will be shown to differ from the ones mentioned so far with respect to certain crucial properties.

2.4. Fragment answers

Not all ellipses have an antecedent that – in the prototypical cases – is uttered by the same speaker (note that all three previous types can have antecedents uttered by another speaker). A very common type of ellipsis one might not immediately think of as such is fragment answers, as in (12). In fragment answers, the whole clause is elided except for the constituent that is the answer to a question, and it is this question that provides us with an antecedent. The most influential analysis of fragments is Merchant's (2004) work (but see also Temmerman 2013), in which he argues that the fragment constituent moves to the left periphery of the clause, and that what follows is deleted at PF (see section 3.2.2 for more on PF deletion). This is shown in (12c).

(12) a. *What did Roy eat? – Strawberries.*
b. *~~Roy ate~~ strawberries.*
c. *Strawberries [~~Roy ate $t_{strawberries}$~~].*

2.5. Stripping (aka bare argument ellipsis)

A type of ellipsis that is very similar to fragment answers in the sense that there is only one constituent surviving the ellipsis in the clause, is stripping (or bare argument ellipsis). The difference is that stripping typically occurs in coordinated structures, and the remnant is usually accompanied by negation or an intensifier:

(13) a. *Roy wanted strawberries, and Jen, too.*
b. *Roy wanted to buy cream, but not Jen.*

Stripping differs from VPE, NPE and sluicing in several respects, as elaborated on in Lobeck (1995). First of all, stripping is only possible in coordination, not subordination:

(14) a. **Roy wanted strawberries because Lola, too.*
b. **Roy wanted to buy cream, although not Jen.*

I illustrate that subordination is possible in VPE, but the same also holds for sluicing and NP ellipsis.

(15) a. *Gonzo ate peas because Lola did.*
b. *Gonzo ate peas, although Lola didn't.*

Another, related property involves what Langacker (1966) called the Backward Anaphora Constraint, which states that an ellipsis site can precede, but not c-command its antecedent. This is shown to hold for VPE in (16a, b). The examples in (16c, d) illustrate that stripping does not allow the ellipsis site to precede the antecedent (which is expected if the first conjunct of a coordination c-commands the second one, and stripping only occurs in coordination, not subordination).

(16) a. *Although Gonzo doesn't [~~like peas~~], Lola likes peas a lot.*
b. **Gonzo doesn't [~~like peas~~], although Lola likes peas a lot.*
c. **Although not carrots, Gonzo ate peas.*

d. **Not carrots, but Gonzo ate peas.*

We will see that the phenomenon discussed in the next section, gapping, patterns with stripping in these respects.

2.6. Gapping

Gapping is very similar to stripping, but instead of a negator or intensifier, a second contrasted remnant remains:

(17) a. *Lola gave her brother strawberries and her sister cherries.*
b. *Lola wants to study in the garden, but Jen in the library.*

Just like stripping, gapping is only allowed in coordinations, and as expected, it does not allow the ellipsis site to precede the antecedent (see Jackendoff 1971; Hankamer 1979).

(18) a. *Gonzo ate the peas, and/but Lola the carrots.*
b. **Gonzo ate the peas, although/because Lola the carrots.*
c. **Gonzo the peas, and/because Lola ate the carrots.*

Although gapping is standardly taken to be an elliptical phenomenon, there are also authors who argue for an account of gapping that does not involve ellipsis at all. Johnson (2009) claims that gapping is derived through low coordination and across-the-board-movement (but see Toosarvandani 2013 for a reply to this view).

2.7. Pseudogapping

A phenomenon that looks like a combination of gapping and VP-ellipsis is pseudogapping. Examples are given in (19), where what is elided is the verb phrase except for one contrasted remnant. The auxiliary verb remains as well, in contrast to what we saw for gapping. Another remarkable difference with gapping and stripping is that pseudogapping is actually best in subordinated structures, such as comparatives.

(19) a. *Roy ate strawberries this morning, and Jen did cherries.*
b. *Roy ate more strawberries than Jen did cherries.*

The most widely accepted approach to pseudogapping views it as a kind of VP-ellipsis, but where the remnant constituent has vacated the VP prior to the ellipsis. There has, however, been a lot of debate on why the remnant moves and where it lands (see Jayaseelan 1990; Lasnik 1999; Gengel 2007b, 2013; Aelbrecht 2010).

2.8. Modal Complement Ellipsis

We have already noted that VP-ellipsis is rather limited in its distribution across languages. It occurs in English, and quite a few other languages such as Hebrew, Irish,

Welsh, Portuguese, Danish, Japanese, Swahili, Serbo-Croatian and Taiwanese, but not in many other languages that are related to some of these, such as Dutch, German, French, Italian, Spanish, or Swedish.

It is remarkable, however, that there is a type of ellipsis in several of these languages that is reminiscent of VPE, as shown in (20):

(20) a. *Ik wil wel helpen, maar ik kan niet.* [Dutch]
I want PRT help but I can not

b. *Je veux bien aider mais je ne peux pas.* [French]
I want PRT help but I NEG can not
'I want to help, but I can't.'

Aelbrecht (2010) shows that this is not actually a case of VP-ellipsis: it is restricted to elide the complements of (root) modal verbs, and what is elided is more than just the verb phrase. For more details on this Modal Complement Ellipsis (or MCE) and its properties, see Aelbrecht (2010), but also Dagnac (2010) for a closer look at MCE in Romance languages.

2.9. Null Complement Anaphora

A last elliptical phenomenon I will touch upon here, is called Null Complement Anaphora (NCA), illustrated in (21).

(21) *I asked Jeff to help me, but he refused [~~to help me~~].*

Depiante (2000) argues that NCA, which elides the entire infinitival complement of a verb, differs from VPE in some crucial respects. We come back to this in the next section where we discuss the various analyses for ellipsis.

3. Analysing silence: various viewpoints

The introduction already mentioned that there are several quite different answers to the first big question one should ask when studying the mismatch between form and meaning: If what you hear is not the same as what you interpret, what is present in the ellipsis site syntactically? Does the syntax match with the phonology or with the interpretation? Merchant (2005: 3) represents this discussion on the syntax of an ellipsis site schematically.

The present section elaborates on these different viewpoints. I first discuss the non-structural accounts, focusing on the recent fully worked-out proposal by Culicover and Jackendoff (2005), and then turn to the structural analyses, which do assume the presence of at least some syntactic structure in the ellipsis site, be it a fully specified structure, a null proform or a structure with empty categories (see also Aelbrecht 2010 for discussion).

(22)

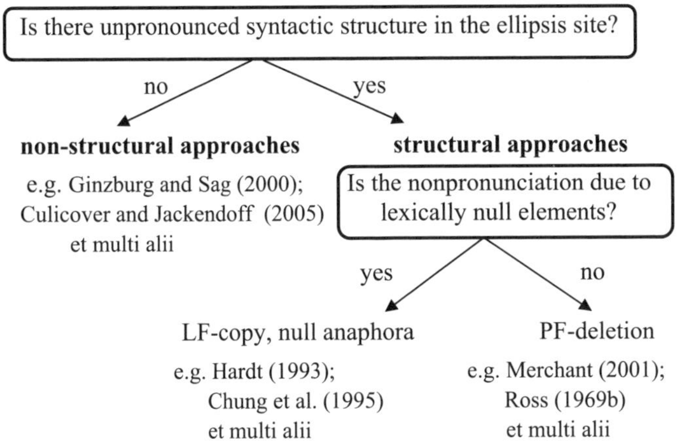

3.1. Non-structural approaches

Non-structural approaches represent what we could call WYSIWYG, 'what you see is what you get' (or rather WYHIWYG, 'what you *hear*…'): there is no more structure in the sentence than what is actually pronounced; no deleted parts, no null elements. However, we know that the interpretation of an elliptical sentence is richer than its actual phonetic realization, implying that the syntax-semantics interface will have to play a significant role in order to get the correct meaning. Some accounts along these lines are Van Riemsdijk (1978), Ginzburg and Sag (2000), Schlangen (2003), Culicover and Jackendoff (2005) and Stainton (2006).

The simplest and most naive implementation of this view assigns the sluice in (23a) the structure in (23b): the verb *know* only selects a wh-phrase as its complement.

(23) a. *Someone had brought strawberries, but I don't know who.*
b. *…but I don't*

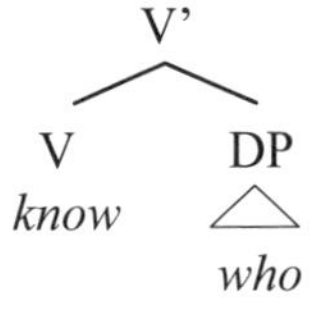

Merchant (2001: 40–54) indicates some immediate problems with such an analysis. For instance, the sluiced phrase behaves like a clausal complement, not a nominal one, with respect to its distribution and the agreement with the finite verb. Moreover, the *wh*-phrase can be shown to not get its case assigned by the verb *know*, but by the verb that is missing inside the ellipsis site (see also section 4).

A more sophisticated implementation of this approach is proposed in Culicover and Jackendoff's (2005) *Simpler Syntax*. They argue for an indirect licensing approach of ellipsis, which 'posits no more syntactic structure than appears at the surface, in conformity with the Simpler Syntax Hypothesis' (Culicover and Jackendoff 2005: 235):

(24) Simpler Syntax Hypothesis (SSH)
The most explanatory theory is one that imputes the minimum syntactic structure necessary to mediate between phonology and meaning.
(Culicover and Jackendoff 2005: 5)

They claim that "if machinery exists that accounts for the interpretation of a fragment of one type, without appealing to covert syntactic structure containing the fragment, then that machinery is available for all types of fragments and constitutes the default hypothesis" (Culicover and Jackendoff 2005: 235). For example, they compare stripping and sluicing to *wh*-movement and topicalisation, and claim that there is an 'orphan' phrase in all these cases that needs to be licensed indirectly. Three kinds of indirect licensing can be distinguished: "matching" – in which the orphan is matched with an existing constituent of the clause –, "sprouting" – where the orphan is a supplement to the clause by spelling out an implicit argument or adjunct (following Chung et al. 1995) – and a third type in which the orphan corresponds to a trace in the clause (Culicover and Jackendoff 2005: 257–258).

I illustrate the mechanism of indirect licensing (IL) with the sluicing example in (23). The sluiced clause is interpreted as an embedded question '(I don't know) who had brought strawberries', even though this question is not pronounced. The *wh*-phrase *who* refers to a questioned argument in an unexpressed proposition P, corresponding to the proposition expressed by the antecedent. Through the connection with this antecedent both the semantic and the syntactic features of the orphan are 'indirectly licensed', resulting in the structure in (25).

(25)

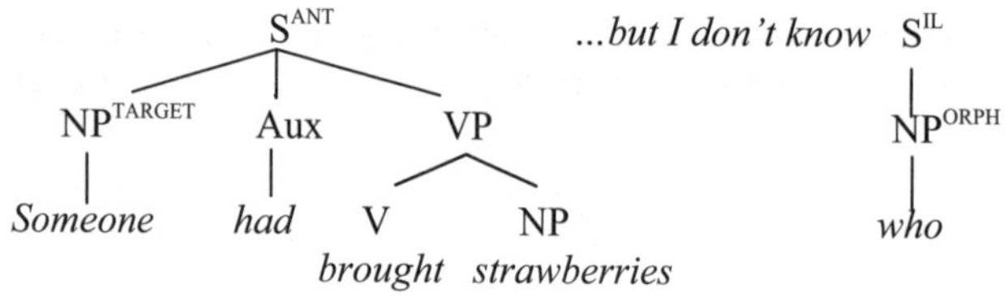

The structure shows that the sluice is of category S but only contains an orphan NP. This orphan finds a target NP in the antecedent from which it receives its semantic and syntactic features, but it is realised as the *wh*-phrase *who*. The semantics of sluicing are given in (26): because there is a question operator Qx binding the *wh*-word, the sluice is interpreted as an embedded question. It acquires its propositional content F through indirect licensing, i.e., via the antecedent in the discourse.

(26) **Sluicing**
Syntax: $[_{S}$ *wh*-phrase$_{i}^{ORPH}]^{IL}$
Semantics: $Qx[\mathcal{F}(x_i)]$
(Culicover and Jackendoff 2005: 270)

This view on ellipsis – and on grammar in general – clearly presupposes less syntactic structure. On the other hand, it requires a much richer syntax-semantics interface to map utterances to the interpretation they receive. There is no more syntax in ellipsis than what is actually realised, but elliptical utterances are processed as full sentences through the mechanism of indirect licensing. In other words, even though the syntax itself might be simpler, this approach requires a much more complex mapping from syntax to semantics, which could be seen as a major drawback of the theory. See also Aelbrecht (2010) for instance, which is essentially an extended argument against a non-structural approach to ellipsis.

3.2. Structural approaches

Unlike non-structural views, structural approaches to ellipsis give an affirmative answer to the question of whether there is unpronounced syntax in the ellipsis site. Even so, there are several approaches still within these accounts. The unpronounced structure can be silent because it only contains elements that were null in the first place, or it can be unpronounced because of deletion of its phonological content, or lack of (late) lexical insertion, at PF. I first discuss the perspective assuming null lexical elements before I turn to the deletion account.

3.2.1. Null proforms and LF copy

A first line of structural approaches argues that there is indeed more in the syntax than what we hear, but that the syntax does not match with the semantics completely either: there is no fully specified syntactic structure in the ellipsis site, but rather, there are null elements which get their interpretation from the antecedent.

Among the accounts assuming null elements two points of view can be distinguished. The *null proform* approach, advocated by Wasow (1972), Shopen (1972), Hardt (1993, 1999), Lobeck (1995) and Depiante (2000), argues that the ellipsis site contains a null proform *pro*. This proform is interpreted like overt pronouns by purely semantic means. The other account, called the *LF-copy analysis*, claims that the antecedent is instead copied into the ellipsis site at LF, providing the null element(s) with the right interpretation in this way (see Fiengo and May 1994; Chung et al. 1995; Wilder 1997; Beavers and Sag 2004 and Fortin 2007). I abstract away from the differences between the two options, however, and refer the interested reader to Winkler (2003) for a detailed presentation of both alternatives.

The proform approach can be represented as in (27) for the sluicing example we saw earlier. In this case, the ellipsis site is a proform that stands for an entire IP, parallel to the overt pronoun *it* in (28) which corresponds to an entire CP.

(27) a. *Someone had brought strawberries, but I don't know who.*
b. *... but I don't*

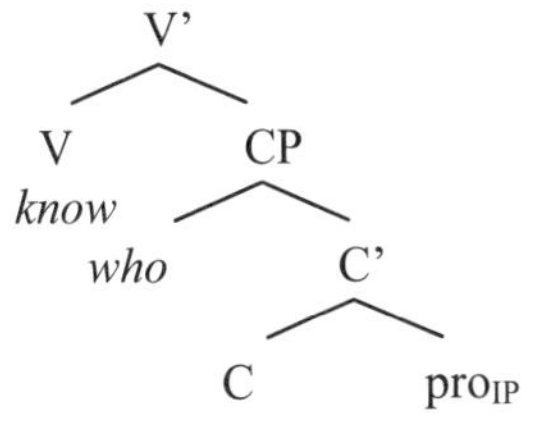

(28) a. *Someone had brought strawberries, and I didn't know **it**.*
b. *it = that someone had brought strawberries*

A first argument in favor of this view is the fact that ellipsis sites behave like overt pronouns in certain respects. For example, pronouns can take split antecedents and so can VP-ellipsis (cf. [29]). Moreover, Lobeck (1995) points out that ellipsis can take a non-linguistic antecedent in some cases, parallel to pronouns (cf. [30]).

(29) a. *Brian$_i$ told Jill$_j$ that they$_{i+j}$ could go away together.*
b. *I can walk and I can chew gum. Gerry can too, but not at the same time.*
(Hardt 1993)

(30) a. [Pointing at someone:]
***He** should do that.*
b. [On receiving a present:]
You shouldn't have!
(Lobeck 1995)

Secondly, the island insensitivity of sluicing indicates that the ellipsis site does not contain any more syntactic structure than a pronoun. Take the sentences in (31), which show that *wh*-movement of *which Balkan language* is ungrammatical out of a complex NP island.

(31) a. *I don't know [which Balkan language]$_i$ Susan speaks t_i.*
b. **I don't know [which Balkan language]$_I$ they want to hire someone who speaks t_i.*

In the sluicing example in (32a), however, no island violation seems to take place, even though the non-elliptical counterpart of this sentence in (31b) is unacceptable (Ross 1969; see Merchant 2001 for an extensive discussion). Therefore, this has been taken as evidence that the *wh*-phrase has not in fact been extracted from the ellipsis site and that the ellipsis site does not contain any syntactic structure but is instead a null proform:

(32) a. *They want to hire someone who speaks a Balkan language, but I don't know which Balkan language.*
b. *They want to hire someone who speaks a Balkan language, but I don't know which Balkan language pro$_{IP}$.*

The same island insensitivity has also been observed in fragment answers by Culicover and Jackendoff (2005) and Stainton (2006).

However, there are also some arguments against this analysis. If ellipsis sites are like pronouns, we do not expect cases such as the one in (33a), where the ellipsis site is contained in the antecedent. Parallel to what happens with the pronoun in (33c, d), interpreting the antecedent in the ellipsis site would lead to infinite regress (as in [33b]; see Sag 1976). Nevertheless, such "antecedent-contained deletion" – or ACD – is allowed.

(33) a. *Christina [read every book Hilary did pro$_i$]$_i$*
b. **Christina read every book Hilary did [read every book Hilary did [read every book Hilary did [read every book ...]]].*
c. **Waldo saw [a picture of it$_i$]$_i$*
d. **Waldo saw [a picture of a picture of a picture of ...].*

Furthermore, there is evidence that an ellipsis site can contain more syntactic structure than a mere pronoun. These data will be discussed in section 4, after we present the PF-deletion approach.

3.2.2. PF-deletion

The previous sections presented approaches to ellipsis in which the syntax matched the form either partially or in full, and the semantics of the ellipsis site had to be retrieved from the antecedent. The third and last account takes the exact opposite point of view: the syntax of ellipsis matches the interpretation, and it is the phonology of the elliptical sentence that deviates from its non-elliptical counterpart. The ellipsis site is a fully-fledged syntactic structure, so at LF nothing much changes compared to non-ellipsis, but PF leaves part of the structure unpronounced, through some kind of operation. One could say it is an extreme form of whispering (p.c. Jason Merchant). This is illustrated in (34) below, where the gray font represents unpronounced material.

This (PF-)deletion approach was first explored in its pre-PF form by Ross's (1967, 1969) seminal work, and further worked out by Lasnik (1999), Merchant (2001, 2004 and subsequent work), Johnson (2001), Tomioka (2004), Gengel (2007a, 2008), van Craenenbroeck (2010), Aelbrecht (2010) and many others. I come back to some of these proposals and how PF-deletion is implemented technically in section 6, where I discuss the licensing of ellipsis.

(34) a. *Someone had bought strawberries, but I don't know who.*
b. *... but I don't*

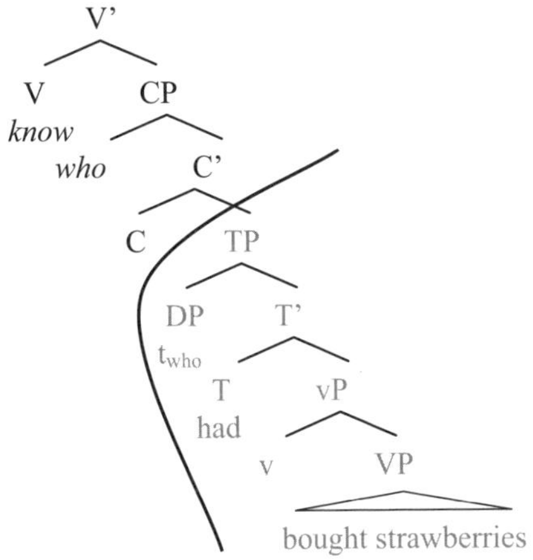

In the previous section I have already mentioned several pieces of evidence that show that the ellipsis site does not contain a full syntactic structure. The problem with this debate is that there are also quite a few data that point in the exact opposite direction. The next section reviews some of the indications put forward in favour of syntactic structure.

4. Deleted structure or not? Diagnostics

Merchant (2001, 2004) provides several arguments supporting the deletion approach for sluicing. What this basically comes down to is proving that there is syntactic structure in the ellipsis site that you cannot see or hear. The only way to be able to do this is to show that this present but unpronounced syntactic material affects its environment in the same way that it would if it were pronounced. Merchant gives several sets of data that point to such so-called connectivity effects in ellipsis. Due to reasons of space I cannot go into all of them, but I refer the interested reader to Merchant (2004), and discuss a couple of the pieces of evidence here. First, the island-insensitivity that was observed for sluicing does not hold for VPE. Second, Merchant shows that there is a correlation between preposition stranding in ellipsis and in non-elliptical *wh*-questions. A third set of data that I discuss involves case marking. And lastly, the fact that elements can be extracted from the ellipsis site indicates that it has to contain enough syntactic structure to host the movement trace.

4.1. Island (in)sensitivity

I first present the island-sensitivity argument. Recall that sluicing is not sensitive to island violations, see (32), and that this was taken to be evidence that the ellipsis site does not contain anything more than a null proform. It turns out that VPE is sensitive to island violations, however, as (35) illustrates:

(35) a. **I don't know [which Balkan language]$_i$ Susan knows someone who speaks* t_i.
b. **Steve knows someone who speaks Romanian, but I don't know [which Balkan language]$_i$ Susan knows [~~someone who speaks t_i~~].*

Relying on the other arguments in favour of syntactic structure inside the ellipsis site (which will be presented below), Merchant (2001) argues that sluicing (high ellipsis) can repair island violations, while VPE (low ellipsis) cannot. I refer the interested reader to Merchant's work and the vast literature on ellipsis repair (Merchant 2001, 2002, 2007; Lasnik 2001; van Craenenbroeck and Den Dikken 2006; Müller 2011; but see also Barros 2012; Abels 2012). What should be clear from this remarkable contrast is that a lot more research needs to be done in the domain of islands and how exactly ellipsis relates to the locality effects.

4.2. Preposition stranding

Next, we look at the argument involving preposition stranding (Merchant 2001, 2004). English allows *wh*-movement to target only the DP complement of a preposition and leave the P head itself behind, as in (36a), while Greek, on the other hand, does not (cf. [36b]).

(36) a. *Who did he talk **to**?*
b. **Pjon milise **me**?* [Greek]
who she.spoke with
(Merchant 2004: 667)

This behavioural contrast between the two languages is mirrored in sluicing: English allows sluicing to strand the preposition in the ellipsis site, whereas Greek does not (cf. [37]).

(37) a. *He talked to someone, but I don't know who.*
b. *I Anna milise me kapjon, alla dhe ksero *(**me**) pjon.* [Greek]
the Anna spoke with someone but not I.know with who
Anna talked to someone, but I don't know with who.'
(Merchant 2004: 667)

If the ellipsis site has a fully-fledged syntactic structure, this can easily be captured: the same restrictions apply in ellipsis as in non-ellipsis (Merchant 2001, 2004). Based on a sample of 18 languages, Merchant puts forward the Preposition Stranding Generalization that says "A language L will allow preposition stranding under sluicing if and only if L allows preposition stranding under regular *wh*-movement" (Merchant 2001: 92).

It should be noted that there have been observed some apparent counter-examples to this generalization by several authors focussing on different languages (Almeida and Yoshida 2007; Fortin 2007; Stjepanović 2008, 2012; Nykiel and Sag 2008; Vicente 2008, van Craenenbroeck 2008; Rodrigues et al. 2009). Most of these authors, however, still provide a structural analysis for ellipsis and argue that the apparent exceptions to the P-Stranding Generalization are only found in certain environments which, for instance, allow for an interpretation of the ellipsis site without the preposition. Again, the last word has not been said on this topic.

4.3. Case-marking

A third set of data in favour of deletion of syntactic structure concerns morphological Case-marking (Ross 1967, 1969; Merchant 2001, 2004). The *wh*-element in the German example in (38a) appears with the structural dative Case that it would receive from the missing verb *schmeicheln* 'flatter' in the non-elliptical counterpart (cf. [38b]). In (39) on the other hand, the verb *loben* 'praise' assigns accusative Case to its object in a non-elliptical sentence, and accordingly, the *wh*-element appears with accusative Case in the sluice (examples taken from Merchant 2004: 665–666). Absence of internal structure in the ellipsis site leaves this difference in Case-marking between these two sluices unexplained.

(38) a. *Er will jemandem schmeicheln, aber sie wissen nicht* [German]
he wants someone flatter but they know not
*{*wer /*wen / wem}.*
who.NOM who.ACC who.DAT
'He wants to flatter someone, but they don't know who.'

b. *Er will jemandem schmeicheln, aber sie wissen nicht*
he wants someone flatter but they know not
*{*wer /*wen / wem} er schmeicheln will.*
who.NOM who.ACC who.DAT he flatter wants
'He wants to flatter someone, but they don't know who he wants to flatter.'

(39) a. *Er will jemanden loben, aber sie wissen nicht* [German]
he wants someone praise but they know not
*{*wer / wen /*wem}.*
who.NOM who.ACC who.DAT
'He wants to praise someone, but they don't know who.'

b. *Er will jemanden loben, aber sie wissen nicht*
he wants someone praise but they know not
*{*wer / wen /*wem} er loben will.*
who.NOM who.ACC who.DAT he flatter wants
'He wants to praise someone, but they don't know who he wants to praise.'

4.4. Extraction

A final piece of evidence for structure in the ellipsis site that I discuss here are extraction possibilities. If the ellipsis site does not contain any syntactic structure, extraction out of an ellipsis site is impossible, as the moved elements would not have a position to be base-generated in. On the other hand, if syntactic structure is present, it can host the movement trace and be deleted after movement has taken place. The example in (40) indicates that the object *which one* can be extracted from an elided verb phrase (see Schuyler 2002 for some restrictions on this extraction).

(40) *I know which puppy YOU should take home, but I don't know* ***which one*** *SHE should [~~take home~~ ~~$t_{which\ puppy}$~~].*

Note that not all types of ellipsis allow (all) extraction out of the ellipsis site. Depiante (2000) shows that no element can be extracted out of the ellipsis site in Null Complement Anaphora (NCA), as in (41).

(41) **I know Dany made a mojito, but I don't remember* ***which cocktail*** *he refused [~~to make~~ ~~$t_{which\ cocktail}$~~].*

She concludes from this data that, unlike VP ellipsis and sluicing, NCA should not be analyzed as PF-deletion, but rather should receive a proform analysis.

Aelbrecht (2010) uses the extraction test for Modal Complement Ellipsis and observes that MCE allows for subject extraction out of the ellipsis site, but not object extraction, as illustrated in (42).

(42) a. *Die broek moet niet gewassen worden, maar die rok mag* [Dutch]
those pants must not washed become but that skirt is.allowed
wel al [~~*gewassen* $t_{die\ rok}$~~ ~~*worden*~~].
PRT already washed become (subject extraction is allowed)
'Those pants don't have to be washed, but that skirt can already be.'

b. **Ik weet niet wie Thomas wil uitnodigen, maar ik weet wie hij niet*
I know not who Thomas wants invite but I know who he not
mag [~~*uitnodigen*~~ t_{wie}].
is.allowed invite (object extraction is disallowed)
'I don't know who Thomas wants to invite, but I know who he's not allowed to.'

She shows that the extraction test should only be used uni-directionally: if extraction is allowed, there is deleted syntactic structure, but if (certain) extractions are blocked, this can also be due to some independent reason (in this case, the timing of ellipsis, see section 6 on licensing, cf. Aelbrecht 2010 for details). In other words, the lack of extraction does not automatically mean that the ellipsis site is a null proform without internal structure, although it can be.

As this section and the previous one have shown, there are several different approaches to ellipsis, and all of them have their advantages and drawbacks. It was also pointed out that many of the arguments for or against syntactic structure in the ellipsis site could go either way, depending on which phenomenon one is looking at. It is perhaps true that not all elliptical phenomena should be given one uniform analysis, but that they come about through different mechanisms, even though from an economical perspective it might seem odd that language would have different strategies at hand to not pronounce part of an utterance. In the next two sections we come back to the conditions that ellipsis is subject to, namely the recoverability condition and syntactic licensing.

5. Recovering what is missing

Ellipsis is subject to the condition of recoverability: you can only leave part of your utterance unpronounced if there is a straightforward way for the hearer to recover its meaning from the context. When uttered out of the blue, the sentence in (43a) is ungrammatical, and the sentence in (43b) can only have the first interpretation. In other words, an ellipsis site has to be recoverable by means of a salient linguistic antecedent.

(43) a. [Uttered out of the blue:]
#I know Theano has.

b. *I found three old coins and Oliver found two.*
=I found three old coins and Oliver found two [~~old coins~~].
≠I found three old coins and Oliver found two [~~small sculptures~~].

Merchant (2004) argues that the antecedent is not necessarily linguistic. An elided constituent can also find an antecedent in the non-linguistic context, parallel to deictic anaphora (but see Hankamer and Sag 1976). I gloss over the different kinds of antecedents, linguistic or non-linguistic, here, but I refer the interested reader to Merchant (2004) on this matter.

In the previous sections, we have mainly addressed the first big research question in the domain of ellipsis, namely what is present in the syntax when there is a mismatch between form and meaning. Now, with the recoverability condition comes the second prominent ellipsis question: we know ellipsis needs an antecedent, but what is the relation between the ellipsis site and its antecedent? Do they have to be exactly identical, or only mean the same thing?

Broadly speaking, there are two main answers to this question: one view sees the identity relation between the ellipsis site and the antecedent as a syntactic identity; and the other considers it semantic. The answers to both this question and the first question on the syntax of the ellipsis site can be summarised in the table above.

There are of course many different implementations for these diverging views and how strict the condition is. The arguments for one approach or the other have been the topic of many a debate, and I cannot cover all of the viewpoints here. Therefore I focus on only a couple of ways of addressing this question in the next two sections.

5.1. A syntactic recoverability condition

Among the authors who view the condition to be a syntactic one are Fiengo and May (1994), who propose the Strict Isomorphism Condition:

(45) Let E be an LF phrase marker.
Then, E can be deleted only if there is an LF phrase marker A, A distinct from E, such that A = E.

(Fiengo and May 1994)

This is illustrated below: the phrase marker A in (46a) is identical to the phrase marker E, so following the Strict Isomorphism Condition, E can be deleted.

(44) Tab. 18.1: Answers to two ellipsis questions in the literature

		Recoverability condition?	
		syntactic	semantic
syntactic structure in the ellipsis site?	yes	Sag (1976); Williams (1977); Chung et al. (1995); Fiengo and May (1994); Kehler (2002)	Hankamer and Sag (1994); Merchant (2001); Aelbrecht (2010); van Craenenbroeck (2010)
	no	NOT APPLICABLE	Dalrymple et al. (1991); Hardt (1993); Ginzburg and Sag (2000); Culicover and Jackendoff (2005)

(46) a. *Snoozy Suzy can [$_A$ dance the cha-cha-cha], but Foxy Freddy can't [$_E$ dance the cha-cha-cha].*
b. *Snoozy Suzy can [$_A$ dance the cha-cha-cha], but Foxy Freddy can't [$_E$].*

Arguments for the strict identity approach can be found in the domain of mismatches: if syntactic mismatches between the ellipsis site and the antecedent are disallowed, even if they have the same meaning, this supports the view that an ellipsis site needs a syntactically identical antecedent. As it turns out, voice mismatches are not allowed in sluicing: sluicing can occur in both passive and active sentences, but the combination of an active antecedent and a passive ellipsis site, or the other way around, is ungrammatical (Merchant 2013):

(47) a. *[$_A$ Ed was murdered by someone], but we don't know by who [$_E$ ~~Ed was~~ murdered].*
b. *[$_A$ Someone murdered Ed], but we don't know who [$_E$ ~~murdered Ed~~].*
c. **[$_A$ Ed was murdered by someone], but we don't know who [$_E$ ~~murdered Ed~~].*
d. **[$_A$ Someone murdered Ed], but we don't know by who [$_E$ ~~Ed was murdered~~].*

Another unacceptable mismatch is found in the argument structure in VPE: the ellipsis site in (48) cannot mean that Steve was reading something other than a book, even though truth-conditionally, if you are reading a book, you are reading. But a transitive VP differs structurally from an intransitive one, and that apparently blocks ellipsis of simply *reading*.

(48) **Jeff was reading a book, and Steve was [~~reading~~], too.*

On the other hand, there are also instances where such mismatches *are* allowed. VPE for instance allows for voice mismatches (in both directions), as illustrated in (49) (see Hardt 1993, but also Sag 1976; Dalrymple et al 1991; Fiengo and May 1994; Johnson 2001; Kehler 2002; Frazier 2008; Arregui et al. 2006; Kim et al. 2011 and Merchant 2008a, 2013).

(49) a. *The janitor should [$_A$ remove the trash] whenever it's apparent that it should be [$_E$ ~~removed~~].*
b. *The problem was to have been [$_A$ looked into], but obviously, nobody did [$_E$ ~~look into it~~].*

And unlike VPE, sluicing allows for argument structure mismatches:

(50) *Jeff was [$_A$ reading], but I don't know what [$_E$ Jeff was reading t_{what}].*

Apart from the much debated voice mismatches, for which Merchant (2013) provides an elegant analysis in favour of syntactic identity (but see Arregui et al. 2006 and Frazier 2008), there are other pieces of data that show that this syntactic identity cannot be taken too strictly, such as the phenomenon that is called *vehicle change* by Fiengo and May (1994: 218) (see also Dalrymple 1991). Vehicle change implies that under ellipsis, nominals can be treated as non-distinct with respect to their pronominal status. This is exemplified in (51):

(51) a. *They [arrested Alex$_i$] even though he$_i$ thought they wouldn't.*
b. *They [arrested Alex$_i$] even though he$_i$ thought they wouldn't arrest *Alex$_i$/him$_i$.*

In non-ellipsis, repeating *Alex* in the embedded clause results in ungrammaticality, but under ellipsis, the R-expression can act as an appropriate antecedent. In the ellipsis site, the referent is simply referred to by means of a different "vehicle": a pronoun instead of the R-expression. One should note, though, that this vehicle change is mainly a description of a problem, and not necessarily the solution.

Another set of data involves non-finite verb forms. The elliptical sentence in (52a) is fine, even though the antecedent and the ellipsis site cannot be syntactically identical.

(52) a. *Decorating for the holidays is easy if you know how [$_E$].*
b. *[$_A$ Decorating for the holidays] is easy if you know how [$_E$ to decorate for the holidays].*
c. **[$_A$ Decorating for the holidays] is easy if you know how [$_E$ decorating for the holidays].*

And of course there are the famous cases of categorial mismatches where a noun acts as an antecedent for VPE, such as (53) from *You'll Never Eat Lunch in This Town Again*, Julia Philips, cited by Hardt (1993: 34).

(53) *David Begelman is a great [$_A$ laugher], and when he does [$_E$], his eyes crinkle at you the way Lady Brett's did in* The Sun Also Rises.

These data are nevertheless still compatible with a syntactic identity approach, as most of the implementations show that the syntactic identity needs to be established at one point in the derivation, but not necessarily in the end result (see for instance Lasnik 1995, and many others). That way the mismatches can be explained, while the unacceptable voice mismatches discussed above support the view that the relation between the antecedent and the ellipsis is of a syntactic nature (see Merchant 2013).

Even though the proponents of the syntactic identity approach have been successful in certain cases, there is also much to say for the view that the ellipsis site only has to be semantically recoverable: it does not need to have the exact same syntactic structure, but it needs to have the same meaning, i.e., truth conditions.

5.2. A semantic recoverability condition

As table 18.1 above showed, there are two different sides to the proponents of the semantic identity view, namely those who do not take there to be any syntax involved in the ellipsis site anyway, and those who argue for deletion of a fully-fledged syntactic structure. I cannot represent the entire spectrum of approaches that can be situated here, but I very briefly introduce one of each side: Hardt (1993) and Merchant (2001).

Hardt (1993: 45–46) views an elided VP as a property variable that is bound in the discourse. Under this approach the antecedent VP is considered an indefinite property P, parallel to an indefinite DP, as it adds the VP meaning to the discourse. The elided VP, on the other hand, is definite, on a par with pronouns, and it selects the relevant meaning from the discourse. This is illustrated in (54).

(54) Harry <u>walked in</u>. Sean did *pro* too.
P

For the exact details of how the ellipsis site is interpreted and the semantics of auxiliary *do* I refer the reader to Hardt (1993). What is important for the discussion at hand here, is that the ellipsis site does not contain any syntactic structure. That makes the answer to the recoverability question fairly straightforward: if the ellipsis site does not contain any syntax, it cannot be syntactically identical to the antecedent, so the recoverability condition is necessarily one of semantic identity.

Merchant (2001) provides another way of implementing a semantic recoverability condition, but in combination with the view that the ellipsis site contains syntactic structure. He argues that a constituent can only be deleted if it is e-GIVEN (*e* for ellipsis). This notion of e-GIVENness is based on the concept of GIVENness found in Rooth (1992) and Schwarzschild (1999). Whether a constituent is e-GIVEN is determined by the presence of a salient antecedent. Roughly, for ellipsis to be acceptable, two conditions need to be fulfilled: (i) the antecedent has to entail the ellipsis site, but (ii) the ellipsis site also has to entail the antecedent (replacing focus-marked parts with ∃-bound variables of the appropriate type; see Merchant 2001: 26 for the relevant definitions).

The examples below illustrate how e-GIVENness works. Consider the VPE example in (55), adapted from Merchant's (2001) (45b). This sentence receives the first interpretation, not the second one, even though the antecedent VP (= VP_A) *call Pat an idiot* does entail VP_E *insult Pat*.

(55) *Alice called Pat an idiot after KIM did.*
= … *after Kim did ~~call Pat an idiot~~.* (VP_E 1)
≠ … *after Kim did ~~insult Pat~~.* (VP_E 2)

According to the second condition of e-GIVENness, however, the entailment must also go in the opposite direction in order for ellipsis to take place. This is the case for the first ellipsis site, so that we can conclude that VP_E 1 is e-GIVEN and can thus be elided. VP_E 2 on the other hand, does not entail the antecedent, since you can insult someone without necessarily calling them an idiot. Therefore this VP is not e-GIVEN and cannot be elided.

Both these approaches take the recoverability relation between the ellipsis site and the antecedent to be a semantic identity condition, as they do not take into account the syntactic form of the antecedent and the ellipsis site (under Hardt's view there is no syntactic form in the ellipsis site), but only the meaning, either determined by the semantics in an entailment relation, or through the discourse. As mentioned above, however, to this date no consensus has been reached: although both the semantic and the syntactic identity approaches have reached some success, the voice mismatches remain a problem for either view (but see Merchant 2013 for a potential solution from a syntactic identity perspective). Therefore, some authors have proposed more hybrid approaches, incorporating both semantic and syntactic restrictions (see Kehler 2002; Chung 2006; van Craenenbroeck 2008; Merchant 2013).

6. Licensing ellipsis

So far we have already discussed the nature of the ellipsis site and the identity relation with the antecedent. The last of the three big questions in the ellipsis literature concerns its syntactic licensing. It is obvious that material can only be left out when its meaning can be deduced from the context, but it turns out that the syntactic environment also plays a crucial role in deciding whether ellipsis can take place or not, as was shown in section 1. We have seen that not all environments allow for ellipsis, even when there is a salient antecedent, and that not all elliptical phenomena occur in all languages. English VPE cannot be reproduced in Dutch or French, even though the verb phrase can be equally e-GIVEN in all these languages (see [3]). And sluicing is subject to restrictions as well: as (56) illustrates, in English it is only allowed in *wh*-questions, not in embedded declaratives or relative clauses.

(56) a. *It was painted, but it wasn't obvious why [~~it was painted~~].*
b. *Someone is singing, but I don't know who [~~is singing~~].*
c. **It was painted, but it wasn't obvious that [~~it was painted~~].*
d. **The octopus predicted that Spain would win, but no-one knew for sure yet whether [~~Spain would win~~].*
e. **Someone is singing, but I can't find the person who [~~is singing~~].*

In short, the syntactic environment plays a role in ellipsis: missing material has to be licensed, and these licensing criteria differ depending on the language and the elliptical phenomenon. The remainder of this section briefly explores some of the proposals that can be found in the literature for ellipsis licensing.

6.1. Lobeck (1993, 1995)

The first proper attempts to capture the syntactic licensing condition on ellipsis date back to Sag (1976), Williams (1977) and Zagona (1982, 1988a, 1988b), but it was the seminal (1993, 1995) work by Anne Lobeck that developed a fully-fleshed out answer to the licensing question. Her approach is a proform analysis, hence the ellipsis site is a null pronoun without any internal syntactic structure, but this proform is subject to both the Empty Category Principle (ECP, see Chomsky 1981, 1986; but also Rizzi 1990) for licensing and a strong agreement requirement for identification:

(57) An empty, non-arbitrary pronominal must be properly head-governed, and governed by an X^0 specified for strong agreement.

(Lobeck 1995: 52)

For Lobeck, a head X^0 is "specified for strong agreement iff X^0, or the phrase or head with which X^0 agrees, morphologically realizes agreement in a productive number of cases" (Lobeck 1995: 51). She develops this account for sluicing, VPE and NPE. For instance, she argues that VPE in English is licensed by strong agreement in I^0: because auxiliaries, modals, dummy *do* and infinitival *to* all sit in I^0, they can license VPE, but main verbs, which do not raise to I^0 in English, cannot, because they do not exhibit strong agreement.

A problem for Lobeck's account, however, is that German and French, for instance, display richer morphological agreement on finite verbs than English and have their main verbs raise to I^0 as well. Therefore, her theory seems to predict that these languages would have VPE with all verbs, while in fact, they do not allow for VPE at all.

6.2. The E-feature (Merchant 2001, 2004)

On the PF-deletion side, Merchant (2001) proposes a different way of licensing ellipsis syntactically: as his analysis is developed within the Minimalist framework, the notion of Government is discarded, and he uses an E(llipsis)-feature on the licensing head instead. For sluicing he puts forward the following entry of an E-feature [E_S]:

(58) a. The syntax of [E_S]: $E_{[u\text{WH}^*,\ u\text{Q}^*]}$
b. The phonology of [E_S]: $\varphi_{IP} \rightarrow \emptyset$ / E _
c. The semantics of [E_S]: $[\![E]\!] = \lambda p$: e-GIVEN(p) [p]

The semantics have already been explained in the previous section, and the phonology is pretty straightforward as well: it means that the phonological representation of the material dominated by the IP node is null when it follows an E-feature. In this sense, ellipsis is "a familiar kind of morphologically triggered syncope", where the trigger is the E-feature and the syncopated element is IP. Merchant's account is a PF-deletion one, and "the non-pronunciation is entirely controlled by the actual phonology" (Merchant 2004: 671). What is of interest to us here, however, is the syntax of E: as Merchant proposes, the E-feature for sluicing has strong uninterpretable *wh*- and Q-features, which need to be checked locally. That means that this E-feature can only occur on the C^0 head that we find in constituent questions. That is, this specific type of head which we call the licensing head. All other environments would leave the uninterpretable features unchecked and the derivation crashes. In other words, the syntax of [E_S] ensures that sluicing in English only occurs in *wh*-questions. How the E-feature works is illustrated in (59).

(59) a. *Addie was reading something, but I don't know what.*
b.

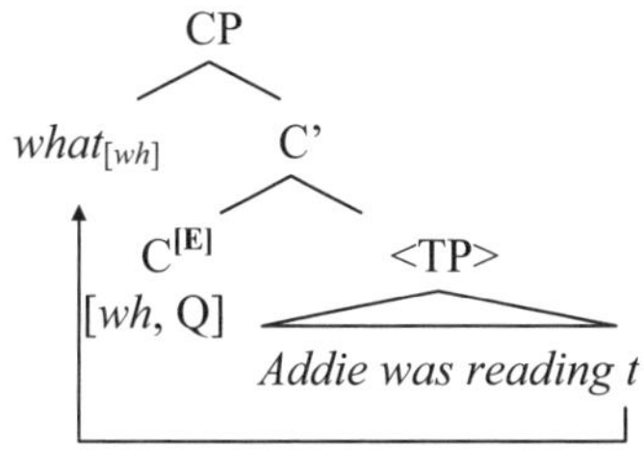

(Merchant 2004: 670)

6.3. Licensing via Agree (Aelbrecht 2010)

Building on Merchant's theory is the proposal for ellipsis licensing in Aelbrecht (2010). This work shows that there can be material between the licensing head and the actual ellipsis site, something that cannot be captured by the original implementation of the E-feature. Therefore, Aelbrecht proposes that ellipsis is licensed via an *Agree* relation between E and the licensing head, hereby allowing for some distance between the two. Moreover, she argues that ellipsis happens during the derivation, as soon as the licensing head is merged and checks the E-feature. The theory is summarised in (60) and represented schematically in (61) (Aelbrecht 2010: 87, 96): E has to check an uninterpretable feature F against the category feature of the licensing head, parallel to what happens in Merchant's (2001) account. However, in Aelbrecht's (2010) analysis, the E-feature does not occur on the licensing head L itself, but on the head X immediately dominating the ellipsis site, thus allowing for material to potentially intervene between the licensor and the elided constituent.

(60) a. Ellipsis is licensed via an Agree relation between an [E]-feature and the ellipsis licensing head.

b. Ellipsis occurs in the course of the derivation, as soon as the licensing head is merged. At this point, the ellipsis site becomes inaccessible for any further syntactic operations and vocabulary insertion at PF is blocked.

(61)

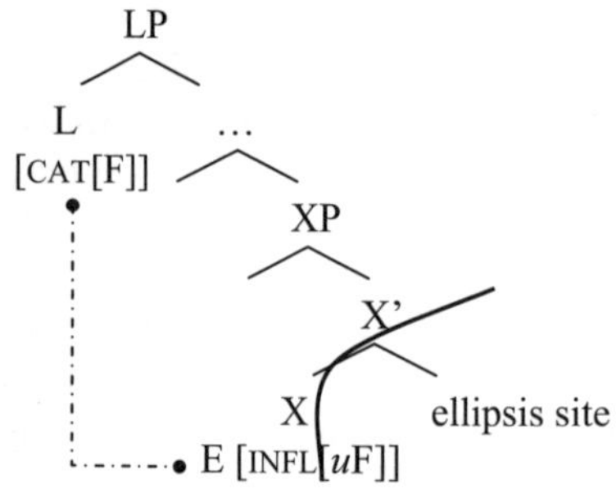

Furthermore, because of the fact that ellipsis occurs derivationally, this licensing theory can account for the extraction puzzle encountered in Dutch MCE mentioned above in (42) and hence interacts with the question in section 4 of whether an ellipsis site contains syntactic structure or not (see Aelbrecht 2010 for the details of the analysis).

6.4. Ellipsis and Phase Theory

The concept of ellipsis occurring in the course of the derivation is reminiscent of cyclic Spell-out and Phase Theory. In the Minimalist framework (Chomsky 1995, 2000, 2001, 2005) parts of the structure – i.e., phasal domains – are claimed to be sent off to PF before the derivation is complete. This is known as cyclic or derivational Spell-out (see also Epstein et al 1998). From this perspective a phrase is accessible to the syntax as long as the domain of cyclic Spell-out that contains it has not been shipped off to PF (Phase Impenetrability Condition or PIC; Chomsky 1999, 2000, 2001). The revised version of the PIC further specifies that a phasal domain is accessible to syntax until the next phase head is merged (Chomsky 2001). In other words, merger of a phase head triggers the domain of the previous phase head to be sent to Spell-out.

It is tempting to see ellipsis as a special kind of Spell-out, as both ellipsis and Phase Theory make part of the structure inaccessible for further syntactic operations when a specific trigger is merged. A direct parallel between ellipsis and phases has been drawn by Gengel (2007a, 2008), who develops the idea that ellipsis is simply part of Spell-out (see also Holmberg 1999, 2001; Rouveret 2006, 2011, 2012; Gallego 2010; Bošković *to appear*; Harwood *to appear*). According to these authors, ellipsis targets phasal domains and is the result of a phase head sending its domain to PF for non-pronunciation instead of pronunciation, as in (62). Under such an account, ellipsis naturally takes place during the derivation as well, parallel to cyclic Spell-out of phasal domains, and the licensing head is a phase head.

(62)

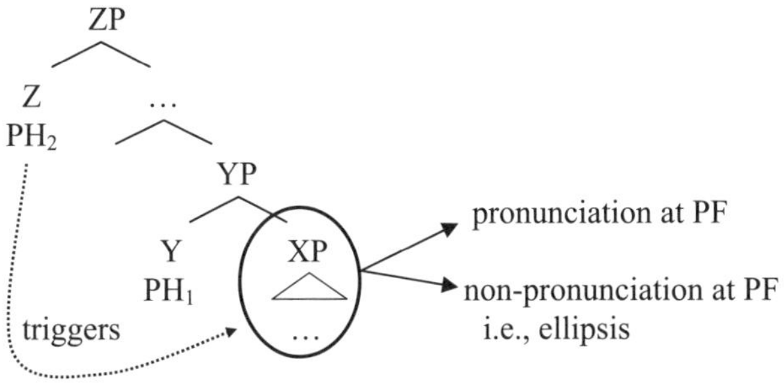

Such an analysis predicts that the same syntactic operations can occur in ellipsis and non-ellipsis, as the difference between the two is only a matter of what happens at PF. Aelbrecht (2010) shows, however, that this is not always the case: for instance, a Dutch *wh*-object can move to [SpecCP] in a non-elliptical sentence, but it cannot in its MCE counterpart (as was shown in [42b]). Therefore, Aelbrecht concludes that the trigger for ellipsis cannot be the same as for phasal Spell-Out.

6.5. Licensing by movement (Thoms 2011)

A last licensing account I introduce here is quite different from the previous ones in that it moves away from the idea of a licensing head. Thoms (2011) argues that the idea of a licensing head is a stipulation which is specific to ellipsis in the current Minimalist framework, where Government does not play a role anymore, and instead, proposes that ellipsis is actually licensed by A'-movement or head movement.

Based on VPE data from different dialects of English, he revives a suggestion in Chomsky (1995: 125–126), and claims that whether or not a recoverable constituent can be deleted – he assumes a PF-deletion approach to ellipsis – should be understood as dependent on general conditions on deletion of lower copies of the movement operation.

More specifically, ellipsis is licensed by non-A-movement (that is, A'-movement and head movement), and should be viewed as a "repair operation": ellipsis deletes the constituent that is immediately dominated by the target of the movement in order to avoid a linearization failure.

Thoms proposes that there are two ways in which a linearization failure as a result of movement can be avoided. The first way is the standard view: if an element overtly moves, the original copy needs to be deleted locally (see also Nunes 2004). However, Thoms argues that there is a second option: when the base copy of a movement chain is not deleted locally, i.e., at the point when it is moved, the entire complement of the landing site of the moved element has to be deleted to make sure that the structure can be linearized. This is what we perceive as ellipsis. Thoms shows that this is only the case in non-A-movement because A-movement, unlike non-A-movement, never allows for multiple copies to be spelled out and therefore the lower copies of A-movement are *always* deleted locally, without the option of ellipsis.

Although there are quite a few problems with the account and much still needs to be worked out, it provides an interesting and refreshing view on ellipsis licensing. This section should make clear that a lot of work still needs to be done before we can reach an answer to the licensing question. As is in fact the case for all three big questions. But that is why research in ellipsis is still so very relevant and alive.

7. Conclusion

This chapter had given some insight in the workings of silence, and has pointed out how the study of ellipsis actually reveals a lot about grammar in general. If natural language is the combination of form and meaning, ellipsis – which is a mismatch between the two – is a valuable subject exactly because it zooms in on the relation between the form and the meaning and how this relation can be established. Studying silence by comparing it to the non-elliptical counterparts can place certain operations in the syntax, or at PF or LF, depending on how ellipsis and non-ellipsis differ. Moreover, the link between ellipsis and other silent forms, such as traces and *pro*, and also overt pronouns, is an important path to explore.

We have seen that there is a whole spectrum of elliptical phenomena, with different properties and varying ellipsis sites. As there are several different approaches to ellipsis, and each account has their advantages and disadvantages, it remains to be seen whether ellipsis should receive a uniform analysis, or whether all – or at least some – viewpoints can occur in language at the same time, in different contexts. The other two questions we have dealt with, the identity condition and syntactic licensing, have been discussed at length in the literature and although no real consensus has been reached yet, the different answers have consequences beyond the domain of ellipsis and the predictions that they make are indubitably worth exploring.

8. References (selected)

Abels, Klaus
2012 Don't repair that island! It ain't broke. *Paper presented at Islands in Contemporary Linguistic Theory.* Vitoria, Spain.

Aelbrecht, Lobke
2010 *The Syntactic Licensing of Ellipsis*. Amsterdam: John Benjamins.
Aelbrecht, Lobke, and Will Harwood
2013 To be or not to be elided: VP ellipsis revisited. Ms. GIST/Ghent University.
Almeida, Diogo, and Masaya Yoshida
2007 A problem for the preposition stranding generalization. *Linguistic Inquiry* 38: 349–362.
Arregui, Ana, Charles Clifton Jr., Lyn Frazier, and Keir Moulton
2006 Processing elided verb phrases with flawed antecedents: The recycling hypothesis. *Journal of Memory and Language* 55: 232–246.
Barros, Matthew
2012 Arguments against Island Repair: Evidence from Contrastive TP ellipsis. Ms. Rutgers University.
Beavers, John, and Ivan Sag
2004 Coordinate Ellipsis and Apparent Non-Constituent Coordination. In: Stefan Müller (ed.), *Proceedings of the HPSG04 Conference*, 48–69. Stanford: CSLI Publications.
Bošković, Željko
to appear Now I'm a phase, now I'm not a phase: on the variability of phases with extraction and ellipsis. *Linguistic Inquiry.*
Chomsky, Noam
1981 *Lectures on Government and Binding*. Dordrecht: Foris.
Chomsky, Noam
1986 *Barriers*. MIT Press: Cambridge, Massachusetts.
Chomsky, Noam
1995 *The Minimalist Program*. Cambridge, Massachusetts: MIT Press.
Chomsky, Noam
1999 Minimalist inquiries: The framework. In: *MIT Occasional Papers in Linguistics 15*. Cambridge, Massachusetts: MITWPL.
Chomsky, Noam
2000 Minimalist inquiries: The framework. In: Roger Martin, David Michaels and Juan Uriagereka (eds.), *Step by Step. Essays on Minimalist Syntax in Honour of Howard Lasnik*, 89–155. Cambridge, Massachusetts: MIT Press.
Chomsky, Noam
2001 Derivation by Phase. In: Michael Kenstowicz (ed.), *Ken Hale: A Life in Language*, 1–52. Cambridge, Massachusetts: MIT Press.
Chomsky, Noam
2005 On phases. Ms. MIT.
Chung, Sandra
2006 Sluicing and the lexicon: The point of no return. In: Rebecca T. Cover and Yuni Kim (eds.), *Proceedings of the Annual Meeting of the Berkeley Linguistics Society 31*, 73–91. Berkeley, CA: Berkeley Linguistics Society.
Chung, Sandra, William A. Ladusaw, and James McCloskey
1995 Sluicing and Logical Form. *Natural Language Semantics* 3: 239–282.
van Craenenbroeck, Jeroen
2004 Ellipsis in Dutch Dialects. LOT Dissertation Series.
van Craenenbroeck, Jeroen
2008 What does silence look like? On the unpronounced syntax of sluicing. *Paper presented at the University of Chicago.*
van Craenenbroeck, Jeroen
2010 *The Syntax of Ellipsis: Evidence from Dutch Dialects*. New York, NY: Oxford University Press.
van Craenenbroeck, Jeroen
2012 Ellipsis, identity, and accommodation. Ms. CRISSP/Hogeschool-Universiteit Brussel.

van Craenenbroeck, Jeroen, and Anikó Lipták
2006 The crosslinguistic syntax of sluicing: Evidence from Hungarian relatives. *Syntax* 9: 248–274.
van Craenenbroeck, Jeroen, and Marcel den Dikken
2006 Ellipsis and EPP repair. *Linguistic Inquiry* 37(4): 653–664.
Culicover, Peter W., and Ray Jackendoff
2005 *Simpler Syntax*. Oxford: Oxford University Press.
Cyrino, Sonia, and Gabriella Matos
2002 VP ellipsis in European and Brazilian Portuguese – a comparative analysis. *Journal of Portuguese Linguistics* 1: 177–195.
Cyrino, Sonia, and Gabriella Matos
2005 Local licensers and recovering in VP ellipsis. *Journal of Portuguese Linguistics* 4: 79–112.
Dagnac, Anne
2010 Modal ellipsis in French, Spanish and Italian. Evidence for a TP–deletion analysis. In: Karlos Arregi, Zsuzsanna Faygal, Silvina A. Montrul, and Annie Tremblay (eds.), *Romance linguistics 2008: Interactions in Romance. Selected papers from the 38th Linguistic Symposium on Romance Languages (LSRL), Urbana- Champaign, April 2008*, 157–170. Amsterdam: John Benjamins.
Dalrymple, Mary, Stuart M. Sheiber, and Fernando C. N. Pereira
1991 Ellipsis and higher-order unification. *Linguistics and Philosophy* 14: 399–452.
Depiante, Marcela
2000 The syntax of deep and surface anaphora: a study of null complement anaphora and stripping/bare argument ellipsis. Doctoral dissertation, University of Connecticut, Storrs.
Emonds, Joseph
1976 *A Transformational Approach to English Syntax*. New York: Academic Press.
Emonds, Joseph
1978 The verbal complex V'-V in French. *Linguistic Inquiry* 9:151–175.
Epstein, Sam, Eric Groat, Ruriko Kawashima, and Hisatsugu Kitahara
1998 *A Derivational Approach to Syntactic Relations*. Oxford: Oxford University Press.
Fiengo, Robert, and Robert May
1994 *Indices and Identity*. Cambridge, Massachusetts: MIT Press.
Fortin, Catherine
2007 Indonesian sluicing and verb phrase ellipsis: Description and explanation in a minimalist framework. Doctoral Dissertation, University of Michigan, Ann Arbor.
Fox, Danny
1999 Focus, parallelism and accommodation. Paper presented at SALT 9.
Fox, Danny
2000 *Economy and Semantic Interpretation*. Cambridge, Massachusetts: MIT Press.
Frazier, Lyn
2008 Processing ellipsis: A processing solution to the undergeneration problem? In: Charles B. Chang and Hannah J. Haynie (eds.), *Proceedings of the 26th West Coast Conference on Formal Linguistics*, 21–32. Somerville, Mass.: Cascadilla Proceedings Project.
Gallego, Ángel
2010 *Phase Theory*. Amsterdam: John Benjamins.
Gengel, Kirsten
2007a Phases and ellipsis. In: Emily Elfner and Martin Walkow (eds.), *Proceedings of the 37th meeting of the North East Linguistic Society*. GLSA: University of Massachusetts, Amherst.
Gengel, Kirsten
2007b Focus and ellipsis: A generative analysis of pseudogapping and other elliptical structures. Doctoral dissertation, University of Stuttgart.

Gengel, Kirsten
2008 Phases and ellipsis. *Linguistic Analysis* 35: 21–42.
Ginzburg, Jonathan, and Ivan A. Sag
2000 *Interrogative Investigations*. Stanford, CA: CSLI Publications.
Goldberg, Lotus Madelyn
2005 Verb-stranding VP ellipsis: A cross-linguistic study. Doctoral dissertation, McGill University, Montreal.
Hankamer, Jorge, and Ivan A. Sag
1976 Deep and surface anaphora. *Linguistic Inquiry* 7: 391–428.
Hardt, Daniel
1993 Verb phrase ellipsis: Form, meaning and processing. Doctoral dissertation, University of Pennsylvania.
Hardt, Daniel
1999 Dynamic interpretation of verb phrase ellipsis. *Linguistics and Philosophy* 22: 185–219.
Harwood, Will
2013 Being progressive is just a phase: Dividing the functional hierarchy. Doctoral dissertation, Ghent University.
Harwood, Will
to appear Being progressive is just a phase: celebrating the uniqueness of progressive aspect under a phase-based analysis. *Natural Language and Linguistic Theory.*
Holmberg, Anders
1999 Yes and No in Finnish: ellipsis and cyclic spell-out. *MIT Working Papers in Linguistics* 33.
Holmberg, Anders
2001 The syntax of Yes and No in Finnish. *Studia Linguistica* 55: 140–174.
Hoyt, Frederick, and Alex Teodorescu
2004 Sluicing in Romanian: A Typological Study. In: Julie, Auger, J. Clancy Clements and Barbara Vance (eds.), *Contemporary Approaches to Romance Linguistics. Selected Papers from the 33rd Linguistic Symposium on Romance Languages* (LSRL). Amsterdam: John Benjamins.
Jackendoff, Ray
1971 Gapping and Related Rules. *Linguistic Inquiry* 2(1): 21–36.
Jayaseelan, K.A.
1990 Incomplete VP deletion and gapping. *Linguistic Analysis* 20(1/2): 64–80.
Johnson, Kyle
2001 What VP ellipsis can do, and what it can't, but not why. In: Mark Baltin and Chris Collins (eds.), *The Handbook of Contemporary Syntactic Theory*, 439–479. Oxford: Blackwell Publishers.
Johnson, Kyle
2004 How to be quiet. In: Nikki Adams, Adam Cooper, Fey Parrill and Thomas Wier (eds.), *Proceedings from the 40th Annual Meeting of the Chicago Linguistic Society*, 1–20.
Johnson, Kyle
2009 Gapping is not (VP) ellipsis. *Linguistic Inquiry* 40: 289–328.
Johnson, Kyle
2012 Recoverability of Deletion. Pre-publication version of paper to appear in Kuniya Nasukawa and Henk van Riemsdijk (eds.), *Identity Relations in Grammar.* (Studies in Generative Grammar.) Berlin: Mouton de Gruyter.
Keenan, Edward
1971 Names, quantifiers, and the sloppy identity problem. *Papers in Linguistics* 4: 211–232.
Kehler, Andrew
2002 *Coherence in Discourse*. Stanford, CA.: CSLI Publications.

Kim, Christina S., Gregory M. Kobele, Jeffery T. Runner, and John T. Hale
2011 The acceptability cline in VP ellipsis. *Syntax* 14(4): 318–354.
Langacker, Ronald
1966 On pronominalization and the chain of command. In: William Reibel and Sanford Schane (eds.), *Modern Studies in English*, 160–186. Englewood Cliffs, NJ: Prentice Hall.
Lasnik, Howard
1995 Verbal Morphology: *Syntactic Structures* Meets the Minimalist program. In: Hector Campos and Paula Kempchinsky (eds.), *Evolution and Revolution in Linguistic Theory.* Georgetown University Press: Georgetown.
Lasnik, Howard
1999 Pseudogapping puzzles. In: Elabbas Benmamoun and Shalom Lappin (eds.), *Fragments: Studies in Ellipsis and Gapping*, 141–174. Oxford: Oxford University Press.
Lasnik, Howard
2001 When can you save a structure by destroying it? In: Minjoo Kim and Uri Strauss (eds.), *Proceedings of the North East Linguistics Society* 31, 301–320. GLSA.
Lobeck, Anne
1993 Strong agreement and identification: evidence from ellipsis in English. *Linguistics* 31: 777–811.
Lobeck, Anne
1995 *Ellipsis: Functional Heads, Licensing and Identification.* New York: Oxford University Press.
Merchant, Jason
2001 *The Syntax of Silence: Sluicing, Islands, and the Theory of Ellipsis.* Oxford: Oxford University Press.
Merchant, Jason
2002 Swiping in Germanic. In: C. Jan-Wouter Zwart and Werner Abraham (eds.), *Studies in Comparative Germanic Syntax*, 289–315. Amsterdam: John Benjamins.
Merchant, Jason
2004 Fragments and ellipsis. *Linguistics and Philosophy* 27: 661–738.
Merchant, Jason
2005 On the role of unpronounced syntactic structures. Paper presented on March 17, 2005, University of Illinois, Urbana-Champaign.
Merchant, Jason
2008a An asymmetry in voice mismatches in VP-ellipsis and pseudogapping. *Linguistic Inquiry* 39: 169–179.
Merchant, Jason
2008b Variable island repair under ellipsis. In: Kyle Johnson (ed.), *Topics in Ellipsis,* 132–153. Cambridge: Cambridge University Press.
Merchant, Jason
2013 Voice and ellipsis. *Linguistic Inquiry* 44.
Müller, Gereon
2011 *Constraints on Displacement: A Phase-based Approach.* Amsterdam: John Benjamins.
Nevins, Andrew, Cilene Rodriguez, and Luis Vicente
2007 Preposition stranding under sluicing. In: *Proceedings of Going Romance.*
Nunes, Jairo
2004 *Linearization of Chains and Sideward Movement.* Cambridge, MA: MIT Press.
Nykiel, Joanna, and Ivan Sag
2008 Sluicing and stranding. Ms. University of Silesia and Stanford University.
Pollock, Jean-Yves
1989 Verb movement, Universal Grammar and the structure of IP. *Linguistic Inquiry* 20: 365–424.

Raposo, Eduardo
1986 On the null object in European Portuguese. In: Osvaldo Jaeggli and Carmen Silva-Corvalán (eds.), *Studies in Romance Linguistics*. Dordrecht: Foris.
van Riemsdijk, Henk
1978 *A Case Study in Syntactic Markedness: The Binding Nature of Prepositional Phrases*. Dordrecht: Foris Publications.
Rizzi, Luigi
1986 Null Objects in Italian and the Theory of *pro*. *Linguistic Inquiry* 17(3): 501–557.
Rizzi, Luigi
1990 *Relativized Minimality*. MIT Press.
Rodrigues, Cilene, Andrew Nevins, and Luis Vicente
2009 Cleaving the interactions between sluicing and preposition stranding. In: Torck and W. Leo Wetzels (eds.), *Romance Languages and Linguistic Theory 2006*, 245–270. Amsterdam: John Benjamins.
Rooth, Mats
1992 A theory of focus interpretation. *Natural Language Semantics* 1: 117–121.
Ross, John Robert
1967 Constraints on variables in Syntax. Doctoral Dissertation, MIT. (appeared as Ross 1986 *Infinite Syntax*. Ablex Publishing Corporation: Norwood, New Jersey).
Ross, John Robert
1969 Guess who? In: Robert I. Binnick, Alice Davison, Georgia M. Green and Jerry L. Morgan (eds.), *Proceedings of the Fifth Annual Meeting of the Chicago Linguistics Society*, 252–286. Chicago, Illinois.
Rouveret, Alain
2006 VP ellipsis in phasal syntax: the case of Welsh. Ms, Université Paris-Diderot and Laboratoire de Linguistique Formelle, CNRS.
Rouveret, Alain
2011 Hallmarks of Portuguese syntax. In: Laura Brugé, Anna Cardinaletti, Giuliana Giusti, Nicola Munaro and Cecilia Poletto (eds.), *A Festschrift for Guglielmo Cinque*. Oxford: Oxford University Press.
Rouveret, Alain
2012 VP ellipsis, the vP phase and the syntax of morphology. *Natural Language and Linguistic Theory* 30(3): 897–963.
Sag, Ivan A.
1976 Deletion and logical form. Doctoral dissertation, MIT, Cambridge, Massachusetts.
Sag, Ivan A., and Jorge Hankamer
1984 Toward a theory of anaphoric processing. *Linguistics and Philosophy* 7: 325–345.
Sailor, Craig, and Grace Kuo
2010 *Taiwanese VP Ellipsis and the Progressive Prohibition*. Ms., UCLA. Presented at the joint meeting of the International Association of Chinese Linguistics 18 (IACL-18) and the North American Conference on Chinese Linguistics 22 (NACCL-22), Harvard University.
Schlangen, David
2003 A coherence-based approach to the interpretation of non-sentential utterances in dialogue. PhD Dissertation, School of Informatics, University of Edinburgh.
Schuyler, Tamara
2002 Wh-movement out of the site of VP Ellipsis. MA Thesis, UCSC.
Schwartzschild, Roger
1999 Givenness, AvoidF, and other constraints on the placement of accent. *Natural Language Semantics* 7:141–177.

Shopen, Timothy
1972 A generative theory of ellipsis: A consideration of the linguistic use of silence. Doctoral dissertation, University of California, Los Angeles; Reproduced by the Indiana University Linguistics Club, Urbana, Ill.
Stainton, Robert
2006 *Words and Thoughts*. Oxford: Oxford University Press.
Stjepanović, Sandra
2008 P-stranding under sluicing in a non-P-stranding language? *Linguistic Inquiry* 39: 179–190.
Stjepanović, Sandra
2012 Two cases of violation repair under sluicing. In: Jason Merchant and Andrew Simpson (eds.), *Sluicing: Cross-linguistic Perspectives*, 68–82. Oxford: Oxford University Press.
Temmerman, Tanja
2013 The syntax of Dutch embedded fragment answers. *Natural Language and Linguistic Theory* 31(1): 235–285.
Tescari, Aquiles Neto
2013 *On Verb Movement in Brazilian Portuguese: a Cartographic Study.* Doctoral dissertation, Università Ca'Foscari Venezia.
Thoms, Gary
2011 Verb-floating and VPE: towards a movement account of ellipsis licensing. *Linguistic Variation Yearbook 2011.*
Tomioka, Satoshi
2004 Another sloppy identity puzzle. In: Hang-Jin Yoon (ed.), *Generative Grammar in a Broader Perspective: Proceedings of the 4th GLOW in Asia*, 209–233. Seoul: Hankook.
Toosarvandani, Maziar
2013 Gapping is low coordination (plus VP-ellipsis): A reply to Johnson. Ms. MIT.
Vicente, Luis
2008 Syntactic isomorphism and non-isomorphism under ellipsis. Ms. University of California, Santa Cruz.
Wasow, Thomas
1972 Anaphoric relations in English. Doctoral Dissertation, MIT, Cambridge, Massachusetts.
Wilder, Chris
1997 Some properties of ellipsis in coordination. In: Artemis Alexiadou and T. Alan Hall (eds.), *Studies in Universal Grammar and Typological Variation*, 59–107. Amsterdam: John Benjamins.
Williams, Edwin
1977 Discourse and logical form. *Linguistic Inquiry* 8: 101–139.
Winkler, Susanne
2003 Ellipsis at the interfaces: An information structural investigation of sentence-bound and discourse-bound ellipsis in English. Habilitationsschrift, Universität Tübingen.
Zagona, Karen
1982 Government and proper government of verbal projections. Doctoral dissertation, University of Washington, Seattle.
Zagona, Karen
1988a Proper government of antecedentless VPs in English and Spanish. *Natural Language and Linguistic Theory* 6: 95–128.
Zagona, Karen
1988b *Verb Phrase Syntax: A Parametric Study of English and Spanish*. Kluwer Academic Publishers: Dordrecht.

Lobke Aelbrecht, Gent (Belgium)

19. Syntactic Effects of Cliticization

Abstract

This chapter discusses the syntax of clitic pronouns and compares them to strong and weak pronouns and full DPs. The peculiar properties of clitic pronouns will be presented, which concern all modules of grammar. To account for these peculiar properties, it will be argued that clitic pronouns are merged as reduced maximal projections which are further reduced to heads during the derivation. Clitic placement is a local movement operation, which places the pronoun in one of the two clitic areas available in the clause and most visible in restructuring contexts allowing clitic climbing. The hosts of clitic pronouns and their mode of attachment (proclisis, enclisis, mesoclisis) are also discussed. Finally, some motivations for the obligatory movement of clitic pronouns will be presented.

1. Introduction

Cliticization is one of the topics (alongside with locality and clause structure) on which most works of the past 40 years have concentrated. For this reason, what follows cannot be an exhaustive overview. For a rich bibliography which collects the studies on clitic pronouns until 1991, the reader is referred to Nevis, Joseph, Wanner and Zwicky (1994).

This chapter restricts its attention to the cliticization of personal pronouns, because this is the area where the most stable knowledge has been attained; mention of other clitic grammatical elements will be made, but unfortunately there are still too few studies of clitic elements other than personal pronouns (with the notable exception of Slavic clitic auxiliaries, see Franks and Kings 2000). Furthermore, this chapter focalizes on Romance languages and in particular on Italian, although many studies exist on clitic pronouns of other language families.

We will analyze special clitics, in the sense of Zwicky (1977). Cliticization of special clitics is not a purely phonological phenomenon. As far as their internal syntax is concerned, clitic pronouns are deficient from all points of view, not only phonologically. As for their external syntax, clitic placement is sensitive to syntactic notions such as finite vs. infinitive, indicative vs. imperative mood, declarative vs. interrogative sentences, noun vs. verb, and so on. Phonological phenomena do not display this kind of properties.

Kayne (1975), the most influential work on personal pronouns in the framework of Generative Grammar, recognized in French two morphologically and syntactically different series of pronouns, clitic and strong pronouns, and elaborated a number of tests to distinguish one series from the other. Since then, comparative research has extended the empirical domain from French to other Romance languages and from Romance languages to other language families, e.g. Germanic, Slavic, Greek, Semitic and Berber, which has brought to light a number of properties of clitic pronouns not instantiated in French (e.g., clitic climbing, clitic doubling, mesoclisis, etc.) and a wide cross-linguistic variation in clitic placement. Furthermore, comparative research has led to the conclusion that clitic pronouns differ not only from strong elements, but also from clitic-like (called *weak*) pronouns, which led to the proposal that natural languages may possess not two, but three classes of personal pronouns (cf. Cardinaletti and Starke 1996, 1999).

2. An overview of the cliticization of verbal arguments

Every complement of the verb can be realized by a clitic pronoun, if such an element is present in the lexicon of the language: a direct object (either accusative or partitive) (1a, b), an indirect object (1c), or a prepositional object (locative [1d–f], manner [1g]). Examples are provided for Italian (note that if not otherwise indicated, all examples in the text are Italian):

(1) a. *Mangio un panino.*
eat.I a sandwich
'I eat a sandwich.'

a′. *Lo mangio (*un panino).*
it eat.I a sandwich
'I eat it.'

b. *Mangio un panino.*
eat.I a sandwich
'I eat a sandwich.'

b′. *Ne mangio uno (*panino).*
of.them eat.I one sandwich
'I eat one of them.'

c. *Parlo a Gianni.*
speak.I with Gianni
'I speak with Gianni.'

c′. *Gli parlo (*a Gianni).*
to.him speak.I with Gianni
'I speak with him.'

d. *Sono uscita da quella situazione.*
am.I gone.out of that situation
'I am out of that situation.'

d′. *Ne sono uscita (*da quella situazione).*
from.there am.I gone.out of that situation
'I am out of it.'

e. *Abito a Roma.*
live.I in Rome
'I live in Rome.'

e′. *Ci abito (*a Roma).*
there live.I in Rome
'I live there.'

f. *Passo sempre per quella strada.*
pass.I always along that street
'I always go along that street.'

f′. *Ci passo sempre (*per quella strada).*
there pass.I always along that street
'I always go through there.'

g. *Mi comporto sempre in malo modo.*
REFL behave.I always in bad way
'I always behave badly.'

g′. *Mi ci comporto sempre (*in malo modo).*
REFL so behave.I always in bad way
'I always behave so.'

In some languages, notably northern Italian dialects, subjects can also be realized by clitic pronouns. An example is provided from Trentino (Brandi and Cordin 1989: 113):

(2) a. *El Mario el parla.* [Trentino]
the Mario he speaks

a′. *El parla.*
he speaks

As the examples in (1)–(2) show, clitic pronouns realize an argument of the verb, bear the same thematic role and the same case assigned to that argument and are usually in complementary distribution with it (but see [2a] and section 5.4 below for cases in which pronouns and DPs co-occur, a phenomenon known as *clitic doubling*).

The same observations hold when clitic pronouns realize secondary complements of the verb, such as the benefactive/malefactive dative complement in (3a) and locative (3b), comitative (3c, d), and instrumental (3e) complements:

(3) a. *A Gianni è nato un bambino.*
to Gianni is born a baby
'Gianni has had a baby.'

a′. *Gli è nato un bambino (*a Gianni).*
to.him is born a baby to Gianni
'He has had a baby.'

b. *Mangio sempre in quel posto.*
eat.I always in that place
'I always eat in that place.'

b′. *Ci mangio sempre (*in quel posto).*
there eat.I always in that place
'I always eat there.'

c. *Ho parlato con Gianni.*
have.I spoken with Gianni
'I have spoken with Gianni.'

c′. *Ci ho parlato (*con Gianni).*
with.him have.I spoken with Gianni
'I have spoken with him.'

d. *Esco sempre con Gianni.*
go.out.I always with Gianni
'I always go out with Gianni.'

d′. *Ci esco sempre (*con Gianni).*
with.him go.out.I always with Gianni
'I always go out with him.'

e. *Ho aperto la scatola con le forbici.*
have.I opened the box with the scissors
'I have opened the box with the scissors.'

e′. *C' ho aperto la scatola (*con le forbici).*
with.them have.I opened the box with the ...
'I have the box with them.'

Non-arguments, such as temporal (4a) (from Cinque 1990: 119, to be compared with [19c]), and causal adjuncts (4b), and frame locatives (4c) (from Rizzi 1988/2001: 541, 1990: 127, n. 9), are never realized by clitic pronouns:

(4) a. *Rimarrò tre settimane.*
will.stay.I three weeks
'I will stay three weeks.'

a′. **Spero di rimaner=le in allegria.*
hope.I to stay=them being jolly
'I hope to stay being jolly.'

b. *Telefono per questo motivo.*
call.I for this reason
'I call for this reason.'

b′. **Ci telefono.*
there call.I

c. *Gianni è felice a casa dei genitori.*
Gianni is happy at home of.the parents
'Gianni is happy at their parents' house.'

c′. **Gianni ci è felice.*
Gianni there is happy
'Gianni is happy there.'

The generalization seems to be that only VP-internal complements can be realized by clitic pronouns, while VP-external complements cannot.

3. On the peculiar properties of clitic pronouns

Clitic pronouns display a peculiar behaviour as far as properties of all grammatical modules are concerned (see Kayne 1975; Zwicky 1977, 1985). In particular, they are deficient from all points of view. Clitic pronouns have a restricted syntactic distribution in that they only appear in specialized non-thematic positions; they are monosyllabic elements which do not bear word stress; their reference is restricted to salient antecedents, and they cannot introduce new referents into the discourse. Clitic pronouns systematically differ from strong pronouns, which behave like regular DPs.

What follows is a survey of their properties, mainly exemplified on the basis of Italian. Most of these properties characterize clitic pronouns in all languages studied so far. They can be taken to reflect a fundamental property of natural languages. These properties also characterize clitic (and clitic-like, i.e., weak) elements of other categories, such as possessive pronouns and adjectives (Cardinaletti 1998), demonstratives (Cardinaletti 1999: 70), adverbs (Cardinaletti and Starke 1999; Cardinaletti 2007, 2011), and wh-elements (Bouchard and Hirschbuhler 1987; Friedemann 1990, 1997; Munaro 1999; Poletto and Pollock 2004, 2009; Sportiche 2011).

3.1. Syntactic properties

A1: *obligatory displacement*: clitic pronouns cannot remain in their merge position, but are obligatorily displaced to a higher position (adjacent to the verb in Italian), a position not available to strong pronouns and full DPs:

(5) a. *Maria conosce *lo / lui / Gianni.*
Maria knows him / him / Gianni

b. *Maria lo / *lui / *Gianni conosce.*
Maria him / him / Gianni knows
'Maria knows him / Gianni.'

A2: *limited distribution*: clitic pronouns cannot appear in peripheral positions (6a) or in isolation (6b):

(6) a. *Lui / *Lo, Maria lo conosce.*
him / him Maria him knows
'Him, Maria knows him.'

b. *Chi conosce, Maria? Lui / *Lo.*
whom knows Mary him / him
'Who does Mary know? Him.'

A3: *limited distribution*: differently from strong pronouns, clitic pronouns cannot be modified (7)–(8), conjoined (9), contrastively stressed (10):

(7) a. *Maria conosce solo lui.*
Maria knows only him
'Maria knows only him.'

b. **Maria conosce solo lo.*
Maria knows only him
b′. **Maria lo conosce solo.*
b″. **Maria solo lo conosce.*

(8) a. *Accuseranno loro stessi.*
will.accuse.they them themselves
'They will accuse themselves.'

b. **Accuseranno li stessi.*
will.accuse.they them themselves
b′. **Li accuseranno stessi.*
b″. **Li stessi accuseranno.*

(9) a. *Maria conosce [lui e voi].*
Maria knows him and you.PL
'Maria knows him and you.'

b. **Maria conosce [lo e vi].*
Maria knows him and you.PL
b′. **Maria [lo e vi] conosce.*

(10) a. *Maria conosce LUI, non voi.*
Maria knows him, not you.PL
'Maria knows him, not you.'

b. **Maria conosce LO, non voi.*
Maria knows him, not you.PL
b′. **Maria LO conosce, non voi.*

3.2. Phonological properties

B1: *lack of word stress*: clitic pronouns lack word stress, while strong pronouns bear one.
The following Italian monosyllabic words form minimal pairs, where one word bears stress, while the other, i.e., the clitic pronoun, lacks word stress: *là* ['la] 'there' vs. *la*

[la] 'her', *né* ['ne] 'neither' vs. *ne* [ne] 'of them', *sì* ['si] 'yes' vs. *si* [si] 'himself/herself/ themselves', etc.

Minimal pairs are also formed by clitic and strong pronouns which have the same segmental content, such as French *nous* 'us' and *vous* 'you.PL':

(11) a. *Il nous voit.* [nu] [French]
he us sees
'He sees us.'

b. *Il ne voit que nous.* ['nu]
he not sees than us
'He only sees us.'

B2: *prosodic status*: Clitic pronouns do not form single phonological words with the host verbs. In Italian, for instance, the process of s-sonorization which is found word-internally in intervocalic contexts (after a prefix, as in *re*[z]*istere* 'resist', *de*[z]*istere* 'desist', and before a suffix, as in *ca*[z]*a* 'house'), does not take place between a proclitic pronoun and the verb (*Lo* [s]*o* / *[z]*o* 'I know it.'), and between the verb and an enclitic pronoun (*mettendo*[s]*i* / **mettendo*[z]*i* 'placing himself'). The verb and the clitic(s) are different phonological words. In Selkirk's (1995) terminology, clitic pronouns are neither internal clitics nor affixal clitics, but free clitics, which are incorporated into prosodic structure at the level of the Phonological Phrase. The same conclusions hold for subject clitics found in northern Italian dialects (see Cardinaletti and Repetti 2009 for discussion).

3.3. Morphological properties

C1: *reduced morphological form*: clitic pronouns are morphologically reduced with respect to their strong counterparts. They are always monosyllabic words, while strong pronouns can be bisyllabic. Since clitic pronouns can also be homophonous to strong pronouns (cf. e.g. French [11]), the generalization on morphological reduction can be formulated as in (12): clitic pronouns are equal or smaller than their strong counterparts (see other examples in Cardinaletti and Starke 1999: 174):

(12) Morphological reduction: clitic $\leq$ strong

C2: *free morphemes*: although they bear no word stress (see B1 above), clitic pronouns must be considered independent words (free morphemes) and cannot be treated as affixes (bound morphemes) – for discussion, see Klavans (1979), (1982), (1985); Zwicky (1977); Zwicky and Pullum (1983). In Romance languages, this is very clear when clitic pronouns appear in proclisis; this is a position where inflectional morphemes are never found. However, the same is true when they occur in enclitic position. See the phonological evidence in B2 above. Note that in grammaticalization theories (Givón 1979; Hopper and Traugott 1993, 2003, among many others), clitic elements are situated between grammatical words and affixes: content word > grammatical word > clitic > affix > zero.

C3: *case distinctions*: although in Italian and French (and other Romance languages), DPs do not display morphological case, clitic pronouns can manifest case distinctions:

accusative (e.g. It. *lo*, Fr. *le* 'it/him'), dative (e.g. It. *gli*, Fr. *lui* 'to him'), partitive/genitive (It. *ne*, Fr. *en* 'of it/them'), locative (It. *ci*, Fr. *y* 'there').

C4: *phi-features*: depending on the features they realize, two series of clitic pronouns should be distinguished: person and non-person pronouns (Kayne 2000b). Cardinaletti (2008), (2010a) further elaborated this distinction for Italian clitic pronouns, which can be categorized as in (13) (note that the morphological make up of clitic pronouns may have consequences, among other things, on the type of clitic clusters that the pronoun can enter, as shown in the quoted works):

(13) a. morphologically simple clitic pronouns which only consist of consonantal morphemes expressing person (the final vowel is epenthetic):
- 1st, 2nd and 0 person clitics: *mi* 'me', *ti* 'you.SG'; *si* 'himself/herself/themselves'; *ci* 'us, there', *vi* 'you.PL, there'
- 3rd person (masculine) dative clitic *gli* 'to him'

b. morphologically complex clitic pronouns which consist of the pronominal morpheme /l/ and portmanteau vocalic morphemes encoding number/gender (also found in the unmarked Italian nominal declension, see [40]):
- 3rd person accusative clitics: *lo* 'him', *la* 'her', *li* 'them.M', *le* 'them.F' (note that in Spanish (pro)nominal system, phi-features are expressed by more than one morpheme: *l-o-s* 'them.M.PL', *l-a-s* 'them.F.PL')

c. morphologically complex clitic pronouns which consist of the pronominal morpheme /l/ and the vocalic morpheme /e/ (also found in the marked Italian nominal declension, e.g. *fiore* 'flower', *felice* 'happy'):
- 3rd person feminine dative clitic *le* 'to her'
- partitive/genitive/locative *ne* 'of them', 'from there'.

3.4. Semantic Properties

D1: *non-arguments (expletives) and quasi-arguments*: clitic pronouns can realize non-argumental and quasi-argumental subjects, which cannot be realized by strong pronouns. Data come from the northern Italian dialect of Trepalle, province of Sondrio (Manzini and Savoia 2005 I: 174). (14a) contains non-argument *al* 'it' co-occurring with the post-verbal subject *i marcin* 'the children' (see the similar Florentine example in [14a′] from Brandi and Cordin 1989: 115); (14b) contains the quasi-argumental *al* subject of the weather verb *plof* 'rain'; (14c) contains quasi-argument *al* co-occurring with the postverbal subject clause *klamel* 'call him':

(14) a. *Dopo al vegn i marcin.* [Trepalle]
later it comes the children
'The children are coming later.'

a′. *Gl' è venuto la Maria.* [Florentine]
it is come the Maria
'Maria came.'

b. *Al plof.* [Trepalle]
it rains
'It is raining.'

c. *Al sarò megl klame=l.* [Trepalle]
it will.be better call.INF=him
'It would be better to call him.'

D2: *benefactive and ethical datives*: clitic pronouns can realize non-argumental datives, i.e., benefactive (15a, b) (see [3a′]) and ethical (15c) datives; the latter cannot be realized by strong pronouns:

(15) a. *Mi parte il treno.*
to.me leaves the train
'My train is leaving.'

b. *Mi è nato un bambino.*
to.me is born a baby
'I have had a baby.'

c. *Mi è saltato dalla finestra.*
to.me is jumped from.the window
'He jumped out of the window.'

D3: *[±human] reference*: (3rd person) clitic pronouns can refer to both human and non-human entities, a possibility excluded to strong personal pronouns which may only refer to human entities (see Kayne 1975: 91; Jaeggli 1982: 41; Rizzi 1982; Berendsen 1986: 38–39; Schroten 1992; Corver and Delfitto 1999; Cardinaletti and Starke 1996, 1999 among others). A verb that implies a non-human object, such as *comprare* 'buy', gives ungrammatical results with a strong pronoun, and is only compatible with a clitic pronoun:

(16) a. *Non conosco / *compro che lui.*
not know.I / buy.I than him
'I only know him.'

b. *Lo conosco / Lo compro.*
him/it know.I / it buy.I
'I know him / I buy it.'

Demonstrative pronouns behave differently in that they can have non-human referents. We show it with the following French example: *Je ne connais / achète que celui-là* 'I only know / buy that one'.

D4: *referentiality/specificity/familiarity*: it is often claimed that clitic pronouns only have referential/specific usages (e.g. Uriagereka 1995a; Sportiche 1996/98). But this claim is not entirely correct. First, clitic pronouns can realize non-referential arguments, such as clitic objects in idiomatic expressions (17a, b), measure objects of verbs like *pesare* 'weigh' (17c), and the object of phrasal verbs (17d) (examples [17c, d] are taken from Cinque 1990: 163, n. 8):

(17) a. *Ce la farò.*
there it will.make.I
'I will manage.'

b. *Ci vuole altro pane.*
there wants more bread
'More bread is needed.'

c. *70 chili, non li pesa.*
70 kilos, not them weighs.he
'70 kilos, he does not weigh them.'

d. *Giustizia, non la farà mai.*
justice, not it will.do.he ever
'Justice, he will never do it.'

Referentiality only matters for discourse grammar, i.e., when the antecedent of the clitic pronoun must be recovered from the discourse. In this case, non-referential clitics are not possible. Consider the contrast between (17c, d) and (18c, d) (examples from Cinque 1990: 162, n. 8):

(18) a. Speaker A: *Io conosco Mario.*
I know Mario
'I know Mario.'
Speaker B: *Anch'io lo conosco.*
also I him know
'I know him, too.'

b. Speaker A: *Io so l'inglese.*
I know English
'I speak English.'
Speaker B: *Anch'io lo so.*
also I it know
'I speak it, too.'

c. Speaker A: *Io peso 70 chili.*
I weigh 70 kilos
'I weigh 70 kilos.'
Speaker B: **Anch'io li peso.*
also I them weigh
'Me too.'

d. Speaker A: *Farà giustizia.*
will.do.he justice
'He will do justice.'

Speaker B: **Anch'io la farò.*
also I it will.do
'Me too.'

Second, clitic pronouns can also have non-specific readings (sentence [19c] from Cinque 1990: 119):

(19) a. *Cerco una segretaria che sappia l'inglese, ma non la voglio troppo*
look.for.I a secretary who knows English but not her want.I too
giovane.
young
'I am looking for a secretary who speaks English, but I wouldn't like a too young one.'

b. *Il bambino che arriverà per primo lo premieremo con un*
the child who will.arrive for first him will.give.a.prize.we with an
gelato.
ice-cream
'The child who will arrive first will get an ice-cream as a prize.'

c. *Ci rimarrò tre settimane. Spero di passar=le in allegria.*
there will.stay.I three weeks hope.I to spend=them being jolly
'I will stay there three weeks. I hope to spend them being jolly.'

Third, a subject clitic pronoun as in (20) can have an impersonal, existential reading. The example comes from an Emilian dialect spoken in Gazzoli (province of Piacenza) (Cardinaletti and Repetti 2010: 130, n. 24):

(20) [*in kula butiga la, i m an vendi:d əl paŋ vɛtʃ*] [Emilian, Gazzoli]
in that shop there they to.me have sold the bread old
'In that shop they sold me stale bread.'

In all the examples seen above except idiomatic (17a, b) and existential (20), clitic pronouns have an anaphoric usage and refer to familiar antecedents. They cannot be used to introduce a new referent into the discourse, for example accompanied by a pointing gesture; in this case, only strong pronouns are possible:

(21) *Conosci ☞lui / *☞lo?*
know.you him / him
'Do you know him?'

3.5. Choice between classes of pronouns

E: In contexts like (22), a clitic pronoun must be used instead of a strong pronoun. In (23), the opposite situation is found: when e.g. modification or coordination occurs, a strong pronoun is the only possibility since these are contexts in which clitic pronouns are independently barred; see (7)–(9) above. This suggests that a clitic pronoun is always chosen over a strong pronoun if possible. The choice preference can be expressed as in (24):

(22) Question: *Conosci Gianni?*
know.you Gianni
'Do you know Gianni?'

Answer: **Sì, conosco lui / Sì, lo conosco.*
yes know.I him / yes him know.I
'Yes, I know him.'

(23) Question: *Conosci Gianni?*
know.you Gianni
'Do you know Gianni?'

Answer: *Sì, conosco solo lui / conosco lui e la moglie.*
yes know.I only him / know.I him and the wife
'Yes, I know only him / I know him and his wife.'

(24) choice: clitic > strong

4. A syntactic attempt to derive the peculiar properties of clitic pronouns

In order to capture the co-variation of syntactic, semantic and phonological properties, a syntactic trigger is needed. Given the current model of grammar, where semantics and phonology are independent of each other, a syntactic trigger will necessarily have both semantic and phonological consequences. The first attempts to derive the properties of clitic pronouns capitalize on their syntactic head status. Since they are heads, their behaviour is expectedly different from that of full phrases, i.e., DPs and strong pronouns (see section 4.1). The discovery of weak pronouns makes this view insufficient. Weak pronouns display the same properties as clitic pronouns, but they are not heads: they do not occupy head positions, but specifier positions, typical of phrases. A more elaborated analysis is needed which captures the parallel behaviour of clitic and weak pronouns. One such proposal is that clitic pronouns (as well as weak pronouns) are reduced maximal projections (see section 4.2 for two different implementations of this idea).

4.1. The head approach

Since Kayne (1975: 81–83) and Baltin (1981), clitic pronouns are taken to be heads. This view is supported by the observation that a clitic pronoun and its host can undergo movement as a unit. Consider French interrogatives (25a, b) (Kayne 1975) and Italian hypotheticals (26a, b) and gerunds (27a) (Rizzi 2000b: 108), in which the verb moves to C, i.e., the position preceding the subject which is occupied by the complementiser in subordinate clauses. In the presence of a clitic pronoun, both the clitic and the verb precede the subject, (25d), (26d), (27b). These data can be interpreted by saying that object pronouns are carried along by auxiliary movement to C; also see (62c–e) below. In (25)–(27) and throughout the paper, the barred character indicates the traces of moved constituents (we assume that clitic pronouns move from the positions typical of the XPs they replace; see section 5 below for arguments to support this analysis):

(25) a. [$_{CP}$ [$_{TP}$ *tu as* [$_{VP}$ *vu Jean*]]].
you have seen Jean
'You saw Jean.'

b. [$_{CP}$ [$_{C}$ *as*] [$_{TP}$ *tu* ~~*as*~~ [$_{VP}$ *vu Jean*]]]?
have you seen Jean
'Did you see Jean ?'

c. [$_{CP}$ [$_{TP}$ *tu l' as* [$_{VP}$ *vu* ~~*le*~~]]].
you him have seen
'You saw him.'

d. [$_{CP}$ [$_{C}$ *l' as*] [$_{TP}$ *tu* [~~*l'as*~~] [$_{VP}$ *vu* ~~*le*~~]]?
him have you seen
'Did you see him?'

(26) a. [$_{CP}$ [$_{C}$ *se*] [$_{TP}$ *Gianni avesse* [$_{VP}$ *programmato l' incontro in anticipo*]]] ...
if Gianni had programmed the meeting ahead, ...

b. [$_{CP}$ [$_{C}$ *avesse*] [$_{TP}$ *Gianni* ~~*avesse*~~ [$_{VP}$ *programmato l' incontro*
had Gianni programmed the meeting
in anticipo]]] ...
ahead
'If Gianni had programmed the meeting ahead, …'

c. [$_{CP}$ [$_{C}$ *se*] [$_{TP}$ *Gianni l' avesse* [$_{VP}$ *programmato* ~~*lo*~~ *in anticipo*]]] ...
if Gianni it had programmed ahead, ...

d. [$_{CP}$ [$_{C}$ *l' avesse]* [$_{TP}$ *Gianni* ~~*l'avesse*~~ [$_{VP}$ *programmato* ~~*lo*~~ *in anticipo*]]] ...
it had Gianni programmed ahead, ...
'If Gianni had programmed it ahead, …'

(27) a. [$_{CP}$ [$_{C}$ *avendo*] [$_{TP}$ *Gianni [*~~*avendo*~~*]* [$_{VP}$ *restituito la busta al*
having Gianni given.back the envelope to.the
direttore]]] ...
director
'Since Gianni gave the envelope back to the director, …'

b. [$_{CP}$ [$_{C}$ *avendo=la*] [$_{TP}$ *Gianni* [~~*avendola*~~] [$_{VP}$ *restituita* ~~*la*~~ *al*
having=it Gianni given.back to.the
direttore]]] ...
director
'Since Gianni gave it back to the director, …'

Other arguments for the head status of clitic pronouns come from their complex interaction with verb movement (giving rise to proclisis and enclisis, see sections 6.2–3).

The peculiar properties of clitic pronouns might be attributed to their head status. Their behaviour is similar to that of elements realizing functional heads, which cannot be focalized, modified, conjoined, and do not bear word stress.

Although clitic pronouns are taken to be heads, the peculiar properties discussed in section 3 cannot be attributed to their head status. Most of these properties also characterize the class of weak pronouns, which, like clitics, differ from strong pronouns, but are not heads: they occur in specifier positions (Cardinaletti and Starke 1996, 1999). One example is provided by the Italian dative pronoun *loro* 'to.them' which, like clitic pronouns, must evacuate its merge position (28), cannot be modified and coordinated (29)–(30), is morphologically reduced with respect to the strong dative form *a loro* 'to them', and is always anaphoric (Cardinaletti 1991). *Loro* however differs from clitic pronouns in that it is a bisyllabic word which bears word stress, as shown by the fact that the tonic vowel is lengthened by a productive phonological rule of Italian (cf. ['lo:ro]); on the syntactic side, *loro* does not share the distribution of clitic elements since it follows the lexical verb (28b) vs. (28c) and is not necessarily adjacent to it (31):

(28) a. **Maria ha dato un libro loro.*
Maria has given a book to.them

b. *Maria ha dato loro un libro ~~loro~~.*
c. **Maria loro ha dato ~~loro~~ un libro ~~loro~~.*
'Maria gave them a book.'

(29) a. *Maria parla solo a loro.*
Maria talks only to them
'Maria only talks to them.'

b. **Maria parla solo loro.*
Maria talks only to.them

(30) a. *Maria parla [a loro e a voi].*
Maria talks to them and to you
'Maria talks to them and to you.'

b. **Maria parla [loro e a voi].*
Maria talks to.them and to you

(31) *Non ho dato mai loro un libro ~~loro~~.*
not have.I given ever to.them a book
'I have never given them a book.'

A common analysis is needed to account for the syntactic and semantic properties which are shared by clitic and weak pronouns and differentiate them from strong pronouns. Taking weak pronouns into account, the morphological and the choice generalizations in (12) and (24) should be reformulated as in (32a) and (32b), respectively:

(32) a. morphological reduction: clitic $\leq$ weak $\leq$ strong
b. choice: clitic > weak > strong

Although clitic pronouns behave as heads, they cannot be merged as such. Kayne's (1994) antisymmetric framework excludes the base-generation of a pure head in complement position, as in (33a) (see Kayne 1994: 61). A more elaborated hypothesis is therefore needed in which clitic pronouns are inserted as maximal projections, as in (33b), and become heads in the course of the derivation. Since its category hasn't been established yet, the clitic pronoun is represented here as X and XP, respectively:

(33) a. *

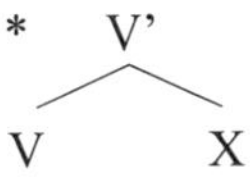

b.

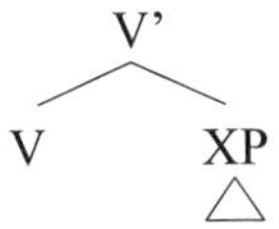

Before turning to the discussion of (33b), the proposal by Moro (2000) is worth mentioning, who assumed Kayne's (1994) antisymmetric approach, but looked at clitic placement in a slightly different way. Moro suggested that clitic pronouns (i) indeed merge as heads and (ii) must move to break down a symmetric configuration, namely a phrase which contains two heads (the verb and the clitic pronoun itself), as in (33a). We have just seen in (28a, b) that obligatory syntactic movement also characterizes weak pronouns, which are not merged as heads. Moro's proposal thus cannot be extended to account for the obligatory movement of weak pronouns. Since it is more desirable to have a common motivation for the obligatory movement of clitic and weak pronouns (see section 6.1), this hypothesis will not be further considered here.

4.2. The maximal projection approach

As we concluded above, a clitic pronoun should be regarded as the realization of the head of an otherwise empty phrase generated in argument position, out of which it is extracted at some point of the derivation (see Torrego 1988 and section 5.6). Two approaches have been explored in the literature: compared to full DP phrases (34a) (see Abney 1987), pronominal projections are reduced from either below (i.e., they lack the NP projection, as roughly in [34b]) or above (i.e., they lack the DP projection, as in [34c]):

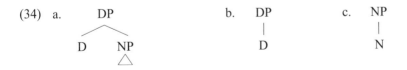

(34) a.

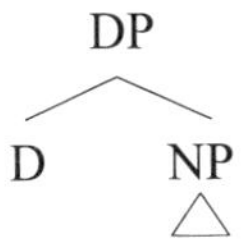

b.

c.

The two proposals in (34b, c) are discussed in sections 4.2.1 and 4.2.2, respectively – note that within a Bare Phrase Structure Theory, Chomsky (1995) suggested that clitic pronouns are both maximal (X^{max}), because they do not project, and minimal (X^{min}), because they do not dominate anything. This proposal does not allow us to distinguish clitic from weak pronouns, hence it will not be assumed here.

4.2.1. The D-hypothesis

Since pronouns lack descriptive content, clitic pronouns can be taken to realize a nominal projection which lacks the lexical portion of the nominal structure, namely NP. In other words, clitic pronouns only realize the head D of the nominal expression, as in (34b).

The fact that in some Romance languages, 3rd person accusative clitic pronouns have the same morphological form as determiners, as shown in (35) for French, seems to support the view that clitic pronouns are determiners (Ds). This proposal builds on Postal's (1969) analysis of English pronouns, according to which phrases like *the linguists* and *we linguists* have the same structure (for Germanic languages, see Cardinaletti 1994: 198–199; for a historical perspective on the D-hypothesis, see Harris 1980a, b and Vincent 1997). Clitic pronouns differ from regular DPs (36a) (see [34a]) in that their complement NP is empty (36b); something like a null pronoun – Torrego (1988); Uriagereka (1988), (1995a), (1996); Corver and Delfitto (1999); Panagiotidis (2002), or absent (36 b′) (i.e., they are intransitive Ds, cf. Cardinaletti 1994; Rizzi 2000b):

(35) a. *Je connais la fille.*
I know the girl
'I know the girl.'

b. *Je la connais.* [French]
I her know
'I know her.'

(36)

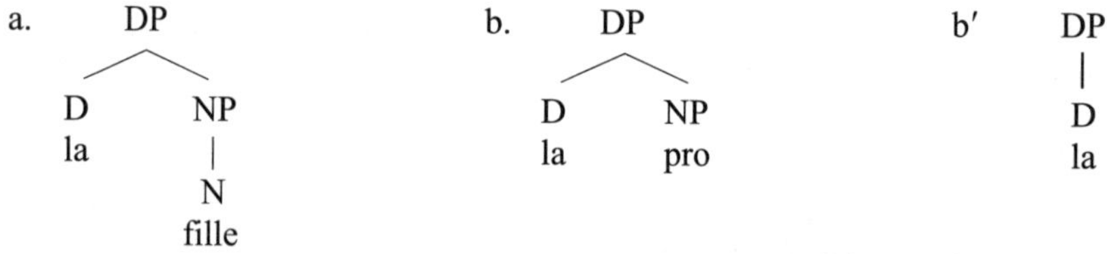

In spite of its *prima facie* attractiveness, this proposal raises many questions, both on the morphological/phonological side and the semantic side of grammar.

First, while in some Romance languages such as French, the paradigms of determiners and (accusative) clitic pronouns are indeed identical, in other languages (e.g. Italian), the two paradigms are similar but not identical, something which is unexpected if determiners and clitic pronouns are listed in the lexicon as one and the same lexical item:

(37)

French			Italian		
determiners		accusative clitic pron.	determiners		accusative clitic pron.
MASC	le	le	MASC.SG	il/lo	lo
FEM	la	la	FEM.SG	la	la
PL	les	les	MASC.PL	i/gli	li
			FEM.PL	le	le

Note that the differences between the two paradigms in Italian cannot be traced back to productive phonological rules. Furthermore, the final vowels of clitic pronouns have a different distribution from those of definite articles in front of vowel-initial words. Note the minimal pairs in (38) and (39):

(38) a. *Lo àmo / ??l'àmo*
him love.I
'I love him.'

a′. *Lo inìzio / l'inìzio*
it.M begin.I
'I am beginning it.'

b. *La àmo / ??l'àmo*
her love.I
'I love her.'

b′. *La inìzio / l'inìzio*
it.F begin.I
'I am beginning it.'

(39) a. **lo àmo / l'àmo*
the.M fish-hook.M
'the fish-hook'

a′. **lo inìzio / l'inìzio*
the.M beginning.M
'the beginning'

b. *?la àmaca / l'àmaca*
the.F hammock.F
'the hammock'

b′. *??la amìca / l'amìca*
the.F friend.F
'the friend'

Final vowels occur on clitic pronouns depending on the phonological properties of the verb: they are preferably kept when the initial vowel of the verb is stressed (38a, b), and optionally omitted otherwise (38a′, b′); note that the gender of the pronoun is not relevant. Determiners display the opposite behaviour in that they are preferably omitted, and gender is a crucial factor. Vowels are obligatorily missing on the article if it is masculine (39a, a′) and preferably missing when it is feminine (39b, b′). The phonological differences between (38) and (39) argue against a common treatment of determiners and clitic pronouns (cf. Cardinaletti 2010a). In phonological theories, clitic pronouns and determiners are analysed as independent lexical entries. For Italian, Repetti (2004) and Cardinaletti and Repetti (2007) take /l/ to be the underlying form of the masculine singular definite article, which explains why final [o] does not occur in (39a, a′), and /lo/ to be the underlying form of the masculine singular (accusative) clitic pronoun.

Second, since determiners do not bear case distinctions in Romance languages, it is surprising that determiners are identical/similar to accusative clitic pronouns. This criticism can be suspended by observing that in some Romance languages, notably northern Italian dialects, nominative clitic pronouns are (often) identical to accusative clitic pronouns. Thus, the lack of case distinctions seems to characterize not only determiners but also clitic pronouns. However, the same observation as above holds: Although nominative clitics are often similar to accusative clitics and determiners, their paradigms are not always identical. This is again unexpected if these three items were the same lexical elements of category D. In the D-approach to clitic pronouns, it is also difficult to understand why one of the Italian allomorphs of the 3rd person plural masculine determiner, namely the one used in front of consonantal clusters (e.g. *gli studenti* 'the students'), should be identical to the 3rd person dative singular masculine clitic *gli* (e.g. *Maria gli parlerà* 'Maria will speak to him'). These homophonous forms can only be explained diachronically. See Vanelli (1996) for the parallel, but not identical historical development of determiners and clitic pronouns from Old Italian to Modern Italian.

Third, the D-hypothesis is also undermined by the observation that some languages manifest one paradigm but not the other: Slavic languages have clitic pronouns but not determiners, Brazilian Portuguese has determiners but no corresponding clitics.

Fourth, the D-hypothesis is hardly extendable to those clitic pronouns whose morphological form is different from determiners, but which share the same syntactic and phonological properties as 3rd person (accusative) clitic pronouns: 3rd person dative clitics (Italian *gli*, *le*), 1st and 2nd clitic pronouns (Italian *mi*, *ti*), locatives (Italian *ci*, *vi*) and partitives/genitives (Italian *ne*) (see [1]). To overcome this difficulty, Uriagereka (1995a) suggests that non-3rd person pronouns are indeed not Ds. The non-uniformity hypothesis concerning clitic pronouns is also defended in Bleam (1999), who suggests that only accusative 3rd person pronouns are determiners, while dative clitics are inflections.

Finally, an observation concerning the semantic side of the grammar: if D is the locus of referential properties (Longobardi 1994), the proposal that clitic pronouns are Ds is problematic in view of the fact that they do not have any autonomous referential capability. Contrary to strong pronouns, they are always anaphoric on a DP present in the linguistic context and cannot be used to introduce new referents into the discourse (see property D4 in section 3 and [21]).

These observations make the proposal that clitic pronouns are Ds highly controversial.

The morphological identity or similarity between determiners and 3rd person (accusative) clitic pronouns observed in Romance languages must be attributed to historical reasons, both classes of elements having Latin demonstratives as their predecessors (Harris 1980a, b; Wanner 1987; Vincent 1997), and cannot be used to argue for a common syntactic status of determiners and clitic pronouns. Historical reasons, but not the D-hypothesis can also explain why in Sardinian, 3rd person clitic pronouns and determiners display different roots: *l-* and *s-*, respectively (Jones 1993). While clitic pronouns derive from Latin *ille*, determiners derive from Latin *ipse*. Also see Jones (1999).

In conclusion, determiners and clitic pronouns are different lexical items: while definite articles occur in D and can be seen as the spell out of copies of the features of the noun (Giusti 2008), clitic pronouns have more structure: they realize (reduced) nominal projections. As we will see in the following section, they may be taken to realize a nominal projection lacking the DP layer, as in (34c).

4.2.2. The structural deficiency hypothesis

The critical observations against the D-hypothesis suggest that the peculiarities of clitic pronouns must be captured in a different way. Here, we explore the alternative hypothesis depicted in (34c) above, according to which clitic pronouns are reduced projections crucially lacking the highest portion of nominal expressions (i.e., the DP layer). Clitic pronouns only realize the nominal functional heads encoding phi-features (person, number, gender) and case features. Note that 3rd person clitics indeed display the same morphemes realizing gender/number features (40a) as in the unmarked nominal declension of nouns (40b) and adjectives (40c) (the same morphemes also appear on quantifiers, demonstratives, and past participles):

(40) a. ***lo*** ***la*** ***li*** ***le***
him.M.SG her.F.SG them.M.PL them.F.PL

b. *bambin**o*** *bambin**a*** *bambin**i*** *bambin**e***
child.M.SG child.F.SG child.M.PL child.F.PL

c. *alt**o*** *alt**a*** *alt**i*** *alt**e***
tall.M.SG tall.F.SG tall.M.PL tall.F.PL

In languages with case morphology, such as Slavic, clitic pronouns realize another DP-internal feature (case) and end up being homophonous to case endings; see for instance the Czech clitic *ho* in (41a), which is identical to the case ending found on the adjective in (41b) (this observation is also true of Germanic language, see Cardinaletti 1994: 198–199; Cardinaletti and Starke 1996):

(41) a. *Videl **ho**.* [Czech]
saw.he him.ACC
'He saw him.'

b. *velké**ho** muze*
big.ACC man.ACC
'the big man'

The projection realized by a clitic pronoun can thus be seen as the nominal counterpart of the clausal IP layer (see Roberts 2010 for the similar proposal that clitics encode phi-features and not the D feature). Like clitic pronouns, weak pronouns also lack the highest functional projection D, but retain some further projection that clitics lack. This can account for the differences between them, in particular their different phonological properties. The representation of full phrases (including strong pronouns), weak pronouns and clitic pronouns is provided in (42) (see Cardinaletti and Starke 1999: 195):

(42) a. Strong Pronouns b. Weak Pronouns c. Clitic Pronouns

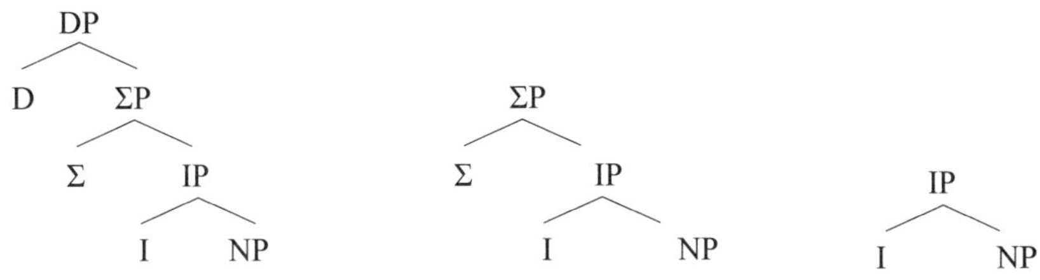

As we have seen in section 3 above, clitic pronouns are deficient on all linguistic levels. Their peculiar behaviour can be reduced to the syntactic properties of the phrase they project. The lack of the highest DP projection can explain their semantic properties and the fact that they cannot be modified, conjoined and contrasted, under the hypothesis that only full extended projections can undergo these operations. The lack of the Σ projection, to which phonological properties are correlated, explains the fact that clitic pronouns bear no word stress. As we will see below, the deficiency hypothesis can also motivate the peculiar syntax displayed by clitic (and weak) pronouns, in particular the fact that they never appear in their merge position and always occur in derived positions – see (5) and (28a, b). For a more detailed discussion of the deficiency hypothesis, see Cardinaletti and Starke (1999).

5. Clitic placement: Derivation or base-generation?

Since Kayne (1975) and Quicoli (1976, 1980), a movement analysis has been assumed for object clitic pronouns: they are merged as arguments of the verb and moved to higher clitic-dedicated positions. In the following sections 5.1–3, I discuss the arguments for taking clitic placement as a syntactic movement rule. In section 5.4, I discuss the evidence, mainly represented by clitic doubling, to analyze clitic pronouns as merged in their spell-out positions. In sections 5.5–6, some recent attempts at reconciling the apparently contradictory pieces of evidence are presented.

5.1. Locality restrictions

Clitic placement displays locality restrictions typical of other movement operations, such as *wh*-movement and NP-movement.

As originally pointed out by Kayne (1975), pronouns cannot be cliticized across the subject of causative constructions (a Specified Subject Condition effect, currently analyzed as a Minimality effect, Rizzi 1990), which can be taken as a piece of evidence for a movement analysis of clitics:

(43) a. *Jean a laissé* [*Pierre parler à Marie*]. [French]
Jean has let Pierre speak to Marie
'Jean let Pierre speak to Marie.'
b. *Jean l' a laissé* [~~*le*~~ *parler à Marie*].
Jean him has let speak to Marie
'Jean let him speak to Marie.'
c. **Jean lui a laissé* [*Pierre parler* ~~*lui*~~].
Jean to.her has let Pierre speak
'Jean let Pierre speak to her.'

Now compare (44a) with (44b): while the nominal expression *la foto* 'the picture' in (44a) contains a determiner in D, *questa foto* 'this picture' in (44b) contains a demonstrative in SpecDP, which blocks movement out of the DP (see Giusti 1997: 111; Sportiche 1989/98: 126, 143, 1996/98: 256):

(44) a. *Ne ho vista* [$_{\text{DP}}$ *~~ne~~ la* [$_{\text{NP}}$ *foto ~~ne~~*]].
of.him have.I seen the picture
'I saw the picture of him.'

cf. *Di chi hai visto* [$_{\text{DP}}$ *~~di chi~~ la* [$_{\text{NP}}$ *foto ~~di chi~~*]]?
of whom have.you seen the picture
'The picture of whom did you see?'

b. **Ne ho vista* [$_{\text{DP}}$ *questa* [$_{\text{NP}}$ *foto ~~ne~~*]].
of.him have.I seen this picture
'I saw this picture of him.'

cf. **Di chi hai visto* [$_{\text{DP}}$ *questa* [$_{\text{NP}}$ *foto ~~di chi~~*]]?
of whom have.you seen this picture
'This picture of whom did you see?'

Clitic pronouns cannot be extracted out of an adjunct temporal PP (45), a CED effect (Huang 1982). Argumental and adjunct locative PPs give rise to contrasts like those in (46): extraction of a clitic pronoun is possible out of an argumental locative as in (46a–c) and ungrammatical out of an adjunct locative as in (46d) – see also (92); cf. Rizzi (1988/2001: 540–542); Siloni (1997: 64, n. 27); Belletti (1999: 557–558). A similar effect is found with partitive *ne*-extraction out of quantified nominal expressions: in (47a) *tre* 'three' is the argument of *passare* 'spend', and extraction is possible – see also (93), in (47b) *tre* 'three' is a temporal adjunct of *rimanere* 'stay', and extraction is ungrammatical (Belletti and Rizzi (1981)):

(45) **L' ho parlato* [*dopo ~~lo~~*].
him have.I spoken after
'I spoke after him.'

cf. **Chi hai parlato* [*dopo ~~chi~~*]?
whom have.you spoken after
'After whom did you speak?'

(46) a. *Gianni le si è messo* [*accanto ~~le~~*].
Gianni to.her REFL is placed next
'Gianni placed himself next to her.'

cf. *A chi si è messo* [*accanto ~~a chi~~*]?
to whom REFL is placed next
'Next to whom did he place himself?'

La ragazza a cui Gianni si è messo [*accanto ~~a cui~~*]
the girl to whom Gianni REFL is placed next
'the girl next to whom Gianni placed himself.'

b. *Gianni le è seduto* [*accanto ~~le~~*].
Gianni to.her is seated next
'Gianni is seated next to her.'

cf. *A chi è seduto [accanto ~~a chi~~]?*
to whom is seated next
'Next to whom is he seated?'

La ragazza a cui Gianni è seduto [accanto ~~a cui~~]
the girl to whom Gianni is seated next
'the girl next to whom he is seated.'

c. *?Gianni le ha mangiato [accanto ~~le~~].*
Gianni to.her has eaten next
'Gianni was eating next to her.'

cf. *A chi ha mangiato [accanto ~~a chi~~]?*
to whom has eaten next
'Next to whom was he eating?'

?La ragazza a cui Gianni ha mangiato [accanto ~~a cui~~]
the girl to whom Gianni has eaten next
'the girl next to whom Gianni was eating.'

d. **Gianni le è felice [accanto ~~le~~]*
Gianni to.her is happy next
'Gianni is happy next to her.'

cf. **A chi è felice [accanto ~~a chi~~]?*
to whom is happy next
'Next to whom is he happy?'

**La ragazza a cui Gianni è felice [accanto ~~a cui~~]*
the girl to whom Gianni is happy next
'the girl next to whom Gianni is happy.'

(47) a. *Ne ho passate [tre ~~ne~~] a Londra.*
of.them have.I spent three in London
'I spent three of them in London.'

b. **Ne sono rimasto [tre ~~ne~~] a Londra.*
of.them am stayed three in London
'I stayed three of them in London.'

Clitic movement cannot take place out of complex NPs (48) and PPs (49):

(48) a. *Ho cominciato [la lettura [di [due giornali]]].*
have.I started the reading of two newspapers
'I have started reading two newspapers.'

b. **Ne ho cominciato [la lettura [di [due ~~ne~~]]].*
of.them have.I started the reading of two
'I have started reading two of them.'

cf. **Cosa hai cominciato [la lettura [di [due ~~cosa~~]]]?*
what have.you started the reading of two

(49) a. *Ho parlato* [*con* [*la madre* [*di Enrico*]]].
have.I spoken with the mother of Enrico
'I spoke with Enrico's mother.'

b. **Ne ho parlato* [*con* [*la madre* [~~*ne*~~]]].
of.him have.I spoken with the mother
'I spoke with his mother.'

cf. **Di chi hai parlato* [*con* [*la madre [~~di chi~~*]]]*?*
of whom have.you spoken with the mother
'With whose mother did you speak?'

Other locality constraints are discussed in Torrego (2002).

It can be concluded that clitic pronouns undergo syntactic movement from the first merge (complement) positions to the positions in which they are pronounced (spell-out positions).

5.2. Locality and Clitic climbing

Differently from *wh*-movement, clitic movement cannot take place long-distance, whether the clause is finite (50) or infinitive (51):

(50) a. *Penso* [*che lo vedrò ~~lo~~*].
think.I that him will.see.I
'I think that I will see him.'

b. **Lo penso* [*che vedrò ~~lo~~*].
him think.I that will.see.I

cf. *Chi pensi* [*che vedrai ~~chi~~*]*?*
whom think.you that will.see.you
'Who do you think that you will see?'

(51) a. *Penso* [*di veder=lo*].
think.I to see=him
'I think to see him.'

b. **Lo penso* [*di veder=~~lo~~*].
him think.I to see

cf. *Chi pensi [di vedere ~~chi~~*]*?*
whom think.you to see
'Who do you think to see?'

In this respect, clitic movement is similar to NP-movement, which also takes place locally:

(52) a. *John seems [~~John~~ to win].*
b. **John seems* [*that it is likely* [~~*John*~~ *to win]].*

Apparent counterexamples to the locality of clitic movement are so-called *clitic-climbing* structures found with modal, aspectual, and motion verbs (*Restructuring* verbs), in which the pronoun can appear cliticized onto the superordinate verb of which it is not a complement (53a′, b′, c′), in addition to being enclitic on the infinitival verb (53a, b, c) – see Rizzi (1982) for the first extensive discussion of the phenomenon, Cinque (2004) for the most recent and comprehensive account, and Bok-Bennema (2006) for an introductory overview of the literature and examples from Italian, Portuguese, and Spanish; also see Strozer (1976) for Spanish; Picallo (1985), (1990) and Fischer (2002) for Catalan; Jones (1988) for Sardinian; Martins (2000) for Portuguese:

(53) a. *Voglio legger=lo ~~lo~~.*
want.I read=it
'I want to read it.'

a′. *Lo voglio leggere ~~lo~~.*
it want.I read
'I want to read it.'

b. *Comincio a legger=lo ~~lo~~.*
start.I to read=it
'I am starting to read it.'

b′. *Lo comincio a leggere ~~lo~~.*
it start.I to read
'I am starting to read it.'

c. *Vado a legger=lo ~~lo~~.*
go.I to read=it
'I go and read it.'

c′. *Lo vado a leggere ~~lo~~.*
it go.I to read
'I go and read it.'

The sentences in (53) are monoclausal structures in which modal, aspectual, and motion verbs are functional verbs (like auxiliaries), merged in the extended projection of the lexical verb (in the sense of Grimshaw 1991) (see Cinque 2004). (54) is a schematic clausal representation where FP stays for the functional projections associated with the lexical verb V, subject to rigid order restrictions (Cinque 1999). Restructuring verbs may realize the heads of such functional projections:

(54) $[_{CP} \ldots [_{FP} \ldots [_{FP}\ V_{restr}\ [_{FP} \ldots [_{VP}\ V_{lex}\ ]]]]]$

The phenomenon known as clitic climbing boils down to the appearance of the clitic pronoun in the high clitic position which precedes the finite restructuring verb, as in (53a′, b′, c′).

To account for the position of the clitic pronoun on the infinitival verb in (53a, b, c), another clitic position must be assumed, located in the (lexical) domain of the infinitival verb. The structure is schematized in (55) (see Cardinaletti and Shlonsky 2004, who also distinguish different classes of restructuring verbs with respect to clitic placement). The high and the low clitic positions encode different features, person/number features and case features, respectively (see section 6.5):

(55) $[_{CP} \ldots [_{FP}$ clitic $[_{FP}$ (V_{restr}) $[_{FP} \ldots [_{FP}$ clitic $[_{VP}$ V_{lex} $]]]]]]$
functional domain lexical domain

Another argument for the existence of the two clitic positions and the movement nature of clitic placement comes from the observation that in restructuring contexts, more than one instance of the same clitic pronoun is sometimes possible, as in (56) (see Kayne 1989b: 257, n. 37 and the references cited there). Similar sentences are produced by children acquiring Italian, both with restructuring verbs, (57a), and imperative infinitival forms, (57b):

(56) *Gianni li vuole veder=li ~~li~~.*
Gianni them wants see=them
'Gianni wants to see them.'

(57) a. *Voglio prova=llo* [= provarlo] *a fa=llo* [= farlo] ~~*lo*~~.
want.I try=it to do=it
'I want to try to do it.'
(Adriano, 4;3.15)

b. *Non ci andar=ci ~~ci~~!*
not there go=there
'Don't go there!'
(Adriano, 4;6.10)

In these sentences, more than one link of the clitic chain is spelled out, both the intermediate link on the infinitival lexical verb and the highest link in the functional domain.

Although two clitic positions are available in the clause, they cannot be occupied by different clitic pronouns. As the Italian contrasts in (58) indicate, two clitic pronouns inside one and the same sentence necessarily have to cluster (see Rizzi 1982). The data show that the cluster is formed in the lower clitic position (58a) and optionally moved to the high clitic position (58b):

(58) a. *Voleva presentar=melo ieri ~~me lo~~.*
wanted.he introduce=to.me.him yesterday
'He wanted to introduce him to me yesterday.'

b. *Me lo voleva presentare ieri ~~me lo~~.*
to.me him wanted.he introduce yesterday
'He wanted to introduce him to me yesterday.'

c. **Mi voleva presentar=lo ieri.*
to.me wanted.he introduce=him yesterday

d. **Lo voleva presentar=mi ieri.*
him wanted.he introduce=to.me yesterday

For the analysis of the syntactic and phonological properties of clitic clusters in Romance languages, see Perlmutter (1971); Bonet (1995); Laenzlinger (1993); Dobrovie-Sorin (1995); Gerlach (1998a, b); Popescu (2000); Cardinaletti (2008); Săvescu Ciucivara (2009), among many others.

5.3. On the nature of clitic movement: XP movement followed by head movement

In previous sections, we have shown that clitic placement displays locality properties shared by syntactic movement and in particular A-movement. Is clitic movement indeed A-movement, namely the movement of a maximal projection? The answer is positive. Consider the fact that e.g. in Italian, accusative and partitive clitic pronouns trigger past-participle agreement; this is true of both lexical verbs (59) and restructuring verbs (60):

(59) a. *Gianni ha* ***letto*** *queste riviste.*
Gianni has read these.F.PL magazines.F.PL
'Gianni read these magazines.'

b. *Gianni le / ne ha* ***lette****.*
Gianni them.F.PL of.them has read.F.PL
'Gianni read them / some of them.'

(60) a. *Gianni ha* ***dovuto*** *leggere queste riviste.*
Gianni has must read these.F.PL magazines.F.PL
'Gianni was obliged to read these magazines.'

b. *Gianni le / ne ha* ***dovute*** *leggere.*
Gianni them.F.PL of.them has must.F.PL read
'Gianni was obliged to read them / some of them.'

If (morphological) agreement is the reflex of a local relation like specifier-head agreement (Kayne 1989a), the data in (59)–(60) show that there must be a step in the derivation in which the pronoun occupies the specifier position of the projection headed by the past participle and is therefore an XP. Past participle agreement is found in other instances of XP-movement, i.e., with passive and unaccusative verbs: *queste riviste sono state lette* 'these.F.PL magazines.F.PL have been.F.PL read.F.PL', *queste riviste sono arrivate ieri* 'these.F.PL magazines.F.PL have arrived.F.PL yesterday'.

In order to reconcile these data with the fact that clitic pronouns are heads at the end of the derivation (cf. section 4.1 above, where it was shown that the verb takes the pronoun along), clitic placement must be seen as a two-step operation: The first step is A-movement of a maximal projection to the specifier of the head realized by the past participle, the second step is proper head movement to the next higher head (cf. Sportiche 1989/98; Belletti 1999; Cardinaletti and Starke 1999; Rizzi 2000b, among others):

(61) a. *[*$_{CP}$ *[*$_{TP}$ *Gianni [*$_{T}$ *le ha] [*$_{PARTP}$ ~~*le*~~ *lette [*$_{VP}$ ~~*Gianni lette le*~~*]]]].*
b. *[*$_{CP}$ *[*$_{TP}$ *Gianni [*$_{T}$ *le ha] [*$_{PARTP}$ ~~*le*~~ *dovute [*$_{VP}$ ~~*Gianni*~~ *leggere* ~~*le*~~*]]]].*

As pointed out in Sportiche (1996/98) and Roberts (1997), the piece of data in (60b) argues against an analysis like Kayne's (1989b) according to which clitic movement proceeds through the C head of the CP complement to restructuring verbs (when this head is empty). (60b) shows that clitic pronouns move as maximal projections at least as high as the participle phrase headed by the restructuring verb.

That XP movement is followed by head movement is also clearly shown by the following French data. In infinitival clauses (62a, b), the pronoun and the verb or the auxiliary follow adverbs such as *pas* 'not'; infinitival auxiliaries can also optionally precede *pas*, as in (62c), similarly to what happens with finite verbs and auxiliaries (62d, e) (cf. Pollock 1989; Belletti 1990; Rizzi 2000b: 117). In (62c–e), the clitic pronoun attaches to the verb in the lower position (seen in [62a, b]) and is taken along by the verb or the auxiliary on their way to the higher position preceding *pas*:

(62) a. ... *ne pas les manger ~~les~~.* [French]
... not not them eat.INF
'... not to eat them.'

b. ... *ne pas les avoir [~~les~~ mangés ~~les~~].*
... not not them have.INF eaten
'... not to have eaten them.'

c. ... *ne les avoir pas ~~les avoir~~ [~~les~~ mangés ~~les~~].*
... not them have.INF not eaten

d. *Jean ne les mange pas ~~les mange~~ ~~les~~.*
Jean not them eats not
'Jean does not eat them.'

e. *Jean ne les a pas ~~les a~~ [~~les~~ mangés ~~les~~].*
Jean not them has not eaten
'Jean did not eat them.'

If past participle agreement is however due to another mechanism, it is no longer strong evidence to support an XP-movement step of clitic movement. D'Alessandro and Roberts (2008) for instance suggest that morphological agreement obtains between elements that are contained in the complement of the minimal phase head, that is, the substructure that is transferred to PF as a single unit (Chomsky 2008). The clitic pronoun moved to the auxiliary and the past participle are contained in the complement of same phase head, namely C.

The view that clitic movement is indeed XP movement at least until a certain point of the derivation is given independent support by the comparison with the derivation of weak pronouns. The first part of the clitic derivation shown in (61) also characterizes weak pronouns. The head movement step is instead peculiar to clitic pronouns (cf. Cardinaletti and Starke 1999: 195–196 for discussion).

5.4. Clitic doubling and the base-generation approach

Some reduplication constructions known as *clitic doubling* seem to challenge the derivational approach discussed so far.

Clitic doubling is the possibility attested in some languages to realize both a clitic pronoun and the associated phrase in one and the same clause. See the examples in (63) from River Plate Spanish and Rumanian (cf. Jaeggli 1982 and Dobrovie-Sorin 1990, 1994, respectively), where the direct object is doubled, those in (64) from Spanish (Demonte 1995) and Italian, where the indirect object is doubled, and those in (65) from Trentino, where the subject is doubled (see [2]):

(63) a. *Lo vimos a Juan.* [River Plate Spanish]
him saw.we to Juan
'We saw Juan.'

b. *L' am văzut pe Jon.* [Rumanian]
him have.I seen ACC Jon
'We saw Jon.'

(64) a. *Le entregué las llaves al conserje.* [Spanish]
to.him gave.I the keys to.the janitor
'I gave the keys to the janitor.'

b. *Gliele ho date a Gianni / Gliene ho date due a*
to.him.them have.I given to Gianni to.him.of.them have.I given two to
Gianni.
Gianni
'I gave them / two of them to Gianni.'

(65) *El Mario el parla.* [Trentino]
the Mario he speaks
'Mario speaks.'

Clitic doubling must be differentiated from Left and Right Dislocation, where the phrases associated to clitic pronouns occur in clause-peripheral positions (see Anagnostopulou 2006: sect. 2 for an overview of the differences):

(66) a. *Gianni, io lo conosco.*
Gianni I him know
'Gianni, I know him.'

b. *Io lo conosco, Gianni.*
I him know Gianni
'I know him, Gianni.'

The observation, known as Kayne's generalization, that in clitic-doubling constructions, a case-marker is in general present on the doubled object DP (such as *a* and *pe* in [63]), has led to the view that clitic pronouns are government / case absorbers (cf. Jaeggli 1982; Borer 1984). See Anagnostopulou (2006) for an overview on the cross-linguistic robustness of this generalization and the actual role of these preposition-like elements. Rizzi (2000a: section 2) addresses the question as to why Kayne's generalization does not extend to subject clitic doubling, as in (65).

Doubling of DPs – as in (63)–(65) – contrasts with doubling of pronouns. This is obligatory in all dialects of Spanish (67a) (Jaeggli 1982). In other Romance languages, doubling is allowed only with pronouns. See the French data in (67b) (cf. Kayne 2000a) and the Catalan data in (67c, d) (cf. Rigau 1988; Fischer 2002):

(67) a. *Lo vimos a él.* [Spanish]
him saw.we to Juan
'We saw him.'

b. *Il m' a vu moi.* [French]
he me has seen me
'He saw me.'

c. *La veig a ella.* [Catalan]
her see.I to her
'I see her.'

d. *M' ho va donar a mi.* [Catalan]
to.me it will.he give to me
'He will give it to me.'

When both the clitic pronoun and the associated phrase are present in the clause, it seems trivial that the pronoun cannot originate in the VP-internal position, which is occupied by the associated phrase, as in (63) and (64), or by a trace of the associated phrase, as in (65) (assuming that the subject DP *el Mario* is merged VP-internally and moved to the canonical, preverbal subject position, SpecTP).

The existence of clitic doubling led many researchers to suggest an alternative analysis of clitic placement: clitic pronouns are generated in their surface position, i.e., attached to their host, and are linked to an empty category in the canonical position of the phrase with the same grammatical function. If a full phrase is merged instead of the empty category, clitic doubling arises. Various implementations of this idea are found in the literature which cannot be discussed here at length (among many others, see Strozer 1976; Rivas 1977; Jaeggli 1982, 1986; Bouchard 1984; Suñer 1988; Roberge 1987, 1990; Rini 1991; Gutiérrez-Rexach 1999, 1999/2000 for Romance, and Borer 1984; Siloni 1997; Shlonsky 1994 for Semitic).

In what follows, we discuss the attempts at reconciling the contradictory evidence coming from locality restrictions and clitic doubling.

5.5. An attempt to reconcile the evidence for movement and the base-generation approach

Sportiche (1996/98) is the most recent base-generation approach to clitic placement in Romance. He suggests that clitic pronouns are merged as functional heads in the clausal skeleton and project CliticVoicePs, as in (68). An empty category (akin to *pro*) is merged with the verb and moved to the specifier of the Clitic-Voice Phrase, in order to satisfy a requirement of spec-head agreement with the clitic (the so-called Clitic Criterion) and to check features such as specificity. Note that if what is displaced is not the clitic pronoun itself, but an empty category associated with the clitic, the locality effects observed in clitic constructions in section 5.1 still follow.

(68)

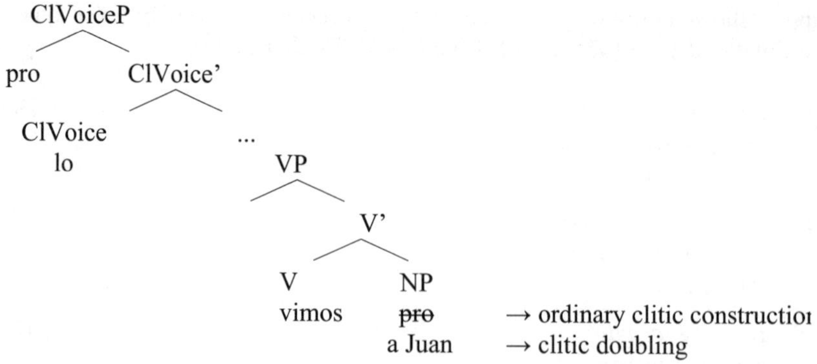

In Sportiche's reasoning, this analysis of clitic placement has the advantage of explaining the phenomenon of clitic doubling in a straightforward way. Clitic doubling can be said to obtain when a noun phrase is generated instead of the null category *pro*. The following would be the relevant portion of the structure of the two River Plate Spanish sentences *lo vimos* and *lo vimos a Juan* (cf. [63a]).

This analysis of object clitics somehow recalls the proposal by Brandi and Cordin (1981), (1989); Burzio (1986); Rizzi (1986) that subject clitics are realizations of the Inflectional head, while the argument of the verb is realized by either a null subject *pro* or a subject DP (for recent proposals along the same lines, see Poletto 2000, 2005; Goria 2004, among others). (69) is a simplified structure of *el parla* 'he speaks' and *el Mario el parla* 'Mario speaks' (see [65]).

(69)

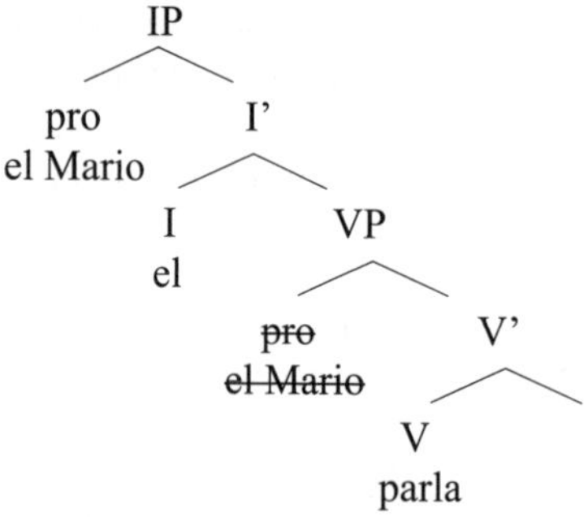

Sportiche's proposal also accounts for two facts concerning doubling and weak pronouns. First, doubling is possible with clitic pronouns and ungrammatical with weak pronouns, which are not heads and therefore cannot be merged as functional heads of the clausal skeleton – compare (64b) with (70a, b), which contain weak *loro*. Second, it predicts doubling of a clitic and a weak pronoun, a correct prediction as shown by (70c) (although a register clash arises: doubling is typical of spoken language, weak *loro* is restricted to the high register of Italian, cf. Cardinaletti 1991):

(70) a. **Ho dato loro le caramelle ai bambini.*
have.I given to.them the sweets to.the children

b. **Le ho date loro ai bambini.*
them have.I given to.them to.the children

c. *Gliele ho date loro.*
to.him.them have.I given to.them
'I gave them to them.'

In spite of its *prima facie* attractiveness, the proposal in (68) however raises a number of questions, for both subject and object clitics – for the criticism of (69) and the proposal that subject clitics like *el* in (65) / (69) must be analyzed as moved verbal arguments along the same lines as object clitics, also see Cardinaletti and Repetti (2008), (2010).

First, it cannot capture the parallel behaviour of clitic and weak pronouns as far as the syntactic and semantic properties are concerned (see section 4.1 above). If clitic pronouns are heads of the clausal skeleton, as in (68), clitic and weak pronouns are now seen as two fundamentally distinct elements. The fact that they share most syntactic and semantic properties should be seen as accidental, and their common properties should be attributed to different reasons, a move which clearly implies a loss in descriptive generalization. Furthermore, the relationships between the two classes of pronouns in terms of morphological reduction and choice would be much more difficult to capture than under the hypothesis that they instantiate two different classes of deficient nominal projections – see section 4.2.2, (12), (24), and (32).

Second, although this type of proposal seems to capture clitic doubling quite easily, it predicts that this phenomenon should be much more common among languages, whereas it is pretty restricted.

Third, there is evidence that clitic doubling structures obey locality conditions on a par with simple cliticization. Compare (71a, b), taken from Belletti (1999: 558), with (46a, d) above:

(71) a. *Maria se le colocò cerca a Juan.* [Spanish]
Maria herself to.him placed next to Juan
'Maria placed herself next to Juan.'

b. **Maria le es feliz cerca a Juan.*
Maria to.him is happy next to Juan
'Maria is happy next to Juan.'

Since in (68) the associated phrase, contrary to *pro*, does not move, the CED locality effect seen in (71) is unexpected. It can only be explained by assuming that clitic movement takes place in clitic doubling as well (Belletti 1999: 558). In conclusion, a purely derivational analysis seems to be the only coherent analysis of clitic placement. The existence of clitic doubling however remains puzzling.

5.6. An attempt to reconcile the evidence for movement and the existence of clitic doubling

In recent years, the attempt has been made to make the movement account of clitic placement compatible with the existence of the clitic doubling phenomenon. Under the enriched nominal structure made available by the DP-hypothesis, it has been proposed that both the clitic pronoun and the associated DP are contained in a big DP merged in argument position – cf. Torrego (1995); Uriagereka (1995a), (2005); Belletti (1999), (2005); Cecchetto (2000). Different implementations of this idea exist in the literature. The doubling phrase is taken to either occur in SpecDP (72a) (Uriagereka 1995a) or in the complement to D (72b) (Belletti 1999, 2005; Cecchetto 2000):

(72) a.

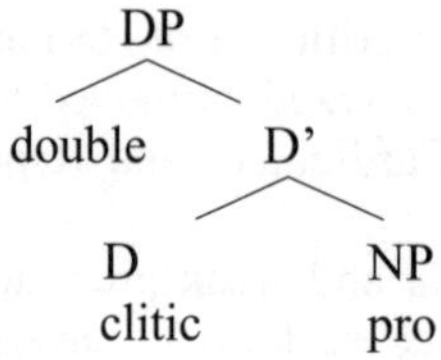

b.

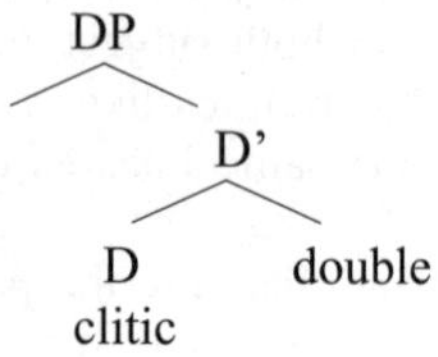

The big-DP hypothesis makes Sportiche's (1996/98) analysis of clitic placement and clitic doubling unnecessary, a welcome result given the problems pointed out in section 5.5 above. Note however that both proposals in (72) have the disadvantage of considering the clitic pronoun as the D head of the big DP. As we have seen in section 4.2, clitic pronouns cannot be considered as determiners. A reformulation of the hypothesis in (72) which is worth exploring is (73a), which takes the clitic pronoun to be merged as a reduced maximal projection in the specifier position of the big DP. Clitic doubling would involve merge of the big DP in (73b):

(73) a.

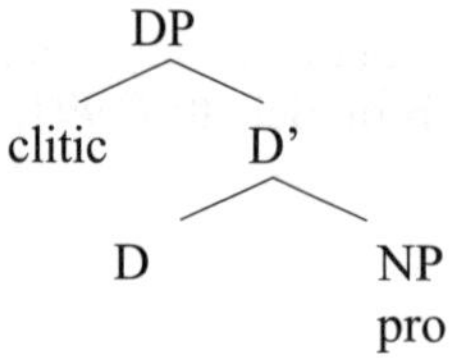

b.

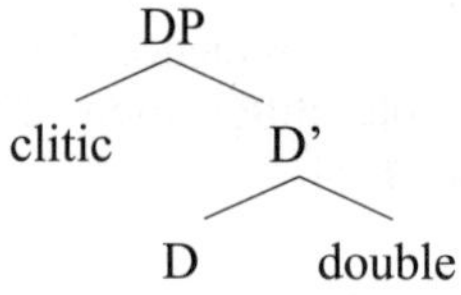

We cannot address here the wide cross-linguistic variation concerning

(i) the type of arguments that allow clitic doubling (e.g. any argument in Rumanian and River Plate Spanish (63), the goal argument in Italian and Spanish (64); Sportiche (1996/98: 302, n. 24) observes that the existence of accusative clitic doubling in a language presupposes dative clitic doubling),
(ii) the semantic conditions under which doubling is possible (e.g. specificity in direct object doubling, Suñer 1988),
(iii) the implicational hierarchy concerning the type of nominal expressions that allow doubling – pronouns > definite DPs > quantified DPs; see (63)–(65) vs. (67) above.

The interested reader is referred to Anagnostopoulou (2006) for a thorough discussion of object clitic doubling and to Cordin (1993); Belletti (1999: 555–557); Poletto (2000) for subject clitic doubling.

6. On the derivation of clitic placement

In the previous sections, we have established that clitic pronouns realize reduced maximal projections which are moved out of the merge position by XP movement followed by head movement. In the following sections, we will try to establish why clitic pronouns have to move obligatorily, and where they move to in the structure. A general answer to the first question is required since that property characterizes clitic pronouns in all languages which displays this category of pronouns. The second question is instead more difficult to answer given that a wide cross-linguistic variation is observed.

6.1. On the motivation for clitic movement

One of the defining properties of clitic pronouns is that they have to appear in displaced position. The question addressed in this section is: why is clitic movement obligatory?

In recent grammatical theories, syntactic movement is motivated by feature checking: elements move to verify their grammatical features against functional heads with the corresponding features. If clitic pronouns move to check their phi-features and case, the obligatoriness issue however remains: while in e.g. Romance languages, DPs may check their features without syntactic movement (via Agree), clitic pronouns can do so only via movement.

One answer to this question takes the obligatory nature of clitic movement to ensue from the fact that they have to check more features than regular phrases. On the one hand, a semantic motivation has been adduced: clitic pronouns move to check the familiarity feature (Corver and Delfitto 1999), or the specificity feature (Sportiche 1996/98) (see property D4 in section 3). On the other hand, a morphological motivation has been used: clitic pronouns display case distinctions and therefore move to check case features (Belletti 1999) (see property C3 in section 3).

Although these proposals can account for many instances of clitic pronouns, there are other cases in which they cannot be used because clitic pronouns do not encode any such features. Consider for instance those clitic pronouns that have non-referential usages in idiomatic expressions (17a, b) and impersonal sentences (20). No familiarity or specificity feature is ever involved in these cases. Since these pronouns share the same syntax as "familiar" and "specific" clitics in above proposals, we cannot appeal to such semantic notions to account for their obligatory movement. Similarly, many clitic pronouns, such as 1st and 2nd person clitics, do not encode case distinctions, still they are obligatorily displaced (cf. Italian *mi* in *mi conosce* 'he knows me', *mi parla* 'he speaks to me', and French *me* in the same contexts: *il me connnaît* 'he knows me', *il me parle* 'he speaks to me').

Suppose that clitic pronouns check features like ordinary DPs and may move. As in other cases, it is desirable to assume that Movement (Internal Merge) is free, and that some interface condition regulates whether it should apply or not. It follows that clitic pronouns move in order to avoid a crash in the derivation.

One proposal is that lack of clitic movement causes a crash at the syntax-phonology interface. Raposo and Uriagereka (2005: 650) assume that "Romance determiners (special clitics or regular articles) are phonological clitics that must find themselves within a well-formed prosodic word at PF". In addition, they assume that the phonological host must be to the right of the clitic pronoun, in other words, proclisis is required. While articles always fulfil this requirement (74a), clitic pronouns staying in their merge position do not (74b); to find an appropriate host, they must evacuate their base position (74c) (in [74] the host is bold; the category of the host in [74c] does not matter here and is marked as X):

(74) a. *No compré* [$_{DP}$ *la* ***aspirina*** *corriente*]. [Spanish]
not bought.I the aspirin normal
'I did not buy the normal aspirin.'

b. **No compré* [$_{DP}$ *la N*].
not bought.I it

c. *[$_X$ la [$_X$* ***compré****-X]]*.

This proposal raises the following questions. First, Toman (1993) has convincingly argued for Czech (a language with second position clitic pronouns which seem to be always enclitic) that "clitics cannot be mechanically described as enclitics" (Toman 1993: 113). The direction of (phonological) cliticization depends on the phonological environment: it "is established locally at the level at which prosodic structure is determined" (Toman 1993: 114). In Czech, pronouns are indeed enclitic most of the times, but if the first position is filled with a heavy phrase such as a clause or a DP containing a relative clause, pronouns become proclitic on the element which follows them. Note also that in Galician, determiners can be enclitic to the verb (Uriagereka 1995a); it is thus surprising that this cannot happen when the N is unpronounced, as in (74b). Second, obligatory syntactic movement is shared by weak pronouns, which do not display the same phonological properties as clitic pronouns: crucially, they are not phonological clitics. As shown for instance by the Italian dative pronoun *loro*, weak pronouns can bear word stress (see section 4.1) and are not necessarily adjacent to the verb (31). In conclusion, the fact that clitic pronouns must move cannot entirely be motivated by their phonological properties (Cardinaletti and Starke 1999: § 6.3 suggest that only the head movement step is motivated by phonological requirements).

The alternative proposal is that lack of clitic movement causes a crash at the other interface. Under the hypothesis that clitic pronouns are merged as (defective) maximal projections (section 4.2.2), obligatory clitic movement is due to their reduced structure. The deficient phrases they head cannot be interpreted at the syntax-semantics interface; only full phrases can. In order to get interpreted, clitic pronouns must occur at spell-out in dedicated derived positions. (An advantage of this proposal is that the same account can be used to explain the obligatory XP movement step of weak pronouns).

Note finally that there is indeed no tension between a deficiency approach and a feature-checking approach to clitic movement. Deficiency tells us that the pronoun must move obligatorily, feature-checking tells us where the pronoun moves to. This is the topic of next sections.

6.2. The host of clitic pronouns

Kayne (1991: 649) assumes "that Romance clitics have the (perhaps defining) property that they must adjoin to some X^0 element" and takes this X element to be a functional head. As noted by Kayne (1994: 18–21), antisymmetry forces the pronoun to be a head in order for it to adjoin to X. Antisymmetry also requires left-adjunction. Cliticization can thus be represented as in (75): The clitic pronoun left-adjoins to a functional head F, and the verb can occur in the same head (75a), or in a structurally lower functional head (75b):

(75)

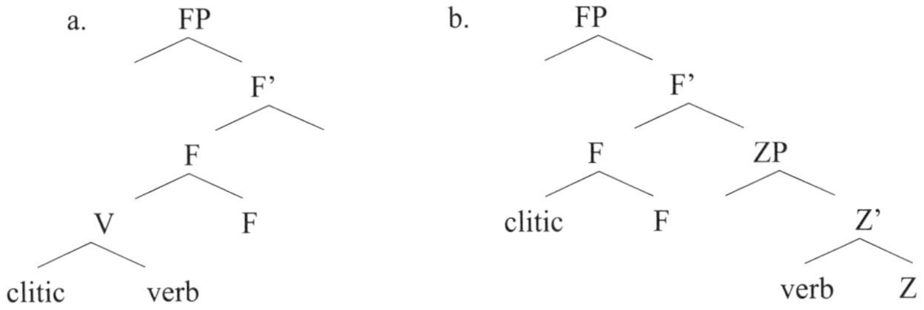

The structure in (75a) accounts for the fact, pointed out in section 4.1 and 5.3 above, that the clitic pronoun and the verb may move as a syntactic unit to functional heads higher than F. The structure in (75b) accounts for cases in which the clitic pronoun and the verb are not adjacent, but separated by various material in the clause. This is the rule in languages with 2nd position clitics such as many Slavic and Germanic languages (cf. Wackernagel 1892). In (76), Croatian examples taken from Ćavar and Wilder (1999) are provided. As can be seen in (76a–c), any constituent can precede the pronoun; furthermore, (76d) shows that the pronoun can be separated from the verb by the subject DP *Ivan*:

(76) a. *Ivan ga je često čitao.* [Croatian]
Ivan it has often read

b. *Često ga je Ivan čitao.*
often it has Ivan read

c. *Čitao ga je Ivan često.*
read it has Ivan often
'Ivan often read it.'

d. ... *da ga Ivan čita.*
that it Ivan reads
'... that Ivan reads it.'

The structure in (75b) is also encountered in languages which usually display adverbal clitics, i.e., clitics adjacent to a verbal form. The phenomenon is known as *interpolation* – see Chereny (1905); Ramsden (1963); Wanner (1992); Rivero (1992, 1997); Fontana (1993) among others. Examples are found in many Old Romance languages – see Rivero (1986) for Old Spanish; Martins (1994, 2002, 2003, 2005) for Old Portuguese; Fischer (2003: 260) for Old Catalan; Ledgeway and Lombardi (2005) and Cardinaletti (2010b: 435) for Old Italian. The phenomenon is still attested in some modern Romance varieties, such as certain northern dialects of Portuguese (Barbosa 1996), Romanian (Dobrovie-Sorin 1994; Rizzi 2000b: 101), Galician (Uriagereka 1995a), Occitan (Kayne

1991: 653–654), and some Italian dialects (see Renzi 1989: 369, n. 12). An example from literary French is provided in (77a), in which the clitic pronoun and the infinitival verb are separated by the adverb *bien* 'well'. The pronoun raises to a higher position with respect to the verb, presumably the same position as in finite clauses (77b) (cf. Kayne 1975: sect.2.3, 1991: 653–654):

(77) a. ... ***en*** *bien* ***parler***. [literary French]
of.it well speak.INF
'... to speak well about it.'

b. *Il* ***en*** ***parle*** *bien*.
he of.it speaks well
'He speaks well about it.'

An example from Galician is provided in (78), where the intervening element is the subject DP (from Raposo and Uriagereka 2005: 649):

(78) *A bon fado a Deus encomende.* [Galician]
to good fate her God entrust
'May God entrust her to a good fate.'

The phenomenon displays different properties in different languages. Variation concerns for instance the type of arguments that can appear between the pronoun and the verb (some special simple adverbs, as in Romanian, any adverb or adverbial phrase, as in French, or any constituent, as in Galician), suggesting that different processes are perhaps at work in the different languages which display the phenomenon.

In all the cases discussed above, the pronoun appears before the verb, either in proclitic position or in a higher position than the verb. Let's now consider how enclitic pronouns, which follow the verb, are represented. Since Kayne's (1994) antisymmetric approach bans right adjunction, enclisis can only be obtained as in (79), i.e., the verb left-adjoins to the clitic pronoun left-adjoined to F:

(79)

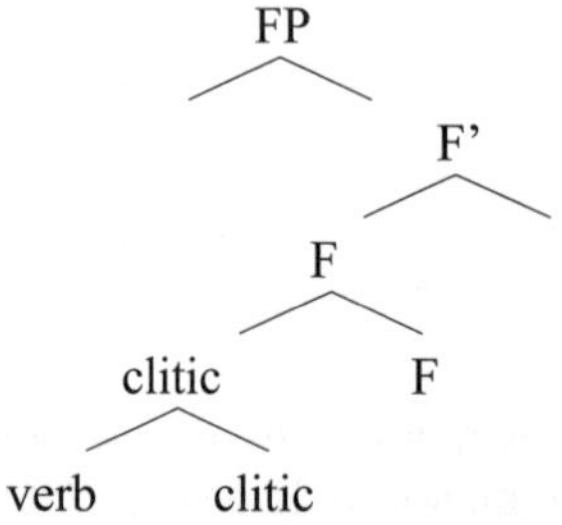

The hypothesis represented in (79) accounts for the following very robust crosslinguistic generalization. While proclitics can appear independently of the verb (see [76]–[78] above), enclitics cannot. In (80) and (81), two possible situations are schematized: the intervening material is either an adverbial XP or the subject DP – see Kayne (1991: 657, n. 27) and Rizzi (2000b: 117–118) for Romance languages, and Starke (1993) for Slavic languages:

(80) a. clitic XP verb
b clitic DP verb

(81) a. *verb XP clitic
b. *verb DP clitic

The generalization concerning enclisis can be formulated as in (82) (Rizzi 2000b: 118) (apparent counterexamples to this generalization are discussed in section 7.2 below):

(82) If the verb moves to a position past the landing site of the clitic, it carries the clitic along.

It is also possible, although rare in the Romance languages, that the pronoun appears between the verb stem and the verbal inflection, a phenomenon called *mesoclisis*. The examples in (83) come from European Portuguese (see Vigário 2003; Luís and Spencer 2005 among others):

(83) a. *Ela levá=**lo**=ia.* [European Portuguese]
she take=it=would
'She would take it.'

b. *Eles dar=**no**=**lo**=ão.*
they give=us=it=will
'They will give it to us.'

The phenomenon is also found in imperatives in e.g. Spanish varieties – Halle and Marantz (1994); Harris and Halle (2005); Kayne (2008). As shown in (84b), a clitic cluster appears between the verb stem and its plural *-n* inflection. This order contrasts with the enclitic pattern of standard Spanish in (84a):

(84) a. *De=n=me=lo!* [Spanish]
give=you.PL=me=it
'Give it to me!'

b. *De=me=lo=n!* [Spanish varieties]
give=me=it=you.PL

Mesoclisis is also found in other Romance and Albanian varieties (see Manzini and Savoia 2009).

6.3. On the landing site of cliticization: Proclisis vs. Enclisis

As mentioned above, typologically there are two main locations for clitic pronouns: either in the second position of the clause (i.e., independently of the position of the verb), as in Slavic and Germanic languages (cf. Wackernagel 1892), or adjacent to a verbal form, as in Romance languages. In section 6.1 we have seen that with 2nd position clitics, as in Czech, proclisis and enclisis is a matter of phonology. The location of adverbal clitic pronouns in proclitic or enclitic position is instead a syntactic matter. In the case of subject pronouns, proclisis and enclisis correlate with sentence types, declarative and interrogative, respectively. Data come from the northern Italian Emilian dialect of Donceto (province of Piacenza) – Cardinaletti and Repetti (2008); for other dialects, see Brandi and Cordin (1981), (1989); Rizzi (2000a); Poletto (2000):

(85) a. *ət 'be:v* [Emilian, Donceto]
you *drink*
'You drink.'

b. *əl 'be:və*
he drinks
'He drinks.'

(86) a. *'be:v=ət?*
drink=you
'Do you drink?'

b. *'be:və=l?*
drinks=he
'Does he drink?'

The difference in placement can be easily captured by assuming that the postverbal position of the clitic in (86) is due to verb movement to a higher position in interrogatives than in declarative sentences (cf. Rizzi 2000a, b; Cardinaletti and Repetti 2008, 2010 for slightly different analyses), similarly to what happens in English and Germanic interrogative sentences and complying with (79). A we have seen in (25), a similar derivation is adopted for the enclitic placement of French subject pronouns in interrogatives (see Cardinaletti and Repetti 2008, 2010 for the comparison of French and Northern Italian dialects):

(87) *Est=il parti?* [French]
is=he left
'Has he left?'

Note that French preverbal subject pronouns (as in *Il est parti* 'he has left') are weak and not clitic – see Cardinaletti and Starke (1996: 49–50), who reinterpret Kayne's (1983) proposal that they are phonological clitics. For the different behaviour of preverbal subject pronouns in French and Northern Italian dialects, also see Brandi and Cordin (1981) and Rizzi (1986), (2000a). For arguments against a morphological analysis of French subject clitics, see De Cat (2005).

As for object clitics, the position varies depending on the finiteness and mood of the verb. In Italian, for instance, clitic pronouns precede finite verbs (88), and follow imperative and infinitival verbs (89):

(88) a. *Lo compro.* indicative
it buy.I
'I buy it.'

b. *Lo comprerei.* conditional
it would.buy.I
'I would buy it.'

c. *Se lo comprassi, ...* subjunctive
if it bought.I
'If I bought it, ...'

(89) a. *Compra=lo!* imperative
buy=it
'Buy it!'

b. *Penso di comprar=lo.* infinitive
think.I to buy=it
'I think to buy it.'

c. *Comprando=lo, Maria ha dimostrato il suo cattivo gusto.* gerundive
buying=it Maria has demonstrated the her bad taste
'By buying it, Maria has demonstrated her bad taste.'

d. *Comprato=lo, Maria uscì dal negozio.* participle
bought=it Maria went.out of.the shop
'After having bought it, Maria left the shop.'

As with subject clitics, enclisis with object clitics is explained by movement of the verb across the pronoun, see (79). The generalization seems to be that enclisis is found if (i) the verb is morphologically complete under the cliticization site, and (ii) the verb must move at least as far as the cliticization site (Rizzi 2000b:109). There have been many attempts at analyzing the enclitic vs. proclitic placement of object clitic pronouns. Since the analyses of the various proposals would exceed the limits of the present paper, I refer the interested reader to Kayne (1991); Benincà and Cinque (1993); Rivero (1994); Rivero and Terzi (1995); Belletti (1999); Rouveret (1999); Terzi (1999); Shlonsky (2004); Ouhalla (2005); Raposo and Uriagereka (2005), among many others, and the references quoted there.

The distribution of proclisis and enclisis is similar in Italian and Spanish. In French, proclisis is also found with infinitival verbs, see (62a, b). In Portuguese and Galician, enclisis is also found with finite verbs.

Various proposals have tried to account for language variation in clitic placement in terms of the different functional heads which host clitic pronouns. For instance, while Romance languages such as Italian and French use the head T as the clitic host (a head that also contains the finite verb, as in [75a]), Slavic languages such as Czech, Slovak and Croatian are said to make use of a structurally higher head which does not contain the verb, called AgrC in Starke (1993), as in (75b) (cf. Rivero 1986, 1994, 1997). This type of language variation is also found Romance-internally. In Galician and Portuguese, a functional head higher than T, probably corresponding to AgrC in Slavic, is said to be the clitic host (Madeira 1992, 1993; Uriagereka 1995a, 1995b; Rouveret 1999; Raposo and Uriagereka 2005 among others; see Galves 1996, 1997 for the history of clitic placement in Brazilian Portuguese).

The assumption of a high number of functional heads in the clause (cf. Pollock 1989; Cinque 1999), gives a potentially broad range of language variation, still to be fully evaluated. The French data in (62) provide an example of more than one location for the clitic pronouns with respect to adverbs and finite and infinitival verbs.

What is striking, however, is that language variation always involves functional heads which are located in the clausal areas either immediately above the VP or between the Comp and the Infl domain. As seen in section 5.2, the two clitic positions are clearly visible in restructuring contexts; especially when reduplication occurs, see (56)–(57). The following sections discuss this generalization and a possible way to account for it.

6.4. Arguments of nouns, adjectives, prepositions, and quantifiers

In most examples so far, clitic pronouns realize arguments of the verb. A clitic pronoun can also realize the object of other categories: nouns (90) (also see [44]), adjectives (91), prepositions (92) (also see [46a–c]), and quantifiers (93)–(94) (also see [47]). These categories do not provide a clitic host internally to the phrase they project (b. examples), and clitic pronouns are adjoined to the verb in these cases, too (c. examples). In restructuring contexts, the clitic pronoun can appear either on the infinitival lexical verb (d. examples) or on the superordinate functional verb (e. examples) (see section 5.2). Note that according to the QP-hypothesis, quantifiers realize the head of the projection QP, which embeds DP, as depicted in (93) and (94) (Cardinaletti and Giusti 2006). This allows us to consider partitive *ne* in (93) on a par with all other clitic pronouns, namely as realizing a (deficient) maximal projection. The phenomenon in (94) is known as *floating quantifier* and is also possible with full DPs: *I ragazzi sono partiti [$_{\text{QP}}$ tutti [$_{\text{DP}}$ ~~i ragazzi~~]]* 'the boys have all left':

(90) a. *Ho visto [$_{\text{DP}}$ il ritratto [$_{\text{PP}}$ di Gianni]].*
have.I seen the portrait of Gianni
'I saw Gianni's portrait.'

b. **Ho visto [$_{\text{DP}}$ il ritratto ne [$_{\text{PP}}$ ~~ne~~]] / [$_{\text{DP}}$ ne il ritratto [$_{\text{PP}}$ ~~ne~~]].*
have.I seen the portrait of.him / of.him the portrait

c. *Ne ho visto [$_{\text{DP}}$ il ritratto [$_{\text{PP}}$ ~~ne~~]].*
of.him have.I seen the portrait
'I saw his portrait.'

d. *Voglio veder=ne [$_{\text{DP}}$ il ritratto [$_{\text{PP}}$~~ne~~]].*
want.I see=of.him the portrait
'I want to see his portrait.'

e. *Ne voglio vedere [$_{\text{DP}}$ il ritratto [$_{\text{PP}}$~~ne~~]].*
of.him want.I see the portrait
'I want to see his portrait.'

(91) a. *Sono [$_{\text{AP}}$ contento [$_{\text{PP}}$ delle tue parole]].*
am.I happy of.the your words
'I am happy of your words.'

b. **Sono [$_{\text{AP}}$ contento ne [$_{\text{PP}}$~~ne~~]] / [$_{\text{AP}}$ ne contento [$_{\text{PP}}$ ~~ne~~]].*
am.I happy of.them / of.them happy

c. *Ne sono* [$_{AP}$ *contento* [$_{PP}$ ~~*ne*~~]].
of.them am.I happy
'I am happy of them.'

d. *Voglio esser=ne* [$_{AP}$ *contento* [$_{PP}$ ~~*ne*~~]].
want.I be=of.them happy
'I want to be happy of them.'

e. *Ne voglio essere* [$_{AP}$ *contento* [$_{PP}$ ~~*ne*~~]].
of.them want.I be happy
'I want to be happy of them.'

(92) a. *Sono saltato* [$_{PP}$ *addosso* [$_{PP}$ *a Gianni*]].
have.I jumped on o Gianni
'I jumped on Gianni.'

b. **Sono saltato* [$_{PP}$ *addosso gli* [$_{PP}$ ~~*gli*~~]] / [$_{PP}$ *gli addosso* [$_{PP}$ ~~*gli*~~]].
have.I jumped on to.him / to.him on

c. *Gli sono saltato* [$_{PP}$ *addosso* [$_{PP}$ ~~*gli*~~]].
to.him am.I jumped on
'I jumped on him.'

d. *Voglio saltar=gli* [$_{PP}$ *addosso* [$_{PP}$ ~~*gli*~~]].
want.I jump=to.him on
'I want to jump on him.'

e. *Gli voglio saltare* [$_{PP}$ *addosso* [$_{PP}$ ~~*gli*~~]].
to.him want.I jump on
'I want to jump on him.'

(93) a. *Ho letto* [$_{QP}$ *due* [$_{DP}$ *giornali*]].
have.I read two newspapers
'I read two newspapers.'

b. **Ho letto* [$_{QP}$ *due ne* [$_{DP}$ ~~*ne*~~]] / [$_{QP}$ *ne due* [$_{DP}$ ~~*ne*~~]].
have.I read two of.them / of-them two

c. *Ne ho letti* [$_{QP}$ *due* [$_{DP}$ ~~*ne*~~]].
of.them have.I read two
'I read two of them.'

d. *Voglio legger=ne* [$_{QP}$ *due* [$_{DP}$ ~~*ne*~~]].
want.I read=of.them two
'I want to read two of them.'

e. *Ne voglio leggere* [$_{QP}$ *due* [$_{DP}$ ~~*ne*~~]].
of.them want.I read two
'I want to read two of them.'

(94) a. *Ho letto* [$_{QP}$ *tutti* [$_{DP}$ *i giornali*]].
have.I read all the newspapers
'I read all the newspapers.'

b. **Ho letto* [$_{QP}$ *tutti li* [$_{DP}$ ~~*li*~~]] / [$_{QP}$ *li tutti* [$_{DP}$ ~~*li*~~]].
have.I read all them / them all

c. *Li ho letti* [$_{QP}$ *tutti* [$_{DP}$ ~~*li*~~]].
them have.I read all
'I read all of them.'

d. *Voglio legger=li* [$_{QP}$ *tutti* [$_{DP}$ ~~*li*~~]].
want.I read=them all
'I want to read all of them.'

e. *Li voglio leggere* [$_{QP}$ *tutti* [$_{DP}$ ~~*li*~~]].
them want.I read all
'I want to read all of them.'

The generalization thus seems to be that in languages like Italian, clitic pronouns attach to verb-related heads, namely functional heads belonging to the extended projection of the verb. We can think of the cases in (90)–(94) as particular instances of clitic climbing in which climbing is obligatory (section 5.2). Note that similar data are also found in languages such as French, in which clitic climbing in the verbal domain is impossible (*je peux le faire* vs. **je le peux faire* 'I can do it'). Semitic languages are different from Romance languages in that clitic pronouns can attach to nouns, prepositions, and quantifiers. See Siloni (1997: 56) and Shlonsky (1994) for the discussion of Hebrew clitic pronouns.

6.5. Person/number features

The fact that in languages like Italian, clitic pronouns can only attach to heads of the clausal skeleton means that the clitic host (F in [75]) necessarily belongs to the extended projection of a verb. This generalization might be related to the fact that only the extended projections of verbs encode case and phi-features.

On the one hand, only verbs assign case, while nouns and adjectives do not. Prepositions, which seem to assign case to their DP complement, might indeed be seen as functional elements of the clausal skeleton (Kayne 2004). On the other hand, the phi-features person and number are relevant in Agree relations only in the case of finite verbs; in other configurations (e.g. nominal expressions and infinitival verbs such as past participles), the phi-features number and gender enter Concord relations – for this important difference between Agree and Concord, see Giusti (2008) and the references quoted there.

It has been suggested that clitic pronouns have to move to the relevant clausal heads to check their case (see Belletti 1999 among others) and/or phi-features against them (see Bianchi 2006 among others). Italian clitic clusters provide evidence that clitic pronouns check both sets of features, and that these features are encoded in the two different clausal areas see in the structure in (55): case is checked against heads in the lexical domain of the verb (what was called AgrO in previous accounts, see Rizzi 2000b), while phi-features are checked in the high inflectional layer of clausal structure, roughly corresponding to the highest portion of the IP layer. The relevant clitic cluster data are however too complex to be summarized here, and the reader is referred to Cardinaletti (2008) for discussion. A reasonable hypothesis is that the heads against which clitic pronouns check person/number features are criterial in the sense of Rizzi (2006). The proposal that criterial heads have freezing effects (*ibid.*) might also explain why clitic movement is not long distance (50)–(51).

If these proposals are correct and if cartographic approaches are correct in assuming that the array of functional projections is universal (Cinque 1999), then language variation in clitic placement cannot be understood in terms of the different functional heads which host clitic pronouns (section 6.4), but rather, it must be attributed to the different scope of verb raising in different sentence types and in different languages (cf. Kayne 1991; Belletti 1999; Rizzi 2000b, among others).

7. Clitic vs. weak pronouns: Two case studies

Some Romance languages display problematic cases for the generalizations on enclisis formulated so far. In the following sections, two such counterexamples are discussed. In section 7.1, we address cases in which clitic pronouns follow prepositions; in section 7.2, cases are presented in which clitic pronouns follow past participles in finite clauses (for past participles in absolute constructions, which allow enclisis [89d], see Belletti 1990). We show that in fact, these cases do not involve clitic, but weak pronouns, which are expectedly found in lower positions than clitic pronouns – see (28b) and (31) above. These cases are therefore only apparent counterexamples to the generalizations discussed in the previous sections.

7.1. Cases of apparent enclisis on prepositions

In Old Italian, clitic pronouns can follow some (lexical) prepositions (Renzi 1989: 369, n. 12):

(95) *(in)controgli* 'against him', *allatogli* 'beside him'

These data are surprising in view of the ungrammaticality of the similar cases in (92b) in Modern Italian. It would be hard to suggest that Old Italian prepositions provided a clitic host PP internally, which is no longer available in Modern Italian (but see Kayne 1991: 649, n. 4). It can instead be claimed that in (95), the pronoun is not clitic, but weak.

Note that the complement of a preposition is a context which differentiates clitic from weak pronouns (see Cardinaletti 1999: 66). As shown by the Italian contrast in (96), the clitic pronoun *lo* 'it/him' is ungrammatical as a complement of P, but the weak pronoun *esso* 'it' is possible. This is true of both functional prepositions such as *di* 'of' in (96a) and lexical prepositions such as *addosso* 'on to' in (96b) (also see [92b]):

(96) a. **Di lo*$_{clitic}$ / *Di esso*$_{weak}$ *abbiamo parlato a lungo.*
of It/him / of it have.we talked at long
'About it, we talked at length.'

b. *Sono saltati *addosso gli*$_{clitic}$ */ addosso ad esso*$_{weak}$.
are.they jumped on to.it/him on at it
'I jumped on it.'

The Dutch paradigm in (97) (due to Riny Huijbregts, personal communication) goes in the same direction: *ze* 'her' is a clitic pronoun, while *r* 'her' and *ze* 'them' are weak pronouns. Also consider the fact that in languages which do not have clitic pronouns, weak pronouns can follow prepositions. In (98a) and (98b), we see data from English and the Rhaeto-Romance dialects discussed in Benincà and Poletto (2005: 228–229), respectively – differently from what is assumed by Benincà and Poletto, the pronoun *el* in (98b) cannot be analyzed as a strong pronoun because it has [−human] reference, see (16):

(97) a. **Ik kijk naar **ze**.*
I look at her
'I look at her.'

cf. *Ik bekijk **ze**.*
I watch her
'I watch her.'

b. *Ik kijk naar'* ***r***.
I look at her

cf. *Ik bekijk'* ***r***.
I watch her

c. *Ik kijk naar **ze**.*
I look at them

cf. *Ik bekijk **ze**.*
I watch them

(98) a. *I count on it.*

b. *Koy figesas kun el?* [Rhaeto-Romance dialect]
what would.do.we with it
'What should we do with it?'

In conclusion, the Old Italian cases in (95) are not counterexamples to the generalization reached on the basis of (96)–(98). The proposal that they contain weak pronouns is not an *ad hoc* solution since there is independent evidence that Old Italian possessed this class of pronouns alongside clitic and strong pronouns. The sentence in (99) is another example in which a weak pronoun (without the functional preposition *a* 'to') occurs in the complement to a lexical preposition (Cardinaletti 2010b:421). Compare (99) with Modern Italian *intorno a lui* 'around him':

(99) *… io vidi intorno lui / quattro donne valenti*
I saw around him four women beautiful

7.2. Cases of apparent enclisis on past participles

In most Romance languages, clitics do not attach to participles in compound tenses and passive sentences (100a), (101a). These are contexts of obligatory clitic climbing, i.e., clitic pronouns appear in the high clitic position (100b), (101b) (see section 5.2):

(100) a. **Ho visto=lo.*
have.I seen=him

b. *L' ho visto.*
him have.I seen
'I have seen him.'

(101) a. **È stato consegnato=gli.*
has.it been delivered=to.him

b. *Gli è stato consegnato.*
to.him has.it been delivered
'It was delivered to him.'

Some apparent exceptions to this very robust cross-linguistic generalization are discussed here.

In Franco-Provençal dialects, a clitic pronoun appears enclitic on the past participle (see Kayne 1991: 660, which reports data from Chenal 1986: 340):

(102) *L' an tot portà=lèi vià.* [Franco-Provençal]
they have everything carried=to.him away
'They have taken everything away from him.'

Two observations suggest that the exceptionality of the pattern in (102) is only apparent. First, as orthography shows, the pronoun bears stress (*lèi*), something which is incompatible with its clitic status (Property B1 in section 3). Second, these dialects allow split clitics, (103). As the Italian contrasts in (58) shows, two clitics must form a cluster (see Rizzi 1982). Note that this is however not the case when a clitic and the weak pronoun *loro* 'to them' co-occur, as shown in (104a) for compound tenses and (104b) for restructuring contexts:

(103) a. *T' an=të prèdzà=nen?* [Franco-Provençal]
to.you have=they spoken=of.it
'Did they speak of it to you?'

b. *T' an=të deut=lo?*
to.you have=they said=it
'Did they say it to you?'

(104) a. *Mi ha presentato loro ieri.*
me has.he introduced to.them yesterday

b. *Mi voleva presentare loro ieri.*
me wanted.he introduce to.them yesterday

The post-verbal pronouns in (102) and (103) can be analyzed as weak pronouns, which occupy the same post-participle clausal area as the Italian dative weak pronoun *loro* – see sentences (28b) and (31) above. The post-participle clausal space can thus be taken to be the typical position for weak pronouns. The question that is raised by the data in (102) and (103) is not why in these Romance languages clitic pronouns occur in a low clausal position, but rather what prevents clitic movement to the high clausal position so that a weak pronoun must be used instead. See the choice generalization in (24) and (32b). The same question is raised by declarative vs. imperative clauses in French. In (105a), the possibility of clitic pronouns blocks the merging of weak pronouns; in (105b) the situation is reversed: clitics are impossible, and weak pronouns are merged instead (Cardinaletti and Starke 1999: 221, n. 32):

(105) a. *Il me donne / * donne moi un livre.* [French]
he to.me gives gives to.me a book
'He gives me a book.'

b. **Donne=me / Donne=moi un livre*!
give=to.me give=to.me a book
'Give me a book!'

A similar analysis might perhaps be offered for the Piedmontese dialect discussed by Burzio (1986: Ch. 2), in which pronouns that follow the past participle, such as *ye* in (106a), are morphologically more complex than proclitic ones, e.g. *y* in (106b). Note that the final vowel on the post-participle pronoun, /e/, is different from the final /a/ displayed by the proclitic pronoun *na* in (106c), which can be taken to be an epenthetic vowel (Burzio 1986: 172, n. 47 observes the different forms of enclitic and proclitic pronouns without analyzing them):

(106) a. *A lé riva=ye dui regai.* [Piedmontese]
A is arrived=there two presents
'Two presents arrived.'

b. *A y riva i client.*
A there arrives the clients
'The clients are arriving.'

c. *A y na riva tanti.*
a there of.them arrives many
'Many of them are arriving.'

Another Northern Italian dialect which apparently displays post-participle clitics is Borgomanerese, discussed by Kayne (1994: 144, n. 8) and Tortora (1997), (2002). In this dialect, pronouns follow not only past participles (107a), but also clausal adverbs such as *più* 'no more' (107b), and the postverbal subject pronoun *mé* 'I' (107c); the contrast between (107b) and (107d) shows that pronouns occur in the clausal area between the adverbs corresponding to Italian *più* 'no more' and *sempre* 'always' (see Tortora 2002, based on Cinque's 1999 adverbial hierarchy):

(107) a. *I o vüsta=la.* [Borgomanerese]
I have seen=her
'I have seen her.'

b. *I o vüst piö=lla.*
I have seen nomore=her
'I haven't seen her anymore.'

c. *I dis mé=vvi.*
I say me=to.you
'I say to you.'

d. **I mœngi sempra=la.*
I eat always=it

e. *I mœngia=la sempri.*
I eat=it always
'I always eat it.'

As shown in (107b, c), clitic pronouns can be separated from the verb by adverbs and postverbal subjects. These data are problematic for the robust cross-linguistic generalization that clitic pronouns can be separated from the verb only if they are higher than it, see (80)–(82) above. A way of making the Borgomanero facts compatible with this generalization is to say that the pronouns in (107) are weak and not clitic (for the order 'verb – adverb – weak pronoun' in Italian, see [31]). Some phonological properties of the data can provide an argument for the weak status of the post-participle pronouns. In (107a), the past participle takes a final vowel /a/, which is not present in (107b), where the past participle does not immediately precede the pronoun. If this /a/ expressed past participle agreement, agreement with a postverbal element would be found, an unprecedented situation in modern Romance languages (see also Roberts 1993 for the same dialect family; past participle agreement with the following complement was possible in Old Italian, see Egerland 1996; Salvi 2010). The fact that the same phenomenon is found with finite verbs and adverbs, whose final /i/ (107d), (108) is replaced by /a/ when they are followed by a pronoun (107e), (109), suggests an alternative analysis of /a/ (data from Tortora 2002: 726–728):

(108) a. *I port**i** la torta.* [Borgomanerese]
I bring the cake
'I bring the cake.'

b. *I porti dent**i** la torta.*
I bring inside the cake
'I bring the cake inside.'

(109) a. *I port**a**=la.* [Borgomanerese]
I bring=it.F.SG
'I bring it.'

b. *I porti dent**a**=la.*
I bring inside=it
'I bring it inside.'

The /a/ could be taken to be part of the pronoun itself, and the sequences in (107a, e) and (110) could be analyzed as *vüst=ala*, *mœngi=ala, port=ala*, *dent=ala*, respectively, where bisyllabic *ala* is a weak pronoun. The vowel /a/ is also found with accusative masculine pronouns (*I trat=alu mal* 'I treat him badly', from Tortora 2002: 731).

Tortora (1997: 23, n. 14) suggests that in cases like (107b), the geminate consonant displayed by the clitic pronoun is due to the presence of a preceding stressed vowel on the adverb *piö*, a phonological phenomenon similar to Raddoppiamento Sintattico in Italian. This phenomenon is not incompatible with the weak status of the pronoun, however, since Raddoppiamento Sintattico also applies to the Italian weak pronoun *loro*: *Gianni parlò* [ll]*oro* 'Gianni spoke to them'.

Note that with the partitive pronoun corresponding to Italian *ne*, a different vowel, /u/, is found both on the finite verb (110a) and the past participle (110b) (data from Tortora 2002: 730 and 1997: 78, n. 49, respectively):

(110) a. *I mœngi**u**=nu.* [Borgomanerese]
I eat=of.them
'I eat some of them.'

b. *I o vust**u**=nu tre.*
I have seen=of.them three
'I have seen three of them.'

On a par with the vowel [a], the vowel [u] cannot be taken to be part of the verbal inflection, since it would imply that the verb (i) agrees with the partitive object, (ii) is sensitive to the accusative vs. partitive status of the complement (see [a] vs. [u], respectively), (iii) has the same inflection when it is finite (110a) or infinitive (110b), which are to our knowledge three unprecedented situations in Romance. As we have done with the vowel /a/ above, the vowel /u/ can be taken to be part of the weak indefinite pronoun *unu* (*I mœngi=unu, I o vust=unu tre*). This indefinite pronoun is parallel to English *one* as in *I have seen three ones*.

That some Romance languages do not possess clitic pronouns at all is not unknown. The Rhaeto-Romance dialects analyzed by Benincà and Poletto (2005) also display only weak and strong pronouns. Note that *el* in a sentence like *Vus amflayas bec el* 'you do not find it' cannot be analyzed as a strong pronoun (*pace* Benincà and Poletto 2005: 228) because it has [−human] reference (see [16] and the discussion of [98b]).

8. Conclusions

Clitic pronouns display a quite intricate array of properties. As far as their internal syntax is concerned, they are deficient from all points of view. As for their external syntax, clitic placement is sensitive to syntactic notions such as finite vs. infinitive, indicative vs. imperative mood, declarative vs. interrogative sentences, noun vs. verb, and so on.

Clitic pronouns must be seen as deficient phrases, which cannot stay in their merge position. They undergo syntactic movement, which displays properties of both XP and head movement. This has led to the view that clitic movement is indeed a two-step derivation, XP-movement followed by local head movement. The first step of the clitic derivation is shared by weak pronouns, which also are deficient phrases.

The landing site of cliticization is a functional head of the extended projection of a verb. Other categories do not provide a clitic host internally to their extended projections. A way to explain this generalization is to suggest that clitic pronouns check case and phi-features against functional heads encoding these features, and this type of functional heads are present in the extended projections of verbs.

Sentences containing restructuring verbs provide evidence for more than one clitic position per clause: one high clitic area corresponding to functional heads encoding person/number features, and one low clitic area corresponding to functional heads encoding case features.

Language-internal and cross-linguistic variation in clitic placement is due to the scope of verb movement in different sentence types and in different languages.

Finally, we have shown that some apparent instances of enclitic pronouns are better analyzed as weak pronouns, the third class of pronouns made available by Universal grammar in addition to clitic and strong pronouns, with the advantage of keeping robust cross-linguistic generalizations on the distribution of enclitic pronouns.

9. References (selected)

Abney, S. P.
1987 The English Noun Phrase in its Sentential Aspect. MIT Ph.D. Dissertation.

Anagnostopoulou, E.
2006 Clitic doubling. In: Everaert, and van Riemsdijk (eds.), *The Blackwell Companion to Syntax, Vol. I,* 519–581. Oxford: Blackwell Publishers Ltd.

Baltin, M.
1981 A landing site theory of movement rules. *Linguistic Theory* 13.1: 1–38.

Barbosa, P.
1996 Clitic placement in European Portuguese and the position of subjects. In: A. L. Aalpern and A. M. Zwicky (eds.), *Approaching Second: Second Position Clitics and Related Phenomena*. CSLI Publications.

Belletti A.
1990 *Generalized Verb Movement*. Turin: Rosenberg and Sellier.

Belletti, A. (ed.)
1993 *Syntactic Theory and the Dialects of Italy*. Turin: Rosenberg and Sellier.

Belletti, A.
1999 Italian/Romance clitics: Structure and derivation. In: van Riemsdijk (ed.), *Clitics in the Languages of Europe*, 543–579. Berlin–New York: Mouton.

Belletti A.
2005 Extended doubling and the VP-periphery. *Probus* 17: 1–35.

Belletti, A., and L. Rizzi
1981 The syntax of *ne*: Some theoretical implications. *The Linguistic Review* 1: 117–154.

Benincà, P., and Cinque, G.
1993 Su alcune differenze tra enclisi e proclisi. In: *Omaggio a Gianfranco Folena*, 2313–2326. Padova: Editoriale Programma.

Benincà, P., and Poletto, C.
2005 On some descriptive generalizations in Romance. In: Cinque, and Kayne (eds.), *Handbook of Comparative Syntax,* 221–258. Oxford: Oxford University Press.

Berendsen, E.
1986 *The Phonology of Cliticization*. Dordrecht: Foris.
Bianchi, V.
2006 On the syntax of personal arguments. *Lingua* 116: 2023–2067.
Bleam, T.
1999 Leísta Spanish and the Syntax of *Clitic* Doubling. University of Delaware Ph.D. Dissertation.
Bok-Bennema, R.
2006 Clitic climbing. In: Everaert, and van Riemsdijk (eds.), *The Blackwell Companion to Syntax, Vol. I*, 469–518. Oxford: Blackwell Publishers Ltd.
Bonet, E.
1995 Feature structure of Romance clitics. *Natural Language and Linguistic Theory* 13: 607–647.
Borer, H.
1984 *Parametric Syntax: Case Studies in Semitic and Romance Languages*. Dordrecht: Foris.
Bouchard, D.
1984 *On the Content of Empty Categories*. Dordrecht: Foris.
Bouchard, D., and Hirschbuhler, P.
1987 French Quoi and its Clitic Allomorph QUE. In: C. Neidle, and R. A. Nuñez Cedeño (eds.), *Studies in Romance Languages*, 39–60. Dordrecht: Foris.
Brandi, L., and P. Cordin
1981 Dialetti e italiano: un confronto sul parametro del soggetto nullo. *Rivista di grammatica generativa* 6: 33–87.
Brandi, L., and P. Cordin
1989 Two Italian dialects and the null subject parameter. In: Jaeggli, and Safir (eds.), *The Null Subject Parameter,* 111–142. Dordrecht: Kluwer.
Burzio, L.
1986 *Italian Syntax: A Government-Binding Approach*. Dordrecht: Reidel.
Cardinaletti, A.
1991 On pronoun movement: The Italian dative *loro*. *Probus* 3.2: 127–153.
Cardinaletti, A.
1994 On the internal structure of pronominal DPs. *The Linguistic Review* 11: 195–219.
Cardinaletti, A.
1998 On the deficient/strong opposition in possessive systems. In: A. Alexiadou, and Ch. Wilder (eds.), *Possessors, Predicates and Movement in the Determiner Phrase*, 17–53. Amsterdam/Philadelphia: Benjamins.
Cardinaletti, A.
1999 Pronouns in Romance and Germanic languages: An overview. In: van Riemsdijk (ed.), *Clitics in the Languages of Europe,* 33–82. Berlin–New York: Mouton.
Cardinaletti, A.
2007 Für eine syntaktische Analyse von Modalpartikeln. In: E.-M. Thüne and F. Ortu (eds.), *Gesprochene Sprache – Partikeln*, 89–101. Frankfurt: Peter Lang.
Cardinaletti, A.
2008 On different types of clitic clusters. In: De Cat, and Demuth (eds.), *The Bantu-Romance Connection,* 41–82. Amsterdam: Benjamins.
Cardinaletti, A.
2010a Morphologically complex clitic pronouns and spurious *se* once again. In: V. Torrens, L. Escobar, A. Gavarró, and J. Gutiérrez (eds.), *Movement and Clitics: Adult and Child Grammar*, 238–259. Newcastle: Cambridge Scholars Publishing.
Cardinaletti, A.
2010b Il pronome personale obliquo. In: G. Salvi, and L. Renzi (eds.), *Grammatica dell'italiano antico*, 414–450. Bologna: il Mulino.

Cardinaletti, A.
2011 German and Italian Modal Particles and Clause Structure. *The Linguistic Review* 28: 493–531.
Cardinaletti A., and G. Giusti
2006 The syntax of quantified phrases and quantitative clitics. In: Everaert, and van Riemsdijk (eds.), *The Blackwell Companion to Syntax, Vol. V*, 23–93. Oxford: Blackwell Publishers Ltd.
Cardinaletti A., and L. Repetti
2007 Vocali epentetiche nella morfologia dell'italiano e dei dialetti italiani. In: R. Maschi, N. Penello, and P. Rizzolatti (eds.), *Miscellanea di studi linguistici offerti a Laura Vanelli da amici e allievi padovani*, 115–126. Udine: Forum Editrice.
Cardinaletti A., and L. Repetti
2008 The phonology and syntax of preverbal and postverbal subject clitics in Northern Italian dialects. *Linguistic Inquiry* 39.4: 523–563.
Cardinaletti A., and L. Repetti
2009 Phrase-level and word-level syllables: Resyllabification and prosodization of clitics. In: J. Grijzenhout and B. Kabak (eds.), *Phonological Domains. Universals and Deviations*, 79–104. Berlin: Mouton de Gruyter.
Cardinaletti A., and L. Repetti
2010 Proclitic vs Enclitic Pronouns in Northern Italian Dialects and the Null-Subject Parameter. In: R. D'Alessandro, A. Ledgeway and I. Roberts (eds.), *Syntactic Variation: The Dialects of Italy*, 119–134. Cambridge: Cambridge University Press.
Cardinaletti A., and U. Shlonsky
2004 Clitic positions and restructuring in Italian. *Linguistic Inquiry* 35.4: 519–557.
Cardinaletti, A., and M. Starke
1996 Deficient pronouns: A view from Germanic. A study in the unified description of Germanic and Romance. In: H. Thráinsson, S. D. Epstein, and S. Peter (eds.), *Studies in Comparative Germanic Syntax Volume II*, 21–65. Dordrecht: Kluwer.
Cardinaletti, A., and M. Starke
1999 The typology of structural deficiency: A case study of the three classes of pronouns, "feature article". In: van Riemsdijk (ed.), *Clitics in the Languages of Europe,* 145–233. Berlin–New York: Mouton.
Cavar, D., and C. Wilder
1999 Clitic third in Croatian. In: van Riemsdijk (ed.), *Clitics in the Languages of Europe*, 429–467. Berlin–New York: Mouton.
Cecchetto C.
2000 Doubling structures and reconstruction. *Probus* 12: 93–126.
Chenal, A.
1986 *Le franco-provençal valdôtain*. Aoste: Musumeci.
Chereny, W. H.
1905 Object pronouns in dependent clauses: a study in Old Spanish word order. *Publications of the Modern Language Association of America* 20: 1 –151.
Chomsky, N.
1995 *The Minimalist Program*. Cambridge, Mass.: MIT Press.
Chomsky, N.
2008 On phases. In: R. Freidin, C.P. Otero and M.L. Zubizarreta (eds.), *Foundational Issues in Linguistic Theory*, 133–166. Cambridge, Mass.: MIT Press.
Cinque, G.
1990 *Types of A'-Dependencies*. Cambridge, Mass.: MIT Press.
Cinque, G.
1999 *Adverbs and Functional Heads*. Oxford: Oxford University Press.

Cinque, G.
2004 "Restructuring" and Functional Structure. In: A. Belletti (ed.), *Structures and Beyond. The Cartography of Syntactic Structures, Volume 3*, 132–191. New York: Oxford University Press.
Cinque, G., and R. S. Kayne (eds.)
2005 *Handbook of Comparative Syntax*. Oxford: Oxford University Press.
Cordin, P.
1993 Dative clitics and doubling in Trentino. In: Belletti (ed.), *Syntactic Theory and the Dialects of Italy*, 130–154. Turin: Rosenberg and Sellier.
Corver, N., and D. Delfitto
1999 On the nature of pronoun movement. In: van Riemsdijk (ed.), *Clitics in the Languages of Europe,* 799–861. Berlin-New York: Mouton.
D'Alessandro, R., and I. Roberts
2008 Movement and agreement in Italian past participles and defective phases. *Linguistic Inquiry* 39.3: 477–491.
De Cat C.
2005 French subject clitics are not agreement markers. *Lingua* 115.9: 1195–1219.
De Cat, C., and K. Demuth (eds.)
2008 *The Bantu-Romance Connection*. Amsterdam: Benjamins.
Demonte, V.
1995 Dative alternations in Spanish. *Probus* 7: 5–30.
Dobrovie-Sorin, C.
1990 Clitic-doubling, wh-movement, and quantification in Romanian. *Linguistic Inquiry* 21.3: 351–397.
Dobrovie-Sorin, C.
1994 *The Syntax of Romanian*. Berlin: Mouton.
Dobrovie-Sorin, C.
1995 Clitic clusters in Romanian: Deriving linear order from hierarchical structure. In: G. Cinque, and G. Giusti (eds.), *Advances in Romanian Linguistics*, 55–82. Amsterdam: Benjamins.
Egerland, Verner
1996 *The Syntax of Past Participles. A Generative Study of Nonfinite Constructions in Ancient and Modern Italian*. Lund: Lund University Press.
Everaert, M., and H. van Riemsdijk (eds.)
2006 *The Blackwell Companion to Syntax*. Oxford: Blackwell Publishers Ltd, 5 Volumes.
Fischer S.
2002 *The Catalan Clitic System: A Diacronic Perspective on its Syntax and Phonology*. Berlin/New York: Mouton de Gruyter.
Fischer, S.
2003 Rethinking the Tobler-Mussafia Law: data from Old Catalan. *Diachronica* 20: 259–288.
Fontana, J. M.
1993 Phrase Structure and the Syntax of Clitics in the History of Spanish. University of Pennsylvania Ph.D. Dissertation.
Franks S., and T. H. Kings
2000 *A Handbook of Slavic Languages*. Oxford: Oxford University Press.
Friedemann, M.-A.
1990 Le pronom interrogatif "que" et la montée du verbe en C°. *Rivista di Grammatica Generativa* 15: 123–139.
Friedemann, M.-A.
1997 *Sujets Syntaxiques: Positions, Inversions et pro*. Bern: Peter Lang.

Galves, C.
1996 Clitic-placement and Parametric Changes in Portuguese. In: *Selected Papers from the 24th Linguistic Symposium on Romance Languages*, 227–239. Georgetown University Press.
Galves, C.
1997 La syntaxe pronominale du portugais brésilien et la typologie des pronoms. In: A. Zribi-Hertz (ed.), *Les Pronoms: Morphologie, Syntaxe et Typologie*, 11–34. Saint-Denis: Presses Universitaires de Vincennes.
Gerlach, B.
1998a Optimale Klitiksequenzen. *Zeitschrift fur Sprachwissenschaft* 17.l: 3691.
Gerlach B.
1998b Restrictions on clitic sequences and conditions on the occurrence of clitics in Romance. *Arbeiten des Sonderforschungsbereichs 282* Nr. 105, Heinrich-Heine-Universität Düsseldorf.
Giusti, G.
1997 The categorical status of determiners. In: L. Haegeman (ed.), *The New Comparative Syntax*, 95–123. London: Longman.
Giusti, G.
2008 Agreement and concord in nominal expressions. In: C. De Cat, and K. Demuth (eds.), *The Bantu-Romance Connection,* 201–237. Amsterdam: Benjamins.
Givón T.
1979 *On Understanding Grammar.* New York: Academic Press.
Goria, C.
2004 *Subject Clitics in the Northern Italian Dialects. A Comparative Study Based on the Minimalist Program and Optimality Theory.* Dordrecht: Kluwer.
Grimshaw, J.
1991 Extended projections. Ms., Brandeis University, Waltham, Mass.
Gutiérrez-Rexach J.
1999 Cross-linguistic semantics of weak pronouns in doubling structures. In: Paul Dekker (ed.), *Proceeedings of the Twelfth Amsterdam colloquium (AC12)*, 115–120. Intitute for Logic, Language and Computation, University of Amsterdam.
Gutiérrez-Rexach J.
1999/2000 The formal semantics of clitic doubling. *Journal of Semantics* 16.4: 315–380.
Halle M., and A. Marantz
1994 Some key features of distributed morphology. In: A. Carnie, H. Harley, and T. Bures (eds.), *Papers on Phonology and Morphology, MIT Working Papers in Linguistics* 21: 275–288.
Harris, M. B.
1980a The marking of definiteness in Romance. In: J. Fisiak (ed.), *Historical Morphology,* 141–156. The Hague: Mouton.
Harris, M. B.
1980b Noun-phrases and verb-phrases in Romance. *Transactions of the Philological Society* 78.1: 62–80.
Harris J., and M. Halle
2005 Unexpected plural inflections in Spanish: Reduplication and Metathesis. *Linguistic Inquiry* 36: 195–222.
Hopper, P. J., and E. C. Traugott
1993 *Grammaticalization.* Cambridge: Cambridge University Press.
Hopper, P. J., and E. C. Traugott
2003 *Grammaticalization.* Cambridge: Cambridge University Press (2nd edition).
Huang, J.
1982 Logical relations in Chinese and the theory of grammar. MIT Ph.D. Dissertation.

Jaeggli, O.
1982 *Topics in Romance Syntax.* Dordrecht: Foris.
Jaeggli, O.
1986 Three issues in the theory of clitics: Case, doubled NPs, and extraction. In: H. Borer (ed.), *The Syntax of Pronominal Clitics*, 15–42. New York: Academic Press.
Jaeggli, O., and K. Safir (eds.)
1989 *The Null Subject Parameter.* Dordrecht: Kluwer.
Jones, M. A.
1988 Auxiliary verbs in Sardinian. *Transactions of the Philological Society* 86.2: 173–203.
Jones, M. A.
1993 *Sardinian Syntax.* London/New York: Routledge.
Jones, M. A.
1999 The pronoun ~ determiner debate: Evidence from Sardinian and repercussions for French. In: E. Treviño, and J. Lema (eds.), *Semantic Issues in Romance Syntax*, 121–140. Amsterdam: Benjamins.
Kayne, R. S.
1975 *French Syntax.* Cambridge, Mass.: MIT Press.
Kayne, R. S.
1983 Chains, categories external to S, and French complex inversion. *Natural Language and Linguistic Theory* 1: 107–139.
Kayne, R.S.
1989a Facets of Romance past participle agreement. In: P. Benincà (ed.), *Dialect Variation and the Theory of Grammar*, 85–103. Dordrecht: Foris.
Kayne, R. S.
1989b Null subjects and clitic climbing. In: Jaeggli, and Safir (eds.), *The Null Subject Parameter,* 239–261. Dordrecht: Kluwer.
Kayne, R. S.
1991 Romance clitics, verb movement and PRO. *Linguistic Inquiry* 22.4: 647–686.
Kayne, R. S.
1994 *The Antisymmetry of Syntax.* Cambridge, Mass.: MIT Press.
Kayne, R. S.
2000a A Note on Clitic Doubling in French. In: *Parameters and Universals*, 163–184. Oxford: Oxford University Press.
Kayne, R. S.
2000b Person morphemes and reflexives in Italian, French, and related languages. In: *Parameters and Universals*, 131–162. Oxford: Oxford University Press.
Kayne, R. S.
2004 Prepositions as probes. In: A. Belletti (ed.), *Structures and Beyond*, 192–212. Oxford: Oxford University Press.
Kayne, R.
2008 Toward a Syntactic reinterpretation of Harris & Halle (2005). In: R. Bok-Bennema, B. Kampers-Manhe, and B. Hollebrandse (eds.), *Romance Languages and Linguistic Theory 2008, Selected papers from 'Going Romance' Groningen 2008*, 145–170. Amsterdam: Benjamins.
Klavans J.
1979 On clitics as words. *CLS* 15: 68–80.
Klavans J.
1982 *Some Problems in the Theory of Clitics.* Bloomington: Indiana University Linguistics Club.
Klavans, J.
1985 The independence of syntax and phonology in clitization. *Language* 61: 95–120.

Laenzlinger Ch.
1993 A syntactic view of Romance pronominal sequences. *Probus* 5.3: 241–170.

Longobardi G.
1994 Reference and proper names: a theory of N-movement in syntax and Logical Form. *Linguistic Inquiry* 25: 609–665.

Luís, A. R., and A. Spencer
2005 A paradigm function account of 'mesoclisis' in European Portuguese. *Yearbook of Morphology 2004*: 177–228.

Madeira A. M.
1992 On clitic placement in European Portuguese. *UCL Working Papers in Linguistics* 4: 95–122.

Madeira A. M.
1993 Clitic-second in European Portuguese. *Probus* 5: 155–174.

Manzini, M. R., and L. M. Savoia
2005 *I Dialetti Italiani e Romanci. Morfosintassi Generativa*. Alessandria: Edizioni dell'Orso.

Manzini, M. R., and L. M. Savoia
2009 Mesoclisis in the Imperative: Phonology, Morphology or Syntax?. In: V. Moscati, and E. Servidio (eds.), *Proceedings of XXXV Incontro di Grammatica Generativa, University of Siena CISCL Working Papers 3*.

Martins, A. M.
1994 Clíticos na história do português. University of Lisbon Ph.D. Dissertation.

Martins, A. M.
2000 A minimalist approach to clitic climbing. In: J. Costa (ed.), *Portuguese Syntax*, 169–190. Oxford: Oxford University Press.

Martins, A. M.
2002 The loss of IP-scrambling in Portuguese: clause structure, word-order variation and change. In: D. Lightfoot (ed.), *Syntactic Effects of Morphological Change*, 232–248. Oxford: Oxford University Press.

Martins, A. M.
2003 From unity to diversity in Romance syntax. In: K. Braunmüller, and G. Ferraresi (eds.), *Aspects of Multilingualism in European Language History*, 201–233. Amsterdam: John Benjamins.

Martins, A. M.
2005 Clitic placement, VP-ellipsis and scrambling in Romance. In: M. Batillori et al. (eds.), *Grammaticalization and Parametric Variation*, 175–193. Oxford: Oxford University Press.

Moro, A.
2000 *Dynamic Antisymmetry: Movement as a Symmetry Breaking Phenomenon*. Cambridge, Mass.: MIT Press.

Munaro, N.
1999 *Sintagmi Interrogativi Nei Dialetti Italiani Settentrionali*. Padova: Unipress.

Nevis, J. A., B. D. Joseph, D. Wanner, and A.M. Zwicky (eds.)
1994 *Clitics. A Comprehensive Bibliography 1892–1991*. Amsterdam: John Benjamins.

Ouhalla, J.
2005 Clitic placement, grammaticalization, and reanalysis in Berber. In: Cinque, and Kayne (eds.), *Handbook of Comparative Syntax,* 607–638. Oxford: Oxford University Press.

Panagiotidis Ph.
2002 *Pronouns, Clitics, and Empty Nouns*. Amsterdam: Benjamins.

Perlmutter D.
1971 *Deep and Surface Constraints in Syntax*. New York: Holt, Reinhart and Winston.

Picallo C.
1985 Opaque Domains. CUNY Ph.D. Dissertation.

Picallo C.
1990 Modal verbs in Catalan. *Natural Language and Linguistic Theory* 8: 285–312.
Poletto, C.
2000 *The Higher Functional Field: Evidence from Northern Italian Dialects*. Oxford: Oxford University Press.
Poletto, C.
2005 Asymmetrical Pro-Drop in Northern Italian Dialects. In: P. Ackema, P. Brandt, M. Schoorlemmer, and F. Weermann (eds.), *Arguments and Agreement*, 159–191. Oxford: Oxford University Press.
Poletto, C., and J.-Y. Pollock
2004 On wh-clitics, wh-doubling in French, and some North Eastern Italian dialects. *Probus* 16: 241–272.
Poletto, C., J.-Y. Pollock
2009 Another look at wh-questions in Romance: A look at Mendrisiotto. In: D. Torck, and L. Wetzels (eds.), *Romance Languages and Linguistic Theory 2006*, 199–258. Amsterdam: John Benjamins.
Pollock, J.-Y.
1989 Verb-movement, Universal Grammar, and the structure of IP. *Linguistic Inquiry* 20: 365–424.
Popescu, A.
2000 The morphophonology of the Romanian clitic sequence. *Lingua* 110.10: 773–799.
Postal, P. M.
1969 On so-called 'pronouns' in English. In: D. Reibel, and S. Schane (eds.), *Modern Studies in English*, 201–224. Englewood Cliffs, NJ: Prentice Hall.
Quicoli, C.
1976 Conditions on clitic-movement in Portuguese. *Linguistic Analysis* 2: 199–223.
Quicoli, C.
1980 Clitic movement in French causatives. *Linguistic Analysis* 6: 131–186.
Ramsden, H.
1963 *Weak Pronoun Position in the Early Romance Languages*. Manchester: University of Manchester Press.
Raposo, E., and J. Uriagereka
2005 Clitic placement in Western Iberian: a minimalist view. In: Cinque, and Kayne (eds.), *Handbook of Comparative Syntax,* 639–697.Oxford: Oxford University Press.
Renzi, L.
1989 Two types of clitics in natural languages. *Rivista di Linguistica* 1: 355–372.
Repetti L.
2004 The masculine singular definite article in Italian and Italian dialects. Ms. SUNY at Stony Brook.
van Riemsdijk H. (ed.)
1999 *Clitics in the Languages of Europe*. EALT/EUROTYP 20–5. Berlin–New York: Mouton.
Rigau G.
1988 Strong pronouns. *Linguistic Inquiry* 19: 503–511.
Rini J.
1991 The redundant indirect object constructions in Spanish: A new perspective. *Romance Philology* 45.2: 269–286.
Rivas A.
1977 A Theory of Clitics. MIT Ph.D. Dissertation.
Rivero M.-L.
1986 Parameters in the typology of clitics in Romance and Old Spanish. *Language* 62: 774–807.

Rivero M.-L.
1992 Clitic and NP climbing in Old Spanish. In: H. Campos, and F. Martínez-Gil (eds.), *Current Studies in Spanish Linguistics*, 241–282. Washington, D.C.: Georgetown University Press.

Rivero, M.-L.
1994 Clause structure and V-movement in the languages of the Balkans. *Natural Language and Linguistic Theory* 12: 63–120.

Rivero M.-L.
1997 On two locations for complement clitic pronouns: Serbo-Croatian, Bulgarian, and Old Spanish. In: A. van Kemenade, and N. Vincent (eds.), *Parameters of Morphosyntactic Change*, 170–206. Cambridge: Cambridge University Press.

Rivero, M.-L., and A. Terzi
1995 Imperatives, V-movement, and Logical Mood. *Journal of Linguistics* 31: 301–332.

Rizzi, L.
1982 *Issues in Italian Syntax*. Dordrecht: Foris.

Rizzi, L.
1986 On the status of subject clitics in Romance. In: O. Jaeggli, and C. Silva-Corvalán (eds.), *Studies in Romance Linguistics*, 391–419. Dordrecht: Foris.

Rizzi, L.
1988/2001 Il sintagma preposizionale. In: L. Renzi, G. Salvi, and A. Cardinaletti (eds.), *Grande Grammatica Italiana di Consultazione*, vol. 1, 521–545 (1st ed. 1988). Bologna: il Mulino.

Rizzi, L.
1990 *Relativized Minimality*. Cambridge, Mass.: MIT Press

Rizzi, L.
2000a Three issues in Romance dialectology. In: *Comparative Syntax and Language Acquisition*, 80–95. London: Routledge.

Rizzi, L.
2000b Some notes on Romance cliticization. In: *Comparative Syntax and Language Acquisition*, 96–121. London: Routledge.

Rizzi, L.
2006 On the form of chains: Criterial positions and ECP effects. In: L. Cheng, and N. Corver (eds.), *Wh-Movement. Moving On*, 97–133. Cambridge, Mass.: MIT Press.

Roberge Y.
1987 Clitic-chains and the definiteness requirement in doubling constructions. In: D. Birdsong, and J.-P. Montreuil (eds.), *Advances in Romance Linguistics*, 353–369. Dordrecht: Foris.

Roberge, Y.
1990 *The Syntactic Recoverability of Null Arguments*. Montreal: McGill-Queen's University Press.

Roberts, I.
1993 The nature of subject clitics in Franco-Provençal Valdôtain. In: Belletti (ed.), *Syntactic Theory and the Dialects of Italy*, 319–353. Turin: Rosenberg and Sellier.

Roberts, I.
1997 Restructuring, head movement, and locality. *Linguistic Inquiry* 28.3: 423–460.

Roberts, I.
2010 *Agreement and Head Movement*. Clitics, Incorporation, and Defective Goals. Cambridge, Mass.: MIT Press.

Rouveret A.
1999 Clitics, subjects and Tense in European Portuguese. In: van Riemsdijk (ed.), *Clitics in the Languages of Europe* EALT/EUROTYP 20-5, 639–677. Berlin–New York: Mouton.

Salvi G.
2010 L'accordo. In: G. Salvi, and L. Renzi (eds.), *Grammatica dell'italiano Antico*, 547–568. Bologna: il Mulino.
Săvescu Ciucivara O.
2009 A syntactic analysis of pronominal clitic clusters in Romance: The view from Romanian. NYU Ph.D. Dissertation.
Schroten, J.
1992 On Spanish definite determiners: Personal pronouns and definite articles. *Recherches de Linguistique Romane et Française d'Utrecht* XI: 9–24.
Selkirk, E.
1995 The prosodic structure of function words. *Papers in Optimality Theory UMOP 18:* 439–469. Amherst MA: GLSA.
Shlonsky, U.
1994 Semitic clitics. *Geneva Generative Papers* 2.1: 1–11.
Shlonsky, U.
2004 Enclisis and proclisis. In: L. Rizzi (ed.), *The Structure of CP and IP*, 329–353. Oxford: Oxford University Press.
Siloni, T.
1997 *Noun Phrases and Nominalizations. The Syntax of DPs*. Dordrecht: Kluwer.
Sportiche, D.
1989/98 Movement, agreement and case. Ms., UCLA, published in 1998 in *Partition and Atoms of Clause Structure*, 88–243. London: Routledge.
Sportiche, D.
1996/98 Clitic constructions. In: L. Zaring, and J. Rooryck (eds.), *Phrase Structure and the Lexicon*, 213–276. Dordrecht, Kluwer; reprinted in *Partition and Atoms of Clause Structure*, 244–307. London: Routledge.
Sportiche, D.
2011 French relative qui. *Linguistic Inquiry* 42: 83–124.
Starke, M.
1993 *En Deuxième Position en Europe Centrale*. University of Geneva Mémoire de Licence.
Strozer, J.
1976 Clitics in Spanish. UCLA Ph.D. Dissertation.
Suñer, M.
1988 The role of agreement in clitic doubled constructions. *Natural Language and Linguistic Theory* 6: 391–434.
Terzi, A.
1999 Clitic combinations, their hosts and their ordering. *Natural Language and Linguistic Theory* 17: 85–121.
Toman, J.
1993 A note on clitics and prosody. In: L. Hellan (ed.), *Clitics in Germanic and Slavic, ESF Working Papers*, 113–118.
Torrego, E.
1988 A DP-analysis of Spanish nominals. Ms., University of Massachusetts.
Torrego, E.
1995 On the nature of clitic doubling. In: H. Campos, and P. Kempchinsky (eds.), *Evolution and Revolution in Linguistic Theory*, 399–418. Washington, DC: Georgetown University Press.
Torrego, E.
2002 Arguments for a derivational approach to syntactic relations based on clitics. In: S. D. Epstein, and T. D. Seely (eds.), *Derivation and Explanation in the Minimalist Program*, 249–268. Malden, Mass.: Blackwell.

Tortora, C.
1997 The syntax and semantics of the weak locative. University of Delaware Ph.D. Dissertation.
Tortora, C.
2002 Romance enclisis, prepositions, and aspect. *Natural Language and Linguistic Theory* 20: 725–758.
Uriagereka, J.
1988 On Government. University of Connecticut Ph.D. Dissertation.
Uriagereka, J.
1995a Aspects of the syntax of clitic placement in Western Romance. *Linguistic Inquiry* 26: 79–123.
Uriagereka, J.
1995b An F-position in Western Romance. In: K. E. Kiss (ed.), *Discourse-Configurational Languages*, 153–175. Oxford: Oxford University Press.
Uriagereka, J.
1996 Determiner clitic placement. In: R. Freidin (ed.), *Current Issues in Comparative Grammar*, 257–295. Dordrecht: Kluwer.
Uriagereka, J.
2005 On the syntax of doubling. In: L. Heggie, and F. Ordóñez (eds.), *Clitic and Affix Combinations*, 343–374. Amsterdam/Philadelphia: John Benjamins.
Vanelli L.
1996 Convergenze e divergenze nella storia del pronome e dell'articolo: esiti di ILLU(M) nei dialetti italiani settentrionali. In: P. Benincà, G. Cinque, T. De Mauro, and N. Vincent (eds.), *Italiano e Dialetti nel Tempo. Saggi di Grammatica per Giulio Lepschy*, 369–386. Roma: Bulzoni.
Vigário M.
2003 *The Prosodic Word in European Portuguese*. Berlin: Mouton De Gruyter.
Vincent, N.
1997 The emergence of the D-system in Romance. In: A. van Kemenade, and N. Vincent (eds.), *Parameters of Morphosyntactic Change*, 149–169. Cambridge: Cambridge University Press.
Wackernagel, J.
1892 Über ein Gesetz der Indogermanischen Wortstellung. *Indogermanische Forschungen* 1: 334–436.
Wanner, D.
1987 *The Development of Romance Clitic Pronouns from Latin to Old Romance*. Berlin/New York: Mouton de Gruyter.
Wanner, D.
1992 The Tobler-Mussafia Law in Old Spanish. In: H. Campos, and F. Martínez-Gil (eds.), *Current Studies in Spanish Linguistics*, 313–378. Washington, D.C.: Georgetown University Press.
Zwicky, A. M.
1977 *On Clitics*. Bloomington: Indiana University Linguistics Club.
Zwicky A. M.
1985 Clitics and particles. *Language* 61.2: 283–305.
Zwicky, A. M., and G. K. Pullum
1983 Clitisation vs. inflection. *Language* 59: 502–513.

Anna Cardinaletti, Venice (Italy)

20. Ergativity

Abstract

Languages show ergativity when they treat transitive subjects distinctly from intransitive ones, treat objects like intransitive subjects, or treat unaccusative subjects unlike unergative and transitive subjects. Ergativity plays a central role in the study of case, agreement, and non-finite clauses. It casts light in addition on the constraints at play in A' extraction. Across these domains, the investigation of ergativity offers a rich arena of crosslinguistic variation against a backdrop of potential language universals. This chapter surveys both the major proposed universals of ergativity and the variety of theoretical approaches which have been applied to them. A central theme is that ergativity is not one but many phenomena.

1. Introduction: three ergativity properties

The study of ergativity is concerned with ways in which languages show one or more of the following properties:

(1) Ergativity properties

a. *The ergative property*
Subjects of transitive clauses behave differently from subjects of intransitive clauses for some grammatical generalization(s).

b. *The absolutive property*
Objects of transitive clauses and subjects of intransitive clauses behave identically for some grammatical generalization(s).

c. *The argument-structural property*
Subjects of unaccusative verbs behave differently from subjects of unergative and transitive verbs for some grammatical generalization(s).

Ergativity properties have been a subject of intense research for over forty years. During this time, the range of data available to syntacticians concerned with ergativity has grown immensely, with important consequences for the way that ergativity is viewed. It is now uncontroversially clear that there is a great deal of syntactic and morphological diversity among languages to be considered ergative in the broad sense of (1). Theories of ergativity are tasked with handling this diversity in a way that balances predictive power with empirical coverage.

This situation is an interesting one for Minimalism and its antecedents, e.g. Government and Binding Theory, which will be the focus of theoretical attention here. In a sense, these theories predict diversity in ergative languages, in that they offer no possibility of a unified formulation of the properties in (1). It is notable in this connection that very little of the description in (1) corresponds to primitive elements recognized by these frameworks. Subjecthood and transitivity must be cashed out in structural terms. So too must the various grammatical generalizations which conform to the broad ergative mold. In each case there will be some range of choices which could be pursued, with different choices potentially appropriate for different languages. This leads us to expect that the net cast by (1) may well bring in a range of species which are different in various ways. Two languages which pre-theoretically both show the ergative property and the absolutive property, for instance, could nevertheless manifest systematic and far-reaching structural differences.

Indeed one of the major results of generative studies on ergativity has been that exactly this situation does obtain. Bittner and Hale's important work in the 1990s on Warlpiri versus Inuit showed that two languages showing similar morphological (1a)/(1b) *ergative-absolutive* patterns nevertheless differ from one another in a range of syntactic and semantic dimensions (Bittner and Hale 1996a, 1996b). There is not just one ergativity, then, but at least two ergativities, the Warlpiri type and the Inuit type – two ways that languages can fall under the joint umbrella of properties (1a) and (1b). And where there are two ergativities there might be more than two. Languages described as ergative in view of the argument-structural property (1c) deserve additional attention. So too do languages showing the ergative property (1a) but not the absolutive property (1b).

What accumulates from ergativity studies then is not an overarching theory of ergativity as a single parameter or a primitive. From a theoretical perspective there is no particular reason why this should exist. Primary concerns of theoretical ergativity studies today are questions of diversity – How many ergative grammars are there? – and of formal unity beneath: What sort of theory can predict exactly these ergative types and no others?

This article will survey two ways of seeking answers to these questions. The first, shorter part (section 2) overviews major results of the typological approach to ergativity. The culmination of this section is a list of some proposed universals, which will play an important role in the motivation and evaluation of theoretical points of view. The second part of the article discusses syntactic and morphological theories of ergativity behaviors, first in relation to case, agreement and control (section 3) and then in relation to Ā-movement (section 4).

2. Ways of being ergative

What is the profile of a language demonstrating one or more of the properties in (1)? When a linguist or a child is exposed to certain evidence of ergativity properties in a given language, what else might he or she conclude? Of the dimensions along which languages showing ergativity properties diverge, let me highlight three:

(2) a. *Variation by ergativity properties*
Which ergativity properties are at play?

b. *Variation by grammatical manifestation of ergativity*
What type of grammatical generalizations reflect ergativity properties?

c. *Variation by scope of ergative patterns*
How generalized or restricted are the ergative patterns?

We will first consider the logical relationships among the ergativity properties, and then consider the scale of variation in their grammatical manifestations and the scope of the patterns they define. Against this varied domain we will then consider a set of unifying correlations, drawing together properties, manifestations and scopes of ergative patterns.

2.1. The relationship among the ergativity properties

What is the relationship among the ergativity properties? The ergative property (1a) and the absolutive property (1b) are logically independent of one another, and indeed, natural languages occupy each place in the possibility space these two properties define. If we consider ergativity properties as seen in morphological case-marking, the following languages represent the four possibilities:

(3) Tab. 20.1: Interactions among (1a) and (1b) (absent [1c])

	Ergative property: yes	Ergative property: no
Absolutive property: yes	Warlpiri	Chinese
Absolutive property: no	Nez Perce	Latin

Warlpiri is a language showing ergativity properties (1a) and (1b). Subjects are marked with a distinct case in transitive clauses – the ergative – while objects appear in a bare form – the "absolutive" – also characteristic of intransitive subjects.

(4) a. *ngarrka-ngku ka wawirri panti-rni* [Warlpiri]
man-ERG AUX kangaroo spear-NPST
'The man is spearing the kangaroo.'

b. *kurdu ka wanka-mi*
child AUX speak-NPST
'The child is speaking.'

c. *kurdu kapi wanti-mi*
child AUX fall-NPST
'The child will fall.'

These data come from Hale (1983), who provides (4b) and (4c) as evidence that Warlpiri makes no systematic division among intransitives. Warlpiri, that is, does not display property (1c). Parallel facts are found in a host of unrelated and geographically diverse languages, including Inuit languages such as West Greenlandic (Bittner 1994) and Inuktitut (Johns 1992), Austronesian languages such as Niuean (Seiter 1980), Australian languages such as Dyirbal (Dixon 1972), Amazonian languages such as Shipibo (Valenzuela 2010), West Nilotic languages Päri and Shilluk (König 2008: ch 3) as well as Eastern Basque (Aldai 2009). Languages showing this combination of ergativity properties are called *ergative/absolutive*.

Nez Perce is a language showing the ergative property (1a) but not the absolutive property (1b). Subjects are marked with a special case in transitive clauses (again glossed ERGATIVE), but intransitive subjects and transitive objects also differ for case purposes. The former appears in a bare form (nominative); the latter takes a distinct case marker (accusative).

(5) a. *haacwal-nim pee-p-Ø-e cu'yeem-ne* [Nez Perce]
boy-ERG 3SBJ-eat-P.ASP-REM.PST fish-ACC
'The boy ate the fish.'

b. *haacwal hi-x̂eeleewi-Ø-ye*
boy.NOM 3SBJ-work-P.ASP-REM.PST
'The boy worked.'

c. *haacwal hi-peeleey-n-e*
boy.NOM 3SBJ-get.lost-P.ASP-REM.PST
'The boy got lost.'

As in Warlpiri, there is no systematic divide among intransitive subjects in Nez Perce. All intransitive subjects appear in the unmarked (nominative) form. Other languages showing this type of pattern include Wangkumara and Pitta-Pitta in Australia (Blake 1987: 22, 59) and Cashinawa in Peru (Montag 1981: 599). Languages showing this type of pattern are sometimes called *three-way ergative* or *tripartite* (Dixon 1994: 39).

This typology of (1a) and (1b) is rounded out by two additional types of languages. Chinese is a language with no morphological case-marking on subjects or objects. The absence of a distinctive mark is (trivially) in common between intransitive subjects and transitive objects, as in Warlpiri, conforming to (1b); but there is no mark on transitive subjects, either, failing (1a). Latin is a language that marks subjects distinct from objects regardless of transitivity, failing both (1a) and (1b). These examples remind us that the ergative property, (1a), and the absolutive property, (1b), are entirely logically distinct.

The relationship of the argument-structural property, (1c), to the ergative property (1a) and the absolutive property (1b) is slightly more complex. The absence of argument-structural effects is compatible with any combination of (1a) and (1b); the four languages just considered all fail to show argument-structural effects in case-marking. On the other hand, the presence of argument-structural ergativity, as applied to particular areas of linguistic generalization (e.g., morphological case), is not compatible with either the ergative property or the absolutive property on a strict interpretation. A system characterized by the ergative property (1a) and/or the absolutive property (1b) treats intransitive subjects as a class, whereas a system characterized by the argument-structural property (1c) bifurcates intransitive subjects. At the same time, whenever argument-structural ergativity obtains, there will necessarily be some intransitive subjects (i.e. subjects of unaccusatives) which behave unlike subjects of transitives, giving a partial case of the ergative property (1a). It can be helpful to think of loose versions of the ergative property (1a) and the absolutive property (1b) as follows:

(6) (1a) (loose) Subjects of transitive clauses behave differently from some subjects of intransitive clauses for some grammatical generalization(s)

(1b) (loose) Objects of transitive clauses and subjects of some intransitive clauses behave identically for some grammatical generalization(s)

In contrast to the (1c)-loose (1a) relationship, the relationship between the argument structural property (1c) and the loose version of the absolutive property (1b) is more flexible. It may or may not be the case that some intransitive subjects behave like transitive objects.

(7) Tab. 20.2. Given (1c), interactions among (1a)-loose and (1b)-loose

	(1a)-loose yes	(1a)-loose no
(1b)-loose yes	Georgian	impossible by definition
(1b)-loose no	Hindi/Urdu	impossible by definition

In Georgian, transitive subjects in the aorist aspect are marked with a distinct case, called the ergative, while objects appear in a bare form. Harris (1981) calls this form the nominative.

(8) *glexma* *datesa* *simindi* [Georgian]
farmer.ERG he.sowed.it.II.I corn.NOM
'The farmer sowed corn.'
(Harris 1981: 147)

Harris shows that the marking of intransitive subjects in Georgian is sensitive to a distinction between unaccusative and unergative predicates. Subjects of unergative verbs mark the ergative case, like subjects of agentive transitives. Subjects of unaccusatives appear in the nominative case, like objects of agentive transitives. Loose versions of both the ergative property (1a) and the absolutive property (1b) are in effect.

(9) *Ninom* *daamtknara.* [Georgian]
Nino.ERG she.yawned.II.I
'Nino yawned.'
(Harris 1981: 40)

(10) *Rezo* *gamoizarda.*
Rezo.NOM he.grew.up.II.2
'Rezo grew up.'
(Harris 1982: 293)

The operative distinction in Georgian splits the class of intransitive subjects into two groups. This type of pattern is therefore sometimes called *split S* (Dixon 1979) or *split intransitive* (Merlan 1985); other names include Active-Inactive, following Sapir (1917), Agentive (Mithun 1991), and Semantically Aligned (Donohue and Wichmann 2008). Languages showing such patterns include Udi and Batsbi in the Caucasus (Harris 2010), Pomoan languages of California (Mithun 1991, O'Connor 1992, Deal and O'Connor 2011), and Western Basque (Aldai 2009).

A final combination of ergativity properties is found in Hindi/Urdu. This language marks transitive subjects with the ergative (in the perfective aspect), and marks certain objects with a distinct case-marker, here labeled accusative.

(11) *yasin-ne* *kʊtte-ko* *dek^h-a* [Hindi/Urdu]
Yassin.M.SG-ERG dog.M.SG-ACC see-PRF.M.SG
'Yassin saw the dog.'
(Butt and King 2004: ex 16b)

Intransitives show a split similar to Georgian. Subjects of unergatives may optionally mark the ergative case; unaccusative subjects must appear in a bare, nominative form.

(12) *yassin(-ne)* *k^{h}ãs-a* [Hindi/Urdu]
Yassin.M.SG-ERG cough-PRF.M.SG
'Yassin coughed.'
(Butt 2006: 147)

(13) *yassin* *gɪr-a*
Yassin.M.SG.NOM fall-PRF.M.SG
'Yassin fell.'
(Butt 2006: 115)

The optionality of ergative case in (12) presents two ways of approaching the Hindi/Urdu facts. Focusing on the version without the ergative case, we see no argument-structural ergative pattern; case-marking is simply 3-way, as in Nez Perce. Focusing on the version with the ergative case, the pattern is argument-structural, entailing a loose version of (1a). Unlike in Georgian, however, the case possibilities for unaccusative subjects and transitive objects remain distinct. The latter may appear in the accusative case; the former may not. A similar profile (also including merely optional ergative marking of unergative subjects) is found in Semelai, a Mon-Khmer language of the Malay Peninsula (Kruspe 2004).

2.2. The grammatical manifestation of ergativity

Where in the grammar do ergativity properties show up? The most intense study has concentrated on morphosyntactic properties of case and verbal agreement, as well as on more narrowly syntactic properties related to Ā-movement and control.

Agreement. Verbal agreement showing an ergative/absolutive pattern is found in Halkomelem, a Salish language. 3rd person subjects of transitives control a special verbal agreement suffix *əs*; subjects of intransitives and objects of transitives control no verbal agreement.

(14) a. *ni ʔíməš* [Halkomelem]
AUX walk
'He/she/it walked.'

b. *ni q'ʷə́l-ət-əs*
AUX bake-TR-3ERG
'He/she/it baked it.'

c. cf. *ni cən q'ʷə́l-ət*
AUX 1SG bake-TR
'I baked it.'
(Gerdts 1988: 47)

The inverse of this pattern is found in Tsez (Polinsky and Potsdam 2001) and a variety of Amazonian languages (Gildea and Castro Alves 2010): subjects of intransitives and objects of transitives control verbal agreement, whereas subjects of transitives do not. In Mayan languages, these patterns overlap (Larsen and Norman 1979): one form of verbal agreement (set B) is controlled by the intransitive subject and transitive object, whereas another is controlled only by the transitive subject (set A). The following examples show this type of agreement in K'ichee.

(15) a. *x-at-war-ik* [K'ichee]
COMPLETIVE-2sB-sleep-PHRASE.FINAL
'You slept.'

b. *x-at-u-ch'ay-oh*
COMPLETIVE-2sB-3sA-hit-PHRASE.FINAL
'He hit you.'

c. *x-∅-war-ik*
COMPLETIVE-3sB-sleep-PHRASE.FINAL
'He slept.'
(Larsen and Norman 1979: 347–348)

Verbal agreement also may reflect the argument-structural property, (1c), in parallel to the case facts in Georgian and Hindi/Urdu discussed above. Languages with this type of agreement include Karuk and Chimariko in California (Mithun 2008), Chol Mayan (Coon 2010a) and various dialects of Neo-Aramaic (Doron and Khan 2012).

Ā-movement. The case- and agreement-based patterns that we have now seen are morphosyntactic in nature. Other manifestations of ergativity properties occur in syntactic patterns, where they are sometimes discussed under the heading of *syntactic ergativity.* The most famous of these concerns Ā extraction, and ergativity properties (1a) and (1b). A variety of languages possess distinct relativization, focalization and/or interrogation strategies for intransitive subjects and transitive objects on one hand versus transitive subjects on the other. An example of this can be seen in Roviana, an Austronesian language. Roviana relative clauses featuring Ā-movement of intransitive subjects or transitive objects involve the same forms of verbal marking as seen in ordinary matrix clauses (Corston 1996).

(16) *Hierana sa tie* [$_{RC}$ *sapu kote taloa*] [Roviana]
this DEF man REL FUT leave
'This is the man who is going away.'

(17) *Hierana sa koreo* [$_{RC}$ *sapu tupa-i-a e Zone*]
this DEF boy REL punch-TR-3SG.OBJ ART John
'This is the boy that John punched.'

Those featuring Ā-movement of transitive subjects, on the other hand, require a specialized form of the verb.

(18) a. **Hierana sa tie* [$_{RC}$ *sapu tupa-i-u*] *Normal verb form
this DEF man REL punch-TR-1SG.OBJ
'This is the man who punched me.'

b. *Hierana sa tie* [$_{RC}$ *sapu tupa-qa rau*] ^{OK}Special verb form
this DEF man REL punch-1SG.NSUF I
'This is the man who punched me.'

Many other Austronesian languages show similar patterns (Aldridge 2004), as do Dyirbal (Dixon 1977), Halkomelem Salish (Gerdts 1988), Coast Tsimshian (Mulder 1994), Chukchi (Comrie 1979), Trumai (Guiradello-Damian 2010), Eskimo languages such as Kalaallisut (Bittner 1994), and Mayan languages such as Mam (England 1983), Jacaltec (Craig 1977) and Q'anjobal (Coon, Mateo Pedro, and Preminger 2012).

Control. An additional "syntactic" area in which ergativity properties have been observed is control. Languages plausibly showing ergativity properties this area are very rare, however, and their existence has been repeatedly called into doubt. For many years the only clear reported example of ergativity properties in control came from Dixon's work on Dyirbal (1994). In this language, according to the generalizations Dixon provides, properties (1a) and (1b) are implicated in the distribution of controlled PRO. PRO may serve as an intransitive subject, as in (19a), or as a transitive object, as in (19b), but not as a transitive subject.

(19) a. *yabu ŋuma-ŋgu giga-n* [*PRO banaga-ygu*] [Dyirbal]
mother.ABS father-ERG tell.to.do-NFUT [PRO return-PURP]
'Father told mother$_i$ PRO$_i$ to return.'

b. *yabu ŋuma-ŋgu giga-n* [*gubi-ŋgu mawa-li PRO*]
mother.ABS father-ERG tell.to.do-NFUT [doctor-ERG examine-PURP PRO]
'Father told mother$_i$ the doctor to examine PRO$_i$.'

Dixon also reports that ergativity properties are manifested in the class of possible controllers of PRO in the main clause (1994: 136). The controller must be intransitive subject or transitive object; it cannot be transitive subject.

Subsequent work on Austronesian has augmented the picture from Dyirbal. Aldridge (2004) reports that for Seediq, property (1a) plays a role without property (1b): only intransitive subjects, not transitive subjects or transitive objects, may be controlled PRO. (Transitivity here must be understood formally, rather than notionally.)

(20) a. *M-n-osa [PRO m-ari patis taihoku] ka Ape.* [Seediq]
INTR-PRF-go [PRO INTR-buy book Taipei] ABS Ape
'Ape went to buy books in Taipei.'

b. **M-n-osa [PRO burig-un taihoku ka patis] ka Ape.*
INTR-PRF-go [PRO buy-TR Taipei ABS book] ABS Ape
'Ape went to buy books in Taipei.'

For Sama Southern, Trick (2006) reports a pattern of control showing both property (1a) and (1b), just as in Dyirbal. In this language, both intransitive subjects and transitive objects may be controlled PRO, but transitive subjects may not be.

(21) a. *Tuli akú* [Sama Southern]
sleep 1SG.ABS
'I will sleep.'

b. *ka-bilahi-an-ku [tuli PRO]*
INV-want-P-1SG.ERG [sleep PRO]
'I want PRO to sleep.'

(22) a. *ni-lengan-an akú leh si Ben* [Sama Southern]
AGR-call-P 1SG.ABS ERG PM Ben
'Ben will call me.'

b. *ka-bilahi-an-ku [ni-lengan-an PRO leh si Ben]*
INV-want-P-1SG.ERG [AGR-call-P PRO ERG PM Ben]
'I want Ben to call PRO.'

c. **ka-bilahi-an si Ben [ni-lingan-an akú PRO]*
INV-want-P PM Ben [AGR-call-P 1SG.ABS PRO]
'Ben wants PRO to call me.'

This type of fact will play a crucial role in the discussion in section 3.2.

2.3. The scope of ergative patterns

To what degree do particular "ergative languages" show ergative properties? Moravcsik (1978) observes that every language that shows ergativity properties shows them to a limited degree. There are no languages where *all* grammatical generalizations distinguish transitive from intransitive subject; group intransitive subject and transitive object together; or distinguish among subjects of unaccusative and unergative intransitives. This means that every language showing ergativity properties has what is sometimes called an *ergative split*, or a division among domains in the grammar which do and do not show ergative behaviors.

The most famous such split concerns a distinction between languages which show ergativity properties only in morphological domains such as case-marking and agreement versus those which show ergativity properties in syntactic domains such as control and

Ā extraction. Based on the data we have seen above, Roviana and Sama Southern can be classified as "syntactically ergative". Languages like Warlpiri have been held up as clear exemplars of the contrasting "morphologically ergative" type (Bittner and Hale 1996a). Only subjects may be controlled PRO in this language, regardless of transitivity (Legate 2002).

(23) *Ngana$_j$-kurra-npa Jakamarra-kurlangu maliki$_i$ nya-ngu* [*PRO$_i$ t$_j$* [Warlpiri]
who-OBJC-2SG Jakamarra-POSS dog see-PST [
paji-rninja-kurra]?
bite-INF-OBJC]
a. 'Who did you see Jakamarra's dog$_i$ PRO$_i$ biting t_{who}?'
b. * 'Who did you see Jakamarra's dog$_i$ t_{who} biting PRO$_i$?'

(24) *Ngarrka-ngku$_i$ ka karli jarnti-rni, PRO$_i$ wangka-nja-karra-rlu*
man-ERG PRS boomerang trim-NPST, PRO speak-INF-SUBJC-ERG
'The man is trimming a boomerang while speaking.'
(Legate 2002: 126)

While both Warlpiri and Sama Southern have ergative/absolutive case-systems, only Sama Southern also shows the ergative and absolutive properties in control. Thus the scope of ergative patterns is broader in Sama Southern than it is in Warlpiri. Distinctions of this type will play a central role throughout sections 3 and 4 below.

Additional limitations on the scope of ergative patterns are found in reflection of two other types of distinctions, which, for reasons of space, will play less of a role in the theoretical survey to follow. First, many languages show a division in ergativity properties among different classes of nominals. It is quite common, for instance, to find first and second person pronouns lacking ergative case or agreement forms, in contrast to other nouns. This type of pattern is seen in Nez Perce, a language with a three-way case system for non-pronominals.

(25) a. ***'iin*** *lilooy-ca-Ø* [Nez Perce]
1SG.NOM be.happy-IPFV-PRS
'I'm happy.'

b. ***'iin*** *cuy'eem-ne 'aa-p-sa-qa*
1SG.NOM fish-ACC 3OBJ-eat-IPFV-REC.PST
'I was eating the fish.'

c. *ciq'aamqal-m hi-ke'nip-Ø-e* ***'iin-e***
dog-ERG 3SBJ-bite-P-REM.PST 1SG-ACC
'The dog bit me.'

Whereas other nominals (including third person pronominals) show distinct ergative, nominative and accusative case forms, first and second person pronouns in this language show only nominative and accusative forms. Silverstein (1976) observes that the reverse of this type of pattern – pronouns, but not common nouns, showing an ergative marking – is not attested. Rather, he posits, types of nominals (pronouns, proper names, animate nouns, etc) are universally organized into an implicational hierarchy with respect to ergative versus nominative case marking. If any nominals lack an ergative form, it will be pronouns; if any nominals possess an ergative form, it will be inanimate nouns. This type of phenomenon is further studied in recent work by Alexiadou and Anagnostopoulou (2006), Merchant (2006), Wiltschko (2006) and Coon and Preminger (2012).

Second, in many languages the distribution of ergative patterns is limited by factors related to clausal properties, in particular viewpoint aspect. This type of pattern is found for instance in Chol Mayan (Coon 2010a). Agreement in this language shows the argument-structural property (1c), but only in the perfective aspect. In non-perfective aspects, for instance the progressive, the same agreement markers are used, but their behavior no longer shows the ergativity properties. All subjects agree using one set of markers (set A), and all objects agree using the other (set B).

(26) Perfective: Ergative

a. *Tyi i-jats'-ä-yoñ* [Chol]
PFV A3-hit-TR-B1
'She hit me.'

b. *Tyi majl-i-yoñ*
PFV go-INTR-B1
'I went.'

(27) Progressive: Non-ergative

a. *Choñkol i-jats'-oñ* [Chol]
PROG A3-hit-B1
'She's hitting me.'

b. *Choñkol i-majl-el*
PROG A3-go-NMLZ
'She's going.'

This type of pattern again reveals an asymmetry which appears to be universal. Where a language shows a split pattern in correlation with viewpoint aspect, it is always the perfective aspect, rather than the imperfective, which shows ergativity properties (Dixon 1994). Recent studies of this type of ergative split may be found in the work of Laka (2006), Ura (2006), Reilly (2007), Salanova (2007), Müller (2009) and Coon (2010b, 2012).

2.4. Six potential ergative universals

The wide variation we have just seen is balanced by a number of potentially universal generalizations. Some of these have already come up in discussion of the relationships among ergativity properties and of ergative splits. Further generalizations concern relations between manifestations of ergativity properties, and relations between ergativity properties and other aspects of particular grammars. Six of these are mentioned below.

The discovery of universals related to ergativity properties is a central project for ergativity investigators, and much attention has focused on particular proposed universals from both empirical and theoretical points of view. Some of this work has brought forward what are apparently counterexamples to the generalizations below. The proper treatment of these cases is clearly of the utmost importance to grammatical theories which take the various generalizations as a starting place. For this reason, I have reproduced or referenced data claimed to be problematic in the appropriate places as an indication of the current state of knowledge on these matters.

1. Syntactic ergativity implies morphological ergativity. The languages that show ergativity properties in Ā-movement or control are all languages which show ergativity properties morphologically – in case and/or agreement. This generalization comes from Dixon (1994: 172).

The only potential counterexample of which I am aware comes from Bajau, the issue of which is raised by Donohue and Brown (1999). The status of Bajau as a language with syntactic but not morphological ergativity is deserving of close scrutiny, though, on the basis of its pronominal paradigm: in a language claimed to lack any morphological manifestations of ergativity, it is telling that the form of pronouns in this language suggests a case-system organized on an ergative/absolutive basis. As Miller (2007) shows, intransitive subjects appear in "Set II" forms, as do objects in transitive clauses with certain verbal morphology. Subjects in such sentences appear in a distinct, "Set I" form.

(28) a. *Ai pungkaw iyo* [Bajau]
PRF wake.up 3SG.II
'(S)he has awakened/gotten up.'

b. *Boi 0-boo=ku iyo pitu.*
COMPL UV-bring=1S.I 3SG.II to.here
'I brought him/her here.'

If clauses like (28b) are indeed transitive (a question made especially difficult by the voice system of the language), then Bajau is not a language that lacks morphological manifestations of ergativity properties. It is rather a language with both morphological manifestations (in case) and syntactic manifestations (in relativization). The counterexample to Dixon's generalization is then merely apparent.

As we will see in more depth in section 4, Dixon's generalization is part of a larger implicational generalization which divides syntactic ergativity into two types. Languages like Dyirbal show ergativity in both control and Ā-movement. Languages like West Greenlandic show ergativity in Ā-movement but not control. There are no languages where ergativity properties are relevant for control but not for Ā-movement. The implicational hierarchy is thus

(29) Ergativity in control > Ergativity in Ā-movement > Ergativity in case/agreement

where the phenomena to the left entail phenomena to the right.

2. In languages showing ergativity in syntactic patterns, the pattern seen in syntax is ergative/absolutive – not just ergative (showing [1a] but not [1b]), and not argument-structural (1c). Austronesian languages showing syntactic ergativity are of the classic ergative/absolutive morphological type, contrasting transitive subject with intransitive subject/transitive object. It is this pattern which shows up in control (e.g. in Sama South-

ern) and in Ā extraction: transitive subjects behave one way, and intransitive subjects and transitive objects behave another way. The Mayan family contains both languages showing syntactic ergativity (e.g. Mam, Kaqchikel, Q'anjob'al) and languages showing argument-structural ergativity (e.g. Chol), but the two patterns do not seem to overlap. There are not, for instance, languages in which only unaccusative subjects may be Ā extracted with normal verbal morphology (in which case Ā extraction would show an argument-structural ergativity property); nor are there languages in which intransitive subjects, but neither transitive subjects nor transitive objects, may be Ā extracted with normal verbal morphology (in which case Ā extraction would show the ergative property [1a] but not the absolutive property [1b]). To my knowledge, this generalization has not been noted in previous work.

The only potential exception of which I am aware concerns languages like Seediq, discussed above in connection with control. Aldridge (2004) reports that controlled clauses in Seediq must be formally intransitive. It is as a byproduct of this transitivity restriction that the distribution of PRO in Seediq shows the ergative property (1a); absolutive property (1b), however, is not involved. I am not aware of any potential exceptions to the generalization from syntactic ergativity in Ā extraction.

It is especially interesting that this generalization should hold given that syntactically ergative patterns do crop up in languages which are not strictly ergative/absolutive on a morphological level. Dyirbal, for instance, is argued by Legate (2012) to show a (partially covert) three-way case system of the Nez Perce type. Nevertheless it appears that control and Ā extraction treat intransitive subject and transitive object as a natural class in this language, even where morphology does not.

3. Ergative case is never unmarked. When verbal agreement shows ergativity properties (1a) and (1b), either transitive subject (ergative) or intransitive subject/transitive object (absolutive) may be morphologically marked. Dixon (1994) observes that the same freedom does not hold in the domain of case-marking. While there are many languages with a null or unmarked absolutive morphological case, there are no languages with unmarked ergative morphological case.

The Nias language of Indonesia provides a potential counterexample, as Donohue and Brown (1999) point out. In Nias, absolutive case is marked by an initial mutation. (The character of this morphology is discussed by Anderson et al. 2006.) There is no morphological marking of transitive subjects, however.

(30) a. *Abe'e sibai g-ehomo n-omo s=e-bua* [Nias]
STAT.strong INTENS MUT-pillar MUT-house REL=STAT-big
'The pillars of the big house are very strong.'
(Anderson et al. 2006)

b. *I-a m-bavi ama Gumi*
3SG.REALIS-eat MUT-pig father Gumi
'Ama Gumi is eating/eats pork.'
(Donohue and Brown 1999)

Thus the subject of (30a) and the object of (30b) are marked in the same way, in opposition to the subject of (30b), yielding an ergative/absolutive system. However, the subject of (30b) – the argument expected to show the ergative case – is distinguished not by any special marking, but by the absence of the initial mutation marking the absolutive.

4. All ergative languages are verb-peripheral, or have free word order. This generalization was perhaps first noticed by Trask (1979) and subsequently popularized by Mahajan (1994, 1997), after whom it is sometimes called. There are certain well-known exceptions. Mahajan (1997) observes that languages like Kashmiri, which show V2 patterns, show ergativity in case-marking despite a preponderance of SVO clauses. Further counterexamples come from languages like Shilluk (West Nilotic), which has basic OVS and SV patterns without a clear case for Germanic-style V2:

(31) a. *byɛ́l á-'rākk*[!] *yī ɲān d̪ájò* [Shilluk]
grain.PL PST.EVID-grind.TR.REP ERG person female
'The woman ground the durra grain.'

b. *māc á-dùŋ áwʌ̄ʌ̄*
fire PST.E-smoke.INTR yesterday
'The fire smoked yesterday.'
(Miller and Gilley 2001: 36–37)

Survey data from Comrie (2008) suggests that some generalization along the Trask/Mahajan line nevertheless holds at least as a statistical trend. Further work is needed to ascertain whether word order correlates with an particular subset of ergativity properties, or particular grammatical manifestations thereof. It remains to be shown, for instance, whether languages showing both (1a) and (1b) are especially likely to obey this generalization, and what the facts are like for languages showing property (1c).

5. Manifestations of ergativity properties never treat derived subjects like basic transitive subjects. This generalization comes from Marantz (1991), a work which focuses primarily on languages showing ergativity property (1c). Marantz's generalization has nevertheless inspired a literature dealing primarily with languages which show ergative/absolutive (1a)/(1b) patterns, e.g. Legate (2008), and so bears discussion in relation to all three properties.

Let us first consider unaccusative subjects, as a prime instance of subjects that are derived. In the simplest cases, the generalization follows by definition. Ergativity property (1c) is manifested where unaccusative subjects are treated unlike transitive and unergative subjects; a process that treated the various subjects the same way would simply not show ergativity property (1c). Ergativity properties (1a) and (1b) call for intransitive subjects to pattern together in a way distinct from transitive subjects, ensuring that the pattern follows in this case, as well.

Things are more interesting when we consider unaccusative predicates made transitive in some way, for instance by addition of an applicative. An apparent counterexample in this domain comes from Shipibo, as Baker (to appear) observes. When an applicative is added to an unaccusative Shipibo verb, the subject of the unaccusative verb obligatorily marks the ergative case.

(32) a. *Kokoti-ra joshin-ke* [Shipibo]
fruit-PRT ripen-PRF
'The fruit ripened.'

b. *Bimi-n-ra Rosa joshin-xon-ke.*
fruit-ERG-PRT Rosa ripen-APPL-PRF
'The fruit ripened for Rosa.'
(Baker to appear)

If the subject of (32b) is indeed a derived subject, the presence of ergative here counter-exemplifies Marantz's generalization.

Another potential test comes from passive subjects, in particular passive subjects of ditransitive verbs. Such subjects – for instance *we* in the English example below – are derived subjects; they do not originate as external arguments. At the same time, there is also a natural sense in which they are subjects of verbs which remain transitive (albeit with transitivity reduced by comparison to the active ditransitive form).

(33) *We were given* t *this book.*

Manifestations of ergativity properties do not classify such subjects with basic transitive subjects. In Nez Perce, for instance, ditransitive constructions are expressed via double object constructions, as in English, but the passives of such constructions feature no ergative marking:

(34) a. *haama-pim cickan pee-'ni-se-ne ki-nye* [Nez Perce]
man-ERG blanket.NOM 3/3-give-IPFV-REM.PST this-ACC
'aayat-ona
woman-ACC
'The man was giving this woman a blanket.'

b. *kii 'aayat hii-wes 'in-yiin cickan*
this.NOM woman.NOM 3SBJ-be.PRS give-PASS blanket.NOM
'This woman was given a blanket (lit. is blanket-given).'

I am not aware of any language showing a passive like (34b) but with ergative marking on the (derived) subject.

Other types of derived subjects – in particular, subjects of raising verbs – have engendered more controversy. These are discussed in section 3.4.

6. If ergativity properties are manifested in verbal agreement, either (i) there is no morphological case-marking, or (ii) case-marking also shows ergativity properties. There is an asymmetry in the scope of ergativity properties in agreement and in case. Languages like Warlpiri show ergative/absolutive patterns in case-marking, but not in verbal agreement. All subjects agree in the same way in this language, e.g. both nominative subject *ngaju* 'I' and its ergative counterpart *ngaju-rlu* control agreement suffix *-rna*:

(35) a. *Ngaju ka-**rna** wangka-mi* [Warlpiri]
I PRS-1SBJ speak-NPST
'I am speaking.'

b. *Ngaju-rlu ka-**rna**-ngku nyuntu nya-nyi*
I-ERG PRS-1SBJ-2OBJ you see-NPST
'I see you.'
(Hale 1983: 18)

Languages like Nez Perce show property (1a) alone in case-marking, but not in verbal agreement. All subjects agree in the same way in this language, too:

(36) a. *haacwal **hi**-x̂eeleewi-Ø-ye* [Nez Perce]
boy.NOM 3SBJ-work-P.ASP-REM.PST
'The boy worked.'

b. *ciq'aamqal-m **hi**-ke'nip-Ø-e 'iin-e*
dog-ERG 3SBJ-bite-P.ASP-REM.PST 1SG-ACC
'The dog bit me.'

Anderson (1977) generalizes that there are no languages showing the reverse pattern: ergativity properties in verbal agreement but not in morphological case (where there is a morphological case system to speak of).

Exceptions to this generalization from the Indo-Aryan family are discussed by Patel (2007). In Kutchi Gujarati past perfectives, verbal agreement is on an ergative/absolutive basis: only intransitive subjects and transitive objects agree. Case-marking, however, treats all subjects identically (leaving them unmarked), and singles out objects of transitive clauses (marking them accusative).

(37) a. *Reena aav-i* [Kutchi Gujarati]
Reena.NOM came-F.SG
'Reena came.'

b. *Reena chokra-ne mar-ya*
Reena.NOM boys-ACC hit-PFV.M/N.PL
'Reena hit the boys.'
(Patel 2007)

An additional reported exception is found in connection with pronouns only. As Gildea and Castro Alves (2010) discuss, pronouns in the Jê language Canela show a nominative-accusative case pattern; other nominals in Canela are unmarked. Despite this, verbal agreement in Canela is on an absolutive basis (just as in Kutchi Gujarati), targeting intransitive subjects and transitive objects.

(38) a. *wa ha i-wrɨk narɛ* [Canela]
1 IRR 1-descend.NF NEG
'I will not descend.'

b. *wa ha iʔ-pɨr na*
1 IRR 3-grab.NF NEG
'I will not grab it (e.g., the knife).'

If the prefixes *i-* and *iʔ-* indeed represent agreement (and not weak pronominals, as in Salanova's 2007 study of related language Mẽbengokre), Canela is an additional example of a language showing an ergative/absolutive agreement system, but nominative-accusative behavior in case-marking. It is striking that such patterns, while extremely rare, are nevertheless apparently found in languages widely separated in genetic and geographical terms.

3. Theories of ergativity in case and its relatives

Moreso than any other manifestation of ergativity, syntacticians concerned with ergative languages have focused on its manifestation in case-marking, agreement and control, a group of phenomena generally held to be closely related. The ideal theory in this domain must face a trio of challenging desiderata. First, it must account for the differences between ergative languages and non-ergative ones. Second, it must allow for differences among ergative languages. Third, it must provide a natural account of universal constraints, to the extent these hold, related to ergativity in case and its relatives. These potentially include the implication from ergativity in agreement to ergativity in case-marking (should there be adequate treatment available for counterexamples such as Kutchi Gujarati) as well as the implication from ergativity in control to ergativity in case and/or agreement.

In this section I introduce a range of theories responding to ergativity in case and its relatives, sorted into three groups depending on the types of explanatory mechanisms posited. A first group makes use of strictly morphological mechanisms; a second, strictly syntactic mechanisms; and a third makes use of both. For reasons that will become clear, I will discuss the workings of the latter two types of proposals before returning to some critiques which potentially apply to both.

3.1 Morphology-based theories

The description of case in a particular language is traditionally a purely morphological description. Given the weight of morphological facts to be dealt with, various theorists have proposed to deal with case and related morphological phenomena in an autonomous morphological representation. As noted by Bobaljik (2008), these morphological representations are autonomous not in failing to make reference to syntax (which, as we will see, they consistently do), but in failing to effect representational changes which are visible to syntactic rules. Two theories sharing this characteristic will be highlighted here: the case theory of Marantz (1991), and the agreement theory of Bobaljik (2008).

3.1.1. Morphological case hierarchies

The morphological case theory proposed by Marantz (1991) is one of a family of approaches, morphological and syntactic, making use of the idea of *case dependency* (e.g.

Yip, Maling, and Jackendoff 1987; Bittner and Hale 1996a, b; Baker and Vinokurova 2010; Baker to appear). Marantz proposes that case assignment falls under the purview of a postsyntactic morphological component, the input to which is syntactic structure. Four types of morphological case are identified, which are realized according to a disjunctive hierarchy:

(39) Marantz's case hierarchy
  a. Lexically governed case
  b. Dependent case (accusative and ergative)
  c. Unmarked case (environment sensitive)
  d. Default case

Lexically governed case covers datives and related cases assigned in a way connected to thematic information. In a given clause, if the conditions are met for a lexically governed case, the case algorithm assigns this case first. Subsequently, the algorithm checks whether the conditions are met for dependent case. The relevant condition considers not just a single DP, but the set of DPs present in a given clause: dependent case is assigned to a DP when *a distinct nominal without lexical case is present.* One nominal is distinct from another if the two are not part of a chain. Languages differ in whether the dependent case is assigned "up", to the subject, or "down", to the object, or (in an extension of what Marantz proposes) both. Finally, unmarked and default cases are realized on nominals not already covered by prior parts of the algorithm.

Several types of case systems can be handled in this way. In English, which lacks lexically governed cases, dependent case is assigned to the object when there is another nominal in the clause – the subject. The subject subsequently receives unmarked case. This produces a nominative/accusative case system. An analysis along these lines has been defended for Sakha by Baker and Vinokurova (2010) and Levin and Preminger (to appear). A language like Warlpiri assigns dependent ergative to its subject when there is another nominal in the clause – the object. After dependent case is assigned to the subject, unmarked case is available to the object. This produces an ergative/absolutive case system. This type of analysis has been defended for Shipibo by Baker (to appear). In Nez Perce, we could plausibly claim that dependent case is assigned both upward to the subject (which depends on the object) and downward to the object (which depends on the subject). Subsequently there remains no nominal in need of realization in an unmarked case. This produces a three-way case system.

This analysis makes a clear prediction for ergative case in clauses where a lexical case is assigned. In a clause with only two distinct DPs, if one of those DPs receives lexical case, the other may not receive a dependent case such as ergative; the conditions for dependent case assignment are not met. While this prediction is often borne out, there are certain well-known problems. One is Warlpiri, which allows ERG-ABS (40), ABS-DAT (41) and crucially also ERG-DAT (42) case arrays (Nash 1980; Simpson 1991).

(40) *ngajulu-rlu ka-rna nya-nyi kurdu* [Warlpiri]
  1SG-ERG PRS-3SBJ see-NPST child.ABS
  'I see the child.'
  (Simpson 1991: 100)

(41) *Ngarrka ka-rla marlu-ku yura-ka-nyi, marna nga-rninja-kurr-ku*
man.ABS PRS-3DAT kangaroo-DAT stalk-NPST grass.ABS eat-INF-OBJC.-DAT
'The man is stalking the kangaroo, (while it is) eating grass.'
(Simpson 1991: 319)

(42) *ngarrka-ngku ka-rla karli-ki warri-rni*
man-ERG PRS-3SG.DAT boomerang-DAT look.for-NPST
'A man is looking for a boomerang.'
(Hale 1982: 248)

Coverage of the Warlpiri facts seems to require that certain lexically case-marked nominals (e.g. the dative in [42]) trigger dependent case for the subject, whereas others do not. In Warlpiri, this is in spite of the fact that the dative arguments in (41) and in (42) behave similarly for a variety of objecthood tests (Simpson 1991). It is notable that this problem does not arise in all ergative languages. It is possible, therefore, that the difference between a language like Warlpiri, which allows ERG to co-exist with a case other than absolutive, and a language like Greenlandic, which does not, will constitute an important parameter dividing one class of ergative languages from another.

3.1.2. Morphological agreement hierarchies

The theory proposed by Bobaljik (2008) extends Marantz's case theory to the domain of agreement. Bobaljik proposes that control of agreement is determined by the following principle:

(43) The controller of agreement on the finite verbal complex (Infl + V) is the highest accessible NP in the domain of Infl + V.

Accessibility in turn is crucially defined in terms of morphological cases, which can be classified into unmarked, dependent and lexical/oblique groups (following Marantz). Building from Moravcsik (1974)'s work on implicational universals in agreement systems, Bobaljik proposes an implicational relationship among case types for accessibility to agreement.

(44) Unmarked < Dependent < Lexical/Oblique

In a particular language, if any of the classes in (44) is accessible to agreement, so too will be all classes to its left. Thus in some languages, only unmarked nominals are accessible; in others both unmarked and dependent nominals are accessible; but in no language are dependent nominals accessible whereas unmarked ones are not.

This theory provides a natural analysis of two types of agreement systems important in connection with ergativity. In one type, only unmarked DPs are accessible to agreement. In a language with ergative case-marking, ergative DPs will bear a dependent case, and thus agreement in a transitive clause will ignore the higher, ergative subject in favor of the lower, unmarked object. This leads to an absolutive pattern in agreement. A language plausibly analyzable in this way is Tsez.

(45) a. *ziya* *b-ik'i-s* [Tsez]
cow.III.ABS III-go-PST.EVID
'The cow left.'

b. *eniy-ā* *ziya* *b-išer-si*
mother-ERG cow.III.ABS III-feed-PST.EVID
'The mother fed the cow.'
(Polinsky and Potsdam 2001: 586)

In a second type of language, both unmarked and dependent-marked DPs will be accessible to agreement. In this scenario, control of agreement will be determined on the basis of structural height. Supposing ergative subject DPs occupy structural positions superior to those occupied by absolutive object DPs, the former rather than the latter will control agreement. This gives an analysis of languages showing a split in ergativity between case and agreement. Bobaljik proposes to analyze Nepali in this way. Transitive subjects are nominative (unmarked) in the imperfective in this language and ergative (dependent) in the perfective. In either situation, the subject and not the object controls agreement.

(46) a. *ma* *yas* *pasal-mā* *patrikā* *kin-ch-u.* [Nepali]
1SG.NOM DEM.OBL store-LOC newspaper.NOM buy-NPST-1SG
'I buy the newspaper in this store.'

b. *maile* *yas* *pasal-mā* *patrikā* *kin-ē*
1SG.ERG DEM.OBL store-LOC newspaper.NOM buy-PST.1SG
'I bought the newspaper in this store.'
(Bickel and Yādava 2000: 348)

A nominative pattern of agreement thus emerges in an ergative-case-marking language because both unmarked and dependent-marked nominals are equally accessible to agreement.

Because agreement rules operate on the output of case-marking rules on this theory, what is not expected are languages which show the reverse of the Nepali pattern: ergativity properties in agreement but nominative-accusative orientation in case-marking. This captures one of the univerals proposed above. The challenges to that universal from Kutchi Gujarati and Canela are therefore challenges to the Bobaljik proposal; these are each reportedly languages with a nominative-accusative case system but an absolutive agreement system. Challenging too are the agreement facts from languages like Halkomelem, which shows agreement only with ergative DPs, rather than absolutive ones. This pattern is not straightforwardly describable if agreement with ergative DPs can arise only in languages where unmarked DPs (such as intransitive subjects) may also control agreement.

For Halkomelem in particular, a potential way out is suggested by work by Wiltschko (2006). Wiltschko analyzes agreement in that language as relating to three distinct syntactic loci – C, I, and *v* – and analyzes ergative agreement in particular as relating to *v*. If we understand Bobaljik's proposal as strictly concerning agreement in I, Halkomelem is then no longer a counterexample. It remains to be seen how the agreement pattern of the language can be handled within the general outlines of the agreement-hierarchical view, once a distinction is recognized between agreement in I and agreement in *v*.

3.1.3. General discussion

The scope of the theories just reviewed is by necessity limited to ergativity behaviors in morphological domains. On each proposal, a constrained range of syntactic facts constitutes the input to a morphological algorithm. The algorithm determines case or agreement behaviors in morphology alone. What these theories by their nature do not do is handle syntactic patterns of ergativity. Other things being equal, this deficit does not speak against the mechanisms just discussed *qua* analyses of the morphological facts; separate principles could be responsible for ergativity in syntax.

It seems quite clear on a cross-linguistic basis that other things are not equal, however. Ergativity in syntactic patterns is only found in languages that show ergativity in morphological patterns as well. For both of the theories reviewed above, this generalization is unexpected. Morphological factors *ex hypothesi* do not influence syntactic rules, and therefore the mechanisms for morphological ergativity cannot by themselves be implicated in syntactic ergativity. There must, rather, be some aspect of the syntax of syntactically ergative languages which requires morphological case and/or agreement mechanisms to kick in. Further development of morphology-based theories is required to elucidate what this connection might be.

3.2. Syntax-based theories

A second group of theories addressing ergativity in case and its relatives seeks to capture these patterns via fully syntactic means. There are two families of approaches in this vein: one which treats ergative marking as reflective of an adpositional structure, and one which treats ergative as a syntactically active feature or feature combination, assigned based on structural relationships between nominals and particular heads.

3.2.1. Ergative as an adposition

In classic instances of an ergative/absolutive case pattern, the ergative subject is marked overtly whereas the transitive object and the intransitive subject remain unmarked. A number of authors have proposed to handle this asymmetry by treating the ergative nominal as structurally larger than the absolutive nominal. In the theory of Bittner and Hale (1996a, b), the additional structure is a KP; other authors proposing additional structure for the ergative have identified this structure as a PP. Notably, the PP analysis immediately makes for a similarity between ergative clauses and passives. Both are syntactic encodings of semantically transitive clauses which involve the realization of the external argument in a prepositional adjunct. Indeed passive clauses are a major source of ergative constructions diachronically (Dixon 1994).

The general outline of this view is lent plausibility by patterns in nominalizations. In languages like Greek, as Alexiadou (2001) shows, adpositional structures are required for transitive subjects only.

(47) a. *i katastrofi tis polis (apo tus Italus)*
the destruction the city.GEN by the Italians
'the destruction of the city by the Italians'

b. *i afiksi tu Jani*
the arrival the John.GEN
'the arrival of John'
(Alexiadou 2001)

This makes Greek nominalizations a particularly revealing example of an ergative pattern on the adpositional view. The transitive subject requires a PP structure, whereas other arguments do not.

Mahajan (1997) extends this type of analysis to ergative arguments in Hindi/Urdu, a language where adpositional status is harder to ascertain. He points out that the Hindi/ Urdu ergative marker is P-like in occurring outside of coordinated subjects – a fact that is handled straightforwardly if ergative marking sits above the DP level. Note that parallel facts obtain in Nez Perce.

(48) a. *Raam or siitaa-ne* [Hindi]
Ram and Sita-ERG
'Ram and Sita' (ergative)

b. *Matt kaa George-nim* [Nez Perce]
Matt and George-ERG
'Matt and George' (ergative)

On the strongest version of the adpositional analysis, one might expect this behavior to obtain for the ergative case-marker only. In this respect Nez Perce coordinations involving accusative case markers prove problematic. Here, too, the case-marker follows the entire coordination.

(49) *Matt kaa George-na* [Nez Perce]
Matt and George-ACC
'Matt and George' (accusative)

This complicates the assimilation of the Nez Perce pattern to the pattern of Greek nominalizations. If coordinations of this type provide a diagnostic for adpositions, then it is sometimes the case in ergative languages that all arguments, not just the ergative, are adpositional. If natural languages contain covert adpositions, such an analysis could in principle hold for a language like Hindi/Urdu, where objects may be unmarked. The ability of the adpositional analysis to account for the ways in which ergative is marked vis-à-vis other arguments thus seems to depend on a theory of covertness in adpositional structure.

An argument for the adpositional analysis from a rather different direction is provided by Stepanov (2004), who also draws evidence from Hindi/Urdu. In ergative constructions in Hindi/Urdu, agreement targets the object, rather than the ergative subject.

(50) *raam-ne roTii khaayii thii* [Hindi/Urdu]
Ram.M-ERG bread.F.ABS eat.PRF.F be.PST.F
'Ram had eaten bread.'

Assuming that this agreement reflects the contribution of a T head, the question arises as to why the higher, ergative subject should be skipped over in favor of the lower, unmarked object. Stepanov proposes that the minimality problem is only apparent: ergative subjects are PP adjuncts adjoined late in the derivation, after agreement between T and the object has taken place. English PP adjuncts fail to intervene in raising constructions in a similar way.

(51) *Mary$_i$ seems [to Sue]t$_i$ to be smart.*

As late-adjoined adjuncts, Stepanov proposes that ergative PPs cannot undergo cyclic syntactic rules. This provides an explanation for the absence of ergative on derived subjects, a proposed universal. The challenges to that universal from applicatives of Shipibo unaccusatives and from raising constructions (section 3.4) are therefore challenges to the Stepanov proposal. Further challenges come from languages where ergative subjects do in fact agree. These subjects would presumably need to be adjoined earlier in the derivation in order to be visible to agreement.

Some of these challenges are taken up by Markman and Grashchenkov (2012) in work on ergative agreement. These authors propose that ergative PPs may enter into agreement relationships with clausal heads just as ordinary DPs may (a view which entails that PPs are not always merged late in Stepanov's sense). The form of agreement

(52) a.
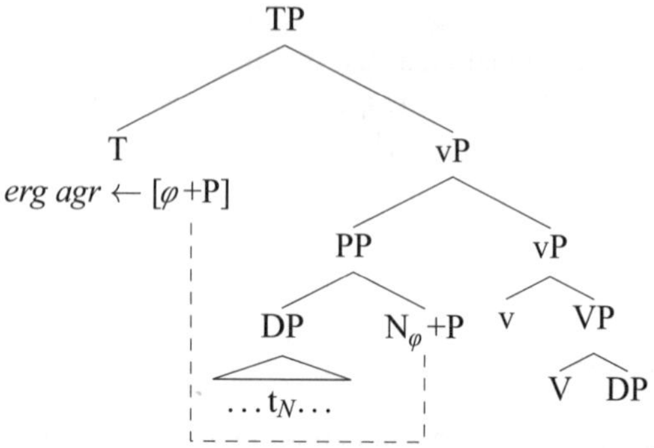

b.
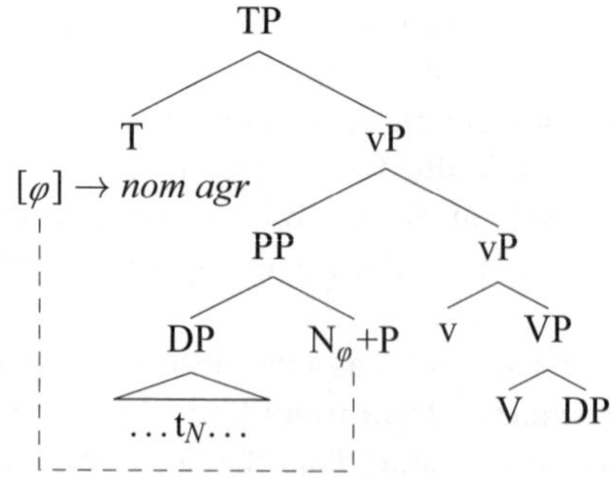

that results will depend on two factors: whether the noun head of the ergative DP incorporates into the ergative P, and whether special realizations are possible for agreement with PP elements. Ergative agreement, which we see for instance in Halkomelem, comes about when the head N of the ergative nominal incorporates into P, and T agrees with the N-P complex in both φ-features and P category, (52a). Nominative-accusative agreement surfaces in connection with ergative case when N incorporates into P, but agreement of the N-P complex with T reflects only φ-features, not P category, as in (52b). Markman and Grashchenkov propose this type of analysis for Warlpiri.

Finally, for languages in which N does not incorporate into ergative P, they propose that agreement with the ergative PP is simply not possible. This is the pattern that we see in Tsez, where only absolutives agree (45a)–(45b). Given that "ergative agreement" requires the presence of the ergative P on this view, we are close to an alternative explanation of the fact that ergative agreement systems are almost entirely absent from nominative-accusative case systems. To derive this effect, we will need a better understanding of covertness in ergative P heads, accusative case-marking, and the interaction between these two.

If the presence of a P head is the major distinguishing property of an ergative case system, ergative patterns in Ā-movement and control must also be able to take account of the P head's presence. Further exploration is required to probe whether the adpositional analysis lends itself to insightful approaches to these effects.

3.2.2. Ergative as a case

The remaining group of theories under the syntax-based umbrella treat ergative marking as realizing a feature assigned by a head. Contemporary work tends to identify the heads which are involved in case assignment as functional ones, and to connect the assignment of case to a nominal with a relationship, sometimes purely abstract, of agreement between the head and the nominal. Theories differ on the particulars of the heads they posit and the relationships that the posited heads enter into. An excellent summary of the different positions authors have taken in this domain through the end of the 1990s is provided by Johns (2000).

An important theme running through this literature is the connection between case assignment and movement. For languages like English, it is now generally assumed that the subject is both assigned case by T and moves to the specifier of the TP projection. The object, by contrast, is assigned case in situ by a functional head *v*. Parameterization of both pieces of this picture have been proposed in connection with morphological ergativity. Three positions can be discerned on what it is that makes ergative languages special:

1. Subjects and objects receive case ex situ from T.
2. Subjects and objects receive case in situ from *v*.
3. Subjects receive case in situ from *v*; objects receive case ex situ from T.

The latter two of these have received the lion's share of attention in recent work, and various authors have proposed that both are indeed correct, for distinct groups of languages. In this section, I present exemplars of all three theories individually, noting in particular their predictions for control. After a discussion of jointly morphology- and syntax-based theories in section 3.3, I return to discuss certain critiques of the shared innovation of theories 2 and 3, namely the mechanism of in-situ case assignment to the subject, in section 3.4.

3.2.3. Subject receives case ex situ, object receives case ex situ

Bok-Bennema (1991) proposes that ergative languages are special in failing to assign case in situ to the object. This means that the object must receive case from another case assigning head, presumably the one which is also involved in assigning case to the subject. In order to receive this case, Bok-Bennema and others propose that the object must undergo movement in ergative languages. A recent exemplar of this type of approach is Bobaljik and Branigan (2006). These authors propose that in Chukchi, both subject and object move to specifiers of a TP projection. Case assignment in the tree below is indicated with dotted lines.

(53) *əʔtvʔet jərʔen-nin mimɬ-e* [Chukchi]
boat.ABS fill-3SG/3SG water-ERG
'Water filled the boat.'

(54)

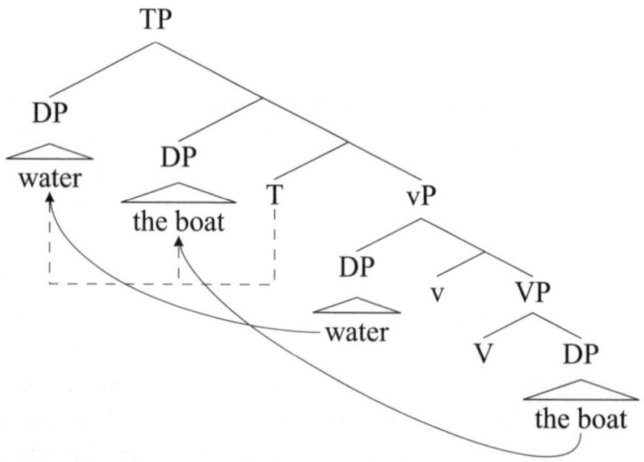

In support of this derivation, Bobaljik and Branigan note that verbal agreement takes port-manteau forms in Chukchi. The port-manteau forms, they propose, realize the features of the two nominals to which T has assigned case.

The derivation just sketched raises the question of how distinct cases can be provided for the subject and the object. Crucial for Bobaljik and Branigan is the order in which these nominals move to TP. The subject is the closest nominal to TP and is therefore, they propose, attracted to TP first. The object is subsequently moved and tucks in below the outer specifier occupied by the subject. Bobaljik and Branigan propose that this type of multiple case assignment by a single head is subject to a markedness constraint. It is always the nominal whose case is assigned first which receives the more marked case, where markedness is to be understood in at least largely morphological terms. Recall that ergative is nearly universally marked overtly when absolutive is also marked. The nominal whose case is assigned second receives the less marked case, which could be identified with nominative.

If the identification of absolutive with nominative is correct – both, on this proposal, would be unmarked cases assigned by T – predictions follow for the treatment of non-finite clauses. A loss of finiteness in TP is associated with the loss of nominative case. Indeed, it is absolutive nominals in opposition to ergative ones which are lost in Dyirbal in purposive control complements, as we saw above.

(55) *yabu* *ŋuma-ŋgu* *giga-n* [*PRO banaga-ygu*] [Dyirbal]
mother.ABS father-ERG tell.to.do-NFUT [PRO return-PURP]
'Father told mother$_i$ PRO$_i$ to return.'

(56) *yabu* *ŋuma-ŋgu* *giga-n* [*gubi-ŋgu* *mawa-li* *PRO*]
mother.ABS father-ERG tell.to.do-NFUT [doctor-ERG examine-PURP PRO]
'Father told mother$_i$ the doctor to examine PRO$_i$.'

Several aspects of this view limit its applicability beyond languages of the Dyirbal type, however. Languages in which absolutive nominals persist in non-finite environments will require a different treatment. Warlpiri has been discussed in this connection (Legate 2008); see for instance the persistence of absolutive DP *miyi* 'food' in the non-finite clause bracketed below.

(57) *Ngarrka-patu-rlu* *ka-lu-jana* *puluku* [Warlpiri]
man-PAUC-ERG PRS.IPFV-3PL.SBJ-3PL.OBJ bullock.ABS
turnu-ma-ni, [*karnta-patu-ku/karnta-patu-rlu* *miyi*
group-CAUS-NPST [woman-PAUC-DAT/woman-PAUC-ERG food.ABS
purra-nja-puru].
cook-INF-TEMP.C]
'The men are mustering cattle while the women are cooking the food.'

Additional distinct machinery will be required for languages in which the ergative is not the more marked of the cases assigned in transitive clauses. This is particularly relevant for languages showing property (1a) but not (1b), as in the Nez Perce facts shown in (5a)–(5c).

3.2.4. Subject receives case in situ, object receives case in situ

An alternative line of thinking locates the source of ergativity in case-assignment not to the object, but to the subject. This approach owes its impetus to Woolford (1997)'s proposal that ergative be treated as an inherent case, a case assigned in connection with θ-role assignment. Woolford proposed that languages showing ergativity in morphology have lexical entries for their verbs which connect the Agent role and the ergative case. This idea connects naturally with the proposals from Kratzer (1996) and others that Agent arguments are introduced by a special functional head *v* or Voice, and from Nash (1996) and Bittner and Hale (1996a, b) that ergative DPs are case-licensed in their base positions. Putting these pieces together, Legate (2002 et seq.) and Aldridge (2004 et seq.) propose that *v* assigns ergative case, in situ, to its specifier argument in ergative languages. It may additionally assign case to the object in such languages, meaning that both arguments are case-licensed in situ by the same head. Let us call the *v* head which assigns case features in this way "transitive *v*", or v_{TR}.

(58)

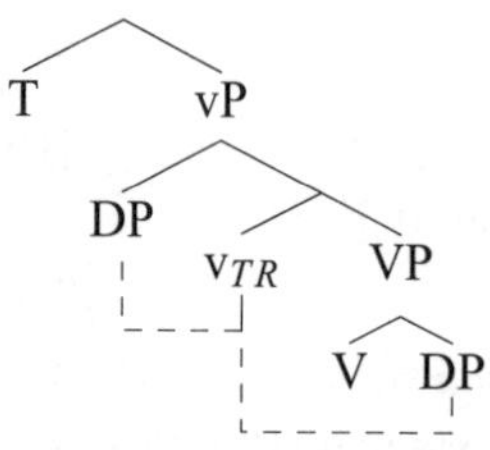

Whereas in a transitive clause *v* assigns case both to the subject and to the object, leaving T with no case-assignment duties, intransitive clauses feature either (i) no *v* head, or (ii) a *v* which assigns no case at all. In either situation, T steps in to assign case to the subject.

(58) a.

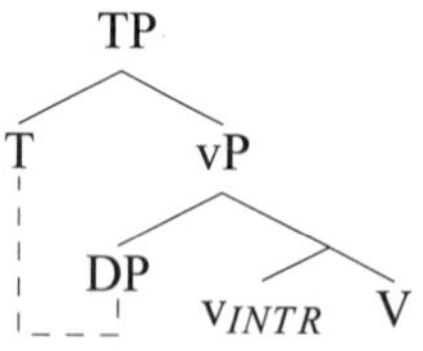

b.

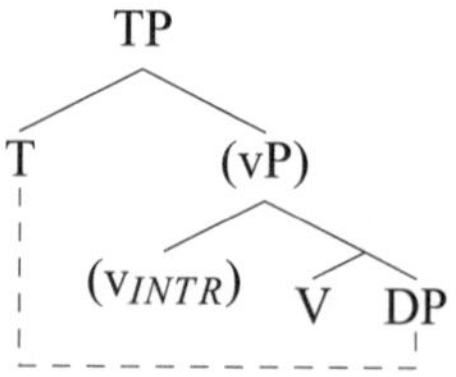

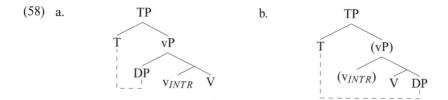

A central feature of this view is that objects and intransitive subjects, despite their similarity in surface case, receive their case features from different grammatical loci. Absolutive on objects reflects case assignment by *v* and not by T. It is therefore expected to persist in non-finite environments; this accounts for Warlpiri examples like (57). Absolutive on subjects reflects case assignment by T, however, and is thus expected to be impossible in non-finite environments. Legate (2008) shows that this is indeed so; a grammatical absolutive non-finite object in (57) contrasts with an ungrammatical absolutive non-finite subject in (60). This pattern is different from the Dyirbal pattern discussed above, and indeed both Aldridge and Legate propose a distinct analysis for languages of the Dyirbal type. This proposal is discussed in section 3.2.5.

(60) **Ngarrka-patu-rlu* *ka-lu-jana* *puluku* [Warlpiri]
man-PAUC-ERG PRS.IPFV-3PL.SBJ-3PL.OBJ bullock.ABS
turnu-ma-ni [*kurdu* *parnka-nja-rlarni*].
group-CAUS-NPST [**child.ABS** run-INF-OBV.C]
'The men are mustering cattle while the children are running.'

Legate (2008) discusses an extension to this view to cover languages like Georgian or Western Basque which show argument-structural ergativity. Whereas Warlpiri differs from English in the ability of v_{TR} to assign ergative case, Legate suggests that languages showing property (1c) are systems where all *v* heads, both in transitive and in unergative clauses, assign ergative to their specifiers (2008: 58). Three groups of languages may thus be discerned:

(61) *v* assigns ergative to its specifier
  a. Never: English
  b. Only when it also assigns case to the object: Warlpiri
  c. Always: Western Basque

The treatment of ergative as a case assigned to the subject in situ, along with in-situ mechanisms for object case, thus is able to account for a broad range of morphological patterns of ergativity, as well as a distinction between absolutive subjects and absolutive objects in non-finite contexts in Warlpiri.

3.2.5. Subject receives case in situ, object receives case ex situ

A final combination of subject and object case assignment mechanisms involves subject case assignment in situ in *v*P and ex situ case assignment to the object. This type of proposal is advanced by Ura (2001) as a general treatment of ergative case-marking; a close cousin of that view is proposed by Müller (2009). Similar ideas are advanced by Bittner and Hale (1996a), Aldridge (2004) and Legate (2008) specifically in light of manifestations of ergativity properties in syntax.

On Ura's proposal, *v* may only assign one case. As on the Marantz 1991 view, this assignment may look either up (to the subject) or down (to the object); ergative case is the name for what *v* assigns to the subject, and accusative case for what it assigns to the object. Assignment of *v*'s sole case to the subject leads to a lack of *v*P-internal case assignment possibilities for the object, as on the Bok-Bennema (1991) and Bobaljik and Branigan (2006) views. The object must therefore move close to the nominative-assigning T head. Ura proposes that the subject moves into an inner specifier of T, receiving no additional case, and that the object receives nominative case in an outer specifier of T.

A closely related analysis is proposed by Müller (2009). The subject receives case from *v* in an ergative language, and the object receives case from T, but the case-assignment relation between the object and T need not result in movement. Whether the *v* head assigns case to the subject (resulting in ergativity) or to the object (resulting in accusativity) comes down to the order in which the *v* head participates in Merge and Agree. If Agree comes first, that operation will take place as soon as *v* is merged. Its specifier has not yet been merged, and so *v* must agree with the internal argument. This results in *v* assigning case to the internal argument; this is the source of accusative. If *v* participates in Merge before Agree, the next step after Merge of *v* itself will be Merge of its specifier DP. When *v* subsequently participates in Agree, it agrees with its specifier DP, the external argument; this is the source of ergative. Müller proposes that *v* must agree with the external argument rather than the internal argument in this case because a specifier of a head is closer to that head than is material contained in the head's complement.

Ura's and Müller's proposals make predictions for non-finite clauses which parallel those of the Bobaljik and Branigan view. Since T is the source of absolutive case for

(62)

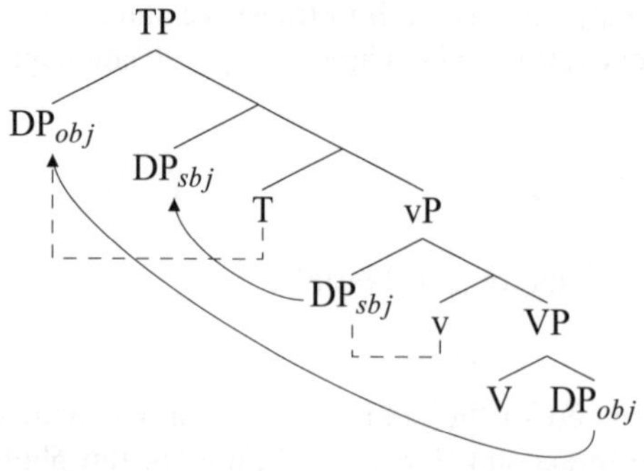

the object, absolutive case should be uniformly lost in non-finite environments. This prediction is appropriate for the Dyirbal facts, as we've seen, but not for the facts of other languages such as Warlpiri. For this reason, Aldridge (2004) and Legate (2008) propose derivations similar to (62) only for languages showing loss of absolutive arguments in non-finite contexts. Languages like Warlpiri are to be handled with in situ case assignment mechanisms for both subject and object according to these authors.

3.3. Jointly morphology- and syntax-based theories

A final group of theories makes use of both syntactic and morphological means to capture ergativity in case and agreement. One of these is the theory of Legate (2002, 2006, 2008), discussed above in connection with syntactic approaches. Beyond the syntactic means of case feature assignment, an essential piece of Legate's proposal involves the interface between morphology and syntax. Case distinctions present in syntax in virtue of syntactic configurations can be lost or obscured by morphological impoverishment. This is generally the situation, Legate proposes, in ergative/absolutive languages showing only morphological ergativity. For Warlpiri (63a), for instance, she proposes that the *v* head assigns accusative case to the object *wawirri* 'kangaroo', and ergative case to the subject *ngarraka* 'man'. In intransitive(63b), the *v* head assigns no case, and the subject is assigned nominative by T.

(63) a. *ngarrka-ngku ka wawirri-∅ panti-rni* [Warlpiri]
man-ERG AUX kangaroo-ACC spear-NPST
'The man is spearing the kangaroo.'

b. *kurdu-∅ ka wanka-mi*
child-NOM AUX speak-NPST
'The child is speaking.'

Case assignment in Warlpiri is then entirely parallel to what we see in a three-way case-marking system like Nez Perce. There is no syntactic category of absolutive that is assigned sometimes by T and sometimes by *v* (cf. Aldridge 2004). Why does the transitive object share the surface realization of the intransitive subject? The key lies in the way that syntactic case features are mapped to phonological realizations. Legate proposes the following list of syntax/phonology pairings for the Warlpiri case system:

(64) Warlpiri case morphemes (partial list)
[ERG] ↔ -rlu/-ngku
[DAT] ↔ -ku
[case] ↔ ∅ (="absolutive")

This list does not provide special exponents for [NOM] and [ACC] cases. These cases, then, have recourse to a default case form. It is their shared realization through default case morphology that leads to the conflation of [NOM] and [ACC] into an 'absolutive' category in Warlpiri.

Evidence for this proposal comes from mismatches in case-marking within a single DP. An interesting example of this is seen in Djapu, a Pama-Nyungan language. Case-marking in this language is generally on a three-way basis, like in Nez Perce.

(65) a. *Mak rlinygu-n galka-y' ba:pa-'ngali-n dharpu-ngal.* [Djapu]
maybe already-IM sorcerer-ERG. spear-PRF
'Maybe a sorcerer has already speared your father.'
(Morphy 1983: 111)

b. *Ngarritj nha:-ma wa:yin-gu.*
Ngarritj.NOM see-UNM animal-DAT
'Ngarritj is looking for animal(s).'
(Morphy 1983: 38)

However, whereas common nouns show specialized accusative case forms, demonstratives lack any accusative morphology. When a demonstrative forms a DP with an accusative noun, the demonstrative appears in the unmarked, default case – a seeming partial emergence of a morphological absolutive.

(66) *Wungay' marrtji-nya* ***ngunhi-ny-dhi yolngu-n*** [Djapu]
honey.ABS go-PST.NONINDIC that.ABS-PRO-ANAPH person-ACC
wapirti-warrtju-na-puyngu-nha-ny *weka-nha.*
stingray-spear.PL-NMLRZ-INHAB-ACC-PRO give-PST.NONINDIC
'We would go and give honey to those stingray-spearing people.'
(Morphy 1983)

Such mismatches are elegantly accounted for via the distinction between syntactic and morphological case permitted by Legate's system. The overall DP 'those stingray-spearing people' is assigned [ACC] by *v*, but the component pieces of the DP present different possibilities for inflection. Nouns which have specialized accusative forms adopt those forms, but demonstratives, lacking any such forms, appear in an unmarked, default morphological case. This default is a constrained example of a pattern that happens on a larger scale in a language like Warlpiri.

A somewhat different example of a mixed syntax- and morphology-based theory is provided by Deal (2010a, b). As on the proposals by Legate and Aldridge discussed above, Deal proposes that *v* enters into a syntactic relationship both with the subject in

Spec*v*P and with the object inside VP. These relationships, however, are understood to be agreement relationships which transfer only φ-features; there are no case features in the syntax per se. Deal also proposes that T enters into an agreement relationship with the subject; in languages like Nez Perce, this additional agreement is realized as a subject agreement affix on the verb. It is agreement relationships, rather than syntactic case assignment, that are indicated via dotted lines in the tree below.

(67)

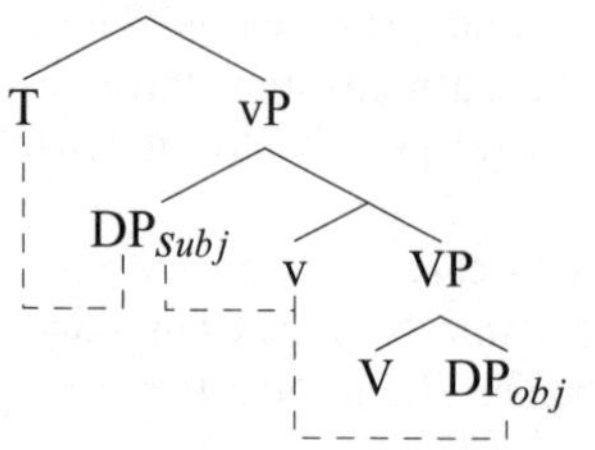

One nominal, then, agrees with two functional heads, in virtue of being closest to T within its c-command domain (agreement down) and being in the specifier of *v*P (agreement up). Deal proposes that this syntactic configuration is interpreted morphologically as ergative case. Morphological interpretation of agreement dependencies first copies the features of the object onto the *v* head and of the subject onto the T head. It then interprets the spec-head agreement relationship between *v* and the subject by sharing the subject's features and *v*'s agreement features, which have been obtained from the object. The subject DP thus ends up endowed with two sets of φ-features, its own and those of the object. The morphological exponent of this complex feature bundle is what we recognize as the ergative case.

(68) Nez Perce case morphemes (partial list)
[φ-T,φ-v,D] ↔ -nim
[φ-v,D] ↔ -ne

This type of approach provides a natural treatment of languages like Sahaptin, a Penutian language, where the appearance of ergative on the subject is conditioned by the person of the object. Ergative case is only expressed on a 3rd person singular subject in the presence of a 1st or 2nd person object.

(69) a. *iwínš-nim=naš i-q'ínun-a.* [Sahaptin]
man-ERG=1SG 3SBJ-see-PST
'The man saw me.'

b. *iwínš i-q'ínun-a miyánaš-na.*
man 3SBJ-see-PST child-ACC
'The man saw the child.'

c. *i-wiyánawi-ya iwínš.*
3SBJ-arrive-PST man
'The man arrived.'

(Rude 1997)

Because the ergative case marker realizes, in part, the features of the object, it is possible for the marker to be different or to be zero only where the object has a certain featural profile.

3.4. Challenges for ergative in situ

Several of the theories considered above have in common the treatment of the ergative case as assigned in situ to the specifier of *v*P. This approach has been quite influential in the recent literature, as witnessed by the papers in Johns, Massam, and Ndayiragije (2006), and work by Woolford (2006), Aissen (2010), Coon (2010a), Coon et al. (2012), and Mahajan (2012). For this reason it is especially important to consider the types of examples that have been raised as possible challenges to it. These concern the correlation between ergativity and thematic role; the absence of ergative case on certain nominals occupying Spec*v*P; and the possibility of raising to ergative.

First, insofar as the *v* head assigning ergative case is connected with agency per se, the proposal makes the prediction that ergative case should not be available on non-agent subjects. There are many languages showing ergativity properties in case and agreement for which this prediction is not accurate (Comrie 1978; Bobaljik and Branigan 2006; Otsuka 2006; Bruening 2007; Deal 2010a; Preminger 2012; Baker to appear). Examples below from Chukchi and Nez Perce underline this point.

(70) *əʔtvʔet jərʔen-nin miml-e* [Chukchi]
boat.ABS fill-3SG/3SG water-ERG
'Water filled the boat.'

(71) *piswe-m 'inii-ne pee-tqe-likeece-∅-ye.* [Nez Perce]
rock-ERG house-ACC 3/3-suddenly-on.top-P.ASP-REM.PST
'A rock fell on the house.'

The standard way to reconcile such data with the *v*P proposal is to weaken the connection between *v* and an agent θ-role. The *v* head may assign a broader class of external or "causer" θ-roles, for instance, including whatever roles are appropriately assigned to the ergative nominals in the examples above (e.g. Monrós 2007; Legate 2012). In this sense the original proposal that ergative is a θ-linked case is crucially modified to highlight the structure in which various roles are assigned, rather than the roles themselves. What is central to the proposal is that ergative is assigned in situ to the specifier of *v*P; a full account of examples like those above is left to await a proper theory of the mapping between this type of structural configuration and observable semantic consequences.

A second challenge concerns whether occupying the Spec*v*P position is sufficient for ergative case-marking. Arguments that it is not come from Basque and from Nez Perce. Between them, Basque dialects and Nez Perce cover three major types of ergativity: ergative/absolutive (eastern Basque), three-way (Nez Perce), and argument-structural (western Basque).

Basque dialects converge on the marking of transitive and unaccusative clauses. Transitive objects and unaccusative subjects appear in an unmarked absolutive case; transitive subjects take a special marker, the ergative.

(72) a. *Nekane-k Miren eta Jon ikusi ditu.* [Basque]
Nekane-ERG Miren.ABS and Jon.ABS seen AUX.3PL_ABS.3SG_ERG
'Nekane saw Miren and Jon.'

b. *Miren eta Jon etorri dira.*
Miren.ABS and Jon.ABS come AUX.3PL_ABS
'Miren and Jon came.'

For the question of the sufficiency of Spec*v*P position for ergative marking, the relevant examples in Basque involve gerundive complements of perception verbs, which contrast with full clausal complements (Rezac, Albizu, and Etxepare to appear). In full clausal complements, such as the bracketed constituent below, transitive subjects must be marked ergative.

(73) [*Katu-ek/*ak sagu-ak harrapatu* [Basque]
[cat-DEF.PL.ERG/*DEF.PL.ABS mouse-DEF.PL.ABS catch
dituzte-la] *ikusi dut*
AUX.3PL_ABS.3PL_ERG-that] seen AUX.1SG_ERG
'I saw that the cats caught / were catching the mice.'

If ergative is assigned in situ in *v*P, the possibility of ergative assignment to the subject is expected to persist in gerundive complements, which possess a reduced clausal structure. This, however, is not the case: gerundive complements show absolutive subjects, rather than ergative ones. (See Rezac et al. to appear for arguments for the constituency represented here.)

(74) [*Katu-ak/*-ek sagu-ak harrapa-tzen*] *ikusi* [Basque]
[cat-DEF.PL.ABS/*DEF.PL.ERG mouse-DEF.PL.ABS catch-ing] seen
ditut
AUX.3PL_ABS.1SG_ERG
'I saw the cats catching the mice.'

On the basis of these facts, Rezac et al. (to appear) argue that position in Spec*v*P alone is not sufficient to condition ergative case assignment in Basque. The involvement of the TP system is required. This conclusion is especially telling to the degree that the contrast above holds across a dialect continuum in Basque, including both dialects showing ergative/absolutive case (where v_{TRANS} would be implicated in case assignment to the subject) and those showing argument-structural ergativity in case (where *v* would always be implicated in case assignment to the subject).

Related arguments from Nez Perce concern reduced clausal structures appearing in the causative. In a full clause in Nez Perce, subjects are marked ergative and objects are marked accusative.

(75) *Annie-nim paa-'yax̂-n-a ciq'aamqal-na* [Nez Perce]
Annie-ERG 3/3-find-P.ASP-REM.PST dog-ACC
'Annie found the dog.'

In a causativized form of (75), however, ergative case on the subject disappears in favor of accusative:

(76) *Meeli-nm* ***Annie-ne/*nim*** *paa-sapa-'yax̂-n-a* [Nez Perce]
Mary-ERG Annie-ACC/*ERG 3/3-CAUS-find-P.ASP-REM.PST
ciq'aamqal-na
dog-ACC
'Mary made Annie find the dog.'

Deal (2010b) argues that the structure of (76) involves a single TP in which the *v*P found in (75) is embedded under a higher, causative *v*P. Just as in the Basque example, when a *v*P whose subject would normally bear the ergative case is not in a local relationship with a T head, ergative case on the subject disappears. This provides another argument that Spec*v*P position is not sufficient for ergative case assignment.

A final challenge to the ergative in situ analysis concerns whether Spec*v*P position is even necessary for ergative case assignment. This question must be handled with some care in view of analyses in which in situ assignment by *v* is in fact definitional of ergative case (e.g. Legate 2002: 143; 2012). The questions that can be addressed empirically are (i) how closely this definition corresponds to the pretheoretical ergative class, and (ii) in cases in which the definition makes distinctions among elements in that class, whether these distinctions in fact track linguistic differences in a useful way. With these questions in mind, let us examine a potential argument for ergative assignment independent of Spec*v*P. This argument comes again from work on Basque.

Basque shows certain raising constructions which result in the assignment of the ergative case to the DP which moves. This holds even in cases when the base position of that DP is not one in which ergative case is assigned. The examples below come from Rezac et al. (to appear), who provide several arguments to show that the structures involve raising (see also Artiagoitia 2001; Preminger 2012). In (77), *Jon eta Miren* raises from the specifier position of a transitive *v*P, in which ergative could be assigned on the in-situ proposal. This provides a possible explanation for the presence of ergative in the matrix clause.

(77) *Jon-ek eta Miren-ek*$_k$ [t_k *lagunei*$_j$ *liburuak*$_i$ *bidali*] *behar* [Basque]
Jon-ERG and Miren-ERG [friends.DAT books.ABS send] must
di-zkii-ej-tek.
AUX-3PL_ABS$_i$-3PL_DAT$_j$-3P_ERG$_k$.
'Jon and Miren must send friends books.'

In (78), on the other hand, *Jon eta Miren* raises from a position in the projection of unaccusative 'come', in which ergative case is *not* assigned. The ergative case appearing on *Jon eta Miren* in its derived position must therefore be the result of raising.

(78) *Jon-ek eta Miren-ek*$_k$ [t_k *etorri*] *behar du-te.* [Basque]
Jon-ERG and Miren-ERG [come] must AUX-3PL_ERG
'Jon and Miren must come.'

This appears to counterexemplify the proposed universal that ergative does not appear on derived subjects.

If ergative is by definition a case that is assigned to DPs in Spec*v*P in virtue of their base-generation in that position, two main avenues remain open to deal with the Basque facts. First, we might treat the case similarity between the raised subject in (78) and the ordinary transitive subject in (72a) as an instance of homophony. The ordinary transitive subject in (72a) indeed receives the ergative case in virtue of its base position, but the raised subject in (78) receives some other case, which happens to be realized in a way identical to the ergative. Just as for the two types of absolutive in Warlpiri discussed above, what must be shown is a distinction in syntactic or morphological behavior between these two case categories in support of the postulated difference. The alternative avenue is simply to deny that Basque makes use of an ergative case. This in turn requires identifying an alternative means of case-assignment for Basque and distinguishing this route from the ergative one by independent means.

4. Theories of ergativity in Ā-movement

We now turn to the manifestation of ergativity properties in the grammar of Ā dependencies. The core phenomenon in this domain concerns a difference in the way that Ā movement is encoded when transitive subjects are extracted versus when other constituents are extracted. Roviana data showed us this pattern above. Object and intransitive subject relativization in Roviana makes use of ordinary verb forms in the embedded clause. Transitive subject relativization makes use of a special nominalized form.

(79) *Hierana sa tie* [$_{RC}$ *sapu kote taloa*] [Roviana]
this DEF man REL FUT leave
'This is the man who is going away.'

(80) *Hierana sa koreo* [$_{RC}$ *sapu tupa-i-a e Zone*]
this DEF boy REL punch-TR-3SG.OBJ ART John
'This is the boy that John punched.'

(81) a. **Hierana sa tie* [$_{RC}$ *sapu tupa-i-u*] *Normal verb form
this DEF man REL punch-TR-1SG.OBJ
'This is the man who punched me.'

b. *Hierana sa tie* [$_{RC}$ *sapu tupa-qa rau*] ^{OK}Special verb form
this DEF man REL punch-1SG.NSUF I
'This is the man who punched me.'

Corston (1996) reports that the type of verbal morphology seen in (81b) cannot be used in object extraction, and suggests that it cannot be used in intransitive subject extraction either. This suggests that verbal morphology is strictly correlated with whether an ergative or a non-ergative is extracted. The literature on ergativity in Ā extraction explores both morphological and syntactic explanations for this type of correlation.

4.1. A morphology-based theory

An example of a purely morphological approach is provided by Stiebels (2006)'s study of Ā extraction in Mayan. Across a range of Mayan languages, a special verb form appears when transitive subjects are Ā extracted. This form is called the "agent focus" (AF) in the Mayanist literature. The AF form does not appear when intransitive subjects or transitive objects are extracted. An example from K'ekchí is given below.

(82) a. *x-at-in-sak'* [K'ekchí]
rec.pst-2sg.abs-1sg.erg-hit
'I hit you.'

b. *ani x-∅-a-sak'*
who rec.pst-3sg.abs-2sg.erg-hit
'Who did you hit?'

c. *ani x-sak'-*[*o*]*-k* *aw-e*
who rec.pst-hit-af-nfut.intr 2sg.erg-dat
'Who hit you?'
(Dayley 1981)

Working in lexical decomposition grammar, Stiebels analyzes the special verbal morphology in (82c) as akin to a form of agreement. Agreement in Mayan languages is generally on an ergative-absolutive basis. The AF morphology is like other ergative agreement markers, Stiebels proposes, but with an additional focus feature (triggering Ā-movement) and impoverished φ-features. When the subject is ergative and has a focus feature, use of AF agreement is obligatory; this is simply because failure to use the correct agreement form generally leads to ungrammaticality. When the subject has a focus feature but is not ergative, use of AF is not possible for these same reasons. Together with additional machinery regulating the form of agreement with objects in AF clauses, this proposal is able to account for a wide range of data from diverse Mayan languages.

The agreement-based proposal, as Stiebels notes, is to a certain degree reminiscent of patterns of agreement in Ā-movement in Austronesian languages like Chamorro. Declarative clauses in Chamorro contain subject agreement in person and number. Note that, according to Chung (1998), Chamorro is not an ergative language.

(83) *Pära bai u-agang* pro *hämyu un pupuengi* [Chamorro]
fut.irr 1sg.irr-call you.pl one evening
'I was going to call you one evening.'
(Chung 1998: 35)

When there is Ā extraction, however, the form of agreement changes, and the change is determined by the case of the Ā-moving element. When a nominative is Ā moved, the infix *um* is inserted; when an accusative is A' moved, the infix *in* is inserted (Chung 1982, 1998).

(84) a. *Hayi f<um>a'gasi t i kareta?* [Chamorro]
who <WH.NOM>wash the car
'Who washed the car?'

b. *Hafa k<in>annono'-mu t ?*
what <WH.OBJ>-eat.PROG-AGR
'What are you eating?'

(Chung 1998: 236–7)

As analyzed by Stiebels, the Mayan AF form is essentially a form of *wh*-agreement in an ergative language. Agreement in Mayan, as in Chamorro, reflects both case and extraction. Extracted ergatives trigger a special overt form of *wh*-agreement, namely the AF suffix, and other instances of agreement with *wh*-phrases are syncretic with ordinary agreement. Now, the Chamorro forms demonstrate the possibility of *wh*-agreement both with subjects and with objects, with roughly equal morphological complexity in the two cases. One might expect to find, then, an ergative language showing special forms of verbal morphology of equal complexity in both ergative Ā-movement and in absolutive Ā-movement. It is striking that such a language appears to be unattested. The generalization seems to be:

(85) When verbal morphology is affected by Ā extraction of arguments in an ergative language, the forms used for Ā extraction of ergatives are always more complex than those used for non-ergatives.

The challenge for the morphological account is to provide a natural account of this type of generalization.

4.2. Syntax-based theories

In contrast to the morphological view, various researchers have posited a structural difference between clauses where ergatives are extracted and those where non-ergatives are. On this view, the standard clausal syntax of some ergative languages makes it impossible to Ā move the subject. Two major threads connect the theories in this domain. The first concerns the involvement of object movement. This movement is frequently, though not always, connected to a second common thread: the idea that the object receives case from T or I. The structure resulting from the object's movement is one in which the subject cannot undergo Ā-movement; or, alternatively, the structure in which the subject Ā-moves is one in which the object cannot be assigned case in the typical way.

4.2.1. The problem is object Ā-movement

A first set of analyses identifies syntactically ergative languages as languages in which objects must undergo Ā-movement in ordinary transitive clauses. This leads to problems in Ā extraction of subjects in transitive clauses. Theories along these lines are proposed by Bittner (1994), Bittner and Hale (1996a) and Campana (1992).

For Bittner and Hale, objects move to an Ā position for reasons of case in a syntactically ergative language. SpecIP, the nominative case-checking position, is to be considered Ā; in ordinary transitive clauses, it is to SpecIP that objects raise. Case-driven object movement interacts with other types of Ā-movement when a limited number of Ā positions are available. This is the situation Bittner and Hale find in Inuit relative clauses, which they propose are formed via nominalization of VP. To fulfill its case needs, the object of a transitive must raise to SpecDP, the closest Ā position. The subject receives ergative case in situ in virtue of case competition with the object. (Details of this are discussed by Bittner and Hale 1996b.)

(86) a. *miiqqa-t* [__ *Juuna-p* *paari-sa-i*] [West Greenlandic]
child-PL [__ Juuna-ERG look.after-REL[+TR]-3SG.PL]
'the children that Juuna is looking after'
(Bittner 1994: 55)

b.

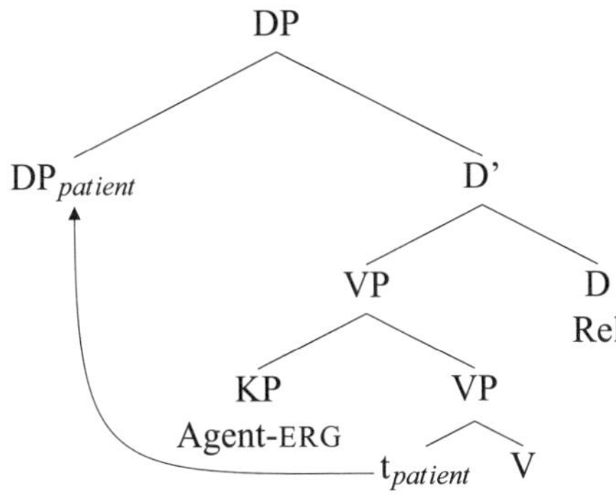

Subject relativization is dependent on transitivity. When an object is not present, the subject may raise to SpecDP for case reasons, (87a). A transitive subject may not do so, however, (87b).

(87) a. *miiqqa-t* [__ *sila-mi* *pinnguar-tu-t*] [West Greenlandic]
child-PL [__ outdoors-LOC play-REL[-TR]-PL]
'the children who are playing outdoors'

b. **angut* [__ *aallaat tigu-sima-sa-a*]
man [__ gun take-PRF-REL[+TR]-3SG.SG]
'the man who took the gun'
(Bittner 1994)

As Bittner (1994: 58) discusses, the problem with (87b) concerns the case filter. When the subject raises to the only available Ā position, the object is left without a source of case. No case is available to it VP-internally.

Special morphology reflects a structure in which the object's case-needs have found a different means of satisfaction. In this structure – the antipassive – the object is able to receive case VP internally, freeing the subject to occupy the sole Ā position available in the relativization structure.

(88) Structure of *(87b): no case for the object

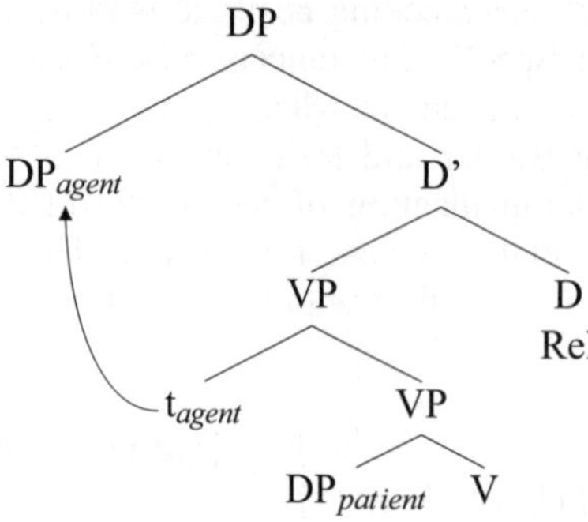

(89) *angut* [__ *aallaam-mik* *tigu-si-sima-su-q*] [West Greenlandic]
man [__ gun-INS take-ANTIP-PRF-REL[-TR]-SG]
'the man who took the gun'

(Bittner 1994: 58)

Additional machinery is required to extend this proposal to ergativity in Ā-movement in full clausal domains, such as relative clauses in Roviana or matrix questions in Q'eqchi. Here, object movement to SpecIP should be possible, fulfilling the case needs of the object; the remaining difficulty in subject Ā-movement to SpecCP remains to be accounted for.

The proposal by Campana (1992) allows for these further examples while carrying over various features of the Bittner and Hale approach. Like Bittner and Hale, Campana proposes that objects must raise for case reasons to an Ā position in ordinary transitive clauses in syntactically ergative languages. He identifies this position as an adjunct position in AgrSP. Subjects receive case below AgrSP. (I show this position, anachronistically, as Spec*v*P in the trees below.) Ā-movement of a transitive subject therefore creates a second Ā-dependency which crosses over the first:

(90) a. Ordinary transitive clause

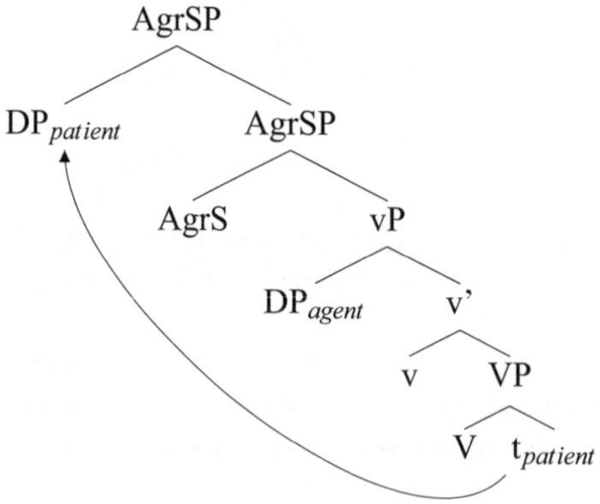

b. Transitive subject extraction

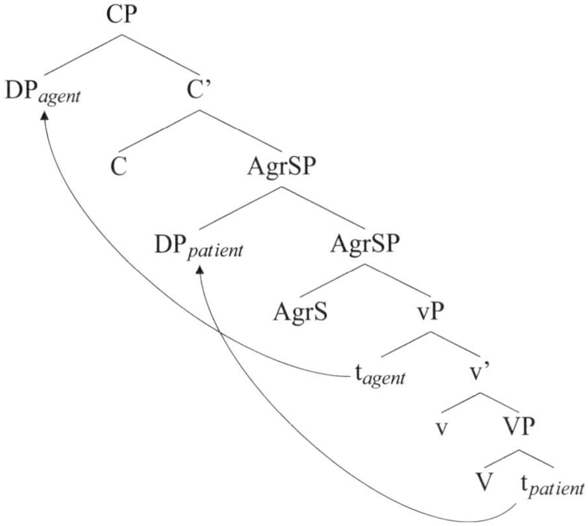

Campana proposes that structure (90b) is ill-formed due to the Empty Category Principle, a principle requiring the trace of the subject in Spec*v*P and its co-indexed antecedent (the subject DP itself) to be sufficently close together. In (90b) the Ā position occupied by the object intervenes between the subject's trace and its landing site, disrupting this locality and producing deviance. Just as on the Bittner and Hale proposal, circumventing this deviance requires finding some way to assign case to the object without Ā moving it. Campana discusses the use of passive and antipassive strategies that achieve this result.

The ECP-based explanation makes for a natural parallel between syntactic ergativity in Ā-movement and the *that*-trace phenomenon. Examples like (91b) are handled on the standard GB approach (Chomsky 1986) in much the same way as Campana treats instances of ergative extraction such as (87b): something intervenes between a trace of the moving subject and its next highest antecedent. In structures like (90b), this is the object DP; in (91b), it is the complementizer *that*.

(91) a. *Who$_i$ do you think* [$_{CP}$ t$_i$ [$_{IP}$ *t$_i$ won the game*]] ?
b. **Who$_i$ do you think* [$_{CP}$ *t$_i$ that* [$_{IP}$ *t$_i$ won the game*]] ?

A major prediction of both Campana's and Bittner and Hale's theories concerns nonfinite clauses – a challenge which will come up repeatedly throughout this section.

Transitive subject movement on these theories is complicated by movement of the object, and object movement is driven by a need to receive case ex situ. The object's case, received from T and its analogues, is the nominative. In non-finite clauses, nominative is expected to become unavailable. This means that languages with ergativity in Ā-movement should be languages where overt objects, modulo some special means of case-assignment, are impossible in non-finite clauses. Structures which are plausibly non-finite in West Greenlandic appear challenging from this perspective.

(92) *Miiqqat* [*PRO Juuna* *ikiu-ssa-llu-gu*] [West Greenlandic]
children.ABS [PRO Juuna.ABS help-FUT-INF-3SG]
niriursui-pp-u-t
promise-IND-INTR-3PL
'The children promised to help Juuna.'
(Manning 1994: 113)

Bittner (1994) proposes to handle such non-finite clauses with mechanisms very similar to those used in finite clauses; nominative-assignment possibilities are dissociated from finiteness. It remains to be seen how a broader range of non-finite clauses, including those of the English and Dyirbal types, can be accounted for under this proposal.

An additional prediction of the Campana theory in particular concerns Ā movement of adjuncts and indirect objects. Movement of such elements out of *v*P is expected to induce an ECP violation parallel to that shown in (90b). Yet languages showing ergativity in Ā movement do not typically show parallel effects in adjunct or indirect object extraction. In Kaqchikel (Mayan), for instance, transitive subjects may not extract when the verb bears ordinary morphology; an AF marker is required.

(93) a. *n-Ø-u-löq'* *jun* *sik'iwuj* *ri* *a* *Carlos* [Kaqchikel]
INCOMPL-3SG.ABS-3SG.ERG-buy INDF book DET CL Carlos
'Carlos buys a book.'

b. **achike* *n-Ø-u-löq'* *jun* *sik'iwuj*
who INCOMPL-3SG.ABS-3SG.ERG-buy INDF book
'Who buys a book?'
(Assmann et al. to appear)

Extraction of low adjuncts and indirect objects imposes no parallel condition. These elements freely extract in clauses with ordinary verbal morphology.

(94) *achoq* *r-ik'in* *n-Ø-u-sël* *ri* *ti'ij* *ri* *a* [Kaqchikel]
what 3SG-POSS-INS INCOMPL-3SG.ABS-3SG.ERG-cut DET food DET CL
Carlos?
Carlos
'With what does Carlos cut the meat?'

(95) *achoq* *chi* *re* *n-Ø-u-ya'* *a* *Carlos* *jun* *sik'wuj*
who PREP DET INCOMPL-3SG.ABS-3SG.ERG-give CL Carlos INDF book
'To whom does Carlos give a book?'

These data come from Assmann et al. (to appear), who observe that this type of theory in effect predicts an "absolutive island" effect in clauses with ordinary verbal morphology. The prediction is contravened by low adjunct movement past an absolutive in (94) and indirect object movement past an absolutive in (95).

4.2.2. The problem is locality

A second set of analyses identifies syntactically ergative languages as those in which transitive subject movement is barred by a principle of locality. Different types of locality conditions are invoked in this literature.

Coon et al. (2012) propose that the relevant principle is one of absolute locality: the Phase Impenetrability Condition (Chomsky 2001). Like Campana and Bittner and Hale, Coon et al. propose that there is no source for object case in VP in the syntactically ergative languages they discuss. Objects must therefore receive case ex situ from IP. IP, however, lies on the opposite side of a phase boundary from the object's base position. The object is therefore required to move into the specifier position of the phase head, which Coon et al. identify as a *v*P above the base position of the subject in VoiceP. Once moved to Spec*v*P, the object may enter into a local agreement relationship with I and receive case.

(96)

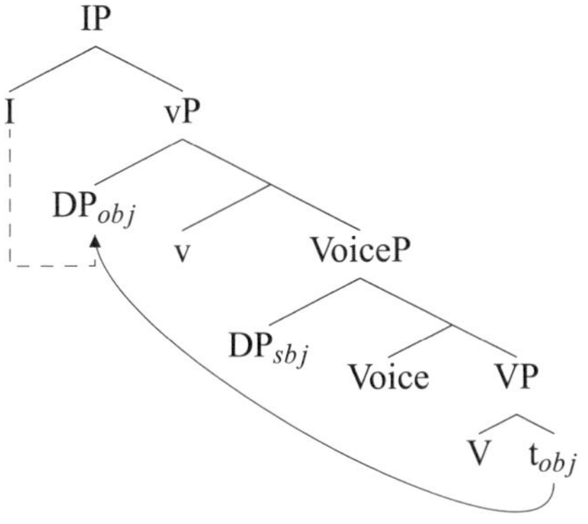

Movement of the object through the specifier of *v*P also comes with consequences for the subject. Ā-movement to SpecCP requires the subject to cross the *v*P phase boundary. However, the object is required to occupy the only specifier position available in *v*P. Ā-movement of the subject is thus ruled out in virtue of the PIC.

Special morphology appearing in Ā-movement of ergatives is again connected to an alternative means of case-assignment for the object – one which operates strictly within the lower phase. One might then expect that this means of case-assignment would appear in other environments in which objects have case-needs that cannot be met in IP; for instance, it might appear in non-finite clauses. Coon et al. discuss evidence from Q'anjob'al showing exactly this type of convergence. The Q'anjob'al suffix *-on* appears in embedded non-finite clauses (97) and in contexts of transitive subject movement (98).

(97) *Chi uj* [*hin* *y-il-on*[*-i*] *ix* *Malin*]. [Q'anjob'al]
ASP be.able.to [ABS.1 GEN.3-see-AF-INTR CL Maria]
'Maria can see me.'

(98) *Maktxel max-ach il-on-i.*
who ASP-ABS.2 see-AF-INTR
'Who saw you?'

Coon et al. propose that the *-on* ("agent focus") suffix is a special Voice head which assigns case to the object in situ. This obviates the dependence of the object on I, and thus makes an overt object possible in a non-finite context in (97). It also obviates the need for object movement through Spec*v*P, and thus opens the way for subject extraction in (98). The view presents a straightforward approach to the fact that the forms used for Ā extraction of ergatives are morphologically more complex than those for extraction of non-ergatives. The Voice head is more syntactically complex under ergative extraction than it would normally be; only in this case does it bear a case feature.

The challenges for this view are similar to those facing Campana's view. Here, too, it remains to be seen how Ā extraction asymmetries can be handled in languages like West Greenlandic, where objects do not seem to depend on IP for case. This raises the question of why objects would have to raise to *v*P in such languages, blocking subject movement. The challenge of adjunct extraction and indirect object extraction also is applicable to this view. The *v*P escape hatch must be unavailable to subjects when an object occupies Spec*v*P, but it must be open to adjuncts and indirect objects.

Aldridge (2004, 2008, 2012) proposes an alternative locality-based account according to which the relevant principle is one of relative locality: Attract Closest. Syntactically ergative languages, she proposes, are those in which transitive *v* possesses an [EPP] features which triggers raising of the object to *v*P's outer specifier. Ā-movement to SpecCP is likewise triggered by an [EPP] feature which attracts the closest DP. Ā-movement of objects and intransitive subjects therefore proceeds straightforwardly; these are the highest DPs in their respective *v*Ps.

(99) a. Basic *v*P structure

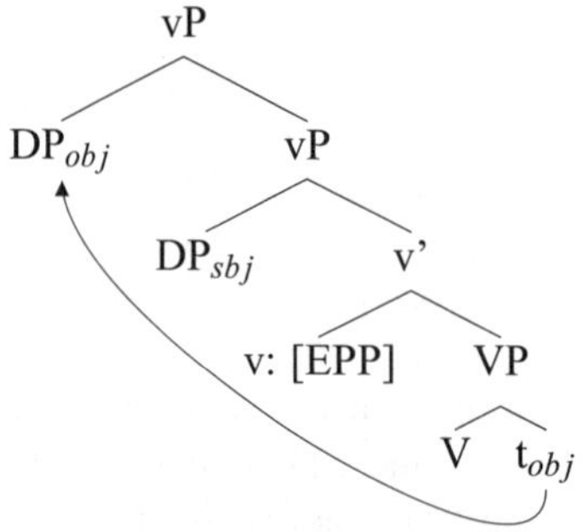

b. Object Ā-movement

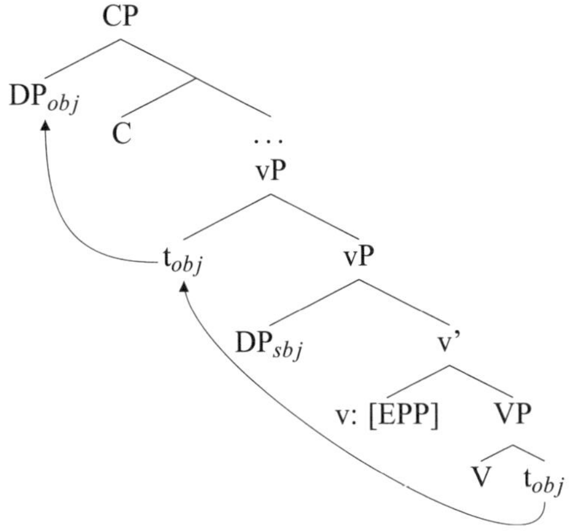

Ā-movement of transitive subjects to SpecCP is forbidden because relative to the object, the subject is not local to C. Only the highest DP in *v*P can Ā move.

(100) *Transitive subject movement: a violation af Attract Closest

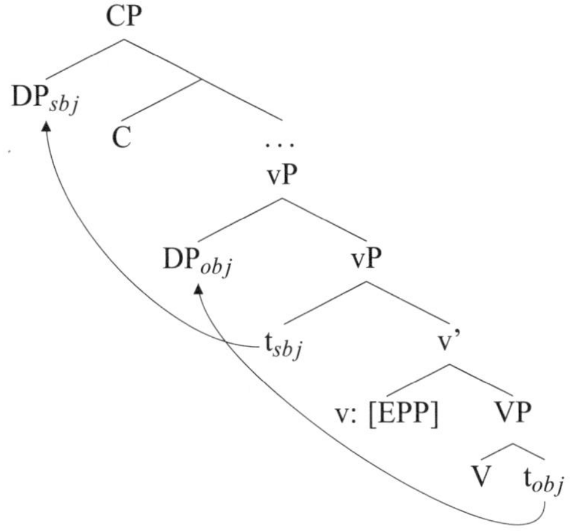

Special morphology appearing in contexts of ergative Ā-movement is connected to a difference in the syntax of the object. Aldridge proposes that antipassive clauses (e.g. [89]) contain a *v* head which does not carry an [EPP] feature triggering object movement. The subject remains the highest DP, and is able to Ā move.

This approach faces a mix of the challenges applying to Stiebel's account and those applying to Campana's and Coon et al.'s. First, like on the Stiebels approach, it remains unexpected why the forms used for Ā extraction of ergatives should be morphologically more complex than those for extraction of non-ergatives. We must somehow assure that transitive *v* is not realized overtly unless antipassive *v* also is. Transitive *v* is furthermore potentially more syntactically complex than antipassive *v* – it contains an [EPP] feature.

One might expect, then, that ergative extraction would feature reduced complexity in verbal morphology, contrary to fact. Second, to the extent that adjuncts and indirect objects behave like DPs in their interaction with [EPP], facts like those in (94) and (95) are also unexpected. Like Campana's and Coon et al.'s proposal, Aldridge's leads us to expect some version of an absolutive island. It remains to be clarified why adjuncts, which are typically less mobile than arguments, are able to extract in cases where subject arguments are not.

A distinctive aspect of this proposal lies in the connection between object movement and object case. Unlike in the other views reviewed here, the connection between these two is only indirect. For languages like Tagalog and West Greenlandic, Aldridge proposes that movement of the object to the outer specifier of *v*P takes place even though there is a source for object case *v*P internally. Ergativity in Ā-movement is therefore possible even when absolutive case (being assigned at the *v*P-level) remains available to objects in non-finite clauses, as we saw for West Greenlandic in (92). The reverse, however, is not possible. In a language where absolutive objects are not possible in non-finite clauses, objects receive their case from T; T, like C, must attract the closest DP. In order for it to be the object that is attracted, the object must first shift past the subject at the *v*P level. Aldridge proposes that a language showing this profile is Seediq. Crucially, there is no language where absolutive objects are impossible in non-finite clauses (as in Seediq) but there is no Ā extraction restriction.

(101) Aldridge's generalization
If a languages does not provide a source for absolutive case in a non-finite clause, then it does not allow transitive subjects in normal clausal structures to be Ā extracted.

The innovation of Aldridge's proposal is that it allows this generalization to be derived as a one-way implication, rather than a biconditional.

Notably, this analysis requires Ā-movement in syntactically ergative languages to work slightly differently than does its counterpart in English. Either subject or object may Ā move in English, despite the fact that the former is systematically closer to C than the latter. The English facts are typically handled by positing that an [EPP] feature on C attracts not just the closest DP, but the closest constituent with a *wh*-feature. This provides a ready account of superiority effects, as in (102c–d).

(102) English: C attracts the closest *wh*-feature
a. *Who ate the pizza?*
b. *What did Susan eat?*
c. *Who ate what?*
d. **What did who eat?*

To produce a syntactically ergative language, then, two independent pieces must come together. First, objects must move to a position above that occupied by subjects. This type of idea is widely explored in the literature on Germanic object shift (e.g. Collins and Thráinsson 1996). Second, triggers of Ā-movement must attract the closest DP without regard to its featural specification. This type of parameter could potentially be useful in dealing with Keenan and Comrie (1977)'s observations regarding languages where only subjects may relativize. Such languages may be examples of closest-DP attraction by a relative C independent of the object shift that Aldridge posits for syntactic ergativity.

4.2.3. The problem is rule ordering

A final type of syntactic approach shares with Bittner and Hale, Campana and Coon et al. the core idea that case assignment to the object is blocked by Ā movement of an ergative DP. Assmann et al. (to appear) propose an implementation of this idea that comes out of the ordering between the operations Merge and Agree.

Assmann et al. adopt Müller (2009)'s approach to ergative case, reviewed in section 3.2.5. Structural case across languages is connected to two loci, *v* and T. Ergativity results when *v* must participate in Merge before it participates in Agree; this has the effect that *v* agrees with the DP in its specifier position and assigns it ergative case. In this scenario the object is assigned case by T. Ergative extraction restrictions arise, Assmann et al. propose, because Ā movement to the left periphery necessarily stops in the SpecTP position (an idea they connect to the proposal that TP is a phase). This means that T, like *v*, participates in both Agree (i.e. case-assignment) and Merge (i.e. attraction of a DP to its Spec). Crucially, if a language requires Merge before Agree at the *v*P level – resulting in ergative case – it also requires Merge before Agree at the TP level. This has the effect of allowing object extraction but not transitive subject extraction to proceed straightforwardly in an ergative language.

Object extraction proceeds as follows. Immediately after T is merged, a DP must move to its specifier position. When it is the object that moves, the structure is altered by Merge as shown in (103). The object, having previously moved to the edge of the *v*P phase, moves to SpecTP. (Note that this tree reflects a copy theory of movement.)

(103)
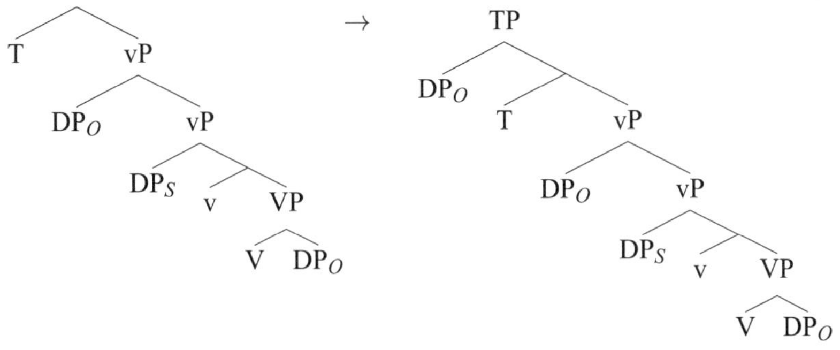

The next step triggered by T is Agree, and this targets the DP in T's specifier. This DP (the object) is thus assigned case. If C is merged, the object can proceed to move to SpecCP. This produces object Ā-movement.

Matters are different when a subject is extracted. Suppose that the initial structure in (103) serves as the input to an alternative, equally available application of Merge. It is the subject DP that moves to SpecTP.

(104)

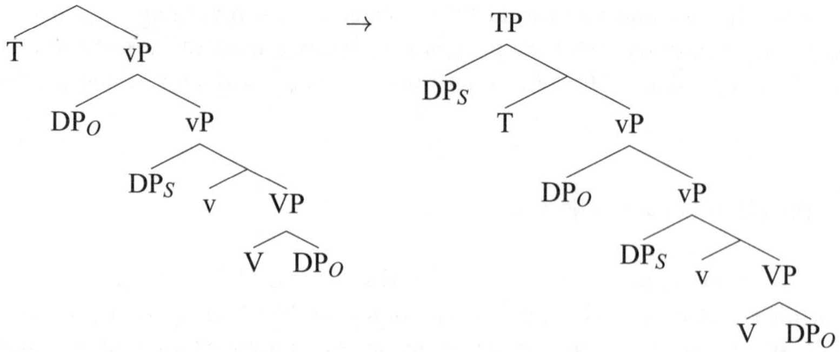

Once again, the next step will be Agree between T and the DP in its specifier position. This DP has already received case from *v*, but it remains a legitimate goal for Agree with T. Agreement of T with its DP specifier, however, prohibits T from engaging in any further agreement with other DPs in its domain. In particular, it may not subsequently agree with the object DP inside its sister *v*P. That object is thus unable to receive case, and the derivation crashes. The requirement that all movement to SpecCP proceed through SpecTP thus interacts with the order of Merge and Agree to produce a prohibition on ergative extraction.

Special morphology appearing in Ā-movement of ergatives is again connected to an alternative, "marked" means of object case-assignment. Assmann et al. analyze agent focus clauses (e.g. [98]) as featuring an additional case-assigning feature, attached to V. As on the Coon et al. approach, this means that contexts of ergative extraction feature more syntactic complexity than those with object extraction. This helps explain the increased morphological complexity of ergative extraction verbs.

A prediction of this approach concerns environments in which both subject and object are Ā extracted. In this case, both DPs move to SpecTP, and the object DP may receive case from T appropriately. Both DPs subsequently raise to SpecCP. No special mechanism of case assignment at the VP level is needed, and thus no special morphology of ergative extraction is expected. This prediction is confirmed by Kaqchikel double questions like (105a) and combined question/focus sentences like (105b).

(105) a. *atux achike n-Ø-u-löq'* [Kaqchikel]
what who INCOMPL-3SG.ABS-3SG.ERG-buy
'Who buys what?'

b. *achike ja ri jun sik'iwuj n-Ø-u-löq'*
who FOC DET INDF book INCOMPL-3SG.ABS-3SG.ERG-buy
'Who buys a BOOK?'

(Assmann et al. to appear)

What is notable about these examples is that transitive subject DPs are extracted with no special verbal morphology.

In tying ergative extraction asymmetries to object case, the Assmann et al. view inherits the challenge of languages like West Greenlandic (as do all views reviewed here, with the exception of Aldridge's). Given that objects do not clearly receive case from T in such languages, it remains to be seen what precise obstacle is encountered in completing a derivation like (104). It is in addition an open question how the view is properly expanded to deal with languages that do not show syntactic ergativity in the first place, like Warlpiri. If ergativity in morphological case uniformly arises when Merge precedes Agree at the *v*P level, as Müller (2009) proposes, and if the order of operations at TP always mirrors the order at *v*P, merely morphologically ergative languages are a surprising exception. Finally, like all of the other approaches reviewed in this section, the Assmann et al. proposal leaves it unclear why indirect object DPs and adjunct DPs should be extractable with ordinary verbal morphology. Movement of an indirect object DP through SpecTP is expected to bleed case assignment to the object in a way precisely parallel to what happens with subjects.

5. Future directions in ergativity studies

It should be clear from the foregoing that ergativity studies offer a great number of leads on the shape of the human language faculty as it relates to syntax and to morphology. The various theoretical approaches surveyed here present different ways of contextualizing the result of ergativity studies in the theory of grammar. Ergativity may be valuable as a source of insight into post-syntactic morphological computation; into the mapping between verbal argument structure and syntactic categories; into the nature of case features in syntax and their distribution across clausal heads; into the shape of Ā dependencies and the distribution of escape hatches in syntax. Most likely ergativity as a broad phenomenon will bear on more than one of these components, given both the diversity of ergative languages and their systematicity in discrete domains.

Future work on ergativity is urgently needed in several areas. A high priority should be accorded to the proper treatment of the proposed ergative univerals and especially their apparent counterexamples. Further work is also required to elucidate crucial questions on which turn promising ideas in the treatment of case and its relatives. Of particular concern is the ergative-in-situ hypothesis and its associated challenges related to raising-to-ergative and the absence of ergative on certain in-situ subjects. Finally, many of the analyses we have seen suggest interesting future work to be done on questions of covertness in ergative languages. If languages may not have the underlying syntax of ergativity without showing it overtly, why should this be? What sort of cues must be overt in the input in order for ergative languages to be learned?

6. Abbreviations

AF	agent focus
ASP	aspect
CL	clitic
EVID	evidential
IM	immediacy clitic (Djapu)
INCOMPL	incompletive
INTENS	intensive

INV	involuntary
KIN.PROP	kinship propriative (Djapu)
MUT	mutation
NSUF	noun suffix (Roviana; see Corston 1996)
OBJC	complementizer indicating control by matrix object (Warlpiri)
OBV.C	obviative complementizer (Warlpiri)
P.ASP	P aspect (Nez Perce; see Deal 2010a: ch 2)
PAUC	paucal
PM	personal marker
PREP	preposition
PRT	second position particle (Shipibo; see Baker to appear)
REALIS	realis mood
REC.PST	recent past
REM.PST	remote past
REP	repeated action
RN	relational noun
STAT	stative
SUBJC	complementizer indicating control by matrix subject (Warlpiri)
TEMP.C	temporal complementizer
UNM	unmarked inflection (Djapu)
UV	undergoer voice (Bajau; see Miller 2007)

20. Acknowledgements

Thanks to Artemis Alexiadou, Jessica Coon and Jason Merchant for helpful comments.

7. References (selected)

Aissen, Judith
2010 On the syntax of agent focus in K'ichee'. In: *Proceedings of FAMLi I.* MITWPL.

Aldai, Gontzal
2009 Is Basque morphologically ergative? Western Basque versus eastern Basque. *Studies in Language* 33:783–831.

Aldridge, Edith
2004 Ergativity and word order in Austronesian languages. Doctoral Dissertation, Cornell.

Aldridge, Edith
2008 Minimalist analysis of ergativity. *Sophia Linguistica* 55: 12–142.

Aldridge, Edith
2012 Antipassive and ergativity in Tagalog. *Lingua* 122: 192–203.

Alexiadou, Artemis
2001 *Functional structure in nominals: nominalization and ergativity.* John Benjamins.

Alexiadou, Artemis, and Elena Anagnostopoulou
2006 From hierarchies to features: person splits and direct-inverse alternations. In: Cedric Boeckx (ed.), *Agreement systems*. John Benjamins.

Anderson, Stephen
1977 On the mechanisms by which languages become ergative. In: Charles Li (ed.), *Mechanisms of syntactic change.* University of Texas Press.

Anderson, Stephen R., Lea Brown, Alice Gaby, and Jacqueline Lecarme
2006 Life on the edge: there's morphology there after all! *Lingue e Linguaggio* 5: 1–16.
Artiagoitia, Xabier
2001 Seemingly ergative and ergatively seeming. In: J Herschensohn et al (ed.), *Features and interfaces in Romance*. John Benjamins.
Assmann, Anke, Doreen Georgi, Fabian Heck, Gereon Müller, and Philipp Weisser
To appear Ergatives move too early. *Ms, University of Leipzig.*
Baker, Mark, and Nadezhda Vinokurova
2010 Two modalities of case assignment in Sakha. *Natural Language and Linguistic Theory* 28: 593–642.
Baker, Mark C.
To appear On dependent ergative case (in Shipibo) and its derivation by phase. *Ms, Rutgers.*
Bickel, Balthasar, and Yogendra Yādava
2000 A fresh look at grammatical relations in Indo-Aryan. *Lingua* 110: 343–373.
Bittner, Maria
1994 *Case, scope and binding*. Dordrecht: Kluwer.
Bittner, Maria, and Ken Hale
1996a Ergativity: Toward a theory of a heterogeneous class. *Linguistic Inquiry* 27: 531–604.
Bittner, Maria, and Ken Hale
1996b The structural determination of case and agreement. *Linguistic Inquiry* 27: 1–68.
Blake, Barry J.
1987 *Australian aboriginal grammar*. London: Croom Helm.
Bobaljik, Jonathan, and Philip Branigan
2006 Eccentric agreement and multiple case-checking. In: *Ergativity: emerging issues.*
Bobaljik, Jonathan David
2008 Where's Phi? Agreement as a postsyntactic operation. In: Daniel Harbour, David Adger, and Susana Béjar (eds.), *Phi theory*, 295–328. Oxford: Oxford University Press.
Bok-Bennema, Reineke
1991 *Case and agreement in Inuit*. Foris.
Bruening, Benjamin
2007 On the diagnostics of structural case and the nature of ergative case: a reply to Woolford 2006. University of Delaware.
Butt, Miriam
2006 *Theories of case*. Cambridge University Press.
Butt, Miriam, and Tracy Holloway King
2004 The status of case. In: Veneeta Dayal and Anoop Mahajan (eds.), *Clause structure in South Asian languages*. Kluwer.
Campana, Mark
1992 A movement theory of ergativity. Doctoral Dissertation, McGill University.
Chomsky, Noam
1986 *Barriers*. Cambridge, Mass: MIT Press.
Chomsky, Noam
2001 Derivation by phase. In: Michael Kenstowicz (ed.), *Ken Hale: A Life in Language*, 1–52. Cambridge, Mass: MIT Press.
Chung, Sandra
1982 Unbounded dependencies in Chamorro grammar. *Linguistic Inquiry* 13: 39–77.
Chung, Sandra
1998 *The design of agreement: evidence from Chamorro*. University of Chicago Press.
Collins, Chris, and Höskuldur Thraínsson
1996 VP-internal structure and object shift in Icelandic. *Linguistic Inquiry* 27: 391–444.
Comrie, Bernard
1978 Ergativity. In: W. P. Lehman (ed.), *Syntactic typology: studies in the phenomenology of language*, 329–394. University of Texas Pres.

Comrie, Bernard
1979 Degrees of ergativity: some Chukchee evidence. In: Frans Plank (ed.), *Ergativity*. Academic Press.
Comrie, Bernard
2008 Alignment of case marking of full noun phrases. In: David Gil and Bernard Comrie (eds.), *The World Atlas of Linguistic Structures*.
Coon, Jessica
2010a Complementation in Chol (Mayan): a theory of split ergativity. Doctoral Dissertation, MIT.
Coon, Jessica
2010b Rethinking split ergativity in Chol. *International Journal of American Linguistics* 76:207–253.
Coon, Jessica
2012 Split ergativity and transitivity in Chol. *Lingua* 122: 241– 256.
Coon, Jessica, Pedro Mateo Pedro, and Omer Preminger
2012 The role of Case in A-bar extraction asymmetries: evidence from Mayan. Ms., Harvard.
Coon, Jessica, and Omer Preminger
2012 Toward a unified account of person splits. In: *Proceedings of WCCFL 29.*
Corston, S. H.
1996 *Ergativity in Roviana, Solomon Islands*. Pacific Linguistics Series B: Monographs.
Craig, Colette
1977 *The structure of Jacaltec*. University of Texas Press.
Dayley, Jon P.
1981 Voice and ergativity in Mayan languages. *Journal of Mayan Linguistics* 2: 3–82.
Deal, Amy Rose
2010a Ergative case and the transitive subject: a view from Nez Perce. *Natural Language and Linguistic Theory* 28: 73–120.
Deal, Amy Rose
2010b Topics in the Nez Perce verb. Doctoral Dissertation, University of Massachusetts Amherst.
Deal, Amy Rose, and M.C. O'Connor
2011 The perspectival basis of fluid-S case-marking in Northern Pomo. In: Suzi Lima (ed.), *Proceedings of SULA 5*, 173–188. GLSA.
Dixon, R. M. W.
1972 *The Dyirbal Language of North Queensland*. Cambridge University Press.
Dixon, R. M. W.
1977 *A Grammar of Yidin*. Cambridge University Press.
Dixon, R. M. W.
1979 Ergativity. *Language* 55: 59–138.
Dixon, R. M. W.
1994 *Ergativity*. Number 69 in Cambridge Studies in Linguistics. Cambridge University Press.
Donohue, Mark, and Lea Brown
1999 Ergativity: some additions from Indonesia. *Australian Journal of Linguistics* 19: 57–76.
Donohue, Mark, and Søren Wichmann, (eds.)
2008 *The typology of semantic alignment*. Oxford University Press.
Doron, Edit, and G Khan
2012 The typology of morphological ergativity in Neo-Aramaic. *Lingua* 122: 225–240.
England, Nora
1983 *A grammar of Mam, a Mayan language*. University of Texas Press.
Gerdts, Donna
1988 *Object and absolutive in Halkomelem Salish*. Garland.

Gildea, Spike, and Flávia de Castro Alves
2010 Nominative absolutive: counter-universal split ergativity in Jê and Cariban. In: Spike Gildea and Francesc Queixalos (eds.), *Ergativity in Amazonia*.
Guiradello-Damian, Raquel
2010 Ergativity in Trumai. In: Spike Gildea and Francesc Queixalos (eds.), *Ergativity in Amazonia*. John Benjamins Publishing Company.
Hale, Ken
1983 Warlpiri and the grammar of non-configurational languages. *Natural Language and Linguistic Theory* 1: 5–48.
Hale, Kenneth
1982 Some essential features of Warlpiri main clauses. In: S. Swartz (ed.), *Work papers of SIL-AAB, Papers in Warlpiri Grammar in memory of Lothar Jagst*, Series A, Volume 6, 217–315. Darwin: Summer Institute of Linguistics.
Harris, Alice C.
1981 *Georgian syntax*. Cambridge: Cambridge University Press.
Harris, Alice C.
1982 Georgian and the unaccusative hypothesis. *Language* 58: 290–306.
Harris, Alice C.
2010 Origins of differential unaccusative/unergative case marking: implications for innateness. In: Donna B. Gerdts, John Moore, and Maria Polinsky (eds.), *Hypothesis A/Hypothesis B: linguistic explorations in honor of David M. Permutter*. MIT Press.
Johns, Alana
1992 Deriving ergativity. *Linguistic Inquiry* 23: 57–88.
Johns, Alana
2000 Ergativity: a perspective on recent work. In: Lisa L.-S. Cheng and Rint Sybesma (eds.), *The first Glot International state-of-the-article book*, 47–73. New York: Mouton de Gruyter.
Johns, Alana, Diane Massam, and Juvenal Ndayiragije, (eds.)
2006 *Ergativity: emerging issues*. Springer.
Keenan, Edward L., and Bernard Comrie
1977 Noun phrase accessibility and universal grammar. *Linguistic Inquiry* 8: 63–99.
König, Christa
2008 *Case in Africa*. Oxford University Press.
Kratzer, Angelika
1996 Severing the external argument from its verb. In: Johan Rooryck and Laurie Zaring (eds.), *Phrase structure and the lexicon*, 109–137. Dordrecht, The Netherlands: Kluwer Academic Publishers.
Kruspe, Nicole
2004 *A Grammar of Semelai*. Cambridge University Press.
Laka, Itziar
2006 Deriving split ergativity in the progressive: the case of Basque. In: Alana Johns, Diane Massam, and Juvenal Ndayiragije (eds.), *Ergativity: emerging issues*.
Larsen, Thomas, and William Norman
1979 Correlates of ergativity in Mayan grammar. In: Frans Plank (ed.), *Ergativity: Towards a Theory of Grammatical Relations*. Academic Press.
Legate, Julie Anne
2002 Warlpiri: theoretical implications. Doctoral Dissertation, MIT.
Legate, Julie Anne
2006 Split absolutive. In: Alana Johns, Diane Massam, and Juvenal Ndayiragije (eds.), *Ergativity: emerging issues*, 143–172.
Legate, Julie Anne
2008 Morphological and abstract case. *Linguistic Inquiry* 39: 55–101.

Legate, Julie Anne
2012 Types of ergativity. *Lingua* 122: 181–191.
Levin, Theodore, and Omer Preminger
To appear Case in Sakha: Are two modalities really necessary? *Natural language and Linguistic theory.*
Mahajan, Anoop
1994 The ergativity parameter: *have-be* alternation. In: Mercè Gonzàlez (ed.), *Proceedings of NELS 24*, 317–331.
Mahajan, Anoop
1997 Rightward scrambling. In: Dorothee Beerman, David LeBlanc, and Henk van Riemsdijk (eds.), *Rightward movement*, 185–213. Amsterdam: John Benjamins Publishing Company.
Mahajan, Anoop
2012 Ergatives, antipassives and the overt light v in Hindi. *Lingua* 122: 204–214.
Manning, Christopher
1994 Ergativity: argument structure and grammatical relations. Doctoral Dissertation, Stanford.
Marantz, Alec
1991 Case and licensing. In: Germán Westphal, Benjamin Ao, and Hee-Rahk Chae (eds.), *Eastern States Conference on Linguistics*, 234–253. Cornell University, Ithaca, NY: Cornell Linguistics Club.
Markman, Vita, and Pavel Grashchenkov
2012 On the adpositional nature of ergative subjects. *Lingua* 122: 257–266.
Merchant, Jason
2006 Polyvalent case, geometric hierarchies and split ergativity. In: *Proceedings of the 42nd Annual Meeting of the Chicago Linguistics Society.* CLS.
Merlan, F.
1985 Split intransitivity: functional oppositions in intransitive inflection. In: Johanna Nichols and Anthony C. Woodbury (eds.), *Grammar inside and outside the clause*. Cambridge University Press.
Miller, Cynthia L, and Leoma G Gilley
2001 Evidence for ergativity in Shilluk. *Journal of African languages and linguistics* 22: 33–68.
Miller, Mark T.
2007 A grammar of West Coast Bajau. Doctoral Dissertation, University of Texas at Austin.
Mithun, Marianne
1991 Active/agentive case marking and its motivations. *Language* 67: 510–546.
Mithun, Marianne
2008 The extension of dependency beyond the sentence. *Language* 84: 69–119.
Monrós, Eva
2007 A neglected foundation for the distinction between inherent and structural case: ergative as an inherent case. *Snippets* 16.
Montag, Susan
1981 *Diccionario Cashinahua*. Number 9 in Serie Lingüística peruana. Instituto Lingüístico de Verano.
Moravcsik, Edith A.
1974 Object-verb agreement. *Working Papers on Language Universals* 15.
Moravcsik, Edith A.
1978 On the distribution of ergative and accusative patterns. *Lingua* 45: 233–279.
Mulder, Jean Gail
1994 *Ergativity in Coast Tsimshian (Sm'algyax)*. University of California Press.

Müller, Gereon
2009 Ergativity, accusativity, and the order of Merge and Agree. In: Kleanthes K. Grohmann (ed.), *Explorations of phase theory: features and arguments*, 269–308. Mouton de Gruyter.
Nash, David
1980 Topics in Warlpiri grammar. Doctoral Dissertation, MIT.
Nash, Léa
1996 The internal ergative subject hypothesis. In: Kiyomi Kusumoto (ed.), *Proceedings of North East Linguistic Society*, 195–210. Amherst: Graduate Linguistic Student Association.
O'Connor, M. C.
1992 *Topics in Northern Pomo Grammar*. Outstanding dissertations in linguistics. Garland.
Otsuka, Yuko
2006 Syntactic ergativity in Tongan: resumptive pronouns revisited. In: Alana Johns, Diane Massam, and Juvenal Ndayiragije (eds.), *Ergativity: emerging issues*. Springer.
Patel, Pritty
2007 Split ergativity and the nature of agreement. Master's thesis, University College London.
Polinsky, Maria, and Eric Potsdam
2001 Long-distance agreement and topic in Tsez. *Natural Language and Linguistic Theory* 19: 583–646.
Preminger, Omer
2012 The absence of an implicit object in unergatives: new and old evidence from Basque. *Lingua* 122: 278–288.
Reilly, Ehren
2007 Morphological and phonological sources of split ergative agreement. *Lingua* 117: 1566–1590.
Rezac, Milan, Pablo Albizu, and Ricardo Etxepare
To appear The structural ergative of Basque and the theory of Case. *Natural Language and Linguistic Theory.*
Rude, Noel
1997 On the history of nominal case in Sahaptian. *International Journal of American Linguistics* 63: 113–143.
Salanova, Andrés Pablo
2007 Nominalizations and aspect. Doctoral Dissertation, MIT.
Sapir, Edward
1917 Review of Het passieve karakter van het verbum transitivum of van het verbum actionis in talen van Noord-Amerika [The passive character of the transitive verb or of the active verb in languages of North America] by C. C. Uhlenbeck. *International Journal of American Linguistics* 1: 82–86.
Seiter, William
1980 *Studies in Niuean syntax*. New York: Garland Publishing.
Silverstein, Michael
1976 Hierarchy of features and ergativity. In: RMW Dixon (ed.), *Grammatical categories in Australian languages*. Canberra: Australian Institute of Aboriginal Studies. [Reprinted 1986 in P. Muysken and H. van Riemsdijk (eds.), *Features and Projections*, Dordrecht: Foris].
Simpson, Jane
1991 *Walpiri morpho-syntax: a lexicalist approach*. Studies in Natural Language and Linguistic Theory. Kluwer.
Stepanov, Arthur
2004 Ergativity, case and the minimal link condition. In: *Minimality Effects in Syntax*. Mouton de Gruyter.

Stiebels, Barbara
2006 Agent focus in Mayan languages. *Natural Language and Linguistic Theory* 24: 501–570.
Trask, Larry
1979 On the origins of ergativity. In: Winfred Lehmann (ed.), *Syntactic Typology: Studies in the Phenomenology of Language.*
Trick, Douglas
2006 Ergative control of syntactic processes in Sama Southern. In: *10th International Conference on Austronesian Linguistics.*
Ura, Hiroyuki
2001 Case. In: Mark Baltin and Chris Collins (eds.), *The handbook of contemporary syntactic theory.* Blackwell Publishers.
Ura, Hiroyuki
2006 A parametric syntax of aspectually conditioned split ergativity. In: Alana Johns, Diane Massam, and Juvenal Ndayiragije (eds.), *Ergativity: emerging issues.*
Valenzuela, Pilar M
2010 Ergativity in Shipibo-Konibo, a Panoan language of the Ucayali. In: Spike Gildea and Francesc Queixalos (eds.), *Ergativity in Amazonia*, 65–96. John Benjamins.
Wiltschko, Martina
2006 On "ergativity" in Halkomelem Salish (and how to split and derive it). In: A. Johns, D. Massam, and J. Ndayiragije (eds.), *Ergativity.* Springer.
Woolford, Ellen
1997 Four-way case systems: Ergative, nominative, objective and accusative. *Natural Language and Linguistic Theory* 15: 181–227.
Woolford, Ellen
2006 Lexical case, inherent case, and argument structure. *Linguistic Inquiry* 37: 111–130.
Yip, Moira, Joan Maling, and Ray Jackendoff
1987 Case in tiers. *Language* 63: 217–250.

Amy Rose Deal, Santa Cruz, CA (USA)

21. Relative Clauses and Correlatives

Abstract

This article provides a survey of a range of relativization strategies: externally headed relative clauses, internally headed relative clauses, and correlative clauses. We examine the syntactic and semantic evidence for the constituency of the relative clause CP, the head NP, and the determiner. The different crosslinguistic strategies used to create relative clause-internal abstraction are investigated. Three different proposals concerning the relationship between the head NP and the relative clause CP, namely the head external analysis, the matching analysis, and the raising analysis, are evaluated. The article concludes with a brief look at contact relatives and appositive relatives.

1. Introduction

Relativization is the name given to a class of operations through which languages can construct expressions that convey arbitrarily complex properties from clauses. Relative clauses, the resulting expressions, are canonically clausal modifiers of noun phrases but can also function as modifiers of other categories. They can be used for restrictive as well as non-restrictive modification.

The study of relativization in natural language is a fertile and rich ground for the exploration of crosslinguistic variation. There seem to be no attested languages that entirely lack relativization strategies (cf. Keenan and Comrie 1977). Concomitant with that, we find considerable diversity in the way languages syntactically construct complex property denoting expressions. We begin with a consideration of this diversity before moving on to a discussion of various analytic possibilities.

2. Three relativization strategies

The relativization strategies found across languages can be divided into three groups based on the surface position of the modified NP with respect to the relative clause: externally headed relative clauses, internally headed relative clauses, and correlative clauses.

2.1. Externally headed relative clauses

The basic components of an externally headed relative clause are as follows:

(1) a. S_{rel} (the relative clause) (which contains a relativized position NP_{rel})
b. A domain noun external to S_{rel} (= the head NP)

(2) Externally Headed Relative Clause:
[$_{DP}$ vo [$_{NP}$ kita:b [$_{CP}$ jo sale-par hai]]] achchhi: hai [Hindi-Urdu]
DEM book REL sale-on be.PRS good.F be.PRS
'That book which is on sale is good.'

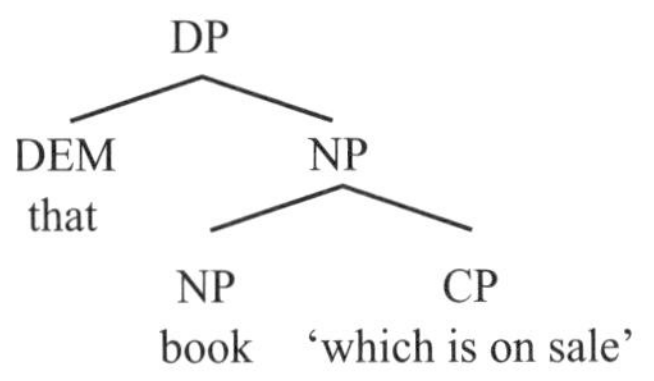

I am assuming here that the NP and the S_{rel} form a constituent that excludes the determiner. We will consider the arguments in favor of this structure when we turn to a discussion of the analytic possibilities. The relative clause can appear next to the NP that it modifies but it can also appear extraposed in a clauseperipheral position.

(3) Right adjoined Relative Clause
[DP vo [NP kita:b]] achchhi: hai [CP jo sale-par hai] [Hindi-Urdu]
DEM book.F good.F be.PRS REL sale-on be.PRS
'That book is good which is on sale.'

On the surface, all six conceivable orders of D, NP, and S_{rel} are attested. Relative clause can be prenominal or postnominal. English relative clauses are postnominal, Mandarin relative clauses are prenominal, and in German we find both prenominal and postnominal relative clauses.

(4) a. D(em) + Head + S_{rel} (English)
b. D(em) + S_{rel} + Head (German participial relatives)
c. Head + S_{rel} + D(em) (Yoruba; Kwa, Nigeria)
d. S_{rel} + Head + D(em) (Basque)
e. Head + D(em) + S_{rel} (Urhobo; Kwa, Nigeria)
f. S_{rel} + D(em) + Head (Mandarin, Korean)

Note that we find orders that do not allow for the NP and S_{rel} to be surface constituents – consider the order in (4e) from Urhobo and the order in (4f), which is found in a number of languages with prenominal relatives. For a detailed discussion of the ordering possibilities, see de Vries (2005).

In addition to their external syntax (prenominal vs. postnominal, extraposed or not), relative clauses also vary with respect to their internal syntax. For example, the relative clause can be finite, participial, or infinitival.

(5) a. finite: *the book [which John reads]*
g. participial: *the book [read by John]*
h. infinitival: *the book [for John to read]*

There is also considerable diversity in how the position inside the relative clause that is semantically abstracted over is marked. One major cut is whether a language uses relative phrases or not. We find languages like Hindi-Urdu where finite relative clauses require relative phrases, languages like English where relative phrases are possible but not obligatory, and languages like Mandarin where there are no overt relative phrases.

(6) a. *vo kitaab [*(jo) Ravi paṛh rahaa hai]* [Hindi-Urdu]
DEM book REL Ravi.M read Prog.M.SG be.PRS.SG
'the book which Ravi is reading'

b. *the book (which) Ravi is reading*

c. *[[dài yǎnjìngr de] nèi wèi xiānsheng] shì shéi?* [Mandarin]
wear glasses LNK that CL mister be who
'Who is the gentleman who is wearing glasses?'
(Chao 1968)

In the absence of relative phrases, the position abstracted over can be marked by a gap or by a resumptive pronouns. The former option is exemplified by Mandarin while the resumptive strategy is used extensively in Modern Hebrew, Arabic, and Persian.

We have examined three dimensions of variation so far: prenominal vs. postnominal, internal composition, and possibility of relative pronouns. These three dimensions are not indepedent. We find the following implicational generalizations between these three dimensions.

(7) a. prenominal relative clauses → no overt relative phrases
(Downing 1978: 392–394; Keenan 1985: 160; Kayne 1994: 93–95)
b. participial relative clauses → no overt relative phrases

Mandarin is an example of a language with prenominal relative clauses and no overt relative phrases. English provides an example of the second generalization – relative phrases are not found in participial relatives (*the book (*which) written by John*). These generalizations only go in one direction though. Not all postnominal relative clauses have overt relative phrases. Nor do all finite relative clauses. This is the case with Persian, which has postnominal finite relative clauses but which systematically lacks relative phrases.

(8) *('un) doxtar-i [ke Ali-ro doust dār-e] 'in-jā-st* [Persian]
DEM girl-REL that Ali-ACC friend have-3SG this-place-is
'The girl who likes Ali is here.'
(Aghaei 2006)

Let us now turn to the definitional property of externally headed relative clauses, which is that they have an NP head that is external to the relative clause. Moreover, they do not have a head internal to the relative clause. This seems to be generally the case with non-extraposed restrictive relative clauses.

(9) a. *the man [who/*[which man] Mina likes]*
b. *the man [whose mother/*[which man's mother] Mina likes]*

(10) a. no internal head:
mujhe [vo aadmii [jo Sita-ko pasand hai]] [Hindi-Urdu]
I.DAT that man REL Sita-DAT like be.PRS.SG
accha: nahī̃: lag-ta:
like NEG seem-IPFV.M.SG
'I don't like the man who Sita likes.'

b. with internal head:
**mujhe [vo aadmii [[jo aadmii] Sita-ko pasand* [Hindi-Urdu]
I.DAT that man REL man Sita-DAT like
hai]] accha: nahĩ: lag-ta:
be.PRS.SG like NEG seem-IPFV.M.SG
'I don't like the man who Sita likes.'

However, the restriction that there is no internal head seems to be too strong crosslinguistically. Varieties of Hindi-Urdu permit "light headed" structures like the following.

(11) internal head, no external head:
%mujhe [vo [[jo aadmii] Sita-ko pasand hai]] accha: [Hindi-Urdu]
I.DAT that REL man Sita-DAT like be.PRS.SG like
nahĩ: lag-ta:
NEG seem-IPFV.M.SG
'I don't like the man who Sita likes.'
(Mahajan 2000; see Junghare 1994 for Marathi)

Exceptions to the *no internal head* requirement have been noted for extraposed relative clauses and for non-restrictive relative clauses. In these cases, the head appears twice, externally and internally.

(12) internal head with external head (for parallel Marathi data see Junghare 1994)
%mujhe [vo aadmii] accha: nahĩ: lag-ta: [jo aadmii [Hindi-Urdu]
I.DAT that man like NEG seem-IPFV.M.SG REL man
Sita-ko pasand] hai]
Sita-DAT like be.PRS.SG
'I don't like the man who Sita likes.'
(Mahajan 2000; see also Marlow 1994)

(13) *I read the New Yorker, [which magazine is one of the finest in the country].*
(Chris Potts, p.c.; see also Keenan 1985 for Latin and Serbo-Croatian.)

2.2. Internally headed relative clauses

When there is no relative clause external NP head, we have an internally headed relative clause (IHRC). The internally headed relative clause (S_{rel}) contains inside it the position that is relativized over; we can refer to this position as the internal head.

(14) a. *?Ewa:-pu-L^y ?ciyawx* [Diegueño; Hokan, Amerindian]
house-DEF-in I.will.sing
'I will sing in the house.'

b. *TEnay ?Ewa:φ ?Ewu:w*
yesterday house-ACC I.saw
'I saw the house yesterday.'

c. *[TEnay ?Ewa:φ ?Ewu:w]-pu-L^y ?ciyawx*
yesterday house-ACC I-saw-DEF-in I.will.sing
'I will sing in the house that I saw yesterday.'
(Keenan 1985)

Generally S_{rel} is sufficiently nominalized to combine with determiners, case-marking, and adpositions. The explicit presence of external markers of quantification can in some cases be used to distinguish between internally headed relative clauses and free relative constructions, whose quantificational force seems to be fixed. However, a more principled and reliable distinction between free relatives and internally headed relative clauses remains elusive. We use the presence/absence of overt relative phrase marking as a working diagnostic for the free relative/internally headed relative clause distinction. Clauses that are called free relatives/correlatives have such marking while those that are called internally headed relatives do not. In many, but not all, IHRC languages, there is an indefiniteness restriction on the internal head as noted in Williamson (1987) for Lakhota and exemplified here by an example from the Kuki-Chin language Mizo.

(15) *Zova-n [Zovi-n lekhabu (*cu) a-lei] kha a-chiar-aŋ* [Mizo]
Zova-ERG Zovi-ERG book the 3S-buy Det 3SG-read-FUT
'Zova read the book Zovi bought.'
(Subbarao 2011)

However this indefiniteness requirement does not hold in Japanese (Shimoyama 1999) or Quechua (Hastings 2004), where the internal head can be universally quantified.

As noted by Hastings (2004), another point of variation between IHRC languages concerns the case-marking of the internal head NP. Some languages do not treat the internal head specially; it bears whatever case-marking it would have had in an unembedded clause. In others, the internal head appears without case. Both cases are exemplified below.

(16) a. head NP bears case (also Imbabura Quechua, see Cole 1987)
[nɨ-nɨ nistarɨ khaŋ sěti ṭhraʔ]-ba-tsə khɨtaŋ tšɨŋle [Sangtam]
you-NOM person to letter write-NMLZ-DEF very tall
'The person you wrote a letter to was very tall.'
(Subbarao 2011)

b. head NP does not bear case: dative marker *hnenaʔ* 'to/for' is missing from the IO (also Cuzco Quechua, see Hastings 2004)
[Lala-n bɔŋ bu a-pek] kha zanikhan a-thi [Hmar]
Lala-ERG cow food 3SG-give DET yesterday 3SG-died
'The cow Lala gave food to died.'
(Kumar p.c.)

The internal head of an IHRC is often not explicitly marked. This can lead to ambiguity. The ambiguity can be resolved in some languages by movement of the internal head.

(17) a. default IO DO word order: ambiguity

[nɔ-nɔ timi yesɨ (pewo) tsɨ]-ke-u-ye ivɔnɔ khušuwo [Sema]

you-ERG person letter ACC give-NMLZ-DEF-NOM very tall/long

'The person you gave the letter to is very tall.'

'The letter you gave to the person is very long.'

b. IO is fronted: ambiguity disappears

[timi nɔ-nɔ yesɨ (pewo) tsɨ]-ke-u-ye ivɔnɔ khušuwo

person you-ERG letter ACC give-NMLZ-DEF-NOM very tall/long

'The person you gave the letter to is very tall.'

(Subbarao and Kevichïsa 2005)

In (17b), the head NP is at the left edge of the relative clause. It is often assumed in the literature on internally headed relative clauses that the head NP undergoes such a movement, be it overt or covert (Cole 1987; Williamson 1987). This would yield a structure that would be very similar to externally headed relative clauses at LF.

(18) Surface: [D [... NP ...]]

LF: [D [NP$_i$ [... t$_i$ ...]]

Basilico (1996) points out that the movement of the head NP in at least some IHRC languages does not need to be all the way to the left edge. In yet other languages with IHRCs, it has been questioned whether the head NP needs to be moved at all; motivated by truth-conditional differences between internally headed relative clauses and externally headed relative clauses, Shimoyama (1999) argues that the link between the internal head and the matrix clause is an indirect one that does not require movement. She proposes that the link is best modeled as E-type anaphora between a silent *pro*-NP that heads the internally headed relative clause and the content of the relative clause. Hastings (2004) proposes a similar analysis for Imbabura Quechua. Striking support for the idea that the link between the *pro*-NP and the internal head can be indirect comes from cases like (19), where the matrix predicate cannot actually be directly predicated of the internal head NP.

(19) a. IHRC:

John-wa [Bill-ga orenzi-o sibot-ta] no-o [Japanese]

John-TOP [Bill-NOM orange-ACC squeeze-PST NMLZ-ACC

non-da.

drink-PST

'John drank the juice from the orange that Bill squeezed.'

b. *#Bill-ga orenzi-o non-da*

Bill-NOM orange-ACC drink-PST

'Bill drank the orange.'

c. Headed Relative:

[pro orenzi-o shibotta] juusu

orange-ACC squeezed juice

'the juice that someone squeezed from an orange'

(Hoshi 1995)

A further intriguing point emerges here: as (19c) shows, certain headed relative clauses might also involve the indirect E-type link needed for the IHRC in (19a).

2.3. Correlative clauses

The third kind of relative clause we will consider is the correlative clause. Correlatives are found in most Indo-Aryan languages (Srivastav 1991; Bhatt 2003), where they are also used to realize conditionals, *when*-clauses, comparatives, and *until*-clauses. They are also found in the major Dravidian languages (Subbarao 2011), Hittite (Berman 1972; Raman 1973), Hungarian (Liptak 2005), Warlpiri (Hale 1976; Keenan 1985); Medieval Russian (Keenan 1985), Old English (Curme 1912) and South Slavic: Bulgarian, Macedonian, and Serbo-Croatian (Izvorski 1996). See Lipták (2009) for a recent survey.

Correlative constructions consist of two clauses: the correlative clause (S_{rel}) that contains the position that is semantically abstracted over, the NP_{rel} and the main clause (S_{main}) which contains the domain NP. The internal makeup of S_{rel} typically resembles that of a free relative. The term correlative is often reserved for instances where S_{rel} precedes S_{main}.

(20) $[S_{rel} \dots NP_{rel} \dots] [S_{main} \dots NP_{ana} \dots]$

The domain NP (NP_{ana}) in a correlative construction is typically marked by devices that indicate deixis. Very often the distal demonstrative is used. No comparable demonstrative requirement holds for externally headed relative clauses.

(21) Simple Correlative:
$[_{CorCP} \dots \text{Rel-XP}_i \dots]_i \; [_{IP} \dots \text{Dem-XP}_i \dots]$

a. *[jo sale-par hai] [Maya* us CD-ko *khari:d-egi:]* [Hindi-Urdu]
REL sale-on be.PRS Maya.F DEM CD-ACC buy-FUT.F
'Maya will buy the CD that is on sale.'
(Lit. 'What is on sale, Maya will buy that CD.')

b. *[Aki korán jött], [azt ingyen beengedték].* [Hungarian]
REL.who early came that.ACC freely PV.admitted.3PL
'Those who came early were admitted for free.'
(Lipták 2005)]

Correlative clauses can appear in the left periphery discontinuous from the NPs they modify. Such correlatives can be multi-headed i.e. they can contain more than one NP_{rel}. This is not an option with externally headed relative clauses or with internally headed relative clauses.

(22) Multi-Head Correlatives:
$[_{CorCP} \dots \text{Rel-XP}_i \dots \text{Rel-YP}_j \dots]_{i,j} \; [_{IP} \dots \text{Dem-XP}_i \dots \text{Dem-YP}_j \dots]$

a. *[Aki amit kér], az azt elveheti.* [Hungarian]
REL.who REL.what.ACC wants that that.ACC take.POT.3SG
'Everyone can take what he/she wants.'
(Lipták 2005)

b. *[jya mula-ne$_i$ jya muli-la$_j$ pahila]$_{i,j}$ [tya mula-ne$_i$ tya* [Marathi]
REL boy-ERG REL girl-ACC saw DEM boy-ERG DEM
muli-la$_j$ pasant kela]
girl-ACC like did
'For boy *x*, girl *y* s.t. *x* saw *y*, *x* liked *y*.
(Lit. [Which boy saw which girl], [that boy liked that girl])

A matching requirement applies to (multi-head) correlatives: the number of relative phrases in the correlative clause must be matched by an equal number of corresponding demonstrative phrases in the main clause. See McCawley (2004) for some principled exceptions to this requirement.

Correlatives differ from headed relatives with respect to the possibility of having multiple heads. Unlike restrictive headed relatives, the head can appear in both the correlative clause and the main clause.

(23) a. 'head' in S_{rel}
[$_{Srel}$ [jo laṛkii] khaṛii hai] [$_{Smain}$ [vo] lambii [Hindi-Urdu]
REL girl.F standing.F be.PRS.SG DEM tall.F
hai]
be.PRS.SG
'The girl who is standing is tall.' (Lit. which girl is standing, she is tall.)

b. 'head' in S_{main}
[$_{Srel}$ [jo] khaṛii hai] [$_{Smain}$ [vo laṛkii] lambii hai]
REL standing.F be.PRS.SG DEM girl.F tall.F be.PRS.SG
'The girl who is standing is tall.' (Lit. who is standing, that girl is tall.)

c. 'head' in both S_{rel} and S_{main}
[$_{Srel}$ [jo laṛkii] khaṛii hai] [$_{Smain}$ [vo laṛkii] lambii hai]
REL girl.F standing.F be.PRS.SG DEM girl.F tall.F be.PRS.SG
'The girl who is standing is tall.' (Lit. which girl is standing, that girl is tall.)
(Srivastav 1991)

Correlative clauses resemble free relatives with respect to their internal syntax and their semantics. They differ in that while free relatives typically appear in argument positions, correlatives typically appear in adjoined positions. Like free relatives, but unlike headed relatives, they cannot be stacked and they allow elements like *ever*. The maximalization based semantics proposed for them by Srivastav (1991) is also similar to the maximalization based semantics proposed for free relatives by Jacobson (1995).

(24) a. Singular:
[jo laṛkii khaṛii hai] [vo lambii hai] [Hindi-Urdu]
REL girl.F standing.F be.PRS.SG DEM tall.F be.PRS.SG
'The girl who is standing is tall.'

b. Plural:
[jo laṛkiyā̃: khaṛii hẼ] [ve lambii hẼ]
REL girls.F standing.F be.PRS.PL DEM.PL tall.F be.PRS.PL
'All the standing girls are tall.'/'The girls who are standing are tall.'
(Dayal 1995)

The singular correlative in (24a) is felicitous only if there is only one standing girl in the context. The plural counterpart in (24b) picks out all the standing girls in the context and requires for truth that they are all tall. Generic interpretations are also available in the presence of appropriate aspectual operators. The Indo-Aryan languages allow very easily for episodic interpretations of correlatives. In some languages, generic interpretations seem to be preferred (see Lipták 2009 for Hungarian). Rebuschi (2009) claims that in Basque, correlatives entirely lack definite interpretations; they can only be used as generic statements.

One major question in the analysis of correlatives has been the relationship of the correlative clause and the demonstrative DP in the main clause that is associated with the correlative clause. Correlative clauses often appear discontinuous from the relevant demonstrative DP but at least for Hindi-Urdu, there is evidence that they can form a constituent with the demonstrative DP. On the other hand, Bhatt (2003) notes that in Bulgarian, correlative clauses can only appear adjoined to clauses. The relationship between the correlative clause and the demonstrative DP varies crosslinguistically. In principle, this relationship could be free from syntactic constraints. More often though we find that this relationship is subject to the familiar island restrictions. In languages like Bulgarian and Hungarian, the source of these restrictions is easy to identify: in these languages, the demonstrative phrase moves overtly to the edge of the main clause in correlative constructions.

(25) a′. [Correlative-Clause]$_i$ [$_{IP}$ Dem-XP$_i$ ... t$_i$ ...]
a. *[Kolkoto pari iska]$_i$ tolkova$_i$ misli če šte i dam* [Bulgarian]
how.much money wants DEM.much thinks that will her give.1SG
'She thinks that I'll give her as much money as she wants.'

b′. *[Correlative-Clause]$_i$ [$_{IP}$ ... Dem-XP$_i$]
b. **[Kolkoto pari iska]$_i$ misli cě stě i dam tolkova$_i$*
how.much money wants thinks that will her give.1SG DEM.much

c′. *[Correlative-Clause]$_i$ [$_{IP}$ Dem-XP$_i$ ... [$_{Island}$ ... t$_i$ ...]]
c. **[Kakto im kazah]$_i$ taka$_i$ čuh [$_{NP}$ sluha [$_{CP}$ cě t$_i$ sa postăpili]]*
how them told.1SG DEM.way heard.1SG the.rumor that are done
'I heard the rumor that they had acted the way I had told them to.'
(Izvorski 1996)

Islands that intervene between the base position of the demonstrative phrase and the edge of the main clause block the necessary movement, leading to ungrammaticality. In Hindi-Urdu, the demonstrative phrase stays *in-situ*; instead Bhatt (2003) argues that the correlative clause is merged adjoined to the demonstrative DP and moves overtly to its surface position. This movement is constrained by islands.

3. The constituency of D, NP, and CP

We have seen that externally headed relative clause constructions consist of a Determiner, an NP, and the relative clause CP. We will consider here the various structures that have been proposed for putting these components together. We can broadly group the proposals based on their tree geometry under the following three rubrics.

(26) structures for D NP CP
  a. the D CP analysis (Smith 1964):
     underlying structure: [[D CP] NP], obligatory extraposition of CP yields surface order
  b. the DP CP analysis: [$_{DP}$ DP CP]
  c. the NP CP analysis: [$_{DP}$ D [$_{NP}$ NP CP]]

3.1. The D CP structure

Motivation for the D CP analysis came from two kinds of facts (see Smith 1964). The first is that determiners seem to differ in what kind of relative clauses they permit. Certain determiners (*a, the*) allow for both restrictive and appositive relative clauses.

(27) both appositive and restrictive:
  a. *They pointed to a dog who was looking at him hopefully.*
  b. *They pointed to a dog, who was looking at him hopefully.*

The putative silent determiner that goes with proper names only allows for appositive relatives.

(28) only appositive:
  a. *John, who knows the way, has offered to guide us.*
  b. **John who is from the South hates us.*

There are also determiners (*any, all*) that only allow for restrictive relatives.

(29) only restrictive:
  a. **Any book, which is about linguistics, is interesting.*
  b. *Any book which is about linguistics is interesting.*

The idea then is that this pattern of selection can be captured by the D CP structure. A similar point is made by Alexiadou (2000: 9) using the German determiner *derjenige* 'the-that/the very'. Another kind of argument for this structure comes from a class of nouns like *way, kind, manner, time, place* that require either a relative clause, a modifier, or a demonstrative determiner.

(30) a. **He did it in a/the way.*
  b. *He did it in that way.*

c. *He did it in a certain way.*
d. *He did it in a/the way that I prescribed.*

In the D CP structure, the NP has a certain need that is satisfied by either the D or the CP. Postulating a D CP constituent allows us to give a non-disjunctive statement of the requirement of the NP.

The D CP analysis was proposed at a time before it was commonplace to use formal semantic explanations to explain certain patterns of grammaticality. With these in hand, the thrust of the arguments for the D CP is weakened. Plausible assumptions about the interactions of the syntax and semantics of DPs with the semantics of non-restrictive modification can help derive the 'selection' facts in (27–29). See Potts (2005) for a worked out proposal of this sort. As for the argument from NPs like *way*, it can also be recasted as a semantic requirement that the reference of such NPs be explicitly restricted; the restriction can be provided by a relative clause, *certain*, or the deictic component of a demonstrative determiner. Without these arguments, the case for the D CP structure with the additional extraposition operation that it requires is considerably weakened.

3.2. The DP CP structure

The DP CP structure was proposed by Ross (1967) as a structure for restrictive relative clauses. This structure was taken to receive support from examples where the determiner and the NP form a morphological unit on the surface that excludes the CP.

(31) a. *someone [who Marika likes]*
(von Stechow 1980)

b. *mus-en som vi såg* [Swedish]
mouse-DEF that we saw
'the mouse that we saw' / (restrictive)
'the mouse, which we saw' (non-restrictive)
(Hankamer and Mikkelsen 2005: 42a)

The strength of these arguments for this structure rests largely upon what we assume the structure of the morphologically complex head to be. If it lacks internal syntactic structure, then we have an argument for a restrictive DP CP structure. But if we allow the morphologically complex head to have internal structure, the argument for the DP CP structure does not go through. Decompositional structures where the relative clause modifies an indefinite NP part of *someone* would eliminate the need for a DP CP structure. The analysis of the data from Scandinavian remains contested. Embick and Noyer's (2001) proposal, which assumes N-D movement and Late Insertion, would allow for an NP CP structure; this is also the case for the Alternative Distributed Morphology proposal discussed by Hankamer and Mikkelsen (2005). They also consider a lexicalist proposal based in Hankamer and Mikkelsen (2002) and that requires a DP CP structure. The arguments against the DP CP structure come from classic constituency tests as well as from considerations of semantic interpretability and we turn to them in our discussion of the widely adopted NP CP structure. The DP CP structure turns out to face many challenges as a structure for restrictive relatives but it has come to be a widely-assumed structure for a family of analyses of non-restrictive relatives, capturing as it does the intuition that a non-restrictive relative is outside the DP proper (see Potts 2005, others, and generalizing somewhat even de Vries' 2006 structure [DP [: CP]] can be seen as related).

3.3. The NP CP structure

We turn finally to the most widely adopted constituency for restrictive relative clauses. This structure is discussed in Chapter 7 of Stockwell, Schachter, and Partee (1973). A very similar constituency was adopted in Montague's PTQ (Montague 1974), who extended ideas in Quine (1960).

Standard constituency tests such as *one*-substitution and coordination provide support for the NP CP structure. *One* can substitute for an NP CP sequence. Further an NP CP sequence can be co-ordinated with an NP sequence (*ruler of much of Gaul*).

(32) a. *Bill admires the very tall [student who came to Tom's lecture today]. Antony admires the very short one. one* substitutes for '[[student] [who came to Tom's lecture today]]'

b. *Clovis was the [[king who unified the Franks] and [ruler of much of Gaul]].*

A different kind of argument in favor of the NP CP structure comes from the Principle of Compositionality (from Partee 1975). To see this let us assume the following plausible assignment of types.

(33) a. D – (*et*)(*et*)*t* (or (*et*)*e* for *the*)

b. NP – *et* (property type meaning)

c. CP – *et* (property type meaning)

d. DP – (*et*)*t* or *e*

Given these types, the NP CP structure is the only one that works out. One attractive property of this structure (and its associated semantics) is that predicts without further stipulation that stacked relatives should be an option.

(34) *Any car that costs less than a hundred dollars that won't break down after a hundred miles would be a bargain.*

It should be noted, however, that a different assignment of basic types would in fact allow for the DP CP structures to be interpreted. A semantics of this sort is in fact proposed in Bach and Cooper (1978) inspired by correlative structures (in Hittite) where the relative clause appears discontinuous from a D NP constituent. More recently, Srivastav (1991) and Dayal (1996) have argued convincingly that correlatives are best given a different semantics but the force of the demonstration by Bach and Cooper remains; a DP CP structure can be given a compositional semantics and so the argument for the NP CP structure from compositionality needs to be supplemented with independent evidence.

4. Relative clause internal abstraction

Any relative clause contains a distinguished position, the position that is semantically abstracted over. Within and across languages there are many different ways of indicating this abstraction. We could start with perhaps the most unrestricted option – the *such that* relative discussed in Quine (1960) (see Ch. 5 of Heim and Kratzer 1998 for a useful discussion).

(35) a. *the book [such that [I bought it]]*
b. *the man [such that [the bell tolls for him]]*
c. *the man [such that [Mary review the book [he wrote]]]*

Even though *such that* relatives are undoubtedly, as Quine put it, unlyrical, they are part of our competence and they help illustrate certain restrictions that apply on other more natural means of abstraction. There are two noteworthy aspects of the *such that* strategy. The first is that the position abstracted over has a suitable pronoun *in situ* (*it, him he* above). The second is a point illustrated by (35c) – *such that* relativization is not subject to the usual island constraints. The position abstracted over is inside a relative clause island. We will see these aspects reappear in the other more restrictive strategies.

Languages vary with respect to the syntactic strategies used to mark relative clause internal abstraction and these strategies in turn restrict the positions that can be abstracted over. A study of these restrictions led to a productive line of work by Ed Keenan and Bernard Comrie under the rubric of Noun Phrase Accessibility (see Keenan and Comrie 1977). They proposed the following Accessibility Hierarchy and associated constraints.

(36) Accessibility Hierarchy (AH)
SU > DO > IO > OBL > GEN > OCOMP

The Hierarchy Constraints:
a. A languages must be able to relativize subjects.
b. Any RC-forming strategy must apply to a continuous segment of the AH.
c. Strategies that apply at one point of the AH may in principle cease to apply at any lower point.

The Accessibility Hierarchy and its associated constraints raise a number of analytical questions. Is the Accessibility Hierarchy a primitive of the theory of relative clauses or can it be made to follow from general syntactic principles? What qualifies as a RC-forming strategy? Since relative clauses have no primitive status in syntactic theory to begin with, we take it that generalizations like the Accessibility Hierarchy should follow from general syntactic principles that govern the derivation of long-distance dependencies. As for RC-forming strategies, we consider three distinct cases here.

(37) a. Non-Local Strategies
i. Overt A-bar movement strategies
ii. Resumptive Strategies
b. Local Strategies

4.1 Local strategies

The first two strategies allow us to abstract over arbitrarily deeply embedded positions modulo any applicable island restrictions. Local strategies typically limit abstraction to the highest argument position in the relative clause. This is the case in Malagasy where only subjects can be relativized. To relativize non-subjects, the non-subject needs to first become a syntactic subject. Once this has taken place, it can be relativized as a subject.

(38) a. main clause:
Nahita ny vehivavy ny mpianatra. [Malagasy]
saw the woman the student
'The student saw the woman.'

b. relative clause on subject:
ny mpianatra [izay [nahita ny vehivavy]]
the student that saw the woman
'The student who saw the woman.'

c. relative clause on object:
**ny vehivavy [izay [nahita ny mpianatra]]*
the woman that saw the student
'the woman that the student saw'

d. passive:
Nohitan-'ny mpianatra ny vehivavy.
see.PASS-the student the woman
'The woman was seen by the student.'

e. relative clause on subject of passive:
ny vehivavy [izay [nohitan'-ny mpianatra]]
the woman that seen-the student
'The woman that was seen by the student'
(Keenan 1972)

Similar cases are found in other Austronesian languages such as Javanese, Iban, Minang-Kabau, and Toba-Batak. Tagalog can also be given a similar treatment if we assumed that its focus position counts as the highest argument position in the relative clause. Participial relatives in Hindi-Urdu display a similar local abstraction restriction. Like in English, present participial relatives only allow for abstraction of subjects. The possibility of abstraction is not affected by the argument structure properties of the predicate of the participial clause.

(39) a. subject abstraction of transitive:
[[phal khaa-taa] bandar] [Hindi-Urdu]
fruit eat-IPFV.M.SG monkey.M
'the monkey [eating fruit]'

b. object abstraction of transitive: *
[[bandar(-kaa) khaa-taa] phal]
monkey-GEN eat-IPFV.M.SG fruit.M
intended: 'the fruit the monkey eats/is eating'

c. subject abstraction of unergative:
[[ro-taa] baccaa]
cry-IPFV.M.SG child.M
'the crying child'

d. subject abstraction of unaccusative:
[[ubal-taa] paanii]
boil-IPFV.M.SG water.M
'the boiling water'

Past participial relatives display a different pattern which at first looks as if it allows abstraction over object positions. A closer examination reveals that the relevant structures are actually passive participles and hence abstraction is indeed over the highest argument. In fact, the participles involved here do not seem to allow for external arguments and hence past participial relatives may only be over objects of transitives and subjects of unaccusatives but not over subjects of unergatives or transitive.

(40) a. subject of transitive: *
[[kitaab paṛh-aa (huaa)] laṛkaa] [Hindi-Urdu]
book read-PFV.M.SG PTCP.M.SG boy.M.SG
intended: 'the boy who read the book'
(literally: *the boy [read the book])

b. object of transitive → subject of passive:
[[Salma-dwaaraa likh-ii (gayii/huii)] ciṭṭhii]
Salma-by write-PFV.F PASS.PFV.F/PTCP.F letter.F
'the letter written by Salma'

c. unergative:
[[aaj subah kuud-ii (huii)] laṛkii]
this morning jump-PFV.F PTCP.F girl
intended: 'the girl who jumped this morning'

d. unaccusative:
[[aaj subah khul-aa] darwaazaa]
this morning open-PFV.M.SG door.M.SG
'the door which opened this morning'
(Subbarao 2011: Ch. 9)

The exact nature of the operation that is implicated in these participial relatives is not clear. But based on its very local character, we can conclude that it is not standard A-bar movement. Short movement of PRO is a promising candidate. Data from so-called "dative subject" constructions reveals further that only nominative positions can be abstracted on in Hindi-Urdu participial relatives.

(41) a. dative subject construction: Dative Nominative
Atif-ko coṭ lag-ii hai [Hindi-Urdu]
Atif-DAT hurt.F feel-PFV.F be.PRS.SG
'Atif is hurt.'

b. no abstraction on dative subject:
**[[coṭ lag-aa] laṛkaa]*
hurt.F feel-PFV.M.SG boy.M.SG
intended: 'the boy who was hurt'

c. abstraction on nominative:
[[Atif-ko lag-ii] coṭ] bahut gahrii hai
Atif-DAT feel-PFV.F hurt.F very deep.F be.PRS.SG
'The injury that Atif has is quite deep.'

One way of interpreting this restriction is to take it to show that dative subjects do not qualify as the highest argument in their clause. The restriction would also follow if participial relatives in Hindi-Urdu involved short movement of PRO given Davison (2008)'s argument that only nominative arguments in Hindi-Urdu can be PRO.

Before we turn to more non-local relativization strategies, it is worth noting that not all participles are created alike, within and across languages. We have already seen in Hindi-Urdu that past participial relatives in Hindi-Urdu seem to be structurally smaller than present participial relatives disallowing external arguments. Other languages display past participial relatives that are not reduced and participial relatives that allow for long-distance abstraction. This is the case in the Indo-Aryan language Marathi.

(42) a. abstraction on dative argument:
[[tyā-ne __ āmantraṇ patrikā dilelī] saglī māṇsa] [Marathi]
he-ERG invitation cards give.PFV all.PL people.PL.M
lagnālā ālī
wedding.that come.PFV.3PL.M
'All the people who he had sent invitation cards had come to the wedding.'

b. abstraction on subject of embedded finite clause:
[[rām-ne [pikle āhet] sāŋgitlele]] ã:mbe] āmh wikat
Ram-ERG ripe are tell-PFV.3PL.M mangoes.3PL.M we buy
ghetle
take.PST.3PL.M
'We bought the mangoes that Ram told us were ripe.'
(Pandharipande 1997: 90, 94)

Only local relativization is possible with participial relatives in a number of familiar languages (English, German, Russian etc.) but it is not a general property of participial relatives crosslinguistically.

4.2. Non-local strategies

Non-local strategies involve A-bar movement of a relative phrase or null operator, binding of a resumptive pronoun, or both.

4.2.1. A-Bar movement of relative operator

Let us first examine cases involving relative phrases and null operators to see that these do involve A-bar movement. In English, the link between wh-movement in question formation and relative clauses is very clear; for the most part, the same set of elements can function as relative pronouns and interrogative pronouns. In many cases, a null operator strategy is also available in English. Both allow for abstraction over arbitrarily deeply embedded positions and license parasitic gaps.

(43) a. *the book [which/∅$_i$ [I like t$_i$]]*
b. *the book [which/∅$_i$ [Mary said [I like t$_i$]]]*
c. *the book [which/∅$_i$ [you thought [Mary said [I like t$_i$]]]]*
d. *the book [which/∅$_i$ [Mary filed t$_i$ [without reading pg$_i$]]]*

The movement in question is subject to the usual island constraints such as the Complex NP Constraint, the Sentential Subject Constraint, and the Coordinate Structure Constraint as well the *that*-trace effect.

(44) a. Complex NP Constraint:
**The hat [which/∅$_i$ [I believed the claim [that Otto was wearing t$_i$]]] is red.*
(Ross 1967: 4.18a)

b. Sentential Subject Constraint:
**The students [whom/∅$_i$ [[that the chairman had sent the information to t$_i$] was assumed by the dean]] .....* (Stockwell et al. 1973: 453: 59b)

c. Coordinate Structure Constraint:
**The lute [which/∅$_i$ [Henry [[plays t$_i$] and [sings madrigals]]]] is warped.*
(Ross 1967: 4.82b)

d. *that*-trace Effect:
*the student [who/∅$_i$ [you thought [(*that) t$_i$ liked me]]]*

It is clear that there is A-bar movement in relative clauses but it is not completely clear what the landing site of this movement is. A commonly held assumption is that relative operators move into SpecCP (like other instances of A-bar movement) while relative complementizers occupy C^0. With this we are able to handle the acceptable cases but we need to appeal to the Doubly-filled COMP filter to block cases like (45d).

(45) a. *the book [$_{CP}$ which$_i$ [$_{C'}$ C^0[$_{TP}$ I like t$_i$]]]*
b. *the book [$_{CP}$ Op$_i$ [$_{C'}$ C^0[$_{TP}$ I like t$_i$]]]*
c. *the book [$_{CP}$ Op$_i$ [$_{C'}$ C^0[that] [$_{TP}$ I like t$_i$]]]*
d. **the book [$_{CP}$ which$_i$ [$_{C'}$ C^0[that] [$_{TP}$ I like t$_i$]]]*

Given the decomposition of the C-domain into a number of distinct projections (see Rizzi 1997), different instances of A-bar movement (relative phrase movement, interrogative phrase movement, focus movement etc.) can target different sites. Unlike English, in many languages, relative phrases and interrogative phrases have different forms and syntactic behavior. Consider the *j*-forms for relative pronouns and *k*-forms for interrogative pronouns in Indo-Aryan languages and the fact that while *wh*-phrases in Hindi-Urdu prefer to be (at least descriptively) *in situ*, relative phrases strongly prefer fronting. Even within English, there are clear differences between relative phrases and interrogative phrases with respect to the availability of null operators and the extent of pied-piping. The motivations that drive the movement of relative phrases and that of interrogative phrases are distinct and this can be used to explain the following contrast in Hungarian. Topicalization in Hungarian can feed relativization but not question-formation or focusing.

(46) a. Topicalization:
Pétert van aki nem ismeri még. [Hungarian]
Peter.ACC is REL.who not knows yet
'Peter, there are people who don't know him yet.'

b. Relativization:
Ez az a fiú, akit van aki nem ismeri még.
this that the boy REL.who.ACC is REL.who not knows yet
'This is the boy who there are people who don't know him yet.'

c *Wh*-Movement:
**Kit van aki nem ismeri még.*
who.ACC is REL.who not knows yet
'Who is it such that there are people who don't know him yet?'
(Aniko Lipták p.c.)

I take this contrast to show that the feature content/semantics of topicalization is incompatible with question formation but not with relativization.

4.2.2 Resumption

Next we turn to strategies that involve resumption. One might imagine that resumption and A-bar movement are in complementary distribution. However, detailed work on a range of languages with pervasive resumption such as Arabic and Hebrew has revealed the important role that A-bar movement plays in the derivation of many cases of resumption. A particularly striking case where we see resumption and movement together comes from Hebrew (Sells 1984).

(47) a. in-situ resumptive:
ha-ʔš še ʔani xošev še ʔamarta še sara katva [Hebrew]
the-man that I think that said.you that Sarah wrote
-ʔlav šir
about.him poem
'The man that I think that you said that Sarah wrote a poem about.'

b. resumptive in *said* clause:
ha-ʔš še ʔani xošev še ʔlav ʔamarta še sara katva šir
the-man that I think that about.him said.you that Sarah wrote poem
'The man that I think that you said that Sarah wrote a poem about.'

c. resumptive in *think* clause:
ha-ʔš še ʔlav ʔani xošev sě ʔamarta še sara katva šir
the-man that about.him I think that said.you that Sarah wrote poems
'The man that I think that you said that Sarah wrote a poem about.'

d. resumptive at the top:
ha-ʔš ʔlav ʔani xošev še ʔamarta še sara katva šir
the-man about.him I think that said.you that Sarah wrote poem
'The man that I think that you said that Sarah wrote a poem about.'
(resumptive pronouns are boldfaced)

(Sells 1984)

Demirdache (1991) takes this paradigm to lend support to her proposal that *in-situ* resumptives move overtly at LF in a manner similar to the overt movement of relative pronouns and the movement of in the above example. However, not all cases of productive resumption involve A-bar movement; using evidence from Complementizer Agreement, McCloskey (1990, 2002) argues that resumptive relatives differ from gap relatives in Irish in not involving A-bar movement. Finally, irrespective of the language in question, cases of resumption inside islands presumably do not involve A-bar movement.

5. The head NP and the relative clause

We have converged on the [D [NP CP]] structure for restrictive relative clauses. But so far we have not touched upon a question that has been central to the analysis of relativization: what is the relationship of the head NP to the relative clause? what information about the head NP is available within the relative clause CP? There are two contrasting intuitions here which have led to very different analyses. One intuition is that the head NP occupies two positions – one in its surface position in the matrix clause and one inside the relative clause. This leads to the head raising analysis. The other intuition thinks of the relative clause essentially as a predicate that combines intersectively with the head: the relationship between the head NP and the relative clause is limited to their sisterhood in the syntax and the head NP is not derivationally/syntactically related to a relative clause internal position. This intuition leads to the head external analysis. The third analysis, the matching analysis, combines elements of both analyses; information about the head NP is available inside the relative clause but the head NP does not itself move out of the relative clause.

5.1. The three analyses

5.1.1. The head raising analysis

The head raising analysis was originally proposed by Brame (1968), Schachter (1973), and Vergnaud (1974). Recent versions include Åfarli (1994), Kayne (1994), Sauerland (1998, 2003), Bianchi (1999), Bhatt (2002), and de Vries (2002) among others. Under the head raising analysis, the head NP originates inside the relative clause CP in the position associated with NP_{rel}. In the particular variant that I am sketching here, the head NP is merged as the complement of a relative operator. The relative operator can be overt or covert in English. The DP that consists of the head NP and the relative operator moves to the SpecCP of the relative clause. From here, the head NP moves on further, stranding the relative operator.

(48) *the [book]$_j$ [$_{CP}$ [Op/which t$_j$]$_i$ John likes t$_i$]*

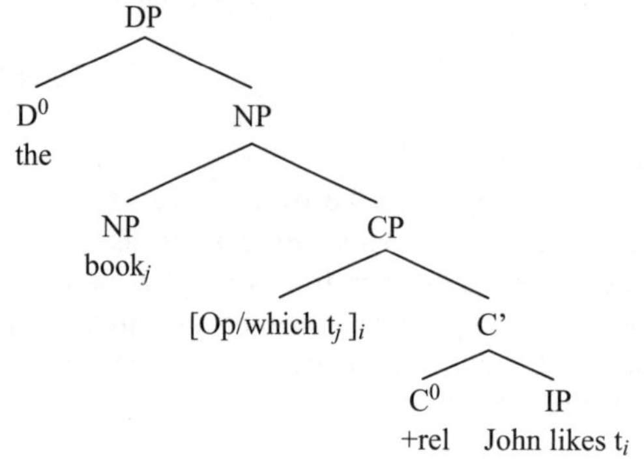

Since the head NP originates inside the relative clause CP, it is possible to reconstruct it inside the relative clause and interpret it in a relative clause-internal position. The movement of the head NP out of the relative clause also explains why the head NP cannot appear with the relative phrase (**the book [[which book] I like]*), something which requires an additional statement in the head external analysis. The particular variant of the head raising analysis sketched here has the head NP raising out of the CP and projecting further. What is important is that the NP moves out of the CP; whether it projects further or moves into the specifier of a functional projection is not essential. Bianchi (1999: 79) proposes a variant where the NP moves out of SpecCP into the SpecAgr$_D$.

(49) *[$_{DP}$ the [$_{AgrP}$ boy$_i$ $_{AgrD}$ [$_{CP}$ [$_{DP}$ who t$_i$]$_j$ C [$_{IP}$ I met t$_j$]]]]*

This variant is compatible with what follows. In contrast, Kayne (1994)'s proposal has the NP staying inside the SpecCP in the specifier of *which*, making *book which* a surface constituent.

(50) *[$_{DP}$ the [$_{CP}$ [$_{DP}$ boy$_i$ [who t$_i$]]$_j$ C [$_{IP}$ I met t$_j$]]]]*

Coordination and extraposition data militate against this constituency.

5.1.2. The head external analysis

The head external analysis is quite ubiquitous in the literature, so much so that its origins are unclear. Quine (1960) seems to suggest it, and it is assumed in Montague (1970),

Partee (1975), Chomsky (1973, 1977), Jackendoff (1977) as well as textbooks like Haegeman (1991) and Heim and Kratzer (1997). The head NP originates outside the relative clause CP. Since the head NP is never inside the relative clause CP, it cannot be reconstructed into a relative clause-internal position. The relative clause CP involves *A′*-movement of a relative operator, which may be overt or covert. The relative clause CP is adjoined to the head NP and the two combine semantically via intersective modification.

(51) *the book [$_{CP}$ Op$_i$/which$_i$ John likes t$_i$]*

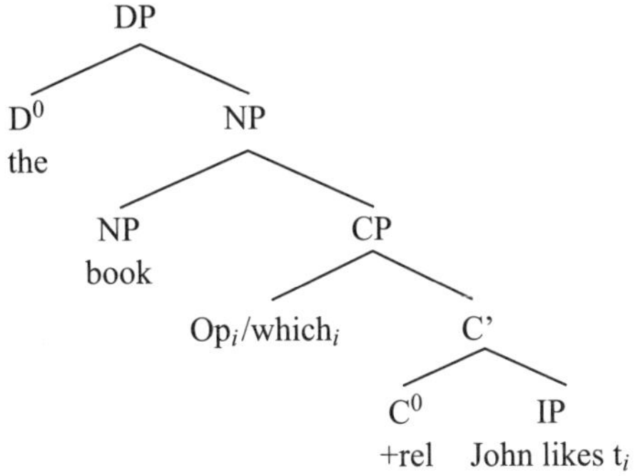

5.1.3. The matching analysis

The matching analysis was originally proposed in Lees (1960, 1961) and Chomsky (1965). It was developed and extended by Sauerland (1998, 2003) and Hulsey and Sauerland (2006). The version sketched here is Sauerland's. The matching analysis can be seen as halfway between the head external analysis and the head raising analysis. The matching analysis postulates that corresponding to the external head there is an internal head which is obligatorily phonologically deleted under identity with the external head. However, the internal head and the external head are not part of a movement chain. In fact Sauerland argues that in certain cases, the lexical material of the internal head and that of the external head do not need to be identical. They just need to be similar enough, thus allowing mismatches of the sort found with ellipsis.

(52) *the [book] [$_{CP}$ [Op/which book]$_i$ John likes t$_i$]*

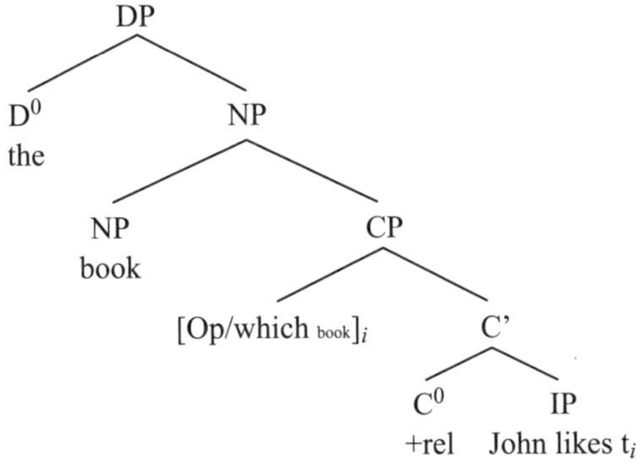

The matching analysis resembles the head external analysis in that the external head does not originate within the relative clause CP. However, the matching analysis does involve a relative clause internal representation of the external head. Since the external head and its relative clause-internal representation are not related by movement, both must be interpreted.

5.2. Choosing between the analyses

On the surface, the head NP is clearly in the matrix clause. In languages where case-marking is visible on the head NP, the case borne by the head NP corresponds to the matrix case and not to the relative clause internal case, which is borne by the relative phrase. The head NP does not seem to be in the scope of relative clause-internal material – consider the possibility of coreference between *John* and *he* in (53).

(53) a. *In [[pictures of Al$_i$] which he$_i$ lent to us], he is shaking hands with the president.*

(from Munn 1994 via Safir 1999)

b. *the picture of John$_i$ he$_i$ likes ....*

(Sauerland 1998: 76)

The issue then is what the motivation is for postulating a relative clause internal origin for the head NP. In this section I will discuss some of the arguments that have been previously adduced in favor of a relative clause internal origin for the external head of a relative clause. What these arguments will tell us is that information about the external head is available inside the relative clause CP. Since both the head raising analysis and the matching analysis make information about the external head available inside the relative clause CP, these arguments will not in general differentiate between the head raising and the matching analyses. When they do so, this will be noted.

These arguments will also be evaluated with respect to the following question: does the external head have to have a relative clause internal representation, or is it is enough to say that it is possible for the external head to have a relative clause internal representation? The larger question is whether the grammar permits more than one analysis for relative clauses e.g. head external as well as raising, or raising as well as matching.

5.2.1. Idioms

The logic behind the argument from idioms for a raising analysis goes as follows: the idiom can only appear as part of a larger expression. The larger expression is shown in the (54–57a). That it cannot appear outside this context is shown in (54–57b). However, the idiom is able to felicitously appear as the head NP of a relative clause, where the position it is associated with inside the relative clause (its trace) is part of the larger expression it needs to appear with. This is shown by the examples in (54–57c).

Under a head external analysis, given the unacceptability of the examples in (54–57b), the acceptability of the examples in (54–57c) is unexpected and vice versa. The raising analysis is able to explain these facts parsimoniously. Idioms need to appear in a particular environments as shown by the examples in (54–57a) and the unacceptability of the examples in (54–57b). The examples in (54–57c) are acceptable because the idiom appears in the relevant environment at some point in the derivation (minimally point of Merge, maybe also at LF).

(54) a. *We made headway.*
b. **The headway was satisfactory.*
c. *The headway that we made was satisfactory.*
(attributed to Brame 1968 ms., ex. 35 from Schachter 1973)

(55) a. *She's keeping careful track of her expenses.*
b. **The careful track pleases me.*
c. *The careful track that she's keeping of her expenses pleases me.*
(ex. 36 from Schachter 1973)

(56) a. *Lip service was paid to civil liberties at the trial.*
b. **I was offended at (the) lip service.*
c. *I was offended by the lip service that was paid to civil liberties at the trial.*
(ex. 37 from Schachter 1973)

(57) a. *He solved the problem in a clever way.*
b. *The clever way in which he solved the problem impressed me.*
c. **The clever way impressed me.*
(attributed to George Bedell, fn. 15 from Schachter 1973)

The argument from idioms is based on an assumption about how idioms are interpreted/ stored in the lexicon. We need to assume that the domain of special meaning is local. In other words, two elements which can be arbitrarily far apart from each other in a structure at the point of Merger cannot be given a special meaning. This assumption is plausible. The alternative requires stipulating that the special meaning of the idiom is available if (i) its parts are merged in a certain local configuration *ID*, or (ii) a part of the idiom is the External Head of a relative clause and the *A'*-moved phrase involved in the formation of this relative clause and the remaining parts of the idiom were merged in the local configuration ID. This alternative is stipulative. That the head raising analysis is implicated in the following idiom cases receives support from binding theory reconstruction data. When the head NP is part of an idiom that is licensed relative clause-internally, we find binding theory reconstruction effects.

(58) a. **[The [headway on Mary$_i$'s project [she$_i$ had made]] pleased the boss.*
b. *[The [headway on her$_i$ project] [Mary$_i$ had made]] pleased the boss.*
(ex. 24 from Sauerland 2003)

McCawley (1981) notes that idioms can sometimes be licensed in the matrix clause.

(59) a. *We made headway that was sufficient.*
(**The headway was sufficient.*)

b. *John pulled the strings that got Bill his job.*
(**The strings/Strings got Bill his job.*)

Such cases do not fit well within a raising analysis as the head NP does not form a unit with the rest of the idiom inside the relative clause. They are, however, less problematic under the head external analysis. Under the head external analysis, the special meaning of the idiom will be licensed at the point of Merge e.g. by being merged as the object of *make* in (59a). Certain questions still remain open. What exactly does the relative clause modify semantically in (59a, b)? A similar issue arises in *We have made sufficient headway.* Once we give an appropriate semantic denotation to the head NP in (59a, b), Sauerland's matching analysis can handle these cases. The identity between the external head and its representation is established at LF under the matching analysis not with the literal form of the idiom, but with whatever its semantic representation is. The matching analysis also does well with cases like *They made the headway that they had hoped to make*, where the idiom is licensed both in the matrix clause and the relative clause.

The argument from idiom tells us different things, depending upon which part of it we look at. If we look at the cases where the idiom is licensed inside the relative clause but not in the matrix clause, we have an argument that supports the head raising analysis but not the head external or the matching analysis. If we look at cases where the idiom is licensed in the matrix clause but not in the relative clause, the picture is reversed. We have an argument for the head external or the matching analysis but not for the raising analysis.

5.2.2. Amount relatives

The existence of amount readings provides another reason for assuming a relative clause-internal representation of the external head. In (60), for independent reasons, we do not wish to entertain a variable following *there be* (cf. Carlson 1977; Heim 1987; Grosu and Landman 1998).

(60) *The very few books that there were on his shelves were all mysteries.*
LF: The very few λd that there were *d*-many-books on his shelves were all mysteries.
(from Heim 1987: 33; also see Carlson 1977)

Under the head raising analysis, it is postulated that the external head of the relative clause is reconstructed in its trace position and the abstraction is over a degree variable. It is possible to interpret the external head in the position corresponding to the trace of the relative clause-internal *A'*-movement only under the raising analysis. This analysis of amount relatives provides independent support to the head raising analysis.

Reconstruction of the head NP in amount readings can take the head NP below another scope bearing element thus producing scope reconstruction effects. This is the the case in (61) and (62).

(61) a. *No linguist would read the many books Gina will need for vet school.*
possible reading: need > many

b. *Mary shouldn't even have the few drinks that she can take.*
possible reading: can > few
(exs. from Sauerland 1998: 54a, b)

(62) *I am worried about the twenty five people likely to come for dinner tomorrow.*
possible reading: likely > 25 people
(Heim p.c.)

The external determiner itself does not reconstruct; only quantificational material that can be part of the head NP reconstructs as shown by the following contrast. A common theme running across various implementations of the head raising analysis and the matching analysis is that what is shared across the matrix clause and the relative clause is the head NP and not the entire matrix DP. The one exception I know of is Koster-Moeller and Hackl (2008).

(63) a. *Ho telefonato ai due pazienti che ogni medico visiterà domani.* [Italian]
have phoned the two patients that every doctor examine.FUT tomorrow
'I have phoned the two patients that every doctor will examine tomorrow.'
(∀ > 2 possible)

b. *Ho telefonato a due pazienti che ogni medico visterà domani.*
have phoned OM two patients that every doctor examine.FUT tomorrow
'I have phoned two patients that every doctor will examine tomorrow.'
(*∀ > 2 not possible)
(Bianchi 1999: 31a, b)

Sauerland (2003) offers binding-theoretic support for the claim that scope reconstruction and amount relativization force the raising analysis. Even though relative clause heads do not in general display reconstruction for Condition C, Condition C effects surface in the presence of scope reconstruction and amount relativization.

(64) a. **It would have taken us all year to read the letters for John$_i$ [he$_i$ expected there would be __].*

b. *It would have taken us all year to read the letters for him$_i$ [John$_i$ expected there would be __].*
(from Sauerland 2003: 27)

We see therefore that the derivation of amount readings requires a head raising analysis. The existence of amount readings does not, however, provide evidence against the existence of the head external analysis or the matching analysis elsewhere.

5.2.3. Variable binding effects, take 1

Quantifiers inside a relative clause are able to bind a pronoun embedded in the external head of the relative clause. Moreover a relative clause internal quantifier is able to bind a pronoun embedded in the external head only if it would have been able to bind the relevant pronoun, were the external head replaced in the relative clause internal gap.

(65) a. i. *[[The picture of his$_i$ mother] that every soldier$_i$ kept ___ wrapped in a sock] was not much use to him.*
ii. *Every soldier$_i$ kept [a picture of his$_i$ mother] wrapped in a sock.*

b. i. *John generally has [[an opinion of his$_i$ book] that every novelist$_i$ respects ___].*
ii. *Every novelist$_i$ respects [John's/an opinion of his$_i$ book].*

c. i. ??*John generally has [[an opinion of his$_i$ book] that ___ is useful to every author].*
ii. ??*[John's opinion of his$_i$ book] is useful to every author$_i$.*

(a–c.i are 70a–c from Safir 1999)

These facts were noticed for Norwegian by Åfarli (1994) and Italian by Bianchi (1995); they receive a straightforward explanation if we assume that the external head of the relative clause can be interpreted in the position of the relative clause internal gap. Such an explanation is unavailable under the head external analysis or the matching analysis. However, the force of such an explanation is undercut by Sharvit (1999)'s observation that not only can the relative clause internal subject quantifier bind a variable in the head NP, it can also do so in the predicate.

(66) *The picture of himself$_i$ that everybody$_i$ likes is gracing his$_i$ homepage.*

She takes these facts as motivation for a semantic mechanism that allows a relative clause internal subject quantifier to bind outside the relative clause eliminating the need for syntactic reconstruction of the head in the cases at hand. Alternatively, one could allow the subject quantifier to scope out of the relative clause syntactically, a possibility suggested in Sauerland (2003). Either option weakens the argument for reconstructing the head NP. However, Sharvit's point is limited to relative clause internal subject quantifiers and Sauerland (2003) constructs cases where a non-subject quantifier binds a variable inside the head NP. Such cases still require syntactic reconstruction resulting in a Condition C violation in (67a).

(67) a. **The letters by John$_i$ to her$_j$ [that he$_i$ told every girl$_j$ to burn ___] were published.*

b. *The letters by him$_i$ to her$_j$ [that John$_i$ told every girl$_j$ to burn ___] were published.*

(from Sauerland 2003: 21)

These facts from variable binding thus support the head raising analysis. Like many of the other tests, they do not rule out the head external analysis or the matching analysis elsewhere.

5.2.4. Variable binding effects, take 2

Another argument that deals with variable binding and its implications for the analysis of relative clauses comes to us from Safir (1999). It is different from all the arguments that we have seen so far in that it actually provides an argument against the availability of the head external analysis in general. Safir (1999) notes that the external head of a relative clause displays a pattern of variable binding that mirrors the one found with non-wh quantifiers in the operator phrases of relative clauses. For non-wh quantifiers in the operator phrases of relative clauses, Safir finds the following pattern:

(68) a. QP is a complement/possessor
i. *[$_{CP}$ [....QP$_i$]$_j$ [Pron$_i$...t$_j$...]]
I respect [any writer] [whose depiction of everyone$_i$]$_j$ he$_i$ will object to t$_j$.
(assuming reconstruction, this is a secondary strong crossover violation)

ii. [$_{CP}$ [....QP$_i$]$_j$ [t$_j$...Pron$_i$...]]
?*I respect [any writer] [whose depiction of everyone$_i$]$_j$ t$_j$ will offend him$_i$.*

iii. *[$_{CP}$ [....QP$_i$]$_j$ [[..Pron$_i$..]...t$_j$...]]
?* *I respect [any writer] [whose depiction of everyone$_i$]$_j$ his$_i$ mother* surely wouldn't recognize t$_j$.
(assuming reconstruction, this is a secondary weak crossover violation)

iv. [$_{CP}$ [....QP$_i$]$_j$ [t$_j$...[..Pron$_i$..]...]]
?*I respect [any writer] [whose depiction of everyone$_i$]$_j$ t$_j$ will offend his$_i$ mother.*
(examples 39a–c from Safir 1999)

Since the QP is a complement/possessor, hence it must be introduced by cyclic merger (i.e. merge before move) (cf. Lebeaux 1990; Chomsky 1993). Hence reconstruction effects surface.

b. QP is an adjunct
i. [$_{CP}$ [....QP$_i$]$_j$ [Pron$_i$...t$_j$...]]
?*Can you think of [a single politician] [whose picture in any civil servant's$_i$ office]$_j$]$_j$ he$_i$ is truly proud of t$_j$?*

ii. [$_{CP}$ [....QP$_i$]$_j$ [t$_j$...Pron$_i$...]]
?*There is [at least one politician] [whose picture in any civil servant's$_i$ office]$_j$ t$_j$ shows he$_i$ is a Republican.*
iii. [$_{CP}$ [....QP$_i$]$_j$ [[..Pron$_i$..]...t$_j$...]]
?*I can think of [several politicians] [whose picture in any civil servant's$_i$ office]$_j$ his$_i$ job depends upon t$_j$.*

iv. [$_{CP}$ [....QP$_i$]$_j$ [t$_j$...[..Pron$_i$..]...]]
?*There is [at least one politician] [whose picture in any civil servant's$_i$ office]$_j$ t$_j$ shows that his$_i$ boss is a Republican.*
(examples 40a–c from Safir 1999)

Since the QP is an adjunct, it can be introduced by countercyclic merger (i.e. merge after move) (cf. Lebeaux 1990; Chomsky 1993). Hence reconstruction effects do not surface.

As can be seen above, the explanation for the pattern of grammaticality in (68a) depends upon the operator phrase which contains the quantifier originating in the position marked by the trace. The contrast between (68a) and (68b) follows from Lebeaux (1990)'s proposal that adjuncts can be merged countercyclically. The same pattern emerges with the external heads of relative clauses.

(69) ___ indicates the relative clause internal gap

a. QP is a complement

i. *[$_{EH}$....QP$_i$] [$_{CP}$ [Pron$_i$....___...]]
*[Pictures of anyone$_i$] [which he$_i$ displays ___ prominently] are likely to be attractive ones.

ii. [$_{EH}$....QP$_i$] [$_{CP}$ [___...Pron$_i$...]]
[Pictures of anyone$_i$] [which ___ put him$_i$ in a good light] are likely to be attractive ones.

iii. *? [$_{EH}$....QP$_i$] [$_{CP}$ [[..Pron$_i$..]...___...]]
?[Pictures of anyone$_i$] [that his$_i$ agent likes ___] are likely to be attractive.

iv. [$_{EH}$....QP$_i$] [$_{CP}$ [___...[..Pron$_i$..]...]]
[Pictures of anyone$_i$] [that ___ please his$_i$ agent] are likely to be attractive.
(= ex. 66 from Safir 1999)

b. QP is a possessor

i. *[$_{EH}$....QP$_i$] [$_{CP}$ [Pron$_i$....___...]]
*[Anyone$_i$'s pictures] [which he$_i$ displays ___ prominently] are likely to be attractive ones.

ii. [$_{EH}$....QP$_i$] [$_{CP}$ [___...Pron$_i$...]]
[Anyone$_i$'s pictures] [which ___ put him$_i$ in a good light] are likely to be attractive ones.

iii. *?[$_{EH}$....QP$_i$] [$_{CP}$ [[..Pron$_i$..]...___...]]
?[Anyone$_i$'s pictures] [that his$_i$ agent likes ___] are likely to be attractive.

iv. [$_{EH}$....QP$_i$] [$_{CP}$ [___...[..Pron$_i$..]...]]
[Anyone$_i$'s pictures] [that ___ please his$_i$ agent] are likely to be attractive.
(= ex. 68 from Safir 1999)

c. QP is in an adjunct

i. [$_{EH}$....QP$_i$] [$_{CP}$ [Pron$_i$....___...]]
[Pictures on anyone$_i$'s shelf] [which he$_i$ displays ___ prominently] are likely to be attractive ones.

ii. [$_{EH}$....QP$_i$] [$_{CP}$ [___...Pron$_i$...]]
[Pictures on anyone$_i$'s shelf] [which ___ put him$_i$ in a good light] are likely to be attractive ones.

iii. [$_{EH}$....QP$_i$] [$_{CP}$ [[..Pron$_i$..]...___...]]
[Pictures on anyone$_i$'s shelf] [that his$_i$ agent likes ___] are likely to be attractive.

iv. [$_{EH}$....QP$_i$] [$_{CP}$ [___...[..Pron$_i$..]...]]
[Pictures on anyone$_i$'s shelf] [that ___ please his$_i$ agent] are likely to be attractive.

(= ex. 67 from Safir 1999)

This complicated set of facts receives a straightforward explanation if we assume that the external head (or under the matching analysis, its relative clause-internal counterpart, see Sauerland 1998, section 2.4.2) is obligatorily reconstructed into the relative clause internal gap position. This assumption captures the similarity in behavior between the operator phrases of relative clauses and the external head of a relative clause. The distinction between complements and possessors (69a, b) on the one hand, and adjuncts (69c) on the other can be related to Lebeaux's proposal that adjuncts, but not complements (and Safir argues possessors), can be introduced via countercyclic merger.

It is unclear how these facts could be explained otherwise. Semantic accounts of reconstruction (e.g. Sharvit 1999) are able to handle cases where the displaced constituent contains a pronoun. They do not, however, extend to the paradigm in (69) where the displaced constituent contains a quantifier. Further, even if the semantic account could somehow be extended to handle cases like (69a, b) on a parallel with cases where the displaced constituent contains a pronoun, it would still not explain why the pattern of ungrammaticality found with complements and possessors (69a, b) is not found with adjuncts (69c). In the absence of reconstruction, the relative clause internal environment is identical in (69a–c). An approach that does not relate the external head (or a relative clause-internal counterpart) via movement to the relative clause internal gap is unable to use Lebeaux's proposal to distinguish between complements and adjuncts.

Thus the argument based on Safir's examples is compatible with the head raising analysis and the matching analysis. Unlike most of the preceding arguments, it is incompatible with the availability of the head external analysis. If the head external analysis were a possibility, we would not find the correlations that we do in (69).

5.2.5. Summing up

Generalizing over the syntactic environments that we have explored in the preceding sections, we see that the raising analysis is a necessary component of any theory of relative clauses. However, we also saw based on the external licensing of idioms and the absence of generalized binding theory reconstruction that the raising analysis cannot be the whole story. We need another component; this could be the matching analysis or the head external analysis. However the Safir facts in section 5.2.4 argued against the availability of the head external analysis. So we are left with the raising analysis and the matching analysis, the conclusion arrived at in Bhatt (2002) and Sauerland (2003). Certain environments will only be compatible with one of the analyses, others might be compatible with both.

6. Further issues

6.1. Contact relatives

Contact relatives is the name given by Jespersen (1956) to a class of relative clauses that lack both a relative pronoun as well as a relative complementizer.

(70) *He has found the key [you lost yesterday].*

The traditional analysis given for these relative clauses is not very different from that given to relative clauses with overt material in the C-domain such as *the key which you lost yesterday* and *the key that you lost yesterday.* The differences are located in how much material is deleted in the C-domain: the relative pronoun, the relative complementizer, or both. However, Doherty (1993, 2000) points out that the traditional analysis is unable to account for two syntactic properties that distinguish contact relatives from other relative clauses. The common feature behind these properties is that they can be seen as stemming from a strong adjacency requirement between the head NP and the contact relative. The first property is that contact relatives cannot be the outer relative clause in a stacking configuration.

(71) a. *the man Mary met who John likes*
b. **the man Mary met John likes*
c. *the book Bill bought that Max wrote*
d. **the book Bill bought Max wrote*
(from Doherty 1993: Ch. 3: 11)

The second property is that contact relatives cannot be extraposed. The intuition is that extraposition would make the contact relative discontinuous from the head NP thereby violating the adjacency condition.

(72) a. *The man (who) Bill knew arrived yesterday.*
b. *The man arrived yesterday who Bill knew.*
c. **The man arrived yesterday Bill knew.*
(from Doherty 1993: Ch. 3: 14)

There is some variability in the data here. Noah Constant (p.c.) notes that the stacked and extraposed contact relatives (in 73 and 74 respectively) are acceptable to him.

(73) a. *Hey, is that the guy who works for Google you were telling me about?*
b. *Who's that guy who works on Finnish I've been seeing around the department lately?*

(74) a. *Later on, a woman's coming by I want to interview.*
b. *Someone came in I'd never seen before.*

Speakers vary in their response to these; the non-contact variant with an added *who* is preferred but these are not unacceptable.

In most other ways – their interpretive properties, the presence of A-bar movement, and coordination – contact relatives behave like other relative clauses. In particular, contact relatives can be conjoined with non-contact relatives.

(75) a. *The man John likes and who Mary can't stand walked in.*
b. *The man John likes and that can't stand Mary walked in.*
(from Doherty 1993: Ch. 3: 17)

Doherty (1993) proposes that contact relatives are not CPs whose C-domain has undergone deletion. Instead he proposes that contact relative clauses are categorially IPs whose head NP undergoes a raising derivation.

(76) D $[_{NP}$ NP$_i$ $[_{IP}$.............t$_i$.............]]

This allows him to derive some of the properties of contact relatives. For example, if extraposition necessarily involves a matching derivation, then its absence in contact relatives would be expected. The proposal that contact relatives are IPs also helps to explain the following puzzling paradigm. Following Jim McCloskey's unpublished work from 1992, we have reason to believe that adjunct clauses reject adjunction.

(77) **I graduated [while at college [without having really learned anything]].*

The adjunction constraint helps explain why adjuncts that modify the relative clausc must follow the relative pronoun.

(78) a. **the officers evidently who the rioters assaulted*
b. *the officers who evidently the rioters assaulted*

(79) a. **the man clearly who the highway patrol assaulted*
b. *the man who clearly the highway patrol assaulted*

But now given the standard proposal, we are unable to explain why the following are ungrammatical as contact relatives.

(80) a. *That's the man *(who) years ago Mary used to know well.*
b. *That's the woman *(who) tomorrow we'll meet after lunch.*

There are in principle two places where *years ago* can be attached on the CP-analysis, to the CP or to the IP.

CP-adjunction would be ruled out by McCloskey's constraint. But nothing would block the IP adjunction. If, however, the contact relative is an IP, then McCloskey's constraint suffices to rule out the contact relative.

The explanation for the absence of stacking is not obvious. Here is a way to make sense of the facts. Assume contra Bhatt (2002) but with Bianchi (1999), that when an NP moves out of a relative clause, it does not project itself but instead moves into a nominal projection (call it XP). The combination of the head NP plus the first relative clause will yield an XP. Now the question is whether this XP can itself raise into the SpecXP. If this could be blocked, we will have blocked stacking. What will allow stacking with non-contact relatives is the fact that their derivation may involve the matching analysis. Since contact relatives are limited to the raising analysis, stacking is unavailable. This suggestion captures the insight behind Jacobson (1983)'s proposal which treats stacking as a kind of extraposition. What we are suggesting doesn't reduce stacking to extraposition but instead explores the idea that they both have the same operation, the matching analysis, underlying them.

A further issue in contact relatives is the treatment of subject contact relatives. Such contact relatives are ungrammatical in many syntactic environments. However, in other environments, something that looks on the surface like a subject contact relative is possible for many speakers leading to structures that have been sometimes called syntactic amalgams.

(81) a. **The key [opens the chest] is missing.*
b. *There's a girl (who) wants to see you.*
c. *I knew a smart Greek fella (who) owns maybe twenty restaurants.*

Subject contact relatives seem to be a feature of spoken English and in the majority dialect seem to be restricted to existentials, possessives, other copular constructions, and the complement of *know*. In other varieties of English such as Appalachian English and Hiberno English, subject contact relatives appear in a wider range of environments including NPs headed by universals as well as intensional environments.

(82) a. *She gave me all the change was in the house.* [Hiberno English]
b. *Everyone lives in the mountains has an accent all to theirself.* [Appalachian English]
c. *I'm looking for someone speaks Irish well.* [Hiberno English]
(from Doherty 1993: 96a, b, 98c)

Doherty concluded that despite their much more limited distribution, the internal syntax of subject and object contact relatives is not distinct. He did not offer an analysis of the distribution of subject contact relatives and even now the proper treatment of the distributional restrictions of subject contact relatives remains an area where more work is needed (see Lambrecht 1988; den Dikken 2005 for significant attempts). It is possible that some of the explanations in this difficult domain will come from processing considerations, as argued in detail by Jaeger (2006) and Wasow et al. (2011).

6.2. Appositive relative clauses

The syntax and semantics of appositive relative clauses have been the topic of much recent discussion. The two kinds of relative clauses differ strikingly in how they make a semantic contribution. Unlike restrictive relatives, appositive relative clauses do not restrict the denotation of the head NP; instead they comment upon the individual or set of individuals independently identified by the rest of the DP. Moreover, as Potts (2005) pointed out, the semantic contribution made by appositive relative clauses is not at issue. Along with this semantic difference, we also find syntactic distinctions. Essentially all of the syntactic differences can be seen as reflections of the intuition that restrictive relatives are closer to the head NP than appositive relative clauses. The following are some of the core effects.

In English, appositive relatives clauses need to have overt *wh*-material in their SpecCP.

(83) a. **This book, that I read thoroughly, is delightful.*
b. *This book, which I read thoroughly, is delightful.*
c. **This book, ∅ I read thoroughly, is delightful.*
(see Kayne 1994; Bianchi 1999: 201)

But in Italian, *that*-relatives allow for appositive interpretations.

(84) *questo libro, che ho letto attentamente* [Italian]
this book that have read throughly
'This book, which I read thoroughly, ...'
(Bianchi 1999: 201)

Cinque (2008) notes that Italian actually has two kinds of appositive relative clauses – the integrated kind, which is shown above, and a non-integrated kind that uses the *il quale* relative phrase. He shows that English only has non-integrated appositives and that *il quale* appositives pattern with English appositives. Much of the work on appositives so far has focused on non-integrated appositives. As a result, most of the properties that are taken to characterize appositive relatives are actually properties that characterize non-integrated appositive relatives. This regrettable practice will largely be followed in the remainder of this section.

When a restrictive relative clause and an appositive relative clause appear together, the restrictive relative clause precedes the appositive relative clause.

(85) a. *The man that came to dinner, who was drunk, fainted.*
b. **The man, who was drunk, that came to dinner fainted.*
(from Jackendoff 1977: 171)

Unlike restrictives, appositives permit a wide variety non-nominal antecedents.

(86) a. *Mary is [courageous], which I will never be.*
b. *Mary has [resigned], which John hasn't.*
c. *[John was late], which was unfortunate.*

But when it comes to DP hosts, there are restrictions on what kinds of DPs can host appositive relatives. Proper names, definite descriptions, and specific indefinites can host appositives.

(87) a. *John, who is from Inverness, came up with this idea.*
b. *The new student, who is from Inverness, came up with this idea.*
c. *A student of mine, who is from Inverness, came up with this idea.*

Non-referential DPs such as QPs and DPs that contain bound variables cannot.

(88) a. **Every 14-year old boy, who is really clumsy, always breaks fragile glasses.*
b. **No 14-year old boy, who is really clumsy/careful, always breaks fragile glasses.*
c. **Every professor$_i$ thinks that [a student of his$_i$], who is from Inverness, came up with this idea.* (vs. *John$_i$ thinks that [a student of his$_i$], who is from Inverness, came up with this idea.*)

In general, it is also not possible to bind into an appositive relative clause or to license parasitic gaps inside one.

(89) a. **Every professor$_i$ saw John, [who she$_i$ had failed].*
(*Every professor$_i$ saw a student [who she$_i$ had failed].*)

b. **John is a man who Bill, who knows, admires.*
(*John is a man [who$_i$ everyone [who knows* pg$_i$*] admires t$_i$]*)

What these diagnostics show us is that certain dependencies – variable binding and parasitic gaps – that can be established into restrictive relative clauses cannot be established into appositive relative clause. Other dependencies that are sensitive to the restrictive/appositive distinction are feeding of ellipsis and standard raising analysis tests. Appositive relative clauses are not copied into the ellipsis site (McCawley 1982; Safir 1986) and appositives fail raising analysis tests like variable binding, idiom licensing, and scope reconstruction (Bianchi 1999: Ch. 4).

None of the competing theories of appositives has them in the same configuration ([D [NP CP]]) as restrictive relatives. At the very lowest, the appositive is attached outside the scope of D. This move derives a number of properties of appositives. Since restrictives are in the scope of D, they must precede the appositive. Attachment outside the scope of D also rules out the raising analysis. Still to be explained is the failure of variable binding, parasitic gaps, and feeding of ellipsis. To account for this lack of dependencies, a number of proposals have been advanced, which can be grouped according to whether the appositive relative clause forms a constituent with the DP (or an extended projection of the DP) or not. The class of analyses where the DP and the appositive do not form a constituent form two subgroups: the high attachment accounts where the appositive is actually attached at the clausal level (Emonds 1979; McCawley 1982; Schlenker 2010 among others) and the radical orphanage accounts where the appositive is not even part of the syntactic structure (Fabb 1990 among others). Under these proposals, the structural location of the appositive blocks the dependencies in question; special operations make the appositive appear adjacent to the DP. Accounts where the appositive is attached to the DP deal with the lack of dependencies in various ways. Safir (1986) proposes that appositives are attached late at a post-LF level he dubs LF′ with the relevant dependencies stated at LF and Demirdache (1991) argues that at LF, appositives obligatorily take widest scope blocking any potential dependencies. Potts (2005) appeals to the special semantics of how appositives compose with the DP they modify. The semantic operation puts the semantic contribution into a separate dimension where it cannot be, for the most part, manipulated or accessed by higher operators.

Finally, we turn to a rather salient distinction between appositive and restrictive relative clauses in English: appositive clauses are separated from the DP that they modify and following material by comma intonation, indicated in the orthography by surrounding commas. While this is an important aspect of English postnominal appositives, it is not found with several instances of non-restrictive modification. English allows for appositive interpretation of adjectives (*the industrious Greeks*) but these do not have a distinctive prosody. Languages with prenominal relatives lack a prosodic break between the relative clause and the NP. It is possible that the prosodic break is a feature of the kind of appositive modification that Cinque (2008) dubs 'non-integrated' but this needs to be established. I believe that an undue focus on this lack of prosodic break in prenominal relatives has led to a pervasive claim in the literature (see Potts 2005; del Gobbo 2005; de Vries 2006 among many others) that there are no appositives in languages with prenominal relatives. Recent work which has set aside the absence of a prosodic break as the signature property of appositive relatives and examined the (prenominal) relative clauses of Chinese (Constant to appear) and Turkish (Kan p.c.) has concluded that these languages do have appositive relative clauses, albeit of the integrated kind.

(90) a. *Politikacı sendika-nın destekle-diğ-i Baykal-ı* [Turkish]
politician syndicate-GEN support-REL-3SG.POSS Baykal-ACC
eleştir-di.
criticize-PST
'The politician criticized Baykal, who the syndicate supported.'
(Baykal is a famous politician.)
(Kan p.c.)

b. *Nèi xiē [bāchéng kǎoshì huì bù jígé de]$_{CP}$ xuéshēng* [Mandarin]
that CLF.PL 80.percent test will not pass LNK student
yīnggāi gèng nǔlì yī diǎnr.
should more make.effort a little
'Those students, who I reckon won't pass the test, should put in more effort.'
(Constant 2011)

6.3. Further reading

In addition to the references in the text, I would like to direct the reader to the very useful survey articles by Valentina Bianchi (2002a, b) and Alexander Grosu (Grosu 2002). Christian Lehmann's *Der Relativsatz* (Lehmann 1984) is an impressive crosslinguistic survey in German. The following dissertations present detailed studies of various aspects of relativization: Salzmann (2006) focuses on resumption and reconstruction, Cardoso (2010) on appositives and extraposition, and Wu (2011) (in French) on prenominal relatives.

7. Abbreviations

The article follows the Leipzig Glossing Rules. The following labels have been added to the standard LGR set:

LNK	linker
OM	object marker
POT	potential mood
PV	pre-verb

21. Acknowledgements

I would like to thank the editors, Tibor Kiss and Artemis Alexiadou, for not giving up on me. Noah Constant, Kyle Johnson, Mark de Vries, and Guglielmo Cinque gave me detailed comments for which I am very grateful.

8. References (selected)

Aghaei, Behrad
2006 The syntax of ke-clauses and clausal extraposition in Modern Persian. Ph.D. thesis, University of Texas at Austin, Austin, Texas.

Alexiadou, Artemis, Andre Meinunger, Chris Wilder, and Paul Law
2000 Introduction. In: Artemis Alexiadou, Andre Meinunger, Chris Wilder and Paul Law (eds.), *The Syntax of Relative Clauses*, 1–51. (Linguistik Aktuell 32.) Amsterdam: John Benjamins.

Bach, Emmon, and Robin Cooper
1978 The NP-S analysis of relative clauses and compositional semantics. *Linguistics and Philosophy* 2: 145–150.

Basilico, David
1996 Head position and internally headed relative clauses. *Language* 72 3: 498–532.

Berman, Howard
1972 Relative clauses in Hittite. In: Paul M. Peranteau, Judith N. Levi and Gloria C. Phares (eds.), *The Chicago Which Hunt: Papers from the Relative Clause Festival*, 1–8. Chicago: Chicago Linguistics Society.

Bhatt, Rajesh
2002 The raising analysis of relative clauses: Evidence from adjectival modification. *Natural Language Semantics* 10 1: 43–90.

Bhatt, Rajesh
2003 Locality in correlativization. *Natural Language and Linguistic Theory* 21 3: 485–541.

Bianchi, Valentina
1999 *Consequences of Antisymmetry: Headed Relative Clauses.* Berlin: Mouton de Gruyter.

Bianchi, Valentina
2002a Headed relatives in generative syntax – part 1. *Glot International* 6 7: 197–204.

Bianchi, Valentina
2002b Headed relatives in generative syntax – part 2. *Glot International* 6 8: 1–13.

Cardoso, Adriana
2010 Variation and change in the syntax of relative clauses. Ph.D. thesis, University of Lisbon.

Chao, Yuen Ren
1968 *A grammar of Spoken Chinese.* Berkeley, CA: University of California Press.

Chomsky, N.
1965 *Aspects of the Theory of Syntax*. Cambridge, MA: MIT Press.

Chomsky, Noam
1975 Questions of form and interpretation. *Linguistic Analysis* 1: 75–109.

Cinque, Guglielmo
2008 Two types of non-restrictive relatives. In: Olivier Bonami and Patricia Cabredo (eds.), *Empirical Issues in Syntax and Semantics*, 99–137. Colloque de Syntaxe et Sémantique À Paris.

Cole, Peter
1987 The structure of internally headed relative clauses. *Natural Language and Linguistic Theory* 5 2: 277–302.

Constant, Noah
to appear Re-diagnosing appositivity: Evidence for prenominal appositives from Mandarin. In: Carissa Abrego-Collier, Arum Kang, Martina Martinović and Chieu Nguyen (eds.), *Proceedings of Chicago Linguistic Society (CLS)*, Vol. 47.

Curme, George O.
1912 A history of the English relative construction. *The Journal of English and Germanic Philology* 11: 10–29, 180–204, 355–380.

Davison, Alice
2008 A case restriction on control: Implications for movement. *Journal of South Asian Linguistics* 1 1: 29–54.
Dayal, Veneeta
1995 Quantification in correlatives. In: Emmon Bach, Eloise Jelinek, Angelika Kratzer and Barbara H. Partee (eds.), *Quantification in Natural Languages*, 179–205. (Studies in Linguistics and Philosophy 54.) Dordrecht, Reidel: Kluwer Academic Publishers.
de Vries, Mark
2002 The syntax of relativization. Ph.D. thesis, University of Amsterdam.
de Vries, Mark
2005 The fall and rise of universals on relativization. *Journal of Universal Language* 6: 125–157.
de Vries, Mark
2006 The syntax of appositive relativization: On specifying coordination, false free relatives, and promotion. *Linguistic Inquiry* 229–270.
Del Gobbo, Francesca
2005 Chinese relative clauses: Restrictive, descriptive or appositive. In: Laura Brugé, Giulian Giusti, Nicola Munaro, W. Schweikert and G. Turano (eds.), *Proceedings of the XXX Incontro di Grammatica Generativa.*
Demirdache, Hamida
1991 Resumptive chains in restrictive relatives, appositives, and dislocation structures. Ph.D. thesis, Massachusetts Institute of Technology, Cambridge, Massachusetts. Distributed by MIT Working Papers in Linguistics.
den Dikken, Marcel
2005 A comment on the topic of topic-comment. *Lingua* 115: 691–710.
Doherty, Cathal
1993 Clauses without ‘that’: The case for bare sentential complementation in English. Ph.D. thesis, University of California, Santa Cruz, Santa Cruz, California.
Doherty, Cathal
2000 *Clauses Without ‘That’: The Case for Bare Sentential Complementation in English.* (Outstanding Dissertations in Linguistics.) London: Routledge.
Downing, Bruce
1978 Some universals relative clause structure. In: Joseph H. Greenberg (ed.), *Universals of Human Language Vol. 4, Syntax*, 375–418. Stanford: Stanford University Press.
Embick, David, and Rolf Noyer
2001 Movement operations after syntax. *Linguistic Inquiry* 32 4: 555–598.
Emonds, Joseph
1979 Appositive relatives have no properties. *Linguistic Inquiry* 10: 211–243.
Fabb, Nigel
1990 The difference between English restrictive and non-restrictive relative clauses. *Journal of Linguistics* 26: 57–78.
Grosu, Alexander
2002 Strange relatives at the interface of two millennia. *Glot International* 6: 145–167.
Hale, Kenneth L.
1976 The adjoined relative clause in Australian. In: R. M. W. Dixon (ed.), *Grammatical Categories in Australian Languages*, 78–105. Canberra: Australian Institute of Aboriginial Studies.
Hankamer, Jorge, and Line Mikkelsen
2002 A morphological analysis of definite nouns in Danish. *Journal of Germanic Linguistics* 14: 137–175.
Hankamer, Jorge, and Line Mikkelsen
2005 When movement must be blocked: A reply to Embick and Noyer. *Linguistic Inquiry* 36 1: 88–125.

Hastings, Rachel
2004 The syntax and semantics of relativization and quantification: The case of Quechua. Ph.D. thesis, Cornell University.

Heim, Irene, and Angelika Kratzer
1998 *Semantics in Generative Grammar.* (Blackwell textbooks in Linguistics 13.) Oxford: Blackwell.

Hoshi, Koji
1995 Structural and interpretive aspects of head-internal and head-external relative clauses. Ph.D. thesis, University of Rochester.

Hulsey, Sarah, and Uli Sauerland
2006 Sorting out relative clauses. *Natural Language Semantics* 14 2: 111–137.

Izvorski, Roumyana
1996 The Syntax and Semantics of Correlative Proforms. In: Kiyomi Kusumoto (ed.), *Proceedings of NELS 26*, 133–147. Amherst, Massachusetts, GLSA.

Jackendoff, Ray
1977 *X Syntax: A study of Phrase Structure*. Cambridge, MA: MIT Press.

Jacobson, Pauline
1983 *On the Syntax and Semantics of Multiple Relative in English.* IULC, Bloomington.

Jacobson, Pauline
1995 On the quantificational force of English free relatives. In: Emmon Bach, Eloise Jelinek, Angelika Kratzer and Barbara H. Partee (eds.), *Quantification in Natural Languages*, 451–486. (Studies in Linguistics and Philosophy 54.) Dordrecht, Reidel: Kluwer Academic Publishers.

Jaeger, T. Florian
2006 Redundancy and syntactic reduction in spontaneous speech. Ph.D. thesis, Stanford University.

Jespersen, Otto
1956 *A Modern English Grammar on Historical Principles*. London: George Allen and Unwin.

Junghare, Indira
1994 Marathi relative clauses revisited. In: Alice Davison and Frederick M. Smith (eds.), *Papers from the Fifteenth SALA Roundtable Conference 1993*, 140–150. Iowa City: South Asian Studies Program, University of Iowa.

Kayne, Richard Stanley
1994 *The Antisymmetry of Syntax*. (Linguistic Inquiry Monographs 25.) Cambridge, MA: MIT Press.

Keenan, Ed
1972 Relative clause formation in Malagasy. In: Paul M. Peranteau, Judith N. Levi and Gloria C. Phares (eds.), *The Chicago Which Hunt: Papers from the Relative Clause Festival.* Chicago: Chicago Linguistics Society.

Keenan, Edward
1985 Relative clauses. In: Timothy Shopen (ed.), *Language Typology and Syntactic Description*, Vol. 2, 141–170. Cambridge, England: Cambridge University Press.

Keenan, Edward, and Bernard Comrie
1977 Noun Phrase accessibility and Universal Grammar. *Linguistic Inquiry* 8 1: 63–100.

Koster-Moeller, Jorie, and Martin Hackl
2008 Quantifier scope constraints in acd: Implications for the syntax of relative clauses. In: Natasha Abner and Jason Bishop (eds.), *Proceedings of 27th West Coast Conference on Formal Linguistics*, 301–309. Somerville, MA, Cascadilla Proceedings Project.

Lambrecht, Knud
1988 There was a farmer had a dog: Syntactic amalgams revisited. In: *Papers from the Parasession on Grammaticalization. (BLS 14.)* Berkeley: Berkeley Linguistics Society.

Lees, Robert B.
1960 *The Grammar of English Nominalizations.* The Hague: Mouton.
Lees, Robert B.
1961 The constituent structure of noun phrases. *American Speech* 36: 159–168.
Lehmann, Christian
1984 *Der Relativsatz.* Tübingen: Gunter Narr Verlag.
Lipták, Anikó
2005 *Correlative Topicalization.* ULCL, Leiden University ms.
Lipták, Anikó
2009 The landscape of correlatives: An empirical and analytical survey. In: Anikó Lipták (ed.), *Correlatives Crosslinguistically,* 1–48. Amsterdam: John Benjamins.
Mahajan, Anoop
2000 Relative asymmetries and Hindi correlatives. In: Artemis Alexiadou, Andre Meinunger, Chris Wilder and Paul Law (eds.), *The Syntax of Relative Clauses,* 1–51. (Linguistik Aktuell 32.) Amsterdam: John Benjamins.
Marlow, Patrick
1994 On the origin of embedded relative clauses in Hindi. In: Alice Davison and Frederick M. Smith (eds.), *Papers from the Fifteenth SALA Roundtable Conference 1993,* 167–186. Iowa City: South Asian Studies Program, University of Iowa.
McCawley, James
1982 Parentheticals and discontinuous constituent structure. *Linguistic Inquiry* 13: 91–106.
McCawley, James
adsentential, adnominal, and extraposed relative clauses in Hindi. In: Veneeta Dayal and Anoop Mahajan (eds.), *Clause Structure in South Asian Languages* Dordrecht: Kluwer.
McCawley, John
1981 The syntax and semantics of English relative clauses. *Lingua* 53: 99–149.
McCloskey, James
1990 Resumptive pronouns, a′-binding, and levels of representation in Irish. In: Randall Hendrick (ed.), *The Syntax of Modern Celtic Languages,* 199–248. (Syntax and Semantics 23.) New York: Academic Press.
McCloskey, James
2002 Resumption, successive cyclicity and the locality of operations. In: Samuel D. Epstein and T. D. Seely (eds.), *Derivation and Explanation in the Minimalist Program,* 184–226. Oxford: Blackwell Publishers.
Montague, R.
1974 The proper treatment of quantification in ordinary English. In: R. H. Thomason (ed.), *Formal Philosophy: Selected papers of Richard Montague,* 188–221. New Haven, CO: Yale University Press.
Munn, Alan
1994 A minimalist account of reconstruction asymmetries. In: M. Gonzàlez (ed.), *Proceedings of NELS 24.* Amherst, Massachusetts, GLSA.
Pandharipande, Rajeshwari V.
1997 *Marathi: A Descriptive Grammar.* (Descriptive Grammars.) London: Routledge.
Partee, Barbara
1975 Montague grammar and transformational grammar. *Linguistic Inquiry* 6.
Potts, Christopher
2005 *The Logic of Conventional Implicatures.* (Oxford Studies in Theoretical Linguistics 7.) Oxford: Oxford University Press.
Quine, William Van Ormand
1960 *Word and Object.* (Studies in communication) Cambridge, MA: MIT Press.
Raman, C.
1973 The Old Hittite relative construction. Ph.D. thesis, University of Texas at Austin, Austin, Texas.

Rebuschi, Georges
2009 Basque correlatives and their kin in the history of northern Basque. In: Anikó Lipták (ed.), *Correlatives Crosslinguistically*, 83–130. Amsterdam: John Benjamins.
Rizzi, Luigi
1997 The fine structure of the left periphery. In: Liliane Haegeman (ed.), *Elements of Grammar*, 281–388. Berlin: Springer.
Ross, John R.
1967 Constraints on variables in syntax. Ph.D. thesis, MIT.
Safir, Ken
1986 Relative clauses in a theory of binding and levels. *Linguistic Inquiry* 17 4: 663–689.
Safir, Ken
1999 Vehicle change and reconstruction in a'-chains. *Linguistic Inquiry* 30 4: 587–620.
Salzmann, Martin
2006 Resumptive prolepsis. Ph.D. thesis, Leiden University.
Sauerland, Uli
1998 The Meaning of Chains. Ph.D. thesis, Massachusetts Institute of Technology, Cambridge, Massachusetts. Distributed by MIT Working Papers in Linguistics.
Sauerland, Uli
2003 Unpronounced heads in relative clauses. In: Kersten Schwabe and Susanne Winkler (eds.), *The Interfaces: Deriving and Interpreting Omitted Structures*, 205–226. Amsterdam: John Benjamins.
Schachter, Paul
1973 Focus and Relativization. *Language* 49 1: 19–46.
Schlenker, Philippe
2010 Supplements within a unidimensional semantics i: Scope. In: Maria Aloni, Harald Bastiaanse, Tikitu de Jager and Katrin Schulz (eds.), *Logic, Language and Meaning: Selected Revised Papers from the 17th Amsterdam Colloquium, Amsterdam, The Netherlands, December 16–18*, 74–83. (Lecture Notes in Computer Science 6042.) Berlin, Springer.
Sells, Peter
1984 Syntax and semantics of resumptive pronouns. Ph.D. thesis, University of Massachusetts, Amherst.
Sharvit, Yael
1999 Functional relative clauses. *Linguistics and Philosophy* 22 5: 447–478.
Shimoyama, Junko
1999 Internally headed relative clauses in Japanese and e-type anaphora. *Journal of East Asian Linguistics* 8: 147–182.
Smith, Carlota
1964 Determiners and Relative Clauses in a Generative Grammar of English. *Language* 40 1: 37–52.
Srivastav, Veneeta
1991 The syntax and semantics of correlatives. *Natural Language and Linguistic Theory* 9: 637–686.
Stockwell, Robert P., Paul Schachter, and Barbara Hall Partee
1973 *The Major Syntactic Structures of English.* New York: Holt, Rinehart, and Winston, Inc.
Subbarao, Karumuri V.
2011 *South Asian Languages: A Syntactic Typology.* Cambridge: Cambridge University Press.
Subbarao, Karumuri V., and Mimi Kevichusä
2005 Relative clauses in Sema. In: Tanmoy Bhattacharya (ed.), *The Yearbook of South Asian Languages*, 255–272. Berlin: Mouton de Gruyter.
von Stechow, Arnim
1980 Modification of noun phrases, a challenge for compositional semantics. *Theoretical Linguistics* 7: 57–110.

Wasow, Thomas, T. Florian Jaeger, and David Orr
2011 Lexical variation in relativizer frequency. In: H. Simon and H. Wiese (eds.), *Expecting the Unexpected: Exceptions in Grammar*, 175–195. Berlin: De Gruyter.
Williamson, Janice
1987 An indefinite restriction on relative clauses in Lakhota. In: Eric Reuland and Alice ter Meulen (eds.), *The Linguistic Representation of (In)definiteness*. Cambridge, MA: MIT Press.
Wu, T.
2011 La relativisation prenominale. Ph.D. thesis, Universit́ e Sorbonne Nouvelle-Paris 3 and Università Ca'Foscari Di Venezia.

Rajesh Bhatt, Amherst (USA)

22. Voice and Valence Change

Abstract

*Voice (*diathesis*) alternations are particular alternations, typically marked as part of the verb's morphology, in the assignment of grammatical functions to the verb's arguments. Voice alternations are of two types: (A) passive, impersonal passive, antipassive, inversion, and (B) middle, including anticausative, reflexive/reciprocal, dispositional middle, impersonal middle, mediopassive and impersonal mediopassive. The alternations of the first type, such as the passive voice, change the grammatical function of the external argument without reducing valence, whereas the middle voice alternation also reduces valence. Various theoretical questions have been raised in the course of the study of issues related to voice, and have been given different answers by recent linguistic theories within typological, functionalist, syntactic, and morpho-semantic frameworks.*

1. Introduction

The term voice is a traditional term (akin to the Greek term *diathesis*) which originates in the grammars of the classical Indo-European languages, where it denotes particular alternations in the assignments of grammatical functions to the verb's arguments. Voice alternations are typically marked as part of the verb's morphology, and accordingly, voice is considered a morpho-syntactic category of the verb. In Classical Greek, for example, there was, in some tenses of the verb, a tripartite morphological voice contrast:

(1)	active voice:	passive voice:	middle voice:	
	lousō	*lousomai*	*louθēsomai*	[Attic Greek]
	'I will wash [somebody].'	'I will be washed.'	'I will wash myself.'	

Voice alternations traditionally subsume processes where there is reduction of the number of *arguments of the verb*, i.e. participants in the event denoted by the verb. Some theoretical frameworks of contemporary linguistics, such as functionalist and cognitivist frameworks, expand the application of the term *voice* also to processes where there is increase in the number of arguments of the verb, as in causative and applicative constructions. In these theories, the term *voice* is used for any alternation of the number of arguments of the verb (Croft 1994; Dixon and Aikhenvald 1997; Shibatani 2006). Other theoretical frameworks restrict the term *voice* to the active-passive contrast, where there is no change in the number of arguments but only their grammatical function, and a different term, *valence alternation,* is used to denote alternation, either decrease or increase, in the number of arguments. Such restrictive approaches are found in typological frameworks (e.g. Haspelmath and Müller-Bardey 2005) and in large parts of generative grammar (explicitly expressed, for example, in Levin and Rappaport 1995; Reinhart and Siloni 2005).

The present discussion endorses an intermediate position, perhaps closest in spirit to the traditional concept, which is also found in formal semantics (Kratzer 1996) and in Distributed Morphology (Embick 1997). Here voice denotes changes in the grammatical function of the so-called *external argument* (typically the subject of the active verb), including the reduction of this argument.

2. Descriptive coverage of voice phenomena

This section lists and illustrates voice phenomena discussed in the linguistic literature. They are classified by whether they change the grammatical function of the external argument without reducing valence, or whether they also reduce valence. In most cases, the enumerated phenomena clearly fall within the boundaries of the notion of *voice* adopted here, and its subclasses. But there are cases which are not clear-cut, and these will be discussed as such. In the case of *inversion* (section 2.1.4), it is not clear whether there is change in the grammatical function of the subject or not. In the case of the *dispositional middle* (section 2.2.3) and the *mediopassive* (section 2.2.5), it is not clear whether or not there is valence reduction.

2.1. Voice alternations which do not reduce valence

2.1.1. Passive

Passive voice morphology marks a change in grammatical function of the verb's external argument without reducing it. The external argument is subject of the active verb, and is suppressed in the case of the passive verb; it is either unexpressed or expressed obliquely. But the suppressed external argument is still the (implicit) external argument of the passive verb.

In (2) below, the external argument of the transitive verb *write* is the subject of the active-voice verb in (2a). In (2b), the external argument is suppressed, but is still an implicit argument: (2b) entails that someone wrote the letter just as much as the active (2a) does. The external argument may be expressed obliquely by means of an optional prepositional adjunct, as in (2c). In (2b–c), the verb's *internal argument* assumes the grammatical function of subject.

(2) a. *John wrote the letter.*
b. *The letter was written.*
c. *The letter was written by John.*

In some languages, the obliquely expressed external argument of a passive verb is assigned the same thematic role which it is assigned in the active voice. In other languages, passive voice assigns the oblique argument the fixed default role of Agent, even in cases where the verb in the active voice assigns it a different role, e.g. Cause, Experiencer, Goal etc. A language of the former type is English, where the passive verb can introduce a variety of thematic roles (Marantz 1984: 129):

(3) a. *The porcupine cage was welded by Elmer.* (agent)
b. *Elmer was moved by the porcupine's reaction.* (cause)
c. *The porcupine crate was received by Elmer's firm.* (goal/recipient)
d. *Elmer was seen by everyone who entered.* (experiencer)
e. *The intersection was approached by five cars at once.* (theme)

Languages of the second type are Greek, Hebrew, Icelandic, where a verb marked by passive morphology assigns only the Agent thematic role to its external argument (cf. Doron 2003 for Hebrew; Jónsson 2003 for Icelandic; and Zombolou 2004; Alexiadou et al. 2006 for Greek). The following examples are from Hebrew:

(4) a. *ha-kluv rutax (al.yedey elmer).* [Hebrew]
the-cage weld.PASS by Elmer
'The cage was welded by Elmer.' (agent)

b. **elmer rugaš (al.yedey tguvat ha-kipod).*
Elmer move.PASS by reaction.of the-porcupine
'Elmer was moved by the porcupine's reaction.' (cause)

c. **teyvat ha-kipod qubla (al.yedey ha-xevra).*
crate.of the-porcupine receive.PASS by the-firm
'The porcupine crate was received by the firm.' (goal/recipient)

Thematic roles other than the Agent role are compatible with the *middle voice* (which will be discussed in section 1.2 below) but not with the passive voice. Grammatical variants can be constructed of (4b) and (4c) with the middle-voice form of the same verbs (glossed as MID), as in (5a) and (5b). (5c) is an example with an experiencer argument:

(5) a. *elmer hitrageš (mi-tguvat ha-kipod).* [Hebrew]
Elmer move.MID from-reaction.of the-porcupine
'Elmer was moved by the porcupine's reaction.' (cause)

b. *tevat ha-kipod hitqabla (al.yedey ha-xevra).*
crate.of the-porcupine receive.MID by the-firm
'The porcupine crate was received by the firm.' (goal/recipient)

c. *elmer nir'a (al.yedey kol mi še-nixnas).*
Elmer see.MID by each who that-enter.MID
'Elmer was seen by everyone who entered.' (experiencer)

In many languages, only transitive verbs can passivize, but in other languages, it is possible to passivize intransitive verbs as well, e.g. in English (Bolinger 1977; Bresnan 1982; Alsina 2009):

(6) a. *The bed was slept in by George Washington.*
b. *The bed has been thoroughly rolled around on.*

2.1.2. Impersonal passive

In some languages where intransitive verbs passivize, the passive construction is impersonal, i.e. no argument is assigned the grammatical function of subject. Some languages require a pleonastic element in subject position in such cases, like the French *il* 'it' in (7a). Others, like German, only require an overt pleonastic element in particular positions, such as the preverbal position in (7b), where the sentence would otherwise be verb-initial. Arabic does not have an overt pleonastic element, but marks the verb in (7c) with default 3.M.SG inflection:

(7) a. *Il a été parlé de vos frères hier soir.* [French]
'It was spoken of your brothers last night.'
(Kayne 1975: 245, n. 51 example [iii])

b. *Es wird hier getanzt. / Hier wird (*es) getanzt.* [German]
it AUX here danced here AUX it danced
'People are dancing here.' Lit: 'There is dancing here.'
(Steinbach 2002: 28, example [17a])

c. *ʔušīra ʔila l-risālat-i.* [Arabic]
point.PASS.3M.SG to the-letter.F-GEN
'The letter was pointed to.' Lit: 'It was pointed to the letter.'
(Peled 1998: 137, example [18]; Badawi, Carter, and Gully 2004: 114)

Some languages, like German and Dutch, allow *by*-phrases in impersonal passive constructions:

(8) a. *Es wurde gestern von uns getanzt.* [German]
'There was dancing by us yesterday.'
(Siewierska 1984: 97, example [7c])

b. *Er wordt door de jongens gefloten.* [Dutch]
'There was whistling by the boys.'
(Kirsner 1976: 387, example [3b])

This is a marked option, not allowed in Icelandic for example (Sigurðsson 1989). Languages which allow by-phrases in impersonal passives also allow them in personal passives (Siewierska 1984).

It was suggested by Perlmutter (1978) and Perlmutter and Postal (1984) that an intransitive verb which has an external argument, an *unergative* verb, can undergo impersonal passive, whereas a verb without an external argument, an *unaccusative* verb, cannot. This is illustrated by the passivizability contrast in Dutch between the unergative verb *run* and the unaccusative verb *fall*:

(9) a. *Er werd (door de jongens) gelopen.* [Dutch]
'There was running by the boys.'

b. **Er werd (door de jongens) gevallen.*
'There was falling by the boys.'
(Zaenen 1988, example [1–2])

Counterexamples to this syntactic characterization have been pointed to by Timberlake (1982) (questioned by Blevins 2003), Zaenen (1988, 1993), Farrell (1992), suggesting that semantic conditions are active as well. One such condition is agentivity, parallel to the restriction on personal passive mentioned in the previous section. An additional condition is telicity. Zaenen (1988) shows that telicity and agentivity reverse the judgments in (9). The telic version of (9a) is ungrammatical, and the agentive version of (9b) is grammatical:

(10) a. **Er werd naar huis gelopen.* [Dutch]
'There was runing home.'
(Zaenen 1988 example [34])

b. *In het tweede bedrijf werd er dor de nieuwe acteur op het juiste ogenblik gevallen.*
'In the second act there was falling by the new actor on cue.'
(Zaenen 1988 example [41], from Perlmutter 1978)

2.1.3. Antipassive

Antipassive is a value of the voice dimension attested mainly in ergative-absolutive languages (Comrie 1978; Dixon 1979). Unlike the original generative analyses of ergativity (e.g. Bittner 1994; Bittner and Hale 1996) where both ergative and absolutive cases are considered to be structural cases, more recent analyses have argued that the ergative subject is assigned inherent (oblique) case by the verb in the active voice, whereas the object is assigned absolutive (= nominative) case by the clausal element which generally assigns nominative case, the verb's tense morpheme (Woolford 1997; Legate 2002, 2008 and others). In the antipassive, like in the passive, the external argument changes its grammatical function. But it is a change in the opposite direction, in some sense, compared to the change in the passive. From an oblique position in the active voice, the ergative subject is promoted to the nominative position. Concomitantly, the internal argument undergoes demotion which is parallel to that of the external argument in passive: it either remains implicit, or is expressed obliquely, as shown in (11b):

(11) a. *biya Jani-ŋgu gunyja.n.* [Dyribal]
beer.ABS John-ERG drink.NFUT
'John is drinking beer.' active

b. *Jani gunyjal-ŋa-nyu (biya-gu).*
John.ABS drink-ANTIP-NFUT beer-DAT
'John is drinking (beer).' antipassive
(Dixon 1994: 149)

Antipassive is similar to the passive in that it does not modify valence. As in the passive, the change in grammatical function of the subject results in the detransitivization of the verb. Yet semantically the antipassive, like the passive, retains both arguments of the active verb: any event of drinking, irrespective of the voice of the verb, involves both the ingesting agent and the ingested liquid. At the level of discourse, the argument which is demoted from nominative to oblique is often less topical, both in the passive and the antipassive. Another semantic characteristic of the antipassive, reminiscent of the impersonal passive, is the aspectual classification of antipassive clauses as atelic (Cooreman 1994; Beach 2003).

Antipassive analyses can be found in the literature for many ergative languages, e.g. Australian languages, such as Dyirbal (Dixon 1972) and Warrungu (Tsunoda 1988), Inuit languages (Kalmár 1979; Fortescue 1984; Bok-Bennema 1991; Johns 2001), Mayan languages (England 1988), Chukchee (Kozinsky et al. 1988), Nez Perce (Rude 1988; Deal 2007). An antipassive analysis has also been proposed for one of the values of the Austronesian voice system (Aldridge 2004; Sells 1995, 1999).

2.1.4. Inversion

The term *inversion* originates in Algonquian linguistics and has been extended to other languages as well. In the words of Thompson (1994), "an inverse construction indicates a deviation from the normal degree of relative topicality between agent and non-agent". In functionalist theories (e.g. Klaiman 1991; Givón 1994a; Shibatani 2006) inverse morphology is considered to mark voice alternation. There may be reasons not to accept the characterization of inversion as voice, in Algonquian languages (cf. Dahlstrom 1991; Woolfart 1991), Athabaskan languages and others (cf. many of the articles in Givón 1994b). The major reason is that inverse clauses are transitive, unlike typical clauses with non-active voice. Yet it is not clear whether the external argument is still in subject position, since, as argued by Ritter and Rosen (2005), Algonquian languages lack any A-positions at all.

Inverse morphology expresses markedness in the proximate-obviate dimension, which grammatically encodes topicality, including a person ranking, where first and second person, which are speech-act participants, are viewed as proximate, and third person as relatively obviate. In direct clauses, the external argument is proximate, and the internal argument is obviate. In inverse clauses, this is reversed. In Algonquian and many other inverse systems, this results in obligatory inverse marking of clauses where a third person agent acts on a first or second person patient. This is different from non-active voice, which is normally optional.

The following example is from the Algonquian Plains Cree language (Dahlstrom 1991), where both direct and inverse morphology is obligatorily marked. In (12a), the direct marker -DIR- indicates that the external argument is a speech-act participant (first person in this example) whereas the internal argument is third person. In (12b), the inverse marker -INV- indicates deviation from topicality – the external argument is third person whereas the internal argument is a speech-act participant:

(12) a. *ni-wāpam-**ā**-w.* [Plains Cree]
1-see-DIR-3
'I see her/him.'

b. *ni-wāpam-**ikw**-w.*
1-see-INV-3
'S/he sees me.'

There actually is some optionality in inversion as well, but it is mostly restricted. For example, inversion is optional in Algonquian when both arguments are third person. The following examples are from the Algonquian East Cree language (Junker 2004, examples [3–5]). Both options (13a) and (13b) are grammatical. In (13a), the direct marker -DIR- indicates a third person object which is obviate relative to the proximate third person subject. In (13b), the inverse marker -INV- indicates that the third person object is proximate relative to the obviate third person subject:

(13) a. *miyeyim-e-u.* [East Cree]
like-DIR-3
'S/he$_{\text{PROX}}$ likes her/him$_{\text{OBV}}$.'

b. *miyeyim-iku-u.*
like-INV-3
'S/he$_{\text{OBV}}$ likes her/him$_{\text{PROX}}$.'

Both clauses in each of (12) and (13) are transitive, i.e. encode two arguments, in comparison with the intransitive passive clause in (14), where agreement to a single argument is marked:

(14) *miyeyim-aakanu-u.* [East Cree]
like-PASS-3
'S/he$_{\text{PROX}}$ is liked.'

The salience of topicality in the description of inversion does not contradict subsuming inversion under voice, since topicality interacts with voice as well. Usually, it is hard to passivize a clause with a topical agent (Bresnan et al. 2001):

(15) **Fries are eaten by me*
(Riddle and Sheintuch 1983, example [110])

Nevertheless, it remains an open question whether inversion should be analysed as a value of the voice dimension.

2.2. Voice alternation which reduces valence: the middle voice

Languages with the middle voice morphologically mark this voice on the verb in various ways. Some languages use reduced forms of the reflexive clitic (Russian: Timberlake 2004; French: Labelle 2008; Spanish: Mendikoetxea 2012; German: Steinbach 2002). Others have designated middle voice morphology (Icelandic: Sigurðsson 1989; Hebrew and other Semitic languages: Doron 2003; Greek: Alexiadou and Anagnostopoulou 2004; Albanian: Kallulli 2006; Georgian: Holisky 1981; Salish: Beck 1997).

Greek and Albanian middle morphology (which shows syncretism with passive morphology) is referred to as Non Active (NACT). In other languages, the middle-voice form of the verb is different from the passive voice. The following example is from Icelandic (Sigurðsson 1989: 268):

(16) a. *Lögreglan drap hundinn.* [Icelandic]
the.police.NOM killed the.dog.ACC
'The police killed the dog.' active voice

b. *Hundurinn var drepinn (af lögreglunni).*
the.dog.NOM was killed by the.police
'The dog was killed by the police.' passive voice

c. *Hundurinn drapst (*af lögreglunni).*
the.dog.NOM killed.MID by the.police
'The dog got killed.' middle voice

The middle voice differs in several respects from the passive voice. The external argument of the active verb is not only suppressed in the middle voice, as it is in the passive, but typically altogether absent from the clause, as shown by the contrast between (16b) and (16c) above. Moreover, unlike the passive voice, the middle is independent of the active voice. Middle-voice verbs exist for which there are no corresponding active-voice verbs (Kaufmann 2007):

(17) *ostat'-sja *ostat bojat-sja *bojat' nadejat-sja *nadejat'* [Russian]
remain-REFL fear-REFL hope-REFL

(18) *notar *yatar hitxaret *xeret hit'aqeš *iqeš* [Hebrew]
remain.MID regret.MID insist.MID

2.2.1. Anticausative

The middle voice derives a verb which does not have an external argument. In the simplest case, this has the effect of an anticausative form which alternates with a transitive active verb.

(19) a. *rebjonok razbil čašk-u.* [Russian]
child.NOM broke.M.SG cup.F.SG-ACC
'The child broke the cup.' active voice

b. *čašk-a razbila-s'.*
cup.F.SG-NOM broke.F.SG-REFL
'The cup broke.' middle voice

(20) a. *ha-yéled šavar et-ha-kos.* [Hebrew]
the-child break.3M.SG ACC-the-cup.F.SG
'The child broke the cup.' active voice

b. *ha-kos nišbera.*
the-cup.F.SG break.MID.3 F.SG
'The cup broke.' middle voice

2.2.2. Reflexive/reciprocal

Some verbs require an agent participant as a lexical property. In the active voice, the agent role is assigned to the external argument. In the middle voice, the agent role is sometimes assigned to the internal argument, in addition to the original role of the internal argument. This assignment of two roles to a single argument gives rise to the reflexive and reciprocal (roughly, group reflexive) reading. The examples in (21)–(22) and the examples in (23)–(24) are familiar examples of reflexive and reciprocal verbs:

Reflexives:

(21) a. *parikmaxer postrig katju.* [Russian]
hairdresser sheared.M.SG Katja.ACC
'The hairdresser gave Katja a hair cut.'

b. *parikmaxer postrig-sja.*
hairdresser sheared.M.SG-REFL
'The hairdresser had a hair cut.'

(22) a. *ha-sapar siper et-dina.* [Hebrew]
the-hairdresser shear ACC-Dina
'The hairdresser gave Dina a hair cut.'

b. *ha-sapar histaper*
the-hairdresser shear.MID
'The hairdresser had a hair cut.'

Reciprocals:

(23) a. *lena i maša vstretili-s'.* [Russian]
Lena and Masha met.PL-REFL
'Lena and Masha met.'

b. *dani ve-dina nifgešu.* [Hebrew]
Dani and-Dina meet.MID
'Dani and Dina met.'

(24) a. *dina i kolja perepisyvajut-sja.* [Russian]
Dina and Kolja rewrite.3PL-REFL
'Dina and Kolja correspond.'

b. *david ve-ruti hitkatvu.* [Hebrew]
David and-Ruti write.MID
'David and Ruti corresponded.'

Sometimes it is not the internal argument which is assigned the role of agent, but rather the argument of an applicative head, an experiencer in the following examples. In these examples, Lena fills both the experiencer and the agent roles in the described event. The prefix *na-* is a perfectivizing affix which has a cumulative interpretation.

(25) a. *lena na-jela-s'.* [Russian]
Lena *na*-ate.F.SG-REFL
'Lena ate her fill.'

b. *lena na-jela-s' kotlet / kotletami.*
Lena *na*-ate.F.SG-REFL burgers.GEN burgers.INST
'Lena stuffed herself on burgers.'

c. *lena na-smotrela-s francuzskix fil'mov.*
Lena *na*-watched.F.SG-REFL French films.GEN
'Lena has watched French films to the limit.'
(Kagan and Pereltsvaig 2011)

2.2.3. Dispositional middle

Some verbs in the middle voice denote a dispositional property of the internal argument:

(26) a. *etot xleb legko rezhet-sja.* [Russian]
this bread easily cut.3SG-REFL
'This bread cuts easily.'

b. *ha-bad ha-ze mitgahec nehedar.* [Hebrew]
the-cloth the-this iron.MID superbly
'This cloth irons superbly.'

c. *Dit boek leest makelijk.* [Dutch]
'This book reads easily.'

There is an ongoing controversy in the linguistics literature concerning the question of whether or not the dispositional middle is reduced in valence relative to the active verb. The question is whether the external argument of the active verb should be considered an argument of the dispositional middle verb (Keyser and Roeper 1984; Hale and Keyser 1987; Condoravdi 1989; Stroik 1992; Lekakou 2004; Bhatt and Pancheva 2005; Schäfer 2007; Kallulli 2007). An indication of the implicit presence of the external argument is the possibility of expressing it obliquely, similarly to the passive. Several languages allow a *by*-phrase with dispositional middles:

(27) a. *afto to vivlio diavazete efxarista akomi ki apo megalus.* [Greek]
this the book read.NACT with.pleasure even and by grown.ups
'This book reads with pleasure even by grown-ups.'
(Condoravdi 1989)

b. *Ces étoffes se repassent facilement par tout le monde.* [Canadian French]
these fabrics MID iron easily by everybody
'These fabrics iron easily by everybody.'
(Lekakou 2005)

c. *ha-bad ha-ze mitgahec nehedar al.yedey kol exad.* [Hebrew]
the-fabric the-this iron.MID superbly by every one
'This fabric irons superbly by anyone.'

Other languages disallow a *by*-phrase:

(28) a. *Walls paint easily (*by anyone).*
(Ackema and Schoorlemmer 1994)

b. *Dieses Buch liest sich (*von den meisten Lesern / irgendwem)* [German]
this book reads REFL (*by the most readers anyone.DAT)
leicht.
easily
'This book reads easily (*by most readers / anyone).'
(Fagan 1992)

Yet even languages which permit a *by*-phrase only allow a very restricted subset denoting human arguments, which are also typical experiencers, and thus may actually be the arguments of the obligatory adverbs found in this construction. Accordingly, the agent may be present in the construction, but not as argument of the middle verb. Middle morphology assigns the verb's internal argument some kind of agentive role, similarly to the reflexive alternation (cf. Kemmer 1993). Under this view, the middle voice attributes to the internal argument the agent-like characteristic of being responsible, because of its inherent properties, for the dispositional property denoted by the verb. The dispositional middle may thus be viewed as a modalized reflexive middle.

A different type of dispositional middle which can also be analysed as a modalized reflexive is found in the Slavic languages. In (29) and (30) below, the verb has two internal arguments, a theme and a goal. The theme is additionally assigned the agent role in the middle voice, and constitutes the argument which the dispositional property is predicated of. The implicit goal is a human argument:

(29) a. *sobaka kusajet vasju* [Russian]
dog bites.3SG Vasja.ACC
'The dog is biting / bites Vasja.'

b. *sobaka kusajet-sja*
dog bites.3SG-REFL
'The dog bites.'

(30) a. *krapiva žžot nogi*
nettle stings.3SG legs.ACC
'The nettle is stinging / stings legs.'

b. *krapiva žžot-sja*
nettle stings.3SG-REFL
'The nettle stings.'
(Timberlake 2004)

2.2.4. Impersonal middle

Impersonal middles are dispositional middles constructed from intransitive verbs. Parallel to the impersonal passive, this construction features expletive subjects. But there are curious differences between the subjects of the impersonal middle and the impersonal passive. In German, the expletive subject is obligatory in the impersonal middle, as in (31a), whereas in the impersonal passive it is unacceptable in subject position, other than in the position preceding the verb sentence-initially (cf. [7b] above). In Dutch, e.g. (31b), the expletive *het* used in impersonal middles is different from the expletive *er* used in impersonal passives (cf. [8b] above). These differences correlate with the structural difference between impersonal passives and impersonal middles. In the passive voice, the verb's null external argument occupies an argument position, whereas the external argument is not part of the structure in the middle construction, which instead features a true expletive subject.

(31) a. *Hier schläft es sich angenehm / *Hier schläft sich angenehm.* [German]
here sleeps it REFL comfortable here sleeps REFL comfortable
'It is comfortable to sleep here.'
(Schäfer 2007: 298, example [60b])

b. *Het zit prima in deze stoel.* [Dutch]
it sits fine in this chair
'This chair is fine to sit in.'
(Lekakou 2005: 100, example [194])

c. *Se duerme bien en los bancos.* [Spanish]
REFL sleep.3SG well in the benches
'One sleeps well on benches.'

In Russian too, there is an expletive null subject, while the argument of the modal/adverbial predicate is realized obliquely:

(32) a. *mne ne rabotajet-sja.* [Russian]
me.DAT NEG works.3SG-REFL
'I don't feel like working.'

b. *mne ne spit-sja.*
me.DAT NEG sleeps.3SG-REFL
'I can't sleep.'

c. *mne xorošo / ploxo rabotajet-sja.*
me.DAT well bad works.3SG-REFL
'I can/cannot manage to work.'
(Timberlake 2004)

2.2.5. Mediopassive

Mediopassive is a form of the verb which has the morphology of the middle voice, but is nevertheless similar to the passive in that it allows the participation of the external argument. Yet unlike the passive, where the external argument is required in the representation of the verb, the mediopassive allows this argument but does not require it. Mediopassives thus also share properties with middle anticausatives, where the external argument is not included in the derivation. The mediopassive is compatible both with interpretations under which something happens on its own and with interpretations where it is brought about by an external argument. It is thus underdetermined for the passive/anticausative distinction (cf. Tsimpli 2006).

In some languages, the mediopassive interpretation of the middle voice depends on the lack of dedicated passive voice morphology, either in the language in general, as in Greek, or at least for particular verbs, as in Hebrew:

(33) a. *O Janis dolofonithike apo tin Maria.* [Greek]
the Janis murder.NACT by the Mary
'John was murdered by Mary.'
(Alexiadou et al. 2006)

b. *Dani nircax al.yedey Dina.* [Hebrew]
Dani murder.MID by Dina
'Dani was murdered by Dina.'

Yet in both languages, the mediopassive interpretation of the middle voice is limited to particular verbs, and is not general:

(34) a. *I supa kaike apo moni.tis / *apo to Jani.* [Greek]
the soup burnt.NACT by itself by the John
'The soup got burnt by itself / *by John.'

b. *ha-gader hitparqa me-acma / *al.yedey ha-mafgini* [Hebrew]
the-wall dismantle.MID from-itself by the-demonstrators
'The wall fell apart by itself / *by the demonstrators.'
(Alexiadou and Doron 2012)

In a limited number of cases, a middle voice verb is interpreted as mediopassive despite the existence of a corresponding passive verb. Interestingly, in the perfective aspect, the same limited class of verbs is found to have this property in French (Zribi-Hertz 1982). The examples below illustrate this class of verbs (restrictions in the perfective aspect are also noted for Spanish by Mendikoetxea 1999):

(35) a. *Le crime s'est commis pendant les heures de bureau.* [French]
the crime REFL.is committed during the hours of office

b. *ha-péša' hitbacéa' bi-š'ot ha-'avoda.* [Hebrew]
the-crime commit.MID in-hours.of the-work
both: 'The crime was committed during office hours.'

(36) a. *Le text s'est traduit en moins d'une heure.* [French]
the text REFL.is translated in less of.one hour

b. *ha-tekst hitargem be-paxot mi-ša'a.* [Hebrew]
the-text translate.MID in-less of-hour
both: 'The text was translated in less than an hour.'

In the imperfective, middle voice verbs can be generally interpreted as mediopassive:

(37) a. *De tels objets s'exposent avant de se vendre.* [French]
such objects REFL.display.3PL before to REFL sell
'Such objects are displayed before being sold.' (generic)
(Dobrovie-Sorin 1998: 422)

b. *Cerkov' stroit-sja rabočimi.* [Russian]
church.NOM builds.3SG-REFL workers.INST
'The church is being built by workers.' (imperfective)
(Blevins 2003: 503, example [32])

c. *Se observan cambios en la economía.* [Spanish]
REFL observe.3PL changes in the economy
'Changes can be observed in the economy.' (imperfective)
(Mendikoetxea 2012: 477)

The mediopassive differs from the passive in several respects. In Hebrew, it often allows the adjunct *by itself,* and non-agentive external arguments, as shown in (38) below, in contrast to the agentive nature of passive external argments (cf. [4] above). A similar argument is made for Greek by Alexiadou and Anagnostopoulou (2004).

(38) *ha-be'aya nocra me-'acma / al.yedey išiyut-o.* [Hebrew]
the-problem create.MID from-itself by personality-his
'The problem was created by itself / by his personality.'

Moreover, mediopassives are derived independently of related active verbs, like middle verbs in general (cf. [17]–[18] above), whereas the passive is typically only derived for a corresponding active. The active verbs *anaš 'punish' and *šalam 'complete' corresponding to the mediopassive forms in (39) are not currently in use in Hebrew, and have been replaced by the related causative verbs *he'eniš* 'punish.CAUS', *hišlim* 'complete.CAUS'. Nevertheless, the mediopassive forms of the non-existing verbs are commonly used:

(39) a. *hu ne'enaš al.yedey yisurey ha-macpun šel-o.* [Hebrew]
he punish.MID by agony.of the-conscience of-his
'He was punished by his guilt feelings.'

b. *ha-haxanot nišlemu al.yedey ha-mištatfim.*
the-preparations complete.MID by the-participants
'The preparations were completed by the participants.'

There are therefore arguments for classifying the mediopassive, as well as the dispositional middle of section 2.2.3, as subclasses of the middle voice. Yet this is by no means a settled issue, and these classes are sometimes referred to in the literature as "passive" and "dispositional passive" instead. One way of settling the controversy is by giving up the characterization of the middle voice as maximally contrastive to the passive voice, i.e. as a voice alternation which reduces valence. Instead, it could be characterized as a voice alternation which optionally reduces valence, while the passive does not reduce valence.

2.2.6. Impersonal mediopassive

There indeed is a middle construction where valence reduction seems not to take place at all, as indicated by the fact that the verb retains accusative case. This is a middle construction with an expletive subject, but, unlike the impersonal middle discussed in section 2.2.4 above, this construction is neither dispositional nor intransitive. Rather, the verb here is eventive and transitive, though the impersonal (human) agent is not explicitly expressed:

(40) a. *Il s'est lu beaucoup de livres l'année dernière.* [French]
it REFL.is.3SG read many of books the.year last
'A lot of books were read last year.'
(Dobrovie-Sorin 1998: [66])

b. *Se curó a los brujos.* [Spanish]
REFL cured.3SG ACC the.PL sorcerers
'The sorcerers were cured.'
(Givón 1990, Ch. 14)

3. General/theoretical discussion of voice

Many general questions are raised by voice. Here is a simple one: If both passive and middle are values of the voice dimension, why are they so different in their productivity? In languages of the world, passive is normally productive. In those languages with passive morphology, passive applies to practically all transitive verbs. But the middle, in languages that have it, is lexically restricted. Does this indicate that the two constructions are of a different character, and that we should not classify both as voice? The answer is probably no, passive is productive because it constitutes a less radical departure from the active voice, as it is not valence changing. The middle voice is valence changing, at least potentially, and may thus clash with the lexical requirements of certain verbs for particular arguments.

Other general and theoretical questions have been raised in the course of the study of issues related to voice. Here are several approaches found in the recent literature which have offered generalizations concerning these issues.

3.1. A typological analysis of anticausatives (Haspelmath 1993)

It is natural to expect language to be structurally iconic, i.e. to expect that in general, a complex linguistic form should represent a complex concept. Haspelmath poses an interesting challenge from the subject-matter of voice to the view that language is iconic: "If the semantic properties of a word are only the objective semantic features discovered by semantic decomposition, then causatives are always semantically more complex than inchoatives and the existence of or even preference for anticausatives is a mystery." (Haspelmath 1993: 106). In other words, since causative events are complex, how is it possible that they are sometimes expressed by unmarked active verbs, while their simpler components are expressed by complex middle-voice anticausative verbs? In his article, Haspelmath demonstrates how iconicity can nevertheless be defended, which allows him to conclude that "the challenge to iconicity coming from cases of apparent reverse word-formation could be answered at least for inchoative/causative alternations. The existence of anticausatives is not a problem because the semantic markedness relationship which iconically corresponds to the formal basic-derived relationship cannot be equated with a basic-derived relationship in the real world. Semantics is conceptual, and our conceptualization of the world reflects it in a way that is profoundly influenced by our conceptual capacities. Only extensive typological comparison has made this conclusion possible." (Haspelmath 1993: 108). Thus, the complexity of verb forms does not directly represent the complexity of events, but that of their conceptualization. Humans conceptualize some events as being likely to be brought about by an outside force, and other as being likely to happen spontaneously. Unmarked causative verbs are iconic in the case of verbs which denote events that are likely to be brought about by an outside force: externally caused. For such verbs, it is less likely that the event will occur spontaneously, and this is expressed by a marked, middle-voice, form of the verb. For such events, the causative is the most probable and expected, whereas the anticausative is marked because it is unexpected. On the other hand, verbs that denote events which normally happen spontaneously will be unmarked in the intransitive form, and marked by causative morphology when they denote the less likely events which include an outside causing force. This does not mean that all languages will categorize each particular type of event in the same way. For example, the verb *finish* encodes an externally caused event in Hebrew, i.e. it has an unmarked transitive *gamar* 'finish.TR' and a marked middle-voice intransitive *nigmar* 'finish.MID' alternant; this is reversed in Turkish, which has an unmarked intransitive *bit* 'finish.INTR' and a causative marked transitive *bit-ir* 'finish-CAUS'. The verb *freeze*, on the other hand, has an unmarked intransitive form in Hebrew *qafa* 'freeze.INTR' and a causative marked transitive alternant *hiqpi* 'freeze.CAUS'; this is reversed in Spanish, where the intransitive is marked by the middle voice: *congelar-se* 'freeze-REFL' whereas the transitive is unmarked *congelar* 'freeze.TR'. Yet Haspelmath shows that these alternations are not arbitrary or completely language dependent after all. A pattern can be detected when one systematically observes different languages. A universal ranking of predicates emerges: ... P_i .... P_j ... (according to "spontaneity of the event") such that in every natural language, if P_i is expressed as an unmarked intransitive verb, then so is P_j, and if P_j is expressed as an unmarked transitive verb, then so is P_i. A section of this ranking is shown here:

(41) Tab. 22.1: A section of the universal ranking of predicates

...	*open*	*finish* ...	*freeze* ...	*boil* ...
	intrans / trans	intrans / trans	intrans / trans	intrans / trans
Spanish:	*abrir-se / abrir*	*terminar-se / terminar*	*congelar-se / congelar*	*hervir / hacer hervir*
Hebrew:	*ni-ftax / patax*	*ni-gmar / gamar*	*qafa / hi-qpi*	*ratax / hi-rtiax*
Turkish:	*aç-il / aç*	*bit / bit-ir*	*don / don-dur*	*pis / pis-ir*

Languages differ in the precise point at which they switch the conceptualization of events from externally caused to spontaneous. Spanish views *open, finish* and *freeze* as describing externally caused events, and thus their intransitive variants are marked by the middle voice. But once it switches to viewing the intransitive verb as unmarked, it will keep on doing so for events which are more and more spontaneous (presumably such as *jump, laugh* etc). This is corroborated by Hebrew and Turkish, which switch to unmarked intransitives earlier than Spanish, and do not switch back.

3.2. A functionalist analysis of the middle voice (Kemmer 1993)

Kemmer's (1993, 1994) achievement is in demonstrating that it is the same verbs which systematically appear with middle morphology across a large number of unrelated languages. Moreover, she shows that these verbs can be classified into a relatively small number of semantically coherent classes:

(42) a. verbs of grooming or body care: dress, wash, shave
b. nontranslational motion: stretch, turn, bow
c. change of body posture: sit down, kneel, get up, lie down
d. translational motion: climb up, go away, stroll, fly
e. natually reciprocal events: embrace, wrestle, converse, speak together
f. indirect middle: acquire, ask, request, take for oneself, desire, crave
g. emotional middle: become frightened, become angry, grieve, mourn
h. emotive speech actions: complain, lament

i. cognition middle: cogitate, reflect, consider, ponder, meditate, believe
j. spontaneous events: sprout, stop, vanish, recover, originate, occur
k. facilitative situations: dispositional middles and mediopassives

Kemmer concludes that there is a conceptual basis which underlies not only the anticausative (as shown by Haspelmath), but the middle voice as a whole. Kemmer views the distinction between transitive and intransitive clauses as expressing the edges of a continuum (following Hopper and Thompson 1980) between two- and one-participant events. She proposes to "add the middle to the event space defined by these situation types and to the parameter along which they differ, namely the degree of discernibility of the participants (...) Two-participant events have maximal distinguishability of participants in that the participants are completely separate entities. The reflexive and middle have progressively lower distinguishability, which means that the Initiator (controller or conceived source of action) and Endpoint (affected participant) are not separate, but necessarily the same entitiy." (Kemmer 1994: 209). Kemmer shows that her proposal subsumes Benveniste (1950), Gonda (1960), Klaiman (1991), who view subject-affectedness as the defining characteristic of the Indo-European middle. In Kemmer's framework, the subject of a middle-voice verb is affected since it is not distinguished from the affected participant.

3.3. A syntactic analysis of the passive voice (Baker, Johnson, and Roberts 1989)

Baker, Johnson and Roberts (1989) establish the status of the passive as a voice which does not alter the number of arguments of the verb. Though arguments had been previously adduced, Baker et al. provide the decisive argument. We first present earlier arguments due to e.g. Manzini (1983), Keyser and Roeper (1984) Roeper (1987). First, passive clauses allow an overt *by*-phrase licensed by the implicit subject, (43a), whereas unmarked anticausative clauses do not, (43b):

(43) a. *The ship was sunk by Bill.*
b. **The ship sank by Bill.*

Second, subject-oriented adverbs may modify the implicit subject of the passive, (44a), though this is not so in the case of the anticausative, (44b):

(44) a. *The ship was sunk deliberately.*
b. *#The ship sank deliberately.*

Third, the missing subjects of rationale clauses may be controlled by the implicit subject of the passive, (45a), though this is not so in the case of the anticausative, (45b):

(45) a. *The ship was sunk to collect the insurance.*
b. **The ship sank to collect the insurance.*

The novel argument provided by Baker et al. (based in part on Williams 1987) which establishes that the passive argument is syntactically active, is that there is a restriction on the interpretation of the understood passive subject. The passive subject is known to be interpreted as existentially quantified, e.g. (46a) is understood as 'Someone/something killed him.':

(46) a. *He was killed.*
 b. *He was seen.*

What Baker et al. noticed is that passives cannot be interpreted in such a way that the understood subject is coreferential with the surface subject, i.e. (46) cannot mean (47):

(47) a. *He committed suicide.*
 b. *He saw himself.*

Baker et al. further note that non-coreferentiality cannot be attributed to a pragmatic effect due to the absence in the structure of the passive argument. Other types of structures with missing arguments do not prevent coreference of an expressed argument with a missing argument. For example, in adjectival passives, such as (48a), the missing subject can be understood as coreferential to the surface subject, i.e. John could have shaved himself. Similarly in (48b), whether it is understood dispositionally or not, there is no ban against John being the one doing the shaving:

(48) a. *John is freshly shaved.*
 b. *John shaves easily.*

3.4. A Distributed Morphology analysis of voice (Doron 2003; Alexiadou, Anagnostopoulou, and Schäfer 2006)

Within a constructional approach to morphology (the Distributed Morphology framework of Halle and Marantz 1993; and the framework of Kratzer 1996, 2005), where words are not constructed in the lexicon but as part of the syntactic derivation of the clause, several proposals have converged to an account of voice (Embick 1997, 2004; Doron 2003; Alexiadou and Anagnostopoulou 2004; Alexiadou, Anagnostopoulou, and Schäfer 2006; Kallulli 2006; Labelle 2008). Roughly, all these accounts include in their syntax a functional head: *Voice*, which regulates the insertion of the external argument required by the verb's root. The values of Voice discussed in these approaches are Active, Middle and Passive. The non-active (NACT) morphology found in Greek and Albanian is viewed as syncretizing Middle and Passive (but see Embick 1997; Alexiadou and Doron 2012 for a different view of Greek non-active morphology).

The active Voice does not interfere with the coocurrence restrictions of the root. For example, the English root *destroy* requires an external argument (with the thematic role of cause assigned by the appropriate functional head *v*), whereas the root *arrive* does not cooccur with an external argument. The roots *dry* and *whiten* allow an external argument, but do not require one:

(49) Active voice

a. *arrive*
dry (intr.)
whiten (intr.)

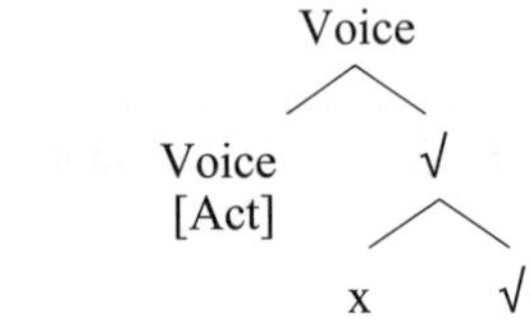

b. *destroy*
dry (trans.)
whiten (trans.)

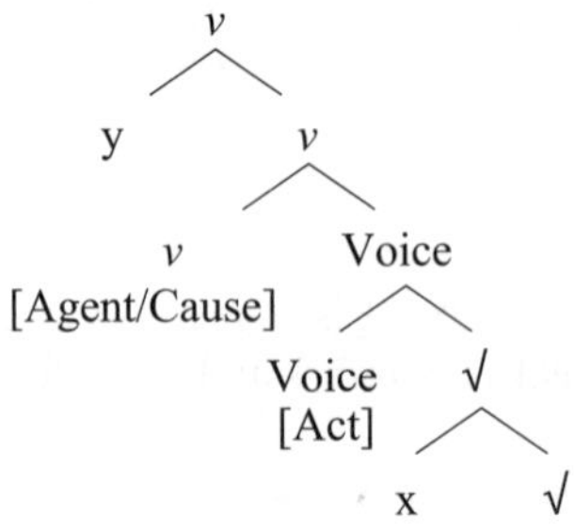

(50) Passive voice

a. * *arrive*

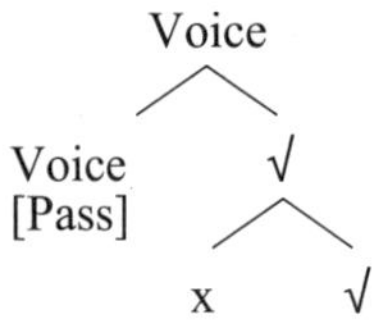

b. *destroy, dry, whiten*

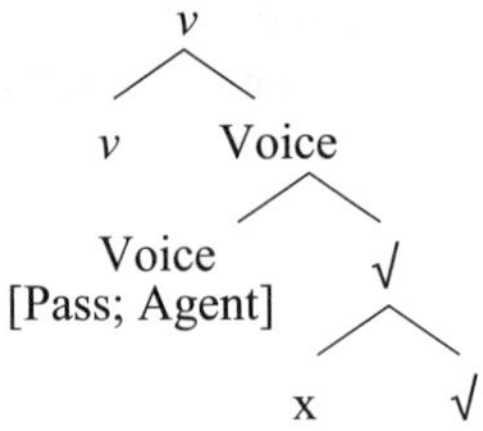

Even in languages with middle-voice morphology, there are active anticausatives constructed as in (49a), e.g. *hilbin* 'whiten' in Hebrew, and *stegnosan* 'dry' in Greek, which are active verbs.

The passive Voice, following Baker et al. (1989), introduces an external argument in the environment of exactly the same roots as in the active, and is thus impossible in (50a).

Similarly to Baker et al., it is the head *v* itself which is the external argument of the passive. In Hebrew and Greek, the argument of the passive Voice is an agent, thus accounting for the fact that the Hebrew *hulban* (whiten.PASS) 'was whitened' and the Greek *stegnothikan* (dry.NACT) 'was dried' can only be interpreted with an agentive by-phrase, though the active can take a cause argument.

(51) a. *Ta ruha stegnosan / *stegnothikan apo ton ilio.* [Greek]
the clothes dried.ACT dried.NACT from the sun
'The clothes dried (*were dried) from the sun.'
(Alexiadou et al. 2006)

b. *ha-kvisa hilbina / *hulbena me-ha-šémeš.* [Hebrew]
the-laundry whitened.ACT whitened.PASS from-the-sun
'The laundry whitened (*was whitened) from the sun.'

(52) a. *Ta mallia mu stegnothikan / *stegnosan apo tin komotria.* [Greek]
the hair my dried.NACT dried.ACT by the hairdresser
'My hair was dried by the hairdresser.'
(Alexiadou et al. 2006)

b. *ha-kvisa hulbena / *hilbina al.yedey ha-kovéset.* [Hebrew]
the-laundry whitened.PASS whitened.ACT by the-laundress
'The laundry was whitened (*whitened) by the laundress.'

The middle Voice head does not co-occur with *v*, i.e. it does not have an external argument. Yet in the environment of some roots, it assigns the agent thematic role to the argument x of the root, such as in e.g. (53b). Since it alters the thematic role of the internal argument, the middle Voice is merged with the root in (53). This is different from the passive voice, which alters the thematic role of the external argument, and thus merges above the internal argument in (50) above. The different level of attachment accounts for the lower productivity of the middle in comparison to the passive, and also for the fact that passive forms are only derived for corresponding active forms, whereas middle verbs are derived independently of related active verbs.

(53) Middle voice
a. *destroy, wash*

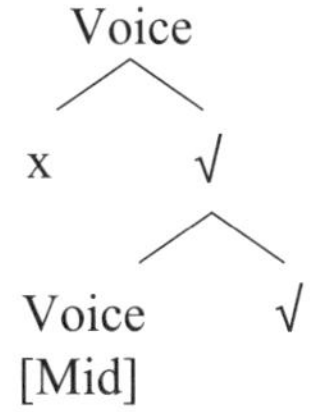

b. *destroy, wash, comb*

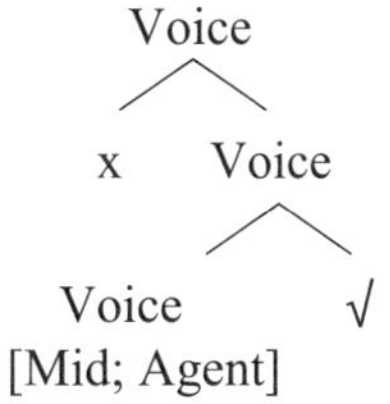

The structure in (53b) derives a reflexive interpretation, for example in the following:

(54) a. *I Maria htenizete kathe mera.* [Greek]
The Mary combs.NACT every day
'Mary combs her hair every day.'
(Embick 2004)

b. *Dina mistareqet kol yom.* [Hebrew]
Dina combs.MID every day
'Dina combs her hair every day.'

Some verbs in Greek require *afto* when the roots appear in the (53b) rather than the (53a) structure. In Hebrew this is sometimes indicated by the contrast between the two middle forms, the simple middle (MID.SIMPL) which tends to be medio-passive, vs. the intensive middle (MID.INTNS) which tends to be agentive:

(55) a. *To hirografo katastrafike apo tin pirkagia.* [Greek]
the manuscript destroyed.NACT by the fire
'The manuscript got destroyed by the fire.'
(Embick 2004)

b. *ha rexovot nirxacu me-ha-géšem.* [Hebrew]
the street washed.MID.SIMPL from-the-rain
'The streets got washed by the rain.'

(56) a. *I Maria afto-katastrefete.* [Greek]
the Mary self-destroys.NACT
'Mary destroys herself.'
(Embick 2004)

b. *ha-yeladim hitraxacu.* [Hebrew]
the-children washed.MID.INTNS
'The children washed themselves.'

According to this analysis, in the case of deponent verbs (middle-voice verbs which may have two internal arguments), the additional internal argument, e.g. a beneficiary, is introduced by an applicative head. The middle Voice may assign the agent thematic role to the applicative argument y in (57):

(57) Middle voice (for Root + Applicative)
use, need

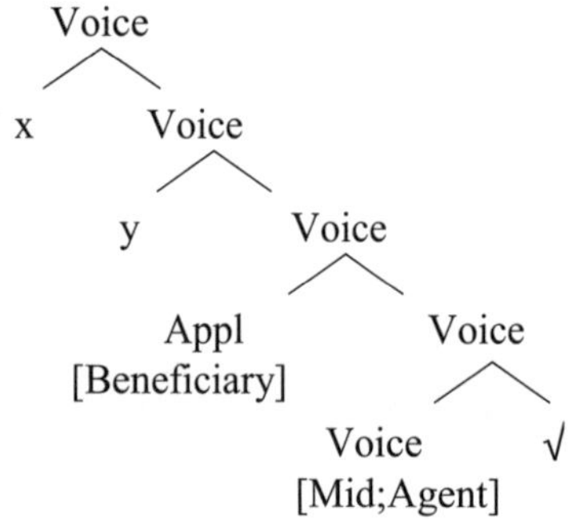

The examples in (58) illustrate the structure (57) in Greek and Hebrew. In Hebrew, the root argument x in (57) is typically oblique in the middle derivation, but it is possible to find accusative arguments, as in Greek:

(58) a. *Metahirizome to leksiko.* [Greek]
use.NACT.1SG the dictionary.ACC
'I use the dictionary.'

b. *Eštameš b-a-milon.* [Hebrew]
FUT.1SG.use.MID OBL-the-dictionary
'I will use the dictionary.'

c. *Ectarex et-ha-milon.* [Hebrew]
FUT.1SG.need.MID ACC-the-dictionary
'I will need the dictionary.'

In conclusion, there is a kernel concept of voice compatible with the different points of view of various linguistic approaches, which denotes alternation in the assignment of grammatical functions to the verb's arguments, often marked by verbal morphology, and driven by change/reduction of the expression of the verb's external argument.

4. References (selected)

Ackema, Peter, and Maaike Schoorlemmer
1994 The middle construction and the syntax-semantics interface. *Lingua* 93:59–90.
Aldridge, Edith
2004 Ergativity and word order in Austronesian languages. PhD Dissertation. Cornell University.
Alexiadou, Artemis, and Elena Anagnostopoulou
2004 Voice morphology in the causative-inchoative alternation: evidence for a non-unified structural analysis of unaccusatives. In: A. Alexiadou, E. Anagnostopoulou, and M. Everaert (eds.), *The Unaccusativity Puzzle: Explorations of the Syntax-Lexicon Interface*, 114–136. Oxford: Oxford University Press.
Alexiadou, Artemis, Elena Anagnostopoulou, and Florian Schäfer
2006 The properties of anticausatives crosslinguistically. In: M. Frascarelli (ed.), *Phases of Interpretation*, 187–211. Berlin: Mouton de Gruyter.
Alexiadou, Artemis, and Edit Doron
2012 The syntactic construction of two non-active voices: passive and middle. *Journal of Linguistics* 48.1: 1–34.
Alsina, Alex
2009 The prepositional passive as structure-sharing . In: M. Butt, and T. Holloway King (eds.), *The Proceedings of the LFG '09 Conference*, 44–64. Trinity College, Cambridge, UK.
Anagnostopoulou, Elena
2003 Participles and voice. In: A. Alexiadou, M. Rathert, and A. von Stechow (eds.), *Perfect Explorations*, 1–36. Berlin/New York: Mouton de Gruyter.
Badawi, Elsaid, Michael G. Carter, and Adrian Gully
2004 *Modern Written Arabic*: *A Comprehensive Grammar*. (Routledge Comprehensive Grammars.) London, New York: Routledge.
Baker, Mark
1997 Thematic roles and syntactic structure. In: L. Haegeman (ed.), *Elements of Grammar*, 73–137. Dordrecht: Kluwer.
Baker, Mark, Kyle Johnson, and Ian Roberts
1989 Passive arguments raised. *Linguistic Inquiry* 20: 219–251.
Beach, Matthew
2003 Asymmetries between passivization and antipassivization in the *Tarramiutut* Subdialect of Inuktitut. In: M. Butt, and T. Holloway King (eds.), *Proceedings of the LFG03 Conference*, CSLI Publications.
Beck, David
1997 Unitariness and partial identification in the Bella Coola middle voice. *Kansas Working Papers in Linguistics: Studies in Native American Languages IX* 22.2: 11–32.
Benveniste, Émile
1950/1976 Actif et moyen dans le verbe. *Problèmes de Linguistique Générale I*: 168–175. Paris: Gallimard.
Bhatt, Rajesh, and Roumyana Pancheva
2005 Implicit arguments. In: M. Everaert, and H. van Riemsdijk (eds.), The Blackwell Companion to Syntax, Vol II. Blackwell.
Bittner, Maria
1994 *Case, Scope, and Binding*. Dordrecht: Kluwer Academic Publishers.
Bittner, Maria, and Ken Hale
1996 The structural determination of case and agreement. *Linguistic Inquiry* 27: 1–68.
Blevins, James P.
2003 Passives and impersonals. *Journal of Linguistics* 39: 473–520.

Bok-Bennema, Reineke
1991 *Case and Agreement in Inuit.* Dordrecht: Foris Publications.
Bolinger, Dwight
1977 Transitivity and spatiality: the passive of prepositional verbs. In: A. Makkai, V. B. Makkai, and L. Heilmann (eds.), *Linguistics at the Crossroads*, 57–78. Illinois: Jupiter Press.
Bresnan, Joan
1982 The passive in Lexical Theory. In: J. Bresnan (ed.), *The Mental Representation of Grammatical Relations*, 3–86. Cambridge, Mass: MIT Press.
Bresnan, Joan, Shipra Dingare, and Christopher D. Manning
2001 Soft constraints mirror hard constraints: voice and person in English and Lummi. In: M. Butt, and T. Holloway King (eds.), *Proceedings of the LFG01 Conference.* CSLI Publications.
Condoravdi, Cleo
1989 The middle: where semantics and morphology meet. *MIT Working Papers in Linguistics* 11: 16–30.
Cooreman, Ann
1994 A functional typology of antipassives. In: Barbara A. Fox, and Paul J. Hopper (eds.), *Voice: Form and Function*, 49–88. Amsterdam: John Benjamins.
Comrie, Bernard
1978 Ergativity. In: Winifred Lehman (ed.), *Syntactic Typology: Studies in the Phenomenology of Language*, 329–394. Austin: University of Texas Press.
Croft, William
1994 Voice: Beyond control and affectedness. In: Barbara A. Fox, and Paul J. Hopper (eds.), *Voice: Form and Function*, 89–117. Amsterdam: John Benjamins.
Dahlstrom, Amy
1991 *Plains Cree Morphosyntax*. New York: Garland.
Deal, Amy Rose
2007 Antipassive and indefinite objects in Nez Perce. In: A. R. Deal (ed.), *Proceedings of SULA*, Vol. 4, 35–47. Amherst: GLSA.
Dixon, Robert M. W.
1972 *The Dyirbal Language of North Queensland.* Cambridge: Cambridge University Press.
Dixon, Robert M. W.
1979 Ergativity. *Language* 55.1: 59–138.
Dixon, Robert M. W.
1994 *Ergativity.* Cambridge, UK: Cambridge University Press.
Dixon, Robert M. W., and Alexandra Aikhenvald
1997 A typology of argument determined constructions. In: J. Bybee, J. Haiman, and S. Thompson (eds.), *Essays on Language Function and Language Type. Dedicated to T. Givón,* 71–113. Amsterdam: John Benjamins.
Dobrovie-Sorin, Carmen
1998 Impersonal *se* constructions in Romance and the passivization of unergatives. *Linguistic Inquiry* 29.3: 399–437.
Doron, Edit
2003 Agency and voice: the semantics of the semitic templates. *Natural Language Semantics* 11: 1–67.
Embick, David
1997 Voice systems and the syntax/morphology interface. In: H. Harley (ed.), *The Proceedings of the Penn/MIT Workshop on Aspect, Argument Structure, and Events*. MITWPL.
Embick, David
2004 Unaccusative syntax and verbal alternations. In: A. Alexiadou, E. Anagnostopoulou, and M. Everaert (eds.), *The Unaccusativity Puzzle: Explorations of the Syntax-Lexicon Interface*, 137–158. Oxford: Oxford University Press.

England, Nora C.
1988 Mam voice. In: M. Shibatani (ed.), *Passive and Voice*, 525–545. Amsterdam: John Benjamins.
Fagan, Sarah
1992 *The Syntax and Semantics of Middle Constructions.* Cambridge: Cambridge University Press.
Farrell, Patrick
1992 A last look at the 1AEX. *Proceedings of the West Coast Conference in Formal Linguistics* 1: 191–206.
Fellbaum, Christine
1989 On the "reflexive middle" in English. *Chicago Linguistic Society* 25: 123–132.
Fortescue, Michael
1984 *West Greenlandic.* London: Croom Helm.
Fox, Barbara, and Paul J. Hopper (eds.)
1994 *Voice: Form and Function.* Amsterdam: John Benjamins.
Givón, Talmy
1990 *Syntax: A Functional-Typological Introduction.* Amsterdam: John Benjamins.
Givón, Talmy
1994a. Introduction. In: T. Givón (ed.), *Voice and Inversion.* Amsterdam: John Benjamins.
Givón, Talmy (ed.)
1994b *Voice and Inversion.* Amsterdam: John Benjamins.
Gonda, Jan
1960 Reflections of the Indo-European medium. *Lingua* 9: 30–67, 175–193.
Hale, Ken, and Jay Keyser
2002 *Prolegomena to a Theory of Argument Structure.* Cambridge, Mass.: MIT Press.
Halle, Morris, and A. Marantz
1993 Distributed Morphology and the Pieces of Inflection. In: K. Hale, and S. J. Keyser (eds.), *A View From Building 20*, 111–176. Cambridge, Mass.: MIT Press.
Haspelmath, Martin
1993 More on the typology of inchoative/causative verb alternations. In: Comrie B., and M. Polinsky (eds.), *Causatives and Transitivity*, 87–121. Amsterdam: John Benjamins.
Haspelmath, Martin, and Thomas Müller-Bardey
2005 Valence change. In: G. Booij., C. Lehmann, and J. Mugdan (eds.), *A Handbook on Inflection and Word Formation*, 1130–1145. Berlin: de Gruyter.
Holisky, Dee Ann
1981 *Aspect and Georgian Medial Verbs.* Delmar, New York: Caravan Press.
Hopper, Paul J., and Sandra Thompson
1980 Transitivity in grammar and discourse. *Language* 56: 251–299.
Johns, Alana
2001 Ergative to accusative : comparing evidence from Inuktitut. In: J. T. Faarlund (ed.), *Grammatical Relations in Change,* 205–221. Amsterdam: John Benjamins.
Jónsson, Jóhannes G.
2003 Not so quirky: on subject case in Icelandic. In: E. Brandner, and H. Zinsmeister (eds.), *New Perspectives on Case Theory*, 127–163. Stanford: CSLI Publications.
Junker, Marie-Odile
2004 Focus, obviation, and word order in East Cree. *Lingua* 114: 345–365.
Kagan, Olga, and Asya Pereltsvaig
2011 Bare NPs and semantic incorporation: objects of intensive reflexives at the syntax-semantics interface. In: B. Wayles, A. Cooper, A. Fisher, E. Kesici, N. Predolac, and D. Zec (eds.), *Formal Approaches to Slavic Linguistics (FASL 18): The Cornell Meeting*, 226–240. Ann Arbor, MI: Michigan Slavic Publications.

Kallulli, Dalina
2006 A unified analysis of passives, anticausatives and reflexives. In: O. Bonami, and P. Cabredo-Hofherr (eds.), *Empirical Issues in Formal Syntax and Semantics* 6, 201–225.
Kallulli, Dalina
2007 Rethinking the passive/anticausative distinction. *Linguistic Inquiry* 38: 770–780.
Kalmár, Ivan
1979 The antipassive and grammatical relations in Eskimo. In: F. Plank (ed.), *Ergativity: Towards a Theory of Grammatical Relations*, 117–143. London, New York: Academic Press.
Kaufmann, Ingrid
2007 Middle voice. *Lingua* 117: 1677–1714.
Kayne, Richard
1975 *French Syntax.* Cambridge, Mass: MIT Press.
Kemmer, Suzanne
1993 *The Middle Voice.* Amsterdam: John Benjamins.
Kemmer, Suzanne
1994 Middle voice, transitivity and the elaboration of events. In: B. Fox, and P. J. Hopper (eds.), *Voice: Form and Function*, 179–230. Amsterdam: John Benjamins.
Keyser, Samuel J., and Thomas Roeper
1984 On the middle and ergative construction in English. *Linguistic Inquiry* 15: 381–416.
Kirsner, Robert S.
1976 On the subjectless 'pseudo-passive' in standard Dutch and the semantics of background agents. In: C. N. Li (ed.), *Subject and Topic*, 385–415. New York: Academic Press.
Klaiman, Miriam H.
1991 *Grammatical Voice.* Cambridge: Cambridge University Press.
Kozinsky, Issac S., Vladimir P. Nedjalkov, and Maria S. Polinsky
1988 Antipassive in Chukchee: oblique object, object incorporation, zero object. In: M. Shibatani (ed.), *Passive and Voice*, 651–706. Amsterdam: John Benjamins.
Kratzer, Angelika
1996 Severing the external argument from its verb. In: J. Rooryck, and L. Zaring (eds.), *Phrase Structure and the Lexicon*, 109–137. Dordrecht: Kluwer.
Kratzer, Angelika
2005 Building Resultatives. In: C. Maienborn, and A. Wöllstein-Leisten (eds.), *Event Arguments in Syntax, Semantics, and Discourse,* 178–212. Tübingen: Niemeyer.
Labelle, Marie
2008 The French reflexive and reciprocal *se*. *Natural Language and Linguistic Theory* 26: 833–876.
Legate, Julie Anne
2002 Walpiri: theoretical implications. PhD Diss. MIT.
Legate, Julie Anne
2008 Morphological and abstract case. *Linguistic Inquiry* 39.1: 55–101.
Lekakou, Marika
2005 In the middle, somewhat elevated: the semantics of middles and its crosslinguistic realization. Ph.D. thesis, University College London.
Levin, Beth, and Malka Rappaport Hovav
1995 *Unaccusativity. At the Syntax-Lexical Semantics Interface*. Cambridge, Mass: MIT Press.
Mendikoetxea, Amaya
1999 Construcciones con *se*: medias, pasivas e impersonales. In: Ignacio Bosque, and Violeta Demonte (eds.), *Gramática Descriptiva de la Lengua Española*, Vol 2, 1631–1722. Madrid: Espasa Calpe.

Mendikoetxea, Amaya
2012 Passives and *se* constructions. In: José Ignacio Hualde, Antxon Olarrea, and Erin O'Rourke (eds.), *The Handbook of Hispanic Linguistics*, 477–502. Chichester: Wiley-Blackwell.
Manzini, Rita M.
1983 On control and control theory. *Linguistic Inquiry* 14: 421–446.
Marantz, Alec P.
1984 *On the Nature of Grammatical Relations.* Cambridge: MIT Press.
Peled, Yishai
1998 *Written Arabic Syntax in Theory and Practice.* Tel Aviv: Tel Aviv University Press.
Perlmutter, David
1978 Impersonal passives and the unaccusative hypothesis. In: J. Jaeger et al. (eds.), *Proceedings of the Fourth Annual Meeting of the Berkeley Linguistics Society.* University of California, Berkeley.
Perlmutter, David, and Paul Postal
1984 The 1-advancement exclusiveness law. In: D. Perlmutter, and C. Rosen (eds.), *Studies in Relational Grammar 2.* Chicago: University of Chicago Press.
Reinhart, Tanya, and Tal Siloni
2005 The lexicon-syntax parameter: reflexivization and other arity operations. *Linguistic Inquiry* 36: 389–436.
Riddle, Elizabeth, and Gloria Sheintuch
1982 A functional analysis of pseudo-passives. *Linguistics and Philosophy* 6: 527–563.
Ritter, Elizabeth, and Sara Thomas Rosen
2005 Agreement without A-positions: another look at Algonquian. *Linguistic Inquiry* 36.4: 648–660.
Roeper, Thomas
1987 Implicit Arguments and the Head-Complement Relation. *Linguistic Inquiry* 18: 267–310.
Rude, Noel
1988 Ergative, passive, and antipassive in Nez Perce: a discourse perspective. In: M. Shibatani (ed.), *Passive and Voice*, 547–560. Amsterdam: John Benjamins.
Schäfer, Florian
2007 On the nature of anticausative morphology: external arguments in change-of-state contexts. Ph.D. Diss. University of Stuttgart.
Sells, Peter
1995 The function of voice markers in the Philippine languages. In: S. G. Lapointe, D. K. Brentari, and P. M. Farrell (eds.), *Morphology and Its Relation to Phonology and Syntax.* Stanford, CA: CSLI Publications.
Sells, Peter
1999 Form and function in the typology of grammatical voice system. In: G. Legendre, J. Grimshaw, and S. Vikner (eds.), *Optimality-Theoretic Syntax.* Cambridge: MIT Press.
Shibatani, Masayoshi
2006 On the conceptual framework for voice phenomena. *Linguistics* 44.2: 217–269.
Siewierska, Anna
1984 *The Passive: A Comparative Linguistic Analysis.* London: Croom Helm.
Sigurðsson, Halldór Ármann
1989 Verbal syntax and case in Icelandic. Ph.D. Diss. University of Lund.
Steinbach, Markus
2002 *Middle Voice: A Comparative Study in the Syntax-Semantics Interface of German.* Amsterdam: John Benjamins.
Stroik, Thomas
1992 Middles and Movement. *Linguistic Inquiry* 23: 127–137.

Svenonius, Peter
2006 Case alternations and the Icelandic passive and middle. In: Satu Manninen, Diane Nelson, Katrin Hiietam, Elsi Kaiser, and Virve Vihman (eds.), *Passives and Impersonals in European Languages*. Amsterdam: John Benjamins.
Thompson, Chad
1994 Passive and inverse constructions. In: T. Givón (ed.), *Voice and Inversion*, 47–64. Amsterdam: John Benjamins.
Timberlake, Alan
1982 The impersonal passive in Lithuanian. *Proceedings of the 8th Annual Meeting of the Berkeley Linguistics Society*, 508–524.
Timberlake, Alan
2004 *A Reference Grammar of Russian*. Cambridge: Cambridge University Press.
Tsimpli, Ianthi-Maria
2006 The acquisition of voice and transitivity alternations in Greek as native and second language. In: S. Unsworth, T. Parodi, A. Sorace, and M. Young-Scholten (eds.) *Paths of Development in L1 and L2 Acquisition*, 15–55. Amsterdam: John Benjamins.
Tsunoda, Tasaku
1988 Antipassives in Warrungu and other Australian languages. In: M. Shibatani (ed.), *Passive and Voice*, 595–649. Amsterdam: John Benjamins.
Williams, Edwin
1987 Implicit arguments, the binding theory, and control. *Natural Language and Linguistic Theory* 5.2: 151–180.
Wolfart, H. C.
1991 Passives with and without agents. In: H. C. Wolfart (ed.), *Linguistic Studies Presented to John L. Finlay: Algonquian and Iroquoian Linguistics*, 171–190. Winnipeg: University of Manitoba, Department of Linguistics.
Woolford, Ellen
1997 Four-way Case systems: ergative, nominative, objective and accusative. *Natural Language and Linguistic Theory* 15: 181–227.
Zaenen, Annie
1988 Unaccusative verbs in Dutch and the syntax-semantics interface. *CSLI Report 123*. Stanford.
Zaenen, Annie
1993 Unaccusativity in Dutch: integrating syntax and lexical semantics. In: J. Pustejovsky (ed.), *Semantics and the Lexicon*, 129–161. Dordrecht: Kluwer.
Zaenen, Annie, Joan Maling, and H. Thrainsson
1985 Case and grammatical functions: The Icelandic passive. *Natural Language and Linguistic Theory* 3(4): 441–483. Reprinted 1990 in: J. Maling, and A. Zaenen (eds.), *Syntax and Semantics 24: Modern Icelandic Syntax*, 95–164. New York: Academic Press.
Zombolou, Katerina
2004 Verbal alternations in Greek: a semantic approach. Ph. D. diss., Department of Linguistics, University of Reading.
Zribi-Hertz, Anne
1982 La construction « se-moyen » du français et son statut dans le triangle: moyen/passif/ réfléchi. *Lingvisticæ Investigationes* 6: 345–401.

Edit Doron, Jerusalem (Israel)

23. Syntax and Grammar of Idioms and Collocations

Abstract

We present a brief typology of Multi Word Units (MWUs) based on criteria including selectional preference, semantic compositionality, and syntactic well-formedness. The bulk of the chapter focuses on Support Verb Constructions and verb phrase idioms. Most MWUs are not the frozen "long word" that can be relegated to the lexicon and marked as impervious to morphosyntactic operations; corpus data attest to their considerable lexical and syntactic variability, which cannot be straightforwardly accounted for in terms of semantic compositionality. Reconciling the fact that so many MWUs are subject to the grammatical rules governing free language with their status as lexical units poses a challenge to prevailing theoretical frameworks. Experimental evidence from speakers' processing of idioms may shed light on the representation of idioms and inform linguistic theories.

1. Introduction

Analyses of spoken and written corpora reveal a high percentage of MWUs including collocations and idioms, both in terms of types and tokens (Jackendoff 1997; Moon 1998; Cowie 1992). MWUs are a compelling subject of linguistic analysis not only because of their pervasiveness and universality, but also because they resist clear-cut integration into any theory of grammar. On the one hand, speakers recognize idioms and collocations as lexical units paired with distinct meanings, a fact reflected in traditional lexicography and the "classical" view of MWUs as merely long, fixed "prefabricated" lexemes. On the other hand, corpus data show considerable variation for many MWUs and present strong evidence that many phrasal units are subject to regular morphosyntactic processes that may operate on the phrase as whole or on internal constituents, independent of their semantic transparency. Semantic wholeness in the face of rich grammatical properties make the lexical representation of MWUs a challenge.

2. Co-occurrence, selectional preference and collocation

Words are selective about their context. For example, an English speaker *brushes* rather than *washes* his teeth, unlike his French counterpart. And he *goes off on a tangent* more often than he *takes off on a tangent*. The idiosyncracies of lexical selection are reflected in the regular and statistically discernable phenomenon of collocation (Firth 1957; Sinclair 1991; Stubbs 2001; Partington 2004; McEnery and Wilson 1998; inter alia).

Church and Hanks (1991) demonstrated the measurability of collocational properties with Mutual Information, a measure that quantifies the idiosyncratic attraction of word forms to one another beyond syntactic and semantic constraints imposed by subcategorization and selectional restriction rules.

Statistical analyses of the phenomena of collocation enable the discovery of collocations (e.g., Bond, Korhonen, McCarthy, and Villavicencio 2003; Baldwin, Bannard, Tanaka, and Widdows 2003; Fazly and Stevenson 2006; Fazly, Cook, and Stevenson 2009; Evert 2004/2005; Schone and Jurafsky 2001; inter alia) and to quantify the strength of their co-occurrence as well as the degree of their lexical and syntactic fixedness, a measure of their lexical status. There are no hard rules to distinguish between preferred co-occurrences and collocations with lexical status, as they are situated on a continuous scale of fixedness.

3. Two types of MWUs: Idioms and collocations

MWUs are characterized not only in terms of their collocational strength but also in terms of their formal properties and their semantic compositionality, i.e., the extent to which the meaning of the phrase derives from the meanings of its constituents. We present a brief typology, focusing on collocations and idioms. Both are statistically significant co-occurrences of specific lexical items, and both fall along a sliding scale of syntactically fixed expressions that are characterized by semantic non-compositionality to varying degrees.

Collocations include Support Verb Constructions (*have a drink/read, take a picture, make a fuss*), phrases consisting of a verb and a bare noun (*in school/prison*), and verb phrases like *answer the door*. While such collocations may be lexically and syntactically idiosyncratic, they are semantically decomposable ("encoding", in Fillmore, Kay, and O'Connor's 1988 terminology) and can be readily interpreted by speakers who are unfamiliar with the phrasal units.

Idioms on the other hand are non-decomposable to varying degrees. *Kick the bucket, bite the dust, rock the boat* and *hit the ceiling* are considered to be opaque, whereas *spill the beans* and *let the cat out of the bag* are at least partially analyzable. (We will not consider here the following classes of fixed expressions: proverbs like *the early bird gets the worm*, statements like *mum is the word, the shoes is on the other foot* and *when the cows come home/when hell freezes over*, routine formulae that often have a pragmatic point (Fillmore, Kay, and O'Connor 1988) such as *thanks a lot, Good morning*, and similes like *sharp as a whistle*.)

4. Collocations

Collocations may be more or less lexically and syntactically fixed. In idiosyncratic compositional collocations like *brush one's teeth* and *confirmed bachelor*, the constituents strongly – and arguably idiosyncratically – select one another, tolerating little or no lexical variation: *#wash one's teeth*, *#affirmed bachelor*; thus, these phrases arguably have lexical status. They are well-formed and are input to all regular rules of grammar.

Other collocations include the class of Prepositional Phrases exemplified by *in class/out of school/to college/in prison/jail/hospital*. The absence of a determiner makes these phrases slightly ill-formed. The singular noun is always bare, and no adjectival modification is possible, i.e., no lexical material can intervene between the preposition and the noun: **in boring class/*out of high-security prison/*to local hospital*. This collocational pattern is productive to a limited degree:

(1) a. *in school/in graduate school/in medical school/in kindergarten/in college*
 b. *in jail/*in penitentiary/*in slammer/*in workhouse*
 c. *in hospital/*in infirmary/*in clinic*
 d. *in court/*in Supreme Court*

5. Support Verb Constructions

Support Verb Constructions (SCVs) or Light Verb constructions (Grimshaw and Mester 1988; Kearns 1998/2002; inter alia) are syntactically well-formed verb phrases that are semantically compositional but exhibit strong lexical preferences. For example, the choice of verb in *take a bow, set in motion* and *keep someone company* does not admit any lexical substitution, even of arguably close synonyms, without a change in meaning: **make a bow*, **place in motion*, **give someone company*. (Some state-denoting complements co-occur with different verbs, reflecting aspectual alternations between causative, inchoative and stative: *put/be/keep on hold, put/be on fire*; however, not all SCVs show all alternates: **go/*get/*keep on fire*.)

Unlike collocations such as *brush one's teeth* and *confirmed bachelor*, which seem to be unsystematically distributed across the lexicon, SVCs constitute a syntactically, lexically and semantically well-defined class found in many languages (see, for example, Grimshaw and Mester's 1988 discussion of Japanese *suru* constructions). SVCs consist of a "light" or support verb and a complement that can be an NP, a PP, a double object, or an NP-PP:

(2) a. *give an explanation, have a drink*
 b. *set on fire, put on hold*
 c. *give the floor a sweep, keep someone company*
 d. *take account of something, make a call to somebody*

The verbs in SVCs come from a fairly small, homogeneous class including *give, take, make* and *do*. These highly frequent verbs are thought to be semantically "light"; Jespersen (1954) asserts that the meaning of the phrase derives largely from the noun. Many

SCVs have a corresponding simplex verb: *take a bow/bow, set in motion/move, make a call/call*, etc. Arguments have been made (e.g., Klein 1968) for semantic differences between the SVCs and the simplex verbs, in particular aspectual differences. For example, the simplex verbs can have an activity reading and tend to be more felicitous with *for*-adverbials:

(3) a. **John gave Mary a kiss for a long time.*
b. *John kissed Mary for a long time.*

5.1. Phrase structure of SVCs

Many SVCs admit only a bare noun (*go to hospital/jail, give chase/voice to*). A large class of SVCs are of the form *have N*, where the noun is a bare verb stem, e.g., *have a drink/read/smoke/look* but not **have a drinking/*reading/*smoking/*looking.*

Wierzbicka (1982) offers a semantic explanation for the limited productivity of this construction, as exemplified by *have a drink* vs. **have an eat.*

5.2. The syntax of SVCs

Storrer (2007) reports on the results of an extensive corpus study of the morphosyntactic properties of German SVCs. Like their English counterparts, German SVCs are semantically compositional but lexically fixed. Storrer notes some morphosyntactic flexibility for German SVCs, and her findings appear to translate fairly straightforwardly to corresponding English constructions. The nouns in many SVCs tolerate little variation of the determiner; those that do allow variation as a rule allow adjectival modification and extraction of the noun, which is referential in these cases (all data from Storrer 2007):

(4) a. *take a/no picture*
b. *take beautiful pictures*
c. *a/two/no pictures were taken*
d. *the picture that I took*
e. *make a couple of calls*
f. *make important calls*
g. *a couple of calls were made*
h. *all the calls that she made*

vs.

(5) a. *give (*a few/*no) smiles*
b. *(*a few/*no) smiles were given*
c. **the smile that he gave*

Storrer's data show that support verbs with a direct object complement are generally freer with respect to morphosyntactic variation than those with a Prepositional Phrase complement. A cursory look indicates that the same appears to hold for English SVCs:

(6) a. *set the building on fire*
b. **set the building on uncontrollable fire*
c. **the fire that the building was set on*
d. *put in contact*
e. **put in casual contact*
f. **the contact that we were put in*

5.3. True Light Verbs vs. Vague Action Verbs

Rather than attribute the apparently unsystematic differences in syntactic behavior to the categorial nature of the complement, Kearns (1998/2002) argues for two distinct types of (English) SVCs. One class consists of "True Light Verbs" (TLVs) like *give the floor a sweep*, *give a groan* and *have a lick*, while another class is constituted by "Vague Action Verbs" (VAVs) such as *make an inspection*, *give a demonstration* and *do the ironing*. A hallmark of TLCs is that their noun complements are verb stems: *give a groan/laugh/cry/snort*; *give the rope a pull/the boiler a stoke/the table a wipe*, *have lick/look/read*. TLVs and VAVs show a number of syntactic distinctions (all data and judgments from Kearns 1998/2000):

(i) VAVs passivize, but TLVs do not

(7) a. **A groan was given by the man on the right.*
b. **A pull was given on/to the rope.*
c. **A sweep was given to the floor.*

(8) a. *A demonstration was given.*
b. *An inspection was made.*

(ii) Nominals can be extracted from VAVs but not from TLCs.

(9) a. **Which groan did John give?*
b. **Which pull did John give the rope?*
c. ??*The groan that he gave startled me.*
d. ??*The pull that he gave the rope had little effect.*

(10) a. *Which offer did the company make?*
b. *Which explanation did the judge give?*
c. *The offer the company made was good.*
d. *The explanation that the judge gave was good.*

(iii) Nominals in VAVs but not in TLVs can pronominalize.

(11) a. **He gave a groan at midnight and another one at noon.*
b. **I gave the soup a heat and Bill gave it one, too.*

(12) a. *The department made an inspection and you should make one, too.*
b. *If you give your presentation, I'll give mine.*

(iv) Nominals in TLVs but not in VAVs must be indefinite.

(13) a. **Who gave the groan just now?*
b. ??*Who gave that groan?*
c. ??*Who gave it the polish?*

(14) a. *Who made the inspection?*
b. *Who gave that demonstration?*

(v) VAVs, but not TLCs, license an argument-denoting NP within their maximal projection.

(15) **John's shake of the bottle/laugh at the chairman's joke.*

(16) *John's inspection of the plant/offer of support/promise to Mary.*

Working in the extended Government and Binding (Chomsky 1981) and Barriers (Chomsky 1981) framework, Kearns proposes that the main property of English TLVs is that the verb projects a phrase according to its Syntactic Argument Structure, but that the Lexical Conceptual Structure of the verb "is not active". Thus, the verb has no semantic content and cannot assign a theta role to the noun. The noun, not being a full argument, cannot undergo extraction operations or pronominalization. (This suggestion has also been made by Szabolcsi 1986.)

In contrast to TLVs, VAVs are like ordinary, full, transitive verbs, though their readings are bleached. VAVs theta-mark the nominals and consequently exhibit the normal syntax of transitive structures.

Kearns argues that the nature of the noun complement determines the status of the collocation. In a TLV, the noun is not fully nominal. Besides the syntactic restrictions listed above, nouns in TLVs cannot have internal arguments: **John gave us a groan that he was sick of the economic crisis* (Kearns 1998/2000).

The difference between the nouns in the TLVs and independently occurring nouns is particularly clear in the TLV subclass formed with *give* (*give a groan*; *give the rope a pull*; *give the floor a sweep*). Kearns argues that structurally similar but freely composed strings like *give Mary a kiss/a pat* refer to giving or transfer events involving a GOAL or RECIPIENT noun. This semantic difference is reflected in a syntactic one: the freely composed double object constructions allow the PP alternate (*give a kiss to Mary*), unlike TLVs (**give a pull to the rope*, **give a sweep to the floor*). However, heavy NP shift is possible in some cases, as the following data from the Web show: *give a tug to every rope in the belfry.* And web data show that the same holds for idioms: *give him the sack/ #give the sack to him/based on the reported results, Putin gave the sack to several special services generals*.

While the distinction between TLV and VAV constructions is supported by formal differences (absence of determiner, bare verb stem), an account of the syntactic differences in terms of an active/inactive Lexical Conceptual Structure, presence or absence of theta marking and semantic role assignment seems somewhat stipulative and is not independently motivated.

6. Idioms

Like collocations, idioms vary in the extent to which they are lexically and syntactically fixed. But unlike collocations, which are always compositional, idioms are semantically opaque to different degrees. Dobrovolskij (1995) describes idioms as a radial category, with non-compositional, frozen idioms as protoypes and idioms that are partly compositional and allow lexical substitution and morphosyntactic operations to varying degrees as "radiating out", i.e., diverging from, the prototype.

6.1. Idioms with irregular phrase structure

Some idioms are syntactically ill-formed and cannot be assigned to a phrasal category. Their constituents are semantically transparent lexemes, but they are "unfamiliarly arranged", in the words of Fillmore, Kay, and O'Connor (1988). It is probably due to their phrasal irregularity that these extragrammatical collocations are resistant to modification and cannot be input to syntactic operations.

(17) a. *nothing doing/nothing much doing/*nothing was doing/*nothing was done*
b. *and then some/*and then more*
c. *say when/*say what/*when was said*
d. *all of a sudden/*some of a sudden*
e. *by and large/*by and very large*
f. *like father like son/*like mother like daughter*
g. *trip the light fantastic/*trip the light totally fantastic*

The last phrase may appear like a well-formed VP, but the original form, *trip the light fantastic toe*, shows that the head of the NP is lost.

6.2. Idioms with cran-morphemes

Fillmore, Kay, and O'Connor (1988) distinguish constructions where "unfamiliar pieces are unfamiliarly arranged". Such "decoding" idioms are non-compositional and unanalyzable. The "unfamiliar pieces" in some idioms may be cran-morphemes, whose distribution is strictly limited to the idiom, as in *kith and kin*, *spic and span*. Because these lexemes cannot be assigned to a lexical or syntactic category, the idioms are syntactically irregular and as a result they are frozen:

(18) a. *kith and kin*
b. **kin and kith*
c. **kith and relative*
d. *spic and span*
d. **spic and very span*

6.3. Partially lexically filled idioms

Many idioms are verb phrases with noteworthy syntactic properties (see Lebeaux 2000 for a comprehensive classification). A large number of verb phrase idioms are discontinuous, where one internal argument is lexically unspecified (Fillmore, Kay, and O'Connor 1988 refer to these as "formal idioms"). These include the many English idioms with a possessive bound to the subject (e.g., *have one's cake and eat it, be on one's last leg, blow one's stack*).

Numerous others include a possessive pronoun bound to a lexically free noun inside the VP:

(19) a. *cook s.o.'s goose*
b. *give s.o. the slip/a hand*
c. *take advantage of s.o.*
d. *put s.o. on a pedestal*

Lebeaux (2000) argues that idioms are not simply constituted of random parts of phrase structure, but rather obey a Constituent Condition that states that an idiom consists of exactly one constituent, "at some level of representation". He cites the apparent absence of idioms that lexically specify the subject and the verb but not an object or PP, in contrast to the large number of idioms that include a verb and its complement(s). However, the Constituent Constraint is more difficult to maintain in the face of the many idioms like *give s.o. the slip*, where an internal argument is not lexically fixed. In fact, Lebeaux acknowledges the non-existence of English idioms of the form V NP NP, where both arguments are part of the idiom, and which would straightforwardly obey the Constituent Condition.

The Constituent Condition can be rescued with appropriate mechanisms, but an apparent majority of English idioms constitute counterexamples to the simplest definition of "constituent".

6.4. Verb phrase idioms with modified phrase structure

In many verb phrase idioms, the argument structure differs from that found in freely formed strings. Verbs may appear with a reduced or augmented number of complements.

6.4.1. VP idioms with reduced argument structure

Verbs that usually select for two arguments occur in some idioms with only a single complement:

(20) a. *You are telling me/tell me.*
b. **You are telling me about a problem.* (idiomatic reading)
c. *give good measure.*
d. **Give me good measure* (idiomatic reading)

Fellbaum (2007) discusses a number of German VP idioms with *geben* ('give') and a bare noun that do not denote transfers. The single argument is not a moved Theme and adding a Recipient or Goal argument results in loss of the idiomatic meaning.

(21) a. *Gas/Gummi geben* (lit. 'give gas/rubber,' 'accelerate') [German]
b. *Ruhe geben* (lit. 'give quiet', 'stop complaining or making trouble')
c. *Alarm geben* (lit. 'give alarm', 'raise the alarm')
d. *Acht geben* (lit. 'give care,' 'pay attention')

A number of German verb phrase idioms headed by *stehen* ('stand') require a singular, bare noun direct object rather than a Prepositional Phrase denoting a Location, the complement of this verb in its literal use:

(22) a. *seinen Mann stehen* (lit. 'stand one's man,' 'stand one's ground') [German]
b. *Schlange stehen* (lit. 'stand queue,' 'line up')
c. *Wache stehen* ('stand guard')
d. *Spalier stehen* (lit. 'stand honor guard')
e. *Pate stehen* (lit. 'stand godfather,' 'be an inspiration')
f. *Schmiere stehen* (lit. 'stand grease,' 'be the lookout')

A Location Prepositional Phrase that is not bound to the idiom can be added:

(23) a. *Im Supermarkt Schlange stehen* ('queue up in the supermarket') [German]
b. *Im Konkurrenzkampf seinen Mann stehen* ('stand o.'s ground in a competition')

The syntactic patterns *geben* + bare noun and *stehen* + bare noun are not productive and seem to be reserved for a limited number of fixed expressions. Arguably, they constitute constructions in the sense of Fillmore, Kay, and O'Connor (1988); Fillmore and Kay (1999) and Goldberg (1995, 2006) (see below), though a common semantic core associated with these structures is not apparent and an account in terms of a regular construction-meaning pairing remains a challenge.

6.4.2. VP idioms with augmented argument structure

There are many cases where the idiomatic reading of a verb phrase requires an argument that is not subcategorized for by the verb. We refer to these cases as Argument Augmentation. A case in point is the German idiom *Baukloetze staunen*, lit. 'marvel toy blocks,' meaning to be so amazed as to produce toy blocks. *Staunen* ('marvel') is an intransitive (unergative) verb that does not take a direct object complement outside it use in the idiom. Similarly, *jmdm. etwas husten* (lit., 'cough something for s.b.', 'give s.o. a piece of one's mind') adds two arguments to a verb ('cough') that is intransitive in its free use.

German has a very large number of idioms that select for an obligatory dative-marked argument. German, like Romance languages but unlike English, can assign such arguments fairly freely in constructions known variously as "personal dative", "ethical dative" or "dative of interest" (Abraham 1973; Horn 2008; inter alia). In the free language, such datives are often pronouns bound to be subject, but in the idioms below, the arguments refer to a lexically unspecified entity that is the Beneficiary or, more frequently, the Maleficiary of an action performed by the subject. Examples are below:

(24) a. *jmdm. den Hof machen* (lit. 'make for s.b. the court', 'court s.b.') [German]
b. *jmdm. schoene Augen machen* (lit. 'make for s.b. pretty eyes', 'flirt with s.b.')
c. *jmdm. die Stange halten* (lit. 'hold the stick for s.b.', 'keep up with s.b.')
d. *jmdm. eine lange Nase machen* (lit., 'make a long nose at s.b.', 'thumb one's nose at s.b.')
e. *jmdm. ein Bein stellen* (lit. 'put a leg for s.b.', t'rip s.b. up')
f. *jmdm. einen Streich spielen* ('play a trick on s.b.')
g. *jmdm. Fussangeln/eine Schlinge/Fallstricke stellen* ('set a trap/snare for s.b.')

The idiomatic reading is not preserved in the Prepositional Phrase alternation that exists for freely composed Benefactive/Malefactive constructions:

(25) a. *jmdm. einen Kuchen backen/einen Kuchen fuer jmdn. backen* [German]
('bake s.o. a cake/bake a cake for s.o.')
b. **fuer jmdn. den Hof machen*
c. **fuer jmdn. schoene Augen machen*
d. **fuer jmdn. Fussangeln/eine Schlinge stellen*

Green (1974) proposes a semantic classification of English verbs participating in the Benefactive alternation. Verbs of creation (*bake, cook*, etc.), performance (*dance, sing*, etc.), acquisition (*buy*, etc.), which denote some kind of transfer, can regularly and productively add a Beneficiary argument. In addition, Green identifies a heterogeneous class of "symbolic actions", performed for the benefit of somebody. In the free language, the double object constructions with "symbolic actions" is infrequent; one of Green's (1974) examples is *God said to Abraham: kill me a son.*

Idioms seem to have appropriated the benefactive/malefactive construction and extended its usage to Green's (1974) "symbolic actions", which are not linked to semantically defined verb classes. The double object construction is thought to express successful transfer of an entity or a benefit (Krifka 1999; Green 1974; inter alia); perhaps this subtle difference meaning difference contrasting it with the Prepositional Phrase alternant can be carried over into the meaning of the "malefactive" idioms.

6.5. Negative Polarity Items

A large number of idioms are Negative Polarity Items; in the absence of a negation expression, these phrases lose their idiomatic meanings (e.g., Lichte and Sailer 2004).

Examples are:

(26) a. *give a damn/hoot/shit*
b. *have a leg to stand on*
c. *horses wouldn't get NP to VP*
d. *be quite right in the head*

A number of NPI idioms are headed by modals:

(27) a. *won't hear of it*
b. *can't take it with you*

Idioms that are Negative Polarity Items are found crosslinguistically.

7. Compositionality in idioms

Many idioms are partly compositional in that speakers can assign a reading to one or more of their constituents. Nunberg, Sag and Wasow (1994) call "idiomatically combining expressions" or "internally regular" those idioms whose parts can be given a literal interpretation; in Fillmore, Kay and O'Connor's (1988) terminology, they are "encoding". For example, in *spill the beans*, *spill* can be interpreted as 'reveal'; and *the beans* as 'information' or 'secret' (see also Fellbaum 1993); similarly, *the cat* in *let the cat out of the bag* refers to sensitive or secret information. Each component of such idioms can be semantically interpreted, and the combination of these meaning constitutes a string whose form and meaning correspond in a one-to-one fashion to that of the idiom.

By contrast, Nunberg, Sag, and Wasow (1994) note that "internally irregular" idioms like *kick the bucket* and *buy the farm* are not compositional, as their constituents cannot be semantically interpreted and re-assembled to map onto the literal reading, 'die'. (Interestingly, idioms in other languages also encode 'die' with transitive verbs; cf. German *den Loeffel abgeben* and French *casser sa pipe*.)

7.1. Metaphors

Metaphorical idioms (e.g., Wood 1986) are compositional in that one or more of their constituents can be interpreted as a metaphor. We define metaphor here as a kind of lexical polysemy restricted largely to simple lexical items. Idiom components like *cat* in *let the cat out of the bag* and *spill* in *spill the beans* are context-specific metaphors, as they receive an interpretation only as components of specific idioms. *Spill* does not mean 'reveal' in phrases like *I'll spill the names of the informants* and *cat* cannot be freely used to refer to 'secret information'; thus separate lexical entries for the idiom components on par with those for freely combinable lexemes do not seem warranted without an accompanying restriction on their distribution (see section 9.2).

Conventional metaphors have a less restricted distribution and their metaphoric meanings are systematically related to literal meanings, possibly based on conceptual metaphors (Lakoff and Johnson 1980). Thus, *fire* in *play with fire* is readily interpretable as a potential or real danger (cf. *pull the chestnuts out of the fire, be in the line of fire*, etc.); the same metaphor is reflected in the meaning of *get burned*, "suffer a setback".

7.2. Idioms with a possible literal reading

Some idioms, like *rock the boat, bite the bullet* and *hold one's horses* can have literal readings in addition to their figurative ones. Others, such as *lose one's head, have feet of clay, build castles in the air* and *hitch one's wagon to a star* can only be interpreted as idioms, as they are egregious violations of selectional restrictions and denote implausible events. Particularly good examples of implausible idioms are German *jmdm. aus dem Gesicht geschnitten sein*, lit. 'be cut out of s.b.'s face', 'be s.b.'s spitting image', and *auf dem Zahnfleisch gehen*, lit. 'walk on one's gum', 'be on one's last leg'.

8. Variation in idioms

Very few idioms are completely frozen. Fillmore, Kay, and O'Connor (1988) note that most idioms allow at least verbal inflection, and variation in tense and number of the lexically unfilled subject; a rare exception are the so-called substantive idioms like *the greater they come the harder they fall* and *it takes one to know one* that are completely frozen (cf. **the greater he came the harder he fell*/**it took one to know one*).

Much of the literature on idioms and collocations is based on data derived via introspection and may not reflect language use by a broader speaker community. Moon (1998) was one of the first comprehensive studies of English idioms based on corpora, and her data challenge a simple integration of idioms into any theory grammar.

Neumann at al. (2004) and Fellbaum (2006, 2007) examine German idioms using a one billion word corpus. Search queries that allow for the retrieval of lexical and syntactic variations of the idioms' canonical forms (Herold 2007) return numerous examples of variations and demonstrate that idioms participate in the regular grammatical processes associated with free language. Strikingly, the data refute the prevailing view that an idiom's variability is entirely conditional on its semantic transparency, as articulated in e.g., Nunberg, Sag, and Wasow (1994).

Cutler (1982) states that the older an idiom is, the more frozen it tends to be. This is not borne out by the oldest idioms in the language, dating back to the Bible, such as *throw pearls before the swine* and *beat swords into ploughshares*, for which the corpus shows numerous variations. Moreover, the data show that even archaic words that cannot be straightforwardly interpreted are subject to modification and syntactic operations.

8.1. Lexical variation

Corpus data (Geyken 2007) show that in many idioms a constituent can be modified. A noun may allow variation of the determiner and insertion of one or more adjectives. Other variations include compound formation, with the "canonical" lexeme as the head; we also find the substitution of semantically related words for a "canonical" idiom constituent.

8.1.1. Determiner and number variation

Number variation is found particularly often with metaphors and nouns that can be mapped onto a referent. An example is the German idiom *den Bock zum Gärtner machen*, lit. 'appoint the buck as the gardener', 'put someone incompetent in charge.'

While a corpus (Geyken 2007) shows that both nouns occur predominantly in the singular, examples with plural nouns, *Böcke zu Gärtnern machen*, where the speaker refers to several specific incompetent persons, are found. But number variation is also found with nouns that cannot be interpreted in the context of the idiom and receive no literal interpretation. *Blatt* ('leaf', 'sheet') in the German idiom *kein Blatt vor den Mund nehmen* (lit. 'take no leaf/sheet in front of one's mouth,' 'be outspoken, speak one's mind') has no obvious referent for contemporary speakers who are unaware of the origin of this idiom. In the following example (Geyken 2007), the speaker emphasizes a spokesman's reluctance to give information (note that the negation is removed):

(28) *Ein Regierungssprecher ist ein Mann, der sich 100 Blaetter vor den Mund nimmt.* [German]
'A government spokesman is a man who puts 100 leaves before his mouth.'

Firenze (2007) and Firenze and Fellbaum (2008) consider the contraction of the determiner with a preceding preposition, a regular process in German. The contracted form that is part of the canonical form of many idioms is often de-contracted, so that the preposition and the determiner appear as individual morphemes. In some cases, the de-contraction is conditioned by the insertion of lexical material such as adjectives between the preposition and the determiner, or number variation of the noun; in other cases, contracted and decontracted forms alternate freely. Significantly, these variations, which reflect the regular grammatical processes of free language, are found even when the meaning of the noun is not transparent: *Licht* in the idiom *jmdn. hinters Licht fuehren* (lit. 'lead s.b. behind the light') has no referent, just like eyes in the corresponding English idiom *pull the wool over someone's eyes.*

8.1.2. Adjectival modification

Corpus data (Geyken 2007) show that noun constituents in idioms are frequently modified with adjectives (e.g., Stathi 2007; Fellbaum and Stathi 2006). For example, German *Karre* ('cart') can in the idiom *die Karre aus dem Dreck ziehen*, lit. 'pull the cart out of the mud', 'straighten out the mess', is often modified with *verfahren* ('lost') or *festgefahren* ('stuck'), where the metaphor of the cart is preserved.

We often find cases of what Ernst (1981) calls "external modification", where the adjective modifies the entire idiom, much like an adverb, as in *den peruanischen Karren aus dem Dreck ziehen*, 'pull the Peruvian cart out of the mud', 'straighten out the Peruvian mess'. Adjectival modification especially of the "external" kind is also found with nouns in non-compositional idioms that cannot be mapped onto a referent can be modified, as these Web data show:

(29) a. *Carter doesn't have an economic leg to stand on.*
b. *Er biss ins texanische Gras.* ('He bit into the Texan dust.') [German]
c. *Many people were eager to jump on the horse-drawn political Reagan bandwagon.*

Ernst's "conjunction modification" is illustrated by the examples such as in (30):

(30) *...having had such fun pulling his cross-gartered leg*

Here, the adjective modifies the literal reading of the noun (*leg*), which belongs to the person whose leg is being pulled, i.e., who is being made fun of. This modification thus mingles literal and idiomatic meanings.

8.1.3. Compound formation

Compounding is similar to adjectival modification in that the head noun is semantically specified. We cite a corpus example from German (Geyken 2007), based on the idiom *jemandem die Butter vom Brot nehmen*, lit. 'take the butter away from s.b.'s bread', 'steal s.b.'s thunder':

(31) *...der Bundesregierung die Argumentationsbutter vom Wahlkampfbrot zu nehmen* [German]
'take the argument butter from the election campaign bread'

Both *Argumentation* and *Wahlkampf* are what Ernst (1981) calls "domain delimiters", i.e., they pertain to the context of the utterance, thus resembling "external" modification.

8.1.4. Lexical variation of cran-morphemes

Cran-morphemes are not exempt from variation. Like non-referential nouns, they can either receive an ad-hoc interpretation in the context of the idiom, or their modification is external or based on conjunction (Ernst 1981).

For example, the noun *Fettnaepfchen* (lit. 'little grease pot') is essentially limited to the German idiom *ins Fettnaepfchen treten* (lit. 'step into the little grease pot', 'commit a gaffe'), and it is difficult to attach a meaning to it that could be mapped onto a free lexeme in the literal phrase *commit a gaffe* or in the idiom *put one's foot in one's mouth*. Yet a corpus (Geyken 2007) shows numerous tokens where the noun is quantified or modified, showing that the speaker assigned it a meaning consistent with the idiom:

(32) a. *er trat in jedes Fettnaepfchen ...*
('he stepped into every grease pot') [German]
b. *ins politische Fettnaepfchen treten*
('step into the political grease pot')

8.1.5. Change of lexical category

Variation extends to change of category. Thus, Moon (1998) cites corpus data where a verb has been turned into a noun (*lose face/loss of face; waste one's breath/a waste of breath, break the ice/ice-breaker*). Similar data are found in German (Fellbaum 2007).

8.2. Syntactic variation

Idioms are also subject to syntactic operations. Moon (1998) cites corpus examples of passivization of English idioms (*Mary's teeth were gnashed as the home team went down in defeat*), relativization (*That is a bullet on which the Arthur Golds of this world have steadfastedly failed to bite*), and pronominalization (*if there is ice, Mr. Clinton is breaking it*). Data from the DWDS Corpus (Geyken 2007) show many similar syntactic variations in German idioms, as well as clefting and topicalization (Fellbaum 2006, 2007).

As with lexical variation, syntactic operations are not limited to constituents that can be mapped onto a referent. An example is the German idiom *kein Blatt vor den Mund nehmen* (lit. 'take no leaf/sheet in front of one's mouth,' 'be outspoken, speak one's mind'); *Blatt* ('leaf,' 'sheet') has no obvious referent. Yet numerous attested corpus examples are found where *Blatt* is passivized, topicalized, questioned, and pronominalized; moreover, this idiom need not always appear as a Negative Polarity Item, as the citation form suggests (Fellbaum and Stathi 2005).

The evidence clearly refutes the common claim that idioms are fixed unless their components can be semantically interpreted. The data also call into question the notion of a continuum of flexibility that interacts with semantic transparency, as proposed by Abeillé (1995), who based her analysis of a number of French idioms, and Dobrovol'skij (1999), inter alia.

9. Idioms in different grammatical frameworks

Idioms cannot be relegated to the lexicon as fixed lexical items; at the same time, they undeniably constitute lexical and semantic entities that speakers recognize and interpret as such, even when they significantly diverge from the canonical, most frequent form. We consider the treatment of idioms within three major theories of grammar.

9.1. Idioms in Generative Grammar

Non-compositional idioms presented challenges to early Transformational-Generative Grammar with respect to their representation in Deep Structure, their introduction into the Phrase Marker, and in particular their idiosyncratic syntactic behavior.

Fraser (1970) is an early attempt to account for syntactic variation found in idioms. He proposes an implicational hierarchy of transformations, distinguishing five levels of frozenness. If a particular idiom allows one kind of NP extraction such as passivization, it will also tolerate other operations extracting the NP. Fraser orders the operations hierarchically, with extraction operations ranked higher and implying permutation of constituents, insertion of lexical materials, etc. Specific idioms are marked in the lexicon with a feature specifying their position in the hierarchy. Idioms marked [+L5] allow all grammatical operations open to a structurally identical freely composed phrase. Fraser's analysis is based entirely on constructed data, and both specific data as well as the value of the hierarchy have been challenged (Newmeyer 1974, inter alia.)

While the theory has undergone significant changes and much of syntax is now thought to originate in the lexicon, idioms still have not received a satisfactory treatment, in particular when it comes to their syntactic behavior, which defies successful description by the same set of rules that handles simple lexemes. As a consequence, idioms – like all constructions – are assigned not to the core of the grammar but to its periphery.

Lebeaux (2000) attempts to integrate idioms into the core. He argues that idioms are constructed like partial phrase markers similar to those characterizing certain stages of language acquisition. Both can be accommodated in a "sub-grammar" framework that is distinct from, but compatible with, the full grammar that defines competence. In the case of acquisition, an operation Merger produces the adult representation; for idioms, Lebeaux distinguishes between a class of "pre-merger" and a class of "post-merger" phrases. Pre-merger idioms, including *take advantage of*, have a variable determiner (*take no advantage of*) and are subject to syntactic operations like passivization (*advantage was taken of Jim*); post-merger idioms like *kick the bucket* include a definite determiner and cannot undergo syntactic operations like passive.

While Lebeaux's analysis is an important step forward in integrating idioms into a theory of grammar, his constructed data are subject to the same weakness as Fraser's. In particular, Web data show clearly that so-called post-merger idioms with a definite determiner are not in fact categorically barred from passivization:

(33) a. **The bucket was kicked.*
b. **The road was hit.*
c. *The beans were spilled.*
d. *The cat was let out of the bag.*

Rather than being correlated with the determiner, passivization appears to be dependent on the semantic transparency of the noun. If the NP functions as a metaphor, either conventional or specific to the idiom context, passivization is possible (though we have seen that semantic opacity does not block syntactic operations).

Lebeaux's work represents a significant advance to move idioms from the periphery of grammar (as in diSciullio and Williams 1987), which cannot be captured by rules, into the core. However, idioms as a class still appear to elude a wholesale treatment based on regular syntax-semantics mappings.

9.2. Idioms in HPSG

Head-Driven Phrase Structure Grammar (e.g., Pollard and Sag 1994) is a monostratal, lexicalist approach to grammar that models language as a system of constraints. Lexical entries are represented as feature structures with attributes for phonology, syntax and semantics of the sign.

As is the case for other theories of grammar, idioms that are lexically and syntactically free to different degrees pose a challenge for the theory that has not been fully met. A core question concerns the representation of idioms as either phonological signs, which would not allow for any variation – including inflection – of the strings, or as lexical signs, which would make them indistinguishable from lexemes not bound to idioms and collocations. A related question concerns the mechanism for the mutual selection of the lexemes that make up an idiom. Finally, accounting for syntactic operations on certain idioms and collocations represents a challenge.

Metaphorical, decomposable idioms like *spill the beans*, whose constituents can be semantically interpreted and that are syntactically free to undergo passivization, pronominalization, *WH*-questioning, adjectival modification, etc. constitute a relatively straightforward case.

Erbach (1992) and Krenn and Erbach (1994) propose to assign each component (V, NP) a transferred meaning that is defined in a lexical entry; these entries can then be combined compositionally, as in freely composed strings. By contrast, frozen idioms should be represented as phrasal signs in the lexicon. However, this would not allow for inflectional variations on the verb or noun, as these change the shape of a constituent of the phrase.

Erbach (1992) proposes an analysis based on the subcategorization of "frozen" complements by the verbal head. He distinguishes fixed, inflexible idioms like *kick the bucket* from freer ones like *take into account*. Syntactic operations like passivization are licensed or blocked depending on whether or not the nouns are assigned a thematic role. (This resembles Kearns's 2002 solution for the nouns in Support Verb Constructions.) Krenn and Erbach (1994) propose a different solution, distinguishing strictly fixed and variable frozen complements by the presence of absence of a feature PHON or LEXEME.

Sailer (2003) constitutes the most detailed and in-depth HPSG account of idiomatic phrases. He, too, recognizes the flexibility of many idioms and categorically rejects a construction-based approach to idioms that considers them as units. He assumes the distinction between internally regular (metaphoric) and internally irregular idioms proposed by Sag et al. (1994) and exemplified by *spill the beans* and *kick the bucket*, respectively. Like Krenn and Erbach (1994), Sailer assumes that the constituents of internally regular idioms are semantically interpreted (i.e., *spill* is interpreted as *divulge*). The requirement for the components to co-occur is captured in the lexicon as a restriction on their distribution. In this way, the principle of combinatorial semantics is maintained. Specifically, a feature COLL – evoking *collocation* but standing for *Context of Lexical Licensing* – assigns a value to a sign, which specifies the possible contexts in which the sign can occur. If the COLL value is empty, the sign has no distributional restrictions. If it is non-empty, the sign may have distributional restrictions. This solution, however, does not allow for lexical variation (e.g., compounding) or adjectival modification of an idiom constituent.

To allow for syntactic variations, locality restrictions specify the syntactic domain within which the idiom components must be found; for VP idioms like *spill the beans* this is usually, but not always, the VP. Sailer notes that in this respect, HPSG and TAG grammar approaches, where trees specify localities (e.g., Abeillé 1995), converge.

Internal irregular idiomatic phrases (like *kick the bucket*) do not obey any rules of regular combination and are licensed by a phrasal, lexical entry. Marked with the COLL feature, they are exempt from the compositional principle as well the requirement for syntactic regularity. Considered to be syntactically fixed, the lexical entry for such phrases states the appropriate restrictions. For *kick the bucket*, the entry specifies that in this VP, *the bucket* must be a direct object, thereby ruling out passivization.

Soehn (2006) calls specific, "frozen", lexemes within a phrase "Listemes", following diScullio and William's (1987) distinction between regular, class-based and irregular, listed items in the lexicon. Constituents of decomposable idioms are encoded in a lexical entry together with a literal string (e.g., *spill, divulge*). The string in an idiom selects its complement (*beans*) via its Listeme value.

Complex mechanisms in HPSG may account for some variation, but the theory is challenged by the rich variations of the core components of idioms, including those that do not receive a semantic interpretation. In particular, it is unclear whether the amazing range of variation shown by corpus data can be captured by a theory that strictly distinguishes free and flexible components within a lexical representation. For example, Soehn's Listeme feature assumes lexical invariance for lexemes that co-occur within an idiomatic phrase; but data show frequent lexical variation of one component when another suffices to evoke the idiomatic meaning. Lexical representation in terms of two mutually exclusive categories (flexible vs. inflexible) may not do justice to the richness of attested data.

9.3. Idioms in Construction Grammar

Construction Grammar (Fillmore, Kay, and O'Connor 1988; Fillmore and Kay 1999; Goldberg 1995, 2006) takes syntactic constructions as the fundamental units from which sentences and their meanings are built. In contrast to other grammatical models, the "radical" version (Nikanne 2008) of this theory (Goldberg 1995, 2006) assigns simple lexemes, MWUs, phrasal categories, and idiosycratic syntactic configurations alike the status of form-meaning pairings and unites them under the umbrella of "construction".

While constructions are units of syntactic representation, they are characterized by often complex semantic and pragmatic properties that cannot be adequately described by general rules of language.

Constructions vary with respect to the degree to which they are lexically filled. Lexically unfilled syntactic configurations like passive, exclamation, resultative, etc., which are traditionally considered the result of operations on basic structures, are constructions with their own semantics and (often) pragmatics. Thus, constructions can be seen as cutting across the traditional levels of linguistic analysis (phonology, syntax, semantics, pragmatics); Croft and Cruse (2003) call them "vertical" structures.

Idioms are considered constructions, on par with simple lexemes, syntactically defined constructions such as the Transitive construction, and collocations. The range of compositionality and syntactic flexibility across different idioms is accounted for by the interplay of the idioms' formal and meaning components.

Prototypical, lexically and seemingly syntactically fixed non-compositional idioms like *kick the bucket* are considered individual constructions associated with a specific meaning. They are not syntactically motivated in that their syntax does not contribute to their meaning. Other idioms form a family by virtue of a common meaning that is contributed by their shared syntactic construction; additional meaning is added by the lexemes specific to the idioms. This is the case for the large number of idioms with double object syntax exemplifying the Transfer construction, e.g., *give someone hell/the axe/a hard time*, all said to refer to a completed, successful transfer. Variations of these idioms, found on the Web, appear in related constructions, e.g. *get the axe/have a hard time*.

One apparent challenge to the theory here is the seemingly arbitrary limitation on the paradigm:

(34) a. *get the goods on*
b. *have the goods on*
c. **give the goods on*
d. *give a hard time (to)*
e. *have a hard time*
f. **get a hard time*

These data would have to be explained in terms of the meaning of the nouns, which constitute a separate form-meaning pair and thus a construction.

Similarly, the many "Malefactive" idioms discussed earlier clearly form a semantic class whose syntax plausibly contributes to their common meaning, roughly 'do something unpleasant to someone.' Their syntax, but not their meaning, is identical to the Beneficiary construction (*John baked Mary a cake*). In view of the fundamental role of a syntactic construction in the theory, one wonders whether both Malefactives and Benefactives should be subsumed under a single shared construction-meaning pairing; however, positing two related constructions with opposed meanings but identical structures seems like a somewhat unsatisfactory solution.

Fellbaum and Stathi (2006) examine idioms from the communication domain; these are generally double object constructions and can be subsumed under a general Transfer (of a Message) scheme. Fellbaum and Stathi (2006) examine the corpus examples showing the usage of the German idiom *jemandem die Leviten lesen*, lit. 'read Leviticus to someone', 'read someone the riot act.' In many cases, the Goal or Recipient is not expressed and the idiom does not strictly represent a Transfer construction but rather a Transitive construction, whose meaning must necessarily differ from that of the double object construction. Construction grammar theory has to explain whether, and by what mechanisms, the two syntactic structures would relate to one and the same idiom; positing two distinct idioms (as there are two distinct form-meaning pairs) is an alternative but – on the face of it – undesirable solution.

Fillmore, Kay, and O'Connor (1988) may be classified as proposing a "medium" (rather than a radical) theory of construction grammar (Nikanne 2008). In this approach, many idiomatic constructions that cannot be described by the rules of the core grammar and are therefore necessarily part of the lexicon-periphery, are assumed into the theory. In particular, Fillmore, Kay, and O'Connor (1988) and Fillmore and Kay (1999) have offered detailed analyses of so-called "schematic idioms". These are specific syntactic configurations characterized by the presence of a few lexical items (usually function words) and specific meanings, e.g., is *the X-er the Y-er*. Schematic idioms are syntactically, lexically and semantically irregular; their properties must be associated directly with the construction and may be extremely complex, as in the case of *let alone* or the "Mad Magazine Construction", as in *Him a doctor?* Such schematic constructions are by definition fixed and show no syntactic variation, though they allow a range of lexemes whose meanings are constrained by the meaning of the construction.

Chang and Fischer (2000), working within a "simulation-based" approach to constructions, aim to account for the flexibility of many idioms. Like Nunberg, Sag and Wasow (1994), they note that partly compositional idioms exhibit more regular associations between the syntactic and semantic structures. They consider the noun in metaphorical idioms like *spill the beans* a separate construction (form-meaning pair) with a context-specific referent. This independent status allows it to be modified. To account for syntactic operations like passivization and relativization that such idioms may undergo, Chang and Fischer stipulate the omission of the constructional constituent "Transitive construction" as well as the addition of a meaning constituent referring to the literal reading ('Spilling Event'). The binding between the idiomatic and the literal constituents allows the idiom the same syntactic flexibility as the phrase with a literal reading.

Chang and Fischer do not address the challenge of idioms that appear to admit only some syntactic transformations rather than behave fully like free constructions. Thus, while passivization is fine, clefting seems odd in the idiomatic reading:

(35) a. *The beans were spilled.* (idiomatic and literal reading)
b. *What was spilled were the beans.* (literal reading only)

10. Towards a grammar of idioms

Any grammatical theory of idioms must provide a motivated account for both the considerable variation found in many idioms as well as the limitations. Given the corpus data that have been reviewed in this chapter, no patterns are apparent that would allow a classification of idioms that could predict their behavior. One might of course simply conclude that each idiom has its own constraints on lexical and morphosyntactic variation, and these must be encoded in the lexical entry with each idiom. (This is essentially the HPSG approach discussed earlier.) But this seems a less than theoretically satisfying solution.

Some linguists (e.g., Sabban 1998) distinguish between the "principled" variation of idioms, which must be accounted for by the grammar, and "occasional" variation, resulting from speakers' efforts to achieve a special effect. But it is not clear how crisp such a distinction might be and whether it is relevant to a grammar of idioms. Corpus data show that all variations follow the rules of grammar, and there is no evidence that speakers resort to a "subgrammar" for the sake of rhetorical effects. There is no doubt that much of the variation is context-sensitive; but in this respect idioms do not differ from freely composed structures.

Although idioms are frequent (e.g., Jackendoff 1997), individual idioms vary in frequency, and it seems safe to say that we do not have enough data for a sufficiently representative spectrum of idiomatic expressions to conclude that idioms cannot be accounted for in a wholesale fashion nor to formulate definitive constraints on idioms. Geyken, Sokirko, Rehbein, and Fellbaum (2004) argue that even a corpus of one billion words is not sufficiently large to yield enough data for a grammar of idioms. We do not have enough data to determine with confidence the lexical and syntactic "canonical" form of idioms, let alone to classify the idioms in terms of their fixedness or the range of their variations.

10.1. A null hypothesis

From the available evidence it is apparent that that discourse and pragmatic factors can account for much of the variation. This may account for the fact that so many examples that are constructed outside a discourse and ruled out by the "armchair linguist" in fact turn up when one searches a corpus. We cited data showing that lexical variation may play on discourse-specific topics. Syntactic variation involving pronominalization or movement of idiom-internal nouns in many cases is attributable to speakers' ad-hoc assignment of meaning to the inherently opaque nouns in particular contexts. A null hypothesis, based on the present evidence, would state that every well-formed idiom can be input to all grammatical operations, independent of semantic compositionality but largely conditioned by the context and speakers' communicative intentions.

10.2. A psycholinguistic approach to idioms

Linguistic theories often make at least implicit claims to psychological theories of language representation and processing. We therefore review the findings of relevant psycholinguistic research concerning the question as to how idioms and collocations might be represented in the mental lexicon and in speakers' grammars.

A number of experiments attempt to determine whether idioms are represented and processed as unanalyzable, fixed lexical units or as partially decomposable strings.

Both comprehension and production of idioms are tested. While the stimuli tend to be constructed rather than based on corpus examples, the conclusions are applicable and relevant to the analyses of attested data.

Familiar, frequent idioms like *kick the bucket* are processed faster in their idiomatic than in their literal meanings and may in fact inhibit them. However, this could simply be a function of their overall frequency and the higher frequency of the idiomatic reading compared to the literal one; a corpus study could test this hypothesis.

Based on idiom production experiments, Cutting and Bock (1997) propose a "hybrid" theory of idiom representation, arguing for the existence of a lexical concept node for each idiom; at the same time, idioms are syntactically and semantically analyzed during production, independent of the idioms' degree of compositionality. A hybrid account is also supported by Sprenger, Levelt, and Kempen (2006), who show that idioms can be primed with lexemes that are semantically related to constituents of the idioms, indicating that the literal meaning is accessed. Sprenger, Levelt, and Kempen propose the notion of a "superlemma" as a conceptual unit whose lexemes are bound both to their idiomatic use and their use in the free language.

The superlemma theory is compatible with Cacciari and Tabossi's (1988) Configuration Hypothesis, which states that speakers activate the literal meanings of words in a phrase and recognize the idiomatic meaning of a polysemous string only when they recognize an idiom-specific configuration of lexemes or encounter a "key" lexeme. In many idioms, the key may be the definite article (*kick the bucket, fall off the wagon, buy the farm*) which suggests that a referent for the noun has been previously introduced into the discourse; when no matching antecedent can be found, another interpretation of the string must be attempted (Fellbaum 1993).

Finally, Kuiper's (2004) work also supports a hybrid representation. Kuiper analyzes and classifies 1,000 slips of the tongue attested in idioms and shows that errors can be attributed to all levels of grammar (phonology, morphology, syntax). Kuiper's analysis, consistent with the superlemma theory, demonstrates that idioms are not simply stored as frozen long words, but are subjected to regular grammar processes.

The experimental findings and resulting theories are consistent with the wealth of data showing speakers use idioms and collocations in full agreement with regular grammatical processes, independent of whether the idioms are semantically decomposable.

11. Conclusion

With a small number of exceptions, collocations and idioms are syntactically well-formed. As lexical items, they may be only partially filled. While we defined collocations as idiosyncratic but fully compositional, idioms are non-compositional to varying degrees. Refuting the assumption that compositionality is a condition for lexical and syntactic variation, corpus data show that all regular grammatical processes operate on a wide range of idioms and in particular on non-referential idiom components.

Their status as lexical units on the one hand, and their considerable flexibility on the other hand make idioms and collocations a challenge for any theory of grammar.

Psycholinguistic work on the comprehension and processing of non-literal language mirrors the ambiguous status of phrasal expressions, but offers a "hybrid" account that is compatible with both the linguistic and the experimental evidence. Further empirical work will bring us closer to a comprehensive account of collocations and idioms.

12. References (selected)

Abeillé, Anne
1995 The flexibility of French idioms: A representation with lexicalized Tree Adjoining Grammar. In: M. Everaert, E. J. van der Linden, A. Schenk, and R. Schreuder (eds.), *Idioms: Structural and Psychological Perspectives*, 15–42. Hillsdale: Erbaum.

Abraham, Werner
1973 The ethical dative in German. In: Kiefer, F., and Ruwet, N. (eds.), *Generative Grammar in Europe*, 1–19. Dordrecht: Reidel.

Baldwin, Timothy, Colin Bannard, Takaki Tanaka, and Dominic Widdows
2003 An empirical model of multiword expression decomposability. In: *Proceedings of the ACL-Siglex Workshop on Multiword Expressions: Analysis, Acquisition and Treatment*, 89–96.

Bond, Francis, Anna Korhonen, Diana McCarthy, and Aline Villavicencio (eds.)
2003 *Proceedings of the ACL-03 Workshop on Multiword Expressions: Analysis, Acquisition and Treatment*. Sapporo, Japan.

Cacciari, Cristina, and Patrizia Tabossi
1988 The comprehension of idioms. *Journal of Memory and Language* 27: 668–683.

Chang, Nancy, and Ingrid Fischer
2000 Understanding idioms. In: Zuehlke, W., and E. Schukat-Talamazzini (eds.), *Proceedings of Konvens*, 33–38. Berlin: VDE.

Chomsky, Noam
1981 *Lectures on Government and Binding*. Dordrecht: Foris.
Chomsky, Noam
1986 *Barriers*. Cambridge, MA: MIT Press.
Church, Kenneth, and Patrick Hanks
1991 Word association norms, Mutual Information and lexicography. *Computational Linguistics* 16.1: 22–29.
Cowie, Anthony
1992 *Phraseology: Theory, Analysis, and Applications*. Oxford: Oxford University Press.
Croft, William, and Alan D. Cruse
2003 *Cognitive Linguistics*. Cambridge: Cambridge University Press.
Cutler, Anne
1982 The older the colder. *Linguistic Inquiry* 13: 317–320.
Cutting, Cooper, and Kathryn Bock
1997 That's why the cookie bounces: Syntactic and semantic components of experimentally elicited idiom blends. *Memory and Cognition* 25.1: 57–71.
diSciullio, Anna Maria, and Edwin Williams
1987 *On the Definition of a Word*. Cambridge, MA: MIT Press.
Dobrovol'skij, Dimitrij
1995 *Kognitive Aspekte der Idiom-Semantik. Studien zum Thesaurus deutscher Idiome*. Tuebingen: Narr.
Dobrovol'skij, Dimitrij
1999 Haben transformationelle Defekte der Idiomstruktur semantische Ursachen? In: F. Bravo, N. Behr, I. Behr, and C. Rozier (eds.), *Phraseme und Typisierende Rede*, 25–37. Tuebingen: Stauffenburg.
Erbach, Gregor
1992 Head-driven lexical representation of idioms in HPSG. In: M. Everaert, E. J. van der Linden, A. Schenk, and R. Schreuder (eds.), *Proceedings of the International Conference on Idioms*, 1–15. Tilburg.
Ernst, Thomas
1981 Grist for the linguistic mill: Idioms and "extra" adjectives. *Journal of Linguistic Research* 1.3: 51–68.
Everaert, Martin, Erik-Jan van der Linden, André Schenk, and Rob Schreuder (eds.)
1995 *Idioms: Structural and Psychological Perspectives*. Hillsdale: Erlbaum.
Evert, Stefan
2004, published 2005 The statistics of word cooccurrences: Word pairs and collocations. Doctoral dissertation, University of Stuttgart.
Fazly, Afsaneh, and Suzanne Stevenson
2006 Automatically constructing a lexicon of verb phrase idiomatic combinations. In: *Proceedings of the Association for Computational Linguistics*, 337–344.
Fazly, Afasaneh, Cook, Paul, and Suzanne Stevenson
2009 Unsupervised type and token identification of idiomatic expressions. *Computational Linguistics* 35.1: 61–103.
Fellbaum, Christiane
1993 The determiner in English idioms. In: Cristina Cacciari, and Patrizia Tabossi (eds.), *Idioms: Processing, Structure, and Interpretation*, 271–295. Hillsdale: Erlbaum.
Fellbaum, Christiane
2005 Examining the constraints on the benefactive alternation by using the world wide web as a corpus. In: Marga Reis, and Stephan Kepser (eds.), *Evidence in Linguistics: Empirical, Theoretical, and Computational Perspectives*, 209–240. Berlin: Mouton de Gruyter.
Fellbaum, Christiane (ed.)
2006 *Special Issue: Corpus Studies of German Idioms and Light Verbs, International Journal of Lexicography* 19.4.

Fellbaum, Christiane (ed.)
2007 *Idioms and Collocations: From Corpus to Electronic Lexical Resource*. Birmingham: Continuum.

Fellbaum, Christiane, and Katerina Stathi
2006 Idiome in der Grammatik und im Kontext: Wer bruellt hier die Leviten? In: Kristel Proost, and Edeltraut Winkler (eds.), *Von Intentionalitaet zur Bedeutung Konventionalisierter Zeichen*, 125–146. Tuebingen: Narr.

Fillmore, Charles J., Kay, Paul, and Mary Katherine O'Connor
1988 Regularity and idiomaticity in grammatical constructions. *Language* 64.3: 501–538.

Firenze, Anna
2007 'You don't fool her' doesn't mean (that) 'you conduct her behind the light': (Dis)agglutination and the determiner in German idioms. In: Christiane Fellbaum (ed.), *Idioms and Collocations*, 152–163. Birmingham: Continuum Press.

Firenze, Anna, and Christiane Fellbaum
2008 Analyse sur corpus d'expressions figées de l'allemand. *Linguisticae Investigationes* 31.2: 158–172.

Firth, John R.
1957 *A Synopsis of Linguistic Theory*. (Studies in Linguistic Analysis.) Oxford: Blackwell.

Fraser, Bruce
1970 Idioms within a transformational grammar. *Foundations of Language* 6: 22–42.

Geyken, Alexander, Alexei Sokirko, Ines Rehbein, and Christiane Fellbaum
2004 What is the optimal corpus size for the study of idioms? Paper delivered at the Annual Meeting of the German Linguistic Society, Mainz.

Geyken, Alexander
2007 The DWDS Corpus: A reference corpus for the German language of the 20th century. In: Christiane Fellbaum (ed.), *Idioms and Collocations: From Corpus to Electronic Lexical Resource*, 23–39. Birmingham: Continuum.

Goldberg, Adele
1995 *Constructions: A Construction Grammar Approach to Argument Structure*. Chicago: University of Chicago Press.

Goldberg, Adele
2006 *Constructions at Work: The Nature of Generalization in Language*. Oxford: Oxford University Press.

Goldberg, Adele, and Ray Jackendoff
2004 The English resultative as a family of constructions. *Language* 80: 532–568.

Green, Georgia
1974 *Semantics and Syntactic Regularity*. Bloomington: Indiana University Press.

Grimshaw, Jane, and Arnim Mester
1988 Light verbs and theta-marking. *Linguistic Inquiry* 19: 205–232.

Herold, Axel
2007 Corpus queries. In: Christiane Fellbaum (ed.), *Idioms and Collocations*, 54–63. Birmingham: Continuum Press.

Horn, Laurence
2008 "I love me some him": The landscape of non-argument datives. In: Oliver Bonani, and Patrizia Cebredo-Hofherr (eds.), *Empirical Issues in Syntax and Semantics* 7, 169–172.

Jackendoff, Ray
1995 The boundaries of the lexicon. In: M. Everaert, E. J. van der Linden, A. Schenk, and R. Schreuder (eds.), *Idioms: Structural and Psychological Perspectives*, 133–165. Tilburg: Holland.

Jackendoff, Ray
1997 Twistin' the night away. *Language* 73: 534–559.

Jespersen, Otto
1954 *A Modern English Grammar.* London: Allen and Unwin.

Kay, Paul, and Charles Fillmore
1999 Grammatical constructions and linguistic generalizations: the What's X doing Y? construction. *Language* 75.1: 1–34.

Kearns, Kate
1998/2002 Light verbs in English. Downloadable from http://www.ling.canterbury.ac.nz/people/kearns.shtml

Klein, Wolfgang
1968 Zur Klassifizierung der Funktionsverben. *Beitraege zur Linguistik und Informationsverarbeitung* 13: 7–37.

Krenn, Brigitte, and Gregor Erbach
1993 Idioms and Support Verb Constructions. In: John Nerbonne, Klaus Netter, and Carl Pollard (eds.), *German in Head-Driven Phrase Structure Grammar*, 265–296. (CSLI Lecture Notes 46.) Stanford, CA: CSLI Publications.

Krifka, Manfred
1999 Manner in dative alternation. In: Sonya Bird, Andrew Carnie, Jason D. Haugen, and Peter Norquest (eds.), *Proceedings of the 18th West Coast Conference on Formal Linguistics*, 260–271. Tucson, AZ: University of Arizona.

Kuiper, Konrad
2004 Slips of the tongue and the phrasal lexicon. In: A. Haecki-Buhofer, and H. Burger (eds.), *Proceedings of Europhras*, Basel, Switzerland.

Lakoff, George, and Mark Johnson
1980 *Metaphors We Live By.* Chicago: University of Chicago Press.

Lebeaux, David
2000 *Language Acquisition and the Form of Grammar.* Amsterdam: John Benjamins.

Lichte, Timm, and Manfred Sailer
2004 Extracting negative polarity items from a partially parsed corpus. In: Sandra Kuebler, Joakim Nivre, Erhard Hinrichs, and Holger Wunsch (eds.), *Proceedings of the Third Workshop on Treebanks and Linguistic Theories*, 89–101. Seminar fuer Sprachwissenschaft, Universitaet Tuebingen.

McCarthy, Diana, Bill Keller, and John Carroll
2003 Detecting a continuum of compositionality in phrasal verbs. In: *Proceedings of the ACL-SIGLEX Workshop on Multiword Expressions*, 73–80.

McEnery, Anthony, and Andrew Wilson
1996 *Corpus Linguistics.* Edinburgh: Edinburgh University Press.

Moon, Rosamund
1998 *Fixed Expressions and Idioms in English.* A Corpus-Based Approach. (Oxford Studies in Lexicography and Lexicology.) Oxford: Clarendon Press.

Neumann, Gerald, Christiane Fellbaum, Alexander Geyken, Axel Herold, Christiane Huemmer, Fabian Koerner, Undine Kramer, Kerstin Krell, Alexei Sokirko, Diana Stantcheva, and Katerina Stathi
2004 A corpus-based lexical resource of German idioms. In: Patrick Saint Dizier, and Michael Zock (eds.), *Proceedings of the Workshop on Electronic Lexicon*, 49–52. Geneva: COLING.

Newmeyer, Frederick
1974 The regularity of idiom behavior. *Lingua* 34: 327–342.

Nikanne, Urpo
2008 Conceptual semantics. In: Oestman, Jan-Ola, and Jef Verschueren (eds.), *Handbook of Pragmatics*, 1–21. Amsterdam: John Benjamins.

Nunberg, Geoffrey, Ivan Sag, and Thomas Wasow
1994 Idioms. *Language 70*: 491–538.

Partington, Alan
2004 Utterly content in each other's company: semantic prosody and semantic preference. *International Journal of Corpus Linguistics* 9.1: 131–156.
Pollard, Carl, and Ivan Sag
1987 *Information-based Syntax and Semantics*. Stanford, CA: CSLI Publications.
Sabban, Annette
1998 *Okkasionelle Variationen sprachlicher Schematismen. Eine Analyse franzoesischer und deutscher Presse- und Werbetexte*. Tuebingen: Narr.
Sailer, Manfred
2003 Combinatorial Semantics and Idiomatic Expressions in Head-Driven Phrase Structure Grammar. Doctoral dissertation University Tuebingen, Germany.
Schone, Patrick, and Daniel Jurafsky
2001 Is knowledge-free induction of multiword unit dictionary headwords a solved problem? In: *Proceedings of the Conference on Empirical Methods in Natural Language Processing*, 100–108.
Sinclair, John
1991 *Corpus, Concordance, Collocation*. Oxford: Oxford University Press.
Soehn, Jan-Philipp
2006 On idiom parts and their contexts. *Linguistik Online* 27.2: 11–28.
Sprenger, Simone, William Levelt, and Gerard Kempen
2006 Lexical access during the production of idiomatic phrases. *Journal of Memory and Language* 54: 161–184.
Stathi, Katerina
2007 A corpus-based analysis of adjectival modification in German idioms. In: Christiane Fellbaum (ed.), *Idioms and Collocations*, 81–108. Birmingham: Continuum Press.
Storrer, Angelika
2007 Corpus-based investigations of German support verb constructions. In: Christiane Fellbaum (ed.), *Idioms and Collocations*, 164–187. Birmingham: Continuum Press.
Stubbs, Michael
2002 *Word and Phrases: Corpus Studies of Lexical Semantics*. Melbourne: Blackwell.
Szabolcsi, Anna
1986 Indefinites in complex predicates. *Theoretical Linguistic Research* 2: 47–84.
Wierzbicka, Anna
1982 Why can you have a drink when you can't *have an eat? *Language* 58.4: 753–799.
Wood, Mary
1986 *A Definition of Idiom*. Bloomington, IN: Indiana University Linguistics Club.

Christiane Fellbaum, Princeton (USA)